THE MASKS OF MACBETH

THE MASKS OF MACBETH

BY MARVIN ROSENBERG

UNIVERSITY OF CALIFORNIA PRESS

BERKELEY, LOS ANGELES, LONDON

University of California Press
Berkeley and Los Angeles, California

University of California Press, Ltd.
London, England

Copyright © 1978 by
The Regents of the University of California

ISBN 0-520-03262-4
Library of Congress Catalog Card Number: 76-14295
Printed in the United States of America
1 2 3 4 5 6 7 8 9

For Mary

Contents

Prologue

To explore the full depth and complexity of *Macbeth*, we must risk to its limits the stance that nothing human is alien to us. All Shakespeare's great tragic characters slide from heights of decency and position to welter in a dark world of proscribed impulse; but only Macbeth and his Lady choose evil, and follow it headlong down. Hamlet, Othello, Lear, all try to resist the void of shame that draws them; the Macbeths instead must resist the slipping hold of civilization that tries to drag them back from the abyss. Macbeth sometimes confesses his struggles in brilliant language, Lady Macbeth is more secretive; but in both the subterranean war goes continuously on, and to know it we must be willing to experience a deepmost turbulence.

In the theatre we can, as spectators, respond to the play from the outside, vicariously sharing the characters' trials through the acting. This way of knowing I propose to recreate in the following pages, from a survey of important critical and theatrical interpretations from Europe, America, Asia, Africa, and Australia. But if we would be swallowed by the play, know it from the inside, as actors do, as Shakespeare made it for them to know, we must try to go deeper. If we can also share, with the actor, Macbeth's impulse to murder, and his impulse to mercy, and feel the two clamoring in us at the same time, we begin to enter the very furnace of the playwright's creation. Civilized, we are comfortable in summoning beneficent impulses to the service of our imagination; to call the forbidden ones from the imprisoned places in our vasty deep takes more daring. We may help ourselves with the actor's technique of exciting our emotional memory, recapturing lost tremors of buried fury. When we can ourselves re-experience the conflicting emotions that simultaneously ravage Macbeth's soul, while at the same time sensing the mask held before his face to hide the inner melee, we begin to know in our tissue something of the complexity of Shakespeare's art in characterization.

As a metaphor for this complexity, I borrow from the great Russian actor,

Mikhoels, whose historic interpretation of Lear helped me in my study of
that play. He wrote:

> [Shakespeare's art] is never a monody, and it is the actor's task to hear the
> separate notes making the character . . . They may be separated by quite an
> interval; on the other hand, contrasting and diametrically opposed notes may
> coincide in time.*

To suggest the many, varied, even contrary strains that Mikhoels and other
actors and critics have found in Shakespearean characters, I will use the word
polyphony. I offer this not as a technical musical term, but simply to convey the
sense of the many notes in the character designs, and their dynamic, changing
patterns. To give a simplified example now: Macbeth knows how wrong it
is to murder a guest-king—and Macbeth murders him. Knowing it wrong
involves clusters of feeling tones, such as conscience, propriety, civilized
manliness. The countering impulse to murder sounds harsher notes, resonant
of ambition, cruelty, fear, the bloodthirst of a different order of manliness,
practical considerations of committing undetected crime. So intricately designed a characterization can never be perceived as a monody, as Mikhoels
observed; sometimes one cluster of notes seems to override all, but even then
countering strains may be faintly heard; sometimes the counterpoint swells,
and overwhelms the original chords, controlling them, but not extinguishing
them.

The same multiplicity—polyphony—pervades the other elements of the
play. No single motif organizes the play's meanings, though critics and the
theatre will sometimes search for one; we are rocked back and forth among
themes. Shakespeare will not comfort us with easy patterns. The evil are
punished, but so are the good; murderers are guileful, but so are those who
bring the murderers to justice. The objects of "real" life may seem less substantial than those of fantasy. If Heaven seems to listen to some pleas, it
seems cruelly to reject others—if indeed Heaven has anything to do with
the *Macbeth* world. Magic may seem malicious, when practiced by witches;
it may seem beneficent, when practiced by a good old king. Disorder is dangerous; but so may be what passes for order. Nothing is sure, in the realms
of man, of witches, of divinity or demons; symptoms of their powers and
dominions mingle inextricably.

Macbeth's language is similarly rich. It is commonly recognized as *equivocal*:
literally, using equal (opposed) utterances simultaneously; "capable of double
meaning" (OED). Many utterances compete in the lines of *Macbeth*, often
denying each other: *Fair is foul; Nothing is but what is not*. Styles of utterance
compete. The chalky rhythms of the witches evoke another world, yet some-

---

*In an interesting critical echo of this, Norman Rabkin applied to Shakespeare's oppositions
the concept, from physics, of complementarity: mutually contradictory elements coexisting.
And Sister Mary Miriam Joseph noted, in Shakespeare's language, his perceiving "simultaneously the multiple meanings of a word like the tones in a musical chord."

times enclose the mundane concerns of everyday. The prose is spare and muscled. The blank verse is Shakespeare's most syncopated: sometimes so abrupt, so erratic in length of line and meter that some have wondered if it is all the playwright's own. The imagery reflects the confusion of the human world, and the mis-match between it and the "other" world. It ranges from the high apocalyptic to the domestic of earth and hearth, sometimes in stately, undulant rhythms, often in monosyllabic staccato. Supple as it is, it suits the chameleon masks that sometimes shelter counter-meaning behind words. Often it speaks loudest in its silences, and in its almost whispered hints of the unspoken, of the unspeakable, of deeds without a name.

The language, verbal and subverbal, is voiced by strange creatures of earth and the regions below and above, predators almost all, from Hecate and kings and noble thanes and hired murderers and servants to the birds that sing at death, and the prowling wolf, and smaller animal familiars. In a great storm, the moans of men asleep mingle with the owl's shriek and the cricket's cry and the wail of cannibal horses. Shakespeare orchestrates accents from the boundaries of imaginable experience—from nature and supernature, from coven, battlefield, wild forest and blasted heath, from courts royal and unearthly. If we are to know the full scale of the *Macbeth* music, we must be tuned to all these harmonics, and taste in our throats the human sounds made: whispers, murmurs, mutterings, shouts, shrieks—and the terrible clamors of silence in those moments of expectation or discovery when the whole world seems to stand still, waiting.

The play's visual imagery—its spectacle—similarly combines many multiple signals, many doubled notes. In faces we may read strange matters, though men try to mask their feelings with mouth-honoring smiles; apparently real figures vanish before the eyes, and images unseen to us are hallucinated; blood will for a while ornament the armor of brave warriors, but will stain irretrievably the hands of murderers; rituals of homage or coronation will say different things when different kings accept them.

Perhaps our most difficult task of all, if we want fully to appreciate Shakespeare's art, will be to try to experience *Macbeth*'s polyphony as only a new audience could. We must not only suspend disbelief; we must suspend memory. We must not look at the play with old eyes; we must not know "what happens next." We must recapture the bewilderment and mystery of the unfolding oracular promises—wonder again about how a forest can move against Macbeth; about what uncanny form of life, not of woman born, could threaten him; wonder if Macbeth will win.

For Shakespeare intended startling surprises for his spectators of *Macbeth*. Only in this one tragedy does he keep major climactic, ironic secrets from his audiences, as only in *Winter's Tale* among the comedy-romances does he similarly palter with us. The first-time—and probably in most cases only-time—spectators at the Globe were not to know how *Macbeth* would "come out." Even if the learned remembered the story from Holinshed, or other

sources, they could only guess at Shakespeare's plan: he so adapted his mélange of source material that he might have ended the play with a Macbeth
who ruled securely, in Tamburlaine fashion, for many years, and still fitted
the given historic frame. Not that old frames restricted this playwright—he
who confidently turned the old *Leir* play, with its happy, romantic ending,
into the darkest of tragedies.

To discover how Shakespeare controlled audience expectation in *Lear*, I
invited spectators who had never read or seen the play—*naive spectators* I call
them—to a performance and reported their often unexpected, often illuminating, responses. With the help of colleagues, I have done the same with
Macbeth, with audiences in England and America. I encountered some of
the same surprises I found with *Lear*. I will report them. They indicate that
we who know *Macbeth* well may know it too well to evaluate fairly and freshly
the art of its plot twists and character configurations; to know the play better,
we must make a sturdy effort to forget what we know.

I would like to progress through the play scene by scene, as if we were all
truly *naive* about "what happens next." This will not be entirely possible.
Perspective must sometimes be extrapolated for the polyphonic interweav-
ings, and echoing motifs must sometimes be anticipated. When I come to the
major roles, I will have to survey the amazing spread of interpretation resulting
from different character emphases, so that we will be able to follow these
through the play. But I will do my best to be surprised where Shakespeare
wants me to be, and so I hope will gentles all.

Ultimately, the interpretation of *Macbeth* this book presents is my own;
but I have fed into it a history of the play in the theatre and in criticism. I am
essentially concerned with the interpretation, only secondarily the history;
but I append a full bibliography for scholars. The materials of the bibliography were pieced, as with *The Masks of King Lear* and *The Masks of Othello*,
from hundreds of books, essays, periodical reports, memoirs, and acting
versions, as well as from my notes on performances and rehearsals attended
and actors and directors interviewed. To manage this mass of material, and
keep it within the bounds of a book, I have used the simple reference technique welcomed in the *Lear* study: the main bibliography lists all sources;
the notes to each chapter list sources consulted for it. After the chapter notes
and the main bibliography, I supply a *Macbeth* Theatre Bibliography: Part I,
on actors and actresses of English-speaking countries, and distinguished performers who have visited these countries; Part II, data on actors
and actresses of non-English speaking countries; Part III, data on stagings
associated with particular producers or places.

I try to cite sources wherever possible, but in some cases I will offer, again
as in the *Lear* study, a synthesis of the insights of too many actors or critics to
identify them individually. Some among the hundreds of sources could not be
identified. Generally I refer to critics by their last names, unless more than

one has that name; I mean this last-naming as a compliment to colleagues so distinguished, and I hope the practice may become standard.

I assume a general accuracy in the observations of reviews and historical reports, though sometimes they disagree with each other, with me, or with comments actors or directors have provided. In such cases, I note the disagreement if it is significant; otherwise I draw into the character syntheses the perceptions that seem most valid. What is important here is how much illumination the synthesized images may lend to our understanding of the play.

Actors and actresses are identified by nationality and by a date of performance, since cultural and chronological contexts may affect interpretation. Some actors are not named because, like some critics, they add nothing to earlier illuminations of the play. A production's contribution may be cited for its director, designer, conception, or for a single role in it. If my selection leaves out bits of interpretation individual readers have prized, I would like to hear from them, from anyone who will teach me.

I use the Variorum edition as my text, since it is the most easily accessible form of the Folio *Macbeth*, the only version of the play endorsed as Shakespeare's by his fellow-actors. I modernize the spelling only the very little that is necessary for easy comprehension. I do not meddle with the lineation: the many broken lines, that offend some editors, seem to me to be deliberate, sensitive accommodations to the rhythms of actors' speech. But I will have more to say about this, and other puzzles in the text, as they arise.

A great gift to my study of *Macbeth* was the privilege of attending rehearsals of the production of the Royal Shakespeare Theatre, when Peter Hall directed Paul Scofield and Vivien Merchant in the major roles. I have found that this experience of either participating in the play, or observing rehearsals, leads to an invaluable intimacy with the work of art. I am grateful to the University of California, Berkeley, Research Committee, and the National Endowment for the Humanities for generous research support.

This study would not have been possible without the help of colleagues, actors, directors and libraries throughout the world. I am particularly thankful to those readers of my *Othello* and *Lear* studies who knew what I was looking for, and responded to my invitation to inform me of interpretations of *Macbeth* I might have missed. I hope any reader of this book with information on interpretations of any of these plays, and particularly of *Hamlet*, my next subject, will communicate with me.

I am particularly obliged to three patient readers of the whole manuscript: James Black, Robert Dent, and Jay Halio. Their suggestions have been invaluable, and I have accepted many of them; though they are not to be held responsible for what follows.

Of the many librarians throughout the world who have helped me, I must first list those who, usually involved with major theatre-history depositories, have had most to bear with my visits and requests: Barbara Hancock, Frau Dr. E. Keppelmüller, Inna Levidova, Paul Myers, Jeanne Newlin, Lindsay Newman, Louis Rachow, and Eileen Robinson. I could not have amassed the theatrical data that helps support my interpretation of *Macbeth* without their aid; but the same is true of other librarians who have welcomed my visits and correspondence, W.A.G. Alison, Celeste Ashley, Robert Atkins, Kathleen M.D. Barker, C. Batt, H.F. Berolzheimer, Jeanette Blanco, Mary Brand, Arthur Bryce, Anthony Carr, P. Casey, Margaret Clark, Jane Allen Combe, A.B. Craven, R.J. Craven, Jo Ann Davies, Desmond Donaldson, Geraldine Duclow, Jean Dyce, Laurence Elvin, Jeanette Fauvel, Betty Gay Gibson, James Gibson, Peter Grant, Collin Hamer, I.G. Hardy, Mark Harris, J. Alan Howe, Mary Ann Jensen, V.J. Kite, G.J. Lang, J. Lilley, Bernard Little, Anthony J.J. MacNeill, Ronald J. Mahoney, Judy W. Nichols, Finola O'Donovan, D. Palmer, J.R. Pike, H.V. Ralph, R.G. Roberts, Janet Russell, Milton C. Russell, Frank Sayer, William S. Simpson, E. Herndon Smith, Monique Tessier, O.S. Tomlinson, D.M. Torbet, F.M. Wilkins, Larry J. Wygant.

The personal reports of *Macbeth* stagings sent to me by colleagues are noted in the bibliographies; but I want to thank particularly some whose assistance from Europe and Asia has sustained my work over many months: Manfred Boetzkes, Edward Carrick Craig, Mladen Engelsfeld, Renée Fisher, Evelyn Gibbs, Jerzy Got, Claus Laurén, M. Martinet, Peter Milward, Nigel Rollison, W. Schrickx, Norair Taschian, and Jürgen Wertheimer. I must thank Marvin Spevack for his computer work; and Keith Sturgess, in England, and Edgar Reynolds, in America, for their stagings of *Macbeth* that made possible my experiments with *naive* spectators. For bibliographic assistance, I am grateful to Elizabeth Key and Deborah Merola; for the final editing, to Peter Dreyer. I have been fortunate to be able to consult on various matters with colleagues at my university. I could not have dealt with information in so many foreign languages, and tangential research, without the assistance of Eric Johannesen, Joseph Kerman, Benson Mates, Walter Schamschula, Grace Smith, Gleb Struve, and Ronald Walpole.

The University of California Press, publisher of my three books on Shakespeare, has faithfully dealt with my complex text. I am particularly grateful to that fine artist, Lloyd Hoff, who has once more provided my book's jacket design and cover emblem.

Most of all, I owe this book to Mary Rosenberg, who helped everywhere with the research and interviews, who tirelessly typed through to the final manuscript, shared in the seemingly endless checking of documentation, and who joined in coaxing the work through the final proofreading and indexing.

MARVIN ROSENBERG
Berkeley, California

When the battle's lost and won.

The Weyward Sisters

Thunder and lightning.

With sound and fury, signifying much, the play is directed to begin. Shakespeare controlled such theatrical means to suggest turbulent storm—pyrotechnics and thunder rolls*—and such verbal means to rouse ready imaginations, that his spectators in the open Globe in midafternoon could experience nature's midnight cataclysms as intensely as night audiences in the public and private theatres. *Macbeth*'s opening storm may not quite match the tempest to come on the night of the murder, for dramatic design prefers the rising accent; but this shock of sight and sound will be fearful, making the earth seem to shudder—and perhaps a wooden theatre to do so in fact. One of Shakespeare's paradoxes is that these ultimate expressions of nature's energy are likely to be perceived by Shakespearean man as "unnatural," as if they bode cosmic disturbances. On this scale the thunder and lightning excite the mind as well as eye and ear, introducing the assault on the senses and thought that, Jorgensen wisely observes, characterizes the play's "sensational" art. In the theatre the thunderous storm, streaked with white and red lightning, may be counterpointed by flashes of fire, war's detonations, drumrolls, trumpets, the cries of the wounded. The air may thicken with smoke or "fog." These are the first sights and sounds in an aural polyphony that will score the music of man's experience from the beast to the supernatural.

Three shapes take form in the "filthy air" on—or above—the stage.

Enter three Witches.

To know these curious figures, that have been visualized by critics and the theatre in amazingly different ways, we must pause to consider their full

*W.J. Lawrence (7) cites a reference to spectacular storm effects for a *Faustus:* "Drummers make Thunder in the Tyring-house, and the twelve-penny Hirelings make artificall lightning in their Heavens." (209) Rolling cannonballs also sounded thunder; and the lightning, Walter Hodges suggests, was contrived of "fireworks running down from the Heavens on a fixed wire." (20f.) Special effects may have been achieved with bursts of resin smoke—*fog and filthy air:* see the discussion of the ghost in 111,iv.

polyphony. I do not want to get far ahead of the action, so I will wait for their
later scenes to fill out their portraits; but we must partly look ahead if we are
to understand their impact when they first appear. They will enter only three
times more, but the mystery and hint of chaos they carry will pervade the
action. If we are to inhabit them, as well as respond to them, we must wonder
how they look, what forces—natural and supernatural—they may represent,
and something of the audience reaction meant to attend them.

Shakespeare shaped them from this hint in Holinshed:

> . . . as Makbeth and Banquho iournied towards Fores, passing thorough the
> woods and fields . . . there met them three women in strange and wild ap-
> parell, resembling creatures of elder world . . . [After speaking] the foresaid
> women vanished immediatlie out of their sight . . . afterwards the common
> opinion was, that these women were either the weird sisters, that is (as ye would
> say) the goddesses of destinie, or else some nymphs or feiries, indued with
> knowledge of prophesie by their necromanticall science, bicause euerie thing
> came to passe as they had spoken.

Some Shakespeareans object to considering these figures "witches," as
demeaning supernatural images of more powerful degree; but the Sisters
are so called by Folio direction, and one is so addressed. *Sisters . . . witches*—
the polarity suggests the wide range of implication the playwright intended.

How much supernatural power, for good or evil, Shakespeare provided the
Sisters is crucial to Macbeth's character and action. If we recognize the three
as simply old crones pretending to be—or thinking themselves to be—possessed of magic, then Macbeth is mainly responsible for his acts, and his
crimes fall heavily on himself—and on Lady Macbeth. Then the two choose—
or find excuses to choose—their fate. At the other extreme, if the Sisters,
perhaps with their "masters," can determine behavior, Macbeth is a man
trapped, helpless to choose good. Every man must answer this: does my
character shape my destiny? Does my destiny shape my character? Do my
witches seek me out because of what I am, or am I this because of my witches?
Do I seek them?

In the Macbeth-witch equation, Shakespeare has created a dialectic between the extremes of control and free will that plays across the whole spectrum separating them. The witches have the same polyphony as the play and
its characters: now one note seems dominant in them, of simple, earthy humanity, now another, of supernatural power, now half-notes of equivocation
and mystery. But always the chord. Some critics have marveled at the complexity. Coleridge, following closely in Schlegel's footsteps (if not indeed
stealing his shoes), partially recognized the multiplicity, in the Sisters, of
classical Fates, Furies, and the sorceresses of Gothic and popular tradition.
Jeffreys suggests a mixture of witches, sorceresses, and Furies. Beyond these
labels are further layers of ambiguity—quite intentional on Shakespeare's
part, Harold Wilson believes.

Nicoll, so early sensitive to Shakespeare's paradoxes:

There is a land, says William Blake, where contraries are true, and that land may be found in Shakespeare's tragic art. The witches form the keynote, the very atmosphere, of *Macbeth*, and yet their power may be reasoned away, must, indeed, be reasoned away, if we are to understand the characters of the thane and his wife aright.

How much of the Sisters' mystery can we penetrate? How many of their powers to rouse, or influence, or control Macbeth can we know? If they are designed to be more than old women, how much more? Are they mad? Seeresses? Sorceresses? Demons? Fates? Furies? Projections of Macbeth's mind? Of all minds?—Archetypal symbols of untamed, dangerous, Dionysian forces? Of unspeakable things?

Interpretations from theatre and criticism can take us, step by step, some way toward the mystery of their relationship with Macbeth. I will consider as if in isolation various strains in their polyphony, but this is only to serve the purpose of discussion: the elements overlap, intertwine, fuse, dissolve into the whole.

THE SISTERS AS WOMEN

We can begin, at the surface level, with Bradley: "Not goddesses, or fates, or, in any way whatever, supernatural beings. They are old women, poor and ragged, skinny and hideous, full of vulgar spite . . ." Bradley sees them associated imaginatively with the magical powers, the supernatural "masters" and the Hecate that popular superstition envisioned, but "there is not a syllable . . . to imply that they are anything but women." They influence Macbeth, but do not determine his action: he must be free to choose and earn his fall in Bradley's concept of the tragedy—indeed, he may have chosen before the meeting with the Sisters.

When the Three are presented as old women in the theatre, they are usually visualized, in their four scenes, as Banquo sees—or thinks he sees—them at the first meeting:

> What are these,
> So wither'd and so wild in their attire,
> That look not like th' inhabitants o' th' earth,
> And yet are on't? Live you, or are you aught
> That man may question? You seem to understand me
> By each at once her choppie finger laying
> Upon her skinnie lips: you should be women,
> And yet your beards forbid me to interpret
> That you are so. (I, iii, 43–51)

Almost sexless "witches" like this bore a resemblance to figures in Shakespeare's world: crones no longer useful to society except as they could extort subsistence by threat or earn it by helpful "magic." The older English co-operative communities had taken some care of their aged; enclosures, and the withering of the manorial system, Thomas observes, led to the casting out of the poverty-stricken old, ugly, decrepit, diseased. For their physical condition alone they could easily be loathsome in the eyes of the healthy and well-fed; the extraordinary rancor these old and helpless ones provoked might also partly reflect, Briggs has suggested, an unconscious impulse toward revenge on parents.

Old women with no resources were particularly likely to "turn"—or be seen as—witches. The remarkable Reginald Scot, brave sceptic of witchcraft magic when it was not easy to be so (1584), provoker (with the Dutchman Johan Weyer) of King James' angry *Daemonology* (1597), describes their sort:

> Commonly old, bleare-eied, pale, fowle, and full of wrinkles; poore, sullen, superstitious . . . They are lean and deformed, shewing melancholie in their faces, to the horror of all that see them . . . These miserable wretches are so odious unto their neighbors, and so feared as few dare offend them, or denie them anie thing they ask: wherby they take upon them, yea, and sometimes thinke, that they can do such things as are beyond the abilities of human nature. (Chapter III)

Presented in the theatre on the "human" level, the Sisters have been charac-terised by Scot's kind of descriptives: grovelling, filthy, wretched, loathsome, perverse, obscene, sinister, repulsive, squeaking, gibbering, hideous, mal-formed. Here we first meet an issue central to the art of *Macbeth*—the aesthet-ics of horror. When is the ugly—or the terrible—physically, spiritually, too ugly? Too terrible? At what point does excess destroy illusion? Or fail it? Ingmar Bergman, looking back on his first spectacular staging of *Macbeth* (1944), thought it "too beautiful," apparently because it did not follow deeply enough the play's descents into its frightful, Dionysian underground to realize Shakespeare's test of the limits of aesthetic tolerance. The witches appear as the immediate symbol of that test.

In a specifically ugly "human" form, the Sisters convey a sense of the nastiness life has enforced on them, and of their helplessness against society except in any power they have—or imagine they have—to injure those who munch on food but give them nothing. Peter Hall (directing Paul Scofield, England, 1967) told his witches he wanted the feeling of the old women, wrapped in ragged paper, hideous, still, peculiar, that he would see in his walk along London's Embankment, or on the Bowery in New York—the withered old crones from whom men seemed instinctively to shrink—from the hair on the chin, from their disturbing cross-sexuality. "You are instinc-tive, animal—you release the sensuality, the drunkenness, the violence under-lying the action."

A director intent on denying supernatural influence to the witches may stipulate a rationale for their prophecies. Thus, in Theodore Komisarjevsky's "modern" *Macbeth* (England, 1933) three filthy old parasites emerged onto a scarred battlefield that the war had momentarily passed over, and, crouched under an abandoned howitzer, were busy looting the dead and dying, and even picking at a booted skeleton. They would linger in the background of the next scene, to overhear Duncan's order to honor Macbeth as Cawdor; this would "explain" their prophecy; as their later oracles would be "explained" in a different way. In Joan Littlewood's "modern" *Macbeth* (England, 1957), her witches, too, were battlefield molls, sneak-thieving from soldiers' corpses; and so were the sluts, obviously camp followers, in a contemporary German production. In Glasgow (1974) the Three scavenged grotesquely in shapeless chemical-warfare suits, "crawling, half-batrachian, half-bat." Peeling off their protective disguises, they emerged in tattered rags suggestive of corrupted flesh. Bergman, in his 1944 staging, made the witches at first mourning widows on a battlefield; one, turning mad, would seem to take on a lunatic's Cassandra-like gift of prophecy. In another realistic pattern, focusing on political oppression, (Canada, 1971), the witches became part of a grey mass of the suffering populace. They emerged from a swaying, faceless peasant crowd as two benign but demented old ladies and an indecent old man in woman's dress. A touch of madness in itself distances a Sister from normality, carrying the archetypal sense of lunatic clairvoyance, and so suggests at least some prescience in the prophecy to Macbeth. No kind of rationalization would do for Tyrone Guthrie (England, 1934): to play the first scene inevitably suggested to him that the witches had a governing influence on Macbeth's career; so he simply cut it.

THE SISTERS AS WITCHES

The craze to persecute "witches" caught fire in the fifteenth century and flamed across Europe into the seventeenth, partly, Trevor-Roper suggests, because it assuaged man's appetite for fear of the strange. Xenophobia is ever an anodyne for the anxiety of ignorant men; and learned men, too, who learn among other things to disguise it in subtle forms. Sartre has pointed out that it may reflect an unconscious Manicheanism: the dream that life is a battle between good and evil, and that if only evil can be eliminated, all will be well. Something of this may lie behind the simplistic criticism that sees *Macbeth* as a clearcut conflict between God and evil, God winning.

One very powerful force behind the witch-hunting craze in England was organized religion, because its thrust to monopoly was threatened. Rome had fought witchcraft because it competed with the magic the church dispensed through priestly intercession with holy figures. In England, with the Reformation, Catholic magic was publicly denied Englishmen who had depended on it; so they turned more than ever for supernatural help to the witches or warlocks, the social castaways they had driven to the occult trade, whom they now both feared and needed.

Here surfaces an important ambiguous element in the figures Shakespeare used. If we can refuse to remember how the play comes out, we must be ready to experience the three figures without preconceiving that they are *evil:* for witches in Shakespeare's time could be "good" as well as "bad." We will not see the Sisters urge Macbeth to any specifically immoral act; they will look into the future, promise him the good, warn him of the dangerous, try to *cheer up* his unhappy spirits. These were prime functions of the 'good' English witches of the period, very much in demand to counter the magic of "black" witches, and also to deal with the ordinary slings and arrows with which outrageous fortune continually bombarded Englishmen. Good old women might have "witchcraft" forced on them. Mother Sawyer of *The Witch of Edmonton*, modeled on an actual Elizabeth Sawyer tried and executed for witchcraft, begins as a very sympathetic, poor old innocent woman, driven to desperation by the suspicious abuse of well-off neighbors. She only submits to a pact with the devil when he threatens violence. To such women, whether suspected of devil-pact or not, the sick and troubled often came. These witches were called "cunning," or "wise."* Scot (V,9): "At this daie it is indifferent to saie in the English toong: She is a witch; or She is a wise woman." Thus Fabian, in *Twelfth Night* (III,iv,114), suggesting a medical diagnosis of Malvolio's distemper: "Carry his water to the wise woman".

Thus also in Heywood's *The Wise Woman of Hogsdon*, where the Wise Woman cites the medical and other specialties of her witch-colleagues:

> You have heard of Mother *Nottingham*, who for her time, was prettily well skill'd in casting the Waters: and after her, Mother *Bombye;* and then there is one *Hatfield* in Pepper-Alley, he doth pretty well for a thing that's lost. There's another in *Coleharbour*, is for Forespeaking: Mother *Phillips* of the *Banke-side*, for the weakness of the backe: and there's a very reverent Matron on Clerkenwell-Green, good at many things: Mistris *Mary* on the Banke-side, is for recting a figure: and one (what doe you call her) in *Westminster*, that practiseth the Booke and Key, and the Sive and the Sheares: and all doe well, according to their talent.

Some thoughtful Christians who saw witchcraft as wicked tried variously to come to terms with the help that witches gave to men. George Gifford (1593) was concerned about the witches' "curious art, either hurting or healing, revealing things secret or foretelling things to come." The witches might distract attention from their mission by such acts as killing swine, but their real purpose was to corrupt men—which they did sometimes by helping. Gifford had the usual corkscrew explanation for an all-powerful God's toleration of evil: in times of trouble, in times of doubt, God is likely to allow witches to run wild—for God uses the devil's acts and minions to test or punish humanity. But Gifford had to face facts:

> Some men reply that this is a common thing and well tried by experience, that many in great distress have been relieved and recovered by sending unto such

---

*See *The Merry Wives of Windsor* IV,v, 26, 68 (the wise woman of Brainford), and *King Lear* II,iv, 75 and III,ii, 13 and 41, where the Fool may be playing on the meanings of *wise*.

wise men or wise women, when they could not tell what should else become of them, and all that they had. Should not men take help when they can find it? Why do men go unto Physicians? Let it be granted that men find help by witches. Yet . . . it is for the most part a plague and token of God's displeasure, when he hath power granted him to heal: for it is a more heavy judgment, which the wicked world hath deserved, that he is suffered to heal . . .

Similarly, the Reverend Thomas Pickering, an enemy to witchcraft, had to acknowledge that if a man were in trouble, he would send to the local "wise" person for help. Pickering conventionally saw Satan at work, as an instrument of God, but he observed that while some bad witches used the devil's help "for doing hurt only," the "good" witch "doth use (Satan's) help for the doing of good only. This cannot hurt, torment, curse or kill, but only cure the hurts inflicted upon men or cattle by bad witches." Pickering's polemic, like Gifford's, obliged him to conclude that the good witches were worse than the bad, for endangering not men's bodies but their souls.

The documented multiplicity of early English "witch" incidents led Margaret Murray to champion the theory of a widespread "old religion," centering on a horned god, and a ritual of death and regeneration. This has been judged by other scholars as more poetry than truth; but that many "witches" existed then, and believed in—and were believed for—their powers, and perhaps the powers of "masters", seems indisputable. The belief has never died. A 1975 news item, reporting the one thousandth anniversary of the death of St. Walpurga, estimated that thousands of British and German witches would celebrate the millennial Walpurgisnacht with ancient rites. That these rites have been traditionally "unholy" has lent them the aura of such power that its very immensity required it to be declared illicit by authorities.

Shakespeare's contemporaries learned, in their desperate moments, that what seemed forbidden, *foul*, in old "cunning women" could bring fair help, as in plays like Lyly's *Mother Bombie*, in which the title character was such a "wise one." This old hag, almost a sister in appearance to *Macbeth*'s Sisters as Banquo described them, was called, the heroine says, "the good woman who yet never did hurt." More glamorous "cunning women" would appear in more fanciful plays, like *The Faithful Shepherdess* and *The Prophetess;* but their skills were cousin: to help and hurt, with magic charms and chants, to hover in the air, and to raise the thunder.

Unfortunately, in the known theatre history of *Macbeth* during its first two centuries, the Sisters would be played as "witches" and yet convey even less sense of significance in Macbeth's life than might simple old women. From Davenant's Restoration abortion of the play to some late stagings by Edmund Kean,* early in the nineteenth century, they function mainly as incidental ornaments. This was a period in retreat from some of the deepest insights of Shakespeare's drama. Stagings of all the great tragedies were "improved" by

---

*Hereafter "Kean" will refer to Edmund; Charles Kean will be identified by his full name.

censorship (*Othello, Hamlet*) and even outright adulteration (*Lear*), to protect
audiences of sensibility from "unrefined" experiences of mortality. *Macbeth*
suffered painfully from this improvement, as we will see, but nowhere more
than in the degradation of the Sisters, transformed from Shakespeare's uncanny images so evocative of guilty, greedy, buried impulse. In England,
the Sisters were customarily played by the unused comedians of the company
(the Porter was cut, as offending "refinement"). The Sisters had come to be
dressed, Hawkins, Kean's biographer, reported, "according to the popular
conception, in tall conical hats, mufflers under their chins, high-heeled boots
and scarlet kirtles, and the . . . crossing-sweeper's broom in their hands."
"Witches rouged up to the eyes, and wizards in jockey boots," the *Monthly
Mirror* complained. Davies was a rare defender of this practice against the
"old complaint of stage critics." Since all the tragic actors of a company were
needed elsewhere in the play, he pointed out, "none but the comic actors are
left . . . but I confess I do not see the propriety of the accusation. There is
in the witches something odd and peculiar, and approaching to what we call
humour . . . more suitable to our notions of comic than tragic action." Garrick may partly have been responsible for the corruption of this good man,
by making a joke of the Sisters. "Beggarly gammers," Oulton called them.
The *St. James Chronicle* (October 1773) scolded Garrick because his "comic
actors are permitted to turn a solemn incantation into a ridiculous farce for the
entertainment of the upper gallery. Every spectator must join in a wish to see
the witches seriously represented." Garrick is supposed to have intended to
try for awe and horror by planning to dress the Three as bearded magicians;
and Kemble later did try to stage them with the mystery they deserved: in both
cases popular demand overruled integrity.

The actor-managers might claim, in apology, that the Sisters' supernatural significance had long been reduced anyway by the continuance, since
Davenant, of the witches' *corps de ballet*, an idea perhaps inspired by the "Black
spirits and white, red spirits and gray" of the questionable IV, i song. In
Kemble's* time full fifty witches danced and sang; an 1864 production would
include twice as many. Tieck, visiting London in 1825, wished these choruses
could at least have projected some mystery, if not menace, as in Germany.
He was particularly annoyed by the conventional intrusion of Davenant's
musicale immediately after Duncan's murder:

> People in our country copied the scene in their production of that tragedy.
> It is totally superfluous. But it did at least not waste as much time as it does
> here in London where it becomes the most prominent of the play. One never
> finds out why enormously many witches of all ages and sizes appear on stage
> where they celebrate the triumph of their sabbath with multi-voiced singing,
> from soprano, alto, tenor to bass. One should at least expect the scene, in the
> manner of Reichard's [German] witches' choirs, to be a wild, screaming, mali-
> cious, horrifying jubilation. But no, these fifty characters (at least that many

*Hereafter "Kemble" will refer to John Philip; Fanny and Charles will be identified by name.

and among them some rather good-looking, charming ones) present a noble, artfully fashioned musical piece . . . And the Englishman . . . hears . . . without protest these wicked and mean creatures sing a long-winded concert, interrupting the tragedy for a long time with choral fugue, and church-like music, turning the theatre into a concert hall.

In 1833 Fanny Kemble could still complain that to act the Sisters "we have three jolly-faced fellows, whom we are accustomed to laugh at . . . in every farce . . . with (a) due proportion of petticoats . . . jocose red faces, peaked hats, and broomsticks."

Ultimately, sometimes under protest,* the Sisters would come into the theatre more than old women or comic caricatures of witches; they would learn to project the aura of danger that belongs to them. They are unquestionably endowed with some power more than mortal: they can see into Macbeth's future, however oracularly. Though they do not directly determine his actions, they enter intimately into the ambiguity of his motivation and behavior. To neutralize them is to empty some of the mystery from the play.

The theatre—and the imagining reader—must decide how the Sisters' uncanny powers are to be reflected in their appearance. Is Banquo's first vision of them—with "choppie fingers . . . skinnie lips . . . beards . . ." what the audience is intended to see? In IV,i Macbeth will call them *secret, black and midnight hags*. Is this description, or only epithet? Hag—or hegge— primarily meant, according to the OED's first two definitions, an evil spirit, daemon, or infernal being, in female form; or a woman supposed to have dealings with Satan and the infernal world. The meaning that has become common—an ugly, repulsive old woman, often with implications of viciousness, of maliciousness—is given third. Might Macbeth's *hags*, who can hover through thick air, who are invisible to such as Lenox, who, Macbeth will say, rise upon the air—might they change shape, color, image from scene to scene? As their concerns differ? Schlegel among others noted the contrast between their "low class" talk together, and their more elevated tones with Macbeth. Might they transform between one appearance and the next?

The only contemporary "report" we have of the Sisters' stage appearance in Shakespeare's time comes—if it can be trusted—from Simon Forman,

---

*Samuel Phelps, in 1847, did away with the Davenant claptrap, at the same time that William Charles Macready, playing in another theatre, included it. *John Bull* (October 4) complained of Phelps' cuts: "We must . . . protest against the omission of the glorious choruses . . . They are . . . so grand, so simple, so characteristic, so full of the spirit of the scene;—they have been so constantly associated with the play during a period of nearly two centuries; that to throw them aside is felt like a mutilation of the drama itself. Mr. Phelps has given some excellent comic effects to the appearances of the witches. But similar effects were given by Mr. Macready, and they are greatly enhanced by the magnificent performance of the music." Artistic scruple motivated the honorable Phelps when he produced the play, and the critical response was mainly in his favor; but when he played Macbeth opposite Faucit in 1864, at Drury Lane, the witches' corps was back. *The Daily News* (November 4): "The wild poetic grandeur of the drama is certainly diminished by the . . . hundred or more pretty singing witches, but . . . managers are bound to be practical, and Locke's music, with Middleton's words, is found to pay."

himself a very doubtful dealer in "magic," a charlatan astrologer-physician. His comments were presumably "found" in his diary two centuries later by an equally doubtful character, the scholar-rascal J. P. Collier, fondly remembered for his clumsy, condescending forgeries of other "found" historical-literary material. Collier may well have forged Forman's commentary.* It seems inept enough to carry his signature. But the stupidities in it might well have been Forman's alone.

Forman says he describes a *Macbeth* performance on Saturday, April 20, 1610; April 20 fell on a Friday that year. What Forman wrote about the other plays he mentions seeing doesn't consistently square with what we know of them; on *Macbeth* he seems to rely more on Holinshed than on Shakespeare, and sometimes on neither. He does not mention the first two scenes of the play, the first of which particularly, with its witches, might have been expected to interest him. He begins (I make him legible) with I, iii:

> . . . ther was to be observed firste howe Mackbeth and Bancko 2 nobles of Scotland Ridinge thorowe a wod there stode before them 3 women feiries or Nymphes . . . [later he calls them "ninnphes"]

The phrases seem almost pure Holinshed: "Passing thorough the woods . . . There met them three women . . . nymphs or feiries." We had better go back to the historian.

Holinshed's picture of the Three in his 1577 edition in no way resembles Banquo's word picture. They seem young rather than old, elaborately dressed (not "strange and wild"), nothing crone-like. We may wonder if Banquo sees what he describes—in his shock and bewilderment he is not certain:

> I' th' name of truth
> Are ye fantasticall, or that indeed
> Which outwardly ye show? (I,iii, 57–59)

For him to look at beautiful "feiries" and be made by magic gesture to see them old crones, as Titania must see handsomeness in an ass, would say something about the power of the Sisters, and about the archetype that lies behind them: of the female figure who, by the power of her person, position, or magic, leads men to destruction. In the theatre the witches have been played as beautiful sirens, notably at Edinburgh in 1965: three lithe, beautiful young blondes, clothed in flesh-colored body stockings so close fitting that the three seemed

---

*Among those for forgery: J. Q. Adams (ed. *Macbeth*, 1931) and S. A. Tannenbaum (*Shakespearean Scraps*). Against: J. Dover Wilson, R. W. Hunt (*RES*. July, 1947). The latter argue, rather ill-temperedly, that Forman's Shakespeare report was not necessarily a forgery; they do not prove it could not have been. I have examined the Diary at the Bodleian, and I believe a forgery was possible. It was just the kind of inefficient impudence that Samuel Schoenbaum shows Collier undertaking. A. L. Rowse has tried to rescue Forman's reputation from charlatanism with arguments such as this: true, on one of the occasions Forman was convicted of malpractice his patient died; but he might have died anyway. Q.E.D.

naked except for their green bikinis, and with knee-length silver-blue hair, squirmed obscenely through floating smoke drifts. The director's conception, he said, came from the art and writing of Shakespeare's period. He wanted his Sisters evil and blasphemous, "creatures half supernatural and half mortal." Hiroshi Akutagawa, a Japanese Macbeth, told Peter Milward he would have liked his witches to be young and beautiful women—but for a different reason. He felt that such witches, personable, intelligent, seeming trustworthy as they hailed Macbeth through the thunder, could seem much more terrible to contemporary audiences. Thomas Heywood, in his re-telling of the Macbeth story in his *Hierarchie of Blessed Angels*, says Macbeth and Banquo met:

> (in a dark grove) three Virgins wondrous faire
> As well in habit as in feature rare . . .
> The first did curtsie low, her vaile* unpinn'd . . .

These would seem more to resemble the trio pictured in Holinshed. Clorin in *The Faithful Shepherdess* (c.1608) would probably have looked so. Sisters of seductive beauty might enhance the fantasies in which learned men dressed—or undressed—witches, the masks of ugly age dreamed away.

The first Shakespeare illustration we have, in Rowe's 1709 edition, shows the Sisters, in IV,i, as rather nondescript figures, not noticeably hairy about the chins, old but hardly crones, dressed in simple robes. They carry the wands that were often their props on the stage, and the drawing may represent theatre tradition at moments not contaminated by Davenant's infusions. Shakespeare has given us no word picture, to help us, of the *other three witches* directed to enter in IV,i and join the ritual. This trio may be a visual punctuation of the witches' chant of *double, double*, duplicating—or contrasting with—the Sisters.** I have copies of nineteenth-century drawings of two sets of witches that may represent a tradition: the evil-looking original trio (men), and a beautiful young three. This makes visual what a mixed three in the theatre has suggested, when two are ugly, one a comely blonde lass: foul and fair. The beautiful young one may be an idiot, perhaps possessed, herself foully fair, as in the Ian McKellen-Judi Dench staging (Trevor Nunn's second *Macbeth*, 1976).***

If Shakespeare intended the witches to have the power of transformation—as for instance Maudlin has in Jonson's *Sad Shepherd*—they might be imagined

---

Vaile: generally carries the same meaning as a veil for the face, though the OED cites the use, in 1634, of a "vaile to cover their privities."

**The Folio, in IV,i, specifies for music the *Black spirits etc.* The first words in Middleton to this music are addressed to these colored spirits. They are not directed to enter in Shakespeare; they exist in the text only in brief words and music, though adulterators from Davenant on would take them as an excuse for a ballet. The first lines, about *invisible* spirits, could fit Shakespeare's scene—see the discussion for IV,i.

***I will refer to this as the McKellen staging, to distinguish it from Nunn's 1975 *Macbeth*.

as shifting from fair to foul, and back. Gordon Craig,† who soaked himself in the play for many years before and after his designs were used for it (U.S., 1928), scribbled a marginal note some ten years after the production: "The witches can and do disguise themselves . . . They have many disguises, and use them in this play." This must be speculation; the text does not order it.

Some clue to the essential ambiguity and equivocation of the witches, marking them as something more than mortal, lies in Shakespeare's terms for them. Named "witch" in stage directions, and by a rump-fed ronyon of a housewife (I,iii), they call themselves "weyward sisters" (I,iii,32). To Banquo and Macbeth they are both *weyward* (I,v,9; II,i,20) and *weyard* (III,i,2; III,iv,132; IV,i,137). Since Theobald's edition, the adjective is commonly tamed to *weird*, by analogy with the noun *wyrd*, which, as early as *Beowulf*, meant a kind of Fate, synonym for the Parcae. *Weyward*—less so *weyard*—is unmistakeably two-syllabled, as it seems to need to be to scan in *Macbeth's* lines— though, certainly, given the play's syncopated rhythms, it is sometimes meeter not to judge by meter. Editors who change the word in Theobald's fashion decide that *weird* is to be pronounced dissyllabically. "Wee-urd." It works. But why assume such a persistent variation of a simple word? The playwright's consistent *weyward*—*weyard* are the only examples of this usage noted by the OED.; they are quite possibly deliberate; Shakespeare may have coined them as a sound-meaning pun, crossing weird and wayward—the latter Hecate's characterization for Macbeth (III,v). No use of *weird* is reported by Spevack in any other place in Shakespeare: *wayward* occurs in many plays and poems. *Wayward* fits the *Macbeth* fabric marvellously: thus the OED definitions:

> One— Disposed to go counter to the wishes or advice of others, or to what is
> reasonable; wrongheaded, intractable, self-willed; forward, perverse.
> Two—Capriciously wilful; conforming to no fixed rule or principle of conduct;
> erratic.

Something of this quality of uncertainty, of the uncontrolled, of reckless forces at work, vibrates in the witches and infects the air men breathe. *Wayward* seems almost to define the *Macbeth* world: as unreasonable, perverse, capricious, non-conforming to fixed rule or principle as the elusive, ambiguous Sisters.

To enhance the aura of the uncanny proper to their prophetic power, the theatre has often framed it in an ambience of mystery. When the Sisters were presented as fortune-tellers, as in a Russian production (Baku, 1936), their intimate relationship with the inexplicable was reflected in the wayward world they entered. They came shadowed in the unknown, into a half-lit heath of uncanny shapes: tortured trees with branches striated into cobwebs,

---

†Hereafter "Craig" will refer to Edward Gordon Craig; Edward Carrick Craig and Hardin Craig will be clearly identified.

or twistedly suggesting a hand of fate. Under Max Reinhardt's (Germany, 1916) yellow-grey, tattered sky, angular forms conveyed a sense of animal skeletons, obscene, naked. *Blasted heath*, Banquo will call the witch country— in the imagination, or on the stage, always more blasted than heath, fit for strangeness. Into it the Sisters may suddenly emerge as from nowhere, with the lifting of smoke, cloud, mist—whatever is used for *fog and filthy air* here and in III,v, when Hecate sees the *foggy cloud*.

In the mid-nineteenth century, in England, Phelps and Charles Kean (1853) used an almost archetypal stage device—gauze scrims—to suggest a thickened ambience in which the Sisters seemed suspended, and from which they emerged. The gauzes, with many folds, drawn up or let down, fold by fold, by invisible threads, served as a thinning scrim: with the light behind it, the air seemed slowly to clear and reveal the witches; with the light before, the air curdled around them, and they vanished. With such gauzes, in their brief first appearance, they might show as vague silhouettes, their faces clouded or hidden until I,iii, when they burst upon the audience as they would upon Macbeth.

Phelps' witches seem to have risen like chthonic figures into the murk from the trap; light poured up from below to bring their features into relief. To a German observer (Theodor Fontane), these Sisters, dark, vague shapes against a darker background streaked with grey drifts streaming in the wind, seemed real apparitions; the scene passed quickly, startling the audience without giving it time to orient itself. Henry Irving's (England, 1889) Three were sudden apparitions above a black and dismal heath, poised "in a lurid and murky sky brindled with unearthly colours. A devil's own rainbow . . . every hue blood-curdling and suggestive of brimstone" *(Evening Post)*. In the Maurice Evans-Judith Anderson (U.S., 1941) opening, silhouettes were projected against a translucent screen, distorted, oversized, with arms elongated and fingers clawlike, floating. Sometimes the Sisters have been no more than shadows, projected on wall or backdrop.

Uncanny movements of the witches themselves, as in a mingling and separation of their forms, in relation to the earth and air, has conveyed an extra-human dimension to realistic figures. In a modern Russian production, as the curtain rose, they lay, tightly against each other and the ground, seeming a solid mass, their limbs barely moving from the center, octopus-like. Little by little their outlines emerged. The First Witch's hand rose into the air, a fist, then a claw, predatory. Then she straightened, a dirty, ugly old woman, in rags, with a beard, moving to a kind of animal chirring from the other two. Sounds begin to come from the first's mouth, strange, jerky, guttural, the words flying out suddenly, like explosives. Then the others, first swarming about her legs, sinister, repulsive, rose to join her in a wild, round dance.

In Germany (1966) the three crawled in like toads from corners of the stage, met and leaped into a single, grotesque silhouette; their words issued from this swaying, amorphous mass.

THE SISTERS AS SORCERESSES

Are the Sisters still a further remove from the human, able not only to predict, but also to interfere with man's—perhaps nature's—behavior?* The magic of sorcerers had been mighty in serious plays up to the time *Macbeth* was written. Respected necromancers might conjure competitively, as in *Friar Bacon and Friar Bungay*—though repentance must follow heretic magic. Wizardry might service megalomanic power, as in *Faustus;* though the invocation of the devil is likely to lead the sorcerer to damnation. Sorcerers would be treated satirically, as in *The Alchemist*, or romantically, as in *The Tempest*. In spite of laws against practitioners (to be discussed shortly), the practice of sorcery was common in Shakespeare's time, and belief in its powers was strong among the credulous in England, even in the highest circles. Some incidents made history. Forman largely built his reputation on his witchcraft; among other adventures, he was implicated in the mysterious death of Sir Thomas Overbury because the Countess of Essex and her confidante employed him to secure, by sorcery, the love of two noblemen. Queen Elizabeth had much respected John Dee, master of a magic glass which he claimed could raise apparitions, and of a holy stone, given him by an angel. When a pierced wax effigy of Elizabeth was found, Dee was summoned to protect the queen with counter-magic. Some twentieth century historians have been impressed by Dee's contributions in mathematics, geography and astronomy, by his familiarity with Vitruvius, and by his capacious library; but coupled with his learning was a very naive faith in magic and in his own magical powers. Dee traveled to the continent with Edward Kelley, and was banished as a charlatan from country after country until he came under the protection of Count Rosenberg of Bohemia (no relation), for whom Dee thoughtfully predicted kingship. Eventually discredited, ordered from Prague by the Pope, Dee made his way back to England. When James was king, Dee petitioned to be cleared of the "slander" that he was, or had been, a conjurer, or invocator of devils. James looked into the case, and denied the petition.**

But James' favorite, the Duke of Buckingham, notoriously employed a sorcerer, John Lambe. Lambe was imprisoned for invoking and entertaining certain evil and impious spirits, when it was proved that he made apparitions emerge from his magic glass. He treated clients while in prison; Buckingham consulted him regularly, and Lambe was believed to corrupt chaste women to serve the duke's pleasure. He himself was charged with seducing an eleven-year-old-girl. He was enthusiastically hated by the populace, and finally killed by a mob; the Duke was assassinated soon after, and this couplet circulated:

> The shepheards struck, the sheep are fled,
> For want of Lambe the Wolfe is dead.

*A popular image of the scope of witch-power is reflected in the full title of Daneau's work (Englished 1575), *A Dialogue of Witches, in foretime called Lottellers, and now commonly called Sorcerers.*

**Dee and Forman are thought to be the models for the *Alchemist's* Subtle, Kelley for its Face.

As Forman, Dee, and Lambe were consulted by the lofty, Englishmen of lower degree commonly sought help, as I observed above, from the run of "cunning" men and women with magic to dispense in matters of love, illness, money, and threats from "bad" witches. *Macbeth*'s Sisters, sounding the note of sorcery, could plausibly be understood to have some of the supernatural powers claimed by the men and women whom Shakespeare's spectators knew by reputation or perhaps consulted.

Some magic the Sisters certainly work. Stage directions stipulate that they—or their masters—can make Macbeth see apparitions, silent and speaking. Shakespeare had used similar legerdemain years before, in *Henry VI* (Part II, 1,iv) where the witch Margery Jordan and a conjurer raise a spirit that utters oracular prophecies which come true. *It thunders and lightens terribly*, the Folio directs, when that spirit rises; and storms again when it departs. "A witch or hegg", William West (1594) was sure, " . . . thinketh she can designe what manner of evil thing soever, either by thought or imprecation, as to shake the air with lightnings and thunder." The thunder that accompanies every entrance of *Macbeth*'s witches may seem to be of their making: and the opening barrage of questions:

> When shall we three meet again?
> In thunder, lightning, or in rain? (I,i, 1–2)

could signalize the Sisters' control of natural forces: so that as Witch 1 mentions each weather she could produce it, as she may activate the winds in I,iii. The theatre here regularly furnishes the invoked thunder and lightning; brave producers, like Charles Kean, provided the rain too.

Always the possibility exists that the witches are using their power to create illusions, even with their storms. *Juggling*, Macbeth will complain of the Sisters in V,vi; Pickering defined this witches' operation as "the deluding of the eye with some strange sleight done above the ordinary course of nature"— so that a man is made to think he sees something he does not. Banquo cannot be sure his eyes are not deceived. Macbeth—and we—sometimes cannot tell hallucination from reality. Control of appearance was made visual in the Charlton Heston staging (U.S., 1975), when, at the opening, only the Sisters' voices were heard, unplaced, over the corpse-strewn battlefield. Then, slowly, the bodies of three slain soldiers began to twitch, and move, and the unlocalized witch-voices began to inhabit the three corpses. These came alive, to provide human integuments for the energizing witch-spirits.

One specific magic the Sisters unquestionably control is the power to *vanish*. Stamm has observed that they are directed to do so only when Macbeth is present, as if to emphasize a special relationship to him; in any case, this capacity to defy spatial logic authenticates their powers. Perhaps in Shakespeare's Globe the witches appeared as if floating in air, as Coghill believes; certainly by Davenant's time,

Hover through the fog and filthy air

was a cue to fly them out. Other spectacular *coups de theatre* have accented their power of magical disappearance. They have vanished in smoke, or stage fog, in blinding lightning flashes, or in the instant dark of blackouts. In one English staging the Sisters seemed suspended like horrible masks, the incantations coming from their disembodied heads, that disappeared into darkness. The Meiningen (Germany, 1867) Sisters, creeping and cringing along the ground, in grey rags, resembled so much the rocks among which they slithered that they seemed to appear by magic when they moved, and to disappear by stopping. Baty's mouse-grey witches (France, 1942) similarly merged into the grim walls of his fortress set. In the Craig-designed *Macbeth* (1928) his gaunt witches appeared by throwing back their cloak camouflages, and disappeared inside them. Caspar Wrede (Norway, 1972) fitted huge batlike wings to his witches, who "vanished" by turning and becoming great boulders. By a skillful use of a trap (England, 1972), one witch seemed to evanesce leaving only a heap of rags on the floor. The ground of the stage itself has been made to stir for the witches—Becks' promptbook reports undulating ground-pieces in the mid-nineteenth century: a kind of visual metaphor for Macbeth's thought that stones have been known to move. This was exploited in the Hall-Scofield *Macbeth*. The whole stage floor was covered with a blood-red rug; as the witches approached their last chant in I,i, the rug began to ripple, as if the earth itself trembled; the Sisters ended their last line, *Hover through the fog and filthy air*, with a high, windy sigh, and, as the air darkened, they dropped into the folds of the earth-rug; meanwhile the last breathy note was sustained by shapes (that turned out to be Duncan's soldiers) struggling out of the obscurity. Though vanishing *down* presents a textual problem: Francis Gentleman, the eighteenth-century pedant who so aptly wrote under the name of *Dramatic Censor* (we will meet him again), complained in his notes to the Bell edition of the practice of using traps here: "A great breach in propriety . . . to make them *sink*, after saying *hover*."

In the theatre, as in criticism, the temptation has been to see the Sisters as malicious only, unmodified by the ambiguity of their apparent favorable interest in Macbeth. They are often presented as instruments of evil, if not as evil itself. They have struck at the human enemy through effigies: a man doll is needled or sliced through; recondite magic hexes are fashioned to the burning of incense; sinister gestures promise wickedness. In the Roman Polanski film (1971), two crones and a dim-witted beautiful but bedraggled blonde girl (fair and foul) stolidly dug a hole in the sand, muttered their lines like a spell, and buried a dagger, a hangman's noose, and a severed hand.

If, as seems likely, the Sisters' scene that begins the play is for them the ending of some kind of witches' sabbat,* they may be ornamented with the

---

*I use the word for convenience; as Kittredge noted, it was apparently not yet in general use. See OED: Sabbat, 1652, sabbath, 1660.

means of their orgy, they may be marked with blood: if not battlefield blood, perhaps the kind we will see them dip into later. They may be curiously dressed.

The evil sorceresses in Jonson's *Masque of Queenes* were, Jonson wrote, by Inigo Jones

> all differently attir'd: some with rattes on theyr heads; some on they'r shoulders; others with oyntment-potts at their girdles; all with spindells, timbrells, rattles, or other veneficall instruments, making a confused noise with strange gestures (Jones devising).

Jonson himself added the kind of objects that Shakespeare will describe in IV,i, and that may accompany the Sisters in the first scene, especially if they convey the sense of a sabbat underway or just completed. Reed suggests that Jonson drew his research on witchcraft mainly from Greco-Roman and Continental sources; but the visual imagery has a homey quality. Jonson: "I prescribed them theyr properties of vipers, snakes, bones, herbes rootes, and other ensignes of their Magick." The overt malice of Jonson's hags, by contrast, emphasizes the apparent benign intentions of Shakespeare's. Jonson's witches wanted to do what Macbeth, in desperation (IV,i), would be ready to demand of his Sisters:

> Let us disturb (peace) then; and blast the light;
> Mixe Hell with Heaven; and make Nature fight
> Within herself; loose the whole henge of things;
> And cause the Endes runne back into theyr springs.

THE SISTERS AS SATANIC AGENTS

There is almost a suggestion by Jonson that the witches represent a third force, apart from heaven and hell; and something of this ambiguity is certainly in *Macbeth*. Sometimes, however, the Sisters are assumed to be unmistakably servants of Satan. He and his hell were a relatively late link to witchcraft that emerged in the Middle Ages. Belief in the magic that would be associated with witches is as old as man's fears and dreams of superhuman or antihuman power—fears and dreams easily displaced onto foreign elements in a society. Norman Cohn notes that the second-century Christian minority in Rome, because it denied the values of the dominant society, was suspected of unspeakable secret practices, including child-killing, cannibalism, and orgies. Once dominant, Christian society could in turn accuse a splinter group like the Waldensians of similar erotic debauchery, infanticide, and cannibalism. This manifestation of society's obsessive fears found convenient shape in Satan. The name, originally meaning "adversary," or "one who plots against," was in the earlier part of the Old Testament associated with human enemies, only later attached to angel figures who tempted men and shamed them before God. Personifying evil in an imagined supernatural adversary trying to infect men and women from without proved a welcome technique for disembarrassing humanity of its antisocial impulses within: so Satan, with his growing legion of subsidiary devils, became a popular and useful enemy. Given the dialectic pattern of human perception, he was magnified to become the adversary of God as of mortals. In the either-or climate of medieval theology, any apparent antisocial behavior could be sensed as serving the prince of darkness in defiance of the Almighty.

Demons were thought by the credulous to be abroad everywhere, in millions. Practitioners of witchcraft—especially the women—were commonly believed to serve the demons, or be served by them: and some later scholars, among them Curry and Walker, determined to see a good-evil Christian-oriented dichotomy in the play, take it for granted that *Macbeth*'s Sisters are instruments of darkness. So did Glen Byam Shaw,* who directed the Laurence Olivier-Vivian Leigh *Macbeth* (England, 1955). He observed that the Sisters first appeared descending from air to earth (Shaw flew the witches), then on earth, and a third time underground, "in fact in hell . . . preparing a hell-broth." Diabolical as they were, Shaw saw them as yet strangely wonderful— "because anything evil is always fascinating and wonderful in some way." His witches were far too evil and intent on destruction to laugh or cackle. But they themselves could not destroy, they were not Fates; that would, Shaw felt—as have many others—destroy the tragedy. Their own stature had to be tragic; as servants of hell, they were "condemned souls."

One reason, very relevant to *Macbeth*, why, in Shakespeare's time, the minions of Satan were expected to be female rather than male is noted caustically by L'Estrange Ewen, after massive searches into their history: learned men agreed that the Devil was the tutor of witchcraft, and that females picked up the lessons more quickly being "more credulous, ambitious, lustful, impressionable, illogical, impulsive, weaker."† Ewen adds, drily, of this chauvinism, "Early opinions of women on this view are not recorded." Women-as-witches served the Dionysian fantasies of proper witchhunters, who spread denunciations of the old women's orgies, and these became material for drama. *Macbeth* will use, as one mask for the play's deep-lying association of sexuality with violence and death, some popular conceptions of the witches' readiness for debauchery.

---

*Hereafter Glen Byam Shaw will always be so identified; George Bernard will be G. B. Shaw or Shaw.

†Scot (Book 12), examining the "art of fascination" by which witches were supposed to control ordinary humans, notes how women were believed able quickly to develop powerful charges of emotion—anger, fear, love, hate—to overpower their victims. Before his own sceptical conclusion, Scot cites an "authority": "For by hate (saith *Vairus*) entereth a fierie inflammation into the eie of man, which being violentlie sent out by beams and streames, &c: infect and bewitch those bodies against whome they are opposed. And therefore he saith (in the favour of women) that that is the cause why women are oftener found to be witches than men. For (saith he) they have such an unbrideled force of furie and concupiscence naturallie, that by no means it is possible for them to temper or moderate the same. So as upon everie trifling occasion, they (like brute beasts) fix their furious eies upon the partie whom they bewitch. Hereby it commeth to passe, that whereas women having a mervellous fickle nature, what greefe so ever happeneth unto them,

Men found it possible to believe, Scot notes, in a witches' ointment that could

> pearse inwardly. By this means in a moone light night they seem to be carried in the aire, to feasting, singing, dansing, kissing, culling, and other acts of venerie, with such youthes as they love and desire most.

The respectable William West, in attacking a typical witch for her shameful pleasure, seemed to leak hints of envy: she would "spend all night with her sweet hart [Satan] in playing, sporting, banquetting, dauncing, daliance, and diverse other devilish . . . and lewd [sports]." In these hot fantasies, Satan was generally imagined the witches' primary lover, in many curious oral, anal, and genital excitements. True, Satan was known to make himself a succubus to seduce males, as well as an incubus to violate females (he apparently scorned homosexuality as not nice), but women were his primary delight. Aquinas, impressed by Satan's astonishing potency with the multitudes of witches supposed to pleasure him, theorized that he managed by discharging as an incubus the sperm he took in as a succubus; the thoughtful King James [*Daemonologie*] sided with those who thought the devil squeezed generative fluid from the sexual organs of dead men in order to carry on so strenuously with the females who served him.

Farnham argues, from intensive research, that women thought to be uncanny, under whatever names—fairies, weirds, weird-elfes, sibils, furies, nymphs—were, like the "hegges" discussed earlier, all considered demons or evil angels. As such, their influence over Macbeth would be oblique; they could tempt him, but not control him.

There is, in fact, no evidence that the Sisters have made a pact with the devil—one requirement of formal discipleship, as Shumaker has observed. *Macbeth* offers no confirmation, explanation, or rationalization of any demonological scheme. However, in Shakespeare's time, witchhunters and the gullible could assume, especially for the purpose of persecution, a tacit compact between witches and their devil-masters; and the playwright, without allowing this possibility to dominate the image of his Sisters, could include

---

immediatlie all peceableness of mind departeth; and they are so troubled with evill humors, that out go their venomous exhalations, ingendred thorough their ilfavoured diet, and increased by meanes of their pernicious excrements, which they expell. Women are also (saith he) monethlie filled full of superfluous humors, and with them the melancholike bloud boileth; whereof spring vapors, and are carried up, and conveied through the nosethrels and mouth, &c; to the bewitching of whatsoever it meeteth. For they belch up a certeine breath, wherewith they bewitch whomsoever they list. And of all other women, leane, hollow eied, old, beetlebrowed women (saith he) are the most infectious. Marie he saith, that hot, subtill, and thin bodies are most subject to be bewitched, if they be moist, and all they generallie, whose veines, pipes, and passages of their bodies are open. And finallie he saith, that all beautifull things whatsoever, are soone subject to be bewitched; as namelie goodlie yoongmen, faire women, such as are naturallie borne to be rich, goodlie beasts, faire horsses, ranke corne, beautifull trees, &c. Yea a freend of his told him, that he saw one with his eie breake a pretious stone in peeces. And all this he telleth as soberlie, as though it were true. And if it were true, honest women maie be witches, in despight of all inquisitors: neither can anie avoid being a witch, except shee locke hir selfe up in a chamber."

it as a minor allusive note in their polyphony by giving them animal familiars.

As scholars have noted, in animal form demons were thought by some Elizabethans to serve witches—and vice versa. Jonson's witches chant a Charme—a charming one—implying this:

> The Owl is abroad, the Bat, and the Toade,
> And so is the Cat-a-Mountaine;
> The Ant and the Mole sit both in a hole,
> And Frog peepes out o' the fountayne.

Macbeth's Sisters are alert for calls, amid the sounds of storm and battle, from their familiars. First Witch answers to the offstage cry of a cat—is it a mew? a love cry? a howled summons? (when the *brinded cat* mews thrice in IV,i, the time for ritual will be near):

> I come, Gray-malkin. (13)

Folio then directs, before their final chant—

> *All:* Paddock calls anon: (14)

Is this Toad? Frog? (or Hedge-pig, as in IV,i?) Impatiently summoning one or all of the Sisters (*Anon*, of course, then meant "at once")? Modern editions since Hudson (1909) often break the speech, putting a period after *calls* and giving *Anon* to Witch 3. She could be answering her familiar, Harpier, the owl—the *obscure bird*, often heard to cry, that *clamor'd the livelong night* of Duncan's murder, startling Lady Macbeth at the very moment of the act; that will again, Witch 3 will say in the IV,i orgy, cry

> 'tis time, 'tis time.

In the theatre, if the Sisters suggest a demoniac link, each may seem to refract the animal nature of her familiar.

THE SISTERS AS FATES

Once an Evil One of any system is involved, Macbeth may be no longer merely awakened to wickedness, or roused to it, or influenced by it. As suggested above, when supernatural force intervenes, the hero's will to act diminishes, in favor of degrees of slavery to fate. Is this power, too, in the hands of the Sisters? Are they Fates? As executive agents of Satan's malice, or of some archetypal or mythic force as represented by Hecate? They engage in no contest with divinity, as would befit Satan's servants, their only adversary seemingly man himself. They—and Hecate—never mention God or Satan, nor does any stipulation link them or the secret "masters" to the Christian Enemy. The main notes they sound are from an "elder world."

"The Weird Sisters are the Norns of Scandinavian mythology," Kittredge declared firmly, accepting Holinshed's impression of "goddesses of destinie."

> They were not ordinary witches or seeresses . . . not hags in the service of the
> devil . . . (but) great powers of destiny, great ministers of fate.

Kittredge argued that Shakespeare made them witches to bring them within
the range of his audience's beliefs and experiences; but adds, almost as if they
have a life of their own, and power to transform: "If they choose to wear the
garb of witches for a time, that is their own affair." (An older argument that
they matched the three Norns because the first of both trios dealt with the
past, the second with the present, and the third with the future, offered neatness; but casual examination shows it not relevant to Shakespeare's three, who
do not follow the pattern.)

If the Sisters are accepted as shaping as well as knowing Macbeth's destiny,
and the tragedy is, as Kittredge saw it, "inevitably fatalistic," then the witchcraft must seem hostile, since Macbeth and his Lady are terribly destroyed.
Then—though the text gives less warrant for this—they can loosely be regarded as Furies too, torturing the guilty whom, as Fates, they have made
malefactors.

Schiller, in his romanticized translation, frankly made his witches malicious
destiny figures. They do not only seek revenge on those who insult them; they
deliberately corrupt poor, cheerful, hardworking men—as they do Macbeth—
because they hate human happiness. They recognize that Macbeth is just
and good, but "the misery of the good and the fall of the fair is shouted with
joy by the powers of hell." Charles Lamb accepted this kind of image of the
Sisters:

> [They] originate deeds of blood, and begin bad impulses in man. From the
> moment that their eyes met with Macbeth's, he is spellbound. That meeting
> sways his destiny. He can never break the fascination. [They] have power over
> the soul.

In France, Ducis (1783), always ready to take Shakespeare's milk for Gaul,
personified this fatefulness by reducing the Sisters to one Scandinavian
sorceress, who, happening to find herself in the highlands, avoids homesick-
ness, and keeps in practice, by turning Scots to evil.

The most obvious theatrical technique for suggesting the Sisters' fatefulness, staged in Germany as early as the late-eighteenth century, and elsewhere frequently since, was to shadow all Macbeth's doing—and even Lady
Macbeth's—with the presence, seen or felt, of the witches. They may hover
in the background as Macbeth gets the news of his new honors, or when
Lady Macbeth invokes the spirits; and from then on, as the protagonists
stumble toward doom, the Sisters, or their shadows, may be seen lurking,
fawning, stroking, whispering; or hovering on high, to suggest a kind of super-
power. Often their voices may be heard. The witches, as Fates, have cackled,
or otherwise let the audience know, by ironic sounds, how foolish are mortals
to imagine they can control their own destiny. James Hackett (U.S., 1916)
used recurrent witch-laughter in his productions because he felt that, as

symbolizing the dominating evil of witchcraft, it gained sympathy for Macbeth. Other intimations of the Sisters' presence have also been suggestive of a supernatural shaping of Macbeth's world. Edward Carrick Craig* (England, 1932) gave one witch a repetitive drumbeat different from the rhythms of the soldiers' drums, and the reprising of this beat, implying an echo of Macbeth's heartbeat under stress, aimed at merging fatefulness with character. Bergman's (1948) witches, when not part of the action, became immobile, grew into the scenery, suggesting that they were part of the destiny of experience.

Fateful Sisters have also mingled directly in the play in various ways. In the Christopher Plummer *Macbeth* (Canada, 1962) realistic crones, playing battlefield ghouls, opened the play dragging in the bleeding captain, unconscious under their spell, but being primed to relate his story. They were not merely to foretell Macbeth's assumption of kingship; they were beginning to arrange it. Coghill found the scene bloodcurdling.

Sometimes the witches, in disguise, have infiltrated the body of performances, actively manifesting their influence. One witch in an English *Macbeth* (1948) reappeared as Lady Macbeth's Gentlewoman. In Norway (1972) the three slid into the roles of Seyton and the murderers. They were dressed as noble ladies at Stratford, Connecticut (1973), moving out of their places in a dumb-show-prologue court scene to become suddenly scheming witches—the voice of the first changing oddly from a social chirp to a malevolent croak. (The play opened with a mime of Duncan leading the court in religious rites; the overtly worshipful witch-ladies, changing to their own ritual, made a mockery of the orthodox rites.) Three elegantly costumed men were "Sisters" and more in Ellis Rabb's *Macbeth;* they seemed able to take on any identity. Edgar Reynolds remembers a chilling effect when, by raising or lowering the hood of a cloak, one of them could suddenly become the bleeding captain, or Ross, or some other pivotal figure.

Symbolically, the fateful power of the witches has been suggested by the presence behind them of looming images of destiny. For the Lionel Barrymore *Macbeth* (U.S., 1921), Robert Edmond Jones swathed the Sisters in crimson—red and midnight hags—fronted them with birdlike masks, and hung behind them three mammoth silver vizards that presided brooding over their witchcraft, in a vast stage that seemed infinite in depth. Somewhat similarly the Michael Redgrave *Macbeth* (England, 1947; U.S., 1948) "double-doubled" the Sisters: three realistic, gibbering, squeaking old crones—Redgrave said the intention was to make them loathsome, but awesome and dignified—were backed by three tall, rigid masked figures, apparently male, seemingly symbolic of the supernatural powers of which the witches were only reflections. In Germany (1959) the hideous Sisters seemed themselves to wear masks; but

---

*He is in fact Edward Anthony Craig; but because he did not want to trade on the fame of his father, Gordon Craig, his professional name in the theatre was Edward Carrick; and he here permits me to designate him by this compromise.

when they turned, they could be seen to be their own doubles—their true faces were apple-cheeked, they wore the witch masks on the backs of their heads. In another doubling mode, three Czech Sisters (1963) shifted between young girlish appearances and sudden transformations marked by spasmodic, haglike speech, grimace and gesture.

THE SISTERS AS PROJECTIONS OF THE MIND

What if the Sisters have no objective identity at all, are only manifestations of Macbeth's inward experience? Then, much more, Macbeth's character becomes his destiny. His will is free. He creates his own oracles. That the witches were "but the personified suggestions of (Macbeth's) mind" was suggested at least as early as Maginn; that they were partly or wholly "projections of Macbeth's evil thoughts, objective presentations of his inward being" was proposed by a critic in the *National Review* (1863) and by some twentieth-century scholars (e.g. E. K. Chambers, Lucas, Nicoll, Pack). But then why do the Sisters appear to Banquo also? Since he is an important—and fated—beneficiary of their prophecy, he has sometimes been conceived as being, like Macbeth, the kind of character to whom the Sisters are drawn, hence as sharing the covert impulses which would evoke their projection. The *National Review* critic noted Banquo's harping on the idea of his children becoming king as evidence of "evil intentions"; and concluded

> The weird Sisters are but outward manifestations of the evil thoughts conceived and fermenting in the brains of Banquo and Macbeth: both high in station, both generals in the king's army, both friends, and both nourishing evil wishes . . . The devils that haunt us and tempt us come out of ourselves, like the weird sisters of Macbeth.

To imply in the theatre that the Sisters exist in Macbeth's mind—and Banquo's—as psychological rather than objective agents, actors have sometimes, while the witches stood aside, spoken to empty air, as if partly at least creating the images that will prophecy to them. Relevantly, a pre-Shakespearean version of Macbeth's story, by George Buchanan, suggested that Macbeth dreamed the witches; Macbeths have sometimes so done in the theatre, particularly in IV, i.

In Freudian terms, the witches could be projections of inner images of the powerful female-mother-figure who suborns the male, driving or luring him to his own destruction. More will be said about this, particularly in the discussions of Lady Macbeth; for now the Sisters themselves, whose femaleness dominates the male side of them, can be seen as immediate visual symbols of mysterious, primeval, but ambiguous feminine influence. Macbeth may be thought to evoke them as screens on which he projects his deep impulse to suffer by calling for the doom-laden oracles. Their very Threeness—there is much of three in *Macbeth*—reflects their equivocation. Veszy-Wagner senses the phallic triad; and he sees the *fair-foul* dialectic as implying that women, who should be fair, are foul—mother, wife, even grandmother (the crones), so that the son's guilty incestuous wishes can be blamed, not on the man, but on woman, especially when so caricatured and distorted as a witch that she must seem below temptation. On the other hand, we have seen that witches served as lascivious sexual agents for the goatish fantasies of proper men; this image then would serve the double purpose of suggesting the shameful seductiveness of a "mother" figure while safely scorning it for its moral or physical ugliness. Such images of witches have been suggested on the stage in the flesh or projected; writhing creatures of the Dionysian id-world, dwellers in a perpetual Walpurgisnacht, slyly or overtly perverse, obscene, lecherous.

THE SISTERS AS SYMBOLS

The witches also can be experienced as projections of wider, archetypal forces, externalizations of the haunting threat of instability and equivocation, the undefined felt experience of chaos that lies beneath the wishfully ordered surface of life; what Coleridge has called the shadowy obscure, the fearfully anomalous of physical nature, the lawless of human nature. To defend himself from the horrifying dread of the unintelligible, the threatening uncontrollable, the human dresses himself in the dream of security—a borrowed robe to hide the lusts, furies, hates, and fears that swarm and consume. Such terrors, at a deep archetypal level, are evoked by dangerous women—particularly old ones, so old their chins show hair, half-men, not one thing or another.

The fantasy of the male storyteller has regularly made of sinister female figures both creator and destroyer. Erich Neumann describes the terrible, archetypal "Uroboric Mother" and her shadowy primeval world that threatens individual consciousness and personality with dissolution: "Insanity is an ever recurrent symptom of possession by the (Mother Goddess) or her representatives." Neumann suggests that the ego learned to convert the frightening facelessness of the primeval Mother into the benignant countenance of the Good Goddess to defend against the "fear of the abyss." Shakespeare asks us to face the facelessness; and the witches are partly visual symbols of it.

As projections of cosmic forces, the Sisters have been seen as transcending easy moral distinctions. Hazlitt, who envisioned them as "hags of mischief, obscene panderers to iniquity, malicious from their impotence of enjoyment, enamoured of destruction," could yet locate them on a grander scale: "unreal, abortive, half-existences, who become sublime from their exemption from all human sympathies and contempt for all human affairs." In such a superhuman climate, Maeterlinck suggested, Macbeth and Lady Macbeth maintain our sympathy despite their crimes because "they breathe in a region so vast that good and evil, viewed from very high, become almost indifferent and much less important than the sheer act of breathing." The Sisters represented, to

Gordon Craig, the whole dialectic of the spirit, from the best to the worst, externalized to test ultimately the two major characters:

> We should recognize the witches as spirits, more terrible because more beautiful than we can conceive except by making them terrible . . . [we should] picture them to ourselves as we picture the militant Christ scourging the money-lenders, the fools who denied Him. Here we have the supreme God, the supreme Love, and it is that which has brought *Macbeth* on the stage. We see in this instance the God of Force as exemplified in these witches, placing these two pieces of mortality upon the anvil because they were not hard enough to resist.

Macbeth and his Lady are "made drunk by these spirits"; then become furtive, alert, fearful as they recognize what has been done to them.

> Yet why, one wonders, should these spirits appear so horrible when a moment ago we were speaking of them as beings so divine as to resemble the militant Christ? and the answer seems obvious. Is it not possible that the spirit may take as many forms as the body, as many forms as thought? These spirits are the many souls of nature, inexorable to the weak, yet obedient to those who obey . . . we [should] see the God, the Spirit, . . . the beautiful spirit, that patient, stern being who demands of a hero at least the heroic.

In the one *Macbeth* Craig "designed," the witches were essentially realistic, but the realism was pushed to its boundaries. Craig saw them as a hypnotic influence over Macbeth directly, and working through Lady Macbeth: if they are not seen with her, he asked, "Are there not moments when one of these three . . . seems to have clapped its skinny hand upon Lady Macbeth's mouth and answered in her stead?" In the reality of performance, the breadth of Craig's imagination was reduced, the director (Douglas Ross) indicated, to

> three tall, thin men, as near cadavers as circumstances would permit . . . the motif of the play is on these premises. Mr. Craig's suggestive drawings of these witches represent and epitomize pure evil, hate, and destruction. They will scarcely be clad at all, and will look positively revolting.

What gave them some of the dimension of Craig's vision was that they were also conceived as aspects of destructive nature: fire, air, earth. The fire witch was veiled, in tulle drapery; the air witch came masked in a great bird's beak, with an inflated bladder on its chest; the earth witch rose like an evil growth from the ground. The opening curtain met a flash of lightning and the maniacal laughter of the witches; one of whom, standing on a bridge, flung stones that exploded on landing in red fire.

Craig had said, from Rome, that he wanted the witches' influence always felt, "impalpable as a shadow of a shadow"; as earlier he had promised, in *The Art of the Theatre*, "I would repeatedly and repeatedly bring upon the stage some reminder of the presence of these spirits." So in the production, after

Macbeth returned from his murder of Duncan, a "Hail!" was heard from the outer darkness; but the reminders of the spirit world were never as insistent as he had envisioned—or as they would be in the production, noted above, by Craig's son, Edward Carrick Craig.

The human form of the witches has sometimes been blurred into an uncanny context to suggest their primeval quality. A striking picture of three Sisters in a Turkish *Macbeth* shows the shapes of women rising out of a white, viscous matrix, as if indeed they are bubbles erupting from a strange earth. In a German version, the three had shaven heads, yellowish-white masks, half-transparent tatters about their bodies; and uttered their prophecies as if in a trance. They first appeared intertwined in a Laocöon grouping, then their naked arms darted out, like the snakes of the Erinyes: they seemed at once the powers of anti-nature, figments of nightmare dreams, and fragments of humanity gone mad.

Mechanical techniques have also been exploited by the theatre to suggest the uncanny qualities of the witches. At least as early as Josef Lange's performance of Schiller's translation at the beginning of the nineteenth century, "optical means" enhanced their mystery—meaning perhaps projections by "*laterna magica*" (used in a Hungarian *Macbeth* in 1832), or reflecting mirrors (used certainly in Vienna staging by 1820). Screened projections since then have often been used to convey elusive and unearthly images of the sort Banquo tried to describe, that *look not like th'inhabitants o'th' earth . . . Are ye fantastical? . . . were such things here?*

In some twentieth-century departures from realism, projections were joined with electronic sound amplification, and occasionally the use of stylized or surreal forms. To suggest the Dionysian characters of the witches, they have transformed into animal-phantasms, or other "symbols of inverted nature" that Brents Stirling sees in them.

The French, particularly, have experimented with impressionistic effects. The T.E.P.—the Theatre de L'Est Parisien—in 1959 superimposed projected images of the witches directly over the flesh and blood Macbeth and Banquo—a visual suggestion of inward fantasy reciprocating with intangible outward influence. In 1965 the T.E.P. conveyed the mystery of the Sisters with cinematic projections of hallucinant images, metamorphosing, decomposing, melting into forms suggestive of reptiles, animals, birds—a faceless, demon world.

In the open at Avignon (1954) at the Palace of the Popes, Jean Vilar began in the darkness with rumbling thunder and lightning, and the hooting of owls, mingled with the shout of trumpets and the wail of bagpipes; then, in the half-light, swarms of nameless beings seemed to lurk in the corners of the stage, until the lights picked out the Sisters, masked in the heads of *oiseaux de nuit*. Stereophonic loudspeakers spread the reverberation of their incantation throughout the palace, so that it seemed to pervade the air and come from every side—to one spectator even perhaps from "inside you—Vilar has succeeded in translating concretely this invasion of the supernatural." Loud-speakers have been used in other productions in France and elsewhere.

Something there is in the threatening image of the bat that has been borrowed to lend a sense of the unearthly to the Sisters. Beerbohm Tree's flying witches, dimly seen in midair through the spindrift of floating clouds, were made to flit about like giant bats, giving a sense of vastness and mystery to the stage. At St. Etienne (1952) the Sisters moved choreographically like bats, skittering and uttering sharp, piercing cries, and sometimes hung, batlike. Three active German witches (Berlin, 1960) were described as acting like bats who had taken a lesson from Mary Wigmore; their hollowed voices followed them from loudspeakers.

Even the projections of subliminal or surreal forms have been too realistic for the dramaturgs, who have created Sisters out of incandescence. Jessner, in Germany, projected three cones of light, three will-o-the-wisps, quivering across the stage while immaterial voices floated behind them. For Sam Wana-maker (U.S., 1964) they were skittering spots of color. In Milan (1948) they were represented as phosphorescent comets, elusive and evanescent. In England (1971) ghostly, formless images twenty feet high were projected, to the musical chants of the Sisters.

We must speculate now on how Shakespeare's audiences—and later ones—might have responded to the Sisters. Speculation, especially for the Elizabethan-Jacobean period, is all we can hope for. Almost no reports survive on how plays were then received. Guesses are sometimes made on the basis of the prose discourse of people who were not essentially concerned with the theatre—indeed were often hostile to it, and to the impulses it released. And even so, "There is no Elizabethan state of mind," as Madeline Doran has written wisely, "only many Elizabethan states of mind"—a wisdom exhaustively demonstrated by William Elton in his remarkable study of *Lear*. The best indication we have of contemporary response is that Shakespeare's spectators had the excellent taste to enjoy his plays—which often resist or deny the orthodoxy of the books from the period which scholars have to study. I have cited books of this kind, and must again; but I feel strongly that what they have to tell us is at best supplementary to what we discover in the primary documents—the plays.

We get our first notion of the response-repertory of Shakespeare's audiences to *Macbeth* as we comprehend the marvelous polyphony the playwright contrived with his Sisters. When this, in its entirety, confronts Macbeth, the deepest tones of his own character—and our reaction to them—can be evoked. To the extent that the Sisters are ugly old women pretending witch-power, they play on his—and our—superstition, imagination, and skill in finding reasons to choose wrong; as seeresses and sorceresses they extort from him—and us—acquiescence to the power of magic to make shame of an "orderly" world; as Fates, they lead him—and us—to a sense of a supernatural design that in human terms is cruel and idiotic; as hints of a diabolic enemy eternally lurking, they terrify us with the tempting vision of power they trade for the human soul, and the even more terrifying vision of what we might do with that power; and beyond all this, they rouse in him—in us—the awesome sense that all the rest may be meaningless, that the chaos lies entirely within us, that all these horrors are of man's making, born of archaic, unspeakable impulses that link us to a nameless awful. *murder ?*

As far as we can tell, the playwright included enough nuances of "witch" power to match all the general beliefs of his Globe spectators. Some of Shakespeare's audience evidently believed devoutly in witchcraft—and any Puritans among them who might have sneaked in to see the play perhaps not long after carried the infection of their barbarous credulity to the New World. The law of England fortified the believers—and tells us how very common "witches" must have been to be so regulated. Three acts, of 1542, 1563, and 1604, declared witchcraft a statutory offense. The first made a capital crime out of any conjuring of spirits, or the practice of witchcraft, enchantment or sorcery—even for so harmless an occupation (apparently a popular one) as seeking treasure. The 1563 law carried the death sentence for the first offense only if a human victim of witchcraft died; if the victim lived, the witch was imprisoned for a year, with visits to the pillory; though on a second offense, for this, or harm against animals or property, the offense became capital. The penalty was less severe now for finding treasure, or provoking unlawful love— another popular demand—but a second offense incurred life imprisonment. Not long before *Macbeth*, the 1604 Act (which remained law until 1736) again ordered the capital penalty for causing injury or death; and also for a second offense in the case of the less mortal practices of witchcraft. The law was specifically aimed at traffic with *evil* spirits—as if leaving a loophole for those magicians who believed they could demonstrate that their business was with good ones.

Shakespeare's audiences, then, were seeing on the stage images of what to them were nominally contemporary lawbreakers—perhaps malicious enemies of life and property, but as likely to be "wise women" of the sort the spectators of all classes sought in times of need. Given this atmosphere, the Jacobeans would probably have been more sensitive than audiences of later times to the full polyphony of the witches: to undertones of diabolic involvement, of the magic of mythology and the "elder world", of the presence and power of a fate at work.

If the dramatization of witchcraft had more implications for the gullible then than now, it was perhaps even less effective on the doubters like Scot, compelled to an aggressive scepticism. Later centuries, not challenged by the issue of belief, may have been more free to suspend disbelief. The eighteenth century might proclaim its rationalism: Gentleman found the witches "an insult to common sense;" and Samuel Johnson was sure that "A poet who would now make the whole action of his tragedy depend upon enchantment

. . . and supernatural agents . . . would be . . . banished from the theatre to the nursery, and condemned to write fairy tales." Johnson condescended to "allow" Shakespeare to "found" *Macbeth* on "the notions that prevailed at the time." (But even for Johnson, a reader of Macbeth's apostrophe before the murder of Duncan "looks round alarmed and starts to find himself alone.")

The comic stage treatment of the witches may have conditioned the bland eighteenth-century response to *Macbeth*'s Sisters; certainly other supernatural effects—as when Garrick's Hamlet was awed by his father's ghost—affected audiences spectacularly. The period was notoriously susceptible to the titillation of gothic horrors—as the hard-headed twentieth-century too would be whelmed in waves of successful "horror films" about the occult, vampires, monsters, possession, exorcism. The enjoyment of *frissons d'horreur*, effected by artistically theatricalized images of uncanny, inexplicable terror, has probably always been one of man's fearful delights.

To make *Macbeth*'s supernatural apparatus at once more "believable" and still frightening, the twentieth-century theatre has tried such anachronistic social contexts as a jungle voodoo climate. Orson Welles, for his "black" *Macbeth* (U.S., 1936) used witchdoctors for Sisters; since then there have been variations of this production idea, including some exciting tribal *Macbeths* from Africa itself. In these curiosities, as in the staging of the true play, one factor is decisive in allaying audience disbelief in the supernatural: the unmistakable belief of the characters themselves in it. If they who portray the "witches"—or readers imaginatively inhabiting them—are deeply involved in the life of the play, and Macbeth and Banquo are understood to believe absolutely in them, then these strange creatures that rise out of the mist and vanish like bubbles have all the "reality" that our need to be aroused requires.

One particular Jacobean's response to witchcraft must be considered since it has sometimes been regarded as crucial to *Macbeth:* King James'—as if Shakespeare was influenced by the king's ideas, or wrote the play to please him. James was at the time thought to be descended from Banquo, an imaginary historical figure invented by Boece at a time when historians were very creative. Contemporaries believed the fiction; thus Holinshed: "Banquo . . . of whome the House of Stuarts is descended." Five accounts tell us how James visited Oxford, and was entertained by three "sibyllae" acting out the prediction that Banquo would start the Stuart line. This may have happened shortly before *Macbeth* was written; but we do not know this; nor need we believe, as Kenneth Muir has pointed out, that it was Shakespeare's cue for his play: he had his Holinshed, and possibly other lesser sources. However, from scraps such as this, the theory exists that James' attitudes more or less strongly influenced Shakespeare. An apostle of the "more" view, Henry Paul, assiduously put together "evidence" for it that had been collected by scholars over the years, and he can be confronted as representative. He asserts that "the philosophy of the play is in truth a fusion of two minds"—James' and Shake-speare's. The notion is itself preposterous, considering the littleness of James' mind, and his even smaller spirit; in any case, the "evidence" proposed may in fact demonstrate that Shakespeare opposed what James believed in, as we will see as we go along.

Paul sets out to prove that *Macbeth* was presented on a specific royal occa-sion—when James was visited by King Christian of Denmark in 1606. All the "proofs" are circumstantial; not a single piece of hard, documentary testi-mony is adduced. Paul cites various witnesses who reported in detail the king's activities and entertainments on this royal occasion: not one mentions Shakespeare, or *Macbeth*, or a play about witches. (More about this in the discussion of IV,i).

Paul's method is to make an assumption on the basis of inference, then proceed as if the assumption is a fact, and then add these "facts" into his "proof." To give one sample now of his logic: Paul notes that James' doctor disclosed that the king did not sleep well; presumably, therefore, Shakespeare meant to please the king when he wrote Macbeth's anguished lament about murdering sleep—as if James would somehow be delighted to relate his in-somnia to the murderer's. Nobody minds speculation, if it is so labeled; but let it not be confused with fact.

James' ideas on witchcraft are sometimes put forward as influencing Shake-speare's treatment of the Sisters, and Paul supports this idea in detail in the later part of his book, citing references from James' *Daemonologie*. The immedi-ate rebuttal to this is the first part of Paul's own book, where, curiously, he has carefully presented testimony that since writing *Daemonologie* in Scotland, James—in one demonstration of kingly wisdom—had begun to realize that "witches" could be among the various mortal cozeners described in such books as "A Declaration of egregious Popish Impostures . . . under the pretence of casting out devils" by Harsnet—who subsequently rose high in James' service. Paul cites evidence that even before coming south, James had relaxed Scotland's official war on witchcraft, and he even cites Thomas Fuller (*Church History*, X, 74), who indeed observed the change in James, as one

> receding from what he had written in his *Daemonologie* grew first dissident of, and then flatly to deny the works of Witches and Devils, as but Falsehoods and Delusions.

There is other evidence. Kittredge, defending James from imputations of witchhunting, notes several instances of royal pardons of "witches" between 1607 and 1610 (the period when—or just after—*Macbeth* was probably writ-ten) and concludes from other evidence that James' contemporaries in fact "thought him sceptical rather than credulous."

Paul has considerable difficulty fitting Shakespeare's witches to both James the witchhunter and James the sceptic. He concludes, as most do who see James' influence, for the former. This is the poorer side of the argument;

Shakespeare had no need of the mélange of credulity, ignorance, superstition, and malice in the *Daemonologie* to make his Sisters; it conveys none of their polyphony. And it puts Paul in the position of arguing that Shakespeare was dramatizing ideas about the power of witchcraft that James was leaving behind—hardly a support for the thesis of propitiation.

James' alleged influence is important to us here only as it may have constricted or enhanced Shakespeare's art; this possibility will be considered at other suspect points; as far as I,i is concerned, the evidence is, at most, inconclusive. The playwright could certainly have written it as he did had there been no King James.

Did Shakespeare write the scene?
Some have challenged its authenticity. Most curiously, Granville Barker thought it neither good Shakespeare nor good theatre:

> Apart from such an opening being un-Shakespearean, the lines themselves are as little like Shakespeare as Hecate is . . . The scene—as better and sterner critical authority allows—is a poor and pointless scene. And Shakespeare did not . . . begin his plays with superfluities . . . therefore it may well be omitted.

Granville Barker's "better and sterner critical authority" means those critics suspicious either of the theatricality of the play, or of its language. Many others have recognized how surely the flashing scene, so startlingly effective in itself, prefigures what is to come. Thus Maurice Morgann, as early as 1777, writing as if attending the theatre of his mind:

> The understanding must in the first place, be subdued; and lo! how the rooted prejudices of the child spring up to confound the man! The Weird Sisters rise, and order is extinguished. The laws of nature give way, and leave nothing in our minds but wildness and horror. No pause is allowed us for reflection . . . We, the fools of amazement, are insensible to the shifting of place and the lapse of time, and till the curtain drops, never once wake to the truth of things, or recognize the laws of existence.

Coleridge, too, was roused to the "invocation made at once to the imagination and . . . emotions; . . . the keynote of the character of the whole play." The theatre has almost always concurred; the scene has been made to begin the assault on the senses that, as Jorgensen noted, characterizes the whole. Guthrie's deletion of the scene to minimize Macbeth's fatalism was exceptional. When other scenes are cut, this one usually remains—though sometimes it suffers the indignity of a dumb show prepended: e.g. as a slow motion war scene, to the sound of battle and the scream of horses, or as mimed religious ritual in Duncan's court.

Macbeth's language, as printed in the Folio, has been suspect to some scholars doubtful that Shakespeare would have intentionally written blank verse so marvelously syncopated, or so irregular in its beats. This play more than any of his others speaks in jagged rhythms; not only do the voices of the natural and supernatural worlds differ sharply, but so do the voices within each world: lines break, tones change. Some scholars contend that the play suffered serious cutting, and point out what seem to them disruptions and lacunae. Some scholars try to normalize the Folio's lovely, ragged lineation. Some believe that the language cannot all be uncontaminated Shakespeare—some other hand may have meddled, or Shakespeare himself may have made later insertions. Most extremely, Henry Cunningham, editor of the 1916 Arden *Macbeth*, found the first two scenes so irregular he could only conclude that, if they *were* by Shakespeare, then "the first act, as we find it in the Folio, was begun by Shakespeare drunk and continued by Shakespeare sober." I will consider the evidence for cutting, mislineation, interpolation or miscegenation at the cruxes; but on the whole, as I have noted, I will accept the Folio version, with a minimum of modernizing, and with line numbers as in the Variorum edition. This will involve me in some controversy with editors I respect, and I will endure that as cheerfully as possible. The Folio text *is* the one preserved for us from Shakespeare's time by his admiring and admirable fellows as essentially authentic, and almost certainly what he and they meant his play to be in the theatre.* I am happy to note that Jay Halio's 1972 edition of *Macbeth* also mainly relies on the Folio; though he and I come to some different conclusions about the lineation, and he believes in a probable first, lost version of the play (proposed by Nosworthy), as I do not. Some disagreement among editors is inevitable given the single original text, and the evidence (from Charlton Hinman, for instance†) of more than one compositor at work on it; but except for learned differences over the specific meaning of words, we must mainly acknowledge speculation. What we *know* is that the Folio *Macbeth* is the text given us as Shakespeare's, whole and entire. To me the very versatility and freedom from pattern of the language argue the mature playwright's own hand: nobody else could so well have tamed poetic form to the varied rhythms of speech suited to this angular play.

---

*Heminge and Condell are specific on this point in their charming note to all the Folio readers: "From the most able, to him that can but spell: . . . where [before] you were abus'd with diverse stolne, and surreptitious copies, maimed and deformed . . . even those are now offer'd to your view cur'd and perfect of their limbes; and all the rest, absolute in numbers, as he conceived them." And they add, as a salutary warning to anyone foolish enough to be dissatisfied with Shakespeare's work: "Read him, therefore; and againe and againe: And if then you doe not like him, surely you are in some manifest danger, not to understand him."

†I generally assume that Shakespeare's punctuation guided his actors: comma, semi-colon, colon and period often seem to indicate different lengths of pause in speech. Assuming the punctuation *was* Shakespeare's: if not from his hand, then from a prompt copy preserving his intentions. Even so, as Bowers pointed out to Hinman (II,p. 250), more semi-colons appear in the *Macbeth* text set supposedly by Compositor A than that set by B. We must try to discover what we can from the text as given.

Act I, Scene i

The first scene, but eleven lines in the Folio, linguistically as well as thematically is of the same blood and tissue as all that comes after. It begins with a *wh-* question—the kind that belongs to Macbeth's wayward world, where a simple yes or no will not answer; where the uncertain future always broods over the elusive present. Sister 1 does not fall into the easy trochaic tetrameter common in chants and charms; she begins almost in marching spondees, and then spills the meter:

> When shall we three meet again?
> In thunder, lightning, or in rain? (5–6)

The importance of the *or* has long since been noticed. Sister 1 is really asking three questions (the two commas may mean substantial pauses). L. C. Knights has observed the disjunction in the lines, this first breaking apart of what is commonly joined together. This is to be a world of many strange options. If this Sister has power over weather, she can show it here, invoking one after another, then all three.

Sister 2 seems to shake them all off. She will speak in the naive trochee beat, but what she says will be wayward paradox, a promise of dissonance:

> When the hurly-burly's done,
> When the battle's lost, and won. (7–8)

Not in noise, but in silence, she seems to say. And, at a time of contradiction, when a thing is its opposite. A battle has been going on, and perhaps its voice may be heard, or perhaps suddenly silenced, so that the senses may experience the shock of juxtaposition that the Sister has verbalized. Other battles than war will be fought in silence in this play.

The witches may be amused by Sister 2's paradox—they will seem to enjoy these dialectical ironies. "Do not let your witches laugh," John Masefield begged. "The kingdom of Satan does not laugh." That depends on your image of Satan and how he and his minions regard the mortal world that often

serves them in the mask of serving God. If the Sisters laugh, their laughter
might well have the same ambivalence as their language and action. Not if they
merely cackle, as with gleeful foreknowledge of Macbeth's painful fate; not
if they giggle at their manipulation of it. This makes too much of their fatefulness, too little of themselves; it *un*-equivocates. Similarly, if the Sisters overtly
blaspheme—as in one staging inverting a cross and pouring ritual blood down
over the Christ—or otherwise proclaim their wickedness at once, then precise
lines are immediately drawn between forces of good and bad, where the playwright intended ambiguity, and mystery dissolves. As noted above, contemporary "witches" or "cunning" or "wise" women, of the sort the Sisters
seem partly to represent, gave generously of help as well as harm. May the
Sisters wish Macbeth well? or at least seem to? May these wayward women
even love this man, to his misfortune? They will be scolded by their mistress,
Hecate, for daring

> To trade and traffic with Macbeth. . . .
>   . . . all you have done
> Hath been but *for* a wayward son, . . . [who]
> Loves for his own ends, not for you. (III, v, 7, 13–14, 16)

Hecate, too, is ambiguous; but one implication here is certainly a complaint
that the Sisters have intended to promote Macbeth's interests. And again, all
that the Sisters say to him, in the play, however oracularly, turns out to be
true, including the warnings to him that he misreads. To be betrayed by the
Sisters' infatuation with him could be more horrible than destruction by their
deliberate malice.

    The crucial factor is that neither love nor malice is defined; the Sisters'
motives are as ambiguous as they are. This is stipulated at the outset of I, i,
in the quick, short lines setting their next rendezvous. The time will be *soon*—
before sunset: we are usually being hurried in this world. The place will be a
lonely heath, *blasted*; and then the line that gives nothing away, only rouses
expectation. Though unmarked, it carries a caesura with the full power of
a colon:

> There to meet with [:] Macbeth. (12)

Why to meet? We must wonder. If we are scrupulous in suspending our
memories, we confront mystery: Is this a planned meeting? an ambush? Who
is Macbeth? From the play's title we know this his tragedy; if we are well-read
Jacobeans we may have some notion of his history, from Holinshed or other
sources—though even so we will also know that this playwright, Shakespeare,
reshapes history to suit his dramatic purpose. We can count on nothing. He
may in fact be playing a game with the learned-judicious among us, who would
anticipate, from Holinshed, Macbeth's long period of peaceful rule. We will
hardly recognize these Sisters, or this Macbeth, his acts and his end.

    If the Sisters carry the marks of a recent sabbat, or if now they complete
one before us, what trains of wonder begin in our minds? If they show the

exhaustion and exhilaration of an orgy, are we led to expect another? Do the Sisters themselves have differing expectations? Sometimes, in both theatre and criticism, they are imagined as three voices with a single intent, and they speak with characterless unanimity. On the stage, more often, they are mingling notes in a chord, sometimes male and female mixed, sometimes differing in voice, in age, size, beauty, or in their rationality, their powers. For Trevor Nunn at Stratford-upon-Avon in 1975, Witch 2 was a pale, frightened novitiate, making her prophecies in a deep trance. The next year she was a distraught, half-witted blonde adolescent, frightened by the unearthly gifts she seemed to possess. The uncanny may have many faces.

To meet with Macbeth. Whatever the Sisters' intentions, whether for rendezvous or surprise, we are given time only to conjecture, not to know, only to experience the mystery and be charged with expectation. As soon as the name is out—Macbeth—our focus is abruptly shifted. The name may reverberate momentarily in the air; but then the atmosphere alters—with a change in the hurly-burly sounds of battle or storm; a shock of silence; an apprehension of men approaching. Then new uncanny notes: the cries of the familiars, Graymalkin and Padock, and perhaps Harpier—warning? promising? coaxing? commanding? and together the three chant their paradox of waywardness:

> Fair is foul, and foul is fair. (14)

In the spreading ripples of dissonance from the Sisters' jarring juxtaposition of incongruities, subliminal impressions take shape: Is it a fair Macbeth who is foul? Does fair-foul relate to the changing weather, next mentioned, that the Sisters may control? To the battle? To the appearance of the Three, whether they look fair or foul, or transform themselves? To any stage property they manipulate? To Fortune? Franco Enriquez, directing *Macbeth* in Verona (1971), thought fair-foul not an antithesis, but a wheel. Does fair become foul? Is fair foul only from the witches' point of view? From a human? A cosmic? Are things *both* fair and foul? Is fair in fact foul? The collapse of the polarity comes with a special shock when the phrase is new; used to it as we are, we may recapture some of the impact from its curious sea-change in the T.E.P. *Macbeth* (1973)—*le beau est hideux.*

May *fair* mask *foul?* Shakespeare played with illusion in the sonnets, particularly in 127:

> For since each hand hath put on Nature's power
> Fairing the foul with Art's false borrowed face . . .

and 137:

> To put fair truth upon so foul a face.

And in *Timon:*

> Thus much of gold will make black white, fair foul.

The polyphony is subtle, with so many notes mingled, some so distanced that they may only be experienced below the level of awareness. Impulses have been loosed; a forbidden world half revealed; shaken the comfortable sense that a thing is what it seems, even that it is what it is. Knights has synthesized a thematic disturbance that *Macbeth* at once rouses: a "kind of metaphysical pitch-and-toss . . . is about to be played with good and evil"—and indeed, with virtually every concept in the play. From now on, we will be uncertain of what is fair, what foul; we will begin to suspect all appearances.

The witches, by Folio direction, *Exeunt;* but their chant boasts that they *hover** in clotting air, so they may well *vanish* in ways we have noted, behind a smoke or gauze, evoking the uncanny;† they leave us, William Empson suggests, in a wild and whirling confusion.

We have never read or seen this play. It begins. In a fierce storm three inexplicable creatures, speaking and acting mysteriously, flash before us, hinting—perhaps demonstrating—supernatural power; they plan a meeting, naming significantly a name that excites them; momentarily they move ritualistically, esoterically, and are suddenly gone, before our thoughts can fix. We feel our way toward their appointed meeting with—Macbeth.

*Hover through the fog and filthy air. Note that Shakespeare blurs the easy beat with the dissyllable *hover,* and with an unnecessary *the.*

†James probably reflected popular myth when he wrote his *Daemonologie,* and could then speculate thus on the disappearance of witches: perhaps the devil's agency did "thicken and obscure" the air, "contracting it strait together, that the beames of . . . man's eye cannot pierce through . . . to see them."

Act I, Scene ii

. . . to meet with *Macbeth*

the Sisters plan, and quickly disappear. We are now alert for Macbeth's appearance, when we hear an intense, troubling question* (the first four scenes all begin with interrogatories, the first three with open-ended *wh*'s):

What bloody man is that? (I, ii, 5)

Is the bloody man Macbeth?

The speaker turns out to be a king: is he Macbeth? We must wait to learn; meanwhile the unease of the human world is felt to match the disturbances reverberating from the world of witches: this king's entourage is in a state of alarm, and his second line tells why: he wants a report

. . . of the revolt
The newest state. (6-7)

The kingdom is in disorder. Witches, images of unreason, lurk in its underworld; human enemies attack it from within and—as we soon hear—invade from without. What hope of stability in this world of men?

Some critics—and some productions of the play—have set aside the unmistakable evidences of a *gor'd state* in favor of an imagined dramatic pattern: Scotland is an orderly place until an evildoer (Macbeth) will bring disorder to it; good men eventually restore order. The pattern is soothing to the mind yearning for equilibrium; to cite Sartre again, it holds the promise that in a Manichean world good may banish bad for ever. Instead of polyphony, it offers one clear tonic tone, of sweet and sonorous assurance, playing against

*We may hear the question before we see the speaker, given the quick cutting between scenes of Shakespeare's theatre. One of the effective devices of that theatre is the succession of shocks achieved by startling changes of direction in the action. We hardly notice this in the well-known plays; but attend an obscure Jacobean drama and observe how the scenes break against each other, so that at each scene-end the mind is challenged with expectation of the unexpected.

a fierce dominant strain that it eventually overrides and extinguishes. Of the
various critics who champion this pattern, Traversi is most explicit:

> The witches . . . prepare the way for the entry of evil and disintegration into
> a state which has been, under Duncan, positive, natural, and orderly.

The play cannot be made to bend to this premise. Under Duncan, the state
has certainly been "natural"—but of the Nature to which Shakespeare holds
a faithful mirror: enclosing all things that happen in it, including the worst
and best that men do and dream of, and that is done to them by this Nature.
Some Shakespearean characters may try to envision "natural" and human
behavior as mutually reciprocating; but almost always they themselves fail
this vision; other Shakespearean personae seem specifically made by Nature
to climb "unnaturally" over the bodies of their fellows. Duncan has allowed
such "natural" men to make Scotland an extremely disorderly kingdom, partly
through sheer failure to understand the motivations hidden behind false faces.
Meanwhile the Sisters, a different manifestation of Shakespeare's commodi-
ous Nature, but a further symbol of the troubled weal, sap the stability of
Duncan's kingdom in their own secret way. Against this disorder at double
levels in the state, the king and his prince—we are given to see—are helpless
to restore even political stability. Unless a great, brave, fighting captain rescues the state, and brings it order, it may collapse in chaos. This is the scene
when a bleeding soldier, come from the battle, reports to the king. Yet Duncan
has been made to symbolize the perfect system that will be restored in Scotland when evil is banished. Eulogies of him range toward the ecstatic: "a
glimpse of an ideal king for an ideal world"; "embodiment of the order which
Macbeth seeks to destroy"; "a saintly king"; "a Christ figure"; and finally the
ultimate ascent: "Duncan represents God, the creative principle."

Such bloodless abstractions would be death to the tragedy. They could
only make sense if, in the premise of one critic, Shakespeare's

> poetic drama . . . is necessarily governed by pattern or design;

or of another,

> the characters in *Macbeth* are not shaped primarily to conform to a psycho-
> logical verisimilitude, but to make explicit the intellectual statements with
> which the play is concerned.

But this is not the way of great tragedy. No series of intellectual statements
could possibly embrace the passion and pain that inform *Macbeth*. Its genius
is to arouse; it deals in blood and anguish; its characters, reflecting the impulses
of mortality, are too alive to be anything so bland as saintly. To deny Duncan
the frailties of the flesh with which Shakespeare endowed him is to occlude
the carefully designed, recognizably human relationship to the associated
roles. Then the emptied design is not in phase with Shakespeare's intensive
interlocking of personae moved to action by ambiguous but unmistakably
mortal drives.

The perception of Duncan as the epitome of good in a good-evil morality pattern is a late sophistication. Early writers ignore or dismiss him. Editing Garrick's version of *Macbeth*, Gentleman found Duncan incidental: "having nothing of consequence to say or act, if he looks like a monarch, on the stage, may do well enough." The first meaningful critical comment I found was in a curious little book that promised *A Key to Drama . . . Containing the Life, Character and Secret History of Macbeth. By a Gentleman* (1768). The estimate was practical:

> Duncan was too soft and easy a disposition to be at the head of a government divided into a diversity of factions.

King James would probably have agreed. In his *Basilikon*, his political-moral guide to kingly behavior for his dear son Henry, he advised:

> Ye have also to consider that yee must not only bee carefull to keepe your subjects from receiving any wrong of others within; but also yee must be careful to keepe them from the wrong of any forraine Prince without . . .

and in *The Trew Law of Free Monarchies* James stipulated the King's duty to "fore-see and prevent all dangers, that are likely to fall upon (the people) and to maintain concord, wealth and civilitie among them." Duncan's failures in these responsibilities are evident in the first visual and verbal impact of his appearance. Good, meek, and gentle he will be called—fair words, better than the "milksop" label Holinshed reports; but, as Christopher Morris says of the Tudors, their kings were not expected to carry holiness to the point of ineptness.

Shakespeare's first example of the *Rex Inutilis* was Henry VI: who shared with Duncan the distinction of being the only British monarch in the canon who does not head his army into battle when war threatens. Even old Lear joined Cordelia to lead his forces. That the medieval king was a fighting ruler who went to battle and brandished his sword was a matter of course, Kantorowicz observes. So the king of Norway fights in the forefront of this war on Scotland. Duncan has seemed to remove himself from battle; yet something curious will emerge in his enjoyment of the reports of violence. Nothing is wholly *fair* in *Macbeth*'s motley: Duncan's fairness, too, is, in this matter, shadowed, as we will see.

When the theatre offers a Duncan without moulding, in the saintly pattern, it usually dresses him in the impeccable white of purity, gives him a halo of white hair, and associates him with a cross, prominently displayed on his breast or borne by one of his retinue. This proclaims him at once as one of the "good"; anybody who opposes him will be "bad," and indeed is likely to be dressed, orthodoxly, in "bad" red or black. (Except in a "Black *Macbeth*," where the colors are likely to be reversed, and Macbeth to say, for instance, "the devil damn thee white, thou cream-faced loon.") The effect of immaculate Duncans in performance, reviews have noted, is so to whiten the character that it becomes bleached. This upsets the dramatic equation by making Macbeth seem much more vicious and inhuman than the lines warrant. The same thing happens in critical interpretation: "pattern" critics are likely to find Macbeth, as the enemy of good, much less sympathetic than those who approach the play unrestricted by axioms.

The best way to experience Shakespeare's design for Duncan, and every other *Macbeth* character, is to enter it as an actor might, fitting the garment not to a pattern, but to the dramatic identity formed by the role's given qualities, actions, and relationships with the others in the play's equations. So Duncan must begin as a king whose kingdom is in turmoil and threatened with defeat; anxious about the disorder within and without, and about the succession to his throne if Scotland survives. His personal and political fate hang on battles under way: he himself can do nothing about them. In the theatre his ineffectuality has been manifest to the point even of senility: a man evidently of good heart and failing authority. To make him the more touching, he has been blind, and so frail he has had to lean on Macduff for support.

His son, the second speaker in I, ii, is a different matter. Malcolm has been linked with his father as a fellow symbol of ideal kingship and orderliness; what needs to be noticed is that he is so unlike his father in design that his pragmatic, shrewd effectiveness will seem almost a commentary on the sponginess of Duncan. The dark moulding to Malcolm's fairness will not for a while appear; but from the first he too must be far from a saintly figure. In this scene he shows the cub; if he fails at least to hint the lion and the fox, as a Russian reviewer complained of a Malcolm manqué (Kirov, 1938), he poses nothing for Macbeth to fear. Later, he will cleverly remind Macduff that he is *young*, compare himself to a weak, poor, *innocent lamb;* but he knows how to use his teeth—and other men's teeth. Dover Wilson sees him posing as "a kind of Jesuit"; Felix Rabb discerns a Machiavellian realism the English could have admired. In the theatre Malcolm has suggested the heroic young savior of his nation; more subtly the Jacobean "new man" (Verona, 1971); a parallel to Antony's young challenger, Octavius (England, 1972); a shrewd politician (England, 1975). If he cannot convey some sense of underlying craft and toughness, he must seem, in Coghill's echo of what Holinshed saw in Duncan, a milksop.

The dramatic equation linking Duncan, Macbeth, and Malcolm is an extremely complex one, obliquely mirroring their common roles. With the nation in danger, Duncan does not fight; Malcolm began to fight, had to be rescued from capture, and we see him withdrawn from battle; Macbeth fights and saves Scotland. In recurring visual imagery, the three will be seen to wear the same symbols of royalty, act similar political rituals, utter regal commands, acknowledge allegiance, depend on loyalty, dispense largesse, fear betrayal. Theirs is an archetypal conflict situation, familially as well as politically: younger pretenders compete for an old man's power—in the *Macbeth* fantasy a king's. The fantasy takes various twists, as in the stories of the

Oresteia, Hamlet, Lear, Zeus-Prometheus, God-Satan-Christ. (The parallels here may partly explain why Milton first considered making his epic from Macbeth's story, rather than Satan's.) Duncan, in this configuration, echoes an archetypal father or father-surrogate figure—Greek king, Judaeo-Christian Jehovah, ruler of Denmark, etc. In religion the god-person may be unassailable—though not so Kronos. In tragic drama, the essential role of the father-figure is to be attacked, and brought down. Entangled with this toppling image is often a seasonal association: the old man is winter-age, yielding to a spring-youth—who in turn may age, and then must give way. These images, which Duncan refracts, that seem to belong to common human fantasy, are in *Macbeth* sensed below conscious level. Shakespeare clouds his archetypes in wreaths of individualized, dialecticized humanity: the "old man," Duncan, speaks of fertility, planting, and growing but applauds savage killing; in the winter of his age, he lavishes gifts with summer's bounty. The echoes of his archetypal role are surds in the Shakespearean polyphony: the ear may not recognize them, but they reach past to stir mind and feeling.

The attitudes of Duncan, Malcolm, and Macbeth, masked and real, that reflect the ambitions, jealousies, and fears of timeless political-familial competitions, will not begin to betray themselves clearly until the confrontation in I, iv; meanwhile we may observe that the three men, in the size of their strengths and weaknesses, lights and shadows, must be worthy of each other.

As the play goes on, other upward-thrusting figures will join in the drive toward power. The Freudian formula, of siblings against a father and each other, accommodates this action; ethology suggests that the drive may be embedded in the very biology of mammals, an Adlerian impulse to dominance, to achieve a status as close to the apex as possible. *Macbeth* certainly deals with this kind of order: *degree,* the comparative place of each man in the hierarchy, will be seen to condition the relationships of the characters. To protect his place, or to rise in degree, man (and woman) will plot, kill, betray, change sides—will, in fact, often act to shatter the ladder which he is trying to mount.

The *bloody man* whom Duncan sees proclaims visually the disorder in the state. The sight of bleeding itself signals immediate alarm; it threatens the source, the fountain of life. Kolbe has counted some hundred references to *blood*—meaning not only the word itself, but also such implications of it as pale cheeks. The computer retrieves twenty-three specific instances, with twenty-five related ones (*bleed, bloody, gory,* etc.). The actual presence of seen blood is more insistent than the sounded word. In many scenes blood is a continuous, mute, terrible witness to the ambience of violence and hostility, and the vulnerability of flesh. It is certainly used by the witches in one scene, and perhaps in all; it marks men who come fresh from killing, as often they do; when not seen, it is hallucinated or dreamed. The visual image, like the verbal, may have several shades. It will not always, as one critic would imagine it, seem a "sickly smear": the blood of a hero may have a different color than that of a ghost, or of the baboon throat-struck by a witch; the new bleeding of a soldier staggering from battle is different from the dried crust on the dress of a general returning in victory. Each will contribute a special note to the polyphony. In both the theatre and the vivid imagination, the articulation of blood into the gathering design of the play's spectacle is essential: the *bloody man* will make a shocking, startling effect; though not so much that later sights—or visualizations—of bleeding lose impact. The motifs caught in these two words of Duncan's first question—*blood, man*—will wind and swell throughout the play.

We have no reasons to suppose, from the Folio directions, that I, ii does not take place in another part of the witches' heath:

> *Alarum within. Enter King, Malcolm,*
> *Donalbaine, Lenox, with attendants,*
> *meeting a bleeding Captain.*

Alarum. Trumpet, drum, perhaps tocsin call men to arms, to battle. The clamant urgency of these sounds follows from the chant of the witches, and the growl and shriek of the storm, overture to the orchestration of animal and natural utterances more frequent in this than any other Shakespearean play. Rowe, in his 1709 edition, domesticated the scene to a Palace, and some others have followed suit, including Garrick and Kemble in the theatre. More often since the nineteenth century the scene has been alive with military men on the move.

The armed camp Charles Kean typically presented, in one of his detailed "archaeological" period reconstructions, broke from the first witches' scene to sudden silence, night had come, "semi-savage armed kerns prowled about on guard."* Wing-flats in such stagings showed tents and a tree; on the back-cloth tents and hills disappeared into the distance. A far-off trumpet called, another closer—another—a drum roll—*alarum.* Suddenly soldiers sprang up from the darkness, many of them—Kean would have over fifty men in the scene. Duncan could enter (and later exit) from one of the tents to confront the bleeding Captain brought in on a litter. In the king's advent, royal panoply may be emphasized: in Sweden (1967) Duncan entered under a blood-red, gothic thronal canopy.

More often Duncan watches the wounded man come on: for good reason. Shakespeare often uses the veteran theatrical device of calling attention to an expected entrance—as noted, the exit of the witches may have been moti-

---

*When curtains were used to break scenes, the theatre could take advantage of Shakespeare's frequent design of alternating intimate scenes, with a few people, with larger public scenes. Thus the first witches' scene could be played in front of a drop, which would be lifted for I, ii; similarly I, iii and I, v and I, vii could play on a shallow forestage, while the more crowded scenes could be played on the deeps behind.

vated by their awareness of intrusion, as they look off—and so the eyes of the audiences are moved to stage left or right. Duncan's alarm and anxiety at what he sees approaching prepare emotionally for the shocking sight and the baroque narration.

When, instead of changing, the scene slides into the previous one or overlaps it, the bleeding Captain often brings his own shock: his scream of pain is heard offstage, or he is dragged in by the witches as part of their scheming, or he is crawling away from their corpse-robber hands; the war seems close offstage. Or Duncan, finding his way over the heath-battlefield, consulting with his entourage—usually only a few men on the modern stage, which can rarely afford the luxury of half a hundred—sees the Captain coming or being borne in. In a Russian production, Duncan stood on a knoll watching a distant battle, à la Napoleon—or Kutuzov—surrounded by staff. In a German *Macbeth* (1928) that rather emphasized the play's animality and violence of war, several impaled heads, whirled aloft on pikes by a soldier gone mad, foreshadowed the catastrophe. In a grim touch in the Polanski film (1971), one trooper went matter-of-factly administering the *coup de grace* to enemy wounded. Duncan and his entourage conveyed in a Czech staging (1963) the climate of a dissolute court, into which the message from battle was an intrusion.

Before Charles Kean, the bleeding Captain generally dashed in with his momentous news as if he had run a long distance, and staggered toward the king. He may not be able to sustain himself, but falls and addresses the king from the ground (Japan). Or his recognition by Duncan, and the audience, may be attenuated (again, is the bloody man Macbeth?), when at first, on a vast empty stage, only a bleeding hand can be seen stretched out beyond the black edge of a rock, and only very slowly the man inches himself into view (Germany). In another German entrance that reflected on Duncan's character, the Captain staggered forward on a plank bridge some six feet above the ground; his bloody sword slipped from his hand and fell, sticking into the ground of the stage just behind the king, passing by. For a moment Duncan was silent in fright; then, looking up at the man, he began to speak.

When the Captain is carried in, his litter is usually a makeshift of hurdles or boughs, to suggest wild country. He is likely to be borne in tenderly; but in a "primitive" *Macbeth* (England, 1949), in a barbaric rush, Scots warriors swirled up the front of the stage bearing a horribly gashed soldier. In Tyrone Power's promptbook (1907), the Captain, on a rough, hide-covered litter, is only semiconscious, awakens at Malcolm's *Hail* astonished to find himself in the presence of the king. Edwin Booth's (U.S., 1881)* litter-borne casualty carried a half-broken sword, a token of the battle. E. H. Sothern's (U.S., 1910) struggled up painfully on his bier to tell Duncan his story.

---

*Hereafter I will refer to Edwin Booth simply as Booth, and provide first names for other Booths.

Because the Captain's speech is figurative and metaphorical, with occasional irregular rhythms, it is sometimes considered to have been interpolated, perhaps by Middleton, or to have been cut in places (see Halio, following Nosworthy). I do not think either supposition is necessary. Let us see.

I call the bleeding man "Captain", as the Folio stage direction does. Malcolm calls him *Sergeant*. "Sergeant" could be the particular title of men who, to cite the OED, are "of knightly rank . . . required to be in immediate attendance on the king's person." The Captain might have been one of Prince Malcolm's bodyguards, acting as a Sergeant when he saved Malcolm from capture. In any case, the title of Sergeant was a worthy one, and this officer of knightly rank would be entitled to speak in elegant language.

Too elegant? Defenders cite Coleridge's suggestion that perhaps Shakespeare deliberately used epic style here to make the tragic style elsewhere, by comparison, seem more "real-life." A parallel is drawn with the "Rugged Pyrrhus" speeches in *Hamlet*. But Pyrrhus' declamations are designedly quite different from the rest of the *Hamlet* language, as if to reflect an older, more stylized form; and Aeneas, the narrator, is not reporting an action on which the present fate of his hearers may hang. The Captain's language is not out of place in the diverse *Macbeth* rhetoric, and he is engaged in direct dialogue with his listeners. In fact, he is tantalizing them with trickles of information—information crucial to their immediate military situation. He could have rushed in shouting "We won!" or reported as concisely as the next messenger (Ross); but not he. His language and style spring from character, as we must know if we would act him. He has the quick individualization of other of Shakespeare's occasional court-attached characters: e.g. Osric, *Lear*'s Gentleman. This Captain is by turns ornate, earthy; soldier, poet; passionately loyal, exulting in violence, angry, triumphant, humorous. He is weak from wounds, a touch hysteric from his bloody ordeal, even in shock; but being a gifted storyteller, with a captive audience hanging on the suspenseful pauses and twists of his roller-coaster plot, one of his auditors even a king (*Mark, King of Scotland, mark* (34)), he summons strength to go on—though not failing to let his hearers sympathize with how wounded he is. Given a good actor, the theatre has no trouble with the speech; it becomes a fine, virtuoso piece, enjoyable partly because the Captain enjoys it so much. The wild excitement of Reinhardt's bloody soldier, Jacobsohn observed, was downright contagious.

The Captain's first line,

> *Doubtful it stood*, (13)

picks up after the leftover syllable of Malcolm's speech (*As thou didst leave it*), but it stands by itself, trochee rocked against iamb, an abrupt warning of uncertainty, of a piece with the action and language of the whole play. So, too, his next metaphor—of the two swimmers—and its extension, reflect the dialectic of oppositions to come: men paired in rivalry, divided but doubled, symbolic of counterforces exhausting themselves in seeking to eliminate each other. Macdonwald is

> Worthy to be a rebel (16)

—a sly oxymoron that will also have its reverberations. The Captain builds up to his first climax: Fortune, smiling on the enemy

> Shew'd like a rebel's whore: (21)

Almost a solid assault of spondees; and then the long pause of the colon, time for his hearers to react, then the change of tone, the reversing *but*—

> . . . but all's too weak: (21)

again the pause, on an ambiguity, until he plunges into praise (doubled), heavy with foreshadowing, for the man whose name we now hear for the second time—to be paired, as he often will be, with a rival:

> For brave Macbeth (well he deserves that name)
> Disdaining Fortune, with his brandished steel,
> Which smok'd with bloody execution
> (Like Valour's minion) carv'd out his passage,
> Till he fac'd the slave:
> Which nev'r shook hands, nor bade farewell to him,
> Till he unseam'd him from the nave to th' chops,
> And fix'd his head upon our battlements. (22-29)

Duncan's profession of warm pleasure at this recital, *O valiant cousin, worthy gentleman* (30), establishes the cultural approval of this Macbeth's violence. From what we learn later, a subtextual ambivalence may discolor in some degree the appreciation of Macbeth's prowess by Duncan—and by Malcolm; the language of the scene now has itself a curious, dialectical ambivalence. Macdonwald is *worthy* to be a rebel, for his war against the state; Macbeth is *worthy* because he kills a rebel, and kills so fiercely. In the interweaving in the play of violence with sexuality, the seductive Fortune serves the rebel like a *whore;* while Macbeth is *valour's minion:* denoting her favorite, her darling, and perhaps also carrying, as sometimes elsewhere in Shakespeare, a sense of erotic service. The Captain's gesture accompanying the "unseaming" must reflect a particular kind of assault on manhood: a savage yerk of the imaginary sword up through the guts, beginning at or near the genitals, then the upper body, to the brain.

The rhythms of the speech trouble some purists, mainly because lines here, and later, are metrically and syntactically irregular. Sceptics have guessed adulteration, later additions, or crude cutting. Thus Dover Wilson called the scene "a real blot upon the play's perfection . . . demonstrably the work of an alien hand." But the roughnesses in the Captain's lines are of the tissue of the play, welcome especially in the theatre. They may suggest, as

Knights and Flatter have noted, the wounded man's pauses for breath and
surcease from pain, and would certainly suit his delight in creating narrative
suspense. Some efforts to make the language in this scene fit the rack of meter
suggest unnecessary torture. Verity wanted the first word in Malcolm's

> . . . Hail, brave friend; (10)

scanned as two syllables—"Hay-ull"—to fill out the line. Several editors
have wanted *Sergeant* made into three syllables for the same reason. But to
the ear that welcomes Shakespeare's brilliant syncopation of *Macbeth*'s verse,
every jagged line, every broken utterance irregularizing the tempo, is a precious gift from the mature poet at work. He had experimented with truncated
verse before—for instance, with several lines in that portentous Pyrrhus
speech, including the wonderfully abrupt one of two words midway that
jerks the whole narration up short:

> . . . Pyrrhus stood
> And like a neutral to his will and matter,
> Did nothing.
> (*Hamlet*, II, ii, 502)

By his *Macbeth* rhythms Shakespeare enforces pauses, as he also enforces,
sometimes, an almost breakneck tempo. The Captain, master showman that
he is, uses both. He hoards his good news; makes his anxious auditors wait,
first frightens them, then dangles the bait of a momentary triumph, then
teases them with hints of disaster, finally relents when he is faint. In making
his auditors believe what has been, but is not now, true, he is a master equivocator. The *knowledge* of the broil he gives is, like most knowing in the play,
double-edged.

Macbeth begins to take shape for us from the reactions of others—as he
will throughout the play. When the Captain cries *brave Macbeth*, we not only
hear his praise, but also see and hear the enthusiastic assent of the army and
his peers. He is admired for his manliness, for his readiness to wade through
blood. *Merciless*, the Captain's word for the rebel, fits this Macbeth, this cousin
of royalty, too; he will disdain Fortune, he will carve out his passage, kill
those who stand in his way. *Which ne'er shook hands* is the Captain's irony—but
it insists on Macbeth's capacity for violence in disregard of courtesy. And
the admiration elicited for this bloody man, from the king down, insists on
the values put on this kind of "manhood" in society.

Before the cheering excitement can die, the Captain explodes another
fair-foul peripety, again bracing it with an oxymoron. Spondees, mainly
monosyllabic, override the iambic:

> So from that spring, whence comfort seem'd to come,
> Discomfort swells: Mark, King of Scotland, mark, (33-34)

An almost Cassandra-like quality accompanies this calling of the perhaps
impatient king to attention: and indeed the two lines are prophetic of Duncan's

own future peripety—though the Captain will now draw comfort from discomfort. Duncan, disturbed as the Captain knows he must be, returns the expected cue. Again the rhythm seems deliberately disjointed for emphasis, the word *Captains* acting as fulcrum to the line, forcing a halt and pause before the repetition of Macbeth's name:

> Dismay'd not this our Captains, [:] Macbeth and Banquo? (40)

Captains may sometimes have been voiced in three syllables; but the jolt of the more accustomed pronunciation suits the *Macbeth* syncopation, and what Elwin called "the slackened delivery of dejection [after] Duncan's more rapid exclamation of joyous admiration." (Do we note the other Captain's name, besides Macbeth's, mentioned and then ignored?)

With his audience at his mercy, the Captain gives them a joke, in short, quick lines, that draws a relieved laugh. He still equivocates, suggesting one appearance while intending another, here using irony, which, like punning, is equivocation pure:

> Yes, as sparrows, eagles;
> Or the hare, the lion . . . (42-43)

and goes on, in his hyperbolic way, to initiate images that will echo through the play, of doubling, redoubling, re-redoubling—reflecting verbally the sense of things more than they are, or can be, of refracted duplicates that mock reality, of excessiveness. The Captain's metaphor fits the overreachers he describes: an overcharged cannon, unable to maintain the explosive force within it, may burst and destroy itself as it lets loose its fury on the world around it. *If I say sooth*, he says; and indeed, again and again, he is soothsayer in the prophetic sense.

Finally comes the terrible vision of Macbeth and Banquo apocalyptic.

> Except they meant to bathe in reeking wounds,
> Or memorize another Golgotha. . . . (47-8)

A horrible image: human heads stripped of flesh on a battlefield—memorized, unforgettable. An agonized churchman contemplating the ghastly possibility of civil war in *Richard II* evoked the biblical image to suggest a kind of ultimate devastation:

> Disorder, horror, fear and mutiny
> Shall here inhabit, and this land be call'd
> The field of Golgotha, and dead men s skulls.
> (*Richard II*, IV, i, 142)

Duncan delightedly welcomes the Captain's bloody words, that *smack of honor*. Even scholars determined to see the symbols of God and goodness in Duncan perceive a dissonance here—but not always its implications. Battenhouse thinks Shakespeare is suggesting, in Macbeth, a "violence unnatural"; and Walker senses that "something is obviously wrong in this story of heroism"; but both see this as reflecting on Macbeth, neither observes how it characterizes Duncan, whose hearty approval smacks of delight in the slaughter. To find Christ, or God, or saintliness in the king's responses is to endow divinity with savagery. Here is no "overflowing love, beneficence, and graciousness" (Siegel). This circumstance has troubled the openminded Maynard Mack, Jr. He sees the Duncan interlude as the brief glimpse of "an ideal king for an ideal world"; yet the king's praise of Macbeth's bloody work

> jars oddly against the violence it approves . . . warns us that Shakespeare has placed his ideal king in a dramatic context that foreshadows and almost guarantees his ruin.

Duncan is much more, much deeper, than a mere ideal king. An actor, inhabiting this representation of mortality, can discover a king's relief from anxiety about the danger and disorder he has permitted in his kingdom, and a mortal satisfaction in the savage defeat of enemies—though perhaps, because he is (we will be told) gentle and meek, he may feel also a squeamishness about the brutality described to him. In this play where so much real feeling is subtextual, his masked reaction may be experienced behind his words.

Perhaps the Captain senses such a reaction in Duncan; perhaps he himself is partly overcome by the horror he hears himself describing as well as by his gashes; perhaps, himself a cannon overcharged, he has spent his great double loading—for he breaks off, and in terse half-lines asks for help. In the theatre he falls back on his litter; or, if risen, staggers, or crumples to the floor. He has groaned or screamed when touched; has fainted—once, when the scene was a court, onto the stairs leading to Duncan's throne. Nunn's old king reached a gentle hand down to the spent man lying before him. One bravura Captain reeled, blood and all, against his startled, recoiling king.

Duncan orders aid—sometimes of the Physician, directed to make his early appearance in some stage versions. Malcolm has sometimes moved to help. The Captain is often supported off, in acting and in regular editions, to clear the way for the next beat, and we lose him. The Folio does not direct his exit, and Shakespeare may have intended his care and bandaging to counterpoint what happens next. This Captain is worth keeping—perhaps attending Macbeth in the following scenes, marking the time passing as he sheds his bandages and recovers from his wounds. At some early point in the play Macbeth will be seen to be served by Seyton, though that faithful man is not named until later. (This may reflect repertory practice; the playwright in rehearsal may have suggested a name for a character, and not bothered to write it down until later: as with the disguised Kent in *Lear*, whose assumed name, Caius, is never mentioned until the very end.) The Captain might well become Macbeth's loyal Seyton, his hyperexcitement of battle over, serving in almost doglike silence, to the end, the terrible man he so much admires. An actor might find the key to Seyton in this.

Using again the classical theatrical device of creating anticipation by drawing attention to an entrance, Shakespeare has Duncan glimpse men rushing in from offstage. Malcolm quickly identifies one as Ross—let us remember this. Lenox furthers anticipation:

> What a haste looks through his eyes?
> So should he look, that seems to speak things strange. (56-57)

Again, alarm! In this disordered kingdom, what disturbing, what uncanny news now? Shakespeare may not be playing entirely fair here (but see below): Ross tells not a strange but a straightforward story, with a few lines about the dangerous enemy, to evoke momentary suspense, but follows with quick assurance of victory. He speaks metaphorically, like the Captain, though without the soldier's teasing "strangeness."

Ross takes his place with the "minor characters," who are sometimes lumped together by critics, at least since Maginn, as flat, or unindividualized, or undeveloped, or uninteresting, or without personality, as functions rather than personae. This underestimates Shakespeare's capacity for compressed characterization in the least of his smaller creations. These "minor" thanes, both separately and in a group, contribute important ground notes to the *Macbeth* music. They are parts of the human "order" that men subscribe to until breaking it is more rewarding. "Degree" conditions their behavior: social and political degree, the place a man has among other men. It will determine where men will sit at a banquet; how close, according to rank, they may station themselves near the king, or awaken him from sleep; to whom they must look up, and upon whom down. Degree both teaches men their place, and dares them to climb higher. Twice in the first act we become aware of thanes who take the dare, defying degree, risking a vault that will upset the given order and replace it with one they can top. One thane has mounted a rebellion, conspired with an invader to take the throne; another will aim at more direct means. The other thanes breathe the same heady air, may likewise dream of playing leapfrog with degree. We will see them change loyalties, think or actively spread disloyalty while mouth-honoring the king they have sworn to follow. They will differ in degree in their defiance of degree. Only a great overreacher will try the ultimate leap; lesser men will seek to rise by finding the right coattails to clutch. These are the *traitors and liars enough* that even a little boy will discern in the *Macbeth* society.

Two thanes in particular, Lenox and Ross, will be weathervanes of courtly winds. Lenox is quite young, a fact that criticism and the theatre generally ignore; he is easily excited, which may explain his anticipation of strangeness from Ross' look (Shakespeare's character-excuse for inserting Lenox' later alarm-note of the uncanny?). Lenox—and Ross—are distinguished not as warriors but as political men, who serve the business of power: a touch in their dress of the diplomat, the "civilian", may set them apart from the fighting thanes.* Lenox' political design will emerge in his ubiquitousness: he is almost always there when courtiers gather in the *Macbeth* world. In every scene with a king, for four acts, Lenox is as close as he can get to the current royal elbow; in Act V he switches to an elbow-elect. His gravitation to power was emphasized in a *Macbeth* at Lincoln (England, 1974) observed by Lois Potter: this Lenox managed early on to be close to Duncan, and then Malcolm, as centers of authority, and to betray a jealousy of the importance of Ross. He would be among the first to attach himself to Malcolm, when the latter (himself clearly a political animal) was named Prince of Cumberland; he would be ostentatiously at Macbeth's side after Duncan's death, until the end when he would ease himself into the role of mentor to the new king, Malcolm.† Ross also keeps turning up at the seats of power—so much so that Libby, in an interesting little book, distinguishes him as a great villain of the play; and at least one acting of *Macbeth* (Polanski's) has made him so. He will bear watching, this figure who keeps himself safe, who can warn a woman cousin of danger, but flee from protecting her; who manages to be a messenger to those who are on top—or who will be; who is called worthy by king and prince. He begins

> God save the King. (58)

God will be often called on in *Macbeth:* how He hears these supplications we will learn.

Ross has come from Fife, to report the final victory by Macbeth, whom he calls *Bellona's bridegroom:* that is, husband, lover, perhaps soldier-servant to a fierce woman—an image that may persist subliminally in our minds. The word-sequence suggests a further subtle sounding of the play's sexuality-violence strain: *Bellona's bridegroom, lapped . . .* The immediacy of the third word, after *bridegroom*, allows an erotic implication, country matters; and the full phrase, *lapped in proof*, suggests a kind of consummation confirming Macbeth's manliness, tested in a great and terrible wedding bed.

The assumption is sometimes made that the Captain's battle was at Forres, impossibly far from Fife; but the Captain never says so, and he seems to have come straight from Fife, for he told of the *Norweyan lord*'s fresh assault there, and it is that conflict that Ross now describes. We learn later that Macbeth after the battle is making his way *to* Forres, so he probably was not fighting there. The geographical details are not crucial, and as Muir suggests, contemporary audiences would probably not have noticed discrepancies; no inconsistency need be found. Shakespeare was busy getting in some exciting, far-off place names.

---

*This impression was effectively achieved in the "modernized" McKellen *Macbeth* with a dapper, shrewd Ross in the striped-pants uniform of diplomacy.

†For all his ubiquity, Lenox's name is never mentioned in the play's dialogue. As observed above, this may reflect repertory practice: the name may have been thrown in by actors where convenient (see also the discussion of Macduff in II, iii). Lenox' very namelessness may be a symptom of his chameleon role.

Ross introduces a new and sinister symptom of disorder in the kingdom: we have heard of a rebel leading a revolt against the state; now we learn of a thane of very high rank—apparently highest below royalty, for his title will be bestowed on the nation's hero—who has turned traitor to help the invader. This is Cawdor—the name is harsh, grating—a prosperous gentleman, we will learn, hence one who had no *need* for aggrandizement, but who was caught up in the striving to overturn degree. He has allied himself with the Norse invaders—led by

> Norway himself, with terrible numbers, (63)

and the commas give moments of pause for response to this alarming news of the foreign king's presence at the head of his attacking army. This king is a fierce warrior, but Macbeth

> Confronted him with self-comparisons . . . (67),

met him man against man, man against king; tested himself as well as his opponent to the utmost, his

> . . . rebellious arm 'gainst arm (68)

curbing Sweno's lavish spirit, and so he triumphed over this holder of the very highest degree, and forced him to crave composition.

Duncan and his entourage are directed in acting versions to respond again as they did to the Captain: "apprehension" when Ross starts his tale, and "surprise" and "alarm" at the news of Cawdor's treachery and Norway's terrible army, ending with admiration at Macbeth's triumphant valor: "a big reaction from all," "laughs of derision and exclamation," and "shouts of joy." In the mirror of *self-comparison* the Scots champion comes away with the noblest of images; his *rebellious arm* is acclaimed for downing a king. By his violent bravery, his manlike fierceness, he has returned order to the state.

No more, Duncan declares, will a traitor practice deception upon his kingship. He will return to this theme: that he trusts, and men betray him. So he lifts Cawdor's title, the lofty symbol of high degree, from the betrayer, and dresses Macbeth with it—putting Macbeth a nearer step to the throne itself.

> . . . with his former title greet Macbeth. (79)

In some stagings, Cawdor himself has been dragged onto the stage, bound or in chains, for execution or to be haled off to it; but not before Duncan, or a designated officer, tears off the thane's badge, usually worn as a pendant, for Ross to take to Macbeth. This junction of the visual symbols of degree, and of disruption of degree, fits Duncan's unwitting echo of the witches' dialectics, and the equivocation of his ironically prophetic gift of more than Cawdor's title:

> What he hath lost, noble Macbeth hath won. (81)

A drum, a drum: Macbeth doth come.

Act I, Scene iii (part i)

Duncan's last words float on the air, echoing the witches' dialectic: *lost . . . won . . . lost . . . won.* Heard too, in productions emphasizing the Sisters' malice, or omnipresence, their laughter or other sounds of their world mingling with the human ones, or, as in Tree's staging, orchestrated to the rising storm.

The king and his attendants exit in formal order, determined by rooted hierarchical rank. Flag bearers, protective sergeants, and chamberlains may lead the advance, but the king is first in fact, then the prince; men of substance fall in behind, according to their degree which—we will be reminded later— they know.

At the last scene end we were for the second time led to expect Macbeth— either to see his acceptance of new honors from Ross, or his meeting the Sisters, or both. Again, expectation is suspended. Men disappear from this emptied world.

Here is the lonely heath again, blasted; death lives here. If one of the witches has been eavesdropping, by some signal she calls the others to her. They appear best separately, since First must ask the others where they have been. They may seem to come from the corners of the world, for this meeting at sunset, appearing, in the same way as they vanished, either suddenly, or almost imperceptibly, heralded by their sounds, or their silence. If, as at the Meiningen, by turning their backs they had disappeared by transformation into boulders, wall, or earth, or into something other native to their wayward world, now they take shape again, by turning back into the open. They may seem to swell up from the ground (Germany) like bladders—earth bubbles. For Phelps and Kean, they materialized as they had melted away, behind layers of gauze. They have flown in or risen from traps; in the Hall-Scofield *Macbeth*, they emerged from the dark red miasma of the stage matting. The expressionistic witches continue as light and shadow or symbolic form; their voices—and the voices of some more realistic Sisters—issue from loud- speakers that, if located throughout the theatre, seem to pervade the whole world.

Sometimes the witches debouch at once, sometimes they come as single spies. Macready's Witch 1 emerged to stand alone at the back, listening, peering into the darkness; then 2 and 3 filtered in from opposite sides of the stage.

As always, they come in storm. *Thunder*, Folio directs; "lightning" the theatre often adds. This new—or renewed—storm will top the first in some way: in sound, or intensity, or ominousness, or in sudden silences—to fit the build of Shakespeare's design. In realistic staging, as brought to climax by Irving and Tree, the wasted heath, in support of the language, is grandly gloomy, made to seem vast and desolate, fitted to the sunset rendezvous with a blood-red sun, streaked by cloud and rain, sinking in the west. The Sisters are sometimes silhouetted against the sky, to emphasize their strangeness, perhaps their gauntness, their odd accoutrements: they may carry their witches paraphernalia, perhaps the fruits of their corpse-robbing—armor, arms, bloody clothes, human remains.

Gordon Craig stipulated a wind machine, to blow in gusts about the Sisters' cloaks, as they stood on the central bridge he designed. He wanted the sense of air, lightness: a leaf or piece of paper was to play in the wind. On one side the sky still light, the other "pretty indigoish and ugly. . . . Let it be gay and light, only the indigo on our side very ominous." The Sisters were to appear in a flash, from a trap. In Beerbohm Tree's spectacular rising, gothic storm, the great backstage tree, struck by lightning, flared and split, then in a loud rush of air swayed and crashed. The Sisters, screaming with the laughter that heralded their entrance—two by flight, one afoot—mounted its ruins.

Various polyphonic associations with witchcraft already discussed may be evoked or imagined in the Sisters' advent. However realistic, beautiful, or ugly they appear, however much woman, or man, something in them is on the edge of human: the strangeness of their coming, of their garments or appurtenances, their movements echo a chthonic if not "elder" world. If they demonstrate magic power—e.g., control weather and wind—the supernatural is explicit; but something of it may reverberate even when they are treated most objectively. The rhythm of their speech, their words, their acts, haunt our reason.

If they are not of the kind that change or transform, they are likely to be recognizably the same as in I, i; even so, as part of an ascending design, they are nerved to a new intensity, a nearer readiness for rendezvous, an awareness of impending climax. Of what they await we may be reminded not only by their looks and listens, but also by the sounds, far off, of approaching drums and such other army manifestations as marching, shouting orders. (Long before the time of modulated electronic sound controls, Charles Kean had his military noise and music issue from the greenroom, the doors of which opened and closed to give the idea of vagrant winds wafting sound.)

Dialogue opens, for the third successive scene, with a *wh-* question. First *When?* Then *What?* Now: *Where?* Degree seems to operate in the Sisters' world as well as in Duncan's: Witch 1 always speaks first, asks the questions of the others, initiates the rituals, commands most power.

> Where hast thou been, Sister?
> Killing swine. (3–4)

Implying, as commonly glossed, the witchcraft of "overlooking"—that is, magically attacking with the evil eye, and so killing, livestock. But the question may also have been prompted by what Witch 1 sees on 2: blood. Pig-sticking is a notoriously bloody business; and the killing would carry the aura of a ritual act, or preparation for it: the Sisters will need baboon's blood later, may want pigs' blood now. Something archetypal may resonate: Neumann describes the slaying of a pig as a central sacrifice in ancient rites.

Only Sister 1, of the three, ever overtly suggests a motive for malice; and it is the malice of revenge, provoked by rejection. In this she is, as we saw, recognizably the contemporary Jacobean old-woman-witch, who practiced the harmful side of her craft on those who mistreated or neglected her. Sister 1 had begged for food, and was denied it by a *rump-fed ronyon*. Rump-fed almost certainly suggests a diet of the best cuts—as Verity suggested—as opposed to "offal." The proposed gloss "fat-bottomed" is appropriately insulting; but *ronyon* was insulting enough, and rump-that-was-fed seems less likely than fed-on-rump; the very well-fedness of this *ronyon** evidently added to Sister 1's provocation, and provided an understandable prick to her revenge. A greedy glutton refusing to share with a hungry old woman, possibly a witch, might expect to pay for it—magic, or the threat of it, being the only power old social relics could use against unfeeling society. The rebuff,

> Aroynt thee, *witch* . . .

serves partly to identify, at last, something of how these creatures are to be comprehended. The formula for exorcising recalls Edgar's "Aroint thee witch aroint thee" in *Lear*; the sound is also close enough to suggest "Anoint thee"— Jonson notes in his *Masque of Queens* that for transporting "from place to place," witches "use to anoynt themselves."

(Note, again, that the revenge the Sister plans *is* motivated and is the only piece of explicit malice Shakespeare gives the three. Left clouded are whatever moves them to engage with Macbeth, and whatever their purpose toward him. Overtly they *grieve his heart* in IV, i, with a show of kings, only when he forces them to it.)

Sister 1's threats to the *ronyon*'s husband bristle with the claimed powers of witchcraft to do harm. These creatures carry an aura of uncanny danger; when they are provoked, they let loose the armory of "bad" magic. The Sister will sail in a sieve, and

> . . . like a rat without a tail,
> I'll do, I'll do, and I'll do. (12–13)

---

*A rather vague term of abuse, which, applied to Falstaff in his woman's dress (MW IV, ii, 160), seemed to suggest someone fat and objectionable, mangy and scabbed.

Mutilated animals might be thought to be devil-marked; but here the implication, perhaps reinforced by gesture, is probably less theological than biological. Rats notoriously indulge in unbridled sexuality; a female without a tail would be lavishly accessible to the mounting male. The verb *do* served Shakespeare elsewhere as a synonym for sexual intercourse, overtly in the naughty exchange between Cressida and Pandarus (IV, ii).* Witch 1 suggests such excess of sexuality that it will become a kind of torture (note again the syncopation of "I will"):

> I'll drain him dry as hay:
> Sleep shall neither night nor day
> Hang upon his penthouse lid:
> He shall live a man forbid:
> Weary sev'nights, nine times nine,
> Shall he dwindle, peak and pine: (21–26)

Here fantasies of witches' lubricity, and of the insatiable succubus, come together in an image of impulses toward satisfaction carried to excess, destroying. The vivid experience of the image, and of the desperation of its victim, is stored in our continuing response to the play; some echo may sound later of another glutted man, sleepless, *forbid*.

The Sister aims, in fact, not at the man, but at his wife, the *ronyon*. Rendering a husband impotent—"ligature"—was one of the chief crimes asserted against sorcerers. Robbins, tracing it back as far as Vergil, offers these primary definitions, from an Italian authority (1608):

1. When one of a married couple is made hateful to the other, or both hateful to each other.
2. When some bodily hindrance keeps a husband and wife apart in different places, or when some thing or phantom is interposed.

That male impotence from witchery was regarded as a significant danger in Shakespeare's time is evident in the attention Reginald Scot gave to the popular beliefs in it. He allots the whole substance of his Book IV to the mythical ravages of the "Incubus," with this titillating preface:

> In so much as I am driven (for the more manifest bewraieng and displaieng of this most filthie and horrible error) to staine my paper with writing thereon certain of their beastlie and bawdie assertions . . . I must intreat . . . readers hereof, whose chaste ears cannot well endure to hear of such abominable lecheries . . . to turne over a few leaves.

(Of course as a scholar I felt obliged to read on.)

Scot deals with the imagined lusts of the Incubus, how it was supposed to

---

*Partridge cites other examples, but misses this one. He seems, also, to have missed the undertow of the sexuality linked with violence in *Macbeth*, which he dismissed as "the 'purest' of the Tragedies and, except for the Porter Scene, pure by any criterion." The purity he speaks of is of course 'moral', not aesthetic.

disable sexuality, and what sorcery was recommended for it. Among the most innocent remedies he mentions are "pissing through a wedding ring," and making an effigy of the bewitched organ and offering it at a saint's altar. Curiously, the one remedy Scot was "ashamed to write" in his catalogue was from "Sir *Th. Moore* . . . for in filthie bawdrie it passeth all the tales that ever I heard."

With a rather surprising "modernity," Scot diagnosed the Incubus as a disease of the imagination. As for the matter of impotence in men, he notes that "manie are so bewitched that they cannot use their own wives; but manie other bodies they maie well enough away withall. Which witchcraft is practised among manie bad husbands, for whom it were a good excuse to saie they were bewitched."

Shakespeare may well have been exploiting the popular beliefs and anxieties with his Sisters and their supposed sensual habits; and perhaps at this or other moments in I, iii, and IV, i, his actors behaved somewhat as witches were supposed to, in fields or woods, according to one of Scot's authorities:

> prostituting themselves uncovered and naked up to the navill, wagging and mooving their members in every part, according to the disposition of one being about that act of concupiscence, and yet nothing seen . . . upon hir; saving that after such a convenient time as is required about such a piece of worke, a blacke vapor of the length and bignesse of a man, hath been seene as it were to depart from hir.

Some twentieth century Sisters, as suggested earlier, have emphasized this kind of sensuality; in one German staging of this scene, the Three, camp-following whores, danced a striptease of what scanty garments they had on.

The Sisters' magic may now again be manifested by what they say they make happen. *I'll give thee a wind*, 2 says; and 3 will give one, too. *Thou'rt kind*, 1 says; and Richepin catches the primary meaning, if extravagantly, with "Oh! Que de gentilesse!"—for witches supposedly could *sell* winds rather than give. But another meaning may subsist: they are all of a *kind*, these three, not of the world of ordinary men and women. Strange.

Do they call the winds forth, by look or sound or gesture? Turn their backsides, to break wind? Pull breezes from pocket, or purse, and fling them into the air, to howl and whistle? Do the winds now seem to rise of themselves, as by coincidence?

Or is the Sisters' magic more mundane? In the theatre besides the gestures above, they have made occult ritual of revenge: they have shaped a doll of the shipmaster, and stuck in pins—e.g., a pin for each cruel word at *dwindle . . . peak . . . pine;* have given tokens for winds; have made cabalistic signs, and curious, laughing, or moaning, sounds; have tapped with wands or sticks in time to the beat of their talk—*do . . . do . . . do.* Their verbal rhythms are tantalizing: never an easy pattern, never a fixed base. The first few lines of the scene have almost the beat of spondees; the few following iambic pentameters give way to shorter, syncopated accents, unmistakably rhythmic but defying easy scansion. The developing, catchy beat and rhyming echo a ritual chant. Sister 1 sometimes voices her promised revenge as if a priestess.

She changes abruptly to her new subject—the pilot's thumb. A great prize; phallic; the Sisters admire it, have made much of it, stroked it, nuzzled it, nibbled. *Thumb*—twice the word will trigger an awareness of Macbeth's coming. Now it rhymes with his drum: and the Sisters go into the ritual preparation for his advent. They call themselves, in Folio, *weyward;* as I have observed, it is a good, polyphonic word that links well to the mercurial image of *Posters of the sea and land;* it need not be changed to the reductively explicit "weird."

The charm to bring on Macbeth gathers speed as it goes along, building to the climax of the last accumulation of threes—the magic number the Sisters themselves incarnate—until it is literally *wound up.* Some special excitement now infects them; some great moment lies ahead. Many notes may sound in their anticipatory chant? song? dance? menace? glee? passion? The rhythm is smooth, but the movements may be—have been—wild and grotesque. Piscator's witches (Germany, 1953) danced as if riding in the wind.

The Sisters in this scene may perform a rite akin to the one seen in I, i, and foreshadowing a later one: mixing strange recipes, shaping and piercing dolls—in the Welles film an effigy was made, to be a stand-in for Macbeth in a mock rehearsal of the ceremony that was to come. What the sisters plan is still mysterious: they may seem to be setting an ambush; preparing for a sacrifice; tracking a victim; greeting a lover; readying a reward; keeping an appointment for witchery. We wait to know.

Enter Macbeth and Banquo.

Macbeth

To dare to inhabit Macbeth, to stretch imagination, feeling, and understanding to the last reaches of this character design, is to adventure toward the limits of artistic experience. Nothing in drama demands more of our response repertory. Into this design Shakespeare has crammed diverse, conflicting, intimate qualities of humanity almost more than any artifact might be expected to bear. In fact more, Bridges has complained worshipfully; a Schücking would argue that Shakespeare never put its incongruous pieces together, a Stoll that the playwright didn't care. No. As Shakespeare's art made the ultimate demands on him, he made them on this design. For all his lavish, centrifugal outpouring of character elements, a center holds. And grows.

The startling diversity of the qualities in the design shows in the descriptives of Macbeth listed below,* collected from comments on the character in criticism, or in reports of acting: note how many must be put together to describe

*Abandoned, abject, absent, abrupt, abstracted, affectionate, aghast, agitated, agonized, almost godlike, almost superhuman, amazed, ambitious, amiable, apathy, appalling, apprehensive, atheist, athlete in evil, authority, awe-inspiring, awesome. Badgered, barbarian, barbaric, beast, betrayed, bewildered, bitter, bloodthirsty, bloody, bluff, bold, bombastic, brainsick, bravery, brawny, broken, brooding, brutalizing, brute, bullies, buoyant, burly, butcher. Callous, catlike, charisma, charm, cheerful, chivalric, clairvoyant, clarity of vision, coarsening, commanding, complex, compulsive, confused, conscience, conscientious, consternation, contemplative, contrition, convulsive, cornered, corrupted, courageous, courtliness, coward, crafty, credulous, cruel, cunning. Damned, dangerous, daring, dark, dauntless, decisive, defender, defiant, degenerates, degraded, dejection, delicate in perception, deserted, desolate, despairing, desperate, despondent, determined, disappointed, disgust, dishevelled, disillusionment, distempered, distracted, distraught, divided, divinely human, dominating, dreamer, driven, dutiful, dwarfed. Earthy, emotional, endurance, energy, envy, excitable, expressive, extraordinary, evil. Faltering, farouche, fatalist, ferocious, ferocity, fervor, feverish, fierce, finely strung, flawed, forlorn, frank, frantic, frightened, furious, furtive. Gallant, gangster, generous, genial, gentleness, gibbering, gladiator, gloomy, goaded, goodness, graciousness, grandeur, granite, great, greed, grief, grim, growing, gullible. Haggard, half-crazed, half-hypnotized, hallucinating, harrowed, harshness, hasty, hated, haughty, haunted, headlong, heartless, heartrending, henpecked, hero, heroic, hesitant, hollow, homicidal, honorable, hopeless, human, humanity, humankindness, hypocritical, hysteric. Imaginative, impatient, impenitent, imperial, imperious, impetuous, impulsive, indomitable, infuriated, ingratiating, instability, instinctive, intelligent,

Macbeth for any single moment. Note, too, how the combinations must change with his moments. The design is a dynamic process, the center masked by a flux of complex, recognizably human responses to new crises.

The shifting qualities congregate and dissolve around the multiple roles Macbeth must play: among them, soldier, general, king, poet, philosopher, player, tyrant, host, father, kinsman, nobleman, hypocrite, liar, traitor, accomplice, murderer, butcher, neurotic, occultist, husband, lover.

Further complicating the design: both the qualities and roles are often polarized, in a furious dialectic. Reciprocation or opposition is implicit in the descriptives: Macbeth is villain and hero, victim and victimizer, manipulated and manipulator, compelled and wilful, noble and vicious. The proper balance is partly in the eye of the beholder, as evident in a sample anthology of comments by critics and by observers of performances—good and ill—in the theatre:

> magnificently great in passion, ambition, imaginative capacity to feel; also poor, vain, cruel, treacherous, snatching ruthlessly over friend and kinsman . . . (the) contrast between his courage when faced with the tangible, and the terror of guilt . . . alternately jealous and generous . . . both vile and heroic . . . his rich voice lends evil a certain dignity . . . lacks neither courage nor sensibility . . . more fire than thought . . . his strong physique illuminates his moral insufficiencies . . . too earthy, no visionary . . . soaring imagination, heroic courage, animal cunning, instinctive nobility, and craven hypocrisy . . . brutal enough to kill, noble enough to feel conscience . . . innately ambitious, religiously humane . . . brave in battle, quaking in imagination . . . inner tenderness, and the ferocity of his age . . . capacity for remorse equal to his capacity for ambition . . . meditates craftily, executes with tigerish

intrepidity, introspective, introvert, irresolute, irresolution, irritable, isolated. Jealous, just. Kindness. Lachrymose, lion, listlessness, lofty, loved, loving, loyal, lying, lyrical. Mad, magnanimous, magnificent, majestic, malevolent, maniacal, malicious, manliness, manly, massive, materialist, melancholy, menacing, mercurial, mighty, monster, moody, morally triumphant, morally defective, morbid, mournful, murderous, muscular. Narcissism, nervous, nimblewitted, noble, nobleman, nonplussed. Observant, oppressed, optimistic, overwhelmed, overwrought. Passionate, paternal, pathetic, pathos, patriot, pensive, perplexed, petulant, philosophical, pious, pitiable, poetic, powerful, preoccupied, pride, primitive, prudent. Rapt, rash, rational, rationalizing, ravaged, raving, reckless, rectitude, refined, reflective, reluctant, remorse, remorseful, remote, repentant, reserved, resolute, resourceful, restless, robust, rough, ruffian, rugged, a ruin, ruthless. Sardonic, saturnine, savage, scheming, secretive, self-aware, selfish, self-regarding, self-torturing, semi-barbaric, sensitive, sensitivity, sentimentalist, sexual, shame, shamefaced, shifty, shivering, shrinks, shuddering, sickened, simple, sinister, sin-laden, smug, solitary, sombre, splendid, stalwart, stateliness, stern, stormy, strong, strongly sexual, stultified, stupefaction, subdued, sublime, subtle, suffering, suggestible, suicidal, sulky, sullen, superstitious, suspicious, sweet. Temperamental, temperate, tempest-haunted, tempestuous, tender, terrified, thoughtful, tigerish, timid, timorous, tired, tormented, torn, tortured, touching, traitor, trapped, treacherous, troubled, turbulent, tyrannical. Unbridled, uncertain, undecided, underdog, uneasy, ungovernable, unregretful, unscrupulous, unstrung, untamed, untruthful, unwhimpering, unyielding, usurper, uxorious. Vain, valiant, vehement, vicious, victorious, vigorous, vindictive, violent, virtuous, visionary, vital, (incandescent) vitality, voluptuous, vulnerable. Wanton, warlike, warrior, weak, weary, wicked, wild, wise, wistful, withering, worn, worried, wretched.

ferocity . . . good on the fatalism, superstition, but not on the terror, rage, despair . . . strength of nerve rather than body . . . from boastful satisfaction to angry discontent . . . intellectual rather than imaginative . . . richly furnished with the good, fatally susceptible to evil . . . the retiring of the human heart, the entering of the fiendish heart . . . the mind sunk by guilt into cowardice and rising with horror to acts of madness and desperation . . . graceful horror . . . the hesitancy of remorseful conscience followed by new and more savage abandonment . . . from burly vigor to paralyzed, fatigued despair . . . ruined by the qualities that made him great . . . lofty ambitions, deep, dark desires, kind affections, treacherous disloyalty . . . the milk of human kindness and bloodthirstiness commingled . . . henpecked at home, a lion on the battlefield . . . from awe-inspiring warrior to cruel tyrant . . . in action a monster, in language a poet, in feelings the greatest of sufferers . . . the face of the primitive cannot hide the courtliness of the warrior . . . needs the imagination of the haunted poet, the physical aspect of the warrior . . . must be both Bellona's bridegroom and a hag-ridden neurotic . . . less the fighting Scotsman than the Dane . . . a sentimental slaughterman who dare not go near the abatoir after dark . . . the ideal Macbeth: a man of action breaking down into a poet . . . the soldier and the murderer too, combines the practicality of the mud-stained warrior with the golden eloquence of the poet . . . the most sentimental of butchers . . . the villainy of Richard III, the reflection of Hamlet . . . half villain, half hero . . . ferocious warrior, sensitive poet, the fear of the haunted, the callousness of a killer, the selfconscious calculation of a thinking man, the pathos of a great figure brought low . . . philosopher rather than butcher . . . the difficulty of reconciling the tough warrior with the superstitious neurotic . . . poet, murderer, dreamer, doer, tyrant, sniveller, warrior, philosopher, Shelley-Himmler, Hamlet-Fortinbras-Claudius . . . intelligent barbarian . . . a giant with a streak of the abject . . . kingliness flawed by greed . . . cut-throat poet . . . poet and dreamer, looking almost Christ-like . . . loving husband, diseased sinner . . . the genius of a war leader, the mind of a king, a man of action penetrating to the core of the idea of power . . . victim as well as malefactor . . . a poet with his brain, a villain with his heart . . . an assassin under compulsion rather than ambition.

Given this opulent polyphony of roles and characteristics, the Macbeth design might have dissolved in chaos: only the sternest artistic control in its creation could embrace such formidable multiplicity. And only the most sensitive and intense inhabitation of the design, in imagination or stage presence, can serve the playwright's intent. Not only must the polar elements be perceived and articulated: they must so interlock that they may be sensed in part and in the whole. So the actor Johnston Forbes-Robertson (U.S., 1898) was once admonished for not distinguishing the sub-roles enough. But the contours must also merge into a total dramatic personality, or the hard outlines may resist "blur"—Farjeon's brilliant complaint of Hackett's (U.S., 1916) Macbeth. So Charles Kean was blamed for playing the parts of Macbeth one by one, but not the whole. Fusion was deliberately avoided, and the multiplicity in the design dealt with trickily, in a Dunlop production (England, 1974) using three different actors as Macbeth: the first playing a wife-dominated conspirator; the second, after the murder, a massive presence with a dark voice, suggesting a majestic adept at magic; and the third, following the banquet, a damned soul past hope. Shakespeare asked one actor to be all of these, and more.

The coherence of Macbeth's design is contrived by a subtle interplay of verbal and visual effects. The language that sometimes starkly reveals Macbeth at other times conspires to mask him. What unifies the dramatic identity is the subtextual personality that exists before, behind, and between the words. Mrs. Montagu recognized this (1810) when she observed

> the art with which Shakespeare exhibits the movements of the human mind, and renders audible the silent march of thought.

Clemen similarly appreciated the nexus supporting the language:

> The words of Macbeth reveal only a fragment of what is taking shape within him. For his demeanour, his silence, his reactions, all allow us to feel what is in progress beneath the surface of the spoken word.

The actor Macready evoked a similar comment:

> Who does not feel, in reading Shakespeare, that the unwritten part of the character is a vastly larger part than the written? That there exist between the speeches vast intervals of passion . . . It is this unwritten portion of the character which Mr. Macready gives us. His acting fills up these chasms, and is the *complement* of the worded part; he not merely tells us what Macbeth thought when he spoke, but shows us all he felt before he spoke.

Macready found in the many human impulses touched in the Macbeth design, and the many roles it offered, a particular emphasis of thoughts and feelings to shape into the dramatic personality. Critics and other actors have been attracted to other combinations, in lavish variety. A study of their differing emphases on particular roles and qualities in the design will help us to discover its possibilities, and how, in its strange complexity, it models the conflict, ambiguity, and mystery of the play itself.

I embark on that study now, beginning with some preliminary consideration of the presence of Macbeth that may be imagined by the reader or be expected to appear on stage.

How old is he to be? Bergman deliberately made his first Macbeth—and his Lady—young, to evoke sympathy. Youth as such cannot guarantee a warm or poignant response—young cutthroats can seem as vicious as older ones, as was demonstrated in a Polish *Macbeth* (1964) where Macbeth and his Lady suggested a young gangster and his moll on the make. But youth can lend a touch of innocence to Macbeth's beginnings, as if he is too unsophisticated to measure fully the enormity of his temptation; and it may, as in Will Quadflieg's portrayal (Germany, 1953), partly explain the immediate snatch at ambition, and the sensuality latent in his relationship with his wife. One advantage of young principals, as in the Polanski film, can be the accumulating signs of maturity forced on the young couple that convey some sense of a long time suffering.* Aging there must be, for Macbeth to feel himself falling into the sere, the yellow leaf; the theatre often makes this visual when, after the long gap since his commitment to violence in IV, i, he appears in V eroded by time and suffering.

Shakespeare is not specific about Macbeth's years. Macbeth's father, Sinel, seems lately to have died, making Macbeth Thane of Glamis. His wife speaks of the infant she has suckled, and he urges her to produce men-children, so she is evidently of child-bearing age. (Historically, the Lady had issue by a previous marriage; but we are not to know that. Shakespeare presents these two as bound together once and for all. See Appendix.)

The tension between youth and age, a familiar motif in Shakespeare, pivots doubly around Macbeth: he is the younger man toppling old Duncan, as he will be the old one overturned by Duncan's son. Certainly at the outset Macbeth must seem older than Malcolm—older enough that his heroic achievement and soldierly capacity contrast sharply with the record of the young prince, whose chief role in the battle to save Scotland was to be rescued: some motivation for Macbeth may be seen in this. Bradley, after thoughtful consideration, visualized Macbeth on the young side of middle age, and so he is frequently played.

Conventionally, Macbeth is represented, or imagined, as embodying at first an image of nobility and heroism in a muscular warrior's form: a man apart by reason of stature, posture, and achievement. His worth will be reflected in admiring faces about him: he must certainly seem at first the most honored man in the kingdom, graced with golden opinions that surround him with an aura of respect and affection. His fellow thanes, when Duncan is dead, will quickly elevate him to the throne; and in appearance he may—like some theatre Macbeths—seem more kingly than the king. His ultimate enemy, Macduff, at first loves him well, Malcolm will recall (IV, iii); Malcolm himself will liken this early Macbeth to the *brightest angel*—who fell. Duncan says he loves him *highly*. His wife testifies to a noble humanity in him.

Yet the Macbeth design demands something more complex than an impressive heroic image. The heart and brain capable of murder will not show a face that is noble only; it will bear other traces of Adam, and, ironically, may most offer a facade of pure nobility when it sets out deliberately to mask its Dionysian impulses. In the theatre, Macbeths have failed from too much honesty, too much nobility. The fine face of Godfrey Tearle (England, 1949), that served so well his lofty, passionate Othello, was to some observers too noble, his velvet voice too emollient, for Macbeth; something apostolic, even Christ-like, in his sonorous despair unsuited the Macbeth darkness. Such a figure

---

*How young can they be? Kate Bateman played Macbeth at the age of six (her Lady Macbeth was her sister, aged all of four). "Those who came to scoff on the first night returned to praise" (Hutton, 241).

moved through a dream, rather than a reality, of evil. Similarly, of a German Macbeth (1960) of heroic dimensions, it was said that his romantic manner would not do—it was suited to Schiller, not Shakespeare. Even in Garrick's time, when, as we will see, Macbeth's goodness was at a premium, Spranger Barry (England, 1746), another grand, fierce, terrible Othello, suffered from his noble front: "the amorous harmony of his features and voice could but faintly, if at all, describe the passions incident to a tyrant."

Macbeth is noble; Macbeth murders. This is the primary polarity of the many in Macbeth's design: between the muscled warrior-killer and the sensitive poet-philosopher; and it offers a gateway to an exploration of the mystery of Shakespeare's creation. We must begin by following a historical path, since a definite chronological shift developed in *Macbeth* interpretation, a shift strongly influenced by cultural milieux, particularly evident in the eighteenth century. Social pressure affecting Shakespearean drama in the 1700s could be treated secondarily in my study of *Lear*, since no decent facsimile of the play worth examining existed in the English, German and French theatre—only the butcheries of Tate, Schröder and Ducis—until almost mid-nineteenth century. Not so with *Othello;* there, to understand contemporary interpretations, I had to examine the play's savaging by critics and actors relentlessly intent on a "refinement" that wore away what was "horrid" or erotic in the atmosphere and substance to suit a society that was "Victorian" almost a century before Victoria. *Macbeth* suffered, too; but different affronts. Eros, so insistent in the other major tragedies, is, except for the byplay of the witches, and the Porter, felt here mainly as undertow, linking sexuality with the violence. This may surface most in the erotic relationship of Macbeth and Lady Macbeth—which was an extremely restrained affair in the eighteenth century theatre. The brutal excision of the Porter was an early concession to propriety. He would be permitted to appear in the early nineteenth century as a lovable rustic singing a sweet dawnsong, in Schiller's translations; but only decades later in his own person. The earthy sting of the witches would be blunted by making them hollow comic characters.

But the play was most affected in the major characterizations. Escape from the urgencies of sexuality, natural function, and the "horrid" in the "proper" literature of the later eighteenth and early nineteenth centuries showed the back of a larger refusal to experience those black and dark desires of humanity reflected in so much of Shakespeare. Some critics would sympathize with Macbeth, or sentimentalize him, as we will see; but others seemed almost frightened of what he represented. Gildon, at the beginning of the eighteenth century, saw both Macbeths as too monstrous for the stage; the only positive quality Johnson could grant Macbeth was courage; Francis Gentleman, true voice of British pre-Victorian taste, was shocked by Macbeth's violence, found him "a detestable monster."

To make Macbeth palatable to the contemporary taste, he had to be re-

fined, as much as possible, into a man of sensibility; the deliberate violence
he engaged in had to be muted. The times were apprehensive of terror in the
theatre: Laetitia Barbauld spoke for a culture (1825) when she attempted to
distinguish "those kinds of distress which excite agreeable sensations from
. . . those painful and disgusting," and she complained of excesses in some
tragedies:

> Full of violent and gloomy passions, and so overwrought with horror, that
> instead of awakening any pleasing sensibility, they leave on the mind an
> impression of sadness and terror. Shakespeare is sometimes guilty of presenting
> scenes too shocking.

The accommodating theatre regularly blunted the "too shocking" deep bite
of Shakespeare's work. One of the saddest examples is the acculturated mis-
carriage of *Macbeth* represented by Garrick, the leading actor of the century.

England was long since accustomed to a *Macbeth* disfigured by Davenant
with insertions of watered lines, characterization, and the witches' ballets;
Garrick, to his credit, restored a portion of Shakespeare's language. However,
a printed edition of his text shows cuts of some 269 lines—more than a tenth
of Shakespeare's text: and a prompt copy of his edition in the Folger Library,
discussed by Stone and Burnim, shows further cuts, quite possibly contemporary, of another tenth. Garrick also kept the claptrap of the dancing and
singing witches, who enter after the murder to suggest a passage of time and
glee in wickedness:

> Above twelve glasses since have run . . .

then a long, dull revel that drains the Sisters of all ambiguity, moving to:

> We should rejoice when good kings bleed.
> . . . nimbly, nimbly dance we still
> To th'echoes from a hollow hill.

But the worst that Garrick did to Macbeth was in characterization. Garrick
was undoubtedly an actor of genius, as he himself readily recognized. In a
letter he wrote that such an actor was distinguished by his capacity to "realise
the feelings of his character, and be transported beyond himself." Yet Garrick
would cut lines and action from the central fabric of Shakespeare's design,
and make up final lines for Macbeth, that defaced with callow embroidery
the austere weave of the original. His interpolated death speech (printed
further on) was a denial of all Shakespeare's text that had gone before; and if
this pious peroration was Garrick's sense of the true "feelings of his character"
his portrayal must have been transported from the beginning toward a hopelessly inadequate realization of what the playwright intended.

Yet it suited the image of a noble Macbeth driven by external forces to
commit crimes he would have shunned if left to himself. That this is Garrick's
own conception presumably appears in *An Essay on Acting, in which will be*

consider'd the Mimical Behaviour of a certain fashionable faulty Actor . . . to which will be added a short criticism on His Acting of Macbeth. This curious piece, ascribed to Garrick himself, is so erratic and ambiguous in its praise and blame of him that explicators are entitled to their confusion and contradiction in interpreting it. The Macbeth character is described as

> an experienced general, crown'd with Conquest, innately ambitious and religiously Humane, spurr'd on by metaphysical prophecies and the unconquerable pride of his Wife, to a deed horrid in itself, and repugnant to his nature.

Then the essay seems to turn on Garrick himself rather inexplicably, though explicators have suggested that this is tongue-in-cheek, or ironically nudging such rivals as the ponderous James Quin (1745) or the stately Barry. If little Garrick did write this, he may have been speaking more truth than parody:

> Valour and ambition, the two Grand Characteristics of Macbeth, form in the Mind's Eye a Person of near Six Feet High, corpulent and Graceful . . . I mention this to prove that Mr. G. is not form'd in the least externally no more than internally for that Character.

This is not all madness.

Certainly the earlier words of the description seemed to suit Garrick's conception, particularly the "religiously Humane" part. Remembrances of his interpretation chronicle almost exclusively the sufferings of a fearful, conscience-riven man. Rare is the suggestion of anything homicidal about this melancholy interpretation. The *Connoisseur* would say in praise of one performance that both poet and player must have been murderers to represent Macbeth so well; and years later the *Monthly Mirror* would remember, in the dagger scene, "the Satanic look of a man resolved on murder." Garrick himself said Macbeth was his most violent role.* But the violence—physically eliminated from the text until the very last fight with Macduff—was, from report, mainly in his feelings: of horror, wild despair, melancholy, despondency, fear.

Mostly Garrick was acclaimed for his suffering in the role—as of a true man of feeling. Hill observed that his gestures were not turbulent, his peculiar talent lay in "pensively preparatory attitudes . . . the propriety and gracefulness wherewith he touches the soft falls of sorrow, terror, and compassion."

An anonymous letter to Garrick raised a rare objection to this soft style: it argued that Shakespeare represents Macbeth as a very bold and daring fellow, "you almost everywhere discovered dejectedness of mind . . . more grief than horror . . . heart heavings, melancholy countenance and slack carriage of body . . . The sorrowful face and lowly gestures of a penitent, which have ever a wan and pitiful look . . . are quite incompatible with the

---

*In 1775, some seven years after his last performance in the role, he wrote, with the wisdom of hindsight, "I am really not yet prepared for Macbeth, 'tis the most violent part I have." He never played it again.

character." Wilkes reflected more faithfully the cultural fashion with this admiring synthesis of Garrick's style in Macbeth: "such a graceful Horror." Garrick's audience wanted a Macbeth to sympathize with, and he gave it to them.

That Garrick's Macbeth should be a sympathetic figure is fair enough. In any theatre, in any age, sympathy is likely to accrue to Macbeth the tyrant-murderer: that is one of the wonders of the play, and one that needs now to be considered. If Johnson and Gentleman could not experience it, others could: critics of sensibility, as Joseph Donohue and others have observed, were prepared to empathize with Macbeth as with other deeply suffering romantic, Gothic wrongdoers. As early as 1746, Upton saw in Macbeth

> a man, not a monster, a man of virtue, till he hearkened to the lures of ambition . . . his mind agitated and convulsed, now virtue, now vice prevailing, how beautifully from such a wavering character.

Richard Payne Knight (1808) tried to explain why we weep for characters like Macbeth: not only

> from our sympathizing, but because of the pressure of rough and turbulent passions upon great and elevated minds . . . [a] most perfect example, Macbeth, in which the character of an ungrateful traitor, murderer, usurper, and tyrant, is made, in the highest degree, interesting, by the subtle flashes of generosity, magnanimity, courage and tenderness, which continually burst forth in the manly, but ineffective, struggle of every exalted quality that can dignify and adorn humankind.

Schlegel, in criticism and in a translation influential on the German stage, would see Macbeth as a truly noble hero unfortunately seduced by hellish temptation.

Most—not all—critics acknowledge Macbeth's spell, and many have tried to explain what it is that pleads for him. Thus: his gift for self-torture and suffering evokes compassion, not only because he endures such enormous pain but also because he is victim as well as malefactor (Gardner, Smidt); even more than the suffering the cause of it captivates us (Flatter); Macbeth is the underdog (Henderson); and he is richly endowed with an underdog's troubles: his yearning for security matched by his need to escape his cabin'd cage; the nighttime insomnia; the daytime nightmares; the bad bargain he has been drawn into; the unequal struggle he faces; the sickness of his wife, and at his own heart (Heilman). Admiration also induces sympathy: for his poetic gift, mammoth sensitivity, rich despair, imagination, resourcefulness, courage, philosophic mind (Wayne Booth).

A close look at Macbeth's vocabulary, as classified by Marvin Spevack's computer, partly explains Shakespeare's secret. From this murderer's mouth come many soft, touching words that hint vulnerability in the speaker: affliction, afraid (3), amen (4), angels, appal (s) (2), a-weary, babe, babes, baby, baby-brow, balm, bless (2), blessed, blessing, cherubin, chuck, dear (2), dearest (2), gentle, grac'd, grace, gracious, heart (s) (14), honor (4), honor'd, honors, hope, humane, humble, humbly, innocent (3), jocund, joy, joyful, kiss, laugh (3), love (s) (11), men-children, mirth, pitiful, pity (2), plead, poor (3), pray (3), prayers, repose, sleep (s) (y) (16), smile, smiles, sorrow, soul (s) (5), sweet (er) (4), tears, tender, thank (s) (5), tremble, trust (2), truth (s) (3), unfortunate, welcome (3), woman (7).

The rewards are considerable if Macbeth can be visualized—or staged—as primarily a noble, sympathetic figure. Shared feeling readily awakens—wants to awaken—in the presence of a troubled central character not specifically designed to alienate: especially a character who pilots an audience through the suffering of many crises of action and emotion in which deeply forbidden impulses, charged with guilt, are avoided. The more sympathetic Macbeth, the easier for the spectator to accept vicarious complicity with his crimes. But to such rewards are coupled aesthetic dangers: given unqualified sympathy for Macbeth, the reach of the play into the reader-spectator's aggressive, hostile—even murderous—layers falls short, and the uncomfortable depths are not stirred. Macbeth—and his Lady—must enable us to discover the most buried impulses. By accentuating the sympathetic aspects of Macbeth, Garrick—and his principal Lady—amputated the thrust of the play.

The degree of sympathy for Macbeth relates to a touchstone I will now adopt to measure the many role-shadings Garrick, and other actors and critics, have found in the character design. This touchstone follows from my first-chapter consideration of the Sisters in terms of their effect on Macbeth's motivation. The more Macbeth is seen as a victim of external forces, a relative innocent, seduced, or driven, or even fated to misdo, the more we may feel for—with—him. Conversely, the more he chooses violence of his own free will, embracing it more than resisting it, the more he evokes alienation. No really distinguished interpretation, critical or theatrical, locates Macbeth at either end of the free-will vs. compelled spectrum. Most more or less recognize an ambiguity of motivation. However, an emphasis on one pole or the other is likely to accompany important conceptions of the character; and to explore the possibilities in the design I will now study these emphases as they developed.

MACBETH WIFE-COMPELLED

In my *Lear* book I proposed the concept of the "dramatic equation": a great Shakespearean character design can exist only as it effectively interlocks with the designs of other personae in the play. Macbeth, for instance, can present a noble murderer only if the whole context, with its diverse characters, is shaped to fit. Lady Macbeth in particular needs to match. I will wait for Lady

Macbeth's entrance for a full discussion of her character; but something will need saying about her equations with various Macbeths, and particularly, now, Garrick's.

Since Garrick chose the way of obtaining sympathy by playing the reluctant victim of external influence, that influence had to be massive enough to justify his submission. He had bowed to public appetite by continuing the witches as semi-comic, broomsticked, song-and-dance figures, so the ominous weight of supernatural force could not account for his conversion from nobility. Almost the whole weight rested on his Lady, most famously acted by Mrs. Pritchard (1773). What he lacked in the cruel, the fierce, the terrible, she had to overflowing. As almost nothing is remembered of evil in his Macbeth, so nothing at all seems set down about any feminine softness, any tender generosity, in her Terrible Woman. One stage direction, in Garrick's edition, for his first meeting with her in I, v, has her *Embracing him;* what else we know of their relation suggests that she must have collared the little man. Other fierce Ladies have yielded some tenderness or generosity in Act III; if Pritchard did, the startling contrast would seem to have gained notice, as did one touch of delicacy in her (V, i) handwashing; but no such notice survives. Her Lady is described as having "a mind insensible to compunction, inflexibly bent to gain her purpose." Boaden called her an "angry Hecate." When she snatched the daggers

> from the remorseful and irresolute Macbeth, despising the agitations of a mind unaccustomed to guilt, and alarmed at the terrors of conscience, she presented a picture of the most consummate intrepidity in mischief.

In the banquet scene, when her "reproving and angry looks" did not control him, she "seized his arm and, with a half whisper of terror assumed a look of such anger, indignation and contempt as cannot be surpassed."

Stupid Mrs. Pritchard may have been, as Dr. Johnson suggested; of Shakespeare's magnificent language in the play she knew, Johnson said, only her own lines; but she said them as an audience wanted them said. Lady Macbeth's complexity was made partly a sacrifice to the popular image of Macbeth the noble murderer: she could not even, for instance, appear after Duncan's murder, to faint. Garrick thought, Davies wrote, that she would be derided if she tried to act the "hypocrisy of Lady Macbeth": given so iron a characterization, hypocrisy could be the only explanation for this moment.

But to return to Garrick: I have been seeking in his characterization for any of the polyphony designed in the role, because he *was* a great actor, and we must learn all we can from him. One possible, curious subtlety in his lugubrious image of Macbeth is hinted in paintings and sketches. In the familiar Zoffany of the elegant room where Mrs. Pritchard, towering a head taller, points commandingly to Macbeth to return the daggers, Garrick teeters on uncertain toes, wonderfully irresolute, almost in a dance of indecision, as if he would move two ways at once. Nobody unfamiliar with the picture's story would guess that this man came fresh from a murder, agonized by fear and remorse. In the larger original—not so easily seen in small photographic reproductions—Garrick's marvelously ambiguous expression hints puzzlement and possibly even a touch of accomplishment. A Fuseli sketch of Garrick grasping at the dagger shows on his face an almost exalted look.

There is little else to suggest that Garrick's Macbeth did project, beneath his exterior of grand remorse and despair, the grim satisfactions of withered murder. His reshaping of the play indicates a flight from Macbeth's darker side. If Garrick did not murder the text, he certainly cut deeply enough to let blood. One deletion might be as small as a line: in the crucial I, vii soliloquy, he banished

> if th' assassination
> Could trammel up the consequence . . .

—as if this early rare defining of the *deed* by Macbeth was still not delicacy enough. Another deletion would gut a scene: thus he erased the killing of Lady Macduff and her children—Shakespeare's deliberate use of a visually horrible act to balance the devices by which he elsewhere demanded sympathy for Macbeth. Garrick further softened the character's violence by eliminating Macbeth's slaying of young Seyward: one journal scolded him for this, we will see, but the cut would become standard practice for a while. What most distorted the whole direction of Shakespeare's work was Garrick's final, defiling death speech.

Shakespeare's Macbeth cried:

> And damn'd be him, that first cries hold, enough.

—and rebuffed the claims of heaven or hell by fighting wordlessly to his death. Not so Garrick's pious craven. In mealy lines that look backward over the shaping of a pathetic murderer who had to end self-pitying and remorseful, Garrick died, excessively, like Bottom:

> 'Tis done! The scene of life will quickly close. Ambition's vain, delusive dreams are fled, And now I wake to darkness, guilt and horror. I cannot bear it! Let me shake it off—'T wo' not be; my soul is clogg'd with blood—I cannot rise! I dare not ask for mercy—It is too late, hell drags me down, I sink, I sink—Oh!— my soul is lost forever! Oh!

OH! indeed. We can hardly say that Garrick "realised the feelings" of and played Shakespeare's Macbeth.

Nor did the best of the actors who rivaled or followed him in his century. They all seem to have been essentially noble murderers, sympathetic because brooding victims of their wives' propelling ambition. True, Charles Macklin (1773) was said in one mean poem to appear "a greater Rogue than Shake-

speare made him"; and in another, "to murder like Jack Ketch"; but a third
poem suggested that the victim of his slaughter was the character itself:

> The witches, while living, eluded Macbeth,
> And the devil laid hold of his soul after death,
> But to punish the tyrant this would not content him
> So Macklin he sent on the stage to present him.

We will still have something to learn from the physical imagery of Garrick
and his contemporaries; at least these English Macbeths did not, in an access
of piety, kill themselves, as in the Ducis version in France, nor suffer as in a
contemporary Vienna production by Stephanie: the play replaced a Don
Juan morality that was traditionally played on All Soul's Day, Macbeth was
appropriately terrified by the ghost of Duncan, then by Duncan's moving
statue; and at last Lady Macbeth, in a fine Gothic denouement, killed her
husband and died in the flames of their burning castle. In Germany, where
Macbeth was most performed outside England, the image of the noble, compelled murderer would die hard. Attempts at more complex interpretations
ran into public and critical opposition. A friend of Tieck's wryly observed
of Reussler's Macbeth (1834),

> rough, confused, half mad with pride . . . not the pattern wanted by the
> audience, which here as everywhere claims that the hero shall sparkle with
> amiability, even if he does cut the king's throat.

Another German Macbeth, Josef Wagner (1856), was seriously criticized for
being only a visionary: "Macbeth should always be presented as a hero."

Garrick's great English successor in the late eighteenth century, John Philip
Kemble, safely played the noble hero-murderer, sympathetic because driven
to crime by his wife. Kemble had hoped to sound more notes of the character's
polyphony, but public taste frustrated him. He wanted, for instance, to add
to Macbeth's motivation the compelling external force of a set of somber,
sinister witches projecting an atmosphere of evil influence; but the clamorous
"gods" of the balcony "would have the dance and broom business," and he
had to restore the customary caricatures. Kemble also tried to emphasize the
imaginative in the Macbeth design by eliminating an appearance of Banquo's
ghost, making it instead an invisible figment of the haunted mind; again he
had to yield to popular pressure, and return the *blood-boltered* phantom.

Kemble stoutly defended Macbeth's nobility and courage against what he
saw as the insults of Whately, who had suggested that the thane was not so
much brave by nature as by the exercise of resolution. Kemble believed
fiercely in the loftiness of Macbeth's intrepidity: his "great heart pants to
meet the barbarous leader of the rebels . . . (with) perfect scorn of danger."
Kemble saw as essential the difference between fear of doing wrong and fear
of external harm—"between the blind animal ferocity that goads the brute,
and the noble motive that inspires the rational intrepidity of man." That

Shakespeare perhaps intended the Macbeth design to experience both extremes was a thought Kemble refused to contemplate.

Like Garrick, he adopted the strategy of the noble mind smothered in remorse and melancholy by the shock of its experience. Kemble at least looked like a man who could have sensed the evil forces in a witches' universe; Hazlitt, pleased by this, called him "the best of Macbeths;" but the description tells us much about the contemporary critical standards:

> a stiff, horror-stricken stateliness in his person and manner, like a man bearing
> up against supernatural influences . . . a bewildered distraction, a perplexity
> and at the same time a rigidity of purpose, like one who has been stunned by
> a blow of fate.

Kemble was involved in the same equation as Garrick, but he suffered more because overshadowed by his customary Lady Macbeth, his famous, formidable sister, Sarah Siddons (1785). We have considerable information about this pair. We know that on a rare occasion Siddons might modulate the fierceness of her terrible Lady, but she was generally so powerful and masterful that Kemble could not have asserted against her any wilful action or independence of spirit, even if he had wanted to. George Fletcher, an early nineteenth-century critic intent on making Macbeth the play's villain, and rescuing Lady Macbeth from the "monster" Siddons pattern, declared that Kemble, in submitting to that pattern, falsified Shakespeare's conception:

> the remorsefully reluctant [and later] repentant criminal is continually substi-
> tuted for [Shakespeare's] heartless slave of more selfish apprehensiveness.

Even Leigh Hunt, who could praise Kemble for "all that there is of stateliness" in Macbeth, could only blame, in "the more impassioned scenes, those methodistical artifices of drooped eyes, patient shakes of the head, and whining preachments."

Half seriously *Macbeth* has been described as a play about a hen-pecked husband—a reference usually to the kind of fierce personality dominance exemplified by Pritchard, Siddons, and their masculinized sisters. But the equation does not require a virago. Any wife may be represented as having some power over her husband: and even when he is frankly weak and uxorious, dependent on a stronger will, as some Macbeths have been, the Lady can dominate more subtly. Such subtlety discovers some of the Lady's polyphony; and inevitably actresses would attempt it. We will see that early in Siddons' own time, in Germany, a daring actress would defy the "monster" convention; and before Siddons was through in England, young ladies would be trying in more "feminine" ways to dominate their Macbeths. Kemble himself, in a performance when he was free of Siddons, played with one such actress, a Miss Smith (1808). He must have enjoyed the relief of being controlled, for a change, by tenderness as well as force; but the actress was scolded for it.

Kean's Lady Macbeth would have more latitude because Kean, the next "star" after Kemble, was determined to bring out a fuller range of notes in Macbeth himself, and the equation required a corresponding flexibility in his opposite. I will discuss Kean's interpretation in more detail later; he is important here for allowing his Lady Macbeth to use gestures of love and coaxing, as well as command, to influence her husband toward murder. A noble Macbeth at the mercy of a Terrible Woman would continue in theatre and criticism, but the pattern of control would begin to change. Lady Macbeth would learn to manage Macbeth with affection, with finesse, with allurement, with insistence that is kind, or will seem so.

Complicating the equation will be the attribute Shakespeare built into the Macbeth design of lover as well as husband. Macbeth's committed love puts in his Lady's hands a gentle force as potent in its intimate way as tigerish ferocity. This softer note in the polyphony vanishes, or is soured, when Macbeth must be submissive to a grim and terrible spouse. When he is compelled to crime by love as well as domination, a different sympathy attaches to him, as still a victim of his wife's will, but on a more inward level.

The tactics of love have been used as manipulatively as those of domination: the feminine power translated into sensual, sexual mastery, Macbeth made victim of passion and even infatuation, the erotic aspect of the Dionysian in him matching the aggressive. In the French theatre, particularly, Lady Macbeth has been the compelling seductress of her lover-husband. The French enjoyed the frank sensuality of Paul Mounet's (1884) Macbeth enamored of his Lady, Mme. Tessandier, and the erotic relationship between Sarah Bernhardt's Lady and her Macbeth (1884). Jean Vilar (1954–5) struck some critics with his "*obsession sexuelle*" for his alluring Lady (Maria Casarès) in an "*envoutement charnel*". Vilar shaped motivation from his "carnal dependence", that drove him, murder after murder, to prove his insecure masculinity before his wife. Vilar's successor in the production, Alain Cuny, also portrayed an attachment to his Lady of unusually strong "carnal ties." In this kind of seduction equation, Lady Macbeth's display of her charms would become, in the twentieth century, quite bold. I, v and I, vii sometimes became explicit bedroom scenes: so the Lady Macbeth of Bergman's first production teased her husband with a sight of her half-naked body in winning him to the murder.

Even though Macbeth may still appear as compelled victim in this kind of submission to his wife, her affection for him often seems real as well as tactical, and this has been an additional means of gaining sympathy for him in association with her. Hackett would turn Macbeth into a fierce overreacher; but to involve the audience sympathetically at the beginning he was deliberately an enamored husband, gentle and tender with his wife, "the most loverlike of Macbeths"—which partly explained his warm reception in Paris.

MACBETH SUPERNATURALLY COMPELLED

Hackett added, as another compulsion to gain Macbeth sympathy, a force that Kemble had hoped to assert, that Kean finally did, and that some actors subsequently learned to emphasize. The witches were made the villain of Hackett's interpretation, wicked figures symbolic of evil, who not only influenced Macbeth with their prophecies, but, appearing in the background throughout the play, pervaded his life.

The effect of the supernatural on Macbeth's action has been touched on in the first chapter. Macbeth must seem even more innocent if he is driven to murder not by his human wife, but instead—or also—by supernatural forces whose power and presence no man can resist. Shakespeare's text does not stipulate such power and presence: the witches may know the future, but are not given control. Yet, as we noted earlier, critics have seen Macbeth as fated by their machinations; and often in the world's theatres, the Sisters have been made, as by Hackett, to hover continuously over Macbeth; or their presence has been known more ambiguously by the sounds they make; so they haunted Hackett's progress and emitted a final cackle at his death. And so is closed off one of the ambiguities in the honeycomb of *Macbeth*'s design; the beckoning, cavernous possible is replaced by the unequivocal, and the playwright's multiplying polyphonies lose some of his most delicate dissonances.

More subtly the continuing impact of the witches is suggested, as Shakespeare intended, in Macbeth's felt awareness—sometimes in raptness—of their enveloping presence. Kemble could convey a sense of being oppressed by the supernatural; but the all-dominating presence of his customary Lady Macbeth, and the foolishness of his witches, offset the projection of supernatural control over his behavior. Though Kean eventually abolished the "dance and broom rubbish," he himself radiated too much inward energy to play passive victim either to wifely or to supernatural influence. Macready was the first, best witches' man—both in his strengths and his weaknesses.

Their first prophecies struck him like a blow. Intermittently he broke out in tremendous bursts of activity, but the shadow of destiny was on him. Reviews suggest a strong man oppressed by messages from a world unseen. He moved toward Duncan's murder almost as if hypnotized: "the glassy eye, the dreamy expression, the uncertain gait, the lapses and trances of thought, all mark one who feels himself a passive instrument in the hands of fate" (*Times*). Macready tried to suggest subtextually, by gestures and looks even when he was silent, that supernatural direction flowed in him, with fresh intimations of his destiny, and continually paralyzed his arm. He moved sometimes as if the real world were annihilated; as if he himself had no steadiness of purpose, no assurance that resolution would result in an act, no will, no self-agency; possessed.

> He seemed to reel through a visionary region where he must stumble on, urged by a mysterious power which he cannot resist and cannot fathom, through a dark, unriddled, portent-laden future.

The submission to the supernatural softened Macready's Macbeth to his wife's influence, without making her entirely responsible for his crime. When he was opposite the gentler Helen Faucit, her touches of solicitude supported him; but even with so domineering a Lady as Charlotte Cushman (U.S., 1858) his acquiescence was a secondary submission; he had already been moved by fate. Macready still conveyed some of the suffering common to the pitiful noble murderer: haggard aspect, piteous dejection of visage, touching melancholy, irresolution before Duncan's murder, desolation afterwards. But not only desolation. Macready touched the bedrock of Dionysian violence in the role: he could turn on Lady Macbeth, in their brief encounters in Act III, with a grim familiarity, even brutality; one observer saw, in his change,

> the hardening of the heart . . . the petrifying of the spirit, as it turns to gaze boldly on guilt . . . from the slave, he became the hero of wickedness.

The Macbeth who, from superstition or credulity, is drugged by the witches' power and promise, who moves hypnotized to their bidding, may well awaken, as Macready did, to a horror and rage, if not at himself, then at the forces that tricked him. Macready, a very intelligent and studious man, understood this, and concentrated his efforts on conveying the passionate depths in the design. As in other roles, he seemed sometimes almost too intelligent to imagine the unknown. The actor himself could not understand—he confided to his Diary—comments asking him for imagination rather than sensibility, and he labored to transcend his technique. A friend, like Lady Pollock, would marvel at his way of "looking at nothing" to create the supernatural ambience he intended to surround himself with. For all Macbeths, but particularly for those motivated by inwardly heard messages from the supernatural, the gift of resonance to the unseen is essential; without it, the role does not work, as one twentieth century Macbeth manqué, Ralph Richardson (1952), acknowledged after his failure:

> I found when I came to play Macbeth—"Is this a dagger that I see before me"— I just damn well didn't see the dagger, and neither did anybody else. Perhaps I haven't the necessary emotional imagination.

Macbeth must convey some sense of being—or believing himself to be—in touch with the supernatural, experiencing, if not complicity, at least some sharing of the dark, Dionysian universe of impulse that serves magical wish. Macbeth has even been seen as a necromancer in IV, i (Paul), commanding the witches and diabolical spirits. A Dryden poem about the Restoration stage complains:

> Witchcraft reigns there, and raises to renown
> *Macbeth*, the *Simon Magus* of the town.

Macbeth does say to the Sisters, *I conjure you* . . . and has been portrayed, even in later times, as a conjurer in his second meeting with the witches; but this, by adding to his powers, diminishes his stature as the troubled hero, trying impossibly to master the mystery of time, grasping at a vision of magic that must always elude him.

Again, equation: the witches and Macbeth meet in a symbiotic relationship, that leads us not to conclusions so much as wondering. The open-ended questions implicit in the Sisters' ambiguous nature depend on the questions that must be asked about Macbeth. Was there a previous connection between him and the Sisters (Dowden)? Were they drawn to Macbeth because he was "temptable" (Dover Wilson)? "Not innocent" (Bradley)? Receptive to metaphysical message (Sisson)? Did the witches home on him because he was already guilty? Had he already contemplated—if not planned—the murder (Flatter)? Did he choose wilfully to misunderstand and exploit the witches' oracles (Wayne Booth)? Or was his consciousness altered as a result of the encounter (Heilman)? Was he haunted? Possessed? Were the witches the origin in him, as elsewhere, of deeds of blood in man (Lamb)? Or was his guilty imagination the source of the Sisters? Were they his projections (Nicoll)? Was it his nature to live at levels beyond human experience (Mack, Jr.)*?

To answer absolutely questions like this would be, again, to close a door on the endless chambers through which the play's equivocations lead us. Who the Sisters are, and what their influence on men's lives, are among the elusive notes that share in the play's beckoning.

MACBETH DAMNED

From a mythology not unrelated to the world of witches comes the suggestion of another compulsive destiny for Macbeth. The Sisters have been considered, as we noted, tools of Satan, that prime antagonist of man, God's enemy-instrument in the theology that envisions sinful mortals as damned. Was Macbeth in a hopeless state of damnation? Was his despair recognizable by contemporary audiences as a fatal stage toward such damnation (McGee)? Did he not only comprehend, but embrace, damnation? Was this the ultimate tragic sin: that having the crucial chance to repent, but his heart hardened (Cunningham), he would finally be impenitent? Stoutly disagreeing critics reject a fated damnation for Macbeth. Is it not remarkable that he never pictures the pains of hell, never thinks of asking forgiveness, is not a rebel defying God (Harold Wilson)? Does it make sense to say that Macbeth is damned when Shakespeare's humanism counters hell as a state of lasting torment after death (Knight)? Do not Macbeth and his Lady breathe in a region so vast and lofty that good and evil become indifferent (Maeterlinck)?

Again, the play abjures answers. It has hints of Satanic evil, but many more of human evil; it touches on heaven's justice, but as much on heaven's injustice. Emphasis on a journey to hell can abort the elements of self-generation in Macbeth's action. So the occasionally staged dichotomies between pale, saintly, Christian-like Duncan and Malcolm, and dark, Satanic Macbeth, or any insistence, as by Garrick, on a Macbeth headed for damnation, reduce

*Hereafter I will refer to him as Mack, Jr., and Maynard Mack as simply Mack.

the polyphony of the play, mute its essential variations on the mystery of men against men, against themselves, and against mystery.

MACBETH, THE INSTRUMENT OF MYTH

A latent archetypal compulsion in the play's action has been noted, at least since Simrock, in the age-youth, yellow leaf vs. green bough imagery of the play. In the ur-magic of the seasons, Macbeth, having replaced one winter king, must himself yield to the thrust of new growth. When in the latter part of the play Macbeth ages and Malcolm grows in power in a green English scene, and advances on the older man behind green Birnam boughs, unconscious responses may indeed be stirred; but again, any explicit attempt to evoke them, by making Macbeth the victim of a fateful process, must call attention to itself, raise the response to consciousness, and lose the hold on archaic depths that Shakespeare exploits so insistently.

MACBETH THE BARBARIAN

A contributory compulsion to Macbeth's crimes has sometimes been seen in his environmental conditioning. Hazlitt placed him in a rude society, in a superstitious age, colored by savagery as well as grandeur. He has been imagined a rough highland chief, a gloomy, fierce Celt, whose trade and indeed obligation was to be bloody, the primitive wildness in his poetry steeping his crimes with savage splendor. In a barbaric world, a leader of barbarians must be first to kill or be killed. Michael Redgrave was one who tried out the rough, rude Macbeth on the stages of London and New York (1947–8). His object:

> to reach back into a world of barbarism, to mirror accurately a primitive people who slept in their boots . . . had no time for haircuts. Our Scotsmen will look what they were, a wild, violent, strange race.

Redgrave saw Macbeth's world kin to the period of his own performances, infected with a spreading fear of something vague and dreadful. The actor sensed Macbeth's sliding from courage into fear to dramatize the play's statement that the "o'erreacher" will have his "come-uppance"; but the play said also to Redgrave that the only way to conquer fear is to find new courage, the unquestioning, noble kind. This nobility was not found in Macbeth himself.

Redgrave's "Stanislavskian superobjective" was Macbeth's compulsion to be secure, to escape the fear that clung to his greedy, ambitious seizure of title and glory.

> Macbeth is described as noble and valiant and during the whole play we see him do nothing that is either noble or valiant . . . I could find none of the noble

resignation, the philosophy, I expected to find in the part . . . You will find yourself appalled at how little the text says in Macbeth's own part that will enable you to build up this great, terrifying figure.

Redgrave found the "tomorrow" philosophy blasphemous, and the final behavior before Macduff ignoble—Macbeth refusing to fight when he no longer believes in his invincibility.

Redgrave's rough, superstitious, fearful Scot made him in some eyes humanized, more pitiable, but not tragic. He was seen as rude, masculine, furious, an assassin who hurried from one bloody outrage to another, a broad-shouldered warrior who might well have survived in a barbarous time; but consensus was that the poetry was quenched. This was partly an artistic choice: Redgrave did not think Macbeth a poet: he deliberately roughened his voice, and seemed to hurl out the lines. In the end he himself was not entirely satisfied with the performance, nor were the critics.

A different aspect of the primitive was suggested by Sarah Bernhardt's Macbeth, Leon-Hyacinth Marais (1884). Here was a natural man of the forests, young, in tune with the supernatural, innocent of morality; no sophisticated restraints of conscience seemed seriously to trouble his mind. The witches' prophecies, and Bernhardt's seductive tempting, released him at once to violent action.

> He advances toward his victim with wild bound and springs; and whenever remorse does seize him, it is never under the form of a moral idea, but . . . of a physical image or spectre.

A lack of subtlety was felt, particularly in a sometimes offended England. A typical comment tells us as much about English taste as about Marais:

> all sound and fury, and violent gestures, but with little or none of that self-contained dignity with which modern English audiences have been trained to believe Shakespearean heroes should be played.

Yet a Macbeth could be condemned for too much gentlemanliness, too— so George Vandenhoff (1860) was called

> too sedate, too self-possessed; too little acted upon; a want of that hurry and tumult of spirits of [one] driven by preternatural spirits . . . a want of that wild spirit of poetry . . . his tone of polished culture and bland modern refinement was not consonant with the harrowed, fiend-driven chieftain.

Vandenhoff conceded that in the eleventh century Macbeth was probably rude and bluff enough; but

> Shakespeare had made him a very courtly person, a man of poetic mind, and considerable culture.

Vandenhoff cited Macbeth's courteous thanks to the thanes in I, iii including this elegantly worded compliment:

> Kind gentlemen, your pains are registered,
> Where every day I turn the leaf,
> To read them.

meaning, of course, in his heart . . . Note also that this rude chieftain never addressed his wife except in terms of the tenderest endearment . . . her death draws from him one of the saddest and most beautiful passages . . . [the poetry places] before us a man of highly pictorial imagination and poetic fancy and cultivated habits of thought and expression, not a rude, unpolished soldier . . . so I play him a feudal lord of high breeding.

Certainly in the *Macbeth* world, as with other societies Shakespeare sets in the long past, notably Hamlet's and Lear's, elegance ornaments a kingly court, men speak graciously in peace, good manners are spontaneous and impeccable, for *humane statute*, as Macbeth will say, has long since purged the *gentle weal*. As in *Lear*, men speak of a rude or barbarian world, of rough people, *kerns and gallowglasses*, as distant to their culture. In *Macbeth* a king honored for meekness can speak lyrically of his subjects and surroundings. He enjoys being welcomed by a gracious hostess, partakes of a feast elaborately served by many attendants, and bestows a fine jewel in token of thanks. The rare references to the time clearly past—about holy King Edward of England, and the inauguration of earldoms—carry with them no sense of a savage age: rather of a mature civilization, continuous with Shakespeare's own time. The only evidence of a coarse and vulgar world is the Porter: and his language is deliberately topical, as familiar as the London streets where Shakespeare's audiences dwelt.

Violence certainly streaks Macbeth's world; but no more violence than in the histories of more recent times that Shakespeare had written. The playwright was used to discovering in the most sophisticated courts men acting like beasts; indeed, for him, civilized man's animal nature itself serves as a kind of fate, emerging to motivate bloody crimes that are truly savage. Among the animals imaged in *Macbeth*, one is Macbeth himself, become a goaded beast. A characteristic Shakespearean irony in Macbeth's animal fury is that he is loved and praised first for the killing which in different circumstances becomes monstrous; Macbeth's traversing of the dizzying range of man's capabilities between "brightest of angels" and jungle animal means as much as it does precisely because it occurs in a specifically "civilized" *gentle weal*.

To make Macbeth a victim of a savage time can be tempting: it both invites shows of violence, and excuses them: hence such spectacular primitives as the "Black" *Macbeth*s noted earlier. Since Macbeth will always, in some ways, belong to now, his timeliness has been squared with primitivism by presenting him in modern "barbarian" dress, usually in the climate of a "world" war, as Barry Jackson (1928) and Joan Littlewood (1957) have done in England—or, in a different way, as in Hamburg (1948), where Macbeth was moustachioed and forelocked to resemble Hitler. The Brechtian director, Peter Palitzsch (Germany, 1963), similarly, though more subtly, projected a cold-blooded manager who liquidated his opponents with the clearheaded calculation of a modern dictator. His Macbeth, as he came under attack from overwhelming enemy power, developed a not-unfamiliar paranoid confidence in the supernatural assurances that he would triumph. To intensify such a political effect, Heiner Müller, in Brandenburg (1972), reshaped the play into a blunt history of a coarse, power-hungry elite. This adaptation, its brutal and erotic aspects strongly emphasized, played elsewhere in Germany, and in Switzerland. In such contrived perspectives, Macbeth is diminished by association with a topical context; or his identity is burdened with a known historical fate that closes down the ambiguous destiny Shakespeare designed.*

We come now to the borderline between Macbeth-compelled and Macbeth acting out of inward impulse or will. From some external compulsion he is never free: rebellion challenges him to become a hero, oracles urge him to a glorious future, new rank conferred invites him, with his wife's urging, still higher: then emergencies of his own making, real and hallucinated, force desperate responses from him. Yet at the core of the design is a readiness, a compulsion, even a determination, to act terribly. Some fierce drive from within seems to move him to violate society's codes, against calls of his own conscience, thought, imagination, prudence, even cowardice.

Macbeth's unrelenting inward drive can itself suggest a strange compelling force. His whole persona may be seen as a vehicle speeding him to his destiny. His body is designed to reflect the tensions of his mind, while the strains on his body, in turn, may be seen partly to explain his mental anguish. On a physiological level, such symptoms as his excessive reactions, his difficulty in making decisions, his mental fugues, may express almost intolerable bodily strain, "battle fatigue." He comes from his exhausting fight with the kingdom's enemies into sudden emotional storms that never give him time for rest. Events happen so fast: the prophecy, the sudden, confirming elevation in rank, the dream of kingship, Duncan's visit making time and place ripe; then rushing—being rushed—into murder. For the rest of his unresting life, in continuous crisis, his body—sometimes intolerably inescapable— reciprocates with the *restless ecstasy* of his mind. In the theatre he has often been represented as wracked in his flesh, particularly after the murder. Then, worn from lack of sleep, he may seem, as did a Japanese Macbeth, almost out of his mind from sheer exhaustion. But always some inward force works in his flesh. He is partly victim as well as governor of a hubristic psyche. Impulses seize him, shake him, paralyze him in raptness. Some he can give a name to; some are unspeakable.

*Other manifestations of the universality of the *Macbeth* material, like the Marowitz and Ionesco variations, are too distant from Shakespeare's text to help with the illumination we seek here.

Macbeth identifies as *ambition* one of the inward forces impelling him; and some critics since Payne Knight have discerned this as his chief motive. The play has even been seen as a morality on the consequences of yielding to this force. But the thrusting Elizabethan-Jacobean soldier was entitled to ambition, as Smidt has observed. The ambitious adventurers who roared out of England to plant the flag across strange seas, and build careers on piracy and war, were much admired national heroes. In any case, what seems to drive Macbeth to and beyond his first "ambitious" murder seems made of darker stuff. Something of which ambition is only the tip, Walter Kerr suggests:

> . . . what a curious way to be ambitious! . . . When an opportunity presents itself to kill the king, he shrinks from it. When he has been all but forced into doing the deed, he is aghast at himself. When he finds himself on the throne, he is at once a model of insecurity . . . Yet Macbeth *is* ambitious—in one small, dark recess hidden far beneath the military integrity, the husbandly warmth, the moral scrupulousness, the nervous sensibility of the man there lies a kernel of ambition just big enough to overbalance him when the scales are properly tipped.

What drives Macbeth, once set on his trajectory, is more consuming than any single fuse. Victor Hugo sensed a ravenous insatiability energizing the design: "*Hunger* . . . some souls have teeth." The Russian actor Simonov (1940) recognized an appetite for omnipotence in the polyphony:

> This genius of a war leader, with the intelligence of a king, the passion of a lover and man of action—this king-murderer, warrior-lover will never be satisfied with a half-victory, half-success. He must have all.

One particular craving in the complex of Macbeth's "ambition" is the commitment to dynasty, a passion that will haunt him, that mainly motivates his murder of Banquo and hence the pivotal unleashing of the forces that must destroy him. Brooks observed this nuclear impetus to Macbeth's action; to Kemble the vision of lineage was the key to the character motivation. No son of Macbeth's ever appears, but it is for this child, after Duncan's murder, that all the blood is spilled, for him Macbeth gambles his kingdom. Macbeth assumes the role of father doubly: not only for the heir who would immediately follow him, on this islet of time, but also for the timeless line of kings he dreams of siring. (See Appendix.)

When he first trembles at the upthrusting forces overcharging him, Macbeth himself recognizes in them powers anterior to anything as explicable as ambition: *my black and dark desires*, he calls them—commands rising from the elemental Dionysian turbulence that drives men to climb over other men because they are there. As he will write to his wife, he *burnt in desire* to know his prospects. He is a man afire.

Deep and black as they are, Macbeth's desires are never made explicit; they seethe beneath words and action. Much of the richness of the play lies in this projection of latent impulses that evoke and release reverberations of ambiguous buried life. Consequently, many varieties have been discerned in Macbeth of the psychological hero, compelled by unconscious or archetypal drives and patterns. Macbeth commits many of the "primal" crimes. Easiest to recognize is the Oedipal fantasy of killing an older man, a "father figure." In *Macbeth*, as noted, the youth versus age *agon* is acted out doubly: Macbeth against older Duncan, then Malcolm against older Macbeth who would destroy—does destroy—threatening younger menchildren, until one destroys him. Similarly, the play exercises the *brudermord* fantasy, the war on siblings: Macbeth against Banquo, against Macduff. Even this is not all: Macbeth kills for us a mother figure (Lady Macduff), too; he also wars against woman. And children.

The tremors of Macbeth's insecure masculinity, and his ultimate commitment to sever his dependence on the female, and sustain his "manliness," are manifested on his surface. At a deeper level, responses may be evoked to Macbeth as the victimized male principle subverted and ultimately extinguished by the destroying female. Of this interpretation more in the discussion of Lady Macbeth, but note here that it assumes a male storyteller working out a male fantasy; criticism has been late to consider how fiction serves the female fantasy. Shakespeare leaves plenty of room; male and female destroy each other in this play, the woman's fantasy working out its course of power and guilt as well as the man's. Archetypally, from the male point of view, magic is associated with woman (as witch as well as wife) who has control of mysteries that are opaque and inimical to man. The most familiar Western form of woman's archetypal guidance of man to destruction is in the Garden of Eden story: as long ago as Hugo, and often after, Macbeth's fate has been likened to Adam's fall from yielding to the persuasion of his wife, who had listened to the Power of Darkness.

As with all other radiations of archetypal fatefulness, Macbeth's buried roles in a primordial equation with a female figure must remain implicit, to excite pre-cognitive response. Efforts to make them explicit, in imagination or in the theatre, risk exchanging the haunting mystery of Shakespeare's polyphony for a flat, clinical monotone. Psychoanalytical interpretation so often suits Shakespeare because both find the most meaningful behavior in the hidden life, the *deep desires*, that can only be inferred from glimpses through the mask of consciousness, or from the mask's telltale grimaces. Shakespeare's treatment of Macbeth's tutoring by female figures, canny and uncanny, needs no magnification to carry resonant echoes of what Freudians discover in the child's helpless submission to the first awesome woman controlling his life. Macbeth's subtext allows both for this formidable subconscious image and for a countering one. The fearsome giantess on whose seeming magical power survival depends is also the first love, for whom the son rivals father and siblings. Macbeth serves as a model for the dialectic that grows from this fantasy. From his doubled motives the manchild, in Freudian terms, is impelled to violate basic taboos, and in acting them out (his sadism) he invokes guilt that drives him to make himself suffer (masochism) to the extent that he may seek self-destruction: by suicide, if necessary, or more subtly by invoking another "good" son to rise up to destroy him. In the Freudian version of the *Macbeth* fantasy, as Holland synthesizes it, the female figure who instigates the crime is, like her archetypal sisters, a projection of the nourishing, seductive, deadly women who live in a man's wishes (again, this is of the *male* fantasy).

The touch of the child in the Macbeth design has been experienced in the theatre: in Macbeth's bewilderment before the uncanny magic that so teases him; in his thrust to win admiration, to do terrible things, dreadful deeds. This grows into his excited visions of omnipotence as if he had himself mastered magic—and withers into dread when his illusions fade, and he knows himself to be helpless.

Almost the worst image of himself that his manliness can tolerate is to be as tremulous as a *baby of a girl* (III, iv, 131); yet he is designed sometimes to turn appealingly to his wife, especially in Act III, with a touch of child-to-mother, asking for support; as in a different mood, he next demands it from the witches. The German actor J. F. Fleck (1788), projected a sense of green naiveté in Macbeth that even had touches of the comic: his terror in the banquet scene turned him childish; and in his later despair a quality of infantilism was sensed. Something of the same innocence and simplicity was felt in Richardson's Macbeth: he moved with a kind of wide-eyed wonder through his crimes, with naive puzzlement, as if this was a nightmare from which he might awaken; and a baffled, child-like pathos softened—too much, critics thought—his despair and suffering.* In neither of these cases was the child in Macbeth made explicit; when that happens, as in Christopher Plummer's interpretation (Canada, 1962), the characterization can be as enclosed as in any morality pattern, and the reverberations of countering forces in the design are stilled. Plummer gave the impression of an "eternally weeping, hysteric, even manic . . . an excitable adolescent." The regressive man whom Plummer saw in Macbeth would fling himself playfully or frenziedly on the ground, chew a plucked root, at the witches' prophecies slap his thigh in laughter that was touched with boyish hysteria. Rushing home to his first meeting with Lady Macbeth, exuberant and tearful, he hurled himself to the floor at her knees, and buried his face in her lap. Later, in despair, he clung to her like a child tormented by nightmare. Sacrificed to the "Freudian" implications of his son's relationship to a mother-queen were important

---

*See also later references to Forbes-Robertson, Walter Hampden (U.S., 1934).

dimensions: he lacked the general's authority of manner, the strength of a determined soldier-killer, the regality of a king, the mind of a thinker.

Lady Macbeth challenges both Macbeth's maturity and his immaturity; by making him sometimes seem a child, she seeks to manage him as a child; but as she demeans his manhood she simultaneously tries to stimulate it and infuse it with her forced strength. The equation demands that he manifest those reserves that raise him to domination as she deteriorates. Shakespeare does not let any pattern, such as the man-by-woman-destroyed, enclose his Macbeth image. The many-layered relations of man-to-woman affect Macbeth's fate, but are not allowed to determine it.

MACBETH THE DIVIDED SELF

Under the pressures that assault Macbeth any man might suffer nervous turbulence; but suppose, as some actors and critics have, that the psychic unease in the character was prior to the traumatic experiences, that Macbeth's was a personality designed in any case to live on its nerves. A man reacting strongly to ambiguous, disabling inner disturbances that alienate him from his surroundings can evoke empathetic recognition, compassion born of shared experience. Several German actors, near the turn of the twentieth century, when "neurasthenia" and the suction of the subconscious were becoming familiar, emphasized the inward tensions embedded in the Macbeth design. They moved through the play with nerves so twisted that raptness, fear, and wild hallucination seemed native to them. Adalbert Matkowsky (Germany, 1901), one of the first of the "psychological" Macbeths, was from the first harrowed, physically and mentally: his head often hung down, he moved restlessly, kept his face averted, his voice in moments of tension hollowing and fading. Under stress, he would seem hardly to have the strength to stand up—in the dagger scene would in fact momentarily collapse. His neurotic indecision pulled him literally back and forth, up toward Duncan's chamber, then away from it, until finally he forced himself forward by pulling hand over hand up the banisters. The same *angst* could drive him to outbreaks of wild violence, or leave him shivering in a kind of fever.

An earlier German contemporary, Friedrich Mitterwurzer (1877), was similarly "psychological": physically as well as mentally undermined by his nerves, always in a fever, never still. The excessive turbulence of his physical imagery demonstrated how the Macbeth design could be thrown awry: he was so lamentable that, as with the noble murderer, Macbeth's bedrock cruelty seemed beyond him. He looked, said one report, as if he could not hurt a fly.

In the same general pattern, Paul Wegener, Max Reinhardt's notable Macbeth (1916), instructively exemplified an actor's deepening perception of the role's inwardness when he performs over a period of years. Wegener had begun as a barbarian Macbeth, brutal, nearly animal, playing in a naturalistic,

Hauptmann-influenced style; his next Macbeth was more of a gentleman, as a king elegant and royal, but troubled by a conscience he could only stifle by new atrocities. Going deeper for Reinhardt, who saw Macbeth as neurotic, Wegener's strong warrior's mask covered a deep, relentless anxiety: at times he seemed almost a somnambulist, at others a son of chaos, yielding in anxiety to physical weakness, consumed by the kind of insatiable turbulence that recalled Matkowsky. Lady Macbeth, in this equation, was worn away and destroyed by the very force of his *angst*.

Something similar developed in the successive Macbeths of Ernst Schröder, who first played early in 1964 a strongly extroverted character-design, bull-necked, furious, ruthless, a maniac of aggression; then, in the fall of the same year at the other extreme, an inward Macbeth, as if a light had gone on behind the scrim of his mask, and through the transparency a helpless inner life was revealed. But now Macbeth's tragedy was touched too much with impotence, magnitude deserted him, he was weak, weepy, malicious. This second performance was in Zurich; and aptly, in this home of Carl Jung, one reviewer wrote: "For this absolutely unheroic man, who exposed himself so indecently, we thought to call a psychiatrist."

The neurotic Macbeth has seemed to be a man of mind, as well as nerves; indeed the power of his mind to confront him with his guilty and endangered self is made partly to account for his instability. This neurotic may come to see himself bitterly, as did Tamás Majór's Macbeth (Hungary, 1950), contemplating his inner tumult with a sour, dry harshness, his outward cruelty a reflection of interior acid. At his worst, this Macbeth becomes a cringing introvert who, disliking what he watches in himself, must go on watching himself.

On the battleground of Macbeth's inner self, no truce is ever called. The multiple options forced on him by circumstance may tear him in opposite directions, but always within him are his most terrible conflicts: part of him believing what part doubts, part wanting what part rejects, part intent on deceiving others, part on deceiving himself, part loving in his wife that which another part fears, part exulting in the dreadful deeds that shake another part with revulsion.

The Macbeth tortured by so many resistances would escape entirely his identity: *Best not know myself*. This is the badge of all the tribe of Shakespeare's most sensitive heroes, as they find their degraded selves nearly intolerable. Lear: *This is not Lear*; Othello: *That's he that was Othello*; Hamlet: *If Hamlet from himself be ta'en away,/Then Hamlet does it not, Hamlet denies it*.

So intense is the inward struggle of the self in all these characters that madness threatens, or beckons as an escape. Lear for a while cannot bear sanity, flees reason; Othello's hysteric rage drives him to the momentary sanctuary of a "fit"; Hamlet's mind whirls, his pretended madness accentuated by a genuine turbulence about his brain. Is Macbeth's intense inner unease a symptom of troubled sanity? The syndrome of his "raptness," his hallucinations, his susceptibility to unbalance—*then comes my fit again*—has been diagnosed as perhaps epileptic (Coriat); he has been seen as verging on madness (Draper), a murderer while under hallucination (Quiller-Couch). Coghill, so sensitively oriented to Shakespeare's theatrical intentions, points out that the text specifies Macbeth's seeming madness; Murry flatly proclaims him mad, adds wryly that in the twentieth century he and his Lady would face the charge of murder while insane. Some innocence would attach to Macbeth if he could claim this defense; or that of a Senecan hero inspired to crazed killing by hallucinatory figures; but he never makes the plea. Often, Mack has observed, in his splendid study of the Jacobean tragic heroes, their madness is Cassandra-like, compounded of punishment and insight; Macbeth sees best, suffers most, in an awful sanity that occasionally darts into unreason and trembles on the edge of madness, but withholds sustained release.

The fierce repression that contains so much inward pressure is sometimes reflected in the theatre by the overreacher's almost continuous hyperexcitement, broken with eruptions of irrational excess. These may be unmistakable "fits of madness" as in the conception of the Italian Almanno Morelli (1849), or in the Pole Witalis Smochowski's (1859) implacable progress toward madness as he prepared to enter Duncan's death chamber. Yet the resilient mind recoils, seeks to snatch Macbeth back to his *here*, his immediate, inexorable sandspit of time. When the outbreaks are paced in mounting intensity, as in the nerve-taut, complex characterization by Paul Rogers (England, 1954), or the grinding toward unreason of Nicol Williamson (England, 1974), ravaged, snarling, aimed toward insanity, the play mounts to follow Macbeth's accelerating battle with derangement. A different kind of madness can make Macbeth, from the beginning, a cold, hard-eyed psychopath. So Macháček (Czechoslovakia, 1969), calculatedly deceiving and abusing the love and trust about him. He was felt to repress his rising anxiety by intensifying his cruelty, indulging it, in a kind of exhibitionism. Such a sinister design, energized by a threateningly "unnatural," twisted mind, can extend the horror of the action. But, as Czech critics observed, it distorts the equation with Lady Macbeth, diminishing her urgency, pushing her into the background; and it rejects the character's ambiguity, particularly its basic human qualities. Macbeth must suffer, while inflicting suffering.

Buried in the design here may be felt the impulse toward self-destruction that is easily fastened to the archetype of the quest-hero, self-doomed. Macbeth refracts the figure's general outlines: he answers a dark call to daring; he accepts magical aid; he endures agony; but he ventures too far beyond normality to return. His search becomes, in effect, a desperate journey toward his own terrible death. He may be spared for a moment of forlorn recognition, but this is all the rebirth he is allowed. Toward such an end the complex, compelled hero, however reckless, must advance with divided soul, divided mind.

The stress rising from Macbeth's *black and deep desires* may be illuminated by Freud's most subtle and effective suggestion about the character*: some individuals cannot stand attainment (a suggestion highly relevant to Lady Macbeth as well). So the Macbeth design might include the subconscious fear not only of what he has done, and what kind of man he is to have done it, but also of the implications of his assumption of absolute power. Since Freud, dread of success has become a commonplace of psychological interpretation: Maslow, for instance, wondered if a "fear of one's own greatness" represents a kind of hubris anxiety: a sense of ominous impudence in assuming impossible, godlike qualities. Certainly Macbeth at first dreads his wish-fulfillment, even while he strides toward it.

Fear itself has sometimes been considered (notably by L. B. Campbell) as a main spur—and lash—of Macbeth's crime. Like many qualities in the design, it is polyphonic. Besides his general psychic apprehension, Macbeth's fear might partly derive, as in Holinshed, from the realistic danger of enemies who surround him. Deeper is the fear, distinguished by Adams, of the crowding terrible images that torment Macbeth. Confirmed Christianizers will have Macbeth fear damnation. He has the decent man's civilized fear of his own wickedness—intensified, in the theatre, by noble murderers, into frightful anxiety and remorse. Is there a touch of the cowardice that Kemble so stoutly defended Macbeth against, that Redgrave sensed in Macbeth's refusal to fight Macduff? A German contemporary of Kemble's, Reineke (1780), shook with a coward's fear from the first moment he met the witches, and he trembled through his crimes—literally afraid of his own shadow when he saw it moving on the door outside Duncan's chamber. A breath of cowardice can dissolve into the complex design; but to base the characterization on so base an aspect of fear is to betray the superstructure—so Reineke was faulted for seeming to show the mind only of a common criminal. Of the essence in the character's dialectic is the energy produced when Macbeth, stipulated a fearless fighter against armed enemies, must at least momentarily quail before the intangible agents of fear, within and without.

MACBETH AUTONOMOUS

Macbeth sees himself as essentially independent, free to act. He does not plead compulsion as extenuation for his crimes, nor insanity as an excuse

---

*More conventionally Freud played with the Jekels idea of Macbeth as part with Lady Macbeth of a single personality, the two halves complementary. The idea has been proposed for other sets of Shakespearean character, by other interpreters without experience of the theatre; but the defiantly individual identities of Shakespeare's creations do not submit to this kind of merging. The dialectic between the two roles creates a dramatic unity, but not a unity of personality: the characters are not halves, but wholes, doomed to dissonance. Their tragedy is partly that the moments when they might harmonize with each other come at different times for each. Each is a unique combination of male and female roles, jumbled and tormenting. In that they are committed man and wife, they meet and reciprocate as intimately as mortals can—"Father and mother are one flesh"—but they cannot dissolve into each other.

for them. He accepts guidance in the oracles of the witches, in the compulsion of his wife—though he never blames her—and in the enticement of a hallucinated knife; but while he will complain of equivocation by the Sisters, and finally of the idiocy of life itself, he acts mainly as if, exposed as he is to multiple influences, he is yet able to choose his way. The more he acts, the more ready he is to act again, full of the sense of will, of a man driving as well as— if not rather than—driven. Macbeth's brain, countered as it may be by his emotional and spiritual resistances, is a directing force that must assay alternatives, make choices, direct action. How if Macbeth is limited in intelligence, as some twentieth century critics decided, his mind commonplace (Macarthy), never acute (Whitaker), lacking (Duthie), manifesting immortal stupidity (Harrison)? If the mind is small, the man must be; in the theatre, interpretations of little magnitude have shrunk Macbeth to flatness. Thus the Polish Macbeth of 1964: "An ordinary rogue and murderer of small calibre." And in Germany (1957), "Not one of Shakespeare's kings, but a dull, earthy peasant Macbeth, making the play a superficial crime story." In a politicized Canadian staging (1971), Ian Hogg seemed hardly more than a petty gangster, in a world where the poor were oppressed by small men, who made even majesty seem trivial. Scotland's rulers were meant to demean the peasants who suffered them, and Macbeth was fittingly dwarfish and weaselly—a cunning, shifty politician.

Such characterizations might seem to make of Macbeth the king manqué Angus describes in V, ii: his title hanging *loose upon him,/Like a giant's robe upon a dwarfish thief*. Maeterlinck literally staged such a giant-dwarf contrast between his Macbeth's dress and person: Macbeth, first appearing riding into the midst of the witches—the play was staged in the grounds of an old abbey— seemed a magnificent, heroic figure, above humanity, an unassailable blockhouse of a man, who almost laughed at the prophecies before he rode on. But when alone in the room with his wife, from beneath the masquerade emerged a little man, a simple assassin, without beauty, genius, or courage.

Reviewers, observing such Macbeths, have sometimes taken them for real. The scholar Bertrand Evans, watching the performance (U.S., 1972) of a hapless thane and his wife (the equation requires that an immortally stupid Macbeth drag his wife down to his own mingy level), decided that they were so intended by Shakespeare:

> Not that the actors are too small for their roles, but that Macbeth and his lady are too trivial for theirs. They are a pair of small-time connivers playing for stakes that are ludicrously beyond their capabilities. Not only that, they are a pair of bunglers. They bungle the murder of Duncan, they bungle the murder of Banquo and Fleance, they bungle their party. They bungle it all, because, of course, they are playing out of their league.

But the grandeur and reach of Shakespeare's words do not fit dwarfed images. In mealy mouths the language proclaims itself alien; it refuses to

serve even as a mask flourished before a shallow soul. It springs from too deep a
suffering, too painful a pondering. The great words, that can stir such universal responses, distinguish a massive stature. They are often the special expressions of Macbeth when he is most autonomous: when he is most aware of
himself in his bewildering world; when he strives for a perspective on the
influences that may shape him; or when he undertakes one or other of the
various roles that come naturally to him, and fit him so well. In these ultimate
moments of intimacy with the self, when a man knows freedom to think, if
not to act, Macbeth asserts the unique selfhood of the design.

MACBETH THE WARRIOR

If anywhere Macbeth seems free to move on his own, it is in the primary
role that criticism and the theatre acknowledge in him: the bold warrior,
described so gorgeously by the bleeding captain. But he is the more the warrior
for having to counter the resistances that deepen the design; his choosing to
battle is edged with a determination that is the other side of an effort of will
that represses or conquers fear and conscience.

The contrast in the theatre is especially striking when the warrior-Macbeth
presents the iron front of a man almost too stalwart to succumb to inward
dismay—succumbing. Stalwart he must be: the role of warrior-killer demands
a physique capable of reckless battlefield slaughter. Less than a military bearing and soldierly assurance seriously undercuts the image. When the rather
slight Maurice Evans played Macbeth (U.S., 1940), his director, Margaret
Webster, complained about the general notion that the warrior-murderer
"must necessarily be a burly ruffian, persistently hirsute and encrusted with
ironmongery." (Webster obliquely defended her Macbeth by citing such
small killers as Napoleon and Attila the Hun.) Evans' limitations were particularly clear in the film he did with Judith Anderson: he never conveyed the
martial force of Bellona's bridegroom; and the obvious doubling for him in
the ultimate hand-to-hand struggles mocked the intercut shots of his face.
On stage, the *New York Times* reported, Evans conveyed "a resolution that
seems fiercer than the body that contains it." His grasp of the role, in Pittsburgh, seemed "more mental than physical."

More than size is involved. A small Macbeth, like Kean, stocky, compact,
exploding with fury, could make up in energy what he lacked in mass; the
limber Sothern (U.S., 1910) could convey the man of armor by the authority
of his bearing and the fierce intensity of his voice and movement; a lean, wiry
Macbeth like Irving* could suggest the nervous power and whiplike strength
to yerk a man from nave to chaps.

Macbeth's physical power sets him apart from Anyman, who generally
leaves spectacular swordplay to others, and so it distances Macbeth as a hero;

---

*One critic (*The Gentleman*) tongue-in-cheekily reported the rumor that Irving had grave
doubts about his physical suitability for the part until he came across the line in the text, "Throw
physique to the dogs."

but the sensitive inwardness, however heightened, cousins him to the whole breed of men, who can recognize in it familiar fantasies and real sufferings.

The archetypal pattern of the soldier-Macbeth was Tommaso Salvini (Italy, 1876). Of colossal physique, he moved across the stage like an army on the march, towering over his fellows, majestic of manner, commanding of accent, his shaggy beard and matted hair the natural accoutrements of a fighting general. "Ready to fight to the end," Salvini wrote,

> like a ferocious lion; you must be ready to succumb to your destiny, and die on the battlefield . . . your excessive ambition—startled and roused by the witches—has ruined your heart and intellect. Even if everyone imprecates you, yet make all admire you.

Obstacles could not intimidate this Macbeth, Salvini felt, only the revolting idea of shedding blood without fair combat. Yet he is so thirsty for honors that to be king he is ready to sacrifice all lives. The committed movement of the Salvini-soldier to his goal, the tremendous physical courage in the face of tangible threat, the sense of the vulnerable spirit within, impressed Henry James and Robert Louis Stevenson. James:

> admirable in sincerity, profundity, imaginative power . . . A Macbeth whom we deeply pity, whose delusions and crimes we understand, and almost forgive . . . Simple, demonstrative, and easily tempted . . . never incoherent or merely violent.

Both writers admired the development of the character design from scene to scene—"the history of a human soul," James thought.

Two particular dangers in the emphasis on the warrior have been noticed. First, so bold, bloody, and resolute a man of war requires a Lady Macbeth of equal stature; or alternatively, of intense enough subtlety in her manipulation to sustain the equation. Salvini was the warrior even in his intimacy with his Lady: even when yielding and passionate, his caresses were more a soldier's than a lover's: a match was not easy to find.

Second, the solidity of the soldier's massive masculine front could suggest an opaqueness that might obscure the consuming inner fires. Thus, too impressive, too impassive a physique seemed to imply an inadequate moral sensibility in the Frenchman, Raymond Garrivier (1959). More subtly, actors have, by the very arrogance of their projection of bodily strength, conveyed a felt hidden insecurity. Salvini's fiery inner life glowed through, reflecting his conception of Macbeth's inward vulnerability: indeed the actor expected, such was his feel for Macbeth's sensitivity, that the thane and not the Lady should have been the one to experience the sleepwalking agony.

Some English critics, though they warmed to the force of Salvini's passionate warrior, perceived him as vibrating only to the fear of superstition, not the ultimate terror of the supernatural: he seemed to them not "haunted" enough, lacked "weirdness and spirituality." In an especially English response, the *Athenaeum* doubted "whether an Italian nature can comprehend the mystic influences to which Macbeth is subject." In Chicago, on the other hand, Salvini's interpretation of Macbeth was much applauded. The *Daily News*, citing critics who held, as above, that "it is impossible for the fiery, impulsive, hotblooded Italian to enter into the spirit of Macbeth," turned the genetic argument back: "The Scots were every whit as impulsive, emotional and gesticulative as their southern brethren . . . indeed to this moment the highlander retains his passionate, volcanic nature and when roused is as animated in his features . . . as the most mobile Italian improvisatores." Salvini's Macbeth was praised as even more subtle than his much acclaimed Othello: it "startles and perplexes by its conflicting emotions . . . its shifting crosslights of purpose and feeling."

Another Italian actor of the same period, Ernesto Rossi (1876), less formidable physically than Salvini, but charged with nervous energy, emphasized in his Macbeth the receptiveness to superstition of a soldier in battle. Rossi saw this warrior, after the excitement of the oracles, feeling himself fully deserving of all that was promised, turning in on himself, savoring what he had done and would do.

> He feels himself to be greater than he is, that his physical strengths and mental faculties have suddenly projected him beyond what he had hoped for. The tribute of high esteem and reverence he pays to himself ignites his fantasy and fires his ambition.

In his raptness over his fantasies, Rossi seemed sometimes as if to move under a spell; but between such moments the warrior's capacity for sudden action would break out in violence of tone and mood. He rejected utterly, with Coleridge, a Macbeth puppeted by supernatural influence. Not the witches, but the witches' oracles, acted on him like a kind of drug; action in rage was his counter-drug, and the more he turned to this refuge, the more intense his soldier's ferocity.

Robert Mantell (U.S., 1905) emphasized the brooding soldier; his involved mind seemed to have considered the murder before the prophecy of kingship stirred him; but very deep inside. Though a rugged warrior, believably bloody-minded and savage in battle, in peace he gave the impression of a man deep in thought, calculating his possibilities—and getting them wrong. Attilio Favorini suggests that Mantell made the subtle distinction between Macbeth's forethought and foresight. He was charged with ambition, but seemed not to know what to do with it; he was a man without direction, after his wife, the focus of his affection, had led him to murder Duncan. His outbreaks were more violent, his control over himself decreased as his power increased, as he left behind the familiar physical genius of the warrior for the greater, different power of a king. He was a Macbeth who needed to fight.

Oppositions of a somewhat different kind disturbed the warrior-Macbeth of Edwin Forrest (U.S., 1908); though he too was comfortable only as a soldier. Until he met the witches, he was an innocent except in the war; a massive, heavily muscled man at home in the costume of a fighter, he first strode on cheerful in victory; from the moment of the oracles, he changed startlingly, was absorbed, abstracted—rapt. The idea of murder oppressed him, like a foreign body infecting him; he tried to purge himself in the first meeting with Lady Macbeth, refusing further talk of the "business" with relief, as if for a moment he could happily be only a soldier again. He was wooed to the murder by his Lady, whom he obviously loved deeply and trusted. The wrench between his commitment to decency, and his commission of murder, was violent, sometimes sapping his energies, sometimes driving him to a frenzy touched with insanity. Surcease came to this warrior only when he could fight again.

Sharp contrast also energized Sam Wanamaker's (U.S., 1964) characterization. Coming from battle, on his first appearance, this warrior-Macbeth was seen to have resumed the manner of peace; his armor had served its purpose, he seemed even gentle. After the murder, his indecision metamorphosed into iron determination, and he himself into a crazed, bloodthirsty killer. A streak of self-pity gave his abandoned killing a note of self-indulgence.

MACBETH MURDERER

For Macbeth the superbly accomplished soldier-killer, whose hand in an emergency may go quickly to his weapons—extensions of the warrior's ego—murder invites the almost instinctive use of his fighting skills. The invitation is accepted: the capacity to kill that resides in the design is exercised. Once exercised, it grows strong through the ill of much usage. If Macbeth reflects the release of murderous impulse that may reside in any man, in him its accelerating quality is terrifying. Hamlet, and even Othello, are able to kill without serious risk to their essential human worth; that Macbeth does not forfeit his entirely, after his succession of bloody acts, remains Shakespeare's miracle, for the design is uncompromising in stipulating the killer role.

When this aspect is emphasized in interpretation, critical or theatrical, Macbeth's determination and energy in action tend to be perceived more strongly than the imagination and introspection disclosed in poetry and subtext. So Wilfrid Walter's thane (England, 1927) was

> the Macbeth of the murders, not the Macbeth of the soliloquies. He always knew what he wanted, and what he was going to do.

The Macbeth determined on murder may even reflect an eminently practical, reasonable man, as did Eric Porter's (England, 1962), an upward mobile nobleman who accepted the witches' oracles as confirmations of his own expectations, who proceeded hardheadedly to consider alternatives, and having decided to murder, looked forward confidently to a successful outcome. Such a Macbeth is frustrated more than terrified by his reverses; he feels swindled by the forces that seemed to guarantee his future.

This Macbeth may be recognizably bourgeois, a henchman on the make, as was Ernst Schröder, in his first 1960 performance, when, in the shrewd words of one reviewer, he played Macbeth's physiology rather than his psychology. The physiology reflected a tyrant intimately known by his German audience: marked by harsh brutality, a corrupted imagination, a disdain for feeling and reason. This Macbeth did not *become* insensitive, or a tyrant—he had always been so; he grinned at men, not to hide his feelings, as would other "player" Macbeths, but because he enjoyed his feelings. Once set upon his murderous path, once free to kill, his easy smiles became brutal laughter, a barbarous mocking of other men and their suffering, issuing from a fat face with watery eyes. The voice, until his collapse, rose to a shrill screaming, that was more than enough clue to its association, as a review noted,

> with the great German rug-biter—

and indeed in the last scenes, though no effort had been made to give the play modern dress, Macbeth's black-robed troops, in a dark square about him, suggested guards in a bunker. Again, the design was crammed into the crippling confines of a limited identity.

The more the murderous potential in Macbeth emerges and controls his actions, the more he takes responsibility for them; and the more he may be seen to choose—leap to—even embrace—his crimes. Sometimes, both criticism and theatre emphasize this note of deliberate, self-generated murderous purpose. Then, as with all the manifestations of the play, evaluations of Macbeth's actions spread across a spectrum. The killing he does outside battle is recognized as evil; but the nature of that evil can be seen as ranging from the mean to the magnificent.

The case for meanness was made in most detail by Fletcher, so intent on rescuing Lady Macbeth from the Terrible Woman image that a Siddons-influenced tradition had visited on her. Fletcher put the primary blame on Macbeth, a scheming conniver, incapable of moral repugnance, afraid only of public odium. Schücking speculated that it was not Macbeth's conscience, but nerves, that hindered an essentially self-regarding, ignoble man; Farnham that Macbeth's grossly imperfect sense of right and wrong, his choice of evil as his good, must evoke antipathy for the villain in him. Villain indeed Macbeth has been classified by others (Nicoll, Kreider); worse than villain: symbol of Evil, of the devil (Jack); implicitly in a pact with Satan (McGee).

Good and evil are delicately balanced in the Macbeth design. Overemphasis on Macbeth's wickedness, as much as on his nobility, can rob the play of its deep reach into secret impulse. Where the "noble murderer" allows us to escape with minimal, almost innocent complicity, the mean villain may be so distanced as not to involve us with him, but only with his victims. Thus the Macbeth of Heinrich George (Germany, 1928): coarse, brutal, animalistic, a massive, sluggish soldier-at-arms, he shouldered his way heavily through a society that was, by contrast, noble and sophisticated. Macbeth's brutishness was underscored, for instance, in the contrast between his and Duncan's royal behavior: Duncan moving majestically to his throne through a court that respected him as he respected it; Macbeth (in III, i) bulling his path past his courtiers and throwing himself on the throne. A picture shows him lolling there, gross, arrogant, lording it over his world. The whole interpretation was awry: it demeaned not only Macbeth, but the Macbeth equation. The golden opinions earned from Macbeth's fellows might possibly be made to seem the intimidated tribute of "gilded butterflies" to an awesome fighting man; but the Macbeth interior alphabet had no relation to George's exterior language. The production was not a success.

More dignity is possible to the murderer-Macbeth when his impulse to destroy is raised at least to the level of the passionate, paranoid drive to supremacy, more often seen in Richard III, that Lionel Barrymore (U.S., 1921) sought to project. Barrymore, preparing for the role, contemplated the complex balancings of qualities in the character design, confessed himself confused, and asked himself the classic questions: Was Macbeth innately evil? Free to act, or driven by ambition? Did the witches inspire him, or only tell him what he wanted to know? Was his wife his inspiration? Or his "unsex'd tool"? Barrymore's very questions pointed to the humpback-Richard type of Macbeth he eventually personated: a self-generating villain, crafty, sinister, committed to a cruel advance toward tyranny from the very outset. And, as with Richard, the concentrated egotism wound in on itself; this Macbeth's troubled sleep, like Richard's, led to a frenetic desperation touched with madness. But his course was unmodulated by the lyric, poetic note, or the philosopher's grieving perception, and neither he nor his audiences were happy with it.

Henry Irving, carefully following Fletcher's interpretation, deliberately played Macbeth as villain. Irving concluded that Macbeth was a cowardly climber, who had thought of murdering Duncan before the play opened, and who cleverly manipulated his wife into persuading him to the act. He accepted Fletcher's notion that Macbeth was not at heart a poet, his verse being only morbid whining. Irving saw Macbeth revelling in the poetry as a self-indulgence; he could, for instance, imagine the character enjoying sentimental tears as he spoke of *pity, like a naked newborn babe*. So the actor lent a touch of hypocrisy to Macbeth's public professions of loyalty and grief that carried an edge of grim, sardonic humor. In 1875, to exaggerate the image of Macbeth as villain, Irving even cut the "bleeding captain" scene with its praise of the great warrior-general. (Fortunately, in later stagings, the moment was restored). Some reviewers reacted to Irving's characterization with shock, calling his Macbeth such names as coward, scoundrel, poltroon, villain— all descriptives they felt should not have been emphasized in the role.

Yet the energy and intensity of Irving's acting, and the very power of his fear and dismay, forced audiences to accept it. Not so much with his first Lady, Kate Bateman; she played in the fierce Siddons pattern, which did not smoothly match the self-generating connivance of Irving's Macbeth; but his next Lady, Ellen Terry (1889), softer, accommodating, following his lead while seeming to prompt him, fitted easily into an equation with his lithe, nervous overreacher. Some observers appreciated its subtlety: "Bravery does not mean insensibility to fear, but the power of conquering it. Macbeth's own account of himself is that he can face the armed rhinoceros or the Hyrcan tiger . . . but that the sense of guilt, reinforced by supernatural visitings, unmans him . . . (Irving) accentuates that side of the character—the nervous or tremulous side." Irving fought intensely at the end: "We shall see presently how a Macbeth with a restless eye, a Macbeth with a spare, nervous frame, a Macbeth with the face of a hungry grey wolf, can fight to the very death with all the power of man and all the fates of heaven against him."

A more formidable villainy informed Donald Wolfit's murderous Macbeth (England, 1957). As he played the role several times, his rigorously desentimentalized Macbeth grew in malevolent power. His massive soldier's body seemed formed for bloody cut and thrust, in peace as well as in war. Once tempted by the witches, once partnered by his wife—who fortified, rather than led him—the imposing nobility of front was made to serve his relentless move from murder to murder. Wolfit's deep voice could be momentarily nostalgic in its reflection on past innocence and tender in its pity for his dead wife; but these were moments that only made more fearful his progress through blood. "Gangster," reviews called him, "unequivocal scoundrel," and "a bloated vessel of corruption"—as his round Mongol mask of a face seemed to yellow with age and desperation. Yet with all this was a sense of tremendous size, of a villainy monstrous in what it did, and falling short only in what it suppressed. So grand that Edith Sitwell wrote to him:

> The greatness of your heart-shaking Macbeth will remain with us all our lives . . . moved to unbearable pity . . . We shall carry with us the memory of that leonine grandeur and terror, the doom implicit in every movement, each tone of voice in the scale of anguish.

MACBETH-LUCIFER

Why are we attracted to splendid evil? Psychologists propose the vicarious delight covertly afforded by surrogate overreachers who perform the wickedness we abjure, who spectacularly but safely let loose the impulses tamped in our own darks. Thus Macbeth's reckless luxuries of violence, the headlong, wanton plunges into the forbidden that only madness or destruction can redeem. This much purpose in wrong has made Macbeth seem, as noted above, a symbol of, even identical with, the Evil One, Satan—himself a magnificent abstraction of antisocial, antimoral forces in man. But where some critics condemn Macbeth for Satanism, others see an artistic configuration that must earn admiration and empathy.

For the other side of the devil-villain is the devil-hero. Thus the description of Macready, moving from being slave to being hero of wickedness. Let

your Macbeth be as magnificent as Lucifer, Mansfield suggested; such Luciferian magnificence in Macbeth, Gardner argued, partly accounts for the
sympathy he engenders. The design radiates a splendor of evil (Leech,
Sanders), the grandeur of a soul in crime, not the ignominy (Knight), carries
immense moral power (Wren); can make even evil seem beautiful, delightful
(Croce). So Milton thought of writing his epic about Macbeth, before turning
to his glorification of the Prince of Evil. Shakespeare, again, has Malcolm
liken Macbeth to the *brightest angel*. The luminous son would topple the father;
the champion turns his arms against Him he should defend; fall he must, but
more dazzling in the blaze of his delinquency and defeat than in his subservience—far more dazzling than any pale Galileans who ultimately crush him
in enormous pain.

The fascination, the admiration, the sympathy that the great wrongdoer
exerts is frustrating to the moralist who would see *Macbeth* as an object lesson
on the evils of ambition, or hubris, or selfness, or various violations of social
and moral codes. Given Macbeth's gigantic stature, the play breathes, as
Maeterlinck suggested, in a rarer air than that of good and evil; so Nietzsche
argued the futility of dwarfing Shakespeare's concept to a moral sermon on
the evil of ambition. Macbeth is too "royal" in his crime:

> From the moment he gains "demonic" momentum, he stimulates empathy and
> emulation in kindred natures. "Demonic" here means in spite of one's own
> advantage and life, in favour of a relentless thought or drive.

As Macbeth's destructive, Dionysian energies become endowed with the
absoluteness and grandeur that make him kin to Lucifer, he approaches the
fine line that distinguishes the heroic villain from the tragic hero.

The heroic villain, by the vastness of his egotistic vision, by the commitment to it of exceptional body and mind and spirit, suiting hyperbolic language and thought to his action, astonishes, excites and releases in audiences
more participation than guilt in his elemental wrongdoing. The design is
tempting; Shakespeare exploited it in such characters as Richard III, Iago
and Edmund; actors of Macbeth have succumbed, making the character a
fascinating virtuoso of villainy. Thus, Irving conveyed so intense and Machiavellian an evil identity that even some critics who resented the desentimentali-
zation yet admired the vision of malign power. But evil, however magnificent,
is only one strain in Macbeth's polyphony. It is the more distinctive because
so persistently countered by the sometimes diminishing but never extinguished notes of humankindness and philosophical perspective.

MACBETH-PLAYER

Even more than Hamlet, Macbeth, with all the roles he plays, must also
assume the role of a player. From the startled moment when he hears the
witches' oracles, and acknowledges to himself the vision of kingship, he must
play a part, toward his king and his peers and inferiors, and partly even toward

his wife and himself. His language reflects his playing: such words as *prologue*, *act*, *false face*, *theme*, *player*, *stage;* his references to putting on of face and garment; to parts of himself—hand, eye—as if telling his body how to perform. There is almost a sense of rehearsal in his director's advice to his wife at the ends of scenes I, v and III, ii. In his set speeches that mask his guilt, he seems to try to be "studied" in his lines, as in his grief over Duncan's death in II, iii, and when he gives the cheer in the banquet scene. To his lips, then, near his end, comes naturally the metaphor of life itself playing pretentiously, meaninglessly. So assiduously does Macbeth play the player that this role has been seen as his essential one: as if all his other personae are part of the repertory of a hollow man, doomed to a life of role-playing. The strong impulse to disconnect from his self, to disconnect from the parts that function to execute his will, to disengage his feelings, has been interpreted as symptomatic of his commitment to the actor's role (Kantak). But his reaction to the role has also been sensed: his image of life as the poor player strutting and fretting may reflect his revulsion against those who act, rather than love (Lawlor); his perspective on life as a bad play may mark a resurgence of a deep identity before his catastrophe.

Once more the spectrum. Macbeth's design moves him between his various roles and his inner self—or, if one does not exist, his self-shell that holds the roles together. If a center of his self is emphasized, the roles he plays may seem forced on him, and distasteful. The more he deliberately indulges in masking, the less innocently does he proceed. The equations are dynamic, open-ended, charged with ambiguity.

Macbeth as player must wear many momentary emotional masks—earnestness, compassion, surprise, shock—and sometimes, in his continuous interaction with others, a smile. A Japanese director characterized Macbeth as a man who does not know how to laugh. But he may laugh savagely from a grim satisfaction in his manipulations and dreadful deeds; and, fusing his torrent of energy and his philosophical perspective, he may perceive the life that ennobles and frustrates him as a kind of running cosmic joke—if sometimes a terrible one. So Ian McKellen's Macbeth (England, 1976). McKellen saw Macbeth as a "superstar," fated to aspire to, and achieve more, than other men, with a mind alert to the irony of existence—able to laugh even in his pain at the succession of surprises and reversals that led him to his destruction. Where Laurence Olivier would find bitter amusement in his first dilemmas, McKellen almost enjoyed his. Often, in this design, a touch of the manic begins to develop: in the great, later crises he laughs to keep from screaming.

Macbeth may *use* a smile or laugh: to mask hostility to king and court, to tease a disclosure from Banquo *(Your children shall be kings)*, to coat a social front, as at the banquet. The many modalities of the player's smile—with superior, equal, wife, inferior—as opposed to the smile of the villain simply enjoying what he is doing, switch off and on with circumstance. It may be a symptom of the player's will fully at work: when Macbeth's mask is consciously put on, he is the manipulator of everybody in his orbit. He plays brilliantly to his "audience"—the others in the play; only the audience in the theatre senses the difference between Macbeth the performer and the Macbeth who retires to the greenroom of his privacy. Denis Quilley (England, 1973), a vital, buoyant, optimistic Macbeth, showed how the false smiles in his first scenes could learn to come so easily that by the time he became king they seemed second nature; he smiled through his "coronation scene," and in V, iii made the soldier-messenger a butt for jokes, enforcing mouth-honor laughter from his court. Alec Guinness (England, 1966) was particularly subtle and quick in projecting, by his ever-watchful look, by his delicate, furtive movements, the role-player's alertness to any uncertain response in his auditors, eye and ear tuned to anything that might be thought or said about him. When he spoke to any but Lady Macbeth, a smile hovered on his lips, seeming sweetest when he was involved in his deepest disguise, as when greeting Banquo in the court after he became king. Guinness suggested the alienation of a player who dare not reveal himself to others. This Macbeth was essentially a loner, an outsider, and once crowned, was more than ever sensitive to the vibrations that he felt threatened him in an alien world. His warm, smiling bonhomie to start the banquet was a slipping vizard that he kept trying desperately to fit back on. But if his smiling was a mask, it still expressed a part of him that emerged in other ways: an excitement about experience, a vibrant readiness to enter into playing: to one observer he seemed to tread the stage like a trampoline.

Behind all the roles Macbeth plays is that deep privacy to which he retreats in his soliloquies. To his wife he is partly opaque, even in their early meetings; later he keeps his own secrets from her, and then she goes from him; he must confide in himself. Sometimes, in violent action, or reaction, he drops his masks, and the quick of the self is laid bare; but only in his solitary awareness does he achieve a perspective on himself free from external influence. Then his will asserts the Macbeth who is usually armored to the world. From these depths in the design emerge the two autonomous roles that most evoke sympathy for Macbeth: of poet and philosopher.

MACBETH POET

"The poet's eye . . . doth glance from heaven to earth, from earth to heaven . . . gives to airy nothing a local habitation and a name." All this Macbeth does, both as poet and near madman; does it so remarkably that Bradley could say that the poet was the best of him. The power of Macbeth's language to express his own emotions and ideas, and to move his audiences with him, had been recognized in many aspects: from the magniloquent, hyperbolic, imperial images (Morozov) to the countering simple, direct speech admired by Maeterlinck. Macbeth's vocabulary of gentle words I noted above; Spurgeon points out images from medicine that are soothing and restful. Macbeth is involved in the conditional mode that tenses the whole play; but he almost alone of the personae turns the language to deeply personal, engulfing poetry.

Yet not all critics and actors allow Macbeth the quality of poet. So Fletcher argued that Macbeth was a "poetically whining villain," his imagery sprung from a morbidly irritable fancy. A century later the actor Redgrave, in connection with his own performances, also insisted, as noted, that Macbeth was not a poet—a quality the actor thought was ridiculously bestowed on Shakespeare's characters. He saw nothing in Macbeth's lines to suggest either the conscious or unconscious making of poetry. Redgrave's essential insistence—which the critics Bethell and Muir (in his Arden edition) would later also assert—was this: the poetry was Shakespeare's, not Macbeth's.

But the poetry is an essential part of the characterization. We are awed and taken by Macbeth, as we are not by Coriolanus, for instance—or, in this play, by Malcolm—not only because of what Macbeth does, or even what he feels, but also because of how he can describe what he does and feels. The sensitivity of the poetic language belongs to the man; it is he who finds words to glimpse his self and world in metaphors that make them achingly real and recognizable. Macbeth's verbal visions that open his soul to us validate his dread of committing murder, and the impact on him of the horror that follows. The poet-Macbeth establishes the identity of a man of action who loves words, caresses them, savors their sounds, invokes their magic for narcotic or spur. Even in his greatest stress, the song of his speech is some extenuation for him—a major source of our empathy with so terrible a man.

The greatest danger is not to deny him his poetry, but to let the harmonics of the poetry mask the residual dissonances in the design. Some actors, as well as critics, tempted by the great language, have so luxuriated in the golden imagery that they have overbalanced the characterization on the side of sensitivity. Though Macbeth may be much of poet and murderer both, the more he is the first, the greater the strain of reconcilement between the two. The poetic Macbeth carries a softer resonance, instinct with pity more than terror; and overmuch of this coloring, if verging on the pastel, risks watering the terror in the design.

Very close to the edge came Beerbohm Tree (England, 1911). He specifically took for his text Bradley's exaltation of the poet in Macbeth. Tree dreamed through the lyrical passages, held them long on his tongue, indulging Macbeth's gift for voicing the beautiful. "A climactic agony of grief" was the ultimate emotional experience Tree sought to share with his audiences. He extended the lyrical note into his entire production, a magnificently romantic vision: to one Victorian it suffered from *too much* beauty. Tree's "bold and fearful Scot" was not to be primarily bloodthirsty; rather a "gallant, honest soldier," innocent before meeting the witches, then half-hypnotized by the vision drawn before his mind's eye. His poet-Macbeth shrank before the murderer-Macbeth: one subtle observation of Tree's characterization was that as he went on continuously discovering new impressions of his self, he felt more horror at his self. With his tormented soul, he became, in the contemporary language, a "nervo-maniac," his hallucinations seeming as much "morbid symptoms" as supernatural visitations. In the moments when Macbeth suffered most—as in Banquo's ghostly eruption—one spectator was impressed by "a low, throbbing hum strongly suggestive of the noises of the head" experienced by persons "subject to optical hallucinations."

Susceptible to imaginative fantasy, the poet-Macbeth is haunted by his uncanny visions of the ambiguous world enveloping him. He is possessed, not only by the witches or other weird stimuli, but also by the visions his own imagination sets in motion in his raw, quivering brain; he is wildly sensitized to sights, sounds, touch, smells, tastes—especially those that are not tangible. What-is-not forces itself on his consciousness as fiercely as what-is; and the assaults are doubly unsettling because in society he must try to mask their effects, and must sometimes fail; when rapt, when the "fit" comes, when he hallucinates, and his face comes unsealed.

Edwin Booth (U.S., 1890) exemplified the poet-Macbeth dominated by imagination. In the banquet scene he could plausibly—as, for instance, Kemble could not—successfully allow Banquo's ghost to remain invisible, and imagine it to the satisfaction of audiences and critics. Booth demonstrated that the highly imaginative Macbeth also *suffered* most highly—from the remorse, the fears, the expectations of the unexpected. Booth himself saw Macbeth "more as a weak man . . . full of the milk etc. than a strong brute." Booth was a slender, supple Macbeth, and at least one observer wished for a thane who could speak like Booth and act like Salvini; though others felt Booth compensated with fire what he lacked in bulk—especially in later performances, where he made himself seem robust and massive as well as haggard. The contrast between the grace of his gentleman Macbeth—likened in a review to the grace of Hamlet—and the frenzy of his murderer's delirium when hallucinating, as well as the maniacal savagery of his final fighting, suggest another face of the Apollonian-Dionysian dialectic Shakespeare designed. As Booth went on playing Macbeth, he seemed to intensify both elements: the whirlwind of horror and fury, and against this the haunted agony of remorse suffered in his private world of imagination.

From his father Booth may have learned to create his imaginative aura. Junius Brutus Booth seemed particularly gifted in experiencing the unseen. When he looked into the air after the vanished witches, he "volatilized their substance"; he made the throne he imagined present to the eyes; he unmistakably heard the imperial theme. Imaginings displaced objective realities; he seemed to live in poetic wonder.

Macbeth as "the most poetic of all murderers" was deliberately and richly realized by John Gielgud (England, 1930). Unlike other actors who played the role more than once, Gielgud felt this performance was truer than a later one that he approached more analytically; because in this first,

I simply imagined it, and acted it for the main development and broad lines of the character, without worrying about the technical, intellectual and psychological difficulties.

Gielgud was the Macbeth called less the fighting Scotsman than the Dane; he resonated with poetic sensibility, projected indulgence in fantasy even before his meeting with the witches. He was gently yielding to his wife, at first seeming too irresolute for a murderer, let alone a commander who aspired to—would be able to—rule the troubled Scotland of the play. Gielgud used the poetic base for a striking linear contrast: conscience might make a coward of such a man; the thought of the deed, and then the gruelling act itself, might shake and then momentarily shatter him—his collapse after Duncan's murder was called "a masterpiece of nerves"; but once embarked upon his bloody course, the qualities of the man of death—the "slaughterman"—made themselves known. Still, sensibility could be seen to worm its way inside him; made him show—a test of the role—how much the ravages of mind, soul, body, went on in the time-gap between his appearance in IV, i and his re-appearances in the last act, when he gave full value to the poetry of the last soliloquies.

MACBETH-PHILOSOPHER

Where the poet-Macbeth's special sensitivity reflects his intense sensual awareness of forces seen and unseen operating on him, that impel him to his luxuriant verbal description, the philosopher-Macbeth is more thoughtful, more introspective, lost in the world of mind more than of fantasy. He is less concerned with the saying than the said; less with finding the words for incomprehensible things than in trying to know the things. He is a step farther outside, less lyrical, thrusting toward perspective. He seeks to give a name to what is immediately and frightfully real to him; and the more his thoughts are twisted from him by bewildering experience, the more earnestly he examines the puzzle of his existence. The philosopher-warrior-killer, by his very nature, manifests oxymoron: the more clearly his inquiring mind comprehends the wrong he does, the more painfully must it observe his awful deeds committed. The philosopher, even more than the poet, would separate himself from the terrible other self that does what he abhors; divide himself between knower and doer.

Something of this dialectic emerged in the earnest Macbeth of Samuel Phelps, who is again worthy of particular remark for daring—temporarily at least—to restore the play's text almost entire in the mid-nineteenth century.

His active and ardent mind passed rapidly from action to thought, and from thought back again to action, while his mind, racked between two opposite impulses—his conscience at war with his conduct—keeps him in incessant anxiety. Hence a succession of profoundly philosophic and tenderly pathetic reflections, intermingled with stern and bloody resolution, which flit across his storm-tossed soul like the wrack of clouds driven by the tempest.

The brooding, introspective Forbes-Robertson manifested the depths and dangers of the philosophical emphasis. Inevitably, much of Hamlet was in this Macbeth. Though he first appeared persuasively as the triumphant general, he was at once oppressed, rather than inspired, by the witches; then, when retreating into his glassy stare of inward raptness, he was restless, sensitive, grimly shadowed by the ongoing thought that undermined his resolution. The image of shedding innocent blood shook him with disgust; he became a murderer who killed on nerve, not brute strength. He would break from his raptness into flaring, exaggerated activity, until thought checked him, and the contemplative mind asserted itself. The sense of mind at work made the characterization seem more intellectual than imaginative—a price the philosopher-Macbeth may pay for his immense introspection. Grein sensed a broad polyphony in this Macbeth:

> great determination and iron will . . . a wilful, lustful murderer, foolhardy yet cowardly, callous yet childish in his breakdown, impulsive, but rather inclined to be meditative . . . a characterisation of conflicting ingredients.

But the critic was particularly challenged by the dimension of thought, evident in the "slow and leisured and deeply reflective" soliloquizing:

> You intended to bring home to us that he was something more than a mere warrior agitated by boundless ambition, that he was a philosopher, a leader of men, a creature of mystical powers.

At first, to romanticize this impression, Forbes-Robertson had worn a noble beard that so reminded the knowledgeable of a familiar head of Christ that the actor felt he had to shave it, letting his own lineaments reflect his inwardness.

When the effect on the Macbeth design of the inhibiting influence of Apollonian thought is not offset by a countering charge of Dionysus, the balance is endangered. The thinking Macbeth is likely to be gentle and thoughtful with his wife, perhaps even to the point—in Forbes-Robertson's case—of uxoriousness. The equation suffered especially when the actor played against Mrs. Pat Campbell's feckless Lady: she was so weak a reed that she did the leaning, and his adjustment, to an even softer and more yielding Macbeth than usual, lost some of the vigor and fierceness by which his murderer had sometimes overridden, as he must, the philosopher.

The philosopher in Macbeth most of all understands the horror of his crimes, and suffers most from doing what he loathes. When fully conscious of his baseness, as the black Ira Aldridge's Macbeth was (U.S., 1858*), his terror at committing murder was less than his revulsion: he found the act

---

*Aldridge was a black American; his great successes were in Europe, where theatres made him welcome.

devilish, disgusting; with a distaste amounting to nausea, he set about making of himself the kind of villain he knew to be everything he hated. This Macbeth would be undermined and destroyed as much by his violated mind as by external assault.

Many philosopher-Macbeths would similarly speak from conscience in their introspection, however violent and bloody their actions. But at the other end of the spectrum is the thinker who takes some refuge from his own corruption in cynicism. The introspection does not resist his ambition, but is made to serve it. Gielgud's second Macbeth was touched with this deliberate discoloration. It was more concerned with "intellectual and psychological" elements, more thought out, and—as noted—less satisfactory to him than his first Macbeth, though it was warmly accepted by critics. Gielgud was inevitably still the poet, but now world-weary, his vision tinged with a sense of meaninglessness from the beginning. Complicating the interpretation was an implied parallelism between Macbeth's tyranny and the effects of Hitler's dictatorship over Europe (this was 1942). Where in his first performance Gielgud had been praised because he was "no neurotic from the Italianate school of Macbeths," now, when he invested Macbeth with a sense of complex psychology, and a sardonic, jaded world view, he was described as a tough Borgia deepening the intrigue but diminishing the pity, giving an Italianate complexion to what was ordinarily northernly bold and resolute. Among other "psychological" facets Gielgud was seen to develop was "a strong vein of narcissism," and the aura of a Macbeth familiar with temptation. To counterweight the intensely intellectual, contemplative projections, Gielgud effectively conveyed a sense of fierce strength in his gaunt, somber image: if he was not rugged, he was lithe, he knew how to project virility by breaking out in crescendos of sound and action that conveyed the eruptive vitality of the soldier-murderer. Yet the roles of poet-philosopher dominated; the rugged contours, the stark Dionysian horror were dissolved in the image of a man who thought more than he could act.

Inevitably, again, the philosopher-Macbeth gravitates towards intellectuality. This has the value of intensifying the dialectic as his searching mind forces him to confront the self he would deny; but the emphatically intellectual Macbeth has never been comfortable in the theatre: he can become thin-blooded, even brittle, almost innocent of the fierce pulse of the warrior-murderer. Walter Hampden (U.S., 1921), whom Towse thought the best Macbeth since Edwin Booth, was enough "intellectual" to perceive that at first he too much represented the reflective, analytic elements in the design. The "ruffianly" note was missing; he knew that Macbeth had the stature of a figure out of Michelangelo; he confided in a letter (still in manuscript) to Furness, "I wish I were built like a Salvini." As with other distinguished actors who had time to return to Macbeth, Hampden grew into sustaining the emotional side:

As strong as the wind that sweeps bleakly over the heath where the witches hover, yet vulnerable as a child on the hearth when memories of poor Banquo's murder come back to him.

He became the philosopher-warrior bitterly at odds with himself, his hesitances of contemplation, self-perspective, and remorse continuing, but interrupted and almost overwhelmed by savage abandonments.

The importance of the philosophic note in Macbeth's polyphony has been conspicuous sometimes, in performance, by its absence. The quieter, deep moments validate the complex, opposition-rich design; without them, the play has again and again degenerated into melodrama. But the introspections do not bear sentimentalization, either. Hazlitt, trained to the noble mellifluousness of Kemble's honorable murderer, charged Kean with not being melodious enough in the later soliloquies; the actor's loyal biographer, Hawkins, pointed out, fairly, that by the very hoarseness of his voice Kean was conveying the sense of Macbeth's stress in these awful perspectives.

Macbeth's philosophy is not consolatory. The world he measures becomes steadily less tolerable to him—as his philosophy is not tolerable to some critics. Those who find Macbeth unintelligent are not impressed by his thinking; some Shakespeareans, like Redgrave and Casson, have been affronted rather by its expression, in the "tomorrow" lines, as blasphemous. On the other hand, Murry so admired these lines he felt they were pure Shakespeare, the world's noblest spirit might have uttered them, they overcharged the play, were, in effect, too good for Macbeth. Santayana, once troubled by Shakespeare's lack of any systematic philosophy or religion, declared,

> If we asked [him] to tell us what is the significance of the passion and beauty he so negatively displayed, and what is the outcome of it all, he could hardly answer in any other words [than Macbeth's in V, v].

By the philosopher-Macbeth Santayana was, as noted, deeply impressed, called him divinely human in his capacity to achieve a perspective on his agonized existence.

For convenience in this discussion of the many roles and qualities compounded in the Macbeth design, I have abstracted distinctive emphases found by actors and critics, and the dialectics provoked by these emphases. All important interpretations, however focused on one or other of Macbeth's roles, are rounded off by interplay with the subordinated ones. The sturdy warrior Macbeth yields to his fears; the tough murderer softens; the poet grows fierce, the philosopher bloody.

A few acting interpretations will be particularly instructive for exploring the complex range of Macbeth's polyphony. I first single out Kean, because he was the first great performer who broke from the noble-murderer pattern to emphasize the inherent violence and darkling fear that counterpointed

Macbeth's brave and generous impulses. "A marvellous compound," Hawkins wrote, "of daring and irresolution, ambition and submissiveness, treachery and affection, superstition and neglectfulness of the future, a murderer and a penitent." To this polyphony Kean added such notes as "the dubious mind, the rapid execution of the soldier, the natural visitations of the man," and— as Kemble did not—Macbeth's gentleness and fear. Even to the end, Kean sustained the dialectic dividing Macbeth against himself: he fought, a reviewer observed, with a combination of ferocity and feebleness.

Hazlitt was not greatly pleased with Kean's Macbeth, because Hazlitt was conditioned to enjoy Kemble's show of noble and stately submissiveness to the critics' much-admired Terrible Woman of Siddons. Nothing so distinguished Kean's contribution as the shift from the Siddons' pattern in his Lady Macbeths. In the Kean equation they became humanized. They could begin to influence Macbeth with tenderness as well as force, offer him love as well as scorn. Kemble, in performances in which Siddons did not appear, might experience an actress striving to portray such a Lady, but we have no evidence that he extended the tones of his own characterization; Kean stretched himself toward the far corners of the design.

Laurence Olivier had the advantage, not frequent in the twentieth century, of playing Macbeth a second time (1937, 1955) after many years of thinking about the role.* Unlike Gielgud, who believed his own later interpretation diminished by too much thinking, Olivier felt he had needed the time to grow:

> If you're twenty-seven years old you can't do it, although you can recite it, you can go through the motions, you can give them a hell of a fight at the end, you can reach all sorts of poetic passages, perhaps. You can reach the humanities to a certain degree, but only to a certain degree, because you have to be of a certain age of life's experience to play parts as enormous as that; you have to know about humanity, you have to know a lot about human relationships. (To Tynan)

In 1955, made up in a dark, almost Mongol mask—false gums to protrude his lips, his eyes slanted, his cheekbones high and touched with yellow, and with black-socketed, brooding eyes—Olivier, on his first entrance, seemed a man already touched with darkness. He himself believed that Macbeth and his Lady had already contemplated Duncan's murder. Yet against this, and Olivier's almost sinister front, countering notes of conscience emanated from his presence, and developed in his subtextual action. The diversity of impressions made by Olivier suggests the extent of his—and Macbeth's—polyphony. Critics saw a nexus of opposites: "the soldier, the unconscious poet, the weakling, the haunted murderer, the tiger trapped"; . . . "capable of angelic exaltation and devilish cruelty, sensitive, imaginative, but dastardly." The

*He had also played Malcolm, in 1928.

different, even contradictory emphases others experienced suggest how many notes were fused:

> "A cool, calculating intellectual" . . . "Frightful spiritual crises" . . . "Brilliant barbarian" . . . "Substitutes introspection for power and barbarism" . . . "A desperate man from the first" . . . "Slow-spoken, reflective, kindly and noble" . . . "Blending of thoughtfulness and controlled power" . . . "A study of nerves" . . . "Fearful ambition, greatness undermined by paroxysms of remorse and despairing outbursts of ferocity" . . . "The philosopher rather than the butcher, suave, cynical, calculating" . . . "Desperate bewilderment" . . . "Lurking there underneath, a sense of humour" . . . "The emphasis of the play is thrown upon his quality of evil" . . . "No man went to kill with such reluctance, and no murderer returned with such horror" . . . "The poetry and the neurotic agony, but not the fierce strength" . . . "Savage, sullen strength" . . . "The very heart of the black and dreadful" . . . "Always a soft thread of conscience."

In his first (1937) staging, Olivier's more explosive Macbeth had made its full impact by the middle of the play, and then had slowed, as easily may happen when the role is not paced as it deserves; in his second (1955) interpretation Olivier deliberately began in a low key, and then, by intensifying the inward resistances to Macbeth's outward climb, accelerated the action relentlessly to the end. Early on could be felt the tremendous inner forces kept leashed; they seemed gradually to build to climax almost of themselves. This inwardness provided a center for the characterization. *The Times:* "The usual difficulty of reconciling the tough warrior with the superstition-ridden neurotic seems scarcely to exist. Attention from the first is fastened on the mind of Macbeth." In this mind lodged the human qualities that gave audiences a developing identity to recognize and intimately share. One such quality was the trait that Olivier had come to believe resided in all Shakespeare's great tragic characters· self-deception. Another, which the *New Statesmen* felt other Macbeths had missed, was "a streak of self-hatred that adds yet another shade to the sombre palette of remorse." Such qualities, with the multiple aspects of the character noted above, fused in a complex but profoundly comprehensible polyphony. As Olivier experienced the character from within, the *Sunday Times* observed, as it developed in his imagination, so did it in the imaginations of the spectators.

Externally, the actor captured the charisma seen in the character by his director, Byam Shaw:

> A superb leader with the courage of a lion and the imagination of a poet. A man of iron discipline and will power and an almost hypnotic personality. There is something marvellously mysterious about him. The sort of man who can make one nervous just by looking at him. No one would ever dare to slap Macbeth on the back or be jolly with him. Even his friends find him a bit overpowering and his soldiers and servants are terrified of his anger. He is tremendously proud

and confident, but never shows off or blusters. When he speaks other people remain silent . . . Apart from his burning ambition, I feel he has a deep sorrow that gnaws at his heart . . . [a dead son]. After he has committed the crime and become King, all that is bad in his character bursts out. He is like a man who is mentally diseased, but the magnificence and courage of his nature remain until the end. He never becomes a brutish villain like Iago or Aaron. He has greatness of soul even though he is damned.

Having deliberately suggested the outer image of a saturnine, even ominous figure, Olivier radiated from within the decencies that modulated his characterization. Scofield's equally complex Macbeth (1967) moved from a different beginning. He represented a front of rock-like integrity, and struggled with the destructive impulses that swam up from within and sought to shatter him. Scofield's Macbeth was tall, muscular, with the bearing of a leader of soldiers, and the face that would honor a crown; cased in slabs of robe and uniform, he seemed impregnable. His austere features, as he first came from battle, carried a kind of weary innocence, until the swarm of black and dark desires fought to drive from his consciousness the fairer ones more native there. His appearance made sense of Malcolm's descriptive, *brightest angel;* indeed Hobson saw him as "Lucifer, but Lucifer with the light of the morning still on him."

This Macbeth's complexity and richly layered inwardness transcended the play's theme as conceived by the director, Peter Hall. To Hall, Christianity was at stake, represented by Duncan, clothed in pious white, and shepherded always by a cross. Macbeth, in black until crowned, and again in final battle, was to incarnate the force of evil—to be, if not the Prince of Darkness, of very high degree in his kingdom. Scofield's Macbeth could almost be seen to force resolve on himself, ordering violence to be done, and himself wielding a bloody sword; there was no holding back. But the lament for Satan: "How art thou fallen, O daystar, son of the morning?" could not enclose this Macbeth: always some deepmost reserve in him seemed to resist final corruption.

Scofield made the poetry his own: especially in the later soliloquies, the words often seemed to come out etched, one by one, from the stone of his mind, in rhythms as distinctive as the grave voice and grave mind that bore them. In these moments Scofield hardly moved; the mask lifted from his face, and Macbeth's whole buried life, with all its contradictions, seemed to be writing itself there. A great actor's face, like a great poet's pen, can reflect, in the subtle working of its lines, many ambiguities, many subtextual implications.* Scofield's eloquent features seemed sometimes capacious enough to

---

*The untrustworthy J. P. Collier "discovered" an elegy to Burbage—of uncertain authenticity, partly because of its awkwardness, and internal contradiction; but it says something about the actor's art, and the almost-impossibility of playing Macbeth:

> Tyrant Macbeth, with unwash'd bloody hand
> We now may vainly hope to understand.

Yet not so vainly, perhaps, when Burbage had acted:

> Thy stature small, but every thought and mood
> Might thoroughly from thy face be understood.

carry at once all the best and the worst of Macbeth—poet, traitor, philoso-pher, butcher, king, tyrant . . . Audiences were magnetized by that graphic face: at the *Tomorrow* lines, as he stood stock still, listening with grim surprise to the philosophy that forced itself, thought by thought, from him, the earth itself seemed to stop and listen.

I return to my first sentence: to dare to inhabit Macbeth, to stretch imagina-tion, feeling, and understanding to the last reaches of the character design, is to adventure toward the limits of artistic experience. Let us forward.

Lesser than Macbeth, and greater.

Banquo

Lesser than Macbeth, and greater (I, iii, 69)

the oracles will say of Banquo. The comparatives underscore the centrality of degree in *Macbeth*. A man is partly defined by what he is in relation to other men. We have so far heard Banquo mentioned just once, by Duncan, who brought the name in across the bleeding Captain's account of Macbeth's triumphs; and it was quickly swallowed up in the panegyrics by the Captain and Ross about the greater warrior. Banquo is not, either in military prowess or rank, the equal of Macbeth, the double thane. What does this mean to Banquo?

Either-or interpretations of the play tend to perceive Banquo as an unwaveringly loyal subject, without ambition, envy, or malice—indeed without dramatic identity, except as a "good" foil to Macbeth's wickedness. That he was the legendary ancestor of King James, whom presumably Shakespeare was propitiating with the play, has provided a reason to support the "good-Banquo" interpretation. If Shakespeare had been intent only on pleasing James, he might indeed have cardboarded the kind of immaculate nobody whom Banquo's extreme apologists discover; so he is sometimes played as a plain, bluff soldier, stolidly loyal, unmoved by the uncanny, or by personal motivation. Fortunately for the density of the play, Banquo is much more: a troubled character, moved by passion—and perhaps purpose—parallel to, if less complex than, Macbeth's. In Holinshed—as the learned among Shakespeare's spectators, and even James, may have remembered—Banquo helped Macbeth kill Duncan; here he is not so active, but by concealing his suspicion of Macbeth's involvement, he becomes a kind of silent accomplice. In his lines, his acts, his feelings, emerge the dark notes that Bradley long ago observed: the polyphony that marks him a true denizen of the *Macbeth* universe. Byam Shaw, analyzing the role for the Olivier production, thought much like Bradley as he wondered why Banquo said nothing of his suspicions about Duncan's murder.

Is it out of loyalty to his friend, or fear of the consequences, or because he feels that he is, to quite a considerable degree, mixed up in the business? Judging by what he says . . . I think his silence . . . is mostly on account of his own interest in the future of the Crown. In which case he is a guilty man and to some extent gets what he deserves. I don't think that it is possible to believe that he remains silent only out of friendship for Macbeth; and if it is fear that prevents him from telling the truth, and he is completely honest, then he could leave the country. Of course he is not a villain, but he is not a simple honest man either. He has his own particular form of ambition.

What Bradley and Byam Shaw suggest would be clear, I think, to anyone who isolates Banquo's words and examines them without preconception. A native to this world of degree, Banquo aims high, highest. The actuality of his characterization seems another reason to doubt that Shakespeare intended it as flattery to James.

Banquo does not reveal himself as readily as Macbeth: neither in the overt behavior men notice in Macbeth, nor in the self-revelation of soliloquy. Banquo's only long solitary speech comes at the beginning of III, i; he speaks briefly of his inner feelings in II, i. But he discloses a great deal in these two speeches; and I think it will be clear that at other times he will share in a phenomenon apparent in other *Macbeth* personae: when seeming to speak to others, he will be saying something to himself. Beyond this, we may know him by his unvoiced interaction with his fellows. Some of his most telling characterization may be subtextual: evidences of impulse and desire that are betrayed by a look or a gesture, perhaps more controlled than Macbeth's, but akin.

What impulses and desires energize the Banquo design? If we enter it from the inside, we experience these things: Banquo is a very good fighting man, but not the best. If his comrade is promised a glorious future, Banquo wants to know his own share. He has a son whom he loves. He will take fire at the thought that his progeny, if not he himself, might ascend to the very highest place of all. Confronted by strange creatures, his instant reaction is that they may not be real, of this world; he doubts his sanity, thinks he may have been hallucinating. The meeting with these creatures, and their prophecy, will invade his mind: he will bring them up in private conversation with Macbeth, as well as in soliloquy; they will haunt his dreams; and so wrack his waking that he will pray desperately for the power to repress his *cursed thoughts* so he can sleep. He is against wrong, as Macbeth at first is, but too expedient to expose it when his own interests are in danger. Macbeth will see him as a rival, a threat to degree, will envy him for some qualities that Macbeth feels he himself lacks. To several *naive** spectators, the two seemed designed to be on a collision course.

---

*Again: I call *naive* spectators those who, having never before read or seen *Macbeth*, reported their reactions for me to performances of the play specially staged for them.

One of the best Banquos I have seen, John Woodvine (England, 1976) slowly developed the characterization of a man of essential decency only beginning to be tested before Duncan's murder. He was evidently troubled by the same ambitious fantasies as Macbeth, but he tried to resist them, even sincerely to warn Macbeth against their implications, playing a restraining counterpoint to the faster-moving Macbeth. Still, his *dreams* and *cursed thoughts* so bedevilled this Banquo that his prayer to be spared them, at the beginning of II, i, was almost convulsive in its intensity. After the regicide, when Banquo seemed to learn by perfectest report that the Sisters' prophecies were coming true, and he guessed how Macbeth had conspired to bring them about, Woodvine knew himself to be wonderfully tempted, as if Fate itself meant him to follow Macbeth's road to the throne. Who knows, Woodvine said, if Banquo had lived longer . . . ?

More will be said about Banquo as we come to his crises. I will try to be fair to those interpreters who do not see him as I do. Mainly I will try to be fair to Shakespeare's complex artwork—beginning at the first meeting with the Sisters.

Act I, Scene iii (part 2)

The witches have pointed our eyes to Macbeth's entrance: *Macbeth doth come* (34); our minds may remember, from immediately before, Sister 1's mutilated *Pilot . . . Wrackt, as homeward he did come.* The drumming that alerted the Sisters, heralding Macbeth's coming, was of troops on the move, approaching: thus economically Shakespeare suggested an army returning from battle. The military drumbeat is designed to arouse and excite the spirit; when sounding under the rhythm of the witches' chant, and building to a climactic approach and pause, it powerfully prepares an audience for an event; "as though," one reviewer wrote of Komisarjevsky's "ghostly drumming . . . an orchestra of all the furies of Hell were playing their diabolical instruments to the downfall of the universe, under the inspired conducting of Hecate herself." The thunder of drums may echo the drums of thunder that accompany the Sisters.

To make Macbeth's entrance more impressive, improvers in the English theatre have added panoply and whole armies.* Macklin wanted Macbeth

---

*Because Forman, of such dubious reliability, wrote—if indeed the writing was not Collier's— that Macbeth and Banquo came upon the sisters while riding through a wood (probably, again, a borrowing from Holinshed's similar description), Sidney Lee speculated that Forman may have seen actual horses ridden across the stage. Wright, considering the possibility of live horses, notes a description by a Spanish ambassador of how, in a comedy at the English court (1522) ridiculing the King of France, "A man came on stage with a great horse [France] very wild and ferocious . . . so wild and untamable he could not make any use of him." The play, also discussed by Graves, was a simple farce-morality in which helpful characters named Friendship and Prudence show the horseman how to bridle and curb the unruly animal, which then, under their ministrations, became quiet and obedient. A horse could conceivably be trained to seem "wild, ferocious, untamable" until a cue to be gentled; but to present such an animal in the confines of a court stage would seem to be taking an impossibly dangerous chance. Even on the Globe platform there would be risk, observes W. J. Lawrence (4), who trusts Forman no more than I do. E. B. Daw points out that in another early morality, *The Trial of Treasure*, for comic relief a character played a fractious horse, and she assumes the same happened in the farce about the French king. My guess is that the animal in question was two men in a horse costume, a time-honored comic device.

E. K. Chambers considered the possibility that Forman might have seen Macbeth and Banquo on hobby-horses; but why multiply entities beyond necessity? Nothing in the lines even remotely suggests equestrianism. In fact, the play carefully avoids it. In III, iii, when horses are heard approaching, and might have been expected to enter, we are told specifically that they go "about," preceded by "officers, drums, fifes, standards, and other warlike characters in insignia of the van of an army on their march." At least since Davenant, to stipulate the approach of many men a shouted order, offstage, was interpolated:

Command they make a halt upon the heath!

and the reprise "Halt! Halt! Halt!" was passed down the unseen line, diminishing in the distance, with the sound of feet coming smartly to attention. Sometimes the troops themselves tramped across the back of the stage: in good order, as with Irving's mail-clad men-at-arms, who seemed in an endless procession, or wearily struggling back after their bloody battle, as in Carrick Craig's *Macbeth*. Battle flags are furled, the wounded helped along. Martial music may speed the march: e.g. Garrick, "Scotch March;" Macklin, "Coldstream March;" Charles Kean, "The Lass of Patties Mill." Variations on Locke's (if it was Locke's) old music are sometimes still heard, or new strains composed to integrate with the other human, animal, and natural sounds of the play.

But all this panoply, staged or imagined, needs to give way to the strangely intimate scene Shakespeare designed: so Garrick's many guards were complained of because their felt presence disturbed the privacy of the exchanges between the witches and Macbeth and Banquo.

We go back to the entrance of two warriors. I will report the initial response of various Macbeths to the Sisters in some detail, since from the action in this first moment much of the character's flow is determined. All the Macbeths will enter more or less tuned to the full polyphony of the design: but they may emphasize different notes in ways that will help us to perceive the full diapason of the character.

Macbeth and Banquo commonly enter together (though they have entered separately from opposite sides). The witches await the two men variously: hiding; merging with bushes or boulders; lurking as if to spring; frozen in

---

to explain why they do not appear; in the marked Padua Folio which G. B Evans considers a pre-Restoration promptbook ("probably dated between 1625 and 1635") the stage direction specifies a sound effect, "Treade." At the end of Act IV,i, Macbeth hears horses that he could not have seen.

A live animal, especially one of any size, used in a serious play, is likely to destroy illusion rather than support it. Horses have been used effectively in *Macbeth* stagings only under special circumstances. Maeterlinck, producing the play in and around a Belgian castle in 1809, could make a dash of horses into his courtyard part of a night spectacle; as could the Turkish *Macbeth* using cavalry near the walls of the river fortress before which the play was staged. At Astley's Hippodrome in the nineteenth century the major part of *Macbeth*—and of other plays—was done on horseback; but here the spectacle was the thing, and none of the horsemen was embarrassed by critical praise for the depth of his acting. *Punch* reported: "We saw General Macbeth, looking very smart and brave and warlike in his new ring'd shirt, accompanied by General Banquo in a crimson cloak of somewhat faded splendor, which had evidently belonged to Count Almaviva; but he looked bravely, too; and it was very pleasant to see them riding over the "blasted heath" and making no more fuss about it than if it had been that of Hampstead. Then followed closely six warriors . . . mounted upon an equal number of 'highly trained steeds.'" Reviews like this tended to evaluate equine and human actors at about the same level.

anticipation; sometimes dark, scrabbling shapes, sometimes only their faces lit; perhaps completing the spell that seems to draw the men from another path to this part of the heath; perhaps setting the stage for ritual—in one case, drawing a magic circle of light for the oncomers to step into. Traditionally the witches knelt: this bothered the gentlemanly Gentleman: "Wholly ridiculous. What reason can be adduced for making these preternatural hags so chock full of loyalty and good breeding?"

The two warriors are evidently leaders of men; but one, as we see or imagine him, is a leader of leaders, a man set apart. Perhaps by the formidable bulk of his presence, as with the giant Salvini; perhaps by the nervous force in his whiplash body, as with Irving; or by the fierce energy bursting the limits of his stocky frame, as with Edmund Kean; or by his silent, dark, almost Oriental intensity, as with Olivier.

The man with him may be very unlike, or very like. When Shakespeare pairs men, he sometimes stipulates differences: thus, in *Lear*, the fiery Cornwall, the restrained Albany. Or he allows for a similarity—even mirroring—of appearances that masks deep internal differences, as with Edgar and Edmund. Clues to appearance are sometimes explicitly given (Cassius, Antony), sometimes implied in character (Coriolanus, Aufidius). In the theatre, where every detail of face and figure makes a statement, the comparative appearance of the two warriors entering will be one signal of their relationship.*

The two must be alike in that they are believably splendid fighters who have come battle-weary from victory. At least one will have marks of blood on him and his weapons; probably both, with one more marked than the other. (They may still be on a battlefield: Heston rolled a dead soldier over—and stained his hand with a premonitory spot of blood.) Here are the nation's two great captains: this both binds them and separates them. In a world of degree, where to be first is to be great, to be second is to be lesser. They are rivals as well as friends. The friendship, or at least mutual support, will be obvious; the rivalry, until it very soon shows itself, may at first be largely subtextual, manifested subtly by the way one of the two may precede the other, or sign to him to go first, in the way one looks at the other, or does not. Perhaps each already dreams of becoming king. The potential may be seen in them: either might become a throne.

One of the two speaks briefly, and then falls silent for many lines to follow. We do not know he is Macbeth; but we may guess it from his manner, from the way the waiting witches single him out with their glances—of hate? love? admiration? malice? mischief? Do they have some special link to him? His first words,

> So foul and fair a day I have not seen (42),

---

*Shakespeare may have intended Banquo to have hair of a distinctive cut and color—perhaps blond, or red, or white-streaked. In Act IV, i, Macbeth will identify the apparitions of Banquo and his descendants by their hair.

echo theirs; but so had Duncan's. Macbeth's words echo with a difference. To the witches, foul *is* fair, fair foul; the polarities are indivisible, interpenetrating. Macbeth can see fair and foul existing side by side—as in him they will. He can experience more than one thing at a time, conflicting things. He is not now a decider.

He describes so much with his words: the changeable battle, the changeable weather, the terrain—have his eyes fallen on the Sisters, too? Walker thought that Macbeth saw them first; or is Macbeth perhaps aware of them and refusing to look? (We still do not know if this is an arranged appointment.) Are they—their faces or postures, or something visible in their turned backs—part of the foulness? In a moment Macbeth will have started, and seemed to fear: how soon? If he did not expect them by appointment, did he in his imagination?

The second man asks a question about locale (Shakespeare gets in another exotic Scots place name) and then, because of what is reflected in the first man's face, or because his own glance is caught as the Sisters move (turn, dance, kneel, wave wands, beckon, approach) or make sounds (sing, moan, coo, whisper, cackle, scream), he sees them and speaks to—and of—them. Does he even, at first, ask *them* the distance to Forres until he sees what they are—or are not? Banquo vibrates to strangeness immediately; his imagination is active, he can at once fancy that what he sees is of another world, or phantasmic.* He does not trust his senses, he perceives things that are, and are not—

> That look not like th'inhabitants o' th' Earth,
> And yet are on't. Live you, or are you aught
> That man may question? (45–47)

The scene is built of many short beats, mounting to fierce pauses as characters confront each other, or themselves, or the inexplicable. One peak comes after Banquo's speech. He may say it in a rough and cynical voice—though the scene seems to demand a tone of mystery approaching awe—but of the trauma of this experience on him there can be no doubt: in a moment he will repeat this searching questioning of their being, he will later dream of them, wonder at their prescience; what they have to say will return to his waking and sleeping mind. Now, though, they will say nothing to him; their *choppie fingers upon . . . skinnie lips* warn him to silence, may half frighten him, as in the Welles film. All their attention, their concern, is for the other, the silent man. He speaks only when the Sisters make it clear, by their rebuff to his companion, and by the concentration of the Sisters on himself, that their business is with him. He too is not certain of their reality. The end of the beat holds until he breaks his silence,

> Speak if you can: . . . (52)

All of the early part of the play has been building to this point: since the Sisters' first commitment to the meeting in I, i, through Duncan's order to honor Macbeth, to their hearing his drum, we have been led to this. It will be a kind

---

*He may already have dreamed of these creatures before him. See pp. 293–4.

of coronation, a ritual to be repeated with variations as the play goes on. In formal fashion the three Sisters give the three *Hails* that, like the beats of the first three scenes, built to this momentary climax. Singly or together, they kneel, or circle Macbeth, or gesture with their wands, crutches, or other paraphernalia to suggest the occult, uncanny character of their obeisance.

Keith Thomas notes that witches were supposed to control people by touch or by "fascination"—the latter probably what Gordon Craig meant by their power of hypnosis. On the stage Macbeth's Sisters have suggested both means. They have pointed their fingers or sticks (wands) in such a way as to seem to transfix the two men; as fortunetellers, they have crowded on one of the men, then the other, to hold and read palms, or otherwise practice divination—and then sometimes have held out their own palms for reward. Occasionally their salutations have been mocking, as if to make clear that they mean no good: but then the dramatic equation must require a stupid, diminished Macbeth and Banquo not to perceive a game played. An important point made in the Eric Porter *Macbeth* was the absolute sense that the Sisters spoke expecting to be believed—and were. Macháček was approached by his Czech Sisters with what seemed genuine veneration—which the hero accepted as his due. Nowhere in the dialogue with the Sisters do the men convey the idea that they regard the strange figures as evil. Only the possibility will occur to Banquo, and that later. If the Sisters have shown themselves entirely malicious when alone (negating ambiguity), they need still to seem utterly persuasive in a doubling now.

An immediate function of their *Hails* is to identify Macbeth for us: by name, by the concentration of the witches on him, and by his reactions. The first *Hail* comes as a shock to him: that such creatures should know who he is, that they should have such power over him as to name him. The second *Hail*, promising him Cawdor, shakes us as well as Macbeth: him because it is a surprise, us because this is solid evidence that the Sisters know more than they have reason to know. Unless, of course, they have eavesdropped on Duncan's order, and then the next—third—prophecy comes from them as a kind of inspired improvisation—what Irving called a "gypsy guess"; but this kind of rationalization undercuts the manifest oracular power Shakespeare gave them. As they were prescient enough to know that they would meet with a triumphant Macbeth after battle, now, with the Cawdor *Hail* they offer him a promise that we know is a certainty; and if elsewhere they may seem to equivocate with Macbeth, their three *Hails* now are without equivocation, including the ultimate one, labeled with a time word that will ring powerfully later:

> All Hail, Macbeth, that shalt be King *hereafter*. (55)

They may complete the ritual by placing a kind of crown—of twigs, or flowers, or witches' materials—on his head. Any man might be amazed; but

the effect on Macbeth is of shock. Again, the beat ends with a climactic pause.
Then his companion:

> Good sir, why do you start, and seem to fear
> Things that do sound so fair? (56–57)

The fear-fair sound-pun mirrors fair-foul; something dark shadows this
golden promise. Genuine as Macbeth's astonishment may be, a small grace
note qualifies his alarm, or his companion's sense of it; in a play where appearance is always doubtful, some ambiguity attaches to "why do you . . . *seem*
to fear?" Does Macbeth feel any sense of needing so soon to show something
other than he feels? For his companion's sake? Is the companion-rival at some
level of consciousness questioning Macbeth's sincerity? Will Macbeth be
partly afraid because his companion has heard the oracle meant for him?
And perhaps guesses his thoughts?* The moment is alive with questions.

The silence holds in a long, brittle moment. Macbeth is looked to for an
answer, and cannot speak. He is rapt. Later we will have some clue to his
overreaction; while we wait to learn more, may we sense a note of prescience
in Macbeth that kingship would be dangerous to him, however he might reach
it? Any tremor that he is the kind of man who, in Freudian terms, perhaps
knows he will be destroyed by the success he woos? Both he and his companion, the only ones in the play ever to see the Weird Sisters, are vulnerable
to the unearthly; we may even be made to feel that the Three have chosen
them for their susceptibility to belief and temptation. Macbeth more than
the other man, more than most men, resonates wildly to a world of the unseen,
the unheard. His imagination can strike him paralyzed: he lives inside himself, dreaming of what might be, or lives beyond himself, seeming in touch
with the powers of nature in darkness. To the offering of a golden mystery,
his complicated response sounds many notes.

The design in both Banquo and Macbeth of a sensitive inwardness cased
in the forms of formidable warriors contributes importantly to the eerie atmosphere of the scene. They may not both be poetic dreamers, as were Bergman's
two in his 1948 *Macbeth;* but their immediate amazement and awe reflects a
sensibility that binds us to the men behind the warriors' armor; and at the
same time will enforce on us the strangeness of an event that could so shake
such figures.

In addition, these Scots thanes, to Shakespeare's London audience, could
convey a sense of a particularly northern vibration to the supernatural. They
may have been dressed in unmistakable Scots costume—in IV, iii, Malcolm
will recognize from far off his *countryman*. Shakespeare apparently intended

---

*In a rehearsal for the Hall-Scofield *Macbeth*, Brewster Mason, as Banquo, asked,
Is it *seem* to fear?
Scofield: No.
Hall: It *is* fear. But notice that Banquo often digs at Macbeth.
(Mason's Banquo kept inquiring eyes insistently on his partner.)

that the garb which Ross—and the other thanes—wore was distinctively national, un-English.

The ambiguous reality of the Sisters, as reflected in the subjective response of Macbeth and Banquo, has been emphasized by special staging techniques. In France, the filmed projections of the Sisters superimposed on Macbeth melded them with him, and they and their loudspeakered voices seemed to belong to him as much as themselves. In an Italian staging, the Sisters stood apart, and Macbeth spoke toward empty space, as if suggesting that the event was in his mind as much as actual. Piscator stipulated Macbeth's thought by projecting over his head a great crown. In another German staging, an enormous veil dropped, carrying the image of the golden round.

Critics and actors, as noted, have long differed over Macbeth's state of mind as he first enters. Was he indeed an honorable man about to be assailed by irresistible influences? Was he temptable? Had he already been tempted, by himself and—or—his wife? Bradley would not believe that murder had been discussed, but: "No innocent man would have started, as he did, with a start of fear at the mere prophecy of a crown, or have conceived thereupon immediately the thought of murder. Either [a fearful] thought was not new to him, or he had cherished at least some vague dishonorable dream, the instantaneous occurence of which . . . reveals to him an inward and terrifying guilt."

The text allows for more possibilities than this. The many varying moods and predispositions imagined for Macbeth's entrance are defined mainly by his visual imagery as he suits the language to it. He acts not only text, but subtext (discussed in the Macbeth chapter), his felt motivations masked as well as revealed by both language and physical movement.

In the theatre, the "noble" Macbeth comes innocently to the Sisters. Dibdin provides the proper eighteenth-century vision of this advent: Macbeth "had gloriously justified his sovereign and preserved his country, his mind was occupied with reflections too noble to have hailed the honors that were thickening about him, otherwise than by their fair and legitimate title; nor, till external forces influenced him, did he in the smallest degree shrink from his fealty." Thus Garrick's primary reaction to the prophecy was intense "astonishment"; he was praised then for the natural way his mind opened to ambition only by degrees. With the kindling of the dream of higher degree, after the oracles, the sensitive, honorable man's conscience promptly appeared: "It is curious to observe in him the progress of guilt from intention to act," Wilkes wrote.

The somber Kemble strode stately down from his army to meet the Sisters, and accepted their surprising prophecies with what seemed a "studied indifference," that suggested an integrity now almost unassailable. Kemble was partly determined to demonstrate—as against Whately and Stevens, who questioned Macbeth's courage—that Macbeth was no more afraid than Banquo. Kemble particularly denied Whately's argument that Banquo showed contempt or disregard for the witches; he granted that Macbeth would be amazed at the vanishing of the witches, but "Banquo . . . is not less moved." As the witches' prophecy took hold of him, Kemble's Macbeth, like Garrick's, shamed by his sense of guilt, would become mournful, melancholic. Neither of these "honorable" men would commit himself to murder until a force far fiercer than that of the foolish eighteenth-century Sisters impelled him.

At the far extreme from the honorable murderers were Macbeths entering shadowed already with some darkness in their souls: with minds that were either ready to do some terrible thing they knew not what, or that had already contemplated a fearful regicide. Seeing a hero carrying this kind of burden, and hearing him hailed as a future king, an audience attuned to plays and a social structure in which non-lineal attainment of the throne implied the killing of a monarch would quickly understand the disturbance in Macbeth, and the possibility that he had already contemplated Duncan's murder.

Irving, so certain that Macbeth had long before broached the act to his wife, entered a romantic, brooding, gaunt figure, armed, helmeted, carrying a great two-handed sword, and stood silhouetted against a blood-red sky, his thin mustaches floating in the wind. The flush of victory that would warm the warrior-Macbeths was not for Irving: his Macbeth was tired, haggard. To an observer in New York Irving seemed to be watching the Sisters before they saw him, as if thinking to take them by surprise *(Sunday Herald)*. His head lifted with alarm at the first *Hail Macbeth:* that these strange creatures knew who he was came as a shock. That, with the next *Hails*, they showed they also knew his thoughts, was frightening to him: "For a moment he is suspicious of himself; if these seeming strangers can read his mind, may not those friends and companions who have fought by his side?" *(Daily Chronicle)* That Banquo was a witness particularly troubled him. Outside of battle Macbeth was not, Irving thought, greatly brave. But to be king! Irving stood as if in a dream, made rapt by the implications of the third *Hail*. "He has longed for it before," was Ellen Terry's note; Kate Terry Gielgud thought that thereafter "the hunted, haunted look never left his eyes."

Mantell, among others, entered with a similar sense of deep brooding: as if the great military victory had already brought to the forefront of his mind the vision of a next triumphant step. Mantell hung back behind Banquo at the entrance, lost in his thought; he started at the witches' *Hail*, partly from the disturbance of his raptness, as well as from what they said. Aldridge, entering, seemed even more shaken by his thoughts: subdued, preoccupied, his gait uncertain, perplexity on his face. Olivier conveyed, to Tynan, the sense that over and over in his mind he had already killed Duncan.

Where these Macbeths seemed oppressed by one terrible imagined act, Booth's poet-Macbeth seemed ridden by imagination itself. His antenna seemed always to be responding to a world of unseen, unheard stimuli, as if possessed, in the folk phrase, of "second sight." This Macbeth was born to sense and suffer the presence of all that was weird, including the Sisters: "to the eye of imagination a pall of ruin is already fluttering in the haunted air" (New York); he responded to the witches "like an Aoelian harp to the wind" (St. Louis). These were sympathetic responses; once when Booth entered, preoccupied and moody, staring at the ground, the unsubtle (and perhaps jealous) Forrest, watching, wondered irritatedly, "What's the damn fool doing? He looks like a super hunting for a sixpence."

Forrest himself represented the sturdy fighting man who seemed, as he entered, cheerful in victory, untroubled by "sinister prepossession" or even susceptibility to it: in Highland Tartan, plumed Scotch cap, his legs bare from knee to ankle, pointed shield on his arm; with his commanding air, and his appearance of elastic strength and freshness, he was a picture of vigorous, breezy manhood. He took off the shield, and handed it to a soldier, before coming down to speak. His first words, to Banquo, *so foul and fair*, were in the easy tone that might be used to describe the weather. The thought of evil had not touched this mind.

He was incarnate the bloody warrior of the Sergeant's tale. The theatric values of this image showed in the contrasting shock of his response to the Sisters' *Hails;* the extrovert at a stroke was made introvert, became agitated, moody, yet abstracted, as if the dark thing in his mind had seeded monstrously and was already swelling.

With Salvini, in the strong-warrior pattern, determination to act was stronger than shock. This giant Macbeth, with his coat of burnished mail, winged helmet, axe in hand, visually the image of a triumphant general, was at first jocund, even jubilant. He came on, Robert Louis Stevenson reported, "fair and red-bearded, sparing of gesture, full of pride and the sense of animal well-being, and satisfied after the battle like a beast who has eaten his fill." His rather slight start at the witches' prophecy was mainly of astonishment—an instinctive jump, Coleman thought—followed soon by tremulous exultation. When he was preoccupied, thoughts of how to act seemed to crowd his mind. He took on the look of a warrior-king, assuming easily an air of authority over Banquo and the clansmen who had followed them; the "moral cowardice" of doubting Macbeths was not strong enough in Salvini to worry seriously his ambition.

Responses to the Sisters' oracles generally vary in the theatre according to the differing emphases on tones in the character design. In a frankly ambitious Macbeth, like the Baku Turk Sharifov (1936), coming from battle with prideful joy, vanity clearly was predominant; he expanded, seeing himself in the witches' words. Phelps' decent Macbeth was horribly shocked. To Wolfit, a soldier-murderer ripe for violence, the implication of regicide was instantly grasped; an observer saw the broadsword that was cradled in the crook of Macbeth's arm seem to rise as if by its own volition, and fall to the stage. A Macbeth in Ulm (1975) was discovered exhausted, clinging to his two handed sword, his naked torso—and Banquo's alongside—smeared with blood; to these killers, as in a trance, came the Sisters' incitement. Sothern, horrified by the image of murder springing into his mind, stood a long time silent, his staff falling from his hand; then he looked uncertainly toward Banquo. Porter's practical Macbeth had unmistakably cherished a deadly ambition before this; his mind, if momentarily surprised, seemed at work at once on plans. The acid implication of the prophecies seemed to eat more slowly into Redgrave's barbarian, anti-poetic Macbeth, as if the mind itself moved slowly toward the murder it would embrace.

These Macbeths were moved or swayed by the Sisters' words; Macready seemed controlled by them. Again, the contrast: he was, Coleman wrote, "a rugged, semi-barbaric chief, a being of another age; a man physically brave, but eerie and superstitious; a believer in wraiths and bogles and witches and warlocks, and all the mysteries of second sight." But this did not at once appear: Macready usually entered in a mood of cheerful triumph. If he lacked the formidable martial air of more stalwart, more fiery Macbeths, he compensated with a studied subtlety and rich detail. In some performances, he began his first line by lifting his sword and pointing it toward the sun—*so fair*—and then let the blade turn so drops of red wax, like blood, showed crusted on the steel, and added *foul* . . . To Leigh Hunt, the line, in an early performance, sounded as casual and untroubled as a routine remark on the climate, when instead "the audience should feel a strange contention of the elements, fit for supernatural appearances . . . and a mood . . . that makes him a fit subject for . . . supernatural soliciting." But Macready too was working for contrast; once he heard the oracular witch-words, the change in him, his subservience to the Sisters as they pointed at him, seeming to transfix him, was striking. They had not read his thoughts, they had planted them, and brought them to bloom, and he seemed helpless to stay the fruit. His mouth dropped open; he fell at once into bewildered agitation; his speech was wandering, unsettled. The rejoicing conquerer became immediately an altered man, the *Theatrical Journal* reported: "The shadow of destiny had fallen on and darkened him, and from that moment he is dragged, inexorably dragged, towards Duncan's chamber." So Coleman, reading Macready's "tell-tale face": "From that moment 'fate and metaphysical aid' seemed to surround him to environ him with death and doom."

Romantic visual images accompanied Beerbohm Tree's poet-Macbeth as he slowly descended into the storm-lit heath where his great tree had been spectacularly lightning split, and brought on a kind of lightning of his own: a high-held torch that waveringly lit up the mountains behind him and the recesses of the barren heath, broken by reflections from silvery pools. He was unmistakably the gallant, honest poet-soldier; he felt the temptation of the oracles, but their most evident immediate effect on his sensitive face was amazement and alarm—alarm not so much at what he heard as at the image of himself that had listened to the Sisters.

The shock of Forbes-Robertson's Macbeth was dominantly intellectual.

His face wore the fascinated look of a man confronted with and trying to comprehend a sinister puzzle—the *Observer* called it a "glassy look of introspection." This expression stayed with him as he moved restlessly, oppressed rather than inspired by the oracles. Where other Macbeths were excited, or terrified, he seemed profoundly interested, as if concerned with making sense of what must happen. His compulsion was to understand as much as to decide.

Gielgud, another "philosopher" Macbeth, seemed to Agate to be deliberately masking his inwardness in his first appearance with a show of picturesque swashbuckling—"low in tone, gaunt and sombre like an El Greco." Gielgud's device for his picturesque entrance was to imitate the portrait of Irving entering romantically with a great, sheathed sword over his shoulder. "I . . . could not think how to get rid of it, until it suddenly occurred to me at rehearsal one day to drop it to the ground . . . to give Banquo a good reason for his line: *Why do you start.* . . . " (Some such "involuntary" response has been standard imagery—the sword or staff or other prop falls, or Macbeth clutches at Banquo, or lifts his helmet and wipes his brow, or betrays subtler subtextual signals of tension, excitement, guilt, alarm in face and body.)

The neurotic Macbeth, twisting in the grip of some inner, ambiguous compulsion from the beginning, has shown his alarm at the oracles as an intensification of the tension already holding him taut. Matkowsky, upon seeing the Sisters, stared speechless, made a circular gesture with his hand as if he wanted to banish them from his mind: the moment they greeted him an acute fright and nervousness erupted. Reinhardt wanted his Macbeth, Wegener, to say *So foul and fair a day* in the same rhythm as the witches; even before this Macbeth saw them he was clearly haunted by the thoughts pursuing him; he stared at the Sisters, unable to speak, until finally he swallowed, gasped for breath, and his voice came in low, abrupt tones. At the *Hail . . . King* he turned pale, and began to shiver; he could not endure Banquo's inquiring look; he lowered his eyes, trembling, unable to move. This kind of "unmanning" has not been unusual: a famous Czech Macbeth, Simonovski (1864), shook helplessly as if with a fever—evoking from the critic Jan Neruda a speculation important in the aesthetics of terror: when does the spectacle of sheer physical stress tend to diminish the mood of horror intended? Neruda was troubled also that the extremity of Simonovski's response came too early for the build of the play.

A different kind of instability threatened Plummer's immature Macbeth. Helpless in a psychic way, he came tired from the battle to fling himself, a "man-child," playfully on the ground, and chew at a root; blandly he eyed the ragged witches waiting for him. At their prophecies, his start was followed by a wild, hysterical laughter, as if at a joke too impossible, too ridiculous, too good to be true.

A more masked image was portrayed by Severin Mars, the Macbeth in Maeterlinck's panoramic production (France, 1809). His invitation to the Sisters to speak was thrown off roughly; he covered his reaction to their prophecies with ironic, half-laughing scepticism. He still seemed an incorruptible block of powerful man, heavy and magnificent in his shining, almost blinding, armor, a fierce warrior who gave the impression that his belligerence had been only partly calmed by the battle he had won. His massive front would seem to absorb the speculations about his darker purpose; what lay behind the mask would not be revealed for some time.

None of the distinguished Macbeths gave himself away completely in the first moments. The play forbids it. The various shades of extremity of shock at the oracle must sustain mystery; whether the dominant note is fear of the witches as such, superstitious panic, alarm at secret thoughts known, the oppression of fatefulness, the anxiety about Banquo's presence, the firing of the overheated imagination, the testing of loyalty, the exhilaration of villainy promised reward, the disbalancing of a tilting nervous state, the blazing of new ambition—whatever the emphasized impulses expressed in words and subtextual imagery, the design is insistently polyphonic, open-ended, vulnerable to ambiguous forces.

Some actors have been notably successful in holding in suspension the compound of roles and impulses compressed into the first appearance. Olivier's semi-Oriental mask enabled him to economize on grimace and gesture: he appeared mounted on a rock, dark, intent, watchful, the image of a dangerous warrior-hero, lithe, sensitive, apparently stoic—except that his controlled face spoke of terrible forces held within. He stood bathed in a strong light, as of a setting sun, that caught the slightest tremor of expression. Banquo lagged a few feet behind, stood lower, his eyes intent on Macbeth's face. To one reviewer, Olivier seemed to have been expecting the witches; to another, the thought of a murderous deed must have been long in this Macbeth's mind. Ronald Harwood remembered that, after the sustained, silent moment during which Olivier stood, arms folded, and waited for the Sisters to speak, and then heard them, "instead of recoiling, as other Macbeths do, he leaned forward as though tugged by some irresistible force." He seemed to radiate a kind of brooding, sinister energy, the *Times* reported, a dazzling darkness, revealing the black abysses in his mind. "From that moment you were aware of a man trapped by a relentless Fate so that, when Macbeth struggles with his conscience before the murder you knew somehow that the decision had already been made: there was something so terrifying about his submission to his destiny at this early stage."

Strange, even contradictory, things too could be read in the face of Scofield, as the witches rose from their blood-colored earth-matting to meet him. His stance and grim countenance belonged to a warrior who could do terrible things; his start of fear was minimal, only enough to alert the everwatchful Banquo. For all his trappings of a fighter, at the still moment of his response to the prophecies Scofield's face and tensed body struggled to contain fearfully conflicting forces. Scofield had accepted the conception of a man susceptible to evil, to fit the director's framework of the play; but evil was not winning in him without a struggle that could almost be felt.

When Banquo, after a strained pause, sees that Macbeth will not—or, from some seizure of raptness cannot—speak, he himself addresses the Sisters. Again, he reflects his uncertainty over their reality. Interpreters who regard Banquo as simply "good" see him here as sceptical, calm and collected, even contemptuous: "He addresses the witches in a spirit of curiosity, even of levity, much as one would address a fortune-teller at a carnival booth."

In fact, Banquo seems the one most bewildered by the Sisters' questionable reality; it is he who wonders if they are real, or imaginary, or hallucinations of the mind, or instruments of darkness. His apostrophe to them is

I' th' name of truth. . . . (57)

It is no casual challenge; the word provokes some start—of fear, anger, confusion, or mockery—among the Sisters; and the very mystery of their response, during the pause provided by the comma, drives Banquo to pursue his baffled questioning:

Are ye fantastical, or that indeed
Which outwardly ye show? (58–59)

Banquo's nervous readiness to perceive imaginary unrealities, illusions, even figments of the heat-oppressed brain feeds the climate of ambiguous otherworldliness Shakespeare enforces. This doughty warrior, as well as Macbeth, feels the presence of something beyond the natural in these bearded women: and they never answer his question, never resolve his doubts, as they do not ours. If Banquo were to make mock of the Sisters, against the clear text, the whole atmosphere of mystery would be seriously diminished.

Character as well as climate is being made. Banquo, as spokesman for the response to the uncanny, establishes the credulousness that will lead him to initiate discussions with Macbeth of this strange experience. When—for the second time—the Sisters refuse to identify themselves to him, he exposes the design of his felt competition with Macbeth. He speaks the simplest form of sibling rivalry: if *he* gets that, what do I get? You promise him *royal hope;* you don't even speak to me.

Banquo concentrates into his questioning the conditional uneasiness that permeates the play, in language, character, action, spectacle, thought:

If you can look into the seeds of time . . . (63)

If. This monosyllable, and various implications of it, thread through all parts of *Macbeth.* Not only *Macbeth,* of course. The word's significance in *Lear* confronted me when I computerized the text of that play. The uncertainty of the *Lear* world was partly reflected by the multiplicity of *if*'s. My computer shows that, in actual numbers, as compared with *Lear, Macbeth* has fewer *if*'s; but *Macbeth* is a much shorter play; when I calculated the average of key words per thousand in the canon, with the help of Harold Weaver, I found that the *if*'s in *Macbeth* exceed the mean frequency of the word in most of the other plays. In *Lear* the *if* environment was conditional on the vagaries of the ongoing "natural" world, mainly as embodied by the people in it, in all their "unnatural" manifestations; any gods that might exist seemed impersonal, cruel, or absent. In *Macbeth*, the conditional is oriented more toward future uncertainty, and is shadowed by the hints of the whimsical or malicious nature of a wayward universe. Aptly, Banquo's first use of *if* is linked with a recurrent image of planting and growth or stunting, that looks to the future:

> If you can look into the seeds of time,
> And say which grain will grow, and which will not. . . . (63–64)

Looking into seeds suggests divination: the metaphor is suitable to the Sisters.

Banquo's bold, brave, final command seems again to glance at his rivalry with Macbeth (and was so played against Scofield's Macbeth):

> Speak then to *me*, who neither beg, nor fear
> Your favors, nor your hate. (65–66)

The comma after *beg* suggests a slight pause, before he goes on to the comparison between his courage and his companion's start of fear. He has already reminded the witches that Macbeth seems paralyzed, *rapt withal*. Macbeth will relive this moment when later he acutely feels the intensified rivalry with Banquo; will remember Banquo "chiding" the Sisters, while he stood mute, and will feel himself shadowed by Banquo's spirit. He may show even now that he senses that darkness over him.

The Sisters at last obey Banquo. They may first consult by looks, or by heads together; as fortunetellers may scan his palm, or perform other "magical" rites of the sort offered Macbeth; finally they tell him what he wants to hear. They tell us, at last, who he is: Macbeth's fellow captain, mentioned once before.

> Banquo, and Macbeth, all hail. (74)

Macbeth is usually shocked to awareness by the Sisters' next oracle. It touches a nerve center: Banquo's children shall be kings. Five father-son relationships work into the structure of this play—Duncan's, Banquo's, Macduff's, Seyward's, and Macbeth's own. The yearning for survival of a line, a continuation of dynasty, will sustain Macbeth's later action. We are to learn how horribly empty is the promise of the crown to Macbeth, if he cannot pass it on to his offspring; now the prophecy that Banquo will *get kings* makes him indeed, in Macbeth's eyes

> lesser . . . greater
> Not so happy, yet much happier. (70–71)

The ambiguity—that recurs in the play—of two dissimilar things the same, here to have and have not, to be and be not, forces itself on Macbeth. *Foul* and *fair*. The intensity of the response that has shown in the actor's face, from bewilderment to disappointment to hate, helps to define both his character and his sharpening relationship with Banquo.

Even the "noble murderer" must react here: Garrick was blamed by the *St. James Gazette* for not sufficiently marking "that disappointment which every one expects from you, and none can represent with a sensibility equal to your own." The Macbeth already on fire with ambition blazes up at the threat to his lineage. If at their entrance Macbeth and Banquo have seemed faithful comrades, as Irving suggested, jealousy toward the father of kings comes with the shock of contrast; if as with Scofield, Macbeth enters separated by several paces from his fellow, if he is a loner, already deep inward, but sensitive to Banquo's insinuations, his smoldering at the golden promise to Banquo deepens the darker tones in his polyphony.*

Brought to himself by the hail to Banquo, and suddenly—as he will write to his wife—burning with desire to know more, Macbeth tries to question the Sisters: usually the more intensely because they have already begun to vanish and he must command—

> Stay you imperfect speakers . . . (75)

Imperfect: because leaving unfinished, him unsatisfied; but perhaps for their message, too; and their own uncertain identities.

Unlike Banquo, Macbeth does not wonder if the Sisters are real or imaginary; women, or phantasms. He is ready to assume their validity; he wants answers, the future explained, security.

> . . . tell me more:
> . . . the Thane of Cawdor lives
> A prosperous gentleman: (75, 77–78)

Irving, committed to Macbeth-as-villain, assumed that Macbeth was designed to be hypocritical here: that he had met Cawdor in battle, and knew him a traitor. But Ross reported only that Cawdor assisted Norway, and Angus will say that perhaps Cawdor supported the rebels, or both enemy forces—nothing in the text stipulates a personal confrontation with Macbeth. Cawdor, in any case, is secondary: the great wonder that enforces the pause of the colon after *gentleman*, as Macbeth gathers breath for it, is

> . . . to be King.

It *Stands not within the prospect of belief* (79), yet he—like others in this play—is willing to believe the impossible: only give me assurances: *whence . . . this strange intelligence? . . . why / Upon this blasted** heath? . . . With such prophetic greeting?* What strange source? Strange force?

In his voice now sounds all his burning desire. The strong Macbeth demands; the guilty Macbeth whispers; the bewitched Macbeth pleads; the

---

*In the experimental productions with *naive* audiences in both England and America, where no effort was made to emphasize rivalry between Macbeth and Banquo, several spectators sensed it here, and expected it to lead to conflict.

**In a "modern" *Macbeth*, staged in a World War I atmosphere, the word *blasted* was used as an expletive.

philosophic Macbeth wonders; the ambitious Macbeth gloats. The voice nearly breaks; or it is hoarse, greedy; or confidential; or eagerly breathless.

The speech builds to the climax of a beat. If Macbeth has arrested the Sisters' going by his *Stay*, they stand to stare at him, as in the Reinhardt staging, motionless, enigmatic, forcing him to offer an appeasing smile, to raise his emotional bid for an answer. They may still be moving to leave him, sometimes in witchlike dance or other configuration, at his desperate, rising, impotent command.

> Speak, I charge you. (84)

Abruptly, the Witches vanish.*

The vanishing is properly spectacular—a *coup de théâtre* authenticating the air of wonder and mystery Shakespeare intended. And, as Gordon Craig suggested, its very legerdemain "must be a delight to see." Realistically, as noted, the Sisters in the theatre have disappeared by merging with the stones and walls from which they came: as for instance when Hampden drove them before him toward a great rock with his questions and suddenly they were not there. They have similarly been lost as they retreated up stairs, or back into the seemingly limitless depths of backstage darkness. With Olivier, Richard David saw this sleight-of-hand: "As Macbeth fixed on the second witch the first slid like a lizard from the scene; when attention shifted to the third, the second was gone; and as Macbeth and Banquo turned on each other in eager surmise the third, too, vanished."

Because the astonished Banquo will say of their dissolving,

> The earth hath bubbles, as the water has, (85)

one guess has them disappearing *down*—into the Globe Theatre's traps—a device made startlingly fresh in 1972 (London) when Banquo, advancing on one of the crones with his sword, found only an empty bundle of rags on the floor where she had been crouching. Macbeth, unlike Banquo, believes the witches *melted . . . into the air*—which suggests that Shakespeare meant the two men to "see" the same thing differently, in different places. Macbeth's perception has been a cue for the Sisters to be flown out—by Tree, hissing, skittering. Irving's Sisters seemed to dissolve in sudden clouds of the well-known Lyceum steam, leaving briefly behind a murky mist—filthy air, impervious to sight. For the momentary distraction all magicians use to cover their tricks, lightning has flared to mask the crucial movement: an old prompt-book instructs "One on a ladder to throw lightning directly on Macbeth's face"—a technique noted in a Kemble version. Hampden, who specified heat lightning for the witches' opening appearance, ordered chain lightning here. Forrest used a distracting whirring sound, and sudden, momentary darkness.

In France (1962) immense spirals of green smoke hid the Sisters' disap-

---

*Irving, by his very violence, seemed to drive them away.

pearance. Popularly in the nineteenth century, as we saw, and later—e.g., in Czechoslovakia in 1939—gauze before the witches, with the light darkening behind, made them seem to deliquesce. Impressionistic witches made of projected light have faded or blacked out. One gambit, used in the Polanski film, transformed the vanishing into an early manifestation of Macbeth's manipulative character: Banquo did not see the hollow into which the Sisters descended; Macbeth did, but pretended to imagine they had disappeared— while evidently making a mental note of their cave should he want to return (as of course he would). Cleverness; at the cost of some of the supernatural climate Shakespeare designed.

In the shocked silence that usually follows the hurly-burly of the superbly architectured climax of the beat, Macbeth, Banquo, and the audience hold a long, frightened pause. Strangeness has been. This world is wayward: that which logic says cannot happen has happened. To do, Oyama suggests, is not to do. The shocking reality of this awesome unreality shows in the faces of the two brave men who try unavailingly to make sense of what is senseless.

Again, their evident fear and awe authenticates the supernatural climate for the audience. In a Macbeth like Macready, feeling the fateful fix of destiny on him, the first response is sheer terror. In one more free to act—one who had long been contemplating violence, like Irving, or was ready for it, like Mantell—the startling moment would give way to characteristic abstraction, the mind working hard ahead. To the imaginative, the poetic, the intellectual, the strangeness of the event itself would hold them for a moment crystallized between amazement and the need to resume the day. No Macbeth could escape the impact of the visitation: the world hereafter must be different, if only because Macbeth has suddenly seen the vast beyond of what he thought were the fixed boundaries of his world.

No wonder the imaginative Banquo, who before suspected that the Sisters were phantasms, now wonders also if the misperception is in his own and Macbeth's unsettled minds:

> Were such things here, as we do speak about?
> Or have we eaten on the insane root,
> That takes the reason prisoner? (90–92)

Banquo speaks as if for both of them; but again, as others will, he speaks mainly to himself, to the trouble in his own mind, voicing the fear of madness that is one motif in the play: Am I hallucinating? Am I insane? Are the things I see real? Sothern's Banquo showed severe fright; and remember Kemble's observation: that Banquo must be as moved as Macbeth. Macbeth will in due course wonder about his own sanity: a foreshadowing may darken his face now. The bewilderment of the two men has been partly rationalized by having them accept a drink from the Sisters' brew that momentarily puts them in thrall; Shakespeare intended the uncanny experience itself to be dazzling enough.

Characteristically, Macbeth speaks conditionally, wishing for something
other than the now:

Would they had stay'd. (89)

The awe of the two men at the wonder of their experience not only contributes to the atmosphere of mystery, but shows, also, that they are the kind
of men who *could* see, now *have* seen, the Sisters. Their gaze from where the
witches were, traveling to where the three vanished, speaks their shock.
Macready was praised for the "innovation" of bewildered agitation now: Lady
Pollock—"His wandering, unsettled tone did more than . . . the witches in
showing the supernatural at work. . . . [His] singular power of looking at
nothing . . . When he spoke 'into the air' we could almost see the hags pass
away, and like a wreath of vapour dissolve into the invisible element." Vandenhoff, Gould wrote, gave body and form to the impalpable air; Junius
Booth made appear the disappearance itself: "with a sudden upward look,
and a sudden springing tone, not musical, but like the whiz of a shaft from
the cross-bow . . . *into the air*. . . . Voice, look, action, conveyed the instant
thought, the vanishing." *Wonder!* was Irving's note to himself for this moment;
Forrest, rapt, spoke with a "dissolving whispering voice"; his Macbeth was
dazed, scared. Reinhardt's nervous Macbeth seemed in a state of physical
shock: he breathed heavily, wiped the sweat from his face and neck; his hands
trembled as he passed them over his face, now grown pale.

The day is different when the witches have gone. Literally different, if their
elements, thunder, fog, and filthy air, pass with them, and the air quiets and
brightens about the two men, as it did, for instance, in Phelps' staging with
the gauzes up. But if nature seems refreshed, not so Macbeth and Banquo.
They will never be the same: toward themselves, toward each other. In the
strained pause that sustains the climax of the last beat, as they digest the
marvel of the Sisters' evanescence, and then begin to appreciate how this
"magic" may validate the prophecies, new tensions constrict their relationship. This was made interestingly visible in the Anthony Hopkins-Diana Rigg
Macbeth (England, 1972): Macbeth and Banquo had drawn their swords before
the witches; after their wonder at the vanishing, as the two men turned face
to face, they found their swords pointing at each other. The same effect has
been achieved with an exchange of looks, or with a deliberate avoidance by
either or both of such an exchange. The strain shows often in the forced casual-
ness, even jocularity, that pretends to dissolve it. Macbeth says, probing,
sometimes summoning a jesting tone:

Your children shall be kings. (93)

As if it is a great joke; or a matter of small—or serious—concern. Kean, full
of hopes and desperate resolutions, afraid to trust himself to say what he felt,
after a searching look at Banquo spoke with affected carelessness. Banquo

responds in kind, with a shrug or a joke: in a Czech staging he made a parody
of kneeling to Macbeth. But the moment has been treated seriously, too, a
tense Macbeth, like Matkowsky, testing Banquo after a long pause with the
abrupt speech. In the Savits staging, Macbeth was frankly suspicious of his
rival, spoke in low, tense tones; and Banquo answered uneasily. Banquo himself has started, almost in fright, at Macbeth's reminder that their two destinies
may collide. Mantell emphasized the rivalry, and his sense of estrangement
from Banquo, by emphasizing the first word: *"Your* children. . . ." Evans
toyed with the twig-crown the witches had put on his head as he spoke.

The note of *children*, first evoked in the prophecy to Banquo, now voiced
by Macbeth, sustains a motif that will wind itself through Macbeth's career
fatefully. Macbeth's first thought, now, is of a dynasty crossing his own line;
the thought will harry him beyond hope. The reminder that he will be *King*
can be almost a bitter shock, in this context; he turns it off, again sometimes
jestingly, sometimes musingly, discounting improbability by minimizing it,
but at the same time ready for reassurance:

> And thane of Cawdor too: went it not so? (95)

Whatever Macbeth may have been before his entrance, from now on he will,
with others, and even sometimes with himself, go on masking his immediate
feelings and thoughts with appropriate words. Banquo sometimes will as well;
now subtextual strains beneath the skin of their language increasingly tense
this brief beat, through Banquo's confirmation of Macbeth's last speech—
that ends with a full stop and a pause before the sudden *Who's here?*

Again, Shakespeare swivels the heads of actors and audience to an entrance—and again an entrance in a moment of suspense: after the witches,
what now? Macbeth and Banquo, still stressed from their supernatural visitation, fresh from battle, may, in reflex, spring to alertness if not alarm at the
sound of an approach. Swords may be out.

Again, the newcomer is the "worthy" Ross. For a courtier, he is once more
in the right place at the right time. He bears a welcome honor to a rising star
in the king's court. His speech suggests covert propitiation to the star:

> The king hath happily receiv'd, Macbeth,
> The news of thy success: and when he reads
> Thy personal venture in the rebel's fight,
> His wonders and his praises do contend,
> Which should be thine, or his: silenc'd with that, . . . (98–102)

Glosses of the last lines usually complicate them in some such way as this:
Duncan is torn between his wonder at Macbeth's deed and his praise of it.
This does not make much sense, seems aimed at avoiding the clear implication,
suggested by H. B. Sprague, that Duncan is deciding which of the wonders
and praises belong to himself as king, which to his general-hero who earned

them. The prerogatives of degree are at stake. The emphasis on Macbeth's
personal venture seems a preparation for the opposition between what is due
to the king, what to Macbeth. Sprague went on to suggest that Ross and Angus
think "the magnanimous king is on the point of abdicating in favor of his heroic
cousin [but] after hinting at such abdication, prudently checks himself,
'silenc'd with that.' "

More likely Ross, a "mouth-honoring" courtier, is ingratiating himself with
his sycophantic interpretation of Duncan's behavior. We need not go so far as
Libby, who finds here further evidence that the villain Ross is "of some ability
but no moral worth, a coward, spy, and murderer." Libby's startling explanation of Cawdor's fate, drawn from nowhere in the text, demonstrates how
close to the brink a critic can come from riding a hobby too hard:

> Cawdor was in fact a loyal gentleman; Ross from a desire to curry favor with
> Macbeth, and from other motives traduced and ruined Cawdor: . . . Macbeth
> and Banquo allowed Cawdor to be ruined, that the words of the witches might
> prove true; . . . Cawdor was in the camp unaware of the plot against him,
> and . . . the conspirators, armed with the hasty command of the king, put him
> to death with complete injustice.

To the extent that Ross can be trusted, we note that Duncan, silenced by the
contention in his mind (for whatever reason), must still continue to hear,
poured down before him, Macbeth's further triumphs:

> Nothing afeard of what thy self didst make
> Strange images of death . . . (105–106)

If Macbeth's mind is designed even now to be populated with strange images
of a particular death, somewhere in the design's subconscious—and perhaps
in ours, as audience—is the wonder if he can escape the fear of it.

We are kept waiting for Ross's mine to explode. Angus, another ready
courtier, makes his little speech. Time was, when extra actors came cheap,
a half dozen more of Duncan's attendants regularly came along to honor
Macbeth. Sometimes Macduff (and Lenox) in the place of Ross (and Angus).
The well-intentioned idea was to improve Shakespeare by establishing Macduff's identity sooner; Shakespeare's craftsmanship was better, as I think I
shall later show. The present scene is still shaped for intimacy—though
under the surface of gentlemanly talk furious forces are barely held down.

Banquo and Macbeth hardly have the chance to shake off their abstraction,
after their experience with the apparent supernatural, when Ross startles
them. Even more than by the magical vanishing does his revelation seem to
validate the Sisters' magic:

> And for an earnest of a greater honor,
> He bade me, from him, call thee Thane of Cawdor: (114–115)

Ross, sometimes placing round Macbeth's neck the pendant badge taken from
Cawdor, or extending a scroll from Duncan, or offering some other visual

token, reprises ceremony as he cries, *Hail*. This clearly enough echoes the recent witches' obeisance; Reinhardt, underscoring, tripled the *Hail*, with Angus joining in, and strokes of thunder accompanying. In a Japanese *Macbeth*, the witches' cackling could be heard—again, an easy irony that undercuts the ambiguity of the Sisters' intentions. Only good so far has come from their prophecies, as far as Macbeth and Banquo can—and should—know.

On them, the effect is stunning. Macbeth may be instantaneously rapt. Banquo responds first, characteristically wondering if some force is working outside their own minds, the speech often a muttered aside or a murmur to Macbeth—whom he continues to watch closely: *What, can the devil speak true?* The line has the ring of a "saying"; the *devil* reference is not pursued, but an implication of the witches' power reverberates. The remark is not entirely generous; a note of envy may hang in the air.

Macbeth, vibrating more intensely to the shock, can only speak after. A start of surprise, like Kean's, was modulated to orchestrate with his earlier amazements; by the working of his face he reflected the new tones drawn into the polyphony. More spectacular reactions were intensifications of earlier responses: with Charles Kean, one clenched fist at his heart, the other opening and closing convulsively. On Forrest, the *hail* acted like an electric shock, Macbeth rigid in face and body. Reinhardt's Macbeth again put up his hand in front of him, as if struck, but also to mask his face; he almost staggered, as he stared at Ross. Other Macbeths built intensity through restraint. Irving, though outwardly courteous to Ross and Angus, had been abstracted, his mind on the immediate past; he was so deep in thought that he was paying little attention to what Ross said, the meaning came to him late, almost as a double take, and he held response down. The more inward Macbeths, like Scofield and Olivier, let slip their shock in the controlled ambiguity of their expressions; or, like Forbes-Robertson, showed what dominated their mind by looking privately at the rival, Banquo; but however restrained, their seismic disturbances could be felt by the audience. We are sensitive to the response because we are prepared for it; we have known more than the hero has. This will not always be so.

> The thane of Cawdor lives:
> Why do you dress me in borrowed robes? (119–120)

Macbeth usually masks with forced calm, as by Irving, the violent feelings that hope and excitement have raised in him. Almost deliberately he avoids expressing any wonder he may have about the implications of Ross' message for that greater honor promised. The image he uses, of a false garment of appearance, discerned by Spurgeon as part of a recurrent pattern in the play, accords with Macbeth's developing process of emotional disguise.

If the thanedom comes with a scroll, Macbeth uses the moment of reading it to cover his excitement. The developing hypertension that often characterizes Macbeth now demands repression or outlet, neither of which may suffice alone. Irving's show of calmness could not cover the signs of inner turbulence; one Macbeth, a warrior capable of terrible violence, turned hotly on Ross, seized him by the shirtfront, and pushed him furiously up against a wall.

Angus intervenes, satisfying Macbeth—and letting us know how Cawdor could have been a traitor without necessarily appearing on the battlefield where Macbeth would have known of his treachery. The main action during this speech continues interiorly, in Banquo and Macbeth, and is communicated through the slow change of expressions, the different tensions of the bodies. Angus' word provides a logical opportunity for the two great captains to draw together, for Banquo to offer a hand in congratulation, however sincerely meant, and for Macbeth to receive it. Their speeches continue their recent fencing: they test each other, watch—or carefully avoid watching— for signs of inner meaning; they speak to themselves, as well as to each other.

The new feelings crowding in on both converge in complex polyphonies; both men fit almost miraculous possibilities into old dreams. Again, the various emphases expressed by different actors suggest the multiplicity of impulses. A nearly innocent young German Macbeth could with naive pleasure say—in what is almost certainly an aside, though it has been murmured to Banquo—

> Glamis, and Thane of Cawdor:
> The greatest is behind. (130–131)

Similarly, Forbes-Robertson, not yet committed to darkness, could speak the words with joy; and Salvini, the stalwart, courageous warrior, was warm with purpose and enthusiasm; no obstacles might intimidate Macbeth, Salvini thought now, but the idea not yet fully born, of crime, of killing without fair combat. Other Macbeths were shadowed in their minds, either moving unclearly toward an idea of violence, or already involved with it. Macready, succumbing to his sense of fatefulness, was so preoccupied, the thick-coming fancies crowding the present out of his brain, that he had to force himself to be conscious of the others: the Sheffield *Iris* was struck by "The counter-currents of emotion, arising from the felt courtesy due to his companions . . . and the snatches of meditation on the prophetic greeting of the witches." Edmund Kean whispered the words of the soliloquy as if not to hear his breeding thought. To Charles Kean, coming to terms with what was in his mind, the thought came out slowly, meditatively. Irving was also reflective, but, he noted, *exultant*. To Reinhardt's Macbeth, the thought seemed to come aloud without his will, unconsciously—he was shocked by his own words, and looked about to see if he was heard; Savits' Macbeth spoke the aside with such fierce inner passion that the suspicious Banquo, watching him, seemed awakened to suspicion; Macbeth checked himself, his hand masked his eyes for a moment, before he turned to the others.

Since Macbeth's encounter with the witches, and his attempt to fix a public face to hide his private one, such has been his absorption with his thoughts that his guard has sometimes dropped, or he has simply withdrawn into the private world unheeding of what he exposed. Othello, Lear, Hamlet, all at times have worn masks and let them slip, out of passion. The deeply inward Hamlet, for instance, has been able usually to protect his essence by controlling his disguise, sometimes by shifting it to an appearance of madness. Like the essential Lear and Othello, Hamlet aims at goodness, but wears a distorted mask that sometimes seems to become his own face. Much of the tension in the essential Macbeth rises from his determination to betray his better nature, and his consequent need to make the old appearance of his person seem still the reality. As the private face, strained by dangerous thoughts, becomes deeply lined, the need is more than ever for the good hero's mask; but while the inner struggle goes on, the mask slips, it slips.

Now Macbeth brings himself back for a moment to remember courtesy to Ross and Angus. A Macbeth with his disguise under control, like Irving, could make a persuasive show of politeness, even exchange bows; an oppressed one, like Macready, would hardly be conscious of the others, his conventional words dropped hurriedly, impatiently, in his "sublime preoccupation" (Lady Pollock). Reinhardt's tense Macbeth was still so abstracted here that he did not see what he was doing, or sense where Ross and Angus were, and paid his respects to empty air.

Macbeth does not draw others into his circle; a primary compulsion is on him now, and he is back to a colloquy with Banquo, gesturing or pulling him closer, testing him again. Holinshed wrote that Banquo jested with Macbeth, and sometimes indeed they begin by trying to speak lightly, as in Sothern's staging; but then they usually become serious in spite of themselves. Macbeth starts harping again on Banquo's children. Partly he is once more being oblique; but partly, too, Banquo's promised dynasty gnaws at him, as if it could—as it will—become his obsession:

> Do you not hope your children shall be kings,
> When those that gave the Thane of Cawdor to me,
> Promis'd no less to them? (132–134)

Again, the affected carelessness, as with Kean, the hidden tremor of anxiety behind the face of fellowship, the searching for assurance. Those that *gave*, Macbeth says—as if, in a wayward world, the future could be a kind of gift of the wayward.

If Macbeth is oblique to Banquo, he is not opaque. Banquo has let us know, and will again, how closely he watches Macbeth; he has instantly noted the first start of fear, the raptness withal. He has remained in the circle of focus with Macbeth; his scrutiny—in some cases staring—even if covert, has mani-

fested to the audience, if not to Macbeth, an intense interest: and the design
seems to require that the interest be edged by awareness of their competitive
destinies. Macbeth's very sense of Banquo's formidable presence, the steady
look, has seemed a motivation for calling Banquo to him for the appeasement
of speech. Irving's note is representative: "Recollecting himself . . . smiling,
with an effort to divert Banquo's thoughts from what Macbeth fears he has
noticed." A nervous Macbeth may be guiltily defensive: Reinhardt's was
pale, his smile distorted; he spoke swiftly, tried to avoid Banquo's insistent
eyes.

Banquo's response seems, to those who find him unimpeachably upright,
a warning directed only to Macbeth. If he is seen as designed to have the
normal ambitions of high-ranking men in this world of degree, excited by
the idea that he may be the founder of a line of kings, concerned about Macbeth's unexplained interposition in this prospect—if the Banquo design is to
be regarded as being more than a monody, but rather composed of the complex, contending notes (amplified in Macbeth) of Shakespeare's best characters, then now, as elsewhere, he is concerned with his own soul as well as
those of his fellows. He begins to speak in the second person:

> That trusted home,
> Might yet enkindle *you* unto the crown. (135–136)

Enkindle, following Bradley, is usually glossed something like, "encourage—or excite—you to hope"; Banquo has shown himself highly imaginative,
and may well suggest, metaphorically, "make you flame as high as." But a
latent meaning might register in Macbeth's mind—and face: "might incite
you so to act."* Something checks Banquo here. So Salvini's jesting Banquo,
seeing something dark in Macbeth's countenance, became grave, with the
significant *but*.

> But 'tis strange . . .

The echoing, uncanny word seems the prelude to a deep personal musing,
and indeed now Banquo changes from *you* to *us:*

> And oftentimes, to win us to our harm,
> The instruments of darkness tell us truths,
> Win us with honest trifles, to betray's
> In deepest consequence. (138–141)

The last lines may be an aside, Banquo's own brooding; for certainly by
their end he has lost Macbeth, who is back deep inside his own mind, too
absorbed to answer, even if he did hear—a Cassandran irony then, since

---

*Coleridge suggested that *enkindle* might be rooted in *kindle* "to give birth to," by extension
"breed," or "raise." Shakespeare does use it this way in AYLI, III, iii, 5; if this meaning is supposed latent in Banquo's mind, it suggests his sensitivity to the issue of issue.

Banquo, whether warning Macbeth, himself, or both, foresees what can happen to both for remaining linked to their future hopes. The warning dissipates: Banquo, finding himself disregarded by his self-absorbed companion, perhaps even gestured away, moves back to the messenger thanes—*Cousins, a word, I pray you*—leaving the full focus on Macbeth.

For a moment, left alone, Macbeth may give himself up to pure delight in his prospect—"exultant," Irving noted again. *Macbeth*'s use of theatre terms is well recognized; it is as if now he is striding across the stage of life to an ultimately meaningful triumph:

> Two truths are told,
> As happy prologues to the swelling act
> Of the imperial theme. (143–145)

Only the Macbeths to whom the future has always been an anxiety, like Matkowsky, or to whom it has now become one, like Macready, refuse themselves this moment of savoring grandeur.

The very flush of excitement brings some warning note, some sense of self-exposure, and Macbeth brings himself back to thank the messengers again, as if he had forgotten that he had already done so. Kemble was noticed for saying this as if fearing that he was surrounded by the thanes who might be watching him: he said the thanks to the air around him, as if the thanes were still there; then he became aware he had been deserted, and returned to his thoughts. An early promptbook provides a business for this moment: a servant enters with refreshment for the thanes, first for Macbeth, then the others; each raises his drink in acknowledgment to the others. This gives the other three something to "do," instead of only miming talk, but is hardly necessary: Macbeth has almost invariably removed himself downstage, and attention—including that of the thanes—is centered on him.

Macbeth has steadily been drawn, as into a whirlpool, by his own thoughts. Inwardness is his pleasure, his retreat, and his punishment. As he revels in it, he is interested in the process of it: how he thinks, how his body responds, how he is to act, the context of time and place and morality in which he meditates. In his world of *if,* he will have some trouble choosing between alternatives; but this indecision is one of the major satisfactions of his kind of mental exercise: when he does cut off his options, his contemplation of his inner process will no longer give him the release it now does.

As the excitement of Macbeth's vision of greatness brings him to inner debate, we are at last given a glimpse of what went on in the moments when we saw him rapt, lost to awareness of the world around him. From now on, we will know that the central action of the play is inward, we will always be party to his sensitive inner process when he becomes immobilized in thought. Never entirely immobilized, for the face, at the surface of the boiling within, will betray, if ever so slightly, repressed disturbance—and sometimes much more: the features of Garrick's noble Macbeth clearly showed the "workings of [a] frightened soul."* Some gesture intimately related to the inward turbulence may be unconsciously manifested: so Reinhardt's Macbeth repeated the gesture of raising a shielding hand in front of him; so with Scofield, early in his raptness, his right thumb unobtrusively rubbed against the near fingertips as if trying to erase something. Such recurrent visual gestures, like verbal ones, take on accumulating meaning, signaling that the body, even when stilled to fend off scrutiny, hides an exquisite sensitivity and a mind furiously active.

As the body at other times betrays the mask of the voice, now, in soliloquy, the voice opens to us the mind's secrets. The convention of soliloquy makes a transparency of the character, letting us into his brain; some stagings, notably in France, have pointed this by issuing the words from loudspeakers while many things are being read from the book of Macbeth's face.

The soliloquy is rich in Shakespeare's insight into the workings of the recoiling mind. Macbeth at first floats on his momentum toward the *imperial:*

> This supernatural soliciting
> Cannot be ill; (146–147)

then he is brought up short by the long pause of the semicolon. The "sickening see-saw" that Knights observed in the language whipsaws the man as well. The counterweighted brain, always alert to discern flaw, confronts itself: *cannot be good.*

That he begins by rejecting anything *ill* in the oracles suggests that he can perceive the Sisters as not *a priori* evil; this tells us something about them. That at a deeper level he begins to sense the effect of the oracles on himself tells us more about him. He is dealing in a moral issue, and at this point in the design his whole self is involved. His brain would persuade him to the "goodness" of the omens: they after all have proved themselves—one honor is already his. But his body's unease warns him otherwise. Here is a kind of inversion of the body-soul debate: the mind argues for what the body knows is wrong. For the great warrior now, the battlefield is within; and one side begins to lose.

The *soliciting* that makes Macbeth *yield* carries a multiplicity of implications—primarily this cluster (OED): to urge, importune, incite, move, persuade; and, as extended, to draw on, allure, tempt, entice, even to affect a person or thing by physical influence or attraction. (Early in the next century the word could stipulate female importuning of men "for immoral purposes"; the implication was already there.) Corollary to this, the word could imply solicitude or care; also, dialectically, it might mean to disturb or disquiet: indeed, the OED's first definition, now obsolete, is "to make anxious."

*Universal Museum, 1762.

The load that this word carries links it to its effect—the fearful *suggestion* darkening Macbeth's mind. "Prompting or incitement of evil," is the OED's first definition (now *obs.*) of *suggestion:* "in extended sense, a prompting from within." To the forces implicit in these two words, Macbeth momentarily *yields*—but not in his knowing body. A *horrid image* devitalizes him. Ever sensitive to the dislocations of his flesh, he feels their disjunctions now: his *hair* unfixed,* his *seated heart*—the central, anchored organ—knocking against his ribs.

Macbeth's perception of "unnatural" phenomena is always likely to lead him to philosophic generalization:

> Present fears
> Are less than horrible imaginings. (153–154)

Then the recoil to the explicit, and he can say while alone, as he cannot aloud to another mortal, even his wife, the word for his *image:*

> My thought, whose *murder* yet is but fantastical,
> Shakes so my single state of man,
> That function is smother'd in surmise . . . (155–157)

The word—and thought—admitted to consciousness, utterly unsettles him. He suffers the boneless helplessness familiar to victims of debilitating anxiety. He apprehends an inner anarchy, waywardness infecting the order of his inner existence: nothing less than, in Traversi's words, the dissolution of his personality. The psychic bewilderment of this fearless warrior confirms the paradoxical nature of his wayward world, inner as well as outer: where different things may be the same, the familiar may be impossibly strange:

> . . . nothing is, but what is not. (158)

The philosopher and poet in Macbeth sound the note of the ruminative and lyrical; but primary is a cry of anguish, not far from madness: an emotional actor like Junius Booth made his audience feel that "the thronging shapes of Macbeth's roused and guilty imagination had displaced the world of objective realities." How intense is Macbeth's anxiety will depend on the actor's—or critic's—imagination. Sometime later Macbeth will speak of his *fit* coming on: this may not mean an absolute seizure, but it suggests at least his own sense of the power of an idea to paralyze his body. Actors not moved enough here, too firmly resolved, have seemed to lack the essential energy—and weakness—that can make the predator a prey to his thought.

An example, again, was Walter, so excellent in Othello, but too unwavering for Macbeth. Two comments are instructive here: "Always too much the man

The Star: "Mr. Irving's hair remains perfectly 'unfixed' throughout . . . he is always pushing his hand through it, or tugging at it."

of action, too little the philosophic, poetically-minded struggler. . . . From the first meeting with the witches his mind was resolved, his courage screwed to the sticking point. . . . There was not much need for his wife's exhortation." And, "It is the poet who must appear in the bloody assassin. There is little of the poet [here]. . . . He is a barbarous chieftain, inflamed by pride, by superstitious longing, by anything but the restless creative energy of his vision."

It is the complex, polyphonic set of urgencies crowding on Macbeth that make the moment of his first soliloquy a fearful crisis, a crisis of survival. All tragic heroes endure this, as they resist the destruction of their self-system, and of the world system to which the self belongs. They summon the strength to act, or think, to survive; or they shatter in madness and death. In the climactic moment in which Macbeth is rapt in—and wracked with—shuddering impotence, in the contrast between a warrior irresistible before an enemy, and the same man helplessly vulnerable to his imagination, Shakespeare is stipulating a brink experience. Since this is one of several such pivotal crises, the play's form demands that however crucial it is, it must scale a peak short of the higher ranges Macbeth will traverse on his way to the ultimate Everest of Act V; but we are not now to know this, and an ultimate collapse of nerve seems imminent.

But the Macbeth design also includes enormous physical reserves and psychological resilience. Another recoil rescues Macbeth from paralysis. He will survive by separating the thought from the act, for an indeterminate time; perhaps he himself will not be responsible for the doing if—when—the thing is done. This thought surfaces, in the Folio, in short, urgent lines, as if the breath for them comes in bursts:

> If Chance will have me King,
> Why Chance may crown me,
> Without my stir. (160–162)

If. He will wait upon the waywardness of the world.

Actors have followed different tortuous roads to this relief. The noble murderer, Garrick, innocent as he was, was shaken instantly, to his depths, by the bare possibility of a looming guilt. His voice trembled with the shock of finding himself allowing terrible images into his decent mind. "Absorbed in thought," he wrote, "and struck with the idea of the murder, though but in idea (fantastical), it naturally gives [Macbeth] a slow, tremulous under-tone of voice." A spectator complained about Garrick's pauses in words, as between *single* and *state*. Garrick: "Though it might appear that I stopped at every word in the line more than usual, . . . my intention was but to paint the horror of Macbeth's mind, and keep the voice suspended a little, which it will naturally be in such a situation." The shadow of horror would never again leave this troubled Macbeth's mind.

Other actors stressing Macbeth's essential decency, who had not considered attaining the throne through violence before meeting the witches, and who were not overcome then by the idea, were more slow to absorb the shocking implications of their thoughts. Pushed toward a decision now to act, some, like Forrest, seemed still able to put it off. He began, balancing the possibilities of good and evil, in tones that were low, but held a suppressed eagerness—the vision of the crown was glorious. Then his conscience rebuked this noble warrior. Yet he was forthright, rather than nervous, in his assessment of his symptoms: when he felt the tremors of his heart, he struck his armed breast firmly with the truncheon Macbeth then conventionally carried, as if to discipline it. He dealt with his *present fears*, left them behind still not a committed regicide. Kean spoke ". . . Why, chance may *crown* me" and paused, as if coming to a full stop; then added, in a low voice, as if disclaiming intent, "Without my stir."

The nervous Macbeths, stressing the note of the design's deep-seated uncertainty, were least in control of themselves. Matkowsky's voice, until the end, was hollow with doubt and seemed to share, with his body, the burden of his anxiety. The *present* fears he experienced seemed very real: as his thoughts and his voice dropped, his head did; his eyes seemed to be searching nervously for something on the earth.

Reinhardt's moody Macbeth showed almost clinical symptoms of anxiety. After his second *Thank you* he watched the other three until he was certain they were safely out of the way, then stepped mechanically down farther from them. "I am Thane of Cawdor" came hissing out of the depths, a fierce self-assurance. But, when he felt his heart knock at his ribs, he swallowed, he had again to gasp for breath, and his hand went to his breast, as if trying to hide the heart's summons. His *state of man* was so shaken a moan came from him, and his hands fell powerlessly to his sides. A young Polish Macbeth (1971) grew violently hysterical, began to shout and throw himself about in a kind of tantrum—almost literally a *fit*.

Savits' Macbeth, on the other hand, resisted his symptom of fear, clenched his fists together, became more and more resolved to the act whose image disturbed him. Mantell, committed in thought, was pale and restless, more aware as he went on of the other thanes, toward whom he shot sudden side glances; but his fear was not of them, it was of himself, what he might do. The fate-oppressed Macready could take little joy from the prospect of the "imperial theme." Marston saw him soliloquize with an "air of brooding reverie, with a strange sense conveyed in the fixed and fateful gaze of impending evil, the insidious encroachment of evil." At—

This supernatural soliciting (146)

he seemed to be trying to deceive himself; then he started as if recognizing the evil he was trying to conceal, and hurried to add, *cannot be good*. When he had shuddered through the dark valley of his images, he wrenched himself back to the relief of rationalization,

> If chance will have me king, . . . (160)

as resigned to be the slave of destiny.

That Macbeth could, in this first introspection, speak of murder as a means to his vicious end seemed to Redgrave contradictory to the "planted" impression of Macbeth as noble, and the actor did not labor Macbeth's conscience. Similarly, Irving, who had frankly discarded inner nobility from his interpretation, dropped in his private communion all the pretense of virtue he made publicly. He concentrated at first on what the oracles meant to his ambition: his whole body twitched with nervous excitement, he ran his hand restlessly through his hair: what is to be done? Then, driving out the contentment that had come with his hopes, the sense of the possible ill transfixed him, a look of horror came on his face. One viewer thought its traces stayed to the end of the play. In a Macbeth so self-seeking, the *horrid image* was not mainly of a dreadful murderous act, as it must be to those wrestling with conscience; it might include more of the terror and danger associated with the criminal moment, and the consequences for the murderer.

By conceiving Macbeth as fearful as well as villainous, Irving was building into the characterization a tension between the readiness to commit the act and the physical fear—rather than the moral fear—of doing it. At the end of the soliloquy, he summoned up his reserves, against his shaken state, by interpolating a "Ha!". Then (Ellen Terry's note) he grasped readily "With such a sigh of relief—at the idea that Chance could decide his course for him—and without the necessity of . . . murder."

The inward Macbeths made the words mainly tell the story for them: against the general restraint of their bodies, their few gestures were startling and powerfully effective. Olivier, grim and dark in his orientalized mask, limited his first perturbation to a "head-shaking puzzlement"—reflecting partly Macbeth the philosopher—until, at *horrid image*, his body betrayed him, and he shuddered. Yet there was no question of his persistence; he did not resign himself to Chance. This Macbeth had too much of the warrior's inner strength; Chance was only another possible mechanism to his end.

To a Macbeth like Scofield, the soliloquy was an opportunity to consider what he had to face. The crime was seeded; and the physical qualms he felt were weighed as doubts of whether he could, as much as would, commit the imagined deeds. Could he conquer his inward resistance? In Scofield's lined face, so capacious with meaning, were implications of spiritual reluctances deeper than Macbeth could admit. Hence the Lucifer with the light of the morning still on him. Though he deliberately shunned the trappings of romantic sentimentality, like Garrick he waited on the words to come, each cut sharply, like crystal, out of the sentences. A powerful pause came as his experience of the *now* suddenly projected one of the darker visions his mind commonly played with:

> Present fears
> Are less . . . than horrible imaginings. (154–155)

His face held in suspension many of the conflicting impulses in Macbeth: violence, human kindness, ambition, wonder: he was a man ready to commit murder, but one who might not be able to do it.

The suspension of certainty here, the seeming dependence of Macbeth's murderous fantasy on Chance, or his use of this as an excuse to free himself of the intention, is essential to the build of the play. Even with Irving, in whose conception the murder had long been thought of, relief had come with the thought that Fate might act for him. With all the Macbeths not absolutely committed, the soliloquy ends with the sense that violence may out, but not unless some precipitating force impels it. The action hangs on an *if*.

When Macbeth has reached bottom in his soliloquy, suffering under the sense that his capacity to act—his function—has been paralyzed by the force of his imagination, Banquo calls his state to the attention of the other thanes:

> Look how our partner's rapt. (159)

The iambic is initially reversed, the first word taking the full weight of his adjuration: *Look*. Banquo had also pointed out Macbeth's fugue to the witches—he has a keen eye for his partner's dissociation. Angus and Ross usually do look, and keep looking, where Banquo tells them; to the party of three, alert for flaw in higher degree, Macbeth's inwardness becomes a naked thing.

In this interval Macbeth may convey the sense of being at some level aware that he is being watched and discussed: at Banquo's speech, Reinhardt's Macbeth suddenly started up, and shielded his face again with his hand, before turning back to consult himself. Under pressure, Macbeth's powers will always revive.

But he is still—or again—withdrawn, and Banquo pursues the quarry, borrowing the borrowed-clothes image Macbeth had used, but, with his own imaginative bent, shaping it to a purpose:

> New honors come upon him
> Like our strange garments, cleave not to their mould,
> But with the aid of use. (163–165)

That is, this hero does not yet know what to do with his distinctions. Macbeth will at various times be reflected in the opinions of others ready to discuss him—and who, in discussing him, will reveal themselves; but here Ross and Angus do not join in, as perhaps not willing to commit themselves to any criticism of the hero, though by their smiling they may seem to say something. Angus may take note of Banquo's speech, since he will later use the image of the giant's clothes on a dwarf.

Banquo's first observation to the others, of Macbeth's raptness, sometimes amused, sometimes as if amazed, might be considered apologetic for his compeer; hardly his gratuitous second remark, far from generous or even defensive, not the kind of golden opinion Macbeth feels he is winning from others. With Scofield, Banquo was unmistakably digging at Macbeth; Savits' Banquo, who had been watching Macbeth suspiciously, frankly sneered.

Again, Macbeth may be responding at least subconsciously to a sense of the watching thanes when he girds himself for the future:

> Come what come may,
> Time, and the hour, runs through the roughest day. (166–167)

Time is not interminable; a crowded day must come to an end, and another will come. The line is aphoristic. A suggestion has been made that by *Time* Macbeth may mean duration, by *hour* opportunity, as in "time and tide." So Macklin was once praised for saying "Time—and the hour runs . . ." as if the first word were a kind of meditative apostrophe, the second suggesting that a moment to act might come at any time. But the antithesis with *Come what . . .* indicates that both terms refer to duration: the first to time eternal, the second to time now, both moving inexorably toward events. Hope and resignation cohabit in the line; a touch of anger or fear may taint it. Sothern spoke it with a great sigh.

Finally, Banquo reproves Macbeth directly: the first words sharp, beginning with the jolt of the trochee, to shock him from raptness, then the slight pause of the comma:

> Worthy Macbeth, we stay upon your leisure. (168)

Macbeth, awakened, turns—sometimes again, mistakenly, to where he thinks the thanes are, but they are not, and he must correct himself. He masks again—this man who has been thinking of murder—as he works out his apology. Scofield's pause told the slow recovery of Macbeth's mind to the now:

> Give me your favour:
> My dull brain was wrought . . . with things forgotten. (170–171)

When Macbeth disguises truth, he sometimes speaks truth.

He must learn better to explain his mental fugues, his moments in a fantasy world. Now he apologizes for his social absence, often with forced affability: Sothern spoke laughingly, and clapped a hand on Angus' shoulder; Macready's manner was personal warmth overdone; Irving, his hand going quickly to his head to explain his abstraction, thanked the thanes almost excessively. Macbeth could hardly be more formally courteous now: his words—*Kind gentleman . . .* —are those cited by Vandenhoff to prove Macbeth's civilized grace, by Masefield to prove Macbeth's "delicate good manners, which make him so winning a man." One profound part of him that may well surface now prizes highly the warmth and security afforded by his *troops of friends*—whose loss he will lament in V, iii.

But Macbeth can speak, also, with the full authority and dignity of the rank, his achievement, and his formidable person. His *Let us toward the king* (175) is an order as much as a suggestion; now he is not only trying out his new garments, but perhaps also anticipating the authority of robes to come; and the others, sensitive to degree, usually accede to his gesture to form a vanguard and precede him.

Booth signaled Banquo back; Savits' Macbeth seized Banquo's arm, and drew him close. The two whose fates are now so entwined are isolated, and Macbeth alludes, again obliquely, to what is in both minds. Characteristically, now, he stipulates an interval before action:

> think upon
> What hath chanc'd: and at more time,
> The interim having weigh'd it, let us speak
> Our free hearts each to other. (175–178)

The next time—the next two times—Banquo will be the one to suggest such a conference. Now his two short words carry a tremendous load of subtext. *Very gladly* may say much more, as may his glance, direct or averted: of readiness, conspiracy, suspicion, apprehension, reluctance, rivalry. He may be ready now to speak further, but is not allowed. Macbeth is in full control again, the commanding captain:

> Till then enough: (180)

This may be followed by a return to abstraction as with Irving, the long pause of the colon giving him time to recall himself; but more often it gives a forceful Macbeth time to repeat in a glance or gesture his verbal direction: "say no more." Guinness took care to explicate this with a finger meaningfully on his lips. Then the confident direction: *Come friends*.

Reinhardt's Banquo lagged behind and looked after Macbeth thoughtfully. Evans, in his film *Macbeth*, was the last to go: he tossed away the witches' crown of twigs; started to leave; lingered; looked back to where the Sisters had been; and tossed a coin in their cauldron for luck.

The intimacies of this scene were, as noted, backed in some elaborate productions, especially in the nineteenth century, by the upstage presence of extra thanes and even the simulacrum of a whole army. As a realistic reviewer of Irving's production said in praise of his impressive troops, "Who indeed could believe that the victorious generals are returning unattended?" The fog, or gauzes, had lifted with the vanishing of the witches, to reveal a panorama of army tents and troops, real and painted; and these had to be got off. Thus Kemble: "The six gentlemen, and the soldiers who are on the stage advance as marching after [Macbeth] while the soldiers on the bridge put themselves in motion." Martial music generally saw the troops off. Phelps, to increase the size of his army, seems to have drafted large numbers of profiled cutout figures that slid out in the general exit. The soldiers, as they go, may repeat the shouts that heralded Macbeth's entrance: thus Tree's army, leaving, cried "Hail Macbeth!"—the "Hail" taking on new meaning from the experience of the scene. In productions emphasizing the omnipresence of the witches, their background appearance, or some reminder of them has been intruded: thus, in Sothern's staging, the army's exit was a background to the last dialogue between Macbeth and Banquo: as one of the marchers fell, and was helped up by the others, the witches hovered behind, laughing. Macbeth and Banquo were on the point of leaving when the eerie laughter was heard: they stopped, looked into the air, then at each other, baffled in a wayward world.

. . . my black and deep desires.

Act I, Scene iv

What it means to be a king is usually made evident—or imagined—as Scene iv begins. The *alarums* of war, sounds of disorder, are silenced; Duncan enters now with the royal *flourish* of horns—signal of order: princes, thanes, and attendants accompany him, in their proper degree. The scene is sometimes set—or imagined—as still in an army camp, the present calm contrasting with the anxious bustle and alertness of Scene ii; but often Duncan is at home in the palace in Forres, toward which Banquo and Macbeth were traveling. This may be a barbarian court; but commonly it is a more sophisticated one that serves multiple purposes. It establishes the opulence and glory that hedge a king, to whet the drive of Macbeth and Banquo for the apex; and it provides a benchmark for comparison with the behavior of any who follow Duncan as rulers of the Scots court.

This last was stressed as noted earlier, with the Macbeth of the German actor George. Duncan's ascent to the throne was a majestic ceremonial: he slowly mounted the stairs, turned, his nobles and soldiers gathered around the throne, flanking him, as he slowly, with great dignity, seated himself. The scene would be repeated in detail in III, i—the outlines of movement exactly the same, and yet, with a brutish Macbeth, the whole disturbingly different. In any case, Duncan's entrance, involving homage paid to a king, looks backward to the distortion of the same ritual for Macbeth by the Sisters, as well as forward to more legitimate reprises. The world is wayward.

When the "palace" is thrown into the backward of time, the emphasis is on the primitive nature of the action, to match the primitivism of the surroundings. Charles Kean, the "archaeologist," had a solidly built hall, with vast round pillars supporting a roof of rough-hewn log beams, the capitals of the columns decorated with old Saxon ornamental ciphers. In 1966, Michael Benthall mounted a great room seemingly made of peaty slabs of oak; braziers threw lights on it, and the shaggy thanes, with horned helmets, seemed to belong to their savage world—as if any one might turn on his old king. With

Redgrave, the rough battle dress and military equipment reflected a semi-barbaric world. These were not gentle weals. In such environments, Macbeth becomes more a creature of a time than of Time.

When the scene is the deliberate elegance of a polished court, it commonly centers on a raised dais for Duncan. Gordon Craig's design is a rich example. To emphasize the throne's magnificence, Craig made it very high and steep. At the very top of the central stairs leading up to it sat Duncan's golden chair, matching his golden crown. At the same high level stood half a dozen court-iers, magnificently costumed, each holding a great staff with a lavish banner, caught in downdrafts of light. To reach this throne, a man had to climb.*

Duncan's authority as king is seen to come from his age and given rank, and occasionally, as in the Hall-Scofield *Macbeth*, where he moved always in white, with a cross held aloft before him, as the symbol of good. Granville-Barker complained, in connection with the character indications in this scene, that Duncan is

> often made older than need be, and sometimes too consistently meek and lachrymose. . . . Duncan's 'plenteous joys' seeking to hide themselves in 'drops of sorrow' are apt to be used to water the character down to an undue depression.

The problem about inhabiting him is to bring into coherence the man who took such pleasure in Macbeth's bloodthirsty fighting, who is so full of senti-ment, who in this scene goes out of his way to publish his failures as a king before Macbeth enters, and then greets Macbeth and Banquo effusively—all as a setting for the contrived climax he engineers. Duncan manipulates this scene; its end—as far as he can know it, which is ironically not far enough—is apparently in his mind from the first.

For the fourth successive time, the scene begins with a question—Duncan's about Cawdor's execution. Malcolm gets his one speech of the scene—his only one until late in the next act—to describe, eloquently, Cawdor's end. His austere monosyllabic prelude—

> But I have spoke with one that saw him die: (7)

—enforces the attention of all around him. In the Hall-Scofield *Macbeth*, Ian Richardson as Malcolm described the death with solemn, almost tearful, amazement. The broken rhythms of the words require an unsmooth speech, from the unmetrical, almost prose first line, to the rough, truncated mid-speech lines, the rhythms edged with weak endings:

> Confess'd his treasons, implor'd your highness' pardon,
> And set forth a deep repentance:
> Nothing in his life became him,
> Like the leaving it. He died,

---

*Craig may have visualized a "highness" metaphor possible in Shakespeare's own staging. Hodges (58–9) notes indications of similar thronal ascent in the London theatre. The evidence for exterior stairs to an upper level in *Macbeth* will be discussed more fully at II, ii.

> As one that had been studied in his death,
> To throw away the dearest thing he ow'd,
> As 'twere a careless trifle. (9–15)

Hall wanted Duncan's court to confront the ambiguity of a villain's admirable death. In rehearsal he said:

> I need from all of you the apprehension, before the speech: is he dead? Then relief. But then a strangeness: this traitor, who died with deep repentance . . . died not well, but very, very well.

There is another strangeness: *Studied* has connotations of the player who has learned a part: to act dying as if life meant nothing. Do we hear this with any presentiments about another thane who will turn traitor? Will we remember it later, as a pattern for a traitor to follow?

Duncan arches a bridge to the future with his musing response:

> There's no art,
> To find the mind's construction in the face:
> He was a gentleman, on whom I built
> An absolute trust. (16–19)

A moment later he welcomes Macbeth in whom he manifests absolute trust and we do not have to know the play to recognize irony. But if it were irony only, the irony would be pretty cheap; Shakespeare is working in character, too. Significantly, Irving wanted his Duncan to accent *face*—as if to emphasize that this is where the king looked. Duncan's son, Malcolm, will someday conduct a clever lesson in how a prince, his own face masked, searches out the mind's construction; Shakespeare seems now to stipulate that Duncan does not know how, and foregoes the responsibility of learning, insensitive to the hunger about him for higher degree. As William Poel put it:

> There was something childish about Duncan's credulity in face of the treachery he had already experienced from the first Thane of Cawdor. In a monarch whose position was open to attack from the jealousy of his nobles, Duncan's conduct showed an almost incredible want of caution. In fact, it was his unguarded confidence which brought about his death.

Actors cannot easily find in Duncan evidences of innate kingly authority, or wisdom; the show of either suggests show. If, as sometimes in the theatre, Duncan turns earnestly to his sons, perhaps puts his arms around their shoulders, to warn them how hopeless it is to detect hidden motivation, he is clearly exposing his own folly. What doubles the irony is that what he says is true: the face may indeed hide the mind's construction. But this truth—this truism—cannot be an excuse for being deceived. A king, who presumably knows this, must look farther, deeper, than the face, as Malcolm will demonstrate. If Duncan speaks in the pathetic bewilderment of an old man betrayed, if even now—as sometimes in the theatre—his ready tears begin to come, the good old man draws sympathy, but not respect as a ruler. Duncan often is represented, as in Savits' *Macbeth*, as having the mildness and dignity of an old man, beyond ruling. So Irving's Duncan, a "hoary old king," spoke philosophically, slowly, dwelling on every syllable. If Duncan is calm and businesslike, or fierce and autocratic, he shows a kind of kingliness that works against the lines that describe him; but something clever is certainly in his mind as he moves the scene along—he is not simple, any more than symbol. He has his own limited polyphony.

Macbeth's entrance is usually timed to follow a moment's pause for the audience to feel the impact of Duncan's confession; but at least one prompt-book has Macbeth entering in time to hear the line and react. In Tree's staging, Macbeth could be seen to wait for a moment behind a pillar, tensely watching the court, before he strode in; this let Duncan's line hold the climax of the first short beat; in the pause, with Macbeth's presence sensed, the implication of Duncan's words could sink further in.

The pause has also been filled with signals of Macbeth's approach: the cheers of the troops, crying "Macbeth! Macbeth! Macbeth!" or, again, reprising past moments with "Hail, Macbeth!" He is the great national hero; as he moves in, he becomes the center of gravity of the court, the courtiers and soldiers (one of the latter the bandaged Captain?) gathering around him.

If Duncan has conveyed a sense of anticipation—even apprehension—of Macbeth's coming, the confrontation of king and captain is the more charged. A reminder of treachery may hang in the air: Macbeth, in the midst of honor, may finger Cawdor's badge, or see it in Duncan's hands ready for presentation; or see, as in Hampden's *Macbeth*, Cawdor's trunk dragged by in a sack. (Piscator made sure the audience was reminded by projecting on his screen an image of the traitor.)

Macbeth's own power is often represented in the theatre: the battle-flags, Scots and captured, carried in by thanes and adjutants, as well as the sounds, glances, and movements of admiration or envy. Macbeth has one of his few chances here, by his warm response to peers and subordinates, to establish the humankindness attributed to him. He must appear the gentleman in whom a king can repose absolute trust.

A Macbeth like Kemble, uncommitted yet to violence, secure in his nobility, can rush in innocently to throw himself at the king's feet; Garrick's honorable murderer, from fear of the violence he might do, would let the audience see how troubled he was—though, as still a good man, his homage and devotion to Duncan could seem free and frank.

Macbeths more fired with ambition, even if afraid of it, move into the court with an appetite, more conscious of their masks. Thus, in the Craig-designed production:

> Macbeth, still covered with mud and blood . . . enters on the lower level [and] looks up at the royal pageant; and something clicks in him and us. His eyes climb the steps of that simple stairway, one by one, until they reach the golden throne; and we know that . . . no power upon earth or in the eerie air can ever prevent Macbeth from climbing that alluring stairway. (Hamilton)

Conventionally, Macbeth first kneels to Duncan; the court may kneel with him. In the Craig production, Duncan first descended, as if to keep Macbeth in the base court. A Japanese Duncan similarly came down to a kneeling Macbeth. The genuflection is one way to cover Macbeth's inner impulses and conceal any indiscretions of his face. Reinhardt's Macbeth could not look straight at the king, could not bear Duncan's generous looks, kept his eyes fixed on the king's throat. Frank Benson (England, 1896) bent his head to kiss the king's hand. Guinness' disguise was his perpetual smile; with Duncan he broke into sudden laughter.

Some ambitions were made of sterner stuff: Olivier was seen covertly to stare hungrily at the crown on Duncan's head; Salvini's persistent "peculiar contemplation" of Duncan was as if at a man in his way: though, to one observer, a sudden gesture suggested that he had put the thought away for the time being. In Scofield the repressed energy hinted something rash and ungovernable, barely restrained: but this could have been seen by the court as the nature of the great warrior, loyal to the king, whom he saluted with studied correctness. Unless Duncan is played as quite senile, he must not be made out a fool by his failure to perceive a murderous mind's construction in a face as revelatory as Macbeth's can be when unmasked. So Rogers' noble bearing at this moment made Duncan's trust understandable.

Duncan's greeting to Macbeth is a masterpiece of comparatives, suited to the world of degree: *worthiest cousin . . . so far before . . . swiftest wing of recompence is slow . . . would thou hadst less deserv'd . . . the proportion both of thanks, and payment . . . More is thy due, than more than all can pay.*

A sincere—or clever—Duncan greets his captain with tears in his eyes, as Savits' did; he is likely to raise the kneeling Macbeth; if Macbeth has not yet been graced with Cawdor's badge, Duncan may present it now, and perhaps some valuable gift; his voice is joyful, growing in admiration, he seems to mean what he says. He may kiss Macbeth on both cheeks, as with Gielgud. This is not in the text; but the implication of it, taken with Macbeth's profession of loyalty, has led Christianizers of the play to suggest that Duncan, as a Christ-figure, suffers from Macbeth a Judas kiss. Again, for any who will see this, it is there; though in the context, one would expect a Christ-figure to see into the treachery building in a mind before it. The idea—nowhere suggested, as far as I know—that Duncan might indeed scent murder in Macbeth's mind, and deliberately come to Macbeth's castle for his fateful slaying, is an interesting one, but has no more source in the text than any other relation of Duncan to Jesus. However, those who would believe it may yet come to think of Duncan between Banquo and Macbeth as between two thieves.

Duncan has greeted Macbeth first by right; the moment of their first locking eyes, of whatever recognition is to pass between them, has brought to a head the first beat, building on the bustle of Macbeth's entrance, the excited moment when he first bursts upon the court, the pause as the great hero faces across to the king. Bergman had them stand and stare for a long moment. Their whole engagement is more political than personal. A kingly embrace is only authorized by the text for Macbeth's rival, Banquo—a point sometimes emphasized in the theatre; it may be a deliberate divide-and-rule gesture of Duncan's, and another spur to the jealousy between the two captains.

Duncan's particular kind of official warmth to Macbeth can reflect the equation between them: the old, insecure Duncan, diplomatic to the giant figure whom he admires and half fears. Macbeth's own expectations bear on what the king may do now. Duncan had sent Ross with the Cawdor title

> . . . for an earnest of *a greater honor*.*

Macbeth had forborne to ask what; and now Duncan again speaks of the *more* that is his due—but that Duncan cannot pay. Duncan may here load Macbeth with tokens of treasure, or scrolls of praise; but Macbeth, fortified by the witches' prophecy, awaits something more—until Duncan ends his beginning eulogy suddenly wishing that

> the proportion both of thanks, and payment,
> *Might* have been mine: (26–27)

There is, in fact, only one ultimate gift, and it is more than Duncan will now give; after the pause of a colon, he makes haste to say so.

Macbeth's first correct response is as masked as his face. "Laboured rhetoric," Bradley calls it; and Coleridge, "the commonplaces of loyalty." The speech is not spontaneous; but we who know the turmoil in Macbeth can share his subtextual wrestling with himself, his listening to his own conventional words as if they are trying to convince him of something. Empson believes that between the last act and this Macbeth had in fact given up the idea of murder. Obvious hypocrisy would be an excrescence here; ambiguity serves better, because it leaves the future open, the battle with the self neither lost nor won. Macbeth's lines . . . *our duties are to your throne, and state, / Children, and servants* (32–33), may well give him pause: he will himself be deeply involved, both from above and below, with the demands of loyalty in service, and even more about the filial relationship. If he has a "real affection for the king," as has been suggested, another note dimensions his emotional response now; he has trembled at his murderous thought about this father-figure now before him. He has also vibrated to the omen that Banquo's *children* would interdict his dynasty.

Children are intimately related to the images of seeding and growth initiated by Banquo; Duncan now picks up the motif with his more formal response to Macbeth's formality, promising—as he often will promise—reward:

> Welcome hither:
> I have begun to plant thee, and will labour
> To make thee full of growing. (36–38)

---

*I follow the Folio on these *or* spellings. Elsewhere, I use the American spellings except when quoting.

Then he turns to Banquo, and the text suggests the warmer welcome, a singling out. The language again emphasizes degree, with its comparatives:

> That hast no less deserv'd, nor must be known
> No less to have done so: (39–40)

but his gesture suggests *more*, a personal affection:

> Let me enfold thee,
> And hold thee to my heart. (40–41)

Is there an emphasis on the *thees*? Whether or not, Macbeth may think so: he may show some jealousy, as did Sothern's Macbeth. This may take the form, as with Scofield, of the slightest of unguarded reactions, instantly controlled, but in that instant revealing the terrible pressure within; or, at the other extreme, of Salvini's shuddering with an overt jealousy he could not for the moment master.

Banquo extends the nurture imagery with a courtier's matching response. In the next scene, he will similarly complement—compliment?—the king:

> There if I grow,
> The harvest is your own. (42–43)

Duncan is moved to the kind of oxymoronic language characteristic of the play: two different things happen to him at once—*plenteous joys . . . hide themselves/In drops of sorrow* (44–6); thus (as with Sothern) he laughs, wiping away his tears of joy. His joys are *wanton in fullness* (45),—the latter word suggesting, possibly, pregnancy—linking the image to the seeding motif.

Then, without any preparation, Duncan nominates Malcolm the Prince of Cumberland. Bradley wondered at the abruptness of the act; J. Q. Adams also questioned Duncan's curious change

> from shedding tears suddenly . . . on this inappropriate occasion, and without explanation [to attempting] to arrange for his son to succeed him on the throne . . . an important proclamation, almost revolutionary in nature.

Certainly Holinshed's account stipulated Macbeth's sore trouble over the violation of the

> old lawes of the realm . . . that if he that should succeed were not of able age to take the charge upon himself, he that was next of blood unto him should be admitted . . . he began to take counsel how he might usurp the kingdom by force, having a just quarrel . . . for that Duncan did what in him lay to defraud him of all manner of title and claim which he might, in time to come, pretend unto the crown.

Henry Irving, among others, has seen here a justification for Macbeth to feel wrongfully deprived of the throne. And Coleman: "[Macbeth] instinctively resented the wrong done him by nominating that feather-bed warrior, Malcolm." The text itself does not let Macbeth verbalize this; and Shakespeare, by not mentioning the disqualification of an underage heir, keeps the audience from perceiving it as a motivation for his tragic hero. On the other hand, the sudden elevation of the *boy Malcolm* is evidently a shock to Macbeth—and perhaps to the rest of the court. Significantly, *naive* spectators, anticipating a fulfillment of the Sisters' prophecy, find their expectations challenged by this apparent peripety. Some response of the sort may have come to Shakespeare's audiences, perhaps sensing that this was not to be a simple dynastic succession. They would not have to know, as Steevens' note tells us, that the crown of Scotland was not originally hereditary, that the title, Prince of Cumberland, might be given to whatever successor the king named in his lifetime. The very fact of Duncan's need, at this time, to make his elaborate announcement of Malcolm's princedom hints a monarchic structure in which the son does not necessarily succeed the father. We may imagine Shakespeare being asked by the actor of Duncan—or Shakespeare asking himself, if he played the part—Bradley's question: why the king's sudden naming of Malcolm? Is this only a conventional ritual, inserted by the playwright for its value as spectacle, and to complicate the plot? Or—as is commonly the case with Shakespeare—does it have implications for character design? Is it motivated? Byam Shaw felt it was.

> I think that [Duncan] senses a certain danger of ambition in Macbeth and that
> is why he names Malcolm as his heir when he does. I don't, of course, mean that
> he imagines for a moment that Macbeth would murder him, but . . . he
> may well feel that, should he die in the near future, the election would fall
> on Macbeth.

So the moment was acted by a Russian Macbeth (Minsk, 1975) who, behind his genial mask of a virtuous, patriarchal ruler was unmistakably a clever politician—troubled that his country faced a new era, alarmed by the swift rise of Macbeth toward power—who was skilfully taking precautions to preserve his royal line. The actor of Duncan can come readily to this kind of motivation, based on the unmistakable emergence of Macbeth as the hero of Scotland, the savior of the nation, the man who has brought order out of national turmoil. His achievements can be, for Duncan—to use the contradictory idiom of the play—an uncomfortable blessing. The court as well as the king may indeed wonder: are Macbeth's praises and triumphs Duncan's, or Macbeth's own? How safe is a weak throne with so strong and strongly supported a thane rising in eminence? Even more: what of the dynasty?—so important a motif in this play involving men who aspire to continuance in the royal degree.

A canny Duncan meets the challenge by stage-managing this whole scene at Forres. The actor's objective may be clear-cut: Duncan knows from the beginning what he will do. He defuses the throngs of Macbeth's cheering partisans by absorbing Macbeth at once into the warm atmosphere of praise and thanks; he then quickly raises Banquo to a parallel value, and prevents any further impulse to Macbeth's ascendancy by an edict from the throne that Macbeth and any followers are not prepared to resist.

If this is Duncan's plan, his concern for its working will be evident in his acting, step by step, to his carefully staged climax. And in his stage properties. Olivier, first coming on, saw waiting a prince's coronet on a pillow. "I looked at it," Olivier told Tynan, "and sort of registered, 'Oh, already, fine.'" Why, indeed, should this not be the greater honor Duncan's emissaries and the witches had promised, coming pat on the heels of the Cawdor title?

If the symbol of princedom is not already on stage, then even more, if Duncan has planned it, he stage-manages now. Perhaps, by his prearranged signal, a trumpet sounds, and an attendant brings the royal objects on: the waiting coronet (Hopkins-Rigg) that Duncan places on Malcolm's head; another trumpet, then a jeweled sword and girdle to be buckled round Malcolm's waist (Craig); or Duncan, giving his scepter to an attendant to hold, takes a prince's chain and puts it around the boy's neck (Gielgud). Tree's Duncan read from a prepared document. Masefield wanted Duncan to keep Macbeth and Banquo on either side of him for the ceremony; this bit of stage-managing would seem to involve them as sharers in the naming.

If Duncan acts by plan, his contrivance will be felt, if not subtly evident, through the sequence of events as he controls them. But what if he is thought to improvise? The basic motivation for the actor would be the same: he sees the immense, threatening popularity of Macbeth; he senses at last the danger to his dynasty, and acts spontaneously to protect his son's future. He may use his own crown for the ceremony, or some other accessible symbol of royalty; or simply make the announcement, with his arm about his son.

Macbeth, listening to Duncan's announcement, cannot know for several lines that he himself will not be the subject of the king's encomium. His thoughts are on himself: if not now, then later. Forbes-Robertson's objective, to this point, was to suggest his haste to get through the ceremony, to discuss the prophecies with his wife. Irving, hearing Duncan address his *Sons, kinsmen, thanes*, wore an ironic smile; a cousin, he did not come first. Then he fell into a "malicious gloom" as the surprise broke:

> We will establish our estate upon . . .
> Our eldest, Malcolm. (48–49)

The courtiers are startled, none more than Macbeth. Now the center of gravity subtly shifts. In the courtly ceremony that follows the promise to *all deservers*, the courtiers, perhaps after a quick, shocked look at Macbeth, make some ritual gesture: kneel as Malcolm kneels for the coronet; raise swords; drink a toast; cry "Hail Malcolm!" (echo of a stranger coronation). Macbeth hears the voices that lately hailed him hailing another. He kneels reluctantly, bows coldly, or late—having to get over his shock (Sothern); must pull himself together to join in the common bow (Irving); raises his sword belatedly (Redgrave); holds his sword so tensely one almost wonders if he plans to use it (Forbes-Robertson); tosses down his drink without ceremony (Czechoslo-vakia); joins in the cry "Prince of Cumberland," but sourly, bitterly (Polanski). The deservers may drift from Macbeth toward the newly magnetized center of power.

A "good" Malcolm accepts his title with modest humility; a more boyish one is astonished and delighted—one is described as so amazed his mouth dropped open and stayed that way. A Malcolm caught up in the struggle for degree, who has already exchanged looks of rivalry with Macbeth, may now look at him triumphantly (in the Polanski film such a Malcolm was himself regarded enviously, inimically, by his misshapen brother, a Richard III–like Donalbain).

The naming is an archetypal example of provocation of sibling enmity; it reminded Northrop Frye of God's displaying of his son before Satan in *Paradise Lost*. For Macbeth, to whom applause for great feats will always be so important, who is so sensitive to rival strength, it must act as a spur.

Duncan may be credited with character enough to sense, if not notice, Macbeth's reaction. Shakespeare perhaps told his actor that the king's impulse to visit Macbeth's castle was a fence-mending gesture: having disappointed his foremost thane, the king makes up for it with a royal visitation.

> From hence to Inverness,
> And bind us further to you. (53–54)

A pause, as Macbeth absorbs inwardly this new shock: the king is putting himself into Macbeth's power. When he can trust himself, he again answers with courtly formality. "Leisure that does not serve you is labor."* He wants to get away: his excuse is to inform his wife of Duncan's coming—and of other things. Not all excuse. He wants to make his wife joyful—Clara Morris as Lady Macbeth (U.S., 1874) felt his primary urge was to be with her—and certainly his husbandly affection for her may be one note sounding.

Macbeth finds it difficult to accept any further friendly gestures from Duncan. Thus the German Dawison as Macbeth: he stammered, was con-fused, eking out the words: he could not endure the king's presence. Duncan exacerbated this by embracing Macbeth, who, embarrassed, reluctantly allowed himself to be pulled to the king's breast: he turned away his head. He forced himself for one moment to look at Duncan, who kept smiling at him . . . and dropped his eyes.

Macbeth's last line, as, conventionally, he kisses the king's hand,

> So humbly take my leave, (58)

suggests the full stretch of the difference between his "doubled" public face now and his private one. Humility is the last of his feelings; humiliation has

---

*Lewis Casson saw a possible double meaning here: "The rest (i.e., the remainder) is labour. . . . not used for *you*." This would point to Macbeth yielding "to the temptation to take the way of violence as a short-cut to power."

a higher rank. Inward forces that he had been keeping down threaten to erupt. He may bow acknowledgment of Duncan's *My worthy Cawdor—worthy* again—but gives back no answer; may, like Olivier, turn his back to the king as he moves away.

Macbeth's last soliloquy has sometimes been made, in the theatre, the last speech of the scene, Duncan and the rest going off. When the text is followed, Macbeth usually comes downstage, while the other characters group up behind and away from him, as in the previous scene. They may be busy felicitating Malcolm, kneeling to kiss his hand, mouth-honorers. Significantly, Duncan keeps Banquo near him, as we learn from the final speech, and their standing together can give Macbeth—watched by them—no comfort. For the few moments that he is alone, he hardly needs business; but he has occupied himself by slowly—grudgingly—putting away the sword he raised for Malcolm; or by meaningfully disposing of the cup used for the toast; even, in one case, kneeling to pray before his journey. Komisarjevsky's Macbeth gave to "Seyton" the letter to be carried to Lady Macbeth, thus establishing the special servant's identity early.

Then for the moment Macbeth is rapt again, inward; the private man is naked to the knowing audience, and partly exposed, too, to the courtiers. Forrest, who forced a show of genial behavior before the court, turning, withdrew into a lowering, agitated gloom. Alger: "His brain seemed sunk in the throes of a moral earthquake." Macready was plunged back into bewilderment and anxiety: the resigned plaything of fate, he had been given one promised honor, had the greater second held out—then denied—then offered again obliquely with the voluntary approach of the king and prince into his power. He would have only to move his hand . . . One of Williamson's recurrent gestures was the contemplation of the hand that might do—and did— so much.

For the form of the play, this second soliloquy must carry Macbeth beyond his first recognition of his mind's *horrid image,* and—except in the cases of Macbeths overtly committed to murder beforehand—move him to deeper consideration of the act while leaving room for the indecision that must later still wrack him. The first lines,

> The Prince of Cumberland: that is a step,
> On which I must fall down, or else oe'r-leap,
> For in my way it lies (60–62)

seem to suggest that the first target of his ambition now must be Malcolm— and so it seemed to *naive* spectators. So, too, to Gentleman, no partisan of Macbeth:

> it appears, that not content with the simple idea of regicide, he determines to cut off the whole family, in return for being loaded with honours by royal favour.

The marvel of Shakespeare's art is that the audience is focused on Macbeth here, and, seeing through his terrible eyes, still shares his troubled mind.

He may here briefly glance at Malcolm, or Duncan; and a complex purpose can be read in his face. Henry Irving saw this moment as

> the pivotal one in the action. . . . Macbeth has his former inchoate intention of murder crystallized into an immediate and determined resolve to do the deed, for he realizes that the King's unconstitutional action will . . . raise an ever-heightening barrier between him and the throne.

But Irving's conception did not allow for Macbeth's later collaboration with, if not persuasion by, Lady Macbeth—Irving's idea was to manipulate *her*. Other Macbeths were not so sure: they mainly reflected not clear intention, but rather an uprush of passion, a Dionysian dissolving of rational connections, reprising the impulse previously noticed toward disjunction. Here it is the separation of Apollonian knowing (the eye) from the unchecked doing of desire (the hand), in a lightless, sightless world where the stars of nobleness Duncan saw shining on all deservers are all blacked out: hide, hide the deep split, the inward doubling:

> Stars hide your fires,
> Let not light see my black and deep desires:
> The eye wink at the hand;* yet let that be,
> Which the eye fears, when it is done to see. (62–65)

(The ear may hear a buried doubling: "the *I* wink . . . the *I* fears. . . .")

Irving had taken leave of Duncan, and rushed out with his sword, as at his first entrance, on his shoulder; after the rest had gone he returned, clutching the door curtain, and spoke the soliloquy fiercely, with violent facial accompaniment. Gielgud here dropped the front of the warrior, and allowed to emerge the "most poetic of all murderers." On the other hand, Tree, who had made the first soliloquy a poetic aria, now stressed the iron in the lines— *for in my way lies*. Forbes-Robertson was preeminently the philosopher: "Thinking, not angry." Salvini seemed to be funneling all his tremendous, frustrated physical energy into the emotional release of the words. In Scofield, the same urgency: after his last words to Duncan he turned at once and drove fiercely into the lines, as if the black and deep desires had barely been contained, the man almost shuddering in the fear of losing self-control. Wild resolve showed in the face and tone of Reinhardt's Macbeth (Wegener): he seemed irretrievably entangled with an evil spirit. At *the eye wink at the hand* he stretched his fingers to their limits, then clenched them into a fist, passed it characteristically over his eyes, and spoke the last words with all the fervor and willpower he could summon. Savits' feverish Macbeth looked quickly at Duncan, then quickly away, his face pale with fury, his hand on the hilt of

*Macbeth has, as it were unconsciously, pulled a glove on his hand here.

his sword. Mantell, left alone on the stage, let a visual symbol enlarge his words: as if by accident, he dropped his battle axe, and it fell on Duncan's throne.

The text keeps Duncan in mimed talk with Banquo. His speech is clearly an answer to what Banquo has just said about Macbeth: perhaps while watching Macbeth's every move, another comment that his partner has been rapt? Banquo's inner state may best be gauged by his visual response to Duncan's praise of Macbeth. Banquo is a player, too. Thus Savits' Banquo stared as before, with intent suspicion—when he was sure Duncan was not looking at *him;* when he exchanged looks with Duncan, his face was of transparent honesty, but it again changed when he glanced back stealthily at his greater rival; old Duncan did not notice. Duncan's last trustful speech is a stipulation that he has not the slightest idea of the construction of Macbeth's mind: the image, combining Macbeth's courage and a banquet, is on a happy note that may have subliminal undertones for the audience later. As their king leads his courtiers out in formal order—they know their own degrees—we may look to Banquo's countenance for the effect of Duncan's last praise of Macbeth:

It is a peerless kinsman. (70)

The qualifier carries buried irony—it unqualifies: in a kingdom, the only man without a peer is a king.

Lady Macbeth

Ellen Terry:
It is ambition that is the true ruling motive . . . ambition first and then love
for husband, and the feeling that, when all is accomplished, they shall be
free—free to rule and to govern, free from all restraint . . . I believe Shakespeare's Lady is essentially feminine, even in the urgency of her appeal to
her husband, and one strong argument is the very feminine way in which,
when all is over—the deed done . . . she faints . . . Mrs. Siddons' Lady
Macbeth could not faint; it would have been inconsistent with her character,
[but] it is an important proof as to the kind of woman Shakespeare intended.
[Mrs. Siddons' Lady] was a remorseless, terrible woman, who knew no
tenderness, and who was already "unsex't" by the enormity of her desires.

Enter Macbeth's Wife alone with a Letter.

Macbeth was hailed by the witches, and Banquo stood by to describe Macbeth's felt shock and its visual manifestations, then and later. But Lady Macbeth comes on alone, in I, v, reading a letter; no bystander to tell how, with
what cries or silences, with what face, feeling, gesture. The lines reveal something of her passion and purpose, but only intensify the mystery of her identity; her full design will not be unfolded until her last words in the play.

Like Macbeth's, her character is a highly complex polyphony. Her roles
are more narrowed: while Macbeth exists in his relationship with his wife,
soldiers, servants, peers, king, later his court, his kingdom, with his ideas,
his conscience, his view of the world, Lady Macbeth exists mainly in relation
to *him*, as wife, lover, co-conspirator, royal partner. She speaks of her inner
distresses to us only once (in III, ii), never to him—as he often speaks his to
himself and to her. Her roles as hostess and queen—and even as suppliant to
the spirits—are transient, and essentially functions of her relationship to
Macbeth, and of her influence on his behavior.

Yet within this narrowed world, her design, too, strains in its polarities
toward the limits of characterization. The harmonics and dissonances in her

polyphony fuse in a progression of marvelous chords; single notes are some-times heard above the rest, only intensified by the counterpoint.

Lady Macbeth's multiple interactions with Macbeth, which mainly define her, demand sharply opposing behaviors. She both scorns and admires him; deeply understands him partly, and partly knows him not at all. She manip-ulates him, but is manipulated by him, too; she begins by seeming to guide him, he ends by overruling her. To realize her vision, she commands him, and finesses him; so acutely questions his masculinity that she has been seen as castrating him; yet is his ultimate shield and staff when he panics. She has been seen as utterly selfish, pluming up her own will; or as utterly selfless, devoted to Macbeth's ambition—but either design reduces her to a silhouette of Shakespeare's intentions. She moves between. Is both. And more.

In some of the shaping of her design she shares dialectic with Macbeth. Like him she sometimes discloses herself, but often is a player in a changing mask; like him she may speak directly, or obliquely; sometimes in baroque, figured language, sometimes tersely, naturalistically; she is sometimes: brave, afraid; splendid, sordid; self-deceiving, realistic; cruelly rational, and so ir-rational she seems touched with madness; mature, childlike; future-oriented, past-oriented; object of terror, and of pity; iron-strong, breaking. "Masculine" and "feminine" impulses struggle in her.

Though she seems the instigator of action, often she is a re-acter; she seems both autonomous and possessed, part witch, part bewitched. In her first appearance (I, v) the inherent dialectic in her character bridges the naked transition in the text between her reading of Macbeth's letter and her deter-mination that he must have what the witches promised; and again, in the next transition, to her fearful invocation of the powers of darkness. In the text she seems so active a force that Macbeth might have remained innocent without her; but critics as well as actors have sensed an interplay between, on the one hand, Macbeth's spoken reluctances that perhaps hid his secret hopes—if not his desires or manipulations—and on the other hand Lady Macbeth's overt, tense determination, masking only for a time the irresolution, vulnerability, perhaps remorse, that destroy her.

Some idea of her polyphony, as with Macbeth, may be sensed from the range of descriptives attached to her.* As with Macbeth, the simpler and

---

*Acquiescent, admirable, affectionate, agitated, agonized, alarmed, alluring, ambitious, amiable, anguished, appalling, ardent, asp-like, authoritative, awe-inspiring. Baleful, barbarian, beautiful, benign, bird-like, broken, buoyant. Calculating, callous, captivating, caressing, cerebrant, charming, chilling, Cleopatra-like, clever, clinging, coaxing, cobra-like, cold, com-manding, competitive, compulsive, confident, consoling, contemptuous, convulsive, coquettish, courageous, cowardly, cruel, cunning. Dalilah-like, daring, dark, dauntless, delicate, demented, demoniac, depraved, depressed, dessicated, desolate, despairing, determined, devoted, dignified, disdainful, dishevelled, domestic, domineering, dreamy. Eager, eerie, enchanting, energetic, enthusiastic, Eve-like, exalted, excited, exhausted, exotic, explosive, exuberant. Faithful, fascinating, fatalistic, feline, feminine, ferocious, fervent, fierce, fiery, firm, flattering, flinty, fluctuant, forcible, fragile, frail, frenzied, full-blooded, furious. Gaunt, gentle, ghastly, glad, glamorous, glassy-eyed, glittering, gracious, grand, grim. Haggard, harsh, hateful, haughty,

clearer the emphasis on any single tonal motif-cluster, the easier to follow the development from one character state to another. Lady Macbeth particularly tempts such a simple linearity. With Macbeth, commitment to a limited tonality reproaches us at once, since we see him wrestle with inward countering forces almost as soon as he appears, when the witches' *hail* rouses a sudden new thought—or a hidden old one; and he promptly asserts his dialectic between conflicting forces, inward and outward. No such struggle is stipulated in Lady Macbeth's early words: it must be found in the subtext of the character design. Some interpreters, particularly among early actors and critics, have not found it. To understand the gradual critical and theatrical appreciation of the Lady's complexity we must again look at the cultural milieus that nourished partial insights.

THE TERRIBLE WOMAN

The first dominant image of Lady Macbeth in both theatre and criticism was of a fierce and terrible instigator of murder. Charles Gildon, again, lumped her with Macbeth (1730): "To say much in praise of this play I cannot; . . . the character of Macbeth and his Lady are too monstrous for the stage." As Macbeth became more ennobled, Lady Macbeth became more responsible, more reprehensible; to Samuel Johnson she was merely detestable; and Lord Kames: "I hope there is no such wretch to be found as is here represented." The pejoration persists; so G. B. Harrison: "Quite unscrupulous . . . no sense of principle, morality, or decency; women of her kind never have."

For eighteenth-century audiences troubled by Shakespeare's ambiguity and counterpoint, this interpretation was highly satisfying, particularly as it interlocked smoothly with the character reductionism of the kind Garrick practiced on his noble-murderer Macbeth.

Sarah Siddons—as the Ellen Terry comment suggests—popularly rep-

---

headstrong, heart-stricken, highstrung, hopeless, horrible, horror-stricken, hospitable, human, hurried, hypocritical. Imperative, imperial, imperious, impetuous, implacable, impulsive, incantatory, indomitable, inhuman strength, inner strength, insidious, insulting, intelligent, intense. Keen. *La Belle Dame Sans Merci*, lovable, loves, loving, loyal. Magnanimous, magnetic, magnificent, majestic, malevolent, malignant, managing, mannish, massive, masterful, materialistic, maternal, melancholy, melodious, merciless, mettlesome, miserable, mournful, moving. Nervous, neurotic, noble. Pallid, passionate, pathetic, petty, petulant, piteous, pitiful, plaintive, poignant, possessive, potent, powerful, practical, presence of mind, prophetic, proud. Rapacious, rapid, realistic, reckless, regal, relentless, remorseful, resolute, resourceful, restrained, rich, rigorous, ruthless. Saccharine, savage, scornful, secret, seductive, self-possessed, self-restrained, sensitive, sensual, serpentine, severe, sexual, sharp-tongued, she-cat, sincere, sinister, sinuous, soft, soothing, sorrowful, spectral, spiteful, spontaneous, splendid, staring-eyed, stately, statuesque, steely, stern, stimulating, stoical, stolid, strident, strong, subtle, suffering, sulphurous, sweet. Taunting, tearful, tender, terrible, terrified, testy, tigerish, tigress-like, tormented, torn, tortured, touching, touch of vulgarity, treacherous, triumphant, troubled, turbulent. Unbalanced, uncompromising, undaunted, unimaginative, unflinching, unnatural, unscrupulous, unselfish, unswerving. Vehement, vibrant, vigorous, virginal, vital, vivid, vixenish. Wan, warm, watchful, wheedling, wifely, wild, will, witch-like, womanly, worn, wracked. Youthful.

resents the archetypal image of Lady Macbeth as Terrible Woman—though other actresses, on the Continent, in America, and in England itself, would be as "terrible." Scream for scream, Boaden said, Mrs. Crawford was many degrees more awful. Siddons' sleepwalking sigh was not as "horrid" as Mrs. Pritchard's, and Siddons' "grief" was compared unfavorably with Mrs. Porter's. But so concentrated was Sarah's passion as she terrorized Macbeth, so charismatic her stage personality, and so chronicled was she, in poetry, prose, and paint, by admirers whose cultural appetites she richly appeased, that she survives as a touchstone of the Terrible design.

Ironically, as we know, this was not her own ideal Lady Macbeth image. Her ideal, and her contrasting acted image together almost define the polarities actors and critics have discovered in the design. Siddons saw Lady Macbeth ideally as a "daring fiend" with a deceptive, almost angelic facade, equipped with "all the charms and graces of personal beauty . . . of that character which I believe is generally allowed to be most captivating to the other sex,—fair, feminine, nay, perhaps even fragile." Only such alluring feminine loveliness, combined with energy and strength of mind, could have seduced the mind of a hero so dauntless, a character so amiable, so honorable, as Macbeth. So Siddons believed. But the public would have none of this soft, seductive image. To Siddons' biographer, Thomas Campbell, "Mrs. Siddons' idea of [Lady Macbeth's] having been a delicate and blonde beauty, seems to be a pure caprice. The public would have ill exchanged [that] for the dark locks and eagle eyes of Mrs. Siddons."

Indeed, Campbell wholly rejected the hypothesis of Siddons that Lady Macbeth could be anything but the figure of "superb depravity" that Siddons acted through the first part of the play. A century later Ellen Terry would suggest that Siddons' Junoesque physique enforced on her the Terrible Woman image; but Sarah could play delicacy and pity when she wanted to: as Desdemona she evoked the startled praise: "This soft, sweet creature cannot be Siddons!" Her public required the Lady Macbeth of the dark locks and the eagle eyes, not only for the sublimity of its power, but also to preserve the image of a "hero so dauntless, amiable . . . honourable" as Macbeth—in order, as Siddons said, that spectators could "pity the infatuated victim of such a thraldom."

Some admirers of Siddons would like to believe that in fact she did not represent the awful lady generally attributed to her. Her most familiar portrait in the role seems to support the defense: George Henry Harlow's romantic image, the soft face softened further by a wimple, the soft eyes more of a doe or a dove than of an eagle. Harlow was aping the gentler style of his master, Thomas Lawrence, disguising in full face the firm, strong Siddons nose, jaw and forehead. What Sarah really looked like is hard to decide, since so many different versions of her face and figure survive in paint and stone; perhaps the most likely image of her Lady Macbeth is the formidable wax bust in the National Gallery of Ireland. That her acting of the role had no connection to her ideal image of the Lady was insisted upon, we will see, by her niece—a later Lady Macbeth—Fanny Kemble.

Siddons' apologists can take some comfort from her own hint of a vestigial layer of humanity even in the early design: " . . . in her bosom the passion of ambition has almost obliterated all the characteristics of human nature." *Almost.* But the obliteration seemed so absolute at her first appearance that no traces of femininity and fragility appeared. Boaden saw, when she read Macbeth's letter, already the "apathy of the demon,"* nor does he or Galt, or Bell, or Marston *(Blackwoods)*, or Siddons herself report any "struggle against virtue."

Siddons could visualize her "daring fiend" as receiving Macbeth's home-coming with "not one kind word of greeting or congratulation . . . so entirely swallowed up by the horrible design." We can understand how the theatrically naive Coleridge could write: "Lady Macbeth evinces no womanly, no wifely joy, at the return of her husband"; but that the great actress herself could read no feeling in the Lady's explicitly admiring welcome, or Macbeth's fond reply, is only explicable in terms of her fierce conception of the role. One wonders how Macbeth could have called this Terrible Woman "my dearest love," or, even more, later, "dearest chuck."

Not until Act III does Lady Macbeth betray, Siddons thought, one "symptom of affection for him." Again, in the actress' description of her manipulation, we get a glimpse of her care to idealize Macbeth: "behold his evil genius . . . by her revilings, her contemptuous taunts, and, above all, by her opprobrious aspersion of cowardice [she drives] before her impetuous and destructive career all those kindly charities, those impressions of loyalty, and pity, and gratitude, which . . . had taken full possession of his mind."

The "perfectly savage creature" Siddons saw in Lady Macbeth indeed savaged her Macbeths. One defense for her is that she needed a great actor opposite. She frightened Pope* as Macbeth out of his wits, the *Monthly Mirror* reported; he only recovered a little after her death in V, i. But granted that a lesser player like Pope or "Gentleman" (William) Smith might, in Boaden's words, "sink under her" at once, what of the great Kemble? Bell, who describes her scene by scene, saw Kemble as playing "only a co-operating part"; a dismissal that no amount of argument can elevate to admiration. How much a dismissal may be sensed from Bell's next sentence, recalling Boaden: "I can conceive Garrick to have sunk Lady Macbeth as much as Mrs. Siddons does Macbeth† . . . she makes [Macbeth] her mere instrument, guides, directs, and inspires the whole plot" (Bell).

A review in the *Monthly Mirror* went further: "She entirely outplays Kemble." Bell, in his detailed account of their performance, will note that a few

---

*I have never seen this properly glossed for the time. The word "apathy" was applied as well to Pritchard's Lady. The contemporary meaning was "insensible to suffering or feeling"; callous.

*Alexander Pope, the actor.

†That Garrick could have "sunk" the mighty Pritchard seems highly unlikely.

times "Kemble plays this well" (and also "not well"), but spared the actor only
the briefest of nods compared with his excited appreciation of Siddons.

Siddons chose not to move between heroic and naturalistic poles in Lady
Macbeth; instead she was able to sustain in the design the awful sublimity
pleasing to her age, seeming supra-mortal. Hazlitt explicated her distancing:
he could imagine "nothing grander, . . . as if a being of a superior order had
dropped from a higher sphere to awe the world with (her) majesty. . . . Power
was seated on her brow, passion emanated from her breast. . . . She was
tragedy personified." To an audience attuned to the gothic, she came as a
visitation:

> Her turbulent and inhuman strength of spirit . . . unrelieved fierceness . . .
> no intercourse with human sensation or human weakness. Vice was never so
> solitary and so grand. The step, look, voice of the Royal Murderess forces our
> eye after them as if of a being from a darker world, full of evil, but full of
> power—unconnected with life, but come to do its deed of darkness, and then
> pass away.

And Marston: "I never saw so mournful a countenance combined with so
much beauty. . . . [Lady Macbeth] seemed made for her . . . the ardour
and boldness mingled with the solemnity and mystery that belonged to the
character of her beauty."

One of the measures of how far the Siddons' pattern was from Shakespeare's
intent is evident in the bloody cuts made in the text. As noted, a Lady Macbeth
like Siddons' could not faint, or seem to, in II, iii, after Duncan's murder is
discovered: as Davies observed, she would have been hooted off the stage for
her hypocrisy. So an essential moment was deleted.

An even more savage surgery denied her audiences the balance to Lady
Macbeth's character provided by the Lady Macduff scene. Apart from its af-
front to refined taste by dramatizing violence, IV, ii had to disappear because
it made Macbeth out to be quite as murderous as Shakespeare intended—
more murderous than the sentimentalized eighteenth- and early nineteenth-
century theatres wanted him. Inevitably the absence of Lady Macduff left
Lady Macbeth without the kind of mirroring by contrast that Shakespeare
excelled in. Lady Macduff belongs to the same world, if not the same nature
of womanhood, as Lady Macbeth; her angers and her tendernesses, in smaller
scale, echo Lady Macbeth's extremes. Without her, Lady Macbeth's evil may
with impunity seem more heightened, but the *Macbeth* world itself shrinks
if the Terrible Woman seems its only important female inhabitant; and some
of the most delicate notes in Shakespeare's polyphony are silenced.

The insistence on the high, clear note of dominance in the theatre's Lady
Macbeth probably both infected critical interpretation and helped evoke the
eventual counter-interpretation. Leigh Hunt, not the best of critics, was
misled: "Mrs. Siddons filled, nay, expanded the idea of the lady, the appropriate grandeur of her person, and the regality of her movements; and

though the part was by no means one in which her greatest powers were put forth—for, *as it is entirely simple and self-sustained, there is no ebb and flow of passion, and the points are too bold and too palpable to be missed* [italics mine], except by the mere want of power to grasp them—still the looks, the tones, the action, were majestic and fearful, as might befit the Clytemnestra of Aeschylus."

Hunt's analysis of the character in fact describes Siddons' simplification of it. She may not wholly deserve Fletcher's comment: "An impassive heroine of antique tragedy," but only very rarely was she reported to descend from "sublimity"—and the rarity emphasizes how insistently she sustained her major tone. Hazlitt was once dismayed suddenly to hear her voice at the end of the banquet scene utter: " 'Go, go' in the hurried familiar manner of Mr. Kean" instead of with her usual "sustained and graceful spirit of conciliation"; he was very sorry for it.

What might have been lost by her sustained "sublimity" is hinted by Galt, who heard her go through one performance "as it were in a suppressed voice that seemed to lend additional poetry to the text." Galt thought afterwards it was because her son Henry, playing Macbeth, was too boisterous, and she was trying to moderate his vehemence. Galt never heard this again.

The alternative to a continuing polyphony in the design was a sequential development Siddons adopted: one major tone partly replaced another. To convey Lady Macbeth's descent to "present wretchedness" in Act III, Siddons tells us, she assumed a "dejection of countenance and manners"; even more important, she allowed "for the first time striking indications of sensibility, nay, tenderness and sympathy" for her husband. Bell describes her as mournful and plaintive here. However, she showed "a flash of her former spirit and energy" when Macbeth talked of the threat of Banquo's existence. In Siddons' own words the murderous impulse returned: she "even hints . . . at the facility, if not the expediency, of destroying both Banquo and his equally offending child. . . . 'In them Nature's copy is [*sic*] not eterne.'"

Siddons' accession of sympathy after Duncan's murder was a revolutionary softening not observed in her predecessors. "Fiend" as she is remembered, others were more fiendish. Of Mrs. Pritchard's conception, until the breakdown in the sleepwalk, few except hard images come down: the cold "apathy" and "confidence" before the murder, contrasted with Garrick's noble anguish; the "horrible force of implacable cruelty, . . . grandeur of imperial manner . . . insensible to compunction and inflexibly bent on cruelty . . . such anger, indignation and contempt as cannot be surpassed." Why should Siddons have ameliorated at all Pritchard's very much admired tigress? Was there any motive beyond Siddons' professed intuitions of the Lady's essential femininity? Michael Redgrave suggests practically that she may have been— in the manner of many actors and critics—searching for some striking originality to distinguish her portrayal.* He cited as a particular instance her

---

*Siddons acknowledged that one of her anxieties in her first appearance as Lady Macbeth in London was "the fear of Mrs. Pritchard's reputation."

business in the banquet scene of seeing a ghost, and forcing down her fears: "She perhaps consciously wanted to do something that her great predecessor . . . had not done [and] she deliberately played the scene . . . in such a way as to draw all the attention to herself."

Nothing established Siddons as the Terrible Woman archetype so much as the backlash when later, gentler Ladies were embraced by the English audience; their tendernesses were regarded as entirely "new," as opposed to the Siddons' interpretation. As Siddons grew older, she seems to have been trapped in her body as well as in her interpretation. In her fifties she became stout and bulky, even unwieldy. She had little chance to change with the times, even if she had wanted to, and audiences had let her.

The eighteenth century might have been astonished to learn that it may have been enjoying in the fierce Lady Macbeth what psychological critics would find, much later, in the role: the exciting fantasy of the fearful, destructive female, particularly in the image of the Bad Mother, the archetypal hated-loved first woman who would wean her son from pity, and conspire with him to kill the father, and assume all power. To achieve her aim, this Lady concentrates a powerful double note: she denies the tendernesses traditionally associated with her sex: and she glories instead in traditionally masculine hardness—in this way echoing the dissonant, masculinized femininity of the witches: different projections of the female in collusion to seize the male power that she covets and destroy the male hero. Buried in this fantasy, Holland has suggested, is the implication that for a man to submit to a woman is bad and dangerous. Others have suggested that Shakespeare's very creation of such Terrible Women as Lady Macbeth implies his own antipathy to womankind: or at least to scheming womankind. Here again, Shakespeare's creative fantasy is interpreted as a projection of the male psyche. It is more capacious. From the female point of view, an archetypally dangerous male has drawn a cooperative woman into an antisocial act that leads to her destruction. So the great artist works out again fantasies that realize covert impulses of both men and women. So in the Bible Eve tempted Adam, but only after she had been herself tempted by a daemonic male figure—acting presumably with the knowledge of an almighty father-God. Sophocles' "Oedipal" fate destroys not only the man who beds guiltily with the mother, but also the woman who satisfies her yearning for the young son. The Lady Macbeth shaken when she visits the bloody bed of the old king who resembles her father touches a psychic destiny as surely as the Macbeth who kills his Old Man.

Shakespeare complicates the polyphonies of Macbeth and Lady Macbeth by sounding in both the elements of "masculinity" and "femininity," in dialectical reciprocation. By the twentieth century, the once clearly defined resistances generally understood to exist between male and female became somewhat dissolved, as women's roles in society changed; Shakespeare had long since explored the human as androgynous. In the *Macbeth* world, male and female characteristics are both easily distinguished and shared across gender. True femininity is associated with nurture, tenderness, and love, but a woman sensitive to these feelings may yet discover in herself traces of "masculinity"—not being a man, which is something else. Lady Macbeth exploits the "male" quality of readiness to take action in a world of men, to plan death, and see it done.

In her "masculinity," in this sense, the Terrible Woman challenges Macbeth's superior capacity for wickedness. Particularly when the equation requires him, by contrast, to decline into mere nobility, she assumes a glory of splendid, Satan-sized iniquity that Leech, Maeterlinck, and Sanders, among others, have sensed in Macbeth's heroic wrong. Bradley, perhaps partly conditioned by what he had long seen on the stage, saw Lady Macbeth "Too great to repent . . . perhaps the most commanding and most awe-inspiring figure that Shakespeare drew." Bradley was sure that Shakespeare meant the predominating impression to be "awe, grandeur, and horror." A female figure so dangerous to man cannot be let off, must suffer in mind and body. In this design, Lady Macbeth provides the double satisfaction of arousing forbidden subconscious impulses (we *want* her to bring Macbeth to murder, Gilbert Norwood suggested) while cursing herself with the guilt for their realization.

The Terrible Woman pattern would long continue, in England and abroad—as in the exacerbation of horror practiced in that German production when the Lady, in her madness, killed her husband before perishing in the flames of her burning castle. Schiller more subtly adapted Shakespeare to the appetites of the time in his romantic version: Macbeth was more than ever the noble man corrupted—by the wicked witches, and the more wicked Lady Macbeth. The translator's intention was served by one of the greatest tragediennes of the German stage, Sophie Schröder (1820), all anyone could wish for in a Terrible Woman:

> The character was completely ruled by a manly will. She never showed weakness or any intimation of female tenderness. . . . She was a powerful, monstrous witch. She interpreted Lady Macbeth as the true creator of all the crimes arising about her.

Schröder sounded from the start the simpler, narrowed note of the masculine, malicious female, stronger than Macbeth and conscious of it—as when she returned boldly and contemptuously from Duncan's chamber after returning the daggers, or when she stood above Macbeth fallen in the Banquet scene, and would not stoop to help him up. Cruelty seemed instinctive to her: her excited thought was translated into unconscious, almost mechanical execution by her body. Similarly, the first Swedish lady, Sara Torsslow (1838) was a model of the Terrible design—a huge, masculine, dominating woman with a furious temper.

Siddons' niece, Fanny Kemble (1832), was at first sensitive to the fused strains of masculinity and femininity, and praised their synthesis in her aunt's written conception: the "fairness of hair and skin" and the "frail, feminine form and delicate character of beauty . . . united to that undaunted mettle . . . constituted a complex spell, at once soft and strong, sweet and powerful." But in maturity Fanny described as her ideal image one much more muscular: and she acted "a fiend," one contemporary said. Then her Lady Macbeth, Fanny wrote, had

> the qualities which generally characterise men, and not women—energy, decision, daring, unscrupulousness; a deficiency of imagination, a great preponderance of the positive and practical mental elements; a powerful and rapid appreciation of what each exigency of circumstance demanded, and the coolness and resolution necessary for its immediate execution.

It followed that Lady Macbeth not only had more of the "essentially manly nature" than Macbeth, but also possessed a remarkable capacity to suppress any consciousness of guilt:

> . . . incapable of any salutary spasm of moral anguish, or hopeful paroxysm of mental horror. The irreparable to her is still the undeplorable—"What's done cannot be undone" . . . never, even in dreams, does any gracious sorrow smite from her stony heart the blessed brine of tears that wash away sin. . . . Intruding a moral element of which she is conscious into Lady Macbeth is a capital error, because her punishment, in its essence, consists in her infinite distance from all such influence.

Fanny's eminently practical lady—"She would not have hesitated a moment to commit any crime that she considered necessary . . . but she would always have known what were and what were not necessary crimes"—is pragmatically ready, after the murder, "to encourage, cheer, and succour with her superior strength, the finer and feebler spirit of her husband." But Fanny, in spite of her sense of Macbeth's great tenderness for the Lady, would not allow her "any special tenderness" for him: rather—the figure is a fierce one—"like the rider whose horse, maddened with fear, is imperilling his own and that rider's existence, [Lady Macbeth] drives the rowels of her piercing irony into him, and with a hand of iron guides, urges, and *lifts* him over the danger . . . her habitual tone, except where [she must] lash and goad him past the obstruction of his own terrors, is a sort of contemptuous compassion towards the husband whose moral superiority . . . she perceives and despises."

Macbeth "may weep"—the noble, remorseful Macbeth—"and wring his hands, and tear his hair, and gnash his teeth, and bewail the lost estate of his soul," but he at least "retains the unutterable consciousness of a soul . . . *She* may none of this: . . . even when prostrated in sleep before the Supreme Avenger, whom she keeps at bay during her conscious hours by the exercise of her indomitable will and resolute power of purpose . . . she may but feel and see and smell blood." What kills her is the

> *unrecognized* pressure of her great guilt. [She has been] destroyed by sin as by a disease of which she was unconscious, and . . . died of a broken heart, while the impenetrable resolution of her will remained unbowed.

Fanny's acting of her conception was approved by the *Times*. Inevitably she was compared with Siddons, not unfavorably, for displaying "throughout a perfect understanding of the nature of that bad, bold woman, the slave of evil passions": though even so the full Siddons power was missed. In Fanny's urging of Macbeth to the murder "she wanted force; she did not give full scope to the wild and devilish suggestions which Shakespeare has set down for her when her passions [have] unsexed her."

No such complaint was made about Charlotte Cushman, an American actress who, like Fanny Kemble, played Lady Macbeth opposite Macready's Macbeth, and whose force Macready admired. She brought to the image of the Terrible Woman a forbidding physical massiveness; tall, she made herself seem taller, towering over Macbeth as the archetypal mother would have loomed over a son. Actors with the strength of Macready and Forrest stood up to her;* others, like Vandenhoff, trembled before the "animal" in her characterization: "She bullies Macbeth, gets him into a corner of the stage and . . . pitches into him. . . . As one sees her large clenched hand and muscular arm threatening him, in alarming proximity, one feels that if other arguments fail with her husband, she will have recourse to blows." Coleman, similarly: "A domineering, murderous harridan . . . browbeats everyone . . . her husband most especially"; after the murder, "drags him off by the scruff of his neck."

Her physique partly determined Cushman's conception. Later in her long career, after other Lady Macbeth styles were introduced, she observed that intellectually she preferred the more feminine Lady, but it did not suit her. For the same reason she kept moving on the stage, always brooding, passionate, with "a restless, swinging way of doing everything." She explained that while Siddons had been beautiful enough to stand still to be gazed at, she, lacking beauty, had to compensate with action. Activity suited her design: she felt that the Lady could work murder as she did only under the influence of drink—and that Macbeth's similar drinking explained the discrepancy between his acts and words. She expected a rugged ferocity in Macbeth to match her own: finding Edwin Booth's conception "refined and very intellectual," she begged him to remember that Macbeth was "the grandfather of all the Bowery villains." She made up the equation, not with vulgarity, but a terrible power. Audiences were terrified, in the scenes up through Duncan's murder, by this "first cousin to Medea." Reports of various observers resound with the tones of thunder in this Lady Macbeth design:

"A woman of infinite pride . . . " "power [that] compelled admiration and wonder . . . " "great physical power and still greater will, and a fierce, implacable, terrible spirit . . . " "awe-inspiring, preternatural horror . . . " "harrowing portrayal of a wicked nature . . . " "full-fledged ferocity of a truculent

*"She acted Lady Macbeth to the Macbeth of Forrest so successfully that after that night the two were never again friends" (Strang).

nature in sight of prey . . . " "a murderous eagerness . . . " "appalling impartment of predestinate evil and sinister force . . . " "deep, thrilling, pitiless tones . . . " "a lurid light of horror spread over the entire performance. . . ." "Not only was she fully capable of killing her own infant at sight, but if occasion offered she could perpetrate by her own unaided efforts another 'Slaughter of the Innocents' merely for the gratification of an insatiable thirst for blood."

England felt the full shock of her fierceness, and generally applauded. The *Atheneum* praised her interpretation (1845) as "the finest thing we have lately seen upon the stage. . . . Not only her hands and fingers pointed, but her entire arms were instinct with the meaning of every passage."

Like Siddons, Cushman changed tones after the king's murder. The "masculine" force of the first two acts yielded to anguish and sympathy as she offered Macbeth, in Act III, an "affectionate solicitude . . . tenderness . . . an indescribable effect of the terrible and the piteous." A biographer: "She coaxed and chided by turns: was now the queen, again the loving wife, and then the suffering, conscience-stricken woman." The *Atheneum* found her "even greater after the murder than before"—though it added decorously of this American: "Perhaps there was an exuberance of power, a plenitude of New-World energy, much of which must be subdued." As her characterization stressed the softer elements, the *New York Times* reported, it "lost the force of passion, [and] gained in tenderness and pathos." Indeed, by the time of a late "farewell" performance (1874), she stressed intensely the softer tones in the polyphony, "suffused the part with a glow of mournful gentleness that brought it nearer to Shakespeare and closer to the universal heart."

That the Terrible Woman could sound a note of love as fierce as her impulse to dominate was suggested by a German actress, Fanny Janauschek (1891). A tigress she was called, with all the qualities of the traditional domineering lady fiend: her person massive, her countenance severe, a "terrible energy and characteristic fierceness tempered with the dignity and majesty befitting a queen." Towse found her a bit less rapacious than Cushman—her "imperious, conscienceless, and indomitable will" seemed less savage, "less inhuman." Amazingly, she overpowered English-speaking audiences, even when she spoke shattered English. She did sometimes attempt the then fashionable experiment of mixing the English of Edwin Booth with her German—she let him know his cues by pinching him—but often she bravely tried to render Shakespeare entire: and the *New York Times* marveled that she could produce her tremendous effects with such speeches as "Gif me dose taggers."

She could, apparently, because of her "fiery vehemence" and "terrible earnestness." Actors as well as audiences were shaken. The young Otis Skinner entered to her as messenger in I, v, and found her massive back turned to him, her eyes fixed on Macbeth's letter, apparently completely unaware of him. Nervous, he jumped his cue, blurted out: "The King comes here tonight." Thereat she whirled like an enraged tiger, her eyes two fiery searchlights, and with a deep vibrato thundered out: "How now, sirrah, vot noos?"

With wilting legs I reiterated my speech and retired clammy. Her eyes had given me a distinct electric shock.

Yet this fierce Lady Macbeth, unrelenting when terrible, only slightly less savage than Cushman, could seem at the same time so enamored of the husband she drove fiercely to murder that the two tones mingled: "power . . . and melting sweetness of feeling." Towse, a skilled observer, wrote, "She loved him passionately, and in her own tigress fashion, tenderly. She indicated this trait constantly"—and he cited some "beautifully compassionate" moments.

One quality that these Terrible Women largely left unemphasized in Lady Macbeth was the cleverness with which she found precisely the right arguments for persuading Macbeth to prove his manliness with murder. They preferred to play the notes of command rather than of craft. But to a later distinguished member of this terrible company, the wiles of Lady Macbeth seemed her truest tones. This was, aptly, the brilliant Italian actress, Adelaide Ristori (1857). She saw Lady Macbeth as having less concern for her husband than for her own ambition, but this was expressed in "a gigantic conception of perfidy, dissimulation, and hypocrisy." She was proud of "identifying myself with Lady Macbeth's type of crafty cunning."

Her power over Macbeth was as great as any, recalling Siddons—whom Ristori much admired—and especially the "sinking" of the men she played against. "Against" indeed describes Ristori's method. The text was "arranged" to make the most of her scenes; typically, in performance, her Italian Macbeth was reduced to "the veriest slave of her will and pleasure. In the murder scene she was everything, he was nothing—in fact, all throughout she overshadowed and extinguished the poor creature." Ristori herself wrote of

the perfidy and cruelty of [Lady Macbeth] . . . monster in human shape . . . difficult to credit a woman of this kind with any of the feelings of ordinary humanity . . . animated less by affection for her husband than by excessive ambition to share the throne . . . She therefore made use of him as a means of attaining her own ends, and took advantage of the unbounded influence her strong masculine nature and extraordinary personal fascination enabled her to exercise over him.

But her "masculinity," though reflecting a "turbulent, inhuman strength of spirit," was Italianate, subtle. In New York she was seen, playing with Edwin Booth, as a "bloody minded virago, without heart, without sensibility . . . in the form of a Lucretia Borgia, an adept at crime." Another observer: "The most unscrupulous of all our Lady Macbeths." "A well-bred *Italian intrigante*; such a woman as Catherine de Medici was." There was felt a pleasure in her Machiavellianism. She was seen to "enjoy her power over Macbeth more than English actresses."

Like Siddons, she turned to a different dominating tone after Act II, of anxiety and wifely solicitude; particularly after the banquet when, with pity, affection, and, in her own words, "gentle violence," she drew Macbeth off to their chamber. The shift between the two tonalities was more than ever necessary with Ristori, for two reasons. Otherwise, a breakdown in the sleepwalk would seem implausible for so crafty and manipulative a design; but even more, the softening rescued the characterization from an ultimate danger. Lady Macbeth, like Macbeth, has been called, in criticism, a villain. To the extent that she is played—or imagined—on the sustained note of self-interest, villain she must be. But if instead she belongs in the rare Olympian company of tragic heroes and heroines, some continuing counterpoint, if not a full polyphony, is necessary; a last-minute, fifth act turnabout comes late. Actresses like Siddons, playing the Terrible Woman, grasped for a largeness in destructive power, an extremity of passion, in their reach for tragic stature; a Terrible *Cunning* Woman, as Ristori's set out to be, aims to corrupt her victim, in the manner of Edmund and Iago, by the magnificence of her subtle manipulation. She assumes toward Macbeth, as well as the rest of the world, the role of "player," is likely to seem—as did Hegerlíková (Czechoslovakia, 1958)—"serpentlike." To attain tragic identity, such a Lady needs to find a self behind the mask, the kind of repressed dimension of womanliness that Ristori was able to radiate.

A French actress, Eugenie Marie Caroline Segond-Weber (1900), admired both Siddons and Ristori, but paced her design differently. Like Siddons, she stressed two elements in the character, but she interwove them—Lady Macbeth as nearly superhuman, and at the same time intensely human.

> She does not love her husband; I am a hundred times in this agreed with Mme. Ristori. . . . She does not love him, because he is her creature; she wants him king because she will be queen. How to suppose that in a soul where all is sacrificed to the desire to rule, love can balance ambition? Even maternal love? A woman capable of saying her abominable blasphemies against children (*I have given suck* . . .), how can she love? She has anticipated the prophecies of the witches; she is herself a kind of fourth witch, a daughter of witches.

Yet this "monster" has still a woman's nerves, that drum in undertone a counterpoint to her overt assurance in action. This Lady Macbeth does not allow herself a moment's hesitation, because she does not want to think. She has Macbeth's weaknesses, but she keeps them latent by an effort of will: she is above all a *will*. "This constant struggle of will against her woman's nerves must be made apparent to the spectator; I take care to show, momentarily, my weakness."

Segond-Weber here raised a crucial problem in the design. Somewhere Lady Macbeth's strength, if not her conscience, must begin to break. Most of the Terrible Women from Siddons on were seen to soften, and begin their decay, after the "Coronation" of Act III, i. An obvious earlier opportunity—

fainting under her strain in the crowd immediately after Duncan's murder (II, iii)—was denied most of these actresses since the scene was cut. (Though Ristori, true to her design, included the moment and made a *show* of swooning—*con intenzione*.) Segond-Weber let slip a break even earlier, as we will see.

The massive contribution made by Siddons and later actresses up through the nineteenth century to our understanding of Lady Macbeth was made possible partly because they played the part many times, and their developing characterizations, reported in detail, could richly illuminate the role. One Australian actress who also was able to develop the role through repeated performance—a rarity in the twentieth century—Judith Anderson, was fated, like Siddons, not to play a fair, fragile Lady. With her own stately nose, dark hair, and eagle eyes, and her gift for intense power, Anderson fitted naturally into the fierce, driving design: "Proud, ambitious, imperious, ruthless. . . ." "A commanding presence, something sinisterly majestic in her carriage, and a voice capable of ranging from a deep ominousness to that sudden stridency which reveals in the character a streak of vulgarity, a touch of the mere hellion." She was, one critic wrote, better fitted for the fierce Lady than any other contemporary actress.

She had the conception in her first performances, with Olivier, in 1937; by 1941, with Evans, she had refined it. She imagined Lady Macbeth as strong at first and determined: "She wants Duncan killed—she is beside herself with wanting it." But she cannot herself plunge the dagger into him. "The opportunity was there and she let it pass." Anderson consulted psychiatrists about Lady Macbeth's mind, particularly as to the etiology of the sleepwalking scene. She concluded that the traumatic episode that broke the Lady was her return with the daggers, when she had to look at the murdered king. "In all mental cases you can trace the trouble back to a moment when the disintegration commenced. With Lady Macbeth it was here."

A century and a half after Siddons this terrible Lady Macbeth could discover in the design an ambition for her husband more than for herself, and sustain compassion as well as scorn for him. If there was no sense of a romantic or deeply passionate love between Anderson and her Macbeth, yet—particularly with Evans in her later performances, and in her film with him—she could suggest a kind of desperate, almost pitying affection for the man to whom she was bonded, a note of care for him that sometimes mingled with, sometimes followed, her stronger domineering motif.

Another twentieth-century actress who repeated the role, Dorothy Green, moved as Judith Anderson did from an embryonic conception to a polyphonic one. Her first, almost melodramatic emphasis on terror, on cunning and iron will, recalled to the *Times*, in 1923, the acting of "an earlier day"; in 1927 this aspect of the role became only part of a "beautifully proportioned" characterization. An indomitable woman, though quite small, with a fearful capacity for evil, yet this Lady sounded the softer notes:

so slight and luscious in appearance, so fervent in speech, so fixed in determination, so ruthless in scorn for her husband's wavering, yet withal so truly
his devoted helpmeet and his loyal wife. Murderess—yes; fiend of cruelty—
yes; yet woman through and through. (*Stage*)

She renounced her sex, and yet it clung to her: "She was very woman: seducing her husband as a woman, standing by him and hiding his guilt as a woman,
commiserating with him as a woman, a wife, and a sweetheart." The subtextual undertones of her womanliness could be sensed from the very beginning, conveying a chord of frailty as well as wifely devotion that made
inevitable her collapse under the constraint of acting the "fiend." Her very
humanity infected her with "a sickness bordering on the grave."

So much force is needed for the Terrible Woman that small actresses have
been doubtful candidates for the role: critics have looked for mass of flesh to
accompany mass of spirit. Dorothy Green demonstrated that power did not
require mass; so did Ann Todd, matching steel for steel against the intense,
near-mad Macbeth of Paul Rogers (1954). Two strong figures met in this
equation, hence there was less of domination, more force against force: the
two magnified by their intensity, by the vehemence of their attack. Todd was
described variously as icy of passion, of commanding authority, magnificent
in pride, courage and ambition, and yet seductive too: in the pivot of her persuasion using not her voice but her hands and body to move her husband to
murder. If anything, to a mid-twentieth century audience she seemed almost
too terrible—in tiger-cat moods showing terrifying claws, cutting edges of
steel. More than one critic accused her of overdoing the inhumanity of the
role; the *Scotsman* reminded her that after all Lady Macbeth was not the Goneril that Todd seemed inclined to make her.

Some special quality of terror seems to attach to the Terrible Woman who
is beautiful as well as fierce: as if the two attributes should be incompatible,
as if a loving nature should accompany beauty—or else nature is guilty of an
unnatural oxymoron. Something of this was felt with Vivien Leigh, Olivier's
second Lady. Slightly built, she compensated with a lengthened stride and
sweeping movements that created an illusion of stature, and she conveyed a
peculiar menace by lowering the voice that issued in steel from her strikingly
beautiful, pale face. Her manner, except in rare intimate moments with Macbeth, and in the sleepwalk, and in her formal courtesy to her guests, was icy,
knowing, cruel. But countering strains sounded: in her rare revelations of the
"soft thread of conscience" which the *New York Times* felt she shared with
Olivier; in her deep-lying concern for her husband, evident in the sudden
gentling of her voice, as she urged him to sleep; in the momentary breaks in her
iron control of face and body before others; and in her final grey wretchedness.

In some such way the subtle dimensions in Shakespeare's design must
emerge. Unless the interpretation allows for moments of yielding, the Terrible
Woman mode seriously endangers Shakespeare's complex image—as it sometimes has done in the theatre. At one extreme, an unrelievedly arrogant "fiend"

has pushed the Lady's persona beyond plausibility, in a *Macbeth* world touched with insistent realism; at the other extreme, the relentlessly realistic, hounding wife has reduced the Lady to a shrew, unfit for the play's soaring spaces. The design insists on contrast and reciprocation between the percussion of Lady Macbeth's incitements of Macbeth and the more lyrical tones of her essential marital relationship with him. Sometimes the emphasis shifts far toward the latter end of the spectrum.

THE LOVING WIFE

At the other extreme from the Terrible Woman is the Loving Wife, whose ambition is all for the husband to whom she is entirely devoted. This design, and its modulations, reflect another archetypal image: of the woman who— sometimes well-intentioned, sometimes not—brings about a man's downfall through temptation, or betrayal. The motif of men betrayed—or thinking themselves betrayed—by women who should love them, is frequent in Shakespeare, especially in the major tragedies. Lear, Hamlet, Othello, and Antony all cry out against the fickleness of women; only Macbeth, who most is tempted, guided, or driven to his doom by the woman he is bound to, ab- stains from blaming her—instead blames the darker female shadows to whom he is linked: the Sisters.

The most familiar pattern in Western thought for the loving woman who betrays is Eve. Like her more terrible counterpart, the temptress Lady Mac- beth partially frees Macbeth from guilt for what he is led to do: Adam's Fall is not all his fault: "The woman tempted me and I did eat." The polyphony of the softer design will depend on how much Lady Macbeth's ambition moves her, how much she needs, in her different way, to exercise control, how much she must resist her innate tenderness and conscience in forcing herself toward the Terrible role for her husband's sake.

Some immediate objection to the image of a delicate, "feminine" Lady comes from scholars reminding us that Shakespeare's women's roles were played by male actors, who might be incapable of the nuances of femininity. This is not the theatre experience. That the actor Kynaston, playing women on the Restoration stage (Pepys called him the "prettiest woman in the whole house") should touch audiences more sensibly than any actress—as John Downes suggested—surprises no one who has watched talented female im- personators. I have reported the moving effect of the man who played Desde- mona at Oxford in 1610.* In Tokyo (1976) a Japanese actor, Tamasaburo Bandō, was cast as Lady Macbeth, because—Toshiko Shibata explains— Japanese men players have commonly been regarded as supremely able to convey femininity.

In the history of *Macbeth* interpretation, Shakespeare critics perhaps learned from the theatre that Lady Macbeth need not be the "fiend" image generally accepted up through the time of Siddons. By the third quarter of the eigh-

*See *The Masks of Othello*.

teenth century, one German actress began to adventure into a softer design; and critics would eventually catch up. The perceptions in the early nineteenth century, by Franz Horn (1823) and Ludwig Tieck (1826) in Germany, and by Mrs. Jameson (1832), William Maginn (1837) and George Fletcher (1843) in England, of a womanly Lady Macbeth's primary devotion to her husband, reflect the pursuit of complexity in Shakespearean character, and the willingness of the culture to de-sentimentalize Macbeth—and perhaps to make up to Lady Macbeth for past insults partly by sentimentalizing her. Her apologists and champions continued into the twentieth century: she has been seen as, "from the beginning spiritually sensitive" (F. R. Hunter). Parrott: ". . . naturally of an affectionate and gentle disposition. She has been a loving daughter and a tender mother. Her whole attitude toward her husband is that of a devoted wife." Hardin Craig: ". . . she has as deep a sense of the sinfulness of the deed as he has, perhaps a deeper sense. . . . What a shame it was that Macbeth, the man who knew the laws of the land, the man inured to war, permitted this delicate creature to engage in dark contrivance and butchery."

Rosalie Nouseul was the German actress who in 1778 seems first to have importantly portrayed Lady Macbeth as a loving wife who (according to a German theatre journal in 1779) "in an ecstasy of mind—caused by flattering visions of royal grandeur—tries to realize a plan from which normally she would have shrunk. Thus she was able to seize our sympathy as well as our interest." An engraving, showing her holding a candle in Act V, scene i, suggests a mild, rather gentle, middle-aged woman. But she was not merely gentle: she was seen to combine enormous strength of will and nervous hypersensitivity with seductive power. Schink suggested the multiple notes in her polyphony: "Lady Macbeth cannot wish to be immortalized by a more royal attitude, by a more royal behavior, by a more royal language. . . . Her humanity [is] visible at every moment. . . . Pride and rage, vengeance and despair, melancholy and weariness of the heart struggle passionately." But her demonstration that, as another writer put it, "Lady Macbeth need not be a terrible fury" was more admired by audiences than by critics, who missed the traditional "fiend."

A grudging explanation for Mrs. Nouseul's warm reception was that she must have misplayed the role:

> People ask, how could spectators' hearts have been moved, when the Lady had fallen into madness? How could such a cold-blooded abnormal villain, such a female image of Richard, acquire our sympathy? If the actress had performed the Lady's part according to Shakespeare's portrayal, she would unquestionably never have gained our sympathy. *That* Lady is a superhuman monster. [But] Mrs. Nouseul humanized this character.

Her softening of the design was not at once popular. The German theatre favored the vision of a wronged Macbeth, particularly as staged by Friedrich Schröder, the actor-butcher who had cut the whole first scene from *King Lear* because Lear's violent temper might seem somewhat to justify his later treatment by Goneril and Regan. As Schröder wanted sympathy for himself as Lear, he wanted it as Macbeth: so he made Lady Macbeth a kind of human evil genius who echoed the demonic witches who pursued him through the play.

Nouseul's "Loving Wife" would not be the popular pattern for German-Austrian Lady Macbeths for a long time to come; but the conception persisted. When Schiller's version, staged at the turn of the nineteenth century, further ennobled Macbeth at the expense of his Lady—realized to great applause by Sophie Schröder in the "monster" image—there was yet an actress, Betty Rose, who played against the translator-adapter's intent enough to be called "too effeminate—too weak and too delicate; instead of the monstrous witch she played a petty seducer." Friederike Bethmann (1809), though a very strong Lady, still informed her characterization with a modicum of love and feminine weakness: she *had* to invoke the spirits to steel her to murder, where mightier Ladies simply commanded their complicity.

By now some critical voices would begin, in Germany, to support the Lady's right to be womanly. Thus Horn:

> All our earlier critics misunderstood our poet. They interpreted the Lady as an extreme example of vaulting ambition who—for the sake of the crown—would not hesitate to commit even the most cruel crime. That is true indeed: only not for herself, but for him, the beloved husband. It might even be said that her passionate love for her husband is the eternal impulse in the Lady's life.

Horn particularly noted, at the end of the banquet scene, a maternal touch to her "loving and noble character: softly she reminds him that he lacks sleep, and like a child, exhausted and obedient, he follows her."

Tieck, the romantic critic, translator, and storyteller, we have met before, complaining in the English staging of *Macbeth* of the tiresomely pretty witches' ballet-chorales. Tieck looked beyond the "monster" dimension in Lady Macbeth, possibly influenced by the innovative German actresses, partly perhaps by a related interpretation he saw by Mlle. George in Paris (1825). She was tall and strong, Tieck reported, with mighty, noble gestures, terrible in expressing fury, disgust, and withering scorn; but in her relation to her husband also charming and tender.

In an extended analysis of the character for von Raumer, Tieck wrote:

> It is an old custom to exaggerate this role and to present it as a fury. Many actresses have gained fame in this way; and thus the poet's quiet, subtle hints, which he often provides, have remained unnoticed. Basically Macbeth and his spouse are noble, wise characters. . . . What happens is that both she and he are torn from their proper place.

Their very nobleness, Tieck felt, evoked the dialectic in their characters, commanded polyphony:

> The noble is fascinated by that which is base; it is charmed and bewitched. The idea that all human passion is an enchantment is here made visible. . . . She

feels the feasibility of their act, and her own woman's weakness; that weakness alone prods itself with those horrible words ["I have given suck . . ."], with the images of the ultimate excess, the most impossible. Were she a fury through and through, she would say nothing, or different words. Great and dignified she must be acted, but not in the way I have always seen it done. Beauty must not succumb, human mildness must shine through. Not without reason does she invoke night, spirits, and all to rob her of just that human mildness, because she has feeling.

Tieck listens to many tones in her orchestration:

One moment she flatters the irresolute [Macbeth], the next she mocks him. Feigned haughty disdain alternates with endearments. Here she has to mobilize all her greatness of heart, all the anger and mockery her eyes and face are capable of. Thus the audience perceives her metamorphosis into an enigmatic creature, which is the more deeply moving, the more the loving woman shows through at times.

His interpretation first puzzled and then rather angered Goethe, too old in the 1820s for the concept. In 1826:

Though I have agreed with my colleague of many years, I nevertheless must confess that I disagree that Lady Macbeth is a tender, loving soul and should be presented as such.

He suggested that perhaps Tieck didn't really mean it, was being paradoxical. Two years later, Goethe was sardonic. "We good Germans cannot rid ourselves of Shakespeare the conqueror. Thorough as we are, we try to penetrate into his nature, his material, his work; we happily attribute every value and depth to it. . . . Recently, even we have been so retrograde as to allow ourselves to be misled into constituting Lady Macbeth a loving wife. We have become so sick and tired of the truth it doesn't seem desirable any more, and we prefer to indulge in nonsense."

When an actress of the Tieck persuasion, Auguste Stich-Crelinger (1834), dared to mingle with her expression of the "demonaic forces of passion" the softer tender notes, an "honest and fervent love," it was to some popular applause, but a critic scolded her and her mentor, Tieck, in Goethe's fashion:

It is a shocking phenomenon, that a very famous critic and dramaturg has revealed all sorts of new findings concerning this character, which can only be perceived with greatest surprise. One of these [is] that love and only love is the motive of all the activity of Lady Macbeth. Unfortunately even celebrated actresses accepted this interpretation [and] this grandiose tragedy becomes crooked and foolish.

Heine was gently amused: "Whereas Lady Macbeth for two centuries has been considered a very wicked person, her renown has improved in Germany since twelve years ago, when brave Franz Horn observed that the poor Lady had been so completely misunderstood: instead she is to be considered a tender, loving wife. And after a short while we saw Madame Stich playing the part: so tenderly did she languish with sentimentality and feeling that eyes flowed with tears."

Inevitably, actresses in England would move in Nouseul's direction: partly with the artist's impulse to originality, to distinguish their interpretations from the Siddons model; partly because acting styles inevitably changed; partly because talented women found other dimensions in the role. Helen Faucit (1846) is generally credited with being the first English player to humanize Lady Macbeth; but at least by the beginning of the century earlier attempts were made—and were generally not well received. When Kemble played Macbeth opposite a Miss Smith (1808), the *Cabinet* generously conceded that she occasionally varied "with advantage" from Siddons; but the Terrible stereotype was reinforced in the criticism of the young actress, with blame for "some faults . . . the most material of which was an emotion of tenderness at times, and a querulous sensibility not proper to . . . Lady Macbeth's cool, deliberate and inflexible resolution by which the poet has distinguished her."

Lady Macbeths to Edmund Kean developed more latitude in the role to match the more complex polyphony that Kean himself was exploring in Macbeth. They met critical resistance. A Mrs. Hill, who played with him in the spring and fall of 1817, was scolded for being "*bit* . . . by the present mania for new readings," and charged with being "the most jovial, open-faced, and unsuspecting-looking Lady Macbeth we ever saw." She was severely scolded for showing "evidences of perfect frankness and guileless good nature." She was advised to pay undeviating attention to the Lady's ambitious character.

A Miss Campbell who played with Kean in the fall of 1817 brought a then startling softness to the characterization. For womanliness that would endear Ellen Terry and others to audiences later in the century, Miss Campbell was reprimanded: she was granted originality, but seemed too tame, insipid: "We have had but one Shakespeare," a reviewer declared, and "but one Lady Macbeth"—Siddons. Miss Campbell was nothing like. She had "none of the dignity, none of the masculine energy, none of the unrelenting cruelty, none of the devouring ambition which belongs to the cool murderess, whose only touch of humanity in the whole play is 'had he not resembled my father.' " Given so marble a standard, Miss Campbell's humanizing was many years premature. "She seemed to coax and wheedle her husband to the commission of the crime, instead of pouring her bold spirit into his milky nature"—a glance at the noble murderer—"or chastizing him with the valour of her tongue." She was even "playful"—a pejorative then for Lady Macbeth, though for Ellen Terry it would sometimes be praise. "This Lady Macbeth was always a mere woman, not unsexed, nor filled from top to toe with direst cruelty."

The very intensity with which reviewers reacted against the interpretation suggests how fixed in England was the Siddons murderess. Miss Campbell was not apparently a great actress; but the main attack was against not her playing, but her conception. Still, she may have dropped a small pebble in the critical and theatrical pond. As in Germany, where the reverberation of Mrs. Nouseul's characterization, and Betty Rose's, may have had some influence on the reevaluation of Lady Macbeth, perhaps Miss Campbell's abortive attempt was a small preparation for the change in critical opinion that encouraged and was encouraged by Helen Faucit's more successful acting of the humanized lady. Some fifteen years after Miss Campbell, Mrs. Jameson, and a few years later Maginn, attempted to exonerate Lady Macbeth from fiendship.

Mrs. Jameson could allow that ambition might be the Lady's "ruling passion," but "less for herself than her husband. . . . It is of him she thinks: she wishes to see her husband on the throne, and to place the sceptre within his grasp." There is no female scorn in such a term as "the milk of human kindness," no "want of wifely or womanly respect and love for him, but "—here Jameson acknowledges Lady Macbeth's greatness—"a sort of unconsciousness of her own mental superiority, which she betrays rather than asserts." Mrs. Jameson sees Lady Macbeth—as others would see Macbeth—as one of the greatest of overreachers:

> Hers is the sin of the "star bright apostate." . . . She reaches at the golden diadem which is to sear her brain; she perils life and soul for its attainment, with an enthusiasm as perfect, a faith as settled, as that of the martyr who sees at stake heaven . . . opening before him.

But it is not the evil itself that involves us; rather:

> Our interest fastens on what is *not* evil in the character . . . something kindling and ennobling in the consciousness . . . of the energy which resides in mind. . . . Many a virtuous man has borrowed new strength from the force, constancy, and dauntless courage of evil agents.

The provocative Maginn, who loved to argue, and who had some good arguments, sensed, as Horn and Tieck did, a capacity for love, and a goodness repressed, in the Lady:

> Love for him is, in fact, her guiding passion. She sees that he covets the throne, that his happiness is wrapped up in the hope of becoming a king; and her part is accordingly taken without hesitation. With the blindness of affection she persuades herself that he is full of the milk of human kindness, and that he would reject false and unholy ways of attaining the object of his desires. She deems it, therefore, her duty to spirit him to the task. . . . Her sex, her woman's breasts, her very nature oppose the task she has prescribed herself; but she prays to the ministers of murder . . . and she succeeds in mustering the desperate courage that bears her through . . . Her language is exaggerated in mere bravado (*A little water clears us* . . .) Does she indeed feel this? . . . She shall answer us from her sleep, in the loneliness of midnight, in the secrecy of her chamber.

Whether or not Faucit was influenced by Mrs. Jameson or Maginn, or by the earlier softenings of actresses like Miss Campbell, she certainly dared to portray successfully in England what seemed then an extraordinary example of the loving wife. Comments tell as much about current taste, and the fading of the Siddons stereotype, as about Faucit. Significantly, *Blackwoods*, in 1834, could not imagine Lady Macbeth in another shape than Siddons; but a decade later, John Wilson (*Blackwood*'s Christopher North) exclaimed, according to Theodore Martin, Faucit's husband, "Mrs. Siddons has misled us." Soon, in his journal, he would confirm this.

A thoughtful Irish observer wrote of Faucit's interpretation in the *Freeman's Journal*:

> I begin to feel as if I had never seen Lady Macbeth's true character before. . . . This woman is simply urging her husband forward through her love for him, which prompts her to wish for the gratification of her ambition, to commit a murder. . . . It is not necessary that she . . . wantonly parade throughout the play that inhuman ferocity by which she has hitherto been distinguished.

Late in the century E. R. Russell would suggest, looking back from a perspective of several decades, that Faucit dissipated, "in the interest of truth and nature, the great Siddons delusion; of showing the world something truer than the massive and monumental style which was all the Kemble school could realise."

Do not assume, though, that Faucit saw in Lady Macbeth only a kind of gentle accessory to Macbeth. The tones of strength and assertion sounded clearly to her:

> I could not but admire the stern grandeur of the indomitable will which could unite itself with "fate and metaphysical aid" to place the crown upon her husband's brow . . . the eagerness with which she falls into his design. . . . If we throw our minds into the circumstances of the time, we can understand the wife who would adventure so much for so great a prize. . . . Deeds of violence were common . . . the moral sense was not over nice, when a great stake was to be played for. . . . Murder often passed in common estimation for an act of valour. Lady Macbeth had been brought up amid such scenes, and one murder more seemed little to her.

Faucit played throughout the British Isles: we read from London of the "fiery decisiveness of her adjurations"; from Scotland of her "aggressive power"; from Dublin how, after the murder, "her ferocity is broken down." "So young and yet so wicked," said one observer. What was revolutionary in Faucit's design was the undertone always of affection behind her force. The polyphony seemed to sound from the beginning: the regality of her air, "overtopping the vicissitudes of her emotions"; her suggestions of passion, "more impressive than its full expression" (this recalls Galt's comment on Siddons' restrained performance); her queenly, though baleful gaze; her domination over the conscience of her guilty partner; but always, the womanly grace, the devotion to a husband whom she worships.

Inevitably some observers were not ready for Faucit's "womanly" design; curiously, one of her bitterest critics was the *Lady's Newspaper*, which granted that

> she expresses care, anguish, and a fiendish vindictiveness with force. This, however, does not accord with our notion of the character, which requires the sublime hardihood and terrible immobility that the greatest actresses have hitherto given. . . . Perfect self-possession and an utter absence of suscepti- bility are the true characteristics of this wicked woman. She enters with a full confession she has drunk enough, and says that liquor has given her life, and made her bold. She is an odious as well as a criminal woman, who could hardly be personated by the most feminine and delicate of our actresses, and the effort to throw traits of tenderness into the part seem to us absurd.

The finesse with which Faucit urged Macbeth to the murder that will gratify his—their—ambition reflected her affection (this kind of subtlety would earn her the description Wingate remembered: "delicate and refined fiend"): "She perceives that he has scruples; and it is necessary that she should work on him so far that he should commit the crime, but at the same time prevent him from feeling revolted at the contemplation of it."

The clear undertones of her love prepared audiences, as the Siddons charac- terization never had, for the Lady's crumbling in Act II after the murder. She actually fainted in the crowd scene, and carried it off—she could act Shake- speare's intention without fear of seeming hypocritical. After the murder, her impulse to tenderness for Macbeth, while it followed the Siddons pat- tern, grew so smoothly out of her earlier characterization, was so much more vulnerable, that it was hailed as an entirely new—and true—design. Siddons had thought that she softened Lady Macbeth in Act III, but "mourn- ful and plaintive" is the best corroboration by observers we have, and Siddons told how she had been quick to reverse and urge the murder of Banquo and Fleance; Faucit was seen as a "naturally generous woman" who "mingled love and pity." She met Macbeth's "hint of a new deed, a new crime, with . . . the weariness of wonder and dread." The polyphony shifted and con- tinued in "the ill-suppressed anguish of a guilty spirit, and a perceptible struggle to subdue the manifestations of that guilt whilst attempting to en- courage and sustain her husband." Her "magnificent" courage in his support through the banquet scene turned, when they were alone, to hopeless sad- ness—a prelude to her sleepwalk. Faucit satisfied even Macready, who pre- ferred fierce Lady Macbeths. Years would pass before her design would be quite respectable in the English theatre, but Faucit's interpretation encour- aged the newer critical interpretation that was enriching European concep- tions of the complexity in the *Macbeth* character designs. Actresses like Mrs. Kean (Ellen Tree, England, 1853) would weave into their strong Ladies touches of softness; and Faucit herself was so accepted that in 1874, some thirty years after she first appeared, Charles Reade, projecting an ideal production of the play, wanted her for his Lady. Wilson's imaginary dialogue in *Blackwood*'s (November, 1849), though dialectic in form, was a handsome apology to Lady Macbeth for his having been "misled" by Siddons' marble pattern. Meanwhile George Fletcher, following Maginn, was justifying Lady Macbeth with his point-by-point indictment of Macbeth's "cowardly selfishness and most remorseless treachery." The terms of the equation shifted toward a more guilty Macbeth, a more innocent and womanly Lady Macbeth. "It has been," Fletcher wrote,

> customary to talk of Lady Macbeth as of a woman in whom the love of power for its own sake not only predominates over, but almost excludes, every human affection, every sympathetic feeling.

Fletcher argued no; she greets Macbeth's homecoming, *contra* Siddons, with "a burst of passionate anticipation, breathing almost a lover's ardour." We are presumably prepared for this: Macbeth had already spoken of the murder—"broached the enterprise"—and she invoked the "spirits" not as a cold-blooded murderess but rather in a "vehement effort to . . . silence the 'still, small voice' of her human and feminine conscience." She covets the "golden round" for *him*, and even considers doing the murder herself—for *him*. She can persuade him, even with sarcasm, because he knows she "devotedly *loves* him."

Siddons was wrong as Lady Macbeth, Fletcher argued, because she missed the multiple tones in the role: it called for "not a *statue-like* simplicity"—Campbell's praise of Siddons' characterization—"but a *picturesque* complexity, to which Mrs. Siddons' massive person and sculptured genius were essentially repugnant." In a later footnote to his essay, Fletcher praised Faucit because her *"essentially feminine* person which . . . Mrs. Siddons herself contend[ed] for,—together with that energy of intellect and of will, which this personation equally demands,—have enabled her to interpret the character with a convincing truth of nature and of feeling, more awfully thrilling than the imposing but less natural, and therefore less impressive grandeur of Mrs. Siddons."

A curious variation of the loving wife was explored in America by Clara Morris (1874). America, also, was generally used to the Siddons pattern, recognizable in Cushman, and a critic could be grateful that Morris' Lady was not "the hereditary idea . . . a species of she-Forrest, with portentous aspect, a corrugated brow, a huge headachy Massachusetts forehead, and a cavernous mouth, which, when the ledge is lifted, emits a deep and dreadful sound. . . . [This], although sanctioned by tradition, has no affinity in nature."

After this stereotype, which Morris herself called "the traditional, martial-stalking drum-major of a woman," her own deliberate humanization of the role came as a relief to many. Her very appearance was daring: the *New York Times* reported, with some astonishment, "she is made a blonde" (Clara saw herself sandy-haired).* As if this were not startling enough, her characterization was accordant: a "fair-haired, pink and white Lady Macbeth," the *Herald* said, "substituting for the masculine impersonations we are accustomed to."

In fact, Morris seemed precisely the "fair, feminine, fragile" Lady of Mrs. Siddons' unrealized dream—and the fragility was deliberately deceptive. Morris was herself small, and not suited to dominating the usual stalwart Macbeth with the physical force natural to Siddons and Cushman; but dominating she meant to be, as a kind of demure Delilah. She reports that Cushman proclaimed herself intellectually "for Clara's kind of feminine Lady Macbeth," but felt obviously unfitted for—and here Cushman presumably described the Morris interpretation—"the coaxing, purring, velvet-footed subtle hypocrite."

But Clara's was not the vicious Machiavellianism of Ristori. She recognized a "devouring ambition," but behind it a capacity for womanly concern, compassion, and repentance. She felt herself ideal for the conception, hypothesizing, much as Siddons had, that Macbeth, as a "fine soldier, big and bluff and . . . brave," would be drawn to someone "fair, soft, tender in seeming, this 'dearest chuck' whose soft body housed a soul of fire." Morris saw Lady Macbeth as very clever, as "her reading of Macbeth's character proves her to have been" (a questionable assumption), and the weapons she chose to assure her ambition were craft and subtlety. An observer reported:

> The woman smiles with the grace and sweetness of a modern drawing room lady while she counsels murder, and she develops a certain shrewdness which places her as it were *en rapport* with audiences, and indicates to them what a fool she is making of the nature on which she works. She seems to tempt evil for the sake of tempting . . . not nerved by any mighty ambition that would give it a Satanic grandeur, but subtle, penetrating, and assured in its own cleverness [proceeding] from some intense spur and motive.

The actress identified the inner drive for the *Brooklyn Daily Eagle:* "What she wants, she wants *now,* and will murder for it." The *Eagle* saw in her design "more metaphysical meaning" than Cushman's mighty "repulsive" characterization, the traditional "barbaric woman, thewed and sinewed like a barbaric warrior."

*Duncan calls Lady Macbeth *Fair and noble hostess*. This could be simple courtesy, a conventional allusion to a beautiful person or personality; but *fair* also meant "blonde," and Duncan could have intended the double meaning, in reference to the Globe actor's yellow wig. To the audience, physical fairness might seem to double, by contrast, the spiritual discoloration.

While Morris' blonde lady now seemed unusual to the *Times*, when Ellen Terry came to Philadelphia some twenty years later the *Philadelphia Times*, seeing her hair more blonde than red, commented "Most of the harm in the world is done by soft, yellow-haired women." Was there always some such belief? Some three centuries earlier Reginald Scot reported that "Maides having yellow haire are most molested" by the Incubus, and so involved in witchery.

Morris sensed, shadowing Lady Macbeth's drive to her goal, a counterpoint of delicacy and even naiveté:

> There is something appalling in her ready faith and eager summoning of the spirits of evil to her aid; and right in the invocation I find my proof that Lady Macbeth was naturally womanly, pitiful, capable of repentance for wrong done.

This subversive womanliness threatened to undermine her; critics noticed with what an evident effort, with "energy unnatural to her," she sustained her mask after the murder of Duncan. She herself wrote:

> When at last it is borne in upon her that they have played her husband false; that all stained with crime they two are left to face an outraged God, how quickly the delicate woman becomes a physical wreck.

The Germans, though looking back with respect to Sophie Schröder's Terrible Woman, were still impressed—if not universally satisfied—with Charlotte Wolter's (1877) interpretation in the Nouseul tradition. She stressed the Lady's femaleness, her charming, tender, passionate nature; this was a wife who loved and admired her great husband, not only as her partner of greatness, but as her man. In moving with him toward Duncan's murder, she seemed to prevail mainly with the warm embracings and tender whispers of a passionately loving wife.

In Czechoslovakia, Kolarová also attempted, in 1852, to establish the softer element in Lady Macbeth's polarity. A critic noted that, unlike Siddons, Pritchard, and Schröder, she emphasized the feeling side, womanliness was always apparent through the translucent mask of the quasi-demonic front she presented. Though Kolarová was praised for making plausible her persuasion of Macbeth to murder and tyranny, traditionalists objected that Lady Macbeth had much more deepseated malice than the actress allowed. The criticism apparently took: six years later, when she played the role, she was murderously coldhearted: she suppressed Macbeth's scruples by grim, unyielding persistence—"in the soul of this Lady Macbeth no corner remained where a guiding angel could hide and appeal to her conscience." Almost exactly a century later, so much had theatrical and critical fashion changed, the Czech Votrubová (1958) was faulted for doing what Kolarová had been scolded for not doing: "She impoverished the role by reducing it toward the demonic, left out the humane feeling which belonged to a wife blindly devoted to her husband, and engaging in crime out of love."

If the "Loving Wife" conception did not quickly become the fashion in the nineteenth century, it was commanding some acceptance. It was known in France, where Mlle. George had softened the role, and where Faucit played in 1845; and it certainly flourished in England: Faucit's own signed copy of Fletcher's essay passed—apparently via Henry Irving—into the hands of Ellen Terry, whose scribbled notes decorate it; and Terry remains surely the most remarkable, if not the most extreme, example of this design.

You would never guess it, looking at the familiar, impressive Sargent portrait of Terry. She looks tall, haughty, forbidding, stiffened with the iron of a murderess. If we did not know, we might take this image as the one acted by Siddons; while the gentle Harlow portraits of Siddons might much better portray Terry's Lady, so soft it was even called "dove-like."

Terry herself stoutly disagreed with that descriptive. In a letter, alive with her passionate punctuation:

> *I* can only see that she's a *Woman*—A Mistaken Woman—& *Weak*—Not a Dove—of course not—but *first of all a Wife*. I dont think she's *at all clever*. . . . She seems shrewd, & thinks herself so, at first [about Macbeth's character] but oh, dear me how quickly she gets steeped in wickedness beyond her comprehension.*

No other actress has written so fluently, with this whimsical sympathy, about the elements in Lady Macbeth: nor so spoken about her, according to her grandson, Edward Carrick Craig, whom as a child she used to charm with readings from the role. She wrote to her daughter: "I by no means make her a gently lovable woman, as some of them say. That's all pickles; she was nothing of the sort, although she was not a fiend and did love her husband." To Clement Scott: "I don't even want to be a fiend"; and Mrs. Scott reports her denying that "Mrs. McB." was a "fiend who urged her little husband against his will to be naughty."

So she presented, the *Daily Telegraph* reported, not the usual theatre picture of the Lady, "no tragedy queen, no hard, harshfeatured woman, with a rasping voice and a forbidding manner, none of the stilted, stagey airs that have attached themselves to the character, but a woman stately, fair, with a clear white face set in a glory of hair Titian red, in the heyday of her beauty, arrayed in apparel as gorgeous as some Queen of Sheba." *The World* also acknowledged that she differed from the traditional Lady, "but [Terry's] is the Lady Macbeth Shakespeare would have drawn had he had an Ellen Terry in his company. . . . We can readily accept this clinging and cajoling enchantress, whose enkindled ambition affects her with a temporary paralysis of conscience."

Pathos was the dominant note in Terry's conception (though she was "awful" too), William Winter thought; and indeed her lectures (rather more sober than her correspondence) included Lady Macbeth among Shakespeare's "Pathetic Women." She would write: "I love Lady M . . . though it is far removed from my temperament, one can't help feeling sorry for the poor creature."

Terry was shrewdly aware of the relation of the role to the particular actress who challenged it. She felt that her own personality, and her physical equipment, determined for her the softer characterization. She sympathized with

*Terry wrote this to William Winter. To his wife: "My Lady Macbeth as 'gentle and dove-like'!!! Lor' a mussy. I feel all the while as if I were 'going on' like a Billingsgate lady." (MSS in Folger library).

Siddons, whose sheer physical appearance, Terry thought, "her nose, her raven hair, her eagle eyes, her commanding form" forced her to abandon her vision of Lady Macbeth's "delicate and sensitive spiritual structure and frail physique." Terry's acted Lady Macbeth was much closer to Siddons' unacted conception, as critics observed—one suggested that it may have been her inspiration. Terry insisted that every line of the part indicated that "the 'dearest partner' is a woman with the nervous force of a woman, the devotion of a woman, and above all the conscience of a woman. . . . [It] kills her in the end."

Many of Terry's annotations on her texts of the play will be noticed later, in context; these suggest that in moving toward a more "womanly" Lady Macbeth she may have finessed the strong notes of power and control that clamor through the first act, made them the ground notes of devotion. The synthesis of her strategy:

> A woman (all over a *woman*) who *believed* in *Macbeth*, with a lurking knowledge of his weaknesses, but who never *found him out* to be nothing but a brave soldier *and a weakling*, until that damned party in the parlour—the Banquet Scene, as it is called. Then, "something too much of this" she says and gives it up—her unmistakeable softening of the brain occurs—she turns quite gentle—and so we are prepared for the last scene, madness and death.
>
> She goads herself on to crime. She feels she has only a *woman*'s strength and calls on "Spirits." The tale of the witches fired her imagination, and kindled her hopes. Under her lonely battlements she dreamed of future splendour— she did *not* realise the measure of the crime.

In her lecture Terry called the "womanly" character compatible with such acts as her fearful taunt that she would kill her baby rather than renege on the kind of oath Macbeth had sworn. "She has never failed her husband yet." They are equals, partners, as partners they engage in crime.

> The wife is compelled to take up the burden of action when the husband, who, being a dreamer, finds it intolerably heavy, lays it down. . . . The frenzied appeal is surely the expression of the desperation Lady Macbeth feels at the sudden paralysis of Macbeth's faculties in the hour of action. He must be roused, he must be roused. Is all they have gone through [to] be for nothing? . . . We really ought not to take her wild words as proof of abnormal ferocity.

Terry demonstrated the dangers as well as the strengths of a design that made Lady Macbeth's love primary. To some she seemed too soft, the deep, fierce tones missing. In America: "More gentle, less self-assertive, tragic and tremendous than we have been taught to think it should be." In England:

> The new Lady Macbeth in her strange green robe and her flame-red hair, with her coaxing ways and graceful movements, it is a creature so fascinating that she might lure a man much less susceptible to outside influences than Macbeth to the doom. . . . Our only difficulty lies in associating her with any crime of the kind. Even in her sleepwalking scene—one of the most beautiful ever seen

on the stage—one never feels that she has really ever had blood on the hands which she moves with restless pathos.

And a more wry English comment:

. . . a Burne-Jonesy Lady Macbeth, who roars as gently as any sucking dove . . . the cultured are prepared to bow before the divinity, and to believe, or make believe, that Lady Macbeth has been much maligned, that the very thought of murder would draw tears from her eyes, that she can exhibit in this character playfulness, tenderness, affection, and conjugal rapture, and . . . make of the sleepwalking scene—which in the hands of Siddons made people shudder—a pretty replica of the mad business of the distraught and dreamy looking Ophelia.

The dramatic equation with her Macbeth—Irving—made it easier for Terry to exploit the "womanliness" of the role. Irving, as noted earlier, felt certain that Macbeth had, long before the play opened, thought of murdering Duncan; so Lady Macbeth did not have to persuade him to do it. Irving's idea, we saw, was that he was in fact manipulating her to expedite his own aims. Fourteen years before, his first Lady Macbeth, Kate Bateman, had been the traditional virago, who seemed to browbeat him; with Terry, his guile worked more subtly, his villainy more rousing because it victimized the wife whom Terry made so appealing in her devotion and support.

Yet many sensed and applauded the notes of strength, determination, and sinister intent as well as femininity in the Terry design. The mysterious "thirst for power" in this "passionate, sensuous and finely strung Lady Macbeth" was seen, by the *Pall Mall Gazette*, to be the function of "some baleful enchantment. . . . We can well understand [how] this strangely impressive, subtle, and exquisite creature . . . should turn her husband round her finger." If she did not project Faucit's ferocity, she did convey a "singleness of purpose, a settled, irrevocable unswerving directness and with a womanliness that made an intelligible and comprehensive whole." Despite her "feminine, soft caressings," the *Pictorial News* observed, she carried "a heart relentless to those standing in the way of her bold project." The *Boston Standard* saw a "womanly horror" emanate from her, a "gluttonous thirst for power flash up and burn until it consumed herself." To the *New York Recorder* she seemed "halfway between the grim ferocity of Cushman and the beguiling suavity of Clara Morris." Her force was especially noticed in America when she played the role a second time, almost a decade after her first appearance: "Miss Terry is far less gentle than of yore, which means that she is a better Lady Macbeth than she ever was." Many notes were heard of Lady Macbeth's polyphony:

". . . such a red-haired, splendid, fearless, stimulating, unscrupulous woman. . . ." "Captivating is not at all the word to apply. Feminine it is; wifely it is; powerful it is; her character, as it were, seizes Macbeth in a vice, and uses it and him by sheer force. All [this] under forms of probable and life-like conjugal compulsion, pretty enough to look at, if the business in hand were less ghastly and the husband not visibly haunted by the most horrible and unnerving apprehensions. . . ." "[Terry] is [a] determined, managing wife, with a keen sense of her husband's native irresolution in matters of high wickedness; full of bright, prompt, fascinating impulse until the sight of her husband's increasing and incurable prostration brings home to her own spirit the essential and inevitable horrors of blood guiltiness."

Of her mingling of light and dark notes, "both awful and pathetic"; ". . . soft smiles preceded and followed terrible utterances; in Macbeth's arms she rested in gentlest womanhood; in the manner of a dove she described the murderous acts of a demon."

> What Miss Terry does is to play this majestic role in sub-tones without sugaring it, and we observe for the first time the stormy, dominant woman of the eleventh century equipped with the capricious emotional subtlety of a woman of the nineteenth century. Fluctuant, dreamy, a creature wholly of sensibility. . . .
> A regal type of self-conflict; the glorious, desolate emblem of a soul at war with itself.

An Englishman wrote of Terry, "The antithesis of the character" had never really been presented on the stage up to that time. But there had been Faucit, whom some remembered, and Nouseul; and very recently a strangely beautiful Frenchwoman whose complex Lady had surprised and rather shocked many Londoners, though, curiously enough, she had pleased more the conservative British north. Sarah Bernhardt.

In a retrospective review, when Terry played the role, the *Times* put the Frenchwoman's Lady in her place, as even less proper than Ellen's: it noted that Faucit had been "blamed" for portraying Lady Macbeth as

> a womanly and to some extent sympathetic personage; but there is no precedent . . . for [Terry's Lady] . . . Madame Sarah Bernhardt's sketch of the character is the only one with which [Terry's] can be compared; and there is a wide difference between the sensuality of the French Lady Macbeth seeking to work upon her lord's nature by means of animal passion and [Terry's] sweet winning womanliness.

More gentlemanly, a Liverpudlian conceded that Bernhardt deserved the comparison, that she "approached very closely to Siddons' [unacted] conception . . . But"—disapproving—"[Bernhardt] made it amorous."

As if for Lady Macbeth to be amorous was somehow shocking. To the French—ah, the French—the way of a woman with a man was likely to involve the erotic. Théophile Gautier is reported, in a French review, to have suggested that Lady Macbeth be "feline, full of the perfidious charm of the temptress, purchasing a murder by a disdainful caress"; at Bernhardt's performance (1884) in Paris *Le Figaro* was delighted at her playing "with an energetic and wild grandeur the . . . infamous and sensual Lady Macbeth."

Madame Tessandier's contemporary Lady was a young and beautiful woman, who dominated her young husband with love and voluptuousness. As we will see, some French actresses have since emphasized sensuality in the design, as have actresses of other countries: the erotic in the relationship will become an increasingly important note in the polyphony.

Conservative English critics were so shocked by Bernhardt's perception in the Lady's design of "animal passion," of "insidious erotic influence," that it distorted their whole view of her performance. Thus the *Saturday Review* could say, "With her husband there is no touch of love or tenderness"—an impression that denies the experience of many neutral and favorable reviews, and other, unfavorable ones. Even the hostile *Times* would observe, "Nothing was more striking than the undertone of tenderness for her husband that pervaded the scenes in which her diabolic determination was at its highest pitch. Even in her scorn for his cowardice there was a touch of love." What some found offensive—five years before Terry would make the Loving Wife respectable—was that Bernhardt, whose benchmark was unconventionality and "natural" acting, also avoided the usual "tragedy queen" aura to portray instead a recognizably "womanly" dear partner to her murdering husband. Her very costume was troubling: a simple skirt and a "tight-fitting jersey that follows every line of the figure, and reaches to the hips"—or, in a more elegant Victorian description, "drape[s] the lithe and undulating form."

The *Times* rested its case on tradition—the tradition of the narrow-toned commanding presence. "The world has agreed to regard [the Lady] as a grand figure, noble even in her wickedness, a woman who dominates her brave but vacillating husband by dint of a stronger will, a higher ambition, and a sterner courage, than his own. Madame Sarah Bernhardt depicts her as an unromantic Cleopatra, who wheedles and cajoles where she should command."

Certainly one essential in Shakespeare's equation is that Lady Macbeth seems to win over—if not "subjugate"—Macbeth through some personal power: and most of Bernhardt's English critics agreed that she was richly endowed with the authority of the "fair, feminine . . . even fragile" charm that Siddons had wished for:

". . . youthful and lovable in appearance—not unlike the pictures of a medieval *chatelaine*, with wavy gold tresses, bound by a golden fillet." "She depicts for the present generation the kind of woman in whom it is strongly interested, the dangerous, siren-like creature by whose fascinations men are enslaved. . . ." "This Dalilah-like character has . . . the merit of being comprehensible. By women of this class the strongest natures have been subjugated. It is very easy to understand that Macbeth in the toils of such a one should prove weak and plastic. . . . "In her support of her husband at a moment when he is closely beset she gives proof of a nature not wholly cruel or base. A Cleopatra-like seductress, with a queenliness and grace of bearing that would also befit the mistress of Antony."

Could there be, in a Lady Macbeth who sounded so strongly the "amorous" note, the countering tones of willful terror and manipulation inherent in the design? *Life:*

> We have, for the first time, a womanly Lady Macbeth, a terrible creature, but still a woman. . . . Hitherto, Lady Macbeth has been played without a conscience. She is usually remorseless and brutal, but Madame Bernhardt has changed all that. There is human nature in all its strength and weakness. . . . Her ascendancy over Macbeth is easily understood; her temper is domination, not domineering, and the infirm Macbeth's is just the nature to be swayed by the resolute will of his wife.

The very dissonance between her evident, innocent beauty and her will to share in murder—one observer saw "the ferocious enthusiasm of a Druidess"—seemed to qualify her as a "fiend," even if a different kind from the Terrible Woman. *World:*

> . . . not the northern virago; from the moral point of view, a southerner, and from the plastic point of view . . . Oriental. Feline, caressing, nervous, intensely womanly . . . the most virginal, the most lovely, and the most subtly fiendish one could wish to see.

One amazing change in the text may have affected Bernhardt's conception. This strange Frenchwoman dared, in the very home of Shakespeare, to reinstate into his play a scene that proper Englishmen—except Phelps, in one staging—had deleted as far back as there is theatrical record: the slaughter of Lady Macduff and her children. By including this scene, Bernhardt's Loving Wife could reflect a commonality in marital relationship as well as the fearful difference possible in it.

Ten years after Terry first played Lady Macbeth, and two years after she won America in the role, the august *Times* would decide that her attempt to control Macbeth by "wheedling affection" was "a curious rather than a plausible experiment, and the Mrs. Siddons tradition of . . . a more or less unsexed virago still dominates powerfully the stage." But if this was so in a corner of England in 1898, it would not remain so even there, and certainly not elsewhere in Europe, though some critics would have wished it so.

Thus, in Moscow, at about the same time (1896), Maria Ermolova, the greatest Russian actress of the day, disturbed a conservative critic, spiritual cousin to the *Times* reviewer, because she portrayed Lady Macbeth as a suffering mortal, then a penitent sinner, instead of the traditional wicked fury untouched by remorse: "Ermolova evoked compassion; the public must be horror-stricken, and not compassionate." Other critical voices were happier that "Ermolova broke with many traditional interpretations: her Lady was not, from the beginning, a demonic fury, nor melodramatic wicked woman, nor a patient from a hospital." Though she created a powerful and majestic image, she sustained the image of wife, too: "Her highest ambition centered in the glory and majesty of her husband, whom she passionately loves. When she saw him suffering from remorse, her tenderness and love become still greater. But she tries to conceal from him her own suffering."

Some decades later in Russia, the attitudes would be mellow: Gogoleva (1955) would be praised because she so ardently loved her husband—though she knew his weaknesses, and exploited them so that he would be able to rise as, in her love for him, she felt he could.

In Germany, even after the success of such actresses as Wolter, a Lady Macbeth could be blamed because she was too ladylike: Louise Dumont (1906) "is a lady in her attitude and gestures: and yet this that is ordinarily an advantage for the actress is [in *Macbeth*] a disadvantage. This [Lady Macbeth] was somehow too soft—her love for her husband was more evident than her demonic component."

Against such views as the *Times'*, another remarkable Continental actress, Helena Modjeska (Modrzejewska) (Poland, 1890), "defended"—so one Polish observer declared—Lady Macbeth. In comments recalling Nouseul, Modjeska was seen as misplaying the text:

> She defended her devil not only against us but also against Shakespeare. In Shakespeare Lady Macbeth does not break down until the end of the play. . . . Lady Macbeth pretends she faints out of horror. . . . Modrzejewska stressed that Lady Macbeth really faints. Of course that would weaken our repulsion for her. But besides that, there was no scene in which she did not emphasize that there was a trace of humanity inside that monster.

Some American critics, used to Terrible Women, missed in Modjeska the fixed qualities, the high, intense, sustained notes; they scented danger in the lack of "imperious will, withering scorn, and dominating temper," in the "viola d'amore" voice.

> "A nervous, excitable temperament not often associated in the common mind with great tenacity of purpose. . . ." "Hysterical excitement rather than self-control and the might of a dominating will. . . . These evidences of womanly agitation are presented with admirable art and exquisite truthfulness, but they are not the commonly accepted attributes of Lady Macbeth."

Others sensed the presence of an "imperious will" expressed subtly, if not insistently. "Modjeska is always a regnant Lady Macbeth. She pleads with Macbeth, and by her pleading forces him to do her will. She commanded by the force of femininity." But should this force not be always sustained? So thought the traditionalists: "She occasionally relaxes the steel-like inflexibility which should be Lady Macbeth's one supreme characteristic; she is too much at the beck and call of her nerves."

As with Bernhardt, Modjeska's range of expression, her projection of a mind at work, and her quick, intense emotional responses, were a test both of the character design and of her audiences. All observers granted her passion, tenderness, melancholy, moments of fierceness and determination, her poignant sensibility; but was she terrible enough? If not, was her failure only seeming so in the eye of a beholder used to other styles—since some saw terror enough? Towse, evaluating her (and the range in the role):

> She can portray hauteur, anger or scorn, but not the frenzy of either rage or despair; she can be infinitely tender, and exquisitely pathetic . . . She can indicate the pangs of suppressed power with admirable and touching truthfulness, but the full expression of tragic grief or horror is not within her range.

To others, her vitality and intensity communicated the force that more traditional actresses conveyed with a higher style. With Modjeska's Lady "a gesture or move of the body discloses the workings of a turbulent mind. No loud speech, no declaiming, no pawing of the empty air, no screams." "She put a fine new edge upon [the] role." These were comments from America, where Bernhardt had not played and Terry would not play for several years. Morris's Lady had only been seen in the East. Modjeska, touring the country, came as a revelation. In California, a critic inured to Lady Macbeths of the "heavy, tragic ambition" welcomed Modjeska's as the only one "who drew from me profound pity." More than pity, and much gratitude, was felt in Boston—and, as usual with the spectator's first experience of a "Loving Wife," we get a sense of a Cortez standing upon an unsuspected peak:

> She conceives the character not as that of a portentous and more or less repellent old woman, but as that of a youngish, ardent, loving wife. It is wonderful what a new illumination is thrown into the beauty of the play, . . . [to] vivify and increase the tenderness and closeness of her relation with the guilty hero and his crimes, and give new meaning to his lines as well as her own. . . . Instead of the traditional grim, consciously important, statuesque, removed and fateful figure . . . Madame Modjeska gives one not less but still more power, but with the power of impulsive, intense action of varied, realistic nuances, of intimate appeal to our common nature, that transform this old stage statue into a human—and very human—being, a living woman, loved and loving, and because she shares every thought and feeling with her husband [played by the poet-philosopher, Booth], going with him every length, . . . keeping him to the sticking point from sheer feminine infatuation with her wifely duty, though she sickens and faints at the tale of the murder and has to brace herself, in order to brace him, with wine, for the murder of Duncan, and finally dies of horror while he lives on.

Like Bernhardt, Modjeska brought a special feminine élan to the character that seemed then almost the special gift of European Lady Macbeths. It could explain the need of—as well as the energy for—the invocation of defeminizing spirits:

> The buoyant eagerness for action, the elastic tension to leap the bloody gap between her and her imperial state, figure themselves in a smile of confident and happy daring, and joy . . . this suffuses her countenance. . . . This

bounding, glad, unhesitating, straining, reckless purpose envelops her like a mystery, and gives sharp meaning to her prayer that the powers of air shall unsex her, for she is not already hard and masculine in disposition, but wholly a woman, with a woman's mentality and a woman's splendid vitality of intent.

In Poland (and perhaps also in Boston, but not commented on there) her "joy" was seen to have a strongly sexual basis:

Modrezejewska enriched her creation with subcutaneous eroticism. Though not explicit, it could be felt. . . . she not exactly incites [Macbeth] but enchants; and in this enchantment the sexuality flowed from the sensual satiety of her voice and from her glance full of promises.

An even more paradoxical polyphony was seen in her 1891 characterization in Czechoslovakia: "Half queen, half predatory animal, Modjeska presses Macbeth to the crime, then supports him when he is weak—a majestic, if evil, goddess."

From the visits of Modjeska and Terry in the United States in the 1890s, American actresses gained new insights into Lady Macbeth and new freedom to express them. In the early twentieth century, Julia Marlowe, fortunate enough to play the role often, discovered variations in the Loving Wife. To audiences that still remembered Janauschek's "rearing, tearing virago," brow-beating her husband into murder, and who were more recently accustomed to Nance O'Neil's masterful, masculine domination of Macbeth (U.S., 1904), in imitation of Charlotte Cushman, Julia Marlowe's loamy interpretation, instinct with pride and dignity, but deepened by an earth-born devotion to her husband, came welcomely as "new." She demonstrated that the aspects of majesty and of a wife's love were two contrasting elements that sometimes could succeed each other, sometimes coalesce:

To the world she is a woman of high place, accustomed to receive the respect and regard of those who are of her rank . . . she is to the world a queen. It is only to her husband that she is the adoring, self-sacrificing, clinging wife.

Her commitment to Macbeth was whole-souled, and by it she made the whole design "comprehensible," according to several grateful observers:

This *new* Lady Macbeth touches . . . the life of our times . . . a woman whose sun rises and sets in her husband, against whose absorbing love for her "man" no moral scruples, no feminine tenderness, no maternal weakness either for her own children or anybody else's would weigh for a moment. Such women may be met with in the world today.

To such a representation of a woman, murderous ambition, instead of being native, came as a kind of aberration of love. Fierce she could make herself, but the only time she seemed approaching the "fiendish" was in the force she brought to images like *I have given suck.* . . . She was temporarily exhilarated by the suggestion of greatness, but thereafter anguish-stricken by the spectacle of the horrors she had precipitated.

> Her haggard, tearful face, her furtive touching of her husband's hand, her constant secret interference to encourage restraint, or remind him in moments of crises . . . showed the part in a new light.

Where Terry had even been playful in her ardor, and Bernhardt and Modjeska youthfully sensual, Marlowe was more mature, "heavy, dark, voluptuous," stipulating a climate of having lived with and loved Macbeth, body and mind, over some years. She was said to have added a breadth of passion beyond Terry's. The equation with her Macbeth made passion easier: Terry had to play against a Macbeth who was unmistakably, by intention, a villain, who manipulated her; Marlowe's Macbeth, E. H. Sothern (her husband), played a brave, introspective soldier turned remorseful murderer, "eager for his wife's caresses, . . . ready to weep" for guilt—an effective pattern of romantic-tragic heroism. Lady Macbeth could meet him on even terms as one who had long been a brave, noble mate and companion.

If Marlowe's Lady was "past her first youth," as a Boston critic delicately put it, "the days of amorous transports behind," her love was still unmistakably alive—perhaps as much so as an American actress could demonstrate then: for the same Boston critic noticed that "she still knows and plies the insinuation of the toying hand . . . her intimate emotions lie a deep pool within."

As well as projecting lover and wife, Marlowe touched a further dimension: "Her love for Macbeth was of a quasi-maternal quality found often in marriage. She soothed and steadied him, and kept guard over his treacherous nerves." Other Ladies would find in the design this touch of the mother.

In the days when actresses established great reputations in tragedy, and, as Lady Macbeth, dominated their noble husbands with power, or love, or both, unless the Macbeth was also a great actor his role might subside, as with Kemble, into the "co-operating part." So it often was with the Macbeths playing opposite Siddons, Schröder, Ristori, Modjeska, et al. But as the dark, murderous tones in Macbeth's score came commonly to be heard, as well as the more kindly ones, and as audiences came to welcome the recognizable humanity of the Lady, her role, except when acted by exceptional women, usually became at most equal, and often subsidiary. This was especially true as the twentieth century wore on, when actresses generally had no more than one try at the characterization, and little chance to establish reputations in tragedy. But Lady Macbeths have gone on exploring nuances in the design, psychological, sexual, occult. The softer side, of the Loving Wife, has usually sounded unmistakably, with emphasis on her vulnerability, her various female roles, even her domesticity.

Too great an emphasis on softness has carried the danger of blandness, and Lady Macbeth's stature has been endangered; particularly when the actress herself regarded the role as secondary. "I do not think that Lady Macbeth is a very great part," Martita Hunt, Gielgud's first Lady (1930) commented. "I used to dream of [it] as one of the most thrilling that any actress could have to interpret . . . one of the most complete . . . [but] the importance of Lady Macbeth is entirely relative to Macbeth himself. She is only significant in the play as an influence on him." Hunt could sense a "great sentiment . . . great feeling as man and wife" between Lady Macbeth and her husband, but not, beyond this, an inherent, heroic capacity for suffering. If only he had continued impervious to the qualms of conscience or nerves: "I still believe that if Macbeth could have treated the whole matter as she treated it [after the murder], she might have remained a contented woman, unharassed by remorse. Listen to what she says to him: 'How now, my Lord! Why do you keep alone . . . Things without all remedy Should be without regard.' "

This would reflect an extreme of the loving wife, not only lacking insight into her husband, but also without tragic depth of her own. She persuades her husband to bite the apple because she thinks this will be the happiest thing for him; and she would be a happy sharer in murder if he would be. She destroys him out of mistaken love, and is destroyed herself by events.

Gielgud's second Lady, Gwen Ffrangcon-Davies (1942) also saw herself mainly in domestic terms, though with a touch of strangeness: "Lady Macbeth is not a Clytemnestra or a Medea . . . she is a wife and mother . . . and a Celt. And being Celtish, she is rather fey." The emphasis on the softer notes evoked from observers some of the old calls for more terror, more mass; indeed the complaints from a half dozen reviewers make up a large catalogue of the dangers facing a small actress with a light voice who plays a bland Loving Wife:

> being tiny, she had none of the usual cold, statuesque dignity . . . never suggesting absolute and unscrupulous wickedness . . . her emphasis shifting from the woman of "undaunted metal" to a lady with a persuasive personality . . . she neither hounded her husband to murder nor was savagely devoted to him. Instead of a tiger burning bright, there was a kitten.

To leave out the darker tones, resonating with the impulse or calculation fierce enough to consider murder, seriously limits the complex chording. Concerned as Ffrangcon-Davies was with the Lady's appeal for Macbeth—"she must have been lovable, or he would not have said 'My dearest love,' his first words to her"—she herself became, in Agate's surprised words, "too likeable" (surprised because she had prepared him for something more sinister). Perhaps the cruellest cut of all was another appraisal of her Lady: "a thoroughly nice little woman."

THE MATERNAL LADY

In the intricate polyphony of the character, as we noted, more than one actress has heard the motherly strain, and sounded it at least softly in the persuasion scenes and at the end of III, ii and III, iv, the Lady's last chances to support Macbeth privately. Some Lady Macbeths, committed to comfort more than castigation, have, like Marlowe, let the mother come out strong. Where the Lady herself is satisfying neurotic emotional needs, she may need to speak to Macbeth as to a child, as the anxious Margaret Johnston (England, 1966) sometimes did. She may be somewhat older—may, as in Czechoslovakia (1958), from her evident maturity guide a young, lyrical Macbeth who seeks in dreadful deeds to win maternal approval as well as marital admiration. The difference in age must have been explicit when Siddons played the role to her son's Macbeth, and also, in the first American staging (1759), when a mother and son played the chief roles.

Where the equation has focused on the wife-mother shelter of the insecure man-child, as with Plummer's Macbeth, Kate Reid (Canada, 1962) infused her mature strength and determination with a kind of patient tenderness for the neurotic husband who hid his face in her lap when he could not face his thoughts. This accords with that psychologically-oriented criticism which has discovered not only a terrible "hated mother" in Lady Macbeth, but also a seductress-mother, to whom the man turns when in fear and frustration he regresses to infantile dependence; here she may also be seen as another face of the witch-mother—cousin to the Weird Sisters—whose solacing magic he also seeks for security, only to be seduced by it into destruction.

In the theatre, when the maternal is sounded, it is usually as a modulating tone in the Loving Wife's personality; if explicit enough to call attention to itself, as in some productions, it troubles observers: it needs to dissolve into the chord. Agate noted that Flora Robson (England, 1934), after asking to be unsexed, promptly began to mother her Macbeth. Most critics and most actresses (except the most Terrible of women) would probably agree that Lady Macbeth in her plea, or command, to be defeminized—that is, to escape womanly tenderness and compunction—is ultimately denied her wish (if it was indeed a wish and not a heavy obligation, perhaps assumed with reluctance and even distaste). Her womanhood keeps insisting on its birthright. So with Judi Dench's young Lady (England, 1976), so intensely devoted to her Macbeth (McKellen) that for him she dared invoke the murdering ministers, though her dread of the act was almost unbearable. When, after Duncan's murder, her husband returned gibbering, near collapse, she comforted him and soothed him in her embrace as she would a terrified child: evidently this Lady had learned motherhood when she had given suck.

THE CHILD LADY

Faintly sometimes, from deep in Lady Macbeth—most often when her mask has dropped in the sleepwalk—sounds a note of the buried child, who lived more innocently in her once. In sleep particularly the eye of childhood, that when awake she scorns, may open on the terror she has made. This has been so even with those Ladies (like Reid's) conspicuously aged between the banquet and the sleepwalk. As if they are suddenly regressed, the note of the bewildered girl mingles with the pain of the woman-wife who knows too clearly what she has done. The bed she would return to may be the image of many beds, infantile, parental, marital, death. Her sudden vulnerability, sometimes hinted in the privacies of Act III, has been voiced by Lady Macbeths of all designs; and with much contrast from those whose mask has most hidden it. (Thus a magnificent barbarian, returning to the voice of childhood; a sophisticated court lady giving way to a girl's anguish; another, her brittle facade broken, lamenting with childish innocence.)

How young the Lady Macbeth is who moves—or moves with—her husband into murder must affect the key of her polyphony. No clues are given to her age, except that she has given suck to a child, that she can still bear children, and that she is married to an accomplished warrior who, near the end of the play, will have fallen into the sere, the yellow leaf (though this may be psychic aging). Bradley locates her, as noted, with Macbeth, as young middle-aged; and she has generally been represented in theatre and criticism as mature. But young actresses have played her; and since Bernhardt, whose youth so impressed observers, the image of a youthful Lady has been frequent in the theatre.

Bernhardt was about forty when she played the Lady, but in her simple, tight-fitting costume she seemed younger; and she was matched with a Macbeth, Marais, who also gave the impression of youth—excitable, impatient, given to roaring out his moments of tension, to counter her sensuous rhythms.

The Danish actress Johanne Luise Heiberg (1860) was herself not young when she came to play Macbeth, but she felt certain, after years of study, that youth was one of the character's primary qualities:

> What in a young Lady Macbeth is a flare of passion will in an elderly, experienced actress appear as a deep-seated, demonic power of evil. This was the way she had always been represented . . . But this tradition . . . is a fallacious conception . . . Macbeth exclaims, when   she passionately exhorts him to murder the king, "Bring forth men-children only." This outburst would be downright comical and unbecoming in front of an older woman . . . [it] seems to me to indicate with certainty that they have not been married for long . . . But if so, then we must see her as a young woman.

Youth would lend to some Ladies the charm of vulnerability, and earn them sympathy, even when touched with evil—like the child-wife, Francesca Annis, in the Polanski film (1971), who cried hurt tears when her young husband denied her the murder that would bring the promised crown, but who grew older in spirit in her young body, and weary in it, as she learned what it was she had begged for. But youth would not necessarily assure sympathy for the characterization: the youthful 1964 Polish Lady Macbeth, Mikolajczuk, was like a girl from a gang, a blonde terror, thirsting for action, sharp-edged in speech and movement. Of such a murderous youngster Grzgorz

Sinko wrote: "A sweet little simperer awaits Macbeth (in I, v). Judging by her carefree, joyful outburst after having received the letter, getting rid of Duncan is small beer." Actresses playing young Lady Macbeths can only do so for a limited span of years. If they go on longer, they must change: thus Wolter, at first very sensual in her interpretation, then, as she grew older, more "heroic," more distanced. Unfortunately, again, most twentieth-century Ladies could not make a career of Shakespeare's tragic roles, and played the part only once.

THE SENSUAL LADY

Young actors were partly essential, Ingmar Bergman believed, to convey Macbeth's sensual dependence on his Lady; and certainly in the twentieth-century Lady Macbeths have made their sexuality an increasingly open weapon in their persuasion of their husbands to murder—and sometimes in support of their husbands afterwards. We saw that Bernhardt's Lady at first shocked some Victorian English tastes; and we can understand that Bradley should find not the "faintest trace in the play of the idea . . . to some extent embodied in Madame Bernhardt's impersonation of Lady Macbeth, that her hold upon her husband lay in seductive attractions deliberately exercised."* But that "amorous" interpretation was often to be followed, and even more "deliberately." By 1972 in Denmark, so essential would sexuality seem to the design that several reviewers faulted an Odense Lady Macbeth who lacked it. The tremendous vitality that almost all actresses have discovered in the role, an imperious energy to dominate, a fierce passion to love, an absolute commitment to the drive for the crown—for Macbeth, if not for herself, or for both—has frequently expressed itself partly in a warm and lavish physical relationship contributory to the play's latent association of sexuality with violence and death.

France, again, provides a fine example in the greatest of its twentieth-century interpreters, Maria Casarès, "all instinct and passion." Casarès played the role in successive years (1954–55) and her sensual equations with her two different Macbeths differed interestingly. Her first, Vilar, indrawn, "reached far too early the 'tomorrow and tomorrow' stage" (Jacquot); when he bade her come to bed, a sad tenderness was mixed with his evident physical desire. The relationship evoked those descriptions cited earlier: "obsession sexuelle" and "envoutement charnel." The implication was, Jacquot observed, that Macbeth killed Duncan to make sure his wife would admit him to her bed. (Jacquot felt that Vilar was deliberately playing to critics looking for eroticism in the play.) Casarès' second Macbeth, Cuny, was brutish and impulsive where Vilar had been introspective and imaginative; and where Vilar's sub-

---

*In Henry James' dialogue, "After the Play," Dorriforth thinks differently: "I should never think . . . of contesting an actress's right to represent Lady Macbeth as a charming, insinuating woman . . . I may be surprised at such a vision; but so far from being scandalized, I am positively thankful for the extension of knowledge, of pleasure, that she is able to open to me."

mission to Casarès' "carnality" had a breath of the spiritual, Cuny's was frankly physical, he clung to Casarès' sensual Lady, held to her by dependence on her strength, but also by powerful "carnal ties."

The Lady who is intensely and sincerely sexually in love with her husband tells us something different about the character than the one who deliberately uses sexuality as a weapon. Derková (Czechoslovakia, 1962) seemed to submerge herself in her vision of glory for Macbeth—whom she served with such sensual devotion it was described as "erotic drunkenness." A manipulating Lady like Wegener's Hermine Korner (Germany, 1916) could couple a lust for power with a passionate love, and use her charms—her blonde hair and her beautiful body—to serve her double purpose. The seductive Lady whose selfish ambition is primary, and who exploits Macbeth's desire, is closer to the deadly temptress shaped by myth and legend, more vicious than the well-intentioned Eve. She is dangerously beautiful, perhaps comes in the mythic form of a hotly erotic female demon, despoiling man with her lust. So the succubus, the siren, La Belle Dame Sans Merci; and deeper in the mists may hover the image of the seductress-mother. Faint undertones of this haunting archetype may undulate from any experience of Macbeth seduced into murder; but where a Terrible Woman who is also voluptuous enthralls Macbeth sexually, the motif asserts itself. Thus Christine Schrader (Germany, 1971), demonic, unscrupulous, boundless in her ambition and her craving for power, yet supple and sensual enough to bewitch into subservience her Macbeth—Horst Mehring, playing a man of strong erotic yearning to balance the equation.

The sensual Lady has also played against neurotic men who would be moving toward madness: so Coral Browne's "voluptuary" opposite Rogers' driven Macbeth (1956), and Helen Mirren's climate of seduction enveloping the anxiety-twisted Williamson (1974). Is there some reverberation, in such equations, of the hot determination of the Sister to drain her victim dry?

As might be expected, stress on the Lady's sexuality would be accompanied by increasing display of nubility. Dress would be deliberately revealing: so with Wanamaker's Lady, first seen in a black "bacchante" gown slit up on either side to the hip, with a neckling plunging to the waist. Rosemary Murphy (U.S., 1973), somewhat similarly dressed, emphasized her physicality by stroking her breasts and thighs. Among other resonances of this kind of physical imagery, the play's deep-lying association between sex and death may be one.

To be *unsexed* in Shakespeare's time would not have all its later connotations of losing not only womanliness but also copulative identity, a most terrible prospect. However, sex did mean that which distinguished women and men; and in this, sexuality is a primary factor. For Lady Macbeth to sustain her sexuality would be one way of resisting her complex, overt wish to abdicate her femininity.

THE "UPWARD-MOBILE" LADY

Inevitably, in a twentieth-century that would come to prize "upward mobility," alike in nature—if not in technique—to Macbeth's thrust to the top, Lady Macbeth would become a kind of "corporation wife," intelligent, calculating, shrewd strategist of her husband's career, skilled tactician with his superiors, a beautiful, charming hostess, good in bed. This design was articulated by Viola Allen (U.S., 1916) who acted with Hackett:

> Lady Macbeth has always been taken as the type of scheming woman . . .
> viciously ambitious and selfishly cruel. But to some she represents the modern
> politician's wife. I do not mean that the wives of the men who administer the
> affairs of our country are murderesses, but being a murderess was not Lady
> Macbeth's chief business after all; it was one of the tragic accidents of her career.
> Everything she did, you know, she did for her husband's sake, and not for her
> own. Certainly he suggested the death of Duncan . . . her resolute fidelity to
> the plan which she thought was in her husband's best behalf, has something
> about it that is distinctly feminine, and in spite of the perverted morals of the
> idea, almost admirable.

Sybil Thorndike somewhat similarly saw Macbeth and his Lady (she told Bartholomeusz) as " 'big capitalists' in a tragic partnership."

Like the Terrible Woman, this Lady may know she knows better than her husband, but will manage, instead of compelling, him. Allen's characterization was protective, tender, sometimes maternal: she coaxed and patronized her Macbeth, treated him sometimes like a spoiled child who must be guided to what he wanted.

This design can convey a cold terror of its own: when, from behind the attractive surfaces of a recognizable social image, something of the same, fixed, fearful determination radiates that energized the more traditional Terrible Woman. So Vivien Merchant, Paul Scofield's Lady (1967), beautiful in a trim, sophisticated way, her mouth tightening into a savage, civilized, triumphant smile as she manipulated her husband, moving herself and him with a crisp, confident certainty—even a kind of soignée brutality—toward their common disaster. For the lost power and magnitude of the terrible heroic image, this design can offer the intense experience of the terrible familiar.

THE LADY POSSESSED

Like Macbeth, his Lady traffics with spirits. Whether she has known them, is in some way one of them, has been visited by them, is now suddenly drawn to think of them, or reaches out in fear, joy, hope, or desperation, she prays for a transaction with them that will expedite her ambition. Once her plea is made, what then? She makes no other move toward them, or even acknowledges their presence—except as they may be sensed as a force in her disintegration. In Germany, in the eighteenth century, as a motivation for a Terrible

Woman she was made to seem a kind of fourth witch; and other actresses since have allowed resonances, if not demonstrations, of their kinship with the evil supernatural—so Segond-Weber saw herself of the witches.

If Lady Macbeth is not a witch, is she possessed by them, or their agents, or masters? Made a "fiend"? Walker and W. M. Merchant see her as indeed demonic, possessed: "a fiend in limb and motion" (Walker); "a willed submission to the demonic" (Merchant). She is called a "fiend" once in the play, but the implication is not supernatural. Malcolm, a perhaps guileful witness, calls her *fiendlike*, on what evidence we do not know, since she is never seen, by others in the play, to do anything even unladylike*; and the attendants at her sleepwalking seem not to know any more than what her dream may imply. Margaret Webster wrote that the spirits "use her, possess her, just exactly as she had prayed them to do; they make of her a creature as relentless as she had desired." Webster saw them as agents of the evil drenching the play: "Evil is alive of itself, a protagonist in its own right." Webster had a chance, when she played the Lady for Edward Carrick Craig (1932), to try to realize her vision; to call the spirits to her so that, in her words "we can almost hear the soft beat of wings." The Sisters in fact visibly hovered around Heidemarie Hatheyer's (Austria, 1964) Lady in her invocation scene. They stretched out their brooms toward her, with a hint of symbiotic infusion. A strong erotic note in her persuasion of Macbeth, noticed by Heinz Kindermann, and the intense urgency of her drive toward murder, could seem partly motivated by the dark impulses associated with witches.

If Eleanor Calhoun (U.S., 1916) had been allowed to produce the play as well as act Lady Macbeth (as she did for Ben Greet), she would have taken the part of Hecate as well (in disguise), she felt such an identification with the spirit she had invoked.

> Only when the deed is done and Hecate has ridden away across the moon does that fire begin to fall back out of her veins and the cold reality come down like snow . . . the glorious palaced realms of the self intoxicated mind utterly vanish and are gone, flown like witches in the night, and simple human truth remains, and takes her by all its bitter stormy way down to the tomb.

The distinctions are delicate between possession and signs like it—trance, obsession, raptness, the blankness of despair, the slavery of somnambulism—and madness. Actresses have ranged among these nuances, some more in spirit with the witches than others. The "Loving Wife" who reaches beyond her normal context to make contact with a dark world she has never known must do so with an uncanny apprehension different from the determined Lady who thinks she acts (as Hatheyer did) from her own cold ambition when in fact her strings move to the witches' pull. And different, too, from the fierce,

---

*Except possibly in her subtextual behavior in the banquet scene; but the design there seems to dictate a managed facade to cover with more or less success her anxiety; and so it has been commonly staged.

Terrible Woman who seems to command the unknown. Where one German actress, Ida Roland (1937), interpreted the Lady as demonic, subtextually in touch with the witches, and acting as if in mysterious communication with their world and another, Ursula Lingen (Munich, 1977) was a *besessene*, possessed by the *Oberhexe* Hecate, a third, Charlotte Joeres (1955), a flaming, voracious overreacher, a "monster grown out of barely Christianised soil," seemed herself a queen of chthonic stuff as she summoned the spirits to her purpose.

THE LADY AS BARBARIAN

Like Macbeth, his Lady has been called a product of a primitive world; but only in her invitation to the spirits does she seem, even to the twentieth century, of a backward time. In Shakespeare's world, where many believed in witchcraft, and "wise women" and men like Simon Forman flourished, her invocation was not archaic. Elsewhere, as with Macbeth, her language and manners belong to as gracious and "modern" a court as that of any of Shakespeare's kings. Efforts to suggest the barbarian in the theatre—as by Flora Robson, against Michael Redgrave's primitive Scot—have failed Lady Macbeth's polyphony. Not only because Robson was a loving, even maternal Lady; but because Shakespeare's "gentle Lady," the "fair and noble hostess" must seem to deserve those lines: surely Macduff and Duncan speak them without irony. Muriel Bradbrook has suggested that Shakespeare learned Lady Macbeth's capacity for violence from Holinshed's account of Scotswomen who carefully suckled their babies, but also went into battle to slay the enemy, then bathe their swords in blood and taste it. Bradbrook sees here the reciprocation of tenderness and barbarity, suckling and bloodshed. Inga-Stina Ewbank observed, however, that the women with children did not go into the fighting; in any case, nothing about the women in *Macbeth* suggests that they belong anywhere but in a civilized court—certainly not on a battlefield. Lady Macbeth may do barbaric things, but not as a barbarian; no amount of dressing her in romantic trappings of the past can disguise a speech and manner suitable for an elegant court. When she is cruel, the essence of her cruelty, like Macbeth's, is that a "civilized" person commits it, it affronts a *gentle weal* long since officially purged of violence by *humane statute*.

THE NERVE-DRIVEN LADY

Some twentieth-century actresses have accentuated a motif latent in earlier characterizations of the Lady—a kind of desperate inner unease. Thus Modjeska: "extreme nervous excitement, almost intolerable tension—her very hair seemed nervous." This unease, intensified, has been expressed as relentless compulsion to act, to escape thought. It may take the form, before the murder, of a kind of manic ecstasy that would give way to depression as well as deterioration.

Freud, again, is relevant here, in his reference to those neurotics who could not stand the success they had labored for. Certainly both Macbeths are restless on their thrones. Macbeth finds himself driven by a need to murder further to ensure security—both Freud and Hecate see that this need can be man's chiefest enemy; but Macbeth, at least, reacts to what seem present dangers, while Lady Macbeth, not feeling threatened as he does, yet painfully senses that too high a price has been paid for the crowns:

> Nought's had, all's spent,
> Where our desire is got without content. (III, ii, 8–9)

The worm that gnaws at the Lady is conventionally called conscience, a sense of guilt, remorse, the agenbite of inwit; was it, or a cousin worm of discontent, at work from the very beginning? Would anything give this Lady's life content? Is she on the edge of madness, as Edith Sitwell suggested?

Another of Freud's suggestions, that Lady Macbeth's worm was her barrenness, was of course faulty: she proclaims that she has "given suck" and she could hardly be imagined serving tenderly as wet nurse to another woman's child (see Appendix). More interesting is the possibility in the design of some compulsion, for instance to destroy—others or, suicidally, herself. A relevant, curiously subtle remark was made of Mrs. Kean's rather unsubtle Lady (1853), who seemed ordinarily a modest mixture of the wilful and the "fascinating": the "appalling intensity" of her face as she lured Macbeth to murder suggested a "hunger for guilt." Freud would have been pleased.

Of the distinguished actresses who made the climate of neurosis a ground note in the design—though, alas, almost none would play it more than once— I will discuss a few whose visual imagery will illuminate some of the lines. All touched the tone of latent terror of a mind that would be—if it was not from the beginning—diseased. The madness that is at least a grace note in all of Shakespeare's overreachers is heard by some critics to sound particularly loudly in Lady Macbeth's end; actresses teach us that the condition for madness, if not its presence, may whisper early in the play. These Ladies may seek it; or beckon it to come.

If the neurosis is far enough advanced, the Lady will seem destined for breakdown the moment she first appears, as was one of Hackett's Lady Macbeths, Clare Eames (U.S., 1924). "She has cut and scratched every inch of softness from the role; there is nothing on the bones of it but twitching, blazing nerves." Her wriggling, nervously intense Lady served as a kind of foil to Hackett's amorous, majestic Macbeth; but her characterization emphasized a danger to the equation: how could so unstable a woman persuade her Macbeth to crime?

Margaret Leighton (England, 1952) escaped this problem because her Macbeth, Ralph Richardson, was so spongy: in Tynan's words, "it would be easier
to strike sparks off a rubber dinghy than Sir Ralph." Against his blandness,
her angular design stood out:

> "a creature taut of nerve, jerky in action, unbalanced in mind and strident in
> voice from the start . . ."; "an unnatural creature, wild, staring-eyed . . . never
> completely in control of herself, she hovers on the verge of madness and hysteria
> throughout the whole play . . ."; ". . . serpentine, petulant, and agonised."

One descriptive, "brittle," would be used for other neurotic Ladies as well as
Leighton; and it suggests to us one of the dangers of this emphasis in the design. The Lady Macbeth who rides on nerves, on the edge of cracking, may
miss some of the tones of blood-chilling awe and terror. "Too much of the
neurotic, and not enough of the tigress." "We recognize this creature of baleful
beauty and serpentine grace as both deadly and doomed. But we watch it with
fascination rather than with awe; it is lethal, it is lovely, but it is not very
large." Some observers found Leighton too delicate of spirit for ruthlessness;
the *Daily Worker*, wishing for a meaner oppressor-queen, claimed that "unfortunately we are offered a Lady Macbeth in whom the milk of human kindness
runs like a flood."

Margaret Johnston's Lady suffered even more from her nerves. From the
very beginning she was "voraciously neurotic and distraught" . . . "turbulent
and unbalanced." She, too, seemed continuously on the edge of a nervous
breakdown:

> never for a moment does she relax . . . Even when not speaking . . . her silent
> screams [suggest] a convulsion of emotion . . . no question of her simulating
> collapse after Duncan's murder . . . a hysteric and amateur murderess . . .
> goading herself as much as her husband . . . the will is Macbeth's, hers the
> appetite which works on it. She is the jackal leading the lion to the kill, quickly
> gorged and sickened by the blood which whets his hunger . . . you feel she
> might *really* go mad.

As if life itself had some revulsion for her, she seemed "in the grip of a permanent nausea." Indeed, when Macbeth came bloody-handed from the
murder, she doubled over, retching. And yet this somber, curdled note was
accompanied by one of passionate love, even lust, for her husband, whom
she incited with a kind of hysteria. Drawn and dragged by her passions, she
did not so much break as follow down into madness.

"Brittle" was the descriptive of choice for Diana Rigg's Lady (England,
1973). Beautiful, but with a controlled, rigid, almost doll-like beauty; quiet,
implacably quiet, cold, rigorous, pale-faced, deadly. She seemed not a lover
to her Macbeth, more a partner in a cruel enterprise, driven to drive him to it.
A profane impulse tightened her resolution: holding her crucifix as she prepared to beg unsexing, she coolly inverted it and spat upon it. Early on her
tension was subtextual, storming under her tight-lipped mask; the very ex-

tremity of her control told of forces that had to be controlled, of insecurity, fragility. After the murder, she seemed inwardly to disintegrate, though she labored to preserve the mask—the sallowing cheeks wildly rouged, the mouth fixed in a grin, the movements almost puppet-like, as if forced through a trance. By the time of the banquet scene, this Lady was clearly on the way from her early compulsiveness to the dissolution of the sleepwalking that then seemed only inevitable madness. This Lady Macbeth did not need success to discontent her.

Rigg's first Macbeth, Hopkins, was at first a nervous match for her—an ambitious, envious thane, shifty and uneasy, planning murder, then caught up in killing and bullying to keep himself safe. Denis Quilley, replacing Hopkins, played an extrovert bully from the first, who used her, body and spirit, as he tried to use the rest of his world. She was not a lover to this Macbeth, either: they seemed "two careerists who happen to live together, rather than a couple. . . . Their collusion in murder was perhaps the greatest intimacy of their marriage."

Actresses and critics have gone far toward exploring Lady Macbeth's polar extremes and much of the deep, complex, tangled terrain that separates them. Moving mainly between the deep base of the Terrible Woman who yields to her humanity, and the higher, more lyrical notes of the Loving Wife who forces herself to be terrible—to do violence to her own nature—for her husband's sake, both theatre and criticism continue to fill in the subtle, many-toned polyphony of the Lady's design.

We will see how this has been done.

Leave all the rest to me.

Act I, Scene v

Again, we cut from large pageantry to an intimate scene. A woman is alone, with a letter. Rarely does a solitary woman appear in the great tragedies, never in her first entrance, never introduced with the self-disclosure this one will now make. We guess she is Macbeth's lady—married to the strange, remarkable Macbeth we have met, who is hastening to make her joyful.

The moment she appears—or is imagined to appear—visual signals begin to shape her character in our minds before she says a word. The room to which she enters says something. At the Globe, it might have been an inner or curtained chamber, opening to her the moment the larger stage was emptied. When, in later times, the room, or other acting area, is large, perhaps another part of a vast castle, the Lady needs commensurate authority to control her space; while a more intimate, enclosed area partly domesticates her, as with Terry and Violet Vanbrugh (England, 1911), and she domesticates it. Margaret Anglin (U.S., 1928) understood this when she asked Gordon Craig to design a small chamber with a door which she could swiftly bolt—so she could stand for a moment before moving to the fireplace to finish reading her letter—the latter business an echo of the imagery of Terry, Craig's mother. The locking of the door would give her a moment to establish her identity, make the room her domain, and declare the importance of privacy for her reading of the letter; Craig liked this, even to adding a key to the door. If the scene opens, as with Komisarjevsky, with the letter delivered by a servant— by a lame Seyton in Japan—the motif of service is sounded, but at a loss of Shakespeare's concentration on Lady Macbeth *solus*.

A woman marching in with a paper gripped in her hand, stinging her fingers, tells something different from one sitting and reading as the scene opens. Sensuous Ladies have been discovered lying on a bed, on the floor, on furs, on animal hides: each couch a comment also on the kind of life and castle they inhabit. This is the interior of a place Duncan will much admire for its serenity, and realistic scenery must take this into account: so G. B. Shaw urged that Pat Campbell bully her producer to make the "scene painter put in a martin's nest or two over the castle windows." On a bare stage the actress can create the atmosphere. Stylized settings, if cold and angular, threaten the irony that murderous thoughts take place in a castle so warm that martlets seek it to procreate—and may be heard to sing outside. Because Duncan speaks in the next scene of the castle's appearance, the time is assumed to be day, and is sometimes so represented. But Duncan will come with torches, the Folio directs, so this could be a dusk scene, and allow Lady Macbeth a candle—a foreshadowing of a light she will later need, when she may again want to look at the paper she now holds. If it is late day, darkness has been seen beginning to come down when the Lady invokes night.

How the Lady appears, her manner of movement, expression, and dress, immediately telegraph an image setting up controlled expectation. By her very formidable appearance, and the haste of her sudden entrance, Siddons' portentous Lady—and others like her—proclaim the dominating force the Terrible Woman must exert. *Blackwood's*, in 1834, tells what we would see:

> Those who beheld Mrs. Siddons could not possibly imagine the [character] embodied in any other shape. That tall, commanding and majestic figure—that face so sternly beautiful, with its firm lips and large dark eyes—that brow capacious of a wide world of thought, overshadowed by a still gloom of coal-black hair—that low, clear, measured, deep voice, audible in whispers—so portentously expressive of strength of will, and a will to evil—the stately tread . . . the motion of those arms and hands, seeming moulded for empiry— all these distinguished the Thane's wife from other women, to our senses, our soul, and our imaginations, as if nature had made Siddons for Shakespeare's sake, that she might impersonate to the height his sublimest and most dreadful conception.

To Boaden she hardly seemed a woman when she came on:

> such was the impression from her form, her face, her deportment—the distinction of sex was only external—her spirits informed their tenement with the apathy of a demon.

To make so awesome a woman *joyful* will require a magnificent Macbeth. For Siddons, magnificence indeed seemed to be in the letter. She hurried in as if she had just glanced over it, and eager to escape from her crowd of attendants to read it carefully alone. Some words quickly struck her; she came forward a few paces and began to read aloud. (Lady Macbeth, breaking into the middle of the message, at once tells us something of Macbeth. *In the day of success*, he writes. Success, great feats, dreadful deeds—such achievements are important to him, and his wife knows it.)

Artist that she was, Siddons kept her excitement in check for a few lines, to build to the climax of her first beat; though she very quickly breathed the supernatural atmosphere of the letter:

> I have learn'd by the *perfect'st* report,
> they have *more* in them, than mortal
> knowledge. (3–5)*

She emphasized *more*. This would almost oblige her to stress the assonantal pun in the succeeding *mortal*. With the commas after *report* and *them*, this gives the prose almost the rhythm of irregular verse, suitable to the adventure in otherworldliness that Lady Macbeth now pursues. Siddons pointed this with her reading of the next words:

> When I burnt in desire to question them
> further, they made themselves air, into
> which they vanish'd. (5–6)

She paused before *air*—"as if", Galt thought, "doubtful of the term employed"; then said it "in a tone of wonder"—with a "little suspension of the voice" (Boaden). Knowles (perhaps commenting tangentially on her fellow actors):

in the look and tone . . . you recognized ten times the wonder with which Macbeth and Banquo actually beheld the vanishing witches.

Blackwood's has her topping this climax with another:

As she was about to pronounce *vanish'd* she paused, drew a short breath, her whole frame was disturbed, she threw her fine eyes upward, and exclaimed the word with a wild force, which showed that the whole spirit of the temptation had shrunk into her soul. Her *Hail, king* . . . was the winding up of a spell, pronounced with the grandeur of one already by anticipation a queen.

From now on, all agreed, she began to loose the torrent of power in her: "the demon of the character took possession" (Galt).

The foremost American Siddons, Cushman, even more massive and foreboding, also hurried on—"in unseemly haste and horror," making no allowance for any "reflection, any ruminations." Here we confront one of the first decisions the actress must make: is she now to read the letter for the first time? Has she glanced at it, and is now absorbing it? Has she read it, and is now deeply experiencing what it says? Siddons had read enough to excite her, and on stage let her excitement mount until, in her words, ambition had all but obliterated her humanity. Cushman came on with

the full-fledged ferocity of a truculent nature in sight of prey . . .

reflecting a mind going over the letter to feed the

explosive, vehement outburst of a preconceived determination.

*The italics are Bell's, to denote Siddons' emphases. I will use them when his report is cited.

Cushman could apparently sustain and intensify a very high level of force through the scene: she could continue mounting Shakespeare's "alps upon alps"; but more commonly the stronger Lady Macbeths, conscious of the dramatic build, like Siddons, began at a lower pitch. Actresses did not need the sheer mass and volume of a Siddons, Pritchard, or Cushman to bring with them the atmosphere of dangerous force. Thus the Russian Gogoleva:

> With animal grace, a beautiful woman moves before us, as though she were created for the purpose of passing through life arm in arm with the devil. There she stands in the gloomy hall of Inverness . . . the image of a carnivore-woman. This is the fourth and more frightening Shakespearean witch, perhaps Hecate herself. . . . The image of sinuousness took the place of strength.

Beauty, again, is threatening when it is not in the service of good, when it is cold, and masks calculation. So Vivien Leigh's cool loveliness was unsettling. She held the letter stretched out between her hands, thinking rather than feeling about it, almost forbidding the spectator to warm to her.

Ristori effectively demonstrated how the subtler ferocity of the character could develop through the letter-reading. In her interpretation, Lady Macbeth had long since heard a prophecy akin to the Sisters', and had thought about making it come true. The actress thought Shakespeare meant Lady Macbeth to have received the note just before she entered, and to have read quickly the descriptions of his battle, and of the Sisters. She would have begun to do this simply and naturally, but the first words would render her anxious and agitated. She would make the audience understand that the letter would change her whole future existence and raise her to the summit of greatness:

> I decided to read the letter straight through . . . only pausing after those sentences which told how recent events had actually seemed to fulfill the prophecies long ago made to her. Thus when I found that the three fatal sisters had vanished . . . after predicting Macbeth's great future, and greeting him with Hail! King . . . my expression was one of mingled awe and superstitious amazement.

Morley thought that, in her deep awe, she was no less sensitive than Macbeth to the terror of the supernatural visitation. But her mind, as it began to work, worked more positively, though not so as to please a British reviewer accustomed to the Siddons pattern:

> as word by word was mastered, ambition rose into the sinister features she put on [but] it was an ambition Medicean in its subtlety as distinct from such more sternly direct purpose as we imagine to have nerved the heart and arm and envenomed the tongue [of Lady Macbeth].

Ristori's *Hail king* was

> a triumphant blast of fiendish joy. Before she spoke the line she paused, then looked at [the letter] again, incredulous as slowly the import of it took shape in her mind, and then came to cry . . . that her dream would be realized.

The Russian actress Andreeva demonstrated a different letter-reading strategy practiced by some Lady Macbeths. Entering, high on a terrace, she stopped at the threshold, holding the letter which she had already finished reading. She looked straight ahead, stood poised, very much agitated by the message; then slowly descending, her perturbation showing as she stopped at each step to reflect, she reached the landing and began to study it. (She would walk these stairs again.) At first she read the pretextual part of the letter under her breath, as if to herself, the movement of her lips and the expression of her face conveying her growing intensity. Gradually, as her voice gained more power, and her emotions rose, the words came ringing out, at last spoken with such force and spirit that they seemed "stamped out of metal."

Marlowe similarly suggested a repeated reading. She entered quickly, absorbed, and by the way she dwelled on the phrases, she made it clear that she was going over it to fit what it said into the plans forming in her mind. She ended with a sigh of satisfaction. Merchant, entering, suggested that she was now savoring the news she had already read; her cooler Lady Macbeth projected a superior, almost condescending consideration of her husband's excitement that would be part of her characterization. Heiberg felt certain Lady Macbeth had already read the letter

> for the twentieth time . . . so I entered with [it] rolled up; only after a pause did I unroll it and read it as one who repeats word by word what has already been read . . . For imagine that the contents are here revealed for the first time—what surprise, what exclamations would not pour from this passionate woman's lips. For here she would have to frame the murderous plot; but we hear nothing of this. On the contrary, she is already resolved. The plan, one feels, has already been thought out.

Dench, obviously from much reading before she entered, had half-memorized the letter. It was clutched in her hand as she came in wonderingly, repeating its first phrases by heart, then referring to it to assure herself. Mme. Maeterlinck was certain the entering Lady already knew the message: she was "lit up with joy."

The "second-reading" strategy has the advantage of showing the Lady's mind already at work, but the disadvantage of giving away the accumulating climaxes of discovery that in the "first-time" readings lead to the Lady's surprise and shock at the Weyward Sisters' ultimate promise.

When Lady Macbeth's power came more from love than from force, her more restrained appearance conveyed at a glance the sense of a "womanly," unthreatening figure, to whom a loving and loved husband might be eager to bring "joyful" news. This Lady may not enter, but be discovered, as Tree's Vanbrugh was in the most romantic of intimate settings: a vaulted Norman room, lighted by a single window that opened on a brightly sunlit vista of Scots heath and blue hills, the more brilliant because contrasted with the grey stone walls. A trumpet sounded far off: a plant for the advent of a messenger.

The Lady looked out, saw nothing, returned to her reading; her gentle face, in this enclosed room, seemed to one critic "over-amiable." Another "discovered" Lady, Piscator's, also sat as she read the letter: while projected on the screen, looking down, was the face of Macbeth.

Ellen Terry felt "it is wretched to be *discovered*"; she wanted the sudden burst upon the audience, and so she entered like a rainbow explosion, in a famous green dress that shimmered with beetle wings,* worn beneath a mantle of claret and gold, her red braids, under a veil that sparkled with silver points, falling down to her knees. But her movement was domesticated—touched, one Victorian admirer said, with "the audacity of realism." She broke into her room urgently, eager to get to the message in her hand. Her notes: "Steady. Breathe hard. Excited. Not too quick." The room had a fire, burning low on the hearth; she went to sit by it, to see by its limited light. Her strategy was to read the letter *twice:* she went over it, silently at first, her lips moving, startled by phrases in it, pausing in astonishment, as the firelight illuminated her nervous, tense face. Her interpretation rested on the curious paradox that she was a tender, loving woman who had already talked with her husband of killing a king; she was now surprised, not by the implications of the letter, but by what had actually happened, which agreeably suited her expectations. Her notes explain that she was lost in dreaming of a splendor to come—"she does not realize the measure of the crime." She began to read the letter aloud, repeating the important phrases as if to persuade herself they could be true—almost crooning them to herself. More than once she interrupted her reading to kiss the miniature of Macbeth on her neck chain; she covered the letter itself with kisses; and when she was through she threw herself back into a long oaken chair, in "a rhapsody of passionate longing," to dream of his coming.

An alternative opening for the more tender Lady Macbeths, establishing at the outset a dialectic between softness and strength, was demonstrated by Faucit in her tenderized version of the Siddons model. The immediate impression she projected, as she read the letter, was of a wild, new inner process, a rush of passion—"invoking with fierce energy the powers of nature to destroy the tenderness within her" *(Glasgow Herald):*

> A strange equivocal fire played in her eye, and we could fancy desires unholy, but as yet half-formed, and a foreshadowing of horror from which she half shrank, all being conveyed in her glance and attitude. As she read, the better part of her nature was vanquished before the darling hopes that thrust themselves upon her . . . and her ecstasy [at the end] was scarcely to be repressed. *(Sunday Times)*

With most of the more frankly Loving Wives, tenderness came first, as with Terry, and secret strength was summoned to serve it. Their lower-pitched beginnings changed the color of their wonder at what had happened

---

*"I am afraid Lady Macbeth, had she seen Miss Terry's dress . . . would have murdered Macbeth himself unless he forthwith presented her with one like it." *(Country Gentleman)*

to Macbeth, and their delight in what must happen; and the contrast as ambition struck them was sharp. Bernhardt particularly, in her simple clothes, and unpretentious manner, began reading the letter quietly, and only slowly increased her excitement; the idea of what was implied "dawned" on her; she was building a very gradual ascent to the invocation. Modjeska, nervous and excitable in temperament—"not often," wrote a critic used to sterner stuff, "associated in the common mind with tenacity of purpose"—came suddenly in the letter to the news of her husband's new thanedom, and a triumphant smile flashed on her lips; a moment later, the thought that he would be king changed her to a lioness, her voice swelled with power, she became the other woman in her, the double; but even here face and voice expressed her deep-felt love for Macbeth, whom she wanted splendidly rewarded; her dreams were all for him. Reinhardt's Lady began to read the letter slowly, grew more excited at *missives from the king;* at *Thane of Cawdor* she was checked, read slowly and with surprise until: *hail King.* She let the hand that held the letter fall, and for a long silence stared straight ahead. (Such a fixed, meditative pause often accents this pulse in the scene.) She raised the letter again, read it to the end, let her hand fall again, and in a deep abstraction stared ahead. The emotions boiling in her began to demand outlet: she again looked at the letter, began to walk, slowly at first, then quicker, quicker, back and forth, her face beginning to harden as her character did. Something of the same growth of ambition informed Bethmann's Lady, but softened by her "female weakness." When she put aside the letter, having read it, she slowly and tenderly passed her hand over it, and in the silence seemed to be enjoying a voluptuous dream; she smiled, her eyes shone; and she, too, began impatiently to walk about her room, thinking. An Austrian Lady, Hilde Krahl (1959), after a staring pause, concentrated her mounting tension in her clenched fists. The slow development of Dorothy Green's thoughts could be perceived in her physical change as she read: her head lifting, her step more majestic, her eyes bolder, her bearing straighter, more proud. Nouseul read straight through to *King that shalt be*—paused suddenly, as the expression of vaulting ambition spread over her face, then repeated the words, very slowly, very distinctly, in a voice full of dark energy and the determination to pursue a terrible decision. The repetition was meant to emphasize that she wanted to be queen, thought of herself as born to be queen.

One startling contrast becomes available to Lady Macbeth if she enters in a high-spirited, happy mood, to confront Macbeth's message. So Casarès, coming in inhabited by her joy in living, in the risk of life, in the daring that is intensified by the predictions of the witches. The promise of her husband's future roused her to a great silent cry—to be echoed by a different kind of cry, much later. Tears came to her eyes, and fell down her cheeks, as she read, as she pondered. The young Polish actress, Mikolajska (1960), came in running, almost dancing, shaking Macbeth's letter in her hand. Bright, modern, girlish, she sat choking with laughter as she read it; she was clearly infatuated with Macbeth, and obviously frantic with waiting for him. In both cases these bright beginnings would lead inevitably to dark endings of tremendous contrast.

The doubling of major tones in Lady Macbeth's polyphony sometimes does not wait for her to read the letter: she is already complex, torn between *would* and *should*. In all the distinguished actresses, some subtextual undertone counterpointed the ferocity, or the love, or the joy of their absorbing Macbeth's report; but the more neurotic Ladies were already nests of contradictory impulses. So with the Russian Fedotova (1890): the seeming embodiment of a demonic woman, reading the letter with excessive, forced, declamatory energy, as if prepared to do anything to achieve her cherished dreams; yet even this soon the occasional tremble of her voice, and her troubled face, hinted of vulnerability, of the torments of conscience to come. Margaret Johnston's Lady was nerve-wracked before even she opened the letter; Rigg, brittle, reading quickly, factually, repressing feeling, seemed already to be living on the surface of madness.

Other actresses brought special undertones to this first introduction of Lady Macbeth to the audience. Segond-Weber read the letter as one who thought of herself as akin to the witches, and felt she knew long before the prophecies that Macbeth would be crowned; the letter was not news, but uncanny confirmation from her Sisters. Clara Morris, though as a Loving Wife at the other end of the spectrum from the Frenchwoman, also gave the sense of clairvoyance, of being in touch with more than words, by a wife's prescience. A foreboding of danger was objectified by Mirren's use of one of the play's recurrent images: as she looked over the letter, held in her right hand, her left hand toyed with a small dagger.

The mounting percussions of Macbeth's letter provide Lady Macbeth a stairway to her first climax, and its aftermath. The initial step is his *perfectest report;* the next lift, his burning desire to know more than mortal knowledge—his childlike dream of mastering the impossible. This builds to the Sisters' magical disappearance; and then, up in a leap, to the confirmation of their first, amazing prophecy. Only after this does he mention the greatest promise of all, *Hail King*, that raises Lady Macbeth to the height of her response, whether of wonder, excitement, hope, ambition, terror, ferocity. Often she pauses here to experience the climax. But the movement is not over; it tapers importantly with an allusion to his feeling toward her—*my dearest partner of greatness.* The Terrible Woman here emphasizes the last words; the more Loving Wife the first ones—"Linger on this," was Terry's note. Similarly with his concern that she not *lose the dues of rejoicing*—is she touched? proud? heedless? impatient? businesslike? Her response, as we perceive or imagine it, teaches us a great deal about the design of the relationship between husband and wife before we can see them together.

Lay it to thy heart . . . (13)

the letter concludes—and the formidable Cushman, who at first crumpled
the letter in her frenzied agitation, softened her image by literally following
Macbeth's urging—she put the letter in her bosom. Mme. James Ponisi (U.S.,
1860) folded it and tucked it under her girdle; Viola Allen put it, like a hand-
kerchief, into her sleeve. Judith Anderson, alarmed by the very voicing of
the words *Hail King*, had looked about the room as if fearful to have been
heard, before returning to read the letter; then she hid it away until Macbeth
came. Ristori, according to one observer, simply threw it away, but I find
no confirmation of this, and it does not seem to fit her own description of her
concentrated mood. Marlowe, after a deep sigh, leaned on a table, almost as
if for support, and dropped the letter there. Lady Macbeth might very well
put the missive together with other similar papers (for she will say she has
received *letters* from Macbeth) and in her handling of them convey something
about her feeling for her husband. Some Lady Macbeths keep hold of the
letter, as if a kind of talisman: Terry brooded over it, Bethmann dreamed,
Leigh held it clutched like a baton as she marshaled her next thoughts. The
sound of a trumpet off is sometimes a cue for the meditators to shake themselves free for the next thought.

The fiercer Lady Macbeths often charge into the next beat. The vision that
flames in their minds already kindled by their inborn ambition, if not by
previous understandings with their husbands, clamors for consummation.
High as they have pitched the tension of the first beat, they move higher now.
So Siddons: "her mind wrought up . . . her eye never wandering, never for
a moment idle, passion and sentiment continually betraying themselves."

Glamis thou art, and Cawdor, and shalt be. . . . (15)

Specific names for things are sometimes avoided by Lady Macbeth, as
Jorgensen—and others—observe; here she has been thought to stick at saying
the as-yet unspeakable—*king*—for the evasive

. . . what thou art promised. (15–16)

Siddons certainly came down hard on *and shalt be*—"with a burst of energy
that electrified the audience . . . the determination seemed as uncontrollable
as fate itself" (Boaden); Bell heard an "exalted prophetic tone, as if the whole
future were present to her soul."

Ristori stressed the same words—she was pleased, later, to learn she had
followed Siddons—but from a different stance. "I had remained for a moment
sad and doubtful, considering and fearing the weak nature of my consort."
Her emphasis was less on vision than on determination.

Marlowe spoke with a kind of relieved triumph, as if she had long thought
of Macbeth's elevation, and how much her much-loved husband was prepared
for the next achievement.

Some actresses utter apostrophes to Time here, or commune with their thoughts. Other Ladies seemed to speak directly to Macbeth, or his image. Anne Römer (Germany, 1953), after a silent interval, head bowed, eyes closed, spoke calmly and tenderly to her husband as if he were there before her. Terry, holding up Macbeth's miniature in her locket, whispered to it lovingly, with affectionate pride. The more austere Anderson addressed his helmet; Piscator's Lady, lying on a couch, stared up at the screened projection of Macbeth that presumably matched her own mental projection. Ristori imagined him by her side:

> I fixed my stern and piercing gaze upon his supposed figure, as though I would wrench from him the most hidden secrets of his soul.

As so often, our perception of Macbeth is filled out by what others experience of him, as well as by what we do. From the Captain's story, and the court's wholehearted joy in it, we had learned to expect a very brave, savage soldier; from the Sisters, a figure suitable for a witches' meeting; then we saw him, and discovered an impressive, highly imaginative, inward personality, quickly prompted to murderous imaginings, but so vulnerable to the alarm of their knowing, or their danger, that he is literally stunned. What we later saw of Macbeth in action was like another, starker photographic image superimposed on first ones; now another image is added. In the multiple exposure we make out the general shape, but the contours are ambiguous, rich in shadings and textures; we who have never seen the play before strain to discern Macbeth's identity in them; they call up in the backs of our minds the conditions under which the first images were minted. Who knows Macbeth?

By her tone of voice and feeling, more than by her testimony, Macbeth's wife, his intimate, his *dearest partner*, exposes the two and their relationship. Even to herself, the task takes some effort, and has its pain. The most loving of wives, Terry, would talk to Macbeth's miniature in loving tones, but it told her, she indicated, "that she must assume masculine strength to support him in [his] fatal purpose." Reinhardt's Lady took a deep breath before she could start, and then spoke very slowly, resolutely, unhappy over what she had to say. Siddons suggested, to Bell, that Lady Macbeth had known about Macbeth's thoughts, wishes, ambitions before this; the "slight tincture of contempt throughout" was for a husband manqué, who lacked the manhood to realize his dreams:

> Yet do I fear thy nature. . . . (16)

Lady Macbeth says *fear* three times in this scene. Even in the Terrible Woman, the design ultimately suggests that she is afraid of being afraid; here the Siddons Lady is not as anxious about her husband's nature as such as about its inadequacy to commit a crime:

> It is too full o' th' milk of human kindness,
> To catch the nearest way. (17–18)

This *milk* is unmistakably gentle, nourishing; whether the gracious life-liquid of all humankind, or the special quality of kindness, it is symbolic of compassion and care. It is one of several liquid images used by Lady Macbeth, and all of these images involve watersheds in her character design. That *milky gentleness* (Goneril) which most of mankind regards as virtuous is to the Terrible Woman a vice in her husband, a foul fairness, to be regarded indeed with contempt. Or, with cool and practical Ladies, like Merchant, with a kind of amused irony.

Some critics read it as meant to be contemptuous (Siegel, Nevo)—or nearly so (W. M. Merchant); Wayne Booth, sympathetic to Macbeth, sees the taunt as a reflection on Lady Macbeth—the unimpeachable testimony of a wicked character deploring goodness. At the other extreme, to the Loving Wife Macbeth's milkiness in this situation becomes, in a different refraction of the play's dialectic, an admirable disability, a noble handicap, to be eliminated only reluctantly. Thus Wolter spoke it with tender care and anxiety; a Czech actress, maternally; Terry, with an affectionate, half-regretful tone, as if her Macbeth was a too-generous person not concerned enough with his own self-interest.

Lady Macbeth's see-saw pursuit of her husband's character echoes his own see-saw rhythms.

> Art not without ambition, but without
> The *illness** should attend it. (19–20)

Illness is another word that looks two ways: a paradoxical symptom of ambitious health to the virago who would impel him to murder; to a partner-wife, a necessary disease a good man requires if he would rise—Reinhardt's Lady smiled kindly. As so often, the characters say much more than they know: the Lady as well as her husband will be wracked by the vicious infection she now would wish on him.

The see-saw continues:

> What thou woulds't highly,
> That wouldst thou holily. (20–21)

Again, strange bedfellows: a godly overreacher. Macbeths in the theatre have occasionally found time to pray, or try to, as if the mask belonged to the face; except in those moments when they reach for transcendence, their words remain below.

Conditional verbs sustain Lady Macbeth's insights, suggesting the equivocation between desire and act:

> would'st not play false,
> And yet would'st wrongly win. (21–22)

*Siddons' emphasis.

The abrupt three-beat thought doubles back on her earlier words. This last is not a true opposition; waywardness surfaces. Not so *holily* does he wish as to keep him from dreaming of winning falsely; the line, in fact, says he would *want* to win in the wrong way. The speech asks slow speaking, with its demands on enunciation, as if the Lady is glimpsing the complexities behind her oppositions.

Then she moves to the word *do*, which, with its variations, winds its way through her thoughts, as it did in Macbeth's last soliloquy. *What* is to be *done*, what wanted, are still masked in innocent words: *it, that*. Again, the climate is conditional:

> Thou'dst have, great Glamis, that which cries,
> Thus thou must do, if thou have . . . *it;* (23–24)*

(This *is* a cry: the whole last line monosyllables, emancipated from the pentameter—almost a succession of spondees; pivoting on an *if*.)

> And . . . *that* which rather thou do'st fear to do,
> Than wishest should be undone. (25–26)

(An echo sounds: *let that be/Which the eye fears, when it is done, to see*.)

How well does she know Macbeth? She is aware of his compunctions, and how they conflict with his wishes; but she ignores—or is ignorant of—his capacity for violence, his readiness to make Golgothas. The terror she might be letting loose does not figure in her calculations.

To the domineering Lady, the contemptuous consideration of Macbeth's irresolution immediately points one way: he must be changed. *Hie thee hither* (26) becomes a command—by Siddons, with a start "into higher animation"— still intensifying intensity. To a devoted Lady—Reinhardt's, for instance— the contemplation of the husband ends on a gentle pause of affection: her

---

*Since Pope, editors have often "corrected" these Folio lines to

> And yet wouldst wrongly win; thou'dst have, Great Glamis,
> That which cries, Thus thou must do if thou have it;

This attempt at regularization seems to me quite unnecessary, and unnecessarily concerned with the language as printed rather than as spoken. The "improvement" is not tidy: the iambic rhythms ending the first line, now joined to the second, make it an awkward, overlong series of off-beats. As given by the Folio (and me), *wouldst wrongly win* finishes one tributary to the main thought; it deserves to stand alone, and let the next thought-branch start a new line. Even more important, for the speaking, the full Folio line *Thou'dst have . . . that which cries* sets up the staccato "cry" to follow, isolates it for Shakespeare's actor to give it full power: *Thus thou must do, if thou have it*. Hanmer and Capell properly, I think, enclosed these words in quotation marks as the "cry": it accommodates the actor's (later, actress') breath control, and sustains the minor climax to which he rises—quite possibly the reason the lines were printed as they are in the Folio. To include, as part of the "cry," the next two lines (ending in *undone*)—as some editors have—makes the whole a very *long* "cry." These later lines, that return to the iambic, seem designed in their rhythms and sense to suggest Lady Macbeth's corollary to the "cry." Perhaps better than the longer quotation is the "cry" shortened to *Thus thou must do* of some editors, though it seems to me not to fit the speech rhythm as well as the full line: it joins the angular beats of *if thou have it* to the following iambics, and it makes less spoken sense.

yearning for him is evident, she calls to him with a tender voice. Here begins
the next pulse of the beat that ends Lady Macbeth's solitude:

> That I may pour *my** spirits in thine ear,
> And chastise with the valour of my tongue. . . . (27–28)

The first line links her with the uncanny. She assumes a kind of power to
nourish a man with her own liquor that can be voiced in the tones of a priestess.
Thus Siddons, in solemn invocation; thus Ristori, emerging from preoccupation with Macbeth's character, desiring his return so she can begin weaving
"[my] web of evil arts and spells . . . [to] imprint my own words upon his
mind in letters of fire." Something of the gesture of a priestess surely informed
Siddons when, envisioning the golden round that her chastisement would
drive Macbeth to, she stood tall, smiled loftily, and raised an arm to draw,
above her head, the royal circle.

Lady Macbeth took her cue for this initiation to a supernatural mood, Clara
Morris felt, entirely from Macbeth's message: she comes to believe she can
rely on the Sisters' power, "and it is her faith in them that sustains her through
the awful ordeals to follow." Similarly, Faucit was seen to draw the inspiration
for her gradual assumption of mystical authority from the prophetic assurances written in the letter she held.

Even the Loving Wife could take on, as Terry did, the aura of a kind of siren
priestess, wooing Macbeth with transcendent, insinuating faith:

> every womanly feeling and thought of self is subordinated to the object of spur-
> ring her lord to that which, in her great love for him, she believes should be his
> by right.

The Lady ends,

> To have thee crown'd withal. (31)

—and almost as if, with a witch's power, she has summoned her lord, his
messenger is there.

He may well knock, as Gordon Craig wanted him to; knocking drums
through the center of the play, and some preparation might be expected for
this entrance upon the Lady, who may then unbolt the door she locked for
privacy. Knock or enter, the action is abrupt, a well-crafted climax to the beat;
but once the servant is on, and Lady Macbeth is shocked from her reverie into
the present, a strong pause holds while he kneels, perhaps catches his breath,
or she hers, before she must ask his news. The lines are staccato—three
accents:

> The King comes here tonight. (33)

*Siddons.

—and then the abrupt, two-foot line, torn away from her, unthinking—rare for her in her waking hours:

Thou'rt mad to say it. (34)

Thus Siddons: loud, with wild excitement, savage exultation; then, alarmed at her display, and as suddenly checking herself to disarm suspicion, she quickly added her question about Macbeth in an abrupt descent of tone:

Soft, as if correcting herself, and under the tone of reasoning concealing sentiments almost disclosed. (Bell)

The temptation for the fiercely determined Lady, whose mind is full of plans for regicide, to break momentarily out of control is great. From Krahl the first line was the shout of a wild beast; for the moment she was herself a witch. Mrs. Benson (England, 1896) screamed. This kind of naked disclosure could indeed make the whole castle suspicious, as Agate observed of one high-pitched Lady. But the Lady can instead be frightened by the news: thus to Bethmann her vague thoughts of achieving Macbeth's ascendancy were challenged before she was ready, the news came too early, time was forcing performance to match desire: her hand came up across her mouth. Marlowe backed away from the news as from a danger; but then she calmed herself and could say the revealing words with delight—they could almost pass for a hostess' show of pleasure at the visit. Viola Allen's greedy note: "Great joy." The cool Merchant responded with a sudden laugh—this was a cosmic joke. Terry deliberately slowed her answer. She had been lounging in her chair, dreaming; as the messenger entered with his news she sat up straight. With the actress' instinct for climactic pause, she looked at him for a moment:

tremble . . . dont believe him except for the first moment . . . impulsively believe . . . scorn the likelihood [her notes]

She spoke kindly to the messenger, as if he must be making it up; then—

with a warm heart she bustles him off.

Like many Ladies she stressed "He brings *great* news."

Beat, beat, beat. At the end of each short movement, focused by a new shock, comes the charged pause, while, in Lady Macbeth's intense face we sense the fuse of idea burning closer to the powder of impulse. Now the fire is touched off. Lady Macbeth is herself aflame.

Her first lines are short, the rhythms sharp, a terrible determination is gathering:

Give him tending,
He brings great news.

Then:

> The raven himself is hoarse,
> That croaks the *fatal** entrance† of Duncan
> Under my battlements. (41–45)

No need to connect the raven with the breathless messenger, as Verity suggested: or, to a sudden, timely cry of the birds; though earlier sounds from offstage of an approach to the castle and the disturbance of bird life have cued the line. The Lady's grim image of the great black bird brooding over the castle threatens enough. It frightens some Lady Macbeths, energizes others, charges them all with tension. G.B. Shaw to Mrs. Campbell:

> Unless you lift that to utter abandonment, how can you drop to the [following] terrible invocation?

But Dench could laugh, as at a cosmic joke; at the other extreme, Anderson's voice "curdled" with a dark ferocity, her throat tightening, the words thickening. Her voicing was suited to the quality in the lines Sitwell called

> rusty, as though they had lain in blood that had been spilt . . . the choked utterances . . . dull and rusty vowels . . . the terrible drumming sound of the assonances—Duncan, under, come, compunction—compunction as a darkened, thickened reverberation of come.

Anderson's intonation signaled the startling change in Lady Macbeth's characterization, as she readies the invocation.

> Come, you spirits,
> That tend on mortal thoughts, unsex me here,
> And fill me from the crown to the toe, top-full
> Of direst cruelty: Make thick my blood,
> Stop up th' access, and passage to remorse,
> That no compunctious visitings of nature
> Shake my fell purpose. (45–51)

The call to murderous spirits seems to put Lady Macbeth in a special relation with the unseen, partly prepared for by her earlier invocation to Macbeth, when she offered her own spirits to him. Rational though she will always try to appear to her husband, alone now she concedes that powers exist which can change her to something other than she is. Scholarship commonly understands the spirits she invokes to be supernatural forces: either vicious, non-theological ones or, after Malone, specifically devils. If diabolical, she must wish to be possessed, and indeed—as Margaret Webster argued—is. Siddons thought she "impiously believed herself up to the excitements of hell." Muir

---

*Siddons.

†Sometimes seen a trisyllable; but "entrance" would slow down the sharp edge of *entrance* that, leaping between *fatal* and *Duncan*, comes with the very sound of incision. The syncopation fits Lady Macbeth's urgency, and also the jagged metrical rhythms that follow, beginning with the two dactyls in the next line.

observes cogently that the supernatural remains ambiguous, and that Lady Macbeth's later behavior cannot always be squared with demoniac possession. Kocher considers the possibility that the *spirits* are "animal"—belonging to the body—as described in Burton's *Anatomy* as a "most subtle vapour . . . expressed from the blood, and the instrument of the soul . . . a common tie or medium betwixt body and soul," and by Petrus Valentinus in this lovely image: "as if it were a starre-beame, which is sent from the brain by the nerues into all the body, to give motion." Kocher suggests that the Lady is in fact asking for melancholy, associated with thick blood, as in *King John:*

> Or if that surly spirit, melancholy,
> Had baked thy blood, and made it heavy, thick. (III, iii, 42–43)

Lady Macbeth indeed asks for her blood to be thickened; that may be a metaphorical appeal for firmness in her purpose. The following injunction, *Stop up th' access* . . . may be an additional request, not necessarily related. Certainly she nowhere suggests that she foresees melancholy as the price she must pay. Up to the moment of the deed she is planning she is almost manic in excitement; but if thick blood was in fact supposed to prevent *compunctious visitings*, then it would have begun to thin by mid-play, eventually allowing access to feelings she feared would come. The very urgency of her crying *Stop up*, F. A. Marshall suggested, indicates how susceptible she knew she was to tender feelings.

Whether with the help of external powers, or by calling on her own deep resources, she is designed to evoke Dionysian forces from within her. She is daring the anarchic, an alienation from her kind, superhuman individuation, existence in the region beyond order and normality that society either dreads or deifies. By calling on spirits of evil, she makes us believe that such things, whether internal or external, can be thought to be; but Shakespeare avoids stipulating diabolic possession, avoids bringing spirits or demons—or even witches—into her presence, as he does to Macbeth (although producers like Piscator, to suggest her kinship with fateful powers, have filtered witches into the background of the invocation). Certainly Lady Macbeth never again makes reference to spirits: like Macbeth she becomes a kind of Jekyll who invokes the Hyde within and has to live with both identities simultaneously. Doubling.

In the theatre, the invocation aims almost always at intangible, extra-human forces. As a woman straining to be something more, the Lady looks into the air about her, appeals with hands and arms—often aloft, as with Bernhardt, though some have beckoned to spirits below. Now more than ever the uncanny note is touched: so Faucit—

> her tall form and sweeping gestures, in union with her terrible intensity, has such a weird and mystic aspect . . . [she] might have [been] Medea, conscious of her power over the preternatural world . . . not merely a tempter, a prophetess.

The Lady may perform enough of a magic ritual to emphasize a link with witchcraft or demonism: thus Krahl, with her toe, drew a magic circle about herself before beginning, and stood in its center, straddle-legged, impudent. The other side of demon worship is blasphemy, and this has sometimes been stipulated. Bergman's (1944) Lady invoked possession while standing under the image, dominating her room, of a bleeding Christ. A Czech Lady knelt in the familiar posture of genuflection, and prayed to *murdering ministers*. Rosemary Murphy, wearing a gown slit from neck to pelvis so as almost to bare her breasts, also began as if to pray—then suddenly ripped off the crucifix, spat on it, and threw it away. Rigg, rigid, pale-faced, tight-lipped, deliberately turned her crucifix upside down and, as noted, spat over it, as a kind of implied contract with the demonic. Mirren objectified this implication by using her small dagger to draw blood from her arm; then she acted as if she were initiating a seance—with gestures that her Macbeth, Williamson, would echo at *Come, seeling night* . . . (III, ii, 56)

What it could mean to Lady Macbeth to invite so terrible an unholiness is suggested by Sheila Allen: "I believe she is frightened and doubtful of pulling off the killing—hence the passion and despair of 'Come you spirits.'" Dench made anguish visual. She could almost be seen thinking what she said was in her mind: "Dare I? Just for this *once?*" Then she slowly knelt, in a circle of light, her hands outstretched, pointing forward and down. Only after a deep, strained breath could she find strength to begin; and as the first words came from her she became more and more frightened at what she was doing. When she reached *topfull/Of direst cruelty*, she could not bear any more: terrified, she broke off, and fled back into the darkness. Only slowly did she regain enough resolution to return and complete, fearfully, the summoning.

Central to Lady Macbeth's characterization is a crux which every critic and actor must confront: what change, if any, must take place in her to make her what she becomes—murderess, and after. For the Terrible Woman, the invocation is less a plea for conversion than for enlargement: strengthen me to do what I want to do. She may speak to the spirits almost as if they are kin; she and they understand each other, may have held commerce before. To the tender Loving Wife, at the other extreme, the call to the supernatural is a desperate, painful, frightened appeal to strange powers for the only kind of strength that might enable her to sustain her new intent—a strength that must end in frightful weakness. Ranging between these poles, Lady Macbeth's polyphony sounds many subtle chords, of mingled ferocity and tenderness, ambition for self and ambition for husband, murderous determination that may be achieved by strenuous suppression of scruple and fear.

The balance of the design will be significantly affected by its answer to a central question mark in the characterization: how much *unsexing* does Lady Macbeth in fact need?

In effect, she is asking to become a non-person, free of human sympathy. To achieve this, must she escape her womanhood? Become man? The masculine-feminine reciprocation is one axis on which the relationship of the Macbeths turns. If she can achieve the kind of sterile sexuality—or ambiguous double sexuality—of the bearded witches, if she can be made unwomanly, then she may make her husband more manly, she herself may be able to do fearful things. The ultimate Terrible Woman of the Siddons-Cushman type, massive, forbidding, seemed to have little femininity to lose: she already seemed very much what she prayed to become. Critics (e.g., Helen Gardner) and actresses (e.g., Morris) have made the obvious point that the Lady's very need to forswear her "sex" testifies to how much womanliness she feels she must abjure. The cost of unsexing will become particularly evident in the markedly voluptuous, sensual Ladies as their erotic relationships wither, and their physical as well as spiritual sexual identities suffer.

In the invocation for help to become something else, Lady Macbeth, like Macbeth, is "doubling"—preparing to play an imposed role; her image must be capacious enough to make plausible the need to evoke Dionysus as well as the impulse and capacity to dare his presence. In the second pulse of this beat, she invites the most rapacious of visitants to intimacy:

> Come to my woman's breasts,
> And take my milk for gall, you murd'ring ministers. (52–53)

Possibly, drink my milk as your gall—carrying connotations of the suspected lubricious association between women and the demonic: an erotic image of devils suckling. In such an aura, the implications of *take* as sexual aggression would fit. More conventional is Dr. Johnson's gloss: put gall—bitterness, rancor—in the place of milk. The appeal seems essentially figurative: the Lady regards herself as having, like Macbeth, too much of the milk of human kindness; and as she hoped her own spirits would masculinize him, she hopes other spirits would masculinize her. But perhaps she is being literal, too; she is aware of perturbing sensations, the prickings of her nipples may agitate her milk (Charlton). May her breasts now carry the milk from which she has been giving suck, to a child, a son? (See Appendix.)

Edwin Booth wondered where *here* was, in *unsex me here*. "Her heart? . . . here—in this place—or now? . . . I think it has reference solely to her feelings. Lady M. usually puts her hands to her two breasts." His Lady touched her heart. Lady Macbeth has also indicated other relevant parts of her body— even, by Robson, her head, meaning compassion—and has sometimes suggested by *here* the whole ambience in which she exists, her world.

Because Shakespeare's Lady was a male actor, some scholars have suggested that audiences then might have felt an irony in a man playing a woman asking to be unwomaned; my belief is that disbelief would have been suspended, as with the Jacobean Desdemona I mentioned in the last chapter, whose pathos made a sophisticated Oxford audience weep. Given such an actor, his sex would not distort the overt response in this scene, or the resonance, at a deep level, to the androgyne image.

The invocation becomes more Faustian as the Lady drives on toward commitment to the dark world, the realm of those ministers:

> Wherever, in your sightless substances,
> You wait on nature's mischief. (54–55)

Does she wait for their response? "They come, those sightless substances,"
Webster believed, "there should be no smallest doubt about that. . . . They
make of her a creature as relentless as she had desired, they shroud the stars
and charge the blackened night with terror." If, from whatever source, Lady
Macbeth can feel new power changing her, she feels it now; now the stiffening, the coarsening, may begin to show; now Hyde may be sensed, if not
seen, in face and body.

Now she mounts to the invocation's final pulse, the prayer for darkness to
hide the deed she plans, to hide it even from the weapon that commits it:

> Come thick night,
> And pall thee in the dunnest smoke of hell,
> That my keen knife see not the wound it makes,
> Nor heaven peep through the blanket of the dark*
> To cry, hold, hold. (55–59)

So the invocation builds to its tremendous climax. In the concealing darkness,
she herself will strike: her word *knife*, as it follows *keen*, sounds bright as a
shining blade, in a rare staccato line set off from the others by its harsh picket
effect—every word a monosyllable, the iambic almost roughed away in an
extended rush of near-spondees.

The Lady seeks, again, what Macbeth sought: a disjunction between conscience and will, knowing and doing; the eye, blindfolded by darkness, is
not to see the hand act. The persona doubles. Macbeth has been seen as meant
to be the Lady's *knife*, but this is straining; she might hold his miniature as
her symbolic weapon, but the clear sense seems to be that she is girding herself
to a murderous purpose with a weapon of her own. She may touch a chatelaine's ornamental dagger in her girdle (a property list for a Swedish *Macbeth*
in 1880 lists for her "two small daggers"). Rigg held her crucifix like a dirk;
but the thing itself is not needed: the cutting word—*knife*—melts into the
play's visual-verbal imagery of flashing, wounding steel.

Now let us go back, and consider the shape of the invocation as it is realized
in the theatre. It almost requires a solemn, low-pitched beginning; and to be
started, as it was by Siddons, only after a long, gestating pause when the
messenger had left. Under *my* battlements, the Terrible Woman has said;
for she means her will to have its murderous way in her castle she now sees

---

*Johnson has been scolded enough for finding this language (*dunnest*, *knife*, *blanket*) too
common; he spoke for the spirit of "refinement" in the culture, as did his contemporary, Gentleman, who felt he "must offer some doubt whether the word *blanket* of the dark, does not convey
a low and improper idea."

as embattled (later she will call it, more domestically, a house). "Let it",
Siddons wrote of her assertion of power,

> be of some palliation, that she had probably from childhood commanded all
> around her with a high hand; had uninterruptedly, perhaps, in that splendid
> station, enjoyed all that wealth, all that nature had to bestow; that she had
> possibly no directors, no controllers, and that in womanhood her fascinated
> lord had never once opposed her inclinations.

As Siddons set out to invoke supernature to her aid, she began in a suppressed
tone that Boaden called a "murmured mysteriousness," Bell a "whisper of
horrid determination." Conventionally, the Lady increases her volume now;
Siddons continued in the intense sotto mood, "Voice quite supernatural, as
in a horrid dream. Chilled with horror by the slow, hollow whisper. . . . "
"A low, deep accent of apprehension, or of conscious conspiracy." She looked
beyond; at *sightless substances*

> the elevation of her brows, the full orbs of sight, the raised shoulders and the
> hollowed hands, seemed all to endeavour to explore what yet were pronounced
> no possible objects of vision. She did not implore the spirits, she commanded
> them. Till then, I am quite sure, a figure so terrible had never bent over the
> pit of a theatre.

Ristori told how she herself let the invocation grow.

> The terrible soliloquy . . . reveals all the perfidy and cruelty of this woman
> . . . a monster in human shape . . . shows with what supernatural powers
> she arms herself. . . . This woman, this serpent, masters [Macbeth], holds
> him fast in her coils. . . . In consequence I uttered the first words . . . in a
> hollow voice, with bloodthirsty eyes, and with the accent of a spirit speaking
> from out of some abyss.

Coleman heard her croon at first, until, lost in passion, she seemed ready
almost to rid herself, by mutilation, of symbols of her sex:

> the voice rose to the swelling diapason of an organ, her eyes became luminous
> with infernal fire, the stately figure expanded, her white hands clutched her
> ample bosom, as if she would there and then have unsexed herself . . . and it
> really required but little stretch of the imagination to conceive that the "dunnest
> smoke of hell" would burst forth and environ her.

Anderson seemed to try to pull the unseen to her—"standing in a spotlight
atop the battlements, her white arms in sensual, psychopathic groping."

Given the ferocity of Ladies like Pritchard, Siddons, and Cushman, no great
change in their characters seemed to take place—or needed to—with the
invocation. This seemed true also of the hard, cold, and intellectual Lady
Macbeths. They knew what they wanted, the supernatural might be of some
help: they would ask. Or it might not. Isabella Glyn (England, 1852) spoke
sceptically, with a touch of scorn, even as she invoked the *ministers . . . in your
sightless substances,*

implying more than a doubt of their visibility and inhabitancy; treating them, indeed, as the fictions of a superstitious fancy—such as that by which her scrupulous lord was hagridden (*Illustrated London News*).

Not so with a more "womanly" Lady like Modjeska:

> She needs unsexing for the deed before her, for she is not already hard and masculine in disposition, but wholly a woman with a woman's mentality and a woman's splendid vitality of intent . . . wholly and absolutely feminine.

To Modjeska, the summoning of the spirits was a daring adventure, that both her spirited, ambitious nature and love for her husband impelled her to:

> The buoyant eagerness for action, the elastic tension to leap the bloody gap [to] her imperial state, figure themselves in a smile of confident and happy daring on her face, and a joy . . . to this great end suffuses her countenance. . . . This bounding, glad, straining, reckless purpose envelops her like a mystery, and gives sharp meaning to her prayer that the powers of the air shall unsex her.

This was the kind of energy Craig urged on his Lady: to be found in bed reading the letter, but at the news of Duncan's coming

> to leap up and begin to dress herself like lightning—here is the fury of her passion—her movement could electrify us, so unconscious the act of dressing, so full of possibilities for you, too.

He wanted the Lady seductive more than commanding:

> I cannot find her even once compelling in the masculine sense . . . cannot hear her calling on [the spirits] in the voice of Siddons, but in the voice of Camille gone a bit crazy. Drunken if you will, but not devastating . . . eyelids covering your eyes . . . in ecstasy—sensual—and immense.

The younger, essentially loving Lady knows she must somehow transcend herself to achieve the aims so uncongenial to her nature; thus Terry: "She feels she has only a woman's strength, and calls on spirits." Terry was uncertain of her capacity to rise to the invocation: "I *must* try to do this, two years ago I would not *even* have tried." She began slowly, straining to suppress her femininity, her voice faltering at the more terrible passages. Her note: "Fear gathers . . . she sparks herself on." She dreads the *direst cruelty* she asks for; her hands try to push away any *compunctious visitings*. At *my woman's breast* her note was "strike with one arm." (Many actresses, like Ristori, brought both hands to their breasts, Mrs. Kean and Siddons after crossing their arms.) Terry summoned the *murd'ring ministers* "from below." All this was done with forced effort; a reviewer noticed that

> when she asks and promises dread things, we can see it is because she is screwing her courage to the sticking place.

She goads herself on with her vision of splendor. Lady Macbeths as early-soft as Terry dramatically double the characterization when they petition seriously

for an infusion of murderousness; but they then must determinedly authenti-
cate their Dionysian descents. Tree's lovely Lady, Vanbrugh, seemed not
even to be genuinely appealing for malicious power; it was as if her character
felt she had to say the words, but could not mean them, a player playing at
playing a double part. If the conflicting tones are juxtaposed, they must make
a plausible dissonance. Agate, observing that Robson asked to be unsexed,

> and promptly gives a display of wifely solicitude and mothering which would
> qualify her . . . for one of Sir James Barrie's plays,

insisted that a fiend in feminine guise had to be sensed.

One very important effect of the invocation on the Lady Macbeth who does
not begin Terrible is what happens to her after her supplication to evil powers:
she cannot be the same. She must show, as was said of a young South African
Lady (1970), that she has lost something as a result. Morris was one of the
gentle—if shrewd—Ladies who felt both the need to invoke the supernatural
and the distortion it must cause:

> In that moment of exaltation, when the promise of the crown was tightening
> every thrilling nerve in mad determination, her first demand of the "murdering
> ministers" is that they shall unsex her. [She] became terrible as a fate through
> her absolute reliance upon the supernatural power of the witches.

Both what Lady Macbeth has been, and what she has now made of herself,
show and are tested with Macbeth's entrance. The waves of the scene have
built architectonically to the crest of

Cry, hold, hold. (59)

Then Macbeth's sudden appearance seems almost an immediate answer to
her prayer: in the atmosphere she has created, anything seems possible. If
the room was not already imagined to be darkening when Lady Macbeth invoked *thick night*, the darkness may now be felt as coming: by a candle's light
in the Globe, or by a show of firelight, as in Irving's production, to throw
strange shadows. (Evans and Anderson would add a true flame's light to the
chiaroscuro when, as if to hide their guilt, they slowly burned Macbeth's
letter.)

The shock of the confrontation often holds the two apart, for a fierce pause.
Sometimes they seem almost driven to each other. In the silence, their actions
speak.

A Kemble promptbook has Lady Macbeth starting to cross right, see Macbeth entering, and return hastily to him. This traditional business gives him
the stage for his entrance, and her the dramatic movement. Ponisi apparently
wanted something entirely new when she asked Forrest, her Macbeth, to allow
the following:

> Instead of going down to the corner of the stage, and then turning to discover
> Macbeth . . .

she held the center till Forrest interrupted her; she turned with a grand gesture of welcome, outstretched arms, and a great, triumphant cry: *Great Glamis* . . .

> It thrilled the house and it astonished and so profoundly affected Forrest that for an instant he stood trembling before her. . . .

But Macbeth has also rushed in breathless to his Lady. He has delayed his entrance to allow her a long pause to point the climax of her beat. He has appeared silently behind her, and watched her finish the invocation, preparing himself to greet her, his face and body expressing his feelings: for himself, of indecision, anxiety, exhaustion, alarm, ambition, excitement; for her, admiration, uncertainty, apprehension, love, sensual need—depending on what he has become in I, iii and I, iv. He has sometimes, before entering, been heralded by trumpets, by the shouts (even the escort) of servants and countrymen greeting the return of the victorious national hero—giving her a long pause to transform her invocatory mood to one of preparation. Ristori had moved to the side of the stage from which he would enter, as if ready to pounce; Krahl, who had toed the conjurer's circle about herself, tried now to toe it out before Macbeth entered (not in time: he approached too quickly, unconsciously entered the charmed area); Loving Wives have made themselves and the room ready for a loving husband—some to rush into his arms, the more erotic to lie on couch or floor, preparing themselves and their dress for an amatory welcome.

Sometimes at once—certainly at last—the two come face to face: though they may avoid each other's glance at first. Two who are doubled: each, below the surface of a partnered relationship, carries impulses and thoughts too private to share easily. Each has thought of murder the moment kingship was suggested—but they meet now not knowing for sure the other's mind.* We (who do not know what these two will do) have some sense of the murderous dreams of both, and of the guilt both hope to detach from it. Will they come together? We know her designs on him, have been introduced to his indulgence in indecision and conscience that she means to eliminate. Will she succeed? Each will strain to hide and to disclose the secret self. Will she recognize something new in him, strange matters, at once? Will he fear a rebuff? Will he see in her the effects of "unsexing"? Or notice anything different in her touch, her embrace?

Our scrutiny is sustained by the tension of forces in the equation. Bell, describing Kemble's inadequacy opposite Siddons, saw that the drama here depends "on the fire which she strikes into him," and his return of flame. With Siddons, if Kemble could play little more than a "co-operating part" the reason partly lay in her. Since she could perceive no sense in Lady Macbeth of sympathy for Macbeth's perils in war, no happiness at his safe return—

---

*Mme. Maeterlinck: "Lady Macbeth has thrown herself into his arms, the door closes upon them, they hold each other in a long embrace, they are alone, they are at home, the massive walls will not betray them, the great secret that eats into their brain quivers in their kiss, is about to escape from their lips, in one breath of love and anguish."

Not one kind word of greeting or congratulation does she offer—is so entirely swallowed by the horrible design—

she must have seemed more a general than a wife, literally intent on chastising him.

Still, Siddons was an artist, modulating her score; her intense, low-pitched building of the invocation paid dividends in its contrast with her outburst now (using language most observers would regard as "greeting or congratulation"):

> Great Glamis, worthy Cawdor,
> Greater than both . . . (60–61)

"Loud, triumphant, wild in her air." Then she moved to dominate him, powerfully, relentlessly. "The commanding majesty of her manner might almost be said to furnish an excuse for the conduct of Macbeth."

The passionate Janauschek similarly unbalanced the equation. Her dignity and majesty, fired by

terrible energy and characteristic fierceness . . . her sanguine, unscrupulous, irrepressible ambition expressed with an eagerness and command that would have roused the veriest craven. . . . Her eager impetuosity dominates the scene completely.

She caught Macbeth physically:

As she seizes him . . . he is made to seem more like a dull country clown in the presence of enraged royalty, than a lusty warrior in the company of his own little wife (N.Y. Mirror).

Almost the same language described Cushman's "violence of manner and speed" as she "seized on (Macbeth) with a murderous eagerness." These Ladies almost seemed bent on disciplining Macbeth with the valor of their muscles as well as of their tongues.

The Machiavellian version of control was demonstrated by Ristori. She had nourished the invocation to a peak of exultation, her voice steadily louder and more resonant, until, ready for his entrance, she changed it to her player's "exaggerated cry of joy at the sight of my husband." The Great Glamis, Kate Field thought, had

a tenderness of tone we never heard before . . . you realise why Lady Macbeth exerted so powerful an influence over her husband. You see that she possesses womanly fascinations, that her heart, so far as he is concerned, it as large as her brain . . . the brightest jewel in her crown is wifely devotion.

But Ristori herself, having tangled him in her web, saw herself enforcing her control with

a cold, dignified and calm demeanour . . . I ignored the trivial scruples with which he received my guilty suggestions as totally unworthy of consideration, confident that his weak and irresolute nature must eventually succumb to my stronger one.

She manipulated him physically, too; but she saved that for the end of the scene.

For Lady Macbeth to make some gesture of affection toward her husband was apparently acceptable even for one so Terrible as Pritchard, who—we gather from that stage direction in Gentleman's edition—embraced Garrick: though, again, the image of that formidable matron enclosing the little man suggests more bear-hug than affection. With Siddons we hear of no trace of tenderness throughout I, v; only at the end, a curiously masculine, "vulgar" gesture. By the time of Mrs. Kean, the Lady "hastily advanced . . . and fondly embraced" Macbeth; so far had the note of the Loving Wife insinuated itself into her polyphony. It persisted in nineteenth-century characterization, and if she was not warm enough, she was scolded—so Irving's first Lady, Bateman—for being unconvincing. Bernhardt and Terry changed that.

Terry achieved her contrast by dropping from the heights of the invocation to a soft, warm valley. Her notes: "Smile. Keep voice down now." "Great Glamis, worthy *Cawdor*, Greater than *both*. . . . " Her welcome was all tenderness, a long, loving, silent embrace: "redolent, pungent with the *odeur de femme*. Look how she rushes into her husband's arms, clinging, coaxing, flattering . . . the rapturous greeting tells what deep affection exists between [them]."

The warm welcome had begun to have passion in it. With a shout of joy Wolter rushed to fold Macbeth in her arms. Bernhardt wrapped her Macbeth in a clinging embrace—she clearly meant to play upon his senses more than his reason.

> We almost see the coils of her serpentine enslavement of him as she clings and leans and winds and coaxes with a demeanour all honeyed passion. . . . A clinging, wheedling caressingness suffuses all (her) dealings with this perilous stuff: this seductive, sweet poison which is at once to weaken his virtue and to intoxicate his will *(Liverpool Daily Post)*.

More explicitly erotic reciprocation—if not manipulation—was introduced into some twentieth-century meetings. Bergman, particularly in his first *Macbeth*, emphasized here the physical passion of his young Macbeth and Lady. The young Polish Lady, Mikolajska, frantic with expectation, threw herself into a passionate clinch with her Macbeth, and between kisses, his hand on her breast, they talked around murder. Almost at the moment he entered, Heinrich George, the hulking German Macbeth, was in a passionate embrace with Straub; as they clung together, she made it very clear with her body that she intended to seduce him to the murder. Similarly, Nicole Heesters (Germany, 1966), young, elegant, in a long black dress, at once insinuated herself into the arms of her more innocent Macbeth. Another German Lady lay on the ground, in lascivious expectation of her husband; they embraced passionately, alternating dialogue and caresses. The Czech

Lady Macbeth who had knelt praying to the spirits, with folded hands, now rose, unbuttoned her dressing gown as Macbeth came toward her, and pulled him down on the bed on top of her.

Lady Macbeth must be lovable, Martita Hunt argued, because Macbeth's first words to her are an endearment:

My dearest love . . . (65)

This is his second *dearest*—following the one in the letter. If the words are designed to be more than a marital formality—which they might seem to be between a Terrible Woman and a Macbeth little more than a consenting adult—a strong bond of affection must be felt to hold these two together: or at least him to her. The compassion she may have shed in "unsexing" may be transformed into a more desperate passion. The dark idea they share may seem, in the more erotic embracings, to drive them to intensify their need for each other, even to the point of discoloration—death and procreation having that strange affinity, as in the milkweed that blooms as it is incinerated, the hanged man's erection. Hence, so often, the coupling of love and sex with death—by pun and more seriously—in the Elizabethan-Jacobean literature. So many mixed impulses—as toward desire and danger, holiness and sacrilege—may fuse in the human polyphony: so the passionate Polish Lady Andrycz (1964) was particularly praised for conveying what is implied in all the cited encounters above, and may be seen to run submerged in the play— a connection between violence and the erotic.

What thrusts the Macbeths together may also hold them apart. So Reinhardt's Lady, glowing with passion, brandished his letters to greet him—*thy letters have transported me*—and Macbeth, touched, came to her for a tender embrace—*my dearest love*—but then they separated for a long pause and exchange of glances. Macready embraced his Lady warmly, but through her opening words he was restless, his lips moving unconsciously with his inward thoughts. Forrest, too, greeted his wife with affection; but with his first words he was abstracted, his mind obviously concentrated on the image behind what he said.

In the theatre, dialogue from a close embrace needs skillful acting. It can, for a time, fill a chambered area of the stage, but not for long a wide platform. Some Macbeths, to spread the space and delay the news—and implications— of the royal visit, have taken the time to remove their battle dress as they prepared to speak (thus Piscator's Macbeth taking off helmet and sword, Mantell giving axe and helmet to Seyton to take away). One housewifely Lady unbuckled her husband's breastplates as they moved toward saying what was uppermost in their minds; another soothed and nursed Macbeth's bruises. A Japanese Lady Macbeth, whose arms had been held high above her head at the climax of *hold, hold,* let them fall, as Macbeth entered, until her hands dropped to his shoulders, and at this distance they began to talk.

A sustained separation between Macbeth and his Lady emphasizes the subtextual tensing of their designs as they skirt the dangerous thought they want to share. The cool Lady Macbeths particularly hold off their husbands while managing them. E. K. Schulz (Germany, 1968), kept a good six yards between herself and Macbeth when he entered. A rationale for this fencing was worked out in Hall's rehearsal, with Scofield and Merchant. Her relationship to Macbeth was kept an unresolved tension throughout the play—a subtle equation, in which the two terms were never quite in balance: power and strength flowed between them, but always one held more than the other, and the difference kept them from union, if not communion. They moved toward each other, they thrust each other off, their embraces restrained and few. In rehearsal Scofield's first appearance to her was sudden, he came halfway into the room before his intense advance stopped. This did not seem right to him, nor did it seem to lead to what came next. Hall wanted to maintain the physical space between the two. Scofield tried stopping dead at the entrance: he looked at her, sitting halfway across the stage. She greeted him with a laugh, wise, triumphant, full of ironic knowing of what was in his mind. Hall liked Scofield stopped at this distance, Merchant's excitement and expectation holding him off until the end, with no embrace until all things had been said. Scofield felt like moving; but he thought that if he advanced at all, it had to be straight toward her; if he moved in any direction away, the scene's momentum stopped. "We are only kept from embracing by what we say."

> Hall (to Scofield): Would it help if you came only partly in?
> Scofield: What would stop me, then? . . . If you could even hold up your hand. Vivien? . . . Would it help if she could make her obeisance to me . . . echo our kneeling to Duncan? That would stop me.*
> Hall: She wants to be sure of you, so she holds off the embrace.
> Scofield: But over the matter of Duncan, I have reason to delay it, too. When I say "Duncan comes here tonight," she knows what I mean. There's fear in it.

Then they experimented with her kneeling, and Macbeth entering with one abrupt step before halting. Now his face held hers: strange matters could be read in its ambiguity: a vision of power, an exultancy, a seeking for guidance, and the underlying fear—not physical, much deeper. Merchant smiled the power and exultancy back at him, smiled with a whetted appetite for greatness. Her cool reassurance stiffened this already rocklike man. "Yes," Hall said, "You've got to take him on a bit. He wants to beguile the time." When Macbeth finally did come to her, it was purposefully: he closed the gap.

The first impulse to off-balance the equation seems by design to belong to Lady Macbeth, since she brings to their first meeting a positive force toward

*Dame Madge Kendal (England, 1888) tells how, to honour her "sovereign," "I went down on my knees and prostrated myself before him." Her Macbeth surprised by the then unusual business, lifted her up. Other Ladies have knelt: Mrs. Benson, Vanbrugh, Rigg.

action against his indecision. But, as the moment above indicates, Macbeth brings his own kind of subtextual strength to poise against hers: whether his impulse to murder, or to withdraw from murder, is dominant, either can be formidable, and the conflict between can itself be of magnificent proportions.

The balance can be of strength against strength: a forthright, soldierly Salvini, coming with murder in his eye and voice, will not need incitement, but cooperation; a Macbeth overtly murderous, like Wolfit, risks defusing his Lady's energy. A shrewd, villainous Macbeth, a Henry Irving, has a more masked purpose, manipulates his Lady under the guise of submitting to her: the energy of his wiliness poises against the power of her devotion. His cowardice can invite her courage. The two may at once understand each other, in their seemingly circuitous journey toward agreement: so Vivien Leigh, cool, self-possessed and steely, seeming to say exactly what the saturnine Olivier wanted her to say, but never supinely.* Macbeth may wear a double face to the outer world that he undresses before his Lady, showing her himself—or at least a more revealing inner mask covering his ultimate privacy. Guinness achieved this transformation by dropping the smile which, in public, normally disguised him.

Maeterlinck's Macbeth wore a massive disguise: the giant figure that had first stalked on stage began to dissolve as he took off his armor. The great gauntlets came off, revealing small hands; then the heavy armor and the huge helmet—and the hero was reduced to a small man, dwarfish.

When a single note in the Macbeth polyphony has been overemphasized, the distortion declares itself at once here, when husband and wife meet. Thus Plummer's reduction of himself from man-warrior to man-adolescent: rushing back to his wife-mother with strangled cries and uncontrolled tears, kneeling before her and burying his face in her lap, he made a Macbeth who forced maternalism on his Lady. As a Terrible Woman can make a mouse of her

---

*The actor works backward from his scene, trying to find seeds of motivation for his speech and action. Tynan said to Olivier:

When I saw the performance, it seemed to me that your Macbeth was a guilty man long before he killed Duncan. He was consumed with his own guilt, and, by killing Duncan, almost overcame his guilt, and was able to become a much more powerful monster.

Olivier: Yes, in a way he knew, he knew. Another thing time gives you is more chance to think about things, to work things out in any Shakespearean tragedy. For instance, we worked it out that it was perfectly obvious that, as Lady Macbeth says about the king 'If he had not resembled my father as he lay', Duncan was her father's brother, so that she really was in direct line of succession. And probably the moot, or whatever they were called in Scotland in those days, turned her down because she was only a snip of a girl. They said 'We can't give the crown to her, we'd better give it to the brother'; that happened constantly in those days. But she was in direct line of succession, I'm sure. She then marries the splendid young Montgomery of the time and they would have shared the pillow with many an intimate thought, 'Of course, dear, you're the fellow who ought to be the next king and, after all, I'm the daughter of the last one.' When they first meet Lady Macbeth says to her husband, 'Your face, my thane, is as a book, where men may read strange matters.' They've talked about it and so when he tries to put it off, he says, 'We will speak further': it's something they both know about.

Macbeth, so a mousy Macbeth, like Bergman's second, a weak-spined poet-Hamlet, invites being overwhelmed—in this case by a cold-blooded murderess who fondled him into violence.

From whatever distances of characterization they come, the language forces the two to converge. Lady Macbeth's triple salute—*Glamis, Cawdor, all-hail*—is a shorthand reprise of the Sisters' greeting: so close to it that some unsought memory of his start, of his fear, may return to him. When Siddons said:

> Greater than both, by *the all-hail hereafter*,
> Thy letters have transported me beyond
> This ignorant present, and I feel now
> The future in the instant. (61–64)

Mrs. Jameson was sure that anyone hearing this *hereafter*

> cannot forget the look, the tone . . . a glimpse of that awful *future*, which she, in her prophetic fury, beholds upon the instant.

What this means is not clear: the Lady's vision only penetrates limitedly ahead; presumably Siddons did not apprehend the ultimate catastrophe—she does not suggest anything of the sort in her writing—for her Lady drove fiercely on. Planché heard her as "exultant." But certainly the sense of nextness is forced on us: every single speech in this scene looks ahead: to what may happen, to how to act. Lady Macbeth, living in what will be, plans volubly for both the immediate practical future and the glorious *hereafter*—the word leaves another trace on our memories. Macbeth, looking forward to—and withdrawing from—the making of a decision, has just three very short lines that commit him to nothing. He speaks mainly with his intonation, his face, his body, and the felt tensions of his battle between to do or not to do.

The resistance or acquiescence of Macbeth's inertia to Lady Macbeth's efforts to shift it shapes the final beat. The first advance to climax after his endearment, and his physical imagery (often, after *dearest love* a long welcoming embrace ensues before he brings himself to the next words) is the implication of his simple

> Duncan comes here tonight. (166)

At one extreme is Forrest—the honest warrior burdened by guilt for his imagining—dropping his eyes, and turning away from his wife's searching glances, or Hackett, averting his face, but his eyes alert for her response; at the other, Salvini, his face alight with purpose and ambition, offering an opportunity for her to help him seize, or Irving, his face masked, his back to her, slowly, suggestively, stressing the last two words. Welles began the line, then paused, not sure of what he could say, until something in her look encouraged him to speak; Hopkins had to wet his lips before he could get the words out; they burst from Macready, came with a "little tremor" from the Maeterlinck Macbeth.

And when goes hence? (67)

Her four-word answer is also loaded with unspoken meaning: from Bernhardt's thoughtful, wifely, "Et quand part-il?" and Modjeska's mild "feeler," to Welles' Lady, speaking very slowly, throwing the darkest implication of the words fully at him, or the "fell significance" of Ristori's "look and tone." Mme. Maeterlinck spoke "In a dead voice . . . merely to dispel the silence." Forrest liked the idea of Macbeth's keeping his eyes averted here, so that he does not become consciously aware of his Lady's fixed stare, her murderous intent. Mrs. Kean, with just such a penetrating stare, laid her hand on her husband's arm, and whispered the words hoarsely. Irving could not get away from Terry, who put her right hand eagerly on his breast, turned him to make him face her, and smiled slowly—"action first," she reminded herself—before she spoke, almost playfully, emphasizing "when *goes* hence?"

Lady Macbeth, though more positive, still fishes for the open commitment she herself would not yet give; he answers in kind—again says much more than his words. And in how many ways he says it! He begins by setting a term to the future about which she asks: *Tomorrow*—a word that will haunt him. Kemble could say the whole four-word line with indifference, as still innocent, still waiting for the Lady to drive him to murder; not so, many later Macbeths. Kean, typically, combined ambiguous intent with innocent words, the tones of voice and manner mixing in a controlled dissonance: his *Tomorrow* was emphatic, but his look was hesitant—"he half divulges the secret in his breast." He paused then, before hesitatingly going on with the last three words—which indeed seem designed to betray the first one—again suggesting a wish countering his speech. Pitoëff's meaning, too, was mainly in the look that undermined his language: conspiratorial, betraying covetousness and fear, cowardice and gratitude to Lady Macbeth for giving him a hint to reveal himself.

Salvini, at least half ready for the murder, paused for a moment, glanced furtively around, then said, very quietly, "Tomorrow . . . as *he* purposes," with a lingering emphasis on the stressed word as he looked straight at his wife, in a grave, intent, wordless interchange. Macready quickly answered *Tomorrow*; then, sensing that his strong wife felt his murderous impulse but also his irresolution, added the rest in a lower voice, slowly, very carefully, his face a "chaos of conflicting emotions" *(Iris)*. Forrest was checked, after his *Tomorrow*, by his wife, who suddenly grasped his arm and looked him in the eye; then he filled out the line. Irving's Macbeth paused, rapt, lost in imaginings again; then avoiding his Lady's eyes, spoke with an affected indifference that gave the lie to his words. Mme Maeterlinck, of her Macbeth: "The Thane of Glamis will not speak at once. He knows that the moment has arrived when the secret, brutally broken by his dauntless wife . . . will burst into shivers around him; he draws a long breath, as though he would retain the last few seconds of a freedom soon to be snatched from him; and, slowly and heavily, he replies." Mantell, who had avoided any embrace with his Lady, his mind full of murderous intentions, left her in no doubt by his intonations that he did not want Duncan ever to leave, and yet he seemed to be sounding her out. Sothern, more conscience-burdened, had broken away from their embrace at her question, so that the two stood facing the audience, as if both waited for a decision to be made. His *Tomorrow*, as he turned away, was a kind of musing. Forbes-Robertson's poet-philosopher wavered in the speech as he wavered to and fro through the scene, unable to make up his own mind, and too involved in thought and vision to yield yet to his Lady. Welles frankly made the speech a question, made the future a question.

Lady Macbeth slashes through the web of implication. Whether the primary note is her impatience to dominate him, from ambition, power or love; or that by indirection she has found his indirection out; or that she is responding to his covert manipulation of her, she now speaks what is in their minds. Again, she avoids the unspeakable: she says, "We will kill him" in innocent words that on their face only express again her dream of controlling the future.

> O never,
> Shall sun that morrow see. (69–70)

The Folio appropriately breaks the apostrophe into two lines, for the first two words bear a great, sustained weight, while the next five march or dance, depending on the Lady. The speech may release a terrible relief: thus Mme. Maeterlinck's experience—"Lady Macbeth's great cry has rent the silence, torn hypocrisy asunder; and, like a dazzling light poured into the darkness of their souls, the truth shows them . . . naked, shaking, and trembling, welded into one by fear, love, and ambition."

For Siddons, the speech became an awful, "imperious injunction," entirely self-involved, trampling over the innocence of a noble Macbeth like Kemble, that deeply impressed Bell.

> A long pause, turned away from him, her eye steadfast. Strong dwelling emphasis on "never," with deep downward inflection, "never shall sun that morrow see" suggesting a repetition and modulation of *never*. Her speaking was very low, slow, sustained almost syllable by syllable.

Bell thought unforgettable, inconceivable, indescribable her "self-collected, solemn energy, her fixed posture, determined eye and full deep voice of fixed resolve," her concentration on "her horrible purpose."

Even a stout warrior like Kemble's Macbeth might be forgiven for blanching under this declaration; what Siddons saw of his mind's construction in his face displeased her.

> Your face, my Thane, is as a book, where men
> May read strange matters. . . . (71–72)

"Very slow, severe, and cruel expression, her gesture impressive." At her soul-searching tones, J. H. Siddons noticed, "Kemble hung his head, as if he could not withstand her penetrating gaze . . . [into] the ambitious whisperings of his own heart." He got no sympathy. She looked at him closely, to see the effect of her words on him; and at *be the serpent* she again spoke slowly, severely, cruelly.

Some Ladies managed their Macbeths in lighter keys. Ristori, the *Sydney Herald* observed, urged Macbeth to murder with "persuasive cajolery;" Mirren made an "enchanting game" of it. Much was unspoken in Terry's sharing of the moment with Irving: "Tender movements rather than verbal expressions; sweet cajolings as if to indicate that the bad business affected the one as much as the other". She heard his subtextual message with a sigh, put her extended arm quickly on his shoulder, then, "her head up, inspired," she cried "Never shall sun *that* morrow see," with "wicked delight." Then she looked at him looking at her: *Your face, my Thane* . . . Irving's expression "unfolded the entire tragedy to come"; her note: "Bright, quick, aflame, alert, smile at him—or a quick exclamation." Observers sensed various impulses in her. "She is persuaded that he will remain moody and discontented until the throne is his." "She indicates that she must assume masculine strength to support him." "Visibly dreading lest her lord should lapse into reflection, smartens her tone, puts life and lightness into her glances, and as it were plucks him by the sleeve, to nudge him onward in the practical present." Irving's note: "Recover. Smile."

In the theatre, a far-off trumpet, heralding Duncan, often cues Lady Macbeth's next push. Terry, advising Irving's Macbeth how to double when the coming on should demand it, herself smiled to show the kind of face she recommended. Observers wondered at the sweetness with which she counselled duplicity:

> Look like the time, bear welcome in your eye,
> Your hand, your tongue: look like th'innocent flower,
> *But be the serpent under't.** (73–75)

The speech, encouraging Macbeth to "act," has itself invited acting: so Terry smiled, so Faucit, her voice exultant, allowed herself a playful moment— she showed how to "look like the 'time' by an action of curtseying about" (*Examiner*).

The recoil of the last line, like the cracking of a whip, has the effect of a theatrical coup; it has been whispered. Lady Macbeth's gestures have similarly worked on Macbeth: her softening of his tensed or clenched fist—*your hand*— and her pressing it against his—or her—knife.

To fool the *time*, the world of other men, smacks of the usual mouth-honoring of the court with its conventional manners; her image for the dysfunction be-

*Siddons emphasis.

tween seeming and intention—*flower* and *serpent*—carries implications insidious rather than terrible. Even the sudden stressing of the sinister first words
is swallowed in her next clever disguising—surely the most ghastly euphemism in Shakespeare, Verity thought—that is often cued by a closer approaching trumpet that spurs the Lady's planning:

> He that's coming,
> Must be provided for. (75–76)

It is not entirely euphemism. She means indeed to "provide" for Duncan
(though again, watching her words, she avoids mentioning either his name
or rank). The language itself doubles, literally equivocates: it talks with two
voices. Savits' Lady made this very clear by speaking very slowly, stressing
each word, letting Macbeth appreciate the ambiguity; recognizing it, he
returned a double signal of his own: he dropped his eyes, but tenderly pressed
her hand. An actress of the Terrible mode, Cushman, was less subtle, snarling
the words as if to say, almost literally, "murder." She seemed to observers
especially appalling when, towering over her Macbeth, she pointed beyond
him toward Duncan's road, and pitilessly spoke the sentence of death.

Terry expected a reaction from her Macbeth here. Her note: "a look like
lightning will help me—I clap a hand on his mouth." To override any resistance, she will "keep fierce." A spectator heard "trumpet tones [that] show
the rising of her soul." The Lady concentrates her attack where he is vulnerable—he is designed to aspire to *great* deeds, and to enjoy recognition for them
(and her cover word, perhaps preceded by a pause—*business*—will shield him
from the reality she intends):

> and you shall put
> This night's great business into my dispatch,
> Which shall to all our nights and days to come,

(Here, "Simmer down," Terry told herself)

> Give solely sovereign sway, and masterdom. (76–79)

Our nights and days. Even in the tenderest Ladies, the undertone of ambition suitable to an overreacher sounds here. For the first time she uses the
first person plural. She allows herself to speak of a future glorious not only
for him, but for her as well. And the sovereignty she expects to share is by
name masculine: *masterdom*.

Through this brief beat, Macbeth's primacy as thane, husband, warrior
has been impinged upon, if not threatened, by her manipulation. To a calculating Macbeth like Irving's, his wife has said exactly what he wishes to hear:
he wants her accumulating, partnering force to impel him to do what he
wishes. But more often Macbeth may be felt still to resist here, as he speaks
of delay; and his procrastination may be designed partly as a defense against
his sense of her encroaching sovereignty and masterdom over him.

So the beat—and the scene—climb to an ambiguity, to intensify toward a suspended climax the whipsaw between the urgings of his wife and his resisting self. His continued irresolution points toward his next appearance, in Scene vii, when he will, in a step higher in intensity, touch the peaks of his agonized indecision. So now Kemble would attempt momentarily to preserve the innocence of noncommitment even under the cruel assault of Siddons; with all Irving's readiness to cooperate with Terry's sweeter promptings, he had, in the words Shakespeare gave him, to insist on putting off a final acquiescence. Macbeths between these extremes, more vulnerable than Kemble, more conscience-troubled than Irving, engage throughout the scene in a subtle interplay in which many overt and repressed notes are sounded. Thus Marlowe, after Sothern moved apart from her on *as he purposes,* went to him, and with her hand turned his face so he had to look at her. When she read withdrawal in his troubled look *(Your face, my thane . . .)* she started to turn away; then it was his turn to move toward her, and seize her hand, before a final embrace—his yielding giving her an implied authority to go on. Wolter achieved leadership through her sensual control of Macbeth. At his entrance she had given her shout of joy, and embraced him hotly. She did not let Macbeth finish *as he purposes;* she broke in abruptly; then, as he paused at this check, she was in his arms again, tenderly whispering *Your face*—literally pouring her insinuating spirits into his ear. She used all the power of her body—an observer noted her glowing, promising eyes, under heavy eyelids— to create a sensuous, langorous atmosphere that slowed his resistance to her.

More sophistication was brought to Macbeth's seduction by Heesters. She tenderly nestled in Macbeth's arms as she denied Duncan any tomorrows; at her husband's troubled reaction she gently held his head between her hands, very close to her, and looking into his eyes told him how much his face revealed. Her voice was low, almost singing. She followed *the serpent* by taking him in her arms again for a passionate embrace. In her black, glittering dress, her body, like the body of a serpent, seemed to wind around him; he had the almost hypnotized look of a serpent's—or a witch's—victim.

Reinhardt's Lady also controlled her Macbeth with beauty and passion; but he was designed to be insistently anxious, and she had to deal with him firmly as well as sensually and tenderly. At *When goes hence,* she fixed him with piercing eyes; he brought out *Tomorrow,* and then dropped his eyes before her as he muttered the rest. She reacted with tremendous energy—*O never . . . ;* but seeing the strain on him, she looked at him tenderly, stroked his forehead softly and lovingly: *Your face. . . .* The energy returned at her thought of *all our nights and days:* the *regiebuch* has

> her bosom, neck and nostrils swell, her eyes sparkle. She seizes his hand and shouts with joy.

Occasionally a visual symbol intensifies the strategies of interaction. Tree's poet-Macbeth, after breaking from a passionate, welcoming embrace, exchanged a long look with his Lady before they spoke. His mind seemed raw with imagined thoughts and visions; after *O never* . . ., when Vanbrugh reached out to touch him, as this Loving Wife often did, he pushed her hand away, and sank back on a seat. She knelt beside him, looked up: *Your face* . . . and, wanting to touch him, as if by accident, brushed his dagger. Macbeth noticed; one of Tree's promptbooks indicates that she immediately withdrew her hand, another directs: "[Macbeth?] "puts hands away." In either case, the dagger had become an objective symbol of their unspoken thought, and of his resistance. The knife similarly proclaimed itself in the Polanski film; Lady Macbeth, helping her husband to dress for Duncan's coming, spoke her *O never* . . . with a laugh, and meaningfully handed him the dagger; he looked reluctance, and her weapon against him, to be exploited more fully in I, vii, was to show the hurt of rejection on her young face. In the Anthony Quayle staging (England, 1949), after Macbeth's tender greeting, during which he stroked his Lady's hair, then turned away at her first incitement, she leaned in his arms, and at *Must be provided for* touched the hilt of his sword.

To intensify the pressure Lady Macbeth is designed to exert on Macbeth now, the theatre may bring the sounds of Duncan's approach to the castle itself. Time, a relentless force in this play, is insistent. Horses' hooves, sometimes stressed as an aural motif, may be heard. The king is coming to the gates.

If we do not know the play, this scene must seem decisive: *naive* spectators expected this to be the pivotal moment when, if Macbeth was ever to be persuaded, he would be persuaded now. Hence the mounting force of Lady Macbeth's vision of their great expectations, as she outtalks him, five lines to one, looking always to the future: look innocent—provision shall be made—I will take care of all—greatness for all our days—tomorrow and tomorrow and tomorrow. . . . Against the power and seduction of her hypnotic attack, he can only take refuge in suspension: *We will speak further* (80). She brushes it away. Again she urges him to clear his face of its strange matters: not only to present a doubled surface, but as if such a surface will assure calm within, will banish the fear she may sense in his uneasy face (this is a kind of prefiguring of the James-Lange theory—that a physical state precedes an emotional). But her strictures seem mainly aimed at asking him to keep well behaved and out of her way: *Leave* . . . *all the rest to me* (perhaps pausing before "all the rest" as she finds another substitution for the deed without a name). The assumption of her responsibility seems absolute.

Siddons made final her power over her Macbeth by leading him out, cajoling him, clapping her hand on his shoulder—a masculine gesture appropriate enough to her characterization, though to Bell it seemed vulgar, as demeaning Macbeth. Bell would have preferred a "higher mental" submission rather than this docile physical one.

Ristori's physical manipulation of her Macbeth was more subtle, but the firm management was the same. His *We will speak further*, she had greeted with a smile, as a half-accomplished purpose: he had not refused her. She meant to go on to absolute control. She

> domineers over him with a show of persuasion, casting her arms about him as about a child, she dandles him, as it were, into obedience to her wishes . . . the weak man still struggling and hesitating.

Ristori was determined to complete the "overwhelming influence I exercised over him, silencing any further remonstrances on his part." She pointed to herself: *Leave all the rest to me;* she drew his left arm around her waist:

> I took his right hand in mine, and placing the first finger on my lips thus swore him to silence. Then I gradually and gently pushed him behind the scenes, towards which his back was now turned . . . accomplished with so much delicacy and so many magnetic looks.—

she added modestly—

> that Macbeth had to own their fascination and yield to my will.

Observers saw: "the heroic disdain of her expression"; "her head nodding slowly at him, the smile of determination on her face"; "he is in her power: he moves at her urging."

Even with a Macbeth as ready to act as Salvini—who spoke his *further* line with divided feelings: concerned by the imminence of Duncan's entrance, but wanting to continue the conversation—Lady Macbeth has the last word. This requires Macbeth to project the line of his indecision to his next inward debate in I, vii—unless he is playing the hypocrite long since determined on murder, as Irving was.

Irving's Macbeth, having brought his Lady to urge what he wanted, could act unhappy here. Her notes to herself for her last speech: "Caution, great change. The charm of the serpent." She could imagine the curtain closing on a tableau with ambiguous implications, that did not leave *all the rest* to her: the two plotting, she kneeling at his feet. One promptbook has her leading him off. But Irving preferred a gorgeous exit: she puts her arm around his neck tenderly; he breaks away, as if going off dejected; then turns, puts out his arms, she comes into them, they go off embracing.

The suggestion that, in spite of Macbeth's final verbal refusal to commit himself, he and Lady Macbeth are already subtextually at one, or very close to it, has been made explicit in other stagings. Thus Porter, a practical Macbeth, said the line as if he did not necessarily reject his wife's urging, but perhaps only wanted to continue it later, at a better time. The two went off with quiet laughter.

Other Macbeths, more committed to indecision than decision, had less control over their leaving. The poets and philosophers are likely to be rapt again, as Phelps was. His Lady Macbeth had started her exit, turned to find him still standing, abstracted, had to urge him off. Countering tensions of irresolution and remorse paralyzed Macready; his Lady, too, had to lead him out. An American Lady Macbeth, faced with a Macbeth awakening to protest, quieted him with a quick kiss, and towed him away. Viola Allen's note for managing Macbeth here: "loving and caressing."

In Macbeths sensitive to the slipping of conscience, the tones of suffering sound. So with an American Macbeth (1962): at *We will speak*, the "sweet, sad, hopeless attempt to put off his own ineluctable thoughts." As Forrest struggled for innocence, his eyes dropped to the ground, then seemed to be looking deeply into the future; the four last words came out low and uneasy, disjointed, as if he were saying "perhaps it is better—that—I—should—reflect—upon this." His irresolution was a torment to him, as he let his Lady guide him off.

Shakespeare seems to instruct Macbeth to drop his eyes, as Forrest did, to cue Lady Macbeth's *Only look up*. . . . But the words carry the doubled implication of degree: look to the topmost, the crown. Merchant said it this way to Scofield, bringing from him a lifting of the vision as well as of the head.

Tree turned his raptness to account. He looked straight into Vanbrugh's eyes to say *speak further*. At her earnest reply, their eyes locked, and then he half pushed her away. They heard the noise of Duncan's approach; she knew she must leave, but at the door she turned to look at him before she went off. He went abstractedly to the window to watch the king's noisy approach, and a slow curtain found him musing there. This focused attention on a brooding Macbeth, in whose mind Duncan's murder was still very much alive: and, by sending Lady Macbeth ahead, it effected a bridge to the next scene's meeting between her and the king.

Something surprising turned up in the responses here of the *naive* spectators, who, having never read or seen the play, did not know that I, vii was still to come. They took Lady Macbeth at her word. She has four times spoken of doing the unspoken, unspeakable act; she has appealed for supernatural help for the unsexing that will enable her to do it. Her last controlling speech, in I, v, pivotal for anyone experiencing the play afresh, seems to confirm her determination: *my* keen knife . . . *my* fell purpose . . . into *my* dispatch . . . now: leave all the rest to *me*. *Naive* spectators in all three experiments—in America and England—expected her to proceed now to kill Duncan, and involve Macbeth in the tragedy that follows. Who is to say no, at this point in the play?

This castle hath a pleasant seat . . .

Act I, Scene vi

The action is continuous. As Macbeth and his Lady exit, perhaps behind the curtains of a chamber, intimacy is again succeeded by pageantry. To the piping of hautboys, the king approaches, with his court. The Folio seems to stipulate the hierarchy of degree in the order of their coming: king, older prince, younger, then the thanes—apparently by rank after Banquo—including one we have not yet seen, Macduff. He has said nothing as yet, and will say nothing now; but something, in his stature, or color of garments, will mark him as different from Lenox, whom he follows, and from Ross, Angus, and the attendants. Shakespeare liked as big a procession as the Globe could mount; remember his innocent stage direction in *Titus:* for the entry of every character he could name, "and as many as may be." Duncan's advent will only be less spectacular than the carefully spaced, increasingly powerful crowd scenes to come.

The Folio prescribes *torches* for the entrance, a sure sign that darkness was at least falling.* Critics and producers who prefer the contrast of sunlight to the darkness of most other scenes suggest that the torches should not be there—though there is no reference to bright daylight. Trusting as I do generally in the Folio editing, I accept darkness coming on, the more so for an implied direction in the previous scene: Lady Macbeth has invoked *thick night*; in this part of the play the wishes and hopes of the Macbeths seem promptly to be realized.

The logic of the action suggests evening, at least. The witches have met Macbeth, after the battle, *ere set of sun*. The day, including the battle, has been a long one. Macbeth and Banquo then go either to Duncan's court at Forres or to his camp (probably the former, to fit the flourish that greeted the king).

---

*One critic suggests that the only explanation for the torches is that "the directions are for an indoor performance (Blackfriars) or for night performances at court, for it is only at court that night performances are recorded at this period." If the Folio here reflects Shakespeare's intention, as I think it does, the torches would have been used to suggest a darkening ambience on both indoor and outdoor stages, whether in daylight or at night. Public performances *did* take place at night "at this period"—see Rosenberg (6).

Macbeth, Duncan, and the court attendants then make the journey to Inverness. (The actual distances are not important; Shakespeare probably did not know them, and did not care about them.) Lady Macbeth's summoning of the night suggests that the darkness may have begun to come down as Macbeth arrived; Macbeth said *Duncan comes here tonight*—and now Duncan is here. All this logic, however, is secondary to the functioning of the work of art. Shakespeare makes time stretch and shrink so flexibly in the gaps between scenes that the mind adjusts without questioning to shifts of place and period.

In the Globe, Duncan would have entered with his entourage to the broad platform imagined as before the castle, or as its courtyard, and mused on the prospect. (Muir suggests that at sundown torches could be needed inside the battlements even with light outside.) In realistic staging, both inside and outside locales have been used, commonly in darkness, to provide the mysterious shadows that promise menace. For economy's sake, the inner courtyard is often preferred because it serves for many scenes besides this one; but when spectacle has been primary, the outer castle has made possible a special richness. For a gorgeous example: Irving brought Duncan to Inverness in deep moonlight. A horn from the approaching party held converse with a horn from the castle. Glimmering lights could be seen from the tall towers of the castle's casements, torches flared under the massive arches of a raised portcullis flanked by greenery. The king and his glittering train of princes, nobles, and soldiers, with their waving tartans and flashing steel, drums beating, seemed to rise from behind an invisible hill, wind their way up a defile, to ascend the stone steps. A large party from the castle, with torches, came to meet them.

It was very dramatic and dark, but it challenged the sense of Duncan's dialogue with Banquo about the castle's surroundings.

> This castle hath a pleasant seat,
> The air nimbly and sweetly recommends itself
> Unto our gentle senses. (5–7)

Duncan could, of course, become aware in his night approach of the castle's location on a knoll, and breathe the cool night breezes—in the theatre he may take a breath before his second line. Banquo's language even more challenges a castle night-hidden, or one with its battlements only silhouetted, as Reinhardt's were; or a grim, inner courtyard with no sense of outwardness, as with Craig's blocks of stone, all angles, lit in green and blue. Similarly, the words have nothing at all in common with stylized settings like Jessner's ravines and precipices, or Komisarjevsky's twisted aluminum pillars—no self-respecting martlet, one critic observed, could be found nesting in such a metal nightmare.

> This guest of summer,
> The temple-haunting martlet* does approve,

*I like the suggestion by A. P. Paton in the *Variorum*, "We think the [Folio] word 'barlet', for which *martlet* is generally substituted, will yet turn up."

By his loved mansionry, that the Heaven's breath
Smells wooingly here: no jutty frieze,
Buttress, nor coign of vantage, but this bird
Hath made his pendant bed, and procreant cradle,
Where they most breed, and haunt: I have observ'd
The air is delicate. (8–15)

The serene pastoral note sounds strongly in these first two speeches. The irony is unmistakable; Duncan, who tells the dangerous castle's mind from its face, greets it with pleasure. Banquo, who might sense the danger, is almost lyric in his description of Inverness' innocence. Some politicized modern productions have tried to empty these speeches of anything but convention. In a German production, described by Brecht, the Macbeths were treated as petty Scottish nobility, neurotically ambitious, and Inverness as a semi-dilapidated grey keep of striking poverty, where the guests' words were obviously false compliments. Welles, in his Black *Macbeth,* worked into the background society's misfits, poor, misshapen, the kind Malcolm would describe in England, *all swoln and ulcerous, pitiful to the eye;* and a Canadian production similarly emphasized an oppressed background proletariat, faceless in grey flannel rags, the upper social level represented by a Lady Macbeth preparing to work like any housewife at her churn when interrupted by the king.

These interpretations scent the degree of rottenness behind the facades in *Macbeth,* but not the kind. The poor "naked wretches" that belong to *Lear* are not primary here; Shakespeare is concentrating on men of the highest rank and culture involved in covert struggles for power and personal identity. More relevant are signs of hunger for degree: Malcolm and Donalbain looking distrustfully at Lady Macbeth (as in the Carrick Craig staging); Banquo studying Lady Macbeth's face as intently as he studied earlier Macbeth's—all beneath the guise of good manners. Inverness, on its face, represents civilization, courtly etiquette, elegant hospitality, the very essence of order. Like so much in the play, it doubles.

As we see—or imagine—Duncan entering the castle, we feel repeated the danger of his trust when Macbeth came to him in I, iii; greater danger, now, because he is entering a house whose mistress is determined he shall not leave. We expect this trust from Duncan; but what of Banquo? Does he carry with him any of his experience with the witches? Any ambitions of his own, if not suspicions of Macbeth? His speech sounds like a courtier's pleasant accompaniment to his king's theme; but also, in a fine fusion of character and language, it speaks feelingly of breeding and procreation, ideas that come appropriately from the subconscious of a man whose children have been promised kingship, who in Shakespeare's design is an important component of the child-seed-growth motif threading the play. Such gentle, procreant birds as he speaks of we will meet again, but not until we visit the castle of the Macduffs—where again violence will lie in wait.

Banquo's speeches, and the soft birdsong that might be heard to cue them, suggested to Joshua Reynolds, and others, a moment of relief from the tension thus far roused. Where Duncan is equated with God, this is a glimpse of Eden, a metaphor for Scotland—even "the well-planned garden of God and Duncan." But as we have seen, Scotland has been turbulent confusion until Macbeth steadied it; and we, seeing or imagining this scene, anticipate against hope a return to violence. Knowles was surely right, as against Reynolds, that perceiving Duncan's unconsciousness of his destined fate must "aggravate in the beholder the feeling of . . . predicament." One of the characteristic ironies of the play is that so much pastoral serenity is associated not with Duncan, but with Macbeth. This is his castle. This quick, bright glimpse of the aura of peace in which he lives measures how much is at stake for him, how much he may lose, may throw away after Duncan enters his walls. For Duncan, the "image of life inviting life" that Knights eloquently discerned in these first speeches is a mirage, floating over a beckoning death trap; waywardly both the raven and the martlet abide here. Again fair and foul come together.

The mirage is more alluring for the personal welcome Duncan receives. The ceremonial seems seductively secure, often staged with great panoply. Thus Macready's Duncan was preceded by five attendants, two with torches, and accompanied by thanes as well as Fleance (frequently present in this scene in the theatre), and six lords. He was met by Seyton, eight servants with torches, eight ladies, and the physician, as well as Lady Macbeth—all glittering in the firelight, while music played off. Producers have invented special treats for Duncan; thus Bergman entertained him with a violent Scots sworddance in the castle courtyard, as torch-bearing men on the battlements, drinking from stoups of wine, cheered and laughed. Among others who come to welcome Duncan is sometimes the Porter, attending the castle gate. Quayle's Duncan was so pressed about by his subjects that Banquo had to quiet them. Duncan may give all his blessing. Such gestures may become the good old man; but reviewers have complained when Duncan, in this, his last appearance, has been so beneficent and innocent that the Macbeths were made to seem even more evil than now they are.

The important welcomer is Lady Macbeth. She has perhaps changed or added to her garments to come out to meet Duncan. Her resolve, we know, is to kill this king she is about to confront. We who do not know the play wonder when she will act. How will she feel as she sees him—this old man who in sleep, she is later to realize, resembles her father? Does anything in his old face check her now, as she prepares to greet him? Will she want still to execute, in reality, the murderous fancy of her solitude?

The Folio directs her to meet Duncan and his entourage alone, the single woman facing all those men. As Duncan moves forward from the rest, this brings the two to focus, and her subtextual responses to the confrontation can be sharply perceived. So, Tree, restraining himself from the romantic grandiloquence of the rest of his production, sacrificed spectacle to concentration on the lonely figure of Vanbrugh, suddenly standing solitary at the entrance to the castle, swatched in a long scarlet veil—and in ambiguity, a "figure of fate"—as she watched Duncan come to her.

Duncan's *See, see our honor'd hostess* (16) may be spoken before the Lady appears, to swing the eyes of actors and audience to her entrance, and hold all poised, wondering. Then the king launches into his own kind of doubling: a whimsical oxymoronic speech, opposites flung together.

> The love that follows us, sometime is our trouble,
> Which still we thank as love. Herein I teach you,
> How you shall bid God 'ield us for your pains,
> And thank us for your trouble. (17–20)

There is a hint of reward in the speech, characteristic of Duncan: some royal token may now be borne to Lady Macbeth, or seem to be promised. Much later Macduff will say that for avarice Scots rulers had been murdered:

> It hath been
> The sword of our slain kings. (IV, iii, 101–102)

(Let us note, in passing, that this will hardly be a compliment to James, whose own avarice was notorious in England.) But Duncan has been lavish with promises, and if he does not bestow anything tangible now, will send a jewel later. For himself, he wants a prayer that God reward him.

Lady Macbeth's response is as conventional as Macbeth's was in I, iv. It is rich in comparatives, quantifying loyalty and service; *all, every, twice, double, poor, single.* Doubled and redoubled, she says, we cannot match the royal largesse, and she promises the persistent prayers to heaven that Duncan asked:

> We rest your hermits. (27)

Actresses have been tempted into playing the scene under a very thin layer of surface: obviously doubling—hiding from Duncan, but making evident to us, the spider game the Lady is playing. Blatant hypocrisy must not only abuse the finesse in the character design, it must also make too much of a fool of Duncan; yet absolute sincerity would also be untrue to the character's action. The Lady *is* doubling; but the subtextual feelings behind her pretensions of loyalty are more complex than the poor and single business of treacherous manipulation. She has had to pray that the power to kill possess her, body and mind; she comes directly from assuring Macbeth that she will see to *all*; now she meets her victim in the flesh she would destroy.

The complexity of the doubling, even on the Machiavellian level, is suggested in Morley's ambiguous description of Ristori here. He saw "much subtlety in the art which makes the spirit of the fox apparent in the manners of these humble or graceful solicitations. It is not overacted, there is a false tone in her voice, a false expression playing faintly now and then across her face, always most intense when spoken words are humblest." But the audience already knows the fox (or serpent) is there; and to refrain from reminding us— and to mask the beast so entirely that not even the most suspicious courtiers could discern it, and warn the king—suggests even greater subtlety. This Ristori was seen to manifest in Sydney: "Her own direction to 'Look like the innocent flower . . .' is absolutely fulfilled, for every suspicion must be lulled . . . [We see] nothing but a seeming cordiality, a plenitude of hospitality."

We may guess at the obvious hypocrisy of some actresses from the praise of Bateman, Irving's first Lady Macbeth, for avoiding "that vulgar by-play, expressions of satisfaction at caging her victim [of] some representatives of the part . . . her reticence makes the scene infinitely more impressive than if any secret hint were conveyed to the audience." One reviewer saw in her Medicean subtlety a "fearful grace."

One subtle sign of the Lady's doubling is sometimes seen in the very warmth of her hospitality. Such a Lady Macbeth comes out showing the charm and élan that must have endeared her to Macbeth, and that have earned the praise Duncan bestows on her. Often she kneels to kiss the king's hand, as Forrest's Ponisi did, or his robe, as Dench did, reprising the visual imagery of homage to Duncan in I, ii; the ambiguous bowing of the Sisters in I, iii; and the genu-flection of Mabeth to the king in I, iv. Mirren sank on the floor before Duncan, and touched his foot. Faucit added a gentle—but ambivalent—touch to the welcome she forced herself to make. She did not like pretending; her courteous mask was such that while the king could not see through it, the audience could detect the difficulty with which it was worn. She turned to Fleance among the courtiers, and graced him with a kind caress. In the reverse language of her seeming, to the audience the signal of affection seemed to promise mischief.

Wolter drew out her entrance by descending a great flight of stairs—the stairs so common in Macbeth staging, for this scene and others—and then enveloped Duncan in a welcome, to all appearances friendly, charming, and completely natural. As she bowed to him, her arms were opened wide in welcome, her voice a melody of hospitality. Marlowe, on the other hand, came out in a rush, suggesting the hurry of her departure from Macbeth, then stopped for the audience to take in the two principals, while members of the royal company saluted her, the attendant soldiers raised their spears, and torchbearers bowed. Then she made her deep curtsy and kissed Duncan's hand. He laughed his compliments to her, she smiled back, laughing gently herself at his *fair and noble hostess.* Terry bowed to the very ground, with a sweep of her great grey mantle; the pause of confrontation was filled, Kate Terry remembered, by the subdued chatter of soldiers and servingmen, and the huddles of curious maids. Terry's notes: "humbly—knowing her place. Most modest . . . sincere, fresh voice . . . the innocent flower—simplicity acted." An observer saw "no trace of her fell purpose . . . under the almost affectionate reverence she pays." But Terry did not think the Lady should seem as innocent as Macbeth, and for all her freshness the shadows showed: one reviewer enjoyed "the bewitching and sinuous grace with all the diablerie that is implied," another "the eyes gleaming, almost gloating, in the flickering torchlight."

Some Lady Macbeths were reserved, particularly the cooler ones, like Merchant, bending to Duncan courteously but without warmth. Reinhardt's emotional Lady was carefully plain and serious, her face impenetrable, as if emphasizing her tempest within by carefully repressing it. Her manner was proper and no more.

Ladies in the Siddons pattern tended to meet Duncan on equal terms, queenly, as Pritchard was said to be. Bell described Siddons as speaking musically, "dignified and simple"—suggesting that she was modulating the fierce tones of her previous scene. A Kemble promptbook indicates that she started to kneel, but Duncan prevented her. Perhaps the most regal of all was Cushman. All the other Ladies that Wingate had seen were fawning:

> Cushman alone, while paying due homage to Duncan . . . and playing the hostess to perfection, never for a moment permitted the audience to [forget] that socially and by birth she was the peer of a king.

Where's the thane of Cawdor? (28) the King asks. Lady Macbeth, by a look or gesture, may indicate that her husband is in the castle. In some productions, Macbeth is seen lurking in a corner, watching. Duncan goes on, using rider-and-spur imagery that echoes the play's offstage sounds of horses as well as its verbal figures.

> We coursed him at the heels, . . .
>   But he rides well,
> And his great love [sharp as his spur] hath holp him
> To his home before us: (29–32)

The Lady answers again in conventional language of service and loyalty, and need not make any show of hypocrisy; Terry was even able, in a visual grace note, to manifest her delight at hearing her husband praised. But we who have heard the Lady a moment before assume command of *this night's great business* may hear the echo in her quantifying, commercial metaphor that everything done for Duncan, doubled and redoubled, were *poor and single business* (Terry's note: "Somebody please put this in plainer words):

> Your servants ever,
> Have theirs, themselves, and what is theirs in compt,
> To make their audit. . . .
> *Duncan:* Give me your hand: (34–36, 38)

He is ready to follow her in; and now that the moment has come for her victim to enter under the battlements, the reality of what she intends forces itself on her. In Ristori, the *Scotsman* observed a "fine, subtle suggestion that conscience in her, even at that stage," had not been entirely extinguished—"by the almost involuntary shrinking she displayed when the good old King offered her his hand." Cushman, too, was momentarily self-betrayed: at Duncan's gracious gesture she momentarily recoiled.

Modjeska, who had begun by being warm and caressing to Duncan, now involuntarily stepped back from the royal gesture, had to force herself to return, take the hand, and kiss it. Leigh hesitated, and only very slowly brought herself to make the salute. Bradley could find "no trace of pity for the kind old king"; but some reservation checked these Ladies, some unwanted doubling of feeling, as they would later be checked at the old man asleep. In the polyphony of impulses projected subtextually, pity might be one undertone of many.

Duncan asks Lady Macbeth to lead him to her husband, again with promises:

> we love him highly,
> And shall continue, our graces towards him.
> By your leave hostess. (39–41)

This last is the royal signal to go; conventionally Duncan, his hand outstretched so she can put hers on it, leads the way—though he may also kiss Lady Macbeth, as in Nunn's staging. If they are outside, he leads her within; the advantage of playing the scene within the "courtyard" is that Duncan can be seen moving toward the room he will occupy—an important focus for future action. His room will be up stairs—for we will learn that a descent must be made from it.

Leigh saw Duncan off with a final Judas kiss. In the Craig staging, the Lady watched him and the others enter the castle; then, as the inner curtain fell behind her, she stood facing the audience, her face reflecting the implications of her entrapment of the king. But often the Lady accompanies Duncan out, as Marlowe did, after a deep curtsy. Siddons, in her mask of respect, bowed graciously and sweetly to the princes and thanes as she followed her royal guest. Now, more than ever, any inner conflict over the Lady's intentions must surface. So Modjeska, after bringing herself to kiss the king's hand, led him to the castle door; then broke away again; then seized a torch from a servant, and holding it high, guided Duncan off.

The Porter, on his way to his giant drunk—noises of celebration may begin, or, having begun, intensify—is sometimes seen closing the gate. The martlet's song may fade, to give way to harsher night noises. In a German staging, on the Inverness that had at first been lighted brightly, to seem bucolic, *thick night* had begun to descend, and shades of black and red began to envelop the battlements. In another, as Duncan entered the castle the sword-like—or tooth-like—blades of a great portcullis slipped silently down behind him, seeming to trap him irrevocably.

Leave all the rest to me, Lady Macbeth had said. Her resolve to kill Duncan has reverberated at a deep level throughout the scene. Now the moment of opportunity has come. By a hostess' gesture, she has sometimes separated Duncan from Banquo and the other thanes. She has sent—or gone with— the king to his private chamber. To what destiny? As far as a *naive* spectator can tell—and this was the expectation in all the experiments in England and America—the fatal moment is at hand. Duncan is going to his death; and Lady Macbeth will wield the knife.

Act I, Scene vii

What is Lady Macbeth planning to do now to Duncan? Where has she led. him? *Naive* spectators anticipated some violent attack on him; and in the bridge between the scenes, with the sounding (as the Folio directs) of the hoboyes— lyrical instruments generally associated with hospitality and elegant social rites (Manifold)—their sinewy song may prick the ear with ironic expectation. But time is compressed again, in visual-aural shorthand, to intensify suspense. While the music sighs, servants laden with symbols of hospitable banqueting pass, in the flare of torches, across the stage. (If the scene is at all realistic, let the appointments seem lavish, as with Macready's silver and gold dishes, and weighty in burden. These servants carry food to a king; scanty provisions cheat the image of lordliness Shakespeare intended for this new example in a succession of civilized rituals.) Noises of people enjoying themselves at food may be imagined, and are usually sounded off, rising and falling with the lilt of music and the flaring of torchlight. Sometimes banqueters are glimpsed when curtains part.

Sometimes Duncan is seen, too, in his *unusual pleasure*, assuring us that he is still safe; but the text keeps him off. Shakespeare did not intend us to see him again. The outer stage grows quiet, pageantry gives way to intimacy, Macbeth appears. He has just come from the banquet, as we will learn, and sometimes we see him backing away from the place he is leaving, perhaps bowing, perhaps bearing on his face a courtly smile wiped off as he turns, sometimes entering deep in thought, sometimes in a rush as if fleeing thought. Sounds—laughter, conversation, song, orchestral music—and lights may rise sharply as he comes through door or curtain, to be muffled again. He has carried a goblet: it has cued him to his thought of a *chalice*; and, as a visual symbol of festive hospitality, has tied this moment to his actions at the later banquet he will give.

If servants dally, Macbeth may send them away—Tree, having directed the traffic of food to the banquet, motioned Duncan's two grooms to the king's room. A weaker or darker Macbeth lurks out of the servants' sight until all are gone. But at last Macbeth is alone, isolated from the social world, free to plunge into introspection. Rapt.

If any symbol of Duncan is visible—royal chair, robe, crown, scepter— Macbeth may come to it, touch it, try it. May finger his dagger. May look up at Duncan's door. But his primary activity is inward: his brain and feelings labor. To suggest this inwardness, Vilar again projected through loudspeakers the thoughts that troubled Macbeth's silent, fretted face, made the voice his conscience—the voice of everyone's conscience, Jacquot felt.

Not until Macbeth speaks do we know for certain that Duncan is safe, that we are being carried to a higher peak of indecision. Then the very first word alerts us: *if*. We are back at once in the maelstrom of a tortured mind.

Macbeth's few lines here have provoked pages of troubled criticism. I must add some. The speech is an extrapolation from Macbeth's last line in I, v: *We will speak further*. Even then he was sliding into the raptness of inner debate; he has not yet learned to look up clear; though he knows the king must wonder, must ask for him, his unease has driven him to leave the king's side, and to struggle privately with his impulses.

The very punctuation of the first line has split critical and theatrical interpretation. To improve the Folio, some actors (e.g., Macready, Irving) and critics have promoted the comma to a full stop after *well*, and demoted the colon in line 2, after *quickly*, to a comma, or deleted it. The bandaged line would now read:

> If it were done, when 'tis done, then 'twere well.
> It were done quickly if the assassination
> Could trammel up the consequence, (5–7)

No improvement results. The whole beginning of the soliloquy pivots on the *if*, the possibility—known from the outset by Macbeth to be impossible—of the thing being ended when performed. The first ten lines all dream of this. Macbeth is only delaying the inevitable *but* as long as he can. His opening line-and-a-half puts the case for the hypothetical possibility with a magnificent triple rhythm—that would be cruelly hobbled by the period after *well*. In proposing the change, White* observed that actors said the speech as if it simply meant "If the murder is to be done, when I do it I had better do it quickly"—as if no apprehension of retribution colored Macbeth's mind. But the whole beginning is only a way of putting off that apprehension. Three implications of *done*—a word, with its cousins, *do*, *deed*, designed to stir reverberations in the mind as the play goes on—are crowded into the first rippling phrases: If it were done (ended) when 'tis done (performed) then 'twere well it were done (got over with) quickly. The first words, all chopped monosyllables, work well in thoughtful whispers or lower tones; they build on the

*See *Variorum*.

w's, the mouth compressed again and again on soft vowels. The *if* is perceived
as an "if only"—*it* could ever be *done*. An even more impossible "if only"
follows, as the rhythms lengthen, the words hiss with sibilants and hard *k*'s.

> If th' assassination
> Could trammel up the consequence, and catch
> With his surcease, success: (6–8)

Some hesitation to say the unspeakable word has been seen in Macbeth,
because of his use of *it;* but his design suggests a reluctance mainly when with
his wife. As *murder* came to his mind in I, iii, *assassination* now comes—though
Macbeth does, with his preceding *the*, partly separate himself from the word
(as, by using the passive verb form, he separates himself from the act). He may
pause before saying it, for it is committing (Garrick's Macbeth, too honorable
yet to acknowledge the word, cut the whole line). The soliloquy may be a
thing of broken mental flashes. It is not thought out, but *felt* out: Macbeth
begins with an attempt at reasoning, and then, as with *Stars hide your fires*, his
thought dissolves into a storm of whirling images.

Again, words impinge jaggedly, unexpectedly, on each other. What will
the assassination do? *Trammel up.* What? *The consequence, . . . and catch/With
his . . .* Catch what? More euphemism: *surcease, success.** The wayward se-
quences reflect Macbeth's mind, and, as well, his world: he would see assassination as more than an act, also as the act's power to wall off retribution. If,
as Cunningham and Mahood have suggested, *trammel* can connote hobble, or
suspend, the sense of *consequence* held at bay is even stronger: time itself might
be trapped.

If-only clause follows clause, the wishful subjunctive explicit, the next line
propelled by the explosive *b*'s. The substantial colon-marked pause after
success indicates the springboard to new imagining:

> that but this blow
> Might be the be all, and the end all. (8–9)

Spoken by Forrest "in such a tone of desire and longing . . . it was almost as
if he said, 'Oh, that but. . . .' "

Editors often improve the Folio grammar by running the sentence on, after
end all; but the full stop accords with the irregular flow of Macbeth's thought.
He could stop now; except that he cannot stop. He is driven to a further qual-
ification: again, "if only"—

> Here,
> But here, upon this bank and school of time,
> We'd jump the life to come. (9–11)

---

*The two near sound-alikes, James Black suggests, demonstrate Shakespeare's talent for
"changing one word into another before our very ears."

Various sensible contenders for the implications of the middle line have been found attractive. *Bank* (as banc) is taken to mean *bench:** *bench* and *school* may suggest that Macbeth feels himself young in deed, still in a learning place in the flow of time—though the inevitable lesson would have to be how impossible indeed are if-only wishes. Alternatively, the *bench* symbolizes a court, and the two terms—court and school—are soon after reprised in the parallel reference to inevitable *judgement* and *instructions*—both to be certainly painful.

Neither implication quite suits the "if-only" fantasy of isolation from temporal cause and effect; rather both seem to deny it. Hence Theobald's rival suggestion, the logical *bank and shoal*,† has seemed preferable to some. It refracts the kind of backwater in time envisioned by Macbeth: insulated from the past, magically free of consequence, safe in the shallows from the onrush of time's river. It may be seen to reverberate, oppositely, to the motifs of wayward wind and water—and of those who ride or are wrecked on these elements—motifs initiated in I, iii, and sustained elsewhere in this soliloquy by the associations of such words as *blow, blast, drown, couriers of the air.* But we must beware of a limiting gloss, however sensitive, that emends the Folio. Shakespeare may have deliberately contaminated his montage with connotations both of escape and punishment to suggest the fever of guilt in Macbeth's fantasy, and the illogic of his process.

Occasionally actors have begun the soliloquy in a deliberate, reasoning style. Kemble's determinedly innocent Macbeth, a cool metaphysician here, began calmly to consider alternatives. Macready, too, seemed at first to be reasoning on the success or failure of the murder, instead of reflecting the turbulence in Macbeth's mind at the prospect of it—though later in the scene he would flee the control of reason for more Dionysian symptoms; and even here his enforcement of a rational discipline could be seen as holding off the fateful powers that drove him.

More often, as the stage Macbeth enters, he is picking up, at a higher pitch, the momentum of nervous indecision that was mounting at the end of his previous meeting with Lady Macbeth. The lines tumble on one another, Richard David observes; the moment cries perturbation, discomfiture, confusion, Knowles felt. Actors sensitive to Macbeth's hidden anxiety have seethed with agitation. Garrick, at this point still the suffering innocent, but enforced to excitement by his actor's nature and style, churned with guilty fear of his thoughts. J. B. Booth conveyed some sense of the mixed notes in Macbeth's troubled polyphony: the "crowd and jostle of inconsequent

---

*Nowhere else does Shakespeare use *bank* in either of the suggested senses of *bench*—though this is not decisive.

†This assumes that *school* may be an error for *shoal*, or a variant. The word carries no such meaning elsewhere in Shakespeare.

thoughts . . . his bewildered mind, his weakened will, his uncertain and post-poning mood." With Kean, the soliloquy "comprised a world of argument" among conflicting forces: "the daring yet dubious mind, the rapid execution of the soldier, the natural visitations of the man." Edwin Booth's poet-philosopher was already haunted in his mind, so frenzied he was momentarily convulsed. Rogers was breathless with tension, near hysteria. Williamson's ever-uneasy hand compulsively flicked a fingernail against his goblet. Reinhardt's Macbeth accompanied his brooding restlessness with an anticipatory gesture that would have visual echoes: his fist, holding an imaginary dagger, thrust forward, phrase by phrase, as if stabbing at a throat.

Some actors emphasized the sense of self-communing: Forrest, beginning in a whisper; Salvini, quietly, intensely, "the wavering of a disordered mind . . . playing with mortal temptation." Matkowsky began slowly, in a low voice, but a word would get away from him: *rasch* (quickly) came out roughly, like a bark. The aura of hypnosis still fixed some Macbeths: Charles Kean began in slow dreamy abstraction; Richardson seemed dazed. The further inward the Macbeths, the more bottled was their force: Scofield, trying to repress his consciousness of the contemplated enormity, weighing whether he *could* bring himself to commit it; Olivier, knowing the price of the act, and haggling with himself over it. *Naïve* spectators responded to a suspense device in the play's design here: the possibility—the hope—that Macbeth will persuade himself to forgo the murder, will escape the forces impelling him to it.

This was true even of Irving—who himself occasionally wavered from his essential conception of Macbeth as a "bloody-minded, hypocritical villain." His inner debate was mainly confined to his head: he spoke slowly, thinking out his options, with "something of the self-distrust of a Hamlet." But his gestures, notorious for their restlessness, suggested to some observers that he was in genuine inner perplexity, that only supernatural and external influence would overbear his personal will and coerce him to the murderous act. He pressed his hands to his head, writhed, trembled, whispered, quavered—an "epileptic hero," he was called. Irving's own analysis:

> Macbeth begins to play with his conscience, after his habit, as a cat does with a mouse; this is after he had made up his mind definitely to commit the murder.

This Macbeth was involved in a subtle self-deception, as we will see, screening from himself his true intent—and he did it so well he deceived many spectators.*

Irving's note to himself for *We'd jump the life to come* was to sneer his disregard for any hereafter. Keightley† suggested (Hoepfner, among others, agreed) that the *life to come* meant the rest of Macbeth's *mortal* days. But Macbeth may

---

*Not all. *Figaro:* "The kindly feeling is utterly out of keeping with the mean-spirited hound [of] other scenes."
†See *Variorum*.

be seen to be contrasting *here* where retribution threatens to some period beyond the reach of temporality (see below). *Jump* is commonly glossed "risk"; but that does not fit the many implications of any of its other uses in Shakespeare—including, as in *Winter's Tale*, of aggressive sexual intercourse (IV, iv, 195), and the more usual "leap over" (Sonnet 44). As Macbeth uses it, the phrase suggests a readiness to dismiss any implications of an otherworldly "life to come."

Much debate has grown about the possible theological implications here. Twentieth-century critics, active in finding Christian references in the play, discover *If it were done . . .* echoing John 13:27, "That thou doest, do quickly"; and Mark 7:37, "He hath done all well." Considering the extreme differences in tense, person and especially situation, I think it doubtful that these fragments would seem relevant, in the ears and minds of Jacobean spectators, to Shakespeare's third phrase in the speech; nor does any effective way of dramatizing the linkage seem feasible. A critic argues, "Thus Macbeth is seen clearly as an antitype of Christ." If so, if he is "clearly" also a Satanic figure; then his scruples must indeed seem hypocritical, his inward action without suspense, and the drama degenerates into morality. "Clearly" seems not to be Shakespeare's way here: more than one thing is being said at once, and the multiple notes complicate tension, rather than simplifying it toward comfortable resolution. Even when a word may, by its special quality, sound a biblical echo—*chalice*—the playwright will qualify it with *poisoned*, shadowing the bright image. Can *the life to come* imply the Christian concept of punishment and reward for the immortal soul in afterlife? Support for this is found in Macbeth's III, i reference to his *eternal jewel* (though about this, too, as we will see, there is argument). On the other hand, Macbeth never manifests—nor does Shakespeare manifest for him—concern for the pains of purgatory or hell; he will speak of the meaninglessness of an existence governed by an idiot-divinity; and the only *damned* he will acknowledge is the man who turns coward in this life. There is not the remotest suggestion that Shakespeare's contemporaries saw Christian allusions here (or elsewhere) in his plays; even the pious Forman, who could be counted on to salvage practical morality out of the plays he saw (if he saw them), reflects no slightest experience of ethical impact from *Macbeth*. The beholder will trust his own ear: as in other places where the playwright shapes a complex polyphony, those of his audience attuned to theological implications will hear some notes more loudly, other auditors will perhaps be sensitive to different sounds. We must listen as well as we can.

The *but* toward which Macbeth's thoughts drive him finally trammels him. Five *buts* jolt the speech, four as intensifiers, interrupting the flow to suit the

speaker's erratic thought; this one reverses the whole direction, starting a
second movement—

But in these cases, . . . (11)

Now that Macbeth confronts *consequence*, he finds himself using more often
the *we* spoken only once so far (*We will speak further*). He will use it four times
in this scene. The first one follows the track of the soliloquy's intimations of
the courtroom—*case, judgment, justice*—

We still have judgement here, . . . * (12)

Various notes sound in the first person plural: perhaps a hint of the royal *we*,
as if he has leaped ahead of his fantasy to the deed accomplished. The *we* may
include Lady Macbeth: *we* is one way of escaping, for a while, the clamorous
I. *We* also manifests the philosophic strain in the Macbeth design: his frequent
extension of his thoughts from his personal involvement to a world view. In
this sense, his soliloquies are both linear and contextual: they flow toward a
conclusion affecting the play's action, but they also pause for eddies in which
the human condition is explored.

Because prudence seems to check Macbeth here, some critics see him as
only self-serving: thus, "not a single thought . . . in any other light than that
of immediate practical consequences." But Macbeth's processes seem designed
to direct the course of the spectators' conscious hopes: these must be nourished
with some reason to believe he may persuade himself not to commit the murder. Certainly he thinks of retribution, his ideas seeming to sprout from the
seed of *school*:

we but teach
Bloody instructions, which being taught, return
To plague th'Inventor. This even-handed justice (12–14)

Even-handed justice fits with the balancing of Macbeth's own reciprocating
thought against thought. But the language is not the fruit of cool prudence;
even at its most philosophic, it is charged with a load of emotional words,
touched with revulsion: *bloody . . . plague . . . poisoned*. So Tree drew back
from the imaginary chalice in his hand as something unbearable. However
much Macbeth may try to reason, feeling forces itself into the design.

What the critic, actor, reader must be aware of is the goal of this soliloquy:
Macbeth bringing himself to refuse the assassination—or at least to say he
does. Partly consciously, partly unconsciously, he has from the very beginning presented himself with a straw man to topple: an impossible *if*. Inevitably
the imagined act collapses before the reasons and the emotions arrayed against

---

*Irving again put his hand to his head, as if this were the seat of judgment. He held his head
repeatedly during the soliloquy to suggest the strain of his indecision.

it; as they gather momentum, reason starts to give way, passion to take over. Rationalization of the resistance to murder becomes emotionalization.

As Macbeth moves into the next phase of the soliloquy, sometimes (as with Sothern) prompted by a sound from the banqueting (Tree went to look), one paradoxical insight into his character by Lady Macbeth is confirmed. He *would* wrongly win; he *would* not play false. Prudence gives way to morality:

> He's here in *double* trust;
> First, as I am his kinsman, and his subject,
> Strong both against the deed: then, as his host,
> Who should against his murderer shut the door,
> Not bear the knife my self. (16–20)

The reverberating *double*, so recently spoken by Lady Macbeth in her doubling-redoubling greeting of Duncan, is interesting also because it is one of the few words of more than one syllable in these taut lines. Two of the few other dissyllables are *against*—itself a symptom of the ongoing dialectic. The only tri-syllable is one Macbeth may well hesitate to say, that by its very length, among the shorter words, gains an ominous distinction: *murderer*. After the longer rhythms preceding, the return to a succession of mainly monosyllables, leading up to the hammering in the last line, signals the shift from a partly generalized to a specific concern with the actual *here*—a word four times spoken. We are brought down to Macbeth's *now*, his personal situation, with the intrusion of *I* and *my*.

To the spectator's ear, "*bear* the knife" sounds like *bare*—a doubled implication which, reawakening the image of bright, cutting steel, intensifies the sense of threat: and which leaves open the identity of the wielder of the knife. Macbeth partly distances himself by objectifying "*his* murderer" and "*the* knife" (as, earlier, "*the* assassination") as if they are extensions not specifically of himself, but perhaps of someone else for whom he might bear—bare?—the blade.

With the actuality of a *knife*—Macbeth may touch or grasp his own, may finger Duncan's robe where the dagger would enter—this movement of the soliloquy climaxes. The weapon is named, the dreadful deed made explicit. Reinhardt's Macbeth checked the impulse to repeat the stabbing movement that seemed to have become almost instinctual, uncontrollable; as if confronting the physical objectification of the treachery he had only contemplated, he became aware of the horror of the crime, and he flung his arms high.

In the pause of self-inspection that follows, the start of the next movement is sometimes cued by sounds of pleasure from Duncan's banquet. A deeper emotional tone strengthens Macbeth's arguments against the act he desires and dreads.

Besides, this Duncan . . . * (20)

*The comma is interesting. *This Duncan* distances the king, makes him someone Macbeth can comment on as another person, find qualities in to save him from murder. The line has been read, "Besides this, Duncan," but the effect, in its different kind of familiarity, is changed.

He is intent on creating an inviolate image of Duncan, as an emotional bulwark against his own impulse to murder—the word for which he again sidesteps, after perhaps the briefest of pauses, with *taking off*—

> Hath borne his faculties so meek; (21)

The line resonates with the play's countering images of the violence and the gentleness that become a man. Ironically, Macbeth now praises the king for meekness—this king who had praised Macbeth for the manliness of his violence. Macbeth's kind words are not wholehearted; *meek* has even been spoken with mockery, but more meaningful is the sense of coexistent implications at odds. Thus Williamson made the word "sound both a virtue and a cursed nuisance, and [wiped] his forehead in an agony of confusion" (*Punch*).

Macbeth moves from his troubled praise to a kind of storm of feelingful association. The puzzle of images he accumulates, as his rhythms lengthen in mounting passion, has fascinated generations of critics and actors.

> hath been
> So clear in his great office, that his virtues
> Will plead like angels, trumpet-tongu'd against
> The deep damnation of his taking off:
> And Pity, like a naked new-born-babe,
> Striding the blast, or Heaven's cherubin, hors'd
> Upon the sightless couriers of the air,
> Shall blow the horrid deed in every eye,
> That tears shall drown the wind. (21–29)

The force of the emotions powering these lines can shake the actor: when Garrick was faulted for making a pause after *hors'd*, he could only say he was

> certainly wrong, and [it] was not so intended to be spoken; but when the mind is agitated, it is impossible to guard against these slips.

Even the most inward of actors breaks out here: thus Scofield, his grim face suddenly vulnerable, his grim voice relenting, working with the effort to contain the upthrust of many conflicting impulses. The desperation of feverish fancy could be heard in the tones of Savits' Macbeth, rising in pitch until, spent, he buried his face in his hands. Macready's passion was terrible, Coleman remembered, but

> it trembled into tears. Who that has ever heard can ever forget his better nature trying to assert itself in the irrepressible wail of agony

of the climax. Reinhardt's neurotic Macbeth, torn physically between the murderous drive and the revulsion against it, groaned wildly, rushed across the stage as if fleeing his thought.

What nourishes Macbeth's good angel now is that milk of human kindness his wife discerned. Theatre Macbeths, like Kean, have seized this opportunity, while Macbeth is still innocent, to assert the nobility in the design: the best of the poet and philosopher straining almost to incoherence for words that can help him believe in his own decency. Even Irving's Macbeth was felt to give a touch of exquisite pathos to the lines; Irving himself saw this as a kind of sincere, if transient, self-deception, to be forgone the moment he allows Lady Macbeth to make the murder seem safe; in these

> poetic imaginings . . . I can see the tears trickling down Macbeth's cheeks as, in the image of pity for Duncan, he pictures the new-born babe tossed about by the tempestuous winds.

Irving used the babe as the object of compassion; an easy way out: the pitiable infant, storm-tossed, the cherub helpless on a fierce steed. But this avoids the crux: the image is the other way around. That which is helpless, or tender—the soft quality surfacing from the underground stream sprung from *meek*—dominates that which is dangerously powerful: an oxymoron in action. Storm and terrible winds submit to innocence. (Sanders hears an echo of "Except ye become as little children.") The image of the babe triumphant will reverberate through the play, as Brooks and Knights have observed. It is central to the action, Brooks argues, because it relates to what helps make Macbeth a tragic hero: his resolve to conquer the future, to achieve more than a personal satisfaction, to establish a line. Macbeth will war on children when his dream of dynasty is threatened (see Appendix); he will finally be brought to account by the offspring of others.

To Brooks, the image of the helpless babe turns into a symbol of strength. The babe and the powerful cherubin are strong and influential in their weakness; the babe will in IV, i, be symbol and agent of Macbeth's equivocal fate. Gardner sees the stress on pity—to Shakespeare the strongest and profoundest, most distinctively human emotion. Imagination and conscience are deeply moved by the vision of "a whole world weeping . . . at helplessness betrayed and innocence and beauty destroyed." Boyle agrees with Gardner, noting that in Shakespeare cherubs are always imaged as tender, winged infants, compared to pity for their helplessness: if they do ride cyclonic winds, some great and supernatural power must have inspired them to act as much against nature as the murder would be. Taylor builds on Brooks' perception of the yoking of seeming helplessness and great power. He observes that great perturbation in nature is usually linked with evil, rather than with the passive virtue represented by babes and cherubs, and suggests that pity is expressed violently not because it influences the real world, but because Macbeth so conceives it. The violence corresponds to the violence of his feelings.

We may go further. What Macbeth is envisioning, in his wild poetry, is in fact a projection of the struggle being fought out in his own interior battleground—his impulses of innocence and humankindness striving to manage and tame the Dionysian storm. The progression of the soliloquy parallels what happens within Macbeth himself; violent impulses are eventually subdued by the more powerful force of a rising tenderness.

This victory is not easily won; it proceeds through fragments of idea and feeling unified by accumulation rather than logical sequence. As if touched on a nerve by his inescapable confrontation with his deep self—the *I* and *my* that forced themselves into his consciousness—Macbeth strains away toward far cosmic abstractions (as Spurgeon and Clemen have recognized). He is again brooding on regions beyond the earthly, and his figures are wayward, surreal. Elusive images hold some associations together, with symbols of strange and multiple meaning of the sort found in paintings by Dali and Magritte. Thus, *trumpet-tongu'd* (how magnificent a concept to the imagination, how surreal to visualization), *blast, blow*. These explosive messages of pity, "broadcast through great spaces with reverberating sound" (Spurgeon), dissolve surrealistically into images of sight unseeable. We do not try to visualize an hour-old infant astride a tempest, but we experience more deeply than in our senses the turbulence, the apocalyptic stresses that Macbeth's mind—and in his imagination, the cosmos—must endure when violence meets tenderness.

In Macbeth's design, one continuing concern is how other people will regard him. This is intimately related to a major motivation in his characterization: to achieve great feats, do dreadful deeds, also to be well-liked, all as part of an impulse for security. The murder of his king, an extraordinary act, may bring him high degree and admiration; but he senses that the thought does not consort easily with his obligations to friends, to the gentle weal, and to his conscience. In this soliloquy the friction between these opposites intensifies the interior back-and-forth that whipsaws him.

He expresses his anxiety in moral terms. Duncan's *virtues . . . plead like angels* to Macbeth himself.* But the terrible, tender younglings, *babe* and *cherubin* (the latter a tributary, after a subterranean passage, of *angel*) will *blow the horrid deed in every eye*, and make the whole world weep so much the fierce winds will be stilled. Battenhouse, committed to Macbeth's devilishness, doubts that he includes his own eye; but the direction of the soliloquy suggests that what is innocent in Macbeth moves toward taming his own tempest; and from Macbeth's eye—as with Macready—tears may indeed flow. This conjunction between what the speaker says and does seems integral to the design here.

The final movement of the soliloquy brings Macbeth inescapably front to front with his personal involvement: again, *I, my*. The mood changes, the words shorten, sharpen.

> I have no spur
> To prick the sides of my intent, but only
> Vaulting ambition, which o'er-leaps itself,
> And falls on th'other (29–32)

*Garrick paused at *angels;* a correspondent foolishly faulted him for transferring the adjective "trumpet-tongued" from *angels* to *virtues;* Garrick patiently replied that "the force of those exquisite four lines and a half would be lost [without] a small aspiration at *angels. . . .* I think it more elegant to give [*trumpet-tongued*] to *virtues*, and the sense is the same."

These lines were, for Irving, a return to firmness. His head, in his hands as he began to talk of Duncan, was now held tensed against a pillar, as if the thinking on pity was unbearable. At the image of *tears* he gave a deep sigh. But he noted a "great change" at the end; he made an impatient gesture, as if to say, "No more of this"; and though, when Lady Macbeth entered, he made the proper disclaimer of murderous purpose, with a persuasive show of immense relief, he was ready to lead her toward propelling him where he wanted to go.

For Scofield, the dominant impulse, countering the compassion he sought to repress, was voiced as a kind of lament, a wish to be spurred. The struggle is often not over: Reinhardt's Macbeth made the lines a fierce self-accusation; but his doubting body belied his voice; as he closed his eyes, he seized a curtain as if to strangle it, and made the stabbing motion again as Lady Macbeth entered. Macready, doom-driven, uttered his wail of agony, as abhorring what he knew he had to do.

Efforts have been made to reduce these last lines to literality: *intent* is seen as a horse, *vaulting ambition* a rider, etc. But again the whole does not bear detailing. Gentleman's literal scoffing may be a lesson:

> To embody *intention*, that *ambition* may be a spur to prick its sides, leans toward burlesque. And then turning the *spur* into another body, that it may vault over. . . .

The images are surreal: one spur pricks both sides of an impulse; *vaulting ambition* does not simply *o'er-leap*, to fit a convenient equestrian figure, but leaps over itself and falls, suggesting a grotesque somersault and crash— projecting the course of Macbeth's present inner process as well as his future career. Macbeth is the center from which the images strike off: the spur, the intent, the ambition, the extravagant, fated leap and drop, all manifest him, as the disjointed actions of a dream all manifest the dreamer. As the images evoke our own early impressions of horses, riding, movement, urgency, we montage their disjointedness without concretizing them. Macbeth may partly wish to be spurred, may fear the spur that does goad him; we share the mood and intent of his words, that reflect emotionally his descent to a feeling of vain purpose. The language reciprocates with the turbulence of his mind. The measure of his determination to return to innocence will be the sincerity of his announcement of it to Lady Macbeth.

Her entrance to Macbeth is a recurrence, in reverse, of his appearance in I, v, when she had completed her soliloquy. The variations in their interaction may indirectly echo the earlier scene. Macbeth may be left for a moment to absorb the shock of his inward struggle. Rapt. The Folio's full stop at *falls on th'other* provides a pause for Macbeth's reflection on the movement of his mind. In such a moment, Tree took time to "wipe his face downward"; Sothern sank on a seat.

Lady Macbeth may enter before Macbeth is through, or while he is brooding. Quayle's Lady came through the curtains, and watched her husband pace out his indecision before approaching. Savits' Lady stood watching, smiling a little, until he raised his head and saw her. Ristori entered in time to hear *I have no spur;* she smiled, as if to say, "But you have me"; then slowly went to him and touched him. He started.

This quiet approach to a Macbeth, and the touch that startles him, can establish the depth of his raptness, and the shock of his return to reality—sometimes a profound disturbance, as with the shaken Tree. Macbeth's soliloquy has been interrupted, too, as when Charles Kean's *falls on th'other* was broken off by the abrupt entrance of his Lady, or when Leigh came in almost running to Olivier. Or at her first appearance, to stress her sense of purpose, the Lady may seem to be desperately searching for him, before locating him in a corner of the stage; in Germany (1928) the urgency was emphasized by the Lady's running on a turning revolve, as if she were hurrying down a long corridor to find Macbeth and pounce.

A curious textual change reported of Marlowe's entrance relates to one mine of suspense in the scene. When Lady Macbeth suddenly appears, and Macbeth asks for news, as if expecting a report of action, some *naive* spectators wondered if she had not already done the deed, as she had promised she would. Marlowe, when the sounds from the banquet had gone silent, flashed into Macbeth, herself whispered:

How now? What news? (33)

and "made her listeners start with the suggestion that the murder was already done, so powerfully had she conveyed her terrible purpose."

The spur to Lady Macbeth's intent, as she enters, is sharpened by more than impatience to get on. Her complex attitude toward her husband, and their ambition, is now complicated further by her immediate past. She has, like Macbeth, only now held or kissed the hand of the old man whom she has thought of killing. However she may have absorbed that experience, we will see that something has happened to her. An actress may already have felt the Lady sensing, subconsciously perhaps, the lineaments of her father in the king's face, and accordingly new—and perhaps only partly understood—tensions have driven her to Macbeth. She will no longer demand, as before, that *all the rest* be left to her. She will not offer to wield the *keen knife* herself. On the other hand, she has seen royalty close up, and now she, too, coming in, may longingly finger the stuffs of kingship left in the antechamber. Some special impulse to get the unspeakable act done may be felt now—Ristori seemed here to be thrust by revenge more than ambition. When the Lady is powerful and dominant, herself a Fate compelling Macbeth, her inexorable beating down of his reluctance structures the scene. Cushman almost physically bullied her husband into acquiescence. Pritchard was so angered at Garrick's tentative resistance that "Her whole ambitious soul came forth in fury to her face, and sat in terror there" (*Universal Museum*). Siddons combined her massive presence with a relentless psychological pressure. Her "intrepidly depraved" determination would overwhelm the inevitably "feeble emotions of gratitude and conscience" that would characterize any Macbeth opposite her. She came charging to him, demanding why he had left the king with "an eager whisper of anger and surprise." Her response to his *no further* was "disappointment, depression, contempt and rekindling resentment." Poor frightened Kemble, Hunt reported, "with what a trembling hand, confessing irresolution of purpose" before his "contemptuous wife," tried to decline to proceed further. To Hunt, Kemble's eye, "yet seemed to gloat and glisten at the visionary crown." But another observer thought Kemble uttered the lines

> with such a sigh of relief and thankfulness, it seemed to bear away with it a crushing load, and leave him renewed and hopeful.

This ambivalence—this double force—in even the extremes of characterization, dimensioning the noblest Macbeths with murderous impulse, the most murderous with some reins of conscience, sustains the spectator's hope that Macbeth may cling to innocence. Reviewing Macready, the *Bath Journal* proposed an image of Macbeth's wavering state of mind "which would and would not—a state that a trifle may turn either way." Macready was urged to realize the "equilibrium betwixt hospitality and treachery . . . so nicely poised" that Lady Macbeth's words would easily tip the balance; Macready allowed his inner feelings so to overwhelm him as to render the success of her eloquence very improbable. The infant struggles against the act, ought to have been exemplified, but so as to be rather more dimly seen through the daring of that vaulting ambition." But in this pivotal moment Macready was holding out the promise of compunction: the *Sheffield Iris* marveled at "How splendid was the portraiture of Macbeth's resolution crumbling away under the influence of conscience;" and only then, "how visibly were his purposes again built up by the fearful promptings of his wife."

In Forrest, reason, honor, conscience and affection seemed certainly to have defeated ambition, and he could say the disclaimer with "a clearing and relieved look." Kean, resisting his darker impulses, seemed genuinely returned to noblemindedness. A veteran critic, hearing Tree's earnest *no further . . .* could write:

> For an instant I thought he wouldn't. . . . I thought for a flash that the play might end differently.

No further in this business. "Business," again, is a relatively popular word with Shakespeare; in *Macbeth's* nine uses it is always either a direct euphemism for a murderous act, as in Lady Macbeth's *night's great business* (I, v), or a mask, as in her disclaimer to Duncan of *poor and single business* (I, vi). Macbeth, now hiding behind it, uses it as a springboard to reasons for refraining from the unspeakable, his language pragmatic (*bought, golden, newest gloss*):

> He hath honour'd me of late, and I have bought
> Golden opinions from all sorts of people,

Which would be worn now in their newest gloss,
Not cast aside so soon. (38–41)

He is not simply shielding her from the word for the deed; he is also trying to shield himself from her scorn by not revealing to her his scruples—perhaps, Empson suggests, out of genuine moral shame. Dover Wilson interprets the practicality as evidence of Macbeth's controlling prudence rather than conscience, and an actor like Phelps could give this impression; but conscience seems to underlie all his protests, as well as expediency.

The language fuses with the doubled character design: Macbeth is driven to want to do well, but also to be *seen* to do well: his appearance, *to all sorts of people*—all degrees—dressed in the golden garments of praise, is precious to him, now, on this momentary bank of time. This is a place where he can stand secure, where what is, is; the formless chaos of uncertainty is held off.

Lady Macbeth's response is to undermine his base, his fortified insecurity. Where she does not simply overpower him, where the equation seems nearly equal, her strategy of approach and withdrawal sustains a risky equilibrium between them up to the moment of decision. Anything, until then, might happen. This seesaw interaction has been made visual. So Heesters, at *no further*, turned her back on Macbeth, as if returning to the banquet hall— again raising the audience's hope that this settled the matter. But Macbeth could not let it go: he began to speak haltingly, and the irresolute note in his voice brought her back, out of the darkness, to look calmly at him, and wait for him to finish his lines under her stare. A Japanese Lady, meeting Macbeth's refusal to proceed, walked silently past him, then turned to laugh at him, rousing his anger, which brought her back. Reinhardt's Macbeth, intimidated by his Lady's first rebuke, tried to pull himself together, moved hurriedly toward the banquet to rejoin Duncan; then hesitated, and came back where Lady Macbeth, as if knowing his mind, waited calmly and firmly. His hands trembling, shaking his head, he took hold of her fiercely to emphasize the vehemence of *no further*. As he went on, *And I have bought* . . . he threw the words at her reproachfully, as if she were partly to blame for his anxiety; but he could not look at her. She was able to quiet him, with her quiet demeanor; but the audience could feel underneath how fearfully uneasy she was, barely managing to contain her own turbulent feeling.

When the equation is between two very strong opposites, strength against strength strikes fiery sparks, and suspense is sustained until one or the other yields. An ego-strong Macbeth does not allow himself easily to submit either to chastisement or seduction—unless he wants to. His Lady's urgings may even seem to intensify his resistance, as if threatening his concern for the manhood she plays upon. Olivier would seem at first stiffened by Leigh's taunts; he turned a stubborn back to her—waiting for persuasion. Scofield's

tough Macbeth matched Merchant's hard anger with anger. They were partners, but were duelists too, protecting their own stakes; love held them together, but ego kept them from easy embrace. Scofield: "We must resist each
other, but not be separate."

The seduction—masked—may be more clearly Macbeth's. He may, like
Irving, be the manipulator playing manipulated. Irving would seem the driven
husband, a man in retreat, when in fact he was laying an ambush. A Russian
critic, Selvinsky, reviewing Tsarev (1955), perceived a similar dynamic shaping the scene—

> usually understood as the confrontation between a strong woman and a weak
> man; but by the most subtle motions he brings his wife around to say to him
> what he would like to hear.

Selvinsky suggested that Macbeth wanted his wife to help him overcome his
superstition, born of the experience with the witches. Olivier found his own
motive for leading Lady Macbeth to do the impelling:

> The man has imagination, the woman has none. The man sees it all, she does
> not. That's what gives her the enormous courage to plot the whole thing, force
> him into it, persuade him, cajole him, bully him, tease him into it. And he allows
> himself, bit by bit, to be teased into it. But he knows the answer, he knows the
> results, and she doesn't.

Macbeth may invite the Lady's countering force in his very speaking of
no further. Macready, cooperating with the fate that drove him toward murder,
demonstrated how the words could be asserted in firm tones—and still come
out almost deprecating themselves, doubling, more question than statement.
With Savits' Macbeth, the line came out so weakly it was obviously pleading
to be denied.

When Macbeth, in the equation, is susceptible to the polemics of softness
and cleverness as well as strength, Lady Macbeth can manage him with diplomacy, or seduction. The impulses may be the same as with Siddons—
ranging from grand ambition to contemptuous resentment—but are enforced
by the softer Ladies with love and tenderness, or shows of it—instead of
cruelty. The dialectic in the character may be even more severe, stretching
between wider poles. So Mlle. George, as Tieck saw her, moving from loving
coaxing to fearsome urging; or Geneviève Ward (U.S., 1893), savage and
soothing by turns; or Faucit, startling for her time in the tenderness she offered
Macbeth, but "when she sees him failing . . . she drops from her sublimity
and descends into the vixen." Or Ristori's splendid "withering scorn with
which she stings away his hesitation . . . But the former sweetness and assurance return with Macbeth's assent."

When sensuality was a major note, the Lady was in Macbeth's arms at once,
as Lily Langtry (U.S., 1896) was. Bernhardt wrapped herself clingingly
around her Macbeth; she was soft, tender, caressing; even in her scornful

words, edged with contempt, undertones of her love sounded—so she was blamed by a conservative critic for never "mastering" her Macbeth. In the twentieth century, physical interaction would sometimes be pushed to its limits: the pairs who embraced hotly in Scene v usually intensified their intimacy now. As Macbeth yields, the Lady perhaps permits him "to treat her body as a reward for obedience" (*Punch* on Mirren).

Much of the complex polyphony of Lady Macbeth's design may be discerned in the emphases of various actresses in the softer mode. Clara Morris smiled gracefully, even sweetly, pleading rather than arguing or commanding, mocking rather than fierce. Modjeska's taunts were described as "silvery." In a different strategy, Wolter looked at and spoke sadly to her Macbeth, as if he had disappointed her; Annis managed at first a wry smile, but spoke out of hurt, and her tears were ready to come because he was refusing her what she—they—wanted. More neurotic Ladies—e.g., Eames—could make their feeling of love rejected seem a threat to their own stability, as if Macbeth did not care if they broke: a different kind of emotional blackmail. The intellectual Lady—e.g., Clara Ziegler (Germany, 1871)—emphasized the note of reason in her persuasion. The more maternal—Mrs. Kean, Reid—sometimes spoke as if to a mistaken youth.

Terry's Lady Macbeth provided a consistent example of the Lady winning her lord to violence with love—a paradox folding smoothly into the play's design. "I love this scene," she noted. It gave her a chance to play the harder side of her role, and yet convey continuously the subtext of devotion. Thus, at Macbeth's *Hath he ask'd for me?* her *know you not, he has?* was quiet, severe, sarcastic, even dangerous—and loving.

Lady Macbeth carries the attack to Macbeth at once, without the fencing of I, v, as if time presses, the time for decision is now. She picks up his clothes image *(worn now in their newest gloss)*, stripping him of the proud array he thinks publicly to present, to show him in a shabbier wardrobe. She aims beneath appearance to the impulses that make appearance so important to him, as a man. She asks questions that sting the more because he cannot answer them with the "yes" or "no" they seem to demand; yet each question assumes that the shameful implication of the previous one has been admitted. The words are mainly monosyllabic and sharp, the second line a succession of hisses:

> Was the hope drunk,*
> Wherein you dressed yourself? (42–43)

As spectators, we will not remember consciously the liquid image; but her use of drink later, and her own drinking, will make insistent the undertone in her polyphony.

*Gentleman: "Suppose we pass over the literal acceptation of *hope* being drunk, surely we must blame a lady of high rank for descending to such a vulgar and nauseous allusion to the paleness and sickness of an inebriated state."

> Hath it slept since? (43)

In the dialectical design of the play even *sleep*, elsewhere so desirable, can be objectionable. The Lady's word—*slept*—comes out strongly after the preparatory *it*. Hungover hope itself awakens cowardly—

> to look so green, and pale,
> At what it did so freely? (44–45)

He does not answer. The physical imagery involved in his silences tells us much. From a dominant Lady, a punishing attack, and his shamed enduring of it, may suggest an habitual pecking. If his mute, shocked speechlessness reveals that these are unexpected blows, the acuteness and uniqueness of this moment is accentuated. When the Lady's sharp words are counterpointed by gestures of love or tenderness, and become appeals rather than attacks, he is helplessly silent in another way. The sensuous wives cling to Macbeth even as they try to spur him, embracing him, even rolling with him on a bed. Bergman (1944) instructed his Lady to raise her skirt to her waist, in her challenge both to Macbeth's manliness and his passion for her.

Lady Macbeth makes such a challenge explicit in the one statement in her series of questions:

> From this time,
> Such I account thy love. (45–46)

He does not reply; or, if he attempts speech or gesture, advance or withdrawal, she keeps control, piling up questions.

> Art thou afear'd
> To be the same in thine own act, and valour,
> As thou art in desire? (46–48)

She is striking at the disjunction he has himself dreamed of, between the mind's conception of an act, and the hand's performance, between wanting and doing. Undertones of sexuality may sound here, in word as well as action, linked again to the primary implication of violence.

Then she brings out the ultimately insulting word, *coward*:

> Wouldst thou have that
> Which thou esteem'st the ornament of life,
> And live a coward in thine own esteem?
> Letting I dare not, wait upon I would,
> Like the poor cat i' th' adage? (48–52)

In Siddons' written interpretation, she saw Macbeth's naturally benevolent and good feelings revived by his awakened conscience: until Lady Macbeth, his evil genius, by the force of her revilings, her contemptuous taunts, above all her "opprobrious aspersion of cowardice," drives from him impulses of charity, loyalty, pity, gratitude. In the theatre, Siddons was relentless. At *the hope drunk:* "Very cold, distant, and contemptuous." At *did so freely:* "Determined air and voice. Then a tone of cold, contemptuous reasoning." Simond saw in her here a "merciless tigress, thirsting for blood and carnage. She goads on her husband . . . with unrelenting ferocity." Kemble, "awed by her scorn," was understandably submissive, as befitted an honorable murderer: so the *Morning Post's* observation, "Her commanding manner might almost be said to furnish an excuse for the conduct of Macbeth." Command came easily to Siddons; Terry, at the other pole, had to win her way by masking her loving coaxing under calculated, forced displays of authority—"fitful spasmodic gusts of power and sarcasm" (*Daily Telegraph*). Her intention was to be "cold and distant" at *Was the hope drunk?* (She described Lady Macbeth's mood in what followed as "white feelings.") She turned from Irving at "Such I account *thy love* (emphasis hers, as also in "live a *coward*," where she added an exclamation point). "Low down voice always," she reminded herself: "Stand still and look at him". The moments of cold reproof this Lady put on only magnified, by contrast, the underlying deep love, glimpsed behind the shows, that in its own way was as compelling as Siddons' commands. Thus, at *What beast was't?* she knelt to Irving. "The changes from mood to mood, from raillery to soft entreaty, are given with irresistible effect, and no one can wonder that the Thane yields in spite of his temporary generous scruples" (*Dramatic Review*).

   Art thou afeard? . . . ? Would'st . . . live a coward? The words challenge Macbeth's manhood, and unless he stands as if drugged or whipped, will manifest some reaction. Lady Macbeth has urged, Dr. Johnson wrote,

> the excellence and dignity of courage, a glittering idea which has dazzled mankind from age to age . . . employed . . . with a peculiar propriety to a soldier by a woman.

And with particular force from a loved and respected wife, the most intimate of the external mirrors in which Macbeth can see himself reflected. In the Macbeth design, courage is integral to his self-image of manliness; when he momentarily loses his courage later, he will feel his *better part of man* is cowed. The intensity of his response is only suggested by his *Prithee peace.* Garrick said this in troubled tones; he was faulted for seeming too motivated by remorse at the thought of Duncan's murder to vent his sense of insult in "a rough way." But Garrick was sustaining the lachrymose tones of his honorable murderer, and would hardly seem to dare to cross roughly the fearsome Pritchard. Other actors have registered the jolt to Macbeth's ego with visual imagery. Olivier stiffened the back he turned to Leigh. Piscator's Macbeth started to leave; his Lady blocked his way, her hands clenched. Forrest started indignantly; Sothern raised a warding arm in protest; Reinhardt's Macbeth listened with eyes closed, his reaction ambiguous: he seemed almost to be welcoming her incitements, but then he broke out against her, harsh and angry. Tree darted his hand to Vanbrugh's face, and covered her mouth to end the speech; more brutal Macbeths have threatened their wives, even slapped them.

In speech, Macbeth now dares air one moral resistance:

> I dare do all that may become a man,
> Who dares do more, is none.* (54–55)

Become suits Macbeth's concern with appearance before his fellows. Critics and actors who find mainly prudence in the line see it as a statement of a man's practical limits; but in context it seems definitely to allude to the ideal of a man touched with the milk of humankindness. The scene builds tension as Macbeth's vision of a man challenges his Lady's: she brings on the climax by retorting with her version of a man's proper commitment. If his statement has been practical, she could answer him practically, as she will his following question; but now she answers "should" with "should," proposing a better manly ideal—again in abrupt words almost all monosyllabic (the only polysyllable is the first of the two euphemisms for the nameless deed, before speaking which she may well hesitate):

> What beast was't then,
> That made you break this . . . enterprise to me?
> When you durst do it, then you were a man: (56–58)

Welles' Lady emphasized *were;* the stress might fall on almost any of the key words, or selected series of them—indeed, each one might be bitten off and spat out as a spondee. A marvelously flexible speech, easily fitted to the wide range of Lady Macbeth designs.

> And to be more than what you were, you would
> Be so much more the man. (59–60)

The man-animal axis runs through much of Shakespeare's tragedies—the animal usually that part of man acting as Lady Macbeth would have her lord act now. She turns the axis upside down: a man must not only be ready to undertake an unspeakable *enterprise*, he must follow through with it because he has agreed to do so. She has challenged his courage and his love for her; now she moves on to challenge the source of both, his manliness; and she cleverly makes it depend on a virtue that indeed all men respect—the keeping of a given word. Thus she appeals to his conscience against his conscience. "You must do it because you promised." Farnham is one critic who has agreed with Lady Macbeth that Macbeth's shrinking from action is touched with

---

*Criticism (see Furness) and the theater (e.g., Reinhardt) sometimes solve the Folio's puzzling second line, "Who dares *no* more," by giving it to Lady Macbeth; but that hardly squares with her own next line ending in *then*. The Folio clearly intended the speech for Macbeth, so Rowe's emendation of *do* for *no* makes sense. While I trust the Folio, I accept that, like all artifacts, it is capable of error.

cowardly irresolution, and therefore baseness, even though it is shrinking from evil and dishonor. Certainly Macbeth's Lady does her best to make him think so.

First *coward*, now *beast*. She is pushing him to the lonely instant when he must reject her utterly, or acquiesce. He has declared a stand at either-or: *all* or *none*, no *more*. She refuses his polarity, her intensifiers insisting on over-reach: *more . . . so much more*. Her words, again almost all monosyllabic, carry the message of attack, and a Terrible Woman voices them fiercely to the husband she would overbear (I have seen a Lady slap her husband to rouse him); but at the other extreme they are appeals by a Loving Wife for marital reassurance. In a Machiavellian Lady, like Ristori, the terrible purpose may be revealed in one moment of flashing eye and mobile face, but then from the earnest-seeming player comes not taunts but reproach, sorrow rather than reviling.

As the Lady pursues Macbeth to this penultimate breaking point, he may again move physically—to resist by speech or action, or to withdraw. Lady Macbeth may be close to her own breaking point, screwing her own courage to the sticking place, as Knights has suggested. If, unlike Ristori, she is masking weakness rather than strength, this may be momentarily exposed to the audience but not Macbeth, as with Reinhardt's Lady. At *what beast was't?*, she had risen to a fierceness that frightened her, and also made her fearful of being overheard; she went quickly to the curtain to see, then hurried back to speak in low tones, sharply. The nearness of the Macbeths to others conditions the dialogue here: actors in this and the next two scenes have been faulted for shouting as if nobody else was anywhere close. Intensity develops not by volume but by pitch, the force often rising as the voice drops toward hiss and whisper.

What Lady Macbeth says, about Macbeth's first proposing, at some earlier time, the deed unnamed, is sometimes cited to demonstrate that he broached it to her before he met the witches. Actresses have also imagined taking the cue from the letter read in I, v, or from one or more of the other letters she mentions—Modjeska waved a paper before Macbeth to remind him of what he had written. Lady Macbeth may be understood, also, to be exaggerating to suit her polemic—a characteristic ploy: how quickly, for instance, she promotes his "breaking the enterprise" to his swearing to do it. Terry explained it to herself thus: "he suggested the murder, she *caught on.*"

A deleted scene of conspiracy between the two has been suggested; but this could only have occurred when it could not have occurred—before I, v; in that scene, in fact, she first seems to have broken the enterprise. When Shakespeare wants us to know for sure of incidents that took place between scenes, he takes care to inform us—as when we will learn from Lady Macbeth that Macbeth has told her about a hallucinated dagger. In I, vii Shakespeare avoids forcing the audience to wonder about the Lady's assertion, leaves it an ambiguity that will only partially be resolved by Macbeth's visual reaction—

admission of her charge, or bewilderment at what is an exaggeration, or shock and anger at an untruth. But resistance, if any, is not given time for articulation: she summons up all her force to sweep aside objection, and obliterate residual scruple, with her horrible example of how a *woman* would keep *her* word.

This ascent to her ultimate argument is usually marked by an abrupt change of tone, expression, and movement. Thus Siddons, who had been pouring her contempt on Macbeth from across the room, now came close to him, and looked intently into his face, before the speech—that is again almost entirely short, brutal monosyllables:

> I have given suck,* and know
> How tender 'tis to love the babe that milks me,
> I would, while it was smiling in my face,
> Have pluckt my nipple from his boneless gums,
> And dasht the brains out,† had I so sworn
> As you have done to this. (63–68)

The Lady's verbal process is reflected in her action, as was Macbeth's soliloquy, but in reverse: where in his mind images of innocence overrode images of violence, and moved him not to act, here innocence becomes helpless before overriding cruelty, in both word and determination.

Siddons was one who felt that behind the horrible declaration was evidence of softer feeling:

> Such a tender allusion in the midst of her dreadful language [demonstrates] that she has really felt the maternal yearnings of a mother toward her babe.

The actress believed that Lady Macbeth chose infanticide, an ultimate example of unfeminine fortitude, as her best weapon to rouse Macbeth:

> the most enormous that ever required the strength of human nerves for its perpetration. . . . she makes her very virtues the means of a taunt . . . "You have the milk of human kindness . . . but ambition, which is my ruling passion, would also be yours if you had courage. . . . I too have felt with a tenderness which your sex cannot know; but I am resolute in my ambition to trample on all that obstructs my way to a crown. Look to me, and be ashamed of your weakness."

Siddons expected that Macbeth might be "abashed . . . humbled before this unimaginable instance of female fortitude." From Boaden's description

---

*Does she emphasize *I*, to make a special point that she breastfed her baby? The spartan Scots mothers who, Holinshed's *History* reports, accompanied their men into battle, evidently suckled their own children; and Shakespeare has such a Roman matron as Volumnia feed Coriolanus her own martial milk (as she said Hecuba had fed Hector); but Lady Macbeth belonged to a station and society perhaps more comparable to that of Lady Capulet, who put Juliet to a wet-nurse.

†Agate warned against one Lady's emphasis on *brains*—as if she were suggesting a choice of injuries to the child.

of her own fierce attack, Macbeth would more likely be frightened. The line itself was filled, Boaden wrote, with direst cruelty; but still he wondered at "the energy of both utterance and action. . . . [Siddons] did not at all shrink from standing before us the true and perfect image of the greatest of all natural and moral depravations—a fiend-like woman." Galt was filled with "mysterious wonder" that there should be "a being of such incomprehensible strength of resolution."

The text yokes again the images of infant innocence with violence as it will later in the play both verbally and visually—Lady Macduff's child will be slaughtered in some such way. In the tradition of the Terrible Woman, Siddons apparently extinguished any submerged note of tenderness. Her milk had become gall. Ristori dared to make the threatened suppression of maternal feeling visual. She began on a softer note, mimed dandling the babe in her arm, smiled on it, clasped it to her breast; then gradually closing one hand into a fist, "She seemed to tear the infant from her nipple and dash it to the earth. In any but a genius," the *Daily News* marveled, "such an act, instead of startling, must have shocked an audience." Ristori seemed to grow in stature as she stood erect, proud and resolute, looking down at what she had done. But she did not glory in the imagined violence; the purpose was not savagery, but encouragement.

Faucit was momentarily wracked by a spasm of pain—"not with any faltering pity . . . But by the conflict of emotions which a tender image called forth." She "appeared to be one who was, or rather who thought she was"—an interesting distinction—"prepared to sacrifice the life of her child, if need be, in obedience to her oath, but not one who would have enjoyed the terrible act she described" (*Guardian*).

Reinhardt's Lady Macbeth, sensing that Macbeth, eyes closed, was listening to her persuasions, forced the last of her effort into the lines, her voice rising from soft vehemence to a wild passion. She could speak of her babe with a kind of ecstasy; but when the theme became violence, she beat her fists against her breasts, pouring out so much energy that she ended exhausted.

Siddons was remembered screaming out those last words, almost as if afraid of her own thoughts. Salvini's Lady did much the same. This was also what Bradley imagined—the voice rising to an almost hysterical scream, in a strained exaltation that the critic saw as vanishing at the same moment, never to return. Some such hyperexcitement seems naturally to accompany the outrage Lady Macbeth contemplates. A limp threat, as Mrs. Campbell's was, would seem to Grein only meaningless lie. Shaw, of the same opinion, wrote to Campbell:

> . . . It is only your second rate people who write whole movements for muted strings and never let the trombones and the big drums go. It is not by tootling to him *con sordino* that (she) makes Macbeth say, 'Bring forth men. . . .' She lashes him into murder.

Lady Macbeth may indeed believe herself capable of the murder of her child, or at least make her audience think she believes it, as Merchant did, with her completely unsentimental, violent, ugly voicing. But if there may be an exaltation of cruelty, an exultation seems excessive, as with a sadistic young Polish moll, who giggled as she said the terrible lines. It is because Lady Macbeth, as well as Macbeth, feels the horror of the infanticide that it so jolts both of them, as well as audiences.

Where fiercer Ladies often tempered the violence of their attack with the hint of suppressed tenderness, the more womanly had to armor their innate softness. Terry is again an example. Her attitude toward the lines is capsuled in her scribble beside them: "Oh!" She reminded herself to begin at *what beast* with a change of tone—"blaze out!"—though with her voice low, deep. She saw herself telling Macbeth bluntly, in the first seven lines, that he was a coward. Then, seizing his arm, the physical action coming before the words, she began the fiercer last lines—"an exaggeration cos she is in a fury." She was careful that her voice was subdued at "I've (*sic*) given suck" and again at "brains."

> This frenzied appeal is surely the expression of the desperation Lady Macbeth feels at the sudden paralysis of Macbeth's faculties in the hour of action. He must be roused. Is all they have gone through to be for nothing? We really ought not to take her wild words as proof of abnormal ferocity.

Terry saw Lady Macbeth as deeply stirred here; and the substratum of her feeling was made apparent to the audience when, speaking of the child, she brushed away a tear. Even more appeal, and less attack, was voiced by Annis' Lady. She wept here, not for the innocent child, but for her husband's failure to keep a promise that was dear to her: he was not being true to their joint purpose.

The husband-wife relationship is a central motif throughout, and here the Lady relates it to their role as parents: she appeals to him as the mother of his child—history reports that she had borne offspring to an earlier husband, but Shakespeare, as I noted earlier, blanks that out completely (see Appendix). This Lady Macbeth has nursed their child herself, as Strindberg took care to observe—and, again, perhaps recently, if she still has milk to trade for gall; the image of wife-mother-child has especial power to move Macbeth, to whom lineage will be so important a motivation throughout the play.

As the complexities of the Lady Macbeth design fuse in the heat of her determination to win her Lord, so the multiple notes in his polyphony sound as he mounts to his decision. In a marvelously compressed polemic, she, as wife, lover, partner, woman, mother, spur, queen-that-would-be, has plucked across all his strings, imaginative, emotional, rational: as man, soldier, husband, lover, father, sworn partner, philosopher, king-that-would-be. He will be convinced; but his design includes the possibility that he may partly have evoked her arsenal of persuasions to nudge him where he wanted to go; may have been waiting for her to confirm the compulsion of fate; may have been ready to go either way; may have been sincerely determined to resist. All of these possibilities lay suspended in the character during the long indulgence in indecision. Now the momentum of her argument, building a wave that must break, floats him from any base he clung to.

He can now reject his scruples real or pretended—though he will find himself dragging them after him. He may be in a near-hypnotic state, or use such a state as a vehicle for his acquiescence: Terry called this the "sudden paralysis of Macbeth's faculties." Rivalry between Macbeth and his Lady, as well as submission of one to the other, may infect the moment. The Lady's resolute will itself, Marston observed—as he scolded Mrs. Kean for its lack—can be part of the fascination that makes her glorious to Macbeth. But the very scorn with which she denounces his weakness may be a source of envy as well as admiration to the warrior in him—thus Lange acted a Macbeth turned murderer to outdo his wife in vigor and strength.

The philosopher in Macbeth is persuaded, the poet is charged with the force of his Lady's energy and the vision behind it. Croce sees his mind recalled to the witches' prophecies

> as a beautiful, luminous idea to an artist . . . [the two] tremble at the creative moment of daring. . . . [Lady Macbeth] makes him feel the necessity of expressing in action what seems . . . beautiful and delightful, making [his will] ashamed of not knowing how to remain at the level of desire which it has encouraged.

The engagement of so many deep notes of character design partly explains the power of this scene. These are gigantic figures, testing the limits of human capacity. He has been seen to be one of the best of men, but touched with the capacities of the worst, an overreacher stretching so far as to be in touch with forces more than human; she, a gracious lovely hostess, a committed wife, also strains far beyond normality toward a terrible, golden dream. The tension is intensified because what seems dominant in each design suffers now a cruel suppression. Macbeth must turn violently on the humankindness that was his bulwark against treacherous violence; Lady Macbeth is even more savage to herself. Macbeth the man tries to deny his other, "womanly" side; Lady Macbeth would sacrifice her feminine, nurturant essence in favor of her secondary, masculine complement. If she crumples before he does, this hollowing of herself will partly explain why. Each will be eroded by the continuing, often subtextual struggle to seal off native impulse.

The contortion of their identities—and the scene—comes to a peak with her avowal of infanticide. Nothing can shock Macbeth more than this particularly horrible violence; and at the same time, no other vision can move him so much, conquer him so. He may stiffen, speechless; instinctively threaten her, then check himself; turn away; cover his eyes with his hand. The submissive Macbeths are staggered by this stark signal of superior force; other

Macbeths, susceptible to a combination of love and chastisement, are persuaded, coaxed, or blackmailed by the startling avowal of ferocity from the erstwhile gentle wives who have shared their beds. Surrender, or acknowledgment of acquiescence, is most difficult in the evenly matched pairs, where ego resists ego, and love may be almost a form of war. Olivier's Macbeth, disposed to advance himself by any means, but fully cognizant of the dangers involved, could not allow himself with grace to yield easily to Leigh's driving adjurations and taunts. His back turned to her, he had managed to seem impervious to her scorn until, torturing herself as well as him, she claimed the strength to kill her child. He swung round to her, David reported, and "laid his hand on her elbow in a gesture at once deeply affectionate and protesting." Scofield, dueling with Merchant, yet needing her, at his *I dare do all*, had reached for her hand, an insistence on relationship. She started to pull it away, he held it, asserting his strength against her polemic. She yielded nothing. Her *I have given suck* was violent, unsentimental, ugly, as if, on the crest of her determination, this Lady Macbeth could indeed destroy her child. Scofield, over his inward shock, recognized and yielded to the force he had forced against himself.

Macbeth, defeated in his moral stand, retreats tactically to a practical one, a final beguiling of time, a last clutch at the safety of indecision, pivoting on an *if*:

> If we should fail? (69)

This is the crest of the scene, as Beckerman has observed. Macbeth has yielded in all but detail; the dialectic has struggled to its apogee, and transcendence follows. In a few short words, Lady Macbeth asserts control.

> We fail?
> But screw your courage to the sticking place,
> And we'll not fail: (70–72)

Siddons ran through three variations of *we fail*: first, "a quick, contemptuous interrogation," then "the note of admiration and an accent of indignant astonishment, the emphasis on 'we'"; then "the simple period, in a deep, low, resolute tone, which settled the issue . . . 'If we fail, well then we fail.' " Bell described this final voicing as unsurprised, with a "strong downward inflection," the actress bowing, her hands down, palms up, accepting (but he italicizes her *not*). Oxberry called this the "calm mildness of a mind prepared for the worst." This "cool promptitude," which seemed to the *Cabinet* too "colloquially familiar for the temper and importance of the scene," followed a suggestion by Steevens; but it was also, perhaps, Siddons' deliberate differing from Pritchard's traditional "daring and scornful" rejection of Macbeth's question. Mrs. Jameson liked Siddons' stoic version best; so did one *Monthly Mirror* critic for its showing Lady Macbeth's resolute mind made up. The main counter-argument, in the same journal, noted the lack of encouragement implied. Such encouragement would be perceived in Miss Smith's intonation, keeping the question mark: Is it to be supposed that we, possessing as we do the power to overcome every obstacle, can miscarry? Terry's note for the lines seemed to call for a Siddons expression: "downward inflection"; she was heard to utter it as a resolute "wail of defiance . . . , then "smilingly urge him in a caressing, coaxing fashion to courage" (*Trade, Finance & Recreation*). In the theatre the line often carries the intensity Bradley sensed: "contemptuous astonishment," ranging in quality from Mrs. Kean's derision at the insupportable notion of failure to Merchant's absolute outrage at the intimation; though at the other extreme a young German Lady could, with an appearance of charming naiveté, seem to say: "We fail? What's that?" Vanessa Redgrave (U.S., 1975) spoke the lines, Stephen Booth reported, "in the manner of someone told there are no cucumbers in the market. 'No cucumbers. Well, send out for some.' "

Lady Macbeth's following line indicates how little hospitality she gives to the possibility of failure. She has broken through his scruple, now she fully expects that he will be as brave to act as she. "Screw *your* courage to the sticking place and *we*'ll not fail" is one intonation that expresses her mood; another stresses *sticking place* and *not fail*.

Her metaphor may turn on the tuning of a stringed instrument—illuminated by Murry's suggestion that, as we may feel "a faint and subtle apprehension lest the (taut) string should snap," we almost hear the crack when Macbeth returns from the murder (II, ii, 14). Or the crossbow, its loading cord strung to firing pitch, may seed the metaphor. But no specific analogy is needed, and indeed may even diminish the sense of Macbeth himself wound to an ultimate stretch. The operative image is *screw:** to twist-drive the self forward until it is absolutely taut—and might break.

Lady Macbeth's sense that she has won is signaled by the colon after *fail*, that marks a sudden change in her rhythms. The last lines of the preceding speech, and the first part of this one, have been fired at Macbeth mainly in monosyllabic bullets, many pointed with hard *k*'s (suck, milk, plucked, screw, courage, sticking). Now the words and rhythms lengthen, the language is softened by *m*'s, *n*'s, and *w*'s, until the triumphant end. She usually has him now: his practical question was the sign that he had delivered himself over; she proceeds practically to show him how they cannot fail. This is a touchy

---

*Garrick used an expurgation for this speech: "But bring your courage to the proper place." What offended? Did *screw* already have its sexual connotation, to go with *sticking place*? The proper O.E.D. is silent on such a meaning. My University reference librarian, however, cites the *Playboy Book of Forbidden Words* (1972) which suggests that the connection may be to the tool called "screw" derived from Middle English "scrue," meaning "to dig." The connotation is probably at least this old. The very propriety with which the eighteenth century censored the metaphor, as it did so many others with sexual implications, suggests that here another subliminal erotic note may be echoing *Macbeth*'s subtle linkage of sexuality and violence.

moment for the actress: she must propose a cunning, cruel scheme for murder and still sustain her stature. When the Polish Wysocka (1904) dropped from dignity into a vulgar cynicism, her wrong kind of dissonance broke the scene.

Liquid images come to the Lady's mind again; and again what she says of the effects of drink will recoil on her own flight to unreason:

> . . . Memory, the warder of the brain,
> Shall be a fume, and the receipt of reason
> A limbec only. (76–78)

She has sometimes carried with her the jug or pitcher of wine meant for the *spungy* grooms—and one or both of the Macbeths may drink, before Lady Macbeth adds, as sometimes now, the drugs she has carried with her. Lady Macbeth can imagine the sleeping to be like the dead—as she can later say both are like pictures. To her, now, sleep can still be pejorative; she will change.

> . . . when in swinish sleep,
> Their drenched natures lie as in a death,
> *What* cannot you and I perform upon
> Th'*unguarded Duncan?** (78–81)

Some of the undertone of the Lady's intensity surfaces here. *You and I.* Since her *leave all the rest to me* she has met Duncan, led him within her castle, eaten with him. Now she is shifting responsibility for doing the unspeakable act onto Macbeth. Though she in fact seems to have broached the murder (*never shall sun that morrow see*), his *if we should fail* has given her the cue to press a joint *enterprise.* In I, v she used the first person plural once only in describing the future glories that would follow the killing; now, for the doing of the act itself, her speech is all *you and I, our* and *we.*

In the end she consolidates her control by appealing to Macbeth's pride in remarkable deeds—again in euphemism: *our great quell.* So these words brought a slow, steadying smile to Welles.

Actresses have emphasized varying tones in bringing Macbeth to the climactic decision (often by intensifying the kind of hypnotic process that seems to glaze his mind). Siddons, who had closely approached Macbeth, looking him in the face, now came so near she could indeed pour her spirits into his ear, in a low, earnest whisper. She watched every effect on him of the first words; with increasing confidence, as she saw his response, she spoke, still in a low voice, but even more earnestly. Bell saw her feeling her way, gauging the wavering of Macbeth's mind, suiting the intensity of her earnestness to it:

With contempt, affection, reason, the conviction of her well concerted play, the assurance of success which her wonderful tones inspire, she turns him to her purpose.

*Siddons' emphases.

In much the same pattern, Ziegler moved swiftly and purposefully up to Macbeth, staring at him with piercing eyes, watching every sign of intention in his face. She spoke slowly but very distinctly, stressing each word. She too kept her voice low, partly out of concern that she might be overheard, but the purpose and effect of hypnosis was unmistakable. When, in this pattern, a Macbeth like Savits' averts or hangs his head, the Lady's passionate speech, if not her hand, brings his face to hers, and his mind yields. Some actresses, like Mrs. Benson, knelt before their Macbeths to command attention.

Lady Macbeth may be overcoming herself as well as her lord: Reinhardt's Lady, near exhaustion, gnawed anxiously at her lip before launching into her final mesmerizing proposal. Marlowe, knowing now that Macbeth was persuaded, at *When Duncan is asleep . . .* had yet momentarily to turn her head away before she could face her husband with her plan. Johnston, strenuously holding herself from breakdown, fed her words to her husband very slowly, very carefully, as if his comprehension and her sanity depended on speaking in words or sounds of one syllable.

Hypnotic charm supplemented hypnotic power in many of the softer Ladies. Terry, again, provided a rationale. She recognized *we fail?* as the scene's climax; from there, after a "great change," the recipe was "charm" ("be damned charming" was one self-caution), "smile"—indeed she was seen laughingly to encourage Irving. "All women are clever at contriving here," she noted. "Now see how here is a beautiful plan which your wife has thought all out (the hell-cat)." Terry, too, watched her man closely: for the moment when she described how she would inebriate the grooms, her note was "pause, observe him." And as she went on, "slowly play with his hands—charm him." One objective was to emphasizes *her* role: "What cannot you and *I* perform . . . ?" Observers saw her as eager but quietly earnest and intense.

Terry played sensually with Irving's hands; other Ladies were even more intimate, coaxing and clinging like Bernhardt, mesmerizing partly with touch and murmur. Wolter linked her arms in Macbeth's, speaking at first in a low, urgent voice, and, like other Ladies sensitive to what might be heard in the next room, led him downstage for the climax of their conspiratorial exchange: there, her arms gently around his neck, she whispered her plans, visibly ensnaring him. Jessner's Lady, passionate, erotic, kissed and embraced her Macbeth as she showed him the way to murder.

During Lady Macbeth's long speech, after Macbeth's defensive *If we should fail?*, he is designed to travel a complex subtextual path. Up to this point he has barely been able to break in on her wash of words before it has overwhelmed him; her power over him, allied by her cunning to the power of his own impulses, has thwarted all his attempts to leave, evade, interrupt, defend his moral stance. The effect of her persuasion has been to move him from vocal resistance to prudential scepticism; now, as his Lady tempts him with the security so important to him, he wavers on the edge of acquiescence.

The multiplicity of tones in the Macbeth design that work to persuade him to—or brake him from—murder may partly be gauged by the diverse emphases of critical interpretation. Somehow the noble thane apparently capable of surrender to the image of babe-pity must be reconciled with the man immediately after persuadable to murder his guest-king. Not if, as with Stoll, Macbeth is found inconsistently made; but Stoll was innocent of how a play works in the theatre, and armored against experiencing dramatic motivation. Fatalists similarly, though from a different approach, by making Macbeth a plaything of nightmare, or fate, miss the insistent self-generating impulses Shakespeare drew into the design.

What does govern Macbeth's action here? Prudence, mainly, Farnham argues. The full case for the practical killer posits a Macbeth ready to rise through murder but, from cowardly irresolution, wanting to be certain he can do it safely; moral considerations are irrelevant; he shows no real affection or pity for Duncan; hence he does not argue effectively with his wife. Stein allows a Macbeth transiently drawing on sources of pity as well as fear, but finally returning to "coldly rational" ambition. Nevo discovers a Freudian ambivalence: Macbeth's very revulsion from murdering Duncan is a measure of the intensity of his desire to commit the act that he finally achieves.

At the other extreme, to Empson, a genuine moral element shelters behind the show of prudence. Rosen perceives a shift from selfness to a broader insight that produces momentarily at least a true compassion for "the other"—Duncan. Bradley allows Macbeth a conscience, sees him held back by an oppressive sense of the "hideous vileness of the deed." Muir, looking deep, believes Shakespeare lets us see, behind Macbeth's pragmatism, a horrified unconscious mind. Fear of a moral kind informed Duthie's image of Macbeth, really appalled by his vision of a last judgment, so terrified of the "life to come" that he would have to jump. Spender intuits a fear of the timeless beyond this bank and shoal, the abyss of infinity.

These sample emphases in critical interpretation, that match theatrical ones, can all find their way into the polyphonic vacillation—Heilman aptly calls it a "medley of moral acumen and practical misgiving"—that brings Macbeth to his moment of decision. The cue for his surrender seems eminently practical: the Lady has seemed to convince him that, by her clever plan, they can *trammel up . . . consequences*, strike a *be-all* and *end-all* blow. Yet Macbeth's conscience will not stay buried for him any more than will all of his victims.

The more conscience Macbeth begins with, the more grudgingly he gives way. So with the honorable Garrick:

With what reluctance he yields, upon the diabolical persuasions of his wife.

Even with a Macbeth more easily persuadable, the visual signs of acquiescence are gradual and accumulating: by the way his face may slowly swivel back to his temptress; by the relaxation of his muscles; by the rigidly held head that succumbs to nodding agreement—sometimes at first reluctantly, then more easily, as with Reinhardt's Macbeth. Irving's successive moods suggest one

itinerary to complicity. His Macbeth was ready to be won over, but his indecision—touched with cowardice—asked for compelling argument. Terry's
adjurations, rising to the fiery assertion of her willingness to sacrifice a child—
the more terrible because uttered with such desperate force by so tender a
woman—seemed to shock and daze this Macbeth. Her notes suggest that she
wanted his *If we should fail* to come very quickly, and she quickly overrode it.
Then, as she began to charm him, outlining the mechanics of a safe murder,
the change came in him: he began slowly to brighten, to listen attentively,
his whole being became more alert, until he "jumped" at her plan, an "evil
gleam," one reviewer reported, lighting his eyes. McKellen seemed, up to the
very last, impervious to Dench's persuasion. He had tried to return to Duncan, only to be stopped by his Lady, who caught him and even shook him to
make him listen. He had moved to the door again when the very practicality
of her evidently extemporized plot suddenly made sense to him, and he paused
of himself. When he turned, and came slowly toward her, he was at first only
speaking hypothetically; but then the idea grew on him, and excited him—as
any new idea could excite this Macbeth.

The tremendous release of resistance that follows the climax of Macbeth's
inward struggle may be signaled by a kind of manic exultation, one form of
the hyperexcitement that often inflames this overreacher. It finds voice in the
curious cry that tells her he is agreed:

> Bring forth men-children only:
> For thy undaunted mettle should compose
> Nothing but males. (84–86)

This reprise of the child-motif sounds Macbeth's own continuing concern
with lineage, and incidentally reminds us that the Lady, who has already given
suck, is still young enough to bear children. And that the child she has nursed
must itself be male (she herself speaks of "*his* boneless gums").
    Fanny Kemble thought Macbeth was shrinking from the

> idea of her bearing *women* like herself, but not *males* of whom he thought her a
> fit mother.

Bernadete sees Macbeth as appalled here. In the theatre, the line may be torn
from Macbeth out of almost frightened admiration. Even when said with a
hint of dismay, that tone usually only lurks under an overt cry of wonder,
as with the nervous Matkowsky, almost shouting in triumph, but conveying
underneath an "uncanny inner tension"; or as with Scofield, his freely given
admiration yet touched by a faint residue of the suppressed horror with which
he heard Merchant speak of infanticide.
    After his last line, if not at the end of the speech, even a restrained Macbeth
has reached out to take Lady Macbeth's hand, or to embrace her, a sign that
he would be at one with her. Macready, still fighting himself, showed the

strain by seizing an astonished Fanny Kemble ferociously by the wrist, and spinning her round to him. Salvini seemed to Stevenson most deeply stirred at this moment,

> in the strange and horrible transport of admiration, doubly strange and horrible on Salvini's lips.

Salvini embraced his Lady "rapturously," Irving his "jubilantly"; Fritz Weaver (U.S. 1973) his with eager sensual caresses. But Olivier, David remembers, said the line "wryly, in almost mocking praise of her lack of scruple," and did not take her hand until, after a pause, he began the words that would help him assure himself of the security she promised. Reinhardt's Macbeth, looking down at his wife, sitting exhausted before him, covered his excitement in a very matter-of-fact tone, but his commonplace manner was belied by his own excited words and by a shiver that suddenly ran down his back.

Macready was faulted by one critic for too much resolution too soon, as he continued:

> Will it not be receiv'd,
> When we have mark'd with blood those sleepy two
> Of his own chamber, and us'd their very daggers,
> That they have done't? (86–89)

—"which we take clearly to be expressive of a lingering wish to go back, and a want of still further heartening up to the 'sticking place'—not the joy of security." The language leaves room here. If there is hesitancy, it subsists not only in the continued avoidance of reference to the nameless deed itself, but also in the interrogative mode of all but the last of the final speeches. Lady Macbeth, triumphant as she is, exultant as she may be, yet shares in the questioning. Her response to *If we should fail?* ended with two questions; Macbeth replied with another; Lady Macbeth will return with a fifth. Both are giving and asking for assurances.

So powerful a Lady as Siddons might not seem to need strengthening. At

> Who *dares* receive it other,
> As we shall make our griefs and clamours roar,
> Upon his death? (90–92)

she had a "look of great confidence, much dignity of mien. In 'dares' great and imperial dignity." She could be sure of her man. Terry felt Lady Macbeth's loving amusement at Macbeth's suggestion about planting the daggers on the *sleepy two.* In this spirit she said her *Who dares* . . . : "Why, you clever idiot, who dares?!!!!!"—with a parenthetical note for *griefs and clamours:* "(act it)." (Macbeth and his Lady will indeed make their griefs and clamors roar, and sigh and whisper too.)

Lady Macbeths have suggested here that Macbeth, for all his surrender, still needs their support and manipulation. Annis, her tears drying as Macbeth acceded to her, turned warm and reassuring again. Savits' Lady, hearing Macbeth develop her own ideas, waited for his smile of triumph before she mirrored it with a smile of her own. Unless she is an iron woman, the Lady herself is under tremendous stress: if she has had to summon strength of cruelty foreign to her, once her object is achieved, her assumed assurance may be threatened with collapse. The Lady who has begun neurotic, suddenly facing the reality of their decision to kill, now twists further toward unbalance. More subtly, the clear-sighted Lady who, at this very instant of her strategic triumph, suddenly glimpses, in Macbeth's commitment, some sense of what may lie ahead, may sound, however faintly, the first unsettling note of the inner dissonance that will shatter her. So Reinhardt's Lady, sitting for a moment pale and drained, opened her tired eyes at her husband's excited speech, saw how far she had taken him, realized what awful force she had set in motion, and had to force herself to *Who dares.* . . .

Strindberg, responding like a *naive* spectator, observed that the end of the scene still does not make clear who will commit the murder. This is part of the design: Shakespeare has Macbeth, like his Lady, now use the plural:

> When *we* have mark'd with blood those sleepy two
> . . . and us'd their very daggers. (87–88)

Our *naive* spectators, who before expected Lady Macbeth to wield her keen knife, now envisioned a kind of partnered murder. This possibility is not contradicted by Macbeth's

> I am settled, and bend up
> Each corporal agent to this terrible feat. (93–94)

He will force his body—previously so out of control, so wayward, that at the thought of murder its function was smothered in surmise—to join in the act; the disjunct will be compelled to merge back into single state. An image of a bending bow has been suggested; but again more impact derives from a direct sense of Macbeth himself constricting his body to serve his will—and he may let us sense the tremendous force he must exert to subdue the reluctant part of himself.

He still does not name the *feat*, but it will be a *terrible* one, suitable to a doer of great deeds. A visual image may assert the magnitude of Macbeth's climactic determination to be at last decisive: he strikes Duncan's throne, or takes up the royal robe or other symbol, or—as in Connecticut (1973)—tears off the crucifix he wears, in a goodbye to all that he would *holily*. (This last gesture linked this Macbeth to his Lady, who had thrown off her own cross; a similar joint commitment to their intention finds them sharing the handle of a dagger—thus also sustaining the ambiguity of who will commit the murderous act.)

Interruptions here to the dialogue sometimes recall the presence of Duncan and his court. Sounds are heard; servants pass; or Duncan himself, with his sons or courtiers, may appear on the way to bed. The Macbeths must then cover their conspiratorial meeting with a show of courtesy. In the most elaborate of these interpolations, Tree and his Lady were about to re-enter the banquet hall when they suddenly came face to face with Duncan coming out. Shock. The king embraced Macbeth, paused to bless the assemblage, and went off to his room, where a minstrel could be heard quietly singing to him.

If no interruption silences the Macbeths, the very sense of what they plan for the guest in the next room may enforce a cautious, whispered last speech and exit. Macbeth, in reverting to how his behavior will be received, seems to be telling his Lady what she has already told him about the importance of playing, masking—doubling—to beguile the time:

> Away, and mock the time with fairest show,
> False face must hide what the false heart doth know. (95–96)

When he does speak directly to her, she may very well, like Ristori, smile to herself with secret irony as he presumes to give her back her own advice. Carrick Craig noted this motivation for such a smile: "I've won. I know how to manage my husband. He thought he could get out of it. Never. I love him."

On the other hand, Macbeth's last line may be another adjuration aside to himself, an attempt once more to still a cry of conscience, or to confess to himself his repugnance and shame for masking foul with fairest show. The Macbeth who was repelled by his Lady's advice to play a flower but be a serpent, now must, with some pain, embrace hypocrisy—if indeed his tell-tale face will allow it. E. R. Russell saw Irving's last speech as

> half vacant, half desperate . . . [knowing] that his face will never be false
> enough to hide his trouble, that Lady Macbeth will have the intolerable respon-
> sibility of keeping up a curtain of fair show before the horrible realities.

Macready's manner suggested that, however he had spoken acquiescence, his inward resistances remained. Committed now to murder, he "presented an impressive spectacle of human misery, the perturbed countenance and agitated frame without giving fearful note of the storm raging within." The evidence of inhibiting conscience the *Bath Journal* had observed still tortured him, though glimpses of ambition drew him mixedly forward: his face, the *Iris* reported, "was as a troubled sea ploughed by the storm, and anon played on by a flickering sunbeam."

A troubled minor Macbeth, Wallack,* startled his Lady when, as if he could bear no more, he suddenly turned and disappeared, leaving her in mute, perplexed wonder. The most confident Lady, watching Macbeth desert her, must show some sense that her husband is not at peace with his commitment to kill. So must we—still uncertain of what he will do next. And she.

*James W. Wallack (England, 1821).

More often the two prepare to leave as a pair, and lead us to wonder if—how—they will together realize their resolve of the moment. If they have not embraced before, they may at last; or may embrace again, as Piscator's Macbeths did, she following him up a staircase toward Duncan's room. In the Quadflieg *Macbeth* (See Germany, 1953) the embrace was long and intimate, one of the most intense moments of the production, Macbeth burying his hands and fingers in his Lady's hair, making love to her as they prepared for murder. In this final embrace, the last before the deed that will so alter their lives, many notes of their relationship come to focus. The moment is designed to make them newly aware of Dionysian qualities in each other. They have yielded to temptation, they are together shedding any innocence they might have had. One has manipulated the other, or each the other, to the brink of the most dreadful of feats. Besides their dangerous knowledge of each other, they know the anxieties and exultations of a civilized man and woman preparing a horrible act. The complexities of the moment were reflected in the clinging of Scofield and his Lady: brought together in arms not so much amorously as for mutual support against apprehension, yet held subtly apart by their new insights into each other and the thing they have agreed to do.

As the Macbeths go off to murder, sometimes a dagger is bared, or if bare, sheathed, sometimes, as with Rigg, the drugged wine carried off toward Duncan's room. Macbeth may take the lead, as with Macready, his hand already firmly on his Lady's wrist, drawing her after him to his fate. Ristori and her Macbeth crept out cautiously, she behind, the smile of accomplishment on her face. Macbeth has returned alone for a moment, to say his final, now self-damning last lines, *False face*. . . . Terry, on the other hand, having preceded Macbeth, to allow him a final moment on stage, came back, after Irving had gone, to make certain he had indeed gone to keep his word. In some stagings the witches are heard, or seen in the background; thus Tree's trio made their presence felt with a hint of wind and storm that was both a choral comment and ominous of the tortured night to come. But this insistence on an infernal machine is false to Shakespeare's text and even more to the mystery of the chief characters' motivation. The scene is designed to end on a pause of dreadful possibility.

Act II, Scene i

For the third time a scene has ended warning of Duncan's imminent murder; is it to be now?

A new act is designated by the Folio, but action may very well have been continuous in Shakespeare's time. To remind us of the gentle victim, the theatre sometimes has (as noted) bridged to II, i with the pageantry of Duncan's movement from banquet to bed. Then he is likely to be enveloped in royal panoply, princes and groom escorting, himself warmly human: he has looked benevolently on the castle, even kissed Macbeth. This pageantry risks evoking sympathies not in Shakespeare's design; and it may make an audience too much aware of the realities of how time must pass before Duncan and his grooms can be dead asleep. Shakespeare's brilliant telescoping of duration is not to be trifled with. Less importunate, and easier to absorb into the background flow of hours, are the dying sounds of the castle's great victory feast. (Of the whole delicate tracery of time in *Macbeth* more will be said later.)

One offstage action must intervene between what we have just seen, and the murderous act to come. Lady Macbeth must drug the drink of the grooms, and look in on the sleeping king: perhaps intending to kill him? The text o'erleaps this moment now—only later the Lady will tell us how she saw the old man, as he lay in bed. The theatre has sometimes hinted the interim, with Lady Macbeth seen moving (Macbeth may distract Banquo's attention from her) toward Duncan's room—up the stairs down which she will later wander in her own sleep, or along an upper gallery. Tyrone Power's prompt-book (1907) suggests details:

> across the silent, empty stage, suddenly, swiftly, stealthily, Lady Macbeth came out from Duncan's chamber, hurrying toward her own room; as she swung the door open, Macbeth was there, confronting her. For a moment they stood, fearful, determined. She let him know, by a gesture, that she had not

succeeded; they heard Banquo's voice; swiftly, afraid, she rushed away up
the stairs; Macbeth, more slow-moving, secreted himself behind the door;
when Banquo's back was turned, he came forward.

A lurking Macbeth is not unusual here.

A great storm will later trouble this night, and the theatre, delighted with
pyrotechnics, sometimes anticipates. Lightning may open the scene, as with
Tree, and then thunder (a cue in this staging for the witches to dance in and
vanish). But the text abjures storm. Wind rising, as with Komisarjevsky, or
even howling, with thunder off, as with Irving, can better fit the premonitory mood, and the sense of clotted darkness into which the characters enter.
(Booth warned wisely that too much thunder would "take the horror from
the time.")

Stillness seems to become the opening best of all. No noise need disturb
the ominous air; the affair cries silence. Stamm observes that the sounds stipulated to be heard—a sleeping man's groan, the owl's shriek, the cricket's
cry—are remarkable in the otherwise dead quiet. Craig wanted "fog to sink
slowly during the scene. Try to keep it cold, queer, and horrible looking . . .
sink the darkness as a veil sinks."

The mystery of the night reigns. It is emphasized by the scene's first visual
gesture: the torch that precedes the entry of Banquo and Fleance. The *Torch
before him* may be carried by a servant, or servants—a common nineteenth-
century stage practice, the torches justifying an accompanying increase of
general illumination on the stage. Tree's Porter could be seen leading the two
in (as a Phelps servant had done) to emphasize the enclosed atmosphere of
the castle. But no servant is mentioned,* as one will be when Macbeth enters;
and the relationship of the father and son, a recurrent motif, is emphasized
if they alone enter, Fleance perhaps carrying the torch.

To a *naive* spectator, Banquo's appearance raises questions. Will he interrupt the planned murder? Discover it? Who is the boy, and what is he doing
here?

Fleance represents a dramatic force out of proportion to his brief appearance and few words. He will say almost nothing; yet his felt presence looms
threateningly over Macbeth and shadows the whole action of the play. He
will disappear halfway through, but we who do not know this may anticipate—as *naive* spectators have anticipated—his return at the very end, the
wonder at his absence coloring late responses.

Banquo calls Fleance *Boy*, and he is usually taken to be quite young, a kind
of visual image of the son Macbeth dreams of putting on a throne; but he is
old enough, agile enough to get away from muscular men who kill his warrior-
father and intend to murder him. He usually is seen very close to his father,
the more so when shrinking from a glance or gesture of Macbeth or Lady

---

*Though Liddell argues that *Torch* was used sometimes in Elizabethan English to designate
a link-boy.

Macbeth. He was a child to Sothern's Banquo, who playfully put his soldier's helmet over the boy's head as they entered; he was a young man in a Prague staging, slightly tipsy, like his father, as they entered from the offstage banquet.

Most stagings agree with Dr. Johnson that the two are to be imagined coming into an inner court, open to the sky, but close enough to Duncan's chamber for the subsequent action. On the placeless Globe stage, the language and action established such an understood, undefined place. In later productions, where versatile stage forms are used, their rearrangement suggests the new scene. Thus at the Meiningen, the rocky platforms of the first act were shifted to become now the stairway to a permanent higher scaffolding housing the door to Duncan's chamber (the importance of an elevated level to Shakespeare's design will be discussed shortly). Such an "upper above" is conventional in realistic, castellated staging; its stairway often attaches to a tower that is part of a turreted wall. Liddell:

> If we recall . . . the castle architecture with which Shakespeare was familiar, . . . we have a large courtyard with a flight of steps in one corner leading up to the sleeping rooms, such as is shown in the cut of Kenilworth in 1620, . . . an upper lobby which opened on the guest chamber. This lobby would be the usual gallery or balcony at the back of the stage. Duncan and his two grooms of the chamber would naturally be lodged in the guest chamber. Such an arrangement would be familiar to an Elizabethan audience, and explains clearly the action of the scene.

Tree and Irving followed this scenic pattern: Tree particularly centered attention on the doors, at the upper level, of Duncan's room.

If the beginning of I, vi was sunlit, now black night has fallen. Light-controlled productions make the most of chiaroscuro: an open fire flicking red and black onto Tree's walls; with Sothern, servants with subdued crimson torches emerging from the depths of gloomy, massive pillars and arches, spectral stairways leading to the mysterious chambers above, formidable gates shutting off the corridors to the outside. Less detail may exercise the imagination even more. The Craig staging banished any sense of place in

> a shadowy, fear-compelling set . . . painted entirely with lights and shadows . . . nothing to localize the scene in Scotland nor to date it in any particular period. We are in the presence only of stark murder. . . . Nothing is discernible upon the stage which might possibly distract from the faces and the voices of the actors. (Hamilton)

O'er the one half world of night, nature herself seems dying.

Banquo carries with him the atmosphere of dread. His mind is burdened; so Reinhardt's Banquo came with heavy steps, he breathed a deep sigh, as did Welles' Banquo. Sothern's glanced back toward Duncan's room, as if to make sure all was well. In a Russian staging (1918), Juriev's Banquo was gloomy, tense, wracked with foreboding; he gazed slowly and searchingly around him into the castle's shadows. Banquo may be weary from the revelling; is certainly oppressed by his thoughts and apprehensions.

But alert, as always, to what goes on around him, Banquo's first words accentuate the torch's signal of darkness: *How goes the night?* He identifies the time as about the witching hour of midnight in his loving-father's small talk with Fleance; but more is on his mind than he can say to his son. Fleance may be in haste to get to bed; he is often seen to be a very sleepy boy here; he has even been "discovered" dozing on a bench, startled awake by the sound of a furtive movement by Macbeth before his father enters.

Banquo's words suggest an interrupting movement—to stop Fleance's departure, or to arrest his own runaway train of thought:

> Hold, take my sword. (9)

A visitor to the castle, a companion to the king, he has been armed before going to rest, and he may well lie down with his weapons close. Now he may part with the sword reluctantly, troubled as he is in mind. The armor seems to be more than ceremonial. Liddell sees Banquo's willingness to let the weapon go as a sign of confidence in his host; but a moment later, alarmed at a sound or movement, he will spring to retrieve it, as if danger might be near in this place.

Banquo usually takes off the sword's harness and hands it, in its scabbard, to Fleance; though Sothern unsheathed the blade and gave it bare to his son. Dramatic form being what it is, this kind of disarming invites expectation that the weapon may suddenly be needed.

Ready with images, Banquo looks up into the dark sky, made darker by his seeing:

> There's husbandry in heaven,
> Their candles are all out. (10–11)

It is an attempt at a joke for his son, to whom he will now give something else: *Take thee that too*. Hackett's Banquo gave his son a loving, fatherly kiss; a fond Banquo may also transfer a coat or blanket to Fleance's shivering shoulders (it is *cold*); more often an object is held out: cloak, hat, most likely the companion weapon, a dagger, perhaps parted with somewhat reluctantly too. *Husbandry* may be heard softly to echo earlier tillage imagery. It has been glossed as suggesting economy,* and even more: one critic hears in the word "wise management. . . . Hence, through Banquo, though obliquely, the irresistible justice of the heavens is being urged." Heaven seems in fact here ungiving, denying light, leaving the world in obscurity; it seems withdrawn before the merciless powers that answered Lady Macbeth's prayers for thick night, Macbeth's for the stars to hide their fires, so that in the darkness terrible deeds might be done. If indeed Banquo can be seen to admire Heaven's

---

*Black wonders if impulses of envy and Scots thrift might be implied, as Banquo looks at the lights of the castle and compares the heavens: "*Their* candles are all out . . ."

way here, later he may learn—after trusting himself to the *great hand of God* (II, iii, 159)—better. But almost certainly he is speaking wryly, as he picks his way with some care through the darkness.

What sits on brood in Banquo's mind must hatch; he pulls away from Fleance, or Fleance dozes, and the uneasy man verbalizes his suppressed *angst*, his urgent prayer:

> A heavy summons lies like lead upon me,
> And yet I would not sleep:
> Merciful powers, restrain in me the cursed thoughts
> That Nature gives way to in repose. (12–15)

Banquo's apologists can conceive him here as mainly concerned with what might happen to Duncan, or what Macbeth might do, as if he himself were untouched by personal fantasies of power: as if the *cursed thoughts* are not his own, as if his dreams, so terrible he cannot dare to sleep, are dreamt for others. I don't see how Shakespeare could more clearly, in these revelatory lines, have mirrored in a flash, in Banquo, Macbeth's extended imaginings of dark means to advance in degree. If at his first entrance Banquo was as worthy as Macbeth seemed, by now (as Nicoll suggests), he may be an altered man— or an altering one. Hackett's note for his Banquo: "Show his antipathy to Macbeth if possible in some way." Libby saw the act of surrendering a sword as a function of Banquo's polyphonic character,

> kindly, conscientious, poetical, but weak and vacillating: he gives up the sword and dagger that he may have no means of defending the king from the fate the witches have predicted.

Westbrook even suggests that Banquo parts with his weapons because afraid

> that if he kept them he would use them on the king . . . he is suffering from a guilty conscience because of his murderous dreams.

Booth's similar note, for giving his dagger to Fleance:

> Banquo is here conscious of the latent power of temptation and seems wishful to rid himself of all incentives to dangerous thoughts, and all the means of mischief.

Certainly Banquo's prayer now to check what has been called his "under nature" is a desperate one. He knows that sleep would further unravel his sleeve of care: he is beginning to incarnate the image of that Sister's victim for whom

> Sleep shall neither night nor day
> Hang upon his penthouse lid. (I, iii, 22–23)

His moment of prayer is almost certainly accompanied by a straining physical gesture beseeching the *merciful powers*. Woodvine's supplicating hands inter-laced so tightly they might have been trying to break each other; and his face was concentrated anguish. This Banquo's *cursed thoughts* were double: he feared what Macbeth might have in mind to do; but he also began to recognize in himself faint stains of the impulses he feared in Macbeth.

Before Banquo has a chance to open himself further he is alarmed by some imminent presence—the more alarmed because he is surprised while in his secret, *cursed* reverie. The Folio directs Macbeth and his torchbearing servant to enter before Banquo springs on guard. So Macbeth may, for a moment, have stood and watched his fellow-captain in dangerous thought, as he himself was earlier watched. Sometimes the theatre anticipates Macbeth's entrance with Banquo's instant defensive action and his urgent order to Fleance:

> Give me my sword: who's there? (17)

Woodvine whispered the first four words to Fleance; drew the boy into the shadows; watched a troubled, resolute figure (Macbeth) stride across the stage; and at an accidental sound in the dark both had weapons out ready for fight. Only then: *who's there?*

In this castle, at this time, in this dark place, Banquo unmistakably feels danger. Until he recognizes Macbeth, perhaps hidden by the flare of the torch, he scents a threat. Olivier's Banquo pushed Fleance around behind him—the heir must be protected. Hampden's Fleance himself shrank back to his father for protection.

We may hear Macbeth's answer before, looking with Banquo into the shadows, we see the answerer:

> A friend. (18)

The phrase is conventional, but not necessarily said conventionally: it carries implications of immediate past experience, and an undertone of irony that Macbeth may intend, or not know. When the rivalry of the two men is masked in jest, Macbeth has laughed the line, forcing a cheerful, casual face. But this will grow increasingly difficult for him, as the enormity of his imminent act presses on him, and he is lured to the escape of raptness. Forrest could not hide the impact of his decision to act; his body—the corporal agent he was bending to his resolution—showed attrition:

> he looked oppressed, bowed, haggard, and pale, as if the fearful crisis had exerted on him the effect of years of misery.

So worn a Macbeth might evoke from a compassionate Banquo the next line,

> What sir, not yet at rest? (19)

More often, Banquo recognizes Macbeth with some relief from immediate danger—but is not entirely relieved. Savits' Banquo was touched with suspicion. The ensuing conversation will be "conscience-troubled," as John Russell Brown observes; it will become hesitant, probing, and end unresolved. Banquo may give Fleance the sword again, as with Benson; or sheathe the drawn blade (Craig); or he may only put the sword up, as Sothern's

Banquo did, his hand still on the hilt. Macbeth will always be half aware of Duncan's room, and what must happen there; but he is tensely alert also to vibrations from Banquo and the boy who may become a king. Trevor Lennam's Fleance dropped his father's dagger; Macbeth picked it up and, as it were jestingly, held its point toward the shrinking boy—until Banquo took it.

Banquo can report that the king is abed, has been in *unusual pleasure*, is shut up in *measureless content*—all signals that time has passed and Duncan will be asleep. He has sent a gift to Lady Macbeth, a *most kind hostess** (may any intonation of doubt enter Banquo's voice?). The gift is a diamond— Banquo holds it out, it glints in the night, a little light in the darkness. Will we later see this diamond as ring, brooch, or pendant, glittering on Lady Macbeth? It may become part of Macbeth's image now: in Sothern's staging, a diamond ring Banquo took from his own finger to give to Macbeth to put on; in Craig's, a jewel pinned to Macbeth's breast. Macbeth's manner of accepting it, seeing it, touching it—or in the slightest shrinking from it— will say much about his mood; and something of this, Banquo may hear in Macbeth's speech.

Macbeth must absorb the shock of Duncan's further generosity; he speaks ironic, double-edged words of apology: we were not prepared to provide for him, or we would have been free to act. Macbeth's will did indeed become the *servant to defect*—an inverted echo of the motif of subject-loyalty. He wears the garment of the player, masking.

All's well. Banquo's abrupt answer, with its full stop, shuts off this line of talk, and leaves time for pause. The two look at each other intently—questioningly, as with Scofield. The silence separates them. Each waits for the other to confide, "like Gaston and Alphonse," Hackett thought. In some stage versions (Irving's, Quayle's) Banquo makes a false exit here, starting off as if having nothing more to say; then turning back to reveal something of what has lain so heavily on his mind. Cowper's Banquo came to whisper in Macbeth's ear. Reinhardt's Banquo looked around carefully, came very close to Macbeth before speaking slowly, significantly, in an undertone. The first half of the astonishing first line is accented lightly, almost apologetically; but the last half is a series of heavy stresses:

> I dreamed last night of the three weyward sisters: (29)

The colon suggests a sustained pause—of inquiry? expectation of an answer? Then, when no answer comes:

> To you they have show'd some truth. (30)

I have called the line astonishing; I am regarding it through the ears of a *naive* spectator. Shakespeare carefully accelerated his action in the first act, hurrying scene after scene, seeming to stipulate Duncan's visit to Inverness the

---

*How wonderfully Shakespeare makes each adjective bear the weight of an entire metrical foot. Does kinship sound in the *kind*?

same day as Macbeth's triumph in battle. No night could then have intervened. Is Banquo confessing that he dreamed of the Sisters the night *before* he and Macbeth met them? Or is Shakespeare stretching time again? In either case, it is Banquo who has brought into the open a worm burrowing in both their minds; and the clear implication is: if so much truth from the Sisters already, why not the rest, for you—and for me? This will, in fact, be his explicit rumination in the next act.

Banquo's allusion to the prophecy clearly connects with his *cursed thoughts* and his reluctance to sleep. His apologists conceive him still entirely innocent of any of Macbeth's kind of dark, ambitious impulses. To do this seems to me to de-humanize, de-characterize the design. One "pattern" critic recognizes this, conceding that the dialogue of the characters is "difficult" as realism; but "as morality play figures who have chosen different sides in the struggle between heaven and hell, there is little difficulty"—Macbeth is the tempter, Banquo refuses the bait. Morality play figures ranged on opposite sides are only "good" or "bad"; their templates lack the flex of human complexity and ambiguity drawn into Shakespeare's dynamic designs. Macbeth and Banquo incorporate within their voices both the good and bad—and not-quite-good and not-quite-bad—angels; when they speak with the voice of the better, they often listen to the voice of the worse. And it is Banquo who, in the present hesitant exchange, speaks first, dangling before both of them the bait of their temptation. We may wonder in passing if King James would be pleased with the image of an ancestor who entertained Banquo's kind of *cursed thoughts* and frightful dreams. Surely *this* was not there because of James' insomnia.

At Banquo's sudden allusion to the witches, Macbeth, already made uneasy by Banquo's interruption of his plans, may well slightly start, as in Reinhardt's staging, his eyes dropping to avoid meeting Banquo's. But Macbeth covers.

I think not of them: (31)

was said conventionally by Irving, with affected carelessness; with a disparaging gesture by Reinhardt's Macbeth. Macready, his mind concentrated on the task ahead, was cold and still, as if impatient to get on. A Macbeth who reacts sharply, even defensively, evokes suspicion—which may affect the manner of the ensuing dialogue.

Again a pause, after the colon: Banquo may start to leave again, as Irving's did, only to be called back. This time it is Macbeth who tempts: as if in afterthought, usually matching Banquo's subdued tones, with a curious use of pronoun:

> Yet when we can entreat an hour to serve,
> We would spend it in some words upon that *business*,

(again that capacious word)

> If you would grant the time. (32–34)

Macbeth seems to use the royal *we*, and the *Times* was impressed with Porter's evident, premature assumption, in voice and manner, of the prerogative—evoking from his Banquo an immediate suspicion. Such a reaction could explain Macbeth's returning to *my* in the next speech.

Banquo's conventional *At your kind'st leisure.*, with its full stop, leaves the initiative with Macbeth. Often a pause follows, a time for the two to measure each other, sounds of storm rising in the silence. Sothern and Hackett went to put a comradely arm around their Banquo's shoulders; but more often a distance is kept. Banquo may stand to Macbeth, outwaiting the pause, as with Reinhardt, until Macbeth, his eyes averted, seeming to search for words, must begin slowly to bring out his next tender. Welles offered it surlily, as if forced to it:

> If you shall cleave to my consent,
> When 'tis, it shall make honor for you. (36–37)

Sometimes Macbeth's effort to get the words out is greater because once more Banquo has begun to leave, as with Irving and Quayle, and then with the words, and the loaded implication of the *If*, Macbeth must stop him, call him back. This pattern of playing Banquo on a line, letting him out, bringing him back, can be seen to be repeated at the beginning of Act III; the visual separation and return intensifies the experience of the covert stresses activating the two characters.

Nothing in Macbeth's words stipulates crime, but both recognize that more than words is being said. Banquo must digest the implications, often, again, pausing, while Macbeth hangs on his answer.

> So I lose none,
> In seeking to augment it, but still keep
> My bosom franchis'd, and allegiance clear,
> I shall be counsell'd. (38–41)

The words, Bradley thought, showed that he feared a treasonable proposal. If so, his response is polite; as he will still counsel politely with Macbeth when, after the murder, his suspicions are inspoken. His doubts now are defined, in his double use of "honor": Banquo says that he would welcome distinction (honor) in degree, though not at the loss of (honor) virtue. He articulates no resistance to what may happen, no warnings. May Banquo think now that, if the witches did show truth, his sons can be kings only after Macbeth has held the throne—and has then been eliminated?

The response gives no comfort to Macbeth, and leaves him nowhere to go. As in many stagings, the men are wary of one another, distrustful. Each takes refuge in his secret thoughts; the conversation flags. On one, time presses; on the other, perhaps, apprehension.

After what was an embarrassed interval, Reinhardt's Macbeth, finding Banquo "impenetrable," finally summoned up a friendly dismissal:

> Good repose the while. (42)

This Macbeth then dared look straight in Banquo's eyes, as if challenging him to make suspicion explicit; Banquo shrugged his shoulders, dropped his eyes to avoid meeting Macbeth's. *Repose* to him, Banquo has just said, means *cursed thoughts;* is there anything wry in his: *Thanks sir: the like to you?* (43)

Hackett and his Banquo each waited for the other to leave—Alphonse and Gaston again; finally Banquo moved, they exchanged "mock bowing, not overdone," and Banquo left. Hackett looked after him, certain that his fellow general was "as rotten as he was."

The subtextual strains on Macbeth, as, in his player's role, he presents the *innocent flower* to Banquo, may be felt to mount to their climax with his covert temptation speech. Arthur Murphy preserves for us Garrick's achievement in this scene by scolding him when the actor fell short of it:

> For a man just going to commit a murder, and so strongly possessed with the horror of the deed as in a moment after to see a dagger—were you not a little disengaged, too free, and too much at ease? I will tell you how I have seen you do it: —you dissembled indeed, but dissembled with difficulty. Upon the first entrance the eye glanced at the door; the gaiety was forced, and at intervals the eye gave a momentary look towards the door, and turned away in a moment. This was but a fair contrast to the acted cheerfulness with which this disconcerted behaviour was intermixed. After saying "Good repose the while"; the eye then fixed on the door, then after a pause in a broken tone, "Go bid thy mistress, etc." . . . Pray observe, that as you assume freedom and gaiety here, it will be also a contrast to the fine disturbance and behaviour, in the night gown, after the murder is committed, when no cheerfulness is affected: I am sure this was the way formerly, and I own it strikes me most.

Garrick "most sincerely" agreed:

> I was indeed not quite master of my feelings till I got to "clutching the air-drawn dagger." I like your description of the state of Macbeth's mind and body, at the time he affects cheerfulness to Banquo. . . . I will not flatter myself I ever played up to your colouring.

As Macbeth watches Banquo off, step by step, sounds and sights of storm may momentarily rise. The witches, in some stagings are superfluously heard or seen. With the going of Banquo and Fleance and their torches the light must be imagined to diminish. In controlled lighting, as with Tree, a moon may break partly through the clouded night. Otherwise, unless a fire flickers in the courtyard stones, as with Tree and Irving, there remains as natural light only the torch of Macbeth's servant. Macbeth may, as Juriev did, take the torch and hang it on a wall. The servant is a quiet figure—often providing our first glimpse of the man we will know as Seyton: so quiet that Macbeth, sliding into raptness, has something forgotten about him. Macbeth may start toward Duncan's room, as Thomas Cooper (U.S., 1810) did, and suddenly, almost running into his Seyton, be shocked into awareness. Kemble, pacing rapt, his eyes on the ground, started as he saw his man. Or Seyton may deliberately move, as with Macready, calling attention to himself. In Tyrone Power's promptbook, a tipsy servant, with a torch, stumbles in, startling Macbeth, who pulls himself together and sends the reveler off. Reinhardt's Macbeth started a move toward Duncan's door, suddenly remembered the servant, cleared his throat to speak, hastily ordered him on his mission:

> Go bid thy mistress, when my drink is ready,
> She strike upon the bell. (44–45)

The speech is surely code, to fix a prearranged signal. Yet it is one more step toward unalterable decision, and the saying of it, the extent to which Macbeth takes care to impress it on the servant, measures his readiness to act. Forrest could only mutter the lines with an absent look and tone, half rapt, "as if the words uttered themselves." Irving, more committed, commanded the servant to go. In Prague, the jocular, drunken Porter, going off behind Macbeth, playfully knocked at the gate, startling his thane. This will be perhaps Macbeth's last chance to be gracious; and there may be a momentary softening as he focuses on the servant and says kindly *Get thee to bed* (45). Or he may pretend a yawn as a pretext for dismissal (McKellen); or, under fateful pressure, snap angrily (Macready).

Now Macbeth is alone. Nothing stands between him and the terrible feat but the knelled signal to act. He listens: to the silence, or the sounds of storm, or to uncanny, unnameable noises heard only, perhaps, in his own head. To wait for the bell is to sit, Dover Wilson suggests; but Macbeth may be too restless for that. He may take precautions: may shut the gates to lock out any possible help for Duncan; extinguish a lamp (Haworth); flex his fingers for action (McKellen); move stealthily along the courtyard wall, to make sure all are asleep (Booth); creep close to Duncan's door (Juriev), even go directly to it, and listen, and come away (Young, C. Kemble); let his wild, restless eye look everywhere *but* at Duncan's room (Cooper).*

The strain of bending each corporal agent to the dreadful task can be felt; the *heat-oppressed brain* wracks the body; in the more imaginative, surmise almost smothers function. Booth, exhausted by inner conflict, threatened by every shadow, returned from his round to fall on some steps; Juriev suddenly turned back from his approach to the king's chamber, fled to a seat and collapsed, weakly. Sothern's Macbeth could not even begin an advance: he looked toward Duncan's room, lit in a sharp flare of lightning; then retreated to a bench, where he sat with his face buried in his hands. These Macbeths seem to have given up the task; only some new, overpowering inducement could move them to murder now.

*Joseph Haworth (US. 1896); Charles Mayne Young (England, 1810).

A more resolute Macbeth may stand to his mission, but the tumultuous forces in him betray themselves, the energies boiling in him enforce action. He paces back and forth, turning away with a momentary shudder when he brings his gaze to the king's chamber (Phelps); he moves restlessly, accumulating momentum toward action (Guinness), or with jerky irritability—so Irving, manifesting a frenetic overriding of strong impulses to retreat that, in lapses of discipline, would make his gait drop to that of an old, feeble man. Macbeth's unease might be seen in the iron determination with which he controlled his resistances, as with Scofield; in the quiet, almost passive acceptance of what he had to do, as with Olivier. A committed romantic Macbeth, Cooper, could start slowly and softly toward Duncan's door, look around occasionally to be sure he was alone, then catch up the skirt of his cloak to mask the lower part of his face, and stride forward to the kill.

Something uncanny stops and shocks Macbeth. He suddenly endures an experience that draws intensely on the full range of his polyphony. This last chance to choose a future in innocence brings to focus a multiplicity of his roles, feelings, ideas and habits. The resulting emotional and mental turbulence drives him to the boundaries of balance, if not over into madness itself. Now comes his "fit" again. The man of action is trammeled by his imagination; the warrior-killer's hand is stayed—and enticed; the thinker, moving between fascination and terror, cannot distinguish what is from what is not. The poet will find haunting words to express his whirling, feverish confusion among what is objective, what supernatural guidance, what the projection of his own murderous thoughts. The inner vortex is externalized in his hallucination—a dramatization of the unconscious, Aronson calls it. To anticipate the Porter's lines, now, even more than in Macbeth's I, vii soliloquy, an image

> sets him on, and it takes him off; it persuades him, and disheartens him; makes him stand to, and not stand to. (II, iii, 34–36)

Macbeth's symptoms of turbulence, in the theatre, have ranged from the masked to the most overt. Garrick would stand in sustained raptness; Salvini would begin in a dream he had violently to break from; Matkowsky's pattern of erratic approach and withdrawal to Duncan's chamber made Bab marvel at its visual orchestration of the zigzag movement of Macbeth's mind. Within such larger designs will be discovered a marvelous intricacy of thought, impulse, and action. And we, as audience, guided in spasms through Macbeth's experience, are not to know until his very last lines if he has the resolution to enter Duncan's chamber with a bared knife.

If Macbeth, left alone after the servant's departure, and facing the actuality of murder, is sunk in irresolution, or determined against acting, he rouses at a weird sight. If he is moving confidently toward murder, he is checked by what he sees. The *naive* audience cannot at first tell what Macbeth is

experiencing. Is this another inner confusion? He is usually looking toward
Duncan's chamber, or with his eyes following a movement in that direction.
(Tree, while Lady Macbeth glided softly along the gallery behind him, looked
out toward the auditorium, tracking something invisible. Hampden also
encountered his illusion over the heads of the audience.) Does Macbeth see
something we cannot see? Does he see something that is not, his imaginative
mind reeling? His first words will tell us:

> Is this a dagger, which I see before me (46)

But the words may come only very slowly, after Macbeth's mind has shaped
the image in the air. Until he speaks, our imaginations are stirred and multiplied by his strange concentration. He may make a clutching gesture *before*
he says a word, as Reinhardt's Macbeth did. What is Macbeth trying to hold?
Why is he so moved? We can tell only that he is beginning to act out the kind
of torment Brutus describes:

> Between the acting of a dreadful thing
> And the first motion, all the interim is
> Like a phantasma or a hideous dream. (*Julius Caesar*, II, i, 63–65)

Some directors, intent on draining the supernatural from the play, in favor
of realistic psychological motivation, have rationalized the image Macbeth
sees. Bridges-Adams's Macbeth came upon the weapon pointing up the stairs
as he looked toward the king's room, and spoke to it. A similar gambit has
Macbeth addressing his own weapon, as did George; a Japanese Macbeth
dropped his dagger, and then communed with it. But the text plainly stipulates a vision Macbeth can see but not touch; truly a dagger of the mind. Time
was, according to a scornful *Monthly Mirror* item in 1807, that the dagger was
suspended on a string, for Macbeth to see; and the Liverpool *Kaleidoscope*
credited Garrick with once and for all abolishing it. Wisely: any suggestion
of a real blade must destroy both the sense of strangeness and of the state of
Macbeth's mind. The subjective experience of the intangible is given objective life only by Macbeth's projection. Even with the resources of film, Polanski could only make a spectral dagger ridiculous; it diminished the grandeur
of Macbeth's imagination. Controlled illumination has sometimes been used
to suggest the presence of the invisible; thus in Craig's *Macbeth* light picked
out a spot on a wall specially painted to catch a muted glow. As a projection
of Macbeth's mind, the dagger can be projected onto a screen, or wall. But
the great power of the hallucination must depend on Macbeth's capacity to
create and react to a figment of his heated brain made almost tangible by fierce
belief in it.

Garrick reflected the pattern, if he did not initiate it, of the brooding, reluctant murderer, his eyes on the ground, suddenly becoming aware of an
hallucination above him. Smollett, in a passage cut from the final manuscript
of *Peregrine Pickle*, describes the actor's sudden, almost mystic sense of "a

dagger which he pretends to see above his head, as if the pavement was a looking glass that represented it by reflection."* Many later actors would similarly, suddenly, look up; more than a century later Irving would be praised for "seeing" the dagger at eye level. One of Garrick's spectators remembered, long after, a satanic, murderous look from the actor as he reached for the dagger; but most testimony suggests a Macbeth almost paralyzed until the end of the soliloquy. "How finely does he show his resolution staggered" (Wilkes). Garrick's hypnotic process was synthesized by Davies:

> the sudden start on seeing the dagger in the air—the endeavour . . . to seize it—the disappointment—the suggestion of it being only a vision of the disturbed fancy—the seeing it still in form most palpable, with the reasoning upon it.

"From the moment he sees the dagger, till he says 'There's no such thing,' his eye is constantly fixed on the vision of his mind," the *Morning Chronicle* reported; and complained:

> Would the phantom of an overheated imagination move slowly before him, and for a tedious length of time, when the nature of the mind, and [of the speech, indicate] that it should pass with the utmost celerity? . . . To trace the tardy progress of a dagger in the air, may give an opportunity of displaying the mechanical use of the eye, but it is not an eye guided by a fiery imagination.

This was partly to defend, by contrast, Macklin's more conventional way of seeing the dagger, turning away to recover himself, then turning back to confront again the hallucination. Garrick, who cherished intense pauses, may have been deliberately differing from Macklin, as he probably was differing from Quin's staccato visualization, apparently alluded to in that curious *Essay on Acting*. Quin was said to have snatched often at the invisible dagger as if trying to catch a fly (other Macbeths, notably Reinhardt's, have also repeatedly snatched for the illusion):

> Macbeth, as a Preparation for this Vision, is so prepossess'd, from . . . Humanity, with the Horror of the Deed [incited by Ambition and] under a promissary Injunction to his Lady, that his Mind being torn by these different and confus'd Ideas, his Senses fail, and present that *fatal Agent* of his Cruelty—the *Dagger*, to him: —Now in this visionary Horror, he should not rivet his Eyes to an *imaginary* Object as if it *really* was there, but should shew an *unsettled Motion* in his Eye, like one not quite awak'd from some disordering Dream; his *Hands* and *Fingers* should not be *immoveable*, but *restless*, and endeavouring to disperse the Cloud that overshadows his optick Ray, and bedims

---

*Garrick's power to make the imaginary terrible here became legendary. Private drawing-room audiences were overwhelmed by his capacity to enter immediately into the hallucination, and portray its horror. In the theatre, a foreign spectator, not understanding a word, was reported to be so moved by Garrick's gesture in clutching at the dagger that he collapsed in a swoon.

his Intellects; here would be Confusion, Disorder, and Agony: *Come let me clutch thee!* is not to be done by *one* motion only, but by several *successive Catches* at it, first with one Hand, and then with the other, preserving the same Motion with his Feet, like a Man, who out of his Depth, and half drowned in his Struggles, *catches* at *Air* for *Substance*.

Whether or not this aims at Quin, the next shaft certainly darts at Davy himself by returning to the theme of his smallness:

The *Daggers* are near an Inch and half too long, in Proportion to the Heighth of the Murderer.

Many actors would start suddenly, as Garrick did, at the dagger image; not all successfully. The abrupt, violent gesture, without apparent motivation, needed unaffected astonishment of the kind Kean would bring to it; Kemble's artificiality here distressed Bell:

Much stage trick . . . [Kemble] walks across the stage, his eyes on the ground, starts at the sight of the servant, whom he forgets for the purpose, renews his walk, throws up his face, sick, sighs, then a start theatric, and then the dagger. Why can't he learn from his sister?

An alternative to the "start," proposed by Bell's brother, paints the dagger in the air by a slower, growing comprehension:

[Kemble] should stand or sit musing, his eye fixed on vacancy, then a more piercing look to seem to see what is still in the mind's eye only, characterised by the bewildered look which accompanies the want of a fixed object of vision; yet the eye should not roll or start.

So intense, but low-pitched, a reaction leaves more room for the build of the speech to the first great climax half-way through. Macbeth, in this last inner debate before the irrevocable act, is starting to move upward in a zigzag to a kind of paroxysm that must either purge him or incite him to murder. His shifts in reaction come like a series of intensifying lightning strikes; but they may begin after a charged stillness. So Rossi was long in pause before his wandering gaze fixed on the air. So Phelps, who had been postponing action, trying to pace out his nervousness, after a silence,

Instead of at once starting at the [dagger], kept his eye fixed on the "painting of his fear" until the brainsick, bewildered imagination made it real; shrinking from its belief and returning to it with a struggling conviction, until it obtained full possession of him (*Lloyds*).

Irving, nerved to a wild excitement as he looked up toward Duncan's tower, seemed to see the imagined dagger without at first really noticing it. "It was the natural outcome of this thought, and at first scarcely aroused alarm or surprise." Then, suddenly, with the kind of "double take" delayed perception and the startling contrast congenial to this actor, he became still, he stared and stared until his eyes seemed to be starting from his head, his face hardened, as if terror were turning him to stone, and his blanched features became paralysed.

One observer was impressed that in his first Macbeth, Irving, though he said *Come, let me clutch thee* (47), at first averted his eyes—*the eye wink at the hand*—and even held back his hand: as if suspicious of the vision's implication, as if he could not trust himself to try to grasp it. Yet finally he looked sidelong at the image, his hand went out, and came back empty; *I have thee not* was charged with disappointment.

Salvini, left alone, fell into a raptness; he looked like a man walking in his sleep, dreaming a horrible dream. This actor, remember, thought that Lady Macbeth's sleepwalking scene really belonged to Macbeth; and here he seemed to anticipate it, making no start at an outward vision, no pretense that he saw a dagger, no effort to clutch it. The experience was internal. His voice and gestures were uncertain, accompaniments to an action working itself out in his mind.

Some outward signs of Forrest-Macbeth's inward stress could be sensed by an audience before Banquo left, but then were highly intensified: he looked half distraught, his movements hushed, stealthy. (At one time the witches appeared behind; but they attracted too much attention from him, and he eliminated them.) Buried in his avalanche of thoughts, he stood and gazed at the floor; then, like Garrick, looked up suddenly, to see the dagger. He tried to blink it away; tried to rub it out of his eyes. Could not clutch it. Then a horror set in, intensified by a warrior's anger at his inability to deal with the intangible by either muscle or mind.

Sharifov, wandering uneasily in his castle, reacted to the vision with a horrible cry. Kean saw the dagger

> with a delirious and fascinated gaze; it grew more and more distinct to his disordered fancy (Hawkins).

The fearful terror that has often been a dominating note in Macbeth's reaction has troubled some observers. One argued against a "delirium of horror" like Irving's, on the ground that if the dagger were so fearful, Macbeth would not have tried to hold or follow it. George Vandenhoff, criticized for not being violent enough, also objected to a conventional stage image of Macbeth so overcome as to "tremble violently, loll out his tongue, and make his knees knock together, . . . old stage tricks." Vandenhoff saw Macbeth merely startled at first, so little thrown off his self-possession that he carefully examines the vision, turns it over in his mind, comes logically to the conclusion that *there's no such thing*, but a product of his overwrought brain and guilty conscience.

The sight of the dagger is certainly no more a terror than a lure to the Macbeths sunk in exhaustion or apathy. So Sothern, looking up listlessly from the bench where he had fallen back, followed with his eye a vision that drew him to his feet, and led him forward. Recognizing it, he staggered back again, but not to fall; he reached toward it. Then he realized it was a fantasy, tried to blink it away, buried his face in his hands against it; but he stood to it. Booth was drawn to his feet, to confront the image, over the resistance of both terror and agony at what the hallucination implied. Juriev, leaning back against a wall, began to look fixedly at an unseen point until he seemed frozen; his eyes were bewildered, then horrified; the vision he stared at compelled him to stand, and pulled him forward.

Where the sense of awe was, as with Macready, uppermost in a Macbeth vibrating to any soliciting that seemed supernatural, the actor subdued his terror to a kind of reverent amazement. Macready had just dismissed, impatiently, his Seyton, and stood poised, "a man on the verge of fate"—when, before his wild, unsettled gaze the hallucination took shape. As he seemed to understand the dagger's message, he threw himself toward the illusion, with a sudden, convulsive grasp. Nothing. Then he spoke—at first in hushed tones. This is one soliloquy that is not exclusively externalized inwardness: Macbeth may also be understood as speaking aloud to his hallucination— the dagger, as Clemen has suggested, becomes a silent partner in a dialogue. Actors have often been careful to speak at first quietly, in muted tones, or hoarse whispers, so as not to be overheard; beyond this Macready seemed to veil his voice out of respect to the otherworldly. *Is this a dagger . . . ?* Now he came slowly toward it, as if not to alarm it into flight, almost coaxing, *Come, let me clutch thee.* Finding himself empty-handed, he averted his face, as if he might deny the image by not seeing it.

To an impressionable Macbeth like Reineke, to whom the illusion could seem an unquestionable reality, the clutch was made with the confidence of absolute conviction—and the shock of encountering illusion was correspondingly violent. Reineke stood stupefied, helpless, his outstretched arm slowly sinking, his voice oppressed: *I have thee not, and yet I see thee still* (48).

A strong Macbeth, perhaps bracing himself as Scofield did before moving purposefully toward Duncan's room, pauses in his stride at the dagger illusion, but does not flinch. If he is afraid, he is also interested in his own inner process, as he was in his first soliloquy: what is happening to me? Scofield looked steadily into a light made of intersecting beams—a cross, a dagger. He saw something in the light that stopped his forward movement. "This is the tension between the imagining, and the summoning up determination to do the murder," Hall, directing, said. "Partly you beguile the time again." In Scofield the energy straining to let loose was briefly contained by the mystery—willed?—of the dagger image. Scofield's seeing of the image made it almost tangible; his words for it seemed to come, in broken fragments, straight from his mind:

Is this a dagger—which I see—before—me?

His firm, single reach for the imagined weapon seemed in fact to grasp something: he had to look at his hand to see it empty. Then he turned inward, puzzling out his process:

> I have thee not, and yet I see thee still.

A less driven, less driving Macbeth, Forbes-Robertson, carrying a heavy burden of thought as he first looked toward Duncan's room, was less shocked than philosophically interested by his hallucination. Indecisive when he found himself alone, he drifted into the illusion slowly, musing in a melodious, meditative voice on the wonder of the image. But the implications, to a thoughtful Macbeth, are not easy to bear: the speech from Tearle reflected the deep agony of "a man quietly sickened by the blackness of his own thoughts."

Olivier seemed almost to expect some kind of projection of his mental fantasy, as his mind filled with the thought of the murder to come. Even while the servant was yet beside him, he saw the dagger image.

> He checks at it like a pointer. With a terrible effort he withdraws his gaze for a moment,

gives the servant Duncan's diamond, and dismisses him,

> then with a swift and horrid compulsion swings round again. (David)

But his reaction was muted, less shock than acknowledgment; he spoke at first with "broken quiet"—

> Far from recoiling . . . he greeted the air-drawn dagger with sad familiarity; it is a fixture in the crooked furniture of his brain. (Tynan)

J. B. Booth, speaking the whole soliloquy in whispers, suggested the emphasis of a Macbeth half-recognizing in the hallucination what he had expected to see, asking himself: "*Is* this a dagger . . . ?" Hackett, intent on suggesting the influence of the supernatural, on first seeing the dagger looked upward into the air, as if questioning invisible witches as to the reality of the vision. Phelps, to one observer, conveyed the specific sense that the image was not so much a creature of the brain as of the powers of hell.

Surprise, terror, expectation must give way, at last, to the insistent reasoning of Macbeth's mind. The more emotional the first reaction, the more difficult the straining toward equilibrium. As the hallucination is a projection of impulse and desire, only by some rational effort can Macbeth achieve a perspective on what is going on in his brain—as if, again, some part of him has asserted a disjunct, independent life.

He asks questions of the image:

> Art thou not fatal vision, sensible
> To feeling, as to sight? or art thou but
> A dagger of the mind, a false creation,
> Proceeding from the heat-oppressed brain? (49–52)

He echoes here the kind of question Banquo asked about the Sisters. Can such things be? Has he eaten on an insane root? Here Macbeths have tried again to touch the illusion, tried to blink it away, or rub it from their eyes; or they have turned away as if to banish it; have held their hands to their foreheads to cool or quiet their fevered brains.*

Now Macbeth bares his own knife, his first unmistakable step toward murder:

> I see thee yet, in form as palpable,
> As this which now I draw. (53–54)

He might be obeying an unspoken command: his dagger† comes from its sheath, normally with the automatic gesture of the trained warrior-killer—though Reinhardt's Macbeth drew a long blade from its hiding place in his cloak, very slowly, voluptuously. Heston's hand went to his dagger for *In form as palpable as this;* then, Stephen Booth noted, the actor paused, and effectively started a new thought, full of intention: *which now I draw*—as if only now impelled to arm himself to kill.

For a moment Macbeth acknowledges command:

> Thou marshall'st me the way that I was going,
> And such an instrument I was to use. (55–56)**

Marshall suggests a military compulsion to action, and Macbeth obeying it, as if abdicating his own will, may move forward. Irving gave a start, then stilled, turned away trying to blank out the image. Matkowsky, whose neurotic Macbeth was jerked back and forth toward and away from Duncan's chamber as his impulses flared and failed, shouted his words as he drew his weapon and rushed ahead, as if he would never stop. But the energy faded as the words faded; he stopped again, the inward struggle paralyzing him. Macklin dropped his dagger here, not to pick it up until *There's no such thing*. Tree slipped, as if some force was drawing him, against his resistance, toward Duncan's room; he recoiled, flung his arms up over his face. Hackett, again looking upward, acknowledged the Sisters as the force he felt to be manipulating the vision—and him. Garrick and Irving emphasized the verb "I *was* to use—"; Garrick meant what *had* been planned, implying that, honorable as he was, he still was withdrawing from final commitment, perhaps in response to the oppressive hallucination. Macbeth's next two lines bring to momentary climax the seesaw of his response:

*Ludlow's nineteenth-century promptbook suggests a practical business for this scene: "Covers his face for 2 or 3 seconds . . . then uncovering . . . take care to ruffle your hair up so as to look wild."

†Almost certainly the murder weapon. Kemble was scolded for drawing a *sword* half out of its scabbard. From the first the image of a knife has been associated with Duncan's death.

**Macbeth's more elegant "dress" dagger will probably differ from the grooms' knives used for the murder. The flashing image is what Shakespeare wants here: jewels may adorn the handle above the shining blade.

> Mine eyes are made the fools o'th'other senses,
> Or else worth all the rest. (57–58)

His other senses tell him he is imagining; but if his eyes are right, if their disjunct perception sees the true reality, why then . . . ? This is a tremendous thought, that Macbeth's "eyes" provide him with clairvoyant insight beyond normal perception. Macbeth may again test, by blinking, turning away, reaching out; or the dagger may seem for a moment to vanish, and when he looks again, *further* toward Duncan's room, it may reappear. Irving made still another attempt to clutch it. Kean watched the dagger into the king's chamber, then saw it come out, his face telling the audience better than words of the image's disappearance, and the intensified shock at something horrible in its new appearance:

> I see thee still;
> And on thy blade, and dudgeon, gouts* of blood,
> Which was not so before. There's no such thing:
> It is the bloody business, which informs
> Thus to mine eyes. (58–62)

Step by step, reversing, recovering, Macbeth is approaching the moment when he must act, or withdraw from the *business*. Now the ultimate challenge, the bloody image, both invites and repels him: this is the face of murder itself. Kean saw it

> at length, palpable and distinct, imbrued with blood, slowly guiding his halting footsteps to the door of Duncan's chamber. Bewildered, terrified, brainsick, he shrank from a belief in its reality, yet returned to it with a struggling conviction until it obtained full possession of him (Hawkins).

The persistence of the dagger drove Forrest's Macbeth

> insane, and as he sees the blade . . . covered with gouts of blood he shrieks in a frenzy of horror.** Passing this crisis, he re-seizes possession of his mind, and with an air of profound relief, sighs "There's no such thing" (Alger).

Kean, who seemed to sense the dagger as a kind of film before his eyes that was finally brushed away, returned to an exhausted tranquillity, and spoke *no such thing* very simply. Casson waved the image away in "a flash of brave defiance," as he would wave at Banquo's ghost. Relief can free the awed Macbeth now: so Tree, who saw the recurring manifestation of the dagger in his courtyard fire, and started to snatch at it, could suddenly draw his

---

*"Gouts" may be a technical term from falconry, referring to small knobs that form on the legs and feet of hawks. If this is Macbeth's allusion, the blood must be imagined to have coagulated into dried blisters. Otherwise he sees the fresh blood dripping.

**The problem of a loud tone here is complex. Realistically, an outcry might wake the castle; and in some moments in this scene and the next, Macbeth and Lady Macbeth will deliberately lower their voices, sometimes after involuntary cries, and listen to make certain they have not been heard. But sometimes, as in this soliloquy, the action seems essentially inward, and a loud cry may imply a greater inner anguish, voiced within Macbeth's psyche. A delicate convention, dependent on the actor's art, governs the effect.

hand back and laugh. Booth turned away from the image as if to flee, then looked back to find it gone; and the fierce power returned to him. Macbeths who lived the experience inwardly returned to the world of now; thus Salvini seemed to wake from his dream; he rubbed his eyes, and made a gesture of casting the illusion away. Hackett held the "dagger" in his hand as if it were real, even tried to wipe the gouts of blood off it; then he denied its existence by throwing the imaginary thing to the ground.

A more resolute Macbeth may be more relieved than shaken by the comprehension that he has seen the invisible, that he must be either hallucinating or clairvoyant. Even the determined Olivier broke into a shrillness at *Mine eyes are made the fools* and *There's no such thing*. Williamson, clinging to reality, fought against hallucination to the end, angrily banging his hand on the table, and shutting his eyes to pretend he did not see it, to make it go away. Scofield's Macbeth stood like granite, showing by the barest of tremors how much he was increasingly disturbed by the experience, and willed the vision gone.

Macbeth's mounting excitement has pointed to some crucial action, some resolution of his anxiety. Anything less than a sense of crisis here has failed the theatre Macbeth: so Bell scolded Kemble when, at *no such thing*, he

> hides his eyes with his hands, then fearfully looks up, and peeping first over then under his hand, looks more abroad, and then recovers—very poor— the recovery should be an effort of the mind . . . not the absence of a . . . corporeal dagger, but the returning tone of a disordered fancy.

Whether Macbeth is purged of fear, or relieved of oppression, or wrenches himself free from his hallucination, he escapes from a deeply interior landscape suddenly to become aware of the strange "real" world about him. To some it brings no comfort. Garrick and Kemble, honorable murderers, still were not resolute, needed a signal to prompt them. Garrick would remain till almost the end in the half-hypnotic state the dagger imposed; Kemble, too—made superstitious by his experience, oppressed by "the time, the witching hour, the decaying sounds of the palace, the feel of loneliness, and the deep enormity of the act for which he is armed" (*Times*). A fate-driven Macbeth, like Macready, was by now visibly degraded by the task imposed on him; he found himself trapped in a world in which his crime belonged, and he whispered his sense of it. Salvini, awakened from his dream of the dagger, looked up at the sky, and seemed almost to grieve at the night's atmosphere of death. Irving, more reconciled, stared about him as if returning to reality, sighed deeply, looked up again at Duncan's door, awaiting him in the night, and sighed again. Irving then indulged in what he regarded as one of Macbeth's perverse delights, revelling in "fervid and poetic imagery"—

> Now o'er the one half world
> Nature seems dead, and wicked dreams abuse
> The curtain'd sleep. (62–64)

Pictures of death, of masking, of troubled sleep, echo in the language. Macbeth's experience of wicked dreams reminds us that he still knows what wickedness is, and links him once more to kinship with Banquo. Are we to sense
him thinking of Sister-created dreams, and their urgencies? Does *abuse* include, in its implication, a succubus note—linking of the erotic with the
dangerous? Macbeth himself now half dreams; raptness is near; though most
of Macbeth's words are still monosyllables, the rhythm subtly changes,
lengthens, the phrases take on an almost ritual cadence; then the words
themselves stretch out, as Macbeth seems fully to enter into his new mood:

> Witchcraft* celebrates
> Pale Hecate's offrings: and wither'd murder,
> Alarum'd by his sentinel, the wolf,
> Whose howl's his Watch . . . (64–67)

Macbeth's perception of the outside world has some of the same uncanny
quality as his introspection: he is in touch with a personified universe, the
poet in him acutely senses the tremors of the intangible, he feels bonded so
osmotically to Nature that he endows her with his own darkling moods.
Whispers, or half-whispers, suit his secretive union with the shadowy unseen,
and often Macbeth so voices the lines.

He names Hecate. Shakespeare may be preparing for her later appearance;
perhaps alludes here to the old usage of leaving propitiations of food at cross-
roads for this witches' goddess, *pale* because of the world of moon and shadows, bloodless, needing no blood. Macbeth's language, in rhythm and word,
is a kind of witchcraft itself; he is charging himself with speech-magic, Stein
suggests, in an archaic ceremony.

Bloodlessness fuses in the image of *wither'd murder*, lean, attenuated, even
anti-life; the root verb, "to wither," carried connotations of hostility and
fierceness (OED). Murder is called to arms by his sentinel, the wolf, whose
howling serves as murder's watch—and among the night noises sounded in
the theatre, as background to Macbeth's speech, or as interjections between
the silences, or mingled with shrieks of owls and drums of storm, has been
the ululation of the wolf, urging Macbeth forward. For the moment, Macbeth
is murder, a depersonalized, destructive force from which the self is detached:

> thus with his stealthy pace,
> With Tarquin's ravishing sides, towards his design
> Moves like a ghost. (67–69)

How the violent Tarquin vision haunted Shakespeare's imagination was
long ago observed. Again, now, images of sexuality and death are linked in
an intended physical assault.

Thus with his stealthy pace suggests how Macbeth may see himself starting
forward. *Strides* (the usual amendment of *sides*) suggests a purposeful advance,

---

*Regularizers have sometimes dampened Macbeth's spring into the line by prefixing a "now,"
to smooth a rhythm that was meant to be unsmooth.

but *slides* more nearly supports *stealthy*, indeed in this context has a stealthy sound (and, as Liddell points out, requires less variation from the corrected form). In Shakespeare's poem, Tarquin's pace varied with the poet's mood: moving toward Lucrece's bed, he *steals*, then *marcheth*, then is a *creeping thief*, finally *Into the chamber wickedly stalks*. Curiously, all these various modes, we will see, have been adopted by various Macbeths advancing on Duncan. The additional image, *moves like a ghost*, suggests Macbeth's oneness with the mood of night's half-world. Something more sinuous than the "martial stalk" of old Hamlet's ghost is intended here. Guinness "slithered forward at great and sinister speed on the word 'stealthy,' high-stepping from wall to wall in a prancing, gliding movement" (*Spectator*). Hunt saw Young "rising slowly and shrinkingly as if preparing to glide without precisely acting the description, which would have been unseasonable and unnatural." Hackett moved with a manic excitement, a touch of the "ecstasy of insanity." Other Macbeths, lost in identification with the night, may only experience the image in a continuous semi-trance, like Garrick or Booth, unmoving; or drag along, like Olivier, in a nightmare raptness.

The first lines after Macbeth's colloquy with the dagger seemed entirely interior; now he reopens communication with the intimate external, his words again mainly monosyllabic, more direct:

> Thou sure* and firm-set earth
> Hear not my steps, which way they walk, for fear
> Thy very stones prate of my where-about,
> And take the present horror from the time,
> Which now suits with it. (69–73)

The lines convey almost impressionistically the climate of mystery enwrapping Macbeth. Stones and earth are entreated personally not to betray the direction of his advance, as if they are alive to him. Hackett's cue was to stumble as he advanced, and then kneel, speaking the lines as a prayer to earth. One Macbeth reached intimately to touch and propitiate his ground. Rogers knelt at the foot of Duncan's stairway. *Sure and firm set* as this earth may seem to be, yet Macbeth may suspect it—for he will remember, later, that *stones have been known to move, and trees to speak* (III, iv, 153), and this apprehension may color his apostrophe now.

In the next clause, *take the present horror from the time* . . . Macbeth may be whispering earth to sustain a dreadful silence: he "relishes his own sense of horror, and to disturb this would be to shatter his irresolution" (Foakes). (This assumes no background sounds—of storms, animals, humans—already disturbing the noiseless night.) However, the verb *take* may, as Knights suggested, be imperative, and, in Johnson's words, aim to "deprive the time"

---

*Sure is the accepted emendation: but the Folio's *sowr* (sour) also carried meanings of *austere* and *sullen*—the latter an adjective Shakespeare twice used with *earth*. In the next line, I accept Rowe's change of the Folio's *which they may walk*.

of the pervading horror—which threatens, in a troubled Macbeth, to inhibit the will. The first implication would sustain the character's determination to encompass a *deed of dreadful note;* the second would allow the actor to initiate a new emotional charge—"Take this enervating horror away!" The latter seems to give more energy to the phrase, which otherwise is rather separated from the preceding line, may lose instead of gain the momentum the conclusion requires.

Either interpretation must bring to climax Macbeth's conspiracy with the night world, as he awaits the signal to kill. Macbeth's dialogue with earth reflects mental state as well as metaphor. Quiller-Couch suggested that Shakespeare made Macbeth commit his crime under the influence of an hallucination—a circumstance that can partly soften the guilt of the murder; and, as we saw, actors have sometimes sustained a strange, dreamlike mood following Macbeth's dagger-vision, from which they only slowly emerge, or do so only at the last minute before invading Duncan's room. Some Macbeths have seemed wrestling with a spell as they approached the fateful act; some so anguished that they had to escape from their minds, or their selves, to admit the compulsion to kill. Olivier's voice sank to a drugged whisper, David reported; he

> moved, as in a dream, toward Duncan's room, but with his face turned away from it . . . and it was already trodden stones behind him that Macbeth, with deprecating hand, implored to silence.

To one observer he conveyed the sense that the world he communed with was the reflection of his own nightmare vision. Booth, who had stood fixed in fantasy, suddenly started forward, activated by a kind of demoniac obsession. The erratic Matkowsky, who had nerved himself toward Duncan's room in jerks, at his first direct advance (*hear not my steps*) lost all resolution again, fell to the ground, groaning; he could only slowly rise from the earth, and even when on his feet he drew back, standing in a wordless struggle with himself. Mitterwurzer was almost as faint; he was fevered, broke into a sweat, repeatedly put his hand to his head. The madness that has been seen to lie at the edge of Macbeth's anguish overwhelmed Smochowski, he became "someone entirely different than before," spoke of himself as of someone else (Got).

The transformation of a man into a different kind of man, a murderer, was stipulated by Macready, in his submission to supernatural direction. Visibly losing his battle with scruple as he lost his first martial dignity, he turned to stealth in body and character as he crept toward Duncan's door.

Other Macbeths actively resisted trances or dissolution by deliberately maintaining a sense of consciousness in action. Rogers, playing against reflectiveness, used the lines as expressing a kind of tactical plan. Reinhardt's Macbeth, wrenching himself from his neurotic indecision, moved quietly but decisively toward Duncan's door, hiding his dagger behind him; listened to make certain of the enveloping silence; then led himself with the words toward the murder chamber.

However Macbeth arrives at this moment, he recognizes it as pivotal. As he listens for his cue, a reluctant murderer, like Garrick, might still be fixed, trancelike, recognizing inability to act; a more positive Macbeth, like Scofield, suddenly angry over his delaying, restless, straining, by the grimness of his determination seems to demand the signal that will summon him to murder. The unrest of inaction, the apprehension that resolution may be chilled by empty talk—*boasting like a fool*—the impatience to act reciprocating in a dialectic with any remaining scruples, affect Macbeth's tone and rhythm, changing it to short, sharp, mainly monosyllabic bursts (McKellen's first line was a series of harsh, angry spondees):

> Whiles I threat, he lives:
> Words to the heat of deeds too cold breath gives. (73–74)

Then, as he waits—a long wait, with Irving—between impatience and indecision, the cue comes. *A bell rings.* Probably twice. This is almost certainly the bell rung by Lady Macbeth as Macbeth had arranged; sounding it ties her, unseen, to the murder. Boaden objected to "the tinkle of a table-bell" here, preferred the "awful and alarming" voice of a clock-tower's "deep-toned summoner"; and Kemble had a clock strike. But Macbeth's cue need not be thought to come conveniently at two o'clock, nor need Lady Macbeth's later sleepwalking reference to *one: two: why then 'tis time to do't* (V, i, 36–37) imply any other memory than that of her own striking upon the bell to give Macbeth the cue he wanted. Presumably she has waited until satisfied that the grooms are deep *in swinish sleep.* The bell she *strikes upon* need not be Bradley's "little bell": deep, urgent reverberations may sound in its muffled tones. When the sound is anticipated, as in Tree's staging—where a few moments before Lady Macbeth was seen crossing the balcony, returning from Duncan's chamber to her own—the audience is partly prepared for it; but it can still come as a shock, both to the ears and to the imagination of an audience keyed to Macbeth's own high pitch. The bell warns us and Macbeth of the symbolic ripeness the signal reports: his *drink is ready.* Hot blood. He must move. Sothern nodded his head to the sound. Even Garrick was finally roused here.

Where does Macbeth go? He will tell Lady Macbeth, in a few moments, that he heard voices as he *descended* from Duncan's room. Subsequently he will take Macduff directly to Duncan's chamber door. If this makes any sense, it means that he leads Macduff up to a gallery level, to a door the audience can see. Hodges, as we saw in I, iv, accepts evidence of visible exterior stairways in cases of stipulated movement up or down. So does W. J. Lawrence. I think a theatre professional would take stairs for granted where appropriate for Shakespeare's upper level, if for nothing else than that they contribute to the dramatic arousal. Movement upward toward transcendence, or downward in retreat, can strongly organize the eye and mind. Richard II's descent to the "base court" would lose the fierce momentum built in the scene if he had to disappear from his "above," make his unseen way down through the tiring room, and then appear; the living imagery of descent would be wasted. The continuity of the speech requires a visual accompaniment. Shakespeare did not need to stipulate "stairs" for a theatrical imagination to understand their dramatic necessity; the stairway structure—which might very well, in the Globe, be temporary for a particular play—is implicit. The physical and symbolic tensions involved in Macbeth's climbing the steps to Duncan's chamber, his later descent, his retracing of the ascent with Macduff, Macduff's horrible announcement from on high, and much later, Lady Macbeth's sleepwandering down these same stairs, have been exploited as a matter of course in suitable theatres—after the eighteenth- and much of nineteenth-century staging, where no upper level was commonly used, so Macbeth had to walk horizontally to his crime.

The Japanese Macbeth, Akutagawa, found himself psychically hampered when an upper level was *not* used; he told Peter Milward, "I wanted to speak the words going up the stairs, in my approach to the king, so my physical action would correspond to my psychological feeling." Only once, when the production was on tour, was he able to say the soliloquy going up steps— "to my great satisfaction."

In some modern stagings emphasis on soaring, higher levels has unfortunately been dangerously exaggerated by designers of what Agate called the "window-cleaning school"—"Macbeth going to murder Duncan, and Lady Macbeth cleaning up, move to their design along a sill so precarious that only a Duncan understood to be good at rock-climbing could have preceded them there." A German reviewer similarly criticized a design that seemed all ravines, across which Macbeth and his Lady had to teeter. When Bergman's Macbeths ran up and down his 1948 set, it shook so that the audience was said to be more concerned for the safety of the actors than the characters. Such designs obviously play against the sense of the great Inverness described by Banquo and Duncan in I, vi.

> I go, and it is done:

Macbeth declares, hoping it will be *done* when done, for himself even if not for *Dun*can:

> the Bell invites me.
> Hear it not, Duncan, for it is a knell,
> That summons thee to heaven, or to hell. (76–78)

The comma after *knell* sets the word apart—it is a sentence of death, as Macbeth moves toward murder. Even at this moment, the drag of his inner reluctance may show: Kean's advance seemed "marked with a conscience-stricken horror of the deed to come." Tree stood trembling before Duncan's great door, before he could force himself to enter. Salvini, crossing the threshold of the king's chamber, shuddered and started back; he had to gather himself to move in again. As Forrest was stealing to the room, a sudden peal of thunder abruptly checked him: he started back, gasped, recovered, and moved forward (storm and animal noises have similarly punctuated the movements of other Macbeths). Rossi, fumbling the curtain to Duncan's chamber, conveyed a sense of horror in the simple physical act; he faltered on the threshold. Booth started at the bell's command, seemed to conjure up visions of a hell to which he was going, and stood paralyzed in thought before he broke free. Aldridge crept toward Duncan's room, but stopped repeatedly, hesitating even at the entrance—a decent man preparing to be a villain. Macready had already changed: the decay of his uprightness sent him almost slinking into the murder chamber. To some observers he seemed too craven now, self-abased, less warrior after a crown than common criminal: "He stood aghast as if dreading arrest" (*Spectator*); but the ocular proof of his degradation was applauded by others for its manifestation of character development—and for the "moral" it pointed. The hesitation that marked Macready's noiseless entry—a "ghastly and impalpable tread"—into Duncan's room was perhaps most evident after most of him had entered: one trembling leg remained behind in sight for what seemed a full half-minute.*

Irving, who played against the image of noble heroism, now seemed laboring under a double fearfulness. His Macbeth was keenly sensitive to the physical danger of an attempt to murder the king—one symptom, noted by Percy Simpson (cited by Dover Wilson):

> As Irving pushed open the door at the bottom of the stair, a draft blew it back and the hinges creaked; he started as if someone were coming down to defend Duncan.

But Irving seemed even more oppressed by his inward apprehension: he gave the impression of being appalled by the direction toward which the dagger led him. As he tiptoed toward the stairway to Duncan's gallery chamber (*hear not my steps*)—one observer thought he staggered, another that his feet seemed to be feeling for purchase, as if he was advancing a step at a time on a reeling deck. He crept up the stairs softly, and silently, breathlessly pulled at the curtain shielding the king. A light from within shone fully on his face before he disappeared inside.*

---

*Macready's friend, Dickens, lampooned this business, Gordon Crosse suggests, in describing a waiter's leg in *Edwin Drood* as "always lingering after he and the tray had disappeared, like Macbeth's leg when accompanying him off the stage with reluctance to the assassination of Duncan."

*Craig's production had a violently lighted door for Macbeth to enter.

Matkowsky had to force himself to respond to the bell signal, and even so he wavered, switching direction as he approached the stairs; and, as noted, he could only mount them by pulling himself up on the banisters, hand over hand. Tree, at *the bell invites me*, seemed to see the dagger in the air again, was drawn by it up the stairway to Duncan's door; but he paused, listening, gathering resolution, before he entered. Such Macbeths, indeed, went to commit murder, in Bradley's words, as a kind of "appalling duty."

The bell finally shook Garrick from his near-trance and set him moving: he obeyed his terrible wife. Reinhardt's Macbeth, having subdued his nerves enough to begin his advance, was momentarily checked by the bell's ring; the hand that held his dagger wiped the sweat from his forehead (and caught a glint of light, as bared blades often did in other productions); he controlled himself again, and could speak calmly his last rites for Duncan. He paused, hid the dagger in his cloak, moved silently like a beast of prey up the staircase, sometimes pausing to listen, and at last disappeared into the darkness. Reineke, similarly transformed from agitated indecision to compulsive action, rushed into Duncan's chamber. To Scofield, straining to move, but constrained to await his Lady's signal, the bell came as a release. Thought dropped from him. He held his hand out, palm up, pointing to Duncan's room as if responding to a self-invitation as well as the bell's; then he strode deliberately on, a man possessed with resolve. Olivier, too, went firmly ahead, under his own spell. To Rogers, the bell was only an incident in his insistent march to the killing. Russell Thorndike, Muriel St. Clare Byrne recalled, made a flying leap to catch the edge of Duncan's balcony, and hauled himself up to it, to invade the king's curtained chamber. Wolfit, murderously intent as he climbed the stairs, evoked tension by emphasizing his warrior's alertness to the sheer physical-political danger of an assassination attempt, encouraging audiences to anticipate the possibility of another interruption like Banquo's. A "feline ascent," Edith Sitwell called Wolfit's, remembering "that leonine grandeur and terror, the doom implicit in every movement."

Not accidentally has Macbeth's wary, soundless ascent to regicide suggested animal stealth. The predator's secret stalking of its prey is part of the common experience. The manchild learns early in play to imitate that silent, sinister assault; the adult leaves off, but the way of it endures in his tissue. So identification with Macbeth's movement comes easily. Any threatened mis-step, any stumbling betrayal of his furtive presence, is shared—as is, also, any precaution to avoid them. If Macbeth's armor makes noise, he softly unbuckles it, lays it down; if a robe or other garment impedes his stealthy motion, or his planned violence, he adjusts it, or sheds it. (This kind of action ties the scene to the next one: the discarded appurtenances must be found, perhaps at the last minute, by Lady Macbeth, and carried off with Macbeth.) At any step Macbeth takes, his ear—so sensitive to sounds made and imagined—may check him; he may start at shadows; turn fiercely on nothing. As long as these gestures emanate from the identity Macbeth has established, are not superficially "theatrical," they serve Shakespeare's design: the outlaw predator, so highly wrought he can hardly contain himself, dare not be discovered. Disappearing into Duncan's room, he hides as well as advances.

The scene is not over. It ends in a pause—of terrible silence, or terrible sound, or both in sequence, sometimes with visual accompaniments. Even, in one nineteenth-century production described in Becks' promptbook:

> distant thunder to give witches time to get down and lower gauze in front of flats—then change scene—slow music, agitato and soft—witches discovered waving Macbeth on . . . then change scene again and discover witches and king and two sleepers. Picture. As Macbeth stabs the king, witches vanish: scene changes to the original dagger scene.

The visible murder of Duncan violates Shakespeare's design of masking, hence minimizing, Macbeth's physical violences until much later; thus the bloody murder visualized in the Polanski film inflicted an experience which inevitably shattered the mediated image of Macbeth that the playwright intended. Even the sound of killing threatens this image. Tree, for all that he sheltered Macbeth in poetic garments, crossed his design in his act of murder. After reluctantly mounting to Duncan's great door, and crouching, lips trembling, on the threshold, he nerved himself to enter, shut the massive portal behind him, and a moment later, a "muffled, gurgling groan" was heard. This kind of signal insists on a response to the murder from Duncan's experience of it, not from the horrified Macbeth's, as Shakespeare designed. We are not yet to know, in fact, that the murder was committed; the *naive* spectator will be uncertain, along with Lady Macbeth in the next scene—until after Macbeth appears, literally red-handed.

The witches, too, have been made to intervene between us and Shakespeare's design by their appearances or offstage sounds (laughing, cackling, etc.) that insist on a fatefulness the playwright left ambiguous. Thus, when Forrest, for a while, used them, they seemed to be floating

> above the fretted embattlements . . . slowly and stealthily rising . . . come to preside over the atrocious crime which they had stimulated their victim to commit.

Such intervention immediately mutes essential strains in *Macbeth*'s polyphony.

If rising thunder has not earlier prefaced the fearful tempest Lenox will describe, it may begin now by accenting Macbeth's entrance to Duncan, as with Forrest—or Charles Kean, whose directions stipulated one clap the moment he put his foot in the doorway, then, as he hesitated and finished his last line, another that accompanied him into the room. Phelps' storm, that began before Macbeth disappeared, now raged: his ambitious, rather endearing stage direction reads, "Rain and thunder as loud as possible." Lightning has flashed, wind risen to howling. The doubtful Forman reported, of the *Macbeth* he says he saw, "many prodigies seen that night and the day before;" but he may have seen these in Holinshed and not at the Globe, if indeed he was there.

The Globe, so skilled at sound and pyrotechnic effects, must have been tempted, as later theatres would be, to create a storm matching Lenox' description; but some lulls would then become necessary for the stillness which seems to shroud the next meeting between Macbeth and his Lady, and to allow for the full effect of Macduff's knocking. The storm may be made, as in a Russian *Macbeth* (1947) of music: the pealing of thunder and the howling of wind sometimes changed into gloomy wailing and soughs, sometimes interrupted by piercing cries, smothered laughter, sighs, the shrieking of an owl—"the musical accompaniments gave the impression of a hell shuddering in horror before such monstrous crime."

For a moment the stage remains empty, and attention focuses on the place where Macbeth disappeared. Shakespeare, again, clearly intended Duncan's door to be visible, since Macbeth will lead Macduff there, so that the whole audience can be fixed upon it. Tree closed the door behind him as he entered; but promptbooks sometimes specify that the door remains open. A streaming light behind the door is sometimes specified; alternatively, Macbeth disappears into a cavelike darkness, as with Reinhardt and Savits. For the moment nothing stirs, except, intensively, the audience's imagination.

Do we want Macbeth to murder? As well as fear he will? We have been led to an ultimate human act. As we wait in expectation, in dread, at what level are we, too, involved in the deed without a name?

This is a sorry sight.

Act II, Scene ii

Lady Macbeth appears, sometimes ushered by a clap of thunder, sometimes by a great storm complete with lightning and rain. Sometimes in silence, in a storm's lull—then her ear is startled with abrupt bird cries and other mutterings of the night.* Charles Kean faded the tempest as the Lady entered, Macready when she reached centre stage. Piscator, fond of his witches, moved them into the background of her entrance; Carrick Craig's symbolic drums followed her to her sudden *Hark*, when they as suddenly stopped.

She ordinarily makes a sudden appearance after Macbeth has gone; though Heesters moved in quietly on the stage level, before the end of Macbeth's last soliloquy, and watched him go up the stairs; she then followed him a step or two, looking upward, listening intently. Sometimes the Lady will herself enter from atop the stairs, as Marlowe and Terry did, and slowly make her way down; she may be carrying a candle—as she will hereafter, when she rehearses this night in her dreams. Cushman emphasized the night's darkness by groping her way into the courtyard—another movement that would be repeated. Lady Macbeth may also enter from below, start slowly up the stairs, as if involving herself with the hidden action—we are not to know that she will not follow Macbeth. But she stops: Reinhardt's Lady, after a few steps, heard a sound, suddenly lay down, and pressed her ear against one of the steps; then, still flat on her belly, slid down again, withdrawing.

Lady Macbeth has had drink, to make her bold. Her characteristic liquid image sometimes is made visual in the goblet she carries—Calhoun portrayed her as mainly drunk with imagination, but meant the goblet to suggest that her mental exaltation was roused by a "wee drappie of the craytur." A "modern dress" Lady came on to down a stiff shot of whisky. The apparent need

---

*Lenox will say, next morning, that the *obscure bird clamored* throughout the loud, stormy night; the Porter will say the castle caroused until the second cock (3.00a.m.). Stagings sometimes punctuate with apt sounds the action of this scene; Shakespeare seems mainly to depend on the suspense of silence.

for "artificial courage" seemed to Mrs. Griffiths some amelioration of Lady Macbeth's wickedness:

> It required two vices in her, one to intend and another to perpetrate the crime.

Cushman, remember, thought the Lady must have been quite drunk to conspire in the murder. In performance the actress did not emphasize this, but a Czech Lady was obviously intoxicated, and others have suggested tipsiness* or hyper-elation—in Dench, a compound of expectation, anxiety, and dread that half-danced her in, laughing feverishly, to await the murder.

That she has had to—or that she troubled to—make herself *bold* with drink may indicate a need that Lady Macbeth can momentarily indulge, perhaps contributing to the sense of exaltation Martita Hunt felt. This is one of the Lady's rare moments of self-communing; briefly now it lets her relive the ambitious excitement of the I, v soliloquy, with its invocation of a different kind of spirit to her aid; never that again. Even now, however flushed with excitement she is, however envisioning the golden round within her grasp, some dark undercurrent flows beneath her confident surface; the troubled Ladies are shaken by it.

She has been in the king's chamber. She has had to pick her way past the drunken grooms to the king's bed, perhaps to raise her dagger to strike. She would have done it, too—except for something she saw in his face. The drink has given her *fire*, but not enough. Here the sage Porter may again be prophetic before the fact about drink that *provokes, and unprovokes: it provokes the desire, but it takes away the performance.* Lady Macbeth left the king alive. She was a coward, Coriat suggested, hence her drinking. Strindberg saw the revelation of a blusterer, lacking the terrible qualities she had dressed herself in. The shock to Lady Macbeth of her failed will—she who had offered to murder her infant rather than back down from a sworn commitment—she carries as a subtextual wound now. She will not admit her retreat yet; but it must color her nervousness at every sound, her apprehension of what may or may not be happening, her sometimes strange elation.

The Lady's primary response may be resentment of herself for her failure—as Byam Shaw suggested when he directed Vivien Leigh. Leigh would not show herself much moved. Ladies of less steel have come away from their glimpse of the old man they would murder with more manifest anxieties; for some this moment would signal the first breaking point.

The strong Siddons entered without compunctious visitings of nature, her interpretation suggests:

> The daring fiend whose pernicious potions have stupefied his attendants, and who even laid their daggers ready,—her own spirit, as it seems, exalted by

---

*Hackett suggested for his Lady "an overcharged, hysterical note, superinduced by alcohol . . . In this way, Lady Macbeth can get great variety, and bring out the fact of her womanliness, which shows in her fainting later in this act, and sleepwalking. The big note is her womanhood asserting itself, between the overstimulation and the subsequent collapse."

the power of wine . . . [enters] in eager expectation of the results of her diabolical diligence.

Bell saw, at her first line, a "ghastly horrid smile"—suitable to the "triumphant fiend," another observer remembered. No remnant of concern for
whether the deed should be done, only care that it be done safely. Yet to this
care the great actress brought layers of uneasiness: the *Edinburgh Courant*
sensed "dread and anxiety" in her look.

The owl cries, startles her. *Hark, peace:* . . . "Hsh! Hsh! Whisper" (Bell).
Lady Macbeth's *peace*—with "the high, doom-haunted tone of the owl's
shriek" (Sitwell)—is to reprove her momentary fear, Dover Wilson believed,
and that fits Siddons; but to calm herself, too, as said meaningfully by Ladies
more deeply anxious: and with them it has implications of a plea to a whole
tormented universe where night birds, like wolves, may signalize the approach of death. The steely Cushman started and shivered at the bird cry.
As tough a Lady as Merchant, startled by the sound, let her goblet fall; the
frightened Annis, after a long, held breath, could lean back against a wall
and laugh at her fears—a laugh touched with hysteria. Bernhardt, who
seemed to one disapproving critic as nervous as Macbeth, quivered long after.

The gentler Lady could armor herself to an unnatural task: so Terry. Her
notes:

> Quite savage for a moment—in the face of possible defeat . . . *much* quicker
> . . . breathe low and hard . . . excited by wine . . .

and, as if borrowing from Siddons, "with a horrid smile." Her intended projection of an enforced resolve carried to audiences

> a woman who has nerved herself . . . simply because she cannot otherwise
> keep firm her liege's purpose . . . success is trembling in the balance and vacil-
> lation now means ruin. If she wavers, he will utterly break down, and though
> her own courage fail her, yet he shall not see that it has done so. (E. R. Russell)

Observers carried away an indelible picture: her face white as a lily, "blanched
with terror," her heavy masses of blood-red—"red-hot"—hair, she supporting herself against a stone pillar, her face sometimes picked out with the
lightning. The *Dramatic Review* saw, in her "every gasping breath, every
despairing glance . . . nothing more terrible, as a picture of subdued passion and agonised anxiety controlled by an iron will." Now a "gleam of fiend-
ishness . . . in the heart-tortured woman" was glimpsed.

The Lady's silence holds the stage: as she strains to listen, her nerve-strung
apprehension of what may—or may not—be happening becomes the spectators' apprehension. Terry crouched against her pillar—an attitude of alarm,
of readiness to move in emergency also adopted by such differing Ladies as
Cushman and Thorndike. Craig, perhaps remembering his mother, recommended such a posture to his Lady:

> Don't be too *erect*—Bend—Listen, not with *straight* head, but with head well
> to one side.

Craig had an elaborate vision of lighting:

a slow but deliberate descending of shadow, . . . shadows . . . on the back-cloth . . . green blue or grey . . . no red or orange . . . [no] spotlights . . . lamps to rake the floor so that actors paddle up to the knees . . . in a bath of one colour, a darker one higher up.

But Lady Macbeth by herself creates the essential atmosphere, by the suspense of her almost painful concentration of listening. Any sense of a change in the accompanying background, any activity of her own, is a distraction unless it underlines her own apprehension. Her need to know exerts a physical force: so Reinhardt's Lady, stretching her neck toward the unheard; Margaret Rawlings (England, 1950), holding shaking hands out to the warmth of a hall fire to try to still her raveled nerves, her ear straining for any sound; Marlowe, daring to mount up toward Duncan's door, stopped and transfixed by the owl's cry, but resuming her ascent, listening, listening; Cushman, advancing to the very threshold of the murder chamber to try to overhear; Siddons tiptoeing forward, bending to the half-opened door itself, so closely that an offstage observer there could feel her breath. Phelps' Lady reached out to the door handle; hesitated, dared to push the door slightly open. These gestures all trumpet one question: Is Macbeth doing *it* (the nameless)?*

An absolute silence best allows the lady to catch the faint sound that momentarily assures her. She sees the open door (that promptbooks sometimes stipulate in II, i for this reason)—sometimes a dark cave, sometimes throwing a bright light to pick out her face. *He is about it*. She is busy reassuring herself: *It* must go well, she had made *it* easy by drugging the possets of the grooms she now hears snoring: *possets*—drinks based on warm milk and liquor, both so apt in her context. Drugged the grooms so powerfully that their very lives—like Duncan's—hang in equivocation:

> Death and Nature do contend about them,
> Whether they live, or die. (10–11)

Lady Macbeth imagines for us Macbeth in the act of doing the killing, perhaps hears a telltale sound, metallic, or muffled. Siddons "breathes with difficulty, hearkens toward the door." Her *He is about it*, a "Whisper horrible." But *it* is being done; Terry allowed herself the relief of the note, "breathes here." Marlowe, restless, started back down the stairs. Merchant waited confidently beside her spilled goblet, watching, listening. The young Mirren, still shielding herself from a sense of the horror underway, could remark with glee Macbeth's going *about it*.

Still, Shakespeare puts off the murder, lets the *naive* spectator wonder if it is really to be done. A dangerous sound alerts Lady Macbeth. She may hide, as Reinhardt's Lady did, fearing an intruder. Macbeth, alarmed, appears

---

*Elwin suggested that Lady Macbeth knew Macbeth was *about it* when she heard snores through the door.

suddenly—almost certainly above, where Lady Macbeth can not see him. He cannot forbear to cry, if softly, in alarm, *Who's there?* (13)* Does he see some image pass before his eyes? Has he heard imaginary voices? Or those he believes to be real that he reports later? Only for an agonized moment is he seen, and he disappears again.

Alack, (14)

Any assurance Lady Macbeth has felt is threatened. Her speech is jerky, abrupt with monosyllables, halted by three long pauses indicated by colons as the direction of her thought changes. She, and we in the audience, must doubt that the act was committed:

> I am afraid they have awak'd,
> And 'tis not done: (14–15)

Not *done*. The word, signal of finality, stops her. In the colon's hiatus, she thinks of the penalty of discovery: the failed attempt *confounds us*. Duncan's supporters will flood the hall, treachery will be punished, as with Cawdor . . . A *naive* spectator wonders if she will try to take charge again. In the long pause of the colon after *us* the Lady listens, listens—*hark:* —and long silent again, hears nothing. She reminds herself again that she did her part—she laid the daggers ready. Then a full stop, as the subtext that must have underlain her anxiety surfaces, in words that speak of much more than self-justification, though that, too:

> Had he not resembled
> My father as he slept, I had done't. (17–18)

Even the mighty Siddons seemed shaken here: "The finest agony. Tossing of the arms," Bell wrote. Then: "Agonized suspense, as if speechless with uncertainty whether discovered." A friend of Walpole's perceived

a degree of proud and filial tenderness . . . that was new, and of great effect.

Siddons herself acknowledged momentarily one "solitary particle of human feeling." Merchant was startled, frightened. This was a delicate pivot in her characterization. She would no longer smile readily; she would be bitter, sardonic, scornful, but the laugh would not easily come. Reinhardt's Lady came from her hiding place, her hands pressed against her lips, and spoke in deadly fear, her voice harassed, the phrases broken with long, tense pauses.

A compunctious visiting the Lady feared has come. "She fails in her fell purpose even *before* the murder," Flora Robson observed, seeing in the lines the "key to the character." Judith Anderson believed that the "father" resemblance was an excuse—"Lady Macbeth simply could not bring herself to do

---

*Quayle had Duncan utter the line; Booth, one of the grooms. Faucit, as Lady Macbeth, said it when playing in Manchester. The Folio is explicit in assigning it to Macbeth. He is sometimes only heard, not seen.

the stabbing." The words are wrenched from deep within; a reluctant, even wondering confessional, they evoke in the audience imagination the Lady's relived experience, intensified perhaps by an abortive dagger-gesture. The imagination's eye shares her bending over the old man, close enough to see his face, the knife in her hand. The preparatory subjunctive clause comes in ragged beats, slowly, recapitulating a graven memory: the iambic muffled, almost prose, haltingly dredging a memory that refuses burial: . . . *My father as he slept*. . . .

Terry's note for this speech-act: *realize*. Reinhardt's Lady began passionately, then slower and more slowly, anxiously. Reverberations of archetypal relationship vibrate in the evoked bedroom image, not only the explicit father-daughter, but also of the mother-child; Wolter, looking up to the old man's room, crossed her hands over her breasts.

This is another one of several moments in this scene where Lady Macbeth may manifest the first sign of breaking, or of crumbling. Most Ladies suggest at least an opening of the soul, the gentler ones as if showing more clearly the hidden face heretofore carefully repressed; the more powerful, like Siddons and Cushman, exploiting the sharp contrast of the momentary descent from power to pathos. The Lady has learned that she cannot kill—this is the essential fact: the father-resemblance may be only a rationalization, as Anderson suggested. Shocked as she may be, yet her resilient spirit and nervous force must sustain her; if "she begins too early to recognize her sin and to become nervous and excited," as Mrs. Benson was seen to do, she may move too far along the delicately articulated path to her despair in the sleepwalk. Certainly what Lady Macbeth does now, and later in this act, may be a foreshadowing of many incidents in the sleepwalk—as when she will remember how much blood the old man, who resembled her father, had in him; the *Times* saw in Sheila Allen an "agonizing premonition" of her final scene.

Those Ladies concentrating—as Terry was—on the wife-husband interaction, or—as Ristori—on manipulation, suppress the moment's trauma until later. With Ristori, for instance, the father-memory was determinedly rushed through—yet the actress conveyed the sense of a repressed impact that would be revived in the next scene when she heard Macbeth describe the bloodied Duncan. In her fainting, half-contrived as it would be, the force of the earlier blow would be understood.

For the Ladies who sought to minimize the Duncan experience, the final, abrupt phrase had less of remorse than regret, or blame—of herself or Macbeth—for the thing un*done:*

I had done't. (18)

Some modern editions complete the line with the next two words, *My Husband?* The Folio appropriately isolates the speech. Lady Macbeth, whatever her governing impulse, whether she mainly looks back or forward, has mounted to a moment of such inward stress and outward anxiety that it holds her, and the audience, poised in the "agony of suspense" stipulated in Terry's scribble to herself. A note of "should it be done" has faintly merged with the apprehensive "has he done it—and if not . . . ?" Shakespeare's mounting design makes the silence of waiting more painful, the uncertainty more intense. The climax of the beat must hold until the startling next one breaks in on it. There have been the reports, in performances with Irving, Tree, and Modjeska, of dying cries overhead; but more often Lady Macbeth is alerted by the soft sound of an approach.

Macbeth may be heard coming before he is seen. If it *is* Macbeth—the *naive* spectator does not know, and Lady Macbeth, waiting in the shadows, may not be sure: *My husband?* may be voiced as the question the Folio makes it. The Lady tracks with her listening ear the sound of steps; if unsure of who it is, she takes shelter in a shadow; if sure she may run halfway to meet him, as Reinhardt's Lady did.

The sounds of Macbeth's approach may begin with a softly reopening door—matched by the sudden shaft of light released; perhaps, then, the closing of the door (these movements may be glimpsed, as with Tree); then the footsteps of a figure sometimes foreshadowed by its shadow—footsteps sometimes with the whisper of stealth, sometimes with the rush of horror, sometimes, as with John Clements (England, 1966), with a heavy repeated clump of dragging feet, proclaiming a body drained of spirit.

The footsteps are one aural hint that Macbeth has at last confronted the act he so intensely feared, and rejected, and desired; now that the terrible *if* has been resolved, his body makes room for the inrush of new obsession, new unease. Revolted—or transported—by what he has done, Macbeth is made nearly hysterical by voices he may have heard along Duncan's corridor, unless they were in his own brain, or from some uncanny "other" world—he cannot now tell, as he will not be able to identify actual sounds that will, soon, again, disturb him. The overt signs of his condition—shock, elation, disorientation, raptness, near physical collapse—describe an abnormal state. Recall, again, that he will later say, in a traumatic moment, *now comes my fit again;* and such a *fit* may shake him now. Both Macbeth and Lady Macbeth, under the pressure of the oncoming events, will suffer the excess of passion approaching insanity that Mack has observed in the Jacobean tragic hero; even now the furies of madness may couch in the wings, avid, close.

Some glimmer of live fear of rousing the palace to retribution still cautions Macbeth, but even care for survival begins to yield to the compulsion to agonize over his act, to relive its irrepressible horror. Still, he may come all the way back to his Lady without letting her—or the *naive* spectator—know what he has done. She—we—must wait for the news. To serve Shakespeare's plot design, Macbeth's speaking, when it does come, will only slowly reveal all. For some moments Lady Macbeth is not to see the daggers he holds. In the dark courtyard they must be hidden from her—and for some time, perhaps, from us, too; or her attention must be distracted; or, like Dench, she will avert her face from the blood she senses on his hands.

Some Macbeths—Mantell, Sothern, Juriev—backed down the stairs, their eyes fixed on the room which they had left—an ironic echo of the ritual backward retreat from royalty. Or Macbeth's whole organism may be concentrated on the survival act of getting away from the murder scene, and Macbeth creeps away straining for any movement or sound that threatens: Tree, surprised by a shadow on the wall, started to strike it. Often Macbeths were so fixed on sights and noises perceived or imagined that, like Garrick, they were not aware of Lady Macbeth, waiting. This could inflict on the Macbeth (e.g., Forrest, Sothern, Booth) an additional shock: the Lady reaches out to touch him, as Juriev's did, alarming him; or he lurches into her, and instantly, reacting with the warrior's killer-reflex, he raises an arm or dagger against her,* an unknown in the dark, perhaps a witness to his deed, an enemy. She stops his wrist, or he jerks it back. However, if Macbeth's reflex now is primarily the guilty criminal's, his immediate gesture is not to attack but, as with Phelps, to hide under his plaid the daggers he carries.

If Macbeth's revulsion toward himself and his crime is violent enough to unhinge the restraints of caution and fear, his escape from Duncan's chamber is touched with panic. Garrick's flight was described by a Philadelphian who claimed to have seen the pattern in the great actor's late eighteenth-century imitators:

> Macbeth appeared, a frightful figure of horror, rushing out sideways with one dagger, and his face in consternation [looking backward] to the door, as if he were pursued, and the other dagger lifted up as if prepared for action. Thus he stood as if transfixed, seeming insensible to every thing but the chamber, unconscious of any presence else, and even to his wife's address of "my husband."

The murderer's alarm is signalized by physical and psychic disorganization, the latter more compelling. Garrick tried reappearing with such external signs as disarranged clothes and a wig awry; he discarded them for startling organic symptoms he knew how to project:

> His distraction of mind and agonising horrors

made him a

> ghastly spectacle and his complexion grew whiter every moment.

Garrick may have wiped off makeup, *The Connoisseur* suggested. This reminds us that the actor, like the king, has two bodies. The first, that becomes one with the character, is indistinguishable from the artifact Macbeth himself,

---

*Forster, Macready's friend and so ever ready to criticise Forrest, saw "a violent start, of throwing his body into one convulsion . . . to the great delight of the injudicious."

in his actual life onstage and his imagined life between appearances. The second is the physical acting instrument, manipulated in appearance and manner to fit the larger artistic design. An actor's studybook (S59) instructed this second Macbeth before returning to the stage, to

> take off paint, whiten cheekbones and blacken under the eyes, also lips . . . hair disordered, blood on back of hands.

So Garrick may have *added* makeup, as may Charles Kean when he appeared "blanched."

Only in imagination will the actor in fact kill Duncan; but a tangible simulacrum of blood must mark him when he returns. In the nineteenth century, when the Porter's scene was cut, and Macbeth would have to return fairly quickly to the stage after exiting with Duncan's blood on his hands, Kean tried a quick-change jacket with sleeves that were of one piece with his gloves, so that he could throw the whole off without needing to clean the "red" from his hands when he returned to meet Macduff and Lenox. While such technical manipulations adapt the actor's second body to his action, the part of him that *is* Macbeth lives its continuing passion: so Macready, imagining his bloody act in the offstage interim, would spend the time standing near a wall and stabbing it again and again with his dagger—in an American theatre he left marks that the impresario Sol Smith would observe with reminiscent admiration years afterwards.

The complexity of the actor-Macbeth's psychophysical state is lampooned in "Garrick's" essay on acting with a curious mixture of sense in the nonsense:

> He should . . . be a *moving Statue*, or indeed a *petrify'd Man*; his *Eyes* must *Speak*, and his *Tongue* be *metaphorically Silent*; his *Ears* must be *sensible* of *imaginary* Noises, and *deaf* to the *present* and *audible* Voice of his Wife; his *Attitudes* must be *quick* and *permanent*; his Voice *articulately trembling*, and *confusedly intelligible*; the Murderer should be seen in *every Limb*, and yet every *Member*, at that instant, should seem *separated* from his *Body*, and his *Body* from his *Soul*. . . .

There is fun in this—Garrick ends by advising a "*real* Genius to wear *Cork Heels* to his Shoes [to] seem to *tread on Air*"; but it is meaningful, too, on the paralysis of Macbeth's functions; and its sense of the disjunction of Macbeth's parts—heart and brain, eye and hand—would find echoes in theatrical and critical insights into the centripetal forces fragmenting Macbeth's identity. Thus Kean, "crept on . . . as if every faculty were for the time unstrung." Observers used "convulsed" and "convulsion" to describe his physical agony, yet did not find it excessive:

> not by strained and struggling gestures,—not by hurried changes of attitude—not by boisterous or vehement expression [but] he shewed . . . in every lineament and muscle of the body . . . the soul-stricken, self-convicted murderer. (*Morning Chronicle*)

Irving crept, terrified, cowering, down his stone stairway, the daggers held well away from him, his body in revolt, near to paralysis. Observers saw him, knees bent, jaw dropped, trembling, reeling, tottering, barely supporting himself, his body swaying as if "already hanging on a gibbet," "positively sobbing with remorse." Booth staggered back from the murder. Macready rushed in, trembling so that the shaking daggers clacked in his hands, his face conspicuously white, and stood arched backward, as if "shot through the breast by an arrow, . . . a dreadful picture of remorse" (*Tallis*). Reineke raced in as if pursued by something at his back, stole looks backward; Charles Kemble seemed to be flying from himself. Charles Laughton (England, 1934) blindly stumbled down, living the "ghastly numb horror of the murderer" (*Punch*), breathless, sweat-covered, looking as if he were really going to be sick; the red on his hands became blood by the way he held his fingers, and smeared his cheeks as he raised horrified hands to his face. He now bore the mark of the criminal, and the awareness that every man's hand was against him, any might find him out. Gielgud's inner chaos was seen in the clumsy way he held the daggers; Agate thought the actor's collapse here a "masterpiece of nerves." The tragic effect of Charles Kean's entrance lingered for years in Henry James' mind: the staggering

> out of the castle . . . blanched, almost dumb, already conscious, in the vision of his fixed eyes, of the far fruits of his deed, he brought with him a kind of hush of terror.

Salvini's great strength seemed all to go into his wild glances, his uncontrolled gestures, remorse more than terror shivering the giant who had by contrast walked so resolutely into Duncan's chamber. "What a different man he returned!" (*Edinburgh Courant*).

We see that this contrast is at the heart of Shakespeare's design. The act has changed Macbeth, however he may try to mask himself. Some changes are obvious: the battle-tried soldier had been *nothing afraid* of the *strange images of death* he had made; the murderer is tortured by them. Still, an essential—if not Luciferian—dignity survives. Kemble's failure here was marked by the Philadelphia observer:

> Macbeth closes the door with the cold unfeeling caution of a practised housebreaker, then listens, in order to be secure, and addresses lady [*sic*] Macbeth as if, in such a conflict, Macbeth could be awake to the suggestions of the lowest kind of cunning.

The change in Macbeth need not be as violent as Garrick's, or Kean's; it may be as subtle as with Scofield, whose return was measured, heavier; he was rapt again, as he strode back, but the élan was lost: with the deed done, something had gone dead in him. Ironically, he held the unholy daggers by the blade, like crucifixes—supporting the production's motif of *sacrilegious* murder. Redgrave conveyed to one observer the impression that he had killed not only the king, but also his own soul. Ernest Milton suggested a poet horrified that he had become a man of action. Wrede's Norwegian Macbeth emphasized one immediately physical symbol of the transformation: the warrior's hands—so conspicuous in the character's design, that had been graceful and athletic, were now deformed, horrible claws.

Blood must mark at least Macbeth's hands, for his Lady will say so—and will remind us later of the *so much* of Duncan's spilled. Red fluid waits in the wings to color the actor. An old promptbook warns Macbeth against touching anything as he enters; but he may seem so deeply rapt, as Redgrave was, as not to seem to care what his hands do. Savits' Macbeth, who staggered down the stairs, clinging to the banisters, passed his bloody hand, in his characteristic gesture, once, twice, thrice, over his forehead, so, as with Laughton, the mark of Cain was on him. Directors fascinated with the power of blood to rouse archetypal responses of terror and pity sometimes spill it lavishly, splashing Macbeth on torso and face. Ristori's Italian Macbeth came rushing hysterically out of Duncan's chamber so daubed he reminded one observer of a butcher from an abattoir.

Even her sight of a bloodied Macbeth cannot immediately tell Lady Macbeth for certain that Duncan is dead. He may carry wounds of his own, want her care. Her face asks: she needs him to tell. Porter, grim and rigidly controlled, could not for some moments speak—his Lady could only look at him with agonized inquiry. But some Macbeths do not withhold: Bernhardt's Marais came running out, almost shouting. While Hackett told what he had done, he was looking up at Duncan's chamber—his note: "Damn you." Olivier spoke in deliberately unemotional tones, denying the feelings that wracked him. Macbeth has even boasted here. But the five monosyllables (again, how much of the great language is built of these small, abrupt blocks) seem scraped from the vitals of many Macbeths, dazed by the unspeakable act they must declare:

I have done the deed. (20)

Done at last is—the equivocation comes hard—the nameless. Jorgensen observes that the *deed* will begin to have a name; but not yet. Often a long pause intervenes, as with Macready; words stick in Macbeth's throat even now. The difficulty of speech underlines the inwardness of Macbeth's process. Salvini's organ voice was piteous in its agony. Garrick, breathless, whispered the words as if to himself.

Torn as he is inwardly, and fearful of discovery from without, Macbeth usually does muffle his voice: so Garrick's "terrifying whispers," Irving's "hollow whisper," Kemble's utterance: "like some horrible secret—a horrid whisper in the dark." Gentleman heard Garrick speak in "low, piercing tones," which suggests voicing "under the breath," as with Charles Kean. Almost the same as a whisper, this suppressed utterance also conveys the moment's special terror and anxiety. Choked speech, a rarity in adult experi-

ence—after childhood we almost never whisper in fear—can awaken re-
verberances that confer an uncanny power: with Macready's sibilants, "all
the terrors of night and crime seemed to pass . . . into the hearer's very soul."

Kean, in his trancelike horror, trembling with apprehension, overwhelmed
with remorse, "in utter prostration of mind, and the stupefaction of one
who had committed his first great crime," had stumbled upon his waiting
Lady without consciously seeing her; "when his timid eye first rested on
[her], his frame was convulsed and wound up to the highest pitch of terror;"
Even when he recognized her, he was still only half assured. He tried to speak,
but at first his voice would not come; then,

> in broken, half-smothered tones, forced from him by violent exertion and
> evident pain, he slowly stammers, "I have done the deed."

The tones of anguish—deepened and broken by agitation—"were almost too
torturing for the sense to bear."

Lady Macbeth's response to Macbeth's condition shapes the next beat of
the scene. In the eighteenth-century equation, the Lady confronted an honorable murderer, who was almost breaking down. Thus Garrick, with horror
and remorse, evoked the scorn of his iron wife, played in the strikingly opposite mood by Pritchard. Again:

> [Garrick's] distraction of mind and agonising horrors were finely contrasted
> by her seeming apathy, tranquility, and confidence.

Kemble found a softer response, Bell thought, in Siddons:

> She displays [Shakespeare's] wonderful power and knowledge of nature. As
> if her inhuman strength of spirit overcome by the contagion of his remorse
> and terror. Her arms about her neck and bosom, shuddering.

But Siddons herself wrote that the "one trait of tender feeling" that had surfaced at the thought of Duncan's resemblance to her father "vanishes at the
same instant"; her notes suggest not the slightest touch of remorse, or fear;
indeed they remark a mounting fierceness.

However controlled the Lady may feel now, or seem to feel for Macbeth's
benefit, at some moment in this scene she is infected by the horror that will
revisit her in V, i. If, earlier in the play, she has even faintly hinted at an inner
disquiet brought on by her need to summon murdering ministers, or by her
meeting with her victim, by her sense of the change in her husband, or by
her glimpse of the sleeping king, the subtextual preparation for her break
may now be recognized. Or some overt, sudden gesture may signal her
awakening to enormity. Thus: the Lady does not expect to see blood on
Macbeth; her first sight of the *so much* of it may begin the haunting that will
emerge in dreamwalking. When Savits' Macbeth returned with his forehead
bloodstained, his Lady, who had only with tremendous effort sustained
herself during his absence in the murder chamber, involuntarily started back;

with brutal self-control she made herself stop, go to him, and wipe the blood from his head: thus first staining—and shocking—her own hands.

Comfort was not available to the Macbeth confronted with a fiend-spouse. When, in the eighteenth century, John Powell's Macbeth (England, 1768) was so distraught as to return from the murder whimpering, seeming more in physical pain than mental, the standard Lady of his time could hardly cosset him. But as the Lady learned to admit underlying sensibility, and to wait for her distraught husband in terror and anxiety, her strength showed as she masked her fears, and bestowed on him the benison of acceptance and a sharing of suffering. So the pioneering Faucit, whom the traditionalist *Reader* scolded here for seeming—as contrasted with Siddons—"as impressionable and almost as feverishly vehement as Macbeth. So far from taking a high pitch above him—so far from thinking little of murder and nothing of omens, she seems as much affected as he is . . . she should be indifferent to all that appals him." On the other hand, the *Sunday Times* was pleased that, "impressionable" as she was, when Macbeth returned "her control over her agitation is admirable; the struggle was perceptible, but the conquest over her dread immediate . . . pallor, and rather more gutteral, are the only outward manifestations of concern." Terry would show her relief that the act was over by the feverish energy with which she tended the shattered Irving. His horror was so intense and overwhelming that by contrast her willowy Lady "seemed almost strong." So loving a Lady as Morris would naturally be soothing; with more contrast Cushman—in her later, compassionate interpretations—transformed her massive force into softness, demonstrating how much the Terrible Lady's score could be modulated: her manner, the *Chicago Times* reported of a reading near the end of her career, was now "infinitely caressing and tender, [proving] how in her love she has partially recovered from her fears and thinks of naught but soothing and guarding her husband." Hackett and his waiting wife embraced; when Henry Ainley (England, 1926) came to his Lady shivering and whimpering, she would take him in her sheltering arms; Sothern and Marlowe instinctively clung to each other; Dench mothered her Macbeth.

With the most loving of couples, what they have done together may now begin to separate them. When Forrest, backing away from Duncan's room, struck against his Lady, and automatically raised his sword, she shielded herself, and the two started from each other, staring in each other's eyes with terror. Tree, faltering down his steps, raising his sword against shadows, his face haunted, his swaying body racked with emotion, exchanged a long, hunted stare with his Lady: they were fixed, beholding a terrible future in the instant. For all their past tenderness, for all her stiffening him still with her resolve, they would never be so close again. Irving intended a different measure of psychic distance: "Don't look at each other," he insisted in one note to himself. Terry, who had at first been so clinging-loving, then strung

up to a high pitch of tension while awaiting Irving, now reacted with a practicality observers found impressive: she controlled her terror, and guided
them through the worst of their emergency.

The more practical the Lady may be here, the further off she holds the
consciousness of what she has done. More brittle Ladies, like Merchant and
Rigg, welcome back their husbands with a feeling of completion rather than
horror. Hunt sensed a mood of excitement, thoughtless of consequence. An
adoring Lady makes much of her Macbeth: Mirren welcomed Williamson
with a proud, jubilant cry—*My husband!* and an ecstatic hug; Bergman's
amorous Lady caressed her Macbeth; in one sensual Bremen production
(1966) when Macbeth dodged back from the murder room and took protective
cover, his Lady went to him exultantly, knelt at his feet, and rubbed her face
against his legs; in another, the Lady (Johanna Liebeneiner, 1975) adoringly
kissed her Macbeth's blood-covered hands.

Accomplishment is not Macbeth's primary concern. He may at first come
to claim his wife's approval for the "manly" thing he has done; even if so,
too many rising notes of apprehension, horror, and mental confusion interdict sustained, prideful satisfaction. Caution mutes Macbeth; his mind
throngs with real and imaginary images and sounds consequent on his deed
that nearly madden him. The pressure within may insist on breaking out,
in an uncontrolled cry: Ristori's blood-covered Macbeth, running in fright
from the murder room, began a scream that she stopped by clapping her hand
over his mouth. She held it until his self-possession returned; but she would
have to repeat the action when his nerves rioted again soon after. Some Ladies
would slap their hysterical Macbeths. Like the suppressed voices, such visual
enforcements to silence intensify the sense that the two are guilty, that discovery is possible, that they now face and fear the machinery of *judgement
here*, if not beyond. The *naive* spectator half expects that they may be discovered. Their secret speech is abrupt, mouth to ear, as they strain for any
sound of alarm or retaliation. Except for pauses to listen, the lines are staccato,
fast. . . . Terry's note for the dialogue suggests overlapping: "Together."
They exchange whispers, muttering, groans, gasps.

Any jubiliation Lady Macbeth may feel for the business done must disperse as she recognizes the strangeness infecting her husband. His questions
at first seem only meaningful practical ones that she can deal with reasonably.
Terse monosyllables answer monosyllables:

> Didst thou not hear a noise? (21)

She thinks he means a sound that men may hear: the owl's scream or the
cricket's cry. But farther sounds—*sorriest fancies* (III, ii, 14)—have begun to
reach his brain, are reaching it even now. The spectator may hear the difference in Macbeth before his Lady does, may sense the something more than
precaution in his far-off listening. Reinhardt's Macbeth showed it in his
wide, staring glance; Mantell in eyes so upturned the whites showed; Garrick
in the "dark colouring" of his voice.

Lady Macbeth still tries to speak reason, breaking into his raptness.

> Did not you speak?
> When?
> Now.
>   As I descended?
> Ay. (23–27)

Macbeth does not respond. The image of descending, with all its implications, takes him: Reinhardt's Macbeth sobbed the words out; Sothern clung more closely to his Lady, as if for protection.

Macbeth hears again the unheard; and again the command to listen that fixes characters and audience:

> Hark . . . (28)

From along the corridor he has traversed, so loud with voices that only he perceived, has come another terrible signal. His hand trembling violently, he may reach out quickly to his Lady, as Reinhardt's Macbeth did; and the Lady, alarmed by what she still thinks may be a real danger, listens—as we do—for a sound. She hears none; we hear none; but Macbeth hears, often shudders: who lies in the room he passed? His Lady, still reacting logically, practically: *Donalbain*. Terry could respond with relief to a reasonable question. But something other than reason is governing Macbeth. Some image recalls him to the enormity of what he has done, and may have to do—Hackett's thought, as he looked toward the prince's room: "Have I got to kill him, too?" Macbeth's torturing mind forces a connection, directs his gaze, and the eye which has carefully avoided seeing his hands can no longer wink at them—"restlessly moves to see the thing it shrinks on" (Macready). The bloody hands. As if Macbeth were disjoined from them, has put off knowing them as his:

> This is a sorry sight. (30)

Ambition forgotten,

> his *Faculties* intensely riveted to the *Murder* alone, without having the least Consolation of the *consequential Advantages*, to comfort him in that *Exigency* (*Essay*),

Garrick stared at the murderous signs of himself. Salvini was as horrified; he conveyed the sense of a warrior shocked by an unforgivable breach of loyalty and hospitality. His gaze through the following dialogue was held on Duncan's door. Tree's glance of terror came down and fixed on his hands hypnotically, and could not break away until almost the end of the scene. Olivier, before so formidably practical, seemed tranced by a flood of images surging in his mind. Scofield's fingers began again to rub against each other, trying to rub off more than blood—they would remember the action and rehearse it secretly in later inward moments. Other Macbeths, from Mitterwurzer on, have also tried so to erase the secret murder sticking to their hands; or, oppositely, have almost mindlessly toyed with the wet, sticky blood.

Macready reacted with "ghastly wildness," flinging his head from side to side in a fear so nearly excessive it tested the aesthetic limits of terror. And, intense as it was, it seemed to Marston too narrow, as if it excluded other notes in Macbeth's polyphony: the

> various mental states seemed too sharply defined and separated. The emotions of shame, terror, remorse, momentary despair, and selfish fear, might . . . have more often flowed into each other.

Marston cited Kean's complex, agonized reaction, which Hazlitt had found an unforgettable lesson in common humanity:

> the hesitation, the bewildered look, the coming to himself . . . the manner in which his voice clung to his throat, and choked his utterance; his agony and tears, the force of nature overcome by passion. . . .

After *This is a sorry* . . . Kean paused for a moment before he could say *sight;* he turned to look at his wife, awful emotions manifest in his face and body.

Lady Macbeth does not see the daggers yet. Sometimes, when Macbeth holds both weapons behind him in one hand, he holds up the other hand, bloody, away from him, and she sees that. Or both, if the daggers are in his belt. This absolute reality may shock her terribly; it is one more possible pivot to breakdown for a susceptible Lady, as it was for instance for Ziegler, terribly frightened, her hands pressed to her heart, breathing heavily, gasping as she spoke—all gestures that would be duplicated in the sleepwalking scene. But even this Lady must summon her strength, in all its polyphony, to support Macbeth. Partner, wife, conspirator, she now hears the cry that some critics have perceived of the helpless child in Macbeth—accentuated in the petulant, almost paralyzed despair of Irving, explicit in Plummer's whimpering. The Lady responds in kind, only beginning to be aware that Macbeth is involved in an inward, rather than outward, event: she sounds the maternal note, corrective, scolding. *A foolish thought*, (31).

The firm Lady is at Macbeth at once, harshly. Siddons, Bell thought, was still shadowed by horror; but her own description suggests the continuance of "remorseless ambition," as she manipulated her man. Other Ladies had to summon their strength. The formidable Cushman, as she developed her characterization, grew more apprehensive, needed more will to will her reproving of Macbeth. Ristori, laboring under great tension, confronted Macbeth with brief, cold responses: "her mental torment is too great for speech." Terry, listening to Irving's broken accents, would seem to apprehend some hidden unease, watched him with "puzzled alarm." She tried to wave off the *foolish thought*. Hackett's loving Lady, smiling, emphasized the implication that the moment was in fact triumphant—"a foolish thought to say a *sorry* sight." The young Annis laughed it away—and yet there was a touch of unbalance in her laughter, and in her response to his bloody hand. Mrs. Kean said the words to Charles Kean with understanding pity. Marlowe, going to Sothern, who had collapsed on a bench, knelt beside him to comfort him, watchful, tender, coaxing, her hand out to him.

Lady Macbeth's primary concern now is to get them away. The sense of urgency, the danger of being overheard, the listening for any threatening sound, all color her desperate responses to Macbeth's almost irrational disregard of the situation. He may break out at any moment, and call attention to them. In the theatre she has tried to push or lead him out. But he is lost from the now, rapt, caught in the half-real, half-hallucinated memory of his passage from the murder chamber. His next line has no connection with his last, except by another subterranean association, with the bloody hands:

> There's one did laugh in's sleep,
> And one cried murder, (32–33)

The speech, almost all one-syllabled, has the simple rhythm of reminiscence. The first words slow and lengthen the meter: *There's one*. . . . The phrases in the next two lines soften into weak endings:

> And one cried murder,* that they did wake each other:
> I stood, and heard them: but they did say their prayers, (33–34)

The meter itself softens:

> And addressed them again to sleep. (35)

Sleep . . . sleep. . . . Men wake to "murder," and return to sleep. There is wonder in it. Macbeth is again trying to make sense of his world; he is talking to himself as much as to his wife. Reinhardt's Macbeth, turning inward at *murder*, closed his eyes, his face disfigured by horror. When the word broke from Hackett, his Lady clapped her hand over his mouth. She has heard the nameless named.

Lady Macbeth's verbal response is curiously tangential, as if she does not know how to deal with his mood, as if she is trying to reach his mind with a simple, appeasing assurance of a reality: *There are two lodg'd together* (36).

He goes on as if he had not heard her, rehearsing the pain.

> One cried God bless us, and amen the other,
> As they had seen me with these hangman's* hands:
> Listening their fear, I could not say amen,
> When they did say God bless us. (37–40)

The rhythm, like the words, is simple, wondering; but as he images himself in the memory, the passion begins to rise. The man who cannot pray, in

---

*One of the curiosities of the Salvini and Rossi interpretations is that the actors essayed to reproduce the tones of the heard voices in these two speeches.

*Hangman's because the hangman had also to butcher his victims. A despicable trade.

Shakespeare, is likely to know a Faustian degradation—so Tarquin before entering Lucrece's chamber, so Claudius. Macbeth reports, with a kind of innocence, his vision of innocence lost forever: a "lamentation . . . fearfully bitter" (Macready).

Now Lady Macbeth is becoming alert to the central danger: that not from without now, but from within Macbeth—and perhaps within her, too—the contagion is spreading. Terry would think:

> 'Why, he is quite ill! Come, come, the danger's *past now* . . .' not stern and angry
> but with some feminine consideration mixed with alarm—

and would say, with a "slight break in voice," *Consider it not so deeply*.

But the Lady's protest is brushed away in the mounting flood of Macbeth's anguish:

> But wherefore could not I pronounce Amen?
> I had most need of blessing, and amen stuck in my throat. (42–43)

Amen may have stuck in his throat in all these last speeches. His intensity is desperate: in Walter's "choked utterance," the word conveyed a raging inner turmoil. So Olivier's "whispered horror." Reinhardt's Macbeth and Tree had to swallow before being able to say the words. *Stuck* itself, so ono-matopoeic here, sometimes comes with slow difficulty from Macbeth's mouth—Macready had to say it twice.* The parent prayer, *God bless us* (again God is called on, and seems not to hear) also is not easily voiced, as with Scofield. Hackett, through this dialogue, spoke resentfully, as if re-proaching his Lady for what happened to him. Her response would be reassuring, maternally comforting, she trying to mask her own nervousness. Parrott suggested that the *God bless us* was a charm against witchcraft and the devil; and some shadow of this may have been felt, in Shakespeare's time, to inhabit Macbeth's prayer; but the essential signal is of the man who had felt a need to ask blessing—even to expect it—and to be denied by some force.

Almost every new speech, every incident, in this scene has provided a cue for Lady Macbeth's start downward. Here is another, as she tries vainly to stem the force of Macbeth's paroxysm. She cannot meet him with reason: he has not been asking of her, but rather of his mysterious world, a question whose answer finally hides within himself, an answer he cannot yet face. She must divert him; the questioning threatens their survival.

In countering Macbeth's anxiety, Lady Macbeth reveals a deep, prescient anxiety of her own: *These . . . deeds* (equivocation still) *must not be thought/ After these ways: so, it will make us mad* (44–45). *Mad.* So close to the edge they come these two. Parrott even saw Macbeth as evidently already half-mad. Lady Macbeth's prophetic fear about herself may be manifested in her phys-

---

*The *Iris:* "We rejoice to see that Mr. Macready eschews that affected mannerism, so common with second and third rate actors, of giving the word "stuck" . . . as though it were written st-t-t-uck. If anything stuck in the throat, it is surely the word "amen.""

ical imagery; even Siddons, according to the Bell notes, seemed to renew the gesture of terrorized remorse she had caught from Kemble: the "arms about her neck and bosom, shuddering." She stressed the final phrase. The gentler Terry was clearly moved: her note, "infected, highly wrought." Reinhardt's Lady moaned, shook her head in dismay.

Two streams of the beat are moving to climax: the passion of Macbeth's account of his hallucinated experience, and Lady Macbeth's fearful awareness that he is out of touch with reality, that madness may be very close. She may at once try to wake him—so Hackett's loving wife-mother soothed her manchild with the first words, then, finding him still rapt, shook him as a parent would a dreaming boy. But even now Lady Macbeth does not fully realize how inward he is. His words are curiously gentle, as if his lament for his lost innocence extends to the loss of the precious good that is soothing and healing and regenerative in life:

> Methought I heard a voice cry, Sleep no more:
> Macbeth does murder sleep, the innocent sleep, (46–47)

(Terry: The most awful line in the play.)

> Sleep that knits up the ravell'd sleeve of care, (48)

Whether this means "sleeve," or a kind of silk thread, or even a kind of bread,* the basic image, here and as the speech continues, is of amelioration, tranquility, sustenance: Macbeth may well dream of a *bath* after *sore labor*, even more presciently of a *Balm of hurt minds*—how bruised their two minds are, and will be, and no ministering to heal them! Macbeth can still image life as a feast, nourishing life. This language of the poet-philosopher, touched with longing and a generous vision, earns sympathy for him, counters the brutal fact of the murder. From that act we have been buffered because it was not present to our senses; this suffering man is so immediate. The voice of conscience cried from within Olivier's resolute mask. Salvini's speech was an anguished wail; Forrest's, too, was "melancholy pathos"; Booth's "piteous," the despairing wail of a lost soul.*

Lady Macbeth's question in response has become a cliché of drama, a "feeder" line. *What do you mean?* But here it intimately serves character and action; it is a compelled step toward her realization of Macbeth's insulation from reality, and the implications for herself of what he has said, and what he has become. All the events that happen now will register on the depths

*I like Robert Dent's gloss, which rescues the primacy of the Folio's everyday meaning: "Emended for two centuries to 'sleave' (variously glossed), but the metaphor refers to repairing a sleeve frayed by labor." Beyond this, Shakespeare may again be cueing a complex response. The primary sense of careworn unravelling can be experienced without a literal imaging of any single object. Sound-alike words from the common memory that are capable of parallel implications may fuse to evoke a cluster-impression—cloth, garment, food, sleep—of things lost to Macbeth.

*One old promptbook has an actor's timely warning to himself: "I am apt to whine here."

of a mind which may now seem not to absorb their meanings, but which will one day shatter trying to expunge them. On a Lady already vulnerable, the psychic and physical impacts trace immediate tremors: even as strong a Lady as Mme. Segond-Weber's is shaken by an almost witchlike foreknowledge:

> On hearing the words (*Sleep no more*) Lady Macbeth succumbs to a feebleness, to a fear that she can scarcely master; for a second she trembles, a vague presentiment grips her, a premonition of retribution. Will *she* sleep? . . . I indicate these vague presentiments, my eye is fixed, haggard, fear seizes me and my hands fall, anticipating thus indistinctly the sleepwalking scene that must be prepared for.

However shaken the Lady is, she must find strength to shore up Macbeth. For he now reaches the climax of his distress, his head rings with a cry that in his imagination echoed throughout the house, naming him, triply, naming him in every way, for himself, for his honors:

> Glamis hath murder'd sleep, and therefore Cawdor
> Shall sleep no more: Macbeth shall sleep no more.* (54–55)

As his intensity rises, it strains against the need for cautious quiet; so Mantell, ringing the words out as he fell to his knees. Olivier's voice rose "to a magnificent resonance"; Hopkins' and Scofield's almost to a deep shout, alarming their Ladies. For such Macbeths the elegy for sleep may be less a lament than a complaint: against a world that would treat a man so; or, in Hackett's case, against Lady Macbeth, as again somehow responsible for his suffering (though he imagined the strange voice to be the witches').† Against the comfort and love shown Hackett by his Lady he broke out with such an intense tone of resentment that she at first recoiled, then tried to hush him with a hand over his mouth; he threw her off brutally.

More often Macbeth, his overcharged mind blown and spent, has subsided into near collapse. His terrible, inexorable vision, as searing as the witches' curse—*Sleep shall neither night nor day/ Hang upon his penthouse lid:/ He shall live a man forbid* (I, iii, 22–24)—has knelled a summons to his own hell. The abyss opens deeper, darker because of the very generosity of his elegiac tribute to sleep: Shakespeare's polyphonic design is of a character whose admirable qualities particularly fit him to suffer from his worst.

So Kean:

> His fit of deep abstraction—so top full of anticipatory horrors—as if the whole of his career had passed in one instant of time, over the mirror of his soul.
> His remorse and terror—the repentant agony and sudden subduing of his

---

*This is the "sleep" speech that, Paul thinks, Shakespeare wrote because James suffered insomnia. That royal circumstance seems, if anything, a further argument against assuming that a play making sleeplessness a curse shared by a murderer could have been written to please the insomniac king.

†Rossi spoke the lines in high, strange tones as if he were trying to reproduce an uncanny voice.

mind—the contrast between the innocent sleep of his victims and the fearful and wretched watchings of their murderer, uttered in a voice broken by terror, inward torment and hopeless despair (*New Monthly*).

So Tree:

terrified by the products of his own imagination.

To muffle his excitement, his Lady put her hand over his mouth, then he relapsed into a kind of trancelike, childish terror. Irving:

the broken and gasping accents . . . mortal affright . . . the very incarnation of despair . . . hollow . . . ghastly, hope bereft.*

Salvini:

full of suffering and dread.

Because so much torment for a misdeed afflicts a character so vulnerable to it, Macbeth's agony evokes compassion: so the "indescribable piteousness" of the voice (Walter), Macready's "piteous and heartrending appearance."

Lady Macbeth, her own tension growing with Macbeth's rising excitement, lost momentarily in the mystery of his hallucination, catches at the possibility of a real, threatening experience.

Who was it, that thus cried? (56)

Siddons stressed *Who?* as if an actual speaker, representing danger, might be identified; and indeed the *naive* spectator cannot be certain that in a world of strange phenomena, some murdering minister might not manifest itself. Reinhardt's Lady even looked about her, as if a presence might lurk somewhere. But a glance at Macbeth, rapt, bewildered, enforces the Lady's belief that he is "brainsickly." She must wake him to reality, for their safety, for his sanity, for hers. Bell on Siddons:

Her horror changes to agony and alarm at his derangement, uncertain what to do; calling up the resources of her spirit. She comes near him, attempts to call back his wandering thoughts to ideas of common life. Strong emphasis on *who*. Speaks forcibly into his ear, looks at him steadfastly. "Why worthy thane, etc." firm remonstrance, tone fit to work on his mind.

What that tone is, Bell does not say; but immediately after he hears her speak with "contempt". Siddons herself saw no touch of agony, alarm, or other weakness, rather "remorseless ambition." Her tone is contemptuous, and suggests the "fiend" pattern already noted, made standard by Pritchard:

the image of a mind inflexible to compunction and inflexibly bent to its purpose . . . she presented a picture of the most consummate intrepidity in mischief. (Davies)

*Terry's note for the end of Irving's speech: "If applause, wait."

So dominating a Terrible Woman must torture Shakespeare's adjectives:

> why *worthy* Thane,
> You do unbend your *noble* strength, to think
> So brainsickly . . . (56–58)

The words are edged differently, in anxious anger, by a brittle Lady like Merchant, furiously trying to drive Macbeth to save their adventure, or like Leigh, her voice malignant with purpose. (The Lady may use force: Rigg caught her Macbeth by the hair, pulled his head back, to try to bring him to himself. He has been slapped, shaken). But to softer Ladies the adjectives have been vehicles for support, and even tenderness. One Lady Macbeth gently put her hands over Macbeth's ears, to silence the cries ringing there, as she sought to bolster him. Dench clapped her hand over Macbeth's mouth. Hackett's Lady soothed and patted him, as she might a child. Marlowe physically supported Sothern, who staggered, function almost smothered in surmise. Terry, concerned with Irving's near-collapse, noted, in a kind of tender vexation, "Upon my soul, you should be ashamed." But more seriously, "Remember the murder is done . . . he's a good fellow and has not failed—dont press him too far—bear with him—humour him."

⌊As she concerns herself with his condition, the Lady suddenly observes a sorry sight—one bloody hand. Her design includes an instinctive "woman's" liquid image:

> Go get some water,
> And wash this filthy witness from your hand. (58–59)

Perhaps with a pause after *this* . . . to find her euphemism. She could once appeal to have her blood made thick; but, skilled in equivocation as she is, she will not yet consciously speak of spilled blood. But what it is, and the smell of it, penetrates to her deeper brain, will not be washed away.⌋

Marlowe probably represented one stage tradition when—Ponisi had done this with Forrest—she reached out to take Sothern's hand, turned him to her, and saw what was worse than the blood alone—the bloody daggers. Sothern was apparently following the old Garrick pattern when, as he turned, he brought his two hands, with the daggers in them, clasped together—a gesture half supplicatory. Gielgud's Lady Macbeth pulled his hand, with the weapons, from behind his back. Macbeth's plaid or scarf, if it has hidden the daggers—as with Phelps and Charles Kemble—may in his desperate movement shift away. Or Macbeth has fallen back on a bench, or to the floor, and so let the blades show. Shakespeare, to multiply the staccato crises of the scene, has brilliantly delayed Lady Macbeth's awareness of the incriminating things; but at last, by the sight, or smell, or touch of blood on them—which perhaps only now she has forced herself to perceive—she knows. She asks, desperately—Siddons stressed every word—a question that probes the very center of the Macbeth design:

> Why did you bring these daggers from [Pause? Equivocation?] . . . the place? (60)

Why indeed? They are the badges of his crime. The plan was to leave them. Commonsense said to leave them. Yet he has not been able to separate himself from them. No Freudian subtlety is needed to perceive here, coated in Macbeth's rapt, hallucinating hysteria, a deep compulsion to discovery and punishment, *judgement here*.

He cannot answer her question. He stares at the daggers, or her, or his hunted eyes look everywhere else. He had not only brought the daggers, he had perhaps concealed them from her. If he knows why, he cannot say.

When she can get no answer, she insists: *They must lie . . . there* (A pun on *lie*—lie and deceive?). She orders him back with the daggers to *smear/ The sleepy grooms with blood* (62). Mechanically, Macbeth may start: so Evans moved toward Duncan's chamber, as if hypnotized, then suddenly stopped dead. Guinness got to the stairs, slipped on the first one, could go no further. When Sothern stood rooted, mute, Marlowe tried to push him, as did Craig's Lady her Macbeth. Merchant pulled at Scofield, as unmoving as stone. Reinhardt's Lady was able to propel her Macbeth a few steps; but when he realized what she was doing, he stopped, and struggled with her, warding her off, his forehead asweat, his teeth chattering.

He will not go. The sense of having *done more* than becomes a man to *dare*— the key words surface—fixes him:

> I'll go no more:
> I am afraid, to think what I have done:
> Look on't again, I dare not. (63–65)

The comma in the middle line marks a pause; and the effect of it was demonstrated when Scofield, so skilled in spacing his words, came to a full stop after *I am afraid*, a halt of deep feelings. Only after a long moment did he finish the line. Farnham sees this speech-act as Macbeth's "most degrading failure in resolution"; and Irving marked it "Cow"—for coward? cower? This was Irving's conception of the role; the *naive* spectator hears the words as an assertion of Macbeth's better part, an access of conscience. Actors generally suggest not physical fear, but moral repugnance. Kean refused the return with "shuddering agony." Rossi could only look at his wife in horror. Matkowsky started back with a cry. McKellen retched. Macready, horrorstruck at the suggestion, rushed to the far edge of the stage, as distant as possible from the murder chamber.

Ristori's Macbeth, too, rushed away from her; she caught up with him, and snatched the daggers, with a terrifying resolution. They must be returned, and urgently, if discovery and retaliation are to be avoided. Macbeth is unwilling, and in his present state unable. She sees him as *infirm of purpose*—sick in will as well as in brain. Lady Macbeth must take over. She says, *"give me the daggers,"* but usually he cannot—will not—do even that; she must take them from his nerveless or resisting or catatonic hands. Usually this is done swiftly—by Bernhardt as "an act of spasmodic audacity," her nerves almost as completely unstrung as Macbeth's. Merchant enjoyed the act: she seized the daggers in a "sensual, ecstatic embrace." But Dench waited: "I didn't believe he would let me take them back; I wanted to give him a chance to do it." She spoke the lines as if half-shaming McKellen into returning; only when she saw he would not—could not—did she take the knives.

Nothing delayed a murderess as determined as Siddons; she saw the Lady "wrenching the daggers from the feeble grasp of her husband [to finish] the act which the infirm of purpose had not the courage to complete." She proceeded "calmly and steadily" to her task. For those Ladies whose unsexing is not complete, or not completely suppressed, the moment is a critical one. Only one other moment later in this scene so much tests her, is as likely to signal her break-up.

She sees blood. And touches it. And smells it.

Siddons, "as bold in action as she had, during speculation, asserted herself to be" (Boaden), might not betray any flicker of troubled reaction; Bethmann, furiously and with great energy, could seize the daggers and stride into Duncan's chamber unhesitatingly, ignoring the blood. On the impassive face of the Japanese Lady in *Throne of Blood*, only calm determination would show, as she slowly worked the murder weapon free of her husband's rigid, paralyzed hands. But the sleepwalk indicates Shakespeare's design of an ineradicable traumatic experience, however repressed, to be relived in awful pain. The violence of the Japanese Lady Macbeth's later anguish even suggested that the more severely repressed, the more eruptive the buried mine.

Other formidable Lady Macbeths have let slip here, at the feel of blood, some sign of faintness, terror, revulsion. Cushman, trembling at the sight of the daggers, had to nerve herself to tear them away from her Macbeth. Holding them, she tottered, had to lean against the gate—where the knock would come. Janauschek, for all her fierce anger—almost leonine, Wingate thought—at Macbeth for his negligence, unrelenting as she was in carrying the murder through, nevertheless, seeing the daggers, had to turn away with a momentary gesture of disgust before resolutely taking them. Welles' Lady seemed in absolute, icy control up to the moment her fingers closed on the bloody hafts; then an almost panic, premonitory shock weakened her face. Anderson, so clearly invulnerable until now, said "The moment she feels the blood—augh! She is nauseated, she wants to vomit. She has a horror of blood. In all mental cases you can trace the trouble back to the moment when the disintegration commenced. With Lady Macbeth it is here. This is the start of all the things that haunt her later."

More feminine Ladies would have to force themselves, as Bernhardt did, to grasp the knives. Morris made the act a visual demonstration of will power over reluctant womanliness, of unnatural energy suppressing timidity. Marlowe, even as she scolded Macbeth for infirmity of purpose, was moved, she said, not by the impatience of a savage woman, but only overmastering ambition for the man she loved. Terry, in the same mood, manifested a determination that, if less Terrible than a Siddons', was in its way as firm and fierce.

Despairing as she was to see her Macbeth so distraught, she did not blench at the bloody daggers, but set about resolutely to save the desperate situation. Her note: "What's to be done? You want shaking." To make sense of her concentration on dealing practically with Macbeth's anguish, she wrote, "Just all about here she realises it [the enormity of the deed] *less than ever* for it's time for prompt action." If this pragmatic attention to external danger missed the emotional power of other Ladies, it had the value of emphasizing the imminent threat of a disastrous discovery. E. R. Russell:

> [She] never missed the greatness, the thrill, the suspense, the dread of the action . . . her keen practical perception keeps hold solely of the one great exigency of concealing the crime and . . . the controlling of her husband's quivering self-betrayal.

Lady Macbeth's exit lines are curious. First,

> the sleeping, and the dead,
> Are but as pictures: 'tis the eye of childhood,
> That fears a painted devil. (67–69)

The speech, loaded with motifs of the play—sleep; death; child; evil; sight and deceptive, artificial appearance—is usually spoken in maternal scorn or encouragement to Macbeth, urging him to be a man, not a boy. Siddons expressed "utter contempt of the dead and of painted horrors. All was self-possession and quietude." But Lady Macbeth has herself recently looked on a sleeping figure, Duncan's, and has been stopped by it from carrying out an intention. The lines may be encouragement less to Macbeth than to herself— perhaps entirely to herself, as with Anderson. So Hackett's Lady: forcing a laugh to bolster herself, quickly kissing Macbeth to comfort him,* or Cushman, faltering at Duncan's door to whisper the words in soliloquy, as a way of quieting her own apprehension.

The final lines have provoked controversy:

> If he do . . . bleed,
> I'll gild the faces of the grooms withal,
> For it must seem their guilt. (69–71)

To achieve the pun, she makes blood—in her first literal acknowledgement of it—golden, as Macbeth will in the next scene: the visual image is of the red gilded by light. But what a strange speech. Is it a ghastly jest (Parrott)? Is she perhaps grinning by now, as Craig's promptbook suggested? Is this a callous gallows humor that perhaps motivated Siddons?

> —As stealing out she turns towards him stooping, and with the finger pointed to him with malignant energy says, "If he do bleed . . ."

*Hackett's note: "The overstimulated feminine mind . . . is trying to brace itself up for the occasion and must show, if possible, that it is her love for Macbeth."

Is she parading her superior "masculine" daring? Muir, believing that laughter was the last thing Shakespeare wanted here, suggests wisely:

> The grim pun is rather a sign of the immense effort of will needed by Lady Macbeth to visit the scene of the crime.

Something of this may have been in Terry's mind when she noted: "This should be to herself, I think."

The "immense effort of will" was particularly manifested by Modjeska as she drove herself up the staircase to the king's chamber. Counterforce waylaid Miss Huddart (Mrs. Warner, England, 1842):

> She moved hurriedly towards the chamber . . . but as she approached the entrance, as if suddenly controlled by some vision of the awful scene that awaited her there, she paused for an instant, and then passed slowly on. (Forster)

Mrs. Campbell ascended her stairs with a slow reluctance that the highly rational G. B. Shaw scolded her for:

> You should not have repeated the exit business by which Macbeth conveyed that he was going to see a ghost on every step of the stairs up to Duncan. You should have gone straight off like a woman of iron.

Reluctance to act, besides qualifying Lady Macbeth's character, contributes in one way to suspense for the *naive* spectator who may doubt that she will in fact bring herself to go—with all that would entail. The sense of time pressing: of Lady Macbeth aware of the urgency of quickly returning the criminal evidence, and of getting the criminals themselves away, intensifies any moments of delay. Conversely, determined, forthright action may also magnify the sense of time dangerously passing, and say something else about character. Ena Burrill (England, 1947) was admired for the precision with which she rolled up her sleeves to the elbow, started to take a dagger in each hand, realized that would doubly mark her with blood, instead took both blades in one hand, and then stole away, softly, gliding, fully capable of smearing the grooms. Terry's movements also proclaimed determination and danger: she dropped her mantle to free her hands to grasp the daggers (Her warning note to herself: "Cuffs"). Then, with the weapons in one hand, she crept up the stairs.

Other Ladies have moved even more quickly, flying to get the business done, as Langtry did. Thorndike "made a bold, almost jaunty exit." Reinhardt's Lady had said *Give Me the daggers* only after she first tried to take them from Macbeth's unconscious hands. She then spoke the words impatiently, as she loosened his stiff fingers; once the daggers were in her hands, she quickly hid them in her garments, looked round to make sure all was still, and flashed up the staircase, intent on escaping detection.

Macbeth is left alone, deep in the trough of his despair. Often he seems half-hypnotized, in a trance of horror, as Macready was. Kean, unseeing, "seemed blinded by the blood that he had shed," his biographer thought. Irving was "utterly unnerved"; Garrick's already paled complexion grew whiter still at every moment, Arthur Murphy noticed. Sothern, groaning in anguish, sat wringing his hands, then burying his face in them.

We who know the play know that Lady Macbeth will return to this defenseless man. The *naive* spectator does not know: wonders—What if she does not return? In time? Will someone else come, and find Macbeth, stunned and bloody? We have never been let to forget that the whispering murderers felt themselves ringed by those who might come upon them, proclaim them, revenge the king. Now, by Shakespeare's design, when Macbeth seems most helpless, his support gone, exposure indefensible, an intruder approaches.

Knock within.

The ominous sound, usually breaking the dead silence of Macbeth's introspection, startles him and the audience. As Stamm observes, to the characters' ears (and ours), straining so long for any threatening sound, the sudden sharp warning of intrusion—always a rousing stimulus—comes with a special jolt. To the Jacobean, Spargo suggested, an extra shock would have been communicated by the connotation of knocking to the collection of the plague dead. Masefield suggested a gentle knocking; but logically the beating at a sleeping castle's gate must be loud, and getting louder—until, given Macduff's impatience, it becomes almost unbearable. Aesthetically, the jolt needs to be visceral. Henry James, dissatisfied with "three or four vague, impersonal thumps" in a Salvini staging, suggested that the actor should have read De Quincey:

> There is nothing heart-shaking in those thumps. They should have rung out louder, have filled the whole silence of the night, have smitten the ear like the voice of doom.

The impatient world outside wants in. At once.

Almost the worst, for him, Macbeth is partly forced out of his raptness to consciousness. In the theatre his alarm is ultimate, physically and psychologically shattering. He hears the sound; and yet he cannot be certain that this is not another of his hallucinations. Forrest was panicked. Reinhardt's Macbeth, convulsed by a terrible fear, held his breath, listening, then tried to flee, but could not move.

Whence is that knocking? (73)

In Macbeth's head? His seated heart knocking at his ribs? Somewhere outside? He cannot locate himself in space or in time:—*How is't with me, when every noise appals me?* (74) (*Appals* could mean, as well as "terrifies," "pales"— literally what was happening to Garrick.) Matkowsky, startled by the first sound, reacted, at each knock, with a reflex rubbing at his hands, as if to wash them. Kean drew his hands out from under his scarf, where he had tried to hide them from himself. Some such action as this starts Macbeth's mind in a new direction. *What hands are here?* (75) The suggestion has been made (Torbarina) that Macbeth may be hallucinating again, seeing—as he saw the dagger—imagined hands: threatening? Swarming? It was so acted at Dubrovnik (1970). But conventionally Macbeth experiences the dapple of blood on his own fingers. If indeed these fingers are his. Or as if they are disconnected from him, as if he cannot—will not—recognize them, he has to ask: *What hands . . . ?* Reinhardt's Macbeth stared at them, turned them over, looked at them from all sides. Smochowski, betraying touches of unmistakable madness, spoke as if the hands really belonged to someone else. But at last Macbeth must own them: *Ha: they pluck out mine eyes* (75). Walker suggests an allusion to Matthew's "If thine eye cause thee to offend, pluck it out." There may be an echo; but the hands are the offenders here, they are what Macbeth can hardly bear to own. So Mantell, holding the hands up before him, "half-idiotically strikes them one against the other with outspread, nerveless fingers." So J. B. Booth, "with starting eyes and a knotted horror in his features," developed the business that some other Macbeths would adopt of "wiping one hand with the other *from* him, with intensest loathing." Sothern and Quadflieg—and some other Macbeths—stretched their hands as far from them as they could. Garrick

> was absolutely scared out of his senses; he looked like a ghastly spectacle, and his complexion grew whiter every moment, till at length, his conscience stung and pierced to the quick,

he spoke the "hand" line in "wild despair" (Murphy). One of McKellen's bloody hands moved to claw in fact at his eyes, as if it had a retributive life of its own; the other hand had to catch it, hold it back.

If the stage holds a well, or other water receptacle, Macbeth may try now to cleanse his offending hands. But literal washing cannot affect the metaphor forced on him by the feel of the blood. Again he relates his personal experience to the universe:

> Will all great Neptune's ocean wash this blood
> Clean from my hand? No: this my hand will rather
> The multitudinous seas incarnadine,
> Making the green one, red.* (76–79)

---

*On the last line, the Folio clearly puts the comma after *one*, indicating that the *green* of all the ocean will become red. On Murphy's advice, Garrick—and some later actors—following Pope, made it *the green, one red*—to suggest the entirety of the changed color. Presumably the antecedent *seas* could not be a *green one*. In Shakespeare it could. When actors use the Garrick alternative, the three words—*green, one, red*—are best spoken as pause-separated spondees, so that a weighted *one* supports a bridge to the final, strong *red*. With the Folio punctuation, the sentence—and the metaphor—come to climax, after the comma pause, with the full weight on the completing word, more insistent perhaps that the murderous hands would stain the whole world's water the color of blood. In either case Shakespeare again contrives a complex response from the deep well of common experience, particularly, here, of nature, water, magnitude, blood, guilt, cleansing.

The rhetoric of the first line is abruptly checked by the monosyllables of the second, beginning with the astringent *clean*. Then flows the third's spectacular, rolling thunder, which is spaced out in the fourth's deliberate accents, beginning with the trochee and ending with a near-spondee effect. The speech climaxes Macbeth's brief, solitary beat, consummating in one metaphor a totality of his physical and spiritual sense of the enormity of his crime. David observed the

> despairing, fumbling abhorrence with which Olivier sought to ward off the multitudinous seas of blood that seemed to be swirling about his very knees.

His tones were heard as

> greasy and slippery with an immense revulsion. (*Sunday Times*)

J. B. Booth's voicing was on the grand scale:

> He launched the mysterious power of his voice, like the sudden rising of a mighty wind from some unknown source, over those "multitudinous seas," and they swelled and congregated, dim and vast, before the eye of the mind. Then came the amazing word "incarnadine," each syllable ringing like the stroke of a sword (Gould).

Lady Macbeth comes upon Macbeth on his lonely shoal of time's ocean, momentarily helpless. He will learn to wade in blood; but for now, in the last open struggle with his conscience, function is so smothered that his Lady may find him on his knees, or even fallen on the ground. Rossi was so lost in remorseful thought that his Lady had to shake him, her hands about his shoulders. Marlowe, finding Sothern collapsed, distraught, had physically to lift him. Tree was frightened by Vanbrugh's sudden irruption, her bloody hands holding the daggers high above her head. Hackett's Lady would return before his speech was finished, and watch him. He turned to her for comfort, wanted an embrace; she avoided it.

Her excuse was her bloody fingers: *My hands are of your colour* (81). But a deeper motivation is the change in the Lady usually marked here. Her experience in the murder room—she has not only smeared the grooms but also gone once more to look at Duncan, and will remember, in her sleep, his bleeding—leaves deep scars, more perhaps than she may now allow herself to feel. Robson, overtly untroubled now, credited delayed shock.* Certainly some Ladies could return as if in personal triumph. Siddons, according to a reminiscence in the *Reader* (1864),

> came leisurely, almost carelessly, across the stage, and held up her bloody hands with something akin to a smile.

---

*"Because by the sleepwalking scene we know how she really felt." Was it the drink that made her bold that carried her through? Or did the necessary haste to hide the crime serve to dull her reactions and to reduce the shock?

She seemed as untroubled as if she had just wakened from sleep—except that she showed even more scorn for Macbeth:

> From the peculiar character of her lip she gave an expression of contempt more striking than any she had hitherto displayed (Boaden).

Siddons herself wrote of the steadiness with which she "returns to her accomplice with the fiend-like boast"

> My *hands* are of your colour: but I shame
> To wear a *heart* so white. (81–82)

The young Bremen Lady came running back breathlessly, holding out her bloody hands with naive pride, to show that she wanted to be her husband's accomplice. As she gave her triumphant speech, Heester's red hands, stretched toward Macbeth, were spread like claws. Robson, and some other Ladies, have signaled their satisfaction by clasping their own bloody hands with Macbeth's, visibly merging complicity. Robson took one of Macbeth's hands in hers; Merchant, who had returned hiding both stained hands behind her back, suddenly whipped them out and clasped them onto those of the startled Scofield. Viola Allen held her hands up deliberately before Macbeth's face, made him look at them when he would have turned away. In the sleepwalk this business would be repeated, as would various gestures by other Ladies in this beat.

For most Lady Macbeths, the experience with the daggers, more than any other, shocks them and foreshadows their breakdown. The compunctious visitings of nature they so feared now trouble them, at least shallowly, and sometimes deeply. Bernhardt returned pale and trembling; Ristori covered her shock with a "wild defiance" in her tone. Some Ladies return already trying to rub the blood from their hands: so Mirren, who would involuntarily repeat the gesture; so Reinhardt's Lady, conveying inner horror, a sense that she would never forget the feel; but seeing her Macbeth so beside himself, she forced calmness on herself, and tried to smile, and speak cheerfully.

Other Lady Macbeths suffered traumas that could not easily be disguised from Macbeth, or from themselves. Bethmann, so strong before the murder, came rushing back breathless, confused, broken, flung herself into a chair. A table was adjacent; she collapsed over it, and a spasmodically clenched fist beat against the table, knocking, knocking. The contrast from her previous formidable front was shocking and moving. After a long moment her mind regained control; she looked stealthily toward Macbeth, saw that in his raptness he was unaware of her break, pulled herself together, and forced herself to speak calmly. Anderson had been able to suppress the impulse to vomit when she first saw the bloody daggers, had steeled herself to take them back; she returned weaving unsteadily down the stairs; she leaned against a wall, retching with nausea, and trying, as Macbeth had done, to rid herself of her gory hands. The startling change in Wysocka's behavior was even more violent. Calmly she had gone into Duncan's chamber; when she came back, the "fumes of madness stirred in her," she moved as if drunkenly to Macbeth, and held out her bloody hands to him like a madwoman.

Caution about the blood only inhibits Ladies with firm control over themselves. The sensible G. B. Shaw scolded Campbell for her undisciplined gestures:

> You should not have forgotten that there was blood on your hand and on his, and that you dared not touch one another for fear of messing your clothes with gore.

But impulsive Ladies do not stop to think: so the Bremen actress, when Macbeth started hysterically to speak, covered his mouth with her hands— and when he turned, his face could be seen stained with blood. As the appearance of complete disregard of bloodiness evokes one emotional response, so does the appearance of meticulous concern. Leigh held the soiled daggers far in front of her. Terry, still very practical, was praised for a "curious, curdling touch of detail" when, returning to the mantle she had dropped, she lifted it with the tips of her fingers. Her note: "Get sleeves out of the way." Irving's note: "*He* lost . . . *she* firm." An observer admired her "air of fearlessness which stood out in bold relief against [Irving's] remorse and fear." Rigg, trying to avoid touching Hopkins with her bloody fingers, used her wrists to make contact with him. A German Macbeth and his Lady, at the point of touching, in a sudden spasm of fear, shot their arms out at full stretch to keep their hands apart.* Caution is involved, and implications of character; but beyond this is the explicit visual image of a step in the separation between the two. This distancing, which may be felt subtextually in less overt avoidances, and in masked emotional tones, may be one of the signals of the end of Lady Macbeth's supremacy. He is at his most helpless, she most dominant, and he needing her to be, but she will never dominate him again after this scene.

Knock.

The sudden, repeated knocking tests Lady Macbeth yet again. Unlike Macbeth, she is in full possession of her senses, locates the source of the sound at once: the *south entry*—outside the castle. The words are cool, but they may mask a growing inward alarm. Faucit was "in an agony of anxiety" lest Macbeth in his wild ravings should betray himself. Bernhardt's nerves, for a moment, seemed as completely unstrung as Macbeth's. For Dorothy Green, "a moment of terrible intensity, beautifully reflected in [her] sudden faltering

---

*Goethe's Lady was apparently not troubled by blood. Producing Schiller's *Macbeth*, Goethe ignored the translator's idea that Lady Macbeth should return with hands so blood-soaked— to make the V, i handwashing more plausible—that she had to "wring out" her hands. Goethe thought this indecent, Deetjen relates (see Germany).

of voice. The thing is done, and for one tragic moment the woman is divested of her power and mortal danger is written upon her."

But the Lady must control him still. Her gesture, now, to lead or guide him to their chamber, again may be reprised in her sleepwalk. So, too, the implication of her repetition of the superficiality of the blood on their hands:

> A little water clears us of this . . . deed. (85)*

Does she try to cleanse their hands now, in some watery bowl, as in the Polanski film? Both feel a need to be purged of pollution quickly; but Lady Macbeth, keenly aware of their perilous situation, urgently wants them away. Given the tension between the two impulses, any effort to get rid of the blood is hasty, makeshift. Lady Macbeth can quickly dip her hands in convenient water, as in *Throne of Blood*, and try to force in Macbeth's hands—in his drugged state, he can hardly move on his own. Evelyn Gibbs remembered how Williamson stared at his hands held before him, half-fascinated, half-repelled; and Mirren, with a napkin of purest white, tried to wipe off the blood. She was not able to clean either her own hands or Macbeth's; they left the stage still bloodstained.

Macbeth is not conscious enough to help; his constancy—his wholeness, his single state—has deserted him, mind and body disconnected. The Lady's middle lines, interrupted by the next *knock*, are short, abrupt. Again, she urges disguise: they must play an innocent part—

> Get on your nightgown, lest occasion call us,
> And show us to be watchers: (89–90)

And, as he stands helpless,

> be not lost
> So poorly in your thoughts. (90–91)

His speech does not answer; he is still talking to himself, wishing again that he could disconnect his self from his doing:

> To know my deed,   *Knock*
> 'Twere best not know myself. (92–93)

---

*The dubious Forman, in his supposed description of the Globe performance: "And when Macbeth had murdered the king, the blood on his hands could not be washed off by any means, nor from his wife's hands, which handled the bloody daggers in hiding them, by which means they became both much amazed and affronted." This description, like others of Forman's, does not begin to fit Shakespeare's play. At best it could possibly relate metaphorically to Lady Macbeth's obsession in sleep, but hardly to Macbeth. Now put this Forman "discovery" by Collier with another "discovery" by the same distinguished fraud, the elegy to Burbage, cited earlier. Two lines carry an echo of the Forman "eyewitness" report:

> Tyrant Macbeth, with unwash'd bloody hand,
> We vainly now may hope to understand.

As with the Forman piece, if this lavatory image is supposed to be literal, it is wrong; if both are metaphor, they can be mainly a tribute to the repetitive inventive fancy of Collier himself.

His lines here are short, as fragmented as his thoughts, the brief pause punctuated by the knocking. Scofield, with his slow return to time passing, let the lines come out in their pieces. They build to the desperate wish that the done might be undone, hammered out in words almost all strongly accented:

> Wake Duncan with thy knocking:
> I would thou could'st. (94–95)

Once more Lady Macbeth must make a gesture likely to be echoed later as she moves to get Macbeth out and to their bedchamber. He may go of his own accord, or willingly allow himself to be guided. Hackett's wife, greatly solicitous, coaxed out her Macbeth, like a child. Gielgud allowed himself to be led. Vilar, too, went out with his lady, heavily:

> He understands that he is a prisoner of the murder. Weighed down with his burden, his arm around his wife's shoulder, slowly, sadly, he is drawn with her into the night, in the solitude of their crime (*Lettres Française*).

Almost mechanically Salvini, terror still full on his face, started staggering up the stairs to his chamber. Mantell stole out, with

> the crouching form and the feline-like tread of the self-debased murderer.

Olivier climbed his stairs in a kind of appalled slow motion, bent double, as if burdened by the enormity of his act.

Other Macbeths were still too rapt to move. Quadflieg's Lady, assuming he would follow her, started out, realized he was still standing fixed, tried with words and gestures to start him, and could not. Such Macbeths needed physical prompting, to be pushed or dragged. Tree had to be pulled away, by Vanbrugh's bloody handclasp, his eyes no longer on his hands but now, to the last moment, riveted to Duncan's door. Irving, too, kept his gaze there, though he had flung himself in his wife's arms; urged off by Terry (her note: "Push him—Pull him off stage") with "feverish energy," he went, reckless and despairing, the last sight of him a curious backward flourish of his right arm.* Booth was at last sensible to the alarm of the final knocking, but was unable to move from the spot; his Lady, behind him, put her hands on his shoulders and forced him out.

Booth groaned his last line; Forrest his, with "lacerating distress." Macready was wakened by the intensified knocking "from his trance of horror to a more mingled and wildering agitation of remorse and terror." He sobbed out the last words: Marston remembered the "terrible agony of his cry—Wake Duncan . . . —as with his face averted from his wife, and his arms outstretched, as it were, to the irrecoverable past, she dragged him from the place." Charles Kean shouted the last line as if he really wanted Duncan wakened: he went then at his wife's prodding, "sorrowfully, she regarding him as though pitying

---

*In 1875 his Lady, Kate Bateman, had emphasized urgency, hurrying him frantically toward their chamber.

his suffering." Sothern, far gone in physical collapse, had to be half-raised by Marlowe, and she supported him off. The stalwart Cushman almost lifted her broken Macbeth from the stage. Dench, pushing her paralyzed Macbeth, was careful not to mark him with her bloody hands: holding them stretched out to the sides, as far from her as she could, she nudged his body with hers, and so shunted him out.

The effect on Lady Macbeth of the night, of the murder, of Macbeth's condition, has been suggested: when she must move him off, and is the last to be seen, her own condition is magnified. Siddons manfully saw to it that final attention was focused on her as she maneuvered her feckless Macbeth off—indeed practically pushed him. Bell saw this:

> Contempt. Kemble plays well here; stands motionless; his bloody hands near his face; his eye fixed; agony in his brow; quite rooted to the spot. She at first directs him with an assured and confident air. Then alarm steals on her, increasing to agony lest his reason be quite gone and discovery be inevitable. Strikes him on the shoulder, pulls him from his fixed posture, forces him away, he talking as he goes.

Siddons herself felt this:

> All that now occupies her mind is urging him to wash his hands and put on his nightgown . . . In a deplorable depravation of all rational knowledge, and lost to every recollection except that of his enormous guilt, she hurries him away.

"His enormous guilt." None of hers. Part of this Terrible Woman's design here is her own "apathetic" separation from compunctious visitings. Other Ladies, we have seen, were shaken by early incidents in the scene; and some almost broken by later ones. On some, deep shock, and the foreshadowing of disintegration, is only felt now. So Faucit's "sudden access of terror" at the moment of escape:

> depicted by her nervous clinging to the husband whom a moment before she had upbraided for lack of resolution.

Hackett's Lady followed her mothered Macbeth out, nearly collapsing from fright and strain. Hackett's note for *her:* "Best not know myself." With Modjeska,

> the break comes after the deed is done, forced by the distracted ravings of Macbeth. As they go off together . . . we see the first signs in Lady Macbeth's face of the horror of mind and the disease of the nervous system which bring her death.

We see them go out, triumphant—and almost shattered. He barely conscious; she marked psychically, if not physically, by that sight, touch, smell of blood. The knocking continues: Will they be able to summon strength to resist discovery? the *naive* spectator wonders. With some ambivalence: partly wanting them, in their suffering, to be undetected, these two by now known so intimately—especially the man, whose last cry, *Wake Duncan* . . . is, in Wayne Booth's words, "the wish of a 'good' man who, though he has become a 'bad' man, still thinks and feels as a good man should." Also partly wanting them punished, these murderers. Our own feelings equivocate.

Knock. Knock. Knock.

Act II, Scene iii

Enter a Porter. Knocking within.

The man shambling across the stage is going to open the great castle door, sometimes apparent at the far end of the great courtyard—in the Globe, perhaps at one of the wing entrances—but he must move slowly to do it. As Capell long ago recognized, Macbeth must have time to change and wash his hands. In the long, proper centuries when the Porter's rowdy interlude was cut,* even when new lines were interpolated (as by Garrick), to delay a respectable servant's opening of the doors, Macbeth offstage was rushed, and would throw on a dressing gown that sometimes betrayed glimpses, underneath, of his armor or other customary garment. The Porter interlude serves importantly, also, to stretch the felt time between the preceding murder scene and what is to come by mocking the actual clock-time with fairest show; but of this more later.

Shakespeare makes a blessing of the necessity of hiatus: using the sound of knocking for a bridge, he begins to bring some faint light into the dark castle, to break for a moment the terrible grip of the murder scene. The knocking signals the awakening of the outer world, as De Quincey sensed; but the outside is allowed in only by a marvelously contrived intermediacy: this sleepy, drunken Porter. At once visually, and in his succeeding language and action, he exploits central motifs in the play. Coleridge certainly nodded when he surmised that another hand than Shakespeare's had written most of these opening moments: they are sterling.

The Porter's character easily authenticates his delay in opening his doors. He has taken full advantage of the great celebration the night before. Like

---

*The restoration, well on into the nineteenth century, of the acted text met with a mixed response. Coleman praised Salvini: "The appearance of this semi-drunken and drivelling idiot, at this supreme moment, is a safety valve for the pent-up hysteria of the audience." But the *Sunday Times* scolded Bernhardt for her inclusion of the scene: "A great mistake." As late as 1927 a producer was applauded for "wisely omitting the less elevated passages of the text." Schiller, as noted, replaced the Porter with an innocent dawnsong.

the king, he has been in unusual pleasure. Granville-Barker takes some pains to rescue the Porter from candidacy in an "inebriates home"—but this door-keeper has certainly drunk his fill. He sometimes hiccups or belches when he speaks. He stumbles on, nursing his hangover, perhaps trying even now to cure it with more of what gave it to him. His appearance, and his various *lazzi*, as he goes through the stage business that fills out his lines, assign him to the great company of Shakespeare's tragic, comic, wise grotesques: Ham-let's gravedigger, Othello's clown, and even, a distant cousin, Lear's Fool. Often in Shakespearean tragedy, Mack has observed, we encounter such a figure from everyday life, seeming at spiritual cross-purposes with the thrust of the play. Then, rocked in the essential dialectic of the tragic experience, we are returned to high tragedy. The Porter bridges us from one moment of tragedy to another, never letting us escape the implications of a murderous world he inhabits, yet dressing them in the rough, humorous language and action of inspired earthy foolery. The actor who played the part for Shake-speare may not have said more than was set down for him—though part of that might have been at his suggestion; he almost certainly "played" more than the Folio sets down, as his comic physical invention thrived; and so have succeeding Porters, finding their own amusing ways—I synthesize some— to delay opening the castle.

Not that the Porter is merely comic. He is a kind of live image of the Dionysian in man, of the naked id, that seethes beneath the masks of the play. In his sensuality he is as open and unabashed as the Sisters. He frankly voices the linkage of the erotic with death that is elsewhere more implicit. He parades none of the courtly manners—the courtly masking—with which the noble thanes disguise their primitive impulses to violence. And as he is himself a man of no false garments, so the types of mankind he chooses to satirize are stripped by him with a grim humor. His laughter can relieve some of his audience's tensions without releasing them. Thus Quiller-Couch: "laughter in which surcharged hysteria breaks and expends itself." Hall, directing, wanted the scene bitter, angry, sardonic; the laughter was to be colored with savagery. His Porter, accordingly, was an ugly, hairy, yellow-ish man, with a knowing sneer for both his real and imaginary worlds, that spread out to include the audience. But, however edged, the Porter's style is low comedy, as Kittredge observed, and he will for a while evoke laughter that is full-throated.

His very appearance is a kind of joke: his below-stairs dress—or undress; his earthiness—he is of the earth, as the Sisters are of the air; his functional, sometimes coarse, movement. He has been played as an old, old retainer; as a sinister, toad-like cripple; as a pure Clown figure; as a kind of comic devil who rises from the trap; but he serves best as a "common man," enclosing a choral voice on the follies of mankind in a dramatic identity too distinctive to be quite Anyman's.

His jesting does not stand by itself; it accompanies his fuddled attempts to get to that door, and open it. The action line must not suffer: a murder has been committed, and may momentarily be exposed. So David praised a Stratford Porter, moving

> with all the time a backward glance for the master and mistress whose stage he was conscious of usurping—an impression re-inforced by the guilty speed with which he made himself scarce on Macbeth's re-entry.

The Porter must not isolate himself—or us—from the sense of that urgent knocking, increasing in intensity to thunder, of visitors determined to get in, quickly. The Porter gets to the door as fast as he comfortably can, given his resentment at being wakened, his hangover, his native humor. One special comic gift involves his developing obstacles that rise up in his way and take him off when he is ready to set on. He may take some pleasure in keeping people waiting while he talks—a mark, *The Era* observed (1898), of the typical Civil Service official.

He must get onto the stage first of all. Craig had him rolling out in his sack bed. From such an obstacle he has to struggle; he can comment on the knocking as he does so. Or he stumbles out, half-blind with sleep and drink, half-dressed, and must throw his clothes on. He tries to move while arranging a kilt, or pulling up his trousers—an immemorial comic action. He may never quite get them right: in the Rigg–Hopkins staging the pants actually fell down at one point—a gag that probably goes back to the time trousers were invented. It is cold, very cold, and the shivering Porter's trouble may be with his coat—sleeves can be intransigent. So too, boots. He may be interrupted by the knocking as he tries to dress, and have to begin all over again.

Then he has to orient himself. He staggers, groping in the dark. If a fire burns in the courtyard, as with Tree, he must try to kick it up, warm himself. He will need a lantern. He must find it; perhaps even light it, if it is not hanging lit. He may be too drunk to find at once the wall where the door is, and feel for it.

Against the wall, his back to us, he may pause to urinate. This seems a universal device for delay: it has been used by Porters in Japan, in Czechoslovakia, in the Polanski film.

After the lantern, he may have to find a key. This is likely to be a large key, and may elude his search for a good part of a speech, until he finds it—perhaps tied around his neck or waist. Having found the key, he must still locate the door. If instead of a keyed door he must turn a winch to lift a gate, he can expend a good deal of his imaginary dialogue finding the mechanism, fitting the handle, and pulling at it. Meanwhile, the knocking may hurt his hungover head, even seem to sound inside it; he may put his hands over his ears, wincing at each rap; may shush the sound.

These are typical large movements. They help provide a spine for his progress to the door, but must never interfere with his dialogue, which comes when his efforts to advance, or get the door open, are interrupted by the knocking. His first lines, usually from across the stage as he starts his sleepy, yawning, long journey to the door, tell his grumbling, ironic mood.

> Here's a knocking indeed: if a man
> were Porter of Hell-gate, he should
> have old turning the key— (4–6)

so many come in.

There is a blank verse meter to much of what he says, as Maginn noted; and the rhythm lends weight to his sustained hell-metaphor. Glynne Wickham makes a case for an echo, here, of the medieval religious drama of the harrowing of hell, where the attended hell-castle's door collapsed at Christ's knocking. Jacobeans conversant enough with the old forms might have heard such an echo. But Wickham wisely disavows an attempt to provide a direct parallel. Again, the sharp, good-bad differentiation of the Moralities and Mysteries dissolves in Shakespeare's compassionate exploration of complex human behavior. Any attempt to find a simple allegorical interpretation of the "devil-porter" scene runs up against the remarkable characterization of the Porter as person, the presence of Duncan in the castle, the nature of those knocking at the door, the result of their entrance.

Shakespeare excels at blur and irony. The Porter is a player, like his betters; talks to imaginary figures, like his betters; fits his behavior to a cosmic frame, like his betters. Murder has been committed in a castle where "Heaven's breath smells wooingly." The place where gentle birds procreate is a scene of violent death. God will be called upon, and keep silence. They who knock at the door have their own faults—the two live thanes, and the Porter's imaginary visitors. It is a complex world.

The Porter's hell-guests belong to the times. The farmer's suicide from producing too much may reflect the steep drop in English prices in 1605—1606. Typical topical pornographic allusions have been scented in all the Porter says, beginning with "sweat" in *you'll sweat for't.* Harcourt relates this to the sweat tub therapy for venereal disease; if so, *napkins* (handkerchiefs) in a special sense were perhaps associated with the treatment. The farmer's fate relates to the action of the play, as well as to the times. He had to die at a time when he was most successful in his growing, because the time was wrong. This is a paradoxical echo of the fertility motif, and extends farther: it may be a mirroring of a greater man, suffering from untimely success. Come to hell *in time.* The Porter may parody pity for the farmer—and other guests: "tsk, tsk."

Porters have had various ways of ushering their candidates into hell. One mock-bows them in, one beckons with a finger, another makes a grand, courtly, Osric-type sweep; another kicks their backsides as they are imagined entering, another prods with a handy pitchfork, real or mimed. One Porter spoke to little bugs he held up after discovering them on the door, as he tried to fit his key to the lock. He would get rid of one, only to find another, before he could get the door open. Speaking of the devils, the Porter has made the horn sign—or excused himself for invoking their names. (He may have trouble remembering *Beelzebub*, as he can't think of *th'other devil's name*). Bergman's 1944 Porter manipulated a small puppet to represent his fantasies.

The Porter hardly gets one "guest" in when the knocking, always louder, more insistent, nudges him toward opening the door—and sometimes toward fortifying himself again from a bottle. He mimics the knock sound, often with a kind of resentful good humor; this is part of the play he is acting. Bernard Dukore remembers one who played with the word itself: "ka-nock, ka-nock."

Now the Equivocator is passed in (and the Porter may, by juggling hands as if balancing weights, image the play's ticklish equilibriums):

> that could swear in both the scales against either scale, who committed treason enough for God's sake, yet could not equivocate to heaven: oh come in, Equivocator. (11–14)

The implication for the character of Macbeth and for the action of the play needs no explication. The play begins and ends with *treason:* "bad" treason, and good. For the Jacobeans, this Equivocator was also, apparently a Jesuitical figure who could evade, in the name of his religion, a truthful answer to a political question. Danks argues that resentment was directed against Equivocators generally (he cites the horrible mutilation and execution of the first Jesuit martyr in England); as Muir and others have observed from the evidence, Shakespeare seems to have meant specifically the Father Garnet who was involved in the "Gunpowder Plot" to blow up parliament and the king. Garnet was said to be called "Farmer," which would link him to his predecessor in the Porter's hell. Garnet's major defense for concealing information through evasion was that he had learned it in confession. He died bravely: his leaving of life became him.* The concept of equivocation itself, Huntley's study indicates, had surfaced far in the past. He cites a curious incident involving St. Francis. Asked where a poor man suspected of robbery had gone, Francis put his hands in his long sleeves, pointed with a concealed finger in one direction, but looked in another, and said, "He went that way." A Catholic in England could equivocate in God's name, by telling some, but not all, of the truth: asked if he worshipped according to his faith, he might exonerate himself by saying, "No, I did not attend Mass yesterday"—but add innocently to himself, "at St. Paul's."

Such deliberate misleading is only one of the kinds of equivocation in *Macbeth*. Macbeth and Lady Macbeth will say and act one thing when they

---

*Hotson observes that Shakespeare knew well some of the conspirators, many of whom were native to his countryside; he would be indirectly connected to them by his daughter Judith's marriage. In this scene he shows no sympathy with treason: but *Macbeth* itself is about a king's assassin who earns some sympathy.

mean another; so will others: thus Lenox to the Lord in III, vi and Malcolm to Macduff in IV, i. The Sisters, as we have seen, practice equivocation more ambiguously: they mean more than they say to Macbeth, but we must wonder if it is they, or Hecate, or their masters, or life itself, or any of its mysterious forces, finally responsible for paltering with him in a double sense. Shakespeare, the creator of all this uncertainty, is himself the Great Equivocator, punning, doubling images and ideas, shifting perspectives on characters and motifs, pointing action in a direction it does not go. Aptly, the playwright uses only in *Macbeth* the words *equivocate*, *equivocates*, and *equivocator*; the play shares with *Hamlet* alone *equivocation*.

The Porter scene reflects—almost, with this second hell-bound figure, stipulates—the motif of equivocation weaving through the play: the doubling of voices, attitudes, images in opposition, or—in Stirling's words—in contradiction. This style and substance validates the scene as Shakespeare's, Muir observes:

> It possesses the antithetical characteristics of the verse, transposed for semi-comic purposes. The whole scene is linked so closely with the rest of the play, in content as well as style. . . . The antithetical style is a powerful means of suggesting the paradox and enigma of the nature of man.*

The Porter's next guest is a robber—and possibly here, too, Macbeth the throne-thief is faintly paralleled.

> Faith here's an English Tailor come hither,
> for stealing out of a French hose. (15–16)

This seems to be a joke against the English for the English to laugh at, like the Gravedigger's joke about a mad Hamlet not being noticed in a land full of English madmen. The joke might be that an Englishman could be so inept as to be caught in hose as large as one French variety notoriously roomy; or so inept as to try to steal any material from the other, notoriously skimpy variety. Sexual connotations may enrich the image. *Stealing* may pun on "staling." Hulme suggests that for Shakespeare's contemporaries *tailor* could carry the sense of "penis" or "vagina." If the former, then the large-mouthed French hose might logically represent the latter; with the implication that the tailor was carried off by the "French disease." This meaning might be confirmed by the Porter's gesture and his final:

> Come in tailor, here you may roast your goose. (17)

*Duthie finds a moral principle in the degree of the play's equivocation: that the notion that any one thing could be two different things at once is essentially abnormal, evil; good involves the normal perception of the differences. This Manichean dichotomy between good and evil seems too sharp for Shakespeare, who deals in the mixtures, in the paradox and enigma of human behavior: it opposes too the concept in physics observed by Rabkin, noted above, of complementarity: incompatible objects do coexist. Paradox is built into reality.

The overt reference is to the tailor's gooseneck iron; but the goose (or goose-neck) easily functions also as a phallic symbol. This tailor's path, then, would surely be the most primrose of the three ways toward the *everlasting bonfire* ("bonfire?")

The Porter dissolves his illusion of hell. The bonfire is as imaginary as the guests, the place is too cold; and he has reached the door, turned the key, slid the bolt, winched the gate, whatever—and the knocking is now peremp-tory. *Anon, anon.* He had thought to let in some of all professions, he says—often pausing to look significantly at the audience. He does, at last, open to the two thanes—with a gesture, overt or behind their backs, that repeats his ushering of his imaginary guests. But in this real world he remembers to say, with open palm or proffered cap:

I pray you remember the Porter. (22)

Hall's sardonic devil-porter let his gaze swing to include the audience, and the line was said more meaningfully to the house than to the other actors. All, all were guests in his hell.

The great door, opening, lets in the two men, and more. The sodden atmosphere emanating from the Porter, following on the nightmare climate of the murder scene, has thickened and soiled the air. It freshens with the entrance of two brisk thanes, the sense of the outside world they bring with them, and perhaps a breeze—the Porter's lantern has been seen blown out in modern productions, and may have been at the Globe. Or there the signs of dawn could have been understood when the complaint was made of the Porter's late lying, and he put his torch out; controlled lighting in later pro-ductions specifies it.

The opening of doors on a closed, secret place, and the letting in of light and fresh men, impart a symbolic as well as realistic effect. New life has the chance to enter—as, in other circumstances, given silence and outer darkness, death may be associated with an open portal. A psychologist suggests that the knocking to enter symbolizes the awakening of the self-preserving con-scious part of the mind to relief from the murderous demands of the id. The passing of the night itself brings an archetypal relief.

Shakespeare, daring to charge his Porter with lying late, again whirls us through time by his compressive art. Various kinds of time serve him. First is measured time, with its varieties: the given time of night and day of the play, and the references to the actual clock time taken by the play's incidents. Sometimes opposed to this is the time *felt* as passing by the spectator. Our sense of clock time is generally suspended with our disbelief, as long as it is not challenged by absurdity. Shakespeare risks the limits: Banquo has said goodnight to Macbeth about midnight, Macbeth goes swiftly to murder Duncan, Lady Macbeth comes urgently to extricate him from the sequel, and at once a knocking is heard heralding, in performance time, the morn. In the murder and post-murder scenes the *felt* passage of time is unmeasured: we experience an agony that stretches out toward doom. This experience dissolves into the Porter's scene; and, as suggested above, one important function of that scene is to hoodwink the time, to cushion our return to the intrusion—in performance time hours later—of the outside world.

Another kind of time we are exposed to is experienced as abstract, measureless: it is the now, or, alternatively, it is eternity—the two concepts of time that had to be considered in Macbeth's I, vii soliloquy. As we are absorbed in the sequence of nows, on momentary banks and shoals of time, we can be transported from one to the other without questioning—as long as the playwright's art strings them into a linear flow that sustains illusion. Often the now in *Macbeth* takes place in the shadow of eternity; the Porter, as immediate as earth, yet involves us in awareness of the life beyond life, in his comic way; as Macbeth has involved us in the universe of time and space in his sterner introspections—those contextual moments when action is temporarily subordinated to an exploration of the human condition.

Macduff eases us into the stress of performance time with his anger for being kept waiting, for the castle's sleeping so late. The theatre has sometimes used Macduff earlier in the play, to carry the news from the king to Macbeth; but Shakespeare meant carefully to save his speaking until now. Until now no other thane except Banquo was designed to carry enough weight to rival Macbeth. Now that Banquo's ambiguous relation with Macbeth is coming to climax, a new figure enters to counterpoise the protagonist. In I, vi we saw him only as an anonymous courtier; now we must get to know him:* by his appearance a prominent thane, visibly a man who can fight well, not one of the politicians. But he belongs to the company of thanes concerned with degree, and we will see him insist on his privileges. A sense of his rivalry with Macbeth has been suggested as early as his entrance. In Hackett's staging a sulky Macduff let his anger at the Porter spill from a deeper resentment to Macbeth, whom he greeted without pleasure. Malcolm will say that Macduff loved Macbeth well; if Macduff indicates something of this now, the more dramatic will be his later recoil. He is called *good*; but he lacks the natural touch, his wife will say; he will grieve for his family's unhappy fate—but he will have left them to that fate. Shakespeare does not spare him complexity.

Lenox has appeared before, but his identity has been absorbed in that of the non-warrior group of thane-aspirants to higher degree. Now that he is brought to our attention, we may remember that a Lenox was King James'

---

*Shakespeare may be faulted here for a failure to identify: the first reference to the name of the important Macduff does not come for more than 80 lines; and then Banquo calls him only "Dear Duff." He is not fully named until the next scene. Lenox' name, as noted, is *never* used in the dialogue. This may not be a mistake: the Globe actors may have ad-libbed the names, as they, again, perhaps did the disguised Kent's (Caius) in *Lear*.

paternal grandfather; James' own first young favorite in the succession of
his dear young men, Esme Stuart, was quickly elevated by him to be Duke
of Lenox. Will this character be a compliment to James? This Lenox is a very
young man—a fact not generally recognized—and a rumormonger, as Nicoll
observes. He is always at the side of the safe, or rising, star; he runs with the
politicians: a man, Walker notes, of enlightened self-interest.

The impatient Macduff, delayed in his privileged opportunity to *call timely*
on his king, is likely to be furiously angry with the drunken servant responsible. In the theatre, this passionate man has seized the Porter, twisted his
arm backwards, pulled his head back by the hair, thrown him down. He
snaps out the first line as he looks beyond to the castle. Where is Macbeth?
Finding his host is his first objective as the scene begins; it is the force that
carries through the next jesting dialogue. Macduff's willingness to pause for
even so much speech may be partly explained by his need, and Lenox', to
shed the traces on their garments of the night's fearful storm, and its muddy
aftermath. The Porter would appease Macduff: help him off with his wet
coat, entertain him with the kind of "allowed" foolery of Shakespeare's
clowns. But it is not all fool. His *carousing till the second cock:* appropriately
ends with the colon; he takes advantage of Macduff's silence to hurry on and
provoke him with a puzzle:

> And drink, sir, is a great provoker of three things. (27)

He may try to count them on his fingers, to show—and have trouble finding
three. Macduff, looking around impatiently, perhaps scraping mud off a
boot, or letting the Porter do it, takes the bait, gives the Porter the opportunity for one of those virtuoso comic bits Shakespeare's clowns were blessed
with:

> Marry, sir, Nose painting, sleep, and urine. (30)

The Porter manages, when he can, to make his pronunciation comic: thus
Hall's spoke the last word "you-rhyne." Speaking it prompted another door-
man to suit action to it: he dashed off to relieve himself, and could be heard
speaking his next few lines off.

The Porter goes on to the meaningful allusion mentioned in the last chapter: the impulse to act baffled, suffering another form of equivocation. Hawkes
scents a kind of echo of Lady Macbeth's lecture to Macbeth on manliness in
I, vii (*Was the hope drunk,/ Wherein you dressed yourself? Hath it slept since?/ And
wakes it now to look so green, and pale . . . ?*):

> Lechery, sir, it provokes, and unprovokes: it provokes the desire, but it takes
> away the performance. (31–32)

The visual conceit that usually accompanies the speech is the miming of an
erection that fails: the Porter's large key is levered up from his waist, then

sadly falls; or some other instrument ups and downs; or his arm jerks up from the elbow, and subsides. The gesture may be repeated, diminuendo:

> Therefore much drink may be said to be an equivocator with lechery: it makes him, and it mars him; it sets him on, and it takes him off; it persuades him, and disheartens him; makes him stand to, and not stand to: in conclusion, equivocates him in a sleep, and giving him the lie, leaves him. (32–38)

Lie again multiplies meanings: seduce him, deceive him, accuse him as false, throw him down (as in wrestling)—all that would sap him of his power—and all echoes of elements in Macbeth's career.

Macduff, amused, angered, disgusted, impatient to get on, would dismiss with the same wordplay the Porter's evident unsteadiness in his hangover:

> I believe, drink gave thee the lie last night. (39)

. . . *i' the very throat on me* is the reply—a fine opportunity for a belch. The Porter manages one more retort, playing on the wrestling image: *though he took up my legs sometime* (42)—suggesting a wrestling throw, with the doubled implication of urinating—*yet I made a shift to cast him* (42–43)—again the wrestling image, again with connotations of vomiting or urinating. The Porter may lift a leg in demonstration, whereupon drink may give him the lie again, and he falls flat.

The impatient Macduff, pressing his duty—he may take the Porter by the shoulder and shake him, or nudge a recumbent one, perhaps already fallen in stuporous sleep, with a toe—asks *Is thy master stirring?* (45). But the Folio has Macbeth enter before this—suggesting a masked entrance, a pause to watch the newcomers and gather strength to confront them. May Lady Macbeth be glimpsed behind him? This is a moment the *naive* spectator has waited for longer than Macduff. How will Macbeth look? Will he betray what has happened to him? Has he recovered self-possession? Will Macduff and Lenox notice anything when they see him—as now they do?

Macbeth must now take over the Porter's "player" role, pretending to be what he is not; equivocating; so no more words from the Porter, J. R. Brown observes:

> The clown disappears without a word; we might almost say that he "vanishes," like the witches, when his many tasks are complete.

He usually scuttles away, sometimes at a sign from Macbeth, grumbling to himself perhaps (Reinhardt). Sometimes he lurks in the background—a visual link with hell, Mullin suggests—and plays a part in the mass scene that follows.

Macbeth begins his playing from the moment he appears, usually before he comes up to the thanes. He is likely to be in a simple nightgown, as Scofield was; though Olivier appeared in a black, monkish gown, with a rope girdle, suggesting a dark, brooding Judas. He stole looks at his hands. Booth came hurrying in, half-dressed, almost at a run—justifying Macduff's observant (and cynical?) *Our knocking has awak'd him* (46). Reinhardt's Macbeth, on the other hand, came slowly, wrapping a cloak around his nightgown, conspicuously rubbing his eyes and yawning, giving himself time to face his visitors. Irving met his guests with studied courtesy, but with his bright red cloak draped over his sword arm—hiding the weapon he might need for defense. Kemble, Walter Scott reported, endeavored to conceal, by "strong exertion" the "rueful horror" of his looks. Charles Kean was able to speak calmly, if forcedly; Reineke, too, managed a constrained calmness; when, unconsciously, he rubbed at his hands, and this caught Macduff's glance, he tried to hide them in his clothes. Macduff's sense of rivalry may surface at once: in the Dunn staging, he looked at Macbeth, then away, then back, with the kind of scrutiny Banquo had practiced.

The greetings exchanged are clipped, abrupt—a staccato sequence. Is there any hint to the relationship of the three men that only Lenox greets Macbeth, that Macbeth in return greets both, Macduff at first neither speaking nor directly spoken to? Hackett felt a snub for Macbeth in Macduff's silence; and he emphasized "Good morrow *both*" to cover it. Macduff responded:

Is the King stirring? (49)

with a tinge of sarcasm on *the king;* but at a reaction from Macbeth, felt constrained to add the rest of the line, conceding the respectful *worthy thane.*

Macduff's question fiercely tests Macbeth's mask; the audience may perceive a layered response, as in Booth's start, quickly aborted, or in the intensity of the terse *Not yet.* Beyond the simple answer, is Macbeth playing for time? Reinhardt's Macbeth made a brief, resistant gesture, as if meaning to keep Macduff back from disturbing the king.

Macduff has a privilege and means to exercise it: the honor of attending on the king. Macbeth, under increasing pressure each step of the way, agrees to conduct Macduff. Their courtly dialogue echoes earlier language, often oxymoronic, associated with Duncan: Macduff speaks of the "joyful trouble" of hospitality to the king; Macbeth speaks of "labour we delight in" that—he uses a medical image that will itself be echoed later—"physics pain."

This conversation gives them time to walk up toward Duncan's door, Macbeth summoning more control, more masking, at every step. Now the ultimate moment of discovery waits. *This is the door* (57), Macbeth must say. As far as the two thanes can tell, this is normal courtesy; but the audience is sensitive, as with Scofield, to the rigidly controlled undertones of the voice, the suppression of dread. Forrest, standing behind the other two, would betray signs of extreme alarm; Salvini managed to say the words quietly and naturally, but contrived to convey an undercurrent of revulsion and terror. Does Macduff sense any of the subtextual stress, look at Macbeth again?

Charles Kean and Sothern, unwatched, shrank from Duncan's door. A Macbeth wishing to go first, to make the discovery himself, may be interdicted by his own reluctance (Irving's note: "Can't go in"); and in any case by Macduff's insistence on the privilege of degree:

> I'll make so bold to call, for 'tis *my*
> limited service. (58–59)

His special honor. Hackett's Macduff made this a taunt. Macduff moves ahead of Macbeth. May stop at the door to try a knock—the sound that recurs so meaningfully in the play. Waits through a silence. Or goes directly in.

Macbeth is left alone with the chatty Lenox, who is beguiling the time with talk, and perhaps, as in Gielgud's staging, still removing from his boots traces of the tempest he will describe. Each moment of waiting for Macduff's discovery turns the screw on Macbeth—and on us: when will the alarm sound? *When?* Macbeth may well, as Booth did, keep his eyes fixed on Duncan's door; or try to pull his gaze away, as Macready did, only to allow it to be drawn back when Lenox is not looking. Kemble specified that the door remain slightly open—inviting a glance, revealing nothing.

Lenox cannot leave Macbeth alone. Another test:

> Goes the king hence today? (60)

Macbeth is sometimes so rapt—"lost and vacant" (Irving)—that Lenox must repeat the question. Or Macbeth forces himself to reply, guardedly in unguarded tones: Reinhardt's feigned a yawn: *He does:* then, after the long pause of the colon, filling time, *he did appoint so* (61).

Lenox, with the babbling extravagance of youth—*my young remembrance cannot parallel/ A fellow to it* (73–74)—describes the excessive storm; then he reports the uncanny manifestations, and here Shakespeare emphasizes that they are not of the youngster's own witnessing, but second-hand, rumors: *as they say,*

> lamentings heard i'th'air
> Strange screams of death,
> And prophecying, with accents terrible,
> Of dire combustion, and confus'd events,
> New hatch'd to th' woeful time. (64–68)

And *some say*

> the earth was feverous,
> And did shake. (70–71)

During the long speech, Macbeth must somehow sustain his stability. Irving's thoughts were obviously far away, as he furtively turned terrified glances at Duncan's door. David reports that Rogers, who had remained at the foot of the staircase, looked up as if almost fainting in anticipation: he stood with one white hand before his eyes; the tension in his racked body hinted at the cruelty of his memory, his restless eyes seemed to be tracking phantoms. Phelps, struggling to appear composed, returned curt and absent answers to

Lenox, listened anxiously for the murder to be discovered, his eyes drifting toward Duncan's chamber. Olivier paced the stage uneasily, moving in fits and starts,

> his guilty hands folded in his long sleeves except when, with a gesture at once furtive and half-automatic, he withdrew them for a moment and hurriedly inspected them from front to back.

As Scofield stood, so unmoving, so evidently molten inside, his thumbs unconsciously rubbed on his fingers. In Carrick Craig's staging, Macbeth stood next to Duncan's red standard, outside the door, and unconsciously his hands tried to clean themselves on the royal cloth, until he came to himself, starting, and forced himself to pay attention to Lenox.

In Kemble's efforts to seem to be listening to Lenox, Scott saw a countenance that seemed "altered by the sense of internal horror":

> When Macbeth felt himself obliged to turn toward Lenox and reply, you saw him, like a man awaking from a fit of absence, endeavour to recollect at least the general tenor of what had been said, and it was some time ere he could bring out the general reply—
>   'Twas a rough night.

This is one of those dangerous Shakespearean lines that risk evoking awkward laughter from the audience. Macbeth must make conversation, and he speaks with a double voice, agreeing with Lenox about the outer storm, but at the same time revisiting his own more horrible tempest. The line comes out in an apparent enormity of understatement, and at a time of such tension verges on incongruity. The saying demands the most careful artistic control. Irving let it come out dully, mechanically, the pain masked in vacancy; Olivier rode hard on the *r* of *rough*, with a touch of Scots brogue; Macready spoke in a tone of affected unconcern under which were fear and misery; the subtextual feeling guarded the line.

The crime is discovered. Macduff re-enters—rushes out, reels out, hardly makes it to the door, almost paralyzed—to cry the horror of what he has seen. It is a triple hail—to the unspeakable:

> . . . horror, horror, horror. (76)*

Hackett suggested the first *horror* was for the murder he had just seen; the second for his suspicion of Macbeth; the third for the glimpse of a "world of horror." The shock must be felt almost too deeply to be spoken. A great roar, to awaken the castle, misses the effect on Macduff himself. The first, primary trauma is to him; he has been appalled to the same degree Macbeth was, though for different reasons; before he can tell others of the enormity, he must himself feel it like a man. He may come out stunned (Hall-Scofield); may have to lean against the door, overwhelmed with dread; need to work

*Will there be any echo later, in *Tomorrow, and tomorrow, and tomorrow?*

to find breath, and words; then, unable to speak, making wild gestures, wringing his hands, finally begin to stammer out his feelings (Reinhardt). He may whisper the words, breathe them quietly in the deathly hush; may gasp them out in a choked, long-drawn anguish; in his rage and horror scream himself hoarse (Ristori); may, in a state of shock, come all the way down the stairs, with a wild look, before he can speak. The deed is, as Macbeth and his Lady first found it, unnameable:

> Tongue nor heart cannot conceive, nor name thee. (77)

The measure of the controlled conventionality of Macbeth's response is that he says the same thing Lenox does: *What's the matter?* But his next response is his own. Macduff, as Jorgensen observes, begins to find words for the deed:

> Confusion now hath made his masterpiece:
> Most sacrilegious murder hath broke ope
> The Lord's anointed temple, and stolen thence
> The life o' th' building. (79–82)

Macduff speaks of disorder, the violation of what is sacred in royalty, and Lenox understands him well enough; but Macbeth's speech, while it answers to the general concern, on another level reacts to a danger to himself:

> What is't you say, the life? (83)

With Scofield, it was a terrible cry: heard by the thanes in its disguise of passionate innocence; heard by the audience for its acknowledgment of what was foreknown, but also for recognition that something unexpected of his own may have been lost too. Macbeth has shaken, even comforted, Macduff here to get him to speak. Macduff still cannot bring himself to name the king's murder, but continues with metaphor, urging the two thanes into Duncan's room, to see what he cannot say. He has caught hold of them, and pushed them, in his frenzy. Macbeth, to dramatize outraged innocence, will want to assert priority here, if he can force himself: so when Lenox started to push past Olivier, Olivier seized his arm, pulled him back, and went in first. But Macbeth, faced with the return to look upon what he has done, may once more be momentarily unable, whatever his conscious impulse: so, with Reinhardt, Lenox rushed on ahead, and then Macbeth followed, wildly.

Then Macduff comes to life. He moves, almost madly; flings himself to a place where he can shout or scream to wake the house, to ring the bell, to summon the castle to look upon what he has seen. He may stamp the floor, hammer on doors with his sword as he passes, beat shields hanging on the wall. Motifs of sleep and death, appearance and reality, nerve his speech, the meters changing and mixing with his passions:

> Banquo, and Donalbain: Malcolm awake,*
> Shake off this downy sleep, death's counterfeit,

*The lines, especially the first two, may appear to have an easy rhythm; but they must crack like shots, the names howled, the cries pounded out in a succession of harsh, heavy accents.

> And look on death it self: up, up, and see
> The great doom's image: Malcolm, Banquo,
> As from your graves rise up, and walk like sprites,
> To countenance this horror. Ring the bell. (90–95)

Like so many speeches at critical moments in the play, this one extends immediate experience to the wide human condition in an apocalyptic metaphor. The last three words of the speech may be a stage direction, as has been suggested; but are more likely Macduff's angry repetition to someone at the bell. He has himself run over to pull the bell rope, and push away a slower servant; in Tree's staging, Macbeth himself started a shrill alarm bell that was taken up by the castle's resonant, booming brass bell. The sound needs to be a massive tolling, trumpet-tongued against the deep damnation of Duncan's taking off.

The proper stage direction follows Macduff's speech:

Bell rings. Enter Lady.

The life of the castle pours into the courtyard as the bell rings—the sound coming on the heels of Macduff's speech, not interrupting it. The specified entrances of characters are few: Lady Macbeth first; then Banquo; Macbeth, Lenox, and Ross (who always manages to be around); Malcolm and Donalbain. The limitation of the stage to these seven, plus Macduff, would have the advantage of narrowing focus on the behavior of the protagonists; but it loses the opportunity for one of Shakespeare's grand spectacles. We may guess that at the Globe Shakespeare took for granted the kind of mass pageantry that, as a young playwright, he had had to stipulate: remember again that innocent *Titus Andronicus* direction, for an entrance of the named cast, plus "others, as many as can be." To toll the bell so furiously to summon only four sleepers would seem excessive. An Inverness full of servants, thanes, and ladies can be let loose to color a live but organized background for the figures in action. Later theatres have taken advantage of the moment to flood the stage with the sight and sound of "extras," all more or less obviously wakened from sleep—not dressed in manly readiness, but the thanes, at least, likely to be partly armed, or arming themselves.

So Charles Kean's terror-stricken castle:

> Crowds of half-dressed men, demented women and children, soldiers with unsheathed weapons, and retainers with torches, streamed on and filled the stage. . . . Wild tumult and commotion were everywhere.

Irving:

> A throng of men, fierce and wrathful, mutually questioning, wondering, threatening; the faces of terrified women, passing down from the corridor above; lights flashing and steel glistening.

Phelps:

> Nobles, knights, squires, pages and vassals armed with every species of ancient weapons picked up on the spur of the moment—here a halberd, there a battle-axe, now a pike, anon a blazing pine torch. . . . [a] thundering tramp-tramp that gathered along the galleries, in the lurid smoke and flame of the torches. . . . With drawn swords and without bonnets.

Becks' proper Victorian promptbook observes that many stagings brought the crowds on

> in partial undress, but always with dubious effect, especially on the part of the ladies;

and remembers that Garrick would not risk the appearance of half, or even disordered, dress. In twentieth-century productions, the disarray has included near nakedness. In *Macbeth*, where the clothes motif is so pervasive, the hasty inrush of alarmed men in *naked frailty*—not fully armed, pulling on clothes—must convey a sense not only of brave common concern, but also of innocence and vulnerability, particularly as they are contrasted with the calculated appearance of unpreparedness presented by Macbeth and his Lady.

The immediacy of Lady Macbeth's entry, after the direction *Bell rings*, suggests how closely she may be hovering in the background, waiting—for the bell to invite her? Since her last exit, the actress as actress has had to put on the shows of womanly unreadiness; the actress as Lady Macbeth has had to anticipate with dread her husband's ability to deal with the crisis of discovery. This must show in her face, as she searches the courtyard for Macbeth—and cannot find him. Beyond this is her own questionable capacity to sustain the image of innocence when she herself has been exposed to terrible trauma.

This was no problem, as we noted, for Ladies up through the later nineteenth century. They did not appear at all. As noted, the Terrible Woman of the Pritchard–Siddons pattern could not, in the imagination of audiences, genuinely faint: one eighteenth-century actress was hooted out when she tried it; even Pritchard, Garrick had to decide, couldn't carry it off. As noted, only her predecessor, Mrs. Porter, Macklin thought, might have effected "the hypocrisy of such a scene."

Actress-vanity also apparently motivated the deletion, we learn from a lament from *The St. James Chronicle:*

> The Piece is maimed . . . a Woman of her personal Courage and deep Dissimulation would [not] fail to summon both these qualities in Aid of her Husband's uncertain Resolution. . . . [One] capital Actress is unwilling to come in only to utter a few Lines, and counterfeit a Swoon . . . so consequential a Being does not chuse to abridge the Time of her Dressing to appear as a Queen.

All honor to the non-English-speaking actresses who were among the first to appear in the scene—and who did not play it only for hypocrisy. Ristori brought it back as early as 1857; the *Athenaeum* thought her greatest effect

> her feigned agony at the shame fallen on the house . . . chequered by the warning and anxious eye with which she commanded the terrors of her accomplice.

Fifteen years later she was praised for the subtlety of her subtextual preparation for the scene, her

> fine rendering of the natural exhaustion of a woman strung to the utmost pitch of nerve by remorseless ambition and indomitable will, and finding security where she had dreaded failure and dismay (*Saturday Review*).

Bernhardt, entering, already showed herself haunted by the feeling that her well-washed hands were bloody, with

> slight gestures, as of drawing her hands up her sleeves, or anywhere out of the way, and furtively looking at them.

Under her practice of grief for Duncan was felt a restlessness that would steadily intensify. At the other extreme, Wysocka stood still as a statue, emphasizing by her rigidity the control she had to exercise over her emotions.

One essence of Shakespeare's design here is the ambiguity between the Lady's—and Macbeth's—playing of disturbed grief and the real core of it. Even so hard-finished a Lady as Merchant would suggest the double level when, in her nervous entrance, she was evidently putting on the face of sudden stress, and yet betrayed a sense that she was more truly hagridden than she pretended to be.

Terry entered half-dressed, her face seeming as pale as the white dress she wore. Other Ladies—for instance, Modjeska—were followed by maids; Terry wanted to be alone. Her note: "Play not the low voiced, commanding Queen, but the frightened 'innocent flower'"; accordingly, as she feigned ignorance of what had happened, she spoke in a "frightened voice."

In Lady Macbeth's first line recurs a word almost synonymous to her with the nameless act:

> What's the business . . . ? (97)

She calls out over the rush and noise of the castle's panic. The stage is still restless: Irving's soldiers, for instance, moved steadily through—his note, "Keep coming till end of scene." Lady Macbeth must at last single out Macduff, and insist on an answer, as Marlowe had to do, when her Macduff ignored her: *speak . . . speak!* He still cannot tell her the worst; and unintentional irony edges his excuse:

> O gentle lady, . . .
> The repetition in a *woman*'s ear,
> Would murder as it fell (100, 102–103),

he says to the woman responsible, for her to absorb. He can finally tell a man, and without the dressing of metaphor, when Banquo comes. *Our royal master's murder'd* (105). Generally, according to Becks, Macduff then threw himself, in grief, on Banquo's shoulder. The whole castle responds, as it will to the succession of shocks in this scene. The words will be the same on many lips: "Murdered!" . . . "The king!" Cries and groans will rise. An impulse to revenge will stir.

Lady Macbeth hears: and it seems a measure of tenuous self-control that her well-calculated show of grief, *Woe, alas:* is followed by the tactless *What, in our house?* (107). The Folio appropriately gives these as separate, short lines, as if to emphasize the change in voicing. Rigg sobbed the first line; followed it with an "uncareful" second that brought an appraising glance from Banquo, and his reproachful:

> Too cruel, anywhere. (108)

Leigh, anxious at her slip, drifted away to the side of the stage, waiting for her Macbeth to appear. Banquo watches. As Craig observes (and Nagarajan) he will not speak again for some thirty-five lines; but he will see everything.

Enter Macbeth, Lenox, and Ross.

The ubiquitous Ross presumably appears from somewhere within the castle; Macbeth and Lenox come from Duncan's room. Macbeth may first be heard lamenting off, with a cry, as by Tree; may even start his speech off-stage, as Forrest did; but usually he begins as he makes his shaken way out of Duncan's room. All eyes move to him, and the noise of the troubled crowd dies to quiet as it sees the shock on his face, gasps—as at Hopkins—at the signs of blood on him, the daggers he again carries (Macbeth sometimes conceals these until his second speech). The silence is the more insistent when, as with Irving, the tolling bell suddenly, finally stops. The sight of a shocked young Lenox, sometimes retching, sometimes unable to stand, authenticates the unseen terror. It is the climax of a beat, a moment for frightful pause: Lady Macbeth—and the *naive* spectator—sees a repetition of Macbeth's action of the night before, and agonizes. What has happened in him? To him? Is he conscious enough to exculpate them?

In the silence Sothern staggered down, fell on a bench. Garrick, projecting innocence and deep concern, carefully avoided meeting anyone's eye. Reinhardt's Macbeth emulated Macduff's grief, raised his arms high, then covered his face with his hands. Salvini rushed from Duncan's chamber, a frenzied figure, waving his bloody sword over the heads of the crowd; Coleman observed, with the eye of a *naive* spectator, that this murderer was prepared to sell his life dearly, if his treachery were discovered. A pale Charles Kean also had his sword high. Scofield stood grimly upright, silent, holding all eyes, as he seemed almost himself to be waiting to know what he would be able to say.

So many relationships are involved in Macbeth's equivocating lament. He is primarily proving his grief to the whole castle, compelling belief; but he is particularly aware of the effect of his words on the silent, watchful Banquo, with whom, in some stagings, he exchanges glances, from whom he may encounter a meaningful stare, as Sothern did. He is also letting a concerned Lady Macbeth know that he is covering for them; as actor, he is sharing with the theatre audience the fact of his equivocation, his secret guilt: but finally he is speaking to himself, more deeply from his heart than he himself may know, so that the audience hears the double voice of pretense and the cry of truth. He may speak slowly, nourishing expectation, letting the theatre audience feel the gathering of his wits, his "feeling round for plausibility," as with Laughton—but giving to the castle audience profound emotion, "a heavy wail of grief," as with Forrest. So much hangs on these moments; three colons mark pauses for the thought to find the richest expression of feeling:

> Had I but died an hour before this chance,
> I had liv'd a blessed time: for from this instant,
> There's nothing serious in mortality:
> All is but toys: renown and grace is dead,
> The wine of life is drawn, and the mere lees
> Is left this vault, to brag of. (112–117)

He might almost be saying *Tomorrow, and tomorrow, and tomorrow* . . . It is a fine elegy from an eloquent philosopher-poet lamenting the meaninglessness of existence—"intended to deceive," as Bradley says, "but at the same time, his profoundest feeling." The castle can only agree, with murmurs, sighs, cries.

The moment holds, giving Macbeth himself a chance to digest what he has said, to glimpse the true horror he has meant to fabricate. This *vault* of remaining life may be the barren underground cellar of his metaphor; may be, also, as Muir notes, an entombment and, by extension, the vault of the sky above arching over a world of the dead. May even echo the vain vault of ambition. Another fused, polyphonic image. Scofield's somber face—as if he was beginning to comprehend all the implications of his contrived vision—reflected a deep inner anguish.

The beat breaks, and the new one starts, with the appearance of the two princes.

DONALBAIN: What is amiss? (119)

Macbeth's answer: *You are, and do not know't* (120) is double-edged: it might be said as well of himself—and he may sense that. Compassion may sound in the words. Lady Macbeth has moved to comfort the young men, seemingly sincere.

They learn that their father has been murdered. One or both may rush to Duncan's chamber to see. Now Malcolm has a chance to establish an identity before his long absence in IV, iii. If treated as only a representative of good, Malcolm can seem the milksop Coghill had thought him (and so Coghill was pleased, in Canada, by the manliness of a Malcolm's response to the news of the murder: the *O, by whom?* (124) had "a real, startled violence and fury"). Ian Richardson, Malcolm with Scofield, after a moment of hopeless shock, instantaneously seized a great, heavy sword, wrenched it aloft, and rounded on the crowd with a fierce cry. It was the visualization of the prince's forced growth from boy to man. He kept the sword.

In Macbeth's way Malcolm lies; the tension between them may be immediately evident. Piscator's Macbeth had been standing behind the two princes; he suddenly thrust forward, between them, forcing them apart. Scofield felt he must confront the princes as soon as they appeared—"my focus must be on them." The young men became another of his main audiences; he was always partly conscious of them. At one apparent movement of Malcolm toward an exit, this Macbeth was suddenly in the way.

Lenox now has a speech of crucial importance. He who has gone into Duncan's room with Macbeth now prepares ahead of time the justification of Macbeth's last, still-unknown, murders. And he validates the alibi for the night before. Macbeth and Lady Macbeth, watching, can only listen with relief. In some stagings Macbeth has begun to make his way toward Lady Macbeth, more often she toward him, in a reaching toward mutual support. Or they have rushed to embrace each other. The two can exchange a hopeful look of assurance when Lenox speaks, detailing better than they could the shifting of the guilt to the blood-gilded grooms. Lenox:

> Those of his chamber, as it seem'd, had done't:
> Their hands and faces were all badg'd with blood,
> So were their daggers, which unwip'd, we found
> Upon their pillows: they star'd, and were distracted,
> No man's life was to be trusted with them. (125–129)

By now, Lady Macbeth may be close to her husband. In Japan, they had drawn so close they were standing back to back. This suggested a common defense; but Milward noted that while their psychological state was the same, they were actually and symbolically looking in opposite directions. Leigh, who had been at the opposite end of the stage when Macbeth returned from Duncan's room,

> instinctively took a step forward to assist him and . . . slowly, inexorably, the two were drawn together by the compulsion of their common guilt (David).

Tree's Lady reached him quickly. Hackett wanted his to fling herself compulsively into his arms, conveying

> her own weakness, her anxiety for him, and the semi-natural impulse of woman. At that time Macbeth should be a rock supporting her.

Terry, approaching her Macbeth, came up behind Banquo, and when Macbeth spoke, would, like a mother identifying with a child, nervously support by nods and gestures and inarticulate lip movements what he had to say.

Lady Macbeth's sense of security must grow as she feels the mood of the crowd against the murderous grooms. Violent passions rise; a movement of angry men toward Duncan's room may begin. The common cry, as with Irving, may be "Revenge!"

But suddenly the Lady, and all the others in the castle—and we too—are checked by a totally unexpected shock: Macbeth the player takes the stage—again perhaps with some deep-dying impulse to truth, doubling. The first monosyllable suggests a cry, though Tree and others have whispered it—

> O, yet I do repent me of my fury,
> That I did kill them. (130–131)

Amazement. In all. In Lady Macbeth the return of alarm. In Macduff and Banquo and the Princes, perhaps, suspicion. It usually informs Macduff's

> Wherefore did you so? (132)

Again, Macbeth the player must find the appeasing words, for all his audiences: for us, who do not share complicity in this new crime; for Lady Macbeth, whose unease he must sense; for those who suspect him; for the crowd he must hold to him.

> Who can be wise, amaz'd, temp'rate, and furious,
> Loyal, and neutral, in a moment? (133–134)

Did he wait for an answer that would not come? And have to give it?

No man: The recurring appeal to manliness: to the Scotland that prized his warrior's valor, to the wife who urged him to a different kind of daring.

> Th' expedition of my violent love
> Out-ran the pauser, reason. Here lay Duncan,
> His silver skin, lac'd with his golden blood,
> And his gash'd stabs, look'd like a breach in nature,
> For ruin's wasteful entrance: (135–139)

Macbeth the poet speaks, painting images that must seize the grieving imaginations of his hearers—and also, perhaps, speaks to his Lady. He imagines Duncan's blood, Mark Van Doren thought, as if it were like no other mortal blood; Murray hears an allusion to a kind of miraculous alchemical tincture, a saintly fluid that would glow as the murderer watched. The *golden* links him to his wife, through her recent image of gilt blood: will they two recognize this?

After the oxymoron ending of the first line, the impression is of awe, of reverence, of deep lament. Words of delicate compassion, of lacerating, tormented vision, ask for pity not only for the dead, but also for the man who had to look on the body. For his hearers in the castle, Macbeth must make his grief seem absolute. But how for us? When he creates his strange image of death, will we feel the edges between his "playing" of sorrow, and a genuine feeling that rises in him?

Irving, forcing the hypocrisy in the design, deliberately *making his griefs and clamours roar*, was certain that when Macbeth "pathetically pictures the aspect of the murdered king" he was being

> a poet with his brain—the greatest poet that Shakespeare has ever drawn—and a villain with his heart, and the mere appreciation of his own wickedness gave irony to his grim humour, and zest to his crime. . . . All through the play his darkest deeds are heralded by high thoughts told in the most glorious word-painting, so that, after a little, the reader or the hearer comes to understand that excellence of poetic thought is but a suggestion of the measure of the wickedness to follow.

In effect, Irving's earnest confession, of pure, unclouded pretense, without dimension, projected a picture "so finely drawn, so intimately plausible" it was completely successful—the "dramatic barrister" had won his "Jury." Other Macbeths have experienced the iron of remorse hidden in the show of it; have at once, as a result, seemed both more earnest in their mourning and less finished in their speaking. In the last lines, where Macbeth, from tender sorrow, wakes to an indignant passion—so Forrest—the Macbeth not fully in control, anxious about the effect he is making, and shadowed by the guilt that becomes heavier with each new pretense, may begin to flounder, as Laughton did; to fumble, as Ristori's Macbeth did, fearful of making a mistake; to betray in his tones that, pressed as he is to justify himself, he is on the edge of protesting too much (Macready, Sothern); he may begin to shrill, to shout (Hampden):

> there the murderers,
> Steep'd in the colours of their trade; their daggers
> Unmannerly breech'd with gore: (139–141)*

He may hold the weapons out, then throw them down, as Hopkins did; or lift his bloody hands (Clements); or pantomime the discovery, as Salvini did; to evoke a reaction from the hearers. He may, at *there the murderers*, look meaningfully at Malcolm and Donalbain.

> who could refrain,
> That had a heart to love; and in that heart,
> Courage, to make's love known? (141–143)

Occasionally stagings (like Phelps', Kean's, Hampden's, Irving's) suggest that most of the inhabitants of Inverness react to Macbeth now with shock

---

*Brooks sees this as symptomatic of the clothes-disguise imagery; it would support the more pervasive visual manifestations of men in nightdress and undress. It has suffered in translation. Sarcey, angry at finding it transformed into "poignards culottes de sang," retorted "culotte-toi, méchant prosateur; car tu n'es que trop souvent deculotte!" The words do carry the masked sexuality that touches other verbal and visual images in the play.

and suspicion. In one version, Macduff lifted his sword to point it at Macbeth, encouraging others to suspect. "All look at Macbeth suspiciously" in Charles Kean's direction. Garrick sensed a general suspicion. Benson had "All men threaten Macbeth with their swords." Given this response, Macbeth must, like Antony, sway a hostile mob—something Irving delighted to do. But this seems counter to the line of Shakespeare's design. Lenox has underwritten the guilt of the grooms; the thanes, with no reason to doubt him, may well have been in a mood to lynch Duncan's murderers; Macbeth did alone what they might have done as a mob. A Macbeth contrived to resemble a Hitler-type might, in his own castle, summon the power to force acceptance of his story; instead Shakespeare's protagonist feelingly pleads his case, precious to the thanes, of a brave man killing in an excess of love—he uses the word three times—the enemy of their king: something he has proudly done in battle. Lenox has seen him kill these men, in whose hands no life is safe, and now stands beside him, approving. The thanes, unintimidated by any show of force, will name Macbeth king. Shakespeare seems not ready yet to initiate the movement toward *judgement here*. Macbeth's deed is accepted, if not warmly praised.

Not by all, of course. Not, perhaps, by the princes, or by Macduff, or Banquo. And most of all, now, Lady Macbeth, when she is allowed to appear here. She must react to Macbeth's new character and actions, either by genuine shock, or a distracting show of it. A pause may hang in the air as Macbeth's final rhetorical question waits for a response, and Lady Macbeth may fill it with her cry—

Help me hence, ho. (144)*

As we saw, the eighteenth century could not ascribe the implied weakness to anything but hypocrisy: the Lady could only be concerned to draw attention away from Macbeth's perilous situation. Later Ladies have acted this motivation: like some critics they take the speech to indicate that she feints. Then she must play to two audiences: the stage one, that must believe in the faint; and the theatre audience that has some hint that it is pretense. One actress, asked how, if she played the faint well enough to be believed by the others on stage, she could let the audience know she was feigning, answered: "I could wink?" In fact, the feint depends on the equation developing between Lady Macbeth and her husband. If she has been strong in dominating him, she is more likely to manage him in this crisis. The early Ristori Lady Macbeth could make it clear that, Machiavellian as she was, she had to act when her Macbeth began to stumble in his confession, betraying an anxiety that could imply guilt. But there was felt in her also the revived memory of the bleeding old Duncan who had resembled her father: shock was mixed with calculation. When her "warning and anxious eye" could not control Macbeth, the horror she half-felt, half-affected, carried her to

*The Scofield rehearsers agreed that this was a rare instance of Shakespeare including a Chinese in his cast. (Lear also calls on this *Ho*, for dinner).

the ultimate perfection of falsehood. When gasping *Deh! chi m'aita?* she faints
into the arms of her attendants (*Morning Post*).

When Hampden's Macbeth began raising his voice, almost shouting in
hysteria, his Lady could be seen by the theatre audience to resolve on some
intervention: she "fainted." Reinhardt's Lady, seeing how intensely all eyes
were focused on Macbeth, deliberately fell to the ground, and gave him the
excuse to come over to her. Joseph Hodgkinson saw a quick visual signal
pass between Macbeth and his Lady, in the Dunlop staging, that cued her
deliberate collapse.

Even the art of so great an actress as Ristori could not always distinguish
for an audience the real from the feigned: when she played in Australia some
twenty years later than the performance in England noted above (1857), her
swoon was taken as genuine. Did Shakespeare intend an ambiguity? May
the balance between feigned and faint be so close even in the pretenders that
the Lady herself may not be sure? Dench felt this: that the collapse was half-
real, half-willed. The event must fit into the total characterization. Much
depends not only on the Lady's strength before and during this moment,
but also on how she will appear as queen in III, i. Will she bear still the impenetrable front of a Terrible Woman? Will she show any marks of a more
human, more "feminine," failing creature, who had learned that under
enough pressure, however the emergency, she might collapse?

Most Ladies follow the latter pattern, though they may find different
motives for their collapse. These add up to a polyphony of impulses that
helps to illuminate the character's complex design.

Faucit, the first important English actress to leaven Lady Macbeth's fierceness with compunction and some tenderness, blamed surprised, frightened
imagination for the collapse:

> The torture she endured while no less to her amazement than her horror,
> [Macbeth recites] with fearful minuteness of detail, how he found Duncan
> lying gashed and gory in his chamber! She had faced that sight without blench-
> ing [later Ladies would not, as we saw] when it was essential . . . but to have
> the whole scene thus vividly brought again before her was too great a strain
> upon her nerves. No wonder that she faints.

Faucit, according to Becks, was carried off by her women,

> in *dishabille*, as having been hastily summoned from their beds.

Modjeska, similarly, was undermined by her horrified imagination but
she learned in Poland to swoon without falling, Got reports.

> Macbeth's very mention of Duncan's name raised up before Modjeska's eyes
> a vision of his crime, terror caught at her throat, she could not speak, she
> choked, tottered and fainted;

but, still on her feet, was supported out by her servants. In America, Booth
as her Macbeth was at her side when she entered the scene, and close by as
her maids half-carried her out.

Terry, on the other hand, was "not horrified by this news," her notes say:

> She stands dead still listening, only drawing her things tightly around her, [listens] until her ears crack, until Macbeth's picture beautifully painted is over.

Strung up as she is, when she realizes that Irving's story has been "swallowed,"

> "Safe, safe" she thinks [and] faints after pent up agony and anxiety from relief.

She fell; Banquo and Macduff were at once solicitous, Irving more concerned with what he had to do next. She was carried out by a thane,

> with her fair head thrown back . . . and her red hair streaming in the torchlight.

Hackett's Lady, with her arms around him, seeing that he stood indomitably on his feet and responded to her unspoken query with a reassuring pressure, also gave way to relaxation and fainted. Hackett thought her resistance was less because her drink had worn off.

Merchant's faint involved a complex dialectic between the real and the strategic. From the crisis in the previous scene, a strained relationship between Lady Macbeth and Macbeth had developed: on the one hand a closer approach when survival demanded it, on the other uncertainty on the personal plane. Merchant's slowly failing strength, following her trauma after the murder, was evident in her harried entrance after the tolling of the bell and as she began slowly to make her way to Macbeth. As his partner she moved to support him; as wife, she felt she should direct toward him her cry for help, should fall toward him; yet was restrained by their new, doubled-edged relationship, and by her awareness that her falling was a public event to be resisted. Her faint was the climax of her slow, weakening movement; her fall was succeeded by a moment of hushed shock—the director wanted a sense of everyone frozen for a moment by this kind of event—and then Scofield moved quickly to her side.

To Judith Anderson, what precipitated the faint was the realization of the terrible events that were suddenly occurring out of control. Her husband was becoming strange to her.

> She faints because she can't help it. Her husband's talk of the king lying there bleeding—

the touch of blood has been enough to nauseate this Lady—

> and she hears him say he has killed the two grooms, something that was not in their plan. Already the deed has got beyond her.

We saw that "delayed shock" had been Robson's explanation for her coolness in managing Macbeth, and returning the daggers, in the murder scene. Now the trauma caught up with her. When she played with Laughton, his very floundering, the danger of the situation for him, for both, overwhelmed her. Guthrie, the director, to emphasize the genuineness of her collapse, designed a spectacular one: she fell down a flight of stairs, to be caught by thanes below.

Gordon Craig, in his own promptbook, suggested another note in the complex motivation of Lady Macbeth's collapse: Malcolm knows on the instant that Macbeth has committed the murder—

> Macbeth's face speaks. Lady Macbeth sees this (in Malcolm), and though Macbeth goes on smoothly and poetically, it is of no avail. She, watching Malcolm, knows quickly that *that lad knows*. Then it is that she faints.

Rarely is the traditional business—real or pretended—of a faint questioned. But the Folio does not stipulate it; indeed does not suggest any exit for Lady Macbeth until the group *exeunt*. Nunn designed this unorthodox business: Duncan's catafalque was brought suddenly down to the stage; Mirren's breakdown under strain was suggested by her approach to it, and by the hysterical outburst with which she virtually attacked the corpse. The moment looked back, Gibbs observed, to *my father as he slept*; as it looked forward to *so much blood in him*. It also made Duncan's body an immediate, tangible object for reverent, piteous regard—something outside Shakespeare's design.* Mirren's outbreak was interrupted by Williamson, who stepped to her, took her by the shoulders, turned her round, and led her to the door.

Most Ladies are carried out, as Terry was: some were passed on, as she was, by her Macbeth; others supported out by attendants, as Modjeska was; some borne by Macbeth himself. Benson, who intensified the sense of suspicion against Macbeth, carried his Lady out while holding off the angry thanes with sword in one hand.

Given a character as complex as the Lady, and an action involving so many notes in her polyphony, no explanation of her "faint" will exhaust all possibilities—as only befits this open-ended play. The various emphases by the individual actresses discussed above did not exclude subordinate impulses. To sum up: all Ladies, even the most fiendish, have suffered psychic shocks, as they must reveal in the sleepwalk. All come to the courtyard in some suspense, if not anxiety: Will there be a discovery? Will Macbeth recover from his helplessness of the murder night? All Ladies, as they make their way through the thanes, to go to the support of their husbands, must be alert to anyone who may suspect. Then, when all seems to be well, when Lenox clears them, comes the unforeseen, almost intolerable shock—Macbeth, whom she feared would again lapse into hopeless inaction, confesses instead to two more murders. Not only is the new violence jolting, it was unplanned, ferocious—this is not the husband she thought she knew, he is moving frighteningly beyond her. Who is he? While she registers this shock, and tries not to show it, he goes so vividly into the details of Duncan's bloody corpse—the old man who resembled her father, with so much blood. She has, with her own senses, experienced the blood of the murdered man; blood in actuality may horrify her. Her imagination may almost be maddened by these images

---

*Langtry was also given an extra-textual cue to motivate her faint. A chorus of monks crossed the stage, carrying a cross, and she was presumably overcome by a sense of her unworthiness before God, a religious note that has no place in Shakespeare's characterization.

that may already have begun to obsess her. Her nerves may have forced
her, in the very beginning, to her monstrous task; to support them through the
crucial night she had resorted to drink, and that by now has worn off; they
are now* stretched to their absolute limits—they must give, if only because
they can do nothing else. She resists as long as she can, torn perhaps between
giving way to distract attention from Macbeth and fearing that a collapse may
deprive her husband of her support and bring suspicion on both.

What we know of the Lady's trouble is her cry to be helped away from
there, and Macduff's:

> Look to the Lady. (154)

After he first says it, Malcolm and Donalbain have a brief interlude, suggesting that attention has been drawn to Lady Macbeth; then Banquo says it,
suggesting perhaps that something has been happening slowly to her; that
Banquo may have summoned help from without, or from others, and it has
just arrived; bystanders have not been able to bring themselves to move to
her, and he insists. After he repeats his call for help, Banquo goes on with a
speech on other things, evidently satisfied that the help has been given.

That Banquo should have been so alert to notice Lady Macbeth's disturbance suggests the watchfulness that so often characterizes him. We may
be pretty sure Banquo suspected the truth at once, Bradley suggested; if
so, this may be felt during Banquo's long silence; he has said nothing, has
watched. So a Czech Banquo (1962) made clear that he knew Macbeth's guilt.

Between those two calls to look to Lady Macbeth—while the concentration is on her, and Malcolm and Donalbain have spoken their fears—
Macbeth's attention, so splintered among his many stage audiences, is now
usually on his wife. He is sometimes first to reach her side; when she recovers, as Leigh did before Olivier, there may be a terrible face-to-face moment
as the two, surrounded by the staring crowd, share a private enduring. If
her faint persists, he may, as noted, carry her out. But he probably never
forgets Malcolm and Donalbain, and certainly by the time Lady Macbeth
is fully off—whether he carries her, and returns, or not—Macbeth has had
time to notice their conference apart. Banquo may see this too; may see something in Macbeth's look that troubles him.

Macbeth, always giving high priority to his sense of Banquo's presence,
may be pulled that way, as Scofield was: for a moment they measured each
other. Banquo is suddenly impelled to assert leadership. To the crowd that
has been successively astonished, furious, bewildered, he speaks with a firm
authority that brooks no defiance. A *naive* spectator wonders here if, in this
highly political situation, Banquo means to take power before Macbeth can;
is Macbeth to be frustrated again? In the theatre Banquo sometimes raises
his sword for attention—and gets it. The thanes rally round.

---

*Each "now" has a concrete existence, and a future.

Banquo's speech sounds menace to Macbeth: an investigation must be held. But, in that it puts off the investigation, ambiguity invests it: he does not denounce Macbeth at once. What the speech implies may be influenced by the subtlest of visual imageries—the exchange of glances, or refusal of them, between Banquo and Macduff, Banquo and the princes, Banquo and Macbeth.

> And when we have our naked frailties hid,
> That suffer in exposure; (155–156)

When we have put on clothes again? Or have masked ourselves, to cover exposed nerves, suspected acts?

> let us meet,
> And question this most bloody piece of work,
> To know it further. (156–158)

Which bloody piece of work? Does he look up at Duncan's chamber? At Macbeth? Or avoid looking?

> Fears and scruples shake us: (158)

Fears, of course. *Scruples* . . . ? The word primarily meant doubt, uncertainty, "a hesitation as to right and wrong," secondarily, suspicion. Suspicion of whom?

Banquo confides himself to God; a God who has not yet, in this play, attended the prayers offered him:

> In the great hand of God I stand, and thence,
> Against the undivulg'd pretence, I fight
> Of treasonous malice. (159–161)

He ends as he began—there may be more to this crime not yet known, a hidden design or purpose that is treacherous. (Macbeth will suspect something of the same sort about destiny.) Again, Banquo often raises his sword as a rallying point; Macduff joins with his, *And so do I* (162), and *All* make it unanimous—*So all*, the courtyard often clashing with lifted swords.

Macbeth, who has been silent for some time, concerned with his Lady, alert to the whispers of the princes, sensitive to the undertones of Banquo's speech and the mood of the thanes, and perhaps for a moment lost in raptness again, rouses himself to assert a contribution:

> Let's briefly put on manly readiness,
> And meet i'th' hall together. (164–165)

Manly readiness requires proper dress, complete arms, the preparation to meet danger. Again the rallying cry: *All: Well contented* (166).

Exeunt, but usually not all at once. Macbeth most often is the last to go—though Irving, having won the thanes to his side with his oratory, now led the thanes from the stage with a wonderful martial stride, dispersing, in the half torchlight, half daylight, the frightened, half-dressed huddle of castle bystanders.

When Macbeth lingers, Banquo may too, and they briefly look into each other's eyes, even nod, as they did at the beginning of the act; Macduff may hang back for a moment too, and the three stare briefly at each other. Macbeth can remain behind as host. He may, as Reinhardt's Macbeth did, look after the others with distrust written clearly on his face, with a deep sigh. As Macbeth looks back over the scene of his crisis, he may sense, without betraying it, the presence of the princes, and withdraw where they cannot see him, but we can.

We return for a moment to the young men. They are sometimes forcefully made aware of Macbeth's menace, more or less overt. Hackett, before leaving, looked at them fiercely, his sword in hand, until one and then the other submitted to bow to him. The princes decide to flee; and as inconspicuously as possible they move toward their escape. Their last exchange helps to establish the shrewdness of Malcolm as he senses the equivocation in his world:

> Let's not consort with them:
> To show an unfelt sorrow, is an office
> Which the false man does easy.
> I'll to England. (168–171)*

Malcolm's words are young and brave, but have also, especially in the last lines, the practical verbal cleverness of the fox:

> there's warrant in that theft,
> Which steals itself, when there's no mercy left. (180–181)

Malcolm may develop his dramatic identity by showing an older brother's care for Donalbain: hug him, perhaps give him money, as in the Rigg–Hopkins staging. There the two picked up the daggers left behind, signals of their planned revenge. In the Hall–Scofield version, Malcolm sent Donalbain fleeing ahead, while he himself backed out, alert for attack, holding at guard the great sword he had seized at first.

If Macbeth lurks behind, he can easily stop the princes; Olivier, watching them, thought better of it, smiled his secret smile as he saw them go. Hampden, more purposeful, as he followed the thanes out, threatened the princes with a glance—daggers in his smiles. They quickly made their plans to escape, and Hampden, returning, saw the last of them with satisfaction. He stood in the torchlight, looking around to see that all was well, on his face a look of triumph.

---

*Gentleman, not partial to this part of Shakespeare's playwriting, described an eighteenth-century response to the scene: "When one says, 'I'll to England' and the other comically replies, 'To Ireland I,' nine times out of ten the audience are thrown into a horse-laugh."

'Tis said, they ate each other.

Act II, Scene iv

Linear impulses move this short scene ahead; but it serves also as a time-stretcher, a rare pause in the rush of the first acts that provides a buffer of indefinite duration between the previous scene and the next.

Enter Ross, with an Old Man.

Something of the lingering mystery of the night before attaches to the Old Man. Why this strange, delphic figure toiling across the stage now? From what as yet unexplored corner of the *Macbeth* world does he come? To do what? In the theatre his hooded eyes can look beyond what he sees, his gestures with hand, stick, or staff hint ageless secrets. Sometimes represented as a kind of holy beggar, sometimes as a monkish figure, a religious father, sometimes as a kind of archetype of ancient wisdom, he speaks almost with the rhythm and perspective of Father Time himself. He is so old. He can remember seventy years—the full life span allotted man—and never a night like the last one.

Ross, who did not speak in the last act, now contributes his part to the strangeness of the night's atmosphere, his speech enriched by more images from the theatre:

> the *heavens*, as troubled with man's *act*,
> Threatens his bloody *stage*; (8–9)

then the familiar antitheses, darkness triumphing: "*day . . . night . . . night . . . day . . . dark . . . lamp . . . darkness . . . lights*" (9–13).

The six months of unnatural phenomena reported by Holinshed are capsuled in these speeches, including the two spectacular examples of order reversed: the owl that killed a falcon, the disobedient, cannibal horses. The peculiar detail in Holinshed that the owl "strangled" the hawk is softened (though night *strangles* the sun). In the source the horses eat each other's flesh, and this in itself would be a wonder; in *Macbeth* the Old Man can report it as a rumor: *'tis said* that Duncan's beautiful horses did *eat each other* (24). This image of ravening mutual destruction matches in strangeness the uncanny response of the heavens to the death of a man, and is perhaps more telling because so immediately domestic. The rumor, broached, absorbs the first shock of the incredible; then Ross confirms that he saw the enormity. To a Globe audience so intimately familiar with noncarnivorous horses, the report must have strained the very limits of the plausible. Was Shakespeare offering another perspective on the superstitition of the Scots?

Ross sees coming *the good Macduff* (28)—the first time that Macduff's full name has been mentioned in the text (surely, again, in performance Shakespeare's actors spoke it in the previous scene?). Macduff seems not only to accept the guilt of the grooms for Duncan's murder, but also to absolve Macbeth by blaming the runaway princes for suborning the grooms. However, if Ross and Macduff exchange meaningful glances as they ask and answer, and let irony into their voices, the significance doubles. Hackett saw Macduff whispering his reply to Ross, with a kind of deliberately childish surprise and sarcasm: *Those that Macbeth hath slain* (32). Ross then would register the implication, and return, *What good could they pretend?* (34)—with emphasis on *pretend*, the speech itself being a pretense. In a later scene, this kind of doubling talk will seem likely. What would be the purpose of it here? Does one test the other? Are they fooling the Old Man? as if he were an eavesdropper? Certainly, if Ross is being double-tongued here, his later apparent allegiance to Macbeth must be colored with pretense.

Against the idea of covert meanings is Ross' comment on the princes, that seems to take Macduff's words at face value, seriously, with a straightforward moral capping that fits the early mood of the scene:

> 'Gainst nature still,
> Thriftless ambition, that will raven up
> Thine own life's means. (39–41)

Like many philosophical observations in the play, its double edge may cut at Macbeth. Ross may point it by indicating the castle they have left. But Ross continues, as if in a counter thought:

> Then 'tis most like,
> The sovereignty will fall upon Macbeth.
> MACDUFF: He is already nam'd, and gone to Scone
> To be invested. (41–44) .

Macbeth will later be called *usurper*, and some critics have used the descriptive; but a usurper takes possession by force, and no slightest suggestion of this colors the end of the previous scene when, as we saw, Banquo asserted leadership in calling a conference of the thanes. Macbeth was evidently freely *named* to be sovereign by the thanes—including, apparently, Macduff, who was present and can report the choice. Shakespeare does not mention tanistry, which made the monarchy elective by near kinsmen, but clearly something of the sort has happened.* The playwright seems to stipulate that Macbeth is safe on the throne, the choice of his responsible peers. No objection is voiced by any of the three present—unless indirectly.

After the news of Duncan's interment—again the ritual note—Macduff reveals that he will not go to Scone for Macbeth's investment. It is his only overt indication to this point that he may not be happy with Macbeth's election, and revives the sense of his felt rivalry. Ross of course will go to Scone— he is not the man to miss such a gathering of the powerful. Now Macduff may let some of his hostility show. He overtly wishes—in the recurrent clothes imagery—that Scotland will wear its new sovereign with better order than its last. This is a good and necessary wish—though irony could creep into his voice:

> Well may you see things well done there: adieu
> Lest our old robes sit easier than our new. (52–53)

That the Old Man senses something unfriendly in this may show in the blessing, in response to the farewell from Ross, that embraces both thanes—and indeed, in the familiar *Macbeth* dialectic pattern, embraces a wider world:

> God's benison go with you, and with those
> That would make good of bad, and friends of foes. (55–56)

E. K. Chambers suggests that this may be aimed at Ross, as a time-server; but it seems more directly to rebuke Macduff's unwillingness to show friendship to Macbeth. Shakespeare is perhaps strengthening the image of Macbeth triumphant. Perhaps doing more than that. The Old Man, still a figure of mystery, may imply more than he can say: in his farseeing gaze, in his speaking that takes in the audience and the wide world, in his slow exit that images an end of life, a crawl toward death.

---

*One may wonder, in passing, if we are to make anything of the fact that Ross, who manages to be everywhere else, missed the meeting that named Macbeth. Are we to sense that he was not of high enough degree? Shakespeare might have saved him for this expository scene; but the playwright has used anonymous "lords" for such purposes.

Act III, Scene i

This is sometimes called the "Coronation" scene, as if Macbeth is even now being invested with kingship. Since Shakespeare provided no text for it, any ceremony must take place in dumb show, except for chants, ritual murmurs, "Hails" and similar acclamations.

The character of the mime depends on the historical context of the staging—ancient, medieval, Elizabethan, "modern"—and whether or not any attempt is made to echo an earlier scene with Duncan. The action is the formal accepting and drawing on of robes, the passing of scepters and other regal paraphernalia, especially the crowns—Rogers and his Lady held theirs high, before lowering them to their heads. Reinhardt's two were acclaimed with the raising of naked swords. The atmosphere may be of a church, as in an Italian staging. In Sweden, Duncan's catafalque was brought to the rear of the stage, the crown taken from it, carried up stairs to Macbeth, and as it was put on his head light reflected the golden circle on a white veil behind. Sometimes Banquo may be seen, with other thanes, kneeling in the coronation ceremony; or it may be seen taking place behind him.*

The scene proper begins with Banquo alone; though even so, normal court action is sometimes seen in the background, giving Banquo a cue for his soliloquy as he withdraws. Conversely, in a Johannesburg staging, Macbeth came up behind Banquo, heard what he had to say, and so had a specific—but artificial and unnecessary—motivation for the murder.

When Banquo is alone, as the text provides, he may begin by sitting on the throne itself, getting the feel of it, as he did in the Nunn staging. This moment most tests the theory that Banquo is thoroughly innocent and untempted. Granville–Barker agrees with Bradley: at the end of II, iii, Banquo

is profoundly shocked, full of indignation, and determined to play the part of a brave and honest man. But he plays no such part. When we next see him,

*For James's coronation, the first that Englishmen would have witnessed for half a century, see *The Masks of King Lear*, p. 70.

on the last day of his life, he has yielded to evil . . . He has not formally, but in effect, "cloven to" Macbeth's consent, he is knit to him by a most indissoluble tie.

Banquo's stance is ameliorated to the extent that he may seem more troubled by his knowledge than made hopefully conspiratorial by it; a "good Banquo" must follow this pattern. But there can be no question that he suspects, and has said nothing at the conference he called; and that he hopes that he himself may benefit from Macbeth's fulfillment of the prophecies. Many *naive* spectators took for granted that Banquo would now try to kill Macbeth, as Macbeth had killed Duncan. The purposefulness of Banquo is sometimes intensified by action: Savits' Banquo was clearly suspicious and envious, spoke in low, hissing tones; Irving's was sardonic; Reinhardt's smiled maliciously, and spoke in an undertone, conspiring with himself.

Banquo acknowledges, as the Sisters had, Macbeth's triple title:

> Thou hast it now, King, Cawdor, Glamis, all,
> As the weyard women promis'd, and I fear
> Thou playd'st most foully for't: (3–5)

The fair is foul (*fear–foully* may hide a pun); but out of the foulness may come fair for Banquo: as before, his notion of his rival's rewards prompts him to compare his own prospects—

> yet it was said
> It should not stand in thy posterity,
> But that myself should be the root, and father
> Of many kings. (5–8)

Here is Banquo's motivation, if it is one, voiced in the growth-fertility pattern, touching on Macbeth's sorest point—the fathering of kingly sons. Banquo refracts Macbeth's *If chance will have me . . .* :

> If there come truth from them,
> As upon thee *Macbeth*, their speeches shine . . .
> May they not be my oracles as well,
> And set me up in hope. (8–12)

Any anxiety he had earlier about *the instruments of darkness* seems now to have disappeared. No debate, like Macbeth's, about *cannot be ill . . . cannot be good.* Banquo scents a *perfectest* report of events. His pivotal *if* has led him to a vision of glory—one that carried for Woodvine, acting Banquo, an intimation of destiny: "If what I fear Macbeth did was in fact foreordained, perhaps I am being pushed toward a similar fateful act?" Woodvine's welcome now to the Sisters' oracles—*May they not . . . set me up in hope?*—ended with a sudden, exhilarated smile, almost as if he could taste dynasty; his emphasis was on *me;* his hands clenched in anticipation.

Banquo now palters with evil, Parrott suggests; certainly Banquo is dreaming of the royal line that the witches promised him—and he may betray this visually. His hand may touch his sword, or dagger. If he has not been sitting on the throne, he may, as he speaks, go to it, stroke it, try it. May sit down heavily—for Banquo is one of the play's sleepless ones, and the night and day drain may show.

Granville-Barker hears no commitment to guilt in Banquo's next terse words. But where an innocent man would use some version of the familiar Shakespearean formula for switching audience attention—"Look where he comes"—Banquo, sensing Macbeth's approach, abruptly censors his thoughts:

> But hush, no more. (12)

An acknowledged "good Banquo" partisan, James Black, suggests that this admonition may imply another *Merciful powers, restrain in me the cursed thoughts.* . . . The thoughts may well be cursed; and only Banquo can know—and convey—how terrible they are as hastily he halts his conspiracy with himself, to present a face of innocence or collusion to the entering Macbeth. He will say nothing, overtly, of his suspicions. We may recall Byam Shaw's production note here:

> I think [Banquo's] silence . . . is mostly on account of his own interest in the future of the Crown. In which case he is a guilty man and to some extent gets what he deserves. I don't think that it is possible to believe that he remains silent only out of friendship for Macbeth; and if it is fear that prevents him from telling the truth, and he is completely innocent, then he could leave the country. Of course he is not a villain, but he is not a simple honest man either. He has his own particular form of ambition.

Dover Wilson could not believe that Shakespeare would let an ancestor of James be touched with evil in a play written for the king. This again demonstrates the danger of trusting an unproved axiom—"*Macbeth* for James"—and making the characters fit it. Future events cannot bear out speculation about Banquo's intentions, since he does not live long enough to manifest them: we must at least say, as Hall did, that for now he keeps his options open. Friendly critics have suggested that Banquo will be trying to get away from Macbeth; but we know he is returning to the feast when he meets his death; and he will himself insist that he is *for ever knit* to a man he suspects of the foulest murder. How this questionable characterization of James' legendary ancestor was supposed to be a compliment to the king is not easy to understand. If that had been Shakespeare's intention, he could have made Banquo innocent of suspicion, innocent of temptation, noble in soliloquy, a chaste victim of Macbeth's ambition, or a heroic nobleman challenging Macbeth with his suspicions now, and dying fighting. Instead, Shakespeare gave us this complex artwork, reflecting recognizable inner conflicts between conscience and commodity.

Now the state entry, directed by the Folio to be preceded by the lordly sound of the sennet, and in production often accompanied by evocative cries of "Hail Macbeth," the raising of swords, genuflection.

Enter Macbeth as King, Lady[,]
Lenox, Ross, Lords, and Attendants.

It is a big, royal show, paralleling perhaps Duncan's court in I, iv, perhaps contrasting with it. The emphasis is still on order: the characters enter by rank, and dispose themselves by their degree. Macbeth and his Lady have sometimes seemed to bear their garments as very heavy—notably in Düsseldorf (1968) where the royal robes were like crusts or cocoons of gold, so that neither walked quite normally: they seemed to drag themselves along. In Paris (1965) the heavy crown, weighing Macbeth down, bristling with points, seemed to *Combat* a reflection of a hideous, criminal power. Anderson's robes seemed weighted with lead, Irene Worth's (England, 1962) so heavy she was weary with them. Gold is a common color for its regality; but often it is contrasted with black, and Macbeth himself may be in black under his crown. Alternatively he—and Lady Macbeth—are sometimes in red, blood color, against black or gold; the single red figures may move through a court of grey, seeming to spill through it. But the symbolism must not be blatant, and sometimes it is deliberately reversed—Salvini entered in silver-white.

The time gap understood to have passed between II, iii, and III, i, is unobtrusive but important. Macbeth will speak of Banquo's advice, presumably for him as king,

Which *still* hath been both grave, and prosperous (28).

Unless we take this to mean before Macbeth's ascendancy, it suggests a passage of time; so does Lady Macbeth's observation, in the next scene:

Why do you *keep* alone . . . ? (III, ii, 13)

and Macbeth's about dreams that have shaken them *nightly*. For the Olivier Leigh *Macbeth*, Byam Shaw assumed three months passed. Skeat traced *solemn* (supper) to a root meaning "annual"; Ellen Terry wondered if a year had passed, and first wrote, for the Lady's entrance, "greatly changed." But Irving wanted to save a marked time-gap for IV, i, so Terry crossed out her first note, substituted "later on."

Sometimes pastness is visually pointed by the sense of some aging in the main characters, particularly the Macbeths. Not too much, for the past must still be fresh. If a coronation is mimed, the time clearly follows soon after II, iv; then the aging will be largely psychic rather than temporal. Either kind—or both—will be evident, if carefully masked, the moment the new king and queen enter.

This is their first appearance since she "fainted" while he justified his killing of the grooms. How we must imagine they have related to each other in the interim will be determined by how they now touch, or exchange glances, or avoid either or both. How did he feel about her faint? A helpful distraction? A weakening that might have caused dangerous suspicion? How does she feel about this man, who now has three murders sticking on his hands? Each must see the other differently than before Duncan's death. Each must sense the anguish that troubles the other. Will they watch with compassion? Solicitude? Distrust? Dismay?

The Lady who enters has lately been under nearly intolerable stain, and in the next scene will speak of her discontent: this may now weigh more than her heaviest clothes. Even Siddons felt burdened:

> The golden round of royalty now crowns her brow and royal robes enfold her form; but the peace that passeth all understanding is lost.

Siddons armed herself in dignity. With other Ladies the stress would show more. Ziegler tried to hide her torment behind a smiling mask, but a German observer saw the muscles of her face resisting her intentions, cramping her face, half-closing her eyes. Faucit's first splendid, aggressive power seemed to desert her under her golden crown; she seemed heart-stricken. Ristori, for all her control, projected an awareness that their new power was not secure, her attention dividing between the court and a distant fate she listened for. Modjeska walked like one in a dream. Modjeska's sensitivity had long ago surfaced; the neurotic Rigg had, until the murder discovery, been impassive in her control; now what was insecure and fragile beneath it showed.

> She looks dessicated, broken, and walks like an old woman, intermittently emerging from self-absorption to present . . . a grin the more ghastly for the rouge she has hopefully daubed on her sunken cheeks. (*New Statesman*)

She kept the smile on her face as long as she was watched; only when she turned her back to the court did her face break.

Some Ladies still, whether by nerve or native force, repressed the anguish that would break out later. Usually this scene marks the intersection of the rise of Macbeth's autonomy and the decline of the Lady; but some actresses held off the change in balance, entering clothed in full authority of the dreamed-of golden round, even exultant for the moment—not a long moment, for even they must soon be checked by their Macbeths. Leigh glowed with power as she marched in. The Polish Andrycz seemed to be the king in fact: her state chair was prominently in the middle of the court, her crown bigger. Determined, resolute, imperious, she could treat Macbeth for this little while still with the old dominance. Terry and Marlowe, who had always played the roles of helpmeets rather than tyrants, were able to continue these roles, taking the immediate stress from Macbeth, and covering his dialogue with Banquo, by moving from person to person in the court with courteous greeting. But this must be mimed, and may be misleading: Lady Macbeth has just one short speech in the whole scene, when she formally greets Banquo. Her silence will partly be explained by her need to watch Macbeth or accommodate herself to his mood; but inward forces are at work as well. Her intuition may be active: Dench only took her anxious eyes from Macbeth when, in his dialogue with Banquo, she sensed a covert impulse; then she looked from him to Banquo and back, apprehension dawning.

What scars does Macbeth bear from his recent experience? He has tasted the power to keep a castle mob loyal to him; he is named and acknowledged king; his people bow to him. But in his mind, as he enters, is one immediate objective: to arrange the secret murder of a rival—and something even worse. However busy with royal courtesies, and with his relation to his wife, inwardly he moves toward this objective. Yet the will is not unimpeded: the planning mind is assaulted by turbulent storms, that must be suppressed or released in private speech and action.

The actor-Macbeth normally looks the kind of man who could be named a king. Finlay remembered Kean in a robe much too large for him, tempting us to an association with the later description of a dwarfish Macbeth in giant's robes; but Finlay was an unfriendly witness—no other report suggests unkingliness in Kean's appearance. More often Macbeth's inadequacies are subtly psychic. In the theatre, again, he may appear "more kingly than the king." He may revel in his royalty; McKellen caressed his rich king's robe.

This is a delicate, pivotal point in Macbeth's development. Temptation to immoral action was in the past resisted, until he was almost paralyzed in mind and body. He is moving toward an action requiring more and more rigorous repression of the moral part of himself. Overtly he will seem more powerful, less vulnerable to subversion by conscience; but that inner dimension is never eliminated, and may sometimes be felt to seethe the more for being lidded.

Hence the demands of the immediate situation inevitably bring out the player in Macbeth. A Japanese, uncertain of his security, was fawning to his courtiers, covertly appealing for support. Irving masked a similar unease with a show of innocence, with touches of humor, and with a ready, continuous smile; but it was dimensioned by a nervous testiness, explained by the subtexts he noted for the scene: "Sleepless! Security!" Plummer, a weak and immature Macbeth, could seem exhilarated by this golden moment; he would regress, shattering, the coat of strength ragged and full of holes.

Where there was no dimension to Macbeth before, none was likely to be discovered now. The German George, emphasizing the brutish in Macbeth, bulled his way through his court to fling himself casually on the throne; the scene, as noted earlier, was designed to contrast his coarseness with Duncan's grace. In Macbeths whose design was already layered, dimension deepened. In Wolfit's strong Macbeth, the naked face showed wear and tear that the mask would have denied—most obviously in the sleeplessness that already drained him. To convey the effect, Wolfit reddened his lower eyelids, Harwood explained, and darkened the patches beneath. Reinhardt's Macbeth was noticeably pale. In an essentially inward Macbeth, like Scofield, the sealed stress told in the lines in his somber face, graven even more deeply. The almost pleading mood of his confession to murdering the grooms was now masked by pride, power, and an assumed unassailability that held him rigid. Olivier kept his mask, but even this seemed already world-weary, the celebration of his kingship joyless.

Macbeth may not at first see Banquo, watching the entry; Reinhardt's Lady had to point him out. Or Banquo may participate in the pomp: he has knelt to Macbeth, has offered the cushion on which the king places his crown and scepter—a close contact with the royalty he dreams for his line. *Here's our chief guest* (15), Macbeth says; but Lady Macbeth adds, in one of several lines in the scene that are loaded with an irony later to explode:

> If he had been forgotten,
> It had been as a gap in our great feast, (16–17)

A formality invests her invitation, and Macbeth's, following. But Macbeth may make the relationship personal; he has taken Banquo aside, put a hand across his shoulder. Macbeth's covert aim is to murder this man; yet they have soldiered together, and ambivalent fellow-feeling has sometimes been felt to color this moment. Garrick "affected" cheerfulness; Irving came to his Banquo smiling; Olivier bantered with his, though an observer could feel a hidden malignancy. Reinhardt's Macbeth, while establishing his new regality, was overflowing with kindness. Now, and throughout the scene, Booth's humanity would undermine his calculated wickedness, as he played friend, meant treachery, and was revolted by it. In Weaver, the sense of his dislike of his manipulation was described as "anguished jollity."

The solemn supper is set for *tonight*. That is the first of many of the restless scene's *time*-words: [this] *afternoon, tomorrow, time, night, hour, tomorrow, night, time, time, seven* [o'clock], *night, time, yesterday, times past, forever, minute, hour, time, moment, tonight, hour, tonight*. Ancillary words powerfully contribute to the sense of rushing, linear movement toward planned murder (e.g., *will, shall, farewell*). The movement will pause in Macbeth's contextual soliloquy when he will project his human condition in the "now" against the ground of the "always," and will dream of dynasty; then the only time-word will be, appropriately, *eternal;* though again supporting words will contribute to pastness and future (e.g., *to be, succeeding*). The scene's resumed linear movement will end in the shadow of the timeless—a *soul's flight*.

Some of the dialogue between Macbeth and Banquo may proceed "apart"; in the next scene Lady Macbeth will ask if Banquo had gone from court, as if she did not know the full substance of their talk. But she may speak then only for reassurance; in the theatre, as we will see, she sometimes participates silently now.

Banquo first responds, as to a sovereign:

> Let your highness
> Command upon me,

but he adds, with a reminder—of loyalty? fellowship? conspiracy?

> to the which my duties
> Are with a most indissoluble tie
> For ever knit. (21–24)

For ever. In hindsight, the words carry more of the scene's irony.

Since Banquo will not live long enough to indicate what he may be planning, the actor must decide if he is offering Macbeth friendship or blackmail; must decide if he is trusting a friend or conspiring with a collaborator, or perhaps refusing yet to decide; must wonder if he waits for Macbeth to die, or perhaps dreams in his *cursed thoughts* of another regicide.

The dialogue between the two men has something of the parrying of the night before Duncan's murder. A scheming Banquo, like Savits', who has let his own ambition and greed show, changes smartly when Macbeth enters to a flattering humility. Macbeth found this puzzling, and responded nervously, his hands playing with his robe. Sothern's Banquo eyed his king with frank suspicion; Sothern carefully refused to recognize it. Woodvine spoke Banquo's words, he said, to a double audience: for the court, he was making a formal submission to his king—in an echo, the actor thought, of Macbeth's formal deference to Duncan in I, iv; meanwhile he was reminding Macbeth of their shared secret.

Usually both men are slightly masked; and if we do not know what is going to happen, we sense fierce undercurrents in the apparently friendly exchange of words and glances. Who is manipulating whom? If Macbeth is tempted to betray to the audience the menace of his questions as to Banquo's ride, he must not be so obvious as to make a fool of Banquo. The pattern of movement generally has Macbeth asking a question as if he has Banquo at the end of a line; Banquo answers, starts to leave, Macbeth stops him and reels him back with another question. Macbeth may take his first cue, *Ride you this afternoon?* (25) from Banquo's equestrian dress—Irving noticed spurs on Banquo's boots. Banquo's *Aye* fits into Macbeth's plans. For form he says

> We should have else desir'd your good advice . . .
> In this day's council: (27, 29)

In the brief pause, Banquo may start to make a gesture of willingness to change his plans; if so, Macbeth forestalls him—

> But we'll take tomorrow. (29)

As Banquo starts to go, *Is't far you ride?* (30). Banquo's answer gives nothing away:

> As far, my Lord, as will fill up the time
> 'Twixt this, and supper. (31–32)

If Macbeth wonders why the ride, he does not ask. He makes gestures of friendly dismissal. Reinhardt's Macbeth offered his hand, then shook hands—but the audience could see that Macbeth was looking at Banquo's throat.

> MACBETH: Fail not our feast.
> BANQUO: My Lord, I will not. (35–36)

Banquo speaks more truly than he—or a doubting Macbeth—can know. Again he makes a false exit; and again Macbeth stops him. Now one of Macbeth's subtextual stresses surfaces. He speaks of the princes abroad—*our bloody cousins*—not confessing their parricide, and

> filling their hearers
> With strange invention. (39–40)

and his masked passions rise, often attracting the court's attention. Then Lady Macbeth must intervene: Tree's Lady caught his eye, to stop him; Marlowe took Sothern's hand, as did Booth's Lady, turning from conversation with her ladies to do so; Macready's touched him on the shoulder; Modjeska, standing behind her angry Macbeth, grasped him quickly. Macbeth drops the matter, for now, in public.

The authenticity of Macbeth's feeling covers what is an important piece of exposition—a hint that some counterforce is gathering. If he has spoken out before all his courtiers—as did Olivier—the information must register with them, as Macbeth recovers his mask:

> But of that tomorrow.
> When therewithall, we shall have cause of state,
> Craving us jointly. (40–42)

The last words perhaps stressed: meaningful reminder of the indissoluble tie. If Banquo's children are to fulfill the prophecy of becoming kings with anything like the immediacy of Macbeth's fulfillment, then the exile of the princes is essential. Having held this out, Macbeth seeks to let Banquo go again: *Hie you to horse* (42). Piscator's Macbeth smiled, put a fellow hand on Banquo's shoulder. Banquo smiled—but his hand went instinctively to his sword. Another false exit; still once more Macbeth brings him back, with a question that may well have been burning in his mind:

> Goes Fleance with you? (44)

Fleance is not directed to enter in this scene; Macbeth may indicate the boy by raising his hand, as Nicol Williamson did, as to say "so high." In fact

Fleance is often present; he may shrink behind Banquo at the state entry, or Banquo may put a protective arm out. Macbeth and his Lady often show kindness to the boy. Pritchard and Siddons might not have softened so; but Faucit developed a business of extending a hand to Fleance's head, and play-ing gently in his hair; when she was praised for acting "smooth treachery," Morley stoutly defended her as knowing her Shakespeare better than that:

> The fingers of a woman who has been a mother, and has murder on her soul, wander sadly and tenderly . . . her own lost innocence is in her mind.

Marlowe had kindly beckoned to Fleance, who came running to her; and Sothern caressed him. Lady Macbeth may have no evil intentions toward the child—as yet, at least—and can be wholehearted; one part of Macbeth's mind sees Fleance dead, as, often, he strokes him. Forrest patted his head, Booth laid a hand on his shoulder. Macready's fondling of the boy was seen to be "cat-like." In the Craig staging, Fleance came running in, saw Macbeth, started back in fear—a common response, often echoing the meeting in II, i. Macbeth put out a hand to Fleance's head, Banquo drew his son back to him.

This extra-textual use of Fleance raises problems. The boy's presence gives Macbeth and his Lady an opportunity to betray their feelings toward a child—especially so Macbeth, seeing the son of a rival. If the boy is obviously intu-itively afraid of Macbeth, and shrinks from him, this posits an effective men-ace, but one that might better stay masked. Fleance's acceptance of caresses, as by Sothern and Marlowe, may, by coating the underlying conflict, make it more effectively ambiguous, and the ensuing events more meaningful. The less obviously Macbeth is planning to trap Banquo, the more the subse-quent action is open to possibility.

Banquo may at last grow impatient—at the attention to Fleance, at Mac-beth's repeated recalls. Scofield's Banquo, Mason, finally snapped out his last line, irritated, giving another impulse to the felt urgency of time's pas-sage: *our time does call upon's* (45). Woodvine took time to remind Mac-beth of their bond. he knelt; then he kissed the king's hand, but only after a long look at him.

At the departure Banquo (and Fleance, if there) must make some obeisance: bow, kiss Macbeth's hand, salute—Craig's Banquo had to nudge his son to make the last gesture. Macbeth's *Farewell* is more final than Banquo can know; it has been made even more so by being delayed, and sent after the departed thane.

Once Banquo is gone, Macbeth has another urgent piece of business to complete. Some hint of its impending may have been given: when Olivier first entered, an attendant started forward with information, but was stopped by the warning look in Macbeth's eye; at such a man Macbeth looks now. But first the court must be dismissed; Macbeth may momentarily be rapt again, lost in thought as Irving was, after the effort with Banquo. He recovered; but he then spoke abstractedly, his mind on other things. But Macbeth must speak, time presses, its passing again specified:

> Let every man be master of his time,
> Till seven at night, to make society
> The sweeter welcome. (49–51)

Guinness easily projected a player's affability; Reinhardt's Macbeth formally walked the steps up to his throne, to turn and make a friendly regal announcement; Scofield, his mind ranging ahead, was polite but haughty.

Macbeth's next line first exposes verbally the changed relationship of Macbeth to his Lady, to whom he directs it. She sometimes has approached him, as expecting mutual support; has even gone to kiss him, as Tree's Lady did; he may pat her affectionately before sending her away, as Sothern did when Marlowe came to protest, or kiss her hand (Hopkins); but more often, as he is deep in his thoughts, Macbeth's manner rejects her as much as his words:

> We will keep ourself till supper time *alone*. (52)

If the surprised Lady lingers, a stern glance may dispatch her. If she is not surprised, if she expects this rejection, much can be seen in that. Irene Worth gave Porter a long, searching glance. Macbeth's habit, as the Lady has been learning, is to keep himself now very much *alone*. Their past interdependence is abridged. Even the strongest matron has to yield to dismissal, with whatever grace or understanding. (How did Pritchard bear this rebuff?) Macbeth, dealing with death, has no time for wife. Where there has been strong affection, the breach is particularly telling: thus Mirren, so sensual, so physically at one with Williamson, seemed now even sexually discarded as he ordered her away. Macbeth and his Lady will have some particularly intimate moments still; but this rejection points ominously to the future, and will partly explain Lady Macbeth's first lines in the next scene. If Macbeth is aware enough of her strain, and he fears for her, or for any danger she may bring to him, he may sign to her gentlewoman, or to Seyton, to attend her off. Macbeth's final line, dismissing his court—and, if she has waited, his wife— (McKellen cruelly rebuffed Dench by turning his back on her as he said it), is a king's blessing, a prayer.

> While then, God be with you. (53)

God may stick in Macbeth's throat, as with Scofield. The blessing will do Lady Macbeth no good.

The words may stick in Macbeth's mind; he may be for a moment rapt again, as Sothern was—to be reminded, by a movement, of the presence of his servant, who then helped him off with his robe. This servant is often familiar by now, may already have the name of Seyton. Irving felt that this man's intimacy with Macbeth was such that he would be the third murderer. Macbeth orders the servant to bring *those men* who attend—grim word here— his *pleasure*.

Alone, Macbeth's mask drops. Did we sense that in the early part of the scene we have been present at a prologue? A deeper action is to begin. The smile slid from Guinness' face. Forbes-Robertson sank back on his throne, and meaningfully handled the scepter that he had earned so desperately. Reinhardt's Macbeth closed his eyes, raised his hands to lift his crown, brought it down, looked at it, sighed deeply. Irving paced; Williamson strode about in a kind of fury. The Japanese Macbeth rose to immediate anger. Scofield stood almost motionless, his face haggard, ravaged.

The whole process of Macbeth's development prepares for the sudden nakedness of his concentrated passion now. No more overt moral debate; no more submission to the inward forces that can so undermine him as to smother his function. There are still self-doubt, self-attack; but now they feed a hostility already nourished from deep sources within the design. These do not at once appear; this soliloquy, like all the others, is an action developing through thought and feeling to resolution, as Macbeth discovers his own motivations.

He begins with the threat he feels to himself, that endangers his dream of *security*—*mortals chiefest enemy*, Hecate will say (III, v, 36)

> To be thus, is nothing, but to be *safely* thus: (59)

The line is jagged; most of the words, small as they are, bear full weight. Much of the rest has the same "quick, sharp utterance" Hackett sensed, as he felt Macbeth hardening through the speech. The inner feeling blazes up, enough to move a man to murder. The first line for McKellen was a sudden fierce outcry, releasing repressed resentments held in until he was alone, that had been only faintly sensed under the smiling mask of his dialogue with Banquo. His whole identity was at stake: "To be thus . . . *NOTHING!*"

As Macbeth found praise for the Duncan he would murder, he finds it now for Banquo. Banquo's best qualities make him the most dangerous. Again the monosyllables hold heavy accents:

> Our fears in Banquo stick deep,
> And in his royalty of nature reigns that
> Which would be fear'd. 'Tis much he dares, (60–62)

Dares. The *man*-word may intimate a mortal threat haunting Macbeth. James Black suggests, "Macbeth seems to see Banquo as murderer—'what I fear from Banquo sticks deep in me.'" Banquo can be a present danger only as he might interrupt Macbeth's kingship. As Macbeth's soliloquized thought progresses in its customary way toward resolve, he anticipates immediate as well as future danger from Banquo. Any action Banquo might take, Macbeth apprehends, would be well thought-out, well covered; he would be *safely* thus. There is a kind of slow pain in the words, the rhythm lengthens:

> He hath a wisdom, that doth guide his valour,
> To act in *safety*. (64–65)

Then the more staccato rhythms again, as Macbeth magnifies Banquo as a
rival, and perhaps exposes a self-image:

> There is none but he,
> Whose being I do fear: and under him,
> My genius is rebuk'd, as it is said
> Mark Antony's was by Caesar. (65–68)

The reference is to Antony and Octavius, and aptly connotes, in this play
involving intangible influences, a fateful inequality between the men's accompanying spirits, or daemons. But the implications may extend to the difference in character: so Antony, with familiar qualities of the tragic hero:
imagination, poetic vision, great dreams, flawed by failure in shrewdness
and adequacy to deal with his own passions; Octavius reasonable, clever,
hard—the typical "new man," who in tragedy often brings down the dreamer.
Macbeth is indeed more like Antony; and he senses himself *under* the more
careful man: *under* echoing again the pervasive climate of degree.

  As his thought develops, Macbeth comes to the heart of his anguish—not
Banquo's threat to himself so much as to the dynasty he dreams of. The Sisters

> hailed him father to a line of kings.
> Upon my head they plac'd a fruitless crown,
> And put a barren scepter in my grip,
> Thence to be wrenched with an unlineal hand,
> No son of mine succeeding: (71–75)

Some have seen in this the implication that Macbeth and his Lady are sterile;
but it is the scepter that would be barren, not this King and Queen: Lady
Macbeth, again, has given suck, has tenderly nursed a child—who may be
alive even now. If Macbeth could have none of the sons he mentions, he would
not be driven, by his envious thoughts, to kill Banquo—it would do him
no good. Kemble, defending Macbeth against what he saw as Whately's
charge of cowardice, insisted that Macbeth was urged to kill Banquo and
Fleance not from fear but

> because they threaten to reduce him and his lineage from the splendours of
> monarchy to the obscurity of vassalage.

(But see the Appendix for a fuller discussion of this.)
  The crown, the scepter, all the symbols of royalty, are live images of Macbeth's passion. Forbes-Robertson's eyes remained fixed on the scepter; Reinhardt's Macbeth clasped the crown to his body, as if protecting it; then put
it on again, with wild energy. Williamson, raging across the floor before the
throne, pounded fist into hand, again and again. The hostility comes out
white-hot, tinged with anguish:

> If't be so, (75)

The *if* is only to hang his anger on; it becomes *so* immediately:

> For Banquo's issue have I fil'd my mind,
> For them, the gracious Duncan have I murder'd, (76–77)

Irving, exulting in the pathos of Macbeth's poetry, indulged a "tender tremolo" that fitted his contrivance of a hypocritical design; but with some other Macbeths a genuine note of grief has mingled with the self-pity. Then the acid bitterness is engulfing:

> Put rancours in the vessel of my peace
> Only for them, and mine eternal jewel
> Given to the common enemy of man,
> To make them kings, the seeds of Banquo kings. (78–81)

Fil'd ripples with polyphony. It is ordinarily glossed "defiled"; it may also suggest "viled"; it may imply the metaphor of the mind rasped—this mind that, we will learn, in another metaphor, is acrawl with stinging things; and it may carry the "degree" meaning of later uses in the play, of being forced into a rank. The spread of connotation may also apply to *eternal jewel*—usually glossed, in Christian framework, as "immortal soul." Dr. Johnson believed that Shakespeare borrowed the image from a pre-Christian context.* Macbeth may be as much poet as theologian here, using the doctrinal reference to support the implication of something most precious—a use to which, elsewhere, he puts *jewel*.

One dimension of Macbeth's furious agony now is rage for his lost innocence, for the time when he resisted immorality, instead of embracing it. Irving's note:

> Savage, great change, no need of his wife now.

Heilman observes that, unlike many tragic heroes, Macbeth emphasizes the price he has had to pay for his action, rather than a self-knowledge, a recognition of what his action had made him. This is certainly true to the text here; though in a sense the whole of the play, from the moment of Duncan's murder, is a record in words and action of how Macbeth comes to terms with what he has become.

Nothing qualifies his hostility now, as he mounts to the climax of his emotion:

> Rather than so, come fate into the list,
> And champion me to th'utterance. (82–83)

This is the warrior, ready to challenge fate itself, perhaps his weapon in his clenched fist. Weaver tore off the cross from around his neck, arming him-

---

*"It is always an entertainment to an inquisitive reader, to trace a sentiment to an original source; and therefore, though the term *enemy of man*, applied to the devil, is itself obvious, yet some may be pleased with being informed, that Shakespeare probably borrowed it from the first lines of the Destruction of Troy, a book which he is known to have read." With Johnson's note Steevens evidently concurred, since it is included in the Johnson–Steevens edition.

self with unholiness. Reinhardt's Macbeth repeated, unconsciously, his earlier stabbing gesture.

The moment holds, and then Macbeth hears a sound—perhaps a knock again. Anticipation: *Who's there?* He may be rapt, as Irving was, and "Start." Sothern went to a table, keeping his eyes on the door, and rested his hand on his naked sword. Tree carefully took off his crown, and laid aside his scepter, wanting to separate from his kingship the dirty business to come. We feel that this is the thing Macbeth has been waiting through the scene for. We see *two murderers* enter, with the servant, who leaves. The murderers may kneel to their king (Hopkins), or bow deeply (Savits). Because they are called simply *murderers*, the two are sometimes represented as the lowest hire-for-pay killers, symbols of human evil. Modjeska had ugly, humpbacked men; Reinhardt's were dull, brutish, depraved; Plummer's stupid, gruesome even before they killed; Irving's common hirelings. Komisarjevsky ran them in a pack: in 1933 he wanted to suggest the topical use of an army to serve a tyrant, so he had a unit of ten depersonalized soldiers, whom Macbeth addressed on a landing until, half way through the dialogue, he dismissed eight, and remained with Shakespeare's two. Savits also used soldiers, but differently, to suggest that his Macbeth would be not a hirer of assassins, but a general whose men obeyed him blindly. In a German staging (1968) that emphasized Hitlerian tyranny, the murderers resembled hardened SS men, in black clothes, jack-booted, brutal.

But Shakespeare's murderers are not the dregs of society, nor faceless. He could have designed killers at the Porter's level, lewd, greedy fellows; instead he presented men of some feeling, and with the verbal ability to give their feeling expression. Granville-Barker cites the first murderer's scene-setting verse in III, iii to demonstrate that they are not "gutter bred." "The text's implication is surely that they were officers, cast perhaps for some misdemeanor and out of luck." Halio proposes "probably disgraced officers." Hall chose simple, troubled men, quiet and determined to improve their lot— obviously an unhappy one. Weaver's murderers were in court dress, though simpler than that of the thanes. Macready used former second and third officers of Duncan's army; Hackett, "trustworthy, impecunious noblemen of the time, soldiers of fortune who would sell their swords to the best bidder."

For the first time we are to see Macbeth uncompromisingly planning murder. Behind his mask is a brain crawling with scorpions, he will say soon; how much of their wriggling, stinging assault will show in the face he turns to his suborned murderers? The theatre Macbeth has sometimes been faulted for betraying nothing of his unease, seeming hardened not only in shell but deep through; the character's effort from now on will be to try to make the shell his self, and the persistent dialectic will be his attempted suppression of anything from within that might erode it. The more Macbeth covers inner resistance to his crime, the more he "plays" his tempter's role; the difference between inner and outer self vanishes when he is committed without reservation.

Benson was able to seem completely indifferent to what would happen to his fellow general; no compunctions visited him; he was the murderer-Macbeth. Mounet, fitted to his fingertips to act the king, played the condescending monarch with mingled bonhomie and majesty. Matkowsky affected haughtiness; Reineke pretended it—but betrayed, with his false dignity, that he was unaccustomed to kingship. Savits' Macbeth played a king made sad by what he had to do, presenting a wry "honest" face as he came down from his throne to speak of the task that made him so unhappy. Irving, playing his conception of the treacherous coward getting others to do his killing for him, would let the audience in on his manipulation of the assassins for his own purposes.

> His subtle caressing manner, as he sits in his chair and surveys them from a kingly distance, looking into their hearts, winding himself round them like a serpent, suggesting a crime which is to gratify *their* evil passions, wreak *their* revenge, and indirectly do him a service—all these touches are refined, courtly, natural, a little bit of pre-Raffealitism [*sic*].

McKellen was the practical politician, now genial, now confiding, now sarcastic, now authoritative, smoothly shifting to the successive moods that most effectively subverted his subjects.

Other Macbeths could not so easily subdue their inner resistances. Aldridge tried, ingratiatingly, to be justifying himself to the murderers for what he wanted them to do, but he could not hide his shame and disgust. Booth's bottled reluctance would finally break out. Williamson's *angst* hid in the impatience and rage which drove him from his "throne" to pace and fume; then to the back of the chair to lean over it to snarl at them—Evelyn Gibbs saw in this the symbolism of the throne abused by villainy. Though Scofield's murderers were decent enough men, he found it hard to deal with them: kingly, he was less politician than general, had to mask his distaste for the work. Chabrol's Macbeth could not bring himself to look at the men, whom he both feared and detested. Olivier, for all his smooth manner, his air of command, conveyed a sense that his immense contempt for the instruments he was using was exceeded by his contempt for himself—"the more arresting because tinged with bitter amusement" (Hobson). He drew laughs from the scene, Harwood noticed, but

> I have the lasting impression that Macbeth found one of those assassins even more evil than he was himself and did his best to keep away from him.

Macbeth had met these men yesterday; but the special business he has to do may check him when he confronts them now. Reinhardt's Macbeth started to speak, had to clear his throat. Juriev deliberately held the pause as his sullen murderers came in (identified in the Russian staging as among the recent insurrectionists against Duncan); he moved slowly toward them, bearing down on them with his personality. Ceremonial sometimes initiates the colloquy: a Japanese Macbeth summoned his Seyton with a bottle of wine and three gold cups; Macbeth poured wine into two cups, and handed them, one at a time, to the murderers; Seyton handed him his own. The men stood, listening as he talked, now not knowing what to do; finally he raised his cup, and they raised theirs. In the echo of a different ceremony, Plummer sat in the center of a trestle table, "rather like a wily Christ-figure," and fed the murderers, one at either side: it looked, a Chicago viewer thought, "curiously like a travesty on the Last Supper." An English Macbeth himself went to fetch a tray of drinks before conspiring. Hackett's murderers were close enough to him in rank that he could go to them graciously, even put his arms around their shoulders.

An uneasy equation brings Macbeth and the two men together: the proportion he can summon of authority, power, persuasion, bribery, and appeal to their natures and interests, as against the strength of their manliness and any shreds of dignity they cling to. If they can be absolutely manipulated, like puppets, then no chance exists for the response Mansfield hoped for:

> Try to rouse the young [only the young? does he mean the *naive* spectators?] in your audience to call to the 1st. and 2nd. M's not to listen to it.

Yet they must acquiesce: the tension derives from the process of their acquiescence, and the virtuosity of Macbeth's persuasion. This is complicated by the fact that he holds something back until the very end; he will avoid as long as possible coming to that point, and so he will find words to fill the spaces in between, words symptomatic of his own suspended state.

Granville-Barker saw Macbeth "pacing the floor and weaving words like spells around the two"; and some Macbeths have so done. Juriev began by speaking slowly, forcefully, very quietly, giving the men no chance to interrupt, as if hypnotizing them. Maeterlinck's Macbeth set a pattern of speaking in whispers, effecting a secret and shameful conversation that allowed no outbreaks of resistance. In this same mode, a Czech Macbeth (1963) betrayed his assimilation into the ranks of the murderers by kneeling with them as he talked.

Macbeth's language here is essentially practical, spare in imagery, as McKellen observed; and a commercial note has entered the relationship. Hopkins held the eyes of his murderers with a money bag, which he dangled as he talked. A Czech Macbeth, his hand in a purse, slowly fed coins to his men.

Olivier's frontal assault, *Well then,/Now*, was described by *Theatre Quarterly* as a masterpiece of mesmerism:

> He stood centre-stage, in his vivid red gown, black-bearded, with his crown at a mere suggestion of an angle on his head . . . Olivier glanced arrogantly from one [murderer] to the other, crooked the index finger of each hand in terrible invitation, and made "well" into a question. He paused. The murderers looked at one another. The index fingers swept downwards and pointed straight at the floor on each side of him. He said "then" as a command. They moved slowly

towards him like frightened stoats. Almost humorously, but with an edge of
impatience, he said "now" and an act of hypnosis was completed.

How much are we to believe Macbeth's insistence that Banquo is the one
who held them *so under fortune,/ Which you thought had been our innocent self*
(93–94)? (Can he say this last phrase, and not wince? How much is he trying to convince himself?)

> This I made good to you . . .
> Passed in probation with you:
> How you were borne in hand, how crossed:
> The instruments: who wrought with them:
> And all things else, that might
> To half a soul, and to a notion craz'd,
> Say, thus did Banquo. (95–101)

He means: "to *only* half a soul, even to a maddened mind, this must seem so".
His own underlying tension may hint at how much it may describe himself.

The First Murderer's answer, *You made it known to us* (102), has a kind of
dignity, acknowledgment without servility. No argument is offered. Macbeth may not allow time. If he is obviously manipulating brainwashed men,
we may doubt the truth of what he says; if they retain some dignity, and he
the sincerity that men of some worth would require, then we may believe
that Banquo may indeed have done some wrong to them. The murderers
have been acted as truly wanting revenge against an enemy. E. K. Chambers
assumes the murderers were Macbeth's victims, since they had thought so;
but they say nothing of this, only he does, and they say they have accepted
his denial. Shakespeare's care to give some individuality to the murderers
suggests that he meant at least to leave the matter ambiguous.

Macbeth moves slowly with them. So much for that. Now:

> Do you find your patience so predominant,
> In your nature, that you can let this go? (106–107)

Then the touch of irony (Irving sneered):

> Are you so gospelled, to pray for this *good* man, (108)

and, more important to Macbeth,

> And for his issue, whose heavy hand
> Hath bow'd you to the grave, and beggar'd
> Yours for ever? (109–111)

Sanders sees Macbeth trying to bully the murderers into such a hatred for
Banquo as to make the murder theirs, not his; this would help explain the
intensity and persuasiveness of his argument. Sanders thinks Macbeth's
try is in vain; but he does rouse them to act. The First Murderer, again speaking simply for them, asserts a man's readiness to kill—which is the other side

of the manliness Macbeth himself declared when he resisted Lady Macbeth's urging.

> We are men, my liege. (112)

Macbeth returns to the attack,

> Ay, in the catalogue ye go for men, (113)

and he likens the hierarchy of men to that of dogs. Shakespeare goes thus to the dogs because of an interest of James', Paul speculates; Muir dismisses this as the main motivation for the passage; certainly it needed no kingly dog-lover to explain at all the relevance of the speech to the play. *Degree* is the subject; Macbeth speaks as if the ranks of dogs, presumably content with their stations, have a parallel with those of men. McKellen, after his catalogue of canines, lumped together with amused contempt the variety of beasts called

> All by the name of . . . *dogs*. (116)

His delay and emphasis on the last word linked to the dog-world those men who were only nominally *men*.

Macbeth had himself breached degree, as had others before him; now he urges these men to prove themselves worth an advanced place in the *valued file* by killing (as he did) someone of higher degree. Granville-Barker points out that this argument could only mean something to men who were already something more than the lowest; men to whom a *man's* status had some meaning—according to his *gift, which bounteous nature*

> Hath in him clos'd: whereby he does receive
> Particular addition, from the bill,
> That writes them all alike: and so of men. (120–122)

Macbeth urges on the men Lady Macbeth's old measure of manliness, but always avoiding the name for the deed:

> Now, if you have a station in the file,
> Not i' th' worst rank of manhood, say't,
> And I will put that *business*

—the practiced euphemism—

> in your bosoms,
> Whose execution takes your enemy off,
> Grapples you to the heart; and love of us,

and then again the plea for sympathy:

> Who wear our health but sickly in his life,
> Which in his death were perfect. (123–129)

The performance is dazzling: he holds out promise of friendship, but no specific bribes (though in the theatre coins have changed hands); subjects them—as he was subjected—to an appeal to a masculinity they must hold dear. He allows them to be partners with him in crime, while challenging them to find a place for themselves not too far below. This is a Macbeth we have not seen before: he has learned how to move men in mass after Duncan's murder, and now he grows more skilled, outwardly a diplomat, whatever seethes inside. So Olivier dominated his men, David noted:

> The murderers, half scared, half fascinated by the now evil magnetism of the king, shrank back each time he approached them in a swirl of robes, while he, pacing the stage between and around them, continuously spun a web of bewildering words about their understandings, about his own conscience, about the crime that between them they were to commit.

His share in murder linked him to them as much as his contempt for them and him: Alan Dent thought he loaded the lines with irony and scorn, a Macbeth who already felt his secret murders sticking on his hands. Williamson, also pacing through the scene, could not subdue his anger to diplomacy when he came to the *dog* speech; he exploded at his murderers, impatient, thwarted. The murderers were hardly worthy of Reinhardt's Macbeth: he was in a fever of excitement, high-spirited, full of passion; they were brutal, matter-of-fact men who nodded with heads and words to all he said.

They are better than that. Agate found the "only absolutely moving moment" in one production when the Second Murderer spoke with authentic passion,

> I am one, my Liege,
> Whom the vile blows and buffets of the world
> Hath so incens'd, that I am reckless what I do,
> To spite the world. (130–133)

The First Murderer speaks similarly, a desperate man. If not Banquo, somebody has certainly made life hard for these two. They are willing to name Banquo their *enemy*. Now Macbeth speaks to them more and more as associates, men to whom he can confide delicate secrets. Banquo is Macbeth's enemy, too,

> and though I could
> With bare-fac'd power sweep him from my sight,
> . . . . yet I must not,
> For certain friends that are both his, and mine,
> Whose loves I may not drop, (142–146)

A curious tone colors this speech: "I could/ With *bare-faced power* . . ." He acknowledges his masking, his hours upon the stage; then, having voiced a capacity to destroy—that the murderers must understand might aim also at them—he juxtaposes to it a request for their *love*. If he is conventional, or pretending, it is not all convention, or pretense: the note of his need for the support and approval of his fellows has sounded, and will sound again later

in unmistakable sincerity. He will not easily give up his ties with human
kindness.

>   thence it is,
>   That I to your assistance do make love,
>   Masking the *business*

Again, the word itself a masking—

>   from the common eye,
>   For sundry weighty reasons. (147–150)

It is a speech that he must be saying partly to himself as well as to the murderers, full of truth, whatever its calculation.

Will the murderers agree to murder? No suspense remains, if the men are
clods, listening aimlessly to a self-serving speech, showing themselves servile
or stupid; or, as Reinhardt's were, impatient, cynical, only waiting to be
told what to do, so they could get on with it; or taking coins, or their eyes fixed
on Macbeth's purse, only waiting to be paid first. If some conviction begins
to move them, at Macbeth's urging for their love to help him; if even they
consult, as Tree's did, or exchange looks, like Irving's, then they are not yet
murderers, and we watch them becoming so, yielding to a personal appeal
without any bribe, except to their manliness. The Second Murderer voices
his acquiescence; and the first, more emotional, begins a speech that seems
to promise commitment, even dedication:

>   Though our lives— (153)

And Macbeth knows that he has won. He interrupts—

>   Your spirits shine through you. (154)

Olivier said it quickly, as if to shut them up, impatient of their protestations,
wanting action. Sothern hushed them, because they were beginning to speak
loudly, and he remembered that his court had ears. Hopkins, who held his
purse ready as a promise, could not hide his contempt. Scofield, continuing
his grim, truly *business*like process, allowed himself—not them—the slightest
flicker of amusement in his words. Savits' Macbeth, who had spoken sadly
all through, as if compelled to an act he really disliked, working himself up
to a high pitch of eloquence, dropped his play the moment the two murderers
agreed. He became matter-of-fact, moved back up to his throne, once more
inaccessible, a king concerned with detail.

Now Macbeth is all action, his *time* words hurrying his speech along: *hour,
time, moment, night, hour*. A touch of excess infects the speech; buried in it
will be the special demand he has held back, that he must shock them with.
Juriev's hesitancies suggested a Macbeth keeping the murderers on a line.
They had started to leave him, on the throne platform; he stopped them:

> Within this hour, at most,
> I will advise you where to plant yourselves, (155–156)

(An inversion of the fertility motif, Duthie suggests; certainly, in that sense, looking back to Duncan's use, ironic.) They descended a few more steps; again he stopped them:

> for't must be done tonight. (158)

Tonight, with Juriev, was like a blow. (Craig's startled murderers repeated, "Tonight?")

> And something from the palace: (159

Macbeth pauses at the colon, then, still not ready to explode his mine—

> always thought,
> That I require a clearness; (159–160)

—*Security*—

> To leave no rubs nor botches in the work: (161)

Again the colon pause—something more to come—and Macbeth rushes through it, no colons till the end,

> Fleance, his son, that keeps him company,
> Whose absence is no less material to me,
> Than is his father's, must embrace the fate
> Of that dark hour: (162–165)

Now the murderers' response forces the pause of a colon, as they consider this new shock. To kill a child, a son. They need to consult, at least with looks. Once more Macbeth must ask for acquiescence:

> resolve yourselves apart,
> I'll come to you anon. (165 166)

Pause. The murderers, because of the fierce frowns Macbeth has given them, or the purse he has displayed, or because they themselves have agreed (one, the worse man, may have been seen to persuade the better), finally declare themselves resolved.

The thing is concluded; Macbeth is ready to send them off. Olivier, Foakes remembers, huddled in his black coat with the two murderers, and the three dark figures carried an echo of an earlier three. The Czech Macbeth, who had been paying out coins, now threw his purse, as did the Japanese Macbeth; Savits' Macbeth had lost all interest in the men, turned away to his own thoughts. When Salvini's murderers, before leaving, tried in obeisance to seize the hem of the king's robe, he repulsed them with an involuntary shudder, and waved them imperiously away. As McKellen watched his assassins go, he wiped his mouth, as if to get rid of a bad taste.

Macbeth has made his murder. He looks into the future. Reinhardt's Macbeth took a deep breath, and slowly let it out. Porter's face settled into a smile of triumph. If any resistance has been stirring in Macbeth against his negotiations with the men, it has been felt to mount as the plans approached resolution. In Scofield's lined face, set deeper in determination, pain could momentarily be glimpsed. A residual reluctance had colored all Booth's action; now, alone,

> repentance and human agony over his own helplessness are seen, for one heart-rending moment, in conflict with the demons that impel [him] to deeper depths of crime and misery. (*Tribune*)

But the thing is done. As before Duncan's murder, Macbeth, with whatever reluctance, sends Banquo and Fleance to doom—the words, short but heavy, ending in spondee-like solemnity:

> Banquo, thy soul's flight,
> If it find heaven, must find it out tonight. (169–170)

Act III, Scene ii

Enter Macbeth's Lady, and a Servant.
She may enter alone, at first, searching for Macbeth, as she may have sought him in I, vii—a German Lady again, on a revolve, seemed to strain through long halls looking. When Lady Macbeth is alone, her mask—her guard—may drop, the numbing despair show. But not before a servant. Then she forces on her queen's face. So Rigg, visibly deteriorated in body, her pale cheeks blobbed with rouge, crouching by herself, still could find the strength to keep up a show when anyone was by.

The Lady may be "discovered" with attendance: Anglin wanted Craig to show her being dressed, and Murphy was so seen; a Czech Lady was having her leg massaged, a reflection of sensuality-malaise. More often the single servant—Seyton, or the gentlewoman, summoned by her, or sent to watch her in the previous scene by Macbeth—bows or kneels, or helps with garment or crown, and awaits her desire.

Dench entered in time to find McKellen ending his last soliloquy. She moved concernedly toward him; he turned away from her and went out. This second rebuff—he had dismissed her with the court at the beginning of III, i—was a blow that would partly motivate her own soliloquy in a few moments, as she let her repressed tears flow.

Lady Macbeth's condition now must be a delicately articulated step in the progression from her trauma after the murder, and her almost silent endurance of the court scene (III, i), through the immediate oncoming intimacy with Macbeth, to the climax of her experience as queen in III, iv. All the forces that converged on her in her "faint"—plus a new one, as we soon learn—are intensified now; they torment her asleep as well as awake, and as we imagine her offstage life, we may wonder if already her night is so troubled that she must leave her bed and walk. Even now, with night coming on, she may have a candle by her, or in the hands of her gentlewoman; has the time already come when she must have light always? The strain on her will be more noticeably overt in her brief moment alone because it will be covert when she is with Macbeth.

Her first question suggests that she may, in the interim, have been thinking about Macbeth's conversation with Banquo in III, i:

LADY MACBETH: Is Banquo gone from court?
SERVANT: Ay, Madam, but returns again tonight. (3–4)

Why does she ask? Will the actress understand her not to have heard the III, i, dialogue? Or to have wondered as Dench had, at Macbeth's motives in learning the details of Banquo's ride? Martita Hunt was sure the Lady did not know of the plan to murder Banquo. Fanny Kemble, writing to Furness, suggested that Lady Macbeth "has undoubtedly been working out in her own mind" what Macbeth intended. Is any new murderous plan in her own imagination? Marlowe put the question anxiously to her Seyton (helping off her cloak) and was relieved at his answer. Marlowe had had enough of killing. But a harder Lady's relief might be ambiguous: because Banquo was safe? Or because he would not be?

Lady Macbeth looks toward Macbeth's chamber, perhaps starts to move there, stops. She has been queen long enough to this moody king, this changing husband, to have learned a different approach. She must ask audience; she has done so resentfully, even sarcastically (with emphasis on *few*):

Say to the king, I would attend his leisure,
For a few words. (5–6)

Left alone, the mask drops, and the dreadful self stares out from under the queen's crown:

Nought's had, all's spent,
Where our desire is got without content: (8–9)

She is surrounded by what she desired; but

'Tis *safer*, to be that which we destroy,
Than by destruction dwell in doubtful joy. (10–11)

In the final oxymoron, the first term, *doubtful*, undercuts and empties the second. There is no *joy*. The thought, voiced in a kind of ritual rhyme, is suicidal: better be with the dead. The face and body sag under it. The difference between the front shown the servant, and the broken one now, measures the Lady's vulnerability to collapse, and the fierceness of will and energy that will be necessary to reassume her mask. She is surrounded by what she thought she desired—this may be accentuated by her burden of regality, in jewels, crown, robes; but for her, too, the dream of commandeering security—safety—is melting away (she confesses it to herself, as she will never to Macbeth). For most Ladies, symptoms of their dissolution would show through, though in different degrees. Some would yield slowly, physically and emotionally; some grieve and tremble; some be so disturbed they evidently live on the edge of madness.

The contrast between the Lady's beginning and now is most striking in those who earlier seemed most invulnerable. Siddons preserved, before the servant, "Great dignity and solemnity of voice," Bell thought, though "nothing of the joy of gratified ambition." The actress herself felt a deep anguish, forerunner of a mind diseased, ominous of the Lady's death. Her Lady is no longer the presumptuous, determined woman who prompted Macbeth to murder Duncan. Cushman yielded even more: she wrung her hands, "hopeless and barren of comfort," exposing "the depths of a soul soon to enter the night of madness, already enduring the torments of hell" (Clapp). Judith Anderson, even more wearied than in III, i by her heavy robes, and being alone free to show it, dragged herself in, a shade closer to the madness fated when she first touched blood on the daggers. Merchant, her eyes searching anxiously for Macbeth, no longer bore the taut, smooth, sophisticated face that had charmed and taunted Scofield; it was crumpling as she went to sit alone on her throne, gazing at his empty one.

One emotional note in Lady Macbeth's design may retard her deterioration: an intense concern, from the beginning, for her husband's welfare. In a Lady who emphasizes this, it momentarily at least masters the swelling of melancholy and despair. But we are not to know this when we see her enter: her depression is such that survival itself may seem questionable. So Reinhardt's Lady, looking despairingly from a window, saying her lines with a real longing for death: her body giving way with her spirit, she closed her eyes and sank down against the wall. Her readiness, since Duncan's murder, to reveal—when unseen by Macbeth—the depth of her shock and dismay made her desperation now seem inevitable. Terry, ironically dressed, she wrote, "for a party" (the banquet) but in deep grief, took her pose from Dürer's drawing "Melancholy," of a seated girl, dreaming, chin supported by her hand. Always, in past crises, Terry's Lady had been impelled to act, not think, for their safety. Now, sighing, she pauses, in deep-seated misery. Her note: "Express here a rooted sorrow." She has a "half-dulled knowledge" that she has been deceived by her husband; "She sees *clearer* now." Faucit's soliloquy was a "pathetic and humbled lamentation"; Bateman's a despairing listlessness; Calhoun's a low moan, as she wandered despairingly about the castle; Thorndike's a cry from the heart of a woman at the end of her tether.

Then Macbeth enters. The infestation in his mind is plain on his face. He too can think of suicide, as we will soon learn. What will happen when despair meets despair? The moment is charged with expectation.

The text suggests that they see and talk to each other at once; but they may not, and then an interesting perspective on their relationship develops. Sothern, his head down as he entered, not aware of Lady Macbeth, crossed

to a table to take off his crown, and sat heavily on his throne. Marlowe's haggard and tearful face, that had been suffused with grief, changed at once as
she watched him. She came to him, knelt on the floor beside him, consoling.

Tree, on the other hand, twisting in his own thoughts, entered quietly to
find his Lady unaware, lost in melancholy. He moved across and slowly
touched her. She turned; he sat down and sighed; her immediate thought
was to strengthen him.

Granville-Barker suggests that Macbeth has kept away from his Lady to
avoid dragging her further into guilt:

> He knows that she is broken and useless. One of the few notes that are let soften
> the grimness of the tragedy is Lady Macbeth's wan effort to get near enough to
> the tortured man to comfort him. But the royal robes, stiff on their bodies—
> stiff as with caked blood—seem to keep them apart.

But Macbeth does come back to her, speaks in intervals more lovingly to her
here than anywhere else; and her comfort, however intended, does seem to
give him strength to pursue his secret murders.

This is the usual pattern: the Lady begins the scene in despair, summons
her strength in the face of his despair, that she must see written large. How
unmistakable it was, when Kemble came to the doorway, Planché thought,
that his mind was full of scorpions; the crown seemed a torturing burden to
him. Siddons could try to encourage Macbeth, Bell thought, "Still [in] accents very plaintive"—which suggests a continuance of her "mournful" tone;
all through the scene she gave an impression of wretchedness in countenance
and manner, as well as in her sad voice, that *Blackwood's* found suited to her
pity for her husband. Siddons herself believed the Lady intended support,
but suffering by now had carried her well on the way to death.

> In gratitude for [Macbeth's] unbounded affection, and in commiseration of his
> sufferings, she suppresses the anguish of her heart, even while [it] is precip-
> itating her into the grave which at this moment is yawning to receive her.

Hence she devotes herself to encouraging—her low opinion holds—"her
weaker, and I must say, more selfish, husband."

Cushman's gentleness, her affectionate solicitude, seemed to Clapp a spectacle of great love, ministering to the loved object; but terror was mingled
with pity, because the Lady herself was so hopeless, and Macbeth beyond
comfort.

Reinhardt's Lady pulled herself up when she heard Macbeth's footsteps;
she came forward to meet him, masked and self-controlled again, smiling
with tenderness at his despondent face. She passed her hand over his forehead, and spoke gently, with great caring.

Savits' Macbeth came bent with the burden of his anguish; his Lady went
tenderly to him, nestled against him, soothing: he hardly heard her; he stood
staring into the distance. Ristori leaned affectionately on her Macbeth, giving support while she seemed to be taking it.

Hackett's misery seemed partly mixed with blame for his Lady, thus echoing his reaction after Duncan's murder; when she went to embrace him, and kiss him, he resisted at first, waiting for more consolation, and then slowly warmed to her loving solicitude. The semi-maternal note was also played by the Russian Ermolova. When her Macbeth came to her crushed and broken, she hid her own suffering from him, and soothed him like a mother trying to dispel her sick child's fears.

Terry's distressing weariness was promptly hidden away when the abstracted Irving stepped into the doorway, silently brooding. Her own heart heavy as stone, she was seen to

> rally her forces, assume exterior fortitude, and resume her accustomed hardness of manner with which to stimulate him with remonstrance amounting to reproach. (S106)

Her scolding was colored with affection: her note, "Reproach with care." She put her arms tenderly about Irving as she spoke, soothing, but ended firmly: "Cautious but not repentant—let everything be damned before we give it up now."

Where the Ladies stronger at first gained contrast by their affection now, the gentler Ladies found contrast in the courage which they drew from deep sources to support their Macbeths. Robson felt she had to act a part for Macbeth: "He had loved her ruthlessness, and she tries to be that woman again," hiding her miserable conscience, cheering him up. Green, her delicate frame deeply drained by the trauma of the murder, was so much more remarkable for the magnificent effort now to manifest strength.

Not all Ladies were successful in consoling their Macbeths; and not all tried lovingly. Merchant attempted her old provocative tone to divert Scofield; she could not engage with the changing nightmare in the man. He stood apart, reluctantly opening his torment as much to himself as to her. Between Heesters and Reincke* the tone was bickering, as in a Strindbergian domestic drama: a mixture of aggression and a vestigial eroticism. The Polish Lady, Mikolajska, had left her sensuality of the first scenes behind, and prodded Macbeth, offering him only iciness, indifference, repugnance. Leigh seemed fully to sustain her hard, calculating dominance—though a sudden shiver betrayed the worn coating of her nerves.

Lady Macbeth's counsel tells much about Macbeth's condition, and her sensitivity to it; but, however intended, it aims wrong:

> . . . why do you keep alone?
> Of sorriest fancies your companions making,
> Using those thoughts, which should indeed have died
> With them they think on: things without all remedy
> Should be without regard: what's done, is done. (13–17)

---

*Hans Reincke (Germany, 1966); not to be confused with Reinecke.

She is not meeting Macbeth's problem; she is projecting on him her own. She is the one who will not let the past lie; her very speech, saying the same thing three times over, as each colon pause brings the thought back to her mind, reflects both her obsession and her need to escape it. She never will. What's *done*, in her mind, will never be *done*.

The overt burden of her message, as Mahood observes, is that Macbeth should accept himself as a murderer. But Macbeth has consciously accepted that. *His* overt problem is to deal not with what was done, but with what remains to do. Where Lady Macbeth copes with her inward distress by trying to suppress it, Macbeth will try to escape his by action. The result will be the kind of hyperactivity familiar in Shakespeare's tragic heroes under stress. The spiders in his brain will excite him to violence; he will momentarily master them, with great effort; and submit again. Without letting a label define the characters—for they are too complex for classification—we can know something about them if we say that Lady Macbeth will be depressive, though making tremendous masking efforts; Macbeth will be depressive and manic. The many contrarieties Harbage observes in the exchanges between these "maimed mortals"—for example, the tenderness and brutality, the insight and opacity—result mainly from Macbeth's inability to sustain a *single state* as he twists between inward torment and outward action.

Macbeth may not even have heard his Lady. He is straining to deal with the now:

> We have scorched the snake, not kill'd it: (18)

Theobald's change of *scorched* to "scotched" is weakening. Both words carried the apt image of maiming with a knife, but *scorched* sounds with more force, suggesting both the violence of the act, and its innocence. Mantell, with a sudden sinuous thrusting of his left arm, conveyed the menace of the undestroyed serpent.

> She'll close, and be herself, whilst our poor malice
> Remains in danger of her former tooth. (19–20)

The poet-Macbeth gives voice in metaphor to his insecurity: the sinister snake, with which Lady Macbeth had identified them before Duncan's murder, now symbolizes the enemy, threatening the high degree Macbeth killed for; now Macbeth can speak as if that killing was somehow in self-defense. "*Poor* malice" carries the connotation not only of inferiority but also of sympathy for it—a meaning that will be more or less primary in Macbeth's other uses of the word.

When Macbeth feels so endangered, his thought turns paranoid, as it will later again. Before we suffer,

> let the frame of things disjoint,
> Both the worlds suffer, (21–22)

The image of disconnection echoes his own earlier sensations of himself, but on a grand scale, again extending his experience to the universe, now with a child's megalomania. Let there be universal chaos, above and below, if I do not have my way, if our life is not ordered, if we must

> eat our meal in fear, and sleep
> In the affliction of these terrible dreams,
> That shake us nightly: (23–25)

The *we* seems mainly used as "personal and affectionate," but the sense of affronted royalty also sounds. And the word may also indicate that Macbeth may know and care that Lady Macbeth is shaken by terrible dreams. Macbeth's dreams may remind us of the cursed kind that made Banquo unwilling to sleep. *Nightly* again suggests a considerable lapse of felt time; nor do we think, carried along by the play, to square it with clock time.

When the Apollonian mainly governs Macbeth, his remorse and self-pity are emphasized: Macready feigned mirth as he threatened the two worlds with chaos before he would show fear; but the mirth was hollow, and his misery pierced through. George Vandenhoff brooded, shadowed by anguish over what he had yet to do; the dominating tone of this gentleman-Macbeth was pathos. Irving spoke mournfully, sighed; he removed Terry's embracing arms, his voice and manner desperate, his hands, in a familiar gesture, holding his head. Tree's Lady tried to cling to him; he shook her off, agonized. Savits' Macbeth had taken his Lady's hand when she came to comfort him; as the torment in his mind returned, he moved away, and spoke in a heavy, rough voice. Reincke began falteringly, his eye on his Lady, then began to speak more and more eloquently, forcefully, trying to convince both her and himself.

When the Dionysian is close to the surface, Macbeth's infested mind finds release in clamor: a Japanese Macbeth, from his fear, began suddenly to shout, in a frenzy. Rogers cried out, beyond restraint, frightening his queen.

If the Lady's dreams are not yet as disturbed as Macbeth's, she may keep her equilibrium better. Terry, not yet night-shaken, still repressing melancholy, could be tenderly solicitous, though she warned herself, "Beware of showing the pathetic result of trouble upon a *good* woman. Lady Macbeth is not too good." She shuddered, looked frightened, but because of the future more than the past: "He thinks more blood." Other Ladies recognized themselves in Macbeth's nightmares. Reinhardt's could not resist a groan. Faucit was sure that Lady Macbeth was haunted as much as Macbeth by dreams, symptoms of "that mental unrest brought on by the recurrence of images and thoughts indicated by her *Nought's had*. . . ." She does not speak of her dreams,

> for hers was the braver, more sustained nature . . . but I always felt an involuntary shudder creep over me . . . when he mentions them as afflicting himself. He has no thought of what she, too, is suffering.

Another dimension to Faucit's despair was her awareness of how much she had mistaken the character she once scorned for too much milk of human-kindness.

⌐ Macbeth lapses into introspection, traced with self-pity. He voices aloud his suicidal thoughts, revealing a further dimension of his mental agony:

> Better be with the dead,
> Whom we, to gain our peace, have sent to peace,
> Than on the torture of the mind to lie
> In restless ecstacy.
> Duncan is in his grave:
> After life's fitful fever, he sleeps well, (25–30)

To lie/ In restless ecstacy. Again the hint of hot, witched dreams: perverse, maddening, defrauding desire with tormenting fantasies of action. The fever that heats Macbeth's blood does not cool, even at night; and so he envies a murdered man. He speaks of the hostile forces against which he had defended Duncan: *malice domestic, foreign levy.* They can never touch the old king again; but the new king seems prophetically to apprehend their approach: only the dead are untouchable. ⌐

The musings of the poet-philosopher are for himself as much as for Lady Macbeth, may even be spoken, as with Olivier, in the raptness of soliloquy. Reincke, as he persuaded himself with his words, looked off into the distance, as if to a private vision. The syncopated meter, and the many *f* and *s* sounds, carry a heavy freight of feeling. The lines should be whispered, Craig thought. Often a mourning tone has been heard: Forrest's of a "moaning wind"; J. B. Booth's "profoundly retrospective . . . mournful music"; and Van-denhoff's "infinitude of desolation." Macready sighed heavily, in hopeless yearning: the words seemed to keep pace, an observer thought, with the beating of his heart. Scofield, so careful usually to mask Macbeth's softer side, mused movingly on Duncan's absolute security, that comes with death: a touch of envy colored the voice, but even more, longing and sadness, the more touching because so rarely allowed to surface in this austere design.

When Olivier spoke apart, his Lady, sitting behind him on the throne, was puzzled by his raptness, did not share the shock of his words. When the Lady is exposed afresh to the image of Duncan's murder, it may revive in her the trauma that caused her to faint. Ristori instinctively shrank from her Macbeth, her face newly haggard with weariness. Shocked, drained from her own tormented sleep, the Lady sometimes cannot summon strength immediately to give support: Reinhardt's at first could only acquiesce in her Macbeth's despairing vision, as her glance showed; Rigg and Hopkins, their bodies stiff with long hours of waking, stood staring past each other, in shared suffering.

But time presses. A public event, a banquet, looms. An effort needs to be made. They must assume the innocent flower. Lady Macbeth tells us something of Macbeth's tortured presence in the kindliest of her addresses to him: he looks *rugged*—meaning with a kind of animal fierceness? Shakespeare uses the word rarely; once in this play to characterize the terrible Russian bear, in *Hamlet* to liken Pyrrhus to the *Hyrcanian beast* (in *Macbeth*, again, the *Hyrcan tiger*)—

> Come on:
> Gentle my lord, sleek o'er your rugged looks,
> *Be bright and jovial** among your guests tonight. (34–36)

Siddons, whose tones were still mournful, managed a "forced cheerfulness." Cushman, in her mood of "mournful gentleness," spoke comfortingly. Even Leigh, usually so consistent in her cold mask, gave way to momentary softness here. The gentler Ladies showed their love: Marlowe caressed Sothern; Piscator's Lady came to Macbeth's side, knelt down and nestled her face to his knees. Terry raised Irving's face to hers, and spoke gently—like Siddons— with "forced cheerfulness." Modjeska hovered behind her seated Macbeth, tender and compassionate. Heesters smiled at her Macbeth, slowly went to him, and insinuated herself into his arms, the erotic note strong. He returned the embrace; but as his thoughts returned to his objective, he loosened himself. Reinhardt's Lady stroked her Macbeth's troubled head, and spoke tenderly; but she also betrayed the deep unrest that must disturb Lady Macbeth now—as she finished, her own mind turned inward, her smile vanished, and she looked down to the ground in a sad raptness.

Macbeth forces himself back to the present. For a moment he may break from his own concerns to look at his Lady, and see the misery she strives to hide, as Reinhardt's Macbeth did, astonished at the sudden quiet in his wife.

> So shall I love, and so I pray be you. (37)

The equation is changing between them. His strength is beginning to equalize hers, and his almost hysterical determination is leaving her behind. Yet he may find pity or tenderness for her, to match his words. Hampden was softly gentle. Macready, always studying his characterization, felt that one of his great improvements was the tenderness he learned to show. This scene gives Macbeth the best chance, in words and action, to manifest a husband's quiet affection. Where love has been a strongly emphasized note, he may embrace his lady, as Sothern did, and Hackett. Where the emphasis has been on sensuality, a different tone may surface now; the erotic, if it does not insist, gives way, or waits for a better time.

Mirren offered her embrace to Williamson; but engrossed in his own thoughts, he ignored her, and she dropped her arms. His *So shall I love* was shallow, submerged under the overmastering idea in his mind.

A divided impulse complicates Macbeth's behavior now. His Lady is not to know that she will not see Banquo alive again. Macbeth will deceive her,

*Siddon's emphasis.

"play" to her (will she recognize his playing, and "play" believing?). Phelps was praised for the double purpose he conveyed here: his excitement at the prospect of Banquo's murder, his care not to let his Lady know.

> Let your remembrance apply to . . . Banquo,
> Present him eminence, both with eye and tongue: (38–39)

The name, the pretending, bring back the storms of insecurity—unsafety— to his brain. Old images come flooding back—water, to wash honor clean; the painful need of a player's masking, to hoodwink the time with appearance:

> Unsafe the while, that we must lave
> Our honors in these flattering streams,
> And make our faces vizards to our hearts,
> Disguising what they are. (40–43)

He has, of course, only this moment disguised his heart to his wife; this may be part of the mounting strain on Macbeth that shows in the Lady's next response, and his rejoinder. He has learned the words of the lesson of seeming that she taught him in I, v; but face and body betray their hollowness. She sees: her alarm shows in her brief line—and in the two remaining allowed to her in the scene.

> You must leave this. (44)

The terse monosyllables usually express the actress' almost desperate attempt to control Macbeth again, since persuasion has failed. Worth's turn away from Macbeth suggested to J. R. Brown a different motive:

> a determination (and a failing power) to find new ways of confronting danger for herself.

Macbeth now puts into words the mental state that he has betrayed physically in moments when his self-control relaxed. It explains why so often actors of Macbeth held their hands to their heads, or shook their heads—or have only resisted such gestures with great effort. The back and forth in Macbeth between his resolute determination to conscious masked action, and his yielding to a deep anguish, involves as much visual imagery as verbal. The connections between his states of mind depend largely on physical expression; so the *Bristol Mercury* admired the way that Macready

> fills up the gaps which the dialogue fails to supply, [conveying] in a tangible form the horrid suggestions, doubts, perplexities, misgivings, and irresolution, which wrack the brain of the unhappy king until, in the delirium of his anguish, he is forced to exclaim,

> *O, full of scorpions is my mind, dear wife.*

His is an ultimate metaphor for the feel of fierce, uncontrollable impulses squirming in the brain, stinging, poisonous, relentless. We must try to ex-

perience the physical anguish of the metaphor to appreciate the paroxysm
that has been seen to shake Macbeth—the savage biting at a lip, the fist beating at the forehead, a hand clawing toward the turbulence of the brain, the
head flung from side to side; or the exhausted seeking for consolation, when
the Lady's arms are open and soothing. Even if Macbeth has begun to feel
himself stronger here, he may, as Hopkins did, momentarily turn back for
the support of an embrace. Forrest frankly turned to his Lady for sympathy
and consolation.

Macbeth's second line may follow the first immediately, as an explanation
of his dismay; but the colons suggest a pause for gathering his own strength,
or his wife's. Then the words come more slowly, meaningfully, perhaps
whispered, almost shyly, as by Reinhardt's Macbeth, an invitation to conspiracy—as if hoping that once more she may push him on to a nameless deed:

> Thou know'st that Banquo and his Fleance lives. (46)

Devlin could not face his Lady as he spoke; they were back to back, and he let
the words go over his shoulder (William Devlin, England, 1946).

The Lady may know, as Fanny Kemble thought, that the murder of
Banquo had been in Macbeth's mind; does she know the full prophecy that
motivates Macbeth? That Fleance must die, too? Much depends on how the
Lady responds:

> But in them, nature's copy's not eterne. (47)

Does she mean—kill them? Walker, among others, thought her "callous
answer" showed that she might be ready to join in more murder; and some
actresses have so acted. Siddons, breaking from her mournful mood, showed
a flash of her "former spirit and energy."* Wolter jerked up like a viper, interrupting Macbeth as he was going on, to make her intention clear to him.
Siddons' niece, Fanny Kemble, was certain of the "hard, unhesitating cruelty"
of Lady Macbeth's response, clearly demonstrating

> that her own wickedness not only keeps pace with his, but has indeed, as in
> the king's murder, reached at a bound that goal toward which he has struggled
> by slow degrees.

This cannot be an isolated moment in Lady Macbeth's design. A Lady
like Fanny's, largely untouched by experience, in full possession of her power,
will be moving towards strength in III, iv. A Lady like Siddons, whose will
has been deflected by a sense of meaninglessness, grasps at action as a way to
meaning. It may sustain her for the crisis ahead; or it may, as with Glyn, be
the last burst of her poor malice, before she sinks into a depression that will
grow more marked behind her mask. To a Lady who had summoned all her

---

*Siddons' note: "She even hints, I think, at the facility, if not the expediency, of destroying
both Banquo and his equally unoffending child."

strength and metaphysical aid for one *great quell*, Duncan's murder was shock enough; the very thought of another saps her further, and will require greater expenditure of will to resist the pressures of III, iv.

This last Lady Macbeth will sense Macbeth's purpose, and may, like Robson, make her line "a horrified question mark." She may hide her dismay in weariness and disappointment, as Faucit did, or with face averted, eyes on the ground (Reinhardt), sit helplessly watching Macbeth pursue his vision. The Lady's only protection from the reality of Macbeth's plan is a determined innocence, like that of Terry, who responded as if to say (her note): "Don't trouble so, for they cannot live forever—that fellow [Banquo] may die any day—*why not!* and the boy may have whooping cough in such a climate as this."

The Lady does not, in any case, flatly reject his implication, and though she may make her misgivings clear, as Reinhardt's Lady did, by her reproving silence, her Macbeth, after a deep breath, will take the comfort he wants from her words; their victims *are assailable*. When she herself seems to suggest the murders, he is of course strongly supported—perhaps almost more than he wishes. Resolved as Olivier was, his Lady pushed him further, and a note of resentment at the necessity of the new murders was heard in the ironic edge he gave to

Then be thou jocund: (49)

As so often, Macbeth gives back to his Lady her own advice: this time, her *be bright and jovial*. But his line is firm, a series of sharp stresses. It may be Macbeth's response to the sudden fear he has seen in his Lady's eyes. He will sweep aside any resistance: whether he does indeed intend gentle comfort to her, as Sothern did, holding her with his eyes as he went to her, or forceful comfort, as Hopkins did, taking Rigg's cheeks firmly in his hands, Macbeth has emerged again from a depth of misery to a near-manic excitement about what he plans to do. His speech, after the colon pause, resumes the almost ritual rhythm that preceded his entrance into Duncan's chamber: he is again at one with darkening night, and with the animals of night; again he acknowledges Hecate's power (another preparation for III, v?):

ere the bat hath flown . . .

. . . ere to black Hecate's summons

The shard-borne beetle, with his drowsy hums,

Hath rung night's yawning peal,

There shall be done a deed of dreadful note. (49–53)

Up to the last, the lines stretch out, the rhythm hypnotic, built on singing words that bear long stresses: *shard-borne beetle . . . Hath rung night's yawning peal* (again, a "bell" will invite murder). As Irving noted, the poet-Macbeth does revel in the music of words.

Macbeth again leaves the *deed* to be *done* unspecified; and this as much as anything may show Lady Macbeth his mind. But his mood is unmistakable, however varied. The resolute Wolfit was ominous: he created a night-climate in which blood must be spilled. Irving could launch into the speech with a cold laugh. Williamson's pose and tone promised violence. Vilar accompanied the line with the swift gesture of a bird of prey diving on its victim. Reinhardt's Macbeth closed his eyes, as if unwilling to see what he described, his voice low and frightening. Macbeth himself may be frightened or dismayed by the world his words create. They broke out from Booth almost of themselves, in a wild delirium; the hoarseness of his voice intensified his pathos. Macready, as if reluctantly forced by fate to his dreadful act, heaved a deep sigh, spoke almost in raptness.

A very determined and malignant Lady may ask with excitement, echoing Macbeth's reverberant word,

> What's to be done? (54)

But often, to Lady Macbeth now, the implication is frightening, and she is likely to ask the question with something of Faucit's weariness and dread. A Terrible Woman who is now revolted by the idea of bloodshed projects a powerful contrast between earlier resolution and present dismay: so Bateman, Irving's first Lady, so urgent for Duncan's murder, and now asked to encourage another, collapsed visibly in nerve and audacity: she asked the question fearfully. A conventional critic scolded her for this, suggesting that instead of despondency she should have manifested "a gleam of triumph." But other Ladies showed even more disturbance. Marlowe, in terror, retreated a step from Sothern. Reinhardt's Lady shifted her head, terrified, and gasped the words. Dench screamed them. Merchant could barely stop the march of Scofield's hypnotic, marching vision of the night: she had to force the line in, alarmed at the nightmare changes in the man. Modjeska made clear that she knew Macbeth's intentions, and was prompting him to an answer with sad-eyed, pitying resignation. This is the last that Lady Macbeth will say in this scene. Fanny Kemble thought, "She knows so well what is about to be done that she ceases all superfluous questioning forthwith."

Macbeth pauses in his word-weaving to notice his Lady. He must decide whether to confide or not. He equivocates. The speech is one of his most tender:

> Be innocent of the knowledge, dearest chuck, (55)

As if she—he—can ever again be innocent. But he likes the word. Bradley thought Macbeth had no thought of sparing her, but was simply beyond needing her any more. Surely he is growing the stronger, the more resolute; he no longer, Robson observed, confides all in her; but he has often, in the theatre, returned comfort with his endearment.

An occasional Macbeth is impatient to get on, as Clements was; others pause. Marston saw Macready turn from his Lady with a furtive look, in guilty isolation, and answer with a "sinister, ill-suppressed laugh" that seemed to mark a "new and dreadful stage" in Macbeth's development: she, formerly dominant, was "now his mere, half-trusted accomplice. His misery had cast off awe; he was become grimly familiar with her." This is impressive; but Marston may not have seen what Macready felt was his "improvement" of bringing more tenderness to his interpretation; a late review found him— wrongfully, it thought—"sweet and tender." Another noticed his deep sigh, his face and "sinking frame," suggesting deep dejection. Reinhardt's Macbeth, responding to his Lady's obvious dismay, was full of pity as he shook his head, and in his turn passed his hand over her eyes, as she had earlier his. Sothern took Marlowe's hand, consolingly.

Macbeth may want his Lady innocent of beforehand knowledge, but he certainly expects her to share in accomplishment:

> Till thou applaud the deed: (56)

Something of the universal child in Macbeth surfaces here: "Wait till you see what I can do!" He will keep the secret only to surprise her, please her. Approval—golden opinion—is important to Macbeth. He will show her what a man can dare. Macbeth sometimes takes her face in his hands to look at her as he speaks (Quayle), may even be hurtful as Quilley was, pulling the sides of Rigg's mouth into a grotesque smile, then chucking her cruelly under the chin; but the gesture is more often gentle. Scofield kept a distance, but he broke from his rapt vision of the night to look at his Lady, and compassion leavened his voice.

The Lady may not be ready for Macbeth's tenderness. Tree, growing visibly dominant now, laughed easily, and tenderly patted his Lady's cheek; she shivered at his touch. Sothern kept Marlowe's hand in his, but she slowly backed away, in fear and wonder. Modjeska, deeply disillusioned, knowing what was in Macbeth's mind, waited through his words. Calhoun's description of her experience of this moment as Lady Macbeth:

> Grief-freighted [they] stand apart, the sweetness gone from the touch of hands that do not meet, and from eyelids that droop to cover eyes that cannot bear to look and see through the other's eyes the measureless desolation. . . . As they stand so, with averted heads and bodies, the words they murmur are old words. Macbeth even uses . . . endearment—"dearest chuck"—but the words are dead.

Macbeth, after the break of the colon, returns quickly to his night mood, with an invocation that echoes both Lady Macbeth's appeal to *thick night*, and his own soliloquy before killing Duncan. The first lines of this speech are at least part soliloquy; he merges himself again with the darkness. The touch of almost childish expectation marks his mood: he is planning a *deed*—a great

quell—for which he wants applause from his Lady: this, as much as anything, may have occasioned her shrinking. He may blow out a light, as Craig
suggested, invoking darkness by sight as well as sound.

> Come, seeling night . . . (56)

Here as elsewhere, Henn suggests, Shakespeare uses the *seeling* image—sew-
ing together a hawk's eyelids—to describe physical or moral blindness. "Once
blinded, the bird is starved . . . denied sleep; until she finally surrenders."
Something hawklike informs Macbeth's later lines: *And with thy bloody and
invisible hand/ Cancel and tear to pieces. . . .* But this fierceness resists another
element in the complex dialectic of Macbeth's design: he is projecting murder,
and yet an image of soft beauty intrudes:

> Scarf up the tender eye of pitiful day, (57)

—a kind of recognition and at the same time denial of the part of him that
could envision the babe of pity. Darkness must extinguish brightness now,
heaven peep not through the blanket of the dark, stars hide their fires, mask,
mask, so cruelty will not be seen. The echoes of Lady Macbeth's first invocation reverberate: let there be no compunctious visitings:

> tear to pieces that great bond,
> Which keeps me pale. (59–60)

The *bond* has been glossed as that connecting him with Banquo: their *tie*, their
shared guilt, their shared prophecy. Or Banquo's own lock on life, or his
witch-promised bond to the future. Halio also suggests Banquo's legal bond,
as vassal to Macbeth. Most inclusive is the ultimate bond, suiting Macbeth's
identification with universals: the bond that made him green and pale in Lady
Macbeth's eyes—the bond to humankindness. This is another bid to say
farewell to that.

Macbeth may wait for his invocation to take effect; when it does, and by
a breath, a gesture, he acknowledges it, he sheds some part of himself. Then,
with his poet's eye, he recognizes in the ambience a co-conspirator:

> Light thickens,
> And the crow makes wing to th'rooky wood:
> Good things of day begin to droop, and drowse,
> Whiles night's black agents to their preys do rouse. (60–63)

Macbeth's communion with the night has again a touch of witchery, of assimilation into the company of *black agents*. Williamson, emphasizing the unholiness of his determination, inverted his crucifix. Olivier seemed to cast
a spell over the whole theatre, David thought—"What a chill was in his
rooky wood!" Macready, for turning to glance offstage, as if to see into the
night, was faulted for introducing realism into an imaginative moment; but
other Macbeths have effectively married gesture with image. So Alec Clunes

(England, 1950), standing at a window, embracing the darkness, his face spotlighted, the words spoken mainly for himself in soliloquy. Richardson was completely rapt. Reinhardt's Macbeth, looking out, began to speak with a wild desire, intoxicated by the idea of murder. In dimming light, Reincke, standing before the window, became a dark silhouette, the words whispered. Booth suggested the flow of night with a wave of hand and arm; Gielgud, in his first Macbeth, gestured with his voice: he rose to the last word of *to their preys do rouse* with a tigerish growl. Tearle, too, gave the word a "wonderful vocal cadenza . . . we were suddenly in a murky forest with no glimmer of light save as it comes from the eyes of wildcats" (*News Chronicle*). All Scofield's words, voiced in slow, broken phrases, were by the intensity of thought invested in them charged with menace: he ended looking straight at his Lady.

Macbeth breaks off when he sees Lady Macbeth's bewildered reaction, in movement or expression. If she is attempting to speak what is in her mind, he prevents her, choosing for himself to interpret her intent:

> Thou marvell'st at my words: (64)

Unless she is still strong to conspire with Macbeth, as for instance Leigh was, the Lady quails at the strangeness of his behavior, if not the horror of his implication. She has not before seen him like this: seen his uncanny communing with the deadly in nature. He has perhaps already told her, as we will soon learn, of the hallucinated dagger; she knows he has heard things unspoken; what is happening to his mind? She sees something new and horrifying, his excitement in anticipating killing. His very echoing of her own invocation to concealing darkness and murdering ministers may be seen to jolt her with self-recognition.

Macbeth, in the colon's hiatus, sees her stress:

> . . . but hold thee still, (64)

Asking her to remain loyal? To be calm? Is she physically restless, ready to flee from him? Again, contrast is striking when a fierce Lady, like Worth, begins to crack visibly here. Even those Ladies sustained until now by their deep love are severely tested. Marlowe, so devoted, could not but draw back in terror before Sothern. He, half-hysterical, agitated, wild, tried to hold her *still* with an arm about her; involuntarily she shrank slightly away, but, terrified and distraught, sought to quiet him.

Macbeth declares a commitment to evil, as if this will encourage the wife he has known:

> Things bad begun, make strong themselves by ill:
> So prithee go with me. (65–66)

Marlowe forced herself to stay with Sothern, hushing him off. Ristori, sensitive to the storm in her Macbeth, went to him, put her hand quietly on his shoulder, and led him out. Reinhardt's Lady stared at her Macbeth. She tried to speak, he signed to her to be quiet, came to her, they embraced, and hurried off, as to an urgent secret deed. Tree met Vanbrugh's eyes, and for a long moment the two stood still as stone at the horror each read in the other's face. They went out silently together.

Other ladies, not quite so ready to go, are carried off by their Macbeths. This may happen when, the imminence of death provoking the life-urge, Macbeth wants her as much as he needs her. Vilar said *go* (translated *Viens*) twice, the first time with regal authority, the second with "sad tenderness and desire" (*Combat*). Hopkins, moving upstairs toward Rigg, pulled her to him, his hands over her breasts; they kissed, kissed again, and holding her hand, he led her upstairs. A Czech Macbeth, lightly slapping his Lady's cheeks to bring her to acquiesce in his intentions, turned the gestures into erotic advances, and the lights went out as they began to make love.

Lady Macbeth may find it impossible to accompany her husband. Faucit avoided her Macbeth as he moved to leave, and mechanically followed him. Dench, horrified by what she now sensed in Macbeth, made a wide circle around McKellen, and exited as far from him as she could. Wallack, after the atmosphere of mystery created by Macbeth's last lines, suddenly went off, as if impelled to act; his Lady, perplexed and wondering, followed slowly after. Irving also went off quickly, Terry watching. His note for her: "No knowledge of his scheme." Her note: "Nervous clutch at his sleeve. Henry goes out. *Sit still.* I think try to find the meaning of his words. Anxious. Uncertain and rather ill."

The relationships implied in the scene's finale project expectations that will be resumed at the banquet. Shakespeare does not let go of us in his interims; one part of our minds will be extrapolating the consequences of these emotional exchanges while the other attends to the events that immediately follow.

Act III, Scene iii

Enter three murderers.

Three. Perhaps not all at once; the two murderers we know may set about preparing their ambush, when the third approaches and alarms them. The scene moves very quickly, almost too quickly: Guthrie complained that often it seems a confused scrimmage of unidentifiable characters shouting incomprehensible sounds. Perhaps this was why, according to Gentleman, it proved laughable in the eighteenth century. But a slow beginning can orient the audience to the abrupt change of frame. The action has escaped from within the palace to a field. Banquo, in Tieck's vision, was to be murdered in a green park, suggesting painted backdrops like Charles Kean's trees and hills with the castle behind. The time is late sunset; we would recognize darkness at the Globe from the murderers' torches or lanterns. In controlled lighting, the torches would illuminate the First and Second Murderers' faces enough for recognition. Waiting to spring on Banquo, they may hide behind a convenient prop—a wing, in Macready's staging, a stone wall in Reinhardt's. But, this is passive ambush: more positively, they may set a trap as they talk. The trapdoor in the stage may become a covered pit—a way of disposing of Banquo's corpse, a necessary act that the text does not provide for. A rope may be stretched across the path. Or one of the murderers may climb atop the gate through which the victims must pass; in the Globe, he could perch over the entrance to an inner below.

The Two Murderers know their job; they are suspicious of the third, often a hooded figure, whom they may accept only after he shows some insignia authenticating him, and they have consulted. Who is he? One far-fetched speculation identifies him as Macbeth, and so he has been played in a Czech staging; Bretislav Hodek observed that this made nonsense of Macbeth's shock at the news he receives in the next scene. The suspicion that Third may be Lady Macbeth is even less likely.* In stagings with omnipresent witches,

---

*Lenore Glen Offord and Bernard Levin propose pragmatic explanations of Third's identity: A relative of Shakespeare or Burbage turned up at the Globe, and a small part had to be found for him.

the Sisters have been one or all of the murderers; Hecate has played the Third. But this is against Shakespeare's purpose: his killers are mortal, though their number—three—is evocative of something more. The Third enters as a piece of the play's mystery, and its promise of violence; and when he huddles with the first two, the trio may evoke images of that other Three.

For this first time, in this violent play, actual violence will break out before our eyes. Shakespeare often saves this kind of shock to the senses until his tragedies move toward their middle: so Gloucester's blinding, Polonius' death. The resolve of the First and Second murderers leaves no doubt that they mean to kill, in front of us. Their daggers or swords may be out; their sense of urgency and danger is reflected in their suspicion of the Third Murderer: Who sent you? Reinhardt's Third answered as if giving a password:

> Macbeth. (4)

Third is almost certainly, as Irving suggested, the trusted attendant who ushered the murderers to Macbeth in III, i; and his name, though not yet in the text, is then almost certainly Seyton (though Libby, alert to ascribe all possible villainy to his chosen scapegoat, suggests Ross). Third may come cloaked and hooded to this meeting, to enhance ambiguity; but, as will appear, he can usefully be someone Banquo knows and trusts. He represents Macbeth's passion for security; he may even be the first hint of Macbeth's intelligence service—a servant fee'd in every house.

The Second Murderer is sulky: Macbeth might have trusted them; they knew what to do. The First Murderer accepts Third, and then with his gentle image sets the time and scene: approaching seven o'clock, the hour of the banquet:

> The west yet glimmers with some streaks of day.
> Now spurs the lated traveller apace,
> To gain the timely inn, (9–11)

Shakespeare has been faulted for putting unsuitable poetic words in a murderer's mouth; but he clearly meant them for *this* murderer, whose reactions in III, i made this speech plausible. The playwright might, again, have made the man like the Porter; he put this touch of sensitivity in the design deliberately, perhaps partly to raise some hope in the *naive* spectator that the killing may be prevented.

Horses are heard,* and then Banquo, off, asking for a light. The murderers get ready, First informing us—perhaps in angry frustration—that the horses are being led *about*, Third knowingly responding that this is the usual path for Banquo, and *all men* going to the palace.

Enter Banquo and Fleance with a torch. The torch was important in the Globe

---

*Forman's supposed eyewitness of the Globe staging tells us Banquo was "murdered on the way as he rode." Shakespeare's text is very specific that this was not the case; and again such a use of horses on stage seems most unlikely. Recall the reference, in my I, iii note, to the marked Padua Folio which G. B. Evans considers a pre-Restoration promptbook. The scribbled stage direction here is for a sound-effect: "Treade."

to remind us of the night; important in indoor theatres to help light the faces, and identify the two. Flashes of lightning to illuminate the two faces were suggested for a Russian staging (Juriev); and in addition, one of the murderers would go up to Banquo and Fleance, and hold a torch to their faces, to make sure.

Here is where the presence of Seyton (or some other person Banquo knows) can give a pause to the action, and clarify it. Second whispers, *A light, a light*. Third (Seyton?) goes forward: Banquo recognizes him, feels safe, may return a half-drawn sword to his sheath. Then Third identifies Banquo to First and Second, speaking aside, *'Tis he*. The murderers prepare, but Banquo, unsuspecting, speaks of the weather. Then, when he has been led by Third under the gate, or above the trap, or wherever the ambush is set, the assault begins. The signal may—though does not necessarily—suggest attack from above, with sword, noose, trammel, or other entrapment.

Let it come down. (27)*

Banquo, with a look at Third, has his cue for *O, treachery!* as he goes down fighting.

He is sometimes stabbed while pulling a murderer off his son. His repetition in his warning to Fleance is touching:

Fly good Fleance, fly, fly, fly (29)

Fleance may have tried to join the struggle; Banquo urges a more realistic purpose, *Thou may'st revenge* (30). Fleance's own life may be seen to be owed to a momentary hesitation of the First Murderer to strike. In some stagings, full *twenty trenched gashes* are brutally given Banquo: savagery is excessive, outrunning the pauser, reason. In a Scottish production (1974), "blood" was arranged to spurt from Banquo's wounds. The Murderers' violence may be seen as a reaction to the loss of Fleance. It may serve to extend and make more comprehensible the fast-passing act. In Japan, the details of killing and escape were articulated in a stylized, slow-motion encounter.

To shield tender audiences from violence, the scene has sometimes been cut, or the killing done offstage, the murderers returning with bloody swords— Kean's First Murderer with blood on his face. Like other similar changes, this dilutes Shakespeare's design, which forces on us, for the first time, a visual stipulation of Macbeth's bloody will.

The last of the torchlight, or a new lightning strike, may be imagined momentarily to illumine Banquo's bloody face; and perhaps the First Murderer's; and then all seems darkness.

Who did strike out the light? (31)

First answers curiously, as if appealing to a murder plan, but perhaps to distract attention from what he has done:

*It is also, as Mary Rosenberg observes, an apt response to Banquo's *It will be rain tonight*.

> Was't not the way? (32)

The darkness may have helped Fleance escape; was the striking out of the light a deliberate act? Is this in the mind of the better of the murderers?

> There's but one down: the son is fled. (33)

The Second Murderer, almost as if sensing Macbeth's true motive:

> We have lost
> Best half of our affair. (34–35)

And First—changing the subject?—urges them off, to report what was (echoing word) *done*.

No stage directions or textual clues indicate the disposition of Banquo's body. He may have been killed in an inner stage, or fallen in the trap; otherwise *Exeunt* indicates that the corpse is dragged off by the three conspirators, who must also take care to remove all signs of their ambush. Though in a Hampden production, Banquo's blood stained the stage floor—and could be seen there through the rest of the play.

Act III, Scene iv (part 1)

In terms of linear design, if the opening of III, i has been imagined as an elaborate coronation scene, then the banquet ritual must be lifted to a higher peak of spectacle. If III, i is a normally impressive court scene, the more opulent banquet marks a natural advance in visual excitement, contributory to the intensifying tension. The scene becomes the objective of a spinal movement begun with Macbeth's first announcement of the solemn supper (III, i) and sustained through the many references to time, the plan to kill Banquo, and the tactics Macbeth and his Lady propose for their behavior this night. Given this development, the banquet builds to the kind of explosive mass spectacle that we saw when the early movements of Act II came to climax with the discovery of Duncan's murder.

Ornaments of royalty, including their majestic *state*, will glorify the king and queen. When curtains are used, the two are sometimes "discovered" on their thrones; but the Folio directs a grand entrance:

> *Banquet prepared. Enter Macbeth, Lady, Ross,*
> *Lenox, Lords, and Attendants.*

The bright scene follows immediately on the disposition of Banquo's corpse: a startling contrast. Once more King Macbeth and his queen lead, in the pomp of procession, the nobility of Scotland—all except two. The effect of this formal entrance is to suggest that the royal pair now firmly belongs at the head of the court. Regal banners may flutter—perhaps including captured Norweyan ones Macbeth brought to Duncan, bloody and war-torn. The courtiers may kneel, or bow, cry "Hail Macbeth"—usually depending on any parallelism designed between this ceremony, Duncan's (with Rigg–Hopkins, Macbeth's royal portrait replaced Duncan's earlier one), and later, Malcolm's; and on the performance style—a Japanese Macbeth used a ritual gesture; hands up forward, palms facing out. Depending on how much military force Macbeth surrounds himself with for security, various guards may stand by, armed. If Duncan's state had been on high, Macbeth's may now be; he may descend as his court gathers below. So Pitoeff's staging: "One sees, all at once, the head with a golden diadem, coming down, luminescent, from the inaccessible heights."

The word "highness," used in the scene insistently, metaphorizes degree; as will, visually, thrones that look down from some elevation, however slight. Degree is further declared as the courtiers form their *file*, according to rank. As if to stipulate this show of order, Macbeth will say, from the altitude of kingship,

> You know your own degrees, sit down: (4)

His nobles will carefully arrange themselves according to their elevation in the hierarchy: any momentary uncertainty or disagreement in taking places will emphasize the importance of degree to these men (and their wives, if included—Kemble and some others after him alternated men and women at table). The thanes may have *limited services*, as Macduff had with Duncan; we may see these in action, as they serve the new king.

That the thanes have come to partake of Macbeth's bread and meat says something of the atmosphere of the banquet. These are the nobles who *named* Macbeth king; they are here to do him and his house honor. Shakespeare does not allow us to see Macbeth the serviceable ruler of Scotland for many years; but to this moment Shakespeare's Macbeth has done no evil thing, as far as the thanes know, to offend or outrage them; he is still their hero as well as king. No words or implied action suggest that they have been forced to come; they are willingly participating in a familiar, intimate ritual of hospitality. The meal is symbolic, as Knights and others have pointed out, of idealized order, in family, tribe, and state: an archetypal gesture of amity and concord. As throughout *Macbeth*, order masks a ferment of its opposite: "This feast in its ritual beginning is a 'ceremony of innocence.'" (Black). The thanes come for peaceful feeding—something men reify in this play. Macbeth would like to eat his meal without fear; the Lord in III, vi will speak longingly, in the same terms, of meat for tables, feasts, and banquets. This now is the *feast* Macbeth promised Banquo in III, i; on stage it is likely to be a grander realization of the offstage banquet in I, vii, when a weight of food was carried through to Duncan's dining.

Symbolism has sometimes framed the staging of the banquet. Bergman, in 1944, set his table, brightly illuminated, under an arch, and suggested an effect of the Holy Supper, with Macbeth central. At the other extreme, a later Swedish banquet (1967) proceeded in what seemed a slaughterhouse, with four huge, skinned, bright red carcasses hanging on a wall that dripped blood. More subtly Robert Edmond Jones, for the Lionel Barrymore *Macbeth*, frankly haunted the feast with distorted and discordant background screens, and great candles, skewed and wizened, that burned with thin flames, and died as the scene ended.

More often the banquet is as realistic as the text asks, with great trays of food and drink, to convey the true sense of proud, hospitable royalty, hopeful of loyal support. Probably never again will we see quite the detail of the nineteenth-century archaeologists; but Charles Kean's setting is worth recapturing, if only to make our mouths water:

> The roughly clad guests . . . sat beneath oaken rafters, supported by . . . Saxon pillars. Rude tapestry hung above the dais, and, instead of the commonplace trumpery of conventional stage feasts, vast haunches of meat, boars' heads, . . . baskets of fruit, and great loaves of bread, set forth the table; while the attendants served the guests with mead and megethlin from strange old vases and from vast horns set in silver; and a band [seven] of bards, clad and bearded like Druids, played wild barbaric music upon rude harps . . . from a gallery above the dais. (*Flattery and Truth*)

Still Kean had to defend himself against complaints that he left out the then customary "gold and silver vessels . . . with the massive candelabra (such as no Highlander of the eleventh century ever gazed upon)" for instead

> the more appropriate feast of coarse fare, served on rude tables, and lighted by simple pine torches. I was admonished that such diminution of regal pomp impaired the strength of Macbeth's motive for murder, the object being less dazzling and attractive. Until that hour I have never believed that the Scottish thane had an eye to King Duncan's plate. I had imagined that lofty ambition, the thirst of power, and desire of supreme command, developed themselves with equal intensity in the human heart (Cole).

We may look ahead for a moment to Malcolm's allusion, in IV, iii, to Macbeth as *luxurious*. By emphasis on the sybaritic and sensual in the court scenes, Malcolm's charge might be made to seem grounded; but the textual evidence insists on a formally mannered, highly proper paradigm of royal courtesy. The violation of decorum, at Banquo's entrance, will be the more shocking for shattering what seems the orderly and even admirable climate established in a dignified court.

Irving would provide a scene of regal elegance. On the deep Lyceum stage he deployed eighty actors, some of the diners so low in degree that they could hardly be seen at the far ends of the many tables: but all ate with "gold" and "silver" tableware. Preparations were going on as the curtain rose: servants carried food, new guests arrived, soldiers put up their shields on the walls before sitting down. It was, an observer thought, a kind of "admired disorder."

At the other extreme of realism is the skimpy "feast," demeaning Macbeth and his court. Burnim believes that Garrick was mocking the meanness of his own banquet—and if it was that mean, it deserved mockery—in that essay on acting:

> *The Banquet* itself, which is suppos'd to be a *Regal* one, should not be compos'd of a few *Apples*, *Oranges*, and such like Trash, but of *hot* costly *Viands*, and large

Pyramids of *wet Sweetmeats*, and *Savoy Biscuits;* this would cast an inconceivable
Grandeur upon the *Scene*, and add greatly to the Horror.

Hot viands do seem essential to a *solemn supper;* and realistic banquets
have tried to suggest steaming, smoking meats, sometimes paraded before
being carved and served. Two practical problems: the diners have a limited
time to eat; and *eat* they must; mimed chewing is a sure destroyer of illusion.
Craig, writing about his designs for the 1928–29 *Macbeth* to Boleslavsky,
hoped the actors would be given a "real nice supper," so that each might act
"like a real guest of Delmonico's at a supper given by Mr. [Herbert] Hoover."
The reduction in larder since Charles Kean's banquet is evident in the rather
lavish, for the time, list of props for the Craig *Macbeth:* brass cups, "gold"
plates, drinking horn; peacock on a platter; boar's head on a platter; large
pudding on a platter; lamb on platter; cake in the shape of a castle; nineteen
stools; four gilded tankards. (Does anyone ever imagine that those still "animals" on platters are to be carved and eaten?) In the Rigg–Hopkins *Macbeth*,
the courtiers, with napkins over their shoulders, seemed very much to enjoy
a five-course banquet served with splendid efficiency—"one might be forgiven for frivolously thinking Scotland had grown in comfort under the new
regime" (*Guardian*). In Holland (1909) only part of the banquet table projected
from one of the wings, conveying the impression that the feast stretched
endlessly offstage—an impression sustainable by sound from the wings
and the angle of Macbeth's face when speaking to the diners both seen and
unseen.

For the massive, populous nineteenth-century banquets, several tables
were often needed—sometimes separate ones for the ladies; and even so,
numerous supernumeraries stood in the background, as pictures of the time
indicate. A royal table, or the throne dais (at side or center), or both, often
dominate the stage. Flanking wing tables might be parallel to the proscenium
arch, but more often were at either side of the stage, slanting downstage.
Macbeth chooses a chair *i'th'midst. Both sides are even* (15), he says: suggesting
that his "middle" seat—usually not his throne, which is saved for later—is
between two tables, or at the end of one of them. What mainly determines
the location will be the strategy of introducing Banquo, who at his first appearance is likely to sit in Macbeth's chosen chair. Kemble employed the
practical two-table pattern of placing at the ends the two speaking thanes,
with Lenox facing—or next to—the "empty" chair he will point out to
Macbeth.

The advantage of the split tables at the stage sides was angrily described
by Fanny Kemble when she had to confront a variation tried out by Macready:

From time immemorial, the banquet scene [was] arranged after one invariable
fashion: the royal dais and throne, with the steps leading up to it, holds the
middle of the stage, sufficiently far back to allow of two long tables, at which
the guests are seated on each side, in front . . . leaving between them ample
space for Macbeth's scene with Banquo's ghost, and Lady Macbeth's repeated

rapid descents from the dais and returns to it, in her vehement expostulations
with him, and her courteous invitations to the guests to "feed and regard him
not" . . . I was much astonished and annoyed to find, at my first rehearsal,
a long banquetting table set immediately at the foot of the steps in front of
the dais, which rendered all but impossible my rapid rushing down to the
front of the stage. . . . It was as much as I could do to pass between the bottom
of the throne steps and the end of the transverse table in front of them; my
train was in danger of catching [the table's] legs and my legs, and throwing it
down and me down, and the whole thing was absolutely ruinous to the proper
performance of my share of the scene. If such a table had been in any such
place in Glamis [*sic*] castle on that occasion, when Macbeth was seized with
his remorseful frenzies, his wife would have jumped over or overturned it to
get at him.

If only Fanny had done so! She yielded, played around the table, content-
ing herself, she wrote, with "a woman's vengeance, a snappish speech" to
Macready.

The emotional atmosphere, as the banquet begins, importantly affects
the play's linear movement. If the thanes are edgy or suspicious, as sometimes in the theater, Macbeth's forward action must seem already blunted,
and his downfall more nearly predictable. But, again, Shakespeare seems to
take care to avoid any suggestion, up to now, of any swell of Scots' resistance
to this *named* king. One of the savage ironies of the play is that Macbeth must
seem now securely unassailable, free to eat his meals in peace, and to sleep
well—if only he could—as a secure, acclaimed king. Except where the intention (mistaken, I think) is to demean Macbeth as dwarfish in his monarch's
robes, the royal manner becomes him. The warrior's bearing, the poet-
philosopher's face, the born leader's grace, all dignify him. For a few fleeting
moments he will seem everything a good ruler may be.

He determinedly "plays" the king. These are the first notes in the deep
polyphony of his design that will sound through the scene. He acts the monarch acting humble host, with words suited to the ritual of breaking bread:

At first and last, the hearty welcome. (5)

He may mean "from beginning to end"; but also, perhaps, from the highest
degree to the lowest. His early language, as does his Lady's, glows with the
warmth of hospitality: *hearty welcome, humble host, hostess, welcome, welcome,
mirth, cheer, feast, welcome, good digestion, appetite, health;* and even after the first
ghostly visitation, *love and health, general joy.* How much is he playing? He
last left us in a strange, excited mood, his mind filled with the image of a
violence to be committed; he enters now anticipating a report of murder,
and part of his attention may wander with his eyes to the doors of the banquet
hall. He may look at the thanes with more than casual attention: in his obsession with security he has, we will learn, planted a spy in every house. But

this is something we are not yet to know; and for now his glances at the guests will lend ambiguity to the design. Macbeth's overt action will be governed again by the ratio between his conscious movement toward his objective and the counterforces—fear, guilt, anxiety, hostility, elation—that threaten his equilibrium. The balance is often delicate.

Hackett silently indicated to attendants that he expected a messenger; the pent-up emotion suppressed in him could be felt in his anticipation. Tsarev was outwardly amiable, if reserved; but he betrayed the seething of his thoughts as he awaited his murderer.

Where Macbeth's excitement and elation dominate him, his counterforces are subdued. So Wolfit entered, obviously enjoying his kingship, his rise to power; he was here to make a night of it, and he began by chucking his Lady under the chin. Scofield experienced a liberating sense of freedom: power became him. He asked his court to be *large in mirth*, meaning it. Guinness' smile seemed to signal genuine bonhomie. Tree, less able to mask his inward tension, seemed so nervous that his Macbeth could be suspected to have a mental disorder; his speech was sometimes gasped, his body contorted. Irving spoke with "forced hilarity"; but in his cowardice he seemed eaten up with fears that he barely masked from his guests.

In clock time Macbeth has passed only a few hours since III, i; but as at that time he had sometimes showed psychic aging, and more in the next scene, now the wear of strain and sleeplessness may further mark him. The more vulnerable to counterforce, the more marked. Mantell's face was haggard, his hair greying, his voice deeper, his manner fevered. Sothern, whose features were already noticeably drawn at the discovery of Duncan's murder, was now grey and careworn. Phelps' face, as well as his Lady's, had grown old.

Lady Macbeth left us last with a new awareness of what her husband had become, and was becoming. She had thought, in the beginning of III, ii, that *all* was spent; she had learned that the spending would go on and on; what was *done* would never rest. Her deepening unrest may be fiercely masked by a Lady as determined as was Leigh or Pritchard to hang on to the golden round; for the more usual Lady Macbeth, the primary force is despair, and though she is still able to will enough counterforce to mask the darkness, her power to do so is to be tested now to the point of breaking. Pressing against control is a new anxiety—what will be the dreadful deed Macbeth promised? She watches everything.

Siddons states the case for the Terrible Woman undermined:

> Surrounded by their court, in all the apparent ease and self-complacency of which their wretched souls are destitute . . . [although] she affects to resume her wonted domination over her husband, yet, notwithstanding all this self-control, her mind must even then be agonized by the complicated pangs of terror and remorse.

Under this kind of tension, Lady Macbeth's psychic aging will keep pace with her husband's. It will show not only in face and body, but also in her manner—and in his toward her. Flora Robson thought Macbeth kept his Lady apart because he was afraid she might betray their secret. The Lady surely reciprocates. Her entrance with Macbeth, their exchange or avoidance of look and touch, how much they will drink, how sleepless they seem, will be a significant comment on what has happened to both, and between both, since their similar appearance in III, i. He at once takes the lead in this scene; and though the balance of strength will shift as her residual strength is called on, his is a power burgeoning so dangerously as to be cancerous, hers intermittent, and when not demanded, waning.

Something of the dynamic Shakespeare intended between them may be sensed in Macbeth's announcement that he will *play* the *host* while

> Our hostess keeps her state, but in best time
> We will require her welcome. (9–10)

Is he protecting her? Separating her?

Is there any sense that even to enter, under the burden of her meaningless royal trappings, has been taxing? Then she sits on her throne because she must save her strength? Siddons thought Lady Macbeth started as early as III, i down the road toward madness and the grave; now when the attention is on Macbeth and she is not observed, the Lady may momentarily let the attrition show. In Faucit the struggle to subdue the manifestations of her inward stress was unmistakable. Modjeska had visibly to rouse herself to play the hostess; without steeling herself, she seemed to have barely enough strength to stand or speak. Dench tried to smile, but could not. Marlowe had begun noticeably to age, along with Sothern. Bernhardt, with her slight compulsive gestures, would even more draw her hands up into her sleeves, or hide them anywhere, then furtively look at them. Reinhardt's Lady stared into the distance. Sleeplessness told with particular contrast on the Ladies from the beginning nerve-strained: Leighton, so brittle and glittering, now carried an air of despairing resignation; the once-glamorous Rigg was at a farther stage on the road from sanity to insanity. Cushman's manners were a queen's, fully equal to her throned dignity, but the audience could sense how fevered was her behavior. Wolter, so formidable earlier, so ready to urge the murder of Banquo and Fleance, forced a cheerfulness now, spoke from her dais with a strange, embarrassed laughter:

> Pronounce it for me Sir, to all our friends,
> For my heart speaks, they are welcome. (11–12)

The thanes stand, they raise their drinking vessels, bow, drink. Macbeth, as if to reassure his Lady, in the language of the heart that he seeks to disjoin from his acts:

> See they encounter thee with their hearts' thanks. (14)

But Macbeth's attention is elsewhere. Hardly had Lady Macbeth said *to all our friends . . . they are welcome . . .* when, pat, in a far corner, a man appears whose face is marked with blood. To Macbeth, who has been looking for him, this "friend" is indeed welcome; but the time must be hoodwinked. Macbeth assigns himself his place among the guests. *Both sides are even* (15), he says—a simple phrase, but in the context of what the Murderer's presence implies, ripples of meaning may flow from it, about the balancing of forces. His world will not be *even* again. He chooses his middle chair, or orders a servant to place one (as Olivier did), and to keep the guests occupied, urges them

> Be large in mirth, anon we'll drink a measure
> The table round. (16–17)

He calls for a vessel—Scofield summoned a large, double-handled goblet—drinks from it, and hands it to the nearest thane to start around the table. Under this cover, he will talk to the Murderer.

For the space of many lines, while Macbeth speaks apart, the banquet must go on, as background. Since of the whole company, besides the king and queen, only two thanes have speeches (except when the Lords speak communally, responding to Macbeth), the rest, however numerous, are there to fill the design and to intensify response. This is the time most of the serving, eating, and drinking will go on, and, inevitably much muted, non-text conversation: a Gielgud stage direction says "Talk (ad lib) but not too much." Toasts may be offered. This may also be a time for vestiges of the banquet's entertainment: thus Kean's harpists, and Tree's troubadours and his spectacular torch dance. A song from *Love's Labour's Lost* was sung in the Craig-designed *Macbeth*. A bagpiper danced and sang for Reinhardt.

Entertainments of this sort contribute to an atmosphere indeed *large in mirth*, confirming the sense of a kingdom up to now content with Macbeth's rule. Laughter may sound from the scene's beginning; with Ernst Schröder it was continuous, rising homerically. Such moods of conviviality and camaraderie, endorsing the image of Macbeth's *innocent self*, builds to a steep peripety when the *mirth* is destroyed.

Alternatively, a suspicious quiet envelops the scene, as with the deliberately sullen Macbeth, George: voices were subdued, the ambience uncanny, foreboding. Similarly, a "strange solemnity" oppressed Reinhardt's feast. Even a mirthful banquet sometimes sobers if the diners are made to become aware of Macbeth's apartness with the Murderer and look toward him. Whether they notice or not, Lady Macbeth, alert for the promised *deed*, but sustaining a hostess's front, must restrain herself from seeming to notice too much.

Ristori's account:

> She alone perceives [the Murderer] speaking in subdued tones to her husband, notes the repressed movements, and keeps him constantly in view. For she fears some imprudence on the part of Macbeth, remembering that he had told

her shortly before that a great thing would soon happen, which would amaze her. I considered that in this scene Lady Macbeth would be terribly afraid lest the guests should observe this strange colloquy, in such a place and at such a moment, and might conceive grave suspicions which would defeat all their projects. Hence I found it necessary to engage in a kind of double by-play, that is to say, with an air of the greatest courtesy to take part in the conversation of the guests, and the toasts they drank to me (remaining, however, always upon their seats) while at intervals I cast furtive and timorous glances towards the group made by my husband and the murderer.

Spectators saw Ristori characterized "alternately by queenly grace and nervous apprehension. She had smiles and greeting for the assembled guests, but the anxiety that was gnawing at her heart . . . was suggested with consummate skill" (*Era*). To distract the guests, Lady Macbeth may now, as Marlowe did, stop eating, come down from her *state*, and cross back and forth between tables, helping the guests and talking to them, while stealing glances at Macbeth.

Meanwhile Macbeth has met his man. Sometimes the Murderer hides behind the servants (Phelps) or mixes with them—may, as with Booth, take a goblet from one of the trays, and approach Macbeth as if bringing him drink. Sothern's Murderer had dressed himself as a servant; he crossed the stage circuitously, keeping his eye on Macbeth, who was sensing his approach. In Tyrone Power's promptbook Macbeth is not aware of the Murderer; the audience sees the man carry a goblet on a silver tray at the cue of Macbeth's *We'll drink a measure* . . . and anticipates the shock when Macbeth looks at the man, gives a slight start, and they talk apart. A promptbook associated with Charles Kean had the Murderer seize a "jug and goblet" and rush up to Macbeth, who quickly turned the man's face away from the court so that the bloodied side did not show. McKellen, when the Murderer approached him, took this as a cue to distract the guests by initiating the ritual of drinking the *table round*. He moved behind the backs of his feasting thanes, smiling as he took the cup from each one who had drunk to give it to the next. In the intervals of drinking he snatched at his conversations with the Murderer, who whispered alongside. McKellen would become so involved in this dialogue that Lady Macbeth would have to remind him to *give the cheer*.

More often Macbeth sees the Murderer looking in at the edge of the banquet space, and unobtrusively moves there. When Sothern caught sight of the Murderer, he quickly exchanged a look with Lady Macbeth for her to take charge, and drifted over. As he spoke, he constantly glanced at the guests, for fear of being overheard. Irving, recognizing his man, slowly made his way to one of the pillars supporting the dais, and leaned against it—a favorite posture—thus masking the Murderer, who was partly behind the arras, while keeping his own face toward his guests.

Reinhardt's Macbeth, who had been trying to relax the serious atmosphere of his banquet with friendly nods to the Lords, laughing, clapping his hands, suddenly noticed the Murderer. Still affecting affability, he moved to fill a bowl of wine for himself, then drifted toward the Murderer, who closed with him. Macbeth, with his back to the man, whispered his *There's blood upon thy face* (17).

The line cracks like a whip, carrying both Macbeth's immense shock and his concern for discovery. The legend has Garrick speaking with such intensity that the Murderer put his hand to his face with a startled "Is there, by God?" The blood may be in Macbeth's imagination, as he may find, trying to touch it. Booth's Murderer had a few red drops on his cheek; others are more badly gashed. Sothern's Murderer wiped the blood from his forehead, then wiped his hands on his clothes. Hopkins wiped his Murderer's face with a napkin. If Macbeth does get the feel on his fingers of Banquo's blood, his response to his friend-victim's death will be even more complex, inevitably will remind him of Duncan's dying.

Irving's note for the moment: "Pause. Sigh. Recover." Reinhardt's Macbeth drew a deep breath; Scofield could close his eyes, his suddenly changed face telling how much tension had fixed it, how ambivalent his satisfaction. For one Macbeth, every mention of Banquo's name from now would bring a wince.

> MACBETH: 'Tis better thee without, than he within. (19)

The line seems to mean, better his blood outside you than in him; or—than Banquo be here. Macbeth praises the cutthroat; then, so much hanging on it:

> Yet he's good that did the like for . . . Fleance: (23)

And the reluctant answer (the murderer has paused to lick his dry lips before giving it):

> Fleance is 'scap'd. (26)

The shock is fearful. The terrible energy suppressed in Macbeth storms to break out:

> Then comes my *fit* again. (27)

It may not, as observed before, be literally a seizure; but as in other of Shakespeare's tragic heroes, the inward pressure becomes almost uncontrollable: this wracking of body and spirit will be of the kind, if for aesthetic purposes more intense, of his earlier raptnesses and spasms. The ratio of force against counterforce will now be conditioned partly by the need to avoid the attention of the guests. Macbeth must contain with tremendous effort the explosive passions within. Reinhardt's Macbeth, who had been masking the conversation with his wine bowl to his lips, had begun to drink when the Murderer told about Fleance. He put the bowl down, his fingers trembling, and stared, agonized raptness coming on. Sothern turned so fiercely on the Murderer that the man knelt, in fear. Scofield's erect, martial form seemed almost to swell with suppressed impulse; but the only overt symptom he allowed was his fierce rubbing of his thumb against his fingers. Williamson, always so close to hysteria, now seemed indeed almost to have an epileptic fit, his eloquent hands stretched, his body ready to fling out, and he barely managed to enforce control. The metaphor Macbeth will use—*cabin'd, cribb'd, confin'd*—will suit his physical caging of emotions; he beats against the bars of self-command, and there is a sense that he might break through.

What Macbeth says is not directed to the Murderer, but is another private exploration of his self. To make the moment a psychological event, Macbeth has sometimes been theatrically isolated, by the freezing of the other characters, or by spotlighting him and darkening the rest of the stage, as with Juriev. But by now we are prepared for these sudden, fierce philosophizings, self-isolating, the mind ranging in an instant from general to particular, from particular to general, identifying with eternals while experiencing the now. The impossible vision of absolute security dissolves; the language, so wonderfully made mainly of monosyllables in the scene, uses a few longer words and rhythms suiting the introspection:

> I had else been perfect;
> Whole as the marble, founded as the rock,
> As broad, and general, as the casing air: (28–30)

This is again the megalomanic dream of the child, to be magically all-powerful. So Olivier was seized with a desperate bewilderment; to have his prize, so close within his grasp, snatched away, was an agony. The verbal image doubly-echoes the child restrained, the man now inhibited,

> bound in
> To saucy doubts, and fears. (31–32)

The emotion, as it must be with a temperament of this design, is in excess of reality. Fleance's survival is not an immediate threat to survival or kingship, but it implies so much: that the Sisters' prophecy has not been controverted, that the cherished dream of dynasty is in danger, all this denying Macbeth's capacity to shape his destiny. His sense of other forces at work against him, that dominated Macready's characterization, may be particularly strong here. *Doubts, and fears*, not what *is*, overwhelm him.

For the first of three times in the scene, Macbeth forces a return to control. Assured that Banquo is *safe*—a word he may pause before, loaded as it is with irony—with *twenty trenched gashes* (34), Macbeth can say, with gratitude? bitterness? pain? *Thanks for that* (36). Salvini spoke with a flash of truculent joy; Welles drunkenly. With returning reason comes the realization that Fleance is indeed not a *present* threat—again Macbeth turns against himself the image of the snake: *There the grown serpent lies* (37). Hackett voiced the image to himself with venom; then, suddenly aware that the Murderer watched him, recovered and was "polite." Booth, with some relief, made as if about to drink his wine; but as he held the goblet up the red color sickened him, and he handed the cup back. The Murderer is dismissed until *tomorrow*.

The banquet has proceeded in the background, with eating and talk that sometimes punctuates Macbeth's dialogue with the Murderer. In Quayle's staging, for instance, at the very moment of the news of Fleance's escape, so shocking to Macbeth, a loud general laugh rose from the tables. Lady Macbeth's awareness of Macbeth's isolation from the dinner will become apparent; she will do her best to distract the guests, as Marlowe did, moving among them; though she may remain seated (Ristori and Siddons), uneasiness visibly growing. Reinhardt's Lady, more and more uneasy, leaned forward from the dais to watch her husband. Was the threatened *deed* near?

The guests, whether catching her concern or not, may look to their host. In Reinhardt's staging, as Macbeth spoke his last word to the Murderer, he was suddenly missed by all, and the whole banquet fell absolutely silent, waiting. Macbeth heard the silence.

Lady Macbeth has gone to speak privately with Macbeth; but this is usually saved for later; her words are of the kind a hostess might speak openly to add warmth to hospitality—

> My Royal Lord,
> You do not give the cheer, (41–42)

She urges the welcoming toast, the conviviality of ceremony. She says the same thing more than once, expressing behind her hostess' words the longing for *content*, given, received. Whether she speaks it apart to Macbeth, or before the guests, will depend upon the development of their relationship. A Loving Wife, like Marlowe, could make it a personal appeal, to be answered personally. Terry's was a gesture of social grace, gently awakening Irving from his raptness. Reinhardt's Lady tried to smile, spoke with forced cheer, Hackett's Lady playfully, but with great tenderness, Ristori with "much ostentation of gaiety," Rigg angrily. Siddons, from the dais, would speak formally, establishing anew a note of dominance.

> *Enter the Ghost of Banquo, and sits in Macbeth's place.*

The Folio direction indicates that the audience receives the shock of the ghost before Macbeth does, and then watches for him to absorb it, while appreciating the irony of his next words. Many later stagings have delayed the entrance, to surprise and shock both Macbeth and the audience. How the ghost has appeared, when he has, will be discussed in a moment; meanwhile we see through the eyes of Macbeth, roused from his inward thoughts, and returning to the banquet to look carefully at the thanes for any signs of suspicion.

Sweet remembrancer (48), he replies to his Lady, the ratio of affection to formality depending, again, on their relationship—Irving kissed Terry's hand, Hackett spoke with "great love." Macbeth gives the cheer, often raising a goblet again, resuming the ceremony of hospitality with a kind of grace before meat:

> Now good digestion wait on appetite,
> And health on both. (49–50)

The lords join in, sometimes rising. Lenox invites Macbeth to sit. Macbeth may look round the table first, see no empty seat, and go on with his *cheer*. If Banquo's ghost is present, the next words mock Macbeth with terrible irony; or Banquo may wait, to appear at the end of his welcome, pat.

> Here had we now our country's honor, roof'd,
> Were the grac'd person of our Banquo present:
> Who, may I rather challenge for unkindness,
> Than pity for mischance. (52–55)

Does the ghost of Banquo, present, smile at this, as he will smile later? Olivier's Banquo, who had been leaning forward, straightened himself here, drawing attention.

Ross, the chameleon, speaks time-servingly: (Hackett—"sycophancy"):

> His absence (Sir)
> Lays blame upon his promise. Pleas't your Highness
> To grace us with your royal company? (56–58)

Then the speeches are abrupt, staccato, building to the top of the beat, when Macbeth gives way to his counterforces, and loses control.

> MACBETH: The table's full. (59)
> LENOX: Here is a place . . . (60)

(Reinhardt's Lenox started toward Macbeth across the stage.)

> Where? (61)

Tree whispered this, already on the rack.

> Here my good Lord.
> What is't that moves your Highness? (62–63)

The control is wearing thin. Is this a trick?

> Which of you have done this? (64)

Macbeth's guards, in the Dunn staging, sprang to the alert, spears pointed. The thanes respond in unison (though not all with the same words, as given):

> LORDS: What, my good Lord? (65)

And then the reason yields.

Shakespeare has built to the ghost slowly. Macbeth and Banquo saw the witches together, when Macbeth first experienced the confusion between the real and unreal that pervades the play's atmosphere. Then, in his soliloquies, Macbeth edged himself toward participation in the ambiguities of both the world he could know physically and the world he communed with that stretched out through nature and the cosmos to the uncanny province of Hecate. Under enough strain, he could hallucinate a murder weapon approaching and withdrawing; but this was privately. He might have puzzled others by escaping, in their presence, into an intense raptness, but publicly he always retrieved control, although with increasing effort. Now he, and he alone, sees a ghost. The explicitness of this is important. The ghost, to emphasize its invisibility, may be made deliberately to walk in front of the unseeing Lady Macbeth and the guests, as it was in Trevor Lennam's staging. As we can in the theatre believe in something as strange as "vanishing" when men are seen to experience it and describe it—as Macbeth and Banquo did with the Sisters—so we can believe in intangibility when something tangible is not seen by those exposed to it.

Is Banquo's ghost "real"? He is designated *ghost* in the Folio direction, and is intended to have an objective appearance; but is he assumed to be a visitation from the dead, or from hell, or is he Macbeth's objectified hallucination akin to the imagined dagger of II, i?* Stoll, fixed against any "psychological" explanation, insists at length that the ghost is meant to be "real"; and Farnham agrees. Curry fits the apparition into his theological framework by finding it an infernal illusion, sent to destroy Macbeth. No textual evidence insists on this: in fact Macbeth claims that the devil himself might be afraid of the sight.

Much interpretation takes the psychological view, as stated by Nicoll: the ghost

> is a material vision in the sense that it rises upon the stage; and yet it is an hallucination in Macbeth's own mind.

R. R. Reed, similarly, classified the image as one of the "second Senecan tradition," having nothing to do with supernatural intervention, and

> no apparent actuality or substance, outside the imagination of the beholder, . . . the ghost of conscience.

Lady Macbeth is certainly on the side of the hallucinationists: that what Macbeth sees is a ghost never occurs to her: she is certain it has no more reality than the dagger he had described to her, a painting of his fear (painted or gilded appearances come easily to her imagery). Macbeth does not name the apparition *ghost;* he will perhaps classify it later with his *strange and self-abuse.*

Shakespeare seems to have intended ambiguity. The "ghost" himself does not force us to examine his "reality" as other ghosts, like Hamlet's father's,

---

*The difference between dagger and ghost may be paralleled in John Webster's *The White Devil,* where Francisco deliberately imagines—and so objectifies—his sister's image (IV, i, 100), while Flamineo seems to be visited by a "real" Brachiano's ghost, who throws earth on him, and shows him a skull (V, iv, 121).

do, by claiming to come from purgatory, or for revenge. He is real to Macbeth, unimaginable to others. Nothing is but what is not. The governing aesthetic consideration is that the image be as uncanny and frightening as possible within the limits of the tolerable. In Shakespeare's time, apparitions were of various kinds: LeLoyer, for instance, differentiated imagined "phantasmes" from "spectres," that had "a substance hidden and concealed, which seemeth to move the fantastique body." Would the imaginary terrify more than the "real"? What counts is what *works* in the theatre. If the spectator can be more roused by the idea of a return from the dead, he may see a "ghost"; if more sensitive to the idea of a risen devil, he may perceive a "hellish spirit"; or the two connotations may mingle. In any case, Shakespeare has built enough terror into the uncanny apparition, and Macbeth's response to it, to evoke arousal enough.

An old myth has it that ghosts never come unless sent for; and Macbeth may have been thought to summon Banquo in thought and then in word. (The corollary, that ghosts never speak unless spoken to, does not apply: Banquo does not answer, and his very silence may imply "phantasme.") The myth may have been grounded in intuitive psychology: the compulsively anxious person can indeed be said to summon the obsessions that haunt him. That something of this sort happens to Macbeth may be suggested by the two stages of his experience with the ghost. It first comes only briefly, it rouses him—but not excessively—then disappears, as Macbeth controls himself. The second appearance is much more terrible, and evokes a strenuous reaction that is almost completely out of control. To this extent it parallels the experiences of the hallucinated dagger. Psychological truth accompanies aesthetic demand here: however shocking the ghost's first appearance, the second will be an intensification, a higher arousal of Macbeth's and the audience's response.

Macbeth's subconscious impulse for calling up the visitation, according to some Freudian interpreters, is Oedipal. Jekels suggests that Macbeth sees Banquo's ghost replacing himself in the seat from which Macbeth himself had driven the father; Otto Rank sees the ghost as a projection of Shakespeare's own impulses toward his father, and the consequent guilt—the ghost functions as a projection of imagined accusations by Shakespeare's father for the child Will's infantile wishes. If a familial source is to be speculated on, I find more likely a repressed impulse of sibling rivalry; the imagined guilt of the competing son who dreams of destroying a brother to secure alone the benefits of the wished-for murder of the father.

Some stagings have attempted to emphasize the subjectivity of the ghost by banishing it. Kemble tried to create for spectators the image of the ghost by staring at an empty chair; he restored the apparition in submission to audience demand, while a futile debate arose as to the value of the visible specter. Salvini, according to his biography, eliminated the ghost because he wanted to make sure the audience felt that he alone saw it; in fact, as reviews indicate, he did sometimes include the ghost's physical presence. Many other Macbeths, of various countries, have imagined the invisible ghost, among them Sullivan, Mantell, Tsarev, George, Williamson. Edwin Booth's imagining seems to have been particularly effective; he made the ghost appear to audiences by the convulsions of fright that shook him, and later, his wild fury as he stared at the "appalling vacancy" of Banquo's chair, in an "intense, horror-stricken concentration of eyes and sense and soul" (*Tribune*). Near the end of the first appearance, he would hide from it with his head in his Lady's bosom.

Substitute illusions for Banquo have also been staged, to convey the "unreal" quality of the ghost. As with the witches, early in the nineteenth century "optical means"—simple projection, or reflecting mirrors—were used; by the end of the century Fitzgerald was complaining about the magic lantern technique and urging a return to the "real" ghost. Irving began (1875) with a transparent painted effigy rising from a trap into a trick chair: while other stage lighting was dimmed, the "ghost" was illuminated by the blue light often used for uncanny spectacle, to focus on Banquo's bloody, matted hair, and to suggest that only Macbeth saw the figure. By the time Irving came to America, twenty years later, the ghost was reduced to a green beam. Irving made the ghost tangible by his show of fear: wild eyes, mouth working spasmodically, lower jaw dropping, hair literally standing on end (*Herald*). Reinhardt thought of using a mirror, ended with a ghost in a blue light. In a rationalized "modern dress" *Macbeth* (1928) Banquo's face seemed to be picked out in the embroidery of a chair back—this not unlike a German device, a wicker chair with a high back woven of concentric circles: the shadows thrown through this pattern on Macbeth's face supplied his hallucination. Evans' ghost was a muted glow. Komisarjevsky, intent on draining all the supernatural from the play, had Macbeth take his own gigantic reflection, thrown on the wall, for Banquo's specter. This Macbeth was literally afraid of his own shadow. Farjeon objected: "It is hopeless to be more reasonable than your playwright."

Shakespeare designed a visible, acted ghost, to evoke a particular response. As Coghill observed,

> What is important is that the audience should see what Macbeth sees, and be identified with him, not his guests.

If Macbeth cowers before nothing, or some invisible figment of his imagination, then to the audience as to the guests Macbeth may seem already insane, as Bergman's Macbeth (1944) did before his imaginary ghost. Moreover, with only Macbeth's response for a clue, the audience knows no better than Lady Macbeth or the guests what is the immediate cause of Macbeth's reaction. If the guests who are, in fact, the most naive of spectators, presumably knowing nothing of what is in Macbeth's mind, imagine a ghost as the unseen stimulus to Macbeth's violence, they are likely to think of Duncan. They know nothing of Banquo's murder; neither does Lady Macbeth, though she may have guessed at it. Only *we* are wholly with Macbeth in this crisis, as we have been with him before. Quiller-Couch:

> Who sees [the ghost]? Not the company. Not even Lady Macbeth. Those who see it are Macbeth and you and I. Those into whom it strikes terror. . . . Those whom it accuses are Macbeth and you and I. And what it accuses is what, of Macbeth, you and I are hiding in our own breasts.

Further, as long as the ghost can be seen, it has a "reality" for Macbeth, and hence for us, that saves him from giving the impression of outright madness. He is on the edge of it, and may seem to slip over momentarily; but as long as he recovers with the disappearance of a seen image, his clutch on sanity is acceptable. He is the more "you and I" that, haunted as he is, he can by an exercise of will sometimes banish his haunts. Yet though Banquo's ghost may seem solid, it must remain acceptable as illusion—as it conspicuously did not when Bridges-Adam's Macbeth gripped Banquo's shoulder, and turned him round in his chair. The essence of the figure—hallucination or ghost—is its immateriality.

Macbeth will describe the apparition's appearance; and the theatre has done its best to make his clues ghastly and terrifying. If Banquo appears in his habit as he lived, the dressing of blood will make him more shocking: the savagery of the many trenched gashes may show, as with a French ghost (1952), by a face all beaten and bloody. Bernhardt's seemed smothered in blood. Banquo may sometimes be fitted out in a wardrobe supposed popular with ghosts. Thus, from *The Puritan* (1607), "Well ha' the ghost i' th' white sheet sit at upper end o' th' table!" Banquo has been so accoutered, notably in Salvini's *Macbeth*. Juriev's Russian ghost glowed with phosphorescence that made lurid his pallid face and feverish eyes. Sothern's ghost was swathed in dark grey chiffon, the red gash of his wounds a startling contrast. Redgrave's was a shrouded figure, hideously mutilated, hounded by the green light effective in eerie scenes. Gielgud's Banquo conveyed immateriality through a miracle of timing: the ghost moved between two tables. The thanes, seated on benches at each table, had their backs to each other, but they continually turned to talk and pass items of food and drink across the ghost's path, so that their extended arms seemed to make a series of barriers before him. Such was the timing, however, that each arm would drop just long enough to let him by, and the impression given was that he was passing through tangible obstructions.

How did ghosts appear onstage in Shakespeare's time? In a puff of smoke? "Comedy," in *A Warning for Fair Women* (ca. 1590), in his sneers at "Tragedy," suggests as much—in an apparent allusion to the *Spanish Tragedy's* wraith:

> . . . a filthy, whining ghost,
> Lapt in some foul sheet, or leather pelch,
> Comes screaming like a pigge half stickt,
> And cries Vindicta, revenge, revenge:

> With that a little Rosin flashes forth,
> Like smoke out of a Tabacco pipe, or a boy's squib.

A poem by Higden (1685), cited by Sprague, speaks of a criminal who "Like Bancoe's ghost . . . stalks in." This may fit the Folio stage direction, and suggests menace as well as surprise. Forbes-Robertson's ghost thus solemnly strode on, in a bluish, spectral costume with which, by contrast, a gash on his face showed vividly. An opposite effect of pace was produced in the second Ernst Schröder staging, when the ghost entered in a kind of tranced slow motion, blood running down his face. The ghost is sometimes peripatetic: Bernhardt's seemed to move in and out of a stage wall; Tree's moved through and behind drapes, and Macbeth's eyes followed it out over the audience. But more often Banquo is nearly still, except for entering and leaving.

When the audience is to be surprised along with Macbeth—the more frequent theatre design—the ghost's sudden appearance must be masked. A common way has been to shield his entrance at the beginning of the scene behind that of the entering lords or servants, and he sits with his back to the house until Macbeth turns and sees him. In the Nunn staging, the audience suddenly became aware, as Macbeth did, that one of the men whose backs were turned had not moved, among all the others busily stirring; there was the sudden shock of the familiar become uncanny. Then the ghost turned. Banquo may enter only after Macbeth designates an empty chair, and then move to it behind a line of entering servants, as with Scofield; the servants then may mask the chair until just before Macbeth makes the discovery. When the ghost sometimes suddenly appears at the dais, he can make his own way to it from behind. Where illumination has been controlled, lights have been lowered and raised for his entrances and exits; blue* and green filters, along with eerie music, have been used to effect ghostly atmosphere.

A more spectacular alternative for the ghost's sudden appearance has him rising from the trap, often as if through the chair itself. Sometimes his ascent is masked by a grouping of servants, or of the lords, when he must appear in an isolated chair. Sometimes he emerges abruptly. Charles Kean achieved a powerful effect when his Banquo seemed to arise out of his center table— only the upper part of the ghost showing, brightly illuminated. In a twentieth-century *Macbeth*, only the spotlighted head glowed on a platter as if disembodied.

The ghost has long been faded in and out behind gauze scrims, as at the

---

*The association of blue lights with specters may be archetypal. In Lyly's *Gallathea* (ca. 1585), Rafe says: "My mother would often tell me that when the candle burnt blue there was some ill spirit in the house." Shakespeare's Richard III, visited by the ghosts that promise his doom, notices that "the lights burn blue." When Tom Sawyer and Huck Finn discuss the haunted house, Tom, eager to explore, says, "Nothing's ever been seen around that house except at night—just some blue lights slipping by the windows—no ghosts." Huck: "Well, when you see one of them blue lights flickering around, Tom, you can bet there's a ghost mighty close behind it. It stands to reason. Becuz *you* know that they don't anybody but ghosts use 'em." Tom: "Yes, that's so."

Meiningen, where he appeared at the side of the stage, so Macbeth's reactions could be seen in profile. The light growing behind the scrim slowly illuminates the figure, the dying light extinguishes it. Technologically, the ideal for the ghost is the hologram, the three-dimensional figure, laser-projected without body into space, that actors can move or strike through. The problem with this, as with all devices that make Banquo appear by surprise, or with ghostly characteristics, is that unless the process is perfectly integrated, it draws attention to itself, and illusion may be dispelled.

The doubtful Forman describes Macbeth drinking a carouse to Banquo when

> The ghost of Banco come and sate down in his cheier behind him. And he turning A-bout to sit Again sawe the goste of banco, which fronted him so, that he fell in-to a great passion of fear and fury, Vttering many wordes about his murder.

This response of Macbeth's could only be that which followed the second, more spectacular, of the appearances (that there are two is not even mentioned in the "Forman" account). Macbeth's first reaction to the ghost is carefully modulated in comparison with the later one. He only speaks twice to the vision. First,

> Thou canst not say I did it: never shake
> Thy gory locks at me. (66–67)

Ross, alert for the politics of the situation, then speaks for the Lords. He may be calling attention to Macbeth; alternately, on the theory that he is one of Macbeth's instruments, he may be trying to protect his chief:

> Gentlemen rise, his Highness is not well. (68)

Ross may rise first and wave them up; they may come up of themselves, almost automatically. Then Macbeth is silent through Lady Macbeth's long speech, breaks into it briefly, and is silent again until his last lines before Banquo disappears. Shakespeare provides him with the *flaws and starts* Lady Macbeth sees, and the *faces* he makes; but not yet the "great passion of fear and fury." He is not yet ready for outright aggression; his comparative silence, his defensive speech, suggests primarily bewilderment, trauma, and recovery.

Multiple impulses tear at Macbeth—the normal man's fear of the insecurity of the inexplicable, the deep common dread of losing reason, the warrior's rage, the philosopher's bewilderment, the king-player's craving to seem imperturbable, the guilt of the murderer not lost to all decency stalked by his victim, the sheer physical revulsion from a horrible sight. All rasp at his mind, his body, and his senses, twisting him at length to the boundary of the bearable.

Macbeth's first shock comes partly from the sudden, jarring immediacy of the ghost-image, when instantaneously thrust upon him. When Banquo's white specter rose from under the table immediately at the feet of Salvini, his Macbeth, at other times so strong and defiant, could understandably express, with every line of his face, agony and dread. A purely physical revulsion for the bloody Banquo activated Salvini as well as the abrupt presence of the uncanny, and his apprehension at his own frightened reaction. Stevenson: "He is afraid of he knows not what. He is abject, and again blustering." For one terrifying moment this bravest of warriors hid his head under his robe. Any Macbeth, let alone Juriev's, so ready to despair, might have been overwhelmed when, putting his hand on his chair, he found himself suddenly face to face with a phosphorescent ghost; and then to recognize his victim, Banquo, deathly pale, blood-covered, with feverish eyes—the actor would write, "I truly felt shivers along my spine."

Macready and the audience were startled together when the ghost, shielded as it rose from a trap, came into view at the moment Macbeth was about to sit. Two bloody wounds marked its pale face—not until it turned did it show the customary cut throat, that seemed to sever head from body. Macready was stricken. Trembling, he tried to shield his eyes from the scorching sight.* Even more painful was the awakening from the spell, after his Lady took his hand. Macready would be able to suggest that the recognition that his mind had yielded, that he had hallucinated, evoked the deepest horror, and he shuddered. The actor experimented once with having the Physician move to Lady Macbeth, and in dumb show question Macbeth's sanity; fortunately he dropped this, to insist on the dialectic between reason and unreason, and the painful triumph of the latter.

Some last thin elastic barrier stretches to allow Shakespeare's tragic heroes to glimpse what madness is, but then usually forces them back to reason. Even Lear cannot escape forever the cruelty of sanity. Macbeth's impulse to yield to a chaos of the mind may be linked in Shakespeare's design with the readiness to invoke a chaos in the universe. But readiness is not all: the mind insists on reason, though the very battle for it may become a skirmish with madness. With a Macbeth like Smochowski, on the rack almost from the beginning, the violent response to the ghost seemed a true insanity physically frightening the thanes; only the summoning of his warrior's courage against an enemy held him from absolute lunacy. The struggle for reason was more surprising when so thoughtful a Macbeth as Forbes-Robertson was suddenly, before the ghost, touched with hysteria. The actor, speaking laboriously, managed to convey again a sense of momentary "nervous disorder," a flight from lucidity; and then, as striking, a quick recovery.

Tree's poetic Macbeth seemed lost to reason in the images he had created.

*Macready perhaps sensed how uneasily Macbeth's eyes could bear *sights:* Hence, to the spirit of Banquo in IV, i (135): *Thy crown does sear mine eyeballs.*

He had been drinking considerably; facing the ghost—whom he first found behind his chair—he seemed mad with wine and the anguish of memory:

> in agony, not fear of what might be, but . . . for what had been and what he had made of himself (*Telegraph*).

His mind seemed weakened by the inrush of complex emotions—

> a wonderful exhibition of the innermost soul of a fear-stricken man . . . of infirmity of purpose, of terror, of remorse. . . . The haunted face, the hunted look, the swaying body racked with every dreadful emotion (*Standard*).

Symptomatic of the poetic hallucination Tree projected was the ghost itself, more insidious than revolting, leaving its seat to move rhythmically along the rim of the banqueting hall. It was here that Tree's projection of "morbid symptoms" was accompanied by

> the low throbbing hum strongly suggestive of those noises in the head to which many subjects to optical hallucination are liable (*Post*).

Introspection, rather than incipient insanity, characterized the first response in some designs. A major problem for Macbeth, as he returns from the murder, is *not* to see Banquo's ghost until ready. He may glimpse the uncanny presence, and not take it in, his eyes moving over the others at the tables; otherwise his eyes must not make contact until the moment for reaction. This is no problem when Banquo's ghost appears suddenly; when he has been sitting there, Macbeth may be seen unconsciously or even consciously delaying recognition, putting off the intolerable. Forrest, his mind deeply inward, moved blindly toward Banquo, and only with slow horror did his brain recognize what his eyes had seen. Guinness, projecting Macbeth's sensitivity to the uncanny in the atmosphere, felt the ghost's presence before he saw it; he was moving away when he slowly turned, with stifled horror, almost as if knowing what he was going to look upon.

Reinhardt's Macbeth was about to drink, the bowl in his hand, at *The table's full*. For some seconds he stood still, as if turned to stone, then backed off. He saw Banquo isolated in a green light, looking like a drowned corpse, with dreadful, bulging fluorescent eyes. The ghost's throat was cut, and its forehead, also gashed, had intimations of the Crucifixion. As Macbeth spoke, in a suffocated voice, the ghost raised a threatening hand.

To preserve Macbeth's dignity before the ghost, and to emphasize his positive courage, actors have sometimes subordinated the note of fear in the polyphony of response. Garrick would look unwaveringly at the ghost—his essay makes fun of a Macbeth looking wildly at the thanes. This firmness accorded with Garrick's determination not to show "pusillanimity." Yet Garrick was arist enough to allow Macbeth momentary surrender, offset dramatically by recovery. The actor wrote to a correspondent that the first appearance of the ghost overpowered Macbeth more than the second, but he was certain that then, as later, Macbeth would resume courage and strength. Kemble, in his writing as well as his acting, insisted on the primacy of Macbeth's courage. This, along with the characteristic dignity of the actor, perhaps explains why Kemble seemed "tame and kindly" during the scene. George Vandenhoff, the later gentleman Macbeth, poised his dialectic between the extremes of awe—not fear—and of courage. The qualities of the warrior Macbeth, nothing afraid of strange images of death, that save him from ultimate collapse, may dominate him at once. So a Macbeth intolerably impatient of repressing impulse, like Piscator's, responded to the first appearance (as other Macbeths would the second) with a warrior's reflex of attack that overruled fear. He leaped upon the table, and jerked out his dagger, as if to do battle with his hallucination.

Kean, exploring the levels in the design, would shadow the moment with the dimension of fear: he drew back, his head averted. Other Macbeths have let the note of fright dominate them, so that any recovery must demand corresponding extremes of control. Dawison (Germany, 1855), recognizing the ghost of his victim, instantly started back, and then was fixed, body arched back away from the specter, arms spread, every nerve taut, so tense with fear that his whole body trembled. A Japanese Macbeth was for a long time unable to make any move at all. Charles Coghlan (U.S., 1889), Langtry's Macbeth, also seemed paralyzed with fear; though, according to an observer, he managed to suggest, with Macbeth's "faces," the dialectic of a man whose senses told him Banquo was there, but whose reason denied it. Savits' Macbeth was so shaken physically by Banquo's ghost, which appeared in silhouette, that he stumbled backward and fell down a step of the central platform. After a few seconds, he recovered and tried to pull himself back up, but his hands trembled too much, and he slipped. When his wife came, he stood behind her, his hands clasping her shoulders, finally buried his face in her neck, until he could look up and see the ghost gone. Charles Kean was a portrait of livid fear: stricken limbs, fixed eyes, palsied lips, all his faculties suspended, he seemed stunned and turned to stone. When his wife came down to him, he clung helplessly to her.

Fleck's response was a see-saw between fearful withdrawal and futile attack. He at once drew back, and averted his glance from the ghost; but at the same time, retreating, his arms moved out as if to strike, windmill fashion. In his overwhelming fright, his inability to bear the sight of the ghost, his frustrated aggression, a touch of childishness was seen. Even more frankly childish, Plummer nestled to his wife-mother, screaming with hysteria at his (imaginary, in this staging) Banquo.

The prince of cowards was, of course, Irving. More than ever he meant, by the very size and dimensions of Macbeth's fear, to project the stature that in other Macbeths was sustained by more heroic resistance. Recognizing Banquo, his first response was to pluck off his crown—as if Banquo had come to claim the ill-gotten prize—and hold it behind his back. But Irving felt that the external threat was secondary to Macbeth's inner experience of desolating fear. Irving wanted the audience to feel

> that horror of the soul, that daemonaical terror of the mind which communicates itself with irresistible power to every expression of the face and voice. The more conscious Macbeth becomes of this irresistible power, by the reappearance of the ghost, the more horror stricken does he grow.

Irving put off the moment of inescapable recognition. He first looked away from the hallucinated seated figure, as if he were not seeing aright, slowly turned again: *The table's full*. When the "empty" chair was pointed out, Irving held a silence, and then said, with a "sharp smile,"

Which of you have done this? (64)

Then the ghost "moved," and Macbeth—his voice "trembling . . . sinking to a whisper"—shuddered, began to give in to frenzies of terror.

The outbreak of fear from Irving would come as no surprise, as it would with a Salvini, for instance; it represented an intensification of an established design. This was also true of Macbeths continuously beset by neurotic anxieties. Characteristically uncertain, explosive, their nerves were on hair-trigger, instantly responsive to symbolic threat. Mitterwurzer turned pale, breathed heavily. For a while he could only stare motionless at the bloody image, only stammer when he needed to speak. Matkowsky resisted noticing the ghost; when he did notice, he was dazzled, as if his eyes could not bear the sight. His voice failed him; his words could hardly be heard.

No design carries more shock than that of the inward Macbeth suddenly forced into uncontrollable self-exposure. So Olivier's, growing from his strategy to build in a low key toward the second half of the play, and from the depth he found in his masked, sardonic characterization. This Macbeth's compressed power had been glimpsed in its few, momentary raptnesses or outbreaks. But these were mainly private; even with his wife, though he had sometimes revealed himself at high tension, as immediately after the murder, he had carefully screened himself, was partly player. All the more his rising excitement during the ghost's two appearances—he would whisper, would shout and scream—betrayed the nakedness of self.

> His hitherto almost privately created apparition of a soul in torment becomes public, flaming across the darkness with terrifying power (*Times*).

Scofield's soldierly, then also kingly, presence had never been a complete cover for his hidden Macbeth: the lined face had labored to become, since the meeting with the sisters, a layered mask carefully suiting itself to Macbeth's audiences; but even in public some shadows of feeling, often conflicting ones, were glimpsed as his rising emotions fought against rigorous repression. In private, and when he exposed aspects of himself to his wife, hints of fearful, reckless, capped energy could be sensed. Even here he seemed to have some perspective of himself, he could after each ghostly visit look at his action with a touch of irony. He had spoken with forced seriousness of how much Banquo was missed: the thanes heard the seriousness, the audience the forcing. The sight of the ghost jerked him out from his mask. The player's role, that he had acted with such control before the lords, dropped from him: as conspicuous as the emotions—fear, horror, revulsion, guilt—that crowded into his face was the sudden absence of self-awareness. He confronted the ghost as if they two were alone in the world. Scofield, through the rest of the play, would powerfully dramatize Macbeth's struggle to return to a perspective on himself, with moments of startling loss of it, moments of crushing return.

To Lady Macbeth, ever watchful of Macbeth, ever apprehensive of his *dreadful deed*, the slightest sign of loss of control is alarming. She has come to recognize now his dangerous raptness, his lostness in his thoughts, the almost mystic elation of his communion with the forces of darkness. A sensitive reader in the book of his face, she may have sensed from it his awareness of the ghost even before he admitted it to consciousness, even before *The table's full*, probably sooner than all the carousing thanes could, though perhaps not much ahead of the alert Ross, urging the lords to rise. Now she must, when she is least able, again become player, assume the innocent flower, attempt to impose a painting of order over the reality of an uncanny hurly-burly. Only her will makes it possible, Segond-Weber thought. She described her emotional problem: to

> preserve a "front calm and cold" in the presence of the terrible behaviour of her husband. This struggle, which nothing in the text helps reveal, must be perceived by the audience. . . . She must recall all her judgment, all her strength to smile at her guests, to lure them from the agitations of Macbeth, to invent some story, a childhood illness, to excuse this terrible perturbation . . . all not achieved without failures, but always redeemed in time, when she feels herself lost.

The Lady's practical problem was demonstrated in Fanny Kemble's

> lynx-eyed caution by which she watched her moody lord, while he is beset by the horrors of Banquo's spectre, her eagerness to prevent the guests from catching any of the wild words which his guilt-haunted agonies made him utter (*Times*).

Her "rapid rushing" down to Macbeth has been described.

Lady Macbeth's language is simple, manly, monosyllabic, suited to the effort she must make. The "invented story," lame as it is, and identifying Macbeth with a childish disease as it does, must serve. She drives the lords' gaze away from Macbeth by insisting that they not note him, but feed. With some awkwardness and reluctance and whispering they turn ostensibly to their eating, and she moves to Macbeth. Now she is in fact split, holding off the thanes' furtive glances while trying to manage Macbeth. She returns to the theme with which she first activated him:

Are you a man? (74)

Pritchard, holding for a long time to her throne, seemed disturbed only by danger, not at all by conscience. Davies described her

admirable art in endeavouring to hide Macbeth's frenzy from the observation of the guests, by drawing their attention to conviviality. She smiled on one, whispered to another, distantly saluted a third; in short, she practised every possible artifice to hide the transaction that passed between her husband and the vision his disturbed imagination had raised. Her reproving and angry looks, which glanced towards Macbeth, at the same time were mixed with marks of inward vexation and uneasiness. When, at last, as if unable to support her feelings any longer, she rose from her seat and seized his arm, and, with a half-whisper of terror, said, "Are you a man?" she assumed a look of much anger, indignation, and contempt as cannot be surpassed.

More dimension deepened Siddons' reaction. Again she saw herself and Macbeth as "wretched souls," the Lady affecting to dominate her husband, but riven by terror and remorse:

What imagination can conceive her tremors, lest at every succeeding moment Macbeth, in his distraction, may confirm those suspicions, but ill-concealed, under the loyal looks and cordial manners of their facile courtiers.

Perhaps to differ from Pritchard, Siddons came down into the arena sooner. Galt remembered the magnificence of her descent; Mangin her brilliant and piercing eyes, that "could be seen to sparkle and glare at an incredible distance." Her variety of expression, "presented . . . with the precision of truth and the splendour of light," amazed the *Edinburgh Courant*:

Terror, rage, contempt, counterfeit hilarity and actual agony, were here combined in a series of looks, and starts, and writhings.

Siddons had reacted sharply to Lenox'

What is't that moves your highness? (63)

"Her secret uneasiness very fine. Suppressed, but agitating her whole frame" (Bell). She descended when Ross asked the thanes to rise, distracted the guests at their level, and "Comes up to him and catches his hand. Voice suppressed." Her question as to his manliness was asked "with smothered terror," Siddons wrote, "yet domineering indignation."

Macbeth's answer, with its echoing *dare*, suggests that by now he dare do more than may become a man—more than the devil. It is not enough. Siddons was "peevish and scornful" in describing the unreality—*the very painting of your fear* (78) of whatever he saw: whether the *air-drawn dagger* (79) or the present vision.

To Lady Macbeth, even his symptoms of terror, his *flaws and starts* (80), are appearances—*Imposters to true fear* (81). They would suit a handed-down, woman's winter's tale, so far are they from relating to reality. The Lady tries to rouse or shame him as a child is roused or shamed. Siddons was again "peevish and scornful" here; then, trying to reduce Macbeth's vision to absurdity—and informing us where his gaze is—

When all's done (84)

by now she must know it never is—

You look but on a stool. (85)

Siddons spoke to her Macbeth

> in his ear, as if to bring him back to the objects of common life. Her anxiety makes you creep with apprehension; uncertain how to act. Her emotion keeps you breathless (Bell).

The star actress knew how to draw attention to herself.

While she had sat on her throne, before descending, her physical imagery, divided between her graces to the thanes and her attention to Macbeth, was such that she "more than divided the interest with the powerful action going on in front." The same was said of the silent layers of meaning conveyed by the seated Ristori—

> her demeanour and her pantomime make her audience almost forget that there is anyone else on the stage. One sees the anxious wife, smiling to her guests in order to divert their attention . . . and yet beneath this she portrays all the agony that fills her mind, and her fear lest he should betray the guilty secret.

She moved from noble hospitality with the thanes to quick anger to Macbeth, then hurriedly back to sustain the composure of the banquet.

Ristori herself "experienced the greatest agitation and dismay at the discovery of Macbeth's incomprehensible and frightful visions." She must try at once

> to hide the hallucinations of her husband, and bring him back to himself by the most bitter though subdued reproofs . . . an appearance of gaiety must be preserved upon the countenance whenever it is turned toward the guests, to excuse the strange demeanour of the husband on the ground of an ancient malady.

The stretch between the two roles the Lady must assume—hostess and wife—severely tests her resilience. So Faucit,

> playing the hypocrite with queenly affability . . . and striving with maddened frenzy to recall (Macbeth) to self-command, and to hide her efforts from their guests (*Glasgow Herald*).

Lady Macbeth meanwhile must make clear to her third audience—the spectators—the tenuous basis of her self-control. So Faucit betrayed

> the ill-suppressed anguish of a guilty spirit, and a perceptible struggle to subdue the manifestations of their guilt whilst attempting to encourage and sustain her husband (*Freeman's*).

The queenly Cushman made her wife's role more real by speaking to the thanes about Macbeth's illness with earnest anxiety. Morris, too, sustained

> with unerring skill the strain of an outward composure maintained by will power under the stress of harrowing anxiety and dread. She signified her distress to the audience while offering a courteous front to her amazed guests *as if the king's seizure were really the frequent infirmity she asserted it to be* [italics mine] (Towse).

Thus, Morris could bend to recall Macbeth to himself while seeming to be attending lovingly to his illness.

The Ladies of gentler design, like Morris, had, as in the beginning, to summon a mixture of anger and scorn into their deep concern. The force of their love was paradoxically reflected in the force of their frustration and anger as they sought to protect their Macbeths. Terry came down to Irving at his first wild speech to the ghost, and calmed the guests until she could get to him and whisper, low and hoarsely, *Are you a man?* Her *O proper stuff* was "quick, peevish"; her note suggests that even in his terror this Macbeth was indeed pretending, his fear part imposture: "She knows he is hysterical, 'giving way' to acting before people." But she coaxed as well as rebuked him. Her note: "Hush, hush, your vision was fancy." The audience was allowed to sense her weariness and exhaustion as she tried feverishly to hide and recall him; if anything, she seemed not queenly enough in her solicitude.

Bernhardt, sitting on her throne, had been seen to give way to a creeping lassitude, from which she had to shake herself to show courtesies to the guests. She was a "sweet and benign" hostess, as suited her "feminine" design for the Lady; but when her Macbeth, Marais, reacted to Banquo's ghost in a frenzy of whirling terror, she moved to him through the court with a formidable majesty and mingled a "little contempt with the love and sympathy" she showed him.

Hackett's Lady found several moments of tenderness in her speech, trying to reassure Macbeth that he was really courageous; but on *Impostors* and *by her grandam* she shook him to bring him to his senses.

Marlowe had been among the guests from the beginning, to cover Macbeth's meeting with the Murderer; courteous as she was to the thanes, her thoughts very unmistakably fastened on Macbeth. When Sothern faced the ghost, dreadfully suffering, she went to him and led him to his throne, giving him her whole frantic attention:

> the alarmed, bewildered thanes were to her almost as much phantoms as Banquo's ghost itself (*Transcript*).

Sothern had sunk back against a table, almost in collapse; when she reminded him of the imagined dagger that led him *to Duncan* he cried out in fear. She had to chide as well as soothe him in her desperate effort to return him to reality.

Reinhardt's Lady kept silence until some of the lords rose, and others shifted in their chairs. Then she made an enormous effort at self-control. Essaying a pale smile, she at first spoke loudly, to draw the thanes' attention. She did not "descend" until *If much you note him* (72), when she moved among the guests speaking in an undertone, confidentially—as to friends of a patient. Then, anxious almost to the limit of her endurance, she advanced excitedly on Macbeth, and the other side of her long care for him showed: she rebuked him angrily, gnashing her teeth with exasperation: *Shame*. Then, looking at his distorted face, she clapped her hands together, frightened by his strange behavior. The sound brought the guests staring at them.

Macbeth has enough hold on reality that he is able to hear his Lady while his mind is filled with his vision. That he can still answer her questions and her goading while keeping his eye fixed on the specter seems to confirm the impression that he is attending to an objective phenomenon. First he answers her, saying the same thing again and again to persuade:

> Prithee see there:
> Behold, look, lo, how say you: (86–87)

Tree followed the moving ghost with his eyes; more often the ghost sits, stolidly, as Fitzgerald reported, continuing to stare, or smile, as it nods. Macready pointed: and the eyes of all the company looked toward the emptiness. Hackett tried really to get his wife to see the image; he grasped her arm, pointed. Then, persuaded and encouraged by her assurance that it was only his imagination, he laughed, *Why, what care I . . . ?*

Now Macbeth gives us his second description of Banquo's appearance. He has seen the ghost shake his *gory locks*. This may have been a minatory side-to-side warning; but perhaps it was already the gesture Macbeth next describes: *if thou canst nod*. If so, the nodding was the immediate rebuttal to Macbeth's first, instinctive disavowal of guilt: *Thou can'st not say I did it*. Or is it now a symbol of the ghost's knowing how vain are Macbeth's bravado, his ambition? Macbeth is desperate enough, or hysterical enough, or brave enough, or angry enough, or enough all of them, to defy the unreal. He cries ironically against a universe that is out of order—for giving a sign of the chaos he himself invited.

> If charnel houses, and our graves must send
> Those that we bury, back; our monuments
> Shall be the maws of kites. (89–91)

The metaphor seems to spring from the habit of kites to disgorge what they have eaten. The underlying image, of the obstinate refusal of the dead to stay dead, will be continued in Macbeth's later speech. Sanders reads, in

Macbeth's words, here and next, a shallowness of rhetoric; not all will agree
with that, but may agree more readily with Sanders' perception of the depth of
Macbeth's courage—that even in its evil it has a Luciferian grandeur. Shocked
by a vision that might make the devil blench, Macbeth can challenge it.

Olivier, intent on holding down Macbeth's response to the first appearance, and still guarding the remnants of privacy, whispered the speech,
backing away. Many Macbeths, having given in to deeper shock, rebounded
more sharply, as Garrick did, recovering from his traumatic horror. But
committed to the reality of their unreal vision, they must break out again
into flashes of irrational energy, physically as well as in words. Macbeth's
speech and manner require him to reach so high a pitch that his Lady must
again question his manhood:

> What? quite unmann'd in folly. (92)

Sothern had broken away from Marlowe's hold, shouting his words. He
tried to crowd the ghost from the seat—and was most horrified to find it
empty. Hackett went furiously to the chair to rip it to pieces; when his spasm
was over, he looked up, with triumph and satisfaction, to see his ghost gone.
Mitterwurzer, breaking out of the spell that had paralyzed him, raised his
trembling hands, shouted, *Why what care I?* (88), and like a wild beast broke
through the row of guests at his table, seized anything at hand—plates and
bowls—and flung them at the ghost. It disappeared, and with a great sigh of
relief he leaned back against the table. Matkowsky demonstrated the opposite
effect on a nerve-ridden Macbeth: he too shouted, threw himself at the table,
and pounded at it. But when the ghost disappeared, he was still frightened,
and answered his Lady's *Shame* with a whisper. Reinhardt's Macbeth, while
speaking, repeatedly passed one hand over his eyes, as if to banish what he
saw. His words, *If charnel houses . . .* were addressed urgently to his Lady.
His other hand, holding a bowl of wine, trembled, so that the red liquid spilled
and "gilded" his fingers. While the guests began to whisper, he stared at his
red hands. Gielgud raised his arms over the ghost, as if to smash it; the alarmed
lords came round to him, to hold him; as Macbeth threw them off, the grouping shielded Banquo's "invisible" exit.

The means of the ghost's first disappearance intensifies the strain on Macbeth's reason. Scofield's Banquo moved slowly toward him during Macbeth's
last speech, with a heavy tread. When Scofield reached his last line, *the maws
of kites*, the bloody face was so close that Scofield had to raise his arms to hide
his eyes—and then the ghost was gone. The show of fear from a Macbeth so
usually fearless was particularly striking.

Tree's ghost, ever in motion when it left its seat, also advanced on Macbeth. Lady Macbeth stood between them, unconsciously protecting Macbeth.
Tree partly shielded his eyes with his hand, as if almost dazzled, and—paying no attention to the thanes, who had risen, disturbed—watched the ghost
out of sight.

Macready's Banquo, after his nodding and Macbeth's defiance, slowly dropped back into the trap, as if sinking into the earth. Pückler-Muskau thought the "perfect" illusion "fearful and thrilling." Macready, still under shock, slumped against the chair. Phelps' ghost also "sank," as it had risen. Salvini's disappeared under the table whence it had issued. Richardson's, with a grand swirl of its great cloak, "vanished" into the background.

Macbeth is unsettled by Banquo's magical disappearance, but even more by the implication that the ghost was perhaps an illusion. The awareness that his mind has worked against him may be the greatest horror: the primary bastion of his security is invaded when brain and senses fail him, when nothing is but what is not.

If I stand here, I saw him. (93)

He has learned again his vulnerability from within, a vulnerability he will increasingly try to counter in wild action. Thus Macready's

> maddening consciousness that his . . . image of horror is the creation of his own brain, and that he is being smitten down and abased before his own being, and that one half of his nature has become a devil to persecute the other half (*New Mirror*).

Macbeth's crisis has forced almost intolerable demands on his Lady. Despairing as she has confessed herself to be, strained by the need to mask her deteriorating emotional strength under the show of innocence, she has now had to summon her last strength for very survival. She continues to monitor Macbeth because she must. Her demeaning *Fie for shame* (94) Siddons kept to a whisper; other Ladies found reserve enough to drive themselves to fierce expostulation, even action. Diana Wynyard (England, 1949) still had strength to browbeat her Macbeth; Wolter became more and more furious as Macbeth's fugue threatened them: she hissed her scornful adjurations at him. So did Reinhardt's Lady, even stamping her foot, still on the wave of her desperate frustration. An Italian Lady (1970) sat in Banquo's chair to rebuke Macbeth's imagination. Gladys Cooper (England, 1935), Sprague remembers, did this to prevent the hallucination returning; Mirren did it to try to exorcise what Macbeth (Williamson) saw. When Dench tried to prove the stool was nothing else by sitting on it, the horrified McKellen snatched her up, and held her bodily away.

Macbeth's hallucination brings some Ladies a marked stage further toward breakdown. These may have seemed toughest, most powerful, in the beginning. Apparently a majestic queen, Gogoleva had been imperious in urging Macbeth toward reality; but beneath her mask she could be seen to be broken. Merchant, whose bright veneer had in III, i begun to show signs of cracking, could still affect before the banquet a brittle, feverish gaiety; when Macbeth first spoke to the ghost, this Lady was strong enough to order, as a queen could, the rising thanes to *Sit, worthy friends*. It was a command, almost snarled; and it was obeyed. But strength began to wane as she came to Macbeth, and tried to understand what went on in this stranger to her. "She is now afraid of him," Hall said. Flora Robson saw the Lady's magnificent response to the intensifying demands of the scene as "her Indian summer of courage. . . . It is her last flare-up."

As soon as Macbeth is freed from the visitation, the Lady's mind reverts to her hostess role, the speed of the transition usually emphasizing the split in her attention, and the consequent stress on her. She moves back through the banquet to the dais—sometimes, as in Marlowe's case, leading Macbeth. But he is rapt, digesting his shock, deeply marveling. The beginning of his speech slows to a contemplative rhythm, even though, again, most of the words are monosyllables. The first line smooths over the iambic,

> Blood hath been shed ere now, i'th'olden time
> Ere human statute purg'd the gentle weal: (95–96)

This is likely to come from Macbeth "aside," as with Garrick, out of a deep inwardness. The philosopher is speaking, putting the present enormity into context—a historical context, as Nevo suggests, not one glimpsing God's Eden, for it is human law that is valued for proscribing violence. The murderer can pause to look back at a revolution establishing order, a triumph of man's Apollonian nature; but it could not banish disorder:

> Ay, and since too, murders have been perform'd
> Too terrible for the ear. (97–98)

He returns to his earlier theme, that murder done is not *done:* the tempo rises:

> The times has been,
> That when the brains were out, the man would die,
> And there an end: but now they rise again
> With twenty mortal murders on their crowns,
> And push us from our stools. (98–102)

Olivier ended with a "compulsive shoving gesture." Macbeth is moving another step toward total irrational outbreak. The speech is an angry cry against the grave's disorder by an architect of disorder.

Once more Lady Macbeth, hearing his morbid thoughts—perhaps at her throne again, watching him rapt—must call him to the present:

> Your noble friends do lack you. (105)

Terry felt keenly the need to play hostess, to fill the king's place. As a matter of tactics, during Irving's "rapt" speech, as she went to the throne, she tried to catch the eye of one of the lady guests, then speak to the others, as she leaned back on her state and called for wine. Her feeling, watching Macbeth, was "Come, come, no more of this." Her reminder to him she meant to be "Not severe but with playful amazement. Are you blind or deaf?" Ristori sent her double message again to guests and Macbeth: mingling an accent of re-proof into

> my half serious, half facetious words. I gave another warning—"My worthy lord . . ." in such a way, however, that I made Macbeth alone understand by the power of my significant glances, what this second appeal really meant.

Cushman, intent on sustaining the "mirth," relaxed her queenly manner, bowed, smiled, also made a show of intensifying the warmth with which she attempted to draw the guests into a sense of conviviality; to Macbeth she was now coaxing. When speech seemed not enough to alert Quayle to the present, his Lady checked him with a touch on the arm; Tree's and Sothern's brought Macbeth wine to drink, and forced it on him.

Some Lady Macbeths showed by their desperation how close they were to breakdown. Reinhardt's, to break through Macbeth's haze, spoke loudly, sharply, anxiously. Mirren, fighting for control, moved compulsively about the room as she reacted to Macbeth's strange raptness; at one point she had to turn her back on the guests, and cling to the back of a chair, to regain self-possession.

Macbeth, with his painful awareness of his doubling consciousness—of both what is, and what is not—wrenches himself back to his host's affability. He cannot avoid the startled, wondering, distrustful faces of the thanes. He craves their golden opinion:

> Do not muse at me my most worthy friends,
> I have a strange infirmity, which is nothing
> To those that know me. (107–109)

He is speaking doubly again—an infirmity does infect him.

> Come, love and health to all,
> Then I'll sit down: (109–110)

Savits' Macbeth started to seat himself in the ghost's chair, was afraid, stopped. Macready looked fearfully around at it, before going on with his toast. Throughout the *cheer*, this sense of the drag of Macbeth's recent experi-ence shows by his hesitation, or alternatively, by his bluff determination to hide it. Sothern put on a hearty manner—so hearty that Marlowe had to touch his arm, to quiet him. Reinhardt's Macbeth lifted his bowl to start the toast, found it was empty. His knees trembled, and again his hand wiped his fore-head, the old nervous gesture.

Macbeth holds his bowl for the servants to pour—

> Give me some wine, fill full: (110)

The last words are sometimes a stressed order, as some wine spills, or Macbeth feels the need of *all* the drink the cup will hold—his tension may drive him to gulp down a great drink compulsively.

Once more the Folio directs Macbeth to proceed unconscious of the ghost's presence: *Enter ghost* precedes Macbeth's elegant *cheer*.

> I drink to th'general joy o'th'whole table,
> And to our dear friend Banquo, whom we miss:
> Would he were here: to all, and him we thirst,
> And all to all. (111–115)

Reinhardt's Macbeth, pulling himself together, said *Banquo* with bravado. Quayle's Macbeth was able to manage a smile to Lady Macbeth; they exchanged a laugh, and as he invited the thanes to join his toast, they all shouted "Banquo! Banquo! Banquo!" Others have hesitated at the name: it stuck in Sothern's throat; Williamson had trouble with it, the word coming out in two broken syllables.

The ghost's second appearance may be less surprising than the first, but is likely to be more terrible. In the first visitation, again, the very shock of the uncanny presence, often startlingly sudden, is powerful jolt enough. Macbeth's limited description of that vision—the gory hair, and the shaking and nodding of the head—suggest that Banquo's back may have remained to the audience, the horror of his appearance reflected in Macbeth's response. Macbeth spoke, after the ghost was gone, of risen corpses with *twenty mortal murders on their crowns* (101), and these seem to match Banquo's *twenty trenched gashes*—Banquo has seemed this bloody, as noted above, on his first appearance; but the description may be Macbeth's impression, not the audience's. In any case, what Macbeth sees the second time is much more fearful—he would rather face *any shape but that*. Shakespeare was saving an ultimate in horror for this second climax in his rising design.

> Avaunt, and quit my sight, let the earth hide thee:
> Thy bones are marrowless, thy blood is cold:
> Thou hast no speculation in those eyes
> Which thou dost glare with. (117–120)

The pitch is higher, the mind inflamed. Macbeth is clearly now looking straight at a glaring image of horrible death itself. Does he—do we—see something other than before? (Akutagawa saw celluloid eyes on his Japanese ghost.) The marrowless bones suggest that Macbeth perceives—if we do not—something transparent, skeletal. Poel staged this second ghost as Duncan's. The stage direction does not specify that the ghost is Banquo's, but it is commonly taken to be, if for no other reason than that once more Banquo has specifically been invited to the feast, and that only Banquo's ghost— later as *the* ghost—is specified.

The very ineffectiveness of Lady Macbeth's final attempt to appease the guests is a measure of the vain desperation of her role-playing, and her own increasing futility, if not disintegration. The thanes are alarmed, restless, whispering, on their feet. Any divided effort the Lady directs to Macbeth, by look or pantomime, is equally useless. He returns to his concern—his obsession, now?—with the daring of manliness:

> What man dare, I dare: (124)

And he catalogues the terrible images, other than this ghost's shape, he will gladly confront; even Banquo alive again.

> If trembling I inhabit then, protest me
> The baby of a girl. (130–131)

That complex sentence, variously glossed, seems to me to mean, "If I live (inhabit) trembling, call me the baby of a girl" (a girl's doll, or girl baby—in any case, a suggestion of the farthest extreme from manliness.* Any image of pity the babe had disappears). *Protest me* suggests his concern for reputation, golden opinion; in this naked moment, his most private thoughts become public. He does not care who hears or sees him battle with what he himself recognizes as phantasmal:

> Hence horrible shadow,
> Unreal mockery hence. (131–132)

This means and place of the ghost's appearance may intensify Macbeth's—and the audience's—reaction. Charles Kean's Banquo was seen mysteriously to "rise" in what looked like a solid stone column—in fact, the front was a gauze scrim, lighted behind as the specter materialized. Hopkins' Banquo erupted from a trap immediately next to Rigg, to stand in Macbeth's place, at the throne. Banquo often appears here, sitting in Macbeth's throne—pushing him from his stool indeed. The ghost has even taken off Macbeth's crown—a tricky test of illusion, the intangible acting on the tangible. He may enter from behind, or be screened by entering servants, or stalk boldly in. With imagined ghosts the audience knows of the second coming by Macbeth's reaction, or by symbols, in light or sound. Blue and green lights on the ghost, and on Macbeth, and "horrid" music have accompanied the second appearance, as before. Lights have dimmed for his entrance, as for his exit.

The aesthetic importance of restraint in Macbeth's reaction to the ghost's first appearance is demonstrated at the second, when a nearly ultimate release of repressed impulse surfaces. For this climax Shakespeare designed a mounting pressure toward eruption (first, the news of Fleance's escape, then the ghost's appearance, now the return). The progression in tension is felt both in the developing excitement in Macbeth, and the attrition bringing Lady Macbeth to her breaking point.

*In *The Puritan*, a man who cannot control his laughing is called a "babe of a man."

The pacing to build intensity through the ghost's two appearances was understood by Phelps. At the first visitation, the ghost, suddenly rising to a chair in the middle of the stage, was deathly pale, but did not show deformity; the second time the wound of the cut throat clearly showed. In a German staging, only the disfigured profile showed at first, promising more horror later. The actor must do his share, as the imagining reader must, to experience the gathering tremors that will break out with the intensification of the spectacle. The growing nervousness and suspicion of the thanes helps; but Macbeth mainly turns the screw. Phelps, for instance, was shaken, but not broken, as he watched through the "sinking" of the first ghost; to test his baffled senses he stood next to Banquo's chair, and gripped it convulsively. The mounting subtextual tension of this gesture continued through his forced *cheer* to the banquet, welcoming Banquo; this time unexpectedly, the ghost suddenly came out silently and quickly from the wings, startling Phelps, and evoking a violent oubreak. Another actor may, in this pattern, make each of his crises—first with the murderer, and twice with the ghost—into a stairway of pyrotechnic displays, as long as each one, as with Hampden, overtops the preceding; or he may, like Piscator's Macbeth, move actively but coolly at the first appearance, wildly and uncontrollably the second; or may more gradually and continuously build tension, as Olivier did, to the final fierce confrontation.

As in all of Shakespeare's major tragedies, a middle crisis savagely challenges the protagonist's heroic control. With Othello, Iago's temptation; with Hamlet, the Mousetrap and his immediate subsequent action; with Lear, the storm. So Macbeth and Lady Macbeth rise to the impossible demands of the joint known and unknown. The whole of their giant beings pour into these moments: as public selves and private; as royal rulers and pretenders; in their mutual relationship as spouses, lovers, and suddenly strangers; as players masking a polyphony of emotions as complex and turbulent as dramatic character can hold. An immediate measure of their mighty size is the contrast to the little men about them. The thanes are limited in language, in passion, in vision: against their gray ground Macbeth and his Lady are flaming daystars, most dazzling when at most risk. Backs to the wall, trying to blind the suspicious mortals around them with a failing finesse, they are fields of great force: even greater in their titanic engagements with each other, and with the corroding impulses within themselves, as they wrestle with the responsibilities of body and spirit to humanity and its systems of morality. What happens *to* them is high theatre; what happens *in* them, high tragedy.

Among Macbeth's many varieties of spectacular response to the ghost's second appearance, three very general patterns may be described, for the purposes of discussion: a frightened Macbeth retreats; a recovering Macbeth stands his ground, and finds courage; a third attacks. The "patterns" are, in fact, not so simple: behind each primary force the dimensions resisting it may be felt. As fear can become attack, attack can become fear, either become hysteria. The unloosed Dionysian energy is many-layered.

A first, almost obligatory gesture marks Macbeth's immediate response to the ghost. He is holding the cup, goblet, or bowl from which he has been drinking to Banquo, and he gets rid of it. Garrick's business was laughed at by Smollett:

> When the whole soul ought to be alarmed with terror and amazement, and all his attention engrossed by the dreadful object in view . . . his friend whom he has murdered, he expresses no passion but that of indignation against a drinking glass, which he violently dashes in pieces on the floor, as if he had perceived a spider in his wine.

Smollett missed the sheer theatrical effect of the gesture; and the sound motivations that may underlie it. Macbeth may drop the vessel, too startled to keep hold; he may revolt from the act of drinking to his ghostly enemy from it; he may use it as a weapon to fling; he may drop it to free his hand for his sword, to attack or defend. The gesture may echo the sometime business of Lady Macbeth's dropping of her goblet when she heard the owl shriek, at the beginning of II, ii.

Shakespeare's own Macbeth may have made the gesture, if the suspected allusion from *The Knight of the Burning Pestle* is apt: Jasper, as ghost, threatens,

> When thou art at the Table with thy friends,
> Merry in heart, and filled with swelling wine,
> I'll come in midst of all thy pride and mirth.
> Invisible to all men but thy self,
> And whisper such a sad tale in thine ear
> Shall make thee let the cup fall from thy hand,
> And stand as mute and pale as Death itself.

If this is relevant, it suggests a ghost creeping up behind Macbeth to whisper, and a reaction in Macbeth of deathly fear. This would be effective in the theatre, and could be made to fit Macbeth's first line, which seems to suggest that his immediate awareness is through seeing. If the shock of the first appearance had been accentuated by the sight of Banquo's bloody head, then an intensified *frisson* might accompany the ghost's next silent approach behind an unsuspecting Macbeth. Garrick evidently intended the violent action with the glass, since in his essay he suggests instead, presumably in satire, that it be dropped gently; but what he says is not nonsense: Macbeth

> should not discover the least Consciousness of having such a Vehicle in his Hand, his Memory being quite lost in the present Guilt and Horror of his Imagination.

Actors have indeed let the vessel fall, out of surprise or dismay: so the nerve-ridden Ernst Schröder, his bowl dropping from his hand (German actors have often used bowls). Reinhardt's Macbeth flung his bowl on the ground. Other Macbeths have seemed to make a weapon of their drink—Evans threw his goblet clattering toward the ghost; Charles Kemble once threw his cup so hard it broke part of a glass chandelier, and almost hit Siddons (who sat still as marble). One practical old stage direction urges a goblet with a square bottom—and Booth wanted a weighted one—so it would not roll when thrown or fallen; Forrest shrewdly obviated mischance by throwing his goblet into the wings, where it was caught.

Garrick's positive act of flinging the glass reflected his sense that Macbeth, having recovered from the ghost's first appearance, now could summon "a stronger assertion of his powers" to be able to say

> Avaunt, and quit my sight, (117)

One of the actor's correspondents, H. H., argued that since, at the end of the visitation, Macbeth finds himself recovered, *a man again*, he must have been "bereft while the spectre was present." This brings into question the full meaning of the key word, *man*. Garrick thought Macbeth was saying "I am a man again, or returning to my senses, which were before mad and inflamed with what I had seen." Garrick was not thinking of fear:

> I make a great difference between a mind sunk by guilt into cowardice and one rising with horror to acts of madness and desperation, which last I take to be the case of Macbeth.

Manhood, in this view, implies more than sustaining courage, or showing daring: it involves also a mastery of impulses roused by incendiary sensations or images. An opposite, latent in the text, is also implied. To be out of control, irrational, acting out a wild, Dionysian impulse is not being *man*. It is something else, uncanny, an inversion in nature, touched with that part of us that is predatory beast—of whose savagery we are triply reminded in Macbeth's speech: *the rugged Russian bear* . . . (reminding us of Macbeth's *rugged* look?), *arm'd rhinocerus* . . . *Hyrcan tiger*. The word-sounds themselves are savage.

H. H. remembered Garrick advancing on the ghost, and would have preferred "a fixed, immovable attitude of horror and amazement." Garrick could not believe he had so moved forward:

> I certainly . . . recollect a degree of resolution, but I never advance an inch, for, notwithstanding my agitation, my feet are immovable.

Pleased as he was with the sign of his firmness, he found a way in the *Essay* to make fun of it:

I must observe that the *Attitude* G———k stands in at the second Appearance . . . is absolutely wrong: *Macbeth* here should *sink* into *himself*, or rather . . . *hide* himself behind himself.

Garrick was evidently saying, in obverse, that Macbeth must, as he did, come out in the open, reveal himself entirely; and to insist on how mistaken any inhibition would be, Garrick insisted on the opposite: Macbeth should imitate the contracting power of a *Snail*, preserving at the *same time a slow awful manly* folding up of his faculties.

Garrick may have been determined to remain immovable to differ with the traditional stage business, involving an advance by Macbeth and a backward retreat by Banquo's ghost.* This would, of course, suit Kemble, the determinedly brave Macbeth. Bell faulted Kemble because he "chid and scolded the ghost out!"; and a *Monthly Mirror* correspondent (1808) wished the actor would not bellow his dismissal of the ghost, preferring "less bravado, and more guilty trepidation." But an answer in the same journal (1809) defended Kemble for portraying Macbeth as

> a character of momentary fortitude, which almost immediately degenerated into despondency. . . . The sudden resolution in [Kemble's] countenance at the word "Hence," . . . as he approaches the ghost, gradually subsides to a fearful horror, . . . the words "horrible shadow" are spoken in a low hurried tone while the actor seems to tremble and shrink at the phantom before him.

The balance between attack and withdrawal, courage and fright, is a dynamic one, depending on the actor's manipulation of the whole polyphony in the design. Some Macbeths have emphasized the aggressive cues implied in the violence of the language. Macbeth begins by seeming to command the *shadow* to get out (he never calls it a ghost); and though it forces its unspeakable presence on him, he defies it, and ends by again ordering it away:

> Hence horrible shadow,
> Unreal mockery hence. (131–132)

Every word bears the weight of fierce demand, the more intense because so many counter-emotions, from fear to guilt, help to impel the anger. Forrest said the six words as if each was a separate ejaculation, shot out with exclamation marks: "Hence! horrible! shadow! . . ."

Sothern exemplified the Macbeth at first terror-stricken—he threw his cup to the floor and, breathing heavily, rushed wildly to his throne, clinging to it, his eyes fixed on Banquo. Then, steadying himself, he drew his sword, and began slowly to approach the ghost—as the thanes rose in alarm, and the women shrank back. As Sothern gathered courage, he thrust forward with his sword, as if through the ghost—and the blade came to rest slashing at a stool, as the ghost disappeared. Sothern dropped the sword, fell on his knees, and beat at the stool with clenched hands, hysterically, until it fell over. The company shrank from him in fright.

If the warrior's conditioning dominates, the attack reflex may come sooner. So Rossi, his rage greater than his terror; so Salvini, his anger overriding

---

*A complaint by Garrick's correspondent suggests that even at that time the theatre seems to have used stylized slow motion to achieve effect: "Banquo . . . should have stepped back much quicker at last; such excessively slow motions are preposterous and unnatural, and keep the spectator in a painful suspense."

horror and fear, his sword quickly out, and in one uncanny moment using it: his Lady's white veil, slipping off, became ghostly to him, and he struck through it with his blade. This seemed to persuade him of his helplessness before the ghost, and momentarily again he hid his face in his mantle. Booth, like Salvini, emphatically projected the warrior image here, and so for both the immediately evident shock of fear came with startling contrast. Mantell, as at the first appearance, started back in fright, hiding his face in his cloak; but the second time he turned back on the ghost, swinging his arms widely, with great waves of his mantle, to blow the specter away. Forrest, cowed at first to abject terror by both ghostly visitations, now raised his robe as if to shelter himself from the sight, and advanced sideways behind the lifted garment, flicking it at the vision—a picture of a man afraid but nevertheless moving against an uncanny enemy. At each fearful step he cried the final "Hence"—some four or five times, before the ghost vanished. Marais, Bernhardt's Macbeth, amazed and impressed British spectators by the Gallic wildness of his letting go: suddenly finding the ghost arisen across the table from him, Marais rushed round, loosing his sword as well as his tirade, and his furious outburst (*Va t'en!*) in a frantic access of courage roused his audience to acclaim. Fear came as aftermath; once the ghost had vanished, Marais' semimaniacal excitement was followed by a paralytic trembling that shook him uncontrollably (and produced a fine pause for applause, and then Bernhardt's consolation).

When Macbeth has not emphasized the warrior in the polyphony, a violent attack on the ghost now can come as a sudden illumination of the contained killing power in the design. Macbeth until now has never been seen to raise his sword to strike an enemy. A sudden explosion now of naked fury is both frightening in itself and ominous of what may come. The reckless assault, finding no animate enemy, may spend itself on the inanimate. Matkowsky, as his passion rose against the ghost, drew his sword and, wildly attacking the apparition, smashed the banquet dishes to pieces. When he saw the ghost was gone, he was swung by his unstable nerves to the extreme of mad relief: he laughed wildly, and shaped a magic circle of safety in the air about him.

With the sword out, Macbeth may be a fearful figure. Hackett played on this. After unleashing his pent-up energy on Banquo's empty chair, he went on waving his sword at the empty air, giving him the assurance to say *I am a man again*. But a weapon may serve, too, almost as a mockery of the craved security. McKellen stabbed and stabbed, violently, at Banquo's stool. Tree thrust repeatedly at the throne where his peripatetic ghost had seemed to be; then, the philosopher in the design dominating, he went to the chair and felt it with his hand, puzzling at its emptiness, shivering. Then his eyes began to follow the passage of the ghost, behind the tapestries, out over the heads of the audience, and he could only await its disappearance, the sword useless in his hand.

Macbeth does not need a striking weapon to suggest the boiling of forces within. His hands and his body can speak for him. Reincke wildly struck at

the table with both fists, roaring at the specter, until his voice broke; at *Hence*—
the ghost still there—this Macbeth buried his head in his hands, hiding.
Frustration does not end for this kind of Macbeth; he does not drive the ghost
away, but, like a child, waits fearfully for the awful nightmare to end; so when
Reincke, after a long silence, raised his eyes, and saw that Banquo was gone,
he slowly brought himself to his feet, breathing deeply. Williamson jumped
on the table and tore off the cloth, shouting and raving as he tried to crawl
across to the wholly imaginary figure. Olivier, as early as his 1937 Macbeth,
had leaped on the table to get at the ghost; in the later production where he
paid out his reaction to the first visitation with restraint, he saved this gesture
for a peak moment. First, in shock, he dropped his cup and backed away;
then, recovering, he sprang upon the table, his words pouring out feverishly
as he strode among the dishes, flourishing his crimson cloak at the specter,
"in a mad fury of desperation" (Byam Shaw), his voice rising to a shout, a
scream. Baty's infuriated Macbeth (and some other actors), blocked by the
table, overturned it, scattering the guests, as he tried to get at his ghost.

Less spectacular shows of violence have sustained force by the intensity
of Macbeth's cold fury: so Scofield's menacing, methodical march, as if he
were bent on coming to physical grips with Banquo—a movement made more
effective by his quick protective gesture of putting Lady Macbeth behind
him as he strode forward. Forbes-Robertson developed a powerful contrast
between his earlier philosophic reserve, after his quick recovery from the first
shock of the ghost, and the audacity with which now, as if trying to understand the vision, he stared as he moved against it, until it disappeared.

As Kean understood when he began to shadow Macbeth's stronger tones
with the dissonance of fear as well as guilt, fright belongs to the complex response—Macbeth will himself speak of his cheeks *blanch'd with fear*. In the
theatre, a fearful Macbeth emphasizes retreat. Thus Kean's second meeting
with the ghost:

> he remained on the spot, or rather recoiled, and covered his face from the ter-
> rific sight (*Sun*).

Caught in a mental agony, when Kean came to urge the ghost away the words
broke, separating (as they would later with Forrest, who may have borrowed
the business): "Unreal! mockery! . . ." Then Kean paused, and with increasing alarm and terror cried "Hence!!!"—feebly motioning the specter away
with his hands.

The debilitating fear Macready showed fitted his design of submission to
the supernatural. Frightened as he was by the first appearance, he looked
cautiously at the empty ghost chair before starting his toast to Banquo. He
had barely raised his cup to his lips when the second alarm overwhelmed him.
Bell, so much more pleased than with Kemble's "bullying":

> Macready began in the vehemence of despair but, overcome by terror as he
> continued to gaze on the apparation, dropped his voice lower and lower till he

became tremulous and inarticulate, and at last [with] a subdued cry of mortal agony and horror, he suddenly cast his mantle over his face, and sank back lifeless on his seat.

The special power of his despair, Lady Pollock thought, was to make the spectator share the feeling that the most daring courage must fail before the terrors of another world. The residue of courage remained and only waited to be revived. Macready cried the final *Hence* three times. After a pause, he looked out to see the ghost gone, and immensely relieved, recovered again his manly spring, and hailed his release in a tone of triumph: *I am a man. . . .*

Like the physical signs of aggressive bravery, the signs of fear have been spectacular. Savits' Macbeth was absorbing the shock of the first appearance, and offering the new toast, when he became aware, behind him, of Ross and Lenox whispering. He turned, saw the ghost, risen from the trap, and pressing his fists against his eyes to keep away the sight, rushed backwards, crying out his words frantically. Agate was impressed with Laughton's "most imaginative horror that I can remember" at *Avaunt*, "bounding away from the ghost and landing half way up the staircase like an indiarubber cat." The sign of fear might be physical panic: so Piscator's Macbeth, relatively controlled before, now running wildly to and fro; pausing as if to approach the ghost, then, unable to endure the sight, frantically moving again. Or Macbeth may be fixed in his response: so Booth, paralyzed, overwhelmed by guilt and remorse, "one incarnate horror."

Irving, again, models the fear-stricken Macbeth. The first disappearance left him appalled, not relieved: he turned a frightening, lingering look of horror at the empty chair. He was able briefly to feign a cheerfulness, but started to slide into raptness, for a moment his hands covered his eyes, and then he looked round abstractedly. Finally, with a desperate effort, he suddenly proposed the toast to Banquo, bringing the guests to their feet.

The ghost, screened in its entrance by the incoming servants, suddenly appeared before him. At once he was trembling, crying out to it to leave, in "frenzies of terror . . . the agony worked up until it grew blood-curdling" (*Evening Post*). His *Hence* was a scream. At last he flung himself, writhing, on the floor of his throne, cowering at Lady Macbeth's feet. He lifted his crimson mantle as a kind of shield, and hid his face behind it in a convulsive effort to avoid the sight.

Whether Macbeth advances on the ghost, or retreats, the violence of his emotion, and the naked exposure of his private experience, with all it implied of secret murders and possible insanity, creates a moment of climactic turbulence, a peak of tension that will hold and intensify until the court is cleared.

Act III, Scene iv (part 2)

Given his double consciousness, Macbeth recovers with the shocking aware-ness both of his interlude of unreality, and of the real situation about him. He sees the thanes, risen, moving, whispering, shouting: they are excited, fearful, possibly dangerous. Sometimes, as with Benson, Lenox and Ross have rushed to Macbeth's side to support him, or to restrain him in what has seemed his maddened rush at nothing. The thanes must feel, Irving noted, the presence of the uncanny. The public player's mask is at least momentarily pulled back over Macbeth's naked face; then, by his kingly authority, or the presence of his guards, or the force of his personality, he controls his stage. *I am a man again:* (133) is spoken mainly to himself; the colon gives him time to breathe before facing down the thanes. *Pray you sit still* (133) is couched in politeness, but the threat of rank, force, or hysteria arms it. Irving made a tremendous effort to recover self-possession; he affected lightness; but chill-ingly he remained, to the end of the scene, only partly present in mind. Hop-kins, oppositely, transformed his frustration into power: he roared the words, freezing the guests with his command. Scofield faced down his court with the same confidence before which Banquo had vanished; but there was a touch of irony in the voice now, of a man who no longer feared anything, and of a king whose polite speech was a blunt order. If a Macbeth's voice trembled, as Sothern's did, his request might carry the authority of the sword, still held, that had stabbed at the intangible. Hackett frankly waved his sword, reminding himself he was a man again; speaking to the thanes, he held it like a warrior's weapon, and his *Pray you* was partly a warning.

The thanes sense, uneasily, how near to madness is their king; and their uneasy queen senses their uneasiness. Let us go back to her.

Unless the Lady Macbeth who returned to her state after the ghost's first appearance was of the iron Pritchard stamp, she has been so shaken by the experience that almost no reserve is left to her. Even in Siddons, Bell discerned "the flagging of her spirit, the melancholy and dismal blank beginning to steal upon her"; and Siddons herself:

> Dying with fear, yet assuming the utmost composure, she returns to her stately canopy; and, with trembling nerves, having tottered up to the steps of her throne, that bad eminence, she entertains her wondering guests with frightful smiles, with over-acted attention, and with fitful graciousness; painfully yet incessantly labouring to divert their attention from her husband.

Siddons sensed that the Lady herself contributed to the turbulence:

> Whilst writhing under her internal agonies, her restless and terrifying glances towards Macbeth, in spite of all her efforts to suppress them, have thrown the table into amazement.

The repeated torments of Macbeth—inexplicable to all but him—caused by the ghost's reappearance* jolts Lady Macbeth at the moment when surcease had seemed possible. She is the more vulnerable when, as often in the theatre, Macbeth has seen the returned ghost on the throne next to her, his horrified stare focused on a vacancy of which she is almost a part, and his attack has seemed almost directed at her.

Still she makes her plea for calmness to the thanes, in the pause of Macbeth's split apostrophe to the specter: a pathetic gesture of hospitality, meant for Macbeth to hear. In addressing the *peers*, she reminds *him* of the need for courtly order; then she tries to call to his mind the importance of this social event: *the pleasure of the time* (123). She repeats the excuse for his aberration that she has improvised, and that he has had the wit to pick up: *a thing of custom* (122). She says more than she knows.

Siddons "Rises and speaks sweetly to the company," Bell reported; the image is almost touching, as if the great Sarah would indeed try to stem the effect of Macbeth's seeming mad passion with saccharine tongue. Perhaps her physical imagery counterpointed her speech, as it did with Terry. Terry would remind herself to speak "sweetly" too; but she wondered, in a note to herself, that the Lady did not go mad; and she meant her face to deny her voice:

> With a ghastly mouth. The mouth tells all—the pain and the effort and the madness.

Marlowe almost shrieked the speech, to distract the thanes, and reach Macbeth's brain. But the words are useless; Macbeth brushes past them in his storming; and the emptiness of the effort may threaten to break the Lady. Reinhardt's was on the verge of tears; Savits' seemed unable to endure any longer: she hid her head in her arms and bent forward over her table, unable to

---

*Siddons could imagine that Lady Macbeth also saw an appearance, a groundless speculation not worth the trouble that her niece, Fanny Kemble, among others, took to dispute it. But Siddons could make it work in the theatre: the *Bristol Gazette* admired her "stretching out her arms in terror, as if she herself had likewise seen the ghost of Banquo . . . [then] recovering her presence of mind, in a hasty, and confused, yet dignified manner."

stand. Yet once more, and still once more, the Lady will have to rise to shield her husband; we may feel how close to the end of her struggle each emergency brings her.

The shocking irrationality of Macbeth's final, visceral *Hence*—again, perhaps, seemingly aimed in her direction—and then the sudden strange recovery, of reason returning, with a jolt or slow wakening, and then Macbeth's confrontation with the thanes, demands of Lady Macbeth an ultimate effort at intervention. All she has been, all she has dreamed of, all she has urged her husband to do, have brought her to this moment. "What imitation," Siddons asked,

> in such circumstances as these, would ever satisfy the demands of expectation? The terror, the remorse, the hypocrisy of this astonishing being, flitting in frightful succession over her countenance, and actuating her agitated gestures.

This will be the Lady's last public transaction with Macbeth; and the last time she will face the thanes whom she welcomed with such pride and calculation when they came with Duncan to find her standing alone at her door. The superb public mask is slipping. As with the other elements in this scene, her inner tension, and its effect on her relation to the others, is closing to a breaking point. She now tries to reach Macbeth at the very summit of his excitement, perhaps moving down again through the lords, as Leigh did to reach Olivier, or speaking meaningfully from her thronal authority. But her words shatter on him:

> You have displac'd the mirth,
> Broke the good meeting, with most admir'd disorder. (134–135)

The speech is aimed again at a double audience: meant for Macbeth, but in language restrained enough for the ear-stretching guests to hear. Terry, standing at her throne, with her ladies around her, allowed herself a tone of "deep and dignified offence, smiling proudly." But the Lady's words have lost their sting, even the alarm implicit in *disorder*, with its archaic threat to the structure of security so dear to Macbeth, does not register in his consciousness. Nothing penetrates him now; and Ladies at the limit of their endurance may stagger, as Reinhardt's did, from the vain effort, the slipping strength.

To bring Macbeth back to awareness, perhaps to make him bold as it did her, Lady Macbeth has sometimes tried to force a drink on him here, as Vanbrugh did Tree. With Dorothy Tutin (England, 1976) this effected a foreshadowing of the sleepwalk: she let a drop of spilled wine fall on Macbeth's hand, and shuddered as she wiped it away. In II, ii her assurance, *A little water clears us of this deed*, had been jaunty; now she was clearly on the way toward that hopeless nightmare when stains would stubbornly resist purgation.

Nothing Lady Macbeth says or does can bring Macbeth to the decorum she begs for, though he may acknowledge her intentions with a bitter laugh, as Scofield did. His mind is full of the astonishment of the moment: he has had a most rare vision. The philosopher surfaces now, ignoring protocol, trying to comprehend for himself his experience, his capacity for fear, his special world. The eased rhythms at first soften the iambic, the gentler *uh* sounds, followed by *m* and *n*, fitting Macbeth's lyrical musing. Reinhardt's Macbeth spoke as if in a dream:

> Can such things be,
> And overcome us like a summer's cloud,
> Without our special wonder? (136–138)

He speaks to himself mainly, but not only; caught up in the reality of the unreal, he no longer pretends a private hallucinatory fit; as he half-believed in a prank when he first saw the ghost, now he begins to suspect pretense from any who do not react as he did to what must have been visible to all. He may mean to speak only to Lady Macbeth; but if so, his disclosure, despite her hushing of him, is public enough for the others to hear, and for Ross to respond. Macbeth may be addressing the thanes as well, wondering if they conspire to make him doubt his identity, estrange him from himself, shake his single state of man. Salvini spoke furiously to the whole company.

> You make me strange
> Even to the disposition that I owe,
> When now I think you can behold such sights,
> And keep the natural ruby of your cheeks,
> When mine is blanch'd with fear. (138–142)

The shock of his public relevation of private fear silences the turbulent crowd; and in the pause Ross asks the terse question that is on every mind:

> What sights, my Lord? (143)

Libby, assuming Ross to be Macbeth's fellow-villain, saw the thane providing his chief with a chance for a reasonable explanation; but what could that be? Hall saw Ross needling Macbeth, and the question was deliberate, slow.

A Macbeth whose hostility is quickly tapped might respond fiercely, as one frenzied actor did, catching Ross by the shirt, and forcing him up against a wall, or like Dunn's Macbeth, drawing a sword in murderous fury, then stopping, aghast at what he might do. A philosophic Macbeth, in a revelatory mood, may pause to find an answer for Ross, or stare apathetically, as Reinhardt's Macbeth did. If Macbeth is not in fact driven by a compulsive aggravation, Lady Macbeth invents one for him, as she intervenes for the last time. The colon-pauses suggest her moving from group to group, trying to disperse them:

> I pray you speak not: he grows worse and worse
> Question enrages him: at once, goodnight. (144–145)

The *admir'd disorder* pervading the whole play, and especially this scene, has sprung from the impulse to disrupt and then to control degree: to top the *file*, and locate each other man in a hierarchy below. Paradoxically, such an order now creates its own confusion; the thanes cannot hurry out in a body if they must observe the degree which, as Macbeth observed, they all knew, where each must follow someone else. By rank they are likely now to begin to line up to kiss the king's hand. Lady Macbeth sees and cuts through, decreeing disorder for order's sake:

> Stand not upon the order of your going,
> But go at once. (146–147)

For the last time—and indeed in the desperate summoning of her will a very *last* effort may be sensed—Lady Macbeth takes command. Survival is again at stake. Terry, covering for Macbeth, who had flung himself bonelessly on his throne, spoke her first lines even before Ross' question was finished (Irving had "Everybody" ask it), overrunning the words in her eagerness to prevent Macbeth's answer—"Voice choked—alarm—hurry. Convulsive fear" (her notes). Getting rid of the guests who moved to surround her came as a sudden afterthought, and with the request she reminded herself to "smile and smile," with the forced politeness some Ladies have been careful to sustain. Craig's Lady Macbeth begged the thanes to go; Cushman, painfully sustaining her courteous queenliness, and the contrast from her earlier awesome strength, entreated them. Other Ladies neglected formality in their haste. Even Siddons learned to emphasize the urgency to act that seems to fit the double *at once* of the speech. Hazlitt disapproved:

> She said 'Go, go' in the hurried familiar tone of common life . . . without any of the graceful spirit of conciliation toward her guests, which used to characterise her mode of doing it.

Curiously, the dismissal by Bernhardt, whose Lady was so unlike Siddons in performance, though closer than Siddons herself to the earlier Siddons' written conception, was criticized also for the familiarity of tone, for her "*Partez! Partez!*" sounding a demanding rather than a "high tragic" tone.

By her urgency Lady Macbeth emphasizes the critical danger of the moment. She may have guessed at Macbeth's horrors, but she is not sure of their source, or which murdered ghosts may fill his brain, how much his hallucinations may indeed become *a thing of custom*, or how much more dangerously the wild energy festering in him may erupt. Anything might happen. Siddons

> Descends in great eagerness; voice almost choked with anxiety to prevent their questioning; alarm, hurry, rapid and convulsive as if afraid he should tell of the murder of Duncan. (Bell)

Ristori remembered the "agony of fear" with which she faced a situation "both impossible and dangerous": but she had another motive for rushing the company away, with a final regal wave of her hand: "to remain alone with him." Mrs. Kean, similarly, spoke in intense haste, in a paroxysm of fear, feverishly clearing the hall so she could return to her Macbeth. Through tears Dench tried desperately to hurry the guests out; she wept for her husband, whom she tried to screen with her body, but also for the wreckage of their royal hopes that she saw reflected in the staring faces about her.

So the show of courtesy often yields to the fact of urgency. Marlowe, her whole concern for Macbeth, cried out the order to leave. Rigg was impatient, angry, jerky; Wynyard was hysterical, her nerves shattered. Merchant's voice was saying bluntly, "Get out!"; Savits' Lady, too, with harsh gestures as well as words.

At least as long ago as Bateman, Lady Macbeth's speech at first ended on half of her last line:

> Stand not upon the order of your going,
> But go! (146–147)

And then—as some thanes dallied, looking at Macbeth, talking with each other—came the fierce, shouted imperative: *at once!* (147) Wynyard thought she was alone, suddenly realized the presence of the delaying thanes behind her, and turned on them with the last angry words. Dench finally screamed at the men waiting awkwardly still to kiss Macbeth's hand.

In the shuffling murmurs of the thanes as they leave, Shakespeare stipulates Lenox' line with the emphasis on *health* that may be ironic:

> Good night, and better health
> Attend his majesty. (148–149)

The Lady's formal reply insists on the clearing out of the whole company, including any lingerers or servants:

> A kind goodnight to *all*. (150)

Janauschek, having in her urgency imperiously ordered the guests to depart *at once*, suddenly recalled her courtly responsibility, and was able to offer a sweet *Good night;* Merchant, impatient of the thanes' crowding still to kiss her hand, made it an order of expulsion.

While Macbeth broods, Lady Macbeth must watch the guests jostle out, witness to the end the ruin of the hospitality which had symbolized her dreamed-of *golden round*. As she endures, behind the best social mask she can put on, the confusion of the forced exit—"a great visual antithesis to the ceremonial entrance," Black observes—the strain on the Lady is ultimate. The most Terrible of iron Lady Macbeths may still convey, primarily, anger and disgust for Macbeth's unmanliness, as Sophie Schröder did: as noted, she stood contemptuously over her fallen mate, and would not stoop to help him rise. Less formidable figures begin—or continue—in some degree to yield, and may betray signs of breaking even before the last of the alarmed, wondering, suspicious thanes has backed out. So Worth:

> She had already shrunk in stature within her great robes, and her mind controlled her voice only by a great dying effort; she stood a long time without moving and then went slowly to her throne (J. R. Brown).

Other Ladies, at the thin edge of collapse, could be felt to sustain themselves by the very last of their strength, as they waited for solitude; and when it came they, too, seemed almost paralyzed, pathetic, sagging. Woltcr, pasting on an enchanting smile for each guest who went out past her, held her poise until the sound of her heavy iron door slamming; her smile vanished, she stood staring hollow-eyed into the darkness, then slowly, wearily, made her way down from her dais, so unsteadily that she almost fell down a step, and had to draw back and try again. Mrs. Kean, after wildly waving the guests away, sank at once into deep dejection, leaned against a pillar and with a wearied, pitying air watched her wretched Macbeth. Römer, after a long silent pause, retreated to a table, rested her arms on it, and let her head fall on her breast.

Some ladies, when the taut hold on their nerves was released, had no strength left. Vanbrugh staggered to Tree, and fainted at his feet. Morris, who had forced a gentle courtesy until the last passing of the last guest, uttered a distressed wail, and surrendered to complete nervous collapse. Mrs. Benson fell down the steps of the throne, gasping for breath. Mirren dropped into a chair, and sobbed like a child.

Lady Macbeth's visual imagery—possibly to be repeated in the sleep-walk—may suggest an exhaustion that transcends the physical. Faucit conveyed a haggard weariness that would be lifelong; "the canker worm of remorse has begun to eat its way into the harder heart of the Queen"; her figure bent, she staggered, grew faint, and as she sat down, rested her face on her hand. The hand touched her crown—the symbol of their dreams and crimes—which she then lifted from her head. Reid, bent over a table, unconsciously unburdened herself of her crown. Modjeska, dead tired, slowly removed her diadem as if this were all she had strength left to do. Gielgud remembered a moment of great beauty when Mrs. Campbell sank back on her throne, and her black hair fell to her shoulders as she dragged the crown from her head. To Leighton, the weight of the crown would seem intolerable; she laboriously lifted it, her taut nerves showing the need for sleep that she would cry out for, for herself as well as Macbeth.

Lady Macbeth's own misery is modulated by her concern for her husband. How she expresses it will condition the expectations that the scene-end must rouse in audiences. The events that since Duncan's murder have begun to drive the two apart may be emphasized by a separation, or even a sense of distaste, between them. Or their misery may point another way by bringing them closer together. Wegener's Macbeths before and after he was directed by Reinhardt suggest opposing possibilities. In a pre-Reinhardt performance, the guests gone, Macbeth and his Lady crouched together, nestling against each other, and suddenly both burst out sobbing, helplessly and bitterly, defeated. In the Reinhardt *Macbeth*, Körner, a stronger Lady, did not approach Wegener, but stood off, watching him as he sat moaning and staring.

The Lady in whom love survives seeks the way to her Macbeth, in the first pattern, to share his dismay. Even when, apparently, she has no strength left after dismissing the thanes, she must somehow find it for her husband. Marlowe, who had seemed to use up her last ounce of will, could yet kneel on the steps of the throne beside Sothern, who seemed paralyzed with horror. Weeping, she searched out his hand, and he put his arm around her, returning consolation. Bernhardt comforted her Macbeth with sad embracing, soft soothing. Even the formidable Janauschek took her Macbeth's head to her bosom, hid it from further sights, and stroked it, her own face pale and drawn with pity.

Love for Macbeth does not serve if, out of their isolation from each other, the two Macbeths must go separate ways. Irving and Terry made this visual; he sat at first in utter collapse, at the opposite end of the stage from her. She moved quickly to take off her crown, as if to unburden herself of some of her load of sin; he sat with dreamy eyes and wan face, oblivious of his surroundings:

> They are two creatures once united heart and soul, now utterly alone and isolated . . . Macbeth, groaning in spirit and demon-haunted, but utterly apart from his wife, who sinks in an agony of dejection into her comfortless throne (*Telegraph*).

Wolter would stare past her Macbeth, speaking her brief answers without looking at him; so Mirren and Williamson were lost in themselves.

The pattern of mutual unhappiness often begins this last beat of the scene. The Lady, usually at first more resilient, as Booth's was, and strong enough to turn from the departing guests to look angrily at her husband with beginning blame, may relent at seeing the sunken Macbeth, fallen on the steps of the throne, seeming utterly crushed. Booth's Lady relented, and came quietly and lovingly toward him. In similar shared moments of weary despair, Gielgud and his Lady, mourned in a sleeplessness that had brought them to the "uttermost nerve edge of exhaustion"; Walter and Green huddled numbly together as in an earthly hell; Mantell, his crown off, his Lady laying her head moaning in his lap, or he holding her face between his hands, partook of hopelessness.

An interlude of deep misery for the two protagonists can effect an intense emotional arousal; but it must not blunt the linear force of the action. A mood of unalloyed despair now almost brings the play to a false close, and nourishes the criticism that the play is not sustained in the second half. This scene is pivotal; it moves not to a full stop, but to a colon: it must point toward a rising action, including an onstage violence, that the playwright has carefully limited up to now. If we remember what we know happens next, we can only look forward to a closed ending with the sleepwalk and the final battles; but if we can remain *naive* spectators at a new play, what will be said and done in the rest of this scene must excite us with intense expectation of almost unimaginable possibilities—and at the same time provide a rich contextual experience of human desperation. What can this puzzled, distraught woman do now? This haunted murderer?

Macbeth must carry the main forward thrust of the scene end; most of the lines, and the resolution, are his; Lady Macbeth speaks only three brief speeches. Once Macbeth is ready to talk, he needs only six lines before he is ready to plan his next move. His first words are of a piece with his semi-mystical speeches before the murders of Duncan and Banquo; he enters the world of the mysterious and speaks its language. Partly he reflects his recent experience of the bleeding ghost returned; but he begins in the future tense, looking to what will be, with the old saying, a warning of retribution with its implication of an endless cycle:

> It will have blood they say:
> Blood will have blood: (151–152)

He often speaks as in his rapt state, but beneath must seethe the excitement and perhaps even deeper the exultation that carries him through the ghostly visitations, and that will very soon surface again. The words themselves suggest that he himself may feel caught in a cycle, where the blood already shed demands of him more shedding. This may be a horror to him, as it was to Booth, for instance; but it is a horror he will soon find himself accepting. "So unstably poised," Alger wrote of Forrest's Macbeth, "was his disposition between his good affections and his wicked desires that the conflict was still repeated." The conflict will go on until the end; but the subordinated side is increasingly subtextual: now Macbeth seems to take strength, as well as fear, from his sense of the strange otherworld, akin to Hecate's where that is which is not, where the living inanimate and the least birds of the field hum to murder. Here the earth is not *firm-set;* and *trees* act unnaturally (Will Macbeth remember that?):

> Stones have been known to move, and trees to speak;
> Augures, and understood relations, have
> By maggot pies, and choughs, and rooks brought forth
> The secret'st man of blood. (153–156)

Schanzer notes the three talking birds, and suggests that Shakespeare refers to the widespread folktale of the Tell-Tale Bird that identifies evildoers. Robert Dent's effective gloss: *Augures:* signs from the flight of birds; *understood:* properly interpreted; *relations:* utterances by talking birds. Beyond these associations, I find Heath's gloss (in Furness) illuminating:

> By *relations* it is not improbable that Shakespeare might understand those hidden ties by which every part of nature is linked and connected with every other part of it.

Macbeth is alive to this hermetic communion.

Suddenly his brooding stops. Lady Macbeth may distract him, as for instance Booth's Lady did with her touch on the shoulder; but the direction of his change of mood suggests that he is yielding to an aggressive impulse that has been growing in him. He has things to do. Time clamors again:

MACBETH: What is the night?
LADY MACBETH: Almost at odds with morning, which is which. (156–157)

What difference does it make? Ffrangcon-Davies seemed to be saying to Gielgud: night or day, dark or light, they live in a world between, a time of no-time. The Lady may despairingly sense Macbeth's yeasting plans: Siddons was "very sorrowful. Quite exhausted"; Cushman dropped passively into a chair, spoke hopelessly, forlorn with a world of weariness. How long a day it has been, since Banquo went riding! But the specification of the time looks both ways—to the crowded past of the last night, and also to the dangerous day ahead. In the Craig *Macbeth*, the first strokes of midnight sounded, as Lady Macbeth told the hour.

Macbeth's specific objective develops in his mind: in a sudden blunt line that is almost prose, he wonders why Macduff did not come *at our great bidding*. The *great* is partly conventional, but it carries, too, Macbeth's sense of his power. The Lady's response is formal, distanced, perhaps from dread:

Did you send to him sir? (160)

Sir.

MACBETH: I hear it by the way: but I will send:*
There's not a one of them but in his house
I keep a servant fee'd. (161–163)

An astonishing trick with time is played by Shakespeare here. Suddenly in the present a history has been inserted into the past. Until the banquet, no firm clue had been given as to the duration of Macbeth's rule; we had no reason to suppose he intended anything untoward, as king, except Banquo's isolated death. Now it serves Shakespeare's purpose to give us a remembrance of things past, because the playwright needs very quickly to establish a climate of Macbeth's past tyranny and immediate fear—made wild and irrational in Williamson's speaking the lines—of insecurity.

In its quicksilver transition from the brooding quality of *blood will have blood*, Macbeth's speech now seems particularly fluid. Again with a marvelous control of monosyllables, Shakespeare changes the length of his rhythms to match his characters' emotional moods. The lines leap to an excitement that will evoke Lady Macbeth's warning of his sleeplessness; it builds on the hurried nervous searching for security, the megalomaniac concern for the self, the self momentarily envisioned deep in blood, the mind's

*See my note at the end of the III, vi chapter.

leaping escape to new action, immediate, *strange*. To salve the self, ego-words abound: *I, I, I, mine own, I, I, I:*

> I will tomorrow
> (And betimes I will) to the weyard sisters.
> More shall they speak: for now I am bent to know
> By the worst means, the worst, for mine own good,
> All causes shall give way. (163–167)

(I use the Folio punctuation, suggesting the swift flow of thought after the colon.)

> I am in blood
> Stepped in so far, that should I wade no more,
> Returning were as tedious as go o'er:*
> Strange things I have in head, that will to hand,
> Which must be acted, ere they may be scanned. (167–171)

In his excitement, he ends on a curious disjunction: the hand must instantly do the head's bidding before even the head has time to consider it. The eye (in doubled meaning) must wink at the hand,† which is to play unrestrainedly its savage part.

The conflict within Macbeth, between what has been and might have been, as against what must be, does not come easy: his manner, as much as his words, will trouble Lady Macbeth. The vision that is flashed into his mind of the blood he wades in—again Macbeth the poet projects the capacious fluid image—is not easy to bear. Sothern moaned, and beat his head; Laughton, Agate thought, said the words with "real heartache"; Booth slowly took off his crown, held it in his hand, looked at it loathingly with a sickening consciousness of what it had cost him. But terrible as the sense of wading in endless, knee-deep blood may be, the core of Macbeth's misery may sound most surely in the word *tedious*. It is always a dreary pejorative in Shakespeare's vocabulary; in this play it takes all life from life. Macbeth has already voiced the deadly "tomorrowness" of it in his lament—so false, so true—on the meaninglessness of life after the death of Duncan. Even if he had the choice of going back through the bloody flood—a whole ocean it may be in his mind, one red—the way would be to the same waterless *dusty death*.

Has he any choice? Macbeth has been thought to contemplate repentance—so *returning* is translated—here. Is repentance possible for Macbeth now? If it is theologically, he does not verbally consider it—as Faustus, for instance, does. Nowhere in the play is the option of a spiritual purging stipulated, or

---

*Stephen Booth heard, in Porter's voicing, a pun, "gore."

†Shakespeare uses *Scan* both to suggest consideration (*Hamlet* III, iii, 75: "And so am I revenged, that would be scanned") and to suggest visual examination (*Pericles* II, ii, 56: "Opinion . . . makes us scan/ The outward habit for the inward man"). Both are suggested in this *Macbeth* sentence.

made to seem desirable—quite the contrary: *returning*, too, would be *tedious*.
No hint is given that not returning would entail pain or suffering. Conceivably, in a theologically-oriented staging, Macbeth might lift a cross to brood
over now; but any commitment to the implication of a formal repentance
must lie in the felt subtext of the actor, or in the perception of the beholder.
Shakespeare avoids this note in Macbeth's polyphony: rather the design reflects that strain in humanity which tries to fight out its battles *here, but here;*
which is driven, by exceptional will, energy, and circumstance, to exhaust
its Dionysian powers against the brake of mind and conscience. Regret, remorse, grief for what has been *done* certainly color the design; but Macbeth
knows it *is done*.

At last (as in all his introspections, however agonized) Macbeth's vision
will end in resolution. Phelps would bring himself to acquiesce in the violence
ahead, Forrest move toward it more readily with a hardening of manner.
A Japanese Macbeth, slumped in the seat where the ghost had been, grimly
worked out his plans. Reinhardt's Macbeth, moving out of a trance-like
raptness, seemed to narcotize himself with the words, fascinated by the image
of further blood: he smiled wildly, his face distorted with murderous passion.
Michael Hordern (England, 1958), suiting action to impulse, drove a knife
into the table. Irving was frankly sinister: he felt that this moment confirmed
his conception of Macbeth as villain, announcing

> his fixed intent on a general career of selfish crime, and this to the wife whose
> hands have touched the crown, and whose heart has by now felt the vanity of
> the empty circlet.

Irving suggested again that Macbeth—this "hypocrite, murderer, traitor,
regicide—threw over his many crimes the glamour of his own poetic, self-
torturing thought." The succeeding tones in the speech, of anxiety, power,
remorse, self-pity, excitement, resolution must all be contained in the design
of the poet-murderer. Even a most resolute Macbeth, like Scofield, in whom
the counterforces to action were sensed only deep beneath his surface, was
for a moment close to tears as he acknowledged to himself the redness of
his crime.

Macbeth once more does not divulge what his deeds will be, and Lady
Macbeth this time does not ask. She responds not to his words but to his
manner:

> You lack the season of all natures, sleep. (172)

Something abnormal, unnatural, impels him. She may allude to a missed rest-
ing time that all growth needs, and also to the lost seasoning that is, as Macbeth had cried after murdering Duncan, the *Chief nourisher in life's feast* (II,
ii, 51). He is, she seems to tell us, living the Sisters' curse.

Surely Lady Macbeth must know by now what he means by the *worst means*, by *strange things;* but she has nothing to say about the great moral and political urgencies his speech stipulates. She sets against them—and in so doing magnifies both them and it—an essential domestic urgency. If he could only sleep . . . if they could . . . Her mind searches for something that could be done now. She may offer him—them—drink, or toy with the sleeping potion given the grooms; by look, gesture, caress, may try to quiet him, while she does her best to sustain her own self-control.

What she disciplines is not only her feelings, but also her need to disclose them. In her sleepwalk she will reveal impulses and stored images that by now are festering. Verbally she has allowed us only a glimpse of this subterranean life—*nought's had, all's spent;* but her physical imagery may well convey the sense, not only of her despair, but also of the pressure to air it, betrayed in abortive efforts to communicate with Macbeth. If she cannot speak to him, yet she may convey some sense of her reliance on him; not until he leaves her to go into the field will her repressed anxiety break out in sleepwalks.

The threads Shakespeare weaves into the final design of the scene are many and complex. As always when the two principals interact, Macbeth's patterns cannot be extricated from Lady Macbeth's; but for the purpose of a deeper look, I will use them alternately as guides, the Lady's first.

Two ways in which she might consolidate the role now were proposed by Ridley.

> She can keep herself completely in hand till the end of the banquet scene, and show no signs of breaking even then, but only an inevitable exhaustion. This, I believe, is what Shakespeare intended . . . the sleepwalking scene comes upon our flagging attention with a shattering surprise. . . . This scene then lifts the whole of the last act from the anti-climactic tedium in which it is in danger of falling. . . . It is possible to present her quite differently, to let her begin to break almost at the moment when Duncan has been murdered; growing wearier, sicker of blood, apprehensive of further murders, almost changing places with her husband as the dominant partner. So presented she is more interesting and more appealing; but the shock of the sleep-walking scene is destroyed, since it is now no more than we can reasonably expect. . . . This is the way a selfish actress, if she is allowed, will present her.

Michael Redgrave agreed with Ridley, arguing that the sleepwalk would be twice as effective if it was not foreshadowed. This seems to assume that an audience will not expect Lady Macbeth to participate in the action until the sleepwalk. But we are not to know that this moment, so crowded with feeling between Macbeth and his Lady, *is* the last we will see of her until much later. This is the fourth time the two have ended a scene together; why not again? Soon? Given the rush of time of the play so far, the *naive* spectator again wonders: what of Lady Macbeth tomorrow? When Macbeth leaves her uncon-

sulted, and goes to those other women? If some thread has seemed to tie the
Lady to the witches, it dissolves now. Her powers—her weaknesses—are
mortal. We who know the play must ask as if we did not: how will the actress
project, or we imagine, the expectations of a next day, an immediate future?
Many *naive* spectators believed now that Lady Macbeth, in a following
action, would begin to resist Macbeth's murderous planning. Perhaps these
spectators were conditioned to the dramatic logic of reversal of original positions—as Shakespeare may well have intended. Some *naïfs* thought Lady
Macbeth would appear next mad.

Most actresses, as we saw, have found in both text and subtext the suggestions of countering dimensions in the Lady that move her to a much more
complex posture than physical exhaustion. That the Lady could have survived the emotional shocks of murder, danger of discovery, and a seeming-
mad husband betraying them in full court, without enduring changes in her
dramatic personality, would seem to argue that she had no personality to
change. Pritchard may have preserved an iron front intact through the banquet scene—Michael Redgrave suggests that Siddons' change to signs of
breaking may have been a deliberate departure for originality's sake. Sophie
Schröder, too, remained iron. But most distinguished Ladies were unmistakably disturbed by the time of the scene ending. In the nineteenth century, so formidable a Lady as Cushman gave way; Leigh, one of the hardest—
in her ice-beautiful way—of twentieth-century Ladies would momentarily
melt in her concern for Macbeth's sleeplessness, would urge him to rest softly,
sorrowfully, by private gesture would reveal her own loss of hope and happiness. Symptoms of the obsessions that would appear later have been seen to
surface, for the first time, by the end of this scene—thus Mrs. Benson and
Mirren began unobtrusively to "wash" their hands, Anderson to make strange
abortive gestures that would later reveal their full meaning in the context of
the sleepwalk.

The whole design of the character, as acted or imagined, must determine
when the cracks begin to show. Siddons' ultimate objective, since the beginning of Act III, was Lady Macbeth's madness and death; now, urging sleep on
Macbeth, she was (Bell) "Feeble . . . and as if preparing for her last sickness
and final doom." Hampden's Lady fainted. Ristori definitely dated the beginning of Lady Macbeth's "mental prostration . . . which ended at last in
total derangement" from the moment the guests left. One report has her suddenly drinking, and drinking again, to sustain her will. Ristori herself:

> I found it necessary . . . to convey an idea of her depression and discourage-
> ment, possessed as I was by the sad conviction that it was in vain to fight against
> destiny. . . . I let it be seen how remorse had begun to torment me.

She dropped her queenly dignity for deep dejection; the "subtlest thing," a
Liverpool observer thought, was

the manner in which, with eyes glazed with despair, she succumbs to her husband's terrors, and feebly craves sleep, the only refuge for those to whom consciousness is intolerable (*Albion*).

Where before she had to find strength to support Macbeth, now she found compassion. She was prepared to upbraid him,

But Macbeth stands unmanned. There is not time for self. The expression passes as quickly as it comes; the fellow feeling made her wondrous kind. Here is the gentlest of all gentle counsellings.

As Ristori spoke of his sleeplessness, she took Macbeth's hand, leaned against him, and

in [my] attitude of sorrowful meditation, now raised to heaven with an expression of dismay, now turned toward my husband with a look full of vivid remorse,

she drew him gently out, as

one would lead an exhausted maniac. . . . I made Macbeth, who was terrified by a fold of his mantle getting between his feet, have another fearful paroxysm.

He rushed away from her.

Frightened, yet forcing myself to master my own terror, I could not help . . . letting the audience see I was shaken; but with a gentle violence

she caught and propelled Macbeth off, her hand on his shoulder, trying to calm him "by affectionate means."

Ristori's equation required Macbeth in this scene to be a subordinate object for her pity. Other Ladies, more equal to their troubled Macbeths, have similarly tried to support them with compassion, sometimes successfully, sometimes not. Vanbrugh, struggling from her faint to bring her strength to the dejected Tree, gently removed his crown, as from the head of a tired child, then quietly stroked his hand. He looked at her, courage returning; moved to take a torch from the wall. He said his last line, and a dead silence followed, as they looked around the empty room. She opened the arras to show that no threat was there; he went to his throne, where Banquo had sat, and examined it. Did he suddenly see the ghost again, over the heads of the audience? She took his troubled hand in hers, and—in a reprise of the exit after the murder, and in a foreshadowing of her last sleepwalk gesture—led him out.

In an atmosphere of lullaby, Laughton's Lady, Robson, rocked with him breast to breast. Marlowe had to deal with a Sothern who sat staring into a future that demanded horror of him; the hope died from her eyes, she moved toward him with a motherly as well as wifely concern, kneeled beside him, and with a tender caress urged sleep upon him. He put an arm out to lift her; but at his grim words, she looked at him with fear and wonder, shrank back, wept passionately, and slowly sank down until she lay on the ground before him. Leblanc-Maeterlinck, sitting crushed in her chair, her crown off, barely listened out her Macbeth, Mars; she swooned, and he would have to drag her away. McKellen had to half-carry out the distraught Dench.

Terry sustained herself partly by forcing attention to Irving: she meant to be "determined, quick, firm" in reminding him he needed sleep, though she herself "is nearly dead from lack of [it]." One observer heard "dull hopelessness," another "sweet and loving tones." This was the one place in the play, she wrote to Mrs. Winter, when she wept. Her promptbook notes: "How about trying to ease his head by taking off his crown which *he* the more firmly plants on his head?" Irving (as we will see) intensified here his coward-Macbeth's frightened dismay; Terry saw, however, that the scene must not end with his fear, but with the implications of his intended action. Her note: "Now she knows him—now Lady Macbeth shall sleep *no more—for she is at last frightened.*" Terry envisioned a scene-ending that was future-pointing: "*He* to go off full of vigour, *blood—more blood. She*, left behind—dazed—turned weary—faint—and stagger to throne—Alone—*Isolation* on the throne. Crown in her lap. Laugh? Dark. Curtain."

An ending like this was indeed reported by Grein in *Revue d'Art Dramatique*:

> The guests have gone, she is alone. . . . Terry seeks to show the futility and indignity of the reward for which she sold her soul. . . . Snatching the crown from her head, she takes it in her hands. She walks slowly behind the empty throne, then sits in desolation. The lights are lowered, the curtain slowly comes down, the spectator forgets, for a moment, the "femme criminelle."

This ending, Terry perhaps thought, would leave open the possibilities of her despairing resumption of royalty, as well as of Macbeth's new resolution. Perhaps she knew of a similar business by Miss Atkinson (England, 1857), who remained after her Macbeth (Phelps) had left. She took off her crown, looked for a long time at it, then went deliberately back to her throne, and seated herself rigidly, like an "Egyptian statue." The light dimmed and went down on this picture, implicit with a sense of destiny. Morris, in America, detailed her own version of this ending: she herself, at the scene-end, was "as physically shattered, shaken, spent as was ever Lady Macbeth spiritually." And the heavy weight of an unpadded metal crown was pressing on her forehead. At Macbeth's *My strange and self abuse* . . . (173),

> the queen, unable to longer endure her suffering, raised both hands and lifted the crown . . . and in the same instant the king, turning, noted the action with such a surprised frown that quick as a flash the queen dropped it to its place again and bravely smiled into his face. . . . He added his suggestive "We are both yet young . . ." and so made exit, and Lady Macbeth kept her forced smile till he was gone. Then it faded. Slowly she removed the crown, and stood looking at it, calculating all its cost, until tears trickled down her wan cheeks,

when, hearing a sound outside, she hastily resumed it, [and] dragged her royal trappings, her misery, and herself out of sight.

Cushman was another who watched her husband out. The impression of rocklike strength in her early scenes had been eroded by her conscience and the vulnerability of her womanliness; now all that seemed to sustain her was the wholehearted compassion she gave to her troubled Macbeth. Left alone after his exit, she incarnated remorse. Something terrible seemed ahead for this very strong, very broken woman. Faucit, haggard and deeply dejected, had also been able to show love and compassion for her husband, rather more as she played the role over a long span of years. In 1846 the *North British Daily Mail* noted, at the end of III, ii, "the attempts the heavy-hearted pair make at consoling each other," with "a touch of melancholy tenderness." Now they leaned for a while on each other; but they ended divided: one report had her leading her Macbeth off but in isolation, averting her head to avoid looking at him; late in her career (1864) she followed him, keeping several paces of distance between them. The final impression was of her deep mournfulness, and a separateness that could perhaps point to conflict. The similar despair of Siddons was

> finely expressed in the dejected and disconsolate air with which she slowly followed her husband. From that moment it is evident that her peace of mind is forever fled (*Caledonian Mercury*).

Some Ladies left perforce after their Macbeths, who strode off intent on moving into the future. Savits' Macbeth finished speaking bluntly to his Lady, with no passion or tenderness, and she went out after his abrupt departure sadly and slowly. Macready, springing back from his shock, steadily hardening in his manner, turned to leave without regard to Lady Macbeth. Quayle, going upstairs ahead, laughed as he turned to look at his Lady; she fell back against the wall, faint. Olivier, leaving, loaded *We are yet but young* . . . (175) with the recognition both of what had been, and the significance of what would be; his Lady watched him go with a gesture of despair, and sank down upon her throne.

Spiritually, if not in fact, Lady Macbeth is being left behind. Whether she leaves last or not, the primary suspense, as the scene ends, will derive from the implications of Macbeth's character and actions. While expectations may be roused by her last moment, they may not point to immediate consequence, and therefore can carry over the rest of Act III and all of Act IV. Macbeth's now dominant impulses augur strange deeds in the nearest future. The next two brief scenes, before he appears again, will prepare us for his spectacular action; but even now the force of his scene-end resolve begins arching toward a next major action.

When he speaks to Lady Macbeth,

Come, we'll to sleep: (173)

many notes may sound: of remorse; of a real fatigue; but also of an impatience
to get on; of a satisfaction with new resolve; of a care and sometimes tenderness toward her; even mingling with a feeling of rising power, of an erotic
note. Whichever tone dominates will condition the complexity of the next
lines:

My strange and self-abuse
Is the initiate fear, that wants hard use: (173–174)

His *strange and self-abuse* may refer to hallucinations of the ghost; and may also
hint at the restless ecstasy, the nightly dreams, of his troubled bed; the impulses within him that weaken him to action by recalling to his conscience
the bloody past. He yields to these things, he says, because he has the timidity
of the initiate, the novice; *hard use* will enable him to transcend the self that
abuses him with visions; or that denounces him to himself—for his cowardice,
he seems to mean, but his self-attack goes much deeper. He is ready to wade
farther into blood:

We are yet but young indeed. (175)

The latent motif of the young versus the old takes on an ironic twist here.
Macbeth identifies himself with the *young;* but he has made himself the old
one now, he will make war on youth, and youth will come in war against him.
He sees himself *young* as a man learning to dare much more than he once
thought became him. Brooks sees Macbeth

> still echoing the dominant metaphor of Lady Macbeth's reproach: He has not
> attained to manhood . . . he has not yet succeeded in hardening himself to
> something inhuman.

Voiced, Macbeth's lines may sound as if he means they are *young in deed*—in
act—and this is certainly one implication; but an emphasis on *indeed* as one
word (as in the Folio) suggests how very naive and unready for ruthlessness
Macbeth feels they have been. All the more frightening, then, is his vision
of what terrible things may now more easily be done. But complex as Macbeth
is, there may be latent notes of discomfort and dismay, as well as resolution
and excitement, in his estimate of their comparative innocence.

As before, the imminence of death may evoke an impulse to the sensual,
to coupling. Macbeth's repeated *we* Leech sees as not necessarily the self-
involved royal use, but a straining for a lost union; and this has sometimes
been stipulated in the theatre. Yet if, now, an erotic aura warms the last meeting of the two, their doing will be shadowed by what is not *done*. So the dis-
colorations of Bernhardt's consolations, which were, as always, essentially
amorous. At *You lack the season* . . . the Liverpool reviewer saw in her "sad
embracings and soft soothing," the

subtle domination of an insidious erotic influence . . . visibly at work as the woman who is the lord tenderly leads away to repose the lord who is her vassal, held enslaved by his heartstrings.

But the strain on Bernhardt, accumulating since Duncan's murder, darkened "the ecstasy of her old luscious craft," which now masked a weariness and dull despair. Still, she nestled the excitable Marais' face in her shoulder as they went off.

Hackett and his Lady remained close to each other through the post-banquet dialogue, ready to embrace. But she began to sob when he began *for mine own good,/ All causes shall give way* (166–167). Reacting, he spoke ambiguously, almost jovially, of his *strange* plans, and kissed her, overbearing her resistances. She responded acquiescently, yielding to his kisses; he held her in his arms, giving a sensual implication to his final *Come, we'll to sleep . . .* and *but young in deed*.

Hopkins looked up at his portrait, as king, that had replaced Duncan's, and pointed to it laughing. On the move, he took Rigg's passive hand, fondled it, and led her up the stairs to their bedroom. Piscator's Macbeth, more direct, picked up his Lady in his arms and carried her off.

Scofield, in rehearsal, saw his Lady's *You lack the season . . .* as an invitation of the kind that would partly be echoed in the sleepwalk.

> She feels if we could only go to bed. . . . She offers it as the only healing thing. Yet I think she draws away from me . . . she is horrified.

He felt, finally, that she was impotent to help him; he now had the power she had at the beginning, and no longer had, and it was in him to use it.

Almost ironically Scofield could return affection, feeling his dominance, and his freedom even to laugh at his fate. Behind him now was the assurance that he could survive even the fact—or the hallucination—of the return of a murdered victim. "Even this final horror can be smothered and stared down," the *Spectator* observed; and of the experience of this Macbeth's Dionysian liberation into action:

> that very rare thing, a performance at once horrible and beautiful: appalling in its naked openness to evil, intensely beautiful in the passion with which the exploration is accomplished.

This surge of a liberating force in Macbeth powers the linear drive of the play past the great middle crisis. As Olivier's director, Byam Shaw, put it, Macbeth

> has recovered and with fantastic energy begins to think of new crimes to commit.

Matkowsky, who had stumbled in word and action in the first shock of the ghost's passage, moved slowly but steadily toward finding strength in his security measures—his spy system; vacillated again as he re-experienced the blood he waded through; but then, as his resolution gathered, the words came hard and angry, rising to a high pitch at *young indeed*.

Salvini's returning assurance was momentarily checked when once again his Lady's white scarf moved, and he started;* but the warrior's momentum carried him past that. Stevenson saw him look about the room, and, seeing nothing, prepare with almost sensual relief to go to bed. At *We are yet but young* . . .

> He is looking with horrible satisfaction into the mouth of hell. There may still be a prick today; but tomorrow conscience will be dead, and he may move untroubled in the element of blood.

Irving, on the other hand, yielded to the fear that fitted his characterization. His vision of the scene-ending was different from Terry's; he meant to be in the picture to the last. He developed a spectacular business, as he was leaving, of seizing a blazing torch from a sconce in the wall, then, suddenly overcome with frenzied fear and horror, dashing it to the floor, muffling his face in his robe, and staggering back against a pillar—with Terry, in sympathetic agony, kneeling at his feet and gazing up at him. He finally changed the business, according to Winter, for a quieter ending, that pointed more forward, was more open-ended. He started to move up the shallow backstage steps, Terry supporting him. Then,

> as though by a horrible, irresistible compulsion, he slowly turned till his gaze could settle on the empty stool, at which he looked with an awful glare of terror, his eyes growing wide and wild, and through contraction of his facial muscles, his long mustache fairly bristling with fright. Picture. Curtain.

Thought, rather than fear, inhibited a philosophic Macbeth like Forbes-Robertson, struggling to silence his Apollonian urgings within. If his nominal, transient triumph over these resistances came slowly, the coming was clearly signaled: he stood at the end grimly determined, a fierce resolution straightening his muscles as he took aim on the future.

The frequent suggestion of a remarkable replenishment of Macbeth's energy, after the cataclysm of the ghost's appearance, reflects one of the most compelling notes in his polyphony. His design includes the deep reserve, as well as the capacity for immediate response, of the Shakespearean tragic hero. Macbeth draws on strength beyond the warrior's trained striking power, the arm of the king's awful authority, and the ultimate resilience that enabled him to survive the fearful testing of his reason. A true overreacher, he is at last almost freed from the nominal restrictions that civilized roles have imposed

---

*This kind of thing seems to have been a favorite piece of business with the Italians. Ristori, as noted above, had her Macbeth made fearful when his mantle almost tripped him. Rossi, who had been soothed into going off with his Lady, also felt his cloak catching at his legs, and starting as if afraid of a ghostly trap, flung both sword and crown at the imaginary figure, and backed off pointing at the spot with horror and loathing. Besides the comment on the character, the action implied a fear of future supernatural pursuit.

on him. His enormous Dionysian force, earlier impatient of such restraints as conscience, pity, judgment, and external opinion, now anticipates license. Macbeth will believe himself capable of such license, and will carry us with him as he tries to realize it with acts of impulsive savagery.

The linear action of the rest of the play will mount on the succession of his excesses. Meanwhile expectation will be sustained in his character, because the deeper resistances within will never be wholly silenced, an inner dissonance will accompany, if only subtextually, his most resolute action. His *strange and self-abuse* will not stop; he will not be able to leave himself alone. He is dialectic alive. He will work actively to destroy the friendship and golden opinions and the power he so much values; the health of the nation he fought to save will make him wish to cure it, yet he will himself be the disease. He will feel his soul charged with the blood he relentlessly spills. The more he exercises power, the more evident to him that *nought's had*.

So with Shakespeare's other major heroes, and one explanation of their hold on us. Hamlet, after the Mousetrap, will be let loose to kill; Othello, after Iago's temptation, will be let loose to kill; Lear, after the storm, inner and outer, is let loose to the *kill, kill, kill, kill* of madness. The normal controls slip; we are on the edge of the dark world of impulse, that beckons. Part of us is impatient to plunge in—the more readily because another part of us is protected by the deep "moral" resistances each hero shares with us.

Security
Is mortal's chiefest enemy.

Act III, Scene v

Thunder. Enter the three Witches, meeting Hecate.
Much thoughtful critical scholarship rejects this scene as Shakespeare's. One single fact is indisputable: near the end of the scene (and again in IV, i) a song is specified that was discovered to be in Middleton's *The Witch*, printed in 1778. "It has, however," Muir notes in his introduction to *Macbeth*, "come down to us in a transcript by Ralph Crane. . . . He states that the play was 'long since acted by His Majesty's Servants at the Blackfriars.'" Muir suggests that this note in the transcript, which is roughly dated 1627, may refer to a period between 1609, when the King's Men first used the Blackfriars, and about 1615. We do not know when Middleton began writing for Shakespeare's company, or when he wrote *The Witch*, but consensus places it after the composition of *Macbeth*.

The common belief is that Middleton originated both songs, and that they were taken over for the staging of *Macbeth*. Even if we accept the guess that Middleton did introduce them, and that they were inserted into *Macbeth* performances, this would remain the only possible piece of objective "evidence" anybody can cite for claiming that the text of III, v, itself is not by Shakespeare. All else is speculation.

On what grounds? I have a feeling that the impulse to deny the authenticity of the scene comes largely from a reluctance, appearing late in Shakespearean criticism, to believe that the playwright would make this use of the supernatural. The usual "evidence" given is "internal," based on style. One authority quoted is D. L. Chambers, arguing that Hecate and the First Witch speak in iambics,

> a strong presumption against their Shakespearean authorship. . . . The metre of these speeches of Hecate—dull, mechanical, regular, touched with favour and prettiness—is in striking and almost amusing contrast with the grotesqueness, the freedom, the bold roughness of the colloquies and incantations of the weird sisters.

Middleton is sometimes proposed as the imagined true author of the scene; though no serious student of the two plays believes that the coarse Hecate of *The Witch* is in character and speech at all like Shakespeare's goddess. A few small echoes of *Macbeth* in *The Witch* may be surmised, but if they are borrowings, then Middleton was almost certainly the debtor. Other playwrights for III, v have been suggested, on no evidence; one speculation has Shakespeare himself doing the writing as a later interpolation after the play was in completed form, to fit around the song. The song may as easily have been borrowed to fit the text.

I very much respect the scholars who believe the scene spurious; and I am particularly grateful to George Williams for patiently trying to persuade me that its tone is not Shakespearean; but I do not now find any reason to reject Shakespeare's authorship of the dialogue as part of the original *Macbeth*. (I am happy to agree with Halio, among other perceptive scholars, on this.)

Shakespeare was quite capable, especially in this play, of putting differing meters—and non-meters—in the mouths of his characters. The First Witch's two speeches, that open and close the scene, have rhythms quite "boldly" and "roughly" different from Hecate's; in fact both are very close to prose. Hecate's rhythms are by contrast usually—not always—as formally rhythmical as the Sisters' own ritualistic chants. Nor are Hecate's lines all dull, mechanical, regular. The rhythms have breaks and changes; the words and ideas have echoes of the play's action, as well as of recurrent motifs in the language; and some of the lines speak with authentic Shakespearean eloquence.

The denial of Shakespeare's authorship surfaced about the same time as disintegrationist critics began to doubt such other scenes as I, i and I, ii, and to assume many cuts in the play. I believe that critical scholarship will tend more and more to accept virtually every word as Shakespeare's text, but this may be as wild a speculation as those I disagree with about III, v. I leave it to get on with a consideration of why Shakespeare, as vouched for by Heminges and Condell, wrote the scene, and why his fellow actors found it playable. (That the company may have inserted the scene after Shakespeare retired is another pure speculation, and must be evaluated as such.)

Technically the scene serves important purposes. First, it helps give a rest to the Macbeth-actor's second body, the physical instrument that has endured almost all the stage time of three grueling acts. And it provides a time-buffer between the end of the banquet scene and the evidence, to follow, of Macbeth's bloody tyranny. Shakespeare had prepared for Hecate, as observed by Flatter (one of the scene's defenders) in two of Macbeth's speeches associated with night and deeds of darkness, that set up expectations of a fateful assignation. The *understood relations* between the strange underworld of the Sisters, and the world of men, could have no better spokeswoman: Hecate suggests, as the play does, that a man may be lured by his Dionysian visions to destruction. She is, in this scene, an embodiment of that part of the Sisters

that touches the supernatural, that broods over human action, and that inter-
feres with it. Her method here is the essence of equivocation: leading man by
what seems the safest way to the worst. The irony is at least as old in the theatre as the *Oedipus*.

Hecate appears in the play immediately after the "other woman" in Macbeth's life begins to lose control of his direction; though he seems to need no
further guidance, she will take him to deeper, darker assurances than Lady
Macbeth did. A psychologist may see, as Veszy-Wagner does, the image of
the "sinister mother" who will not let her son get away with his Oedipal
crimes—the female is the instigator, and becomes responsible. The "fair"
sex, Veszy-Wagner suggests, is made essentially foul. Aronson, with his
Jungian orientation, sees Hecate as an archetypal matriarchal figure who
plays, as the "mother" does, paradoxical roles: preserver and destroyer.
Hecate makes her appearance at midnight, Aronson observes, the dark time
of the unconscious, associated with the female image; certainly she prepares
Macbeth for a descent into his underground, the pit from which he will try
to rise "bloody, bold and resolute."

Hecate is specifically a figure out of the ancient mythology, and as such
Shakespeare seems to have used her in this scene, as in Macbeth's earlier references, deliberately to provide many implications, beyond the diabolical,
of mysterious dread. In Neumann's scheme, as we saw, Lady Macbeth fitted
the image of the terrible "Great Mother"; and one of the "Mother's" classical
forms was Hecate, "the dread goddess, . . . the mother of the man-eating
Empusa and the lamias who suck the blood of young men and devour their
flesh." To this

> triple-bodied, uroboric Hecate, mistress of the three realms—sky, earth and
> underworld . . . is attributed the power to enchant and change men into ani-
> mals, and to smite with madness, which gift belongs to her as to all moon
> goddesses.

The connotations of Hecate are capacious enough that Walker, in whose theology Lady Macbeth is "the fiend in limb and motion feminine," can also see
in the goddess a figure in whom Lady Macbeth can be recognized—not as a
living presence, but as a reflection, as Banquo's ghost reflected Banquo living.
(We may remember that Eleanor Calhoun wanted to double as Hecate when
playing Lady Macbeth. Sprague and Trewin report a Lady who, in 1869 and
1870, doubled as Hecate "with gauze wings, fair hair waving and streaming
into a cloud, and various emblems of incantation woven picturesquely into
the costume"). Flatter suggests that Shakespeare used Hecate to specify a
non-Christian demonology. To me the pagan element is part of the deepening ambiguity of the play's supernatural. Hecate, besides advancing
the mystery, intensifies the interaction between the symbolic and the
psychological.

Hecate's tripartite form projects a special kind of midnight terror: so Luciano, in Hamlet's Mousetrap, of his deadly poison:

> Thou mixture rank, of midnight weeds collected,
> With Hecate's ban thrice-blasted, thrice-infected. . . .

She may well have appeared in the Globe as a figure of horror. In Jonson's *Masque of Queenes* the witches' "Dame" appeared

> naked armed, barefooted, her frock tucked, her hair knotted, and folded with vipers: In her hand a torch made of a dead-Man's arm, lighted: girded with a snake.

Even so, her horror in the masque may have been softened, as Lion's roar was mewed in *Midsummer Night's Dream*, so as not to fright the court ladies.

Unlike the Sisters who appear, to mortals at least, as old women, Hecate is frankly supernatural, and was meant to inspire dread. She may even have appeared with three heads: in *As You Like It*, Shakespeare has her described as the "thrice-crowned Queen of Night." Part of her terror is in her multiple-equivocal nature, made of so many fearful images that her whole is indefinable, unplaceable in any familiar context. Hideousness in images of evil, Neumann suggests, is an expression of the ego's inability to experience the featurelessness of the primal deity. The face of evil plain would be unbearable, and is fortunately beyond the capacity of man to picture, but for those willing to try, Hecate's face—or facelessness—is a kind of ultimate challenge.

Unfortunately she was made rather more pretty than dreadful during much of the eighteenth and nineteenth centuries in England, following the meretricious Davenant pattern of musical spectacle: and the scene itself was sometimes followed by a shift to a distant sylvan prospect, or was merged with IV, i. Kemble's Hecate entered with the witches from the wings, but was flown off: the "moon" rose, a cloud car with six spirits descended to fetch the goddess, while witches flooded the stage to join in singing "We fly by Night," from a phrase in Middleton's sensual song.* Macready was somewhat more elaborate. Hecate rose from a trap onto a darkened stage accompanied by the Folio's *thunder* and streaks of lightning. Unseen spirits beneath the stage and in the flies called Hecate's name. Amid stage clouding, the car came down for her. Four white-clad child spirits, according to one prompt-book, flew up with Hecate; but a *Spectator* critic, complaining that Hecate "should be less of a concert singer in her jubilant strains," also observed that "the one 'littley airy spirit' who calls Hecate is quite enough to 'sit in the foggy cloud,' especially as she [Hecate] talks of toying, culling, and kissing [part of Middleton's song]. . . . A solitary tiny sprite would be more picturesque than a row of tall figures filling an omnibus of clouds." Downer notes instances where "Come away" was sung; one Macready promptbook names the

*Cutts includes Middleton's music and words in his *Shakespeare Quarterly* article.

song "We fly. . . ." The chorus was large, and the *Spectator* wished there had been young as well as old women in it. Hecate "descended" to begin the scene for Phelps: who had "Come away" sung in a spectacular ending:

> The flight of Hecate (with one "little airy spirit") in a vaporous car is so contrived that the ascending figure, illumined by limelight, is traced through broken masses of clouds (*Telegraph*).

Charles Kean made particular use of gauze scrims, as he had for the witches and Banquo's ghost: the moment the banquet scene ended, the stage faded into a mist behind the gauzes. Hecate and the other three witches appeared out of the mist, as light picked them out, to the accompaniment of thunder and "horrid" music. As the mist darkened again, Hecate was flown off, and the witches sank through a trap.

Twentieth-century stagings largely avoided the scene, as unnecessary and unlikely to sustain the continuing illusion for sophisticated audiences—though sometimes it has been included for shock and terror. Hecate's sinister, female, *La Belle Dame* aura has been emphasized—as a "beautiful frosty she-devil" delighting in wickedness (Gribble); even appearing nude (Scotland, 1974). Her fearful triple nature was incarnated in a production in Rome by an awesome female goddess who seemed to have six arms—two actresses waving their arms as they stood behind the third, representing Hecate. The Hecate in Welles' Black *Macbeth* held a bull whip and lashed the witches. Reinhardt staged for dread that was mystic as well as physical. His Hecate, at first a dark shade, emerged as very tall, her head just touching the clouds that hung from the flies. She towered over the witches, who made her seem taller by crouching before her, humble, whimpering. Furiously angry, Hecate, with arms that seemed very long, seized the throats of the witches, and fiercely lectured them. At the end she spread her arms voluptuously upward, a cloud came down as at her command and covered her, and when it lifted, she had vanished.

Hecate's whole angry speech furthers the motif of equivocation. She scolds the Sisters—in language made for scolding—for daring

> To trade, and traffic with Macbeth,
> In riddles, and affairs of death; (7–8)

Yet she will herself take charge of drawing him to *confusion** through illusion. She introduces another motif: degree operates in the witches' world as well:

> And I the Mistress of your charms. . .
> Was never called to bear my part, (9, 11)

*The OED cites this to illustrate the first meaning of *confusion:* "Discomfiture, overthrow, ruin, destruction, perdition." The third meaning, from *Hamlet,* "he puts on this confusion," and the fifth, "a confused and disordered condition," are relevant to Macbeth's inner experience.

Order has not been observed.

Hecate's characterization of Macbeth throws some doubt on the Sisters' motives and on his character:

> . . . all you have done
> Hath been but for a wayward son,
> Spiteful, and wrathful, who (as others do)
> Loves for his own ends, not for you. (13–16)

As suggested earlier, "*for* a wayward son" intimates a beneficent motivation, as if the Sisters intended something, in their terms, *fair* for Macbeth, whose love they wanted. It also implies, as Wayne Booth argues, that Macbeth is not a true son of evil; and Hecate seems to confirm this by insisting that Macbeth's "love" is for his own human goals, not for the witches. On the other hand, Irving, in the same lines, found evidence, in *wayward . . . spiteful, and wrathful* . . . to confirm his conception of Macbeth as villain. The *wayward* is particularly interesting: it suggests the human impulse to uncertainty that matches the waywardness of the *Macbeth* world itself.

Hecate sets the meeting for the next day at the *pit of Acheron*. Dover Wilson has the perfect answer for editors who objected that this river was in Hades, not Scotland:

> Hell itself is clearly implied, a meaning gen. given to Acheron in Eliz. lit.;
> and Hell may be reached as readily from Scotland as from any other country.

It is a placeless place, an underground locus of evil; and there—

> Great *business* must be wrought ere noon. (25)

The word, earlier mouthed so meaningfully by Macbeth and his Lady, echoes their euphemism, links Hecate to their world. She speaks of the magical illusions planned, to draw Macbeth on to his confusion. Her rhythms roughen in the next four lines, ending in two that have the true trace of Shakespeare's pen:

> He shall spurn fate, scorn death, and bear
> His hopes 'bove wisdom, grace, and fear:
> And you all know, security*
> Is mortal's chiefest enemy. (33–36)

So Hecate puts for a moment into brief words one of the basic thrusts in the Macbeth design—and indeed in the human design. Even if I discounted—I do not—the other links to the rest of the play in this scene, in language, action, and idea, I would want to hold it Shakespeare's for those last two lines.

---

*The OED., in its third definition, cites this line as an example of two significant meanings of "security." First: "Freedom from care, anxiety, or apprehension." Second—with some of the ambiguity of our play—"a *feeling* of safety or freedom from or absence of danger." (Italics mine)

The end of the beat is pointed, in the Folio, by the *Music, and a Song* that calls Hecate:

> my little spirit see
> Sits in a foggy cloud, and stays for me. (38–39)

Then, *Sing within. Come away, come away, etc.* The full text as Davenant used it was

> Hecate, Hecate, Oh come away:
> Come away Hecate, Hecate! Oh come away.

Shakespeare himself was fully capable of writing these two lines; Middleton may have picked them up from him; the song goes on in *The Witch*, as almost certainly not in *Macbeth*, since Middleton's naming of characters (Puckle, Hoppo, Hellwaine) is meaningless to Shakespeare's play—and would interrupt the swift flow Shakespeare intended—as evidenced by the hurry of the Sisters: thus Witch One will say, again in a reversion to prosaic rhythm,

> Come, let's make haste, she'll soon be
> Back again. (41–42)

Why the song at all? If it was limited, as I think, to the urgent calling away of Hecate, and her swift uprush into the "foggy cloud," it would manifest her magic as the Sisters' chant did, and forward the play's flow. Possibly when Shakespeare wrote the scene, the fashion of masques was already important enough for him to make a gesture toward it—and more than a gesture in IV, i. But I believe Shakespeare and his fellows were too professional to allow a diversion, only for fashion's sake, to slow the powerful march of Macbeth's action. The scene was there because it intensified the climate of terror with remarkable spectacle. It worked. When later it was corrupted into the balletic, operatic frill Davenant brought forth, tinseling Shakespeare's terror with prettiness as the scene rolled straight on into IV, i, it worked for the kind of audience that wanted to be protected from deep penetration, that enjoyed, as Pepys did, diversion; that welcomed Garrick's horribly pious death speech for Macbeth—and the gutting "refinements" visited on *Othello* and the Nahumtatite castration of *Lear*.

Shakespeare's Hecate represents a dimension of evil more deliberately malicious, more intent on destruction, than in the ambiguous witches; she appears at a crucial time, when Macbeth leaves his Lady to visit the Sisters; and any possibility that the Three may mean him well is threatened by the counter-commands of the fearful goddess. We now know better than Macbeth what danger lies ahead.

Act III, Scene vi

At the end of the banquet scene, Macbeth spoke of going early the next day to see the Sisters. Then Hecate appeared at her midnight "witching" hour, to confirm the expected meeting. In clock time, III, vi should take place in the morning of the next day. But felt time has been stretched. Now it is the next day, and also long enough afterwards for the murder of Banquo to be known, and for Macbeth's tyranny to be widespread. Once this is stated, the news of the long tyranny becomes dissolved into the present, much in the same way as when Macbeth suddenly spoke at the end of III, iv of his history of spying on his thanes. Past duration is telescoped and inserted into the now.

The messenger of time is Lenox, and not accidentally. At the banquet the "loyal" Lenox sat closest to the seat reserved for Macbeth. In the next scene we will see that Lenox is Macbeth's aide in the visit to the witches. Now we are to hear him talking behind his king's back. The doubling of his loyalty will be emphasized in both his words and manner. Empson saw from the beginning the ambiguity of the lords:

> we feel any of them may be playing his own game in this period of confusion, though we never get it clear . . . it is what people really feel in times of civil war.

I believe Shakespeare's intentions about the lords to be deliberately pointed in this scene. Empson calls it "mutually suspicious gossip between persons hardly worth naming"; and this last applies to the anonymous "Lord"; but Lenox should be signaled out for special treatment.

The atmosphere of his speech is conspiratorial. He is going to speak subversion, as he has several times in the past:

> My former speeches,
> Have but hit your thoughts (3–4)

He may look over his shoulder, before speaking, and speak quietly at first. Until he is sure of his man, his speech itself equivocates: anyone listening could not tell for certain his true attitude toward Macbeth. He may raise his

voice at ostensibly loyal statements, for the benefit of any who may hear;
and lower his voice for the passages where his sarcasm is to be made clear.
The lord, Lenox mutters, could himself *interpret farther* from Lenox' earlier
remarks; Lenox himself *Only* says *things have been strangely borne* (6). Only he
says much more. Anyone might hear him, with full voice, add

> The gracious Duncan
> Was pitied of Macbeth: (6–7)

but only the lord hears, after the sly colon pause, *marry he was dead* (7). The
next line about Banquo walking too late might also be outspoken; not so
the sarcastic sequence, perhaps accompanied by a gesture indicating a very
small boy:

> Whom you may say (if't please you) Fleance kill'd,
> For Fleance fled: (9–10)

The next clause, prepared for by the colon, is ominous in its succession of
spondee-like monosyllables, each a warning:

> Men must not walk too late. (10)

The following lines, about Malcolm and Donalbain killing Duncan, can again
be spoken aloud, and perhaps for that carry even more irony. Lenox most
nakedly reveals his own doubleness now:

> How it did grieve Macbeth? Did he not straight
> In pious rage, the two delinquents tear,
> That were the slaves of drink, and thralls of sleep?
> Was not that nobly done? (14–17)

And then the muttered recoil:

> Aye, and wisely too:
> For 'twould have anger'd any heart alive
> To hear the men deny't. (17–19)

This is the same Lenox who saw the grooms killed and, standing beside Macbeth afterwards, endorsed the act: *no man's life/ Was to be trusted with them* (II,
iii, 129). Now the applauded act has become criminal. By pointing the loose
loyalties of the man, Shakespeare both individualizes him and locates him
among the mouth-honorers. The hollowness of the courtier design is furthered
by the quality of Lenox' sarcasm: aimed against a tyrant, it might evoke empathy, but it is too clever, too unfeeling about the terrible things described.
He goes on in his cynical doubling, some words for any to hear, some for his
special listener:

> So that I say,
> He has borne all things well, and I do think,
> That had he Duncan's sons under his key,

> (As, and't please heaven he shall not) they should find
> What 'twere to kill a Father: so should Fleance. (19–23)

Then Lenox puts a direct question to the lord: Where is Macduff, who failed Macbeth's feast, and so lives in disgrace? The Lord, in direct and sympathetic language—and sometimes, in the theatre, referring to a written report he brings out—tells of Duncan's sons at the pious English king's court. *Thither Macduff/ Is gone* (33–34), he says, to rouse the English to help overturn Macbeth, and return

> to our tables meat, sleep to our nights:
> Free from our feasts, and banquets bloody knives; (38–39)

Here speaks the yearning for the familiar, homely domestic order that Macbeth and his Lady also dreamed of—and they two are not excluded in the lord's *All which we pine for now* (41).

> And this report
> Hath so exasperate their king, that he
> Prepares for some attempt of war. (41–43)

These lines have provoked critical confusion. Some editors, after Hanmer, have read *their king* to be *the king*, meaning Macbeth, preparing for war. Presumably, then, Macbeth would have already learned of Macduff's flight to England; hence this scene should follow the next, IV, i, where Macbeth gets the information. However, the Folio clearly says *their king*, which could mean no other than England's, as Liddell observes.* The lord does say that Macduff *is gone* to England; but he apparently means "on the way," from what follows.

Lenox asks, *Sent he to Macduff?* (44), meaning now, by *he*, Macbeth—this was emphasized by Reinhardt, whose Lenox with a disdainful gesture of the thumb pointed to Macbeth's rooms, thereby distinguishing Macbeth from the earlier reference to *their king* of England.

When Lenox learns that Macduff refused to obey, he prays that

> Some holy angel
> Fly to the court of England, and unfold
> His message *ere* he come. (51–53)

Which clearly indicates that Macduff is en route, and cannot be there yet. Presumably the lord meant that *their* (English) king had already heard *this report*—this news of Scotland's suffering—and was indeed, as we will learn he was—preparing for war; only later will we hear of Macbeth's mobilization.

If this scene followed the end of IV, i, Lenox would not need in it to ask about Macduff, because he himself (in IV, i) tells Macbeth of Macduff's flight to England. Lenox might ask now anyway, given his duplicity, to test the

---

*Query: "Would holy Edward be 'exasperate'?" Since, however holy, he was ready to share in a war, I think we may allow him susceptibility to provocation in a righteous cause.

lord; but this unlikely speculation does not outweigh the advantages of locating the scene where the faithful Heminges and Condell left it, as Shakespeare and his company evidently played it.*

Even the final dialogue says much about the two speakers: while the lord takes on some of Lenox's coarser tone, Lenox, apparently taking some coloration from the lord's more earnest speech earlier, begins to talk seriously and even reverently. This change, too, seems part of the chameleon design Shakespeare drew in his mouth-honorers. Finally, Lenox' note of prayer matches the old man's apostrophe that ended the previous act.

The scene may close with Macbeth coming to a door,† and signing to Lenox to follow, for Lenox will be in attendance when Macbeth goes to meet the Witches. The low sounds of thunder may already sound.

*The problem arises that the Lord has heard of Macbeth sending to Macduff—though Macbeth, at the end of III, iv, tells Lady Macbeth he has not done so, but would. Shakespeare seems to be taking every advantage of felt time. We are not forced to wonder how, between midnight and early morning, Macbeth could have sent the summons to Macduff, and received the answer. Again, the time-buffer of the Hecate scene helps relieve us of a compelling clock sense, and so the sending to Macduff fits into the felt context.

†In the Polanski film, the courtiers spoke in a room in the palace, while a distraught Lady Macbeth, sitting apart, caught their tone of voice and looks; and though she heard no words, sensed disaffection. This was a visualization of a stage toward the agony of her sleepwalk.

You secret, black, and midnight hags.

Act IV, Scene i

Thunder. Enter Three Witches.

Gordon Craig, at the age of eighty-four, after nearly an artist's lifetime at working and reworking his ideas for staging *Macbeth*, thought he was *beginning* to solve the puzzles of this scene. The essential problem: to break free from the romantic aura that had often prettied the witch-action, to find instead how to project the horror Shakespeare designed, and plumb deeply enough the human impulse to indulge in it.

The scene begins a second cycle in the action, but at a much darker level. The first appearance of the Sisters, in their witch-world, was a threat to the innocence of the human world; now the two worlds are in collusion. So Shakespeare makes us confront the deeps in ourselves. We exercise the sinister energies of our malice, then, horrified to find it so devious and destructive, externalize and personify it, call it Evil. Macbeth began by trying to resist the malice, then yielded to it; now Shakespeare unites him and the images of externalization in a common, horrible purpose.

From the Restoration through the stagings of Irving and Tree, a kind of gothic beauty masked the scene's darker impulses. Davenant's interpolations of music and dance, and Middleton's full, silly lyrics, were usually presented operatically, with large groups of "spirits." The Folio will direct only Hecate to enter with *the other three witches;* but Charles Kean, for instance, specified groups of "Black and White imps"; "Red and white imps"; "Ladies of the Ballet"; and "Singing Witches." When the Davenant–Middleton material was cut, some applause greeted the "experiment," but it did not become common for a long time. Gentleman, in the Bell edition, reports on

> a very bad alteration of this play by Betterton [with this] emendation . . .
> making the witches deliver all the prophecies; by which the surfeiting quantity
> of trapwork, ghosts, phantomes, &c. is judiciously lessened.

But public opinion demanded the witch extravaganzas, as I noted earlier; not even Kemble could teach it better. The daring Phelps eliminated the junk in his 1847 staging, but perhaps frightened by such comments as *John Bull*'s that he was too extreme, restored it later. Creswick's return to the text in 1871 was not followed by the leading end-of-century managers.

I will not spend much space on the vestiges of the Davenant pattern, since they distract us from what Shakespeare intended; but I will describe briefly the stage contexts that were developed to evoke audience pleasure; and relate them, where I can, to usages of later periods. From the beginning, stagings were light-limited by the Sisters' locale. Thus the "ougly Hell" in Jonson's *Masque of Queenes*, "flaming beneath, smoaked unto the top of the roof." Garrick's *Macbeth* atmosphere was basically the same: "A dark cave, in the middle a great cauldron burning." This has remained a standard setting, though the forms might differ. A Japanese *Macbeth* would use it, in mid-twentieth century, intensifying the effect of smoke and flame with a great bubbling from the cauldron. With Porter, the cauldron was a hole in the floor; with Guthrie, who wanted to de-emphasize the supernatural, it was a small kettle. The flames in the cauldron are likely to be spectacular: for flare-ups, "magic" powders may be used, as with Scofield, fireworks, as with Irving. The flames may cast shadows on the walls, may seem to redden the whole cavern, as with Redgrave, or cast the only light in a dark and dreary cave, as with Macready. The nineteenth century audience generally wanted something more romantic than a dark hole, and often, as the scene went on, the stage would open out into a moonlight prospect, for the Davenant business. The sense of nearby water has contributed to the visual effect: Sothern's staging suggested a cavern on a lake lit by the moon—and later, in Germany, Reinhardt offered a green pool, with the cauldron in the centre, a black path for the witches leading to it from fore-stage.

Witch Two's *Open locks, whoever knocks* clearly suggests a door, and Macbeth will say later, *Come in, without there*, stipulating an enclosed area. This is generally assumed to be a "cavern," as Rowe decided, if not the pit of Acheron Hecate promised.

This subterranean place has been made to seem vast, with high arching space above. Phelps, in 1864, showed a

> lofty and lengthened vault of rocks . . . (with) its wreathing vapour . . . its misty moon that only struggles through the aperture at back, to steep the cavern in a hue as strange and spectral as its doings. (*Weekly Dispatch*)

The light was ghostly bluish, appropriate for Phelps' atmosphere of wild incantation, picking out his witches in the moonlight. Tree's cavern, flame-lit from the boiling cauldron—from which steam rose to shift shadows on the rocky walls—was roughly terraced so that his congregation of singing witches could sit high on tiers. Craig's "pit" gave the impression of a cathedral—a hellish one. He would have liked, as well, three high gibbets. In Robert Edmund Jones' design for Barrymore, a tall, tapering, white pillar, that suggested to observers a phallic image, enclosed at its base the embers around which the Sisters crooned their rites.

Irving was not satisfied with the limitations a roof imposed: his witches gathered at a high mountain crater, rimmed with jagged rocks flanking a defile of steps down which Macbeth would descend. The witches were intermittently illuminated by flashes of lightning and the flames that rose, mingled with steamy air, from the bubbling, hissing hell-broth of what seemed an unfathomable pit.

But the scenic effects must not be too explicit: the Sisters move now in a deeper underground than any place man can define. We first saw them hovering in "fog and filthy air," Byam Shaw observed: the second time on the earth; "now we see them below the earth or as though they were in hell." A particularly "ougly hell"—the locale of man's forbidden; a descent into the most shame-hidden recesses of the unconscious; the deep cellarage of the id, where unspeakable crawling things writhe and sting; the lair of Dionysus grinning over secret lusts and cruelties. The ingredients of the witches' brew are associated, as Goddard observes, with dark, cruel human qualities: thus the voracious shark, the poisonous adder, the ravenous wolf, the venomous toad, the fiery dragon. Shakespeare had mentioned a few of these ingredients in *Titus Andronicus* (II, iii, 91), to create a climate of horror; here the long catalogue supports not only the atmosphere and action, but also the motif of disjunction that elsewhere terrorizes the *Macbeth* world. The cauldron stews with shocking fragments of torn animals (including the human)—shocking partly because slivered and disbranched, partly because associated with hurt, danger, vulnerability, death: *tongue, maw, finger, nose, lips, wing, baboon's blood, tooth, scale, sting, gall, liver, eye, entrails, toe,* even—in name so innocent, in texture so horrible, felt under the fingernails—*wool of bat.* Disjointed scraps of deadly plants also belong: the root of the killing hemlock, a sliver of the poisonous yew, taken in the moon's eclipse, all light gone, the world dark. The several phallic-symbol organs are, by their amputation, rendered impotent. Death itself is mixed in—*witch's mummy.* So the cauldron boils with symptoms of anti-life chaos. As it evokes a sexuality it interdicts, so it invites us to a macabre feast that is, as Knights observed, a destructive counter-image of the kind of hospitality intended by Macbeth and his Lady in their banquet.

We enter from the beginning something of an intense sensuous witches' sabbat that was perhaps ending an emotional orgasm when we first met the Sisters. With this third meeting since—threes, threes—by Shakespeare's art we have been both prepared for a more arduous experience of the uncanny, and still unprepared for the trauma of this enveloping horrible.

Something beyond the confronting of these strange creatures with Macbeth is about to happen to us. We breathe in the dark world hinted at in their first brief, ambiguous appearance, and in the witches' gossip and prophecy of their second. To the Jungian, the scene is a refraction of the archetypal plunge into psychic depths that is pivotal in the human experience, pointing to destruction or rebirth. The hero confronts both the terrible female and the babe that promises manhood. A Freudian, like Veszy-Wagner, can interpret the cauldron as a projection of the kind of fearful mystery the man-child fantasies as stirring in the pregnant mother's abdomen. But these can only be deep, latent resonances in our response; the Sisters have too much identity to function only as symbols. While they stir deeper levels, their characteristic action and spectacle sustain the mystery and expectation of drama.

The full polyphony of the Sisters sounds in this scene. They usually appear as before: old hags, or beautiful images seen as hags (though stagings that presented them at first as projections, shadows, or electronic phenomena continue to do so). They work "real" magic, they prophecy, they are linked to familiars and superiors who suggest the diabolical and the mythical. They require multiple definition—and indefinition.

They also can seem to exist partly as the creations of a mind tempted, as was Macbeth's—and Banquo's. They confirm, Piteöff suggested, Macbeth's latent desires. To emphasize their aspect of interiority, and to avoid supernatural implications, stagings have sometimes made the whole scene a dream in Macbeth's mind. The German Macbeth, George, was seen to retire to bed at the end of III, iv; and his encounter with the witches in this scene was a projection of his stormy sleep. Webster, directing Evans, said she handled the scene as if it was a "half dream of Macbeth's, a creation of his own mind," built from the suggestions and atmosphere of his early meeting with them. Webster meant to de-emphasize the externals of the witches, to drive instead for the sense of spiritual power of witchcraft; in fact, in performance, the whole action took place as Macbeth dreamt. Littlewood's Macbeth also dreamed the scene, a product of his disordered fancy, as he writhed on the bed and spoke in nightmare. Both Bergman's Macbeths dreamed: in 1944, Macbeth tossed restlessly, his upper body naked, and, asleep, communed with his horror; in 1948, as Macbeth and Lady Macbeth lay in their bed, the Sisters, young, with depraved, immobile faces, crept out from under it, and played out the dream. Komisarjevsky, committed to an anti-supernatural treatment of *Macbeth*'s supernatural, made the witches, like his Banquo, shadows that Macbeth projected as he slept—his bed located where Banquo had been murdered. Macbeth began by muttering "Blood, blood, it will have blood", and the shadow witches rose to haunt him, their voices loudspeakered. Douglas Campbell, defending dreamed witches, argued that Macbeth's mind had been stripped to its lower depths, he lives in "restless ecstasy," his mind "full of scorpions"; he hears voices, sees Banquo's bloodless ghost, his words are the surfacing of his unconscious; hence he dreams "or, half-waking, has a vision" of the Sisters.

"Half-dream" and "half-waking" allow for the sense of sleeplessness that must haunt Macbeth, and suggest a confused, nightmare quality that makes the projections plausible. But they entirely interiorize images Shakespeare meant to appear as externalized but ambiguous forces reciprocating with

Macbeth in his decisions. The Sisters' existence is clearly independent of him, even though perhaps they exist only to appear to a man as dark of soul as he—and Banquo?—may be; Lenox cannot perceive them. They are— and are not—part of the spectrum of Macbeth's visions, more "real" than the outright hallucinations of dagger and ghost, yet only partly occupants of his "real" world of kings and murderers. They seem weird old women—who can vanish. To suggest the multiple nature of the Sisters here, Ashwell suggests that controlled lighting from one angle of vision might make them appear beautiful fates, from another repulsive hags practicing black magic.

Depending on their earlier appearances, the Sisters may fly in, rise from traps, creep in, dance in, to find the cauldron rising, or already risen. Sound often bridges their entrance: the triple mew of the *brinded cat*, our old acquaintance, Graymalkin. *Brinded* is usually glossed for color: fiery, as if burned, or branded, which would fit a witch's cat; the verb came to mean, too, irritated, and something of burning impatience may certainly sound in cat-cries. The Sisters listen for the calls of the next familiar: the obscene hedge-pig, who may be Paddock heard in the first scene. Why thrice and once instead of four? To maintain the magical power of the odd number, as Elwin suggests? To fend off the danger of evenness to their equivocal world? Have we watched the second Sister count the calls to three, and awake to the special significance of the unexpected fourth? The impatience mounts, and Harpier—possibly from Harpy, but I believe the owl, the fatal bellman— commands action. If the Sisters are "discovered," they may echo their positions of earlier scenes. Macready dispersed them, in a pattern Irving copied: one at the mouth of the cavern on watch, one cowering over the flames beneath the cauldron, one across the stage, rocking in impatience. They may be already about the fire, itching for the signal to start their revel, or already worked up to it, in a Bacchic frenzy. Hopkins' Sisters could be seen to start by cleaving a baby in two; in an earlier English staging (1970), the three slaughtered a sacrificial babe, and smeared their arms and legs with blood.

Many threads will again be intertwined and made visual in this scene: birth, death, sexuality, violence, the uncanny. The Sisters may again begin with the kind of erotic play, described by Scot, cited in Chapter I, iii. As they circle *round about the cauldron*, and begin to throw in the juicy, poisoned entrails, the emphasis may be on selected notes in the polyphony. Where the "real" earthy end of the spectrum is stressed, the witches are practical old women—so Hopkins' crones mixed their brew from a witches' cookbook, Williamson's took their ingredients from a tray. The Sisters have hugged their precious ingredients to them, or unpiled them from heaps, or—magically—snatched them from the air. Gielgud's found the things in their bosoms. In a more formal pattern, Craig's Macbeth introduced now the Folio's *three other witches* who are directed to appear later, and these came forward one at a time as each stewstuff was designated, to drop it in the cauldron—so providing a visual image of doubling. The uncanny insists, and is often enhanced with an atmosphere of magic, of ritual, that gives a curious sense of timeless formality to the Sisters' sensual riot.

The naming of the ingredients, as the Sisters drop them in the stew, may become a meaningless gabble unless each item is distinguished, and enjoyed for its shocking quality. The recipe book device was a way of dealing with this; more often each thing is held up, named, gloated over, as with Olivier's Sisters. The language does not hurry: thus the measured pace of

> Toad, that under cold stone,
> Days and nights, ha's thirty one:
> Sweltred venom sleeping got, (8–10)

Regularizers have wanted *cold* to become "coldest" or "the cold," or "a cold," or "cold cold," to smooth out the rhythm; but the stretched *cold*, carrying along the lengthened *o* sound, takes a heavy emphasis that conveys frigidity as no qualifier could. *Sweltred* and *sleeping* echo the slow hissing of the cauldron; the words between, *venom* and *got*, provide a rhythmic balance of word-speed as well as metre.

How do the Sisters make meaningful *Double, double, toil and trouble?* Some editors follow the eighteenth-century notion of removing the comma after the second "double." This changes the meaning to "double toil and trouble"; this perhaps makes sense as an echo of earlier uses of *double* to suggest intensified effort: the Captain's *doubly redoubled strokes* (I, ii) and Lady Macbeth's obeisance to Duncan: *All our service . . . twice done, and then done double* (I, vi). Are we reminded, faintly, of some resonance of Duncan's own doubling of *trouble?*

> The Love that follows us, sometime is our trouble,
> Which still we thank as love. Herein I teach you,
> How you shall bid God-eild us for your pains,
> And thank us for your trouble. (I, vi, 17–20)

If the comma after the Sisters' second *double* is deleted, they might, in accompaniment, dance faster, blow harder on the coals under their stew, stir more fiercely to make the *fire burn, and cauldron bubble*. But the Folio's repeated comma does well to isolate *double*, with its implication of equivocation, and its aural doubling of the rhythm: the separated word suggests chanting magic, perhaps a doubled use of fingers, hands, bodies, signs, artifacts to accelerate their boiling. Hands may make the sign of the devil's horns, thumb concealed, middle fingers folded, index and little finger pointed. Gestures and movements may oppose and cancel each other, or be reflected in mirrors, visually imaging the play's dialectical style. Duplicates of images of things may be made to appear and disappear, a doubled thunder and lightning may be involved.

To the music of the chant, so full of hissing "s's," "sh's" and "f's," sharp "k's" and "t's" and the resonances of "m's" and "n's," the Sisters prepare their feast with sensual delight. The cauldron boils and steams indeed like a hell-broth, so that anything dipped in it is seen to shrivel; but the Sisters may plunge their fingers unburnt into the poisonous stew to sip and taste, as new ingredients thicken it; they will not feel the heat. The orgiastic nature of the revel, always popularly associated with witchcraft, moves toward its climax as human fragments, with erotic-violent associations, are offered to the cauldron.

> Nose of Turk, and Tartar's lips:
> Finger of birth-strangled babe,
> Ditch-deliver'd by a drab, (31–33)

Noses and lips surface in Othello's sensual fit; what the Sisters gloat over may not be the organs the Sisters name. The human parts also suggest the cannibalism that was imagined to accompany witch orgies; so in Reinhardt's staging, when Witch Three mentioned the *finger*, the others, excited and greedy, began to fight for the mutilated member, biting, tearing, pushing, shrieking. The *a* in *babe* may have had the sound of "grass as pronounced in the United States" (Liddell), rhyming with *slab;* "baby" can still be heard as "babby" in some regional English speech. The mutilated image of the *babe* is part of the miracle of the play.

The stew is complete with tiger's entrails, and the final, slow ecstatic pouring:

> Cool it with a baboon's blood . . . (39)

The animal kingdom, from the least crawling thing to the human, is represented in the cauldron's charm. It is *firm and good*—the Sisters may taste it greedily, to make sure.

Now the Folio directed Hecate to enter with the *other three witches*—so the figures on stage now mount to another powerful number: seven. Some scholars find this incident spurious, interpolated, as was III, v, to fit the Middleton song mentioned soon after: *Black spirits, &c.* Twentieth-century stagings generally cut the moment if they have cut III, v, believing both to invite disbelief. I am willing to suppose that Heminges and Condell knew their Shakespeare better than we do, and that the bit is his. I would have been skeptical if the Folio directed the kind of large ballet scene Davenant apparently borrowed from *The Witch*, where, as the music ends, Hecate calls her "sweet sisters," of whom there are evidently many, to dance and leave with her. Shakespeare's Hecate, magnificently alone at the top of her order, does not demean herself to the level of the Sisters; she enters with just three attendant witches; there is no suggestion that she dances or sings with them—though she may make one elevated point of a seven-pointed rite. She is still a figure of terror, though now, in contrast to her anger in III, v, she is gracious, endorsing with her power the witches' magic. With her changed mood, her verbal rhythms change and dance. Yet the fearful authority remains. Tieck envisioned a huge Hecate, draped in black veils that could not hide her face, pale as death; on her head the image of the new moon. He also could imagine her royally attended by many specters, small and dwarfish, whirling about her. Kemble used four groups of little children as goblins; the story goes that the boy Kean, playing goblin for Kemble, once tripped up the child next to him so that the whole line tumbled, one after another, like dominoes.

English stagings tended to emphasize a strange sensual beauty in their use of Hecate's minions; a few examples will indicate how elaborate were their digressions. In Charles Kean's gleaming moonlight, a rock wall opened at the back for Hecate's entrance, amid an impalpable mass of shadowy limbs and flying garments, a myriad of white arms uplifted, moving in what was then described as a "Bacchic frenzy." Phelps' moon-goddess rose from a trap, in green light, to a sound of thunder, and a wild reaction from the Three. Tree's Hecate, hovering over the cauldron fumes, seemed almost to rise from them. Irving's soared up the deep sky above the flames of his crater, a bright star gleaming on her head, sometimes half-eclipsed by the hell-broth steam. Her spirits, clad mystically in greenish white gauze—sixty of them but seeming hundreds—moved in gestures of "strange, unhallowed worship" under a "bewilderingly beautiful moon" (*Morning Post, New York Times*). Irving mixed gothic mystery with romance: "in grateful contrast comes the exquisite choral setting of 'Black spirits . . .'" (*Sporting and Dramatic News*), "the haunting wail of Hecate's invisible elves . . . in a chorus of exquisite delicacy" (*Lady's Pictorial*).

Other stagings have been more faithful to the Folio text. Poel distanced his Hecate simply, with three masque figures attending her. Reinhardt's formidable Hecate was again a towering terror, before her the crouching witches; given permission to dance, they leaped up, shouting with joy, took hold of each other's hair, and moved in a frenzied round that grew wilder and wilder, until one had stripped off her clothing. Staccato, jagged music, of the sort Bergman used, suits such a mood better than the sweeter and more langorous rhythms of the nineteenth century.

Like elves and fairies in a ring, the triple-queen orders her six witches to dance. Elves and fairies, as Farnham and McGee point out, could refer in Shakespeare's time to creatures of the same order of uncanny power as witches or devils. One of the OED's tributary definitions for "fairy" is "One possessing more than human power. An enchantress." (The reference to *Antony and Cleopatra* [IV, viii, 12] is metaphorical.) Recall that in Holinshed the "common opinion" about the weird women who first met Macbeth and Banquo was that they were "nymphs or feiries" (and Forman, when—if—he saw the play, called them "feiries or Nimphes"—though this apparent borrowing straight from Holinshed is one of the reasons his authenticity may be doubted). So the *elves and fairies* might be supposed dark spirits; if not, if "spirits of another sort" (*MND* III, 2, 378) of the kind frolicking with Oberon and Titania, then the Sisters, who would certainly dance widdershins, could in all other movements be perversely parodying their more innocent counterparts (see Jonson's *Masque of Queenes* description later). Hecate has been presented realistically, as a sinister eminence (Germany, 1964). She can give to her lines the force and awe due to her mystic image: a Johannesburg Hecate (1970) was applauded for the brilliance with which she chanted in a whisper, "like a priest bestowing the cup at Mass." This kind of effect explains why the King's Men would have wanted Hecate in the scene.

My assumption is that Shakespeare and his fellows, working for the awe surrounding Hecate's familiar image of dread, used only the first lines of the "Middleton" song—as would Irving and other, later producers. These lines seem appropriately to conjure the spirits in the cauldron to blend themselves (the music is called in Middleton, "A Charme Song"):

> Black spirits and white: red spirits and gray,
> Mingle, mingle, mingle, you that mingle may.

In Middleton, named spirits apparently entered into the ballet, as so many would from Davenant into the nineteenth century, and the song could single them out personally in such grotesque and suggestive terms as "Titty, Tiffin, keep it stiff in. . . ." Middleton's chorus sings of throwing into their stew extracts of bat, toad, and adder that besides being redundant to, would only have diminished the horror of the Sisters' stirring, and would surely have offended the artistic taste of Shakespeare and his players. (Perhaps the one ingredient worth its own kind of immortality is Middleton's fifth and last:

> Here's three ounces of the red-haired wench.)

Hecate and her second trio may have vanished after this interlude; if they remained, it was for background, Hecate brooding over the Sisters' mysteries, most likely from above, though Garrick placed her at one side. Kemble, in his brave but abortive effort to change the witch and spirit figures to beings of preternatural horror—before popular taste made him resume broomstick caricatures—had serpents writhing over the "evil spirits": with striking effect, Oulton reported.

We may suppose that the King's Men staged a dance that emphasized the unnatural, the sinister, the dark magic of odd-ness. Jonson's idea a few years later for his *Masque of Queenes* revel suggests the tone:

> full of praeposterous change, and gesticulation, but most applying to their property: who, at theyr meetings, do all things contrary to the customs of men, da... daun... hip to hip, theyr hands join'd, and making theyr circles backward, to the left hand, with strange phantastique motions of theyr heads, and bodyes.

The popular theatre may have emphasized the sensuality of gesture and movement to deepen the reverberations, so pervasive in the play, of the linkages among sexuality, strangeness, violence, and death.

The rising beat of the incantation over the cauldron, moving through—if the Hecate moment is included—the excitement of the music and dance, breaks off at a peak. Witch Two suddenly jerks at her *pricking thumb*. The member may seem to move of itself, as if automatically responding to *something wicked;* and in the dead silence, all look at it. (A *thumb* preceded Macbeth's first entrance, perhaps not accidentally isolating this part so essential to the operation of the human hand, and so ready to serve for phallic imagery.)

Weaver's Sisters put their three thumbs together, and used them as a kind of divining rod to point to Macbeth's approach. Then, the sound of knocking. The Sisters surely know who, wicked, is coming; their enjoyment of their charm may hint this:

> Open locks, *who ever* knocks. (50)

The word suggests conjuring gestures for a magical opening to a cave door, the kind of "charm to open locks" described by Scot. But in the theatre the knocking can grow fierce, echoing the hammering at Macbeth's gate. Even evidence of force has been suggested: Tree could be heard working a crowbar against stone, to effect an entrance.

A shaft of light from above signalizes an aperture, a shadow across it the presence of Macbeth, who often "descends." Lenox may appear momentarily with Macbeth, to establish his proximity: Sothern's, carrying Macbeth's shield, came in half way, looked with wonder at the witches, and was waved away. Guinness' Lenox stood apart, but close enough to see what ensued: yet he saw nothing except Macbeth—to whom, only, the Sisters and their magic was perceivable.

This is a different Macbeth from the one who first met the Sisters. Again, he may be both physically and psychically aged. Irving, ignoring Macbeth's III, iv timing of a next morning meeting, decided here to suggest an interim during which Macbeth had ruled—seventeen years, according to the chronicles Irving consulted. So he ordered a change of beards for the male cast; his own hair and moustache were white streaked, and his face lined. More often Macbeth waits until the gap between this scene and V, iii for massive signs of physical erosion. What distinguishes Macbeth now is the focussed hyperenergy that began to rise at the end of III, iv. He comes determined to take for his good anything that will serve him, and he seems to know that the choice will be evil, and to be excited by the knowledge.

Behind Macbeth's feverish elation may be sensed his fear of the uncanny scene he confronts. He may not reveal it as openly as Tree, who was unmistakably frightened; but as in I, iii, his felt apprehension will be one of the guarantees of the terror of the scene. He will make a show of anger; though threats with his sword can only amuse the Sisters. He may try to cast a spell on them, as if he is their master—has even acted (as noted earlier) in Faustian robes. Cowper's promptbook: "Conjure, as if by magic." Paul suggests that Macbeth is indeed a controlling necromancer here. If Macbeth believes he is, he learns differently: he has no power even to interrogate the apparitions evoked by the Sisters. The Sisters themselves claim other governance, besides the Hecate from whom they may be seen to take invisible, unheard cues. Macbeth's nearly hysterical, apocalyptic speech, in his effort to dominate the supernatural, masks not only his latent fear, which surfaced so nakedly in III, iv, but also other subtextual impulses. Macbeth has been found thoroughly wicked now (Lynch), and, in his readiness to invoke chaos, self-aligned with the devil (Jack); or—in synthesis—he has contracted into a butcher, has cast all doubts behind, acts now only as he consciously intends to act—in straightforward, bold, bloody resolution. Certainly this is his conscious determination; and the spectacle in which he engages may seem on the page so to dominate him as to diminish his inner complexity. The play's overt acts can be absorbing now. Granville-Barker believed Shakespeare "outdoes even his own accustomed mastery in . . . marshalling the play's action to its end"—from, in this scene

> the whipping up of the evil in Macbeth to the top of its fury, immediately followed by the most savage outbreak (IV, ii) . . . sudden and short . . . (to the) elaborate and weighty preparation for the play's counter-action

of the fifth act. But what happens *within* Macbeth in the magnitude, the magnificence of his impulsive thrust, and its smash, is even more compelling. A terrible life-force drives him, as Bradley observed; Sanders sees him resisting the evil of contraction, of the unfreedom of a cribb'd, confin'd state, to be free as the casing air—at whatever cost, he will recover integrity of impulse and action. So the dimension of his resolution is broad and involving: we are "surprised into an attitude of secret, perhaps unconscious, complicity," Emrys Jones suggests. While the very grandeur of Macbeth's over-reaching assault on the future asks sharing, his hyper-excitement, hinting of the crowding counter-impulses he represses, absolves us from identification with unalloyed wickedness.

Macbeth's salutation to the Sisters is peremptory; he finds himself, as at their first meeting, wondering at their mystery, resorting to question: *How now, you secret, black, and midnight hags?/ What is't you do?* They answer in the masking language he and his Lady have used, refusing to define the unspeakable:

> A deed without a name. (54)

Macbeth may stop to speak at his entrance; but, partly perhaps because he recognizes his own past equivocation, partly because his mood can bear no pause, he often storms down, demanding impatiently, as Garrick did, for an immediate revelation of his destiny. One correspondent in the *St. James Chronicle* complained that when "you precipitate down the steps which lead to the Cavern, you have never appeared enough struck with the Solemnity of (the) scene"—as apparently Macklin was. The writer would have preferred "A Pause of silent Wonder." A Garrick defender observed that "A Pause and a Start would take off from the abrupt and Disordered state of [Macbeth's] mind."* Macbeth's passion is on the rise, he is moving toward the height that, at the end of the scene, will sustain an arch of expectation until his next appearance, far off in V, iii. He comes in force, and the force, in the face of a series of shocks, intensifies.

Tree forced his way through a cleft in the rock. Phelps strode on, the warrior on attack. Irving was already bloody, bold and resolute, Williamson angry and violent. Olivier, showing his care for lifting the play's last acts, rushed in as one fanatically eager to learn his fate. Vilar, driven on to prove himself, "needed the witches' predictions like a man who needs drugs to be a man" (*Figaro Littéraire*). John Wilkes Booth (U.S., 1860), too urgent for steps, leapt down from a ledge of rocks some twelve feet high to the pit floor (O terrible leaper!).

The counter-impulses in Macbeth may be manifested in the violence of manner with which he seems to deny them: so Forbes-Robertson momentarily discolored his philosophic design with moods of boastful satisfaction and angry discontent. A Macbeth obviously physically weakened by lack of sleep, as Mantell was, his face lined, neck knotted, seeming fifty pounds thinner, spoke with an intensity that was feverish, and that would grow more so through Act V. A Macbeth who sustains an instant of shock at the first sight of the Sisters' darksome lair may, as Reinhardt's did, strenuously pull himself together, intent on his purpose. When the emphasis is on Macbeth's superstitition, he comes, as Salvini did, absolutely trusting the Sisters; and the impact of their revelations is correspondingly traumatic. The Macbeth like Macready, fearfully acceptant of a fateful destiny, grimly learns what he has to do: Macready's hardening resolution at the end of III, iv is extrapolated into a fierce commitment: "the voice changes . . . his manner . . . is decided and firm; from the slave, he has become the hero of wickedness." But the counter-currents could be sensed:

> In the first three acts, almost as sensitive as Hamlet, in the last two, he is almost as ruthless as Richard [III]. Yet still his ferocity is very distinguishable from [Richard's]. His vigour is passion; his severity is impulse; his courage is the frenzy of shame. To the last, through the rings of the steel-armour of sternness with which he has encased his breast, you catch a glimpse of the same, susceptible, excitable, quick spirit, which, in the morning of his days, had made his appreciation of virtue so intensely keen, and his sense of the departure from it so fierce an anguish. (*The New Mirror*)

---

*Garrick's critic also complained of the actor's contemporary dress, that made him look like a "*modern fine Gentleman* . . . a Beau who had unfortunately slipped his Foot and tumbled into a Night Cellar where a Parcel of old Women were boiling Tripe for their Supper." Garrick's defender could only say he was sure Garrick made other arrangements for his dress.

   The Sisters, whether or not under the eye of Hecate, greet Macbeth with an intensification of their earlier welcome. More than ever, Macbeth must not be made a fool by their condescending cackling or sly contempt. He is not to know, nor are we, the nature of his entrapment. The ritual hushing, bowing, kneeling, circling, fawning seem to honor him. The Sisters may even bestow a kiss on him, as did Williamson's. Tree's Three further solemnized the moment by mantling Macbeth's shoulders with a garment of black, making gestures of the cross before his face, and giving him—as other witches have given their Macbeths—a mock "communion" chalice of their brew to drink. McKellen's Sisters stripped him to the waist before the blonde Third, the tranced idiot girl, who seemed strangely in love with him, kissed him and slowly poured the drink into his mouth. In these libations the audience can almost taste the sour venom (or may magic make it seem sweet to Macbeth?).

   Macbeth's violent demand for answers echoes his megalomanic declaration in III, ii: . . . *let the frame of things disjoint*. For this speech Macbeth has been accused of aligning himself with hell; but his child's cry for all or none unless he is satisfied reflects the archetypal human frustration of the second murderer (III, i, 130), *reckless what I do/ To spite the world*; or of Lear, commanding wind and water to avenge his suffering by destroying the earth, and man's structures on it. Lear calls for an end to humanity: *all germens spill at once*; Macbeth uses comparable language:

> Though the treasure
> Of Nature's germaine, tumble altogether,
> Even till destruction sicken: (63–65)

Till destruction sicken is prophetic for the speaker; the pause following suggests that for a moment Macbeth himself may have an insight into what he would welcome; then he goes on to demand answers, racing to outrun the pauser reason. The quality and intensity of Macbeth's mood may partly be known from his language, thick with the polysyllables that Shakespeare saves for particular moments in the design, building, block by block, to the ultimate vision of chaos. The speech has itself a terrible destructiveness; Kemble, concerned with his image of the honorable murderer, deleted it, as did many nineteenth-century actors, thereby muting one of the ground notes in the *Macbeth* polyphony.

   Macbeth demands to know; the Sisters one by one, in ritual procession, accede, emphasizing various possible notes in their design: submission, adoration, affection, mystery, power. Sister One's offer, in slow prose, is intimidating:

> Say, if th'hadst rather hear it from our mouths,
> Or from our masters. (70–71)

Almost as if he takes a dare, Macbeth, however apprehensively, calls on the darker powers. The Sisters' invocation, though shorter than the earlier ones,

is a shade more awesome, more ominous. The killing of a pig—a witches'
trade, as we remember from I, iii—had, as Neumann noted, archetypal ritual
roots. Is there an echo of the vulnerable babe? Of the mother ready to destroy
her issue? This one has *eaten/ Her nine farrow**—again the odd number, three
times the sinister three. So unholy was a pig that ate its young that by a Scots'
law (cited in Holinshed's *History*), it was to be stoned to death and buried.
Craig suggested that in front of Macbeth the pig be killed, screeching—"not
particularly pretty." The *sow's blood* is poured in; and then the *greaze* (note the
slithery z) sweated from the gibbet—scraped off even now from a gallows
looming over the stage, if one is there, as Craig suggested. Besides the connotations, the *blood* and the *greaze* convey an experience of texture, as they are
put into the cauldron, which may respond with hissing, steam, smoke, fireworks, an explosion. The atmosphere of perverted feast, as the Sisters stir—
and likely sip—their brew enriched by the cannibal potion, and the tincts
of dead men, intensifies the strange, discolored light that has played about
the sensual verbal and visual imagery of drink and food: nurture inverted,
milk become gall, a king banqueted while being marked for murder, liquor
drugged or cheerless, meals eaten in fear. A woman prays to be filled with
cruelty, drinks to become bold, and ends tasting discontent; a man affects to
believe the wine of life is drawn, discovers that in fact goblets filled full might
as well be empty; the chief nourisher at life's feast, the seasoning, is gone.
He will sup *full of horrors*—and think he has almost forgot even the *taste
of fears*.

   Come high or low, the Sisters charge, invoking the terrors of the thunderous
air and the vasty deep to make their show. Sky and earth answer the beckoning. *Thunder*, the Folio directs; and up into the filthy air above the cauldron,
from deep below, an armed head appears.†

   This, and the following apparitions, have been staged as a psychological
event: Macbeth facing front, the figures emerging behind him as he envisions
them. More often he responds to objective sights, however distorted or surreal. Since the early nineteenth century, disembodied images have been
reflected in mirrors and by projection—which, growing sophisticated, has
learned to filter images of the apparitions through prisms (Mexico, 1967) or
other mediums of distortion, to intensify mystery and ambiguity.

---

   *Victorian English audiences were somewhat taken aback by Bernhardt's "neuf petits cochons."
   †That "Sooth saying wizards"—and their masters—had the power to raise apparitions was
accepted by the credulous in Shakespeare's time—and long before. West's *Symboleography* told
how they "divine and foretel things to come and raise up evil spirits by certeine superstitious and
conceived formes of words. And unto such questions as be demanded of them, do answers by
voice, or else set before their eyes in glasses, christall stones—(we recall Dr. Dee)—or rings,
the pictures or images of things sought for." The fantasy is surely as old as the dream of magic.
In Macbeth's visit to the Sisters may be heard an echo of Saul's (Samuel 1:28) to "the woman that
hath a familiar" at Endor who, invoking the dead Samuel for her visitor, said, "I saw gods ascending from the earth."

Carrick Craig's witches tipped their cauldron backward, and the apparitions seemed to spring from it in giant figures on the cyclorama. Stagings faithful to the Folio's tangible images have varied in intensifying and revealing the apparitions. Tree's were luminous, the 1918 Russian staging's phosphorescent. Olivier's Sisters plunged their hands into the boiling cauldron to bring up each oracle. More often the images are seen to rise of themselves— as they probably did at the Globe—out of the smoke and steam of the cauldron, through a trap (the repeated ascents and descents in rapid succession may require a double trap. Things can go wrong: Sir Walter Scott tells of an *armed head* that got stuck, and the strenuous effort to free him from below shot a whole man, shabbily dressed, onto the stage, to much amusement.) The cauldron itself sets a delicate problem in visual definition: the apparitions must be discerned for what they are, but preserved in some aura of unreality. If stage fire throws too much glare, as happened once with Kemble, recognition is difficult; similarly with too much obscurity from mist, smoke or steam. One of Kean's critics observed that Shakespeare's text did not require the apparitions to emerge from the stew; Irving's flitted past him; but the *hell-broth* has seemed their most suitable womb. If, at each appearance, Macbeth must steel himself to stand to a new startling, supernatural effect, the momentary pause helps give time for recognizing the figures.

In some stagings the Sisters have imposed on Macbeth apparitions that were crude dummies, or effigies held on sticks, or dolls brought out from hiding places, and have spoken through them ventriloquially. In Brussels (1970–71) gigantic puppets, towering over Macbeth, created an ominous contrast to the small human figure. To enhance a mystical climate, the Sisters have gone into trances, raised the images as in a seance, and have let each figure's voice come through their own mouths, until they ended exhausted. When the apparitions rise as by magic, with a life of their own, their voices have sometimes been the unidentifiable uncanny, sometimes the voices of the play's personae. Walker argued that the apparitions have no connection with the play's characters; but more often critics have looked for umbilical relationships. The armed head, so symbolic of the warrior's kind of manhood, and encouraging Macbeth in it, has been interpreted at least since the mid-eighteenth century (Upton) as a foreshadowing of Macbeth's decapitation, and has been so staged. Booth made up the head to look like his own; Byam Shaw similarly raised an image to look like Olivier, with his agonized expression: as the figure's lips moved the voice issued trancelike from Olivier's mouth. Scofield's voice came back at him from the monstrous iron mask that rose and faced him above his cauldron, seeming, against the black background, to hang in the air. The *head* may seem impersonal, archetypal: so Reinhardt's huge metal vizard, hovering in steam, sharply lit from below. For Komisarjevsky, a recognizable Macduff stood behind a transparency to speak for the helmet projected in Macbeth's dream.

Banquo, tempting Macbeth beyond man's daring, may be suggested in the image. But we had better not consciously recognise any such concrete identities, for they might betray the mystery of Macbeth's future. We are not to know how Macbeth is misled until he knows it. All of Shakespeare's intention that we can reasonably assume is that a man inhabited the *head*, and probably rose from below stage and returned there, for the Folio finally directs *He descends.** Hackett found a way to represent Macduff in the apparition, but avoid present recognition: what appeared was a distinctive headgear that Macduff would be seen to wear in his final conflict with Macbeth. This could also be done with a helmet that would later be recognized as Macbeth's.

Macbeth, insistently daring, carries his challenge to the mysterious *unknown power* itself: *Tell me*. He is rebuffed—perhaps by some sign: lightning, a puff of smoke, a fearful sound. Sister One:

> He knows thy thought: (81)

To Macbeth, so intent on shielding himself from penetration, the idea must be alarming. And the Sister is right: after the apparition's triple hail, *Macbeth . . .* comes the anticipated warning against Macduff, that harps Macbeth's fears aright. It ends, *Enough*. (Will there be any resonance of this when Macbeth ends his own final speech damning him who first cries *Hold, enough?*)

The *head* disappears as it came—or as manipulated by the Sisters. Macbeth tries to call it back—Tree would look deep into the cauldron—but again is rebuffed by some fearsome sign. Sister One announces, ominously, a *more potent* spirit: *Thunder. 2 Apparition. A Bloody Child*—a newborn infant in some stagings. Bloody it must be—Reinhardt's was smeared with gore on face, neck, arms, shirt—but not so bloody as to make recognition of childhood difficult. In its weakness this is again (as in the I, vii image) the powerful, tiny child embodying the archetypal fantasy of the triumph of the youngest who proves most *potent*.

Macbeth recovers from the shock of this gruesome show, and its triple hail, with resurgent exultancy, even sometimes a touch of humor covering his apprehension:

> Had I three ears, I'd hear thee. (93)

The child's identity has been debated: this is Macduff untimely ripped; or Macduff's slaughtered babe; or the naked new-born babe Pity, whom Macbeth has tried to ignore; or the child Lady Macbeth would have savaged rather than forswear herself. Or the babe is one composite image of all the play's echoes of childhood and of life endangered. Interpretations rest on connotation: the spectator's experience, as with the *armed head*, is of something strange and awesome, resonant with past verbal and visual images, and tantalizing but not revealing in its foreshadowing:

---

*Halio suggests that the *He* in Elizabethan usage could mean "it."

> Be bloody, bold and resolute:
> Laugh to scorn
> The power of man: for none of woman born
> Shall harm Macbeth. (94–97)

What then? The very assurance of safety implies a riddle, hiding a warning of *more potent* danger. If we can forget what we know will happen, what will we imagine can endanger Macbeth? Can we possibly remember our young guesses, when we first saw—or read—the play? Many *naive* spectators were instantly agreed: no *man*, but a *woman*, should kill Macbeth. Others imagined a child, a natural catastrophe, an animal, or some supernatural intervention. A few (here and after the next oracle), citing the accuracy of the Sister's earlier prophecies, believed Macbeth would survive, only to experience increasing misery. Some were mystified—and this is certainly part of the complex response Shakespeare intended.

The second apparition, too, *Descends;* Macbeth may see it go with a shuddering breath of relief. He can speak now of his repressed *fear*—he uses the word twice. Why *fear* Macduff? But Macduff will be killed, anyway (this seems to confirm that Macbeth does not yet know of Macduff's flight). Macbeth will make assurance *double* sure (the *double* an ironic assertion of certainty in a time—in a world—of "doubling" equivocation). Then Macbeth may tell pale-hearted fear it lies (Hackett: "a thump on his heart to summon up false courage"); and will no longer be shaken nightly—an urgent need voiced from the depth of his ravelling being

> And sleep in spite of thunder. (102)

Pat on the last word, the Folio directs, *Thunder* sounds, and the third apparition rises, the Child, crowned, with a Tree in his hand. This figure is sometimes taken to reflect Malcolm; in terms of literal age, Fleance seems more likely; even King James has been suggested, holding his "genealogical tree" (Parsons), though nothing in the text hints this. In fact, again, the image absorbs past allusions to childhood, growth, fertility, and seems to look forward innocently; and again we must not recognise any identities that might give away the future. Coming after the bloody image, this one seems to promise Macbeth the serenity of perennial vegetation. Again, it urges him to extreme daring, to the excess of fighting manhood, to hubris:

> Be lion-mettled, proud, and take no care:
> Who chafes, who frets, or where conspirers are:
> Macbeth shall never vanquish'd be, until
> Great Birnam wood, to high Dunsinane hill
> Shall come against him. (108–112)

Macbeth, doubly encouraged, repressing his past fears of the hostile inanimate (*Stones have been known to move, and trees to speak*), is further strengthened in his dangerous security, rises to a peak of confidence. His relief may be

almost manic: Reincke erupted in wild joy; Plummer cavorted like a school
boy; even Scofield's austere face allowed itself a victorious smile. Reinhardt's
Macbeth uttered a shout of triumph, Quayle a great laugh; Tree, too, laughed,
and was joined by the witches, as he cried

> That will never be:
> Who can impress the forest, bid the tree
> Unfix his earthbound root? (113–115)

Macbeth speaks almost in the witches' rhyme, but not their rhythm, accepting their magic. Unlike Macbeth, we may suspect a trick again in the oracle,
and wonder what it is. The presence of the branch in the crowned child's
hand has seemed, from one critical point of view, an obvious clue to the trick;
but *naive* spectators were mystified: the alternatives they could guess for the
previous oracle seemed not available here. Only some cataclysm could transport a rooted forest. In fact, a forest will *not* move—nor will a man not of
woman born endanger Macbeth: only by quibbles can these be said to happen,
and Shakespeare has skilfully unprepared us to outguess quibbling equivocation—his Sisters' early prophecies were realized so unequivocally. Indeed,
the Sisters, if they seemed before to favour their *wayward son*, may now be
felt to mislead Macbeth only under Hecate's duress; her brooding presence
may be sensed. Still the aura of ambiguity, the tint of evil, makes us doubt
the Sisters, whatever their affections. The trick might later be recognized as
relating to Malcolm if in V, iv, cutting the first branch of Birnam wood as he
explains his strategy, he holds it up in a gesture clearly reminiscent of the
apparition's: but such explicitness is, again, limiting.

These riddling oracles, and their tantalizing opacity, have a quality of timelessness, and of the kind of fateful irony that trapped Oedipus. There are
closer classical precedents. Joseph Fontenrose has described some for me:

> In Herodotus, King Croesus of Lydia heard from the Pythia of Delphia that
> his reign would last until a mule should become king of the Medes, so he felt
> secure, as did Macbeth; but Cyrus was the mule, being half Mede and half
> Persian. Likewise King Tarquin of Rome was told that he would lose his throne
> only when a dog spoke with human voice: the dog was Brutus, whose name
> would indicate a dumb beast (Zonaras, *History*). The Birnamwood theme
> appears in an oracle supposedly spoken either to the Amphictions or to the
> people of Crisa in the First Sacred War: the Amphictions would not take Crisa
> until the sea should touch Apollo's sanctuary, which was five miles from the
> sea at a higher altitude. The Amphictions finally consecrated the whole plain
> next the sea to Apollo, thus including it within his sanctuary. (Polyaines,
> *Strategemata*, 3,5).

Macbeth, having learn'd by perfectest report that the Sisters have more
in them than mortal knowledge, grows hubristic in security. He speaks with
a kind of exultation about himself as of some exalted person now safe from

the returned dead (the suggestion has been made that this should be a witches' speech, but the elated disjunction complements Macbeth's earlier images of separation):

> Rebellious dead*, rise never till the wood
> Of Birnam rise, and our high plac'd Macbeth
> Shall live the lease of nature, pay his breath
> To time, and mortal custom. (116–119)

And yet a worm still gnaws in him. To live out his own *time* has never been enough. His *heart throbs*—characteristically he is aware of his body—*to know one thing:*

> Shall Banquo's issue ever
> Reign in this kingdom? (121–122)

He does not command now, he again asks—*if your art/ Can tell so much*. For this most important question, a momentary note of pleading sounds. Because they want to shelter him from knowing, or to keep their secrets, or to lure him on, they resist. His fierceness returns, he *will be satisfied*—the *will* rings out, as with Irving—or

> . . . an eternal curse fall on you: (125)

The Sisters have laughed at the threat: not so much to demean Macbeth, as to make him realize, as Mephistopheles might, how meaningless a curse must be to the damned. Alternatively, they have been grieved, or frightened. The colon allows pause for either reaction, before Macbeth's insistent command: *Let me know*.

The scene has developed in waves, with each apparition intensifying the spectacle, and with Macbeth's rising reactions. Now his arrogant demand evokes an abrupt punctuation, in sight and sound—Macbeth's startled, fear-resisting question:

> Why sinks that cauldron? And what noise is this? (126)

He sees, in a climax of silence, the amazing spectacle of the disappearing vessel—shielded, if illusion requires, by the Sisters, with last bursts of smoke, steam, and flashes of fire (Kemble), perhaps leaving behind, as with Carrick Craig, a continuing glow of embers. Then, to refill the quiet, the sound: sometimes indeed, *noise*—a shriek, for Kemble, "Thunder and discordant sounds, shrieks, etc." for Booth; for the Craig production, "all the noise possible." The Folio direction suggests the strange, the eerie: *Hoboyes*—the music played for Duncan's banquet at Inverness (I, vii), but now probably in a distinctively minor key.

---

*The proposed emendation to "head" never made sense. Dover Wilson, who had earlier accepted it, effectively presided over its extinction in a letter (to *TLS*) calling the change "sheer editorial sleepiness."

The Sisters will spur the ominous, intensified quality of the final episode. Hopkins' gave him a potion from the cauldron, he drank it, was revolted and felled by it. His Sisters, with their backs to the audience, slipped on skull masks, turned for the moment of shock and vanished into the floor, leaving Macbeth to face their show. Olivier's witches knelt, and moaned their triple prologue: *Show. Show. Show.* McKellen's Third Sister, the possessed idiot girl, writhed in pain, as if she were the reluctant transmitter of visions she already foresaw would be painful to her beloved victim. Sothern, at the sinister implications of his Sisters' preparation, threw his arms up to shield his face from what would come.

What is the witches' motivation?—as they, pursuing the disjoining motif, warn

> Show his eyes, and grieve his heart, (130)

Do they exult in his grief? Or, for their *wayward son*, do they themselves grieve?

We see their *show*—

> A shew of eight Kings, and Banquo last,
> with a glass in his hand.

Shakespeare had found the three preceding oracles in Holinshed, and had fitted them to his *Apparitions;* the pageant of kings was his own. It is the only substantial element in the play that may be taken specifically to relate to King James. One "Walter", a supposed descendant of James' imaginary ancestors, Banquo and Fleance, began the Stuart line, and one of his descendants, another Walter, married the daughter of the Scots king Robert Bruce to give birth to Robert II, the first male Stuart king. The eighth Stuart ruler, Queen Mary, is sometimes assumed to appear in the *show* last, and so Bridges-Adams paraded her. But Mary was not a *king*. Then was the last to be James himself? A living King was not likely to be represented on stage, especially in a play about the killing of a king, even in a masquelike interlude. Dover Wilson and Flatter suggest that since James could not be shown, the eighth, holding a "glass" (mirror) would be held up for James to see himself. (The *glass*, in Shakespeare's time, could also mean the kind of magic crystal John Dee and other sorcerers used.) The text itself complicates matters, since, in contradiction to the stage direction, it has the eighth king, not Banquo, holding the glass. Davenant, perhaps following custom, stipulated eight kings and then Banquo. Liddell suggests this punctuation: ". . . eight Kings, and Banquo: (the) last with a glass." Other editors resolve the problem by directing Banquo to be first and also last.

The confusion is not important. Banquo may have been the eighth figure, holding the glass; or have followed the eighth figure. Most of the members of the Jacobean audiences would have been as ignorant of the myth that James had descended from Banquo as audiences of later centuries were. Jacobean

spectators probably took at its face dramatic value Macbeth's shock at seeing
the *treble scepters*. They would have been pleased to recognise that this signified a British monarch. This was incidental to the primary emotional state
evoking empathetic response: Macbeth's dismay when he accepts the truth
that his rival's children will rule in Scotland—and then in England, too, if the
last of the kings wore recognizably English royal robes (otherwise Macbeth
could hardly be expected to foreknow the meaning of the scepter).

The theatre—perhaps from the time of the Globe—has been sensitive to
the expectation of audiences that Fleance should appear here, and though
even as an imaginary figure he was not a king, he has sometimes been seen in
the procession—to the discomfiture only of any rare pedants who know too
well the true (false) history. (Though any spectator might cavil, as one did,
when Irving placed Fleance last in the procession, as if the heir of his seven
descendants.)

Was the scene designed to please James? The question is only relevant if
it leads to illumination—or distortion—of our perception of the play, and
our understanding of the playwright's intentions. I believe the poetic and
dramatic meanings are more available to us if they are not obscured by the
shadow of James' taste; and my doubts as to the reality of that shadow persist. Even assuming James did go to see *Macbeth*, we may wonder if, from
what we know of his spectator's habits, as reported in detail when he visited
Oxford in August, 1605, he would still have been watching—if awake—
when Act IV came around.

As noted earlier, in the Oxford "Progress" James—preceded, incidentally,
by the Duke of Lenox—was welcomed by three boys, dressed as "Nymphes,"
who presented a brief series of verse recitations about the prophecy that
Banquo's children would be kings. This presumably pointed to James' succession, and he enjoyed hearing it. That evening James attended a pastoral
comedy, which he did not enjoy: "If the Chancellors of both Universities had
not intreated his Majesty earnestly, he would have gone before half the comedy had been ended." The next day he attended a Latin version of Sophocles'
Ajax and "was much wearied by it." The next night he went to another comedy: "After a while he distasted it, and fell asleep; when he awaked, he would
have been gone, saying 'I marvell what they think me to be,' with other such
speeches showing his dislike thereof." On the next and last day of his visit
another play was offered: James went to a library instead.

These performances certainly were not of the quality provided by Shakespeare's company, nor the plays as entertaining, but the subject matter was
apparently not offensive. *Macbeth*'s might well be. That James should have
been pleased with a play about the killing of two Scots kings, however followed by retribution, when he objected strenuously to the idea of deposing
even the most monstrous of tyrants (as we will see), seems to me highly argu-
able. Finally, again, if this IV, i scene had been tailored for James, and especially for the visit of the Danish king, surely one of the court gossips so busy

reporting the visit to Oxford and the other royal pleasures would have mentioned it—Harington, perhaps, who described in such delighted detail the drunken orgy of the two monarchs (see IV, iii chapter). Why multiply entities beyond necessity? We *need* no further explanation for the scene than that Shakespeare, indulging his flair for spectacle with his *show of eight kings*, was appealing to a wider Jacobean audience by bringing a touch of England into the Scots story, as he would do intensively in the rest of the play.

The spectacle is a grand one, worth the hocus-pocus of the Sisters' prelude. It moves the scene higher than the cauldron incident through Macbeth's greater intensity, and also through the strange magic, and the ritual aura of ceremonial awe associated with it. The line of great kings projected into Macbeth's future carries also for the audience resonances of time, passing and present; of the power and sanctity of lineage; and the visualized extinction of Macbeth's future hopes. After the excitement and thunder of the apparitions, this procession, piped across the stage with haunting music, by its very restrained solemnity grasps attention in a new and more powerful hold. The unreality of sorcery mingles with the fact of prophecy. A hint of retribution is experienced without being moralized.

We know that as early as Garrick a filmy transparency, lit at the back of the theatre, distanced and magicked the kings. The 1763 Bannerman engraving, noted by Burnim, shows Garrick center-stage, Hecate and the witches watching as the procession crossed the rear translucency. Kemble similarly, according to Scott, "diminished their corporeal appearance" by passing the kings (who uttered groaning sounds) "behind a screen of black crape," emulating some lines from Collins:

> Before the Scot afflicted and aghast
> The shadowy kings of Banquo's fated line
> Through the dark cave in gleamy pageant passed.

A "gleamy" effect seemed to be achieved by flashes of fire, a "moony vapour" and the employment of backlighting reflectors. One report, from the *Monthly Mirror* in 1803, describes Kemble using a single king, made to seem eight by repeated flashings of light upon him. One twentieth century staging managed somewhat the same effect by using a revolving searchlight on Macbeth to suggest his perception of the procession, the light speeding up as the line of repeated images matched Macbeth's growing intensity. And the apparitions have been luminous, clothed in fluorescent materials.

The "cavern" itself, in the indoor Blackfriars, may have dissolved to allow for a mirage procession in the rear. As early as Henry VII's reign, British theatre mechanics who mounted the pre-masque "disguisings" were moving stage mountains; Inigo Jones' designs for Jonson include various instances of rocks opening to reveal "sights." This kind of transformation would delight nineteenth-century audiences. On Macready's dark stage, with very soft music playing below, as the lights came up, the back of the cave split open, the backing was removed from the transparency there, and "the kings walk through 3 gauzes." (A century and a half later, at Stratford, Connecticut, the rear wall would similarly split, the jagged teeth of each half framing the spectacle.) Charles Kean and Phelps similarly used gauzes; Phelps' kings were cut-out fingers in profile that moved on a track, lit from below.

Were gauzes used in Shakespeare's time? The material itself is described in a thirteenth century OED entry; for Jonson's masques, such items as the "transparent front of a castle" are mentioned; I am ready to assume that artists like Inigo Jones understood the principle of backlighting scrims, certainly for use in the indoor Blackfriars, possibly in occasional outdoor night performances at the Globe;* even—given an enclosed, darkened inner space— in daylight ones. In any case, in the Globe the kings may have been distanced in recessed spaces above or below. Macbeth, at his sight of the first Banquo-like king, will cry, *Down*. He may only be trying to crush a vision; but he might also be adjuring the figure to vanish through the earth (the trap) or from the air (the above).

To further the sense of mirage, the kings have, in some stagings, seemed to pass suspended, as if gliding without taking mortal steps, achieving the dream-like effect Phelps may have intended with his cut-outs. With scrims, the back-lighting has been limited to the upper bodies, the walking movements disguised. Reinhardt's kings, aloft, seemed to hover through the air, their feet hidden in clouds. Savits achieved a similar effect by dressing his actors in long robes that masked their strides, making them seem to move motionlessly. For Irving, the kings crossed veiled in steam; dry ice smoke has more recently framed their passage. Tree turned his figures on a giant wheel where, in visual metaphor, each rose to the highest before giving way to his successor. With Scofield, the procession rose from the stage matting of blood-colored earth, and moved past a reflecting glass that indeed made them seem to go on forever.†

In a Japanese staging, the figures, all in stark, pure white, surrounded Macbeth. Piscator's kings slowly descended the staircase up which Macbeth had gone to kill Duncan. Hopkins, standing in shadow, faced a chilling, supernatural change of scene that carried particular power from its contrast with the grotesque, semi-comic puppet-show of apparitions that preceded. On the stairs where first had been seen a portrait of Duncan, there now appeared, after a thunderclap that darkened the stage, the portraits of Macbeth and Lady Macbeth—as skeletons; then the parade of ermine-robed kings, wearing gilded death's heads, and made ghastly in the ultra violet light, moved on the stairs as Hopkins watched. Booth, to give the kings a common identity with Banquo, thought of marking each with a bloody lock of hair.

*Again, see Rosenberg (6).
†James Black suggests a kinship between the tableau figures in these parades and the ritualistic effigies that move in solemn procession across the faces of some European clocks.

A different, frightening sense of commonality was achieved in an English staging (1969): the figures wore stocking masks that conferred on them the kind of ominous facelessness of marauders.

Projections have long been used to suggest the half-fantasy of the procession. The 1832 Hungarian *laterna magica* imagined the figures in varying colors. The kinds of filtered distortions noted above for the three apparitions have also skewed the kings. The reflecting mirrors used in Vienna in 1820 could similarly have altered the realistic perspective. Projection and mirroring effectively multiply images to convey the impression Shakespeare intended with his "magical" *glass:* duplications of Banquo in an eternal procession of kings that—after the first eight have passed—stretches out *to the crack of doom*—a timeless tomorrow and tomorrow and tomorrow.

A moment before this show, Macbeth was at the very height of his assurance, exulting in his power. At this acme of *hubris* he himself forces this traumatic visual rebuff to his future hopes—as if, latent in his design, may be a dialectical impulse to self-hurt. At once an image confronts him *too like the spirit of Banquo*—hence Booth's idea for a benchmark of blood. The image wears a crown, that—again the body awareness—sears Macbeth's eyeballs.

> And thy hair
> Thou other gold-bound brow, is like the first: (135–136)

Some editors prefer "air" to *hair;* but, as noted earlier, the Folio word may intend a helpful identifying feature to make Banquo's image easily recognizable and duplicatable. Macbeth goes on telling us what he sees: suggesting that the procession was meant to pass in the deep upstage area, with Macbeth's words filling in the detail blurred by smoke or steam or darkness.

As previously Macbeth's exultation mounted, now so does his angry, frustrated passion. Each time he believes he has seen the last Banquo-copy, a new one appears. Though he has asked for the show, he complains—echoing the unhappiness of the frustrated child:

> Filthy hags,
> Why do you show me this? (137–138)

Again he can hardly bear the seeing, again his bodily sense impinges: *Start eyes!* As the images come on, he looks away, or covers, or shuts his eyes: *I'll see no more:* and yet he must, as if drawn to what would destroy him.

The climax comes as he identifies Banquo, appearing like all the others except dressed in the old habit, and in blood. It is a tremendous moment of recognition, an *anagnorisis* in the extended if not the literal Aristotelian sense: *Now I see 'tis true* (the words so like Othello's (III, iii, 444) at the climax of his false *anagnorisis:* "Now I do see 'tis true.") This is not only a bitter resignation to the present, it is also an agonized experience of the wasted horror of the past, and a vision of the future in an instant. Macbeth must now assume that he would have been King of Scotland *without* his *stir*. Yet even as he glimpses this perspective down the corridor of the past, he is being simultaneously further blinded to the path before him: this demonstration of the Sisters' "truth" will only persuade him more wholly to believe in the apparitional equivocations that draw him on to his confusion. Doubled notes go on sounding.

When Macbeth is made to dream this "cave experience," his response is measured in the twisting of his body, as he agonizes over what the audience may see projected. Komisarjevsky did not bother with the parade of kings: there was only Banquo, behind a scrim, and Macbeth's nightmare imaginings of the rest; at the end this Macbeth grovelled on the floor, a mass of "unkingly flesh." The procession was similarly a psychological event for Williamson, blindfolded by the Sisters, hysterically envisioning what could not be seen.

But Shakespeare stipulates the *show*, to make the audience as well as Macbeth marvel; and to provide the series of mounting stimuli to Macbeth's climactic *anagnorisis*. In one manifestation, Macbeth reacts as if pounded by many blows, the introspective element dominating, his force contained as his dismay and dread increase. So Craig's Macbeth, like a man lost in a dream state; Laughton, hypnotized, trancelike; Booth, unable to bear the sights, burying his face in his hands. A Macbeth like Irving could recover from the initial shock, then, divided between attack and retreat, struggle with horror, and despair, and finally dread certainty. Scofield, standing stiff as a ramrod to the repeated shocks, rasped his anger at the cosmic joke played on him. Other Macbeths raged more demonstratively: Reinhardt's, at first staring fixedly at the vision of his fate, and wanting not to believe it, pressed his hands against his eyes to blot it out, then raged and stamped at its inevitability. Byam Shaw saw his Macbeth, Olivier, tortured and driven to fury by the vision. When the aggressive component supervenes, Macbeth takes action, as Piscator's Macbeth did: emphasizing the warrior's instinctive response, he rushed up the stairs to seize Banquo's image—and it seemed to vanish in his hands. Salvini similarly, his rage mastering his anxiety and his control, drew his sword and charged at the figure, to be halted in mid-act, amazedly, by a power he could not touch.

Helpless in the face of the inevitable, Macbeth can only ask:

> What? Is this so? (146)

He may be hope-haunted—as we may be—by the experience that *nothing is but what is not*. We are perhaps even more uncertain, as the *naive* spectators were: if a trick could be suspected in the prophecies of the apparitions, is some trick encased here? Is Macbeth being misled by appearance to misadventure? If the kings' procession is authentic, does that endorse the validity of the apparitions' oracles? Or vice versa? What can he—we—believe?

The Sisters promise that *all this is so*. Unequivocally. Finally. They have predicted so accurately in the past. Now in immediate juxtaposition they have raised Macbeth high with assurances of long life, brought him low with a denial of dynasty. No wonder he stands *amazedly*, stricken with confusion.

The Sisters offer to cheer up his spirits, charming the air with sound, his sight with a round,

> That this great King may kindly say,
> Our duties, did his welcome pay. (153–154)

These lines are found spurious by those who suspect the Hecate scenes. I am ready again to trust Heminges and Condell. The irony of a "cheering" dance for the man the Sisters have led to desperation serves as a tributary to the play's clouded stream of equivocation. Especially this is true if the witches have seemed in fact to want, in their dark way, only good for this wayward son. But for his insistence, they would have saved him from his last destructive *sight*. That our last vision of them should be this ironic, even—in the circumstances—ghastly, "cheering" ritual dance, that it may recall the first sight of them, suits these ambiguous figures. They dance—surely widdershins—an *antique round*, a mannered movement that might itself be of equivocal cheer to Macbeth.*

The Folio direction is simply: *Music. The witches Dance and Vanish*. If Hecate and the *other three* had remained through the *show*, they probably disappear first, leaving the Sisters for a momentary, reminiscent image—the music, movement, and perhaps words recalling the initial *When shall we three meet . . .?*

We are not to *know* that Macbeth—and we—will not see the Sisters again in the play; *naive* spectators invariably speculated on their next appearance. We, if we forget what we know, will look forward to a return; and, not encountering the Sisters again, will understand retrospectively that we have seen a farewell with perhaps cyclic implications of a return in another time.

Some stagings have spelled out the Sisters' evil intentions by a scornful cackling, as with Irving, a "paroxysm of laughter," as with Bernhardt; Reinhardt's figures, before disappearing into vapor, sneered at Macbeth, shouted hypocritically, danced about him making vulgar gestures. But these stipulations disperse the mystery and destroy an important element of suspense Shakespeare drew into the design. More appropriately Craig wanted the last sound to be as ambiguous as the Sisters: "a long and fearful laugh—or was it the wind?" Macbeth, standing *amazedly*, is not to be sure. He utters a solemn curse on this *pernicious hour*—this shoal of time.

Amazedly could mean, for Shakespeare, deep shock: even "stunned or stupefied" (OED). Traumatized as Macbeth has been, the magic of the Sisters' disappearance may come as a climactic blow. Their power—and stage

---

*Liddell cites Ascham's scornful description of an unscholarly pastime: "To go on a man his tiptoes, stretch out th'one of his armes forwarde, the other backwarde, which, if he blered out his tunge also, myght be thought to daunce anticke verye properlye."

means—to disappear has been noted earlier; now, again, they may turn and transform themselves into boulders, or otherwise merge into the background, sink through traps, fly aloft—sometimes behind a puff of smoke or steam, or stroke of lightning, sometimes accompanied by the tympani of thunder. Shakespeare, intensifying the design, has made this the most stringent of Macbeth's experiences with the supernatural, and Macbeth's response is proportionate. Scofield, moving to challenge the Sisters, suddenly found one looming above him: even his iron courage failed momentarily, and he shrank back; when he looked again, all were gone. Reinhardt's Macbeth turned pale, staggered, held to the rock wall for support. Salvini, twisted to an unbearable pitch, fell fainting on the ground, the Sisters dancing about him before they vanished. Others—Sothern, Polanski's Macbeth, Piscator's—similarly collapsed. Williamson grovelled on the floor. Saul at Endor supplied a precedent: he fell "straightway all along on the earth." Saul faced an immediate catastrophe; to Macbeth no threat could be more final than the denial of a dynasty.

One of the recurrent ambient sound-signals for swiftness that is often joined with verbal images to haunt the play is of horses galloping, including, possibly, not only horses of the earth. This sound now may wake Macbeth from his raptness, or from his physical collapse. He comes to awareness; finds himself alone. He had threatened the Sisters with an eternal curse if they did not show him the future; now that they have shown him, he voices the curse. His consciousness of his daring may check him as the echoes of thunder, of sky horses, startling him, intervene. Holloway suggests that the sounds may carry implications of the four horsemen of Revelation. Hackett shivered, waved his sword wildly, started at imaginary shadows, and, unnerved, cried out—

Come in, without there. (159)

—the call of an agitated man suddenly needing the security of company.

Answering the call is the corkscrew Lenox, whom we saw applauding Macbeth for killing Duncan's "murdering" grooms, then turning on him in private gossip, but still serving where power is. Shakespeare's use of him here, directly after the III, vi dialogue, seems not accidental. Lenox would have watched Macbeth thoughtfully, if not suspiciously, during the king's inexplicable behavior toward the invisible at the banquet; now he comes upon a Macbeth evidently shaken by a somewhat similar experience: at one extreme rapt, lost in a dream, as Scofield was; at another, Williamson cringing under a table. The Seyton of a Japanese Macbeth (Seyton is sometimes substituted here, with the loss of Shakespeare's character-point about Lenox) came in to find his master lying as if dead. Hackett, still panting and overcome, clutched his startled Lenox to ask:

Saw you the weyard sisters? (161)

Again Lenox has perceived nothing that Macbeth saw; he may look at the tense, questioning Macbeth with a curiosity reminiscent of his scrutiny in III, iv. Then, perhaps from far off, Macbeth may hear the fading thunder of hoofs—or the hoofs of thunder—that may cue his outbreak, whether spoken to himself or to Lenox:

> Infected be the air whereon they ride,
> And damn'd all those that trust them. (165–166)

The irony is almost too easy. Macbeth both curses them and trusts them; for trusting them, he damns himself. What saves the line from obviousness is Macbeth's passion, erupting from his lost dream of founding a dynasty, that blinds him to what he does. Yet he may pause, with some glimpse of the implications for himself of what he has said; he may move quickly between concentration and raptness now. A last echo of hoofs may again cue him to recall hearing *the galloping of horses*.

> LENOX: 'Tis two or three my Lord, that bring you word: (168)

Lenox seems meant to take the full colon pause, watching Macbeth, hesitating at the name, as Reinhardt's did: who then spoke in lower tones,

> Macduff is fled to England. (169)

Because Macbeth is still half lost in his thought, or because his mind refuses at first to accept unwelcome news, he can only repeat, questioningly, the last three words. The furious Hackett seized his Lenox, and shook him, forcing confirmation from him. Lenox speaks in formally respectful language that may mask an opposite intention (will we remember Banquo's repeated use of the same phrase (in III, i) to the Macbeth he suspected of foul means?):

> Aye, my *good* lord. (171)

Frustration piles on frustration. The first response is shock: Reinhardt's Macbeth fell back, and stared at Lenox. But fury is likely to dominate: the philosopher in the overreacher gets a further glimpse of a world that is not only equivocal but also perverse; he will in time find it even worse—meaningless. He rages now at the image of eternity that seems to have circumvented him by some hours:

> Time, thou anticipat'st my dread exploits: (172)

He calls on his warrior's prowess to be strong in him; the Macbeth not afraid, in war, of making strange images of death, who can promise his wife a private deed of dreadful note, means now to focus his energy in violent force. He declares a watershed resolve. He imagines now—again—that he can cut loose entirely from that bond that kept him pale, be entirely a man of action, unhindered by scruple. The moment is pivotal, likely to be charged with fearful emotion, however held under. Porter's practical Macbeth fiercely controlled his fierce resolve. Reinhardt's Macbeth drew a deep breath, clenched his fist, spoke with a compressed wildness that grew into a desperate frenzy. Williamson was at once wild-eyed, slashing at the servants come to help him, hysterically determined on blood. Hackett believed the "insane streak is commencing to show."

Macbeth cannot easily cry farewell to that disjunction of his *heart* from his *hand* that has so much impeded him. Consciously determined to fuse thought and deed, he must try to assure himself, again and again, in different ways, that indeed surmise will no longer smother function, that the eye will bear to see the hand's business:

> The flighty purpose never is o'ertook
> Unless the deed go with it. From this moment,
> The very firstlings of my heart shall be
> The firstlings of my hand. (173–176)

Firstlings. Firstborn. Images of infancy, related subterraneously to flashes elsewhere of babes and birds; shadowed here by the imminence of blood and destruction implied in the old commitment to a dreadful *deed*.

> And even now
> To *crown* my thoughts with acts: (176–177)

a king's image for commitment—

> be it thought and done: (177)

If only *it* could be *done* with the terrible thought of *it:* to surprise Macduff's castle, slaughter *wife* and *babes* and

> all unfortunate souls
> That trace him in his line. (180–181)

Determined as he is to play Herod, unfeelingly to deny lineage to his peers because his has been denied, yet the words after *babes* seem to betray him: *unfortunate souls*. A note of pity lurks in the polyphony dominated by rage and frustration. Checked perhaps by his own awareness of the latency he seeks to repress, he for the fourth time in the speech insists on action untinged with reflection:

> No boasting like a fool,
> This deed I'll do, before this purpose cool, (181–182)

But the very insistence is qualified by his apprehension that he may think better, that follows the slight pause of the comma—*before this purpose cool*. The door of thought is opened momentarily, and the trauma of the recent experience shakes him:

> But no more sights. (183)

The thought was a sudden blow to Irving, who spoke it with concentrated intensity, and, after a quick order to Lenox, hurried out. Reinhardt began, *But* . . . then looked around, his hand hid his eyes, and he shuddered, before he finished. Scofield's controlled voice suddenly rose to a fierce, agonized outburst, his hand also across his eyes; only after a deep breath could he master himself, and order Lenox to bring him to *these gentlemen*. Hackett, who had been struggling with himself, trying to bolster his courage, suddenly with a wild cry, as if warding off more apparitions, almost collapsed; he pulled himself together, laughed half-hysterically, then assuming a soldier's dignity, he forced a final tone of absolute firmness—though, on his exit, he threw one fearful look back at the witches' chamber.

Macbeth carries us now to the apex of his murderous resolve—and we will not see him again until V, iii. Hamlet makes a similar resolve at the end of IV, v: "My thoughts be bloody, or be nothing worth," and also disappears for a long period; and Coriolanus, after committing himself to action with the Corioli, also is not seen for some four hundred lines. Critics may be tempted to draw, from such parallels, generalizations about Shakespeare's writing habits, or guesses that Burbage told the playwright to please give him a rest at this point in the plays. But Shakespeare will not fit neat patterns: Othello likewise resolves, in IV, i, to act—to kill Desdemona—but he continues to appear through most of the remaining scenes; while Lear, who is also absent through the long gap after III, vi, is too feeble for resolve. Antony, unstable of resolution, is in and out of *Antony and Cleopatra* until his death. In each case, Shakespeare finds a different thrust that sustains interest in the hero during any hiatus: Hamlet's advance into the danger of the English voyage; the murderous pursuing of Lear, who can flee only by the help of friends; with Coriolanus the ominous prospect of war against his home; with Antony, the tug of war with Rome and with Cleopatra. With Macbeth, attention and expectation are kept alive by his bloody resolve, as it will affect others—including his wife—and by the mystery of the oracles.

Act IV, Scene ii

From the spectacular turbulence of the witches' pit, we are transported, in a flash, to simple domesticity. In the Globe the Sisters, with their super-natural paraphernalia, may have vanished in an inner compartment, leaving Macbeth bewilderedly on the outer platform; at his exit, with Lenox, the stage clears for the sudden transition to an unexpected glimpse of two strang-ers, and a familiar thane:

> *Enter Macduff's wife, her son, and Ross.*

Shakespeare's quick cut to the unexpected scene forces the spectator's mind to engage, to adjust to a new situation and assimilate it into the play's past. Nowhere in this scene is Macduff's name mentioned; but warned as we were of Macbeth's intention, our challenged minds begin to identify place and strangers. The Lady's first, meaningful monosyllabic line helps, relating the present to echoes of remembered dialogue:

> What had he done, to make him fly the land? (3)

This, then, must be the castle of Macduff. His wife's thought is that he must have *done* something: *doing*, in *Macbeth*, can imply crime, and imminent punishment. So Macduff had to *fly*—the word intensifies the motif of speed, confirms the Lady's suspicion that her husband has had to escape for some act committed. She, like Lady Macbeth, does not fully know her husband's plans.

Shakespeare characterizes Macduff in patches: a glimpse here, a glimpse there. Now, the abandoned, bewildered Lady Macduff angrily conveys one such glimpse. In refutation, since Macduff becomes a heroic avenger, apol-ogists have looked for noble explanations for his flight. Thus Bradley, often so insightful about Shakespeare's characters, but tempted sometimes to imag-ine for them extra-textual personality attributes, proposes that Macduff de-parted without a loving leavetaking for fear his purpose would give way.

Another critic, fitting the case determinedly into a Christian context, deviates even further from sense. He assumes that Macduff lets his "dear wife" think that he loves his family not, to "leave her the unconscious possessor of her best defense against the instruments of darkness, her innocence of his plan. His wisdom is unavailing . . . but when the news of the slaughter comes he has his reward. He knows at last the spiritual identity of his enemy." No such impulses—even as rationalizations—occur in the text to Macduff, who calls himself sinful for what he has done, and who never shows himself willing to pay so high a price to recognize an enemy he had already identified.

From the design Shakespeare has drawn to this point, Macduff is a highly emotional man who, for motivations (some canvassed above) that the actor and critic must intuit in terms of the whole play, has refused to join in Macbeth's investiture, or attend his court, long before Macbeth's tyranny has surfaced. To whatever impulses have been sensed then—of quick hostility, resentment, envy, suspicion—is now added the understandable questioning of his nature by his wife. Furness cites W. Leighton as objecting to the authenticity of the scene, partly because Macbeth

> should be opposed by a spotless champion of good and right, and not by one
> suffering in reputation under such accusations as his wife makes against the
> fugitive thane.

But Shakespeare, in his significant characterizations, is too much an artist to dabble in spotlessness.

Lady Macduff has her whole portrait drawn in this one brief scene. She is furious at her husband; and yet, if the son's intuition is true, as it seems to be, Macduff is far from dead to her. She can complain forthrightly to Ross; deal tenderly and humorously with her son; ask God's protection for him; after the warning of danger to her, grasp a vision of the world in which innocence is defenseless; speak bravely and boldly to ruffians; and run in fright. She is someone to be trusted, both in her overt declarations, and in the occasional subtextual implications of the opposite in her masked feelings.

In her likenesses and differences, she importantly refracts Lady Macbeth in Shakespeare's design. She is a wife being separated from a husband driven to manipulate power. Like Lady Macbeth, she has known what it is to nurse a child. Neither entirely understands her husband, and here similarity and difference interlace: Lady Macbeth believes her husband is overfull of the milk of humankindness, and learns better; Lady Macduff believes her husband lacks natural affection, and does not live to learn better. The two Ladies interestingly exemplify the complexity of Shakespearean character dialectic. We first see Lady Macbeth thinking of her husband's ambition, and how to further it; she must deny her femininity to help him—them—to the highest degree; she turns ruthless in pursuit of their joint ambition. We first see Lady Macduff blaming her husband, thinking of herself, and her children; yet her "femininity" remains uppermost in her design.

To Strindberg, Lady Macduff seemed like a fishwife, with low, shabby language; more often she is seen, by contrast with Lady Macbeth, as exclusively a gentle, tender mother, a "representative," in Fletcher's words, of "loyalty and domestic affection." But Lady Macbeth is this, in her own way: Shakespeare is not showing two extremes of female personae, but, as so often with his complex characterization, two who share some basic qualities and impulses, but diverge in others. Poel speculated that if Lady Macduff had been Macbeth's wife, Macbeth would never have murdered Duncan; but, as Speaight observed, Poel was careful to avoid the easy contrast between a woman and an Amazon, rather projected the more subtle contrast between two who were alike in domestic affection, and even, possibly, their physical habit, but who differed in their moral sensibility. Guthrie imagined Lady Macduff a big woman, much like Lady Macbeth, who would give the murderers a good run for their money; she has been played as a "spirited Highland lass" (Canada). Hall envisioned her as different from Lady Macbeth in being an essentially instinctive woman, who speaks what she feels, without the overlay of calculation: his Sheila Allen was a shower of many quick feelings. Byam Shaw's notes for his Olivier *Macbeth* imagined her "simple, sweet" (and so she has been played), but under his direction Maxine Audley, far from a "sweet, appealing soul," was impressively characterful, a woman of noble bearing, with a passionate, sometimes even strident, resentment against her husband, yet with a "scarcely hidden pride" in him.

The domestic climate of the scene is affirmed immediately at the entrance, showing for the first time a mother and child together—archetypal images of filial affection. For the first time, as Byam Shaw noted, we will hear childish laughter. The Folio stipulates here only one Son, but since elsewhere the Messenger, and Macduff, will speak of pretty—or little—*ones*, some stagings have introduced two or even three children to intensify the mood of innocence that will be terrorized. A babe particularly has been included as—even more than Macduff's sturdy boy—the living symbol of the hope that mortal nobility is possible; and as an echo of the infant in IV, iii. Rocked in arms, or prepared for bed, the child is a promise of sweet sleep and carefree wakening. So, in the Weaver staging: a young boy and a girl playing with a ball, a babe given a sponge bath by a nurse. Byam Shaw also brought on his Lady with three children, two sons and a babe cradled in her arms. In Nunn's chiaroscuro staging, Lady Macduff, dressed in pure white, standing in front of an archetypal white plaster madonna that she seemed to resemble, held as her second child an infant—also in a white wrap. Children of any age to play, do: so a daughter entered first in the Rigg–Hopkins scene, humming a tune; the boy crept in behind her, surprised her, made her jump; she cried, a servant soothed her, and both left; the boy sat down to read, awaiting his mother.

More often stagings follow the Folio direction, saving the evidence of other children until final offstage cries. The one boy is young, may be reminiscent in age of Fleance, whom Macbeth also meant to kill. He very often carries a wooden sword, in his hand or belt: Byam Shaw's entered bashing chairs about with his toy weapon. Gielgud's carried a real sword, as if his father's, which he polished as he listened to his mother and Ross. Or other toys occupy the boy: Quayle's trailed a ball on a string, and jerked it along after him; Tree's played gaily on a garden swing, in a sunny orchard; a boy in Rome rode a rocking horse.

Ross' answer to Lady Macduff measures the intensity of her reproach of Macduff for his flight: *You must have patience. . . . He had none:* she retorts, impatiently, her phrases short, sharp. He was treacherous to his family out of fear, she says. Ross adopts the play's dialectic mode, avoiding statement, inconclusively balancing opposites—

> You know not
> Whether it was his wisdom, or his fear. (9)

Ross acts as ambiguously as he speaks. He clearly knows—or suspects—more than he will say. Most charitably, he may be intuited as caught in the courtier-politician's need to avoid commitment to a side not in power; at the other extreme is Libby's conviction that Ross the villain came to lead Macbeth's gang of murderers—and Polanski, on this cue, showed the scoundrel piously wording Lady Macduff, then arranging for the castle's doors to be opened to the assassins. Shakespeare's clues again suggest another man—a small one—divided between conscience and commodity.

Lady Macduff, given no reason to see wisdom in her husband's unexplained flight, continues her attack, sustaining threads begun in her first speech. Her first *fly*, which she now repeats, suggests fear and flight; but it also leads her to the bird images by which she proclaims the unprotected vulnerability of the *wife* and *babes* (this reminds us there are several) left behind. For a moment we return to the innocent, procreant—but precarious—climate of the temple-haunting martlet of I, vi.

> He loves us not,
> He wants the natural touch. For the poor wren
> (The most diminutive of birds) will fight,
> Her young ones in her nest, against the Owl: (12–15)

Like Ross, she speaks in opposites: *all . . . fear, nothing . . . love; little . . . wisdom . . . against all reason*. Macduff will spearhead the revenge on "unnatural" Macbeth; but in the tangled yarns Shakespeare weaves, Macduff seems "unnatural" to his wife—he who was, we will learn, born "unnaturally."

Ross calls her *dearest cuz*, but can speak only roundabout regarding Macduff, whom he calls noble, judicious, best knowing. Ross hardly comforts the Lady by taking up one of her own dark words, seeming to confirm Macduff's treachery (though he may aim at himself, too):

> . . . cruel are the times, when we are traitors
> And do not know ourselves: when we hold rumor

> From what we fear, yet know not what we fear,
> But float upon a wild and violent sea
> Each way, and move. (23–27)

This voices Ross' own turbulence as well as his world's—and reflects, at a remove, Macbeth's experience. Action seems fateful, controlled by wayward incomprehensible forces that confuse us even as to whom we are, what we should do and be. From our uncertain, indefinable fears we know only rumor; we drift helpless *each way, and move*. Complicating Ross' immediate situation is a familiar Shakespearean uncertainty that underlies much of the play's later action: what is "loyalty," what "treachery," to a king unfit to rule?

Ross' last lines have given trouble, and if syntactical emendations are felt necessary, Capell's "And move each way" or Steevens' "And each way move," will do. But the Folio makes sense as conveying Ross' upset mind, that grows more troubled as his metaphor grows, so that his saying . . . *and move* becomes a verbal and aural correlative to his felt sense of a restless, threatening instability. That the phrase does bring his feeling to a climactic apprehension that may force him to interrupt himself (so some editors have followed the line with a breaking—) seems evident in his sudden switch to the decision to leave.

He promises to come again, offering what little consolation Lady Macduff may get from the assurance that *Things at the worst will cease*—that is, they will get no worse—or perhaps return to what they were. He turns then to the boy, who has often been kept apart in staging, so that he will not hear the adults' anxieties—though his dialogue will suggest that his ear has been attentive. In the first of the scene's many invocations to heaven, Ross blesses the *pretty cousin*, and is sometimes seen to kiss the boy, who welcomes affection. Tree's boy had come close to get his kiss, had then knelt caringly at his mother's feet; Quayle's crept up to Ross, and rubbed his face on Ross' sleeve, the gesture hinting at how much he missed his father.

Lady Macduff does not miss the chance, in the antinomic pattern, to blame Macduff:

> Father'd he is,
> And yet he's fatherless. (32–33)

Ross suggests that he is so moved he is ready to weep—though his words may suggest to the Libby-minded a level of darker meaning:

> I am so much a fool, should I stay longer
> It would be my disgrace, and your discomfort. (34–35)

For whatever reason, he will hurry to take his leave *at once*, after, sometimes, exchanging a quick kiss with Lady Macduff. He may take one last look back, as Piscator's did. In Japan, the boy waved his wooden sword to Ross in farewell.

Mother and small son are left together, in a rare scene for Shakespeare. Only Hermione's exchange with Mamillius in *Winter's Tale* matches its tone, and that passes almost as soon as it begins. This scene is the more domestic for its prose, of the kind, Milton Crane observes, that ordinary people might use. And indeed the Folio identifies her simply as *Wife*, the boy as *Son*.

As Lady Macduff watches her boy, her feelings are divided between her anger-love for Macduff, and her care for her child. The complex of her emotion is channeled into her bitter-humorous first words:

> Sirrah, your father's dead,
> And what will you do now? How will you live? (37–38)

Her gestures often belie her overt declaration: so Phelps' Lady fell on her knees to the boy; Bernhardt's was tender, trying to hide her sad fears and forebodings in cheerful prattle; Reinhardt's, at first musing, looking into the distance, scratching the boy's hair, turned to him with a face made merry, and pressed his head to her cheek. A Japanese Lady gave her Son an apple, he put his arm around her neck, and sat beside her.

The boy answers, innocently enough, *As birds do,* which she turns into her joke: *What with worms and flies?* * The winged imagery is pursued through several lines, from different angles. *Poor bird,* the Lady says, meaning pathetic, easily trapped; but this time he turns her meaning against her, giving *poor* the meaning of insignificant:

> *Poor* birds they are not set for: (46)

Under her acknowledging, melancholy chuckle, and in words that reprise the motif of difference between what is said and meant, he brings up a subject lying deeper in his loyal heart:

> My father is not dead for all your saying. (47)

Yes he is, she says; and turns away further talk of Macduff with her sad jesting about how to get another father. At length he must ask a question that may have been seen to lodge in his mind when he overheard the earlier talk:

> Was my father a traitor, mother? (55)

Dover Wilson assumed this talk was specifically included in reference to the conspiracy involving Father Garnet discussed in connection with II, iii. Empson thought the atmosphere of civil war was warrant enough for the dialogue. But certainly it needs no topical reference for its feeling, its power, and for the joke it prepares:

> the liars and swearers are fools: for there are liars and swearers enough, to beat the honest men, and hang up them. (66–68)

---

*Her entirely practical answer seems to controvert the suggestion that the son is thinking of Matthew 6:26: "Behold the fowls of the air . . . your Heavenly Father feedeth them." If the Biblical allusion *was* intended, and the son makes some allusive gestures to Heaven or its Book, this would be another instance in the scene of a misplaced trust in divine protection.

The boy is witty, but plausible in the simplicity and repetition of his words and the violence of the thought behind them (Reinhardt's, for instance, did not simply cap the Lady's line, but considered carefully, finger to cheek, before he made his *mot*).

Once more an appeal is made to heaven that will be ignored:

Now God help thee, poor Monkey: (69)

Lady Macduff prays, and returns to her own obsession: *How wilt thou do for a father?* The boy is shrewd enough to know that she would weep for his father, dead; and this very wisdom may start her tears. *Poor prattler.* . . . Reinhardt's Lady turned her eyes up, as it were silently imploring heaven, and put her hands protectively round the boy's head; he nestled against her.

This peak moment of tender warmth is broken, urgently, by the inrush of the Messenger. He will twice wish the Lady and her children heavenly protection, beginning

Bless you fair dame: (76)

On stage he has been a young servant, an old man (*the* Old Man), an ancient shepherd. In a Prague *Macbeth*, Seyton brought the warning—a touch Hodek thought very effective. The Messenger's blank verse suits his simple person, as does his naive concern. There is dignity in his offer of a *homely man's advice:* in a way different from a killer's, he dares do what becomes a man. When his urgent warning that she and her *little ones* (again a tender reminder of more than one) must leave the place frightens her, he is apologetic, thinks himself *too savage;* but not to warn her would be worse. The McKellen Messenger, in his zeal, tried to seize the Lady and her child, to move them forcibly to escape; when, frightened, she resisted and drew away, he made his apology. The man senses imminent assault (his urgency to get away parallels Ross') and he must hurry out, but not before he once more calls upon divine protection:

Heaven preserve you . . . (83)

Lady Macduff is alarmed, and we with her. Some sound is often heard, off— a whistle, with Reinhardt—to intensify the mood of encroaching danger. The Lady becomes a visual image of vulnerability, looking about her, to her child, to the heavens—a *poor wren. Whether should I fly?* repeats the image of a winged fugitive, perhaps with a reminiscent emphasis on *I.*

> I have done no harm. But I remember now
> I am in this earthly world: where to do harm
> Is often laudable, to do good sometime
> Accounted dangerous folly. (86–89)

It is a bitter philosophy, ending with her awareness that professing harmlessnes is a vain *womanly defence.* In her reverse mirroring of Lady Macbeth, this is the most ironic moment.

Sometimes the Lady attempts flight: so Gielgud's began to ready her boy, taking his sword and putting it down, throwing his cloak around him, and kneeling to fasten it; Reinhardt's started up the stairs, heard a whistle in that direction, came down uncertainly, tried to fly across the stage. It is always too late.

The invasion of the murderers is sometimes ominously suspended. In Tearle's *Macbeth*, the audience could watch the slow, sinister creeping of the murderers, from the pit and from the wings, toward their victims. In the Meiningen, Lady Macduff was paralyzed by the sight of the intruder coming down on her, step by step. Huge horned shadows darkened the wall behind Welles' Lady, signaling encroachment. Or the marauders burst into the room (Olivier), facing their victims in an intense, startled hush.

What are these faces? (92)

Lady Macduff asks, in a voice that may well break with fear (Reinhardt). We may recognise the men as the murderers of Banquo—or as other men seen about Macbeth—with Seyton sometimes in the lead. Or they may be vizarded: Nunn's were faceless, thick stocking masks blurring their features. Lady Macduff herself may recognize, and be shocked by, the faces. In this house, as in all others, Macbeth keeps a *servant fee'd*. We make the connection if we see such a man, at a signal, open for the murderers the barred gate through which Ross left, and then join them. The attack on the family may even come from the servants. Travis Bogard remembers, in the Hordern *Macbeth*, the castle's guards standing as if protectively during the first part of the scene; and then, after Ross and the Messenger had left, ominously transforming into murderers, closing in ruthlessly on the frightened innocents.

The threat in the Murderer's question, *Where is your husband?* rouses the protectiveness of the wife: she answers, as all actresses have, boldly, bravely, however much fear underlies her audacity.

<blockquote>
I hope in no place so unsanctified,
Where such as thou may'st find him. (95–96)
</blockquote>

The suggestion is that in a sanctified place Macduff will be safe: again an allusion to the protection of heaven, she trusting it. She can only be answered with violence. Shakespeare, having built to a moment of horror, compresses his climax, the echoing words and motifs jammed into a few short, abrupt lines, and convulsive action. When the speaking Murderer calls Macduff a traitor, the boy fires out like a young warrior:

Thou liest thou shag-ear'd villain. (98)

The Murderer's abrupt, rough speech projects the familiar babe-bird imagery (that Macduff will resume in the next scene):

               What you egg?
               Young fry of treachery? (99–100)

Like an egg, the boy is smashed.

Visually as well as verbally Shakespeare orchestrates, in cruel dissonance, the counter-struggle of the young against the old—the other side of Macbeth's killing of the patriarch. The horror of the scene is explicit, lacking even the cover of darkness imagined for Banquo's quick murder. Shakespeare tests the aesthetic limits of terror for a specific purpose: to visualize Macbeth's violence. For Banquo's murder there had been at least the explanation—if not excuse—of ambition, and the lurking threat of a dangerous rival; here killing is pitiless, meaningless, wild. The eighteenth century could not easily bear the scene: Garrick's version cut off at the Messenger's warning (following the pattern of Davenant's unspeakable adulteration here), but the prompter-marked Folger edition eliminates the whole scene, and it was generally deleted until Phelps tried to revive it in the next century, and had to drop it. Bernhardt deserves credit for insisting on its restoration in the 1880s; but as late as 1904 Parrott could note that the scene was usually cut, "since our modern nerves would be too greatly shocked by the murder of a child."

At stake, clustered around the image of the babe, is, as Brooks observed, the survival of those enlarging forces which make life meaningful. When they are threatened with extinction, the audience itself is. Our hopes move with the boy and his pitiful wooden toy against the image of terror. We dread the unbearable, hope for some miracle, perhaps some relenting, some victory of babe-won pity. In staging, this is always one of the play's most powerful moments. Thus the Olivier scene:

> The boy made his ungainly run across the stage, a puny, unplanned, forlorn attempt at defence. A blow with the hilts, a thrust. The murderer hung back, as if himself aghast at what he had done, leaving the boy standing in midstage, with both hands huddled over his wound. For a long moment he hung, wavering, then crumpled slowly to the ground. There was a still silence, a long, shocked silence, before the first animal scream broke from his mother. This was hitting below the belt, but that is precisely what Shakespeare intended to do. It is not until this moment that the full horror of Macbeth's actions bursts upon the audience. (David)

The violence of the child-murder, Granville-Barker thought, should be very deliberate:

> The thing is so abhorrent that we are apt to try and gloss it over in action. This is a mistake. The dramatic enormity is belittled by the open-eyed, heroic readiness with which the child faces death. This heroism strikes the note on which the scene must end.

That the boy's heroism makes the final impression, rather than the tyrant's violence, is questionable; but the point of the explicit killing is well-made. As with Banquo's murder, the action must be swift but not blurred, with moments allowed for reaction to the acts of violence.

At the first sight of the Murderers, Lady Macduff has drawn her boy to her instinctively (Reinhardt), put protective arms around him (Phelps). The Son, at the first frightening advance, may have momentarily retreated, if only to stand before his mother (Hopkins); with Olivier, when the younger brother dropped his sword and ran to the refuge of his mother's skirt, the older boy shielded both of them before attacking. Often the Son charges at the assassins, with his wooden sword, or with his fists. Reinhardt's Murderer laughed at the boy's rush, stabbed him, and pushed the body away with his foot. The killing itself may be attenuated, one Murderer holding the Lady's hands behind her back, a second seizing the struggling boy, laughing and teasingly ruffling his hair—then deliberately stabbing him (Hopkins). Somewhat similarly, McKellen's Murderer began by dandling the boy on his knee, then suddenly knifed him in the back. Quayle's murderer caught and upturned the little boy, and stabbed him, holding him by the heels, suggesting the image of the newborn infant. When Gielgud's boy jumped on one of the Murderers, the man killed him and threw the body to his accomplice, while he moved toward Lady Macduff. In Japan, two Murderers, led by Seyton, articulated the scene by killing the Son in slow motion, as he stood against them holding a sword in one hand, his apple in the other.

The dying boy calls out

> He has kill'd me, Mother,
> Run away I pray you. (101–102)

This reversal of Banquo's murder, where the parent urged the child to flee, delicately challenges Lady Macduff. She is now the *poor wren* whose young are threatened by the murderous *owl*. The stage direction has her *Exit crying Murder*. One simple technical condition facing Shakespeare was the need, unless an inner curtain was drawn, to get dead bodies off stage. The Murderer could easily and plausibly carry off the boy; the larger actor playing the Lady might be more of a problem. Stagings have avoided the killings on stage with the murderers dragging both the mother and boy off, screaming (Phelps), or with the mother snatching up the son and fleeing, their death cries heard offstage (Rogers). But the boy's plea to his mother is a character test that must not be shirked. Her courage may well falter in the face of these fierce men. She may be momentarily paralyzed by the horrible sight of her son's murder; then have to flee for her life (Reinhardt). She may go to clasp the dying boy, find him dead, and then flee (Hopkins). She may start toward him, face the menace of the resolute murderers, and run to save the lives of her other children. If the others are on stage, she may catch up one, and pull the other along with her, the murderer pursuing (Olivier).

Lady Macduff herself is sometimes seen killed. In a particularly violent staging (Weaver), one murderer strangled her, one picked up the little girl and seemed to break her back, one held the boy in the tub where he was bathed, and slit his throat. In one staging (England, 1966) the Lady was killed on stage, and the scene ended as, dying, she reached out for her son's hand.

This kind of effect is possible in stagings using curtains or blackouts for ending scenes. Under these circumstances, the Son may be left on the stage: so Reinhardt's, whimpering as he died. Diverse comments have been made by closing gestures. Violence and vandalism have been gratuitous: the white plaster statute that in Nunn's staging resembled Lady Macduff was smashed; in the Polanski film, the children's toys were knocked about. One of Gielgud's Murderers paused as he was leaving, to steal a ring from the dead Lady Macduff's finger. But a "good" murderer, in Dunn's staging (the same who resisted the idea of Fleance's killing) stopped at the Son's body, picked up the boy's wooden sword, looked at it, at the boy, then slowly, gently, lifted the child and carried him off.

Whatever the violence on stage, Macbeth's savagery is aurally confirmed from offstage as well, partly in Lady Macduff's screaming exit, often in other shrieks and dying cries off: the stifled wail of an infant (Hopkins), the moan of ravaged women—rape, made explicit in the Polanski film, may be extrapolated in the theatre from the behavior of the murderers as they pursue Lady Macduff, in another association of violence with sexuality. The cry of persecuted children or women announces innocence defiled and destroyed: a silent Tearle murderer, left holding the corpse of the dead boy, stiffened at hearing such sounds offstage. They may hang in the air: only dying as Malcolm and Macduff enter for the next scene (Quayle).*

Some critics have regarded IV, ii unfavorably, and even doubted that Shakespeare wrote it. The violence partly explained its long absence from the stage: Gentleman called it "farcically horrid . . . with great justice omitted." The "prattle" of the boy has particularly offended "decorum." Strindberg found the dialogue absurd; to Liddell it, and the murder "in broad daylight in full sight of the audience," does not sound like Shakespeare; if the playwright wrote it, he was, like Homer, nodding. Cunningham considered that the scene perhaps "violates the modesty of art." Paul called it "a disagreeable scene at best, written without fervor." L. B. Campbell evaded

*Where stage curtains are not used, any remains of the scene must be shifted before the audience's eyes. Twentieth century audiences, used to this, were still somewhat taken aback when the Murderers in the Guinness *Macbeth* became scene-changers; curiously English audiences some eighty years before were similarly surprised when Bernhardt's assassins performed the task. *Plus ça change* . . .

the issue squarely: "Whether Shakespeare could write badly enough to write [this scene] I shall leave others to dispute."

Campbell did allow that it sustained her favorite theme: fear. It also carries on multiple other threads woven throughout the design, as observed in my discussion. It poses an image of womanhood that enriches, by likeness and dissimilarities, the characterization of Lady Macbeth, and of the human condition itself under stress. For a moment it charmingly relieves the fierce tension of tragic action, only to twist it tighter. It insists on that savagery of Macbeth that has been half-hidden from us; we are made to confront the darkness in a figure whose crime as well as suffering we have been drawn to share. And it intensifies the motif, intermittently touched on earlier, of the silence of God. Time and again, in this scene, surely not accidentally, the blessings and help of the Heavens are implored—perhaps even with ritual gestures of the cross, of prayer, or of benediction—for these innocents; but if God looks down, he does not take their part.

Act IV, Scene iii

Enter Malcolm and Macduff.

Now the pounding rush of what has gone before decelerates. Quiet meetings ended the previous two acts, but neither involved anything like the sustained encounter that will now develop. The scene's relative austerity led Chateaubriand to single it out as an example of great writing; but the sharp change in mood has tempted some critics to find it inferior as drama: Shakespeare only wanted to give the Macbeth-actor a rest; or the characters are not meant to be motivated, or convincing as realistic personae; or the scene abandons realism for symbolic experiment; or its unity is poetic or historical rather than dramatic; or it provides choral comment rather than dramatized action.

This criticism is based on hindsight. If we know the outcome, we may be tempted to agree that Malcolm's antics with Macduff are "tedious," a "dull . . . perfunctory paraphrase from Holinshed"; a conventional exercise in deception leading without suspense to a foregone conclusion. To the *naive* spectator, however, the first half of the scene points dangerously to possible disaster, and the later part is charged with emotion.

Visually the scene promises immediately a changed quality of experience. We are in England: and we may know this not only by the presence of Malcolm, to whom Macduff is come, but perhaps also by English flags, and guards in distinctive English uniform, who may intensify the sense of danger to Malcolm by the way they watch over him. He may have to gesture them away to confer with Macduff. Traditionally, as with Kemble and Macready, the English countryside has been suggested; specifically a lovely lane, for Tree; with a summery pool and foliage, for Irving. A green world fits this first image of the burgeoning of resistance to Macbeth; and a place in the sun is implied by Malcolm's first melancholy urging that they seek instead *some desolate shade*. The garden sense of England has been made real with vernal properties and backdrops; or stylized, as in Hall's staging, with an enormous green veil, dropped from the flies, backing a simple warm wooden bench and table.

Alternatively, stagings sometimes follow the Garrick pattern of a palace interior: though here, too, an English brightness may illuminate the scene: Reinhardt displayed distinctive heraldic ornaments and, for the first time, pleasant colors. The absence of lightness was objected to in the Vilar *Macbeth:* Jacquot wished for some touches of "pure air," something to match the gracious exterior of Inverness. Among unusual settings was one in Prague, in a sailor's tavern; Bergman's 1948 background was a graceful courtly dance; in a German staging (1834) influenced by Tieck, Malcolm mourned indeed in the shadow of a tree.

Malcolm immediately sets the tone of the scene. He will act the fox so well that Macduff, a man represented as easily sceptical, absolutely believes him. Casson wanted Malcolm to play his guile as fairly broad comedy, so the audience can know he is pulling Macduff's leg; but this would diminish Macduff, and seems far from the spirit of the scene, as well as the craftsmanship. More likely Shakespeare intended, as Hall suggested, that the audience as well as Macduff be deceived by Malcolm's surface. The young prince may be seen as more mature than in II, iii; where a substantial passage of time has been suggested, he will have grown in years, may be played by an older actor, as in Craig's staging.

Even as Malcolm first urges a dark retreat, where he and Macduff can *weep our sad bosoms empty,* he is convincing, but—we will understand later—deliberately acting his chosen role. However noble his motive, guileful he remains, his behavior of a piece with the equivocation pervasive in the play. He now says what later he will say is not; when can we trust him? At the scene end, we may look back and realize how calculatedly he now manages Macduff, and how carefully—or guiltily—he has watched for his effects. Olivier's Malcolm could be seen to give Macduff a "mental look" as he began his dissimulation; Sothern's Malcolm could not face Macduff, but looked away.

We first see in Malcolm only the sad young man—nothing of the shrewd diplomat who will after a while reveal that he has already arranged for English military support. Macduff's response—he will briefly reverse positions later—is to urge battle rather than grief, to retrieve the terrible suffering of *our downfall birthdom*—the babe image comes fittingly to his lips. Malcolm at once switches from mourner to sceptic, mixing passionate reason and self-pity. In a world of equivocal appearances, he will believe only what he knows. In light of his own masking, there is buried irony in his reminding Macduff—and us—that men are not what they seem:

> This tyrant, whose sole name blisters our tongues,
> Was once thought honest: you have lov'd him well,
> He hath not touch'd you yet. (16–18)

This partly explains Shakespeare's variation from Holinshed, in having Macduff leave Scotland *before* the massacre of his family: it gives Malcolm more reason to doubt. He is able to see himself, in self-pitying, apocalyptic terms, as potentially a sacrifice to wicked collusion:

> a weak, poor, innocent lamb
> T'appease an angry God. (20–21)

The *angry God* is a curious, powerful image, suggesting a dark divinity countering beneficence in the play. Macduff angrily denies treachery; Malcolm knows Macbeth is treacherous, and suggests that any man might be—a verbal statement of what we have seen dramatized—if high enough degree is at stake:

> A good and virtuous nature may recoil
> In an imperial charge. (24–25)

Macduff is affronted; Malcolm adroitly craves his pardon; he cannot tell the mind's construction in the most honest face; innocence must look fair, but fair may mask what is most foul:

> Angels are bright still, though the brightest fell.
> Though all things foul, would wear the brows of grace
> Yet Grace must still look so. (27–29)

Macduff, hopeless, is ready to leave, as he will be twice again. Malcolm plays him on a string, in a way that may be reminiscent of how Macbeth played Banquo. He checks Macduff with the terrible, inescapable question:

> Why in that rawness left you wife, and child?
> Those precious motives, those strong knots of love,
> Without leavetaking. (33–35)

Full stop. A pause for an answer. There is no answer, except silent, subtextual pain. This is Malcolm's second reference to the abandoned family: Shakespeare is insisting on this troubled note in Macduff's design. Macduff reacts bitterly, and Malcolm, citing his concern for his own safety, offers as appeasement a hollow apology:

> you may be rightly just,
> Whatever I shall think. (37–38)

It is in fact an insult: "You may be all right—for all I know." Almost as if avoiding the question about leaving his family, Macduff fires at the insinuation that he may not be *just;* he bids farewell—

> I would not be the villain that thou think'st . . . (43)

Malcolm reels him in again. *Be not offended:* . . . and shifts his tactics. "Young and unsure," Byam Shaw saw Malcolm; certainly the prince may be seen to be finding his way with Macduff, trying out grief, self-pity, suspicion. As the apparent sincerity of his passion grows, as he both rejects Macduff, and holds him from going, we sense some underlying objective, and now he seems to reveal it. (Later we will understand this next tactic as a ploy toward a still further goal; but for now, as Malcolm comes to a revelation about himself, it seems to be the point to which he has been moving.) The weak, poor, innocent lamb now discloses that he has in fact had the offer of *goodly thousands* of English troops for help, and believes he can count on support in Scotland; but alas, his *poor country* would suffer more from him than Macbeth—who would then be the one to seem the lamb compared to Malcolm's *confineless harms*. Macduff is bewildered at Malcolm's *It is myself I mean*. Sothern's Macduff laughed incredulously.

Shakespeare follows the drift of Holinshed here closely enough that he is sometimes accused of doing little more than putting the historian into blank verse. He does much more. Malcolm's "confession" curiously refracts our experience of Macbeth, in its mixture of boasting and self-denigration. Not only Malcolm's own self-comparisons with Macbeth, and his paralleling of both their vices; but also the very nature and intensity of his passionate admissions of corruption may rouse echoes of the grander figure. If Malcolm only pretends to Luciferian maldoing, he must pretend so trenchantly that for the time we must believe him as much as we believed Macbeth.

Later, when Malcolm reveals his duplicity, we will have been so convinced of his vices that we may doubt his recantation, as Macduff will. We may wonder at his superb skill as a player, and still sense something deeper. That Malcolm's design enables him to own, even in his imagination, the images of vice that come so readily to him, indicates that he is meant to know them in fantasy, if not in reality. The verisimilitude of his passion will not all be playing. Ian Richardson could be seen to blush as he asserted his vices; he said the blush came from the awareness of his (Malcolm's) capacity for corruption.

Malcolm is quick to suspect his own imagined vices in Macbeth. When Macduff argues that no devil in hell could top Macbeth's evil, Malcolm grants him

> bloody,
> Luxurious, avaricious, false, deceitful . . . (69–70)

As observed earlier, neither Shakespeare's words nor implied actions have given—or will give—any evidence of Macbeth's lasciviousness or avarice. Neither attribute seems fitted to the Macbeth of the introspective, doubt-ridden soliloquies, the Macbeth earnest to win golden opinion, the poet-philosopher, the king so concerned for courtly manner. The speech may be seen as deliberate deceit, a reflection of the spread, in Knights' words, of the central evil of the play. Malcolm may even be trying the questionable adjectives out on Macduff, and hurrying on when they are not instantly received. Hurry on he will, and we see why he chose these qualities—they are also the ones he will first claim vividly for himself. Thus he begins by describing his own voluptuousness, *The cistern of my lust*, right voluptuously.

Immediate problems in expectation have concerned *naive* spectators here. First: must Scotland face these alternatives for a king—satyr or tyrant? (Is there a third possibility . . . Fleance?) And then: how will Macduff take Malcolm's vice? Not easily, if he is as decent as we could wish: and we watch him hunt for his reaction. He begins with a kind of formal sermon against intemperance; having made that bow to morality, he proposes masking, echoing the cautions of Macbeth and his Lady: *seem cold* (the innocent flower); *the time you may so hoodwink* (beguile the time). Macduff—with some pain? some cynicism?—assures the prince that there will be willing women enough for his lusts. What kind of man is Macduff? What vision of order in Scotland are we presented?

Malcolm absorbs this. The audience does. Perhaps Malcolm was right:

> Better Macbeth,
> Than such an one to reign. (77–78)

Malcolm will not let Macduff rest. He challenges further, again testing Macduff's loyalty and compromising his morality. Malcolm's avarice is the subject, and it indeed fits a monster whose greed must destroy his kingdom, forging

> Quarrels unjust against the good and loyal,
> Destroying them for wealth. (97–98)

He is already, in fact, promising to *Pour the sweet milk of concord into hell;* and again Macduff—and we—are challenged by this confession of corruption in a young prince. Malcolm's avowal must seem, from its voicing, and from Macduff's response, worse than the first. After the pause in which Macduff swallows and assimilates his shock, he must note that this *sticks deeper;* then he moves by association from the penetration metaphor to a dark variation of the growth one: avarice does not have a passing season, but grows perversely stronger with time—

> with more pernicious root
> Than summer-seeming lust: (100–101)

Then Macduff launches into a perspective of Scots history that may have given some satisfaction to the English in the Globe audience, but, as observed earlier, (I, vi) could surely only have offended James: avarice

> . . . hath been
> The sword of our slain kings: (101–102)

That Shakespeare might have included, in a play specifically intended to please a Scotland-bred king, Holinshed's reference to the deadly crime— avarice—of Scots' rulers seems to me most unlikely, particularly considering James' own greedy absorption of English wealth.

The colon pause suggests that Macduff may be battling with himself before he yields; but yield he does, again in terms of growth imagery. To fill Malcolm's will, *Scotland hath foisons*—which suggests abundance, but Shakespeare's several uses in other plays have specific reference to growing things and their harvests. This vice in Malcolm, Macduff sighs, can be "endurable"—assuming a balance of better qualities.

The prince is forced to an even more rigorous test. The Malcolm-actor may feel that the design by now includes a justifiable suspicion at Macduff's readiness to accept so vicious a claimant to the throne; how can he paint himself any blacker? A sense of almost desperation may be felt to gather in him.

An irony that seems unintended in Holinshed has Malcolm assert, as an ultimate vice, his capacity for deceit, for dissimulation, for telling "leasings"—lies. This is the final straw for Holinshed's Macduff: it becomes clear to him that the choice must be between a bloody tyrant and a prince "so replete with the inconstant behaviour and manifest vices of Englishmen that he is nothing worthy." In another context Shakespeare might have used the Holinshed allusion to the English for a laugh; but the playwright is serious now; and he may have rejected deceit as the unacceptable acme of vice because he didn't think English audiences would believe it so important. The idea would be undercut anyway by young Macduff's joke about the liars and swearers outnumbering honest men. Shakespeare may have avoided the emphasis on deceit, finally, because Malcolm is even now engaged in highly skilled "leasings" and could hardly deny later that he was inexperienced in all the vices he had so convincingly enumerated.

Going beyond Holinshed's key vice, Shakespeare, to move Malcolm to the climax of the three-step beat, and test Macduff to the uttermost, has the prince deny *any* of his catalogue of kingly graces. This is a list more applicable to a saint than a ruler—and certainly almost conspicuously ill-fitting King James at some points.* It leaves out, among other essential qualities of kingship,

---

*Particularly at the time when, according to Paul, *Macbeth* was supposed to be prepared for the special delectation of James and his guest, King Christian of Denmark, James' reputation for *temperance* and *stableness* could hardly be high. Could court spectators have seriously compared Malcolm's ideal image with James, knowing what had happened at a recent royal dinner? By G. B. Harrison's(1) dating, this notorious event took place July 28, 1606. That would be just three days before *Macbeth* was possibly presented for the two kings at Greenwich, according to Paul, or ten days before the performance Paul imagines more likely for them at Hampton Court. Here is Sir John Harington's letter to Mr. Secretary Barlow:

  A great feast was held, and, after dinner, the representation of Solomon his Temple and the coming of the Queen of Sheba was made, or (as I may better say) was meant to have been made, before their Majesties. But alass! . . . The Lady who did play the Queens part, did carry most precious gifts to both their Majesties; but, forgetting the steppes arising to the canopy, overset her caskets into his Danish Majesties lap, and fell at his feet, tho I rather think it was in his face. Much was the hurry and confusion; cloths and napkins were at hand, to make all clean. His Majesty then got up and woud dance with the Queen of Sheba; but he fell down and humbled himself before her, and was carried to an inner chamber and laid on a bed of state; which was not a little defiled with the presents of the

the kind of practical "wisdom" Malcolm is now practising, and the insight into character that might have helped Duncan discover traitors and rebels, and protect his kingdom from disorder. Malcolm names the sweetly "fair" qualities to contrast with his succeeding catalogue of his almost every thinkable foul failing; he is testing Macduff with a self-portrait of absolute corruption. In so doing, he projects a paranoia that curiously echoes Macbeth's preference to chaos over frustration. The ostensible passion of Malcolm's pretended avowal, to be plausible, will show some of the same intensity in the mixture of boast and self-disgust, in the compulsive commitment to megalomanic satisfaction. Malcolm, like Macbeth, claims willingness to

> Uprore the universal peace, confound
> All unity on earth. (114–115)

Can even the iron-stomached Macduff—can we—accept this Malcolm-monster as an alternative to Macbeth? Macduff's first great wail, *O Scotland*, extends the moment of doubt. Does he only lament the inevitable? Will he yield again? Malcolm presses: is such a man *fit to govern?*

To what must be the player-Malcolm's evident relief, this final test Macduff passes, fiercely—sometimes, in the theatre, with an outburst almost equal to his reaction to Duncan's death.

Queen which had been bestowed on his garments; such as wine, cream, jelly, beverage, cakes, spices, and other good matters. The entertainment and show went forward, and most of the presenters went backward, or fell down; wine did so occupy their upper chambers. Now did appear, in rich dress, Hope, Faith, and Charity: Hope did assay to speak, but wine rendered her endeavours so feeble that she withdrew, and hoped the King would excuse her brevity: Faith was then all alone, for I am certain she was not joyned with good works, and left the court in a staggering condition: Charity came to the King's feet, and seemed to cover the multitude of sins her sisters had committed; in some sorte she made obeysance and brought giftes, but said she would return home again, as there was no gift which heaven had not already given his Majesty. She then returnd to Hope and Faith, who were both sick and spewing in the lower hall. Next came Victory, in bright armour, and presented a rich sword to the King, who did not accept it, but put it by with his hand; and, by a strange medley of versification, did endeavour to make suit to the King. But Victory did not tryumph long; for, after much lamentable utterance, she was led away like a silly captive, and laid to sleep in the outer steps of the anti-chamber. Now did Peace make entry, and strive to get foremoste to the King; but I grieve to tell how great wrath she did discover unto those of her attendants; and, much contrary to her semblance, most rudely made war with her olive branch, and laid on the pates of those who did oppose her coming.
A footnote in the 1804 edition of Harington's *Nugae Antiquae* adds, "Sir Edward Peyton [*History of the Stuarts*] makes a very sottish report of King Christian, and says that King James got so drunk with him at Theobalds, he was obliged to be carried to bed."
Assuming that this bibulous Danish king would sit through an English blank verse tragedy, and could understand it, we may wonder how he—and James—and the court—might have responded to a list of kingly qualities that included some so foreign then to either monarch. Indeed, if topical reference is to be hunted, Macduff might even be seen alluding reprovingly to the recent behavior of the two rulers:

> Boundless intemperance
> In Nature is a tyranny: it hath been
> Th'untimely emptying of the happy throne,
> And fall of many kings. (79–82).

No not to live. (119)

Into his outrage Macduff may be seen to release the suppressed revulsion evoked by Malcolm's first-and-second-step "confessions." His passion, that surges so instantly in his design, overflows: in grief for Scotland, and for the betrayal of Malcolm's good parents. Now indeed the furious Macduff—he has snarled, shouted, screamed his words—is ready to leave. On the stage only Malcolm's active physical intervention may stop him long enough to make him listen; and even so, Malcolm may again and again have to hold him from breaking away in his *noble passion*.

Malcolm begins his long speech of explanation as if he expects to win Macduff simply by saying his own doubts are dissipated. But he must do more: must claim again that Macbeth tried to trick him, offer to put himself into Macduff's *direction*, disavow any touch of all the vices he had claimed, declare that he had never before spoken falsely in his life. The virginal picture he projects is itself as extreme as the earlier corrupt one. Macduff may well still be sceptical; Malcolm finally holds out the promise of Siward's ten thousand men to march with them.

Macduff is stopped, but he does not respond. *Why are you silent?* Malcolm asks—as if he cannot understand how shocked the emotional man may be, trying to digest the kind of trickery Malcolm exposed him to, trying to distinguish the real from the pretended. Like Malcolm, Macduff wants to know before he believes. Macduff's answer, coming slowly, without acquiescence, paradigms the equivocal nature of the *Macbeth* world itself:

> Such welcome, and unwelcome things at once
> 'Tis hard to reconcile. (155–156)

Macduff may make a gesture of reconciliation, but he more effectively remains in evident doubt. His line, often spoken, Granville-Barker noted, with "tame puzzlement, is really the passionate half-choked utterance of a man still torn between hope and despair"—and, we may add, by an injured scepticism. Reinhardt's Macduff, when Malcolm smiled at him, tried to return the smile, but he was confused, his words came only slowly. When Benson's Malcolm extended a hand, Macduff refused to take it. Sothern's Macduff at first only looked at Malcolm, who finally dropped his offered hand; slowly, after speaking the last line, Macduff did shake hands.

Shakespeare apparently intended an incomplete ambiguous tension at the beat's end; for immediately after Macduff's non-committal response, the sudden diversion of the *Doctor*'s entrance prevents any resolution of the relationship with Malcolm. Macduff will make no avowal of loyalty to Malcolm in this scene—not, indeed, until the very end of the play—and he may resent some of the prince's forthcoming gestures. The playwright seems careful to preserve dramatic identity within the larger movement of men against Macbeth.

Why the Doctor interlude? It has sometimes been regarded as another sop to James, since it introduces the theme of the good English king who cures invalids with the "touch" of a pendant golden coin. This would more likely be a compliment to English custom than to James. James himself had the good sense to find touching "distasteful." He did not like, in any case, to be close to the common people: "Their caresses made him impatient that he often dispersed them with frowns, that we may not say with curses." He particularly disliked the diseased; and he came to the insight that "touching" was a superstitition—if not a blasphemy—in attributing divine power to a mortal. One of the conditions of his coming to England was that he would not touch for scrofula. But since the act was associated with English kingship, he was persuaded to it occasionally, though he would never make the sign of the cross over a sore, as Elizabeth had. He touched (but evidently not the diseased part) and came to hang coins—golden stamps—about the necks of the sick he treated. Paul, very fairly, went thoroughly into this matter, and inevitably observed James' dislike of the practice. But how does this square with Paul's thesis that Shakespeare wrote *Macbeth* to please James? The solution: "The king's councilors wished help in their effort to bring the king to their way of thinking concerning the royal touch." The hypothesis: the Acting Master of the Revels "told the author of the play of the king's disinclination to use the coin, and asked him if he would help to overcome these scruples . . . Perhaps [Shakespeare's lines] eased, even if they did not wholly set at rest, the king's scruples." Presumably James would be pleased to be instructed in kingship by the playwright, by being treated to a glorification of a practice he distasted. I find this unlikely.

A better explanation of Shakespeare's intent might be that, in his usual encompassing way, he was exploring in *Macbeth* every nuance of superstitious belief in the magical, and he recognized the concept of miraculous healing as one variation on the theme. So did intelligent contemporaries. Thus John Donne's curious catalogue of paradoxes, *Biathanatos*, glances at the irony that royalty can practice the magic of healing that otherwise was prohibited (although as we have seen in the case of Forman and "white witches," many Englishmen patronized outlawed medical sorcerers). Thus Donne's marginal note to his paradox: "Laws forbid ordinary men to cure by extraordinary meanes, yet the kings of *England*, and *France*, & *Spaine* cure so." The "cunning folk" (witches) used essentially the same technique as the kings—thus West's *Symboleography:*

> Juglers and Sleightie . . . for the curing of all sicknesses and sores of man and beast, use either certeine superstitious words or writings called charmes or spelles hanged about the neck or some other part of the body.

Reginald Scot describes some of these popular remedies:

> *To heale the King or Queens evill* . . . Remedies . . . is first to touch the place with the hand of one that died an untimely death. Otherwise: Let a virgine

fasting laie her hand on the sore, and saie; *Apollo* denieth that the heate of the
plague can increase, where a naked virgine quencheth it: and spet three times
upon it.

Clearly, as Thomas observes,

The religious ceremonies which surrounded the royal power of healing were
merely a protective framework for a more primitive piece of magic.

That some illnesses are beyond ordinary medical practice is a point Shakespeare will make differently in the next scene, to sustain the sense of separation between the mortal and the mysterious.

The complex dialectic of the play is further exercised in this "doctor"
interlude. Shakespeare now more and more will bring in touches of England
for his spectators, to their country's credit: by contrast with old Scotland,
where the king is a source of infection, old England is ruled by a saintly
leader-king, in a healthier kingdom. But Shakespeare dimensions fair with
foul even here: healthy as England seems, yet a disease—metaphorical as
well as literal?—*called the Evil** infects it. Extraordinary, ambiguous medicining, solicitations to heaven, are required to cure *strangely visited* Englishmen,

All swollen and ulcerous, pitiful to the eye,
The mere despair of surgery, (172–173)

Many are afflicted with the uncanny bane, for Malcolm has *often* seen the cure
effected (stagings have sometimes shown a crowd of the deformed here).
Though good presides, in the person of the English king, an *Evil* flourishes,
despite the good monarch's mysterious, occult power (*How he solicits heaven/
Himself best knows*). In a secondary paralleling of high and low magic, Malcolm
allows the English king a *heavenly gift of prophecy*—a glorified mirroring of the
Sisters' illicit, unheavenly gift. Heaven has apparently given sanctity to this
English king's hand; this same heaven will be questioned, in a few moments,
for looking down unmoved on the slaughter of innocents. Shakespeare can
almost always be counted on to see at least two sides of every coin he handles.

Before Macduff can question further, he notices an approach, and gestures
off—again, Shakespeare's classic way of moving audience eyes to an entrance.
Ross is at first far enough off for Malcolm to recognise him only, by the distinctive Scots dress, as *My countryman*. Macduff speaks directly to Ross,
anxious for news—of Scotland first. He is likely to rush to his *ever gentle
cousin*, and greet him warmly with word and touch and anxious look.

Ross' lament reprises insistent motifs. His first line ascribes to the nation
the uneasy identity of individuals (like Macbeth):

Alas poor country,
Almost afraid to know itself. (189–190)

---

*Various diseases were named "Evil"; but Shakespeare stipulates one: "*the* Evil."

Death is everywhere, growth frustrated; men die before their plucked flowers turn sere and yellow.

What happens now to Macduff becomes in the theatre one of the play's most effective, affecting scenes. He finally asks about his family: the sense may be that he has hesitated for fear of what he may learn. Ross is at first terse, equivocating—looking down, looking away. He cannot yet bring himself to tell the truth, so he speaks of the Macduffs as *well . . . well at peace:* if not lying, then in the double sense that the dead are well (thus Cleopatra, *Antony and Cleopatra* II, v, 33), free of life's fitful fever.

When Macduff presses, Ross changes the subject, still unable to break his news; he comes back to it, but still only indirectly, after his extended exchange with Malcolm, in a speech that, as Styan observes, demands a hushed voice:

> But I have words
> That would be howl'd out in the desert air, (224–225)

Macduff senses, in Ross' hesitant and evasive manner, what is unsaid, presses again, often seizing Ross:

> If it be mine
> Keep it not from me, (233–234)

I guess at it. So Ross tells the most terrible of facts. The shock to Macduff is seismic. Phelps' Macduff—in a day when gestures were large—fell insensible; he sank into Malcolm's arms. Sothern's fell back on a log, sat with his face in his hands. The most restrained Macduff winces with a pain readily shared by an audience in shock from the last scene's slaughter.

The incompleted reconciliation between Malcolm and Macduff may only be strained by Malcolm's response to Macduff's shock, dismay and silent grief. To hide the trauma and its accompanying tears, Shakespeare makes the stoical Macduff shield his face with his hat, in sorrow too deep, too private for words. Malcolm, again, cannot understand silence. Apostrophizing *Merciful heaven,* he urges the stricken man not to hide, but to speak, unload his grief.

Macduff ignores Malcolm. Instead he presses for any crumb of amelioration: *My children too? . . . And I must be from thence. My wife killed too?* Again, Malcolm tries to divert Macduff's honest grieving, to transform it to Malcolm's own purpose:

> make med'cines of our great revenge . . . (252)

In this context my intuition suggests that Macduff next means Malcolm as—again ignoring the prince to speak to Ross—he says:

> He has no children. (254)

Bradley, in his notes, considers three possibilities here: first, that Macduff means Macbeth, and is angry because he cannot in revenge kill Macbeth's children—an idea promptly dismissed. Second, that Macduff means Macbeth, who could never have ordered the killing of children if he had had any of his own. Third, the line refers to Malcolm who, if he had children, could not at this moment talk so easily of curing such a grief by revenge. Bradley decides for the third, partly because he sees a persuasive analogy to Constance's reply (*King John*, III, iv, 91) to Pandulph's remonstrance that she grieves too much: *He talks to me that never had a son.* "What Macduff does is precisely what Constance does." Beyond this compelling model, Bradley cites the bereaved father's feelings: "What could be more consonant with the natural course of the thought, as developed in the lines which follow, that Macduff, being told to think of revenge, not grief, should answer, 'No one who was himself a father would ask that of me in the very first moment of loss.'?"

The Variorum, canvassing a spectrum of criticism, cites about as many who refer the *He* to Macbeth as to Malcolm. I have already argued that Macbeth must be assumed to have children, in the absence of any denial, considering Lady Macbeth's declaration of her mother's role—a point which Leigh Hunt, among others, long ago made. In the theatre some Macduffs have alluded to Macbeth, some to Malcolm. The *New Monthly Magazine*, in 1828, complaining about one stage Macduff's implication that Macbeth was meant, argued for Malcolm, "who is so forward with his counsel to a heartbroken father"; Macduff means "that none but a stranger to the affections of a parent could talk of revenge as a cure for his sorrows." Hunt, too, saw Macduff turning away from Malcolm "as unable to understand a father's feelings," rather to Ross, for sympathy. When a Macduff of Kean's played it as Hunt suggested, the critic was impressed at the "deep and true effect . . . far beyond that which can be produced by any denunciation of impotent vengeance." What is conclusive, I think, is the context of tension already existing between Malcolm and Macduff, that continues as the younger man persists in misreading the depth and nature of his elder's grief. Youth is to conquer age in *Macbeth*, but is not always right; may be wrong, cruelly.

Macduff's broken speech touchingly echoes some child-and-bird images from the scene in his castle.

> Did you say all? Oh Hell-kite! All?
> What, all my pretty chickens, and their dam
> At one fell swoop? (255–257)

The last words have become a cliché; but to contemporaries accustomed to seeing a predatory bird's *fell swoop*, the image must have been terrifying. Macduff, pleading for better news, has fallen on his knees as if imploring Ross to say "No."

Again Malcolm tries to break into Macduff's private anguish with his didactic *Dispute it like a man*—a boy telling a tried warrior what manhood means, implying the kind of denial of feeling (though different in degree) that Lady Macbeth urged. What becomes a man, in Macduff's eyes, includes the emotional depth and sensitivity of one who loves. This speech, and the preceding, bring Macduff to a climax of his spoken grief that has moved audiences to tears and often thunderous applause in every country where its acting is recorded. Reports of performances that may mention no other detail will often comment on the heartfelt audience response to Macduff's laments. The words are simple, mainly monosyllabic, but they seem torn from the heart—in tortured sentences broken by four colons, as well as a question mark and semicolon.

> I shall do so:
> But I must also feel it as a man;
> I cannot but remember such things were
> That were most precious to me: did heaven look on,
> And would not take their part? (259–263)

One critic, intent on vindicating the ways of divinity to Shakespearean man, argues,

> Heaven took their part by leading Macduff to 'no place so unsanctified' that assassins could find him before he has done heaven's justice here.

This suggests that the murderers were doing the work of heaven, which was siding with the innocents by arranging for them to be slaughtered as the other side of a beneficent saving of Macduff to fight Macbeth's wrong. I doubt if the critic really believes in this kind of uneven-handed divine "justice"; surely the sense of uneven-handedness, whether heavenly or not, pervades the play, and never more than in the killing of the unoffending Macduffs, after the many pleas to divinity to preserve them. Macduff's own theology does not see divine justice, but another kind of dispensation. First he instinctively wonders that heaven could allow such slaughter; then, immediately, as if apprehensive of further harm from above, he finds a nearer scapegoat. So a Phelps Macduff had thrown up his arms as if to challenge heaven; then, with a thrill of horror at his blasphemy, crossed his arms in penitence. Macduff must try quickly to transfer the blame to himself: heaven allowed his dears to die because *he himself* was wicked, let them not be pursued with wrath beyond the grave:

> Sinful Macduff,
> They were all struck for thee: naught that I am,
> Not for their own demerits, but for mine
> Fell slaughter on their souls: heaven rest them now. (263–266)

Still once more Malcolm presumes to coach Macduff, urging that he *let grief convert to anger*, to *enrage* his *heart*. And again Macduff turns Malcolm off. He does not care for this instruction from the boy, and his feeling shows as he alludes to Malcolm's earlier adjuration to speak his grief:

> O I could play the woman with mine eyes,
> And braggart with my tongue. (269–270)

He prefers to address himself to the now *gentle heavens*, from whom he asks
nothing for Malcolm, or even Scotland, but only for the imminent chance to
confront Macbeth urgently:

> Within my sword's length set him, if he scape
> Heaven forgive him too. (273–274)

As observed earlier, Malcolm has been acted as the young Augustus,
shrewd and practical, under whose genius the imaginative, passionate Macbeth will be rebuked. Those two will not meet again; but in the encounter
between Malcolm and Macduff, a similar difference may be seen: Malcolm
the young but skilled fox, playing whatever role suits his purpose—sinner,
innocent, leader, mentor; and Macduff, emotional, impulsive, impatient
with unfeeling counsel. Shakespeare does not make a point of the absence of
any mention of Malcolm's own grief at the loss of a father; but the actor building the role will take note of it. Immediately after Malcolm learned of Duncan's
murder, his primary thought was to get away: his *strong sorrow*, like Donalbain's unbrewed tears, was not yet in *motion* (II, iii, 152). Moments later he
said, as if mistrusting the emotion of all the thanes,

> To show an unfelt sorrow, is an office
> Which the false man does easy. (II, iii, 169–170)

These are the only references of any kind to his father's death. When IV, iii
begins, Malcolm urges Macduff to weep with him for Scotland's fate, but
this mood is hard to separate from the guile he begins at once to practice. He
will not share—unless subtextually—the personal pain of Macduff's loss; on
the other hand, at the end of the play, as we will see, he will seem to become
capable of some empathy, some felt sorrow. As the actor of Malcolm must find
the threads tying these moments together, the actor-Macduff must explore
his ambivalence toward the Prince. Macduff will fight loyally at Malcolm's
side, but a tension might well persist between the impulsive warrior and the
man who has manipulated him.

Macduff, in the theatre, has made his last speech of this scene a prayer—
kneeling, with his sword out, to apostrophize the heavens; and such a prayer
would seem to repeat the ending-pattern of the previous two acts. Tree's
Macduff kissed the elevated hilt of his sword, as did Gielgud's; Sothern's
uttered a groan of vengeance and grief, his arms raised aloft. Forrest's flung
his hat to the ground, knelt for his appeal to the heavens, drew his claymore,
and rushed out.

Malcolm, having achieved his purpose, his idea of manhood satisfied, is
ready for action. *This time goes manly*, he says, still Macduff's mentor. Sometimes, his own sword drawn, he leads the other two forward. In seasonal and
diurnal imagery, he projects Macbeth's late autumn (as Macbeth himself will)

in words that recall Macbeth's own on the inexorable passage of time (*Time, and the hour, runs through the roughest day*): Macbeth

> Is ripe for shaking, and the powers above
> Put on their instruments: Receive what cheer you may,
> The night is long, that never finds the day. (278–280)

Malcolm assumes that he is acting for the *powers above*. Though he represents the needful force of retribution, his success is not assured in the minds of *naive* spectators (some of whom wondered where Fleance is). Heaven has not conspicuously supported innocence, despite repeated appeals; and witchcraft has promised Macbeth security. As the three Scots and their entourage set out to overthrow Macbeth, they—and we—must not know that they will win.

No justification would seem to be needed to depose a tyrant; but, as Shakespeare demonstrates in all his plays about the killing of any king, complex moral and political considerations are involved. Some currency still was given to the idea of divinity hedging the monarch—who, in the chain of being, took a place under God. Lesser man's contract with heaven presumably obliged him to accept the ruler given him. Moody Prior cites John of Salisbury's medieval work on tyranny, *Polycraticus*:

> Since all power is of God, tyrants also are of God . . . hence to be endured.
> God will judge and punish tyrants.

Could nothing be done? John provided a loophole: God might find a hand to remove a tyrant. However, it should not be of one who had sworn an oath of fealty (which, in this system, would specifically absolve Macduff). Even so, Prior notes, John counseled prayer and dependence on God, instancing David's sparing of Saul.

King James was more absolute on this matter: *no* action against a tyrant was justified. James' attitude needs citing here, in the face of suggestions that Shakespeare tailored the play to the king's taste, and "took care that nothing in (it) would run counter to James' political views." James had himself been in danger of deposition in Scotland; and his wish to sanctify the doctrine of divine right was unmistakably self-protective. In his *The Trew Law of Free Monarchies*, he repeatedly insisted that the worst of rulers must be left untouched.

Thus he used Saul as an example of the terrible tyrant, "however intollerable his qualities," that the people must accept. "We neuer reade, that euer the Prophets perswaded the people to rebell against the Prince, how wicked soeuer he was." James went through various arguments for deposing, and disposed of them all. He returned to the theme that no prophets employed

> their credite to vproares & rebellions against these wicked kings . . . as many
> of our seditious preachers . . . stir up rebellion vnder the cloak of religion.

James cited *Jeremie* against Nebuchadnezzar, who

> although he was an idolatrous persecutor, a forraine King, a Tyrant, and
> vsurper of their liberties; yet in respect they had once receuied and acknowl-
> edged him for their King, he (Jeremie) not only commandeth them to obey him,
> but even to pray for his prosperitie.

To demonstrate that even the most awful depravity in a king must be tol-
erated, he recalls that Paul

> Bids the *Romanes obey* and serue for *conscience sake* . . . Nero, that bloody tyrant,
> an infamie to his age, and a monster to the world, being also an idolatrous
> persecutor. . . .

James propounded this recipe for the people's behavior toward a king:

> Praying for him as their protectour; for his continuance if he be good; for his
> amendment if he be wicked; following and obeying his lawfull commands,
> eschewing and flying his fury in his vnlawfull, without resistance, but by
> sobbes and teares to God . . . I have at length prooued that the King is aboue
> the law.

The understandable alarm James had felt for his kingly safety in Scotland,
reflected still in his care in England to wear padded garments against assassins' swords, may well have been exacerbated by the recent Gunpowder Plot.
The killing of Duncan could hardly have appealed to him; and considering
his philosophy against deposing even Neros, the organized assault against
Macbeth would seem not to be to his taste.

Act V, Scene i

From the rousing mood of belligerence set in the exit, by daylight, of the three revengeful Scots, the atmosphere shifts abruptly to a heavy quiet, emphasized by the whispers of two figures in half darkness (at the afternoon Globe, one or both holding candles). The scene may duplicate that of the murder-night in II, ii, Lady Macbeth sometimes appearing with the same nightgown and general movements she used then. Though not always: in Germany (1928) she walked on the battlements; when the Yugoslav fortress was the setting, Mladen Engelsfeld reports, two doubles for the Lady were used: the first seen high atop the walls—where the witches first appeared; the second then seen on an intermediate terrace below; and finally, a few moments later, the Lady Macbeth at courtyard level.

> *Enter a Doctor of Physicke, and a Waiting*
> *Gentlewoman.*

The Gentlewoman's appearance here is her first, unless she has been seen to attend Lady Macbeth earlier. Few as her lines are, she will establish an identity: loyal, concerned for her Lady, with some intuition of an unspeakable wrong, she is also shrewdly self-protective, and able to be impatient with the ineffective Doctor. He also achieves identity: he knows the limitations of his skill; he cares about his patient; he is shocked by what he learns of her, but is compassionate if not helpful. He knows his place: superior to the Gentlewoman (if she will let him be), servant to his king—and like so many of this king's servants, uneasy and self-concerned. Between the Gentlewoman and Doctor may be felt a common purpose, but also a touch of distrust: she has called him in because she had to, he is not comfortable with her dangerous knowledge of the Queen's secret life. The Gentlewoman may enter first, to protect propriety, before waving the Doctor in.

The two quickly convey a great deal of bald, compacted exposition. They have watched two nights. The Doctor is slightly sceptical of what the Gentlewoman has asked him to look for. She tells him what she must have told him two nights ago. Macbeth has gone into the field (a reminder that time passes). Macbeth has not necessarily begun war, but he is away from the castle; and Lady Macbeth, left alone, is seriously, secretly disturbed. The Gentlewoman's prose details steps in a cleanly visualized activity, articulated phrase by phrase, almost as if memorized for accuracy:

> I have seen her rise from her bed, throw her nightgown upon her, unlock her closet, take forth paper, fold it, write upon't, read it, afterwards seal it, and again return to bed;

then, the details reported, the rhythm can relax:

> yet all this while in a most fast sleep. (7–11)

The Doctor gives a professional opinion, in the dialectical pattern of the play:

> A great perturbation in Nature, to receive at once the benefit of sleep, and do the effects of watching. (12–13)

He names it wonderfully, in the same pattern, *slumbry agitation*. He wants to know what the Lady has said; the Gentlewoman refuses to take the responsibility for telling.

Enter Lady, with a Taper.

Shakespeare may have meant the Gentlewoman's *Lo you, here she comes* to be said first, and move the audience's eyes to the place where the Lady would enter; but in this case the usual moving light in her hand could draw the same kind of sudden attention. The sleepwalker's approach may be a long one, as if seen from far off: Robert Edmond Jones had her making a way through twisted screens before the waiting two—and audience—saw her; Byam Shaw envisioned only the light at first approaching from the end of a long corridor.

Upon my life fast asleep, the Gentlewoman reminds us. How does a sleepwalker act? In one popular image, the somnambulist moves slowly and trancedly in straight lines, and speaks in hushed, sleepy monotones, avoiding sudden cries or movements that might cause wakening. This does not make for intensely physical dramatic activity; when Langtry sleepwalked in this mode, one cruel review acknowledged the effect of somnolence—on the audience. A theory, more congenial to *Macbeth*, from a German critic cited by Furness, accepts the popular image of the somnambulist proceeding with outstretched hands, seeing "as it were, with the . . . fingertips," and able to walk safely on the rim of ledges without danger; but it also allows for an increase during sleep of muscular power and convulsive activity, so that Lady Macbeth might move more erratically and energetically than in the waking state. The Lady's physical torment may bring to mind Macbeth's gestures after Duncan's murder, when he was so convinced that no ocean could cleanse his hands.

Lady Macbeth's activity in the presence of the watchers can ironically confirm that she is indeed fast asleep. The Gentlewoman urges the Doctor to *stand close*, which can be taken (Liddell) to mean stay hidden—and so Reinhardt's Gentlewoman pulled the Doctor back, and they remained behind a curtain; but the Gentlewoman may mean "stand close enough to see": so Polanski's Doctor waved his hand before Annis' eyes, and she passed openeyed, unseeing. Casarès, at one point, walked with hand outstretched directly at the Gentlewoman who had to arch her head out of the way. Merchant, walking close past, held out the candle in her hand as if to drop it on a nonexistent table; only the Gentlewoman's quick grasp of it kept it from falling to the floor. This kind of obliviousness to "reality" is akin, in reverse, to the illusion confirmed when Macbeth's banqueters were not aware of the passing before them of Banquo's ghost.

Of the many different character designs completed by the sleepwalk, I will concentrate on the most distinguished and representative, drawn from the hundreds of reports of this spectacular virtuoso scene. In all portrayals the principle of contrast is at work: the Lady who appears is recognizably the woman last seen; but in her strange reappearance the enduring of time and of harsh experience will be variously imaged, and the future variously anticipated.

Sophisticated twentieth-century research in sleep and dreaming seemed to confirm the hypothesis of intense activity. Usually in sleep, according to the findings of William Dement at Stanford University, we are physically benumbed in the dream state: "Dreaming involves an awake brain in a paralyzed body." The brain fires at a rapid rate, but the motor nerves in the spinal cord are inactivated, so that normally the dream is not acted out, in voice or movement. During non-dreaming sleep, muscular activity is not inhibited; but the brain is slow-firing, and sleeps in a relaxed body. Dement's research leads him to believe that sometimes, in the period before dreaming begins, the brain begins firing actively before the muscles are paralyzed. This imbalance, Dement theorizes, explains sleepwalking: there may be tremendous nervous activity, the sleeper sweats, talks, cries out, stares glassily.

Whatever the realities of sleepwalking, Shakespeare's somnambulant image must be our guide; and it certainly demands activity. We learn at once that Lady Macbeth rubs her hands—a gesture of washing that may go on for a quarter of an hour. The text suggests cries, sighs, starts, coaxings, commands; and though her visual sense is *shut*, she seems to "see" a great deal, as well as hear, smell, touch—indeed experience all sensations, even taste: if Rachel had acted the role, she would, she said, have tried to cleanse her hand by licking it; Siddons, Beerbohm Tree was told, sucked at the imaginary blood; Dench bit at it.

Governing all interpretations is the complexity and range of the inner

forces combining to torture Lady Macbeth. Common human experience
suggests that a major note in the polyphony of her suffering is the thunder
of conscience, sounding a moral imperative. Partly depending on our individual histories, we recognize conscience as either the inevitable fruit of a
native (or divinely inspired) sense of right and wrong, or of a socially conditioned sense of moral guilt—or, perhaps, of both. Conscience connects with
compassion—for a slaughtered wife, for the Lady's own lost innocence, for
her suffering husband. Some observers deny Lady Macbeth the benison of
remorse. Bradley, who saw her in one sense as too great to repent, found her
also untouched by contrition. But whatever the grandeur of the Lady's
wickedness, it is not proof against some form of mortal anguish, psychic and
physical. Lady Macbeth's stature is accentuated, not diminished, by the
intensity of her sealed agony.

For critics who rule out remorse of conscience, what tortures the Lady is
a form of fear (L. B. Campbell, Arnold). Certainly fear is manifested and may
itself be partly a symptom of psychic distress: remember Freud's suggestion
about those achievers who cannot bear their achievements—what they have
done. Such psychic pain may manifest itself in the Lady's physical torment, as
well as in diffuse anxiety. The fear may be akin, also, to the archaic animal
apprehension of capture and destruction—and certainly this has been one
strain in the polyphony. Sounding, too, is the "civilized," metaphysical dread
of judgment after—of a murky hell; and a more or less practical concern for
safety from discovery now, for herself and her husband—the more for him
in Ladies who emphasize the love in the design. The complex, turbulent
experience makes enormous demands on the actress—and on the imagining
reader—willing to inhabit the characterization, to share Lady Macbeth's
sensations: of the prop that must be held—a small light glittering in the darkness; of seeing sightlessly; of the feel of blood on the hand, ineradicable; of
the images of more blood flowing, and unforgivable violence; of the dangers
of retribution from without, of agony within.

"Every nerve is stirred," wrote Louise Heiberg:

> When I rehearsed this scene in the solitary hours of the night . . . I was often
> seized with an inexplicable horror, as if the room was filled with demons mov-
> ing closer and closer. My breath was taken away, and they seemed to be press-
> ing me out of the room, so that I was as if forced to seize the lamp and hurry
> away. And yet, I could only rehearse this scene at night.

She saw herself, in the sleepwalk, moving "petrified, like a ghost."

Significantly, the crowding, conflicting forces that jerk the Lady back and
forth emerge in her sleep. In her waking life she has struggled to keep her inner
resistance under control; only once, in the first three acts, has she allowed
herself, in a moment of solitude, to acknowledge the emptiness of her life—
and then a suicidal thought flashed in her mind. Otherwise she has striven,

by strenuous discipline, to seal up her inward voices—of despair, remorse, guilt, shame. When Macbeth opened to her his own secret dismay, she was able to respond with counsel and care, still trying to conceal her own traumas. Something of the mounting rigor of her repression will have been sensed; now, suddenly, in sleep, the containment breaks and her demons ravage her. As Macbeth's visit to the witches was his descent into a world of the subconscious, so now she visits her dark, writhing underworld, where her naked nerves are flayed by her memories and impulses. Mind, body, and feeling suffer attrition; the Lady seems worn to the edge of insanity, and her life itself is under attack. Yet always the fact of her sleep separates this experience from the "reality" of her waking life, and encloses it in a gauze of ambiguity. That she may awake, repress her nightmare life, remains one of the open possibilities that sustain expectation.

Most resistant, even in sleep, to inward torment are those Terrible Women who had shown few signs of breaking even during and after the disastrous banquet. Their tragedy, if they can make it one, may be not that they deny compunction, but that they cannot know what it is. Hence Fanny Kemble, who inherited the conception, enviously comparing Macbeth's capacity for remorse, however painful, with Lady Macbeth's crippling inability to feel it:

> He may be visited to the end by those noble pangs which bear witness to the pre-eminent nobility of the nature he has desecrated . . . But *she* may none of this: she may but feel and see and smell blood; and wonder at the unquenched stream that she still wades in—"Who would have thought the old man had so much blood in him?"—and fly, hunted through the nights by that "knocking at the door" which beats the wearied life at last out of her stony heart and . . . impenetrable brain.

The formidable Pritchard apparently represented archetypally the unfeeling "fiend" of "apathy" (in the eighteenth-century sense). Compunction knew better than to visit her; she opened only to the knocking of horror. Bell's "Garrick" edition perhaps records, in Gentleman's prescription for Lady Macbeth's action, Pritchard's business:

> Speak in a low anxious voice, keep moving slowly about, with fixed, glaring, open eyes, and horror-struck features.

Davies, who described Pritchard as an "angry Hecate" perceived her sleepwalking wholly in terms of the "terrors" of a guilty mind: her acting resembled "those sudden flashes of lightning which . . . discover the horrors of surrounding darkness." For so adamant a figure, the signs of yielding could be small: Wilson, of *Blackwood*'s, heard that her handwashing was limited to touching one palm with the fingertips of the other hand—which held its candle throughout. One finger was held on the spot, the *Monthly Mirror* remembered. In so iron a design, even a small crack could seem a breach in her nature, and point a moral, so dear to the age: fiends end badly. This fitted comfortably with Garrick's execrably pious interpolated dying speech.

In the twentieth century the coldly fearsome Leigh sustained through most of the sleepwalk her grim hold on her feelings; only small clues signified the feeling woman within who cried to escape the hard outer shell. The previously elegant Lady with the handsome red wig now emerged from a long corridor of arches in disarray, in a shapeless sack, her mouse-coloured hair hanging lank. At first she breathed with the horrifying stertorousness of desperately troubled sleep. Since, in her waking hours, she had managed almost without a wince the convulsions of her husband, and the threatening confusion of a roomful of thanes, her naked dream life came with sudden shocking contrast. Even in sleep, though, she seemed to resist disclosing herself. Byam Shaw, her director, noted that no torture in the world would drag from this Lady Macbeth the things she said now; she seemed tortured at revealing them, in a panic, wringing her hands viciously but secretly. (This pattern has been marked in other Ladies: Wolter, particularly, pacing the stage wearily, deadly pale, seemed to try to hide her thoughts, that came as if forced from her.) Occasionally a tone of Leigh's voice betrayed her: she would speak firmly, fearlessly, then would let escape faint childlike tones, of an innocent despair too deep for control. (This touching, regressive note would mingle in the polyphony of many interpretations.)

When a Lady Macbeth who has been cold and ruthless before the sleepwalk now is quite broken, the contrast is jolting. In *Throne of Blood*, the Lady's face had been as smooth and impassive as enamel as she wrenched Macbeth's bloody murder-spear from him, to return it to Duncan's chamber; now she was in helpless, unbalanced anguish, desperately laving from her hands, in a bowl of water, the blood that she had before seemed to ignore. When Macbeth, who was present, took the bowl away, she went on mindlessly with her hand washing. The dramatic shock was powerful; though it came at the cost of some unrevealed dimension in Lady Macbeth's early characterization.

In modifying the Pritchard pattern, Siddons' Terrible Woman had preserved the "fiend" facade up to the murder of Duncan; but in her next appearance, in III, i, had moved toward the second part of her two-step characterization; we recall that then she was already pointing to what she would become in this scene: "The peace that passeth all understanding [was] lost to her for ever." Siddons' Lady Macbeth, hiding her sufferings from Macbeth, while letting the audience perceive them, thought "the anguish of her heart . . . is precipitating her into the grave which at this moment is yawning to receive her." This trajectory toward death is made implicit in some stage interpretations: either by anticipation of the suicide that the doctor fears (and the rumor of which Malcolm reports), or, more often, by accumulating physical and psychic attrition. Siddons saw the deterioration as far advanced:

Behold her . . . wasted form, with wan and haggard countenance, her starry eyes glazed with the ever-burning fever of remorse, and on their lids the shadows of death. Her ever-restless spirit wanders in troubled dreams about her dismal apartment; and whether waking or asleep, the smell of innocent blood incessantly haunts her imagination.

Denied the relief Macbeth had found in "unloading (his) weight of woe" through talk, "Her feminine nature," Siddons believed, "her delicate structure . . . are soon overwhelmed by the enormous pressure of her crimes." Siddons' very stare, Leigh Hunt thought, was deathlike.

This suggests physical frailty, but Siddons would not be frail, any more than she would realize her original conception of the role—"fair, feminine, nay perhaps even fragile." Bell described her now as "Feeble . . . as if preparing for her last sickness and final doom"; but his and other descriptions suggest a convulsive vitality. Bell wishes, for instance, that she would enter "less suddenly . . . she advances rapidly"—suggesting the frantic rush, almost as if to escape some hound of heaven or hell, of some later Ladies. She was unmistakably asleep, and conveyed impressions of unconsciousness, of bewilderment: pale, her lips seeming to move involuntarily, her gestures involuntary and mechanical, she moved like an apparition, the body asleep, the mind awake. Boaden found her much more active than previous actresses, who had felt that the perturbation of sleepwalking did not exert "full power upon the frame"; they had "glided rather than walked . . . every other action had a feebler character" than when awake, they "kept perpendicularly erect, the eye, though open, studiously avoided motion." Siddons, Boaden observed, seemed to conceive that the sleepwalker's imagining had "power over the whole frame, and all her actions had wakeful vigour." She dared to express her feeling with faces that were "horrid, even ugly." She bent to listen to imagined sounds, moved actively to inner prompting, as in her hand washing. Where Pritchard had decorously paddled with the palm of her hand, Siddons—perhaps, again, partly to differ from her remarkable predecessor—energetically engaged both hands. To do this, she had to set her candle down—an innovation that at first shocked her manager. Her hands freed, Siddons "laded the water from the imaginary ewer over her hands" (Boaden) so realistically that the *Monthly Mirror* complained that she scrubbed her hands as if "diligently employed at a wash-tub"; though the *Examiner* allowed its "dribbling and domestic familiarity" was "not unnatural in a person so situated."

"Enveloped" in white drapery, she seemed to Boaden "lovelily dreadful"; though the white evoked some protest from spectators accustomed to associate that non-colour on the stage with madness. Siddons moved obliquely toward unbalance, where some Ladies would do so directly—indeed the sleepwalk has been called, as in a review of Ermolova, Lady Macbeth's "mad scene." The sense of borderline rationality could endorse Siddons' sense of the awareness of remorse and guilt. She began with a great shuddering sigh, and spoke in stifled tones. A true somnambulist, she moved among stage objects as if completely unaware of their existence, her essential life inward; contrasting "the most terrible working of the soul with the deathlike stillness of the medium" (*Edinburgh Courant*). How vividly contemporary spectators experienced her Lady is suggested by a dialect description in *Blackwood*'s:

> Onward she used to come—no Sarah Siddons—but just Leddy Macbeth herse' . . . gliding wi' the ghost-like motion o' nicht-wanderin' unrest, uncon-scious o' surroundin' objects—for oh! how could the glazed yet gleamin' een see aught in this material world?—yes, by some mysterious power o' instinct, never touchin' ane o' the impediments that the furniture o' the auld castle micht hae opposed to her haunted footsteps,—on she came, wring, wringin' her hauns, as if washin' them in the cleansin' dews frae the blouts o' blood . . . Lord save us! that hollow, broken-hearted voice, "out damned spot" was o' itsell aneugh to tell to a' that heard it, that crimes done in the flesh . . . will needs be punished in the spirit during eternity.

This was in 1827. As we have seen—and will see—some who watched Siddons thought her acting too "real," not queenly enough. But by the 1840s, as theatre fashions changed, *Blackwood*'s would recall a more portentous, dis-tanced interpretation, wanting

> the agitation, the drooping, the timidity. She looked like a living statue. She spoke with the solemn tone of a voice from a shrine. She stood more the sep-ulchral avenger of regicide than the sufferer from its convictions. Her grand voice, her fixed and marble countenance, and her silent step, gave the impres-sion of a supernatural being.

The sleepwalking seemed, in retrospect, too unreal:

> Nothing so solemn, so awful, was ever seen upon the stage. Yet it had one fault—it was too awful. She more resembled a majestic shade rising from the tomb than a living woman, however disturbed by wild fear and lofty passion.

By this time Charlotte Cushman, in the Siddons pattern, could seem more human in her two-step descent from the early figure of terror to a remorseful, broken woman. She had conveyed the sense that she would have died a thou-sand deaths before letting the world, or even her husband, know her deep sense of guilt; but alone, in sleep, her will was powerless, she "inexpressibly mournful." The contrast between the grim murderess of Act I and the weak, hurt, burdened, unstrung creature of the sleepwalk, trembling "on the brink of the opening grave" (*Evening Mail*), was both shocking and touching,

> making us totally forget our horror at the brutal and bloody business for which she is so largely responsible. (*Graphic*)

In the twentieth century, Anderson similarly changed the mood of her audiences from terror to a terrible pity. In 1937, with Olivier, she had seemed too feverish, too fast. By 1941 she had deeply thought about the role; now she made her Lady's fierce early ambition almost unrecognizable in the pitiable, wretched woman who sleepwalked. Anderson had consulted a psychiatrist about sleepwalking, and had watched while Johns Hopkins doctors hypnotized a female mental patient. The actress said of watching the woman walk barefoot:

> She set each foot down most carefully, with the muscles seeming to grip the floor. Her feet were feeling their way by instinct, and they didn't venture to step without making sure of the ground under them. Well, that is the way my Lady Macbeth walks.

When the patient was told to try to remove from her hands lipstick that would not come off, the motions were the kind the actress expected to use:

> Over and over she rubbed the flat palms of her hands, always making the strokes away from her.

Anderson's harsh, almost brutal handwashing was in this manner, and her walk was similarly influenced; her tottering steps were called "sleep-locked"— a dazed, dragging gait, the more burdened because, though she wore a thin nightgown, she seemed in her imagination to be pulling the long royal train that had already begun to bear heavily on her in III, i. A chilling horror was felt, but a poignancy too, in the broken utterance of her cracked voice, in the stiff, unnatural, almost cataleptic jerking of her gestures with her "bloody" hands. The "glaze of lunacy" was perceived in her voice and gesture, manifestations of the actress' explorations into mental illness.

Anderson made explicit what many Ladies had learned to suggest: that the sleepwalk repeated crucial gesturings from the murder scene (II, ii). Siddons had seen herself moving within her own "dismal apartment"; and apparently only in her imagination acted "over again the accumulated horrors of her whole conduct." In the nineteenth century Ladies began to indicate that they had come from their bedchambers to the scene of the murder-night. By 1884:

> Modern actresses uniformly come in dragging the sheet of their bed after them, and evolve as much terror as they can out of a mixture of tumbled linen and back hair ostentatiously let down. (*Studio*)

Then the locale would become, again, the courtyard where Lady Macbeth had waited in II, ii for Macbeth, and from which she went with the bloody daggers to Duncan's chamber, and returned. Anderson, with the help of her director, Webster, emphasized the real and imagined details. She came down the same stairs of the earlier scene, to await her Macbeth; carried much the same kind of candle, put it down in the same place; stood over an imaginary Macbeth on the bench where he had collapsed; made the motion of taking the daggers from him, and going to Duncan's chamber; then, as she recalled the trauma of the feel of blood on her hands, she choked again, as if the blood was in her throat and nostrils; she climbed back up the stairs as she had before.

One source of the sympathy for Anderson was that, like Siddons, she had not been afraid to look unpretty as, graceless and shattered, she wandered and jerked through her agony. This visual fall from pride of place and health provides a contrast that was even more emphasized in some Ladies. Thus in the Craig-designed *Macbeth*, Florence Reed, so ornamental and enchanting in the first acts, dragged down the great spiral staircase in a loose-fitting, coarse nightgown, an untidy old woman, slopping about in straw slippers. Her hair, that had been red, braided, was turned white, hung slack on her shoulders; she carried an old oil lamp. She was not quite as wretched as Craig's sketch of a frightened woman in tattered rags; Craig had written to Anglin, who was to have been his Lady:

> I may horrify you by the drawing I've made of Lady M. . . . because it's ugly. It makes her ugly . . . it makes her untidy . . . she is not impressive she is merely almost daft and uncouth.

So the moving "show" of Reed's tragic fall, as she wandered shabbily, pitiably on the stairs, touching unseeing with her outstretched fingers the objects in her way.

Since Ristori had chosen to show her power over Macbeth not with the fierce dominance of the Terrible Woman, but rather with the subtle manipulation of the player, the change she projected was also more subtle. Hers was not the resistance—or submission—to the collapse of a "fiend"; rather she mainly showed the other side of the sensitivity and intelligence with which she had managed her warrior husband. The mask she had carried superbly for so long, even as it had begun to slip in Act III, was now entirely gone, and the naked self showed. Ristori herself:

> Behold her! reduced to the ghost of her former self by the effects of that remorse which gnawed like a vulture at her heart, her reason disturbed until she became so unconscious of herself as to reveal her tremendous secret in sleep. *Sleep*, did I say? It is rather a fever which mounts to her brain.

She was not broken so much as crystalized in shattered pieces. She came from deep recesses of darkness into a shaft of moonlight, in a white robe and coif, bewildered and grief-stricken. In her pallid, emaciated face, framed in her blue-black hair, her glazed eyes were wide open and so rigidly and unrelaxedly fixed that tears came (Ristori believed this "forced immobility" caused her subsequently weakened eyesight). Her stertorous breathing was oppressively naturalistic: Terry was upset by its realism, and the *Saturday Review* decided "It is ugly; and tragedy should not be ugly."

Ristori's voice was uncanny, a low, mesmeric muttering, almost a whisper from beginning to end, "which conveyed most powerfully the notion of something mysterious, strange and terrible." It might have come from "the depths of a sealed charnel house."

Her movements were mechanical, but painfully energetic, with the impatient restlessness of a "tortured spirit torturing itself." Spectators had not before seen handwashing like hers. Her basic gesture, repeated several times during the scene, was to lift imagined water from a basin into the hollow of her hand; then, with a frighteningly real terror she desperately rubbed it against her hands, so spasmodically, even convulsively, to cleanse the blood from skin and soul that it seemed her flesh must crack.

Then a moment later, as a movement of her hands roused an old thought, she was in the past, rehearsing the murder scene, in "ghostly repetition." Ristori seemed to re-enact the crises of II, ii, involuntarily; the memories forced themselves on her, she would shudder, stand up and repeat spasmodically her gestures of the traumatic night, now in a paroxysm of alarm, her mouth open in horror, now her hands bloody, now urging dissimulation, coaxing or leading her imaginary husband. Momentarily she would struggle for repose, then the nightmare would engulf her again.

Under so much attrition, this Lady moved unmistakably toward death, almost as if death were already upon her.

> The hands and fingers were as of one risen from the grave. (*Era*)
> There was death as well as sleep in those low whispers, in that awful glassy stare. There was the grave, not the bed, waiting to receive the guilty one . . . and that grave *not* the grave of the holy quiet! By what shades of tone, by what tremulousness of gesture, by what management of steps and drapery, the idea of the soul that could not rest in a body about to be a corpse was conveyed, it passes words to tell. But the impression was there. (*Atheneum*)

Imminent death also supplied Segond-Weber's primary objective. She entered breathing so harshly her lips were ruffled by her exhalations—with too great effort, according to the otherwise admiring Sarcey, who felt that it undercut the force of the great climactic sigh Shakespeare designed for later. But Segond-Weber wanted to suggest genuine physical symptoms preceding her death, held off only by the Lady's will—

> She sees nothing around her, hears nothing, even thinks of nothing; she wills . . . Her nerves [become] the master, these terrible demons . . . she is now another person, broken morally and physically [in] the great agony of a great criminal; and all this while she is sleeping, her gait heavy with sleep and the death which is coming. Slow gestures, painful, the eye haggard, fixed without seeing, the regular breathing of profound sleep, mixed with the sobs of the sleeper who cries and rattles, the prelude to death . . . I play it as simply as possible, without a cry, without any gesture violent enough to waken me from this lethargy. I re-enact the scene of the crime, saying almost the same words, making the same gestures, repeating the same inflections, but all without life, without force, monotonous in voice and movement.

Faucit, as we saw, was one of the first of distinguished actresses, after Nouseul, to find the freedom to project from the beginning tenderness and love for Macbeth as well as a fierce impetus to his ambition. All the tones she had discovered in the polyphony of the character were sounded in her sleepwalk.

> Every word of the few sentences she utters was surcharged with one or other of the contending emotions of a chequered lifetime compressed into the almost momentary compass of a dream.

Thus the *Manchester Examiner*, going on to note her terror at "the abiding proofs of her guilt," her taunts at Macbeth's cowardice, her promptings to the murder, and her reasoning about its results, her horror at Duncan's blood, her compassion for Lady Macduff, her self-pity. Observers noted the surfacing of "tenderness," the re-emergence of a womanliness coated over when she urged Macbeth to murder:

> The gentler nature of the woman is beautifully shadowed forth and there is a world of hidden meaning in the wailing tone that speaks of a heart ill at ease, looking back, perchance, at those early days of innocence when it needed not the perfumes of Arabia to sweeten that little hand. (See *Guardian*, *Sporting Life*)

By her very physical imagery, her "action and gesture . . . [Faucit seemed] to disclose the history of a whole life." "The parched mouth, that told of the burning tortures within." . . . "The low moans." Like Segond-Weber, she was careful to avoid any starts that might seem incompatible with sleeping. Faucit was pleased when Macready acknowledged that she

> gave the idea of sleep, disturbed by fearful dreams, but still it was sleep . . . in my walk, which was heavy and inelastic, marking the distinction—too often overlooked—between the muffled voice and seeming mechanical motion of the somnambulist, and the wandering mind and quick, fitful gestures of the maniac, whose very violence would wake her from deepest sleep.

But her action was not all repressed: she wailed and cried; she was observed to display some of the feverish agitation associated with Siddons. The effect was powerful: an Irish observer experienced

> Such a frightful reality of horror—such terrible revelations of remorse—such struggles to wash away, not the blood from the hand, but the blood from the soul, as made me shudder from head to foot, and the very hair to stand upon my head (*Freeman's*).

Faucit, too, with "corpse-like hands" seemed on the burdened way to the grave.

Faucit's sleepwalk mined below an early fierceness that had complemented her more tender side; Terry, early representative of the primarily loving Ladies who had to impose fierceness on themselves for their husband's sake, returned in sleep to her relative innocence before Macbeth's letter stimulated her to urge the murder. She was likened to Ophelia; not because she was mad, but because, in her fair and fragile way, she perceived the horrors of the past in a haze of sorrow and regret. Her nerves were broken. She gave the impression of a suffering that had spiritualized her and returned her to the conscience of her childhood. Her notes suggest her image of the Lady's vulnerability:

> Remember she is *weak and asleep* . . . She took to sleepwalking when Macbeth went into the field . . . Macbeth preyed on her mind more than the deed. This might be some time afterward and grey hair would be pathetic. For both of them have been through enough to make them grey.

The Lady would die of remorse, Terry thought.

In performance her hair was blanched white, matching her gown, of soft, thin, white woollen, falling away in many folds that followed every movement of her body. Her physical weakness showed in her slow gliding onto the stage. Her long pale hands—after she hung her lamp on a stairway bracket—trembled as, rubbing them and wringing them, and re-enacting events of the night of murder, she tried to erase or shake off her guilt. Her body swayed, her hollow eyes had a lost, faraway look: an observer felt they hypnotized the whole house. She murmured brokenly, sometimes with the longdrawn muttering of a sleeper, her syllables slowly articulated; sometimes with hopeless weary cries that lapsed again into a dreamy mood.

The experience, to one spectator, was Burne-Jones impressionist. To many others, it was a deeply moving, realistic triumph. The gentlemanly *Gentleman* heard

> one of those voices which speak to the very soul, and linger on in the memory as the tones of some sweetest harmony. I saw big unemotional Englishmen crying like children.

For critics hungry for sterner stuff, the deep sympathy Terry evoked was too touching, not terrible enough. The *Evening News:*

> Terry's dreaming horror suggests anything but stern and unrepentant wakefulness. One begins to sympathise with her; it is pathetic, and that is bad enough; it is sympathetic, and that is fateful.

The hedging *Liverpool Daily Post* explained: the scene was infinitely touching, but

> the solemn splendour of the grander Lady Macbeths lingers too impressively in the mind to give tender realism its chance.

Much later Terry herself would write, in retrospect (*McClures*):

> My ideas have changed since I played Lady Macbeth more than twenty years ago. I know I struck no note of horror.

The later English actress, Vanbrugh, who portrayed the Lady in the Loving Wife mode, found in the scene darker shades of physical and mental disarray. She was deeply lost in a kind of narcotic sleep. She stumbled down a high, narrow, perilous stairway, so perpendicular it seemed almost a ladder; and her unawareness of danger seemed to confirm, as she blindly felt her way, that somnambulists can teeter safely on dangerous edges. (Vanbrugh moved unscathed; Wynyard, less lucky, in one of her distraught, hysterical descents on a similarly narrow stairway at Stratford, though her hands guided her down the wall, fell several feet, smashing the lamp she held. A trouper, she rose, still deep in sleep, and proceeded with her nightmare.)

Vanbrugh still had her bright red hair, now startling against her dark robe and the whiteness of her set face. When she had dragged herself halfway down the stair, she stopped to leave her candle on a ledge, and moved again in the flickering blue light. Once on the ground, she fell in a wailing heap, then slowly raised herself and rocked back and forth, like a child. As she re-lived II, ii, she would break from her half-anesthetized dreaminess to a tormented, disordered, hysterical anguish. Her voice went from a hoarsely whispered agony to cries and then sobs—to one observer the whole speech was a series of sobs, punctuating her broken half-sentences.

Marlowe, who with Morris in America developed the Loving Wife image, emphasized low-key continuity between her growing misery in the banquet scene, and her intensified, subconscious agony now. In her long white robe she came slowly, gently, step by step, down her stairs, in absolute silence, her fixed eyes staring ahead, seeing nothing. She drifted blindly against a table, and as without volition put her candle down on it. As she washed her hands, she moaned softly—

> a low, insistent, penetrant moaning. It was a sound that seemed to . . . mean the fateful fulfillment of that horror and remorse she had begun to show in the Banquet scene.

She spoke gently, in whispers—

> the last accents of the last woe of a mortal frame wrenched and racked beyond endurance . . . "Out damned spot" seemed made of pure pain and to quiver with a weary sorrow. (C. E. Russell)

Grief dominated from the first Dench's intensely loving, intensely troubled Lady. She had been weeping in her sleep before she entered, and the tears ran down her cheeks to the very end of her nightmare. Her sorrow had a terrible immediacy, as if she were agonizing afresh through a series of unexpected, intolerable moments. She seemed to be wearing the simple black gown of the previous acts; in fact, it was different. Made of softer cloth, it had been rolled up and thrown in the corner of a closet, where it was trampled upon until the very threads were tortured. It looked unmistakably slept in—by a dreamer who had writhed through many nightmares. On it she rubbed her hands even before she dared look for the spot she knew was on them; once she started to scrub her hands, she never stopped, even when her attention was on some other fragment of her anguish. This act would never be *done*.

Some five years before Terry's Loving Wife, as noted above, Bernhardt introduced her French version; and as the amorousness of her manipulation of Macbeth shocked some English tastes—"totally at variance and distinctly antagonistic to our English ideas"—so her sleepwalk in some eyes "outrages all British notions" (*Land and Water*). A French comment (*Revue d'Art Dramatique*) preferred her temperamental violence to Terry's softness: and even some English applauded: the *Liverpool Daily Post* in a perceptive comment on the scene itself:

> The acting is entirely new and entirely great. Most Lady Macbeths are aged and as it were aggrandized in this episode. They are magnificent wrecks. Madame Bernhardt avoids this expansion . . . ennobling instead a weird dignity of somnambulism. What [Bernhardt] has been awake she is asleep, with the single exception that her feminine wiles and lures and seeming ardors are all gone.

What took their place was violent activity—Bernhardt's Lady was more manic than somnambulist. To the late Victorian theatre, used to Lady Macbeths gliding on, in a comatose state, Bernhardt's frantic invasion of the stage, on naked feet, her face and clinging white nightdress deadly white, was unnerving. Frail and slender, her morbidly bright eyes fixed on vacancy, her hair dishevelled, she seemed driven from bed by a feverish, hysterical nightmare that compelled her, by its "hideous illusion" to re-enact her crime. Though, the *Times* observed, she never lost the abstracted air of the somnambulist, some spectators missed the accustomed dreamy tones:

> No fierce whisper denoted the inward struggle; [instead] cries of pain and terror and a palpitating restlessness of affright [conveyed the] underlying emotion. (*Pall Mall Gazette*)

Her voice ranged from a terrible scream, at the first sight of blood, to "wonderfully earnest and pathetic tones" and groans.

The half-hidden hand-examining gestures audiences had glimpsed in the scenes after the murder had become a mechanical handwashing now, but so fiercely compulsive as to be frightening:

> With a nervous grinding strength in her slender fingers . . . she incessantly rubs her hands.

She rubbed for a full half-minute after she had entered, and had put her large Pompeian lamp on the table. Then her eyes, that had been staring sightlessly ahead, seemed to fix on the spot on one hand: she lifted it high and scolded it. Then, the *Edinburgh Courant* observed, as she moved restlessly across the stage, she stretched out her *other* hand, and seeing the spot transferred there, staggered back shrieking. She returned to the chair, exhausted. But her tormented body did not leave her alone:

> With swift movements and flashing countenance—in spite of the sadly worn expression in which may be read her death-doom—she re-enacts the incidents of the murder night. (*Liverpool Daily Post*)

The compulsive, even maniacal action stayed in Ellen Terry's remembrance: a quarter of a century later she would recall it as "something strange, something aloof, something terrifying. It was as if she had come back from the dead" (*McClure's*).

Madness in sleep was suggested more restrainedly by Modjeska. The Polish actress had projected a highly emotional woman, as amorous as Bernhardt, but not as seductive about it. As she had been more a strong, dominant Juliet than a beguiling Cleopatra, now, as she came sick in conscience, she conveyed in quieter rhythms "the deep lyricism of the demented" (*Tygodnik Ilustrowany*). She brought many notes into her polyphony: of the mental and physical decay symptomatic of death; of the almost unbearable remorse; of her unavailing flight from conscience in sleep; of her continued care for Macbeth; of her resurgent caution to clear them of guilt; of the Ophelia note of the child rediscovered in madness; of the strangeness of the somnambulistic act. Jerzy Got:

> Her movements were automatic and tottering, as if she were led by a strange will; her breathing laboured and gasping, often whining, at times lost altogether amidst a hoarse rattling; her voice sometimes recalled that of a child frightened by a nightmare. Her look was glassy, her face altered beyond recognition, shaded by deathly signs. It was a moving and heart-rending insanity, but it made the impression of an insanity caused by the unhappiness which enveloped her rather than by any crimes she had committed.

The horror of the moment was softened more than some observers liked by the aura of romanticism about her figure, and her piteous face, made the more haggard by the white band enclosing it, the whole creating an effect of "almost unearthly beauty, weird, agonized, spectral, and profoundly pathetic" (*N.Y. Tribune*).

An austerity far from Bernhardt's restive sleepwalk characterized Casarès, France's distinguished Lady Macbeth of the mid-twentieth century. An amorous wife, she, too, had governed her Macbeths more by sensuality than fiendish authority; but in her lonely sleepwalk she emphasized the scene's strangeness with an aura of mystery and even solemnity. Her "mad delirium" (*Lettres Françaises*) had a fragility in it that was yet touched with the superhuman. At Avignon she rose from behind the empty stage, like some chthonic figure, in a dark gown with curious cabalistic designs on its hem that caught and glittered in the light. She carried a three-headed candlestick—the triplicity seeming to carry a significant echo of the elder world—which she slowly, almost ritually, put down. Casarès stared straight ahead—not only as if she saw nothing, but as if her blind eyes were trying very hard to see. She might have been hypnotized. She began to rub her hands palm to palm, and then, as she felt the contamination spread, she slid one hand up to her upper arm and rubbed the whole length trying to rid herself of the disgust. Her face, as she was involved in nightmare with herself, refracted the mask of tragedy, she seemed defeated, shattered, a dead woman, her features breaking at agonized moments; but when her thoughts returned to Macbeth, she was persuasive, tender, loving—the Lady who had first welcomed him home. As he "disappeared," there was emptiness on her again.

Intimations of madness came as a surprise with those Ladies who, though earlier highstrung and then despairing, had managed their Macbeths with an evident resilience of mind and personal strength. The neurotic Lady Macbeths, whom we found appearing with some frequency in the twentieth century, had manifested from the beginning an inner instability that located them from the beginning on the edge of sanity. Events pushed them increasingly farther off balance, until only the most strenuous efforts enabled them to support Macbeth through the banquet. Then in the sleepwalk, if the tenuous control gives way, the madness is engulfing. Thus Leighton, hovering "on the verge of madness and hysteria throughout," now in "sheer insanity . . . wild, staring-eyed . . . terrifying to watch" (*Leamington Spa Courier*). "New and harrowing . . . no frigid statuesque interpretation here; instead . . . a writhing, restless, cringing figure" (*Birmingham Mail*). She was likened to Ophelia—but an Ophelia with memories too savage to escape. Physically as well as psychically she fell to pieces:

> The brittle creature breaks. The proud little head cannot carry the weight of the diadem . . . Though she is still capable of bursts of febrile energy [which] leave her collapsed, so that the sleepwalking mutters through the night as the last echo of destruction. (*Stage*)

Gaunt, pasty, haggard, compulsive, she looked "as if her long, frail body would snap in two at any moment under the weight of its intolerable guilt" (*Sunday Times*). She made "little drooping runs" for the curtains, and clung to them. The end would be utter disintegration. Rigg, too, was almost completely broken physically. The decline that had begun in Act III had accumulated: her rouged cheeks looked even more garish against her pallor as, in her nightgown, she trembled down the stairs, her clothes seemingly almost more than she could bear, and then collapsed on the floor, in an abasement of the soul as well as of the flesh. In this dissolution of the mask she had maintained with such effort, a motif sounded that we have seen to inform other personations of the scene: "most moving . . . was a childish innocence that came with her breakdown, somehow discernible beneath the doll-like circles of rouge on her corpse-like cheeks" (*Telegraph*). Rigg groaned often in her anguished speech; with some reserve of caution would try to calm herself, and give way again.

A similar note opened a window onto the brittle, hard-finished Lady portrayed by Merchant. She had struggled to sustain her outer veneer, though the cracks had been implicit in the higher pitch of her conduct at the banquet, and in the touches of hysteria with which she had increasingly tried—and failed—to communicate with her Macbeth while alone. She had begun to retreat into the hollowness behind her mask; and at last, in the sleepwalk, she discovered in the hollowness a deep well of feeling, for the first time passionate emotions sounded. She rolled up her sleeves desperately for the hand washing and when she knew it was useless she began to cry in the frightened hopeless agony of a child in despair.

I will begin now, moving through the scene, to draw on the physical imagery of many actresses to project a montage of Lady Macbeth's progress through her crisis. We must refuse to remember that this is her journey's end; we must, like the *naive* spectator, experience it as an ongoing exigency that will not necessarily come to a stop, but rather may point to sinister, even explosive turmoil and uncertainty. In her dreaming she experiences a twisted, episodic past; we experience in her a tormented being capable of strange and perhaps dangerous future impulse. Our first glimpse of her at entrance, by the playwright's design, evokes expectation as well as wonder; as will our last glimpse.

Whether she enters quickly, as if in flight from pursuit, or in a strange, compulsive rush to scourge her bloodstains; or staggers in, weak under her load of memory; or drifts in trancelike, deep in a dream; the striking evidence of disturbance and disarray will contribute—along with the tension of the watchers—to the atmosphere of potential outbreak that might lead anywhere. Some behavior of hers—which may be made explicit—will make the doctor fear a suicidal act; other, nameless deeds may seem possible. The Lady will re-experience her most terrible acts, will re-live moments of care and love for her husband, will reach back into a past so remote that then her *little hand* was without taint. Whipsawed among her memories, she may seem worn and broken unto dying; but as we will learn, in V, iii, her movement is toward unbalance, not, immediately, the grave. Actresses may make this a pre-death scene, as their own farewell to audiences; but Shakespeare clearly intended to sustain the Lady's dramatic possibility into the future.

The evidence of physical strain will be unmistakable, even when the Lady is sustained by manic hyper-excitement. She may obviously have come from a disordered bed, her hair matted, her nightgown in disarray, like Ffrangcon-Davies. She may cling to a wall as she feels her way, or supports herself, her pale hands slipping on the stone (Vanbrugh) or, as with Hampden's Lady, her fingers scratching along white tile that reflected her shadow as she moved (a similar shadow was cast by Leblanc-Maeterlinck as she walked along a castle wall, her lamp held aloft). Or she may fling herself in: Stephen Booth saw Vanessa Redgrave race down the stairs at "improbably high speed," her feet seeming not to touch the steps. The energy is erratic, and may fail, as the Lady stumbles, or falls: so a Japanese Lady collapsed as she moved up to her platform, and she made her hand-washing gestures with hands hanging over the edge.

Lady Macbeth often re-enacts her entrance of the murder night; Quayle's, to emphasize this, began by coming from the room that had been Duncan's chamber. In Poland (1966) Lady Macbeth did not enter at all, but was seen to imagine the whole incident while trying to fall asleep on her huge bed, in a kind of perverse love scene, the Lady writhing compulsively, whispering hoarsely, while a tight spotlight picked out her white hands.

The text was seen in action in the Polanski film; acting out the business with the paper that the Gentlewoman described, Annis was seen to go to her desk and handle her secret writing. "Lady Macbeth tries to get rid of the oppression of her secret by committing it to paper," E. K. Chambers supposed; Liddell suggested that she may be re-enacting a time before I, v, when Lady Macbeth wrote to Macbeth to suggest the murder of Duncan. Nothing so explicit could be assumed from the words, or the gestures, if played out; but some intimidation of re-enactment, related to the one letter Lady Macbeth received, could be perceived. Annis was seen nude, through a filmy curtain, until the Gentlewoman covered her with a gown; her nakedness unobtrusively echoed the nudity of the witches' cavern of IV, i. The Lady has appeared unclothed in other twentieth-century stagings. Justification presumably derives from the old Scots habit of sleeping without clothing—hence the *Nightgown* which Lady Macbeth, according to the Gentlewoman, throws upon her. Given this, the only moments the Lady could appear completely unclothed would be when—if—she is indeed seen the moment after leaving her bed.

Mirren wore a stark white robe as she acted out the movement to her desk, from which she took her paper. She turned half-front as she began to speak, still seated, working hard at her hand washing. She seemed to lick or spit on a handful of robe which she rubbed fiercely against her palms. She was wildly urgent in the scene, her anxiety-ridden voice returning to the tones of childhood.

Lady Macbeth's handwashing, once she has entered, generally follows the Siddons' pattern: the two hands are freed, candle or lamp out of the way. Though not always: Miss Smith, playing with Kemble once when Siddons did not, like Pritchard kept her light in one hand, which she rubbed with the other; and Nico Kiasashvili recalled that the Georgia actress, Tariel Anjaparidze, rubbed with her left hand her right, which held a candlestick—"so remorse is shown through the awareness of the hand that killed."

The Lady "seems" to wash her hands, the Gentlewoman says, and so usually she uses imaginary water—actual fluid might be thought to waken her. But Anglin, preparing for the role in the Craig-designed staging, wished for a well to wash in on the stage. The entranced Lady in *Throne of Blood* was seen to lave her hands in water without waking—and, as noted, to go on laving when the water was taken away. Got reports that one Polish actress entered with a red candle in her right hand and a bucket of water in her left. She put the bucket down, and let the drops of red wax fall from the candle into the water. She then plunged her hands into the water, lifted them dripping, and with her eyes fixed on the drops, in a kind of trance, spoke "Out damned spot . . ."

After Reinhardt's Lady, Körner, came groaning and staggering down her stairs and put her candle down, she examined her quivering hands searchingly, even "candling" them—holding them against the light, as if to look through them. Then she pulled back her sleeves, and washed her hands, until she focused the scrubbing down to a spot, which she rubbed intensely. Some Ladies have courted the danger of seeming so involved with the physical washing act as to scant the sense of spiritual purgation: one was scolded for resembling a surgeon preparing for an operation. We have seen the refined complaint on Siddons; Bernard Shaw was hard on Mrs. Campbell's technique similarly. She had wandered and wavered onto the stage, groping her way, murmuring and sighing; then her washing was, he thought, too literal: "You should not have scrubbed your hands *realistically*." Agate, too, objected to a Lady who struggled as if to cleanse a "real defilement" like pitch—"the stain is on the soul." But Shakespeare's visual metaphor does suggest a pollution that Lady Macbeth must try desperately to remove with her *little water*— and try, and try. Strenuous rubbing can imply the ineradicable filth on the conscience. Robson was praised for working agonizedly at her hands as if they were sticky with resin—murder sticking to her hands. Reid rubbed her fingers along her sides, back and thighs; one Lady scrubbed her hands against her long hair; another laboriously scoured each finger separately.

At Lady Macbeth's first words—*Yet here's a spot**—startled, anguished, fearful, desperate, resigned, beaten—the Doctor decides to set all down in his tablets—another manifestation of the suspicion and watching that have become endemic in Scotland. Then the Lady speaks, in the form of prose in the Folio, but in clearly articulated, though much mixed, rhythms that suit her shifts of attention. The first of the mainly monosyllabic words are imperative, spondee-like: *Out damned spot:*† (then the pause, as the rubbing goes on) *out I say.* The words were whispered by Terry; spoken with a shuddering sigh by Siddons, Bernhardt fell back shrieking hysterically—the reaction perhaps partly explicable by the old notion that a strange spot on the body may mark a witch. Lady Macbeth's horrified, unseeing eyes can make her

*Siddons: "Yet here's a *spot*."
†Cushman was careful to voice the final *ed* in *damned*, as the Folio gives it; this was found by one reviewer "a very judicious alteration on the common mode of reciting this speech . . . Miss C., by pronouncing the last syllable at full length, and raising the voice, in some degree, upon the word, converted (to our ear) a profane expression, not likely to fall from the lips of a lady, even in a "mesmeric state," into one of fervent remorse of conscience."

stigma seem as real as Macbeth's stare could his hallucinated dagger. Thus "Ermolova looking down on her hand, peering at the imagined bloodstain . . . I see this hand smeared with good Duncan's blood—dried-up and faded blood, violet at the edges, circled by yellowish rings. Exactly as when a Hindu fakir throws up a stick and you see a snake—so Ermolova's hand, this clean, white, fine and noble hand . . . looks to you bloody and dirty" (Kugel).

Then, as the Lady's blind eyes see the unseeable, the deaf ears hear the unhearable: two strong beats, broken by a pause—*One: Two.* Terry stretched the sounds out, with a long pause between, hinting the reverberations of a bell. Siddons, after sounding the first word, listened eagerly to mark the second; she stressed both, heavily. Casarès heard the tolling with a shock— time for murder. Reinhardt's Lady herself signaled the imagined countdown to action, lifting the fantasied bell, and swinging it once, twice. Her speech grew sleepy, as if her tongue were heavy; her lips hardly opened for the next words. From Savits' Lady also the words came more and more slowly, until they seemed to have no syntactical context. Her steps became halting, directionless.

> Why then 'tis time to do't. (36–37)

Addressed in fancy to Macbeth, the line is pure iambic speech. It may sound the resurgence of her will, after the traumatic blood-memory. But it may also be dismaying: Siddons, on her way to unbalance, spoke it in a "strange, unnatural whisper." Casarès' face showed the shock, as if now she could not bear the ceaseless cycle of murder she was caught in. Reinhardt's Lady tenderly passed her hand over the imaginary Macbeth's forehead. Now the Lady may, as she imagines events, watch Macbeth move up to Duncan's room, and listen again, as she did that other time, for the sounds of murder, and her husband's return. This may motivate her sudden, seemingly inconsequent, *Hell is murky.* Another suggestion has her confirming something Macbeth has, in her fantasy, said to her, and she replies "Hell *is* murky." Leigh spoke it firmly without fear. But the speech, again in verse rhythm, seems another recoil on what preceded, as if the resolution that followed dread is itself succeeded by dread. Casarès suddenly started as if looking on very hell itself: her face contorted, she turned away with a shriek.

Lady Macbeth's erratic stops and starts may be accompanied, as by Savits' Lady, with movements in one direction aborted by counter-movements: concentration on her hand may start the thought of the murder being done, and the hand closes; the clenched fist may signal hell; a gesture to abolish that association may bring on the new one. But the linkages are not all obviously explicable; they have a mysterious, subterranean sequence that is experienced rather than comprehended. Lady Macbeth's movements have both the logic and illogic of a dream; Chabrol's anguished Lady traversed the stage in what seemed almost a dance.

In the next recoil, the woman is dominating, or guiding; and the familiar "man" theme is reprised, still in metrical language. She has imagined Macbeth fearful, and suddenly she is a great queen:

> Fie, my lord, fie, a Soldier and affear'd?
> what need we fear? who knows it, when none
> can call our power to accompt: (37–39)

The Lady has often repeated in detail, here, her tones and gestures of scorn and assurance. Or, in sleep, the mood may change. Casarès turned to persuade her imaginary Macbeth earnestly, her hand on her breast. Then again, the briefly recaptured force collapses into the horrible, accentuated image of blood. Sometimes the Lady has motivated it by moving, in her sleeping walk, towards Duncan's chamber, to come trembling back. As the vision attenuates her pain, the speech rhythms lengthen, though still supported by a metrical structure (which I will suggest):

> Who would have thought
> the old man to have had
> so much blood in him. (39–41)

It is a fearful thought, linked in memory with the *old man*'s resemblance to her father. Bradley found it the most horrible speech in the tragedy. Liddell sensed "an inhuman jest," that an old man should be so rich in vital fluid; but actresses have shuddered. Terry's note: "haunting." Faucit heard herself with "surprised horror." Ristori pointed agonizedly to her bloodspot, indicating the link between it and Duncan's death, "the real cause of my delirium." Siobhan McKenna (in U.S., 1959), as if afraid of her thought, ran suddenly in terror across the stage, her voice rising to a shriek at *so much blood*. Reinhardt's Lady inhaled painfully through her teeth, then moaned, deeply.

For the first time the Doctor learns the depth of Lady Macbeth's secret horror, and cannot repress his shock. The Gentlewoman, as with Casarès, cautions him to silence. But Lady Macbeth hears nothing. She may even, for a moment, stand dead still, almost as if stupefied, as was Savits' Lady. Zeigler, too, became motionless for several seconds, absorbed in her thoughts, breathing only slightly.

Once more the Lady's rhythm changes; a childlike rhyme structures her prose as she alludes—without naming her—to another murdered:

> The thane of Fife,
> Had a wife:*
> where is she now? (43)

Liddell somehow scented demoniacal laughter at the Lady's thought of the murdered mother—"the joy of a triumph over her hated rival." Actresses have usually made the line one of the saddest in the scene. Faucit rendered the

*Bell heard Siddons stress all seven words, leaving out the comma.

"pathetic inquiry" with a "touching tenderness." The words came to Terry
with terrible surprise—as if she had just learned of a murder Macbeth had
kept from her. Her emphasis: "*Where* is she now?" Reinhardt's Lady whispered the question to her Macbeth. Rigg cried out, loudly. Siddons: "Very
melancholy tone" (Bell). Savits' Lady broke suddenly from her stillness to
sing the first two lines wildly, to the tune of a ballad, then checked herself
at the last line. Even Leigh's usually armored voice yielded to a "sudden high-
pitched quaver" (David). Piscator's Lady turned round and round, looking:
"Where is she . . . ?"

Lady Macbeth again associates to her own guilt.

> *What will these hands*
> *ne'er be clean?** (44)

⌈It is the third of her four awarenesses of the ineradicable bloodstains, and
rises in intensity—if not volume—above the first two, in anguished sound
and tortured gesture.⌋ Siddons' mind grew more strange: she spoke, Bell reported, with "melancholy peevishness." Casarès, like many Ladies, repeated
her earlier cleansing gestures, scrubbing a hand down over the whole length
of her contaminated arm. The hands are sometimes flung out, away; even
Leigh could not prevent their "secret, vicious wringing." Rigg cried out again,
washed compulsively, obsessively. Nothing serves. Terry's note: "Rubs
them. Gives it up." The Lady's own starting, and her confrontation with
herself, may turn her again to her earnest—taunting? frightened? tearful?—
confrontation with Macbeth, this time in a memory-leap back to his flaws
and starts at the banquet, her gestures and tone of voice recalling a crucial
moment:

> No more o' that my Lord,
> *no more o' that:*
> you mar all with this starting. (44–46)

Again, the mood may repeat the remembered moment, or may contrast with
it, more desperate, or softened: Casarès pleaded lovingly, Siddons with an
"eager whisper." Ristori, sharp and angry, feigned to be whispering into
Macbeth's ear.

The troubled doctor is alarmed at what the Gentlewoman has known of
the queen's privacy—Reinhardt's looked at her with horror. The Gentlewoman ironically answers with the voice of masking society: *She has spoke
what she should not.* . . . Speaking should be separated from knowing. *Heaven
knows what she has known.*

⌊For the fourth and most terrible time the bloodstained hands recall the
Lady, this time not by sight, but odor:

> Here's the smell of the blood still: (51)

*Siddons' emphases.

The accumulated, obsessing experience of the blood becomes almost intolerable. Rigg groaned, held her head, tried to calm herself. Ermolova's voice winced with pain and repulsion. Marlowe extended her hand, palm away from her, as far as she could, then fell back weakly on a stool. Vanbrugh tried to wipe her hands on her breast, then still smelled the blood on them, gave the great sigh, sank on her knees and like a little child rocked to and fro. The tradition of actually smelling the hands was first reported for Mrs. Cibber (England, 1752), though it probably began with the first performance. It insists on the reality of the sleep-walking experience. It could seem too "real" to a delicate taste: when Siddons did it, Hunt felt a want of "refinement . . . she made a face of ordinary disgust, as though the odor was offensive to the senses, not appalling to the mind." Siddons was, of course, working toward a sense of both psychic and physical unbalance, and was daring the limits of the aesthetically ugly. Anderson's voice, as she spoke before of her bloody hands, had had the "curdled" quality, as if the blood was in her throat; and as she choked on her words, again her nostrils, too, seemed filled. Somewhat similarly Ermolova, whose voice had been before melodious and passionate, suddenly turned thick—"something was gurgling in her throat." Marlowe's sustained sound of *still* was a note of "final, hopeless despair and of the ending of a long struggle."

The experience of guilt, shame, remorse, self-disgust fuses climactically with a womanly lament, accompanied perhaps by a gesture of applying scent that may recall similar gestures since Act III:

> All the perfumes of Arabia
> will not sweeten this little hand.
> Oh, oh, oh. (51–53)

Little hand, as Bradley observed, does not necessarily mean that she was small; it is a diminutive, contrasting the littleness with the ocean of Arabia's perfumes (a "feminine" image, as opposed to Macbeth's vision of the inadequacy of *multitudinous seas*). And it often carries the implication of a tender diminutive: Ladies often see—and voice—a cry for the innocent girl's hand that was, that seemed incapable of the great crime. Something of this, as well as horror and remorse, seem to inform the great triple sigh that the Doctor remarks. In Faucit's lament was heard even "A tender womanly pride in a point of beauty" (*Manchester Examiner*). Her sighs came with a "dreamy pathos."

Terry's *Oh's* diminished, with a deep, mourning pity, down to a soft, third, breathed sigh. Zeigler's, too, became more and more repressed, sighs not loud but deep. Ponisi's apostrophe to her hand was "wonderfully and regretfully tender, (the) three 'ohs' as of painfully cracking heartstrings—as if endurance could bear no more" (Becks). Tessandier spoke the "three famous sighs . . . in rising cadence . . . in a gentle voice like the cries of a child . . .

with a child's gesture, the arms above the head." Eames, too, cried like a child; Reinhardt's Lady wept; Piscator's hid her face in her hands; Robson seemed "a forlorn girl." Viola Allen's note: "*Lips and chin trembling.* Mental and physical torture." Ristori's *oh's* were "exclamations . . . wrung from me as though a grasp of iron were laid upon my heart which would hardly allow me utterance, and I remained with my head thrown back, breathing with difficulty, as if overcome by a profound lethargy." Cushman's "abject, desolate suspiration" (Winter) had an inwardness that touched audiences: "The fearful sigh, the agonized "oh! oh! oh!" of grief, madness and despair . . . was almost the utterance of supernatural sadness" (*N.Y. Times*).

Harsher notes in the Lady's dismay have also been emphasized. Pritchard's sigh was remembered because so "horrid," suggesting a continuation of her stress on horror. Siddons' sigh was remembered as only less horrid than Pritchard's, though Bell remarked a curious tone in it: "This is not a sigh. A convulsive shudder—very horrible. A tone of imbecility audible in the sigh." Siddons herself felt Lady Macbeth moving toward collapse, and some observers sensed gestures of deterioration. Here it was, Tree heard, that she would raise her hand to her mouth, try desperately to suck the imaginary blood and spit it out. In Edinburgh she was seen to strike "the poor hand, that conscience had conjured up as a witness of her guilt, with a fretful and hopeless peevishness." (The action "was followed by so many rounds of applause, that we really ceased to reckon them"—*Courant*). Bernhardt, violent in a different mode, uttered a deep groan, and rushed vehemently across the stage, fleeing the image in her mind. Casarès' low, slow groans sounded a desperation and protest intense enough to recall Lear's "Howl, howl, howl"; she stretched her hands out, palms forward, as if to push encroaching images away. Dench's hoarse sigh shook her whole body: it began in the depths, and drew on her last ounce of breath—on one occasion she was so deprived of oxygen she momentarily blanked out. "That cry comes from the gut," she said. She tried to bite away the stain on her hand.

The Lady must sustain some action—or agonized inaction—to cover the five next speeches of the onlookers. A choral tone has been heard in their dialogue; but it remains characterful, charged with compassion and wonder and, still, expectation. The Gentlewoman's relief that she has not *such a heart* in her bosom seems to evoke the Doctor's admonishing *Well, well, well;* though this has been said ruminatively, and also as a prologue to a next speech. In any case, the Gentlewoman rather tartly responds to an equivocal meaning in the tripled *well: Pray God it be, sir.* The Doctor diagnoses—*this disease is beyond my practice.* After a colon pause, he covers himself, for the benefit of the Gentlewoman: sleepwalkers *have died holily in their beds;* but the impact of his speech is that something terrible, incurable, is at work. This meaning may partly be evoked by Lady Macbeth's actions. During their dialogue she has been working through the grief and dismay of her recognition that she will

never be cleansed again. Yet in spite of this terrible *anagnorisis* she still finds
enough courage, love, terror—all—to break into another direction, to think
of Macbeth's safety, and hers. Her actions again may be very close to those at
the end of II, ii. She is clearly dealing directly with Macbeth, in voice and
gesture. Her mind switches in its disjunct way back to the first murder, then
to the second. She may emphasize caution, as Terry did, whispering; may
recapture an exultancy of the past, in shocking contrast to her preceding dismay. Thus Ristori—who chose this moment to imagine Macbeth's first
return from killing—breaking her phrases with long, half-stifled gasps to
preserve the sense of disturbed sleep:

> I was transported in my delirium to the scene of the murder of Duncan, and,
> as the cause of my change of expression might be the sight of the King's apart-
> ment, I advanced cautiously, with my body bent forward towards . . . where
> I imagined the assassination had taken place. I fancied I heard the hasty steps
> of my husband, and I stood in an attitude of expectation, and with straining
> eyes, apparently awaiting his arrival to assure me that the dreadful deed was
> accomplished. Then, with a cry of joy, as though I saw him approach to an-
> nounce the complete fulfillment of our plans, I exclaimed, in violent agitation,
> > [I break down the lines]
> > Wash your hands, put on your nightgown,
> > look not so pale: I tell you yet again
> > Banquo's buried; he cannot come out on's grave.

A name is out: *Banquo*. It broke from Bernhardt, trying to convince her Macbeth, in a sudden shout that startled her audiences. Reinhardt's Lady, after
at first warning Macbeth with a suppressed nightmare shriek, changed to
calmness to assure him Banquo was buried; paused, listened, shook her head,
and insisted, *He cannot come out. . . .*

At the naming of *Banquo*, the Doctor cannot keep still—though, perhaps
with a quick look at the Gentlewoman, he may wish he had. We may assume
now, though Macbeth did not confess it to her in our presence in III, iv, that
Lady Macbeth has learned—or guessed—of the murder, has perhaps tried
to reassure Macbeth about it, and now the second crime mixes in her mind
with the circumstances of the first one. The confusion of time reflects the
confusion of her thought: her brain fires erratically. Some warning signal
starts her:

> > To bed, to bed: there's knocking at the gate;
> > Come, come, come, come,
> > give me your hand: (66–67)

Komisarjevsky sounded real external knocks for each *Come;* but no evidence
of approach follows, and the alarm, like many of the other cues in the sleepwalk, seems surely self-generated. Janauschek, in her urgency to escape,
moved against a table, and this called to her mind the knocking; one of Phelps'

Ladies backed up against a chair, and paused terrified; but no external cue is needed for the tormented mind to hear the unheard.

Many impulses are felt to gather in the Lady as she now coaxes, urges, commands, physically impels the imaginary Macbeth to bed: maternal, marital, sexual, fugitive-criminal. They fuse in her yearning to return to an older relationship, whether mainly to dominate or love. If only the past could be retrieved, before all meaning in life had been spent. But—

> What's *done*, cannot be *undone*.
> To bed, to bed, to bed. (67–68)

Done, in Lady Macbeth's mouth earlier, was an insistence or a wish that Macbeth accepted finality—most notably in *What's done is done*. Now she cries the mangled phrase as much to herself as to him, vainly; as in her sleep she is compelled repeatedly to try both to undo what was *done* and to do it over and over. Others of her words may similarly haunt her: she lives a denial that the sleeping and the dead are but as pictures; Nature's season, sleep, does not restore her; she looks on everyday things like stools, and sees images of hell. All of her miseries fuse in her final vision of irremediability—which at last drives her back to her bed.

Two descriptions of Siddons suggest something of the range of variation in the exit. Leigh Hunt heard her whispering her last words anxiously: "as if beckoning her husband to bed, [she] took the audience along with her into the silent and dreaming horror of her retirement." Boaden, seeing somewhat differently, had noticed how she "hurried to resume the taper where she had left it, that she might with all speed drag her pallid husband to their chamber." One account had her picking up her lamp by feeling for it, her staring eyes keeping the audience fixed—and making her exit backwards (an action of some other Ladies, usually to repeat a retreat from Duncan's room in II, ii).

Terry was very much impressed by a reported contrast created by Siddons' hurried departure. In the earlier part of the scene, Terry had heard, "*She never moved!* . . . The effect of the whirlwind exit must have been tremendous after that immobility." Terry herself went feebly back to the balustrade where she had left her lamp, and slowly, lonelily, walked up and out of sight—to die of remorse, Terry thought. Rigg, too, went exhaustedly up her stairs, stooping over her candle. Reinhardt's Lady, after again listening to her imagined Macbeth, shook her head, as if answering, pressed her hands against her eyes, listened again to the imagined knocking, held out her hand to Macbeth to come with her, stamped impatiently when he did not; then taking up her candle, and whispering some inaudible words that resolved into *To bed* . . . she went out, weeping softly. Merchant, too, after taking back, unseeing, the candle in the Gentlewoman's hand, left weeping; she had shed all her early hardness, and was begging her husband to come *To bed, to bed.* . . . "It is all she has left, to reach me," her Macbeth, Scofield, said.

Wolter suddenly picked up her lamp again, and, as if someone were trying to take it away, pressed it with both hands against her breast, so that her face was lighted from below. She slowly staggered backwards, and disappeared with a deep sigh—more a cry than a sigh. Anjaparidze also backed out—the last thing seen of her was her hand, outstretched, beckoning Macbeth to follow.

Zeigler's last words, *To bed* . . . were all sighs. In her erratic progress, whenever this Lady had sagged, some resilience had brought a spasm of returning strength; now she sank deeper into weakness, no resurgence came, and as she wavered toward the door, she seemed unmistakably on her way to death.

Worth's *"What's done* . . ." was emphasized by a held, crucified attitude; on leaving she went towards Duncan's room and not the conjugal bed; and then, realizing her mistake, she turned in horror and ran out. Guilt was the last impression: "To bed! . . . spoken only for fearful haste" (J. R. Brown).

Vanbrugh could only whisper the last words tonelessly as, weary to death, she dragged herself back along the high, narrow stairs. Campbell left with a low, long, mournful cry, desolate, despairing, tortured. The desperate Annis, when her outstretched hand found the old Doctor, took him for Macbeth and tried to drag him with her.

In Cushman's triple *To bed*, the words softened until they sank into a dying whisper. Anderson's voice was dead as she pointedly dragged herself out the same door she had used in II, ii. Leblanc-Maeterlinck's going was a prolonged lamentation: eyes still unmoving, her gestures stiff, she suddenly disappeared by a door lost in the shadows from which she had come. The voice of a Baku Turk Lady, who had been whispering, rose to an "inhuman cry" that seemed a certain prelude to death.

Other Ladies' exits were more charged with the kind of energy Boaden ascribed to Siddons. Faucit's was described as a "flight . . . weird and startling," unlike the traditional "stilted" exit. Bernhardt, suddenly overcome with remembered dread, snatched up her lamp, screamed her *"Au lit, au lit* . . ." and rushed frantically out. I have been told of a minor actress who conveyed a resurgence of her physical love for Macbeth: *To bed* was filled with hope and desire. Tutin's risen agony strained the controls of sleepwalk: The *Daily Telegraph* saw "her face wrenched by anguish, her body writhing on the ground, in a welter of self-disgust, and finally her voice crying out, 'To bed . . .' [when] suddenly, unexpectedly, she wakes up." *She wakes up!*

Some Lady Macbeths, in replaying the murder night, took particular care to mime their earlier exit with Macbeth. Casarès did this very lovingly, her face suffused with tender resignation. She stretched out her hand to her imagined husband, *Give me your hand*, lifted her triple chandelier, and went off saying, wearily, *"Au lit.* . . ." Hampden's Lady changed her candle from one hand to another so she could take her husband's imaginary hand; but in her sleep she came up against a closed steel door, and hammered on it wildly until she found her way out. Bethmann repeatedly stretched her hand out to Macbeth. Segond-Weber deliberately reprised the end of II, ii, when

> I dragged Macbeth off with all the force of my nerves; I wish to recapture, sleeping, this exit, but more nervous, more force . . . I leave the scene dragging Macbeth, and because I am afraid of shadows, instinctively sleeping, I take up my lamp again for light . . . I take it mechanically, and leave it only to make a supreme effort to try again to snatch this frightful stain which dirties my hand.

There was finality in her last movements; this Lady, too, was by design, on her way to death.

Ristori, rehearsing her murder-night exit, left her candlestick behind as she helped her imaginary Macbeth off. By the "old gesture, half leading, half cajoling" (*Sydney Morning Herald*) she moved him with her into the outer darkness. Ristori:

> I changed to a more coaxing and persuasive tone of voice . . . Then, terrified by the knocking that I fancied I heard . . . and fearful of surprise, I showed a violent emotion, a sudden dismay. I imagined it was necessary to conceal ourselves in our apartment, and turned toward it, inviting Macbeth to accompany me . . . "Come, come!" in imperative and furious tones; after which, feigning to seize his hand, I showed that I would place him in safety in spite of himself, and urging him on with great difficulty, I disappeared . . . saying, in a choking voice, "To bed . . ."

Since the Lady has heretofore always needed light by her, Ristori's act of leaving it behind is suggestive. Other Ladies have more definitively been separated from light. Langtry extinguished her taper before finally ascending her stairs; Marlowe blew out her lighted candle, put it down, and holding only an imaginary light drifted out. As Craig's Lady left, her dying lamp flickered and went dark.

This moment can foreshadow Macbeth's requiem two scenes later. Thus Robert Edmond Jones:

> The candle flame lives in the theater. It becomes a symbol of Lady Macbeth's own life—flickering, burning low, vanishing down into darkness. *Out, Out, brief candle!* . . . The dramatist . . . has seen deep into the meaning of this terrible moment, and the taper is part of it . . . little flame, little breath, little soul, moving before us for the last time . . . And the shadow on the wall behind "that broken lady" becomes an omen . . . a dark companion following her, silent and implacable, as she passes from this to that other world . . . we remember, not only the dreadful words and the distraught figure, all in white like a shroud; we see vast spaces and enveloping darkness and a tiny trembling light and a great malevolent shadow.

The Lady's anguish and the shocked compassion of the Doctor and the Gentlewoman almost inevitably create some sympathy for her. Her original ferocity may now, Harbage suggested, even seem false to her essential nature; this would certainly be true of the Lady who unmasks a true capacity for remorse that may be understood, in retrospect, to have been repressed before. Compassion for her, Mack observed, can spread over to Macbeth, who is present in all but body, and who must be felt to suffer with her. His ghostly presence serves, also, to keep the audience aware of him until he appears again.

As observed above, Lady Macbeth is often portrayed as being about to die. But, as I suggested, we are not to *know* that this lies ahead. Shakespeare does not put a period to the scene, but a colon. The Doctor fears suicide, but he does not otherwise anticipate death. His next line,

> Will she go now to bed? (70)

confirms the sense of a cyclic behavior, that may go on indefinitely, tomorrow and tomorrow. Expectation is not cut off; again—if we do not know what will happen—we must wonder what this troubled woman, at the edge of madness if not touched by it, may do. Remember that *naive* spectators speculated that she might be the woman—no *man* of woman born—who might kill Macbeth. This illusion is confirmed, if anything, by the next reference, as she endures offstage, to her *mind diseased.* (We may remember that in a late eighteenth-century German version a mad Lady did destroy her husband.) Shakespeare deliberately compacted in the scene many notes in her polyphony, and the polyphony of the play, to sustain possibility. The design is open-ended still, charged with dynamism. If the Lady is weak and exhausted by thoughts of guilt, remorse, fear of apprehension, she still can be aroused, even in sleep, by demands of her care—if not passion—for her husband, or by cues of danger and exposure. If she regresses to the fearfulness of childhood, and the visions of a lost soul, she also is a proud queen whom nobody can call to account. Her variety and potentiality remain dazzling; strange things may yet happen when she wakes from her tormented sleep, and reaches again for the power to control her wayward counterforces. Implicit in her repeated night experience is her unawareness that she is enduring it. This implication happens to be confirmed by sleep research: somnambulists do not remember their night-wandering. But we do not need to know this to allow for the possibility of a resurgence of will in the morning.

The Doctor's speech contributes to the ambience of dread possibility, of *troubles* to come. His first word, *Foul*, signals a reminder of the play's pervasive underlife; the second line reprises the motifs of perverse growth and illness, his change to verse emphasizing the deeper, darker tones.

> Foul whisp'rings are abroad: unnatural deeds
> Do breed unnatural troubles: infected minds
> To their deaf pillows will discharge their secrets: (72–74)

Again the Doctor denies that medicine can deal with the strangeness of Lady Macbeth's case—

> More needs she the divine, than the physician: (75)

He repeats a word as he speaks—one way Shakespeare at a stroke draws character in a minor role—as he joins in the appeals to divinity with what has sometimes been a formal, kneeling prayer:

> God, God forgive us all. (76)

He urges the Gentlewoman to *look after her*, and—the hint of the danger of suicide, possibly cued by some seen physical imagery—

> Remove from her the means of all annoyance. (77)

The Doctor confesses his confusion, indicated in the text by the colon pauses in more than half these last lines. He can hardly believe what he has seen and heard, and he is worried by what may be. Reinhardt's sweating Doctor uneasily wiped his forehead.

> My mind she has mated, and amazed my sight.
> I think, but dare not speak. (79–80)

Again the motif of masking, of suppressing the unspeakable. The Gentlewoman, who has dared to consult the Doctor, and who has received no more help than this, has sometimes in the theatre touched with sarcasm the *good* in her farewell, as if glad to get rid of the man:

> Good night good doctor. (81)

Act V, Scene ii

The dread silence ending the last scene is interrupted by the sounds of war first heard as the play began:

> *Drum and Colours. Enter Menteth, Cathnes,*
> *Angus, Lenox, Soldiers.*

The troops may come on with a roar, as if all ready for battle, uttering war cries, as Dunn's did. More often the scene specifies preparation: these are unmistakably Scots officers (to distinguish them from the English later) moving their army to a strategic meeting with the English.* They may be consulting maps. Directors have sometimes added historical colour by accompanying the men with the baggage of war, including even the women who historically followed their Scots fighting men. In the Hopkins *Macbeth*, however, Michael Blakemore had the thane-leaders hold a furtive, candle-lit meeting for a growing band of conspirators, who filtered in from the darkness; and to suggest a moral theme, an enormous curcifix hung over them.

Two of these four thanes have been mentioned by name in stage directions as having already appeared—Lenox and Angus. We remember that the dialogue never mentions their names, but Shakespeare's actors may well have; and all four were probably included among Duncan's *Attendants*, so we can recognize their faces. Lenox we know best: he has always been present near power, and his appearance here suggests his jackal's facility for switching. Angus is specified once in stage directions, when he went with Ross (I, iii) to greet Macbeth with Duncan's message. His speech will connect with that early scene.

While preparations for march and battle sustain the background, Menteth and Angus provide exposition, plausibly if they and Lenox come from one direction to meet Cathness entering oppositely. Menteth carries us back to the end of IV, iii, telling us what we know: Malcolm will be coming, with

---

*To further distinguish Malcolm's Scots from Macbeth's, Gielgud, directing, dressed the former in brisk, clean tunics, the latter in tatters.

Seyward and Macduff, at the head of an English army. Shakespeare's audience would welcome the imminent appearance of England's power; though a faint echo may be sensed of that earlier invasion of Duncan's Scotland, based on an alliance with two rebellious Scots and a foreign warrior against Scotland's king. The Scots are roused against Macbeth:

> Revenges burn in them: for their dear causes
> Would to the bleeding, and the grim alarm
> Excite the mortified man. (6–8)

Muir sees an extension of disease imagery: *burn* being associated with fever, *dear causes* capable of meaning "sore diseases" and "grievous wrongs" as well as "grounds of action." The implication seems to be that a man benumbed, even dead, would be roused.

Angus drops an ominous word: the allied meeting will occur near *Birnam Wood*.

Cathnes is the uninformed "straight" man, apparently most recently come from Dunsinane, who must be enlightened by the other three: his question about the whereabouts of Donalbain gives Lenox a chance to sound the motifs of the young against the aged, of man as warrior: *many unrough youths*, in their *first of manhood* are coming to fight the old man. Young Seyward is specified— for we will meet him. Lenox, characteristically, knows all: he has collected intelligence: *a file/ Of all the gentry*. *File* echoes Macbeth's ranking by degree of dogs and men when he used the word twice to the murderers (III, i).

What the three now have to say about Macbeth is sometimes accepted as gospel, partly because it fits the play's clothes imagery pattern; but truth is undercut by the emphasis on rumor:

> CATHNES: Great Dunsinane he strongly fortifies:
> *Some say* he's mad: *others*, that lesser hate him,
> *Do call it* valiant fury, but for certain
> He cannot buckle his distemper'd cause
> Within the belt of rule. (17–21)

And Angus, who heard Banquo's image in I, iii, about Macbeth's new garments cleaving not to their mould, now extends it, diminishingly. He first describes a condition easy to believe, from what we know:

> Now does he feel
> His secret murders sticking on his hands, (22–23)

(we know how Macbeth has felt about his hands—and have seen how some actors unobtrusively rubbed them). Some irony seems implicit in the next line, which speaks of the breaking of faith—an act Angus now shares with Lenox, at least:

> Now minutely revolts upbraid his faith-breach:
> Those he commands move only in command.
> Nothing in love: (24–26)

Then the garment image:

> Now does he feel his title
> Hang loose about him, like a giant's robe
> Upon a dwarfish thief. (26–28)

Do we accept this as a valid report? Is it to whet our expectation for when we see Macbeth? To see if this giant has as king indeed shrunk, contracted (as some critics believe) to a dwarfish man? Do we perceive that these men are dwarfish compared with Macbeth, mouth-honorers who, their previous golden opinions having turned to dross, now try to outdo each other in calumny? In any case, we are likely to see Macbeth differently than they do, as we see with his eyes rather than theirs. The tension between the two ways of seeing will persist to the end of the play.

Menteth, who first asked *What does the tyrant?* now joins in with an analysis of Macbeth's divided self. The last speech about Macbeth, it edges away from criticism of Macbeth's actions to an experience of his inward suffering, and so retrieves some sympathy, as it prepares for his appearance:

> Who then shall blame
> His pester'd senses to recoil, and start,
> When all that is within him, does condemn
> Itself, for being there. (29–32)

The four finish their talk in time for some signal that the army is ready to move out; and as they go they resolve that, with Malcolm, himself

> the med'cine of the sickly weal, (35)

they will give their last drop to *purge* the country, or enough at least, Lenox says, as will *dew the sovereign* (royal, curative) *flower, and drown the weeds.* On these compressed images of medicining, cleansing, growth and liquidity they set off, in military order—*Exeunt marching*—drum and colours active again.

> Make we our march towards Birnam. (40)

The last word rings out, for the second time, ominous, full of possibility to us who have heard the oracles: *Birnam.*

For simplification these army scenes—V, ii, V, iv, V, vi—are sometimes merged, sometimes cut—Garrick eliminated V, ii altogether, thus minimizing implications that Macbeth was anything but an honorable murderer. This deletion, along with that of the killing of the Macduffs, almost made Macbeth inoffensive. The army scenes are part of the grand design, establishing temporal insulations that measure the progress of Macbeth's downfall, and providing quick shifts between the miseries in Dunsinane and the attacking force without, until the two fuse in the "grand battle."

I have lived long enough.

Act V, Scene iii

As the sight and sound of the marching Scots dies away, the scene shifts abruptly to Dunsinane. The sense of speed will be sustained through the scene—in sudden entrances, in emotional language, in the atmosphere of preparation for climax, most of all in Macbeth as a vortex of energy.

Macbeth is sometimes seen on the battlements (in the Globe, perhaps in the "above"); sometimes, as specified by Rowe, at the Castle—implying a room within, and then often the throne room. The mood is usually of war, often with banners aloft, drums urgent. Macbeth's *Attendants* will be armed men as well as courtiers. We last heard of Macbeth going into the field; he may only now be returning, perhaps on purpose, as Strindberg thought, to enquire about his wife's mental state (and perhaps for his own as well). If so, his felt objective will be to get through his early lines—as he takes off his armor to breathe, and reassure his men—to confer with the Doctor, who is directed to enter with him. The first battles have not yet been specified; but if Macbeth is accompanied by wounded men, as with Tree, the Doctor may at first be busy with them, helped by the fit soldiers.

The first shock to our eyes may be Macbeth's appearance. Even if he has begun to show age in earlier scenes, now he has unmistakably lived longer— harder—than when first seen. Irving, who had begun to grey earlier, was now even more grizzled, his lean figure seemed more lean, he summoned a fierce, full-toned voice that proclaimed defiance, but a half-mad defiance. Irving's note: "a deadly heartsickness over him now." Terry saw in him a "gaunt, famished wolf." That was the effect Gielgud specifically strove for, making up his actor's second body "with whitened hair and bloodshot eyes." Agate, appraising Gielgud, provided a good touchstone for Macbeth's appearance:

> Mr. Gielgud . . . came on the stage as though he had lived the interval. Macbeth has to say: "I have supped full of horrors," and the actor must make the audience realize that this supper-time has been the time of the interval.

Akutagawa's complete change of make-up was radical: he appeared almost a madman: hair dishevelled, face pale, clothes disarranged. Milward thought he looked like a beast. Akutagawa:

> Yes he does; or rather, like a god of the plague. Yet he is not inhuman, but only an invalid . . . the country becomes sick, and Macbeth himself is completely diseased. He is not only the source of the plague, but is himself the victim and is infected with it.

Macbeth's hair may be turned entirely white (Rogers); or hang lank and grey on dark patches of cheek in his gray face (Clements). He may be haggard, self-tormenting (Benson): "lost too poorly in himself" (Hazlitt on Kean). He usually is marked by some harrowing of sleeplessness.

With some Macbeths, the physical symptoms of attrition were subordinated, and by contrast the psychic wear was startling. Thus Stevenson on Salvini:

> There is still the big, burly, fleshy, handsome . . . Thane; . . . the same face which . . . could be superficially good-humoured and sometimes royally courteous. But now the atmosphere of blood . . . has entered into the man and subdued him to its own nature; an indescribable degradation, a slackness and puffiness, has overtaken his features. He has breathed the air of carnage, and supped full of horrors. Lady Macbeth complains of the smell of blood . . . Macbeth makes no complaint . . . but the same smell is in his nostrils. A contained fury and disgust possesses him.

Anger is sometimes the mask now for the complex of Macbeth's emotions. It comes with great contrast in an interpretation like that of Sothern, so markedly a gentleman in the early part of the play, now quick to strike an underling—so that his troubled attendants withdraw from him, leave him alone to his soliloquies. With Scofield, who seemed almost to be more toughened with age, stiff as a seasoned tree against the wind, his sudden, violent, unusual rages at the reports brought him had an edge of uncertainty: something was wrong in this world in which he had been promised certainty. On the other hand, Macready ostensibly wore the confident armor of a Macbeth trusting in the supernatural assurances of security: with a proud, haughty self-complacency he tore the latest report, which he had been reading as he entered, and tossed the fragments aside.

The Macbeth who had been operating on nerves might now move by contrast to a depleted mood. The philosophic reserve and poetic sensibility, which had before returned Forbes-Robertson to stability, were worn thin:

> the old sensitive nerves have frayed out under the stress of all that had gone before, until they vibrate only fitfully. The old restlessness sinks into a settled gloom, flaming now and then into an exaggerated activity. The old morbid irirritability has become a grim brooding. Except at rare moments, (he) no longer feels all things as keenly as he did . . . The capacity to do so has gradually, and to him unconsciously, dried and hardened within him. (*Transcript*)

Evans sat bowed on his throne, emphasizing his aloneness from the rest, the isolation that was to be his fate. On the floor before him were scraps of paper, reports he refused to look at.

Hyperactivity may also signal the deep inner unrest, emphasize Macbeth's patrol of the boundary of madness. Reinhardt's neurotic Macbeth seemed by now almost completely deranged: he paced restlessly, trying to intoxicate his attendants—and himself—with big talk. The others watched him, standing in a little group. He listened to the first report, stared for a moment, and dismissed it with a great, contemptuous gesture. Kemble, who was intent, both in his writing and acting, to defend Macbeth against any charges of cowardice, insisted:

> His original valour remains undiminished, and buoys him up with wild vehemence in this total wreck of his affairs.

The young face of Polanski's Macbeth had become brutalized: half mad, he burned unread the messages brought to him. Quilley's Macbeth intensified the exhilarated, laughing exterior he developed earlier: a manic touch enlivened the sallies of his opening speech, and he was elated with the mouth-honoring smiles he forced from his attendants. Maháček, achieving the same effect, was bitterly amused.

A rare implication that Macbeth might have deserved Malcolm's condemnation—"luxurious"—was dramatized by Bergman in 1944. He staged a "wild-renaissance-picture" drinking party,

> with furiously laughing wenches, and shady men, damped for a moment by the doctor, dressed in a black robe, who glides down a winding staircase like a shadow. Then . . . bellowing and screaming (they) dance an intoxicated and absurd gavotte (and) out of the dusk of the room through a blood-red cone of light (*Stockholmstidningen*).

But the "party" was described as "horrid, cheerless . . . a feast for sadists" (*Dagens Nyheter*), presided over by a strained Macbeth with white, furrowed face and staring look; it seemed to present not so much a characteristic trait of Macbeth's as an aberration.

This Macbeth we meet after the long delay embodies opposites reflected in our reactions to him. The killing of the Macduffs, the intense reaction of Macduff himself and the comments of the thanes, have harnessed our resistances to the butcher king. At the same time, we have identified with Macbeth's capacity for a moral perspective on his acts; we have shared the poetry of his pain, directly and —more recently—through his wife's nightmare. We have never been allowed to see Macbeth himself do violence to anyone. He remains the character with whom our own impulses and passions and guilts are most involved; now the sight of his aging in suffering is some bond between us. We will be moved between the poles of antipathy and sympathy as Macbeth himself is whipsawed between his harsh resolution to action and his grief for a discolored lifetime. The butcher has sometimes been perceived as dominant, even fully in control—all "manhood" gone in him, filled with direst cruelty, a dwindled, hardened figure, incapable of a recognition of what he has become. Conversely, his suffering and remorse have been emphasized to the point of sentimentality, his bravery has been seen as heroic, his recognition of what he has done truly tragic. These are verbalizations of separate tones that sound together in the final polyphony. The dissonance among them helps to sustain expectation. However Macbeth may be wracked, he believes in his charmed life, aims himself at destiny, prepares to kill savagely, speaks disillusion but does not accept defeat; what will happen in him vitalizes what is happening to him.

He usually enters brushing away, tearing up, or rebuffing written or spoken reports—reports that, we may gather from his reaction and from the covert attitudes about him, are unfavorable. With a show that may range from bravery to bravado he denies any fear, citing—partly to remind us— the Sisters' assurances. The speech may be said apart, after he has sent off a messenger with a last report; then he is isolated from his attendants. Or he speaks it to them, to instil confidence in his magic; and their open and masked responses convey the context of his terrorized world.

Like so many of his pivotal speeches, the words—except for names—are mainly in sharp monosyllables, fitted to Macbeth's assertive, aggressive theme.

> Bring me no more reports; let them fly all: (3)

—Reinhardt's Macbeth, with a shrill laugh—

> Till Birnam wood remove to Dunsinane,
> I cannot taint with fear. What's the boy Malcolm? (4–5)

Macready's proud lip curled at this last. But the words reverberate: with echoes of the infant apparitions of IV, i, of the child-motif threading the play, of the recently repeated *Birnam*. The *boy*-child comes to Dunsinane; and Macbeth's very distinction between *boy* and *man* as he repeats the Sisters' oracle hints at a buried mine:

> The spirits that know
> All mortal consequences,* have pronounc'd me thus:
> Fear not, Macbeth, no man that's born of woman . . . (6–8)

*I see no reason to drop the *s:* the six beats sustain the portentousness of the line, with its slowing polysyllables. It still echoes *Trammel up the consequence . . .*

The words teased the wondering minds of *naive* spectators with the possibility that the *boy* (Malcolm)—not a *man*—may be the instrument of Macbeth's downfall. If not Malcolm, then Fleance?

The speech becomes an exercise in hubris, that asks for a recoil:

> Then fly false thanes,
> And mingle with the English epicures . . . (9–10)

Epicures. Shakespeare perhaps took the word from Holinshed's reference to English gourmandizing corrupting the Scots, though it implies as well over-refinement, the effete; the Globe audiences were probably amused.

> The mind I sway by, and the heart I bear,
> Shall never sag with doubt, nor shake with fear. (11–12)

The primary meaning of *sway* here is rule; but Macbeth's phrase also hides the implication of an unsteady, swaying mind; and as in immediate, ironic challenge to this connotation the *Servant* enters, usually showing, by his fearfulness, how dangerous it can be now to approach Macbeth with bad news—Reinhardt's entered deadly pale, trembling with fear, as if expecting violent rebuff; Macbeth stalked before him, watching maliciously, but appearing to take no notice, until finally the man swallowed and spoke.

Garrick, preserving Macbeth's gentlemanliness, cut the first retort, *The devil damn thee black*—though he did bring back the rest of the line, which had languished while actors spoke Davenant's callow words.* Macbeth's mind sways; the brain fires as erratically as Lady Macbeth's did in sleep:

> . . . thou cream-fac'd loon:
> Where got'st thou that goose-look. (14–15)

The servant is likely to stutter his *t*'s and *th*'s—

> There is ten thousand. (16)

An aesthetic problem faces the Macbeth-actor now. He will catch the Servant up savagely: but this response will be one of a series leading to his climactic confrontation with Macduff. However fierce his outbreak, the next, in V, v, must modulate it somehow, usually with more ferocity; and the pitch of tension, if not the tempo or volume, must still intensify to the ending.

One interpretation sees Macbeth himself as infected with the messenger's fear, an idea Kemble stoutly rejected:

> But it is clear, from the angry contempt with which he treats both [the Servant] and the report of the approach of Malcolm's army, that the coward's countenance has no dejecting influence on his own mind.

*"Now friend what means thy change of countenance?" (!) This was so familiar, the story goes, that Quin, hearing Garrick's use of Shakespeare's words, asked where he had found them.

Yet Macbeth becomes terribly uneasy, if not from fear then from the tension between his belief in the promises of the Sisters and the mounting evidence of force brought against him.

Macready thundered at the Servant; Richardson hissed; Olivier stood over him; Reinhardt's Macbeth made as if to beat the man; Hopkins struck the face of his boy-messenger, and pushed it away; Evans, in a sudden violence, jerked his scuttling messenger upright, held his face close, then pushed him away; Quayle's direction: "Kicks Loon out of his way. Loon crawls backward and runs off." Sothern's "Servant" was an officer, who knelt: Macbeth kicked him, and put a foot on him, evoking evident resentment from the knot of men watching, and sympathy for the man, who rose angrily.

Macbeth wrenches out the news, upsetting himself more at every word he forces himself to hear: *Soldiers . . . The English force.* He senses his effect on his own men, already alarmed by the news. The frightening white cheeks of the servant particularly anger him: *Counsellors to fear.* He drives the man away. He calls for his most personal attendant, and for the first time the name enters the text: *Seyton*—generally assumed to be a variation of Seton, the name of a family of armor-bearers to Scots kings, pronounced "See-ton." "Say-ton" (Satan) has also been proposed, but this, in its sound so unequivocally diabolical, seems too unsubtle for Shakespeare, who does not indicate devilish qualities in the design. This Seyton has probably appeared before, as Macbeth's chief attendant, and as such may have been recognizable as the third murderer (III, iii). He has been played as a black, sinister shadow to Macbeth; but his actions, especially in V, v, suggest only loyal, trusted service, not limited to armor-bearing—again, I can see the admiring Bleeding Captain become Macbeth's aide, by now mainly healed of his wounds, perhaps limping.

Macbeth's swaying mind, unpoised by the messenger, swings from hubris to a dark vision of reality. His impulse to action, signaled by his calls for Seyton, is broken by his old need for self-communion, for locating his self in a turbulent world. Reinhardt's Macbeth motivated the first shift in dialogue with physical imagery: when his servant ran away, he stretched his arm out after the man, stumbled down several steps, called *Seyton*, and pressed his hand against his heart as the next lines came out. But the breaks in speech direction are well enough explained as reflections of the zigzag of Macbeth's mind:

                              Seyton, (24)

the command is shouted; but the old raptness is coming on—

                         I am sick at heart,
                    When I behold: (24–25)

Pause, the thought remains unfaced, as the brain fires across; back to the summons.

Seyton, I say, (25)

and now the full recoil into raptness, and a return to the mind and spirit of the man with whom our fantasies and sympathies have been deeply linked:

this push
Will cheer me ever, or disseat me now. (25–26)

(Perhaps a pun: cheer—chair—for throne; though that might imply more mind at work than feeling, which now dominates.) The meter takes the edges from the iambic beat:

I have liv'd long enough: my way of life
Is fallen into the sere, the yellow leaf, (27–28)

Garrick said "my May" for *my way*, and Johnson so emended his edition; the seasonal metaphor is neater but I am not sure neatness is the proper measure here. Shakespeare often poises one metaphor against another. *My way of life* has a universality about it, a sense of the long journey, that may spread more ripples. Duration stretches out, words and expressed feeling hymning the passage of time: *ever . . . now . . . long enough*. And Macbeth uses *way* elsewhere: *the way that I was going . . . the way to dusty death*. The primary image, in any case, is the wintry season to which Macbeth sees himself coming. Shakespeare has elsewhere used the seasonal metaphor for a life's passage through time, most wonderfully in the sonnet (73),

That time of year thou may'st in me behold
When yellow leaves, or none, or few, do hang
Upon those boughs . . .

In the context of the play, as Simrock observed, Macbeth's metaphor fits the seasonal myth of the old king who must die with the dying year, to be replaced by rising green youth. He seems, in Malcolm's words, *ripe for shaking*. But the play never wholly submits to the myth; Macbeth sustains an identity that resists any pattern; he may still survive. His musing now belongs to the moral Macbeth who long ago wrestled with the true value of a man:

And that which should accompany old age,
As honor, love, obedience, troops of friends,
I must not look to have: but in their stead,
Curses, not loud but deep, mouth-honor, breath
Which the poor heart would fain deny, and dare not. (29–33)

Perhaps most touching and most terrible of all is the last confession, once more a repression of truth: he *dare not*—he who dares do all that may become a man, and more—fully admit how tarnished are the golden opinions he once won, how false the protestations and smiles that even now we may see evoked as he turns suddenly to look at his attendants—perhaps surprising them in furtive whisperings that turn to servile grins.

Macbeth's allusion to his own *poor heart** gives to himself some of the sympathy he could sense for the *unfortunate souls* who had to die with the Macduffs. Self-pity enters here, but it is not craven; it is absorbed into the despair of a realistic vision of what he has become. The words of the soliloquy are marvellously simple, seeming to come from the poor heart itself; again they are mainly monosyllabic—but how different from the shrapnel of the scene's opening bluster. These words linger in the mind, and on the tongue; the mood in which they demand to be spoken, and are almost always spoken on the stage, is of melancholy.

Hazlitt remembered the "thoughtful melancholy" of Kemble's retrospection, Hunt how Kemble's "voice fluttered among the fond images of decay, and clung with melancholy grace to the blessings 'which should accompany old age.'" Charles Kean's voice, in the same tradition, "trembled like a leaf fluttering in the wind." Macready exploited the contrast between his haughty assurance at first and the sudden boneless slump, his face cheerless, his voice a deep, melancholy pathos, the words, instinct with the dreariness of desolation, echoing "the knell of a better life" (*Morning Post*). Irving's first afflatus, too, was gone: he had turned nervous at the first appearance of the *Servant*, and now, his mask completely dropped, he sagged with doubt into a picture of weariness and despair, musing vacantly on his despair, sighing, projecting an infinite sadness.

More than melancholy sounds in the speech. Macbeth is partly moving toward his ultimate glimpse of meaninglessness, and a measure of protest informs his lament. If he has brought himself to this, it is yet a terrible place to be. Olivier gave the impression of resurgent nobility bewildered, haunted. The conscience and decency that had been only momentarily glimpsed behind his almost sinister surface was suddenly exposed to the quick. He spoke in a breaking voice, his forehead furrowed.

> You would swear that Macbeth, for all his wickedness, has a right to feel that the universe has monstrously betrayed him. (*Sunday Times*)

Scofield made his admission to himself grudgingly, bitterly, breaking off the two lines beginning *I have lived* almost as a series of spondees. The speech ended grimly, the *poor heart* touching in its mingled pity and irony. Kean, conspicuously avoiding the melodious melancholy of his contemporaries, was hoarse and restless, unrelieved from strain. Wolfit's vision was intolerable: "'I have lived long enough' was the desperate cry of a trapped animal, evoking horror, rather than pity" (Harwood). Krahulikův's (Czechoslovakia, 1963) lament seemed dominated by a deep, nostalgic longing for the man he once was.

Seyton, summoned, asks: *What's your gracious pleasure?*—the last word tainted in its context, as it has been before. Macbeth's hyperactivity is fully

---

*One editor suggests that the *poor heart* belongs to the mouth-honorer; but in the context of the lament Macbeth seems, painfully, to mean himself. If the sycophant is intended Macbeth is finding some bitter compassion for him.

roused by the time Seyton enters. Now he wants more reports; Seyton confirms what has been told; Macbeth grasps at relief in action. He who has taken pride in being unkillable now envisions himself butchered:

> I'll fight, till from my bones, my flesh be hacked.
> Give me my armor. (39–40)

'Tis not needed yet, Seyton answers, introducing a sense of duration, a slowed measure against which Macbeth's frantic urgency must seem irrational. The renewed horse-speed image suits the pace of his mind:

> I'll put it on:
> Send out more horses, skirr the country round,
> Hang those that talk of fear. Give me mine armor: (42–44)

The repeated demand forces Seyton to comply: Macbeth's sequent putting on and taking off his outer garments will complement in visual imagery the pervasive verbal imagery of the effect of clothes on appearance. If he has regal robes, making them too large for him would sacrifice metaphor to demeaning literality: his very restlessness in whatever he wears, as suggested in the text, unobtrusively supports his language. He is beginning to reassume the heroic warrior's outer image that he first presented when returning from victory in battle; but he does so by degrees, as if unwilling to leave off his regal garments, slow to return to no more than what he was. He may be wrestling with his robes, uncertain whether to keep them or leave them off, even now as he talks to the doctor.

> How does your patient, Doctor? (45)

In many stagings the Doctor does not enter until this moment, since he has had no lines; Shakespeare's intention in bringing him on with Macbeth, as the Folio directs, was perhaps to establish him as an observer of the husband, as he was of the sleepwalking wife. He may stand in the same place as before. The Doctor would not, until now, have had an opening to speak of his patient, however much he may have tried; and while Macbeth's objective was to speak to the doctor, he may, from fear of what he might learn, have welcomed the putting off forced by the messenger. As Macbeth asks now, another major note in his polyphony sounds: his care for his wife. The degree of earnestness and urgency with which he asks connects back to any shows of affection in the past to his "dearest chuck"; and looks ahead to his leavetaking of her.

None of Macbeth's sudden transitions in the last act is more abrupt than this shift from the almost hysterical order for armor to the inquiry of the doctor, and an actor may be tempted to make too much of it. Macready to some observers, overdid, moving from stormy chiding in the "ultra colloquial"; but the *Sun* was impressed at how

> amid the din and confusion of the advancing enemy Macbeth seeks of the physician the state of his wife's health; the same breath that a minute before was hoarse with battle orders . . . slides into an exquisite suavity, communicative of pain and condolence . . . a chivalric tenderness characterises this touch.

Mantell's voice dropped to a quiet solicitude; Irving turned from his imperious command to cast a pathetic look upon the doctor, as he made his inquiry. Salvini asked, Stevenson thought, with "something like a last human
anxiety."

The Doctor's diagnosis opens the possibility of Lady Macbeth's reappearance; her mortality seems not in danger:

> Not so sick my Lord,
> As she is troubled with thick-coming* fancies (46–47)

All that the Doctor has to say of Lady Macbeth may be felt by Macbeth to
apply to himself. His immediate response is terse, abrupt: *Cure her of that:*
touched with threat (Irving: "cold and imperious").

Macbeth's images echo central urgencies not only in Lady Macbeth, but
in himself: images of cleansing, purging, eradicating the records of the *done*.
Characteristically, Macbeth speaks of the body, and his language, however
demandingly spoken, is sensitive, compassionate, the occasional polysyllables and soft "s" sounds lengthening and solemnizing it:

> Canst thou not minister to a mind diseas'd,
> Pluck from the memory a rooted sorrow,
> Raze out the written troubles of the brain,
> And with some sweet oblivious antidote
> Cleanse the stufft bosom, of that perilous stuff
> Which weighs upon the heart? (50–55)

Some complaints have been made that, in the next to last line, *stuff* repeats
stufft. I do not find it objectionable. I can imagine Macbeth feeling for his
words, and after *perilous* avoiding anything more dangerously specific by
using a word that conveys so widely a sense of the breast stopped up, both
literally and metaphorically—congested, plugged, choking. That Macbeth
was pleading not only for his Lady was suggested by a note in Charles Kean's
promptbook:

> the feelings with which he describes the sensations he wishes to be removed;
> the longing he expresses for the means of doing it; the plaintive measure of the
> lines: and the rage in which he bursts, when he says, "Throw physic . . ."
> evidently show that in his own mind he is all the while making application to
> himself.

Olivier conveyed as much gesturally: he

> not only showed us the bond of affection between husband and wife but also
> (his hands gesturing dumbly and half-unconsciously toward his own breast)
> included himself in the plea for mercy. (David)

---

*Multiple implications accumulate—profusion, turbidity, acceleration—as in *thick as tale;*
thick night; gruel thick and slab. And we remember that Lady Macbeth prayed for *thick . . . blood*.

A touch of pleading for himself entered even Scofield's austere voice, as he looked directly at the doctor.

The doctor may pause, in one of Shakespeare's powerful, pointed silences, before responding. Will he not recognize the latent as well as the overt plea? "The doctor has watched two nights," the Tyrone Power promptbook directs: "He must sense something of what crimes were committed. He looks straight into Macbeth's eyes." Now there is no referral to a consultation with a divine. The doctor's short speech, when he makes it, breaks into two abrupt, comfortless phrases.

> Therein the patient
> Must minister to *him*self. (56–57)

Another crucial pause, as Macbeth absorbs the implication. One view of Macbeth finds him conscious now of damnation. The text suggests, rather, his acknowledgement of judgment here. Does Shakespeare deny Macbeth a recognition of his condition, and his responsibility for it? Certainly actors here—and elsewhere—indicate that they glimpse the enormity of what they have become: but their Macbeths do not accept passively as long as there is strength to *do*. Whatever Macbeth has done, he looks forward. He fires back at the doctor:

> Throw physic to the dogs, I'll none of it. (58)

Macbeth may laugh, as Quayle's did, but it is a brutal laugh, more often a snarl, as with Reinhardt's Macbeth; Hopkins spat. Macready turned his back. Williamson angrily threw the black cloth, which the witches had used to blindfold him, over the doctor's head. The line is a signal for the full return of Macbeth's escape into hyperactivity. He *will* have his armor on; no, his staff; no, Seyton must dispatch troops. (Seyton signals off? Macbeth does not let him go.) Macbeth speaks a few anguished words to the Doctor, then to Seyton again, then, while he is wrestling with his armor, to the Doctor again. Colons point his erratic directions.

> Come, put mine armour on: give me my staff:
> Seyton, send out: Doctor, the thanes fly from me: (59–60)

This last is an unexpected confession of vulnerability, though coated sometimes in sardonic carelessness, as if unimportant, or fired with anger. Murphy cherished a memory of Garrick's saying the line with a "strong, involuntary burst of melancholy"; but Garrick intended something else:

> Macbeth is greatly heated, and agitated with the news of the English force coming upon him; his mind runs from one thing to another, all in hurry and confusion: would not his speaking in a melancholy manner in the midst of his distraction be too calm?

And the actor cited all the short, sharp orders, sometimes contradictory, to Seyton, as evidence of Macbeth's frenetic state.

Macbeth, perhaps finding no sympathy from the doctor, embarrassed, frustrated, turns again to Seyton: *Come sir, dispatch.* Becks' promptbook suggests that by now the armor is buckled, and Seyton is now to offer "surcoat, hat, sword, gauntlets, truncheon," and to follow Macbeth off with the shield. The text suggests that Macbeth will not allow the armor fully to be emplaced. While Seyton tries to buckle it, Macbeth, turning again to the doctor, may make the job difficult, as in the Kumo production: and Seyton must fumble as best he can.

Macbeth may even stop Seyton, so intent does he become on the next, only sustained, thought in the speech, entreating for Scotland's health. He is deeply earnest, as again he mingles images of medicine, purging, cleansing:

> . . . If thou could'st, Doctor, cast
> The water of my land, find her disease,
> And purge it to a sound and pristine health . . . (61–63)

The irony has cruelty in it: Macbeth is himself a disease that the Scots, as we have just seen, mean to purge. As if this may enter his consciousness, he becomes impatient with Seyton—*Pull't off I say.* Scofield, raging impatiently at Seyton for an imagined delay, tore off the unfastened armor, as did Irving; Sothern's Seyton fell to his knees as Sothern threw the armor to him; Olivier meant his cloak, which Seyton took.

Macbeth becomes specific: he wants a purgative that

> Would scour these *English* hence: hear'st ye of them? (67)

The doctor, who gives nothing away, answers dryly:

> Aye my good Lord: your royal preparation
> Makes us hear something. (68–69)

It is another speech that may give Macbeth pause; he has no reply, other than an angry or bewildered look. He may find it hard now, finally, to part with his royal robes. He orders the cast-off armor to follow—*Bring it after me*—sometimes as his answer to a gesture from Seyton: Olivier's offered a helmet, Tree's a shield. Irving, fiery energy in every movement now, with a desperate desire to drive away thought and apprehension, flung the proffered armor violently on the ground; Sothern, still furious, struck his Seyton for making the offer.

Macbeth strides off, his rhyming couplet suggesting almost a charm:

> I will not be afraid of death and bane,
> Till Birnam forest come to Dunsinane. (71–72)

Sothern's Seyton, on his knees gathering up Macbeth's armor, looked at the Doctor, who shook his head, ominously. The Doctor's couplet is a kind of charm of his own, and reveals his only motivation for serving Macbeth:

> Were I from Dunsinane away, and clear,
> Profit again should hardly draw me here. (73–74)

The sense of haste energizing Macbeth picks up the drive toward climax. Not accidental to Shakespeare's design, probably, was Macbeth's hurried exit, more or less unprotected by armor: the *naive* spectator, alert to some impending catastrophe, wonders if Macbeth will now be vulnerable to some unimagined stroke.

The Doctor returns to his patient; Seyton goes after Macbeth with Macbeth's soldier-attendants. The evidence of their fidelity will condition expectation now. Sometimes they follow loyally, cheering Macbeth, as Tree's did; more often they begin to melt away, by back doors.

We go with Macbeth. Heilman wisely observes that we are moved to fellowship by the dignity of Macbeth's style, expressing experience with which we feel kindred, and the capacity for human feeling (*sick at heart*); by the universality of the mediation on his approaching winter; by his intellectual candor; by the burden of his sick wife, and his concern for her; by his role as underdog, deserted by his thanes. He feels deep fear, and tries to talk it down; he turns grief into contemplation. We do not articulate these attractions, as we do not their opposites—the near-hysteria, the violent or sardonic outbreak against attendants, the history of delegated cruelty. All are experienced in a dramatic identity that absorbs our antisocial as well as our social impulses. The design permits us vicariously to release hostility and yet deeply grieve. If the design is distorted in either direction, Shakespeare's grasp on our involvement is frustrated. If, as with Garrick, we have not seen the slaughter of the Macduffs, and meet only a mainly noble murderer aimed at ending in a pious expiation of his past, our own darker strings are not touched. If, on the other hand, as in post-World War II Germany, Macbeth becomes recognizably a ranting Hitler, the grieving introspection meaningless in the mouth of a monster of cruelty, he evokes only antipathy. The design demands an artistry that will convey its full force, yet preserve its delicate balance.

We go with Macbeth. Because our own polyphony responds to his.

Act V, Scene iv

Hardly has Macbeth swept out, followed by his own colors and sounds of war, than the stage is full of the invading armies.

> *Drum and colours. Enter Malcolm, Seyward, Macduff,*
> *Seyward's Son, Menteth, Cathnes, Angus, and*
> *Soldiers Marching.* *

Two armies are meeting here, Scots and English. They will be distinguished by their uniforms; and will probably be seen coming from different directions to meet, for an emotional alliance. But this must happen quickly: the tempo is on the rise; these men are on the march. They may be seen to stop in a forest; perhaps, with controlled lighting, under a bright evening sky (Reinhardt) or in moonlight (Irving). To Shakespeare's Globe audience, the glimpse of the English uniforms would be pleasantly arousing: the Marines have landed.

Maneuvering enough men on the stage to make them acceptable as "armies" is complicated. Audience disbelief must be suspended in any case, but more easily when the theatre does not try to pretend more than necessary. Token color carriers, drummers, and spearmen supporting their generals, as presumably the vanguard of troops heard offstage, have worked more effectively than small groups in formation intended to represent masses of men. One technique developed in the twentieth century frankly recognizes the war scenes as conventional, and stylizes them, as with slow motion or projections; this, if calling attention to itself, has risked disturbing the mood of the rest of the play.

After Malcolm's welcome, only three half lines are needed to identify the place as *Birnam wood,* and Malcolm has his masking idea—to use the branches to

*For the first time Lenox is missing; Ross also is not named. We may assume Lenox is included in the "thanes" mentioned in V, vii (Ross is mentioned there)—unless we are to imagine Lenox now playing a double game, appearing on Macbeth's side to betray him?

> shadow
> The numbers of our host, and make discovery
> Err in report of us. (11–13)

As Knights has observed, the cutting of Birnam's boughs for camouflage again associates the opponents of evil with deception, the unnatural, disorder. Guile from Malcolm is not unexpected now: it has become one of his skills. He develops his brilliant idea of military disguise with the same cool competence with which he played masked roles for Macduff. His associates must admire him for it.

It shall be done, a Soldier assures him; the grim echo of *done* seals for the *naive* spectator the realization of the trap waiting for Macbeth. So much for the Sisters' promise. After the surprise and comprehension—so Birnam Wood *will* come to Dunsinane—the spectator's mind begins to puzzle again over the other oracle: no man of woman born. . . ?

Our full attention is not required for the next few lines. We hear the soldiers cutting the boughs, usually offstage, partly covering the dialogue of Malcolm, Macduff, and Seyward as they exchange sober, expositionary military talk: *the confident tyrant/ Keeps still in Dunsinane. . . . none serve with him, but constrained things*. Macduff, and particularly old Seyward, solemnly speak of war. Shakespeare seems deliberately to have minimized their inward character energies: the personal excitement has gone out of Macduff's speech, and Seyward's lines are a conventional summons to battle. Never more than now do these men deserve McElroy's description, "the lacklustre defenders of the right." They exist, but we hardly have been given to know them, apart from the few intimate moments with Macduff and Malcolm; and except as those moments reverberate in subtext, the emotional lives of these righteous men do not draw us. By contrast Macbeth, all fire and energy and danger and despair, is the more a magnet.

The action is sustained by the tempo, the charge to war, and the surprise in—and then the anticipated consequence of—the Birnam camouflage. The green boughs may begin to appear with the exit march: for Wanamaker, they cast elongated shadows across the stage; some were brought on by Tree, and as the drums began to sound, distant cries along the line signaled the march to begin, Malcolm lifted one Birnam branch, and the soldiers followed him off.

Act V, Scene v

*Enter Macbeth, Seyton, and Soldiers, with Drums
and Colours.*

The Macbeth charging onto the stage to the sound and trappings of war
has suddenly become a different figure in our eyes. As in the first act, we
know an ominous secret he does not know. This time the secret had been
kept from us, too, until a few moments before. Now, as Macbeth enters in
the armor of a warrior, breathing courage and defiance, we know that a kind
of cosmic joke is being played on him. One of the two essential props to his
security will be snatched away. A touch of compassion enters into the *naive*
spectator's perception. Expectation is focused, both by our sense of the cam-
ouflaged advance of Malcolm, and by Macbeth's warlike determination,
toward the moment when the Birnam boughs will be seen. The other surprise Shakespeare plans for us will come with its own sudden shock.

Macbeth's troops man a defensive position, usually somewhere on the
battlements. As a practical matter, the Dunsinane soldiers will be distinguished in some ways from Malcolm's Scots. When Gielgud directed, as
observed above, Macbeth's men were in tatters, clothed already in the symbols of defeat, as opposed to Malcolm's trim troops; more often a different-
colored accessory (scarf, ribbon), matching the general's personal banner,
separates the two forces.

Even before the scene opens the far-off sounds of war may herald Macbeth's preparations. From offstage, sentinels may shout, "They come!" The
shouts are likely to be "distant" or "low," as with Phelps; the scene must not
develop too intensely too soon, the noise usually controllable enough to drop
to silence at Shakespeare's next surprise. These outer cries may be a cue for
the troops to rush on, as with Komisarjevsky. Or the troops enter as per the
Folio to the beat of drums; Hampden added the menace of thunder to his
mood of war. The ringing of an alarm bell brought Tree's soldiers to the
walls, the sun rising behind them until the whole sky was red.

Macbeth, sometimes markedly older now, usually carries one step higher the hyperactivity of V, iii; though he may still modulate his intensity toward the climaxes ahead. Macready sustained expectation by the force of his will, now inflamed by the compulsions of fate. Gielgud entered radiating nervous energy, yet it was still under control; stage by stage his desperation and distress was increasing, but, the *Spectator* observed, he had been able to come so far "without having shouted himself hoarse and without having thrown away the final 'hysterica passio' with which Macbeth must meet the successive revelations of the equivocation of the fiend." Scofield, too, was pacing himself; the fuse to his final explosions was burning, the violence could be sensed near flash point, but still contained. Olivier was markedly, grimly restrained, still moving upward toward the convulsions that his capped, inward tension made inevitable. Porter's seething anger pointed to imminent outbreak. In a Macbeth tortured throughout by nervous excitement, like Matkowsky's, the imminence of a clash in reality lifted him to a new pitch of strain: on his castle tower, in a fever of expectation, he paced back and forth, shivering with an expectation communicated to the audience. Williamson's Macbeth, raging at the boundary of madness, teetered toward the beckoning edge.

Many tones in the Macbeth polyphony come together in this scene, as mind and emotion, will and body, strain to meet inward and outward stresses, and multiple roles converge. Macbeth enters primarily the soldier-general-king; but the philosophic note heard in V, iii, will sound again, in the voice of a poet. Wolfit, so dangerous a fighter, seemed now not to find surcease in the battle to come: older, his Mongol mask yellowed, his eyes bloodshot, he seemed drained by the effect of inward emotion. In a Macbeth as sensitive as Booth, a kind of battle frenzy coated the evident heartsickness of the man; similarly with Forbes-Robertson's introspective philosopher.

Macbeth's overt readiness for battle sounds in his first command, that overrides the iambic in its fierce pace:

> Hang out our banners on the outward walls,
> The cry is still, they come. (4–5)

The first line has sometimes been stopped (as by Kean, Sullivan, Irving) at *banners,* on the assumption that flags would fly on the less accessible inner keep, not on the outer ramparts. But logic must submit to drama here; the unbroken Folio line rings with power, locates the scene, and vitalizes Macbeth's mood—he wants his flags flying in the enemy's face.

Tree, striding on with one of his pennants, threw it to an aide to mount on the walls. Reinhardt's Macbeth, on stage, was roused by the sound of drums and trumpets off; while his soldiers moved to guard the battlement loopholes, he seized a mighty banner, brandished it, and gave it to an aide to post. Kean, according to Dame Kendal's report of her father's memory, shouted the first line

in a voice of thunder. Suddenly he paused, dropped his double-handed sword
. . . and leaning on it, whispered "The cry is still they come . . ." at the
same time seeming to become ashy grey with fear.

I find this hard to fit into the Kean design; no other report suggests this kind
of physical cowardice in his Macbeth.

As Macbeth speaks, looking toward where the advance must come, and
the audience waits for him to see Birnam Wood, he seems absolutely assured:

> our castle's strength
> Will laugh a siege to scorn: Here let them lie,
> Till famine and the ague eat them up: (5–7)

The speech, again mainly monosyllabic, is confident, contemptuous, the
abrupt words at first hissing with *s*'s, then snapping. Shakespeare has Macbeth
emphasize the point that strategy dictates an invulnerable defensive siege; but
also that Macbeth the fighter would gladly do battle, except that so many Scots
had gone over to the enemy—

> We might have met them dareful, beard to beard,
> And beat them backward home. (9–10)

The successive, explosive *b*'s sound an arrogance, even a bravado, that almost
asks for recoil, and at once that comes—but not in the form of the Birnam-
masked attack from without that we have been led to expect. Alarm sounds
from another direction; this new assault is from within.

A cry . . . of women.

A wail, a mournful lament, an animal moan, a banshee shriek, perhaps with
a faint echo of the Sisters' cries—the sound shatters the air. Macbeth and all
his men are jolted by it. Phelps: "All slightly start and look toward left." Irving
reminded himself to start, pause, and then ask what the noise was. Seyton,
unbidden, goes—often rushes—to find the cause—so manifesting his personal service to Macbeth.

In one of the scene's several spectacular transitions, Macbeth's ferocity
fades, he slides into a raptness that brings him, almost full circle—perhaps
better, by downward spiral—close to his first soliloquy in I, iii. Once more
the awareness of the body at a stressful moment; once more the experience—
now, non-experience—of fear, which could before *unfix* his *fell of hair*. The
language slows; the underlying iambic beat persists, but it is modulated to
fit the nostalgic mood shaped by the backward-looking verbs: *I have almost
forgot . . . The time has been . . . would have cool'd* (how the monosyllable
stretches out) *To hear a night shriek . . . Would at a dismal treatise. . . .*

As in all the soliloquies, the mood intensifies, as if Macbeth must notice
his incapacity for feeling with growing feeling. The echoed ritual of feasting
is inverted, touched with nausea:

> I have supped full with horrors, (17)

Unusual polysyllables, beginning with a trochee, reflect the depth of inwardness aborted:

> Direness familiar to my slaughterous thoughts
> Cannot once start me. (18–19)

Seyton returns—usually very slowly: Savits' crouched under the burden
of his news. Seyton is gone just long enough for Macbeth's soliloquy—
Craig's Seyton only went to the door, where three women had been coming
out with their news; he listened and pushed them back. The lament that has
continued softly offstage may rise in the pause. It will continue to be heard;
perhaps along with the beginning drumbeats of a dead march, as with Komisarjevsky. Seyton calls Macbeth's attention to himself by kneeling, or other
movement. Hopkins' Seyton brought back with him a bloody dagger—a
stipulation of suicide—and showed it.

> Wherefore was that cry? (19)

For the first time Lady Macbeth is named by her royal title:

> The Queen (my Lord) is dead. (20)

Macbeth's famous response has evoked a wide range of critical interpretation. Two main problems are involved. The first: what are Macbeth's feelings about his wife at her death? Many critics find him negative, to the point
of brutal indifference, on the basis of either of two possible readings of the
first line:

> She should have died hereafter;
> There would have been a time for such a word: (21–22)

Shakespeare used *should*, in *Macbeth* and elsewhere, either to denote *ought to*,
or as a variation of *would*. Here, as *ought to*, it has been seen to imply that
Macbeth is thinking only of inconvenience to himself—she died at the wrong
time for him. Alternatively, as "would," it is seen to imply that she had to die
anyway, Macbeth didn't care.* "His wife's death, it has often been observed,
means nothing to him," one critic noted, and others have agreed, thus: "(His)
callous remark on the inopportuneness of her death"; "His wearied unconcern . . . callousness"; "Insensible even to the death of his wife"; "She was
dead to Macbeth before she died"; "Her loneliness is attested by Macbeth's
coldness"; "Callous indifference to everything but his own danger"; "The
death of his wife cannot touch him with either grief or regret"; "She had to
die sometime or other, and it makes no difference when." Macbeth's indifference to his wife's death has also been extended to his response to the world:
"He has lost his capacity to feel"; "Almost complete failure to respond emo-

---

*Murry suggests that Shakespeare may have meant "a plunge across a new abyss into a Here-
after." The context does not nourish this interpretation.

tionally"; "The desolate coldness of one who has renounced all particular affections." Bradley, more sympathetic, could allow that "he has not time now
to feel," as if Macbeth were thinking that at some time hereafter he would
have. Mary Rosenberg suggests a parallel with Brutus' touching au revoir
to the dead Cassius:

> Friends, I owe moe tears
> To this dead man than you shall see me pay.
> I shall find time, Cassius, I shall find time. (*Julius Caesar*, V, iii, 101–103)

The most extreme view of Macbeth's attitude toward his wife's death
ascribed to him not too little feeling, but the wrong kind: thus, the actress,
Robson: "When Macbeth is told of her death, we learn that he has grown to
hate her." Certainly Laughton, who first played Macbeth to Robson's Lady,
showed no grief at her death; and Michael Redgrave, who played with her
later, seemed at the news past grieving, harshly barked his soliloquy; but
mostly the theatre Macbeth has reacted as Lampson has suggested he must,
with shock, as well as mourning, and even tears. An actor scanting the poetic
lament in the speech has been faulted (Redgrave); while a Macbeth like
Cowper, who invested his soliloquy with deeply felt grief, would be specifically praised (by the *Liverpool Porcupine*) for avoiding the coldness urged by
critics.

Traditionally, Macbeth's instant dismay at Seyton's news was reflected
physically: thus Macready let fall, from his extended arm, his commander's
truncheon; Phelps dropped his "baton," Booth a staff, Dawison the cup he
held. Forster scolded Forrest for pacing about in anguish, "As if Macbeth
should not . . . stand rooted to the spot"; but other actors too were moved
to body imagery. Charles Kean's battle axe slipped from his grasp and, sad
and thoughtfully, he laid his hand on his heart. Salvini fell back into his seat,
his face in his hands: "As though overwhelmed by the fatal news (in) utter
heartsickness" (*Scotsman*). Matkowsky, at Seyton's report, closed his eyes,
stood in a long pause before finally speaking, in a weary voice. Hackett registered a tremendous shock; in Paris he was seen to drop his head, fixed for a
while in immobility. He dismissed Seyton with a gesture, so he could mourn
alone; and with emphasis on the pathos of what-might-have-been he spoke
the first two lines to suggest that he was confident he would soon have defeated their enemies, and she could have lived in peace. Sothern put his hand
over his eyes, turned his back to the audience, and slowly, sorrowfully, measured out the soliloquy. Kemble, Macready remembered, "seemed struck
to the heart; gradually collecting himself, he sighed out, 'She should have
died. . . .'" Macready himself, seeming "soul-struck with absorbing grief",
conveyed "exquisitely touching pathos." One observer asked, "When did
these words ever fall upon the ear with a deeper or more mournful cadence?"
Mantell's melancholy, afflicted voice was "fraught with desolation"—the

voice of a "seared, hopeless mind and broken heart." Irving, though he said "She *would* have died . . . ," mourned sadly for his dead Lady.

Booth noted that a lament by Macbeth fitted the dialectical pattern in the character now. The actor, during a Chicago appearance, referred to Bulwer-Lytton's thoughts expressed at Macready's farewell banquet:

> Macbeth . . . alternates perpetually between terror and daring . . . a trembler when opposed by his conscience and a warrior when defied by the foe. Fierce and tender by turns, his wretched soul is at last torn by a frenzy (of) wild and conflicting passions . . . in the midst, a pause to word a tender apostrophe to his dead wife.

Tenderness came naturally to Booth's poetic Macbeth, as it did Forbes-Robertson's thoughtful one, returning to his philosophic mood, his expression of deep affection for Lady Macbeth becoming naturally one of the most poignant and touching moments of the play.

More contrast accompanies the descent to grief of the grim-surfaced Macbeths whose passionate inward impulses are more sensed in their repression than in sudden revelatory flashes. For Olivier, who sustained a fierce, if controlled, nervous intensity that had mounted inexorably to this scene, the moment of introspection at the women's cry turned, with Seyton's news, to an anguished, restrained pity, "a quiet, sad beauty," a "profundity of despair," a "shattering pathos." "To watch him receive the news with resignation to a drooping, tearless profundity is to be compelled to appalling fear" (*Truth*). Scofield seemed to look into a hereafter when Lady Macbeth might still be alive to him; his stern voice softened with compassion—for fools, for himself—and a touch of longing.

Particularly striking was the contrast in Wolfit's lament for his wife. The burly, brooding warrior's response to Seyton's news was

> great bemused pity . . . tells us, with infinite clarity, that Macbeth had loved his wife with a deep unquestioning affection, a manly love and sacrificing of self (*Catholic Herald*).

Macbeth, departing from the text, has even gone to hold his Lady in his arms, as he spoke of her too-sudden death (Robards; Bergman, 1944).

To most actors, then, Macbeth's *should have died* clearly indicates a sadness that death had to come so soon. A scholar with theatre experience shares the latter response: thus John Russell Brown: "However spoken, (the line) must suggest pain and loss." Brown senses Macbeth saying less than he feels: "There is perhaps a reticence in these words, and Macbeth is excusing his inability to speak, or more probably, his unwillingness." Strindberg was thinking like a playwright when he also suggested tension between the spoken and unspoken, a playing against the words—Macbeth seems to become angry at Lady Macbeth's death, and to say that the time was inconvenient, but he may not mean that because he has shown himself so affectionate to her.

A grieving Macbeth reflects a subtext that would have developed through all his relationships with his Lady. I see his first line as a poignant wish that Lady Macbeth could have lived longer. The last word, *hereafter*, may be thought to evoke reverberations of memory: her promises (I, iv) of the *all-hail hereafter*. The last word may carry his mind back to the Sisters' earlier assurance; but the subterranean association may also link him to his own first *Tomorrow—Tomorrow as he purposes*. Such connections may not be perceived by the spectator, or if so, only subliminally; but if the memory-linkage helps the actor to fill out the design, the spectator will experience the fullness in the implications of Macbeth's language.

To Dr. Johnson:

> it is not apparent for what "word" there would have been "time," and that there would or would not be a *time* for any *word* seemed not a consideration of importance sufficient to transport Macbeth into such an exclamation.*

The *word* Macbeth longs for could be of ultimate importance, as synecdochic for the many, many words he would have liked—now too late—to exchange with his *dearest partner of greatness*, his *love*, his *dear wife*, his *dearest chuck*, about whose health he has been so concerned. There is, Ecclesiastes preaches, a time for all things; Macbeth may mourn the better moment, now missed forever:

> There would have been a time for *such* a word: (22)

So much has been left unspoken. So much to say. Macbeth will not, primarily, see his Lady's death as part of the meaninglessness of life; rather will finally see life so meaningless because she had died, and too soon.

Actors have sometimes run *such a word* into the first *Tomorrow*, as if Macbeth would rather have heard the news the next day. But he expects a long siege; to specify this near time diminishes the sense of infinite stretching out that fits his deepening distress. The Folio's colon after *word* directs a pause; providing a transition from Macbeth's withdrawal into another raptness—his last contextual introspection on the human condition.

The implications of Macbeth's philosophic statement now have been a second center of critical disagreement. From one judgmental point of view, it has been seen as a sign of moral violation: Macbeth voices the "hopelessness of a hardened sinner." Redgrave and Casson, of the theatre, concluded that the speech was atheistic nihilism, "the greatest blasphemy that man can utter." Casson even saw God answering back, with the approach of Birnam Wood. This puts Macbeth in direct, Faust-like relation with a god ruling the world, or with identifiable gods, as Oedipus was. The theological issue, and the man-to-personal-god relationship, are not so drawn here. Unless, in a

---

*So Johnson proposed the irrelevant "world."

contrived religious context, Macbeth indulges in some such non-textual blasphemy as breaking or desecrating a cross, his vision seems at least to preserve ambiguity, a challenge to nameless power—or to powers or mechanisms—responsible for the human condition. Even when a Macbeth looked up deliberately toward heaven, as Porter did, and hurled at it the accusation *idiot*, he seemed not—and meant not—to specify the Judaeo-Christian God, but rather the impersonal author of meaninglessness.

Another critical interpretation emphasizes Macbeth's personal, rather than theological, downfall. He is in "abject collapse," insensible to all natural feeling, in a "mindless state." Certainly Macbeth sees the world as wasteland; but the very energy of his seeing, and saying, establishes a human force that denies meaninglessness. The speech is so treasured, so fondly remembered, because it voices so truly and humanly a universality of despair. Macbeth puts into words the mortal frustration with a world that seems to lie in wait to baffle and enervate the trusting. Macbeth has played his part in the tragic force; he does not disclaim responsibility; but that he is what he is seems to him part of the scheme of meaninglessness.

Not only what Macbeth says, but how he says it, helps explain the enormous impact of the lines. This is Macbeth the poet at his best: the words so suited to the rhythms of contemplative dismay; the images, piled one on another, reflecting the agonized, roaming mind; the depth of feeling; the language, so close to that of life, yet enough distanced; the slow build to climax. If our response is to judge Macbeth, we may indeed see him as damned, or spiritually or psychically failed; but if, as in the theatre, we continue to share his dramatic life, we participate in the magnificent experience of a disappointed soul that has not,—in Bradley's words—lost all its native goodness and grandeur. How its splendor—though perhaps, as Leech observes, of the darkest kind—contrasts with the commonplaceness of Macbeth's righteous enemies!

Critics who find wisdom in the soliloquy relate it to other wisdoms, theological, philosophical, archetypal. Roland Frye suggests that Macbeth's glimpse of the frailty and transience of living was familiar in the contemporary Christian context, though not itself Christian. Frye cites biblical references and sermons using the metaphors of life as a guttering candle, a passing shadow, a tale that is told. Thus John Donne preaching to the unwise:

> Thou passest through this world as a flash, as a lightning, no man knows the beginning or ending, as an *ignis fatuus*, in the air, which does not only give light for any use, but does not so much portend or signify anything.

Frye:

> That [Macbeth] should have realised the true nature of his life and of all human life at this particular point in his own existence . . . is one of the most brilliant strokes of Shakespeare's tragic genius.

Santayana could see Macbeth as "divinely human" in his capacity to examine the spoilage of life. Santayana could find no more religion in Shakespeare than in Macbeth, hence the philosopher's famous equation of the two:

> If we asked [Shakespeare] to tell us what is the significance of the passion and beauty he had so vividly displayed, and what is the outcome of it all, he could hardly answer in any other words than Macbeth's *Tomorrow, and tomorrow*. . . .

Santayana could perceive Macbeth's process as rational; but it penetrates so deeply by the charge of emotion that impels it.

Eternal time, present duration, and felt time—or timelessness—fuse in Macbeth's melancholy perspective. Past, present, and future come together on the treadmill of time. The old, human longing for a re-done past, for a better future, dissipates in the desert of the now. Time and the hour run through the roughest day, but now there's not an end, with night and sleep; time and the hour run on . . .

Tomorrow . . .

The word may come out as a single thought; though a theatre Macbeth, like Macready, may speak the first word as if, as so often, he is looking ahead, planning some action:* *Tomorrow,*—and then hold the slight pause indicated by the comma while the sense of future meaninglessness takes his brain, and he articulates the glimpse of the endless procession of barren days—

and tomorrow, and tomorrow, (23)

Each tomorrow becomes a phrase, with its feminine ending and the breaking comma pulling down and slowing the movement, overriding the iambic. The words accommodate themselves to the reflective message, the monosyllables in the first line separating themselves, the following polysyllables lengthening the rhythm:

> Creeps in this petty pace from day to day,
> To the last syllable of recorded time:
> And all our yesterdays, have lighted fools
> The way to dusty death. (24–27)

All our yesterdays. The *all* bears the weight of the whole life gone by: the fair glory, as well as the foul crime, all pursued along the path lit by the beckoning *ignis fatuus*, the "fool's light." The *our*, if emphasized, as by Hackett, includes Lady Macbeth in the betrayed past. The comma after *yesterdays* provides the slight pause for Macbeth to set apart his backward vision before he turns forward to the grave.

Out, out brief candle, (27)

*Thus, almost his last speech to Lady Macbeth: *I will tomorrow/ (And betimes I will)*.

The image is a natural one, and may have occurred to the first primitive human with a metaphorical mind who watched by a flame as another human died. Proverbs 24:20 and Job 18:5–6 declare that the candles of the wicked shall be put out, though the references do not specifically imply the end of life. Shakespeare twice used the candle image to suggest the slow (*Henry IV, Part II*, I, ii, 156) or close (*Henry VI, Part III*, II, vi, 1) approach of death. Liddell suggests that the words indicate Macbeth's "immediate purpose to take his life"; but almost certainly it refers back to the fact of Lady Macbeth's death, that has set his train of feeling in motion. If a single spine is to be sensed in the mosaic of images, it is the effect of her death on his thought.

Garrick's correspondent, H. H., faulted him because, at "Out, out. . . ."

> You gave two starts . . . each with a strong action of both hands: is not this wrong? . . . The whole train of Macbeth's reasoning tends to enforce the insignificance of life, which he slights as of little value, and not worth preserving, under the figure of the candle, which is easily extinguished, and whose existence cannot, in the nature of things, be very permanent, as it is incessantly consuming.

H. H. thought the words should be spoken with "philosophical contempt"—which is what Garrick himself thought:

> I must have spoke [sic] those words quite the reverse of my own ideas, if I did not express them with the most contemptuous indifference of life.

But as he went on, one spectator heard the lament for the *poor player* "pronounced by the softest voice that ever drew pity from the heart of man."
Kemble's voicing Hazlitt found particularly striking,

> as if he had stumbled by an accident on fate, and was baffled by the impenetrable obscurity of the future.

Hazlett disagreed with the *Times* ("which seems to be written as well as printed by a steam engine") for comparing Kemble to

> the ruin of a magnificent temple, in which the divinity still resides . . . The temple is unimpaired; but the divinity is sometimes from home.

Macready remembered Kemble, "as if with an inspiration of despair," hurrying out the speech, "pathetically, rising to a climax of desperation."
Macready seemed immobilized again by the awareness of a fateful trap: in his "brief interval of sad repose," his delivery conveyed

> in its withering calmness a controlled agony of feeling . . . a voice of chill despair, a look of blankest desolation . . . in the highest degree pathetic . . . the source of its pathos "too deep for tears" (*Examiner, Theatrical Journal*).

Irving's note for the speech was "very determined," but it came across with "A world of fancy and reflectiveness" (*Daily Telegraph*). Salvini raised his head from his hands, and with one hand on his forehead, spoke with a mixture of mourning and cynicism, of affliction and disillusion; though Stevenson thought it was a dirge more for himself than for her.

The verbal figure of the candle awakens the lingering image of the light Lady Macbeth must always have by her, that may have been emphasized visually as early as the night of Duncan's murder, again through Act III, and so recently in Act V, when it would flicker as her life did. Even now, sometimes, the visual image may be revived. Dawison, while he had waited for Seyton to investigate the cry of women, had drunk from a cup, and as he finished he turned the cup over a lighted candle, extinguishing the flame; now his eye fell on the dead wax. Macbeth has held a candle, has blown one out. Furness cites a report of Macbeths striking their breasts to indicate the flickering of their own life-lights.

The idea of light gone dark, or the visual result, may be thought to lead to the next figure, of the shadow. But logical connections are not primary here, as they were not in earlier soliloquies; indeed they might interdict the felt experience of subterranean life throwing off, in a crisis of pain, images connected mainly in the identity of the sufferer, Macbeth. Subtle verbal threads certainly underweave the images together, in the texture Armstrong saw as "clotting": walking, struts; hereafter, time, tomorrow, yesterday, brief, hour; lighted, candle, shadow; fools, idiot; shadow, player, stage; heard, told, sound; syllable, recorded, tale, signifying. The outcrop of a poet's passion, and a philosopher's wonder at the meaning of existence, the images echo Macbeth's earlier introspections, particularly those on time, and on the stage: indeed, as the V, iii soliloquy came round again to his final physical responses to stress, now this one circles back to his first images of the theatre of life where he was to enter his part: the

> happy prologue to the swelling act
> Of the imperial theme.

His theatrical references in between have dealt with the player in action (e.g., *Ourself will . . . play the humble host*); this one laments an exit:

> Life's but a walking shadow, a poor player,
> That struts and frets his hour upon the stage,
> And then is heard no more. It is a tale
> Told by an idiot, full of sound and fury
> Signifying nothing. (28–32)

In Verona, Melchiori remembered, Lady Macbeth's body was brought on, and Macbeth alluded to her as the *poor player;* but this is extra textual, and misses the wider implications of the figure. Kantak observes the continuance, in the "actor" image, of the sense of a mask world without reality, barren of the substance of fertility and growth posed in the earlier images of child and seed. The world is resolved into appearance, symbolized by the posturing player saying meaningless lines. Lawlor reads also in the metaphor another example of the disconnection between desire and act: we are not what we would be. To Lawlor the essence of the futility expressed is not time stretching unendingly but

A different notion of futility . . . of man going round and round in his tracks,

of a repeated, empty cycle. Lawlor finds in *poor player*

not the pitiful human lot [but] the player as incompetent performer.

The pathos is not in being cast to act, but in being inadequate for our roles. To Lawlor this is distinctively Shakespearean: men tear a passion to tatters, strut and bellow like Hamlet's detested hacks, speaking with empty sound and fury; so Macbeth would disengage himself from the sterile action, be spectator instead of player—failed player.

If the implication is incompetence, the emphasis must be on the "*poor player*"; if the emphasis is, as commonly, approximately equal between the words, or more on *player*, it carries the implication of Macbeth's earlier uses of *poor* as unfortunate. The latter meaning has more pity in it, the former more cynicism and anger. If it is the player who at first seems inadequate, he becomes responsible for his failures; but the last lines imply that the part, not the player, is bombast, that what is acted out in life is an idiot-author's making. So Kittredge felt the impulse was to pity, "Macbeth's contempt [is] not for the actor, but for life."

The touch of self-pity is stronger in Macbeth as he identifies the string-pulled player with life, and, at the same time, in a metaphysical transmutation, *is* the player manipulated. This enters into the brooding pain that fires his last line. Depending on Macbeth's mood, the soliloquy moves toward either of two extremes. Anger may predominate—though this may be restrained, as with Scofield, the words breaking off like clubs against the impersonal nemesis that was demeaning him. The resentment at a felt manipulation may be fiercely personal. Savits' Macbeth, from a quiet beginning, began to edge a hostile contempt into his voice, building in rage until he spat the final *nothing*. Williamson was sneeringly contemptuous from beginning to end, intensely manic now. Porter, as observed before, virtually shook his fist at the heavens, snarling defiance at the "idiot," some "god imagined over his head," in "a savage burst of existential atheism" (J. R. Brown). A Czech Macbeth, Hodek reported, made furious throwing gestures upward, as if hurling stones against heaven.

Angry Macbeths have been described as outraged by the swindle practised on them, deeply wronged by the theft of their happiness, reacting violently to a fraud of Fate. The angry Macbeth usually builds the soliloquy to a climactic *nothing*. Wolfit first let the words come out in a slow, grim drumbeat, building a sense of doom that rose to a sudden, final explosion of disgust. Hackett's note for the end: "Crash of steel and fury." A touch of savage laughter edged McKellen's disgust with experience. The actor thought of Macbeth's *walking shadow* as akin to the insignificant "walking gentleman" of the old theatres, given no more than "walk-on" parts. McKellen's Macbeth, feeling now the loneliness and the hollowness of his ambition, could see the great joke of life, but raged at being its butt.

An alternate mood moves Macbeth toward sadness and resignation. Salvini, weary with loss, mourned movelessly through the soliloquy. So did the Kumo Macbeth in Japan, spotlit alone in the center of the stage, silent for a long pause before he began his lament, spoken quietly through, emphasizing Macbeth's deep feeling. The poet in Gielgud's Macbeth mused through the lines, conveying a sense of nobility, of deep personal tragedy; he dropped into quietude, Agate reported, letting "the sound have it." In Olivier's voice Billington heard "a profound and almost unbearable regret." Rogers, who had been shaken at the end of the banquet, and nearly manic during his visit to the Sisters, was moved again to a sharp contrast in mood:

> Lost in grief at the death of the Queen, [he] sank to a seat, with all fight gone out of him, pausing between the words as if shattered in mind, and breathing the hushed lines until they dwindled into the bleak whisper of "signifying nothing."

This choked ending is characteristic of the Macbeth subdued, in sad, poetic, philosophic moods; long ago George F. Cooke (England, 1811) was marked for his long pause after *signifying:*

> he sunk his voice, and with a tone of suppressed feeling, and heart-breaking disappointment

uttered the *nothing* (Dunlap).

The image of Macbeth's response to his wife's death refracts, soon after, Macduff's. Both wondered at the force that could contrive their disasters: the one to question, and then submit to, a higher power; the other to upbraid whatever power there be. They will not again pause to mourn their losses; but in Shakespeare's orchestration the surds of their grief will inform, subtextually, their movements toward their interwoven destiny. Their emotional bruises will condition all that they do.

The inrushing messenger hesitates to speak to the king before him: an angry Macbeth is too formidable, a Macbeth rapt in sorrow uninterruptible. Macbeth must shake himself free. The pause while the intimidated messenger waits may be extended, as with Hackett, who mused long over his "dead wife." When Macbeth finally notices an intrusion into his thoughts, he may speak with the risen anger of his recent defiance, with the moody disinterest of disillusion, with the controlled calmness of a general's official manner. The continued fear and confusion of the Messenger must rouse in Macbeth some apprehension of grim news—Charles Kean held a long pause before speaking again, almost as knowing what he would hear. The prompting, when it comes, is terse, controlled, has carried a sardonic, angry edge. *Well, say sir.*

The Messenger's cataclysmic report emerges, probably after a long, confused pause, and hesitant between phrases:

I look'd toward Birnam,

The very word is ominous, jerking Macbeth to full attention—

and anon me thought . . .
The wood began to move. (39–40)

Liar, and slave. Macbeth's words have traditionally been accompanied by an instantaneous physical menace, if not attack, directed at the messenger. Rowe's 1702 stage direction was "Striking him," probably a traditional business; by the time of Macklin, one customary business was for Macbeth to hit the slave with a truncheon—which, being half-sawed through, would break— as a visual gesture of Macbeth's strength and passion. A comment in the *St. James Chronicle* praising Macklin for avoiding the business indicated that his "competitor," Garrick, had used it; a reply from a not-too-helpful friend argued that Garrick certainly had not done so for "these ten years," having seen the action made ridiculous in a farce. Garrick now "Put his Hand upon his Sword and, with a Look of Terror mixed with Dispondency, pronounced his threat." Macklin did seize his man's arm, and force him to the ground. The image of a gentlemanly Macbeth striking a servant impinged on some eighteenth-century sensibilities: Gentleman, accepting Rowe's stage direction as authentic, sniffed, "Shakespeare was too fond of blows, especially from royal hands"; and Kemble sustained the nobler image by discovering in Macbeth a restraining emotional life:

Such outrageous violence does not belong to the feelings of a person overwhelmed with surprise, half-doubting, half-believing an event . . . most strange, and to himself of the most fatal importance.

So Kemble's passion was turned inward more than outward, Macready remembered:

He staggered, as if the shock had struck the very seat of life, and in the bewilderment of fear and rage could just ejaculate "Liar and slave," then (lashed) himself into a state of frantic rage;

and Hunt:

The thrilling suddenness of [Kemble's] agony in the utterance of the words . . . and the terror of his eye cowering over the messenger who had half dispelled his charm, yet haunt me.

The moment brings to a climax the tension between the man of action— killer, warrior, general, king and leader of men—and the man of thought and feeling, the philosopher seeking to understand, the poet to verbalize. The turbulence may be measured partly by the gigantic force needed to restrain it, as in the confrontations above, and in later ones. Olivier, still pacing his rising intensity, crushed his man, Agate observed, using "the edge of his brain," with "cold malignity." Scofield's constrained power, as he loomed over the messenger, promised annihilation if it were but let loose from its iron bridle.

Often the emotional volcano finds abrupt release in a furious eruption of the warrior's violence—akin, in its intensity, to Othello's attack on Iago in the third act, to Lear's against the storm. From Macbeth's rapt retreat in a timeless, contextual introspection on the condition of man, he sometimes flashes fiercely into the present; his multiple emotions—rage, astonishment, terror, incredulity, foreboding, superstition, despair—have been seen to drive him almost to a murderous action that made Rowe's "striking" seem tame by comparison. Sullivan whirled a giant two-handed sword above the man, as if ready to split him from chaps to nave. Of Charles Kean's vehement assault the *Spectator* wrote "We thought he would have literally exterminated the fellow." Irving, with a shrill cry—one observer heard a shriek hinting at the superstitious fear infecting his rage—bodily attacked his officer-messenger, while a huddle of frightened soldiers peered at the scene from a doorway. A Japanese Macbeth beat his nuncio; Benson whipped his man with a dagger; McKellen held his young servant's chin, and deliberately slashed his cheek.

The primary attack has been, sometimes, at the throat, as if Macbeth's instinctive impulse is to seize the hostile life in his hands. Macready first drew his sword, towering over his trembling, terrified Messenger, who knelt before him; but the blade was only half drawn, and a promptbook has Macready going on to seize the man by the neck, forcing him to his knees. Komisarjevsky's Macbeth leaped on his soldier-messenger to strangle him; so also Evans. The brawny Forrest, though he first staggered back, "as if his brain had received a blow" (Alger), recovering, lifted his messenger high, choked him, and "fairly flung him off the stage" (Forster).

The longer rhythms of Macbeth's alternate hyperactive and brooding states now contract, so that outbreak and introspection almost coalesce. So Macklin delivered the first lines of the next speech "in a tone and look of such terrible menace as almost petrified the audience: while in the last he fell into such an air of despondency" (Cooke). Double possibilities still whipsaw Macbeth as he tries to judge reality from appearance, his whole existence pivoting on the *ifs:*

> If thou speak'st false,
> Upon the next tree shalt thou hang alive . . .
>   If thy speech be sooth,
> I care not if thou dost for me as much. (45–48)

Macbeth's fierce beginning with the Messenger thus ends with a half-aside, suicidal note, at the full stop. Then he is back inside himself:

> I pull in resolution, and begin
> To doubt th'equivocation of the fiend,
> That lies like truth. (49–51)

It is a moment of terrible perspective. In his *Tomorrow* . . . Macbeth has looked back on a life without meaning, an idiot's scenario; now, with a deeper sense of betrayal, he must sense a conscious malicious design: the life-actor's script has been devised to trick him to destruction with false appearances. A faint irony may have been in Shakespeare's mind as he himself wove this tale trapping Macbeth, and then made his character blame his fate first on an idiot, then a fiend.

Macbeth ruminates as, however reluctantly, he moves to look out over the castle—Matkowsky dragged his messenger along the floor after him. The speech has the beat of stunned remembering. The rhythm rolls out until brought up short by the last heavy words:

> Fear not, till Birnam Wood
> Do come to Dunsinane, and now a wood
> Comes toward Dunsinane. (51–53)

Again the zigzag ascent to passionate action, the flight from Apollonian reason to Dionysian impulse:

> Arm, arm, and out . . . (53)

Seyton or another officer may attempt to dissuade Macbeth from open battle, to emphasize the impulsive folly of leaving impregnable Dunsinane for an uneven fight; Macbeth will only sweep resistance away. His command is relayed down a line—first picked up by Seyton in the Evans' *Macbeth*—as the bustle of the preparation for war begins (perhaps some soldiers begin to slide away). Macbeth muses again, his rhyming lines hinting a kind of formal confrontation with experience. A last faint hope for options sounds in the flicking *if*:

> If this which he avouches, does appear,
> There is nor flying hence, nor tarrying here. (54–55)

And now he may have at last brought himself to look out of turret or loop-hole or window; and on his face, reflecting the approach of Birnam, we see the shock of realization: a long, slow moment that reprises his sense of meaninglessness, and his readiness to see chaos come again if he is to be unfairly treated. For Olivier, letting go his control a notch, the next lines "held the very ecstasy of despair, the actor swaying with grief, his voice rising" (*Observer*).

> I 'gin to be aweary of the sun,
> And wish th' estate o'th' world were now undone. (56–57)

But Macbeth knows better: what's done cannot be *undone*. The grandeur of the design flames in his burst of resilience: drear as the world may seem to him, he is a man who can rise to battle, who cannot submit to apathy. Tricked by an oracle, over-reacting to the sudden recognition that security has been a chiefest enemy, Macbeth, in a final pyrotechnic transition, leaps to serve the heedless firstling of his heart. The violence in his mind is reflected in the sound and fury of his cries, which end in the detonations of the vicious *k*'s.

> Ring the alarum bell, blow wind, come wrack,
> At least we'll die with harness on our back. (58–59)

Theobald suggested that the order for the bell was a stage direction; but it clearly fits rhythm and meter, and fittingly gives to Macbeth the second ordering of an alarm that Macduff had before, in a crisis, commanded. Evans, seeing no soldiers springing to his order, leaped to strike the bell himself, as he shouted his last commands. The echoing bell suits the apocalyptic mood in which Macbeth asserts his will to battle whether the chaos he wishes for comes or not: *blow wind, come wrack*.

Granville Barker did not see how, without too much subtlety, to stage a merger of the contemplative Macbeth who begins to weary of the sun, and the warrior ready to fight till the flesh is hacked from his bones. "A character cannot be effectively developed in two directions at once." But this is the essence of the tension in this character design: by now these notes in the Macbeth polyphony have been established. As they come into evermore simultaneous fusion, each, in its rising sound, reaches deeper into our response: the warrior's resolve evoking, however, fearfully, respect and admiration for the courage and resilient power, while the heartsick introspection, as in *I 'gin to be aweary*, touches profoundly the universal ache at life gone grey. In the *Macbeth* world, nothing is easily reconcilable, the uneven is dominant, fair is foul, and never more so in Macbeth than at this focal moment. The fever within is masked in the feverish belligerence of the great captain.

The warrior's resurgence may partly require a conscious effort, as with Tree, whose castle was already under assault—an arrow from Malcolm's army flew in to strike one of the soldiers. More often Macbeth acts out of violent, instant impulse. Juriev remembered Rossi shouting his charge with the frenzy and despair of a man staking his all on fate. Swinging his sword he turned now toward the soldiers, now toward the battlefield, as he led the advance into the wings. Farjeon saw Hackett worked into "such a state of abandoned exaltation that he actually dances off the stage like a madman." Gielgud's gathering momentum through the scene burst into a "flabbergasting" explosion of nervous energy. Olivier's capped tension, until now felt most in its containment, suddenly broke out: his "throttled fury switches into top gear, and we see a lion, baffled but still colossal." (*Observer*). Scofield's iron restraint also gave way to a startling panache: the sweeping gesture of a great general beckoning his troops to follow. The Macbeth who had returned from his Act I victory was there again, as, flashing his sword high above his head, he summoned his men, reviving unmistakably the image of his power to command a great army into battle.

Act V, Scene vi

In the Globe, the preceding scene may have been staged "above," presumably on the battlements, where the banners would be hung, and Macbeth could look out to see the approach of Birnam Wood. Hardly would he and his men have disappeared aloft when a forest would appear below. Only the greenery would be seen, perhaps; or, as with Macready, Malcolm would appear, in front of what looked like a solid thicket. Macbeth—and we—would see no more.

Beyond the uncanny experience of an equivocation come to reality, a further shiver might perhaps have been enjoyed by Shakespeare's audience; a further shock felt by Macbeth. What Malcolm had seemingly done belonged presumably to the power of witchcraft. Thus West's *Symboleography*, II, 3, 24:

> A witch or hegg . . . by a league made with the devil . . . thinketh that she can designe what manner of evil things soever, either by thought or imprecation, as to shake the air with lightnings and thunder, to cause haile and tempests, *to remove* greene corne or *trees to another place*. [italics mine]

Properly displayed, the moving forest makes a fine, startling moment. But it must be substantial: skimpy branches are worse than none, cannot—to quote one disappointed observer—deceive "a Wolf Cub or a Brownie." For a long stage run, the branches must be either refreshed or artificial; drying ones, cut long before, destroy the illusion. Hence such stylized silver leaves as in the Weaver staging.

Drum and Colours. Enter Malcolm, Seyward, Macduff,
and their Army, with boughs.

Malcolm, standing before the "forest" (the young man, and the greenery, evoking subliminally the archetypal image of the rise of the spring king), gives his order to decamouflage—to dispense with the guile of illusion (How neatly the Prince's design is fitted into the action—working out with characteristic deception the Sisters' equivocal oracle!). Malcolm may at the same time signal for a whistle, or trumpets—and suddenly the boughs go down, the army appears, perhaps with a great shout, as with Phelps. It is a spectacular effort. To intensify the spectacle the nineteenth century theatre drew on stage machinery: the branches held by live soldiers were multiplied behind by painted branches on a backdrop that seemed to stretch out into the distance; when the boughs fell, to disclose live soldiers, new backdrops that shifted into place now showed a multitude of (painted) soldiers behind the live ones. Thus Macready and Charles Kean; Phelps slotted in cut-out profile figures in the background to suggest the many lines of troops behind his flesh-and-blood men in front.

Malcolm disposes his army—perhaps with his war map in hand. He assigns the first attack to old Seyward, *with my Cousin your right noble son*. Young Seyward is not mentioned in the entering personae, but he must surely be present to acknowledge Malcolm's designation, so that we may recognise him in the next scene. Malcolm assigns to Macduff and himself *what else remains to do*.

Seyward and Macduff again end the scene, as they did in V, iv; but now their brief couplets move briskly, suited to the martial mood, as Shakespeare intensifies the approach to conflict. Macduff's coda, spoken with the energy of his discovery of Duncan's body, calls out the full-throated cry of war:

> Make all our trumpets speak, give them all breath
> Those clamorous harbingers of blood, and death. (15–16)

Act V, Scene vii

As Macduff led the charge at the end of the last scene, the concluding stage direction,

Alarums continued.

orders the sounds of war to go on reverberating. As the two armies engage in battle, the snatches of confrontation and struggle specified for the stage now flash off and on against a background—seen or implied, through sound—of the larger war. For this montage of incident, the Folio stipulates only one final scene, embracing Macbeth's last moments of musing and anagnorisis, his fights, and the accession of Malcolm.

Some editors have broken the scene in two, and even three, on the assumption that when Malcolm entered the castle, and later acknowledged his kingship, new locations were necessary. Probably not in the Globe, where the diverse incidents would easily have coalesced, as the men swarming in and out of various stage areas would have identified their positions in relation to the Dunsinane imagined as central. Some theatres have sustained the continuity (e.g. Garrick, Phelps, many twentieth-century stagings), some have broken it (e.g. Macready, Charles Kean). I believe Shakespeare, as per the Folio, intended a single, unbroken intensification of battle and duel up to a climactic struggle, followed by a brief coda.

Malcolm's forces are to assault Dunsinane in a night action (Old Seyward, V, vi, 12), which provides an opportunity for the spectacle of flashing lanterns moving among the weaponed men and their banners. Thus Irving's set: dark, threatening skies, touched here and there with the fires of an angry sunset, the rushes of armed men across the shadows. (Rather than changing backdrops, as was then the custom, Irving rolled a moving panorama behind the action.) With Randle Ayrton (England, 1931), the silhouettes of horn-helmeted men broke the line of the fading sunset. With Ernst Schröder, Malcolm's troops, unseen behind the shields they carried, seemed a walking metal wall, moving against Dunsinane.

Sounds for the battles have been war cries and groans, and the crash of metal on metal, and the marshalling drums, often mixed with storm-thunder. Irving's seeming thousands of troops were applauded for their war songs as they fought. In "modern" twentieth century productions heavy artillery, dive bombers, and rifle fire also sounded; one of Komisarjevsky's directions called for a "bombardment record."

The theatre is often not content with the noise of offstage war, but seizes the opportunity for gorgeous visual display of men in battle. The logic of the last two scenes, with Macbeth's determination to rush out to meet Malcolm's approaching men, suggested, at least as early as Macklin, a see-saw battle,

> so manoeuvred as to make the Scotch first appear to defeat the English and drive them off the stage—the English must beat them back and totally rout the Scotch.

Of the many stagings that followed this plan, Phelps' was the most authentic and spectacular. Thus, in one battle seen from a perspective at the castle walls,

> A sally of the defenders . . . now driving out their besiegers; anon a fierce rally of the English soldiers beating back the troops of Macbeth; while forth from the *melee*, with difficulty disentangling themselves from the fighting, rushing crowds—now Macbeth, now Macduff, now Siward would struggle forward for a more conspicuous place. (May Phelps)

The battle scenes were commonly played then before backdrops, but not in Phelps' ambitious setting for his staging with Faucit in 1864;

> The Castle of Dunsinane, towers, arches, drawbridges . . . are all perfect, and through the solid masonry of the building a breach has been rendered practicable by the warlike engines of attack. Large portions of the crenallated wall have been levelled . . . Over the ramparts and through the breaches . . . the troops of the invading army comes pouring by hundreds [attacking] beneath the protecting smoke of a conflagration which has been effected in lower wards of the fortress [and amid] the continual clangour of trumpets calling, as clamorous harbingers to death.
> (See *Sunday Times, Sporting Life, Telegraph, Era*)

Phelps' engaging stage directions: "Everybody is disc. on stage fighting"; and later, "All the characters and forces, everybody on." It was a time when masses of extras contributed as much to theatrical spectacle as they would later to "historical" films.

The later theatres of the twentieth century, like Shakespeare's, would generally have to learn to suggest *Macbeth*'s final battles with more limited troops—barring exceptional circumstances, as when, in the Turkish staging before a river fortress, volunteers from the army's 66th Division fleshed out the opposing forces.

Macbeth and his men are at once on the defensive in some productions as, following on Macduff's call to advance (V, vi), Malcolm's troops move against Dunsinane. They may be seen creeping up the battlements, as with Tearle; or rushing against the castle. Thus, with Sothern:

> *Malcolm* and *Siward* and their men fought their way into it step by step. As they battered down great doors there appeared a distant prospect of the sea, and arose the din of battle from other parts of the fortress. *Macbeth*'s men are slowly driven back until they are forced to surrender. Only the wild, tiger-like Macbeth is left . . . (C. E. Russell)

In such mass confrontations, Macbeth is likely to be seen, as Marais was, rallying his men, but with little effect, as they fall away, or join Malcolm, who can say, in the play's paradoxical mode:

> We have met with foes
> That strike beside us. (39–40)

With Sothern, the surrender of Macbeth's troops was like the end of a civil war: they knelt to Malcolm, who raised them, and they could then be seen making friends with the attackers.

When a mass battle erupts on the stage, it usually fades away, or recedes into the background, so Macbeth may be singled out for his first one-to-one duel. Alternatively, he appears, after a sound-bridge of *Alarums*, alone on the stage, as the Folio directs, his physical fatigue extrapolating the unseen fighting that he must have shared. He is unmistakably an older man now, even the Old Man, who must confront Youth in a climactic battle. To emphasize his ritual role, and the importance to him of the throne, he may be wearing the crown, and other royal regalia; or he has fully returned to his armored image of a titan-soldier, as Hackett had, in his battered garments of the first act,

> looking with affection . . . at the indentations on his shield and nicks on his sword . . . so that we see him finish as we saw him beginning.

When Macbeth does appear alone, his stark presence can tell much about the fighting he must have done. Thus Sullivan, appearing on a bare stage between wings of wild rock and heather:

> At the back was Macbeth's castle . . . seen in perspective. It was supposed to be vast, and occupied the whole back of the scene. In the centre was the gate, double doors in a Gothic archway of massive proportions . . . The stage was empty, but from all around it rose the blare of trumpets and the roll of drums. Suddenly the Castle gates were dashed back and through the archway came Macbeth, sword in hand and buckler on arm. Dashing . . . down to the footlights he thundered out
> > They have tied me to a stake, I cannot fly,
> > But bearlike I must fight the course.

Macbeth's feeling of being tethered echoes a frustration that has before beset him when *cabin'd, cribb'd, confin'd*. He frees himself with a psychic wrench—perhaps accompanied by a physical one—meant to lift him to safer ground:

> What's he
> That was not born of woman? Such a one
> Am I to fear, or none. (4–6)

Duthie perceived as a pitiful lack of intelligence the failure to realize that since there had been the one equivocation—Birnam Wood—there might be two. This sees Macbeth from the outside; if we share Macbeth's uncertainty, his leap to assurance is primary. And it makes the *naive* spectator wonder, again, at a cerebral level, what trick might be hidden in the identity of any possible destroyer of Macbeth: a woman? a child? a beast?

Shakespeare partly gives Macbeth the speech so we will be reminded of his promised invincibility; and this may well be visually confirmed. If Macbeth is in the midst of battle, he will slay many men, and emerge unharmed. Even now, when he is alone, enemy soldiers may come at him, and he may kill several, as in the Craig staging, before he meets young Seyward. In any case, his meeting with this youth stipulates his apparent invulnerability. Young Seyward, as Hall decided, must be a fine fighter, strong, fearless, visibly a worthy opponent of the old king he challenges, a match for almost any stalwart swordsman.

The cutting of the scene to protect the nobler image of Macbeth, as committed by Garrick certainly and often thereafter, doubly mutilated Macbeth's character. It denied him the only specific visual evidence, before his meeting with Macduff, of his prowess as a fighter; and frustrated Shakespeare's intended illusion of Macbeth's charmed life. So the *St. James Chronicle*, scolding Garrick for the "material Injury" of the omission:

> The Poet meant to *shew* that *Macbeth* was invincible til he encountered Macduff . . . so graceful a Fencer as Mr. *Garrick* has no excuse for refusing to gratify us with the two Rencontres instead of one.

And the *Chronicle* had a further objection:

> On account of this Mutilation, the beautiful Reflection of the elder *Siward* is left out.

In Macbeth's brief dialogue with young Seyward sounds the clipped arrogance of a warrior to whom killing is almost too easy. Weaver chuckled at the idea of this single young man challenging him; Reinhardt's Macbeth, raising his visor with a scornful laugh, thundered his identity. As Scofield straightened himself for the necessary work of slaughter, he spoke in a dry, weary voice, that yet had a note of compassion in it, as if he would as soon not kill.

With all the energy and muscle of youth Seyward attacks; and an amused or unroused Macbeth may casually parry a blow or two, as a further manifestation of his assurance. When he decides to strike mortally, he does so without great effort, using sword or dagger or, in a sudden movement, seizing his enemy bodily and hurling him from the battlements (a gambit more often saved for Macbeth's later duel). To the *naive* spectators who wondered if young Seyward might represent the oracle's equivocation (will a boy, not a man, destroy Macbeth?), an easy victory over him seemed to confirm the Sisters' assurance that Macbeth may in fact be invulnerable to human battle.

Macbeth convinces himself of this as he looks down on the dead young man. The epitaph he pronounces extends to all men:

> Thou was't born of woman; (19)

However triumphant, the words may be colored with the note of pity Scofield gave them; even with the special concern implied by Tom Baker (England, 1973), who in II, i had gently caressed Fleance, and who now paused briefly to bend and touch the dead young Seyward's corpse, with a fatherly "restrained melancholy." Even so, Macbeth also acknowledges a satisfaction, however grim, in this proof of his charm against woman-born man.

The *alarums* call Macbeth to fighting elsewhere; and his exit to the battle offstage will be marked by the rising sounds of struggle which will in a moment attract Macduff, now entering:

> That way the noise is: (23)

He pauses to affirm his resolution to avenge his family, or—the image of Banquo's return from the dead is faintly reprised—

> My wife and children's ghosts will haunt me still: (25)

Macduff will not strike at hired kerns, only Macbeth, whose magnitude and centrality to the battle, he affirms:

> There thou shouldst be,
> By this great clatter, one of greatest note,
> Seems bruited. (29–31)*

Macduff's plunge into the offstage battle rouses new *clatter;* and under cover of this Malcolm and Seyward enter. They do not see the body of Young Seyward; he may have been slain above, as Granville-Barker suggested, or in the "inner below." No provision is made anywhere for the removal of his body, though Ross will say later that he was brought off the field. I have seen him left on the stage, unnoticed now by his father, until later, when old Seyward is told of the death; this was a very moving moment, as the father knelt over the dead son. Shakespeare, so knowledgeable about evoking emotion may have been tempted to include the bit; but instead he made sure young Seyward was off, so as not to distract from the tidal emotion centering on Macbeth's ending.

---

*A pun on "brute" is scented here by Coursen.

Old Seyward informs Malcolm, who seems not to be involved in the fighting, how the battle has gone: it is almost over, Dunsinane has been taken, will he step into the castle? They go in; the *Alarums* continue.

Here Dyce suggested a break for a new scene, but any suggestion of delay or intermission after Seyward's last speech seems wrong. The war is almost over: Shakespeare does not let the continuous momentum of the action slacken for a moment. Macbeth's fate, the first priority, demands immediate consummation. So in the Folio, Macbeth returns at once to the stage, he still fighting, alone, his castle lost, his men mainly surrendered or gone over to the enemy. He may still be killing: Craig's Macbeth stabbed one attacker; Tearle threw a soldier over the stairwell, caught and hurled a thane over the back rostrum, and killed another soldier coming over it. The Power prompt-book has Macbeth killing three men, and toppling a fourth over a parapet. Even Seyton has been seen to turn on Macbeth, as in Japan, where he limped up for the kill, and was himself brutally stabbed to death.

This kind of continued violence visually reawakens the image of the heroic warrior-Macbeth, once honored for his bloody sword. Ironically now his superb professional killer's genius, that seems without the need of supernatural aid to confer invincibility on him, only gains Macbeth a little time. Almost he may convey the sense now that he would as soon be killed as kill.

Certainly, when he is alone—and the Folio direction suggests nothing else—his thoughts are again on suicide, if only to reject it, as he wavers still between options:

> Why should I play the Roman fool, and die
> On mine own sword?*

The lines evoke earlier intimations of life as theatre and particularly Macbeth's image of the *poor player*, assigned an absurd part, and of his later realization that by the equivocation of an Idiot playwright his own part had been made mock of. To Empson, *fool* here primarily implies "lunatic clown," with the stress on *Roman* to suggest one variety of *fool*—Macbeth has to play some kind of clown's part anyway, but not this one. But commonly both words share the stress with the weight toward the second word. Macbeth decides that as long as he has enemies to strike, suicide would be foolish.

But the thought of killing himself has come to his mind, and sometimes, in the theatre, the gesture to his hand. Charles Kean and Phelps rushed in as if determined on self-slaughter, and knelt, swords to chest; Hampden, kneeling more thoughtfully, propped his sword as if to fall on it; so did McKellen, the point at his throat; Richardson's hand held the naked blade toward his heart. A *naive* spectator does not know the suicide will not be consummated; only at last does a thought stop it. "What am I doing here?"

---

*The Variorum text, which I am following, breaks the last scene into two, and the lineation is therefore confused. Since only relatively few lines remain, I will not number them from here on.

was what flashed through the mind of McKellen as Macbeth, when he felt the point against his skin.

The moment passes. Macbeth will fight. *Alarums* offstage may have distracted him from the suicidal act, as with Sothern, who, at sudden shouts, dropped his chested sword, then lifted it again in a second attempt, finally as the shouts once more rose, changed his grip to one of attack.

Or inward, not outward, inhibitions, as with Hamlet, may check Macbeth's move to suicide: the philosopher may see, sardonically, the pointlessness of the act; the poet may find the reason in metaphor for clinging to life; the warrior perhaps puts off his own end only temporarily *whiles* he sees *lives* that challenge him to one of his purposes in life.

A deep-lying irony and a searing suspense can enrich the moment. The Macbeth-actor may feel it when he faces his own sword's point: as a man of woman born, he is presumably not dangerous to himself—though the *naive* spectator, seeing Macbeth's first gesture toward self-destruction, and expecting that he will go on to commit suicide, wonders if this may explain the Sisters' oracle: no *man*, but Macbeth himself, threatens Macbeth.

Stagings have sometimes obscured Macbeth's final, introspective solitude by filling the background with searching soldiers, or glimpses of battle. Nineteenth-century elaborations might first crowd the stage as prelude to the sudden focus on a two-man duel, as when McKee Rankin played Macbeth (U.S., 1886). The staging followed the Folio's directions for a first duel between the adversaries, their exit, and a second round of fighting:

> Macbeth's castle on a veritable hill of Dunsinane filled the background. From an open gate Macbeth descends by a steep path to the bridge in the middle mistance, where he meets Macduff; in one corner of the foreground, with their war engines, a party of besiegers watch the conflict, and a similar group of Macbeth's men stand under the castle walls above. The duel proceeds and the principals and men vanish from the scene. Hand-to-hand fights follow on . . . three levels at once. Bands of soldiers rush up the hill and disappear around the walls. Macbeth and Macduff now appear in the foreground and continue their duel.

Shakespeare, having built to the ultimate man-to-man conflict, gave Macbeth, and then Macduff, the whole stage. Macbeth, a solitary figure, having cast off the pall of irresolution, looks off—perhaps moves off—toward the sound of enemies when Macduff enters behind him.

> Turn, hellhound, turn.

Macbeth's response has evoked argument. He begins:

> Of all men else I have avoided thee:

and indeed, in the war scenes, he may have been seen to turn away, seeing Macduff. But the reason he gives for avoiding confrontation has been questioned.

> But get thee back, my soul is too much charg'd
> With blood of thine already.

Macbeth's words now speak remorse, and so Chambers, Dolora Cunningham, and others have heard it. Farnham discerns no pity, only concern about possible retribution. Muir asks, "Or is he rationalizing his fear?", and Heilman finds much to be said for that interpretation. Redgrave discovers, in Macbeth's later unwillingness to fight, a lack of bravery. Does fear stay his hand? Certainly Macbeth has been warned by the Sisters against Macduff, and some deeply felt reverberation of distrust may underlie his reluctance. But the warning did not seem to point to physical danger; *none of woman born* can harm Macbeth, and Macduff seems still unmistakably some mother's offspring. That Macbeth should see Macduff as the victim of his shameful cruelty harmonizes with the note of humankindness so strong in the earlier characterization, and fits the pattern of recurrence of inward scruples. Kean, Hawkins reported, repelled with horror the idea of fighting with the man he had so injured. Scofield looked at his Macduff with a weary pain, as if feeling the full weight burdening his overcharged soul, and unwilling to add to it. A deep remorse was sensed in Booth, that he would with some difficulty suppress. Dramatically, the abrupt shift from Macbeth's slaughter of enemies to this sudden, brooding reservation makes a startling contrast. It shapes emotional response; the *naive* spectator, accustomed now to expect another victim of Macbeth's bloody sword, hoped Macduff would have the sense to escape. This response follows from Macbeth's demonstration, to himself as well as to his audience, of how invincible, how invulnerable, he is. Shakespeare designs him to know that he can easily strike down the Thane of Fife, and not only because of the oracle. "If their fighting reputations mean anything," as Quiller-Couch observes, "Macbeth should kill Macduff. The Seyward duel emphasises this."

In the theatre, Macbeth's superior power may quickly become visual. Macduff has called Macbeth *villain*, lifted his weapon—*My voice is in my sword*—and, as the Folio directs, they *Fight: Alarum*. Amid the sounds of battle, as the swordplay begins, Macbeth may, as Irving did, confidently, almost casually, ward off attack. Alternatively, he may strike so heavily as to hold Macduff at his mercy. In the Kumo staging in Japan, Macbeth easily knocked the sword from Macduff's hand, then allowed him to pick it up, while warning him against further battle. A Prague Macbeth, after disarming Macduff, kicked the fallen sword back to him. A fiercer Macbeth gives Macduff no quarter, after the *villain* epithet. Thus Sothern, now a haggard echo of the heroic image of the first act: his eyes feverish, his tangled hair over his eyes, his voice like the cry of a cornered animal. His attack so endangered Macduff that one of Malcolm's soldiers heard, and rushed in to try to help: Sothern, "raging and frothing," struck him lifeless with a blow, and turned to beat Macduff to his knees. Macduff, wounded, was allowed to stagger off, while another soldier, running in, engaged Macbeth and was driven off. Then Macduff returned, for the final encounter.

Macbeth has time, while the wounded, or winded, or down-beaten Macduff recovers, for the extended declaration that reveals how profound is his belief in his invulnerability. *Thou losest labour* has been spoken with the tone and gesture of sarcasm (Kean), or contemptuous smiling confidence, the sword held at careless ease, or even thrown off (Macready); but it may carry a dry compassion (Scofield), or pain: Reinhardt's Macbeth laughed wildly, Rogers spoke almost as if regretting his own immunity. Kemble meant sincerely that Macbeth did not want to use, on Macduff, the special power he believed he possessed. An ebullient self-assurance may color the words: Hackett, in manic excitement, could see himself throwing aside his sword, seizing Macduff, and holding him as he would a baby. He laughed at the insistence that a mortal sword could as easily wound the air as make him *bleed*.

> I bear a charmed life, which must not yield
> To one of woman born.

Now the ultimate joke is played on Macbeth. However desperately Macduff may be defending himself, now he is suddenly armed with a terrible psychic weapon.

> Despair thy charm,
> And let the angel whom thou still hast serv'd
> Tell thee, Macduff was from his mother's womb
> Untimely ripp'd.

The evidence of equivocation is the more devastating for being so shabby. Macduff has of course been born of woman, if perhaps not "naturally." But in the context of the oracle, his birth suddenly sets him apart from ordinary men, in our eyes, and Macbeth's. Macduff becomes an instrument of the ironic forces manipulating Macbeth, as if fated by his Caesarian irruption to play the part often assigned to legendary heroes strangely birthed. He incarnates, as Brooks observed, the motif of the triumphant babe, mighty, bloody.

That Macbeth's *angel* should have been the agent of Macbeth's misleading is a bitter stroke, that Macduff may well load with sarcasm, as with Hackett. The word could mean, neutrally, "spirit" or "demon," but here suggests the kind of discolored image associated with the brightest angel who fell. Fanny Kemble:

> What a tremendous vision of terrible splendour . . . What a visible presence
> of gloomy glory . . . the great prince of pride, ambition and rebellion seems to
> rise in lurid majesty.

Macbeth, in the next to last of his spectacular transitions, now experiences the full horror of his ironic trap. A kind of value now more precious than life has turned false to him. Death he has been able to contemplate, even as self-inflicted; this betrayal strikes at his psychic survival, disjoins his self-image:

> Accursed be that tongue that tells me so;
> For it hath cow'd my better part of man:

Muir interprets this last as "the mind, soul, or spirit: not 'the better part of manhood' (Clarendon)." Perhaps in Macbeth's sense now the two meanings resolve. He may well feel the loss of both his spiritual energy and the masculine strength that served it. The subversion of his manhood, for which he has dared more than man should dare, strikes at his center. The shock, in the theatre, is traditionally seismic, and the disturbance Macbeth manifests enhances the new, special aura about him.

Kemble, careful as he was to protect an image of Macbeth's courage, nevertheless shrank away from his enemy.* Macready, a moment before overglowing with assurance, reacted even more violently—he fled to a far corner of the stage, stood shrinking before his nemesis, in agonized, hopeless despair. Irving's "sword arm falls senseless . . . Macbeth reels like a drunken man" (*Telegraph*). Sothern started back, horror-stricken, knees shaking, sword half let go. Charles Kean responded with a suppressed cry, and his sword shook in his hand until it jangled—an effect the *Spectator* had also observed in Forrest. Reinhardt's Macbeth staggered and his guard dropped. The unbalanced Williamson retched in panic.

Other Macbeths have reflected their shock more in still, silent response, the impact inward. In Salvini's reaction Henry James saw "A wonderful picture . . . of the blind effort of a man who once was strong to resist his doom and contradict his stars"; but then "All virtue goes out of him," Stevenson observed, "and though he speaks sounding words of defiance, the last combat is little better than a suicide." Kean startled audiences as he stood for a moment petrified, then loosed his "terrific and deadly glare" on Macduff. Rossi, too, stood frozen for an instant, his eyes, full of horror, fixed on his enemy. Hackett's reaction was tremendous rage. Scofield remained standing solidly, giving no ground; but his glance at Macduff seemed to look beyond him to the mystery and horror of equivocation; the most sounding note was the philosopher's, comprehending what had happened to him.

Macbeth's shock gives Macduff time to recover from a defensive posture; and Macduff's recovery gives Macbeth the pause for his rumination, voicing to himself his glimpse of his trammeled life.

> And be these juggling fiends no more believ'd,
> That palter with us in a double sense,

---

*Kemble: "Was retreat ever thought disgraceful, when the superior numbers and resistless great fortune of the foe made all further struggle useless?" But Kemble would return to the duel when, in his view, despair roused Macbeth's "palsied powers"; and he fought, Macready remembered, with "most heroic defiance."

> That keep the word of promise to our ear,
> And break it to our hope.

It is the lament familiar to all human experience, and characteristic of the heroes who, from the time of Oedipus and before, bring themselves by their best means to the worst. Speaking it, Macbeth may well slide for a last time into the raptness of his first encounter with the Sisters. If so, an abrupt move from Macduff will bring him alert.

Macbeth does not want to fight. He seems to withdraw, not from Macduff, but from the treacherous universe of the kind Scofield glimpsed beyond his adversary—as if man can ever disengage, short of death, from the ironic traps laid for him. The withdrawal usually follows at once on the rumination. Rossi, however, impelled by desperation, rushed in at once to cross swords with Macduff; a Belgian observer was impressed by the superstitious fear of his utterance—*Accursed be that tongue*—and then the increasingly slower and more dragging blows of his sword. Only after he felt drained of strength by Macduff's avowal, and its implications, did Rossi disengage himself from the fight. Juriev, in Russia, saw him stop, walk apart, and wipe the sweat from his face, and only then, after a pause, say

> I'll not fight with thee.

It is a difficult, demeaning line for a great warrior, carrying echoes of the childhood complaint, "It's not fair. I won't play." Because Macbeth *is* acknowledged to be so great a warrior, he can speak with dignity, determination, anger; but still he is confessing a defeat, and this may come hard: Booth could only stammer the words. Terry's notes on Irving: "Tremor, then throw it away . . . white as death."

Macduff offers Macbeth the only alternative to fighting: imprisonment, and a poor player's last frettings, in a public cage,

> the show, and gaze o' th' time.

The exhibition to be advertised with a sign: *Here you may see the tyrant*. But the word that touches Macbeth most cruelly, as it did from his wife's mouth, is *Coward*; if Macbeth has been turning away, as Forrest had, this insult checks him brutally.

The offered part Macbeth refuses to play. Though he has been misled by equivocations—and he repeats them in a last cry against unfairness—he will *try the last*. If his confidence has collapsed, his courage has not:

> Lay on Macduff,
> And damn'd be him, that first cries hold, enough.

He clings to his manhood; cowardice is the only kind of damnation he acknowledges. Now he begins to fight again, and the tempo changes to something quite different from the first exchange. Now Macbeth fights under a double shadow: the knowledge first that he has believed in an illusion, has played a part designed to lead him to disaster; and second that this man whose revengeful sword he now confronts represents the unnatural threat held over him. He has been doubly warned against this enemy.

In some stagings Macbeth's freedom has been further constricted by an enclosing ring of Malcolm's soldiers—a whole army seemed to surround Porter. Ernst Schröder was hemmed in by the faceless shields held up before encircling soldiers that made a wall of steel wherever he looked. In another German staging (Berlin, 1968) Malcolm's men did not merely make a circle for the duel, but menaced Macbeth with their spears as they closed in upon him. In defense he struck and killed one; and as he guarded himself from the others' spear-points, Macduff slew him. In Brandenburg (1972), in the Müller distortion, the soldiers themselves killed Macbeth with their lances. The danger with this kind of visual imagery is that it suggests a final fight wholly enforced on Macbeth, he battling an army, not only the strangely born Macduff. The text indicates rather that Macbeth *chooses* to stay and engages in the kind of lonely, archetypal battle that is still fought out in Western and costume films. Macbeth's death, in the face of strange odds, will become him; he will not let life slip away like a careless trifle.

The vicious struggle makes severe demands on the actors' two bodies. As Macbeth, the actor must convey the illusion of being in fact in a spontaneous, wild, life-and-death encounter. But the second, trained body performs in a carefully calculated choreography. Only when actors are so rehearsed in their movements that they can trust each other to make mortal thrusts harmlessly can they dare to exchange mortal thrusts. If not, they must suffer the kind of verdict passed by one observer on Tree's duel: "The two warriors seemed to lay on as though desperately afraid of hurting one another" (*Truth*)*; or they may be scolded for seeming to engage in a mannered duel, like Hamlet and Laertes; they are trying to kill, they are warriors rather than swordsmen, an animal ferocity fires their fight.

The choreography that lies behind what will seem a heedless fight to the death, is sometimes set down in cold print. Olivier's elaborate schedule of thrust and counter, preserved in the Stratford Shakespeare Centre, indicates the difference in the duel before and after Macduff's revelation: in the first part, parried "cuts" high and low on the body, clinches, broken when one pushes the other away; then, after *untimely ripp'd*, Macbeth fighting "desperately," the cuts and parries building to large movements across the stage, and close infighting:

> Macduff retreats up steps and Macbeth lunges. Macduff disarms, and draws dagger (R hand) stabbing down.

*Though *Stage* was impressed by the brutality of the final combat, the two hurling their shields at each other and then discarding swords for knives "used ferocity in savage and determined grappling." The *Daily Telegraph* thought the scenes "admirably devised, admirably played."

Macbeth draws dagger with L hand, transfers to R hand, catching Macduff's stab with L hand. Macduff kicks Macbeth's dagger with R foot. Macbeth lunges with dagger. Macduff grabs Macbeth's dagger wrist. LOCK. They struggle up to level. ON LEVEL. They struggle and Macduff gives way, going down on R. knee. Macbeth falls over him on steps. Positions reversed. Macduff pushes Macbeth's dagger with his own, grabs his wrist with L hand and pushes his R forearm under Macbeth's throat.

The best laid plans, congealed in print, have been upset by the rising passions of the players. Reports from as early as the Restoration* tell of men wounded or even killed in this final battle—which partly explains the myth of jinx associated with the play in the theatre, and why its name is supposed not to be mentioned backstage by the superstitious. The actor playing Macduff absorbs fearfully the murderous motivation. The actor inhabiting Macbeth has reached a peak of emotion rarely matched in Shakespeare, and the whole passion of his mimetic self, infected with many strains—among them fear, confusion, violence, the need to hurt—is focused on destroying or being destroyed. The reader who seeks to understand the character, and who does not breathe more quickly here, who does not feel his hand tighten on his imaginary sword, who does not almost hear and feel the clash of steel, and the sharp point near his throat, is not yet sharing Shakespeare's design. The actor may forget himself in the role. Macready remembered Kemble lashing himself into such a rage (ending in a "perfect triumph") that Charles Kemble (who as Macduff had "killed" him) "received him in his arms, and laid him gently on the ground, his physical powers being unequal to further effort." The opposite happened to Cooper:

He would not die. Macduff had to kill him three times before he would yield, and seemed actually at a loss how to dispose of him. Macbeth, the more he fought and was wounded, became the more lively, and at last became so infuriated as to seize his sword with both hands to knock his antagonist down.

In Macready's encounters with his Macduffs may be sensed how fierce can be the determination to invest the image of battle with reality. None knew better than the intellectual Macready how much of acting could be the product of technique; none struggled harder for the truth of spontaneity, for such identification of the actor's first body with his character that, as was said of Burbage, the personator became the personated. Macready's violent action in battle inevitably overflowed his choreography, which in words seems so simple: "Six cut and lunge—six cartwheel (circling)—Macd.: cut at head and cross L.—six lunges—stab." In an early duel with Phelps as Macduff, Macready, pressing for more intensity in the swordplay, cursed Phelps who,

*Harris as Macduff was reported to have stabbed his Macbeth through the eye, killing him (*Shakespere Allusion Book*). Many accidents have been reported to accomplished actor-swordsmen Macbeths. Booth, for instance, was once badly hurt by his Macduff (Otis Skinner); Ristori's Macbeth, George Rignold (England, 1882) was so severely cut he had to be replaced. Beware Macduff indeed.

though a pious man, cursed back—and afterwards Macready praised him for his fighting. Coleman, playing Macduff against Macready, was even more roused:

> The fury of his first onslaught . . . staggered me, and I recoiled. When, however, he continued to let drive at me, growling, "Come on sir, come on!" I responded to the best of my ability, and at last, losing my head, gave him a crack on the wrist, whereat he emitted a scream like a wounded horse, and shrieked, "Kill me! Kill me!" I needed no second invitation, but let him have it with such a will that the impact of the pommel of my sword brought him a cropper.

In this last of Macbeth's appearances, the character intensity becomes almost intolerable. The tension may manifest itself, at one extreme, by hysteria (Plummer), or manic laughter (Quilley), at the other by clenched determination (Scofield), or furious snarl (Porter), or madness (Rogers), but underlying all has been the experience of life at the boundary of possibility.

These crucial moments require in Macbeth a profundity of feeling that will magnetize an audience's full mental and emotional involvement. Macbeth has been seen, by some scholars, as

> unsympathetic; alienating; damned; reduced to a beast; shrunken in body and spirit; a human mind dwindled down to one faculty: faith in force against all sense and conscience . . . without any of the finer quality of a courage . . . a soulless man, a beast, chained to a stake and slaughtered like a beast; . . . he dies less a demigod than a gangster.

The great visualized images in the theater do not square with this, but rather with more positive critical impressions:

> a triumphant failure . . . with his mighty human strength he wins back his manliness; the grandeur of a soul meshed in crime; death befits a man who for all his crimes has not lost our good will . . . like Siward, he has parted well and paid his score.

The primary tone of the warrior-killer in Macbeth's polyphony certainly rises to a dominating pitch in his last moments; but it is always modulated by the complex of other tones implicit from his whole journey to desperation. Macbeth is felt to struggle not only against Macduff, but against higher odds: against the equivocating world, hence suffering the disillusion of the poet and philosopher and king and widower seeing all lost but persistently implicated in the struggle for life. The whole design surfaces in the new tempo of Macbeth's attack, that was before so superbly assured, now at the last ungoverned, wild, with a recklessness almost suicidally careless of safety. The rich, dense subtext can be felt informing Macbeth's death with a touch of apotheosis.

"Appalling" was Coleman's descriptive for the reckless bravery of Macready's final *agon*.

So might the fallen star of morning have confronted the archangel in the last dread conflict. His hair stood up erect, his eyes flashed fire, and his frame dilated to almost preternatural proportions. As he himself has finely said, "One would have thought almost that his soul would have lived on from the very force of will." Death could not have been felt by a man so resolute.

"His physical energy was terrific," Marston noted, "and took grandeur from the desperate mind. He turned upon Fate and stood at bay."

Macready attacked violently, rushing madly at Macduff: with the sweep of an avalanche, one observer remembered, with the deadly spring of a tiger, another. Leaving himself, in his charge, more open to attack, Macready was stabbed again and again, at last mortally. Still he resisted:

> Nothing can possibly be grander than his manner of returning, with that regal stride, after he has received his mortal thrust, to fall again on Macduff's sword, in yielding weakness. The spirit fights but the body sinks in mortal faintness. Still, as it sinks, Macbeth survives and Mr. Macready's attitude in falling, when he thrusts his sword into the ground, and by its help for one moment raises himself on one knee to stare into the face of his opponent with a gaze that seemed to concentrate all Majesty, Hate and Knowledge, had an air of the preternatural fit to close such a career. (Forster)

This last expression of Macready's, defiant, proud, unyielding, as he rested for a moment on one knee, had tremendous impact on observers:

> Collecting all the old heroism of his character, he fixed a look full of resolution and defiance on his enemy . . . and instantly fell dead. (*Morning Post*)

In Kean's great climax, primary strains in Macbeth's polyphony sounded. Finlay, who made little of Kean's shortness, mocked the actor's large crown, for its weight, which must "have galled his leaden brow" and its height which "appeared almost as tall as himself." Finlay was obviously no friend; nothing midget in the Kean's finale is suggested by better observers. Quite the contrary. Challenging Macduff for the last time, Kean's voice

> seemed almost choked and stifled by his overwhelming emotions; he rushed to the clash with a frightful eagerness compounded of the determination of fighting to the death, and of the desire of flying for ever from the development of those horrid mysteries which open one after the other, merely to distract and destroy him. The ferocity of rage and the agony of appalling doubts were equally conspicuous.

After the deathblow,

> there was a fine contrast of fierceness and feebleness—the energy of the soul resisting the destruction of the body; his strong volition kept him standing for some moments . . . as the expiring flame burnt brightly at the last, he aimed a final blow at his antagonist . . . still retaining his erect position by several half-expressed writhings followed by a certain indescribable stiffness of the trunk and limbs . . . At length Macbeth feebly lifted his sword and appeared to aim

a stroke at [Macduff]. The effort was unavailing—the point of his sword
dropped—his body rested for an instant on the hilt.
(See *Examiner*, Hawkins, Hazlitt, *Sun*)

He finally fell forward on his face, as if to cover the shame of his defeat—the
pose suggested to Kean by a soldier's figure on a St. Paul's monument; but
one spectator saw the actor, after falling, crawl on the floor to reach his sword,
and die touching it.

Booth's ending reflected his warrior's triumph over the deep remorse he
showed in his first warning to Macduff, and over his superstitious shock after
Macduff's revelation. His final battle seemed to Winter,

frightful in its maniacal vitality . . . the recklessness of defiant valor and the
fury of desperation. When he was beaten down and bereft of his sword he
wildly fought on.

Dying, he threw his dagger at Macduff, went on stabbing the air toward him
with his hand, finally

reared himself for a moment in agony, and then plunged forward dead, at the
foot of his antagonist

in a "strange, weird" death. (See *Brooklyn Times, Daily Alta, New York Times,*
Winter).

Often, as schematized in the Olivier choreography, Macbeth loses his
sword, and Macduff does too; or one drops his sword and the other, chival-
rously, lets go his; and they take to daggers. Both weapons, flashing in the
light, as they seek out enemy flesh, continue the verbal and visual imagery of
metal against life, spilling blood, that runs through the play. The short knives
carry a special resonance: not only for Duncan's death, but also because killing with them involves a close, intimate savagery, an animal clinching that is
embrace as well as grapple; as of *two spent swimmers, that do cling together,/ And
choke their art*. Sothern, the once gentlemanly Macbeth, then frustrated and
bitter, especially over the loss of his Lady, clawed at Macduff furiously, with
any weapon at hand.

He beat Macduff to his knees . . . His sword was knocked from his hand; he
whipped out his dagger and threw himself upon [Macduff], and when at last
the fatal thrust passed through him, he died with a wild beast's scream, still
struggling to get to his feet. (C. E. Russell)

Sometimes even the dagger is lost by one or the other man, or both, and
the fighting may be with fist and claw, or with any clublike thing, or with
shields, or with muscle against metal. Wolfit, his magnificent strength worn
down, eyes red, hair unkempt, his nerve-tortured face haggard, when his
weapons were gone flung his shield violently at Macduff, and closed in on
him. Hampden, disarmed, fought his Macduff's blade with bare hands (a
business of Kean's as Richard III) and, as he staggered back in his death throes,

his bloody hands stained the white walls of his castle (an echo of his blood-stains when he returned from murdering Duncan).

In extended duels, graced by expertly savage swordplay, Macbeth may suffer many woundings before the final one. Each more serious stab builds forward the last. Young, Kean's contemporary, was repeatedly cut. With just sufficient strength to support himself on his sword, he helplessly "trem-bled with shame and indignation at being no longer able to cope with his ad-versary" (*Dramatic Magazine*). Aldridge bled from many wounds, Russian and German observers noted: at the end, like a wounded bear, he dragged his sword after him, tried to draw his dagger, and sank down impotent from loss of blood. Charles Kean

> Proved a very glutton of steel; he insisted on being run through twice, and seemed disappointed at not getting a third mortal thrust, for he looked up re-proachfully as he lay on his face, as if imploring the *coup de grâce*. (*Spectator*)

The *Sun* saw a clear suicidal impulse:

> With desperate lion-mettle he twice impales himself on his antagonist's sword and then falls . . . forward in a death sprawl toward his adversary, hungry after annihilation.

Something of the same self-destructive impulse, that Stevenson sensed also in Salvini, underlay the deaths of some twentieth-century Macbeths. Hradilák (Czechoslovakia, 1967) seemed, existentially, to choose death: he deliberately opened himself to a mortal attack. Eric Porter, angry as he was with his unfair world, subverted by the knowledge of the Macduff trick, too proud to surrender, fought wildly, sensible of the ring of Malcolm's men pinning him in with swords implacably pointed to his heart. One enemy now was his enigmatic Seyton, played as his shadow with sinister ambiguity—he had been third murderer—by Ian Richardson. Porter, his weapons finally lost, hemmed in, seemed to beg for death: "panting, eyes pleading, throat contracted to animal sounds before he is butchered" (*Stratford-upon-Avon Herald*). He almost flung himself, at last, on Macduff's sword. William Devlin spectacularly embraced death by leaping down from a high rostrum to impale himself on Macduff's upturned blade.

When a single mortal blow ends Macbeth's life, instead of a succession of woundings, the preliminary fencing spirals directly to a final climactic act. The giant Salvini, fighting with a massive two-handed sword against a Macduff armed with rapier and dagger, yielded, after only a few exchanges, to a single stroke through his coat of mail. Mantell and his Macduff fought a furious broadsword fight around the stage, both finally losing their major weapons and drawing daggers. As they struggled to close quarters, Macduff maneuvered himself downstage, concealing Macbeth from the audience, and was then seen to raise his dagger high and plunge it down. He stepped back. The dying Mantell dropped his dagger and began to collapse; but even falling, he flailed out with his hands in a dying attempt to throttle Macduff.

The killing of Macbeth on stage can function as an almost sacrificial slaying of a man (scapegoat?) betrayed by circumstance, supernatural influence, and his mortal impulses; and involve a kind of warrior's rebirth for a Macbeth of any essential worth.

Even a nerve-twisted, neurotic Macbeth, facing death in battle, finds his way back toward the self he was first proclaimed by all to be. Thus Matkowsky, who had become so shaken by Macduff's *untimely ripp'd* that he seemed at the point of collapse. Yet now, slowly, as he moved from paralysis to confront Macduff, he found his voice, and himself, and built both to a crescendo of sound and action, that graced again the hero he had been at first. Even the rare coward-Macbeth—Irving's conception—found the fighter's courage at his core, as his manhood revolted at the charge of cowardice. Irving seemed at last to redeem the descriptive *brave Macbeth*. He wore no helmet when he began to fight—he wanted no masking of his expressive features as he recovered reeling from the shock of Macduff's revelation. His dishevelled grey hair floated wildly in the wind. His dark, hunted eyes glared out of his pale, determined face. In his recklessness, he gave a special meaning to

> Before my body,
> I throw my warlike shield:

by casting the shield away and grasping the hilt of his huge sword with both hands to attack Macduff in blind, unguarded fury—only the desire to strike seemed left in him. In his armor, all shining, that "made the doomed king gleam afar like a tower of gold" (Winter), wild, haggard, anguish-stricken, "at once brave and prescient of evil" (*Saturday Review*), the "great famished wolf" fought out his "splendid despair." "Destiny seemed to hang over him," Terry remembered, "and he knew there was no hope, no mercy." He fought on, though he was weary with age, and even more "weak with the weakness of a giant exhausted, spent as one whose exertions have been ten times . . . those of commoner men of rougher fibre and coarser." He lost his sword, and in a burst of fury, while collapsing from a mortal wound, hurled his dagger at Macduff,* and then fell forward, as Kean had done, face down.

Variations in the ritual of onstage death have been introduced both for the sake of spectacle, and to emphasize notes in Macbeth's character.† Macbeth had mounted his stairs to the murder of Duncan, and the kingship; the stairs have been the pathway of his ultimate destruction. Komisarjevsky's Macbeth, locked in a wildcat grapple, rolled down a long stone flight before

---

*This was in 1889, In 1875 he had pulled himself to his knees, wrenched out his dagger, and with a dying effort had attempted to stab his enemy (or himself perhaps—the *Evening Standard* was not sure. This was an old business that Forrest had used.)

†I will not again enlarge on Garrick's shameful "dying speech," which demeaned the character by trying to tidy it up with a show of repentance. Somewhat similar diminutions of Shakespeare's design are effected when Macbeth accepts the *coup de grâce* passively: e.g., Charles Dillon (England, 1869), covering his face like a Roman to await the killing thrust; a later English Macbeth (1969) offering his neck to Macduff's axe, to hint a parallel with Cawdor's execution. These submissions imply a silent cry of *Hold, enough*, inviting the secular damnation that Macbeth so fiercely abjures.

Macduff did the killing. Ernst Schröder, slain at the top of his steps, himself rolled down to his death. Bergman's Macbeth (1948), wounded at the upper landing, tottered down his stairway, dying as he descended.

In the Kumo staging, Macbeth finally threw down his sword, and was exposed to Macduff, who picked up the fallen weapon and held that and his own, ready to attack. Then he threw away the advantage, as Macbeth had done earlier; he dropped the swords, and the two fought at close quarters with daggers. As the battle approached climax, the stage was suddenly blacked out, leaving Macbeth's death to darkness. For Craig, as Macbeth died a small red pinspot grew on his face, spreading like blood.

Macbeth has been pursued beyond defeat. Tree's Macduff planted his foot on his dead adversary's chest; but he then summoned soldiers to bear Macbeth off on a shield. After Irving fell, Malcolm's soldiers lavished execrations on his dead body. Such excessive attacks can function in the theatre as dark tributes to the grandeur of Macbeth's overreaching. A more extreme symptom of awed hate for him was visualized in Edinburgh (1970) when Macbeth's stricken body, seeming dead, stirred slightly:

> The nobles pounced on him to administer a terrible coup-de-grace. . . . The concerted ferocity [of] their revenge showed what a monster they were dealing with. Seized with frenzy, they appear to be battening down the powers of darkness which Macbeth had let loose. (*Scotsman*)

The action, inevitably, was also a comment on the thanes. In Canada, after Hogg was killed, George House remembered, the herd of grey commoners rose from his killing with blood-smeared cannibal lips.

The duel has been distanced in style, as if to avoid testing, with realistic swordplay, the audience's suspension of disbelief: so Hopkins fought his Macduff in a surreal, slow motion minuet, ending with Macbeth's throat cut before the audience's eyes. One German encounter was played out, an observer reported, as a "ballet of death." As indicated earlier, Macbeth's clinging to his kingship has sometimes been emphasized in the royal garments he has worn, and his death in crown and robes then carries a special ritual impact. Cooke "fell like a ruin of the state, in full regalia."

Macbeth's visible death, providing an ultimate climax, physical and spiritual, to his career, obeys the second of the Folio's apparently confused stage directions, alluded to above:

> *Exeunt fighting. Alarums.*
> *Enter fighting, and Macbeth slain.*

Dover Wilson at one time accepted the critical notion that these were alternative endings; later he saw, as Greg did, that Shakespeare might have intended an extended, exciting swordfight that moved in and out of the audience's view. Wilson suggests that the fighting began on the main stage, at *Exeunt* moved into the tiring room out of sight—*Alarums* indicating the sounds of the duel—then concluded in the inner stage. Granville-Barker envisions the two fighting their way offstage to reappear for the killing in the above. Harbage proposes an action that seems unnecessarily demeaning: Macbeth fleeing from Macduff, and Macduff making the kill in his back—as a contrast to the death of Seyward, who had his hurts in front. Directing Scofield, Hall experimented with having Macduff drive a retreating Macbeth off, and it seemed wrong, both in terms of character and the building of expectation, and instead they fought off on even terms.

Either Wilson's or Granville-Barker's visualizations would work. While the men are fighting offstage, the last *Alarums* of the larger battle rise in sound, with perhaps a skirmish across the stage (*Alarum* may be a direction for the shows of war as well as noise), and then the re-entry of the two antagonists. The break would have the effect of suggesting the unyielding courage of both fighters, and it would give the impression of a very long duel, without dulling the edge of visual excitement—a swordfight seen to go on too long begins to invite attention to technique, rather than to drama, as in Polanski's seemingly interminable battle, fought by "armored" men who looked—and sounded—as if encased in tin cans.

The theatre, we saw, has on occasion followed the Folio direction for two rounds of struggle between Macbeth and Macduff, as with McKee Rankin (noted above); though usually a single, uninterrupted battle has been fought, ending in Macbeth's onstage killing. Sometimes, however, to facilitate Macbeth's stipulated decapitation, he is killed off. Then his peak moment is cut short. Hence Marston's tribute to Phelps for so playing the scene:

> To relinquish the usual close, in which the death of Macbeth in his desperate fight with Macduff concentrates attention on the former, was a piece of self-sacrifice . . . that cannot well be overrated.

Few moments are more satisfying to actors—and audiences—than death scenes. Some Macbeths would find solutions that could allow them both spectacular seen deaths and, if desired, decapitations. Thus Olivier's end, typically spectacular. In his second interpretation (in 1937 he had died onstage after valorously fighting Macduff with his bare shield) he had, as noted, carefully paced the mounting intensity of his characterization to its climax now: "The smouldering anger with a universe that had betrayed him" (*Times*), "flashes into flame and throws over the end of the bloody tyrant a sense of tragic sublimity." At *Lay on Macduff* Olivier seemed inexplicably to grow in height: he was seen as a lion, turning grandly at bay, a "trapped soul" reminiscent of Macready's, at war with Fate. He fought with a haunting desperation to the end, but Macduff and destiny were together too much for him; he was driven up a long flight of his castle's stone steps, to the battlements, and from there, mortally wounded, he fell, out of sight, to the imagined depths below.

Other stagings also took this way to hold Macbeth visible to the very moment of his death, and then discharge him spectacularly into the void. A frenzied Macduff, with a final stab, forced Evans to the edge of a parapet, over
which he fell with a piercing shriek. Redgrave's fall, after a fierce and sweaty
combat that prowled down and up the stage, was remembered for the "sickening thud" of his body, heard as it "landed" off, and for the sight, next, of
his head and headless body lifted into view. In the Bridges-Adams and Carrick Craig productions, expectation was cunningly extended when both fighters, grappling at close quarters, went over the battlements, and the audience had to wait to learn the outcome of the struggle. This, of course, is the
suspense tactic inherent in the first of the Folio's two stage directions for the
duel, that sends the combatants off with the issue in doubt.

To extend the battle while avoiding Macbeth's onstage death, final thrusts
of the fight have been seemingly continued offstage in projected shadow
play. Thus Williamson, whose Macbeth traced a progress to distintegration
by a step-by-step intensification of madness, found himself at the end poised
dementedly atop a grotesque throne built of thrown-together pieces of furni-
ture. Williamson moved crazily up and down this structure, toward and away
from the giant shadow, dwarfing him, of Macduff. Finally he clambered
down to *Lay on*. The combat, masked upstage by the "throne," was reflected
in silhouette on a black screen. Somewhat similarly, Tearle's killing was
projected in shadows against a rock.

In the Globe, the act of severing Macbeth's head could be imagined offstage. In light-controlled theatres it can be projected in shadow. It has been
made to seem to happen on the stage. In Welles' "Black" staging, Macduff
drove Macbeth up to the battlements and, momentarily out of sight, hacked
down with his sword, and from where he stood threw down the head.

In a more spectacular action that was much applauded, Rogers' Macbeth
seemed to be decapitated before the very eyes of the audience. Rogers, aging,
white-haired, but still a towering martial figure, rushed into his final battle
touched with a madness that gave him superhuman strength. He, too, seemed
to engage in a duel with his whole fateful world as well as with Macduff; he
fought in "the half-crazy exaltation of the born fighter," with "demented,
heroic splendour" (See *Times, Scotsman, Tribune*). The fury of his fighting
against the single enemy attracted Malcolm's men to the scene. What happened then, at the ending of a "very vigorous and dangerous fight with broad-
bladed claymore type swords and daggers," Rogers described for me:

> The staging was flooded by Macduff's victorious followers just at the moment
> when in the hand to hand grappling fight Macduff had brought Macbeth to
> the ground. The thanes and soldiers swirled into a group hiding the fallen
> Macbeth from the audience; but by some of them crouching, the better to see
> the fallen tyrant, Macduff was clearly seen to hack down at where the audi-
> ence had a split second before clearly seen Macbeth's head (a bit of swift roll-

ing in the right direction and great faith in Macduff was called for here on my part), the thanes/soldiers let out a huge yell of triumph and "my head" (which had been secreted in the general movement onto the stage) was raised aloft on the head of a spear.*

However Macbeth dies, on or off stage, the battle must have the quality of the apocalyptic: as if our whole emotional investment in the play to this moment is at stake. We have been living in Macbeth's world all this time; and that world must collapse with him. Its fall should make a great crash, that leaves his conqueror drained, as it will us.

And still we cannot breathe easily. Climactic as the peak moment is, spent as we may be with our share of Macbeth's enduring, and with Macduff's pain and purpose, we are not to be let off yet.

Macbeth's death, on or off stage, will not bring an end to his terrible presence in Scotland. The young prince, now to be king, will enter; the winter king seems dead; the survivors of his tyranny all seem to unite in hailing the successor. Storm sounds may die with war sounds, and the sky may suddenly clear, as with Olivier. Yet the Old Man may still come between the prince and the light.

Since the battle was fought as night came on, as Seyward said, it is over in a darkness, that is lit perhaps by torches, and a moon. A momentary hush, startling after the suddenly truncated noise of combat, may frame the preceding, climactic beat, and provide a border for the next to begin, in full dazzle:

> *Retreat, and Flourish. Enter with Drum*
> *and Colours, Malcolm, Seyward, Ross, Thanes and Soldiers.*

This is rich pageantry: almost everybody is on. In the Globe the actors who played the women may have returned as spear carriers. Malcolm's soldiers may rush in, fresh from battle, may push prisoners ahead of them. English uniforms will be prominent among the victors. Captured Macbeth flags may be among the trophies of war, the scene reversing Macbeth's own great moment of I, iv. Malcolm's speech becomes a prince: he is concerned for the dead, for missing *Friends*. A brushstroke fills in the Spartan character of the great English general: soldiers must die—

> Some must go off: . . .
> So great a day as this is cheaply bought.

Malcolm misses Macduff—a reminder that in one possible ending the final

---

*The realism of a decapitation posed no serious problem for film: for the crucial moment Polanski, for instance, cut to a full sized effigy of a fighting Macbeth, activated from inside by a small person who came up to the effigy's waist; Macduff could be seen actually to cut this "Macbeth's" head off, with a grand-guignol effect.

duel with Macbeth was indeed to continue offstage, leaving the audience, as well as Malcolm, in suspense as to the fate of both warriors. Macduff's absence is not pursued; Malcolm has also asked about Seyward's son: Ross, in reporting the young man's death, revives the image of manhood achieved in fighting:

> He only liv'd but till he was a man, . . .
> But like a man he died.

Seyward's grief is muffled in his soldier's bearing. He absorbs the shock: *Then he is dead?* and, verbally, only troubles to make sure his son was wounded in front. As I have noted, if young Seyward's body remains on stage, his father's bending over him could be very touching; Shakespeare's avoidance of any demonstration of tenderness here seems deliberate. Seyward's ostensible concern is clearly more for his brave son's manliness than for his son; satisfied on that score, he can pun

> Had I as many sons, as I have hairs,
> I would not wish them to a fairer death:
> And so his knell is knoll'd.

If Seyward is bluffly masking grief, he does it well enough for Malcolm, altered (grown?) since his rebuff to Macduff's mourning, to insist, *He's worth more sorrow*. Seyward will not have it so; he manifests a touch of the excessive in his refusal, as a "man," to grieve:

> He's worth no more,
> They say he parted well, and paid his score,
> And so God be with him.

In the theatre, the moment can be ambiguous. While the contrast with Macduff's sorrow is not pointed it may be experienced. Seyward's iron concentration on courage in battle as the measure of a man turns back to the first eulogies of *worthy* Macbeth, the slaughterman. "Manly" and "heroic" as this English general is made, in him Shakespeare seems to be echoing something about the limitations of this kind of manliness.*

It may be a subtle emphasis of this intention that Seyward is chosen to see approaching the fighter whose response to family loss so differs from his ostensible own. *Here comes newer comfort.* The comfort Seyward takes is both in the man welcomed and the gruesome object carried:

> *Enter Macduff; with Macbeth's head.*

How can Macduff *enter* with the severed head if he has only a moment before slain Macbeth on stage, as per that second Folio directive? If anywhere

---

*He is perhaps saying something else, too, by showing Malcolm having successfully invaded Scotland to depose a Scots king—only because he had the help of a tough English general. This would please an English audience—but James?

a nominal scene-break might be justified, it would seem to be after the slaying, to allow for Macbeth's body to be drawn off under cover of Malcolm's
large entrance. But the Folio instructs us in no scene change. I can believe
that at the Globe the duel had moved, near its end, upstage, and the decapitation went on perhaps as far back as the inner above or below; and Macduff
would take the time, while Malcolm and his entourage filled the forestage
and talked, to recover from the fearsome exhaustion of his struggle before
producing Macbeth's head.

In Prague, Macduff barely held himself upright until he could welcome
Malcolm, then collapsed. In Berlin (1968) Macduff staggered on, his grief,
sealed in stone until now, beginning to find outlet; he was almost in tears.
Macduff's sorrow is not assuaged by a killing.

For the severed head to achieve the impact Shakespeare intended, it must
seem Macbeth's indeed. We may suppose that Shakespeare's company
counted on an artist who, as early as *Titus*, could counterfeit heads that conveyed both identity and characterful expression. The Globe's spectators
could judge critically: they knew the real thing in piked heads. In the play's
theatre history, unlike or obviously ersatz images have properly been faulted
for destroying illusion, and were better left unseen. Perhaps partly to avoid
the challenge of meaningful verisimilitude, the head is not always exposed.
In Berlin, for instance, Macduff was seen to drop the bloody object in a white
cloth, which, blood-spattered, he carried on. In another staging, what Macduff brought was a heap of bloody tissue that might as well be a disembowell-
ment, and flung it on the ground. But when the head will bear scrutiny, it
has been made chillingly to face the audience. In Düsseldorf (1966) Macduff
stood at the rear of the stage, under a glaring light, holding up the head in a
fixed Perseus grip for all to confront. But Macduff says

> Behold where *stands*
> Th'usurper's cursed head:

suggesting that it is supported in some way. So it has been held up at the point
of Macduff's sword, though more often "standing" at the top of a spear or
pole. It may even be placed where Macbeth fixed Macdonwald's head, so
long before, *upon our battlements*.

Malcolm has been seen to enter above: in Sweden (1967) he stood looking
down as Macduff raised his spear, with Macbeth's crowned head on it, for
Malcolm to take the crown for his own. (Macduff, in other stagings, has taken
off the crown to hand to Malcolm; and the Thane's experience of holding it
for a moment can convey something of Scotland's future.)

Malcolm and his followers usually enter at ground level, and find themselves looking up to where Macbeth's head "stands." The fastening of the head
on its pole may be carried out before the audience; and here its weight and
solidity are an important part of its reality. I remember still the *frisson* that

went through the Scofield audience as a loaded head, with its jagged neck, was jammed with effort down on the point of a lance. The brittle "thunk" that implied a piercing of brain, tissue and bone was felt viscerally. This last reprise of the recurrent motif of bladed metal penetrating flesh may be one of the most kinesthetically experienced sensations in the play, as Macbeth's head is almost literally painted on a pole.

With Hopkins, three other heads besides Macbeth's were piked aloft, for corollary effect; but the one that counts is the fierce, complex, tragic skull whose face, if the sculptor well those passions read that yet survive, is a book in which men may read the legend of a life. Shakespeare brought Macbeth back in this guise not only for Malcolm's ceremony of triumph, but also as a presence brooding over that triumph, as it broods back over the whole play.

Tyranny has been defeated with Macbeth's death: but as many critics have observed, how pale and diminished are the survivors, in contrast with the size and grandeur of the dead. Malcolm and the surviving thanes speak formal language that has none of the grace, muscle, and temperature of the man they have defeated. This is a greyer world, as Leech notes. To capture the larger image besides which Malcolm seems dwarfed, much is sometimes made of his victorious moment. The Folio tells Macduff to call for voices to join him in his *Hail King of Scotland*. In the theatre the soldiers' cries often follow, thick as Hail—sometimes in echoing threes. The men around Malcolm may kneel, salute with swords, wave their banners, rush to lift Malcolm on a great shield (Kean, Sothern) or on their shoulders. He has even been accorded a coronation ritual that may echo Macbeth's and be reminiscent of Duncan's ceremonial. Sometimes, in stagings emphasizing the triumph of white purity over black evil, the end is ornamented with religious paraphernalia and personnel. But none of this is in the text. Shakespeare is in a hurry to clear the stage; the Folio directs a *flourish* to accompany Macduff's *Hail*, and a final one, but no more; Shakespeare has Malcolm neutralize the highly charged atmosphere with a conventional speech that enunciates relevant recurrent motifs, but formally.

Malcolm mentions *time* thrice, the first almost a promise by the playwright to an emotionally wrung audience that this valedictory will be short:

> We shall not spend a large expense of time,
> Before we reckon with your several loves,
> And make us even with you.

He names his thanes Earls—a rare indication, in the play, of past time. It functions to suggest, at the end of a dead reign, the beginning, spring-growth of a new one, with a new nobility:

> the first that ever Scotland
> In such an honor nam'd:

Then Malcolm speaks of the present, in the continuing growth imagery his father had used:

> What's more to do,
> Which would be newly planted with the time,

To heal the disjunction in the state, to punish the cruel ministers

> Of this dead butcher, and his fiend-like queen;
> Who (as 'tis thought) by self and violent hands,
> Took off her life.

Why fiendlike queen? Why the report of another rumor—*'tis thought*—another of the several allusions to the uncertainty that thickens the ambience of ambiguity in the play: *as they say . . . some say . . . 'tis said . . . 'tis most like . . . I hear it by the way . . . I hear . . . This report . . . we hold rumor from what we fear . . . Foul whisperings are abroad . . . some say . . . others call it . . . make discovery err in report of us . . .?* Malcolm may presumably have learned some suspicion of the Queen's complicity, from someone who knew of her sleepwalking confessionals; but that the suicide can only be rumor seems certain from the absence of any information to Macbeth in V, v that Lady Macbeth laid hands on herself. Does the actor assume that the fox Malcolm once more, to ensure his own position, is involved in the false speaking he claims to abhor? The text guards its enigmas; we cannot *know;* what is important is that the actor—or the identifying reader—from his experience of the whole character design, senses and conveys the impulse behind the words as they are to be spoken.*

Malcolm's final statements are all proper, as, in his third reference to time as future, he promises decorum in all:

> by the grace of grace,
> We will perform in measure, time, and place:

and he invites all to his coronation.

The whole speech is highly proper; and yet we may be uneasy about it, as some critics and stagings have been. In Malcolm's view of the world is, Mack Jr. observes, a shallowness of comprehension. The imaginative energy capable of conceiving trumpeting angels, and infant Pity astride the storm, has been displaced, leaves an emptiness behind. Nothing of Duncan's naiveté

---

*Malcolm speaks as the unquestioned ruler now of Scotland; but in doing so he leaves unfulfilled an expectation raised by the play. What of Fleance? His absence in this scene puzzled Brecht, as it did almost all my *naive* spectators. Banquo's heirs, in the play, were supposed to become the Scots kings, indeed were imaged as such in IV, i. Historians might, in Shakespeare's audience, have known that the beginning of the Stuart succession would have to wait many years; but most of Shakespeare's spectators would not have been so knowing. Was this one of the playwright's final tricks played on an audience, to leave it wondering? Or something he simply did not bother to explicate? Mlle. Martinet reported that in the 1973 Paris staging, after all the characters were set for the play's finale, Fleance walked down the stairs and to the forestage, where he was picked out by a spot. This was an attempt to deal with Brecht's point, but it was not much admired.

survives in Malcolm. He has sufficiently demonstrated his capacity for
shrewdness and practicality and fantasied vice, in conjunction with his
avowed commitment to the ideal. The dialectic within him may be a source
of dramatic tension that Malcolm himself may be understood to feel. If he
has grown toward kingship (as in his response to Seyward on the son's death),
he will have grown also in awareness of the inextricable shadow and sun in
himself, in humanity. Even in the atmosphere of religious triumph of the
Hall-Scofield finale, Malcolm (Richardson) could be felt to manifest a self-
doubt, his assurances of devotion to Grace coating an anxiety about his adequacy to deal with a world tainted with tempting evil. The instruments of
power he held, held dangers for him.

That the political-social world has not been purged of danger by the death
of a man and woman, that in it men will continue the mortal struggle for degree, is emphasized when Malcolm leads the way off, and the new Earls work
out, with some edginess, the hierarchical order of their going. In other ways
the final moment may seem less than triumphant, rather discolored by fatigue
and disillusion. In the Lincoln *Macbeth* observed by Lois Potter, a jackal
Lenox—now clearly Malcolm's tutor and henchman—handed his pragmatic
politician-king a prepared statement to read. Malcolm reeled it off. "Macduff,
who had been exhilarated and exhausted by his victory, gradually realized
what he had let Scotland in for, and stood dazed as the new Fascists marched
away." The Minsk Malcolm, once sure he was king, looked on his associates
with cold calculation. When Macduff, warm in victory, moved with open
arms toward his new monarch for the embrace he had earned, and would have
expected from Duncan, Malcolm rebuffed him with a curt, whipcrack gesture. The young king coolly drew to his side the courtiers he sensed would be
his creatures. "The long awaited morning dawning over Scotland was very
dark—greeted with relief, but very little joy." In the McKellen *Macbeth*,
Macduff's *Hail* to Malcolm was tired and drained, and the thanes limply
echoed it as, dispirited, they sat watching a Malcolm whose last speech,
that attempted to rouse them, became tentative and then frustrated at their
apathy. The lights went down on a circle of drear men, eyeing each other and
their new king without hope.

It is the same world as before: and one symptom, characteristic of its dialectic, that counters Malcolm's imagery of fertility, is the fearful note of steril-
ity that, as I pointed out in my *Lear* study, reverberates in the endings of all
the major tragedies—no mortal woman of rank or importance remains alive
to carry on the race.

Conversely, no sign has been given that the spiritual equivocation resonating in the Sisters has been silenced. These uncanny figures who appear at the
moment of a man's triumph, are never far away in this world. To underline
this, some stagings have deliberately invoked extra-textual returns of the
Three. In Munich (1977) they were clearly already at work to influence the
new king. In versions that overplayed the element of Fate by manifesting their

continuous presence, the Sisters were likely to make themselves known at least once earlier in the scene, laughing or "hailing" Macbeth's shock at the news of Macduff's "unnatural" birth (e.g., Prague, Tree). Similar background cackling has sounded at the end at Malcolm's assumption of power, or at his leaving.

The Sisters have even appeared at the side of Malcolm—three young, beautiful ones in Poland. If they are obviously supernatural, they are presumed to be invisible, but they have also been disguised as members of Malcolm's entourage, and as all others leave the scene, the three may turn and reveal themselves, as Carrick Craig's did. The implied threat to Malcolm was spelled out by Polanski's Donalbain, who, at the end of the film, was seen visiting the place where Macbeth and Banquo had first met the Sisters.

The Three have also focused their relation to the dead Macbeth. After a crash of thunder, the Tyrone Power promptbook ordered, "*Every light* goes out—the cry of witches heard in demoniacal glee—lightning vivid for one moment—we see the witches hovering over the body of Macbeth—in the darkness the curtain descends swiftly." Not hate, but grief, has motivated the Sisters' return to Macbeth, too. Bergman's Three (1948) fell with mournful howling upon Macbeth's corpse; others have crawled on stage to carry off tenderly Macbeth's butchered remains. To these Sisters, he is indeed their wayward son, lost.

These are all directional intrusions that stipulate a fatefulness Shakespeare intended to leave ambiguous. The text since IV, i has alluded to the Sisters' oracles, but has carefully kept them offstage, while Macbeth determined his own final actions. Supernatural influence remains a subdued note in the polyphony of inner and outer strains accompanying mortal behavior in the play. Recognizing this, some stagings have tried subtly only to intimate the continuing existence of the Sisters. Hackett wanted Malcolm to be ushered offstage by a rising wind, in which a faint hint could be heard suggestive of the Sisters' crooning. The *Hails* that greet Malcolm's accession to power themselves inevitably echo the Sisters' first strange *Hails* to Macbeth, and this likeness has been nourished by sounding them in threes, sometimes with haunting undertones of the voice of witchcraft. The effect has been strengthened when Malcolm, at the height of his honors, has seemed to hear a note not of the earth. Macduff may listen too. But none of this needs be explicit: we are not likely to forget the wraiths of mystery and mischief that shadow the world of man.

For all that the end of the play seems to be Malcolm's, his moment is carefully made too brief to diminish the fiery image of the man he overthrew. Our experience of the journey of Macbeth, and of his Lady, through temptation to death, goes on reverberating, while Malcolm is remembered as an incident on the track. The panoply may be all Malcolm's now: his, if any, the drums,

the banners, the crown and scepter, he heading the parade of thanes, all carefully fitted into the order of their going—with only at the last, now ironically
below degree, the head of the dead king carried; but, as Coghill observes, "We
are still thinking of Macbeth and what has become of him in the dark universe
of ambiguities and equivocation, and of how he fought and died." As if to
make sure of this, Shakespeare—who allows his other tragic heroes to lie
down when they die, their rest earned—keeps Macbeth's anguished countenance center stage.

In our experience, if not before our eyes, the play ends with Macbeth; and
before our eyes, too, if—as I think Shakespeare intended—that great, noble,
terrible head, with a mortal history graven on the face, is, aloft on its lance,
the last thing we see, looking down on the little men leaving below. And on us.

Tomorrow, and tomorrow, and tomorrow . . .

Epilogue

We stand back from the experience of *Macbeth*, shaken by the two hours of passion, violence, ambiguity and suffering we have shared.

Then, sometimes, a familiar human impulse, central to the action of the play itself, moves us to try to organize our experience in reasoned Apollonian terms: to look for what the play is *about*. Conventionally, we consider the action in terms of its outcome, to discover a pattern in the completed succession of events. We may locate the pattern in a socio-legal framework: *Macbeth* is about crime and punishment; about the restoration of social order; about the roles of kings and subjects; about violence breeding violence. Or we may locate the pattern in an ethical-theological context: *Macbeth* is about sin; about evil; about damnation; about disorder attempting to overthrow the divine order of nature; about heavenly justice triumphing over human wickedness (or failing to suppress it); about Nature defeating the unnatural; about the hopelessness of the hardened sinner; about moral man in an immoral universe; about immoral man in a moral universe; about moral-immoral man in an amoral universe.)

We may discover propitiations to the god of Irony: what Macbeth strives for excessively destroys him; he and Lady Macbeth are their own worst enemies; their best qualities bring them to ruin; in pursuit of social approval Macbeth isolates himself; he who lives by the sword dies by the sword; what does it profit a man to gain the whole world . . . ?

We may extract a fateful design: forces beyond Macbeth's control lure or drive him to disaster; man proposes, but an infernal—or divine—machine disposes. Or we may discern an absurdist design: what Macbeth does, and dreams of doing, are irrelevant in an impersonal (if not hostile) world.

The theatre, as well as criticism, has sometimes been more comfortable rejecting *Macbeth's* ambiguity in favor of such simplified patterns: hence Garrick's attempts to reduce Macbeth to a cringing recreant, or the twentieth-century adulterations that translated the play into reflections of topical tyranny. *Macbeth* does not reduce to such constrictions: there is too much in it. Like all great tragedies, it asks questions rather than gives answers; it is centrifugal, throwing out ripples of experience that cannot be boundaried.

The moral, theological, and historical formulas for explaining *Macbeth* generally commit Shakespeare to the narrowed axioms of various sober thinkers or religionists of his time. But no other mind then, nor the highest common denominator of them, could match Shakespeare's special artistic vision of the human condition: as it may be, not as it should be, informed primarily with the truth of passion, not of wishful thought. The playwright's vision may allude to, but will not depend on, the conventional religious or philosophical dogma; his lens is much broader. Our confidence in Shakespeare's art relies on a sense that underlying his confrontation with the worst, the most tragic in humanity is a devotion to honest seeing, and to universal, positive values that struggle to survive in a real world of terrible experience. Hate, greed, violence may shake the *Macbeth* universe, and even seem to rule it; but the worst is seen steadily, if with grief; and a faith in counterforces of decency—as in babes, in pity, in loyalty—however vulnerable, persists. Given the breadth of Shakespeare's perspective, with its commitment to truth as well as compassion, any simplifications we find the play to be "about" will serve what we want to see in it.

We may try to go deeper than a pattern, to penetrate to the infrastructure, and discern evidence not of Apollonian statement, but of underlying psychic impulse: so the Freudian, Jungian, and mythological inferences touched on in my text. All great drama resonates with these deep-lying energies. Barthes, guiding on Darwin and Freud, could find "the whole of Racine's theatre" in the tribal experiences suggested in *Totem and Taboo*, that revolve around the desire of the sons for the sisters and mothers controlled by the father, the suffering and mutilation of the sons under the father's savage autocracy, the overthrow of the father, the internecine warfare of the sons, and finally their tabooing of incest as a means of supporting a rational alliance. The implications are provocative, and probably relate to any great artwork—including *Macbeth*—with a family configuration.

But even this kind of X-ray of substructure misses what is unique in a great tragedy's gradual development of muscle, nerve, and tissue. A drama as polyphonic as *Macbeth* cannot be described from the hindsight of what happened. It must be re-experienced in terms of what *happens* from moment to moment; in terms of its *process*. *Macbeth* is about all that goes on in it. In this tragedy, particularly, the end is kept in doubt, as if—and indeed this is the case—that end will be significant as it continues the whole mysterious process of experience we first meet in Act I, scene i. We first meet it there, but unmistakably as part of a world already in flow; as the end becomes an eddy in a tide whose flow we feel about us long after the stage has been emptied.

The impulse to capsule the meaning of the play—to fit it to a recognized pattern, to see the raw safely cooked, the Dionysian domesticated—itself reflects the ordering energy that shapes *Macbeth*. This I think is as close as it is meaningful to come in describing a principle behind the tragedy's persistent play of opposites: the tension between the reckless forces inherent in the human condition and the countering, timeless human effort to tame them. As in all the major tragedies, we see at last in *Macbeth* the rebel impulses momentarily controlled; but any social order restored rests uneasily in a gored state; maldoers may have been eliminated, but the world is not purged, it is a drear place, no childbearing women left alive, only fallible men. And we of the audience must be for both sides of the equation: for those terrible-pitiful scapegoats who act out our forbidden fantasies, as well as for the policing that must make them sorry for their spectacular misconduct.

Is there no "moral"? There is this: as our own impulses, covert and acknowledged, are exercised through the action and characters, particularly Macbeth and Lady Macbeth, and we share the violence, frustration, and despair, we may sense in our tissue the alarm and danger of liberating anti-social energy. This is a morality felt more deeply than the brain can know. We are not always in sympathy with Macbeth and his Lady, we may sometimes spend pity on them while recoiling with terror and even repulsion; but either way our response to them, if we yield to the genius of the artwork, is primarily emotional and spiritual, only secondarily intellectual, judgmental.* We see almost all the action through their agonized eyes, we endure their disasters as they do. We get under their skin; they get under ours. Their crimes are ours; our crimes—perhaps repressed so deeply we do not recognize kinship—are theirs. Afterwards, with cool perspective, we might isolate some threads of the action, and fit the play to such formulas as "crime and punishment" or "sin and retribution"; but surrendered to the special ecstasy of the dramatic moment, we are more likely to experience it from the inside, as we did our own first punished misbehaviors, as "error and suffering," or "act and agony." Only because we care so much is *Macbeth* the *tragedie* we—and the Folio— call it.

We are roused at levels of experience so long-ago absorbed that our responses may be below awareness. Great tragedy can do this to us: its multiple stimuli provoke not only to the easily recognizable reactions:—indignation, terror, awe, pity, anxiety—but also seek out the distant corners of the psyche and stir the dust of experience forgotten or repressed. So *Macbeth* builds on deep substructures that reflect an amazing spectrum of human enduring. Shakespeare draws from the earliest matrix of sensation of the human organism to the most complex socio-metaphysical dilemmas of maturity. None

---

*L. C. Knights puts it this way: The logic is not formal but experiential [demanding] sensation and feeling as modes of understanding. Only when intellect, emotion, and a kind of sensory awareness work together can we enter freely into [the] exploratory and defining process (4).

of these experiences is isolate or static: they overlap, interweave, fuse, in a polyphony that mimics the polyphony of life. Recognizing them in *Macbeth* brings us closer to what the play is "about":

- *the beginning of life: birth, childhood, seeding—the power and harmony of tender growing: but also the opposite, symbolized in bloody interruption of infancy, untimely bringing forth, untimely ending.*

- *the early, and lastingly intimate, experience of the live body—of its head, hair, skin, face, eyes, ears, tongue, brain, hand, finger, thumb, heart, heartbeat, its vital fluid of life—blood. This familiar body, so full of life and fair in appearance, so trusted in function, yet may be helpless to act, is often sensed with dismay and even revulsion, may be stricken by disease—sometimes strange and undiagnosable—may seem in a hurry for death.*

- *the primal anxieties, physical and psychic: experienced inwardly from a hypnotic raptness to the sensation of a brain acrawl and function paralyzed; outwardly the flesh shaking; or cut, bleeding, pierced by sharp metal; or stained or fouled indelibly by some ugly stigma, that may never be cleansed, whatever the effort: or suffocated, confined, chained, unfree; or disjunct, dismembered, no center holding (the psyche and the soma share in the dread and fascination of the fantasy of violent death—a fantasy fed in Shakespeare's time by the butchery in public executions, piked heads displayed.) Behind all, the nameless, unnameable, swarming mysteries that lie below consciousness, the blurred, censored, indefinable Dionysian images that threaten reason, uncontainable phantasms that the mind seeks to contain in words like* hell, hellish.

- *the early experience of, and familiarity with, the natural world: the friendly sun, light, day, gentle birds, tame animals, solid earth, water, fire, sweet air, musical sounds, spring—but also the multiplying villainies of nature, the hostile wind, rain, thunder, lightning, darkness, night (the whole sinister world in the unseeing dark, with its imagined accompaniments of the horrible, the undefined, the murky, murderous), leaflessness, winter, decay, stench, an earth that may quake, redness in tooth and claw, harsh alarums, animal cries and screams, the terrible dreams that nature gives way to in repose.*

- *the primitive need to recognize a self, to construct a center of personality, an identity—resisted by the shock of recognizing thoughts and acts foreign to the constructed identity:* How is it with me? *(In tragedy a recognition—anagnorisis—may be single, climactic, as in* Oedipus Rex*—though Oedipus' recognition there recedes by the time of the* Colonus. Macbeth, *like others of Shakespeare's heroes, experiences a succession of perspectives on the self—and we more keenly share that process because it is the painful process of life.)*

- *the common, life-sustaining rituals: eating, putting on and taking off clothes, entering shelter, going to bed, sleeping, waking, washing clean—all so beneficent, so traumatic when violated.*

• *the nuclear family relationships: child-mother, child-father, child-child, held together by "motherhood," "fatherhood," "friendship" (brotherhood, sisterhood), the breeding of kin—all components of an ideal mutual-support system, but with built-in possibilities for disintegrative (almost selfdestruct) forces. Trust is learned and betrayed. Associated with the parental images, some uncanny figures, gifted with secret, inexplicable powers: uncommon, gigantic men and women, sometimes ancient, sometimes with a sinister beauty, wise, terrible, prophetic, dangerous in beneficence as well as in hostility, felt to be capable of unspeakable acts. Beyond them extended reflections of parental power, the ultimate vision of "good," God—countered by that of "evil," the devil.*

As relationships grow, so does the complexity of approved interpersonal, social behavior, in dialectic with impulse. *Macbeth* develops, and tests, out of some of the primitive notes of individual growth, motifs that refract such "values" of maturity as honor, manhood, worth, hospitality, faith in divinity. Such values, the symbols of the order humankind seeks to impose on Dionysian experience, are resisted by various counterforces in the human condition. As time passes:

• *the central adult relationship, of husband and wife—the intimacy, affection, sexuality, mutual commitment—tenses and strains under the pressure of emotional clamor and outer demands, is tested in the interdependence of the two when they function as a loving pair, in their isolation when not, in their understandings of each other and their failures in understanding and communication. They whom no man may put asunder may, as impulse governs mind, sunder themselves.*

• *sexuality and aggression become conscious forces to be experienced, used—and for social approval, controlled. Even when repressed, they find their way, symbolically and metaphorically, into the language, the objects, and the relationships of men and women. Sometimes they themselves intertwine, as if the erotic and aggressive energies reciprocally rouse each other. Biological pressures, joined to social ones, mould distinctive male and female roles, and so partly distort personality, partly suppress inherent androgyne qualities; sometimes these struggle to surface, sometimes gender roles and social roles clash intolerably. To contain the inner vortex, restraints of conscience and of practical societal discipline will combine to articulate political, commercial and theological "moralities" that command compliance to a group structure; a dialectical resistance may, instead, provoke an attempt to conquer the structure, or overturn it.*

• *a growing need for approval, a reward of golden opinions for achieving great deeds, builds the urge to outdo peers, often close by ("father," "brother"), to be the best, the highest. In the doing, the great daring deeds (in fantasy or reality) may be dreadful ones, proscribed, but native to the human capacity for violence, battles, killing; dreams of grandeur may be sullied, innocence surrendered. "Civilized" values may complicate and magnify the release of violence: killing many in war, for national aggrandizement, is worthy, approved; killing one in peace, for personal aggrandizement, horrible, forbidden.*

● *the straining against ordered relationships outside the family—social, political, personal—involves the necessary interlacing and simultaneous incompatibility of the daring individual and the group. The great man—or the great dreamer—is impelled to outrun the "petty pace" of ordinary mortals; his very greatness, as much as what he does—or fantasies—may make him unbearable to society. He threatens the structure of social degree, even if he saves it. If it is subverted by the savior, it may be saved by subversion.*

● *for action to be taken, decisions must be made: between demanding, often equivocating, alternatives; individual values poise against social, impulse opposes mind. A competitive vision of doing more than may become a man, overreaching, of invulnerability of magic power, is resisted by social and inherent restraints: the fear—and wish—to be the same in act as in desire, the dread of failure, of insecurity, of the detection of wrongs done, and punishment now or later—so stealth, masking, spying are learned.*

● *the maturing self studies disguises to go with its several roles. Ordinary social behavior becomes so much "acting" that the* process *of the stage, as well as its content, imitates life. (The stage repays by providing philosophers—and playwrights—with a grand metaphor: the theatre of the world; and lends to scholarly disciplines a model for studying human "roleplaying.") When among many people, a "public" self is on display, and—except for moments of uncontrolled action or passion—must often find ways not to say what it means, not to express what it feels or thinks; backstage, with a few others, or with only one, the semi-private self discloses more; only in the innermost dressing room will the mirror be scanned in solitude for the core identity. If there is such an identity—an ultimate self, whole, or divided, or splintered; and if there is one, perhaps best not to know it, instead try somehow to separate from it and what it has done, disjoin the inner self from the outer.*

● *time becomes a pressure: both the now, with its hourly contradictions requiring emergency decision and action, hence doublecharging the tensions in personality and performance; and eternity, against which the now may be glimpsed in perspective. The ego, uncertain of its ability to control its destiny, may submit tentatively to influence from without—from wife, friend, custom. It may trust in a deity, discovered or invented; in supernatural intimations and hints of fateful guidance—trust that can be undermined by apprehensions that decision and action are in fact meaningless, that the questing ego may be the victim of an indifferent god, or a cruel, teasing, or idiot power that hides ugly reality in fair show, paltering equivocatingly with human hopes and dreams, until nothing seems sure, and madness threatens.*

● *as the inevitability of death is confronted, one adult impulse—that may become a need—is for immortality: by achievement now, through generations of children later.*

● *such need and impulse, frustrated, may evoke a countering motivation to try to make people, society, the whole universe, sorry. In fantasy or act, suicide may be considered; or violence be acted out to a manic degree; if urgent desire is enough unsatisfied, a paranoid passion may even welcome, in revenge, universal chaos. Under this strain, the mind and body may break down; may resort to drink and drugs. The brain curdles, the flesh droops, and the normal restorations—sleep, food, companionship—do not serve.*

● *the yearning comes to express the search for meaning, for making sense of a bewildering universe. The philosopher in the self struggles to manage with thought the assaults of life: Who am I? Why have I done what I have done? Why does this agony happen to me? What forces move me? And my world? Do all men have their witches? What do I feel? How will I end? What is real, what illusion? The poet seeks for words for his pain, in images drawn from the totality of human experience, from nature and society: thus life-time seen as a flow of waters, status as a function of costume, human actions as stageplaying. Ironically, the most beautiful expression may convey the most of anguish and despair.*

● *the flesh blooms, and withers; the spirit soars, and sinks. Death comes, always. All ways.*

These are some of the wordable things that *Macbeth* is "about." They are enough to suggest how extensively the play evokes primary human experience. Yet in themselves they have power for drama only as they are experienced through the mighty characters in action speaking *Macbeth's* timeless language—particularly Macbeth and Lady Macbeth. Consider the range of figures with whom the two have been compared. Lady Macbeth has been likened to such diverse images of womankind as Medea, Clytemnestra, Dalilah, Eve, Cleopatra, the Ur-Mother. She shares contradictory elements of their fierceness, ambition, passion, seductive misguidance, and a capacity for the care for child and mate, and for tender, passionate, marital love.

In Macbeth a multitude of timeless images of great and terrible and vulnerable male figures have been seen: among them Saul, Ahab, Cain, Phaeton, Adam, Judas, Herod, Faust, Richard III, Richard II (and Richard II or Hamlet in combination with Henry V), Aaron, Claudius, Satan, Hyperion, Quixote. Macbeth relates himself to Tarquin and Antony. These linkings suggest the magnificence and maldoing, the daring and degradation, the imagination and delusion, the introspection and violent overt action, the compassion and ruthlessness that help stretch the Macbeth design to the boundaries of dramatic characterization.

Macbeth may have some qualities of all these figures he is compared to, but he is not *like* any one of them: he is *another one* of them, a unique design. The same is true of his Lady. Both resonate with archetypal undertones, but these are absorbed by a marvelous compression, in unique characterizations, of the essential human experience noted above. In the Macbeth designs are packed all those echoes of life from childhood to the grave, all the interpersonal, sexual, social and political substructures, as well as the mythic shadows they throw. Thus the image of the Mother figure, as discussed in I, v, looms behind Lady Macbeth, but it fades into a design that ends with the simplest and most immediate of human activities—grieving, handwashing, going to bed.

Macbeth's characterization almost classically exemplifies the Freudian son-man-father images. He refracts, as well, a double role as the mystic challenger of spring (so amply documented by the anthropologists and scholars like Simrock and E. K. Chambers) who overturns the winter king—and is then himself, in the latter role, made by Shakespeare to succumb. In this design, also, are touches of the Lord of Misrule, the "named" monarch of a topsy-turvy world who must pass quickly from the scene. Macbeth adumbrates too the fallen man, misled by a woman, losing his glimpse of paradise; and the romantic overreacher foiled by the practical man. But however Macbeth reflects the archetypal, he is most recognizable—if larger than life—as "man," a focus for the play's tremendous expanse of the "natural"—and the "unnatural" and supernatural—in the human condition. In the mightiest of the many roles he plays—including that of playing roles—he verbalizes his experience in the most elementary of terms, in monosyllables that any man might choose but that no "man" has ever been able to put together in so moving and meaningful a way.

The lamentable humanity of the two tremendous figures balances against their audacious violation of social and moral codes. We have seen that Shakespeare has burdened them—especially Macbeth—with the heaviest of primal crimes: the killing of a father figure, a brother figure, a mother figure, child figures. So terrible are these crimes that Shakespeare avoids showing them, until later in the play, with the killing of Banquo and the slaughter in Macduff's castle: even so, Macbeth only continues the atmosphere of Dionysian unrest established at the outset with the news of revolution and treachery in the state, the offstage violence, and the ambiguous force of the Sisters, all cues to an archaic disorder in the *Macbeth* universe. The play skirts the absolute limits of acceptable aesthetic terror, just short of forcing audience disinvolvement. Only the playwright's firm command of the language and the character keeps disbelief suspended through the horror that increases to the end.

For committing the primal crimes that most human beings allow themselves only in fantasy, if then, Macbeth and Lady Macbeth must be made terribly sorry. They must die: Lady Macbeth, from an inward agony that perhaps drives her to suicide; Macbeth, after recognizing how equivocation has paltered with him, finally suffering physically, in his decapitation, the kind of disjunction haunting him through the play. The deaths fittingly conclude the tragedy because they manifest the crowning dialectic between man's vision of order and the reality that resists it. To the thrust of active human life, death is the ultimate anti-order; to nature, death is order itself.

I return now to a theme in my Prologue. Shakespeare indeed composed his polyphonic play, and its major character-polyphonies—Macbeth and Lady Macbeth—from nearly the whole diapason of human experience. So great an artwork demands a corresponding greatness in the instrument of communication. This is normally the actor. He has (as I suggest elsewhere), like the king, two bodies: the second is the physical one that must have the skill and strength to endure the technical demands of the role; this is the Macbeth body that must, in intervals offstage, change clothes, age, be marked with blood: must, onstage, speak, mask, hallucinate, fight, sometimes die. A first body *becomes*, in spirit, Macbeth: experiences in the very cells of its flesh all that Macbeth experiences, resonates to his polyphony from the low-est of his notes, in the base, to his highest. The second—mortal—body must convey the keyboard-wide range of tones experienced by the first, immortal part, the living Macbeth. Unless, like a great instrument, the actor can vi-brate to the least grace note of the artwork he is put to, and can convey it all, the whole of the tragedy will not be transmitted. Competence can project the shell of Macbeth, but only an artistic commitment comparable to Shake-speare's, the heart.

Macbeth was written to be seen; but reading the play has its own special satisfactions. The reader, like the actor, has two bodies. If his second, phys-ical body, like the actor's, wills to inhabit the immortal part of the role, the eternal Macbeth, he lavishes on himself a unique double experience: both the cruel transport of the actor who lives the triumph and pain of the char-acter, and the dazzle of the spectator exposed to the play's pyrotechnics. The reader's second body may sit comfortably in an armchair; but the first will enter more deeply into Shakespeare's art if the mortal part assists: if it at least senses an imagined knife in the restless palm, the felt movement of fisted blade striking past bone, the touch of blood sticking on the fingers, the use-lessness of water to cleanse, the thickness of the dark closing in, the almost unbearable agonies of hope, doubt, fear, despair. Better still if the second body actually handles, in movement, the stage properties; best if, too, the words are spoken aloud as they were written to be, their tasted, heard tex-ture and music making even more immediate the recreative moment.

For experiencing the whole play, the reader has one enormous advantage over the actor. He who plays the king in his study may play all the other roles, too, particularly Lady Macbeth—and so may know intimately, as Shake-speare's actors of women's parts did, the summoning of the androgyne quali-ties woven into the *Macbeth* characterizations: what it is to call murdering ministers to the breast where a babe has suckled, and to sense there the heavy milk offered in exchange for gall; what it is to pretend fair female courtesy to a king marked for killing, how to agonize over a seeming-mad husband with-out letting guests see beyond a hostess' hospitality, the mystery of rising unconsciously from bed in sleep, putting on a gown, and haunting castle

corridors with stained hands and conscience. She who plays the queen in
her quiet room may also enter imaginatively into the man's world: to sense
the heft of a murderous sword, the weight of armor, the murderous stroke,
the heavier burden for an introspective man of making a decision that will
affect a lifetime, and lifetimes to come; the excitements and horrors of a
heated imagination, the experiences of hallucinations and of the uncanny.
And these are only the two major roles: we come even closer to Shakespeare's
art if we resonate also to such lesser polyphonies as the bleeding captain,
the drunken porter, the clever prince, the revengeful father.

   If, to the greatness of the play, we bring whatever greatness is in us; if—
actor or reader—we can exercise to their limits our emotional, spiritual,
intellectual, and physical sensitivities to the language, character, and action,
and to the wide experience of humanity they reflect, we begin to be worthy
of *Macbeth*.

If more thou dost perceive, let me know more . . .

Readers of this book will be aware of how much it has been helped by personal reports of performances of the play. I will be grateful for other such reports about *Othello*, *Lear* and *Macbeth*, but especially now about *Hamlet*, my next study.

Appendix

Every Shakespearean is entitled to an imaginative speculation now and then, as long as he labels it speculation. This appendix speculates on an *extra-textual* possibility in the staging of *Macbeth*. Anti-speculationists are warned.

I have found no instance of such a staging. I would be interested in hearing of any.

LADY MACBETH'S INDISPENSABLE CHILD

Of course Lady Macbeth has at least one child: she reminds her husband that she has "given suck," and knows "How tender 'tis to love the babe that milks me." History may insist that the child was not sired by Macbeth; but Shakespeare carefully censored Lady Macbeth's earlier marriage,* and no spectator—except the few burdened with excessive learning—could possibly, in the playwright's time or subsequently, have suspected it. Shakespeare begins with a loving pair, and tells us unequivocally—in a play full of equivocation—that they have had a child.

I suggest that a sense of this Macbeth-child's existence in crucial scenes might intensify our experience of Macbeth's inner and outer struggles.

That a babe is *Macbeth*'s most powerful symbol has been suggested by L. C. Knights and Cleanth Brooks. Let us dare further. A highly-charged child-image, persistently challenging a father-image of like force, drives this tragedy on. *Five* fathers and sons populate *Macbeth*. Two fathers—Duncan and Banquo—are murdered; two sons—young Macduff and young Siward—are killed; Macbeth, who causes all these deaths, is killed by one of the surviving fathers, Macduff. Macbeth is a wheeling pivot in this depth-upon-depth exploration of man's archetypal impulses to cherish and destroy begetter

---

*Bradley's note: "If Shakespeare had followed history in making Macbeth marry a widow (as some writers gravely assume) he would probably have told us so."

and begotten: not only does he first defend and then kill a father figure—
Duncan—and befriend and then make war on rival sibling-surrogates—
Banquo and Macduff—and their children; he becomes in turn a father figure
who must be assaulted by children, the *unrough youths* led by the boy Malcolm.
But even further, and central to his action: all of Macbeth's violence is in the
service of a son of his own.

After Duncan's death, Macbeth sits securely on the throne. Crowned at
Scone, supported by the sworn fealty of all the thanes but one, this first
soldier of the kingdom has become its first lord and accepted ruler. His bravery has been matched, as far as men know, by his large share of humankindness; no external circumstance need prevent him from ruling easefully and
well for many years, as he did in history.

Except for one thing.

The witches, who clearly knew the future, had predicted that Banquo's
issue, not his own, would reign in Scotland; and a fierce impulse drives Macbeth on to the murder of Banquo and Fleance—and to the breaking point of
Macbeth's own career—so that the Macbeth-child Shakespeare invented
can succeed to the throne. If Macbeth were childless, the succession of Fleance
would be no great matter, it could come after Macbeth had peacefully paid

> his breath
> To time, and mortal custom. (IV, I, 118–119)

But Shakespeare does stipulate a child-Macbeth with a father driven more by
ambition for the son's royalty than for his own.* This pattern in his design,
as we shall see by following its track, might be enriched by a sense of his
living son.

The child's felt presence might deeply color the experience of the first
scene in Macbeth's castle, when Lady Macbeth reads the letter. She has perhaps just now given suck to the babe (that she has milk, to trade for gall, may
reflect a recent accouchement) and put it in a cradle that is there when Macbeth comes. What emerges, for a moment that will have curious echoes later
in Lady Macduff's touching domesticity, is the softer woman whom even
Sarah Siddons sensed in Lady Macbeth's nature: the woman to whom Lady
Macbeth may return in the sleepwalking scene. Macbeth's letter will change
her. The cradle's rocking stops; her terrible prayer to be unsexed, to give
up her mother's milk for the juice of anger, shocks the more because voiced
in the presence of the babe. And now may be sensed the first sounds of the
child, sounds that can orchestrate with the play's scattered animal cries of
cat, toad, owl, cricket, of the child-apparitions in the witches' cave, the ravaged child in Macduff's castle.

---

*Macbeth's urging to his Lady, *Bring forth men-children only*, seems to indicate that this is
what she has done so far, as noted earlier. See p. 282.

Macbeth's visual care—when he enters in I, v—for his son* (now, in his mind, a king-to-be) will deepen the implications of the dialogue with Lady Macbeth. Macbeth, as father, will speak circuitously about the killing of a father-figure, while his own "Prince of Cumberland" lies before him. The babe's existence now, as later symbolically, will be a tug to his conscience; Macbeth may well be gazing into the cradle when, refusing the commitment to murder, he says

We will speak further.

The child as an image of compassion will force itself into Macbeth's consciousness in his next soliloquy (I, vii); the child's felt presence can put an edge on all Macbeth says, evoking the innocence he knows he risks forever losing. For his child, as much as for himself, Macbeth is designed to embrace a *Vatermord*. Now the child-image both pushes him and pulls him back; pulls him back more, fills his mind with visions of mercy: *pity, like a naked new-born babe . . . heaven's cherubin. . . .* Under this influence, he would dare no more than what he can feel becomes a man. Then the wife-mother comes, and turns Macbeth's mind with different images of maleness, of bloody promises to be kept, murderous plans executed. Macbeth himself is instructed almost like a child by an angry mother. To kill is what it is to be a man. She says,

I have given suck,

and there beside her is the suckled babe; the power—and the horror—of her willingness to crush a living child to keep a murderer's oath is intensified by the child's presence. Intensified, too, is the shaming of the man before his manchild—

What beast was't . . . ?

Lady Macbeth's persuasion—her scorn, love, hurt, pride—transforms the image Macbeth had clung to of a man and manchild; now he will be the warrior first. Warriors kill without conscience, they are praised for it.

Every allusion from now on to innocence, babes, dynasty might be enlarged by the proximity of the Macbeth child. Fleance, alone with his father in the night-blackened courtyard, becomes more than an abstract threat; he, alive, rivals the seen babe. Actors of Macbeth have sometimes, in II, i, offered significant gestures to Fleance—have patted his head kindly, for instance, or would have if Fleance had not drawn back or been sheltered by Banquo. This

*Kemble, defending Macbeth against Whately's charge that Macbeth killed Banquo out of personal fear, not to secure the crown for his own issue, argued: "'Thou shalt get kings, though thou be none'—this is the worm that gnaws his heart; this is the 'hag that rides his dreams'; this is the fiend that binds his soul on the rack of restless extasy; and this is the only fear that makes his firm nerves tremble, and urges him on to the penetration of crimes abhorrent to his nature. . . . Banquo and Fleance . . . threaten to reduce him and his lineage from the splendours of monarchy to the obscurity of vassalage."

can represent a genuine symptom of Macbeth's human kindness, though shadowed by an hostility to his son's rival. The tension between the two, man and boy, begins really to sting when Macbeth's mind is felt moving between Banquo's Prince of Cumberland and his own, so recently left.

Even more, after Duncan's death, must Macbeth, suddenly so powerful, confront the uncertain fate that awaits any child of his. If Macbeth's son will not be king, he may not be allowed to live at all. There will be echoes here of Malcolm's doubtful fate in the questionable future of the young Macbeth; and King Macbeth, fencing verbally with Banquo in III, i, must find his eyes coming back to Fleance, whose life seems to threaten the very existence as well as the succession of his child.

Motifs of *Brudermord* and *Kindermord* mingle in the design.

> Goes Fleance with you?

Macbeth asks, as he watches his friend and the friend's boy who would supplant his own son, unless killed first. When Macbeth is alone, he speaks the resolve that only the imminent sense of his son-prince's fate can drive him to. He fears, and envies, Banquo; but this in itself is not made motive enough for murder. Macbeth's restless mind is designed to search for motives to murder; but he keeps coming back to this central one. What he cannot bear is the consequence of the Sisters' prophecy that Banquo would be father to a line of kings:

> Upon my head they plac'd a fruitless crown,
> And put a barren scepter in my gripe,
> Thence to be wrencht with an unlineal hand,
> No son of mine succeeding: if't be so,
> For Banquo's issue have I fil'd my mind,
> For them the gracious Duncan have I murther'd,
> Put rancours in the vessel of my peace
> Only for them, and mine eternal jewel
> Give to the Common Enemy of man,
> To make them kings, the seeds of Banquo kings.
> Rather than so, come fate unto the list,
> And champion me to th'utterance.

Typically an action as well as a soliloquy, the speech moves Macbeth from idea to resolution. From initial apprehension of insecurity there comes to him a realization of his underlying impulse: he must kill to ensure his hope of dynasty. One critical reading has found, in the line *a barren scepter in my gripe* an implication that Macbeth is confessing impotence. But again, Shakespeare, for his own purpose, improved history by making Lady Macbeth's offspring Macbeth's. The crown is barren, not Macbeth. His talk of dynasty would be absurd, as Empson observes, if the Macbeths had no issue of their begetting. To Brooks, it is this hope of Macbeth's for a line of kings that gives him tragic stature.

The *son of mine* Macbeth mentions may be present to his eye, as well as his mind; he has asked to be alone; and perhaps, looking into an inner chamber, he may again gaze on the cradled child whose life demands Fleance's death. *To be thus is nothing* if there is no safety, if the crown is fruitless, if the manchild cannot succeed the man.

Macbeth would leave the child to go to speak to the murderers; in the next scene the distraught Lady Macbeth, if again at the cradle, can take no joy in her babe—nor the babe, any more, in the mother's milk. Lady Macbeth must ask for Macbeth to come to her, so she may comfort and counsel his distraught mind; instead his frenetic anxiety mounts as the burning mineral in his brain, the image of Banquo, takes fire. *You must leave this*, she urges, sensing his thrust, and the scene climaxes:

> O, full of scorpions is my mind, dear wife:
> Thou know'st that Banquo and his Fleance lives.

. . . *and his Fleance*. It is another glance verbally, if not visually, at his own son.

Up to this moment, there has been no whisper of a threat to Macbeth's kingship. Banquo alone suspected Macbeth's means to the throne, but Banquo had easily accepted his role as counsellor, had reminded Macbeth meaningfully that he was to Macbeth

> with a most indissoluble tie
> For ever knit.

He had sustained this role for some time, apparently; Macbeth desires his good advice

> Which *still* hath been both grave and prosperous.

All seems well in the kingdom; only Macduff, among the thanes, is noticed as having avoided Macbeth's coronation. Then comes the attempt to assure the dynasty through the killing of Banquo and Fleance; this evokes the deterioration in Macbeth's outward world that will parallel his inward break.

That Fleance's death, and the assured succession of his own son, has dominated Macbeth's design comes sharply clear when the murderer reports *Fleance is scap'd*. Macbeth replies:

> Then comes my fit again:
> I had else been perfect;
> Whole as the marble, founded as the rock,
> As broad, and general, as the casing air:
> But now, I am cabin'd, cribb'd, confin'd, bound in
> To saucy doubts, and fears.

Until the discovery that Fleance survives, that the succession is in danger, there is no evidence of Macbeth's tyranny. That does not surface until III, vi. The authenticity of the intervening Hecate scene, III, v, has often been questioned; but, as observed in my text, the episode can be seen structurally as providing a sense of a long, evil duration after Macbeth's banquet. The country's discontent has only been provoked after Macbeth's despairing recognition that his royal line may end with him. Until then, he was only *young indeed*—(still glimpsing innocence?).

Macbeth's overt violence finally erupts only after he visits the Sisters for an ultimate answer to his obsession with dynasty. He is comforted by child images, but they leave him unsatisfied. Warnings and assurances about his own security exhilarate but do not content him. He might now tell pale-hearted fear it lies, and sleep in spite of thunder: he has been guaranteed the safety he yearned for; but another impulse continues to control the design:

> Yet my heart
> Throbs to know one thing: . . .
> shall Banquo's issue ever
> Reign in this kingdom?

He *will* be satisfied, or will curse the Sisters forever; when they finally confirm his fear, when he has learned by worst means the very worst, he does curse forever the hour of their revelation. Nothing is left for hope. Herod-like, to crown his thoughts, he carries on his war against children—other men's children.

Now all he has to live for is death. His Lady is misting from him, and will soon be gone altogether. So from now the tone changes; there is disillusion and despair, and the elemental struggle of the splendid warrior trained to live until killed. The young men come against him; the children fight back. Behind their green boughs they advance on the bare, ruined choirs hung with yellow leaf.

For Lady Macbeth, in her sleepwalk, the manchild's cradle may be a cue for her visual as well as verbal imagery; the V, i scene can be made to recall her invocations in I, v, and her relationship to her babe may be part of the dark reverberations. For Macbeth, enduring a time grown meaningless, the unmothered, futureless manchild will exist as one of the sounds of hopeless life in the castle, among the cries of women, dying soldiers and the voices of battle. A little cry, a final little cry, may herald Macbeth's death knell.

Notes

These notes refer to (1) the books and articles; (2) the promptbooks; and (3) the periodicals that contribute to the chapters in the text. The works of cited authors may be found in the main bibliography. For the identity of the promptbook numbers, see Shattuck in the main bibliography. The periodicals are part of the individual lists for each actor or production in the theatre bibliography following. This consists of three parts:

Part I.   Alphabetical lists of significant actors and actresses from English-speaking countries, and distinguished visiting actors from other countries.

Part II.   Chronological lists of stagings of *Macbeth* in non-English-speaking countries.

Part III. Stagings of *Macbeth* associated with particular directors or productions, listed alphabetically.

This organization was developed to keep the mass of data and comment to manageable proportions, provide documentation to scholars, and supply theatre historians with useful information on *Macbeth's* stage career. (I include, for the historian, citations to meaningful periodical reports even though they may not specifically refer to stagings related to the major actors or productions described in the text.)

For the chapters dealing with Macbeth and Lady Macbeth, I list only the major books and articles consulted. The syntheses of the stage characterizations are amalgamated from too many sources—periodicals, memoirs, interviews, etc.—for effective identification of the parts. The significant contributions to these character syntheses are identified elsewhere in the text and notes.

Act I, Scene i

BOOKS, ARTICLES AND PERSONAL
REPORTS

Becks, S106*
Bradley, "Macbeth"
Briggs, 23
Chambers, E. K., edition
Coghill, (4) 223ff.
Cohn, 31
Coleridge, Notes on Lecture II
Craig, G., (1) 274; (6)

Cunningham, edition
Curry, 59
Davies, (1) 118ff.
Doran, M., (2) 426
Ewen, (1)
Falk, see Germany, Reuss prod., 1927–28
Farnham, (3) 100
Gifford, Sig. *Hiv*
Granville-Barker, (2)
Hall, see Rosenberg (2)
Hawkins, (1) 280 (Kean)

*Hereafter promptbooks are listed by the Shattuck numbers. See end of each section.

Jonson, *Works*, Vol. 7, 282ff.
Jacobsohn, (2) 120ff. (Reinhardt)
Jeffreys, 42
Johnson, Dr., edition
Jorgensen, (2)
Kittredge, edition
Knights, L. C., (1) 6, 18f.
Lazarus, (Salvini)
Loeb, see Falk above
Lucas, 62ff.
Maeterlinck, M., 696
Masefield, 143ff.
Muir, edition
Neumann, 324ff.
Nicoll, 116–20
Oulton, 135ff. (Kemble)
Pack, 538
Paul, *passim*
Pickering, 3ff.
Reed, 165
Schoenbaum, *op. cit.*
Schumacher, 114–15, 130, 166 (see Germany)
Shumaker, 72f, 90
Stamm, 54ff.
Stirling, (2) 152
Thomas, 562
Tieck, (1) vol. 3, 40ff.
Trevor-Roper, *passim*
Towse, 301 (Irving)
Walker, 106–137
West, R., 18ff.
West, W., part II, section 24
Wilson, H., 72
Unidentified sources

PROMPTBOOKS

Shattuck: 7, 8, 13, 25, 27, 29, 35, 44, 47, 48,
  59, 63, 70, 77, 89, 94, 106, 108, 109, 112,
  117, 118, 123, 133, 137, 146
Hampden
Welles, filmscript

  Note: Promptbooks consulted for each scene are referred to in these notes, as indicated, by the Shattuck number where available. The full list is in the bibliography. The following promptbooks will be frequently cited by the name of the artist associated with it, and will not be repeated in the notes: Booth, Craig, Hackett, Piscator, Reinhardt, Savits.

PERIODICALS

Athenaeum, July 11, 1857 (Ristori); Oct. 2, 1875
  (Irving)

Berliner Borsen Zeitung, Nov. 12, 1922 (Jessner
  prod., Germany)
Birmingham Gazette, April 19, 1933 (Komisar-
  jevsky)
Birmingham Mail, June 8, 1955 (Olivier)
Birmingham Post, April 19, 1933 (Komisarjevsky)
Birmingham Weekly Post, June 10, 1955 (Olivier/
  Leigh)
Boston Evening Transcript, Feb. 21, 1921 (Barry-
  more); Sept. 17, 1935 (Merivale)
Boston Traveler, Oct. 28, 1941 (Evans/Anderson)
Bristol, Sept. 6, 1955 (Olivier/Leigh)
Combat, July 23, 1954 (Vilar, France)
Daily Chronicle, Aug. 25, 1909 (Maeterlinck);
  Feb. 7, 1928 (Maturin)
Daily Express, Sept. 4, 1957 (Littlewood)
Daily Herald, Sept. 4, 1957 (Littlewood)
Daily Mail, June 8, 1955 (Olivier)
Daily News, Nov. 4, 1864 (Faucit/Phelps);
  Feb. 7, 1928 (Maturin/Merrall)
Daily Telegraph, Dec. 31, 1888 (Irving/Terry);
  Sept. 6, 1911 (Tree)
Echo, Sept. 27, 1875 (Irving)
Edinburgh Evening News, Aug. 24, 1954 (Rogers/
  Todd)
English Illustrated Magazine, Dec., 1888 (Irving)
Etudes Anglaises, July–Dec., 1954 (Vilar, France)
Evening Post, Dec. 31, 1888 (Irving)
Evening Standard, Sept. 27, 1875 (Irving); July
  5, 1884 (Marais/Bernhardt); Sept. 19, 1896
  (Forbes-Robertson); June 8, 1955 (Olivier)
Financial Times, Jan. 16, 1975 (Dunlop prod.)
Guardian, Feb. 18, 1971
Göteborgs-Tidning, March 13, 1948 (Bergman,
  Sweden)
Illustrated London News, Jan. 13, 1968 (Scofield)
Jewish Chronicle, Nov. 1, 1974 (Dunlop prod.)
Literary Gazette, Feb. 19, 1846 (C. Kean)
Mid Sussex Times, Oct. 10, 1974
Monthly Mirror, N. S., vol. 5, 1809
Morning Advertiser, n.d. (Redgrave); May 15,
  1955 (Olivier)
Morning Chronicle, Feb. 16, 1853 (C. Kean)
Morning Post, Dec. 31, 1888 (Irving/Terry);
  April 19, 1933 (Komisarjevsky)
Net Nieuws van de Dag, Sept. 7, 1909 (Nether-
  lands)
New Statesman, Jan. 12, 1968 (Scofield); Nov.
  8, 1974 (Williamson)
New York Daily News, July 16, 1973 (Kahn)
New York Evening Post, Oct. 30, 1895 (Irving)
New York Herald, Feb. 18, 1921 (Barrymore)
New York Herald Tribune, June 2, 1962; June 20,
  1962 (Plummer)
New York Mail, Feb. 18, 1921 (Barrymore)
New York Sun, Feb. 8, 1916 (Hackett/Allen);
  Feb. 18, 1921 (Barrymore)

New York Times, March 8, 1874 (Janauscheck); Oct. 30, 1895 (Irving/Terry); Feb. 18, 1921 (Barrymore); June 20, 1962 (Plummer); July 15, 1973 (Kahn prod.)

New York Telegram, March, 1924 (Hackett)

New Yorker, April 10, 1948 (Redgrave/Robson)

North Devon Journal, April 1, 1971

Notes and Queries, July 13, 1889 (C. Kean)

Nottingham Evening Post, Nov. 4, 1967 (Scofield, Hall prod.)

Les Nouvelles Littéraires, Jan. 27, 1955 (Vilar, France)

Observer, Dec. 30, 1888 (Irving); Nov. 3, 1974 (Williamson)

Philadelphia Evening Bulletin, Nov. 27, 1941 (Evans)

Plays and Players, August, 1955 (Olivier)

Queen, Jan. 5, 1889 (Irving)

Redditch Indicator, Nov. 1, 1974 (Williamson)

Saint James Chronicle, October, 1773 (Garrick)

Scotsman, Aug. 23, 1965

Scottish Daily Press, Aug. 25, 1965

Shakespeare Survey, 1949 (Redgrave/Robson); 1956 (Vilar, France)

Source and Satirist, December, 1814 (Kean)

Spectator, Feb. 11, 1928 (Maturin/Merrall); Dec. 29, 1961

Stage, Jan. 4, 1889 (Irving); Sept. 7, 1911 (Tree); June 9, 1955 (Olivier); Oct. 10, 1974, Nov. 4, 1974 (Williamson, Nunn prod.)

Stratford-Upon-Avon Herald, April 22, 1927 (Green)

Sunday Mercury, June 12, 1955 (Olivier/Leigh)

Sunday Telegraph, Aug. 20, 1967 (Scofield)

Sunday Times, Dec. 31, 1888 (Irving); June 12, 1955 (Olivier/Leigh); Jan. 7, 1968 (Scofield)

Teatralny Almanakh, 1947 (Juriev, Russia)

Theatre Arts, February, 1925; February 1942 (Gielgud, Komisarjevsky, Tree)

Theatre Quarterly, vol. 1, no. 3, 1971 (Garrick, Guthrie, Kean, Komisarjevsky, Tree)

Theatrical Inquisitor, November 14, 1814 (Kean)

Times, Oct. 2, 1875 (Irving); April 19, 1933 (Komisarjevsky); June 8, 1955 (Olivier); Dec. 19, 1958 (Hordern); July 24, 1967 (Scofield)

Toronto Star, June 10, 1971 (Hogg)

Vanity Fair, Sept. 13, 1911 (Tree)

Weekly Dispatch, Jan. 6, 1889

Windsor Slough and Eton Express, Aug. 5, 1966 (Clements)

Act I, Scene ii

BOOKS, ARTICLES AND PERSONAL REPORTS

Battenhouse, 71
Coghill, (1) 19; (3)
Elwin, edition
Flatter, (3) 99
Halio, edition
Kantorowicz, 259
Knights, (1) 19f.
Kolbe, 2ff.
Libby, *passim*
Loeb, *op. cit.*
Morris, C., (1) 104
Nosworthy, (1) 126–27
Potter, personal discussion
Rabb, 40f.
Traversi, 152
Walker, 31
Wilson, J. D., edition, Introduction
Unidentified sources

PROMPTBOOKS

Shattuck: 8, 15, 16, 35, 44, 47, 48, 54, 63, 112, 118, 123, 137, 144, 147

PERIODICALS

Birmingham Mail, April 11, 1949 (Tearle)

Boston Evening Transcript, Oct. 1, 1928 (Craig); Sept. 17, 1935 (Merivale)

Daily Express, Nov. 10, 1972 (Hopkins)

Daily News, Feb. 7, 1928 (Maturin); May 5, 1949 (Tearle)

Daily Telegraph, Dec. 31, 1888 (Irving)

Divadelní noviny (Czechoslovakia, 1963)

Düsseldorfer Nachrichten, June 4, 1960 (Germany)

Financial Times, March 6, 1975 (Williamson)

Gentleman's Magazine, 1889 (C. Kean)

Göteborgs-Tidning, March 13, 1948 (Bergman, Sweden)

Göteborgs Handels och Sjofarts Tidning, March 18, 1967 (Lundh, Sweden)

Irish Times, Nov. 16, 1973

New Statesman, April 23, 1949 (Tearle); Aug. 12, 1966 (Clements); March 14, 1975 (Williamson)

New York Times, Feb. 28, 1971

Notes and Queries, July 13, 1889 (C. Kean)

Plays and Players, January, 1973 (Hopkins)

Stage, April 28, 1927; April 27, 1934 (Komisarjevsky)

Sunday Times, Nov. 6, 1864 (Faucit); April 8,
    1934 (Laughton/Robson); Oct. 23, 1966
    (Guinness)
Theatre, Feb. 1, 1889 (Irving)

Times, Sept. 10, 1954 (Rogers); Dec. 19, 1958
    (Hordern); Nov. 11, 1972 (Hopkins/Rigg)
Universal Review, Jan. 15, 1899 (Irving)
Weekly Scotsman, April 23, 1849

Act I, Scene iii (parts 1 and 2)

BOOKS, ARTICLES AND PERSONAL REPORTS

Agate, (1) 227ff. (Laughton, Olivier, Gielgud)
Alger, 743 (Forrest)
Bab, 252ff. (Matkowsky)
Coleman, (1) 237
Craig, G., (6)
David, op. cit.
Downer, (1) 316 ff. (Macready)
Evans, edition
Farjeon, 132 (Hackett)
Garrick, (3) 133ff.
Gentleman, edition
Got, letter (Poland)
Gould, 120 (J. B. Booth)
Grossman, 98 (Edwin Booth)
Grube, 82 (Meiningen)
Harwood, letter (Olivier, Wolfit)
Hodek, letter (Czechoslovakia)
Knights, (1) 20ff.
Lawrence, (4)
Marshall, 32 (Aldridge)
Marston, J. W., 72
Masefield, 152
Milward, letter (Kumo prod.)
Murdoch, 326 (Forrest)
Oyama, 34
Partridge, 103
Phelps, 100 (Phelps)
Pollock, Lady, 118ff. (Macready)
Robbins, 305
Robinson, E., Personal report (Olivier)
Salvini, (2) 211–12
Schumacher, 198 (Germany)
Sprague, H. B., see Variorum
Spurgeon, 244
Steevens, edition
Stevenson, op. cit.
Terry, (1); (5) (Irving)
Thomas, 437
Traversi, 156
Tynan, Observer, June 8, 1955 (Olivier)
Vandenhoff, G., 190
Walker, (2)
Wilkes, 248 (Garrick)
Wright, op. cit.
Unidentified sources

PROMPTBOOKS

Shattuck: 8, 10, 11, 15, 16, 25, 27, 28, 29, 44,
    47, 53, 54, 63, 70, 72, 89, 112, 118, 123, 127,
    137, 144, 146, 147
Hampden

PERIODICALS

Academy, April 15, 1876 (Salvini)
Belgravia, Nov., 1875 (Irving)
Birmingham Gazette, April 19, 1933 (Komisar-
    jevsky)
Birmingham Post, June 6, 1962 (Porter/Worth)
Birmingham Weekly Post, June 10, 1955 (Olivier)
Boston Evening Transcript, Sept. 17, 1935 (Meri-
    vale)
Boston Record, July 31, 1959 (Robards)
Catholic Herald, March 26, 1953 (Wolfit)
Comoedia, Dec. 12, 1912 (Baty)
Daily Chronicle, Dec. 31, 1888 (Irving)
Daily Express, Sept. 4, 1957 (Littlewood)
Daily Herald, Feb. 7, 1928 (Maturin/Merrall)
Daily News, Sept. 27, 1875 (Irving); Dec. 31,
    1888 (Irving)
Daily Telegraph, March 10, 1884 (Salvini); Dec.
    31, 1888 (Irving); Sept. 6, 1911 (Tree)
Dramatic Review, Jan. 5, 1889 (Irving)
Edinburgh Dramatic Review, Feb. 22, 1825 (John
    Vandenhoff)
English Illustrated Monthly, December, 1888
    (Macready)
Era, Jan. 5, 1889 (Irving)
Evening, Nov. 20, 1895 (Irving)
Evening Standard, Sept. 27, 1875 (Irving);
    March 10, 1884 (Salvini); Dec. 31, 1888 (Ir-
    ving); Sept. 10, 1954 (Rogers)
Evesham Journal, April 23, 1949 (Tearle)
Examiner, Nov. 3, 1814 (Kean); Dec. 3, 1964
    (Phelps)
Figaro, March 15, 1884 (Salvini)
Figaro Littéraire, June 20, 1959 (Garrivier,
    France)
Financial Times, June 9, 1955 (Olivier/Leigh)
Gentleman's Magazine, March, 1889 (Macready)
Göteborgs Handels och Sjofarts Tidning, March 3,
    1948 (Bergman, Sweden)

Illustrated London News, June 25, 1955 (Olivier/Leigh)

Literary Gazette, March 12, 1823 (Macready)

Litteratur und Theater-Zeitung, April 14, 1780 (Reinecke, Germany)

London Magazine, Jan., 1967 (Guinness)

London News, Oct. 16, 1875 (Macready)

London Tribune, July 28, 1955 (Olivier)

Manchester Guardian, April 20, 1933 (Komisarjevsky)

Morning Herald, June, 1819 (Macready)

Morning Post, Sept. 27, 1875 (Irving, Macready); April 19, 1933 (Komisarjevsky)

Narodni Listy (Czechoslovakia) n.d.

New Statesman, April 23, 1949 (Tearle)

New York American, Feb. 8, 1916 (Hackett)

New York Herald, Oct. 29, 1868 (Forrest)

New York Herald Tribune, June 20, 1962 (Plummer)

New York Post, Jan. 22, 1833 (Forrest)

New York Sun, 1889 (Coghlan); Feb. 8, 1916 (Hackett)

New York Times, Jan. 22, 1889 (Coghlan); Oct. 30, 1895 (Irving); Feb. 18, 1921 (Barrymore); Nov. 23, 1941 (Evans); June 20, 1962 (Plummer)

Notes and Queries, July 3, 1889 (C. Kean)

Le Nouvel Observateur, June 5, 1965 (Garrivier, France)

Observer, Feb. 24, 1845 (Forrest); Dec. 30, 1888 (Irving); Sept. 10, 1911 (Tree); Feb. 12, 1928 (Maturin); June 10, 1962 (Porter/Worth)

Philadelphia Evening Bulletin, Nov. 27, 1941 (Evans)

Il Popolo, Aug., 1952 (Strehler)

Punch, Jan. 10, 1857 (Astley's); Nov. 13, 1974 (Williamson)

Queen, Jan. 5, 1889 (Irving/Terry)

Saint James Chronicle, Oct., 1773 (Garrick)

Saturday Review, Jan. 5, 1889 (Irving); March 30, 1889 (Irving); Feb. 11, 1928 (Maturin); U.S.: April 17, 1948 (Redgrave)

Scotsman, April 6, 1876 (Salvini)

Le Siècle, May 26, 1884 (Marais/Bernhardt)

Shakespeare Survey, 1956 (Vilar, France)

Sheffield Iris n.d. (Macready)

Sketch, July 2, 1952 (Richardson)

Spectator, Aug. 12, 1966 (Clements); Oct. 28, 1966 (Guinness)

Stage, n.d. (Kean); Sept. 7, 1911 (Tree); Dec. 6, 1928 (Craig)

Star, Dec. 31, 1888 (Irving)

Stockholmstidningen, March 3, 1948 (Bergman, Sweden)

Stratford-upon-Avon Herald, April 22, 1927 (Walter)

Sunday Mercury, April 17, 1949 (Tearle)

Sunday Times, Sept. 10, 1911 (Tree/Vanbrugh); Dec. 5, 1937 (Olivier); July 12, 1942 (Gielgud); Aug. 7, 1966 (Clements)

Tablet, July 18, 1942 (Gielgud)

Theatrical Journal, Aug. 8, 1840 (Macready); April 2, 1842 (Macready)

Theatre-Royal, July 7, 1837 (Forrest)

Times, Oct. 2, 1875 (Irving); Dec. 31, 1888 (Irving); Jan. 15, 1929; April 19, 1933 Komisarjevsky); July 9, 1942 (Gielgud); March 20, 1953 (Wolfit); July 28, 1955 (Olivier)

Vanity Fair, Sept. 13, 1911 (Tree)

Macbeth

BOOKS, ARTICLES AND PERSONAL REPORTS

Adams, edition
Bethell, (2) 66
Booth, W., (2) 188, *passim*
Bridges, 13f.
Brooks, 192ff.
Burnim, 108
Campbell, L. B., (1) 69, 209ff.
Clemen, (2) 78, 158
Coghill, (1)
Coriat, 45, 64
Croce, 223ff.
Cunningham, 41ff.
Davies, 129ff.
Donohue, (3) *passim*
Draper, (4) 19ff.

Duthie, (2) 128
Evans, Bertrand, (2)
Farnham, (2) 107, 118f; (3) 81
Favorini, dissertation
Flatter, (2) 92, 99
Fletcher, *passim*
Freud, 323ff.
Gardner, 55
Gentleman, edition
Hall, see Rosenberg (2)
Harrison, (2) 190f.
Heilman, (1) *passim*
Henderson, 14
Holland, N., 325ff.
Hugo, 240–41
Hutton, 241
Jack, 180ff.
James, H., 170f.

Kantak, (1) 50
Kemble, J. P., (1) 161ff.
Knight, G. W., (4) 250, 289; (5) 155
Knight, R. P., 351–52
Kreider, *passim*
Lawlor, 186f.
Lamb, *op. cit.*
Leech, 29
McCarthy, 35
McGee, 63
Mack, Jr., 116
McKellen, personal discussion
Maeterlinck, M., 696
Morozov, 90
Murry, 322ff.
Nicoll, 113
Nietzsche, *op. cit.*
Partridge, 103
Pollock, Lady, 118ff.

Quiller-Couch, 19
Rank, 209ff.
Robinson, E., personal report (Olivier)
Sanders, (1) 256
Santayana, 142
Scofield, personal discussion
Sitwell, see Harwood, 154
Sisson, 16ff.
Smidt, 247
Stevenson, R. L., *Academy* review
Stone, (2)
Upton, 46
Vandenhoff, G., *op. cit.*
Whateley, *passim*
Whitaker, 291ff.
Wilson, H., 70
Wilson, J. D., edition
Wren, 19f.
Unidentified sources

Banquo

**BOOKS, ARTICLES AND PERSONAL
REPORTS**

Shaw, Byam, notes
Woodvine, personal discussion

Act I, Scene iv

**BOOKS, ARTICLES AND PERSONAL
REPORTS**

Alger, 741 (Forrest)
Casson, Introduction
Empson, (1) 88
Frye, N., *op. cit.*
Gentleman, (2) 84
Hamilton, *op.cit.* (Craig)
Hodges, (1) 58f.
Masefield, 154
Poel, (2) 62
Shaw, Byam, notes
Tynan, (2)

PROMPTBOOKS

Shattuck: 8, 10, 22, 25, 29, 44, 48, 54, 108,
    118, 123, 127, 133, 144, 146

PERIODICALS

Academy, April 15, 1876 (Salvini)
Bath and Wilts Chronicle, Oct. 20, 1969

Berliner Morgenpost, Feb. 28, 1928 (Germany
    Reuss prod.)
Daily News, Dec. 31, 1888 (Irving/Terry)
Edinburgh Courant, April 6, 1876 (Salvini)
Evening Dispatch, June 8, 1955 (Olivier)
Evening Standard, March 10, 1884 (Salvini)
Frankfurter Allgemeine Zeitung, Dec. 5, 1955
    (Germany)
Financial Times, March 24, 1975
John O'London's Weekly, Jan. 9, 1948 (Redgrave)
Mail and Express, Oct. 31, 1895 (Irving)
New York Herald, March 29, 1870 (Booth)
Nordwest-Zeitung Oldenburger Nachrichten,
    March 22, 1971 (Germany)
Notes and Queries, July 13, 1889 (C. Kean)
Observer, Aug. 7, 1966 (Clements)
Plays and Players, Feb., 1967 (Guinness)
Spectator, July 18, 1840 (C. Kean)
Stage, Dec. 6, 1928 (Craig); March 13, 1975
    (Williamson)
Stratford-Upon-Avon Herald, Jan. 24, 1931
Sunday Telegraph, Aug. 7, 1966 (Clements)
Sunday Times, July 12, 1942 (Gielgud); Oct. 23,
    1966 (Guinness)
Times, Sept. 10, 1969
Toronto Star, June 10, 1971 (Hogg)

Lady Macbeth

BOOKS, ARTICLES AND PERSONAL
REPORTS

Agate, (1) 245ff.
Anderson, personal discussion
Bartholomeusz, 226 (Thorndike)
Bell, G. J., see Jenkin
Bradbrook, 40
Calhoun, 299ff.
Campbell, T., 55
Coleman, (2) 300
Craig, G., (6)
Craig, E. C., op. cit.
Craig, H., (2) 55–57
Curry, 38
Dench, personal discussion
Downes, 19
Ewbank, 86ff.
Faucit, 238ff.
Fletcher, 193
Freud, op. cit.
Galt, 304
Goethe, 22ff.
Harrison, G. B., 194
Hazlitt, (1) vol 4, 188–90
Heiberg, (see Krabbe)
Heine, 162f.
Holland, 325ff., and passim
Horn, 51
Hunt, L., (4) 231

Hunt, M., Interview, The Listener
Hunter, 233ff.
Johnson, Dr., edition
Kames, vol. 2, 189f.
Kemble, F., (2) 56ff.
Kindermann, see German bibliography, 1808
Leech, op. cit.
Maeterlinck, op. cit.
Martin, T., (1) 160
Marston, Memoirs, 710f.
Merchant, W. M., 73ff.
Norwood, 188
Parrott, edition
Ristori, 249ff.
Robinson, E., personal report (Leigh)
Russell, E. R., (2)
Sanders, op. cit.
Schink, see German bibliography
Scott, C., 118
Shibata, personal discussion
Skinner, 62
Strang, op. cit.
Tieck, (3) letter to Rauber
Towse, 211f., 265ff.
Walker, (1) 43
Webster, (3) 172
Wingate, 202
Winter, (6) 283, passim
Unidentified sources

Act I, Scene v

BOOKS, ARTICLES AND PERSONAL
REPORTS

Agate, (1) 232, 235
Alger, 741 (Forrest)
Allen, Sheila, letter
Anderson, personal discussion
Anglin, see Craig, G., (4)
Bell, op. cit.
Boaden, 256ff., 308ff.
Booth, S., (2)
Booth, W., 188
Capell, op. cit.
Charlton, 167ff.
Coleman, J., (1) 232 ff. (Salvini, Ristori)
Craig, E. C., personal discussion
Craig, G., (4) 9
Crane, M., 173
Crosse, (1) 66 (S. Thorndike)
Dench, personal discussion
Durylin, 323–25 (Ermolova, Russia)

Falk, op. cit. (Germany, 1928)
Field, 500
Frye, R., (2) 102
Galt, 303
Gardner, 54
Gentleman, edition; (2) 85
Grzymala-Siedlecki, 83–85 (Modjeska, Poland)
Hanmer, edition
Hodek, letters (Czechoslovakia)
Jacobsohn, (2) 120f. (Körner)
Jacquot, passim
Johnson, Dr., edition
Jorgensen, (2) passim
Knowles, 20f.
Kocher, 347ff.
Laurens, personal discussion (Bergman)
Maeterlinck, Mme., op. cit.
Malone, edition
Marshall, edition
Merchant, W. M., (2) 73ff.
Morley, 159f., 185ff.

Muir, (9) 151
Nevo, 222
Richter, 193 (Wolter, Germany)
Ristori, 254
Robinson, E., personal report (Leigh)
Schink, 244 (Nouseul)
Scofield, personal discussion, see Rosenberg (2)
Selvinksy, 66–74 (Gogoleva, Russia)
Segond-Weber, *op. cit.*
Shaw, G. B., (1) 246ff. (Campbell)
Siddons, J. H., *op. cit.*
Siddons, S., *op. cit.*
Siegel, (2) 147f.
Sitwell, (2) 29
Skinner, 62 (Janauschek)
Sothern, *passim*
Terry, (1)
Verity, edition
Unidentified sources

PROMPTBOOKS

Shattuck: 8, 13, 16, 29, 59, 63, 70, 108, 118, 122, 123, 127, 132, 133, 137, 144, 147

PERIODICALS

Athenaeum, July 11, 1857 (Ristori); March 1, 1845 (Forrest); Jan. 5, 1889 (Irving)
Belfast Newsletter, Oct. 19, 1802 (Siddons)
Bell's Life in London, July 9, 1884 (Bernhardt)
Birmingham Post, Sept. 24, 1947 (Wolfit); June 6, 1962 (Worth)
Birmingham Weekly Post, Feb. 1, 1928 (Merrall)
Blackwood's Edinburgh Magazine, Sept., 1834 (Siddons)
Boston Daily Advertiser, Nov. 7, 1866 (Ristori); April 22, 1881 (Salvini)
Boston Evening Transcript, n.d. (Janauscheck); Nov. 16, 1910 (Marlowe)
Boston Herald, Nov. 5, 1910 (Sothern)
Chicago Daily News, April 28, 1942 (Evans/ Anderson)
Country Gentleman, Jan. 5, 1889 (Terry)
Courier, Nov. 15, 1871 (Faucit)
Court Circular, July 12, 1884 (Bernhardt)
Dagens Nyheter, March 13, 1948 (Bergman, Sweden)
Daily Chronicle, Dec. 31, 1888 (Irving)
Daily Express, Sept. 6, 1911 (Vanbrugh)
Daily Mail, March 6, 1975 (Williamson); Sept. 6, 1911 (Tree)
Daily News, Sept. 27, 1875 (Irving)
Daily Telegraph, July 5, 1882 (Ristori); July 5, 1884 (Bernhardt); Dec. 31, 1888 (Terry)
Dramatic Review, Jan. 5, 1889 (Irving/Terry)

Düsseldorfer Nachrichten, June 4, 1960 (Germany)
Edinburgh Courant, July 16, 1785 (Siddons); April 6, 1876 (Salvini)
English Illustrated Magazine, Dec., 1888 (Siddons)
Evening Post, Nov. 20, 1928 (Craig prod.)
Evening Standard, Sept. 27, 1875 (Irving/Bateman); July 5, 1884 (Bernhardt); Dec. 31, 1888 (Terry); Sept. 19, 1898 (Campbell); March 6, 1975 (Mirren/Williamson)
Examiner, Dec. 3, 1864 (Phelps/Faucit)
Financial Times, Nov. 10, 1969
Glasgow Herald, Dec. 22, 1843; Nov. 4, 1846; Feb. 19, 1861 (Faucit)
Globe, Dec. 31, 1888 (Irving)
Jewish Chronicle, Nov. 1, 1974 (Mirren)
John O'London's Weekly, July 31, 1942 (Ffrangcon-Davies)
Lady, Jan. 30, 1975
Lady's Pictorial, Jan. 5, 1889 (Irving)
Leamington Spa Courier, June 10, 1955 (Leigh)
Listener, March 29, 1933 (Gielgud)
Literary Gazette, April 12, 1823 (Macready)
Liverpool Daily Post, June 28, 1884 (Bernhardt)
Lloyd's Weekly London News Paper, Oct. 9, 1875 (Bateman); June 28, 1884 (Bernhardt); Jan. 6, 1889 (Terry)
Manchester Courier, Nov. 15, 1871 (Faucit)
Manchester Examiner and Times, Nov. 14, 1871 (Faucit)
Manchester Guardian, Nov. 15, 1871 (Faucit); April 18, 1949 (Wynyard/Tearle); April 23, 1964 (Wolfit)
Mask, Vol. 15, 1929 (Craig)
Le Monde, June 19, 1952 (France)
Monthly Mirror: see under Siddons
Montreal Star, June 19, 1962 (Plummer)
Morning Advertiser, Dec. 31, 1888 (Irving)
Morning Leader, Sept. 6, 1911 (Tree)
Morning Post, Sept. 27, 1875 (Bateman); Sept. 27, 1885 (Irving); Dec. 31, 1888 (Irving)
Neue Zeitung, June 5, 1952 (Germany)
New Statesman, Feb. 26, 1971; Nov. 8, 1974 (Mirren)
New York American, Feb. 8, 1916 (Hackett)
New York Daily News, July 16, 1973 (Weaver/ Murphy)
New York Evening Mail, Oct. 26, 1874 (Cushman)
New York Herald, Oct. 19, 1870 (Janauscheck)
New York Herald Tribune, June 20, 1962 (Plummer)
New York Press, Nov. 3, 1895 (Irving)
New York Sun, Nov. 7, 1814 (E. Kean); Feb. 8, 1916 (Hackett); Nov. 20, 1928 (Reed)
New York Times, Oct. 8, 1955 (Olivier); Oct. 30,

1956 (Rogers); Feb. 7, 1962 (Clements/Jeffords); June 20, 1962 (Plummer/Reid); July 15, 1973 (Weaver/Murphy)
New York Tribune, Feb. 6, 1899 (Langtry)
New York World, Jan. 22, 1889 (Langtry)
New York World-Telegram, Nov. 12, 1941 (Evans/Anderson)
Observer, Dec. 30, 1888 (Terry); March 23, 1930 (Hunt); June 10, 1962 (Worth)
Overland Monthly, February, 1886 (Rankin)
Philadelphia Post, n.d.
Pittsburgh Post, Oct. 29, 1917 (Mantell); Dec. 4, 1920 (Mantell)
Pittsburgh Sun-Telegraph, April 2, 1929 (Craig)
Przeglad Polski, No. 533, 1910 (Wysocka, Poland)
Queen, Jan. 5, 1888 (Irving/Terry)
Rand Daily Mail, Aug. 21, 1970 (Sonnenborn —see Theatre Bibliography III, South African productions)
Redditch Indicator, Nov. 1, 1974 (Mirren)
Saturday Review, May 20, 1876 (Rossi/Pareti); June 14, 1884 (Bernhardt)
Sheffield Iris, n.d. (Macready)
Spectator, July 17, 1942 (Ffrangcon-Davies); Aug. 25, 1967 (Scofield)
Sportsman, Dec. 31, 1888 (Irving/Terry)
Stage, Feb. 27, 1848 (F. Kemble); Dec. 31, 1888 (Irving); Jan. 1, 1889 (Irving); Sept. 7, 1911 (Tree/Vanbrugh)

Stratford-Upon-Avon Herald, April 22, 1927 (Green)
Summary, July 12, 1884 (Marais/Bernhardt)
Sunday Times, July 5, 1840 (Kemble); July 12, 1842 (Terry); Feb. 27, 1848 (F. Kemble); Nov. 6, 1864 (Faucit); Dec. 30, 1888 (Irving); Sept. 10, 1911 (Tree); April 8, 1934 (Laughton/Robson); Dec. 5, 1937 (Anderson/Olivier); July 12, 1942 (Ffrangcon-Davies); Dec. 21, 1947 (Burrill)
Sydney Morning Herald, Oct. 23, 1975 (Ristori)
Tallis Dramatic Magazine, December, 1850, June 1851 (Glyn)
Teatr, No. 15, 1964 (Poland)
Teatralny Almanakh, 1947 (Andreeva/Juriev, Russia)
Theatrical Journal, Aug. 8, 1840 (Macready)
Times, Oct. 2, 1875 (Irving/Bateman); June 28, 1884 (Bernhardt); Jan. 6, 1889 (Terry); Sept. 6, 1911 (Vanbrugh); April 21, 1927 (Walter/Green); March 18, 1930 (Gielgud/Hunt); June 6, 1962 (Porter/Worth); Aug. 1, 1966; Dec. 31, 1888 (Irving/Terry)
Universal Review, Jan. 15, 1889 (Terry)
Vanity Fair, Sept. 13, 1911 (Tree/Vanbrugh)
Weekly Times and Echo, Dec. 20, 1888 (Irving/Terry)

Act I, Scene vi

BOOKS, ARTICLES AND PERSONAL REPORTS

Agate, (1) 231 (Robson)
Bell, *op. cit.*
Craig, E. C., personal discussion
Craig, G., (6)
Grein, *op. cit.* (Irving/Terry)
Jacobsohn, (2) 120 (Reinhardt)
Knights, (1) 22; (5) 238
Knowles, 23ff.
Morley, 186f.
Muir, edition
Phelps, 100 (Phelps); *op. cit.*
Richter, 194 (Wolter, Germany)
Wingate, 218
Unidentified sources

PROMPTBOOKS

Shattuck: 8, 13, 25, 29, 44, 47, 66, 70, 108, 112, 118, 122, 123, 127, 133, 144, 147

PERIODICALS

Athenaeum, March 1, 1845 (Cushman)
Birmingham Post, May 20, 1962 (Porter)
Daily Chronicle, Dec. 31, 1888 (Irving/Terry); Aug. 25, 1909 (Maeterlinck)
Daily Telegraph, Dec. 31, 1888 (Irving)
Dramatic Review, Jan. 5, 1889 (Terry)
Evening Post, Dec. 31, 1888 (Irving)
Financial Times, Feb. 15, 1975 (Heston)
Göteborgs-Tidningen, March 13, 1948 (Bergman, Sweden)
Illustrated London News, May 7, 1949 (Tearle); July 5, 1952 (Richardson)
John O'London's Weekly, May 13, 1949 (Tearle)
Liverpool Daily Post, Dec. 31, 1888 (Irving)
Manchester Examiner and Times, Nov. 14, 1871 (Faucit)
Morning Leader, Sept. 6, 1911 (Tree)
Morning Post, Sept. 6, 1911 (Tree); April 19, 1933 (Komisarjevsky)
Nottingham Evening Post, Oct. 30, 1895 (Irving)
Observer, Oct. 25, 1955 (*Joe Macbeth*)

Overland Monthly, Sept. 6, 1911 (Tree)
Przeglad Polski, No. 453, 1904 (Wysocka, Poland)
Queen, Jan. 5, 1889 (Irving)
Scotsman, Nov. 27, 1883 (Ristori)
Stage, Sept. 7, 1911 (Tree)
Stockholmstidningen, March 13, 1948 (Bergman, Sweden)

Sunday Times, Nov. 6, 1864 (Faucit); Feb. 18, 1945 (Wolfit)
Sydney Morning Herald, Oct. 23, 1875 (Ristori)
Theatre Arts, February, 1925
Times, July 5, 1884 (Bernhardt)

Act I, Scene vii

BOOKS, ARTICLES AND PERSONAL REPORTS

Agate, (1) 231, 235 (Laughton)
Alger, 741–42 (Forrest)
Anderson, personal discussion
Battenhouse, 197
Boaden (3) 310 (Siddons)
Booth, S., personal discussion (V. Redgrave)
Booth, W., 183f.
Boyle, 130
Brereton, (1) 190 (Irving)
Brooks, 184
Brown, J. R., (1) 149 (Porter/Worth)
Clemen, (1) 98–99
Coleman, (1) 222
Craig, E. C., personal discussion; promptbook
Croce, 224ff.
Cunningham, edition
David, 128 (Rogers)
Davidson, (2) 92
Davies, (2) 183 (Pritchard)
Dench, personal discussion
Duthie (2) 123ff.
Empson, (1) 90, 97ff.
Ewbank, 113f.
Farnham, (2) 107ff.
Fletcher, (2) 193 (Siddons)
Galt, 303
Gardner, (1) 248ff.
Garrick, (2) 133; (3) 20
Gentleman, (2) 88
Gould, 123f (J. B. Booth)
Grein, (1) 56ff. (Irving)
Heilman, (3) 94ff.
Hoepfner, *op. cit.*
Hunt, L., (4) 231 (J. P. Kemble/Siddons)
Irving, (2) 98, (5)
Johnson, Dr., edition
Kemble, F., (2) 60
Knowles, 25
Laurens, personal discussion (Bergman)
Mahood, *op. cit.*
Manifold, *op. cit.*
Marston, J. W., 228
Muir, (3) 46–47, (8) 478

Murry, 325ff.
Nevo, 225ff., 324
Olivier, Tynan interview
Rowe, edition
Russell, C. E., 487 (Marlowe)
Salvini, (2) 212f.
Sanders, (1) 330f.
Shaw, G. B., *op. cit.*
Siddons, S., *op. cit.*
Simond, 131 (Siddons)
Spender, 120f.
Spurgeon, 172, 327
Steevens, edition
Stein, 273
Stevenson, *op. cit.*
Strindberg, 168, 170
Taylor, M., (1) 337
Terry, notes
Theobald, edition
Tieck, (1) vol 2, 286ff.
Towse, 178 (Salvini)
Vandenhoff, 196 (Cushman)
Walker, (1) 54
Wingate, 210ff.
Wilson, J. D., edition
Unidentified sources

PROMPTBOOKS

Shattuck: 8, 66, 70, 89, 108, 112, 122, 123, 127, 137, 144, 146, 147, 183

PERIODICALS

Academy, April 15, 1876 (Salvini)
Athenaeum, March 1, 1845 (Cushman); Oct. 2, 1875 (Irving)
Atlas, Dec. 4, 1836 (Forrest); June 11, 1840 (C. Kean)
Bath Journal May 26, 1823; March 12, 1832; Jan. 12, 1835 (Macready)
Belgravia, Nov., 1875 (Irving)
Bell's Life in London, July 9, 1884 (Bernhardt)
Bell's Weekly Messenger, Nov. 2, 1875 (Bateman)
Birmingham Gazette, July 10, 1942 (Gielgud/ Ffrangcon-Davies)

Birmingham Mail, June 11, 1952 (Leighton)
Birmingham Post, May 20, 1942 (Ffrangcon-Davies)
Boston Daily Advertiser, Nov. 7, 1866 (Ristori)
Boston Herald, Nov. 21, 1895 (Irving)
Bristol Mercury, Jan. 23, 1847 (Macready)
Cabinet, June 1808 (J. P. Kemble/Miss Smith)
Caledonian Mercury, March 15, 1810 (Siddons)
Chicago Sun-Times, Feb. 13, 1957 (Rogers/Browne)
Chicago Tribune, March 9, 1873
Cincinnati Commercial, Jan. 2, 1910 (Sothern/Marlowe)
Coventry Evening Telegraph, June 11, 1952 (Richardson/Leighton)
Daily Chronicle, Jan. 17, 1907 (Bourchier)
Daily Mail, June 11, 1952 (Richardson)
Daily News, July 4, 1857; July 4, 5, 1882 (Ristori)
Daily Telegraph, Dec. 31, 1888 (Irving/Terry); March 6, 1975 (Williamson)
Daily Worker, June 13, 1952 (Leighton)
Deutsche Zeitung (New Orleans), March 7, 1867
Dramatic Review, Jan. 5, 1889 (Irving/Terry)
Edinburgh Courant, April 6, 1876 (Salvini); June 25, 1884 (Bernhardt)
Evening Standard, Sept. 27, 1875 (Irving); July 5, 1884 (Bernhardt); Sept. 27, 1885 (Irving); Dec. 19, 1948 (Redgrave); Sept. 10, 1954 (Rogers)
Evesham Journal, April 23, 1949 (Wynyard)
Financial Times, April 7, 1973 (Quilley)
Frankfurter Allgemeine Zeitung, Jan. 2, 1967 (Germany)
Freeman's Journal, Aug. 8, 1822; March 6, 1833 (Macready)
Kurier Lubelski, no. 90, 1964 (Poland)
Leamington Spa Courier, June 10, 1955 (Leigh/Olivier)
Listener, March 29, 1933 (Hunt/Gielgud); Feb. 2, 1967 (Signoret/Guinness)
Literary Gazette, Feb. 19, 1846 (C. Kean)
London Ontario Free Press, June 10, 1971 (Hogg)
Lumir (Czechoslovakia), 1858
Mail and Express, Oct. 31, 1895 (Irving)
Manchester Guardian, Nov. 15, 1871 (Faucit); Nov. 23, 1937 (Wolfit)
Monthly Mirror, Oct., 1808 (Siddons)
Morning Advertiser, July 5, 1884 (Bernhardt)
Morning Leader, Sept. 6, 1911 (Tree)
Morning Post, June 10, 1816 (Siddons); Sept. 28, 1847 (Phelps); Sept. 27, 1875 (Macready, Irving); Sept. 6, 1911 (Tree)
Neue Freie Presse (Vienna), Nov. 24, 1922 (Kortner)
New Statesman, April 23, 1949 (Tearle/Wynyard)
New York Daily News, July 16, 1973 (Kahn prod.)

New York Evening Mail, Oct. 26, 1874 (Cushman)
New York Herald, Nov. 21, 1895 (Irving)
New York Herald Tribune, Nov. 17, 1962
New York Sun, Jan. 22, 1889 (Langtry)
New York Telegram, Oct. 8, 1935 (Merivale/Cooper)
New York Times, Nov. 26, 1874 (Morris); Jan. 22, 1889 (Coghlan/Langtry); Nov. 19, 1889 (Modjeska); Feb. 8, 1916 (Hackett/Allen); Nov. 20, 1928 (Reed/Craig prod.); Nov. 23, 1941 (Evans/Anderson); April 11, 1948 (Redgrave/Robson); Oct. 8, 1955; June 20, 1962 (Plummer/Reid)
New York Tribune, Oct. 24, 1897 (Modjeska)
New York World, Jan. 22, 1889 (Langtry)
News Chronicle, April 25, 1949 (Tearle); June 8, 1955 (Olivier)
Observer, Dec. 30, 1888 (Terry); Sept. 10, 1911 (Tree/Vanbrugh); Nov. 3, 1974 (Williamson/Mirren)
Plays and Players, Nov., 1969
Punch, Nov. 13, 1974 (Williamson)
Saint James Gazette, Sept. 30, 1875 (Irving)
San Francisco Chronicle, Oct. 22, 1876 (Booth)
Saturday Review, Jan. 5, 1889 (Terry)
Sheffield Iris, n. d. (Macready)
Le Siécle, May 26, 1884 (Bernhardt)
South London Press, March 12, 1971
Spectator, April 9, 1842 (Macready); Oct. 2, 1875 (Irving/Bateman); Jan. 5, 1889 (Irving/Terry)
Spirit of the Times, April 2, 1870 (Booth)
Stage, Sept. 7, 1911 (Tree/Vanbrugh); April 28, 1927 (Walter/Green)
Summary, July 12, 1884 (Bernhardt)
Sunday Times, Dec. 30, 1888 (Irving); Sept. 10, 1911 (Tree); Dec. 26, 1926; Feb. 12, 1928 (Merrall); April 8, 1934 (Laughton); Aug. 7, 1966 (Clements/Johnston)
Sydney Morning Herald, Oct. 23, 1875 (Ristori)
Teatr, no. 15, 1964 (Poland)
Theatre, Dec. 1, 1888 (Siddons)
Theatrical Inquisitor, July, 1820 (Macready)
Theatrical Journal, April 2, 1842 (Macready)
Times, July 5, 1884 (Bernhardt); Dec. 31, 1888 (Terry); Jan. 4, 1889 (Terry); Aug. 1, 1906 (Bourchier/Vanbrugh); April 21, 1927 (Walter/Green); Nov. 22, 1932 (E. Carrick Craig prod.); Oct. 31, 1974 (Williamson)
Il Trovatore, July 18, 1857 (Ristori)
Truth, April 29, 1949 (Tearle/Wynyard)
Vanity Fair, Oct. 2, 1875 (Irving); July 12, 1884 (Marais/Bernhardt)
Vossische Zeitung, March 27, 1913 (Triesch, Germany)
Weekly Dispatch, Jan. 6, 1889 (Irving)
Unidentified clippings

Act II, Scene i

BOOKS, ARTICLES AND PERSONAL
REPORTS

Agate, (1) 242 (Olivier)
Alger, 742–43 (Forrest)
Akutagawa, (Milward interview)
Aronson, 25
Bab, *op. cit.* (Matkowsky)
Bell, *op. cit.* (Siddons)
Booth, S., personal discussion (Heston)
Brereton, (1) 190 (Irving)
Brown, J. R., (2)
Byrne, (2) letter (R. Thorndike)
Clemen, (2) 158
Coleman, (1) 223 (Macready)
Crosse, (2)
David, 125ff. (Rogers, Olivier)
Davies, II, 88 (Garrick)
Fischer, 363 (Reinecke)
Foakes, edition
Forman, *op. cit.*
Garrick, (1) *passim;* (2); (3) 113, 363–64
Grube, 83 (Meiningen)
Hamilton, *op. cit.* (Craig)
Hawkins, (1) 272 (Kean)
Hodek, letters (Czechoslovakia)
Hodges, (1) 58, 78, 88
Hunt, L., *Examiner,* January 15, 1809
Kemble, J. P., (1) 128–29 (Kemble)
Knights, (1) 23
Lawrence, (2) 61ff.
Lennam, personal discussion
Lewes, 34–35 (Macready)
Libby, *op. cit.*
Liddell, edition
Marshall, 33 (Aldridge)
May, personal discussion
McKellen, personal discussion
Milward, personal discussion
Murdoch, 325 (Forrest)
Murphy, A., (2) vol 1, 81ff. (Garrick)
Nicoll, 123
Odell, 165–66 (Cooper)
Phelps, 102 (Phelps)
Quiller-Couch, 19
Robinson, E., personal report (Olivier, Leigh)
Robinson, H. C., 462–63 (Kemble, Kean)
Robson, W., 21 (Siddons)
Russell, E. R., (1) 476; (2) 146 (Irving/Terry)
Sitwell, see Harwood, 154
Smollett, see Buck, 155 (Garrick)
Stamm, 61
Tynan, (1) 98
Vandenhoff, *op. cit.*
Westbrook, 220
Wilkes, 248 (Garrick)

Williamson, (1) 35 (Devlin)
Wilson, J. D., edition
Woodvine, personal discussion
Unidentified clippings

PROMPTBOOKS

Shattuck: 8, 15, 44, 48, 66, 108, 118, 122, 123,
127, 133, 137, 144, 146

PERIODICALS

Academy, May 13, 1876 (Rossi, Irving)
Aftonbladet, March 13, 1948 (Bergman,
Sweden)
Atlas, Dec. 4, 1836 (Forrest)
Belfast News Letter, Feb. 20, 1824 (Macready)
Bell's Life in London, May 20, 1876 (Rossi)
Bell's Weekly Messenger, Jan. 5, 1906 (Irving)
Birmingham Post, June 10, 1955 (Olivier)
Business, Sept. 27, 1875 (Irving)
Champion, July 17, 1830 (Macready)
Christian Science Monitor, June 18, 1955
(Olivier)
Daily News, Sept. 27, 1875 (Irving); Dec. 25,
1888 (Irving); Dec. 31, 1888 (Irving)
Daily Texan, Jan. 1, 1929 (Leiber)
De Tijd, Feb. 24, 1937 (Netherlands)
Detroit News, April 26, 1934 (Hampden)
Dramatic Censor, n.d. (Garrick); Sept. 18, 1811
(Kemble)
Dramatic Review, Feb. 9, 1852
Edinburgh Courant, April 6, 1876 (Salvini)
Edinburgh Dramatic Review, Jan 13, 1825 (J.
Vandenhoff)
English Illustrated Magazine, Dec., 1888
(Kemble)
Era, Jan. 5, 1889 (Irving); Sept. 24, 1898
(Forbes-Robertson)
Evening Post, Dec. 31, 1888 (Irving)
Evening Standard, Sept. 27, 1875 (Irving);
March 10, 1884 (Salvini); Dec. 31, 1888
(Irving); Sept. 27, 1895 (Irving); Dec. 19,
1947 (Redgrave); April 22, 1949 (Tearle)
Examiner, Jan. 15, 1809 (Young); Oct. 4, 1835
(Macready); May 2, 1846 (Macready); Oct.
2, 1875 (Irving)
Financial Times, Oct. 21, 1966 (Guinness)
Fortnightly Review, July, 1924
Freeman's Journal, Aug. 8, 1822
Galveston News, April 5, 1872 (Janauscheck)
Illustrated London News, Jan. 13, 1968 (Sco-
field)
Irish Times, Nov. 1, 1974 (Williamson)
Kaleidoscope, July 17, July 19, 1821 (Garrick)

Lloyds Weekly London Newspaper, Oct. 9, 1875 (Irving)
London Magazine, Jan., 1967 (Guinness)
Manchester Courier, n.d.; July, 1814; Nov. 7, 1814 (Kean)
Manchester Guardian, Dec. 20, 1947 (Redgrave)
Monthly Mirror, Nov., 1807 (J. P. Kemble)
Morning Advertiser, Sept. 27, 1875 (Irving)
Morning Chronicle, Oct. 30, 1773 (Macklin/ Garrick)
Morning Leader, Sept. 6, 1911 (Tree)
Morning Post, Sept. 27, 1875 (Irving)
New Statesman, June 21, 1952 (Richardson); Nov. 8, 1974 (Williamson)
New Theatre, n.d. (Redgrave)
New York Daily Mail, May 8, 1885 (Booth)
New York Herald Tribune, June 19, 1961
New York Post, Jan 22, 1833 (Forrest); Oct. 30, 1895 (Irving)
New York Sun, April 9, 1870 (Booth); Jan 22, 1889 (Coghlan)
New York Times, Jan. 22, 1889 (Coghlan); April 16, 1916 (Calhoun)
New York Tribune, Nov. 2, 1874 (G. Vanden-hoff); Oct. 24, 1897 (Modjeska)
New York World, Jan. 22, 1889 (Coghlan)
Notes and Queries, July 8, 1916 (Macready)
Observer, Feb. 26, 1844 (C. Kean); Feb. 24, 1845 (Forrest); Dec. 30, 1888 (Irving); Dec. 2, 1928 (German prod.); June 15, 1952 (Richardson); June 12, 1955 (Olivier); Oct. 25, 1955 (*Joe Macbeth*)

Overland Monthly, Feb., 1886 (Rankin)
Pall Mall Gazette, Sept. 6, 1911 (Tree/Van-brugh)
Pittsburgh Post, Dec. 4, 1920 (Mantell)
Public Advertiser, Feb. 4, 1785 (Kemble)
Saint James Chronicle, Oct. 28, 1773 (Macklin)
Saturday Review, March 15, 1884 (Salvini); June 14, 1884 (Marais); Jan. 5, 1889 (Irving)
Scotsman, April 6, 1876 (Salvini)
Spectator, April 9, 1842 (Macready); Oct. 28, 1966 (Guinness)
Stage, n.d. (Garrick, Kemble, Quin); Sept. 7, 1911 (Tree); Dec. 6, 1928 (Craig); Dec. 24, 1947 (Redgrave); June 12, 1952 (Richardson)
Sun, Nov. 7, 1814 (Kean)
Sunday Times, Dec. 5, 1837 (Macready); July 5, 1840 (C. Kean); Dec. 21, 1947 (Redgrave); April 17, 1949 (Tearle)
Teatralny Almanakh, 1947 (Juriev, Russia)
Theatre, Feb. 1, 1889 (Irving)
Theatre Quarterly, vol. 1, no. 3. 1971 (Macready)
Theatrical Inquisitor, Nov., 1814 (Kean); July, 1820 (Macready)
Times, Sept. 19, 1811 (J. P. Kemble); June 11, 1952 (Richardson); June 6, 1962 (Porter)
Universal Review, Jan. 15, 1889 (Irving)
Woman's Magazine, Feb., 1896 (Irving)
World Oracle, Oct. 17, 1788 (Kemble)

Act II, Scene ii

BOOKS, ARTICLES AND PERSONAL REPORTS

Agate, (1) 233–34 (Gielgud)
Alger, 743 (Forrest)
Anderson, personal discussion
Ashwell, (1) 72
Bell, *op. cit.*
Bergman, interview
Boaden, (1) 63 (Siddons)
Booth, W., 183f.
Brereton, (2) 144, 190–91 (Irving)
Brown, J. R., (1) 150 (Worth)
Calhoun, *op. cit.*
Craig, G., (4)
Craig, E. C., personal discussion
Coriat, 45ff.
Crosse, (1) (S. Thorndike)
David, *op. cit.*
Davies, (1) 148, 183 (Garrick, Siddons)
Dench, personal discussion

Dent, edition
Elwin, edition
Engelsfeld, personal report (Yugoslavia)
Farjeon, 135 (S. Thorndike)
Farnham, (2) 120
Favorini, 205, 465 (Mantell)
Finlay, 282 (Kean)
Forster, 35, 37, 77 (Forrest, Huddart)
Frenzel, 305 (Ristori)
Gentleman, edition; (2) 110 (Powell)
Gibbs, personal discussion
Got, (2) 87–88 (Modjeska)
Gould, 125f. (J. B. Booth)
Grossman, 49–54 (Booth)
Grzymala-Siedlecki, *op. cit.* (Modjeska, Poland)
Guglia, 86 (Mitterwurzer, Germany)
Hawkins, (1) 273–74, 279 (Kean)
James, H., 37 (Irving), 47 (Rossi), 176 (Salvini, C. Kean)
Irving, (1) 31
Jorgensen, *passim*

Kemble, F., (2) 61
Lazarus, 116 (Salvini)
Mack, *op. cit.*
Marshall, 32–34 (Aldridge)
Marston, J. W., 76–77 (Macready, Kean)
Milward, (Akutagawa)
Muir, (3) 54ff.
Parrott, edition
Pollock, Lady, 120 (Macready)
Redgrave, 135, 337
Richter, 195 (Wolter)
Robinson, E., personal report (Olivier, Leigh)
Robson, F., Introduction
Russell, C. E., 487 (Marlowe)
Russell, E. R., (3) (Terry)
Scott, 120 (Terry)
Segond-Weber, *op. cit.*
Selvinsky, (Gogoleva, Russia) 1955
Shaw, G. B., *op. cit.*
Sitwell, 32–33
Smith, S., 184
Spargo, 269
Sprague, A. C., (1) 241ff.
Stamm, *op. cit.*
Strindberg, 168
Torbarina, *op. cit.*
Towse, 87 (Booth), 178–79 (Salvini), 304 (Irving)
Walpole, 316ff. (Siddons)
Williamson, A., (2) 111 (Rogers); (3) 273 (Clunes)
Wilson, J. D., edition
Wingate, 223 (Janauschek)
Winter, (2) 189 (Booth); (7) 468 (Kean), 469 (Macready)
Wrede, personal discussion (Norway)
Unidentified clippings

PROMPTBOOKS

Shattuck: 8, 10, 15, 16, 25, 27, 44, 47, 48, 59, 63, 66, 70, 77, 89, 106, 108, 118, 122, 123, 127, 133, 137, 144, 146

PERIODICALS

Academy, April 15, 1876 (Salvini)
Aftonbladet, March 13, 1948 (Bergman)
Athenaeum, March 1, 1845 (Forrest); Feb. 19, 1853; July 11, 1857 (Ristori, Siddons)
Atlas, Dec. 4, 1836 (Forrest); July 11, 1840 (C. Kean)
Bath Journal, March 12, 1832 (Macready)
Belfast Newsletter, Oct. 19, 1802 (Siddons)
Bell's Life in London, n.d. (Irving)

Bell's Weekly Messenger, Jan. 5, 1806; Sept. 27, 1875 (Irving/Bateman); Oct. 2, 1875 (Irving/ Bateman); May 13, 1876 (Rossi)
Birmingham Mail, May 20, 1942 (Gielgud)
Birmingham Post, June 6, 1962 (Porter)
Blackwood's Edinburgh Magazine, June, 1843 (Siddons)
Boston Daily Advertiser, April 22, 1881 (Salvini); Oct. 13, 1875 (Irving)
Boston Evening Transcript, April 29, 1904 (O'Neil); Sept. 17, 1935 (Merivale)
Cambrian, Sept. 20, 1834 (Macready)
Champion, July 17, 1820 (Macready)
Chicago Daily News, April 28, 1942
Chicago Times, n.d. (Cushman)
Chicago Tribune, Feb. 13, 1957 (Rogers/ Browne)
Christian Science Monitor, June 18, 1955 (Olivier)
Combat, April 23, 1965 (T.E.P. prod.)
The Connoisseur, Sept. 26, 1754 (Garrick)
Daily Express, March 4, 1934 (Laughton)
Daily News, July 4, 1857 (Ristori); July 5, 1884 (Bernhardt); Dec. 28, 1926 (S. Thorndike)
Daily Telegraph, March 6, 1975 (Williamson)
Dramatic Censor, n.d., 1810 (Garrick); Sept. 18, 1811 (Kemble); Sept. 29, 1829 (Kean)
Dramatic Review, Feb. 9, 1852, Jan. 5, 1889 (Irving/Terry)
Drury Lane Journal, March, 1752 (Mrs. Cibber)
Edinburgh Advertiser, Feb. 26, 1825 (Kean)
Edinburgh Courant, July 16, 1785, Feb. 24, 1812, Nov. 28, 1815 (Siddons); April 6, 1876 (Salvini)
English Illustrated Magazine. Dec., 1888 (Garrick/Pritchard)
Era, May 14, 1876 (Rossi)
Evening Advertiser, June 30, 1936 (Welles)
Evening News, Nov. 27, 1937 (Anderson)
Evening Standard, Sept. 27, 1875 (Irving); July 5, 1884 (Bernhardt); July 6, 1884 (Marais); Sept. 6, 1911 (Tree); Aug. 5, 1944 (Milton); Dec. 19, 1947 (M. Redgrave); June 8, 1955 (Olivier)
Examiner, Oct. 2, 1875 (Irving); Oct. 2, 1875 (Kean); Nov. 13, 1814 (Kean); June 26, 1820 (Kean)
Financial Times, April 7, 1973 (Quilley)
Galveston Daily Bulletin, April 4, 1872 (Janauschek)
Gazette de France, May 24, 1884 (Bernhardt)
Glasgow Herald, Nov. 4, 1846 (Faucit)
Globe, Dec. 31, 1888 (Irving)
Illustrated London News, Oct. 16, 1875 (C. Kean); Jan. 13, 1968 (Scofield)
John O'London's Weekly, June 27, 1952 (Richardson)

Kaleidoscope, July 17, 1821 (Macready)
Kurier Lubelski, no. 90, 1964 (Poland)
Lady's Pictorial, Jan. 5, 1889 (Irving/Terry)
Leamington Spa Courier, June 10, 1955 (Olivier)
Lettres Françaises, July 29, 1954 (Vilar)
Life, March 13, 1884 (Salvini)
Listener, March 29, 1933 (Gielgud/Hunt)
Lloyd's Weekly London Newspaper, Oct. 3, 1847 (Phelps)
Manchester Daily Express, June 11, 1952 (Richardson)
Manchester Examiner and Times, Nov. 14, 1871 (Faucit)
Mirror of Taste, 1810 (Garrick, Kemble, Cooper)
Mirror Magazine, January, 1849
Morning Advertiser, March 10, 1884 (Salvini); June 15, 1955 (Olivier)
Morning Chronicle, Nov. 7, 1814 (Kean); Feb. 16, 1853 (C. Kean)
Morning Herald, March 15, 1831
Morning Leader, Sept. 6, 1911 (Tree)
Morning Post, Nov. 7, 1814 (Kean); June 10, 1816 (Siddons); Feb. 16, 1853 (C. Kean); Sept. 27, 1875 (Irving, Macready); Dec. 31, 1888 (Irving/Terry); Dec. 28, 1928 (Ainley)
Münchner Merkur, 1807 (Germany)
New Monthly Magazine, Dec. 1, 1814 (Kean)
New Statesman, July 18, 1942 (Ffrangcon-Davies); Dec. 27, 1947 (Burrill); Jan. 12, 1968 (Scofield); Nov. 8, 1974 (Mirren)
New York Herald, Nov. 19, 1889 (Modjeska)
New York Herald Tribune, Nov. 23, 1941 (Anderson); April 1, 1948 (M. Redgrave); June 19, 1961
New York Post, Jan. 22, 1833 (Forrest); Oct. 30, 1895 (Irving)
New York Times, Nov. 10, 1895 (Irving); Dec. 11, 1910 (Marlowe); Nov. 12, 1941 (Evans/Anderson); Feb. 7, 1962 (Clements/Jefford)
New York Tribune, Oct. 30, 1895 (Irving); Oct. 24, 1897 (Modjeska)
New Yorker, April 10, 1948 (M. Redgrave)
News, Nov. 13, 1814 (Kean); April, 1831 (Macready)
Notes and Queries, July 13, 1889 (C. Kean)
Observer, Feb. 26, 1844 (C. Kean); Aug. 7, 1966 (Johnston)
Overland Monthly, Feb., 1886 (Rankin)
Pall Mall Gazette, July 5, 1884 (Bernhardt)
Pittsburgh Post, Oct. 29, 1917 (Mantell); Jan. 13, 1923 (Mantell)
Philadelphia Times, April 15, 1896 (Irving)
Public Advertiser, Feb. 14, 1875 (Siddons)
Punch, April 11, 1934 (Laughton); Dec. 31, 1947 (M. Redgrave/Burrill)
Reader, Nov. 12, 19, 1864 (Faucit/Siddons)

Saturday Review, May 20, 1876 (Rossi); March 15, 1884 (Salvini); June 14, 1884 (Bernhardt); Jan. 5, 1889 (Terry); Oct. 1, 1898 (Forbes-Robertson); U.S.: April 17, 1948 (Redgrave)
Scotsman, Feb. 28, 1825 (Kean); April 6, 1876 (Salvini); June 25, 1884 (Bernhardt)
Sheffield Iris, n.d. (Macready)
Sketch, June 8, 1955 (Olivier)
Spectator, Oct. 2, 1875 (Irving); Aug. 12, 1966 (Clements); Oct. 28, 1966 (Guinness)
Spirit of the Times, April 2, 1870 (Booth)
Sporting Gazette, Oct. 2, 1875 (Irving)
Stratford-Upon-Avon Herald, April 22, 1927 (Walter)
Summary, July 12, 1884 (Bernhardt)
Sun, Nov. 7, 1814 (Kean); April 1, 1948 (Robson)
Sunday Express, Oct. 23, 1955 (Joe Macbeth)
Sunday Times, July 5, 1840 (Kemble); Nov. 6, 1864 (Faucit); March 23, 1930 (Gielgud); April 8, 1934 (Laughton); Dec. 6, 1937 (Olivier); July 12, 1942 (Gielgud); Dec. 21, 1947 (Redgrave); June 12, 1955 (Olivier); June 10, 1962 (Porter); Aug., 1966 (Clements); Aug. 20, 1967 (Merchant); Jan. 7, 1968 (Merchant)
Stage, Sept. 7, 1911 (Tree); April 27, 1933 (Komisarjevsky); Dec. 2, 1937 (Anderson); June 7, 1962 (Porter)
Standard, March 10, 1884 (Salvini)
Star, March 20, 1953 (Wolfit)
Studio, n.d., 1884 (Bernhardt)
Sydney Morning Herald, Oct. 23, 1875 (Ristori)
Tallis Dramatic Magazine, November, 1850 (Macready)
Teatr i Zhizn, Jan. 19, 1890 (Russia)
Teatralny Almanakh, 1947 (Russia)
Theatrical Inquisitor, Nov. 1814 (Kean); July 1820 (Macready)
Theatrical Journal, Aug. 8, 1840 (Macready)
Time and Tide, July 18, 1942 (Gielgud); Dec. 27, 1947 (Redgrave)
Times, Aug. 1, 1866; Aug. 11, 1866; May 12, 1876 (Pareti); Dec. 31, 1888 (Terry); Sept. 6, 1911 (Vanbrugh); May 17, 1923 (Green); April 21, 1927 (Green/Walter); June 6, 1962 (Porter); June 11, 1952 (Richardson); Nov. 20, 1973 (Sheila Allen)
Torquay Times, July 11, 1884 (Bernhardt)
Tribune, Oct. 26, 1874 (Cushman); April 30, 1876 (Salvini); July 28, 1955 (Olivier)
Universal Review, Jan. 15, 1889 (Terry)
Vanity Fair, Sept. 13, 1911 (Tree)
Yorkshire Post, March 18, 1942 (Gielgud/Ffrangcon-Davies)

Act II, Scene iii

BOOKS, ARTICLES AND PERSONAL REPORTS

Anderson, personal discussion
Boaden, (1) 310 (Siddons)
Brooks, 191
Brown, J. R., (2) 48
Capell, *op. cit.*
Coghill, (1) 177ff.
Clarence, 92 (Irving)
Coleman, (1) 226–27 (C. Kean, Irving, Salvini)
Craig, G., (6)
Craig, E. C., personal discussion, promptbook
Danks, (2) 289
David, 129 (Olivier, Rogers)
Dukore, personal report
Duthie, (1) 26
Fischer, 364 (Reinecke)
Faucit, 234ff.
Garrick, (3) 135–36
Gentleman, (2) 91
Gibbs, personal discussion
Got, letter (Poland)
Granville-Barker, *Preface*
Gryzmala-Siedlecki (Modjeska, Poland)
Hall, (See Rosenberg [2])
Harcourt, 393ff.
Hotson, 196–97
Hulme, 722
Huntley, (1) 390
Irving, (2) 98
James, H., 177 (Salvini)
Kittredge, edition
Lubowski, E., 20f. (Modjeska, Poland)
Maginn, *op. cit.*
Milward, personal discussion (Japanese stagings)
Muir, edition
Mullin, *op. cit.*
Murray, 34ff.
Nagarajan, 375
Nicoll, 120f.
Phelps, *op. cit.* (Phelps)
Quiller-Couch, 33ff.
Rabkin, (2) *op. cit.*
Robinson, E., personal report (Olivier, Leigh)
Ristori, *op. cit.*
Sarcey, *op. cit.*
Scott, *op. cit.* (Kemble)
Stebbins, *op. cit.* (Cushman)
Terry, notes
Walker, 74
Wickham, G. (2) 68f.
Williamson, A., (2) 110 (Rogers)
Unidentified sources

PROMPTBOOKS

Shattuck: 8, 15, 25, 27, 29, 44, 47, 48, 53, 54, 59, 63, 66, 70, 77, 108, 116, 118, 122, 123, 127, 133, 137, 144, 146

PERIODICALS

Athenaeum, July 11, 1857 (Ristori); Oct. 2, 1875 (Bateman); March 15, 1884 (Salvini)
Belfast Newsletter, Oct. 19, 1802 (Siddons); Feb. 20, 1824 (Macready)
Bell's Weekly Messenger, Oct. 2, 1875 (Irving/Bateman)
Birmingham Post, Aug. 25, 1954 (Rogers)
Boston Daily Advertiser, April 22, 1881 (Salvini)
Boston Evening Transcript, Nov. 15, 1910 (Sothern/Marlowe); Dec. 21, 1934 (Hampden)
Boston Herald, April 22, 1896 (Irving)
Christian Science Monitor, June 3, 1967 (Sole production, Mexico)
Daily Chronicle, Dec. 31, 1888 (Irving)
Daily Mail, June 8, 1955 (Olivier); April 5, 1973 (Quilley)
Daily News, July 5, 1884 (Bernhardt); Dec. 31, 1888 (Irving)
Daily Telegraph, March 6, 1975 (Williamson)
Dramatic Review, Feb. 9, 1852; Jan. 5, 1889 (Terry)
Dublin Evening Herald, June 6, 1972 (Brandenberg production, East Germany, Müller version)
English Illustrated Magazine, Dec., 1888 (Siddons)
Era, Jan. 5, 1889 (Irving); Oct. 15, 1898 (Forbes-Robertson)
Evening News, Nov. 14, 1969
Evening Standard, Sept. 27, 1875 (Irving); Dec. 31, 1888 (Irving); Dec. 19, 1947 (M. Redgrave); Sept. 6, 1911 (Tree)
Examiner, Oct. 2, 1875
John O'London's Weekly, May 13, 1949 (Tearle)
Listener, Feb. 2, 1967 (Terry)
Lloyd's Weekly London Newspaper, Oct. 9, 1875 (Irving)
Mail and Express, Oct. 31, 1895 (Irving)
Malvern Gazette, Oct. 31, 1974 (Williamson)
Morning Advertiser, July 5, 1884 (Bernhardt)
Morning Herald, Feb. 15, 1853 (C. Kean)
Morning Post, Nov. 7, 1814 (Kean); July 4, 1857 (Ristori)
New South Wales Agriculturist and Grazier, Oct., 1875 (Ristori)
New Statesman, Aug. 12, 1966 (Porter)

New York Herald, Nov. 10, 1895 (Irving)
New York Herald Tribune, Nov. 23, 1941 (Anderson)
New York Press, Nov. 3, 1895 (Irving)
New York Times, Oct. 17, 1871 (Cushman); Dec. 29, 1888 (Irving); Jan. 22, 1889 (Coghlan/Langtry); Feb. 8, 1916 (Hackett); April 20, 1921 (Hampden); July 15, 1973 (Weaver)
New York Tribune, Jan. 22, 1899 (Coghlan)
New York World, Jan. 22, 1889 (Coghlan)
Notes and Queries, July 13, 1889 (C. Kean)
Observer, Feb. 26, 1844 (C. Kean); Feb. 24, 1845 (Forrest); July 5, 1857 (Ristori); Aug. 7, 1966 (Clements/Johnston); Aug. 20, 1967 (Scofield)
Overland Monthly, Feb., 1886 (McKee Rankin)
Pittsburgh Dispatch, Dec. 4, 1920 (Mantell)
Punch, April 11, 1934 (Laughton); June 4, 1969
Queen, Jan. 5, 1889 (Irving)
Revue d'Art Dramatique, June–Sept., 1889 (Irving/Terry)
Saint James Chronicle, Oct. 30, 1773 (Garrick)
Saturday Review, July 8, 1882 (Ristori)
Scotsman, March 20, 1850 (Phelps); Aug. 25, 1954 (Rogers)
Spectator, July 17, 1942 (Gielgud); Jan. 12, 1968 (Scofield)

Stage, Jan. 4, 1889 (Irving); Sept. 7, 1911 (Tree); Dec. 6, 1928 (Craig); April 5, 1934 (Laughton); Dec. 24, 1947 (M. Redgrave); n.d. (Faucit, Siddons)
Stockholmstidningen, Nov. 20, 1944 (Bergman, Sweden)
Stratford-Upon-Avon Herald, April 27, 1924; June 8, 1962 (Porter/Worth)
Sunday Times, July 6, 1884 (Bernhardt); July 5, 1840 (F. Kemble); June 12, 1955 (Olivier); Aug. 20, 1967 (Merchant)
Sydney Morning Herald, Oct. 23, 1875 (Ristori)
Theatrical Journal, April 2, 1842 (Macready); April 19, 1916 (Irving)
Times, Sept. 6, 1911 (Tree); Feb. 7, 1928 (Maturin); March 25, 1954 (Rogers); Sept. 10, 1954 (Rogers); June 6, 1962 (Porter); Aug. 3, 1966 (Johnston); April 5, 1973 (Quilley)
Weekly Dispatch, Sept. 18, 1898 (Irving)
Weekly Times and Echo, Dec. 30, 1888 (Irving)
Unidentified clippings: Feb. 14, 1853 (C. Kean); Dec. 31, 1888 (Terry); Nov. 12, 1910 (Sothern); Dec. 11, 1910 (Sothern)
Other unidentified clippings

Act II, Scene iv

BOOK

Chambers, edition

PROMPTBOOKS

Shattuck: 8, 29, 108, 118, 122, 123, 133, 144

PERIODICALS

John O'London's Weekly, May 13, 1949 (Tearle)
Saint James Chronicle, Oct. 30, 1773 (Garrick)
Sunday Times, Nov. 6, 1864 (Phelps)
Teatralny Almanakh, 1947 (Juriev, Russia)

Act III, Scene i

BOOKS, ARTICLES AND PERSONAL REPORTS

Agate, (1) 223, 228 (Gielgud)
Bab, *op. cit.* (Matkowsky)
Chambers, E. K., edition
David, 120, 127–29 (Rogers, Olivier)
Dench, personal discussion
Dent., A., (3) 50
Finlay, 248ff. (Kean)
Foakes, edition
Garrick, (2); (3) 358–59
Gibbs, personal discussion
Granville-Barker, *Preface*

Got, (2) 87 (Modjeska)
Harwood, letter
Heilman, (1) 14ff.
Johnson, Dr., edition
Kemble, J. P., *op. cit.*
Loeb, *op. cit.* (George, Germany, 1928)
Mack, Jr., 169f.
Mansfield, 132, 165–66
Marshall, *op. cit.* (Aldridge)
Morley, 354
Muir, (3)
Parrott, edition
Paul, (2) 198
Robinson, E., personal report (Olivier, Leigh)

Sanders, (1) 257
Shaw, Byam, notes
Siddons, *op. cit.*
Skeat, see *Variorum*
Steevens, edition
Terry, notes
Williamson, A., (2) 110 (Rogers)
Winter, (7) 458, 488 (Salvini)
Wilson, J. D., edition
Woodvine, personal discussion

PROMPTBOOKS

Shattuck: 8, 70, 77, 108, 118, 122, 123, 127,
133, 137, 142, 144

PERIODICALS

Academy, Dec. 23, 1876 (Irving)
Athenaeum, Jan. 5, 1889 (Irving)
Belfast Newsletter, Oct. 19, 1802 (Siddons)
Blackwood's Edinburgh Magazine, Sept., 1834
(Siddons)
Boston Globe, April 22, 1896 (Irving)
Christian Science Monitor, June 18, 1955 (Olivier)
Chicago Tribune, June 19, 1962 (Plummer)
Combat, April 29, 1965 (TEP Production,
France)
Dagens Nyheter, March 18, 1967 (Lundh,
Sweden)
Daily Chronicle, Dec. 3, 1888 (Irving)
Daily News, March 10, 1884 (Salvini)
Daily Telegraph, Nov. 5, 1864 (Phelps); Jan. 1,
1889 (Irving); April 5, 1973 (Quilley)
Dublin Evening Mail, Nov. 4, 1846 (Faucit)
Edinburgh Dramatic Review, Jan. 13, 1825 (John
Vandenhoff)
Evening News, July 5, 1884 (Marais)
Evening Standard, Sept. 27, 1875 (Irving); Sept.
19, 1898 (Forbes-Robertson)

Examiner, Dec. 3, 1864 (Faucit)
Figaro, Jan. 20, 1954 (Chabrol prod., France)
Financial Times, Sept. 11, Nov. 10, 1969
Kaleidoscope, July 17, 1821 (Macready)
Leamington Spa Courier, June 10, 1955 (Olivier)
Le Theatre, 1909–1910 (Maeterlinck prod.,
France)
London Magazine, Jan., 1967 (Guinness)
Magazine of Art, vol. 4, 1881 (Irving)
Morning Advertiser, June 15, 1955 (Olivier)
Morning Post, April 19, 1933 (Komisarjevsky)
München Merkur, vol. 15, 1803 (Germany)
New Statesman, April 23, 1949 (Tearle); Nov.
17, 1972 (Rigg); Nov. 8, 1974 (Williamson)
New York Press, Nov. 3, 1895 (Irving)
New York Tribune, Oct. 24, 1897 (Haworth/
Modjeska), see also E. Booth
New York Times, Dec. 11, 1910 (Sothern); Nov.
24, 1941 (Evans); July 15, 1973 (Weaver)
North British Daily Mail, Dec. 6, 1870 (Faucit)
Observer, Feb. 12, 1928 (Maturin); Aug. 7, 1966
(Clements)
Rand Daily Mail, Aug. 21, 1970 (see Theatre
Bibliography III, South African productions)
Scotsman, July 14, 1962 (Porter); Sept. 7, 19,
Nov. 2, 1974 (Williamson)
Spectator, Jan., 1968 (Scofield)
Stage, Sept. 7, 1911 (Tree); Dec. 6, 1928 (Craig)
Sunday Times, Dec. 30, 1888 (Irving); June 12,
1955 (Olivier)
Theater Heute, June, 1966 (Reincke, Germany)
Theatre Magazine, April 19, 1916 (Irving)
Theatre Quarterly, vol. I, no. 3, 1971 (Olivier)
Times, June 15, 1955 (Olivier); April 5, 1973
(Quilley); Oct. 31, 1974 (Williamson)
Toronto Daily Star, June 19, 1962 (Plummer)
Western Daily Mercury, July 7, 1884 (Marais)
Unidentified clippings: June 8, 1955 (Olivier);
Oct. 26, 1895 (Irving)
Other unidentified clippings

Act III, Scene ii

**BOOKS, ARTICLES AND PERSONAL
REPORTS**

Agate, (1) 219, 276
Alger, 744 (Forrest)
Anglin, letter to Gordon Craig
Bell, *op. cit.*
Brown, J. R., (1) 149 (Worth)
Clapp, 85–86 (Cushman)
Craig, G., (6)
David, *op. cit.*
Durylin, 323–25 (Ermolova, Russia)
Faucit, *op. cit.*
Favorini, *op. cit.* (Mantell)
Fletcher, (1) 38 (Siddons)

Gould, 128f. (J. B. Booth)
Granville-Barker, *Preface*
Halio, edition
Harbage, (3) 387ff.
Henn, 25
Ihering, (Germany, 1927–28)
Kemble, F., (4)
Mahood, 137, 140
Marston, J. W., 78 (Macready)
Planché, 23
Richter, 196f. (Wolter, Germany)
Robinson, E., personal report (Olivier, Leigh)
Robson, F., Introduction, *passim*
Siddons, *op. cit.*
Terry, notes

Theobald, edition
Winter, (7) 491 (Vandenhoff)
Unidentified sources

PROMPTBOOKS

Shattuck: 8, 66, 70, 118, 122, 123, 137, 144, 146

PERIODICALS

Athenaeum, July 11, 1857 (Ristori)
Birmingham Weekly Post, June 10, 1955 (Olivier)
Blackwood's Edinburgh Magazine, Sept., 1834 (Siddons)
Chicago Daily News, April 28, 1942 (Evans/ Anderson)
Chicago Sun Times, Feb. 13, 1957 (Rogers/ Browne)
Combat, July 23, 1954 (Vilar, France)
Country Life, March 29, 1930 (Gielgud)
Daily Chronicle, Dec. 31, 1888 (Irving)
Daily Mail, April 5, 1973 (Quilley/Rigg)
Dublin Evening Mail, Nov. 4, 1846 (Faucit)
Edinburgh Dramatic Review, Jan. 13, 1825 (John Vandenhoff)
Examiner, Oct. 5, 1835 (Macready); Dec. 3, 1864 (Phelps/Faucit); Oct. 2, 1875 (Irving)
Figaro Littéraire, Aug. 11, 1962 (France)
Financial Times, June 6, 1962 (Porter/Worth)
Illustrated London News, Jan. 3, 1852 (Glyn)
Lady, June 26, 1952 (Richardson)
Listener, March 29, 1933 (Hunt); Feb. 2, 1967 (Irving/Terry)

Morning Post, Sept. 27, 1875 (Irving)
New York Times, Nov, 19, 1889 (Booth/Modjeska); Dec. 11, 1910 (Marlowe)
New York Woman's Magazine, Feb., 1896
News Chronicle, April 23, 25, 1949 (Tearle)
North British Daily Mail, Nov. 4, 1846 (Faucit)
Nottingham Journal, June 6, 1962 (Porter/ Worth)
Observer, Dec. 26, 1926 (Ainley/Thorndike); Aug. 7, 1966 (Clements); April 8, 1973 (Quilley)
Pittsburgh Gazette, April 22, 1868 (Forrest)
Queen, Jan. 5, 1889 (Irving)
Scotsman, July 14, 1962 (Worth)
Spectator, Oct. 2, 1875 (Bateman)
Stage, Sept. 11, 1911 (Tree); Dec. 6, 1928 (Craig)
Stratford-upon-Avon Herald, April 22, 1927 (Green)
Tallis Dramatic Review, Nov., 1850 (Macready)
Theatre, Dec. 1, 1888 (Siddons)
Times, July 9, 1942 (Gielgud); March 20, 1953 (Wolfit); June 8, 1955 (Olivier); Sept. 5, 1957 (Littlewood)
Tribune, Oct. 20, 1871; Oct. 26, 1874 (Cushman)
Universal Review, Jan. 15, 1889 (Terry)
Yorkshire Post, March 18, 1942 (Gielgud/ Ffrangcon-Davies)
Unidentified clippings: March 14, 1853 (Mrs. Kean); Dec. 28, 1870 (Glyn); Sept. 6, 1911 (Tree); Nov. 15, 1941 (Evans/Anderson), 1955 (Olivier)
Other unidentified clippings

Act III, Scene iii

BOOKS, ARTICLES AND PERSONAL REPORTS

Evans, G. B., op. cit.
Forman, op. cit.
Gentleman, (2) 94
Hodek, letters (Czechoslovakia)
Irving (4) 328–29
Koneczeny, op. cit. (Modjeska, Poland, 1890)
Unidentified sources

PROMPTBOOKS

Shattuck: 106, 108

PERIODICALS

Beckman and Penge Advertiser, Oct. 19, 1966 (Guinness)
Daily Chronicle, Aug. 25, 1909 (Maeterlinck)
L'Europa, March 12, 1953 (Italy)
Financial Times, Oct. 21, 1966 (Guinness)
Il Giornale d'Italia, Feb. 26, 1953 (Italy)
Morning Post, April 19, 1933 (Komisarjevsky)
New York Times, Oct. 23, 1966 (Guinness)
Observer, Oct. 23, 1853 (Brooke); Sept. 5, 1957 (Littlewood prod.); Aug. 7, 1966 (Clements)
Saint James Chronicle, Oct. 30, 1773 (Garrick)
Scotsman, March 16, 1974
Sunday Telegraph, Aug. 7, 1966 (Clements)
Times, May 22, 1966 (Guinness)

Act III, Scene iv

Note: "Books and Articles" are in two parts: "Promptbooks" and "Periodicals" combine the two parts.

Act III, Scene iv

BOOKS, ARTICLES AND PERSONAL
REPORTS: Part 1

Agate, (1) 231ff. (Laughton), 238 (ghost), 242
   (Olivier)
Akutagawa, Milward interview
Alger, 744 (Forrest)
Baty, op. cit.
Bell, op. cit.
Black, J. personal discussion
Boaden, (1) 312 (Siddons, Pritchard), 411ff.
   (Kemble)
Brown, J. R., (1) 148–49 (Worth)
Byrne, see Price, J., 39ff.
Craig, G., (1) 279; (5)
Curry, 67ff.
Davies, (1) 148; (2) 184 (Garrick, Pritchard)
Dench, personal discussion
Falk, op. cit. (Reuss prod., Germany, 1928)
Farjeon, 57, 137f. (Laughton)
Farnham, (1) 123ff.
Favorini, op. cit. (Mantell)
Finlay, 282 (Kemble, Kean, Macready)
Fitzgerald, (5) 39–40
Fontane, 100 (Phelps)
Galt, 304 (Siddons)
Garrick, (1); (3) 20, 134–36
Gibbs, personal discussion (Gielgud)
Got, (2) 77 (Smochowski), 87–88 (Modjeska)
Guglia, 86 (Mitterwurzer, Germany)
Hall, see Rosenberg (2)
Hübner (Poland, 1958)
Irving, (5)
Jekels, (2) 371ff.
Kean, C., see Cole, 380f.
Kemble, F., (2) 67
Knights, (1) 25
Le Loyer, 1a
Lennam, personal discussion
Loginova, 20–21 (Tsarev, Gogoleva, Russia,
   1955)
Mangin, 85
Martin, (1) 177ff. (Faucit)
Milward, (Kumo prod.)
Neiderle, 120ff. (Wolter)
Oulton, 140 (J. P. Kemble)
Pollock, Lady, 120 (Macready)
Price, W. T., (1) 154 (Cushman)
Pückler-Muskau, 219 (Macready)
Quiller-Couch, 14–15
Rank, 219 (see Holland)
Rees, 266 (Forrest)
Richter, 191 (Wolter, Germany)
Ristori, op. cit.
Robinson, E., personal report (Olivier, Leigh)
Robson, F. Introduction

Russell, C. E., 484ff. (Sothern, Marlowe)
Russell, E. R., (1) 425–26 (Macready, Irving)
Sanders, (1) 257, 261ff.
Segond-Weber, op. cit.
Shaw, Byam, notes
Siddons, op. cit.
Smollett, see Buck, 155
Sprague, A. C., (1) 154
Stevenson, review (Salvini)
Stoll, 107, 206
Terry, notes
Towse, 41 (Phelps), 155 (Morris), 211 (Janau-
   schek), 302 (Irving)
Williamson, A., (2) 111 (Rogers); (3) 271 (Giel-
   gud), 273 (Clunes)
Wingate, 211 (Langtry)
Winter, (2) 190 (Booth); (7) 453 (Macready),
   480ff. (Irving), 488 (Salvini), 496 (Mantell),
   512 (Terry)
Unidentified sources

BOOKS, ARTICLES AND PERSONAL
REPORTS: Part 2

Agate, (1) 231–32 (Laughton), 242 (Olivier)
Alger, 744 (Forrest)
Bab, loc. cit. (Matkowsky)
Bell, op. cit.
Black, J. personal discussion
Boaden, (1) 312 (Siddons); (2) 409ff. (J. P.
   Kemble)
Brooks, 197ff.
Brown, J. R., (1) 148–49 (Worth)
Coghill, (1) 963
Coleman, (1) 226ff. (C. Kean), 228 (Salvini),
   279 (Cooke), 285 (Macklin)
Craig, E. C., personal discussion, notebooks
Davies, (1), 148; (2) 184 (Garrick, Pritchard)
Dent, R., edition
Favorini, op. cit. (Mantell)
Galt, 304 (Siddons)
Gielgud, (2)
Got, (2) 77 (Smochowski), 87–88 (Modjeska)
Grein, (1) op. cit.
Guglia, 86 (Mitterwurzer)
Hall, see Rosenberg (2)
Hawkins, (1) 274 (Kean)
James, H., 37 (Irving), 47 (Rossi)
Kemble, F., (2) 67
Maeterlinck, Mme., op. cit.
Libby, op. cit.
Martin, op. cit., (1) (Faucit)
Nicoll, 120
Redgrave, 135
Ridley, (New Temple Shakespeare)

Ristori, *op. cit.*
Robinson, E., personal report (Olivier, Leigh)
Schanzer, 225
Shaw, Byam, notes
Siddons, *op. cit.*
Stevenson, review (Salvini)
Terry, notes; letter, Folger Library
Unidentified sources

PROMPTBOOKS: Parts 1 and 2 combined

Shattuck: 8, 13, 25, 27, 28, 44, 47, 48, 59, 63,
   66, 68, 70, 77, 106, 108, 109, 112, 118, 122,
   123, 127, 133, 137, 144, 146

PERIODICALS: Parts 1 and 2 combined

Academy, April 15, 1876 (Salvini); May 13,
   1876 (Rossi); Jan. 5, 1889 (Terry)
Aftonbladet, Nov. 20, 1944 (Bergman, Sweden)
Albion, Liverpool, Oct. 20, 27, 1866 (Ristori)
Athenaeum, March 1, 1845 (Forrest); Oct. 2,
   1847 (Phelps); Oct. 5, 1850 (Phelps); Oct. 2,
   1875 (Irving); July 8, 1882 (Rignold); March
   15, 1884 (Salvini); Jan. 5, 1889 (Irving)
Atlas, July 11, 1840 (C. Kean)
Belfast Newsletter, Oct. 19, 1802 (Siddons); Feb.
   20, 1824 (Macready)
Belgravia, Nov., 1875 (Irving)
Bell's Weekly Messenger, Oct. 2, 1875 (Irving)
Birmingham Daily Post, Dec. 31, 1888 (Irving)
Birmingham Gazette, April 20, 1927 (Walter/
   Green)
Birmingham Mail, June 6, 1962 (Porter)
Birmingham Post, April 19, 1933 (Komisarjev-
   sky); May 20, 1942 (Gielgud); Sept. 24, 1947
   (Wolfit); June 15, 1955 (Olivier); June 6,
   1962 (Porter/Worth)
Blackwood's Edinburgh Magazine, June, 1843
   (Siddons)
Boston Daily Advertiser, Oct. 13, 1875 (Irving);
   April 22, 1881 (Salvini); Nov. 15, 1910
   (Sothern/Marlowe)
Boston Record, July 31, 1959 (Robards/McKenna)
Boston Transcript, Nov. 7, 1866 (Ristori); April
   29, 1904 (O'Neil); Nov. 15, 1910 (Marlowe);
   Nov. 16, 1910 (Sothern/Marlowe); n.d. (Jan-
   auschek); March 18, 1921 (Barrymore);
   Sept. 17, 1935 (Merivale)
Boston Traveler, Oct. 28, 1941 (Evans)
Brooklyn Daily Eagle, Nov. 25, 1874 (Morris/
   Cushman); Nov. 28, 1874 (Morris)
Chicago Daily News, March 2, 1906 (Mantell)
Chicago Tribune, March 9, 1873 (Booth); June
   19, 1962 (Plummer)
Christian Science Monitor, June 18, 1955 (Olivier/
   Leigh); June 3, 1967 (Mexico)
Comoedia, Dec. 12, 1942 (Baty, France)

Court Circular, Oct. 2, 1875 (Irving); July 12,
   1884 (Marais/Bernhardt); July 27, 1895 (Ir-
   ving)
Court Journal, Jan. 5, 1889 (Terry)
Coventry Evening Telegraph, June 11, 1952
   (Richardson, Gielgud)
Critical Review, March, 1816 (Kean); March,
   1861 (C. Kean)
Current Literature, Aug., 1906 (Morris)
Czas, 1891 (Modjeska, Poland)
Dagens Nyheter, Nov. 20, 1944 (Bergman,
   Sweden)
Daily Alta California, Oct. 22, 1876 (Booth)
Daily Chronicle, Aug. 25, 1909 (Maeterlinck);
   Feb. 7, 1928 (Maturin)
Daily Mail, Sept. 19, 1898 (Campbell); Sept. 6,
   1911 (Tree); June 8, 1955 (Olivier); April 5,
   1973 (Quilley); March 6, 1975 (Williamson)
Daily Mirror, Feb. 8, 1928 (Maturin)
Daily News, July 4, 1857 (Ristori); Sept. 27,
   1875 (Irving); Sept. 5, 1884 (Bernhardt);
   Dec. 31, 1888 (Irving); Feb. 8, 1928 (Maturin)
Daily Telegraph, Dec. 31, 1888 (Irving/Terry);
   Sept. 19, 1898 (Irving); Sept. 6–7, 1911
   (Tree); Dec. 20, 1961; Feb. 19, 1971; Oct. 3,
   1974
De Groene Amsterdammer, Nov. 25, 1916 (Neth-
   erlands)
Dramatic Censor, 1810 (Garrick/Pritchard); 1811
   (Siddons)
The Drama or Theatrical Magazine, Oct., 1824
Drury Lane Journal, March, 1752 (Mrs. Cibber)
Echo, Sept. 27, 1875 (Irving)
Edinburgh Courant, see Theatre Bibliography I
   for Siddons; Nov. 20, 1815; April 6, 1876
   (Salvini)
Edinburgh Dramatic Review, Feb. 9, 1824, Feb.
   22, 1825, (John Vandenhoff)
English Chronicle and Whitehall Evening Post,
   June 10, 1820 (Macready)
English Illustrated Magazine, Dec., 1888 (Mac-
   ready, Mrs. Pritchard, J. P. Kemble)
Era, May 14, 1876 (Rossi); July 8, 1882 (Ris-
   tori); Jan. 5, 1889 (Terry)
European Magazine, July, 1812 (Siddons)
Evening News, March 10, 1884 (Salvini)
Evening Standard, Aug. 27, 1875 (Irving);
   March 10, 1884 (Salvini); July 5, 1884 (Bern-
   hardt); Sept. 27, 1875 (Irving); Dec. 31, 1888
   (Irving); Sept. 19, 1898 (Forbes-Robertson);
   Sept. 6, 1911 (Tree); April 22, 1949 (Tearle/
   Wynyard); June 13, 1952 (Richardson)
Evesham Journal, April 23, 1949 (Tearle)
Examiner, Jan. 15, 1809 (Kemble); June 16,
   1816 (Siddons); Oct. 4, 5, 1835 (Macready);
   Oct. 2, 1875 (Irving); Oct. 21, 1875 (Irving)
Figaro, March 15, 1884 (Salvini); June 23, 1958
   (Festival D'Angiers, France)

Financial Times, Aug. 25, 1954 (Rogers/Todd); June 6, 1962 (Porter/Worth); April 7, 1973 (Quilley)

Flattery and Truth, Feb. 14, 1853 (Kean)

Frankfurter Allgemeine Zeitung, Dec. 5, 1955 (Darmstadt prod.)

Freeman's Journal, Dec. 16, 1846 (Faucit)

Galveston Daily News, Jan. 26, 1883 (Booth)

Gazette de France, May 24, 1884 (Bernhardt)

Glasgow Herald, Feb. 19, 1861 (Faucit)

Globe, April 20, 1921 (Hampden)

Goteborgs Handels & Sjofarts Tidning, March 18, 1967 (Sweden)

Graphic, Oct. 2, 1875 (Irving); March 6, 1890

Guardian, April 23, 1964 (Clements/Wilson); Sept. 20, 1970; Nov. 10, 1972 (Hopkins/Rigg); Oct. 20, 1976 (Tutin)

Illustrated London News, Oct. 16, 1875 (Macready)

Illustrated Sporting and Dramatic News, July, 1884 (Bernhardt)

Irish Times, Nov. 1, 1974 (Williamson)

John O'London's Weekly, May 13, 1949 (Tearle/Wynyard)

Kaleidoscope, July 17, 1821 (Macready)

Lady, Nov. 14, 1974 (Mirren)

Lady's Pictorial, Jan. 5, 1889 (Terry); n.d. (Macready)

Leamington Spa Courier, June 10, 1955 (Olivier)

Life, March 13, 1884 (Salvini)

Listener, March 29, 1933 (Gielgud/Hunt); Feb. 2, 1967 (Terry/Siddons)

Literary Gazette, June 17, 1820 (Macready); Nov. 8, 1823 (Macready)

Liverpool Daily Post, June 20, 1884 (Bernhardt); Dec. 31, 1888 (Irving/Terry)

Lloyd's Weekly London Newspaper, March 4, 1850 (Glyn)

London Magazine, Jan., 1967 (Guinness)

Lumír (Czechoslovakia), 1858

Magazine of Art, 1889 (Irving)

Maly Theatre, the Year Book of, (*Ezkegodnik Malogo Teatra*), 1955–56 (Tsarev, Russia)

Manchester Courier, Feb. 16, 1853 (C. Kean); Nov. 15, 1871 (Faucit); n.d. (Kean); Sept. 19, 1898 (Siddons)

Manchester Guardian, April 20, 1933 (Komisarjevsky prod.); Nov. 23, 1937 (Wolfit); June 19, 1942 (Gielgud); April 18, 1949 (Tearle/Wynyard)

Manchester Herald, n.d. (Macready)

Mask, vol. 15, 1929 (Craig)

Le Monde, June 19, 1952 (France)

Monthly Mirror, 1798; Dec. 1803 (Kemble); Nov. 11, 1807 (Kemble); 1808; 1809 (Kemble)

Morning Advertiser, April 10, 1854 (Salvini); July 5, 1884 (Bernhardt)

Morning Chronicle, April 22, 1794 (Kemble); Feb. 16, 1853 (C. Kean)

Morning Leader, Sept. 6, 1911 (Tree)

Morning Post, June 10, 1816 (Siddons); Feb. 16, 1853 (C. Kean); Sept. 27, 1875 (Irving); July 25, 1895 (Irving); Sept. 6, 1911 (Tree); April 19, 1933 (Komisarjevsky prod.); April 3, 1934 (Laughton)

New Mirror, Dec. 9, 1843 (Macready)

New Statesman, July 18, 1942 (Gielgud); June 21, 1952 (Richardson); Aug. 12, 1966 (Clements); Nov. 8, 1974 (Williamson)

New York Clipper, Feb. 19, 1881 (Salvini)

New York Dispatch, Nov. 3, 1895 (Irving)

New York Herald, May 12, 1881 (Salvini); Nov. 10, 1895 (Irving); Feb. 18, 1921 (Barrymore)

New York Herald Tribune, Nov. 19, 1889 (Modjeska); April 1, 1948 (Redgrave/Robson); June 20, 1962 (Plummer)

New York Post, Jan. 22, 1833 (Forrest); Aug. 30, 1895 (Irving)

New York Press, Nov. 3, 1895 (Irving)

New York Telegraph, March 17, 1924 (Hackett/Eames)

New York Times, Jan. 24, 1885 (Booth); Dec. 29, 1888 (Irving/Terry); 1889 (Coghlan/Langtry); Oct. 30, 1895 (Irving); Dec. 11, 1910 (Marlowe/Sothern); Feb. 8, 1916 (Hackett/Allen); Nov. 20, 1928 (Craig prod.); April 15, 1936 (Welles); April 11, 1948 (M. Redgrave/Robson); June 20, 1962 (Plummer); Oct. 23, 1966 (Guinness)

New York Tribune, Nov. 18, 1889 (Booth); Nov. 14, 1905 (Forrest)

New York World, Jan. 22, 1889 (Coghlan); April 20, 1921 (Hampden)

New Yorker, April 10, 1948 (M. Redgrave/Robson)

News, Nov. 13, 1814 (Kean); March 19, 1924 (Hackett)

News Chronicle, Nov. 27, 1937 (Anderson); June 11, 1952 (Gielgud prod.)

North British Daily Mail, Dec. 6, 1846 (Faucit)

Notes and Queries, July 13, 1889 (C. Kean)

Novaya Petrogradskaya Gazeta, July 26, 1918 (Juriev, Russia)

Le Nouvel Observateur, June 5, 1965 (France)

Observer, April 8, 1823 (Kean/Macready); Feb. 26, 1844 (C. Kean); Feb. 26, 1844 (Kemble); Feb. 24, 1845 (Forrest); Oct. 2, 1875 (Irving); March 9, 1884 (Salvini); Sept. 18, 1898 (Forbes-Robertson); Sept. 10, 1911 (Tree); Dec. 2, 1928 (German prod.); June 5, 1955 (Olivier); Sept. 5, 1957 (Littlewood); Aug. 7, 1966 (Clements); Oct. 23, 1966 (Guinness)

Overland Monthly, Feb., 1886 (Rankin)

Pall-Mall Gazette, July 5, 1884 (Marais/Bernhardt)

Petrogradskaja Pravda, no. 212 (Juriev, Russia)

Philadelphia Evening Bulletin, Nov. 27, 1941 (Evans)

Pittsburgh Post, Oct. 9, 1913 (Mantell)

Pittsburgh Sun-Telegraph, April 2, 1929 (Craig); May 7, 1929 (Leiber)

Plays and Players, Feb., 1967 (Guinness); May, 1974 (Williamson)

Punch, April 11, 1934 (Laughton); July 22, 1942 (Ffrangcon-Davies); Dec. 31, 1947 (M. Redgrave); Aug. 10, 1966 (Clements)

Queen, June 8, 1882 (Ristori); Jan. 5, 1889 (Irving)

Referee, Dec. 30, 1888 (Irving)

Revue d'Art Dramatique, June–Sept., 1889 (Irving/Terry)

Saint James Gazette, Sept. 31, 1875 (Bateman); Dec. 31, 1888 (Irving)

San Francisco Chronicle, Oct. 22, 1876 (Booth)

San Francisco Daily Post, Oct. 21, 1876 (Booth)

Saturday Review, July 11, 1857 (Ristori); Dec., 1861 (Barry Sullivan); May 20 1876 (Rossi); June 14, 1884 (Bernhardt); March 15, 1884 (Salvini; U.S., April 17, 1948 (Redgrave)

Scotsman, Feb. 29, 1825 (Kean); April 6, 1876 (Salvini; Nov. 2, 1974 (Williamson)

Le Siecle, Oct. 26, 1884 (Marais/Bernhardt)

Sovetskoe Iskusstvo, Sept. 22, 1940 (Simonov, Russia)

Soviet News, Oct., 1955 (Gogoleva, Russia)

Spectator, Oct. 2, 1875 (Irving/Bateman); Jan. 5, 1889 (Terry); Feb. 11, 1928 (Maturin/Merrall); April 6, 1934 (Laughton); Aug. 12, 1966 (Clements); Jan. 12, 1968 (Scofield)

Spirit of the Times, April 2, 1870 (Booth)

Sporting Gazette, Oct. 2, 1875 (Irving)

Sporting Times, Jan. 5, 1889 (Irving)

Sportsman, Dec. 31, 1888 (Irving)

Stage, Jan. 4, 1889 (Irving); Sept. 7, 1911 (Tree/Vanbrugh); April 27, 1933 (Komisarjevsky); June 7, 1962 (Porter); n.d. (Atkinson)

Star, Dec. 31, 1888 (Irving); March 20, 1953 (Wolfit)

Stratford-upon-Avon Herald, April 22, 1927 (Walter/Green); Sept. 21, 1933 (Komisarjevsky); April 22, 1949 (Wynyard); June 13, 1952 (Richardson/Leighton); June 10, 1955 (Olivier)

Summary, July 12, 1884 (Marais/Bernhardt)

Sunday Telegraph, Aug. 7, 1966 (Clements); Oct. 23, 1966 (Guinness)

Sunday Times, Nov. 6, 1864 (Phelps); April 8, 1934 (Laughton); Dec. 6, 1937 (Olivier); July 12, 1942 (Gielgud); June 12, 1955 (Olivier); June 10, 1962 (Porter); Oct. 23, 1966 (Guinness)

Surrey Dailey Advertiser, Oct. 13, 1976 (Tutin)

Svenska Dagbladet, April 24, 1975 (Sweden)

Sydney Morning Herald, Oct. 23, 1875 (Ristori)

Tablet, Oct. 27, 1962 (Porter/Worth)

Der Tag, n.d.. (Bernhardt)

Teatralny Almanakh, 1947 (Juriev, Russia)

Theatrical Inquisitor, Nov., 1814 (Kean); July, 1820 (Macready)

Times, April 16, 1832 (Fanny Kemble); Feb. 15, 1853 (C. Kean); Oct. 2, 1875 (Irving); June 25, 1884 (Bernhardt); July 5, 1884 (Marais/Bernhardt); Dec. 31, 1888 (Irving); Sept. 19, 1898 (Forbes-Robertson); Sept. 6, 1911 (Tree/Vanbrugh); April 19, 1933 (Komisarjevsky); April 16, 1936 (Welles); Sept. 10, 1954 (Rogers); June 8, 1955 (Olivier); Sept. 5, 1957 (Littlewood); Dec. 19, 1958 (Hordern); May 5, 1966 (Clements); Oct. 21, 1966 (Guinness)

Torquay Times, July 11, 1884 (Marais)

Tribune, Oct. 26, 1874 (Cushman); Nov. 9, 1874 (George Vandenhoff); Nov. 26, 1874; July 28, 1955 (Olivier)

Truth, July 13, 1882; April 29, 1949 (Tearle/Wynyard)

Universal Review, Jan. 15, 1889 (Irving)

Vanity Fair, Sept. 13, 1911 (Tree)

Vossische Zeitung, Nov. 12, 1922 (Jessner, Germany)

Weekly Dispatch, Oct. 8, 1975 (Irving)

Western Daily Bristol, Sept. 6, 1955 (Olivier)

Wolverhampton Express and Star, June 6, 1962 (Porter/Worth)

World, Jan. 2, 1889 (Irving)

Unidentified clippings: July, 1820 (Macready); Oct., 1820 (Kean); April 11, 1826 Macready); Feb. 27, 1848 (Macready); Feb. 14, 1853 (C. Kean); Feb. 26, 1853 (C. Kean); 1875 (Macready); May 20, 1876 (Rossi); May 29, 1876 (Rossi); March 10, 1884 (F. Kemble); March 10, 1884 (Salvini); Nov. 4, 1898 (Forbes-Robertson); 1898 (Forbes-Robertson); Dec. 12, 1906 (Bourchier); Sept. 18, 1909 (Maeterlinck); Nov. 12, 1910 (Sothern); Dec. 11, 1910 (Marlowe); Sept. 6, 1911 (Tree); Sept. 3, 1913 (Mantell); Dec. 28, 1926 (Ainley); 1937 (Olivier/Anderson); n.d. (Marais/Bernhardt); n.d. (Garrick); n.d. (Janauschek)

Other unidentified clippings

Act III, Scene v

BOOKS AND ARTICLES

Aronson, 24ff.
Booth, W., 180ff.
Chambers, 11–12
Cutts, (1) 208–9
Downer, (1) 333
Empson, (1) 90ff.
Flatter, (4) 201
Gribble, *op. cit.*
Halio, edition
Hanmer, edition
Irving, (2) 101 (Irving)
Jonson, *op. cit.*
Liddell, edition
Muir, edition
Neumann, 82–83
Sprague, A. C., (5) 39
Veszy-Wagner, L., 250ff.
Williams, G., personal discussion
Wilson, J. D., edition
Unidentified sources

PROMPTBOOKS

Shattuck: 8, 25, 44, 47, 122, 123, 127, 133, 144

PERIODICALS

Birmingham Daily Post, Dec. 31, 1888 (Irving)
Daily Telegraph, Nov. 5, 1864 (Phelps/Faucit)
Era, Nov. 6, 1864 (Phelps/Faucit)
Flattery and Truth, Feb. 14, 1853 (C. Kean)
Kaleidoscope, July 17, 1821 (Macready)
Literary Gazette, Feb. 19, 1846 (C. Kean)
Morning Advertiser, Dec. 31, 1888 (Irving/
    Terry)
North British Daily Mail, Dec. 6, 1846 (Faucit)
Revue d'Art Dramatique, June–Sept., 1889
    (Terry)
Scotsman, March 16, 1974
Spectator, April 9, 1842 (Macready)
Stratford-upon-Avon Herald, June 13, 1952 (Rich-
    ardson); June 10, 1955 (Olivier)
Unidentified clipping: Nov. 12, 1910 (Sothern)
Other unidentified clippings

Act III, Scene vi

BOOKS AND ARTICLES

Empson, (1) 90ff
Hanmer, edition
Liddell, edition

PROMPTBOOKS

Shattuck: 133, 144

PERIODICALS

Saint James Chronicle, Oct., 1777 (Garrick)
Spectator, Aug. 12, 1966 (Clements)
Tribune, Nov. 9, 1874 (Cushman)
Unidentified clippings

Act IV, Scene i

BOOKS, ARTICLES AND PERSONAL
REPORTS

Agate, (1) 232 (Laughton)
Ashwell, (2), 124f.
Bell, edition
Black, J. personal discussion
Booth, E., (1) letter, Sept. 8, 1878
Booth, J. W., (see Weichmann)
Burnim, 121–22 (Garrick)
Campbell, D., *op. cit.*
Craig, G., (6)
Craig, E. C., personal discussion
Cross, L. and R., personal report, Stratford,
    Conn., 1974 (Weaver)
David, 127 (Olivier)
De Vos, (2) 291ff. (Belgium)
Elwin, edition

Farnham, (3) 86
Favorini, *op. cit.* (Mantell)
Fiske, 114ff.
Flatter, (4) 201
Fontenrose, letter
Garrick, Bell edition,
Gentleman, (2) 96
Goddard, 127
Granville-Barker, *Preface*
Halio, edition; personal discussion
Jack, 180, 190
Jones, E., 69
Jones, Inigo, see Orgel
Jonson, *Masque of Queenes* (*Works*, vol. 7) 301
Lazarus, *op. cit.* (Salvini)
Liddell, edition
Lynch, 603–4
McGee, 55ff.

Mullin, *passim* (Komisarjevsky)
Neumann, 82–83
Oulton, 139–40 (J. P. Kemble)
Parsons, *op. cit.*
Paul, 272f.
Pitoeff, 32f.
Poel, see Speaight (3) 185
Robinson, E., personal report (Olivier)
Salvini, (2) 213
Scofield, personal discussion
Scot, *op. cit.*
Scott, Sir Walter, *op. cit.*, 277
Shaw, Byam, notes
Tieck, (2)
Towse, 302 (Irving)
Upton, 39
Veszy-Wagner, L., 253ff.
Walker, (1) 14, 125ff.
Webster, (1) 19 (Evans/Anderson)
West, R. H., 21–23
West. W., Second part, Section 19
Wilson, J. D. (2)
Winter, (7) 466–67 (Kean), 488 (Salvini)
Unidentified sources

PROMPTBOOKS

Shattuck: 10, 25, 27, 29, 35, 44, 46, 47, 54, 70,
  77, 106, 108, 116A, 118, 122, 123, 127, 133,
  137, 144, 146, 147

PERIODICALS

Academy, April 15, 1876 (Salvini)
Aftonbladet, Nov. 20, 1944 (Bergman, Sweden)
Allgemeine Theaterzeitung (Vienna), vol. 17
  (1824) 192 (see Germany)
Athenaeum, July 8, 1832; Oct. 2, 1875 (Irving)
Belgravia, Nov., 1875 (Irving)
Birmingham Daily Post, Dec. 31, 1888 (Irving)
Birmingham Gazette, April 19, 1933 (Komisar-
  jevsky); April 18, 1949 (Tearle)
Birmingham News, June 14, 1952 (Richardson)
Birmingham Post, April 19, 1933 (Komisarjev-
  sky); June 8, 1955 (Olivier); Dec. 19, 1958
  (Hordern); Aug. 3, 1966 (Clements); June 3,
  1975 (Williamson)
Bolton Evening News, June 6, 1962 (Porter)
Boston Evening Transcript, Nov. 15, 1910
  (Sothern)
Boston Herald, Nov. 15, 1910 (Sothern); Oct.
  28, 1941 (Evans)
Boston Record, July 31, 1959 (Robards)
Boston Traveler, Oct. 28, 1941 (Evans)
Chicago Daily News, Dec. 2, 1964 (Wanamaker)

Christian Science Monitor, June 3, 1967 (Sole
  prod., Mexico)
Comoedia, Dec. 12, 1942 (Baty prod., France)
Daily Chronicle, Aug. 25, 1909 (Maeterlinck
  prod.)
Daily Mail, Sept. 6, 1911 (Tree)
Daily News, March 10, 1884 (Salvini)
Daily Telegraph, Nov. 5, 1864 (Phelps/Faucit);
  Dec. 19, 1958 (Hordern); Oct. 30, 1974
  (Williamson); March 6, 1975 (Williamson)
Drama Survey, vol. 6, no. 1, 1967 (Guinness)
Edinburgh Courant, June 25, 1884 (Bernhardt)
Edinburgh Dramatic Review, Feb. 9, 1824 (John
  Vandenhoff)
Era, Nov. 6, 1864 (Phelps); Jan. 5, 1889 (Ir-
  ving)
L'Europa, March 12, 1953 (Italy)
Evening Advertiser, June 30, 1936 (Welles prod.)
Evening Post, Dec. 3, 1888 (Irving); Nov. 20,
  1928 (Craig prod.)
Evening Standard, March 10, 1884 (Salvini);
  July 5, 1884 (Bernhardt); Dec. 31, 1888 (Ir-
  ving); Aug. 5, 1944 (Milton); Sept. 10, 1954
  (Rogers/Todd)
Examiner, Oct. 2, 1875 (Irving)
Figaro, March 15, 1884 (Salvini); May 22, 1884
  (Bernhardt)
Figaro Littéraire, June 20, 1959 (Rétoré prod.,
  France)
Financial Times, Oct. 21, 1966 (Guinness);
  March 6, 1975 (Williamson)
Il Giornale d'Italia, Feb. 26, 1953 (Italy)
Globe, Dec. 31, 1888 (Irving)
Götesborg Morgonpost, March 13, 1948 (Bergman)
Guardian, Oct. 21, 1966 (Guinness)
Illustrated London News, June 25, 1955 (Olivier)
John Bull, Oct. 3, 1847 (Phelps)
John O'London's Weekly, Jan. 9, 1947 (M. Red-
  grave)
Kaleidoscope, Sept. 9, 1823
Lady's Pictorial, Jan. 5, 1889 (Irving)
Leamingham Chronicle and Warwickshire Pictorial,
  Feb. 26–March 1, n.d.
Leamingham Spa Courier, June 10, 1955 (Olivier)
Liverpool Daily Post, Dec. 31, 1888 (Irving)
London Magazine, Jan., 1967 (Guinness)
Manchester Courier, April 22, 1794 (J. P.
  Kemble)
Manchester Guardian, June 7, 1962 (Porter)
Monthly Mirror, Dec., 1803, Nov., 1807 (J. P.
  Kemble)
Morning Post, Sept. 27, 1875 (Irving); Dec. 31,
  1888 (Irving); Sept. 6, 1911 (Tree); April 19,
  1933 (Komisarjevsky); April 3, 1934 (Laugh-
  ton)
Newcastle Upon Tyne Journal, Aug. 9, 1962
  (Porter)
New Mirror Dec. 9, 1843 (Macready)

New Statesman, Dec. 27, 1947 (M. Redgrave/ Burrill); Aug. 12, 1966 (Clements); Nov. 8, 1974 (Williamson)
New York American, Feb. 8, 1916 (Hackett)
New York Clipper, Feb. 19, 1881 (Salvini)
New York Evening Post, Oct. 30, 1895 (Irving)
New York Herald, May 12, 1881 (Salvini)
New York Herald Tribune, April 1, 1948 (M. Redgrave)
New York Post, July 16, 1973 (Kahn prod.)
New York Times, Oct. 17, 1871 (Creswick/ Cushman); Oct. 25, 1874 (Vandenhoff/ Cushman); Dec. 29, 1888 (Irving); April 15, 1936 (Welles); June 19, 1961; July 15, 1973 (Weaver)
New York Tribune, Aug. 29, 1909 (Maeterlinck)
New York World Telegram, Nov. 12, 1941 (Evans)
Night and Day, Dec. 9, 1937 (Olivier)
Le Nouvel Observateur, June 5, 1965 (Rétoré prod., France)
Observer, Feb. 26, 1844 (C. Kean); April 8, 1934 (Laughton); June 12, 1955 (Olivier); Sept. 5, 1957 (Littlewood prod.); Oct. 23, 1966 (Guinness)
Overland Monthly, Feb., 1886 (Rankin)
Pall Mall Gazette, Dec. 31, 1888 (Irving)
Philadelphia Evening Bulletin, Nov. 27, 1941 (Evans/Anderson)
Plays and Players, Nov., 1969; Jan., 1973 (Hopkins/Rigg)
Punch, Nov. 13, 1974 (Williamson)
Quarterly Review, 1826 (J. P. Kemble)
Queen, Jan. 5, 1889 (Irving)
Rand Daily Mail, Aug. 21, 1970 (see Theatre Bibliography III, South African productions)
Redditch Indicator, Nov. 1, 1974 (Williamson)
Revue d'Art Dramatique, June–Sept., 1889 (Irving)
Saint James Chronicle, Oct. 30, 1773 (Garrick)
Saturday Review, Dec., 1816 (Sullivan); March 15, 1884 (Salvini); June 14, 1884 (Bernhardt); March 30, 1889 (Irving); April 17, 1948 (M. Redgrave)
Scotsman, April 6, 1876 (Salvini); June 25, 1884 (Bernhardt); April 21, 1933 (Komisarjevsky); Nov. 2, 1974 (Williamson)
Sketch, July 2, 1952 (Richardson); June 8, 1955 (Olivier)
Spectator, July 10, 1936 (Welles prod.)
Sporting and Dramatic News, Jan. 5, 1889 (Irving)
Stage, Jan. 4, 1889 (Irving); Sept. 7, 1911 (Tree); April 27, 1933 (Komisarjevsky); April 5, 1934 (Laughton/Guthrie prod.); April 21, 1949 (Tearle); June 11, 1955 (Olivier/Leigh); May 29, 1958; Nov. 7, 1974 (Williamson)
Stratford-Upon-Avon Herald, April 21, 1933 (Komisarjevsky); June 13, 1952 Richardson); June 8, 1962 (Porter/Worth)
Sunday Telegraph, Oct. 22, 1966 (Guinness)
Sunday Times, Dec. 30, 1888 (Irving); Sept. 10, 1911 (Tree); April 8, 1934 (Laughton)
Theatre, Feb. 1, 1889 (Irving)
Theatrical Inquisitor and Monthly Mirror, Nov. 14, 1814 (Kean)
Times, April 19, 1933 (Komisarjevsky); Sept. 10, 1954 (Rogers); Sept. 5, 1957 (Littlewood); June 6, 1962 (Porter/Worth)
Toronto Daily Star, June 19, 1962 (Plummer)
Vanity Fair, June 13, 1911 (Tree)
Volksblatt, March 3, 1964 (see Germany)
Weekly Dispatch, Nov. 6, 1864 (Phelps)
Windsor Slough and Eton Express, Aug. 5, 1966 (Clements)
World, April 22, 1794 (J. P. Kemble)
Unidentified clippings: April 11, 1826 (Macready); Feb. 14, 1833 (C. Kean); July 5, 1884 (Bernhardt); Dec. 11, 1910 (Sothern/Marlowe)
Other unidentified clippings

Act IV, Scene ii

BOOKS AND ARTICLES

Allen, Sheila, letter
Bogard, personal discussion
Brooks, 197
Campbell, L. B., (1) 230
Capell, E., *op. cit.*
Crane, M., 175
Cunningham, edition
David, 131 (Olivier)
Empson, (1) 91

Garrick, Bell edition
Gentleman, (2) 97
Granville-Barker, *Preface*
Hodek, letters (Czechoslovakia)
Libby, *op. cit.*
Liddell, edition
Milward, (2) (Kumo prod.)
Muir, (9), 155
Parrott, edition
Paul, (1) 195, 388
Poel, (2) 61f. (Siddons)

Speaight, (3) 185f.
Steevens, edition
Strindberg, 178
Weiner, 130 (Phelps)
Williamson, (2) 110 (Rogers)
Wilson, J. D., edition
Unidentified sources

PROMPTBOOKS

Shattuck: 118, 122, 123, 144, 146, 147

PERIODICALS

Beckenham and Penge Advertiser, Oct. 13, 1966 (Guinness)
Birmingham News, June 11, 1955 (Olivier/ Leigh)
Birmingham Post, Sept. 15, 1954 (Rogers/ Todd)
Birmingham Weekly Post, June 10, 1955 (Olivier)

Boston Evening Transcript, Sept. 17, 1935 (Merivale)
Daily Graphic, April 18, 1949 (Tearle/Wynyard)
Daily Telegraph, Oct. 13, 1884 (Marais)
Il Giornale d'Italia, Feb. 26, 1953 (Italy)
Guardian, Oct. 21, 1966 (Guinness)
London Free Press, June 10, 1971
Malvern Gazette, Oct. 31, 1974 (Williamson)
Montreal Star, June 10, 1971 (Hogg)
New Statesman, April 23, 1949 (Tearle)
New York Times, June 19, 1955 (Olivier); Oct. 23, 1966 (Guinness)
News Chronicle, April 25, 1949 (Tearle)
Saturday Review, June 14, 1884 (Bernhardt)
Shakespeare Quarterly, vol. 25, 1974, 828
Spectator, Feb. 11, 1928 (Maturin/Merrall)
Stage, Sept. 7, 1911 (Tree)
Theatre, June 1, 1887 (Phelps)
Toronto Globe, June 11, 1971 (Hogg)
Truth, Sept. 13, 1911 (Tree)
Unidentified clipping: Feb. 7, 1928 (Maturin/ Merrall)

Act IV, Scene iii

BOOKS AND ARTICLES

Brown, J. R., (1) 145
Casson, Introduction
Coghill, (4) 230ff.
Donne, 216–17
Granville-Barker, *Preface*
Harington, Vol. I, 348–9
Hunt, (4) 235
Jacobsohn, (2) 120ff. (Reinhardt)
Jacquot, (1)
James I, (1), *op. cit.* (see also Fraser, A., 94)
Knights, (1) 23f.
Paul, (2) 360ff.
Redgrave, M., see Burton, H., *Great Acting*
Robinson, E., personal report (Olivier)
Shaw, Byam, notes
Styan, 152
Thomas, 200
West, W., Second part, Section 22
Unidentified sources

PROMPTBOOKS

Shattuck: 27, 63, 66, 70, 118, 123, 127, 144, 146, 147

PERIODICALS

Belgravia, Nov., 1875 (Irving)
Birmingham Post, Dec. 31, 1888 (Irving)

Boston Herald, Nov. 15, 1910 (Sothern)
Daily Mail, Dec. 12, 1906 (Bouchier)
Dramatic Magazine, Oct. 12, 1829 (Young)
Edinburgh Dramatic Review, Feb. 22, 1825
Era, June 5, 1889 (Irving)
Etudes Anglaises, vol. 8, no. 1, 1955 (Vilar prod., France)
Evening Post, Nov. 20, 1928 (Craig prod.)
Evening Standard, Dec. 31, 1888 (Irving)
Götesborgs Morgonpost, March 13, 1948 (Bergman prod., Sweden)
Literary Gazette, Feb. 19, 1846 (Kean)
New Monthly Magazine, July 1, 1828 (Young)
New Statesman, Jan. 12, 1968 (Scofield)
New York Daily News, July 16, 1973 (Weaver)
Observer, Oct. 3, 1847 (Phelps); Sept. 10, 1911 (Tree)
Plays and Players, Nov., 1969
Stage, Dec. 24, 1947 (M. Redgrave)
Stratford-upon-Avon Herald, April 22, 1927 (Walter/Green)
Sunday Times, Sept. 10, 1911 (Tree)
Tatler, no. 68 (Wilks)
Times, Sept. 19, 1898 (Forbes-Robertson); Feb. 7, 1928 (Maturin); Feb. 18, 1971
Unidentified clipping: Dec. 11, 1910 (Sothern/ Marlowe)
Other unidentified clippings

Act V, Scene i

BOOKS AND ARTICLES

Agate, (2) 235–36
Anderson, personal discussion
Arnold, 61
Boaden, (1) 314–15
Booth, S., personal discussion (V. Redgrave)
Brown, J. R., (1) 149 (Worth)
Byrne, letter (Rigg)
Campbell, L. B., 233ff.
Chambers, E. K., edition
Craig, G., (4)
David, 127
Davies, (1) 184
Dench, personal discussion
Drozd, (Nouseul, Germany)
Engelsfeld, letter (Yugoslavia)
Ermolova, see Russia, 1896, all references
Faucit, 288
Freud, op. cit.
Gentleman, edition
Got, letter (Poland); (2) 86 (Modjeska, Wysocka)
Grein, op. cit. (Terry, Bernhardt)
Gryzmala-Siedlecki, 154 (Modjeska, Poland)
Harbage, edition
Hazlitt, (1) vol. 5, 307 (Siddons)
Heiberg, op. cit.
Hunt, (1) 72 (Siddons)
Jacobsohn, (2) (Reinhardt)
Jones, R. E., (1) 633 (see also Young, 100)
Kemble, F., (2) 54–55
Kiasashvili, N., personal report
Koneczeny, 381, 583–86 (Modjeska, Poland)
Lubowski, 154 (Modjeska, Poland)
Liddell, edition
Mack, 24
Marston, J. W. 229 (Mrs. Kean)
Neiderle, 52f. (Wolter, Germany)
Redgrave, M., see Garrett, 139ff.
Richter, 198 (Wolter, Germany)
Ristori, op. cit.
Robinson, E., personal report (Leigh)
Robson, W., 21 (Siddons)
Rogovsky, (Marzia, Russia, 1936)
Russell, C. E., 484 (Marlowe)
Sarcey, op. cit.
Schink, op. cit. (Nouseul, Germany)
Segond-Weber, op. cit.
Simond, 131 (Siddons)
Shaw, G. B., op. cit.
Shaw, Byam, notes
Taylor, J., 26 (Siddons)
Terry, notes (Siddons, Terry)
Towse, 212 (Janauschek)
Tree, H. B., op. cit.

Wilson, J., op. cit.
Wingate, 202 (Faucit); 212 (Langtry)
Winter, (7) 501ff. (Cushman, Modjeska)
Unidentified sources

PROMPTBOOKS

Shattuck: 8, 16, 66, 70, 77, 106, 118, 122, 137, 146, 147

PERIODICALS

Academy, May 13, 1876 (Pareti)
Annalen des Theatres, vol. 1, 1788 (Germany)
L'Arsenal, 1885 (Tessandier, France)
Athenaeum, March 1, 1845 (Cushman); Oct. 2, 1847 (Phelps); July 11, 1857 (Ristori/Siddons); March 15, 1884 (Salvini/Piamonti); July 12, 1844 (Bernhardt)
Bath and Wilts Chronicle, Oct. 20, 1969
Belgravia, Nov. 1875 (Irving)
Bell's Life in London, July 9, 1884 (Bernhardt)
Bell's Weekly Messenger, Oct. 3, 1875 (Bateman); May 13, 1876 (Pareti)
Birmingham Gazette, June 11, 1952 (Leighton)
Birmingham Mail, May 20, 1942 (Gielgud/Hunt); June 11, 1952 (Leighton); June 8, 1955 (Olivier/Leigh)
Birmingham Post, April 22, 1949 (Wynyard) June 11, 1952 (Leighton), Dec. 19, 1958 (Hordern/Lehmann)
Black and White, Sept. 30, 1911 (Tree/Vanbrugh)
Blackwood's Edinburgh Magazine, 1827 Siddons); Sept., 1834, p. 363 (Siddons); June, 1843 (Siddons)
Boston Daily Advertiser, Nov. 15, 1910 (Marlowe)
Boston Evening Transcript, April 29, 1904 (O'Neil); Nov. 5, 1910 (Marlowe); Nov. 15, 1910 (Sothern); Sept. 17, 1935 (Cooper)
Boston Record, July 31, 1959 (McKenna)
Bournemouth Daily Echo, June 3, 1942 (Ffrangcon-Davies)
Bridlington Free Press, Oct. 3, 1928 (Craig)
Cabinet, June, 1808, p. 408 (Kemble/Smith)
Chicago Daily News, March 10, 1896 (Terry); Nov. 8, 1899 (Modjeska)
Chicago Daily Tribune, Feb. 13, 1957 (Browne)
Comoedia, Dec. 12, 1942 (Baty prod., France)
Country Gentleman, Jan. 5, 1889 (Terry)
Courier, June 30, 1812 (Siddons)
Court Circular, July 12, 1884 (Bernhardt)
Coventry Evening Telegraph, June 8, 1955 (Olivier/Leigh)
Daily Express, Sept. 6, 1911 (Vanbrugh)

Daily Mail, Sept. 19, 1898 (Mrs. Campbell); Sept. 6, 1911 (Vanbrugh/Tree)

Daily Mirror, Feb. 8, 1928 (Merrall); April 1, 1948 (Robson)

Daily News, July 5, 1884 (Bernhardt/Siddons/ Ristori); Dec. 31, 1888 (Terry)

Daily Telegraph, July 5, 1882 (Ristori); Oct. 13, 1884 (Bernhardt); Dec. 19, 1958 (Lehmann/ Hordern); Aug. 3, 1960; Nov. 10, 1972 (Rigg)

Daily Worker, June 7, 1962 (Worth)

Dramatic Censor, Sept. 18, 1811 (Siddons)

Dramatic Magazine, Oct. 12, 1829

Dramatic Review, Jan. 5, 1889 (Terry)

Drury Lane Journal, March, 1752 (Cibber)

Eastern Daily Press, Nov. 22, 1969

Echo, Sept. 27, 1875 (Bateman/Irving)

L'Echo du Parlement, Oct. 8, 1884 (Bernhardt)

Edinburgh Courant, Feb. 24, 1812 (Siddons); Nov. 20, 1815 (Siddons); June 25, 1884 (Bernhardt)

Edinburgh Dramatic Review, Feb. 22, 1825

English Illustrated Magazine, Dec. 1888 (Siddons)

Era, July 8, 1882 (Ristori)

Etudes Anglaises, vol. 7, 1955 (Casarès, France)

European Magazine, July 1812 (Siddons)

Evening News, Sept, 6, 1911 (Vanbrugh); March 10, 1884 (Piamonti); July 5, 1884 (Bernhardt); Dec. 31, 1888 (Terry)

Evening Standard, Sept. 6, 1911 (Vanbrugh); June 13, 1952 (Leighton); June 8, 1955 (Leigh)

Evesham Journal, June 11, 1952 (Leighton)

Examiner, July 5, 1812 (Siddons); June 16, 1816 (Siddons)

Express en, March 13, 1948 (Bergman prod., Sweden)

Figaro, Aug. 20, 1909 (Leblanc-Maeterlinck); Jan. 20, 1954 (Chabrol prod., France)

Figaro Littéraire, Aug. 11, 1962 (Lise Delemare, France)

Financial Times, Nov. 10, 1969 (Leigh)

Freeman's Journal, Aug. 31, 1857 (Faucit)

Gazette de France, April 25, 1884 (Bernhardt); May 24, 1884 (Bernhardt)

Gentleman, Jan. 4, 1889 (Terry/Irving)

Glasgow Herald, March 23, 1970 (Eyre prod.)

Globe, May 23, 1884 (Bernhardt); May 24, 1884 (Bernhardt); July 5, 1884 (Bernhardt); Dec. 31, 1888 (Terry)

Gloucester Echo, June 8, 1955 (Leigh)

Graphic, Oct. 26, 1874 (Cushman); May 8, 1882 (Ristori); July 8, 1882 (Ristori); April 18, 1949 (Wynyard)

Guardian, Sept. 20, 1970

Illustrated Sporting and Dramatic News, July, 1884 (Bernhardt)

Kurier, Sept. 19, 1899 (Ermolova, Russia)

Lady, Sept. 14, 1911 (Vanbrugh/Tree); Nov. 14, 1974 (Mirren)

Lady's Pictorial, Jan. 5, 1889 (Terry)

Land and Water, July 12, 1884 (Bernhardt)

Leamington Spa Courier, June 13, 1952 (Leighton)

Lettres Françaises, July 29, 1954 (Casarès, France)

Licensed Victualler's Gazette and Hotel Courier, Sept. 15, 1911 (Vanbrugh)

Listener, March 29, 1933 (Hunt); Feb. 2, 1967 (Siddons, Terry)

Literary Gazette, April 12, 1823 (Ogilvie)

Liverpool Daily Post, June 28, 1884 (Bernhardt), Dec. 31, 1888 (Terry)

Lloyd's Weekly London Newspaper, Nov, 13, 1864 (Faucit); Oct. 9, 1875 (Bateman)

London Magazine, Jan., 1967 (Signoret)

London News, Jan. 5, 1889 (Terry)

Manchester Examiner and Times, Nov. 14, 1871 (Faucit)

Manchester Guardian, Nov. 15, 1871 (Faucit); Nov. 23, 1937 (Wolfit); Jan. 19, 1942 (Gielgud/Ffrangcon-Davies); April 18, 1949 (Wynyard),

Mask, 1929 (Craig prod.)

Mid Sussex Times, Oct. 10, 1974

Monthly Mirror, Nov., 1807 (Siddons); May, 1810 (Pritchard)

Morning Advertiser, July 5, 1884 (Bernhardt); June 15, 1955 (Olivier/Leigh)

Morning Chronicle, Sept. 19, 1798 (Siddons); Feb. 22, 1848 (F. Kemble)

Morning Leader, Sept., 1911 (Vanbrugh)

Morning Post, Feb. 3, 1785 (Siddons); Feb. 16, 1853 (Ellen Kean); July 4, 1857 (Ristori); Sept. 27, 1875 (Bateman); Dec. 31, 1888 (Terry); Sept. 19, 1898 (Campbell); Sept. 6, 1911 (Tree/Vanbrugh)

Newcastle-upon-Tyne Journal, Aug. 9, 1962 (Worth)

New Republic, April 2, 1924 (Eames)

New Statesman, July 18, 1942 (Ffrangcon-Davies); June 21, 1952 (Leighton); Jan. 12, 1968 (Merchant)

New York American, Feb. 8, 1916 (V. Allen)

New York Evening Mail, Oct. 26, 1874 (Cushman)

New York Herald, Jan. 3, 1885 (Ristori)

New York Herald Tribune, Nov. 19, 1889; Nov. 23, 1941 (Anderson); June 19, 1961 (Tandy); June 20, 1962 (Reid)

New York Post, April 1, 1948 (Robson/Anderson)

New York Sun, 1889 (Langtry); Nov. 12, 1941 (Anderson); Nov. 14, 1941 (Anderson)

New York Times, Dec. 29, 1888 (Terry); Jan. 22,

New York Times (continued)
1889 (Langtry); Nov. 19, 1889 (Modjeska); Feb. 8, 1916 (Hackett); Oct. 8, 1935 (Cooper); Nov. 12, 1941 (Anderson); Nov. 24, 1941 (Anderson); Oct. 30, 1956 (Browne); June 19, 1961 (Tandy); Feb. 7, 1962 (Clements/Jefford); Feb. 28, 1971 (Polanski film); July 15, 1973 (Murphy)

New York Tribune, Oct. 24, 1897 (Modjeska); Feb. 16, 1898 (Modjeska)

New York World, March 17, 1924 (Hackett/Eames)

New York World-Telegram, April 1, 1948 (Robson)

The News, July 5, 1812 (Siddons); Oct. 26, 1817; Jan. 5, 1889 (Terry)

News Chronicle, June 11, 1952 (Leighton); June 8, 1955 (Leigh)

North British Daily Mail, Dec. 6, 1846 (Faucit)

Notes and Queries, July 13, 1889 (Ellen Kean)

Nottingham Evening Post, Oct. 30, 1895 (Terry)

Observer, Sept. 8, 1898 (Mrs. P. Campbell); July 5, 1857 (Ristori); Sept. 10, 1911 (Tree/Vanbrugh); Dec. 2, 1928 (German prod.); March 23, 1930 (Hunt); April 27, 1958; Aug. 20, 1967 (Merchant)

PM, Nov. 12, 1941 (Anderson); April 2, 1948 (Robson)

Pall Mall Gazette, July 5, 1884 (Bernhardt)

People, Dec. 30, 1888 (Terry)

Petersburgskaya Gazeta, Feb. 23, 1904 (Ermolova, Russia)

Pittsburgh Post Gazette, March 7, 1929

Pittsburgh Sun-Telegraph, April 2, 1929 (Craig prod.)

Philadelphia Evening Bulletin, Nov. 27, 1941 (Anderson)

Punch, April 11, 1934 (Robson); Dec. 31, 1947 (Burrill)

Queen, Jan. 5, 1889 (Terry); April 18, 1934 (Robson)

Russko Slovo, no. 257, 1899 (Ermolova, Russia)

Saint James Chronicle, Feb. 5, 1785 (Siddons); Feb. 8, 1785 (Siddons)

Saint James Gazette, Sept. 6, 1911 (Vanbrugh)

San Francisco Daily Alta, Nov. 3, 1885; Feb. 8, 1889 (Langtry)

Saturday Review, July 11, 1857 (Ristori); July 8, 1882 (Ristori); June 14, 1884 (Bernhardt); March 15, 1884 (Salvini); Oct. 1, 1898; March 15, 1934

Scotsman, June 25, 1884 (Bernhardt); April, 1933 (Komisarjevsky); Aug. 25, 1954 (Todd)

Spectator, July 18, 1840 (Warner); April 9, 1842 (Ellen Kean); Jan. 5, 1889 (Ristori); Aug. 12, 1966 (Johnston)

Sporting Life, Nov. 9, 1864 (Faucit); Dec. 31, 1888 (Terry)

Stage, Jan. 4, 1889 (Terry); Sept. 22, 1898; Sept. 7, 1911 (Vanbrugh); Dec. 6, 1928 (Reed); April 27, 1933 (Komisarjevsky prod.); Dec. 2, 1937 (Anderson); Jan. 22, 1942 (Ffrangcon-Davies); Jan. 24, 1948 (Burrill); June 12, 1952 (Leighton); May 29, 1958; June 7, 1962 (Worth)

Stratford-upon-Avon Herald, April 22, 1927 (Green); April 21, 1933 (Komisarjevsky prod.); April 22, 1949 (Wynyard); June 10, 1955 (Olivier/Leigh)

Stockholmstidningen, Nov. 20, 1944 (Bergman, Sweden)

Summary, July 10, 1884 (Bernardt/Faucit/Ristori); July 12, 1884 (Ristori/Faucit)

Sunday Times, Nov. 6, 1864 (Faucit); July 6, 1884 (Bernhardt); Dec. 3, 1888 (Terry); Dec. 16, 1906 (Vanbrugh); Sept. 10, 1911 (Vanbrugh); June 15, 1952 (Leighton); June 12, 1955 (Leigh); June 10, 1962 (Worth)

Svenska Dagbladet, April 24, 1975 (Sweden)

Sydney Morning Herald, Oct. 23, 1875 (Ristori)

Tatler, no. 68.

Telegraph, May 23, 1884 (Bernhardt)

Le Temps, March 4, 1883 (Segond-Weber, France)

Theatre, Dec. 1, 1888 (Siddons)

Theatre Arts, Sept., 1928 (Reed)

Times, June 24, 1884 (Bernhardt); June 25, 1884 (Bernhardt); July 5, 1884 (Bernhardt); Dec. 31, 1888 (Terry); Sept. 19, 1898 (Campbell); Sept. 6, 1911 (Vanbrugh); April 21, 1927 (Green); Feb. 13, 1945 (Wolfit prod.); April 18, 1949 (Wynyard); Aug. 25, 1954 (Todd); June 6, 1962 (Worth); Aug. 1, 1966 (Johnston)

Toronto Daily Star, June 19, 1962 (Reid)

Torquay Times, July 11, 1884 (Bernhardt)

Tribunal, n.d. (Janauschek)

Tribune, Oct. 1, 1954 (Todd)

Il Trovatore, July 18, 1857 (Ristori)

Truth, July 13, 1882 (Ristori); July 10, 1884 (Bernhardt)

Tygodnik Ilustrowany, (Modjeska, Poland)

Vanity Fair, July 12, 1884 (Bernhardt); Sept. 13, 1911 (Vanbrugh)

Windsor Slough and Eton Express, Aug. 5, 1966 (Johnston)

The World, Nov. 19, 1889 (Modjeska)

Yorkshire Post, March 18, 1942 (Ffrangcon-Davies)

Zycie Warsowy, no. 273, 1960 (Mikolajska, Poland)

Unidentified clippings: Feb. 14, 1853 (Ellen Kean); 1884 (Bernhardt); July 5, 1884 (Bernhardt); Nov. 4, 1898 (Mrs. Campbell); Dec. 31, 1888 (Terry); Jan. 31, 1911 (Marlowe); Sept. 6, 1911 (Vanbrugh); June 8, 1955 (Leigh); June 6, 1962 (Worth)

Other unidentified clippings

Act V, Scene ii

BOOKS AND ARTICLES

Agate, (1) 225ff., see also Tynan, (1) 24 (Gielgud)
Garrick, Bell edition
Muir, edition
Unidentified sources

PROMPTBOOKS

Shattuck: 122, 144

PERIODICALS

Financial Times, Jan. 16, 1975 (Dunlop prod.)
New York Evening Post, Oct. 30, 1895 (Irving)
Scotsman, July 14,. 1962 (Porter); Aug. 23, 1965
Stratford-Upon-Avon Herald, April 21, 1933 (Komisarjevsky)

Act V, Scene iii

BOOKS, ARTICLES AND PERSONAL
REPORTS

Agate, 227 (Gielgud)
Alger, 795 (Forrest)
Akutagawa, Milward interview
Armstrong, E., 11ff, 57ff.
Coleman, (1) 224 (Macready)
Favorini, *op. cit.* (Mantell)
Garrick, (2); (3) 364; Bell edition
Gielgud, (2) 168 (Gielgud)
Harwood, *op. cit.*
Hawkins, (1) 279 (Kean)
Hazlitt, *Champion*, Nov. 13, 1814
Heilman, (1) 15ff., 20
Hunt, (4) 232 (Kemble)
Irving, (1)
Johnson, Dr., edition
Kemble, (1) 49ff.
Kemble, F., 54
Marston, J. W., 79 (Macready)
McKellen, personal discussion
Milward, personal discussion
Murphy, see Garrick (3) 363
Robinson, E., personal report (Olivier)
Rowe, edition
Simrock, *op. cit.*
Stevenson, review
Towse, 179 (Salvini)
Unidentified sources

PROMPTBOOKS

Shattuck: 8, 11, 29, 66, 106, 118, 122, 123, 137, 141, 144, 147

PERIODICALS

Academy, April 15, 1876 (Salvini)
Aftonbladet, Nov. 20, 1944 (Bergman)

Belgravia, Nov. 1875 (Irving)
Birmingham Post, June 8, 1955 (Olivier/Leigh)
Boston Daily Globe, April 22, 1896 (Irving)
Champion, Nov. 13, 1814 (Kean)
Chicago American, Feb. 13, 1957 (Rogers)
Dagens Nyheter, Nov. 20, 1944 (Bergman, Sweden)
Daily Mirror, Feb. 8, 1928 (Maturin/Merrall)
Daily News, Dec. 31, 1888 (Irving); Dec. 26, 1926 (Ainley)
Echo, Sept. 27, 1875 (Irving)
Era, Jan. 5, 1889 (Irving)
Evening Standard, Sept. 27, 1875 (Irving)
Financial Times, Oct. 21, 1966 (Guinness)
Frankfurter Allgemeine Zeitung, n.d. (Germany)
Graphic, June 5, 1897
Illustrated London News, Jan. 13, 1968 (Scofield); March 6, 1971
John O'London's Weekly, Jan. 9, 1948 (Redgrave)
Morning Post, Sept. 27, 1875 (Macready, C. Kean)
New Statesman, Aug. 12, 1966 (Clements); Nov. 8, 1974 (Williamson)
New York Times, Nov. 23, 1941 (Evans/Anderson)
Notes and Queries, July 13, 1889 (C. Kean)
Obergische Volkszeitung, Sept. 21, 1963 (Germany)
Observer, Feb. 26, 1844 (Fanny Kemble); Dec. 21, 1947 (Redgrave)
Scotsman, July 14, 1962 (Porter)
Son Posta, Aug. 18, 1962 (Turkey)
Sketch, July 2, 1952 (Richardson)
South Wales Echo, May 6, 1972
Spectator, Oct. 2, 1875 (Irving); Aug. 12, 1966 (Clements); Jan. 12, 1968 (Scofield)
Stockholmstidningen, Nov. 20, 1944 (Bergman, Sweden)
Sun, Nov. 7, 1814 (Kean); April 5, 1842 (C. Kean); April 5, 1842 (Macready)
Sunday Times, June 12, 1955 (Olivier)

Times Educational Supplement, Jan. 24, 1975
  (Williamson)
Ulus, Sept. 27, 1962 (Turkey)

Unidentified clippings: Sept. 27, 1875 (Irving),
  Feb. 3, 1913 (Mantell); n.d. (Maturin), Nov.
  4, 1888 (Forbes-Robertson)

Act V, Scene iv

BOOKS AND ARTICLES

Coghill, (4) 234ff.
Knights (1) 23f.
McElroy, 215
Unidentified sources

PROMPTBOOKS

Shattuck: 118, 122, 123, 137, 144

PERIODICALS

Chicago Daily News, Dec. 2, 1964 (Wanamaker)

Act V, Scene v

BOOKS AND ARTICLES

Agate, (1) 227 (Gielgud), 243 (Olivier)
Alger, 745 (Forrest)
Billington, 61
Brown, J. R., (1) 146, 149 (Porter)
Byrne, see Price, J., 39f.
Casson, Introduction
Cooke, 285 (Macklin)
Clement, 82 (Cushman)
Coleman, J., (1) 223 (Macready)
Cooke, W., 285 (Macklin)
Craig, G., (6)
De Vos, (1) 245 (Bernhardt)
Drozd, *passim* (Nouseul, Germany)
Dunlap, *op. cit.* (Cooke)
Durylin, 232ff. (Ermolova, Russia)
Erskine, 81f. (Cushman)
Falk, (Reuss prod., Germany, 1928)
Farjeon, 132 (Hackett)
Forster, 36
Frye, R., (3) 144f.
Garrick, (2) 134, 137
Gentleman, edition
Granville-Barker, *Preface*
Gould, 132 (J. B. Booth)
Gryzmala-Siedlecki, 154 (Modjeska, Poland)
Hazlitt, (1) V, 308 (Kemble)
Hodek, letters (Czechoslovakia)
Iwasaki, 151
Jacobsohn, (2) 120ff. (Reinhardt)
Juriev, 221 (Rossi)
Kemble, (1) 110f.
Kendal, 7
Lampson, *op. cit.*
Lawlor, 186ff.
Lazarus, 110, 116 (Salvini)
Macready, (2) 1, 148
McKellen, personal discussion
Melchiori, personal discussion (Italy)
Murry, 336ff.

Robinson, E., personal report (Olivier)
Robson, F., Introduction
Rowe, edition
Santayana, 142, 270
Scofield, personal discussion
Stevenson, review
Strindberg, 170
Theobald, edition
Williamson, A., (2) 111 (Rogers)
Unidentified sources

PROMPTBOOKS

Shattuck: 9, 29, 66, 108, 118, 122, 123, 133, 137

PERIODICALS

Academy, April 15, 1876 (Salvini)
L'Arsenal, n.d. (Hackett)
Athenaeum, Oct. 2, 1847 (Phelps); May 2, 1876
  (Rossi)
Belgravia, Nov., 1875 (Irving)
Bell's Weekly Messenger, Oct. 2, 1875 (Irving)
Birmingham Post, June 18, 1952 (Richardson);
  Dec. 19, 1958 (Hordern); Aug. 3, 1966
  (Clements)
Boston Record, July 31, 1959 (Robards)
Catholic Herald, March 26, 1953 (Wolfit)
Champion, July 17, 1820 (Macready)
Christian Science Monitor, June 18, 1955 (Olivier)
Daily Mail, March 6, 1975 (Williamson/Mirren)
Daily Telegraph, Dec. 31, 1888 (Irving); March
  6, 1975 (Williamson)
The Drama or Theatrical Magazine, n.d. (Kean)
Edinburgh Dramatic Review, Feb. 19, 1824 (John
  Vandenhoff)
Era, March 15, 1884 (Salvini)
Evening Standard, Sept. 27, 1875 (Irving)
Examiner, n.d. (Macready); May 2, 1846 (Mac-
  ready)

Financial Times, Aug. 25, 1954 (Rogers); April 7, 1973 (Quilley); Jan. 16, 1975; March 6, 1975 (Williamson)
Glasgow Herald, March 10, 1975 (Williamson)
Gloucester Citizen, Oct. 30. 1974 (Williamson)
Illustrated London News, March 6, 1971
Inquirer or Literary Miscellany, Nov. 3, 1814 (Kean)
International Herald, March 6, 1975 (Williamson)
John O'London Weekly, June 27, 1952 (Richardson)
Lady, June 26, 1952 (Richardson); March 20, 1975 (Williamson)
Leamington Spa Courier, June 10, 1955 (Olivier)
Liverpool Daily Post, Dec. 31, 1888 (Irving)
Liverpool Porcupine, n.d. (Cowper)
Literary Gazette, Nov. 8, 1823 (Macready)
London Ontario Evening Free Press, June 19, 1962 (Plummer)
Manchester Guardian, Nov. 23, 1937 (Wolfit); June 17, 1942 (Gielgud)
Monthly Mirror, 1807 (Siddons)
Morning Advertiser, Sept. 27, 1875 (Irving); April 10, 1884 (Salvini); June 15, 1955 (Olivier)
Morning Chronicle, Sept. 19, 1798 (Kemble)
Morning Post, Nov. 7, 1814 (Kean); Sept. 27, 1875 (Irving); April 3, 1934 (Laughton)
New Statesman, n.d. (Siddons); Nov. 8, 1974 (Williamson)
New Statesman and Nation, July 18, 1942 (Gielgud)
New Theatre, n.d. (Redgrave)
New York Daily Tribune, Oct. 30, 1895 (Irving)
New York Herald Tribune, April 1, 1948 (Redgrave); June 19, 1961
New York Times, Aug. 1, 1959 (Robards); June 20, 1962 (Plummer); July 15, 1973 (Kahn prod)
News Chronicle, June 8, 1955 (Olivier)
Notes and Queries, July 13, 1889 (C. Kean)
Nottingham Journal, June 6, 1962 (Porter)
Observer, Feb. 26, 1844 (Charles Kean); March 23, 1930 (Gielgud); June 6, 1952 (Richardson); June 12, 1955 (Olivier); Nov. 3, 1974 (Williamson)

Pittsburgh Post, Oct. 12, 1909 (Mantell)
Pittsburgh Sun, Feb. 1, 1928 (Mantell)
Saint James Chronicle, Oct. 28–30, 1773 (Macklin/Garrick)
Saint James Gazette, Sept. 3, 1875 (Irving)
Scotsman, April 6, 1876 (Salvini)
Spectator, April 9, July 18, 1840 (C. Kean); Oct. 2, 1875 (Irving); Jan. 1, 1889 (Irving); July 17, 1942 (Gielgud)
Sporting Gazette, Oct. 2, 1875 (Irving)
Sporting Life, Dec. 31, 1888 (Irving)
Stage, Sept. 7, 1911 (Tree); Dec. 24, 1947 (Redgrave); June 12, 1952 (Richardson); March 26, 1953 (Wolfit)
Stockholmstidningen, Nov. 20, 1944 (Bergman, Sweden)
Stratford-Upon-Avon Herald, April 22, 1927 (Walter); June 13, 1952 (Richardson)
Sun, Nov. 7, 1814 (Kean); July 4, 1840 (Kemble); April 5, 1842 (Macready)
Sunday Times, Dec. 5, 1937 (Olivier); June 12, 1955 (Olivier)
Surrey Comet, March 12, 1975 (Williamson)
Tablet, Oct. 27, 1962
Tan and Korum, Oct., 1936 (Turkey)
Telegraph, Oct. 30, 1974 (Williamson)
Le Theatre, June 8, 1921 (Hackett, France)
Theatre Royal, Jan. 7, 1837 (Forrest)
Theatre World, Aug., 1942 (Gielgud)
Theatrical Inquisitor, Nov. 14, 1814 (Kean)
Theatrical Journal, Aug. 8, 1840 (Macready); April 2, 1842 (Macready)
Time and Tide, July 18, 1942 (Gielgud)
Time Magazine, March 31, 1975 (Williamson)
Times, March 29, 1842 (Macready); March 10, 1884 (Salvini); March 20, 1953 (Wolfit); Feb. 21, 1971
Truth, June 17, 1955 (Olivier)
Yorkshire Post, Oct. 31, 1974 (Williamson/Mirren)
Unidentified clippings: Dec. 31, 1888 (Irving); June 8, 1955 (Olivier); March 10, 1884 (Salvini)
Other unidentified clippings

Act V, Scene vi

BOOKS AND ARTICLES

Knights, (1) 33
Unidentified sources

PROMPTBOOKS

Shattuck: 8, 27, 29, 112, 118, 122, 123, 127, 133, 144

PERIODICALS

Birmingham Mail, June 13, 1952 (Richardson)
Boston Daily Advertiser, Oct. 13, 1875 (Irving)
Düsseldorfer Nachrichten, June 4, 1960 (Germany)
Evening News, March 10, 1884 (Salvini)
Evening Standard, March 10, 1884 (Salvini)
Financial Times, April 7, 1973 (Quilley)
Frankfurter Neue Presse, June 4, 1960 (Germany)

Licensed Victualler's Gazette and Hotel Courier,
    Sept. 15, 1911 (Tree)
Morning Advertiser, June 15, 1955 (Olivier)
New Statesman, April 23, 1949 (Tearle)
New York Times, Nov. 10, 1895 (Irving); June
    19, 1961
Observer, Sept. 10, 1911 (Tree); April 8, 1973
    (Quilley)
Saint James Chronicle, Oct. 1773 (Garrick)

South London Advertiser, Feb. 26, 1971
Spectator, July 18, 1840 (C. Kean)
Standard, March 10, 1884 (Salvini)
Stratford-upon-Avon Herald, June 13, 1952
    (Richardson)
Svenska Dagbladet, May 10, 1909 (Sweden)
Times, Sept. 10, 1954 (Rogers)
Unidentified clippings

Act V, Scene vii

BOOKS, ARTICLES AND PERSONAL
REPORTS

Agate, (1) 240–41 (Garrick); 243 (Olivier)
Alger, 745 (Forrest)
Bab, *op. cit.* (Matkowsky)
Brecht, (4); see also citation in TEP program,
    France, 1973
Brooks, 199
Brown, J. R., (1) 146–47 (Porter)
Chambers, edition
Clarence, 92 (Irving)
Coleman, 223–24 (Macready)
Coursen, 376
Cunningham, D., 43f.
De Vos, (1) 258 (Rossi)
Duthie, (1) 122ff.
Dyce, edition
Empson, (3) 120
Farnham, (2) 130f.
Favorini, *op. cit.* (Mantell)
Findlater, 78 (M. Redgrave)
Finlay, 248
Forster, *Examiner,* Oct. 4, 1835
Gentleman, 103–4 (Garrick)
Gielgud, Kate T., 96 (Irving)
Granville-Barker, *Preface*
Greg, (2) 394
Harbage, 398
Hawkins, 275 (Kean)
Heilman, (1) 20–23
House, personal discussion
James, H., 177 (Salvini)
Kemble, F., 78
Kemble, J. P., (2) 78
Leech, 30
Mack, Jr., 184
Marston, J. W., 79 (Macready), 175 (C. Kean)
Martinet, Mlle., personal discussion
Milward, Kumo prod.
McKellen, personal discussion
Muir, (3) 47
Potter, personal discussion
Pücklar-Muskau, 41 (Macready)
Robinson, E., personal report (Olivier)

Rogers, letter
Rosenberg, (2) (Scofield)
Scofield, personal discussion
Siddons, *op. cit.*
Stevenson, review
Terry, *passim* (Irving)
Wilson, J. D., edition
Williamson, A., (2) 110 (Rogers); (3) 272
    (Tearle)
Winter, (7) 465 (Kean), 479 (Booth), 484
    (Irving)

PROMPTBOOKS

Shattuck: 8, 11, 16, 29, 47, 53, 66, 90, 108,
    112, 118, 122, 123, 127, 137, 144, 146

PERIODICALS

Academy, Apr. 15, 1876 (Salvini); May 13,
    1876 (Rossi, Irving)
Athenaeum, Oct. 2, 1875 (Irving); May 2, 1876
    (Rossi)
Atlas, July 11, 1840 (C. Kean)
Bath Journal, March 12, 1832 (Macready)
Belfast Newsletter, Feb. 20, 1824 (Macready)
Bell's Life in London, May 20, 1876 (Rossi)
Bell's Weekly Messenger, Oct. 2, 1875 (Irving);
    May 13, 1876 (Rossi)
Berliner Morgenpost, Oct. 12, 1968 (Germany)
Birmingham Mail, Dec. 2, 1947 (Redgrave)
Birmingham Post, Dec. 31, 1888 (Irving); Aug.
    24, 25, 1954 (Rogers); June 6, 1962 (Porter)
Boston Daily Advertiser, Oct. 13, 1875 (Irving)
Boston Globe, April 22, 1896 (Irving)
Boston Transcript, Sept. 17, 1935 (Merivale)
Brooklyn Times, Nov. 2, 1881 (Booth)
Champion, Nov. 13, 1814 (Kean)
Chicago Daily News, Jan. 13, 1934
Chicago Tribune, Feb. 13, 1957 (Rogers); June
    19, 1962 (Plummer)
Daily Alta California, Oct. 22, 1876 (Booth)
Daily Chronicle, Feb. 7, 1928 (Maturin)
Daily Express, Sept. 4, 1957 (Littlewood)

Daily Herald, Feb. 7, 1928 (Maturin)
Daily Mail, Feb. 7, 1928 (Maturin); March 6, 1975 (Williamson)
Daily Mirror, Feb. 8, 1928 (Maturin)
Daily News, Sept. 27, 1875 (Irving); Dec. 31, 1888 (Irving)
Daily Telegraph, Nov. 5, 1864 (Phelps); Sept. 27, 1875 (Irving); Dec. 31, 1888 (Irving); Sept. 6, 7, 1911 (Tree)
Derby Evening Telegraph, Oct. 11, 1967 (Scofield)
Dispatch, Dec. 30, 1888 (Irving)
Dramatic Magazine, Oct. 12, 1829 (Young)
Dramatic Review, Jan. 5, 1889 (Irving)
Düsseldorfer Nachrichten, June 4, 1970 (Germany)
Edinburgh Dramatic Review, Feb. 9, 1824 (John Vandenhoff); Feb. 22, 1825 (John Vandenhoff)
Edinburgh Evening News, Aug. 24, 1954 (Rogers)
English Illustrated Magazine, Dec., 1888 (Macready)
Era, Nov. 6, 1864 (Phelps); May 14, 1876 (Rossi)
Etudes Anglaises, Aug., 1954 (Vilar, France)
Evening News, March 10, 1884 (Salvini); Nov. 27, 1937 (Olivier)
Evening Post, Dec. 31, 1888 (Terry)
Evening Standard, Sept. 27, 1875 (Irving); March 10, 1884 (Salvini); Dec. 31, 1888 (Irving); Sept. 6, 1911 (Tree); June 13, 1952 (Richardson)
Evesham Journal, April 23, 1949 (Tearle)
Examiner, Nov. 13, 1814 (Kean); Oct. 5, 1835 (Macready); Oct. 2, 1875 (Irving)
Financial Times, Aug. 25, 1954 (Rogers); June 6, 1962 (Porter); Nov. 10, 1969; March 6, 1975 (Williamson)
Freeman's Journal, Aug. 8, 1822; March 6, 1833 (Macready)
Glasgow Herald, Oct. 20, 1970
Globe, Dec. 31, 1888 (Irving)
Gloucester Echo, Dec. 9, 1938 (Wolfit); June 8, 1955 (Olivier)
Guardian, May 21, 1969 (Marowitz)
Jewish Chronicle, Nov. 1, 1974 (Williamson)
John O'London's Weekly, Jan. 9, 1948 (Redgrave)
Lady, June 23, 1955 (Olivier)
Lady's Pictorial, Jan. 5, 1889 (Irving)
Literary Gazette, Feb. 19, 1846 (C. Kean)
Liverpool Daily Post, Dec. 31, 1888 (Irving)
Lloyd's Weekly London Newspaper, Oct. 3, 1847 (Phelps); Jan. 6, 1889 (Irving)
Magazine of Art, 1889 (Irving)
Manchester Guardian, Dec. 20, 1947 (Redgrave)
Morning Advertiser, April 10, 1884 (Salvini); June 15, 1955 (Olivier)
Morning Chronicle, Oct. 5, 1947 (Macready)

Morning Leader, Sept. 6, 1911 (Tree)
Morning Post, Nov. 7, 1814 (Kean); Oct. 5, 1847 (Macready); Sept. 27, 1875 (Garrick); Sept. 22, 1875 (Irving); Sept. 27, 1875 (Macready); Feb. 7, 1928 (Maturin); April 3, 1934 (Laughton)
Pittsburgh Dispatch, Dec. 4, 1920 (Mantell)
Pittsburgh Post, Oct. 12, 1909 (Mantell)
Pittsburgh Sun-Telegraph, April 2, 1929 (Craig prod.)
Plays and Players, March, 1969; July, 1969; Jan., 1973
Punch, April 11, 1934 (Laughton); July 22, 1942 (Gielgud); Dec. 31, 1947 (Redgrave)
Reading Evening Post, June 6, 1972 (Germany)
Saint James Chronicle, Jan. 18, 1768 (Garrick); Oct. 30, 1773 (Garrick)
Saturday Review, March 30, 1889 (Irving); April 23, 1898; Feb. 11, 1928 (Maturin)
Scotsman, Feb. 28, 1825 (Kean); April 6, 1876 (Salvini); Aug. 25, 1954 (Rogers); March 23, 1970; March 16, 1974; Nov. 2, 1974 (Williamson)
Le Siecle, May 26, 1884 (Marais)
South London Press, March 12, 1971
Spectator, July 18, 1840 (C. Kean); Oct. 2, 1875 (Irving); Jan. 5, 1889 (Irving); Aug. 12, 1966 (Clements)
Sporting Gazette, Oct. 2, 1875 (Irving)
Sporting Life, Nov. 9, 1864 (Phelps)
New Monthly Magazine, Dec. 1, 1814 (Kean)
New Statesman, April 23, 1949 (Tearle); June 21, 1952 (Richardson); Aug. 12, 1966 (Clements); Jan. 12, 1968 (Scofield)
New York Daily News, July 16, 1973 (Weaver)
New York Herald Tribune, Nov. 12, 1941 (Evans)
New York Times, July 29, 1873; Dec. 29, 1888 (Irving); Nov. 19, 1889 (Booth); Feb. 8, 1916 (Hackett); April 1, 1948 (Redgrave); July 15, 1973 (Weaver)
News, Nov. 11, 1814 (Kean)
News Chronicle, Nov. 27, 1937 (Olivier)
Notes and Queries, July 13, 1889 (C. Kean)
Nottingham Evening Post, Oct. 30, 1898 (Irving)
Nottingham Journal, June 6, 1962 (Porter)
Observer, Feb. 26, 1844 (C. Kean); July 9, 1882 (Rignold); Jan. 20, 1929; April 27, 1958 ("Throne of Blood"); April 8, 1973 (Quilley)
Overland Monthly, Feb. 1886 (Rankin)
PM, April 2, 1948 (Redgrave)
Philadelphia Evening Bulletin, Nov. 27, 1941 (Evans)
Sportsman, Dec. 31, 1888 (Irving)
Stage, Jan. 4, 1889 (Irving); Sept. 7, 1911 (Tree); Dec. 30, 1926; April 28, 1927 (Walter); March 20, 1930 (Gielgud); Nov. 24, 1932 (Carrick Craig prod.); Jan. 22, 1942

Stage (continued)
(Gielgud); April 21, 1949 (Tearle); March
26, 1953 (Wolfit); June 9, 1955 (Olivier)
Stockholmstidningen, Nov. 11, 1944 (Bergman);
March 13, 1948 (Bergman)
Stratford-Upon-Avon Herald, June 10, 1955
(Olivier); June 8, 1962 (Porter)
Suddeutsche Zeitung, Mar. 11, 1977 (Germany)
Sun, Nov. 7, 1814 (Kean); April 5, 1842 (C.
Kean)
Sunday Times, Nov. 6, 1864 (Phelps); July 9,
1882 (Rignold); Dec. 31, 1888 (Irving); Sept.
10, 1911 (Olivier); Aug. 7, 1966 (Clements)
Tablet, Oct. 27, 1962 (Porter)
Der Tagesspiegel, Oct, 12, 1968 (Germany)
Theatre, March 1, 1844 (Phelps); Dec. 1, 1888
(Irving)
Theatre Royal, Jan. 7, 1837 (Forrest)
Theatrical Inquisitor, Nov. 14, 1814 (Kean)
Theatrical Journal, Aug. 8, 1940 (Macready);
April 2, 1842 (Macready)
Times, March 29, 1842 (Macready); Oct. 2,
1875 (Irving); Dec. 31, 1888 (Irving); March
18, 1890 (Booth); July 24, 1917 (Hackett);
Aug. 25, 1954 (Rogers); June 8, 1955
(Olivier); May 22, 1966 (Guinness)

Toronto Star, June 19, 1962 (Plummer); June
10, 1971 (Hogg)
Tribune, Oct. 1, 1954 (Rogers); July 28, 1955
(Olivier)
Truth, Sept. 13, 1911 (Tree); June 20, 1952
(Richardson)
Universal Review, Jan. 15, 1889 (Irving)
Vanity Fair, Oct. 2, 1875 (Irving)
Weekly Dispatch, Oct. 10, 1847 (Macready)
Yorkshire Post, Oct. 31, 1974 (Williamson)
Unidentified clippings: April 11, 1826 (Mac-
ready); Dec. 23, 1827 (Cooper); Feb. 14,
1853 (C. Kean); Sept. 27, 1875 (Irving); Dec.
31, 1888 (Irving); Oct. 30, 1895 (Irving); Jan.
21, 1911 (Sothern); Sept. 6, 1911 (Tree);
Nov. 15, 1941 (Evans); June 6, 1962 (Porter)
Other unidentified clippings

APPENDIX

This essay first appeared in *Educational Theatre
Journal,* Spring, 1974.

Main Bibliography

Anonymous. (1) *An Estimate of the Theatrical Merits of the Two Tragedians of Crow Street.* 1760.
———. (2) *A Letter of Compliment to the Ingenious Author of A Treatise on the Passions.* 1760.
———. (3) *Glimpses of Real Life as Seen in the Theatrical World.* 1864.
Abercrombie, Lascelles. *The Idea of Great Poetry.* 1925.
Adam, B. J. "The Real Macbeth: King of Scots, 1040-1054." *History Today* 7 (1957) 381–387.
Agate, James. (1) *Brief Chronicles.* 1943.
———. (2) *These Were Actors: Extracts From a Newspaper Cutting Book 1811-1833.* Selected and annotated by James Agate. 1943.
———. (3) *The Amazing Theatre.* 1939.
Agate, May. *Madame Sarah.* 1946.
Akutagawa, Hiroshi. Interview given to Peter Milward and Tetsuo Anzai, January 16, 1972.
Alger, William R. *The Life of Edwin Forrest.* Vol. 2. 1877.
Amneus, Daniel. "Macbeth's Greater Honor." *Shakespeare Studies* 6 (1967).
"An Actress." *The True Ophelia: and Other Studies of Shakespeare's Women.* 1913.
And, Metin. "Shakespeare in Turkey." *Theatre Research* 6 (1964) 75–84.
Anderson, Judith. Personal discussion.
Andrews, John F. "*The Ipissima Verba* in My Diary?" *Shakespeare Studies* 8 (1975) 333–368.
Anglin, Margaret. Letter to Gordon Craig. See Craig, Gordon, below
Appleton, William W. *Charles Macklin—An Actor's Life.* 1960.
Archer, William. (1) *Eminent Actors.* Vols. 1–3. 1890.
———. (2) *William Charles Macready.* 1890.
Archer, William, and Robert Lowe. (1) *The Life of Henry Irving: The Fashionable Tragedian.* 1883.
———. (2) "Macbeth on the Stage." *English Illustrated Magazine*, Dec., 1888, 233–252.
Armstrong, Cecil P. *A Century of Great Actors—1750-1850.* 1912.
Armstrong, Edward A. *Shakespeare's Imagination.* 1946.
Armstrong, W. A. (1) "The Elizabethan Conception of the Tyrant." *Review of English Studies* 22 (1946) 161–181.
———. (2) "The Influence of Seneca and Machiavelli on the Elizabethan Tyrant." *Review of English Studies* 24 (1948) 19–35.

Arnold, Aerol. "The Recapitulation Dream in *Richard III* and *Macbeth*." *Shakespeare Quarterly* 6 (1955) 51–62.

Arnott, James F. "Shakespeare and the Marvellous." *Revue d'histoire du théâtre* 15 (1963) 21–28.

Aronson, Alex. *Psyche and Symbol in Shakespeare.* 1972.

Arthos, John. "The Naive Imagination and the Destruction of Macbeth." *English Literary History* 14 (1947) 114–126.

Arthur, Sir George. *From Phelps to Gielgud.* 1936.

Ashwell, Lena. (1) *Myself a Player.* 1936.

———. (2) *Reflections from Shakespeare.* 1926.

Atherton, J. S. "Shakespeare's Latin, Two Notes." *Notes and Queries* 196 (1951) 337.

Auden, W. H. *The Dyer's Hand and Other Essays.* 1932.

Auerbach, Erich. *Mimesis.* 1946.

Aycock, Roy E. "Shakespearian Criticism in the Gray's Inn Journal." *Yearbook of English Studies* 2 (1972) 68–72.

A Warning to Fair Women. Anon. 1599.

Bab, Julius. *Adalbert Matkowsky, eine Heldensage.* 1938.

Babb, Lawrence. *The Elizabethan Malady.* 1951.

Babcock, Weston. "Macbeth's 'Cream-Fac'd Loone.' " *Shakespeare Quarterly* 4 (1953) 199–202.

Bache, William B. " 'The Murder of Old Cole': A Possible Source for *Macbeth*." *Shakespeare Quarterly* 6 (1955) 358–359.

Baird, David. "Some Doubtful Points in *Macbeth*." *Notes and Queries* 173 (1937) 224.

Bajocchi, Fedele. "*Macbeth*, I, ii." *Times Literary Supplement*, March 23, 1940.

Baker, Henry Barton. (1) *English Actors from Shakespeare to Macready.* 1879.

———. (2) *The London Stage.* 1889.

———. (3) *Our Old Actors.* Vol. 2. 1881.

Baker, Herschel. *John Philip Kemble.* 1942.

Bald, R. C. (1) "*Macbeth* and the 'Short' Plays." *Review of English Studies* 4 (1928) 429–431.

———. (2) "Shakespeare on the Stage in Restoration Dublin." *PMLA* 56 (1941).

Barbauld, Anna Laetitia. *The Works of Anna Laetitia Barbauld.* Vol. 1. 1825.

Barker, Felix. *The Oliviers.* 1953.

Barnet, Sylvan. "Coleridge on Shakespeare's Villains." *Shakespeare Quarterly* 7 (1956) 9–20.

Barrault, Jean Louis. (1) *Apropos de Shakespeare et du Théâtre.* 1949.

———. (2) *Nouvelles Reflexions sur le Théâtre.* 1959.

Barrett, Lawrence. *Charlotte Cushman.* 1870.

Barrie, J. M. "What the Pit Says About the Lyceum." *London Times*, Feb., 1889.

Barron, David B. "The Babe That Milks: An Organic Study of *Macbeth*." *American Imago* 17 (1960) 133–161.

Barrymore, Lionel. *We Barrymores.* 1951.

Bartholomeusz, Dennis. *Macbeth and the Players.* 1969.

Barton, Margaret. *David Garrick.* 1948.

Battenhouse, Roy. *Shakespearean Tragedy, Its Art and Its Christian Premises.* 1960.

Baxter, Peter. *The Drama in Perth.* 1907.

Beckerman, Bernard. "The Life of the Scene." Paper read to the Modern Language Association. 1973.

"Bede, Cuthbert." "Macbeth on the Stage." *Notes and Queries.* July 13, 1889.

Bell, G. J. Notes on Sarah Siddons as Lady Macbeth. See Jenkin, Fleeming, below.

Bell, Mary. "Walter Whiter's Notes on Shakespeare." *Shakespeare Survey* 20 (1967) 92.

Bellamy, G. A. *Apology for the Life of G. A. Bellamy.* 1785.

Benson, Sir Francis R. *My Memoirs*. 1930.

Benson, Mrs. G. C. *Mainly Players*. 1926.

Bergman, Ingmar. Comments in interviews on stagings of *Macbeth*, 1944, 1948.

Berlyne, D. E. *Aesthetics and Psychobiology*. 1971.

Bernadete, J. A. "Macbeth's Last Words." *Interpretation* (The Hague) 1 (1970) 63–75.

Bernard, Michael A., S.J. "The Five Tragedies in *Macbeth*." *Shakespeare Quarterly* 13 (1962) 63–75.

Bernhardt, Sarah. *Memories of My Life*. 1908.

Berry, Francis. *The Poet's Grammar: Person, Time and Mood in Poetry*. 1958.

Bethell, S. L. (1) *Shakespeare and the Popular Dramatic Tradition*. 1944.

———. (2) "Shakespeare's Imagery: The Diabolic Images in *Othello*." *Shakespeare Survey* 8 (1952) 68.

Bevington, David. *Tudor Drama and Politics*. 1968.

Biggins, Dennis. " 'Appal' in *Macbeth*, III, iv, 60." *English Language Notes* 4 (1967) 259–261.

Billington, Michael. *The Modern Actor*. 1973.

Biswanger, Raymond A., Jr. "More Seventeenth Century Allusions to Shakespeare." *Notes and Queries* 2 (1850) 301–302.

Black, James. Personal comments.

Bland, D. S. "*Macbeth* and the 'Battle of Otterburn.' " *Notes and Queries* 194 (1949) 335–336.

Blissett, William. "The Secret'st Man of Blood. A Study of Dramatic Irony in *Macbeth*." *Shakespeare Quarterly* 10 (1959) 397–408.

Bloch, Marc. *Les Rois Thaumaturges*. 1961.

Boaden, James. (1) *Memoirs of Mrs. Siddons*. 1893.

———. (2) *Memoirs of the Life of John Philip Kemble, esq.* 2 vols. 1825.

———. (3) *Mrs. Jordan*. 2 vols. 1830.

———. (4) Ed. *The Private Correspondence of David Garrick with the Most Celebrated Persons of His Time*. 2 vols. 1831–32.

Bodenstedt, Friedrich. "Mrs. Siddons." *Shakespeare Jahrbuch*, 1 (1865) 341–361.

Bodis, Klara. Letter, 1973. On *Macbeth* in Hungary.

Bogard, Travis. Personal report on Hordern *Macbeth*.

Boll, André. *Le Théâtre Total*. 1971.

Booth, Edwin. (1) *Between Actor and Critic: Selected Letters of Edwin Booth and William Winter*. Daniel J. Watermeier, ed. 1971.

———. (2) *Edwin Booth: Letters to His Friends*. E. Grossman, ed. 1902.

———. (3) Letter to H. H. Furness, University of Pennsylvania Library.

———. (4) *Promptbook*, William Winter, ed. 16 vols. 1878-90.

Booth, Stephen. (1) Personal Report on Charlton Heston *Macbeth*, 1975.

———. (2) "Shakespeare in California." *Shakespeare Quarterly* 27 (1976) 94ff.

Booth, Wayne. "Shakespeare's Tragic Villain." *Shakespeare's Tragedies: A Selection of Modern Criticism*. 1963.

Bourdon, Georges. *Les Théâtres Anglais*. 1903.

Boyd, Catherine B. "The Isolation of Antigone and Lady Macbeth." *Classical Journal* 47 (1952) 174–177, 203.

Boyle, Robert R., S.J. "The Imagery of Macbeth, I, vii, 21–28." *Modern Language Quarterly* 16 (1955) 130–136.

Bradbrook, M. C. "The Sources of *Macbeth*." *Shakespeare Survey* 4 (1951) 35–47.

Bradley, A. C. *Shakespearean Tragedy*. 1904.

Bragaglia, Leonardo. *65 Anni di Storia del Teatro Rappresentato*. n.d.

Brahms, Caryl. "Perils of Trying to Be 'bloody, bold, and resolute.' " *Times*, Oct. 17, 1966.

Brandes, George. *William Shakespeare*. 1905.

Brandl, A. "Zur Vorgeschichte der Weird Sisters in *Macbeth.*" *Forschungen und Charakteristiken*, 1936, 82–97.

Braun, Felix. "Über Macbeth. Eine Ansprache." *Die Eisblume*. 1955. 84–91.

Brecht, Bertolt. (1) *Brecht on Theatre: The Development of an Aesthetic*. Translated by John Willett. 1964.

——. (2) "A Model for Epic Theatre." Translated by Eric Bentley. *Sewanee Review* 57 (1949) 425–436.

——. (3) Program note for T.E.P. production, Paris, 1973. Quoted.

——. (4) "Vorrede zu Macbeth." *Schriften zum Theater*, I, 1819-1913 (1963).

Brereton, Austin. (1) *The Life of Henry Irving*. 1908.

——. (2) *Henry Irving: A Biographical Sketch*. 1883.

——. (3) *The Lyceum and Henry Irving*. 1903.

Brereton, Geoffrey. *Principles of Tragedy*. 1968.

Bridges, Robert. *The Influence of the Audience*. 1926.

Briggs, Katharine M. *Pale Hecate's Team*. 1962.

Brindley, D. J. "Reversal of Values in *Macbeth.*" *English Studies in Africa*. n.d.

Broadbent, R. J. (1) *Annals of the Liverpool Stage*. 1908.

——. (2) *Annals of the Manchester Stage* (in manuscript).

——. (3) *Stage Whispers*. n.d.

Brock, F. H. Cecil. "Oedipus, Macbeth and the Christian Tradition." *Connecticut Review*, 1950, 176–181.

Brockett, O. G. *Studies in Theatre and Drama*. 1972.

Brooks, Cleanth. "The Naked Babe and the Cloak of Manliness." *The Well-Wrought Urn*. 1947.

Brown, John Mason. (1) *Dramatis Personae*. 1963.

——. (2) "When the Hurly-Burly's Done." *Saturday Review of Literature* 21 (1948) 42–46.

Brown, John R. (1) "Acting Shakespeare Today." *Shakespeare Survey* 16 (1963).

——. (2) *Shakespeare: The Tragedy of Macbeth*. 1963.

——. (3) *Shakespeare's Plays in Performance*. 1966.

——. (4) *Free Shakespeare*. 1975.

Browne, E. Martin. "Review of Guinness' *Macbeth.*" *Drama Survey* 6 (1967) 81–82.

Bruford, Walter Horace. *Theatre, Drama and Audience in Goethe's Germany*. 1950.

Bryant, Joseph Allen. *Hippolyta's View*. 1961.

Buck, Howard S. *A Study in Smollett*. 1955.

Buck-Marchand, Eva. "*Macbeth*, ein Charakteranalyse." *Shakespeare Jahrbuch* 77 (1941) 49–73.

Buland, Mabel. *The Presentation of Time in Elizabethan Drama*. 1912.

Bulthaupt, Heinrich. *Shakespeare und die Virtuosen*. 1890.

Burnim, Kalman A. *David Garrick, Director*. 1961.

Burton, Hal, ed. *Great Acting*. 1961.

Burton, Robert. *The Anatomy of Melancholy*. 1624. Floyd Dell and Paul Jordan Smith, eds. 1968.

Byrne, Myrtle, St. Clare. (1) "The Stage Costuming of *Macbeth* in the 18th Century." *Studies in English Theatre History in Memory of Gabrielle Enthoven* (1952) 52–64.

——. (2) Letter on A. Russell Thorndike as Macbeth. Feb. 2, 1974.

——. (3) "Dramatic Intention and Theatrical Realization" in *The Triple Bond*, 1975.

Caine, T. Hall. *Richard III and Macbeth: The Spirit of the Romantic Play in Relationship to the Principles of Greek and Gothic Art and to the Picturesque Interpretation of Mr. Henry Irving*. 1877.

Calhoun, Eleanor (Princess Lazarovich-Hrebelianovich). *Pleasures and Palaces*. 1915.

Calvert, Louis. *Problems of the Actor.* 1918.

Calvert, Walter. *Sir Henry Irving and Miss Ellen Terry.* 1897.

Campbell, Douglas. *Macbeth.* Three Filmed Lessons, Color Series No. 47570. Encyclopedia Britannica Educational Corporation.

Campbell, Lily B. (1) "*Macbeth:* A Study in Fear" in *Shakespeare's Tragic Heroes: Slaves of Passion.* 1930 (reprinted 1963).

———. (2) "Political Ideas in *Macbeth,* IV, iii." *Shakespeare Quarterly* 2 (1951) 281–286.

Campbell, Mrs. Patrick. (1) *Bernard Shaw and Mrs. Patrick Campbell: Their Correspondence.* Alan Dent, ed. 1952.

———. (2) *My Life and Some Letters.* 1922.

Campbell, Thomas. *Life of Mrs. Siddons,* including "Remarks on Lady Macbeth" by Sarah Siddons. 1834.

Capell, Edward. *Notes and Various Readings to Shakespeare.* 1779.

Caraman, Philip. *Henry Garnet, 1555-1606, and the Gunpowder Plot.* 1964.

Carlisle, Carol J. (1) "The Macbeths and the Actors." *Renaissance Papers,* 1958-1960, 46–57.

———. (2) "The Nineteenth Century Actors Versus the Closet Critics of Shakespeare." *Studies in Philology* 51 (1954) 599–615.

———. (3) *Shakespeare from the Greenroom: Actors' Criticism of Four Major Tragedies.* 1969.

Carter, Huntly. *The Theatre of Max Reinhardt.* 1914.

Casson, Lewis. Introduction to *Macbeth.* Folio Society, 1951.

Chambers, David L. *The Meter of Macbeth and Its Relation to Shakespeare's Earlier and Later Work.* 1903.

Chambers, Sir Edmund K. (1) *The Elizabethan Stage.* 4 vols. 1923.

———. (2) *William Shakespeare.* 1930.

Charlton, H. B. *Shakespearian Tragedy.* 1952.

Cheramy, Paul Arthur. *A Favorite of Napoleon: Memoirs of Mlle. George.* 1909.

Church, Tony. Personal discussion, 1975.

Clapp, Henry Austin. *Reminiscences of a Dramatic Critic.* 1902.

Clarke, Asia Booth. *The Elder and the Younger Booth.* 1882.

Clarke, C. C. "Darkened Reason in Macbeth." *Durham University Journal,* n.s. 22 (1960) 11ff.

Clayden, P. W. "Macbeth and Lady Macbeth." *Fortnightly Review* 8 (1867) 153–168.

Clemen, Wolfgang. (1) *The Development of Shakespeare's Imagery.* 1951.

———. (2) *Shakespeare's Dramatic Art.* 1972.

Clemeshaw, Isabel B. "Literary Notes: *Macbeth.*" *Theosophical Forum* 28 (1950) 291–297.

Clunes, Alec. *The British Theatre.* 1964.

Clurman, H. "Trouble with Shakespeare." *New Republic* 118 (1948) 30–33.

Coe, Charles Norton. *Shakespeare's Villains.* 1957.

Coghill, Nevill. (1) *Stratford Papers on Shakespeare.* B. W. Jackson, ed. 1962.

———. (2) *Shakespeare's Professional Skills.* 1964.

———. (3) Personal report on *Macbeth* stagings.

———. (4) "Macbeth at the Globe, 1606-1616" in *The Triple Bond.* Joseph Price, ed. 1975. See under Price, J. below.

Cohn, Norman. *Europe's Inner Demons.* 1975.

Cole, J. W. *The Life and Theatrical Times of Charles Kean.* 2 vols. in one. 1859.

Coleman, John. (1) "Facts and Fancies about Macbeth." *Gentleman's Magazine.* 1889.

———. (2) *Fifty Years of an Actor's Life.* 2 vols. 1904.

———. (3) *Memoirs of Samuel Phelps.* 1886.

———. (4) *Players and Playwrights I Have Known.* 1888.

Coleman, Marion M. *Fair Rosalind: The American Career of Helena Modjeska.* 1969.
Coleridge, Samuel Taylor. *Shakespearean Criticism.* T. M. Raysor, ed. 1931.
Collection of the Institute für Theaterwissenschaft, Cologne.
Collier, John Payne. (1) *History of English Dramatic Poetry.* Vol. 1. 1831.
———. (2) *New Particulars Regarding the Works of Shakespeare.* 1836 (reprinted, 1973).
Collison-Morley, Lacy. *Shakespeare in Italia.* 1916.
Comyns Carr, Alice. "Ellen Terry: Recollections of a Long Friendship." *Fortnightly Review* 112 (1922) 230–243.
Comyns Carr, John. *Macbeth and Lady Macbeth.* 1889.
Connolly, Thomas F. "Shakespeare and the Double Man." *Shakespeare Quarterly* 1 (1950) 30–35.
Cook, Dutton. (1) *Hours with the Players.* 1883.
———. (2) *On the Stage: Studies of Theatrical History and the Actor's Art.* 2 vols. 1883.
Cooke, William. *Memoirs of Charles Macklin.* 1804.
Cookson, George. "*Macbeth.*" *English* 1 (1937) 431–432.
Copeland, Charles T. *Edwin Booth.* 1901.
Coriat, Isador H. *The Hysteria of Lady Macbeth.* 1912.
Cormican, L. M. "Medieval Idiom in *Macbeth.*" *Scrutiny* 17 (1950) 186–298.
Cossons, Judith. "*Macbeth* I, vii [6.]" *Notes and Queries* 196 (1951) 368.
Cotton, William. *The Story of the Drama in Exeter.* n.d.
Cottrell, John. *Laurence Olivier.* 1975.
Coursen, Herbert R., Jr. "In Deepest Consequence: *Macbeth.*" *Shakespeare Quarterly* 19 (1967) 375–388.
Cowell, Joe. *Thirty Years Passed Among the Actors and Actresses of England and America.* 1844.
Cox, H. Gatti. *Shakespeare nei Teatri Milanesi.* 1968.
Craig, Edward Carrick. Personal discussion and private notebooks. 1973–1974.
Craig, (Edward) Gordon (1) *The Art of the Theatre.* 1912.
———. (2) Collection in Bibliotheque de L'Arsenal. No. 231 in the Gordon Craig Exhibition Catalogue, 1962.
———. (3) *Henry Irving.* 1930.
———. (4) Letter to Margaret Anglin, theatre program. 1928.
———. (5) Letter to R. Boleslevsky. Craig collection, L'Arsenal.
———. (6) Personal notebooks and promptbooks, Edward Carrick Craig collection.
———. (7) Ms. draft of letter to Mme. Meyerhold about Lady Macbeth, Humanities Research Center, Dallas.
Craig, Hardin. (1) *The Enchanted Glass: The Elizabethan Mind in Literature.* 1960.
———. (2) *An Interpretation of Shakespeare.* 1948.
———. (3) "These Juggling Fiends: On the Meaning of *Macbeth.*" In *The Written Word and Other Essays,* 49–61. 1953.
Crane, Milton. *Shakespeare's Prose.* 1951.
Crane, Ronald S. *The Language of Criticism and the Structure of Poetry.* 1953.
Croce, Benedetto. *Ariosto, Shakespeare, Corneille.* 1920.
Cross, Linda and Roger. Personal reports on *Macbeth* stagings.
Crosse, Gordon. (1) *Shakespearean Playgoing.* 1953.
———. (2) "A Reminiscence of Macready in *Edwin Drood.*" *Notes and Queries* 161 (1916) 25.
Crusty, Thomas. "Desultory Reminiscences of Miss O'Neill." *Blackwood's Magazine* 27 (1830) 47–58.
Cunningham, Dolora G. "Macbeth: The Tragedy of the Hardened Heart." *Shakespeare Quarterly* 14 (1963) 39–47.

Curry, Walter C. *Shakespeare's Philosophical Patterns.* 1959.

Cutts, John P. (1) "The Original Music to Middleton's *The Witch.*" *Shakespeare Quarterly* 7 (1956) 203–209.

———. (2) "Who Wrote the Hecate-Scene?" *Shakespeare Jahrbuch*, 1958, 200–202.

Daly, Frederick. *Henry Irving in England and America: 1883-1884.* 1884.

Daly, Joseph Francis. *The Life of Augustan Daly.* 1917.

Daneau, Lambert. *A Dialogue of Witches . . .* trans. 1875.

Danks, K. B. (1) "Macbeth and the Word 'Strange'." *Notes and Queries*, n.s., 1 (1954) 425.

———. (2) "Shakespeare and 'Equivocator' Etc." *Notes and Queries*, n.s. 2 (1955) 289–292.

Darroll, G. M. H. "The Tragic Stupidity." *English Studies in Africa* 5 (1962) 49–58.

Das Gupta, Arun Kumar. "A Note on *Macbeth*, II, ii, 61-63." *Notes and Queries* 7 (1960) 332–333.

Davenport, A. "Shakespeare and Nashe's *Pierce Penilesse.*" *Notes and Queries* 198 (1953) 371–374.

David, Richard. "The Tragic Curve." *Shakespeare Survey* 9 (1956) 122–131.

Davidson, Clifford. (1) "Full of Scorpions Is My Mind." *Times Literary Supplement*, Letter to Editor, Nov. 4, 1968.

———. (2) *The Primrose Way: A Study of Shakespeare's Macbeth.* 1970.

Davies, Thomas. (1) *Dramatic Miscellanies.* Vol. 2. 1783.

———. (2) *Memoirs of the Life of David Garrick, esq.* 1784. Thomas Davies, ed.

Daw, E. B. "Two Notes on the 'Trial of Treasure.' " *Modern Philology* 15 (1917) 53–55.

Dawson, Giles E. "The Catholic University *Macbeth.*" *Shakespeare Quarterly* 3 (1952) 255–256.

Day, Muriel C., and Trewin, J. C. *The Shakespeare Memorial Theatre.* 1932.

Debax, J. P. "*Macbeth* et la tradition de la moralité avec reference particuliers aux images vestimentaires." *Caliban* 5, no. 1, pp. 15–29.

Delderfield, Eric B. *Cavalcade by Candlelight: The Story of Exeter's Five Theatres 1725-1950.* 1950.

Dench, Judi. Personal discussion, 1976.

Dent, Alan. (1) *Mrs. Patrick Campbell.* 1961.

———. (2) *Preludes and Studies.* 1942.

———. (3) *World of Shakespeare: Animals and Monsters.* 1972.

Dent, Robert. Personal comments.

De Quincey, Thomas. "On the Knocking at the Gate in *Macbeth.*" *Miscellaneous Essays.* 1854. 9–16.

De Vos, Josef. (1) *Shakespeare in Flanders.* 1975.

———. (2) "Shakespeare in het Zuidnederlandse theater." *Wetenschappelijke Tijdingen* 30, no. 5 (1971) 291–302.

Dickens, Charles. *All the Year Round.* Oct. 16, 1875.

Dibdin, C. *A Complete History of the Stage.* Vol. 3. 1800.

Doak, H. M. "The Supernatural in *Macbeth.*" *Shakespeariana* 5 (1888) 341–347.

Donne, John. *Bianthanatos.* J. William Hebel, ed. 1930.

Donner, H. W. (1) "Rebellious Dead." *Times Literary Supplement*, September 28, 1949.

———. (2) " 'She should have Died Hereafter.' " *English Studies* 40 (1959) 385–389.

Donoghue, Denis. "Macklin's Shylock and Macbeth." *Studies: An Irish Quarterly Review* 13 (1954).

Donohue, Joseph W., Jr. (1) "Kemble and Mrs. Siddons in *Macbeth*: The Romantic Approach to Tragic Character." *Theatre Notebook* 22 (1968) 65–86.

———. (2) "*Macbeth* in the Eighteenth Century." *Theatre Quarterly* 1 (1971) 20–24.

———. (3) *Dramatic Character in the English Romantic Age.* 1970.

Donohue, Joseph W., Jr. (4) *Theatre in the Age of Kean.* 1975.

Doran, John. "Their Majesties' Servants." Vol. 2. In *Annals of the English Stage.* 1888.

Doran, Madeleine. (1) "On Elizabethan Credulity." *Journal of the History of Ideas* 1 (1940) 151.

————. (2) "That Undiscovered Country: A Problem Concerning the Use of the Supernatural in *Hamlet* and *Macbeth.*" *Philological Quarterly* 20 (1941) 413–427.

Douglas, Mary. *Witchcraft Confessions and Accusations.* 1970.

Downer, Alan. (1) *The Eminent Tragedian.* 1965.

————. (2) "Macready's Production of *Macbeth.*" *Quarterly Journal of Speech*, April, 1947, 172–181.

————. (3) "The Making of a Great Actor: William Charles Macready." *Theatre Annual*, no. 5 (1949).

————. (4) "Nature to Advantage Dressed: Eighteenth Century Acting." *PMLA* 58 (1943) 1002–1037.

————. (5) "Players and the Painted Stage." *PMLA* 61 (1946) 722–776.

Draper, John W. (1) "The 'Gracious Duncan.'" *Modern Language Review* 36 (1941) 495–499.

————. (2) "King James and Shakespeare's Literary Style." *Archiv* 171 (1937) 36–48.

————. (3) "*Macbeth* as a Compliment to James I." *English Studies* 72 (1938) 207–220.

————. (4) "*Macbeth*, 'Infirme of Purpose.'" *Bulletin of the History of Medicine* 10 (1941) 16–26.

————. (5) "Patterns of Humor and Tempo in *Macbeth.*" *Neophilologus* 31 (1947) 202–207.

————. (6) "Political Themes in Shakespeare's Later Plays." *Journal of English and Germanic Philology* 35 (1936) 61–93.

————. (7) "Scene-Tempo in *Macbeth.*" *Shakespeare Studien, Festschrift für Heinrich Mutschmann*, 1951, 56–63.

————. (8) *The Tempo Patterns of Shakespeare's Plays.* 1957.

Drew, Edwin. *Henry Irving On and Off the Stage: His Macbeth, Faust, Etc., Etc.* 1889.

Driver, Tom. *The Sense of History in Greek and Shakespearean Drama.* 1960.

Dryden, John. *Of Dramatic Poesy and Other Critical Essays.* 1668.

Dukes, Ashley. "The Gielgud *Macbeth.*" *Theatre Arts Monthly* 26 (1942) 615–619.

Dukore, Bernard F. "Bernard Shaw: *Macbeth* Skit." *Educational Theatre Journal*, 1967, 343–348.

Dunlap, William. *Memoirs of George Frederick Cooke.* 1813.

Durian, H. *Jocza Savits und die Müncher Shakespearebühne.* 1937.

Durylin, S. N. *Maria Nicolaevna Ermolova, 1853-1928.* 1953.

Duthie, George Ian. (1) "Antithesis in *Macbeth.*" *Shakespeare Survey* 19 (1966) 25–33.

————. (2) "Shakespeare's *Macbeth*: A Study in Tragic Absurdity." *English Studies Today* 2 (1961) 121–128.

Dyson, J. P. "The Structural Function of the Banquet Scene in *Macbeth.*" *Shakespeare Quarterly* 14 (1963) 369–378.

Echeruo, Michael. "Tanistry, the 'Dye of Birth' and Macbeth's Sin." *Shakespeare Quarterly* 23 (1972) 444–445.

Eliade, Mircea. *The Sacred and the Profane: The Nature of Religion.* Translated by Willard R. Trask. 1959.

Elliot, George. *Dramatic Providence in Macbeth.* 1960.

Ellis, Ruth. *The Shakespeare Memorial Theatre.* 1948.

Ellis-Fermor, Una Mary. "Shakespeare, the Dramatist." In *Modern Writings on Major English Authors*, James R. Kreuger and Lee Cogan, eds. 1963.

Elton, William. (1) *King Lear and the Gods.* 1967.

————. (2) "Timothy Bright and Shakespeare's Seeds of Nature." *Modern Language Notes* 65 (1950) 196–7.

Elze, Karl. *"Hamlet* in Frankreich." *Shakespeare-Jahrbuch.* 1865.

Empson, William. (1) "Dover Wilson on *Macbeth." Kenyon Review* 14 (1952) 84–102.

————. (2) *Seven Types of Ambiguity."* 1930.

————. (3) *Structure of Complex Words.* 1951.

Englesfeld, Mladen. (1) Personal report on *Macbeth* in Yugoslavia.

————. (2) Report of press talk by Valdo Habunek, 1975.

Enthoven, Gabrielle. Collection of Playbills and Cuttings. Victoria and Albert Museum.

Erenstein, Marianne. Personal report, *Macbeth* in the Netherlands.

Ervine, St. John. *The Theatre in My Time.* 1933.

Evans, Bertrand. (1) *Gothic Drama from Walpole to Shelley.* 1947.

————. (2) Review of *Macbeth, San Francisco Chronicle.* 1972.

Evans, B. Ifor. *The Language of Shakespeare's Plays.* 1952.

Evans, G. Blakemore. *Shakespeare Promptbooks of the Seventeenth Century, the Padua Macbeth.* 1960.

Evans, M. S. "Free-Will in the Drama." *Personalist* 18 (1937) 273–291.

Ewbank, Inga-Stina. "The Fiend-like Queen: A Note on *Macbeth* and Seneca's *Medea."* *Shakespeare Survey* 19 (1966) 82–94.

Ewen, Cecil Henry L'Estrange. (1) *Witchcraft and Demonianism.* 1933.

————. (2) *Witchcraft in the Star Chamber.* 1938.

————. (3) *Witch Hunting and Witch Trials.* 1929.

Farington, Joseph. *Diary.* Vol. 7. 1927.

Farjeon, Herbert. *The Shakespearean Scene.* 1940.

Farnham, Willard. (1) *The Shakespearian Grotesque: Its Genesis and Transformations.* 1971.

————. (2) *Shakespeare's Tragic Frontier.* 1950.

————. (3) *The Medieval Heritage of Elizabethan Tragedy.* 1936.

Faucit, Helen. *On Some of Shakespeare's Female Characters.* 1888.

Favorini, Attilio. *The Last Tragedian: Robert B. Mantell and the American Theatre.* Unpublished Dissertation, Yale. 1969.

Fell-Smith, Charlotte. *John Dee: The World of an Elizabethan Magus.* 1909.

Fergusson, Francis. "*Macbeth* as the Imitation of an Action." *English Institute Essays,* 1951 (Columbia University Press, 1952) 31–43.

Fergusson, Sir James. *The Man Behind Macbeth.* 1969.

Fidler, Anne. *Shakespeare Criticism 1919-1935.* 1965.

Fiedler, Leslie A. *The Stranger in Shakespeare.* 1972.

Field, Kate. "Adelaide Ristori." *Atlantic Monthly,* 1867, 500ff.

Filon, Augustin. *The English Stage.* 1897.

Findlater, Richard. *Michael Redgrave: Actor.* 1956.

Finlay, John. *Miscellanies.* 1835.

Fiske, Roger. "The Macbeth Music." *Music and Letters* 45 (1964) 114–125.

Fitzgerald, Edward. *Letters of Edward Fitzgerald to Fanny Kemble, 1871-1883.* 1895.

Fitzgerald, Percy. (1) *Sir Henry Irving. A Record of Twenty Years at the Lyceum.* 1893.

————. (2) "Letters to Fanny Kemble." *Macmillan Review,* Jan. 3, 1937.

————. (3) *The Life of David Garrick.* 1868.

————. (4) "Our Play-Box." *Theatre* 13 (1887) 101–104.

————. (5) *Shakespearean Representation.* 1908.

Flatter, Richard. (1) "The Dumb-Show in *Macbeth." Times Literary Supplement,* March 23, 1951, 181.

————. (2) "The Question of Free Will, and Other Observations on *Macbeth." English Miscellany* 10 (1959) 87–105.

————. (3) *Shakespeare's Producing Hand.* 1948.

Flatter, Richard. (4) "Who Wrote the Hecate-Scene?" *Shakespeare Jahrbuch*, 1957, 196–210.

Fleming, W. H. "Shakespeariana." *Werner's Magazine*, June, 1893.

Fletcher, George. (1) "Macbeth." *Westminster Review* 41 (1844) 1–72.

———. (2) *Studies in Shakespeare*. 1847.

Florence, Yves. "Le reste est silence." *Revue des Deux Mondes*, 1972, 291–295.

Fontane, Theodor. "Die Londoner Theater." *Samtliche Werke*. Vol. 22. 1967.

Fontenrose, Joseph. *The Ritual Theory of Myth*. 1966.

Foote, Jesse. *The Life of Arthur Murphy, esq.* 1811.

Forman, Simon. *Book of Plaies and Notes Thereof.* Ms. in the Bodleian Library, Oxford.

Forster, John, and George Henry Lewes. *Dramatic Essays*. William Archer and Robert W. Lowe, eds. 1896.

Foss, George. *What the Author Meant*. 1932.

Frank, André. *Georges Pitoeff*. 1958.

Fraser, Lady Antonia. *King James VI of Scotland, I of England*. 1974.

French, Yvonne. *Mrs. Siddons*. 1936.

Frenke, Lewis, ed. *Actors Talk About Acting*. 1962.

Frenzel, K. *Berliner Dramaturgie*. 1877.

Freud, Sigmund. "Some Character Types". In *Collected Papers*. Vol. 4. 1959.

Frye, Northrop. *Fools of Time*. 1969.

Frye, Roland Mushat. (1) "*Macbeth* and the Powers of Darkness." *Emory University Quarterly* 8 (1952) 164–174.

———. (2) "Macbeth's Usurping Wife." *Renaissance News* 8 (1955) 102–105.

———. (3) " 'Out, Out, Brief Candle,' and the Jacobean Understanding." *Notes and Queries*, n.s. 2 (1955) 143–145.

———. (4) *Shakespeare and the Christian Doctrine*. 1963.

Gaines, Barry. "Shakespeare in Tennessee: Anthony Quayle's Macbeth." *Shakespeare Quarterly* 27 (1976) 58ff.

Galt, John. *Lives of the Players*. Vol. 1. 1831.

Gardner, Dame Helen Louise. (1) *The Business of Criticism*. 1959.

———. (2) "Milton's Satan and the Theme of Damnation in Elizabethan Tragedy." *Essays and Studies*, n.s. 1 (1948) 46–66.

Garrett, John, ed. *Talking of Shakespeare*. 1954.

Garrick, David. (1) *An Essay on Acting*. 1744.

———. (2) *Letters of David Garrick*. David M. Little and George M. Kahrl, eds. 1963.

———. (3) *The Private Correspondence of David Garrick*. James Boaden, ed. 1831–1832.

Gautier, Théophile. *Histoire de l'Art Dramatique en France depuis vingt-cinq ans*. 1839.

Genest, John. *Some Account of the English Stage*. 1832.

Gentleman, Francis. (1) "David Garrick and Other Contemporaries in *Macbeth*." In Agate, J., *English Dramatic Critics*, 1933, 55–60.

———. (2) *The Dramatic Censor*, Vol. 1. Republished, 1969. *Macbeth*, 70–113.

———. (3) Editor, Bell edition of *Macbeth*—Garrick acting version.

Gerstner-Hirzel, Arthur. *The Economy of Action and Word in Shakespeare's Plays*. 1957.

Gibbs, Evelyn. (1) Personal report on John Gielgud's and Komisarjevsky's Macbeths. Jan., 1969.

———. (2) Personal report on Nicol Williamson's Macbeth, 1974.

Gibbs, Wolcott. (1) "Salvador Dali Interprets *Macbeth*." *New York Times Book Review*, Dec. 15, 1949.

———. (2) "*Macbeth*." *New Yorker* 24 (April 1948) 48ff.

Gielgud, John. (1) "Before Macbeth." *Theatre Arts Monthly* 26 (1942) 113–117.

———. (2) *Early Stages*. 1939.

————. (3) Personal discussion, 1974.

————. (4) *Stage Directions*. 1963.

Gielgud, Kate Terry. *An Autobiography*. 1953.

Gifford, George. (1) *A Dialogue Concerning Witches and Witchcraftes*. 1593.

————. (2) *A Discourse of the Subtill Practises of Devilles by Witches and Sorcerers*. 1587.

Gilbert, C. G. "*Macbeth*, V, iii, 22." *Notes and Queries* (1960) 333–334.

Gilder, Rosamond. (1) "Evans' *Macbeth*." *Theatre Arts Monthly* 26 (1942) 80–81.

————. (2) "Shakespeare in New York: 1947-1948." *Shakespeare Survey* 2 (1949) 130–131.

Gildon, Charles. (1) "An Essay on the Art, Rise and Progress of the Stage in Greece, Rome and England." *The Works of William Shakespeare*. Alexander Pope, ed. Vol. 8, 173ff.

————. (2) *The Life of Betterton*. 1710.

Giordano-Orsini, G. N. "Macbeth." *Times Literary Supplement*, April 6, 1940, 171.

Goddard, Harold C. *The Meaning of Shakespeare*. 1951.

Goethe, Johann Wolfgang von. (1) *Selections from Conversations with Eckermann*. Translated by John Oxenford, 1964.

————. (2) *Sämtliche Werke*. Vol. 38. 1902.

————. (3) See also German bibliography, 1800.

Goldman, Michael. *Shakespeare: The Energies of Drama*. 1972.

Goll, A. "Macbeth and the Lady as Criminal Types." Translated by J. Moritzen. *Journal of Criminal Law and Criminology* 29 (1939): 645–667.

Goodale, Katherine Molony. *Behind the Scenes with Edwin Booth*. 1931.

Goode, Bill. "How Little the Lady Knew Her Lord: A Note on *Macbeth*." *American Imago* 20 (1963) 349–356.

Got, Jerzy. (1) Personal letters on *Macbeth* in Poland. 1974, 1975.

————. (2) *Polish Actors in Shakespearean Roles*. n.d.

Gould, Thomas. *The Tragedian*. 1968.

Gow, Gordon. "Shakespeare Lib." *Plays and Players* 20 (1973) 19–21.

Granville-Barker, Harley. (1) *On Dramatic Method*. 1956.

————. (2) "Preface" to *Macbeth*, Players Edition. 1923.

Graves, T. S. "Allusions to Religious and Political Plays." *Modern Philology* 9 (1912) 431–434.

Greg, Walter W. (1) *The Editorial Problem in Shakespeare*. 3rd ed. 1954.

————. (2) *The Shakespeare First Folio*. 1955.

Grein, J. T. (1) "*Macbeth*: M. Irving et Mlle Terry au Lyceum." *Revue d'Art Dramatique* 13 (1889) 103–111.

————. (2) *Dramatic Criticism*. 1899.

Gribble, Dorothy Rose. "Our Hope's 'Bove Wisdom, Grace, and Fear. An Account of a Tour of *Macbeth*." *Shakespeare Quarterly* 5 (1954) 403–07.

Griffith, Elizabeth. *The Morality of Shakespeare's Drama*. 1775.

Gronowicz, Antoni. *Modjeska, Her Life and Loves*. 1956.

Grossman, Edwina. *Edwin Booth. Recollections by His Daughter*. 1902.

Grube, Max. *The Story of the Meiningen*. 1963.

Guglia, Eugene. *Friedrich Mitterwurzer*. n.d.

Guinness, Alec. Personal discussion, 1973.

Gustafson, Zadel B. *Genevieve Ward*. 1882.

Guthrie, Tyrone. Introduction to *Shakespeare: Ten Great Plays*. 1962.

Hadas, Moses. "Clytemnestra in Elizabethan Dress." *Classical Weekly* 32 (1939) 255–256.

Hahn, Renaldo. *Sarah Bernhardt*. Translated by Ethel Thompson. 1932.

Hales, John W. *Essays and Notes on Shakespeare*. 1892.

Halio, Jay. (1) "Bird Imagery in *Macbeth.*" *Shakespeare News Letter* 13 (1963) 7.
————. (2) See editions.
————. (3) Personal comments.
Hampden, Walter. (1) Letter to H. H. Furness, University of Pennsylvania Library.
————. (2) Promptbook. Players Club, New York.
Hamilton, Clayton. "Shakespeare and Gordon Craig," *The English Journal* 18 (April 1929) 286.
Harbage, Alfred. (1) "Elizabethan Acting." *PMLA* 54 (1939) 685–708.
————. (2) *Theatre for Shakespeare.* 1955.
————. (3) *William Shakespeare, A Reader's Guide.* 1971.
Harcourt, John B. " 'I Pray you, Remember the Porter.' " *Shakespeare Quarterly* 12 (1961) 393–402.
Harding, D. W. "Women's Fantasy of Manhood: A Shakespearian Theme." *Shakespeare Quarterly* 20 (1969) 245–253.
Harington, John. *Nugae Antiquae.* 1804.
Harris, B. Kingston. "Martlets in *Macbeth.*" *Times Literary Supplement*, March 16, 1951.
Harrison, Gabriel. *Edwin Forrest: The Actor and the Man.* 1889.
Harrison, George B. (1) *A Jacobean Journal, Being a Record of Those Things Most Talked of During the Years 1603-1606.* 1941.
————. (2) *Shakespeare's Tragedies.* 1951.
Harsnet, Samuel. *A Declaration of Egregious Popish Impostures. . . .* 1603.
Hartwig, Joan. "Macbeth, the Murderers, and the Diminishing Parallel." *Yearbook of English Studies* 3 (1973) 39–43.
Harwood, Ronald. (1) *Donald Wolfit.* C.B.E. 1971
————. (2) Personal letter on Wolfit and Olivier as Macbeth. 1972.
Hatcher, Orie Latham. *A Book for Shakespeare Plays and Pageants: A Treasury of Elizabethan and Shakespearean Detail for Producers, Stage Managers, Actors, Artists and Students.* 1916.
Hawkes, Terence. *Shakespeare's Talking Animals: Language and Drama in Society.* 1973.
Hawkins, Frederick W. (1) *The Life of Edmund Kean.* 1869.
————. (2) "*Macbeth* on the Stage." *Theatre* 12 (1888) 282–287 and 13 (1889) 1–6.
Haydn, Hiram. *The Counter Renaissance.* 1950.
Hayward, A., ed. *Diaries of a Lady of Quality.* 1864.
Hazlitt, William. (1) *The Complete Works of William Hazlitt.* P. P. Howe, ed. 1930.
————. (2) *View of the English Stage.* 1821.
Hedgecock, F. A. *A Cosmopolitan Actor: David Garrick and His French Friends.* 1912.
Heilman, Robert B. (1) "The Criminal as Tragic Hero: Dramatic Methods." *Shakespeare Survey* 19 (1966) 12–24.
————. (2) *This Great Stage: Image and Structure in King Lear.* 1948.
————. (3) " 'Twere Best Not Know Myself'." *In* J. McManaway, ed., *Shakespeare 400.* 1964.
Heine, Heinrich. *Shakespeare's Mädchen und Frauen.* 1919.
Henderson, Archibald. "Macbeth as Underdog: Central Villain, Tragic Hero." *Forum* 11 (1967) 14–17.
Henn, T. H. *The Living Image.* 1972.
Henneberger, Olive. "Banquo, Loyal Subject." *College English* 8 (1946) 18–22.
Herman, G. "Macduff's Boy: A Reply to Professor Syrkin." *The Use of English* 9 (1957) 40–42.
Heuer, Hermann. (1) "Shakespeares Verhältnis zu König Jacob I." *Anglia* 66 (1942) 223–227.
————. (2) "Zur Deutung von Shakespeares *Macbeth.*" *Zeitschrift für neusprachlichen Unterricht* 41 (1942) 201–209.

Heywood, Thomas. *Apology for Actors*. 1612. Reprinted 1841.
Heywood, Thomas, and Richard Brome. *The Late Lancashire Witches*. 1634. In *Collected Works of Heywood*. 1874.
Hiatt, Charles. *Henry Irving*. 1899.
Hill, Aaron. (1) *The Prompter*, no. 92, Nov. 12, 1734–July, 1736.
———. (2) *The Works of the Late Aaron Hill, Esq.* 1753.
Hill, John. *The Actor*. 1755.
Hillebrand, Harold N. *Edmund Kean*. 1933.
Hinman, Charlton. *The Printing and Proofreading of the First Folio of Shakespeare*. 1963.
Hobson, Harold. Reviews cited from the *Sunday Times*.
Hodek, Bretislav. Personal report, *Macbeths* in Prague. 1972.
Hodges, C. Walter. (1) *The Globe Restored: A Study of the Elizabethan Theatre*. 1973.
———. (2) *Shakespeare's Second Globe: The Missing Monument*. 1973.
Hoepfner, Theodore C. "Shakespeare's *Macbeth*, I, vii, 1–28." *Explicator* 7 (1949) item 34.
Hogan, Charles Beecher, et al., eds. (1) *The London Stage, 1600-1800*. 1960–1968.
———. (2) *Shakespeare in the Theatre*. 2 vols. 1952.
Holinshed, Raphael. *Chronicles*. 1587.
Holland, Henry. *A Treatise Against Witchcraft*. 1590.
Holland, Norman N. (1) "Macbeth as Hibernal Giant." *Literature and Psychology* 10 (1968) 37–38.
———. (2) *Psychoanalysis and Shakespeare*. 1964.
———. (3) "Realism and the Psychological Critic; or, How Many Complexes Had Lady Macbeth." *Literature and Psychology* 10 (1968) 5–8.
Hollingshead, John. (1) *Gaiety Chronicles*. 1898.
———. (2) *My Lifetime*. 2 vols. 1895.
Holloway, John. *The Story of the Night*. 1961.
Horn, Franz. *Shakespeare's Schauspiele Erläutert*. 1823.
Horne, R. H. *A New Spirit of the Age*. 1844.
Hort, Jean. (1) *Les Théâtres du Cartel, et leurs animateurs*. 1944.
———. (2) *La Vie Heroique des Pitoëff*. 1966.
Hotson, Leslie. *I, William Shakespeare*. 1937.
Howe, Henry H. "An Actor's Note-Book." In Clement Scott, ed., *The Green Room* (1881).
Huffman, Richard. Personal report on *Macbeth*, Stratford, Conn. 1973.
Hughes, Pennethorne. *Witchcraft*. 1952.
Hugo, Victor. *William Shakespeare*. 1864.
Hulme, Hilda. (1) *Explorations in Shakespeare's Language*. 1965.
———. (2) "Three Notes." *Journal of English and Germanic Philology* 57 (1958) 721.
Hunt, Leigh. (1) *Leigh Hunt's Dramatic Criticism, 1808-1831*. L. Houtchens and Carolyn Washburn, eds. 1949.
———. (2) *Critical Essays on the Performers of the London Theatres*. 1807.
———. (3) *Autobiography*. 1860.
———. (4) *Dramatic Essays*. 1894.
Hunter, Edwin R. "*Macbeth* as a Morality." *Shakespeare Association Bulletin* 12 (1937) 217–235.
Hunter, G. K. "*Macbeth* in the Twentieth Century." *Shakespeare Survey* 19 (1966) 1ff.
Huntley, Frank L. (1) "*Macbeth* and the Background of Jesuitical Equivocation." *PMLA* 79 (1964) 390–400.
———. (2) Reply to "Some Notes on Equivocation." *PMLA* 81 (1966) 146.
Hyman, Lawrence W. "*Macbeth*: The Hand and the Eye." *Tennessee Studies in Literature* 5 (1960) 97–100.

Ingram, William. "Enter Macduffe: with Macbeth's Head." *Theatre Notebook* 26 (1972) 75–77.

Inkersley, Arthur. "Modjeska's Life in California." *Overland Monthly*, Feb., 1911, 175–182.

Ireland, John. *Letters and Poems by the Late Mr. John Henderson, with Anecdotes of his Life.* 1786.

Ireland, Joseph. *Records of the New York Stage from 1750 to 1860.* 1866–67.

Irving, Sir Henry. (1) *A Book of Remarkable Criminals.* 1918.

———. (2) "The Character of Macbeth." *Werner's Magazine* 18 (1896) 96–102.

———. (3) "My Four Favorite Parts." *Forum* 16 (1893) 34–35.

———. (4) "The Third Murderer in *Macbeth.*" *The Nineteenth Century* 1 (1877) 327–330.

———. (5) "Irving on Macbeth—The Actor as Critic Before the Students of Columbia." Nov. 20, 1895. Newspaper clipping, unidentified.

———. (6) "The Art of Acting." *English Illustrated Magazine* 2 (1885) 643–653.

Irving, Laurence. *Henry Irving: The Actor and His World.* 1930.

Irving, Washington. *Salmagundi.* 1857.

Isham, Rev. Robert, trans. (from Latin). *Journal of Thomas Isham.* 1673. Extract Norwich, 1875.

Itzin, Catherine. "*Macbeth* in the Restoration." *Theatre Quarterly* 1 (1971) 14–18.

Iwasaki, Soji. *The Sword and the Word: Shakespeare's Tragic Sense of Time.* 1973.

Jaarsma, Richard J. "The Tragedy of Banquo (By William Shakespeare)." *Literature and Psychology* 17 (1967) 87–94.

Jack, Jane H. "*Macbeth*, King James, and the Bible." *English Literary History* 22 (155) 173.

Jacob, Monty. *Deutsche Schauspielkunst. Zeugnisse zur Bühnengeschichte Klassicher Rollen.* 1913 (references to Rosalie Nouseul, Friedrike Bethmann, Sophie Schröder, Auguste Crelinger and Charlotte Wolter as Lady Macbeth).

Jacobsohn, Siegfried. (1) *Die Schaubühne.* 1919.

———. (2) *Max Reinhardt.* 1921.

Jacquot, Jean. (1) "*Macbeth* au Palais de Chaillot." *Etudes Anglais* 8 (1955) 39–90.

———. (2) Personal letter on Casarès' Lady Macbeth, 1973.

———. (3) See also French bibliography.

James, Henry. *The Scenic Art.* 1948.

James I, King of Great Britain. (1) *The Basilikon Doron of King James VI.* 1599, 1603. 2 vols.

———. (2) *Daemonologie.* 1597.

———. (3) *The Political Works of James I.* C. H. McIlwain, ed. 1918.

Jameson, Mrs. Article in *Blackwood's Magazine*, Sept. 1834, 363–69.

Jankelevitch, S. "Le délire onirique dans les drames de Shakespeare." *Psyche* 5 (1950) 305–324.

Jefferson, Joseph. *Autobiography of Joseph Jefferson.* c. 1890.

Jeffreys, M. D. W. "The Weird Sisters in *Macbeth.*" *English Studies in Africa* I (1958) 43–54.

Jekels, Ludwig. (1) "The Problem of the Duplicated Expression of Psychic Themes." *International Journal of Psycho-Analysis* 14 (1933) 300–309.

———. (2) "The Riddle of Shakespeare's *Macbeth.*" *Psychoanalytic Review* 30 (1943) 361–385.

———. (3) "Shakespeare's *Macbeth.*" *Imago* 5 (1917) 170–195.

Jenkin, Fleeming. "Mrs. Siddons as Lady Macbeth." *Nineteenth Century*, 1878, 296–313.

Johnson, Samuel. (1) *The Rambler.* Numbers 156, 158.

———. (2) See also under Shakespeare, *Macbeth*, editions.

Jones, David. *The Plays of T.S. Eliot.* 1960.

Jones, Emrys. *Scenic Form in Shakespeare.* 1971.

Jones, Henry Arthur. *The Shadow of Henry Irving.* 1931.

Jones, Robert Edmond. (1) "The Artist's Approach to the Theatre." *Theatre Arts Monthly* 12 (Sept., 1928) 629–634.

———. (2) *The Dramatic Imagination.* 1941.

Jonson, Ben. *Complete Works.* C. H. Hereford and Percy and Evelyn Simpson, eds. 10 vols. 1925–1950.

Jorgensen, Paul A. (1) "A Deed Without a Name." *Pacific Coast Studies in Shakespeare.* 1966. 190–198.

———. (2) *Our Naked Frailties.* 1971.

———. (3) "Shakespeare's Dark Vocabulary." In *The Drama of the Renaissance, Essays for Leicester Bradner.* 1970. 108–122.

Joseph, Bertram. (1) *Acting Shakespeare.* 1960.

———. (2) *The Tragic Actor.* 1959.

Joseph, Sister Miriam. *Shakespeare's Use of the Arts of Language.* 1947.

Jung, Carl. *The Archetypes and the Collective Unconscious.* In *Collected Works.* Vol. 9. 1953.

Kames, Lord (Henry Home). *Elements of Criticism.* 1762.

Kantak, V. Y. (1) "An Approach to Shakespearian Tragedy: The 'Actor' Image in *Macbeth.*" *Shakespeare Survey* 16 (1963) 45–52.

———. (2) Personal reports on *Macbeth* stagings in India.

Kantorowicz, E. H. *The King's Two Bodies: A Study of Medieval Political Theology.* 1957.

Kellett, E. E. "*Macbeth* and Satan." *London Quarterly and Holborn Review,* July, 1939, 289–299.

Kelley, John Alexander. *German Visitors to the English Theatres in the Eighteenth Century.* 1936.

Kemble, Frances A. (Butler, Mrs. Fanny) (1) *Journal.* Vol. 2, 1835.

———. (2) *Notes on Some of Shakespeare's Plays.* 1882.

———. (3) *Records of a Later Life.* 3 vols. 1882.

———. (4) Manuscript letter, H. H. Furness Library, University of Pennsylvania.

Kemble, John Philip. (1) *Macbeth and King Richard III: An Essay in Answer to Remarks on Some of the Characters of Shakespeare.* 1817.

———. (2) *Macbeth Reconsidered.* 1786.

Kendal, Dame Madge. *Dame Madge Kendal by Herself.* 1933.

Kennedy, H. Arthur. "*Macbeth* at the Lyceum." *Universal Review* 3 (1889): 134–140.

Kernan, Alvin B. (1) (ed.) *Modern Shakespearean Criticism: Essays on Style, Dramaturgy, and the Major Plays.* 1970.

———. (2) "This Goodly Frame, The Stage: The Interior Theater of Imagination in English Renaissance Drama." *Shakespeare Quarterly* 25 (1974) 1–5.

Kierkegaard, Soren. *Either/Or.* Translated by David F. Swenson and Lillian Marvin Swenson. 2 vols. 1959.

Kirk, John Foster. "Shakespeare's Tragedies on the Stage." *Lippincott's Magazine* 33 (1884) 604ff.

Kittredge, George L. (1) *Witchcraft in Old and New England.* 1929.

———. (2) *Shakespeare* (an address). 1916.

Knepler, Henry. *The Gilded Stage.* 1968.

Knight, G. Wilson. (1) *The Imperial Theme.* 1931. Reprinted 1951.

———. (2) *Myth and Miracle.* 1929.

———. (3) *Principles of Shakespearean Stage Productions.* 1936.

———. (4) *The Sovereign Flower.* 1958.

———. (5) *Wheel of Fire.* 1954.

———. (6) "The Milk of Concord: An Essay on Life-Themes in *Macbeth.*" *Critiques and Essays in Criticism, 1920-1948,* 1949, 119–140.

Knight, Joseph. *Theatrical Notes.* 1893.

Knight, Richard Payne. *An Analytical Inquiry into the Principles of Taste.* 1808.

Knights, L. C. (1) "How Many Children Had Lady Macbeth?" In *Explorations.* 1951.

———. (2) "On the Background of Shakespeare's Use of Nature in *Macbeth.*" *Sewanee Review* 64 (1956) 207–217.

———. (3) "Poetry and Philosophy in *Macbeth.*" In *The Literary Criterion,* Shakespeare Quatercentenary Number, 1964, C. D. Narasimhaiah, ed.

———. (4) "Shakespeare's Tragedies and the Question of Moral Judgement." *Shenandoah Washington and Lee University Review,* Spring 1968.

———. (5) "Some Contemporary Trends in Shakespearean Criticism." *Some Shakespearean Themes.* 1959.

———. (6) "The Thought of Shakespeare." *The Hidden Harmony: Essays in Honor of Phillip Wheelwright.* 1966.

Knowles, James S. *Lectures on Dramatic Literature . . . Macbeth.* 1875.

Kocher, Paul H. "Lady Macbeth and the Doctor." *Shakespeare Quarterly* 5 (1954) 341–349.

Kökeritz, H. "Thief and Stealer." *English and Germanic Studies* 3 (1949–50) 57–60.

Kolbe, Frederick Charles. *Shakespeare's Way.* 1930.

Komisarjevsky, Theodore. *Myself and the Theatre.* 1930.

Kott, Jan. *Shakespeare Our Contemporary.* 1964.

Krabbe, Henning. "The 'Time-Server' in the Porter's Speech in *Macbeth.*" *Notes and Queries* 20 (1973) 141–142.

———. (2) "A Danish Actress and Her Conception of the Part of Lady Macbeth." *Shakespeare Survey* 29 (1976) 145–50.

Kreider, Paul. *Repetition in Shakespeare's Plays.* 1941.

Krutch, J. W. "*Macbeth.*" *Nation* 166 (1948) 421–422.

Kuckhoff, Armin-Gerd. "Shakespeare auf den Bühnen der DDR im Jahre 1971." *Shakespeare Jahrbuch,* 1973, 176–179.

LaGarde, Fernand. "A Note on *Macbeth* I. vii. 4." *Caliban* 6 (1969) 15.

Lamb, Charles. *The Works of Charles Lamb.* Vol. 4. 1818.

Lampson, Robin. "Macbeth's Response to the News of His Wife's Death." *CEA Critic* 34 (1973) 33–34.

Langbaum, Robert W. *The Poetry of Experience.* 1957.

Lange, Josef. *Biographie des Josef Lange.* 1808.

Laurens, Claus. Personal reports on Bergman *Macbeths.* 1944, 1948.

Lavater, Lewes. *Of Ghostes and Spirites Walking by Nyght.* 1572.

Lavin, J. A. "Shakespeare: Bibliographical Spectrum." In *Review of National Literatures* 3 (1972) 163–184.

Law, Robert Adger. "The Composition of *Macbeth* with Reference to Holinshed." *Texas Studies in English* 31 (1952) 35–41.

Lawlor, John. "Mind and Hand: Some Reflections on the Study of Shakespeare's Imagery." *Shakespeare Quarterly* 8 (1957) 179–193.

Lawrence, W. J. (1) *Barry Sullivan, A Biographical Sketch.* 1893.

———. (2) "Bells on the Stage." *Fortnightly Review* 112 (1918).

———. (3) *The Elizabethan Playhouse and Other Studies.* 1912.

———. (4) "Horses Upon the Elizabethan Stage." *Times Literary Supplement,* June 5, 1919.

———. (5) *The Life of Gustavus Vaughan Brooke.* 1892.

———. (6) "The Mystery of *Macbeth* (A Solution)." *Fortnightly Review* 114 (1920) 777–783.

———. (7) *Pre-Restoration Stage Studies.* 1927.

Lazarus, Emma. "Tommaso Salvini." *Century Magazine* 23 (1881) 114ff.

Leach, Joseph. *Bright Particular Star*. 1970.

Leavis, F. R. (1) "Education and the University." *Scrutiny*, 1941, 316–319.

——. (2) *How to Teach Reading*. 1932.

Lee, Sidney. *Life of Shakespeare*. 1898.

Leech, Clifford. "The Dark Side of *Macbeth*." *Literary Half Yearly*, Jan.–June, 1967, 27–34.

Lees, F. N. "A Biblical Connotation in *Macbeth*." *Notes and Queries* 195 (1950) 534.

LeLoyer, Pierre. *A Treatise of Specters or Strange Sights*. 1605.

Lennam, Trevor. Personal report on his staging of *Macbeth*.

Lenormand, H. R. *Les Pitoeff*. 1943.

Leslie, Amy. *Some Players*. 1906.

Letters Respecting the Theatre Royal. Edinburgh, August 6, 1798.

Lévi-Strauss, Claude. *Structural Anthropology*. 1963.

Levin, Harry. "Shakespeare and the Revolution of the Times." *Tri-Quarterly*, nos. 23, 24 (1972) 288ff.

Levin, Richard. (1) "Some Second Thoughts on Central Themes." *Modern Language Review* 67 (1972) 1–10.

——. (2) "My Theme Can Lick Your Theme." *College English* 37 (1975) 307ff.

Lewes, G. H. *On Actors and the Art of Acting*. 1875.

Libby, M. F. *Some New Notes on Macbeth*. 1893.

Lichtenberg, G. C. *Visits to England*. Translated and annotated by Margaret L. and W. H. Mare, 1938.

Lilly, William. *Mr. Lilly's History of His Life and Times*. 1721.

Llorca, Raymond L. "*Macbeth* and the Use of Appetite in Tragedy." *Silliman Journal* 15 (1968) 151–189.

Lloyd, Robert. *The Actor*. 1760.

Lombardo, Augusto. *Lettura su Macbeth*. 1969.

Loomis, Edward Alleyn. "Master of the Tiger." *Shakespeare Quarterly* 7 (1956) 457.

Ludlow, Norman. *Dramatic Life as I Found It*. 1889.

Ludowyk, E. F. C. *Understanding Shakespeare*. 1964.

Lucas, F. L. *Literature and Psychology*. 1951.

Lyle, E. B. "The Speech-Heading 'I' in Act IV, Scene i of the Folio Text of *Macbeth*." *Library* 25 (1970) 150–151.

Lyly, John. *Mother Bombie*. 1594.

McCarthy, Mary. "General Macbeth." *Harpers* 224 (June 1962) 35–39.

McFarland, Thomas. *Tragic Meanings in Shakespeare*. 1966.

Macfarlane, Alan. *Witchcraft in Tudor and Stuart England*, 1970.

McGee, Arthur R. "*Macbeth* and the Furies." *Shakespeare Survey* 19 (1966) 55–67.

Macgowan, Kenneth. "The Jones-Barrymore-Hopkins *Macbeth*." In *The American Theatre as Seen by Its Critics*, 1934, 202–205.

Mack, Maynard. "The Jacobean Shakespeare" in *Jacobean Theatre*. John Russell Brown and Bernard Harris, eds. 1960.

Mack, Maynard, Jr. *The Killing of the King*. 1974.

Macklin, Charles. (1) *An Apology for the Conduct of Mr. Charles Macklin, Comedian*. 1773.

——. (2) Ms. notes in Kirkman's *Life of Macklin*. Harvard Library.

McElroy, Bernard. *Shakespeare's Mature Tragedies*. 1973.

McKellen, Ian. Personal interview, 1976.

McManaway, James G. "Review of the *Macbeth* edited by John Dover Wilson." *Shakespeare Survey* 2 (1949) 145–149.

McNeal, Thomas H. "Shakespeare's Cruel Queens." *Huntington Library Quarterly* 22 (1958) 41–50.

Macready, William Charles. (1) *The Diaries of William Charles Macready 1833-1851*. William Toynbee, ed. 1912.

———. (2) *Reminiscences and Selections from His Diaries and Letters*. Sir Frederick Pollock, ed. 1813.

Maeterlinck, Maurice. "The Tragedy of *Macbeth*." Translated by Alexander Teixeira de Mattos. *Fortnightly Review* 93 (1910) 693–701.

Maeterlinck, Mme. (Georgette Leblanc). "Macbeth at Saint-Wandrille." *Fortnightly Review* 92 (1909) 605–618.

Maginn, Walter. *Shakespeare Papers*. 1860.

Mahood, M. M. *Shakespeare's Wordplay*. 1957.

Malloch, A. E. "Some Notes on Equivocation." *PMLA* 81 (1966) 145–146.

Majór, Tamás. "Lady Macbeth—The Stage Manager's Letter to the Actress." *New Hungarian Quarterly* 5 (1964) 68–70.

Mandel, Jerome, and Bruce A. Rosenberg. *Medieval Literature and Folklore Studies*. 1970.

Mangin, Edward. *Piozziana*. 1833.

Manifold, J. S. *The Music in English Drama*. 1956.

Mantzius, Karl. *A History of Theatrical Art 1903–1921*.

Marder, Louis. "Shakespeare's Musical Background." *Modern Language Notes* 65 (1950) 501–503.

Markels, Julian. "The Spectacle of Deterioration: *Macbeth* and the 'Manner' of Tragic Imitation." *Shakespeare Quarterly* 12 (1961) 193–303.

Marowitz, Charles. (1) Personal discussion. Feb., 1975.

———. (2) " *a macbeth*." Calder and Boyars Playscript No. 45. 1971.

Marshall, Herbert. "Further Research on Ira Aldridge, the Negro Tragedian." *Center for Soviet and East European Studies*, Monograph No. 2, 1973.

"Marston; or, the Memoirs of a Statesman," Part 1, *Blackwood's Edinburgh Magazine*, June, 1843.

Marston, John Westlake. *Our Recent Actors*. 2 vols. 1888.

Martin, Graham. "*Macbeth*, Act I, Scene vii, Lines 1–28." In *Interpretations: Essays on Twelve English Poems*. John Wain, ed., 1955.

Martin, Theodore. (1) *Helena Faucit*. 1900.

———. (2) "An Eye-Witness of John Kemble." *Nineteenth Century*, 1880, 276–296.

Martinet, M. Personal report on T.E.P. *Macbeth*, 1971.

Marwah, Swarah. "Evil in *Macbeth*." *Quest* 55 (1967) 45–51.

Masefield, John. (1) *A Macbeth Production*. 1945.

———. (2) *Shakespeare and Spiritual Life*. 1924.

Mates, Julian. "Macbeth's Head." *American Notes and Queries* 10 (1972) 152–153.

Matthews, Brander, and Laurence Hutton. *Actors and Actresses of Great Britain and the United States*. 1886.

Maxwell, J. C. (1) "Ghost from the Grave: A Note on Shakespeare's Apparitions." *Durham University Journal* 17 (1956) 58.

———. (2) "*Macbeth* IV. iii. 107." *Modern Language Notes* 51 (1956) 73.

———. (3) "Montaigne and *Macbeth*." *Modern Language Notes* 43 (1948) 77–78.

———. (4) "The Punctuation of *Macbeth*, I. i. 1–2." *Review of English Studies* 4 (1953) 356–358.

———. (5) "The Relation of *Macbeth* to *Sophonisba*." *Notes and Queries*, n.s. 2 (1955) 373–374.

McElroy, Bernard. *Shakespeare's Mature Tragedies*. 1973.

Mehl, Dieter. "Visual and Rhetorical Imagery in Shakespeare's Plays." In *Essays and Studies (In Honour of Beatrice White)*. T. S. Dorsch, ed. 1972.

Merchant, W. Moelwyn. (1) *Creed and Drama*. 1965.

———. (2) " 'His Fiend-like Queen.' " *Shakespeare Survey* 19 (1966) 75–81.

Meyerhoff, Hans. *Time in Literature*. 1960.
Middleton, Thomas. *The Witch*. 1950. Edited from the Bodleian Mss. Malone 12, pre-
pared by W. W. Greg and F. P. Wilson.
Milward, Peter. (1) Interview with Hiroshi Akutagawa.
———. (2) Report on *Macbeth* in Tokyo, 1972, 1976.
Mitford, John, ed. *Correspondence of Thomas Gray and William Mason*. 1855. 2nd ed.
Montagu, Elizabeth R. *An Essay on the Writings . . . of Shakespeare*. 1769.
Moore, Robert E. "The Music to *Macbeth*." *Musical Quarterly* 47 (1961) 22–40.
Moorthy, P. R. (1) "All Is the Fear." In *Studies in Elizabethan Literature (A Festschrift for
Professor C. C. Bannerjee)*. 1972.
———. (2) "Fear in *Macbeth*." *Essays in Criticism* 23 (1973) 154–166.
Morgann, Maurice. *An Essay on the Dramatic Character of Sir John Falstaff*. 1777.
Morhardt, Mathias. "*Macbeth* à le Theatre Pitoeff." L'Arsenal collection.
Morley, Henry. *Journal of a London Playgoer*. 1866.
Morozov, Mikhail M. (1) "The Individualization of Shakespeare's Characters Through
Imagery." *Shakespeare Survey* 2 (1949) 83–106.
———. (2) *Shakespeare on the Soviet Stage*. 1947.
Morris, Christopher. (1) *Political Thought in England, Tyndale to Hooker*. 1953.
———. (2) "Shakespeare's Politics." *Historical Journal* 8 (1963) 293–308.
Morris, Clara. (1) *Life on the Stage*. 1901.
———. (2) *The Life of a Star*. 1906.
Morris, Harry. "*Macbeth*, Dante, and the Great Evil." *Tennessee Studies in Literature* 12
(1967) 26.
Morris, James. *Recollections of Ayr Theatricals*. n.d.
Moulton, Richard Green. *Shakespeare as a Dramatic Artist*. 1888.
Mowatt, Barbara. "The Beckoning Ghost: Stage-Gesture in Shakespeare." *Renaissance
Papers*. 1970.
Muir, Kenneth. (1) "A Borrowing from Seneca." *Notes and Queries* 194 (1949) 214–216.
———. (2) "Buchanan, Leslie and *Macbeth*." *Notes and Queries*, n.s. 2 (1955) 511–
512.
———. (3) "Image and Symbol in *Macbeth*." *Shakespeare Survey* 19 (1966) 45–54.
———. (4) "*Macbeth* and Sophonisba." *Times Literary Supplement*, Oct. 9, 1948.
———. (5) "Seneca and Shakespeare." *Notes and Queries*, n.s. 3 (1956) 243–244.
———. (6) "Shakespeare and Dante." *Notes and Queries* 194 (1949) 333.
———. (7) *Shakespeare's Sources*. Vol. 1. 1965.
———. (8) "The Uncomic Pun." *Cambridge Journal* 3 (1950) 472–485.
———. (9) *Shakespeare's Tragic Sequence*. 1972.
Mullin, Michael. "Augures and Understood Relations: Theodore Komisarjevsky's
Macbeth." *Educational Theatre Journal*, March, 1974, 20–30.
Munro, J. J., ed. *Shakespeare Allusion Book*. Vol. 1. 1932.
Murdoch, Dugald. "The Thane of Cawdor and Macbeth." *Studia Neophilogica* 43 (1971)
221–226.
Murdoch, James. *The Stage*. 1880.
Murphy, Arthur. (1) *Gray's Inn Journal*. Vol. 2. 1756.
———. (2) *The Life of David Garrick, Esq*. 1801.
Murray, Margaret. *The God of the Witches*. 1933.
Murray, Patrick. *The Shakespearean Scene: Some Twentieth-Century Perspectives*. 1969.
Murray, W. A. "Why Was Duncan's Blood Golden?" *Shakespeare Survey* 19 (1966)
34–44.
Murry, J. Middleton. *Shakespeare*. 1936.
Nagarajan, S. "A Note on Banquo." *Shakespeare Quarterly* 7 (1956) 371–376.
Nathan, George Jean. *Theatre Book of the Year*. 1947–1948.
Nathan, Norman. "Duncan, Macbeth and Jeremiah." *Notes and Queries* n.s. 1 (1954) 243.

Nehring, H. "Macbeth ein Bruder Hamlets?" *Neuphilologische Zeitschrift* 4 (1952) 361–364.

Neilson, Francis. *A Study of Macbeth for the Stage.* 1952.

Neumann, Erich. *Origins of the History of Consciousness.* 1954.

Nevo, Ruth. *Tragic Form in Shakespeare.* 1972.

Nicholson, Brinsley. "The Number of Witches in *Macbeth* IV, 1." *New Shakespeare Society Transactions* 7 (1880) 103–108.

Nicoll, Allardyce. *Studies in Shakespeare.* 1928.

Nielsen, Elizabeth. "Macbeth, the Nemesis of the Post-Shakespearian Actor." *Shakespeare Quarterly* 16 (1965) 193–199.

Nietzsche, Friedrich William. "Morgenröthe 240" in *Werke in Drei Banden.* Vol. 1. 1966.

"Noctes Ambrosianae." *Blackwood's Edinburgh Magazine* 21 (1827) 481f.

Noble, Richmond. *Shakespeare's Biblical Knowledge and Use of the Book of Common Prayer.* 1935.

Northbrooke, John. *Breefe and Pithie Summe of the Christian Faith.* 1579.

Norwood, Gibert. *"Euripides and Shaw" with other Essays by Gilbert Norwood.* 1921.

Nosworthy, J. M. (1) "The Bleeding Captain Scene in *Macbeth.*" Review of *English Studies* 22 (1946) 126–130.

———. (2) "The Hecate Scenes in *Macbeth.*" *Review of English Studies* 24 (1948) 138–139.

———. (3) *"Macbeth* at the Globe." *The Library* 2 (1947–1948) 108–118.

———. (4) *Shakespeare's Occasional Plays.* 1965.

Notestein, Wallace. *A History of Witchcraft in England, 1558–1718.* 1909.

Noverre, Jean Georges. *Letters on Dancing and Ballet.* 1951. Translated by C. W. Beaumont.

O'Dea, Richard J. "Vehicle and Tenor in *Macbeth.*" *Coranto. Journal of the Friends of the Libraries* 5 (1967) 26–28.

Odell, George. (1) *Annals of the New York Stage.* 2 vols. 1927.

———. (2) *Shakespeare from Betterton to Irving.* 1963.

Ogden, Dunbar. Interview with Ben Albach, Amsterdam. 1975.

O'Keefe, John. *Recollections.* 1826.

Olivier, Sir Laurence. *"Macbeth:* Fight Between Macbeth and Macduff." Ms. in Shakespeare Centre Library, Stratford-upon-Avon, 1955.

Orgel, Stephen, and Roy Strong. *Inigo Jones.* 1973.

Ornstein, Robert. (1) *A Kingdom for a Stage: The Achievement of Shakespeare's History Plays.* 1972.

———. (2) *The Moral Vision of Jacobean Tragedy.* 1960.

Orrell, John. "The Bellman in *Macbeth* II, ii, 3." *Notes and Queries* 13 (1966) 138.

Oulton, W. C. *The History of the Theatres of London, Containing an Annual Register of All the . . . Tragedies, etc.* 2 vols. 1796.

Owst, Gerald. *Literature and Pulpit in Medieval England.* 1933.

Oxberry, W. *Oxberry's Dramatic Biography.* 1825.

Oyama, Toshikayu. *The Tragic Cycle in Shakespeare's Macbeth.* 1968.

Pack, Robert. *"Macbeth:* The Anatomy of Loss." *Yale Review* 45 (1956) 533–548.

Palmer, Cecil, and others. *We Saw Him Act: A Symposium on the Art of Henry Irving.* 1939.

Par, Alfonso. *Representaciones Shakespeariana en Espana.* 1936.

Parker, Barbara L. *"Macbeth:* The Great Illusion." *Sewanee Review* 78 (July–Sept., 1970) 476–487.

Parry, A., ed. *Theatrical Portraits of Charles Macklin.* 1891.

Parsons, A. E. "Macbeth's Vision." *Times Literary Supplement,* Oct. 24, 1952.

Parsons, Howard. (1) "*Macbeth:* Emendations." *Notes and Queries,* n.s. 1 (1954) 331–333.
———. (2) "*Macbeth:* Some Emendations." *Notes and Queries* 197 (1952) 403.
———. (3) "Shakespeare Emendations." *Notes and Queries* 196 (1951) 27–29.
Partridge, Eric. *Shakespeare's Bawdy.* 1960.
Paul, Henry N. (1) "The Imperial Theme in *Macbeth.*" *J. Q. Adams Memorial Studies.* 1948.
———. (2) *The Royal Play of Macbeth.* 1950.
Penley, Beville S. *The Bath Stage.* 1892.
Perkins, William. *A Discourse of the Damned Art of Witchcraft.* 1608.
Phelps, W. May, and J. Forbes-Robertson. *The Life and Life-work of Samuel Phelps.* 1886.
Pickering, Reverend Thomas. "Epistle Dedicatory to William Perkins." See Perkins, W.
Piscator, Erwin. Notes from Erwin Piscator Center.
Pitoëff, Georges. *Notre Théâtre.* 1949.
Pitou, Augustus. *Masters of the Show.* 1914.
Planché, James R. *Recollections and Reflections.* 1901.
Playfair, Giles. *Kean: The Life and Paradox of the Great Actor.* 1950.
Plowman, Max. "Notes on *Macbeth.*" *Adelphi* 15 (1939) 238–242, 287–291.
Poel, William. (1) *Letters.* 1929.
———. (2) *Shakespeare in the Theatre.* 1913.
Pollock, Lady (Juliet Creed). *Macready as I Knew Him.* 1884.
Pollock, W. H. *Impressions of Henry Irving.* 1908.
Porter, Eric. Personal discussion. 1968.
Potter, Lois. Personal report on *Macbeth* in Lincoln, England, 1974.
Price, Cecil. *Theatre in the Age of Garrick.* 1973.
Price, Joseph, ed. *The Triple Bond.* 1975.
Price, W. T. (1) *A Life of Charlotte Cushman.* n.d.
———. (2) *A Life of William Charles Macready.* 1894.
Prior, Moody (1) "The Elizabethan Audience and the Plays of Shakespeare." *Modern Philology* 49 (1951) 101–123.
———. (2) *The Language of Tragedy.* 1947.
———. (3) *The Drama of Power.* 1973.
Proctor, B. W. *The Life of Edmund Kean.* Vol. 2. 1835.
Pückler-Muskau, H. L. H. *Briefe eines Verstorbenen.* 4 vols. 1831. *Tour in England,* Vol. 4, translated by Sarah Austin, 1832.
Purdie, Edna. "Observations on Some Eighteenth Century Versions of the Witches' Scenes in *Macbeth.*" *Shakespeare-Jahrbuch,* 1956, 96–109.
Purdom, C. B. "Comment on Richard Flatter's 'The Dumb-Show in *Macbeth*'." *Times Literary Supplement,* April 20, 1951, 245.
Pyle, Fitzroy. "The Way to Dusty Death." *Notes and Queries* 19 (1972) 129–131.
Quiller-Couch, Sir Arthur Thomas. *Shakespeare's Workmanship.* 1918.
Rabb, Felix. *The English Face of Machiavelli.* 1965.
Rabkin, Norman. (1) *Approaches to Shakespeare.* 1964.
———. (2) *Shakespeare and the Common Understanding.* 1967.
Raby, Peter, ed. *The Stratford Scene 1958–1968.* 1968.
Ralli, Augustus. *A History of Shakespeare Criticism.* 1932.
Ramsey, Jarold. "The Perversion of Manliness in *Macbeth.*" *Studies in English Literature* 13 (1973) 285–300.
Rank, Otto, *Das Inzest-Motiv in Dichtung und Sage.* 1912.
Ransom, John Crowe. "On Shakespeare's Language." *Poems and Essays.* 1955.
Redgrave, Michael. *The Actor's Ways and Means.* 1953.

Reed, Robert R., Jr. (1) "The Fatal Elizabethan Sisters in *Macbeth.*" *Notes and Queries,*
    n.s. 2 (1955) 425–427.
———. (2) *The Occult on the Tudor and Stuart Stage.* 1965.
Rees, James. *The Life of Edwin Forrest.* 1884.
Reid, B. L. "*Macbeth* and the Play of Absolutes." *Sewanee Review* 73 (1965) 19–46.
Reinhardt, Max. *Regiebuch zu Macbeth.* M. Grossman, ed. 1916. (See also Shakespeare:
    Promptbooks.)
Remy, Nicholas. *Demonolatry.* 1930.
Retore, G. "*Macbeth.*" *Pas à Pas* 152 (1973) 68–72.
Rexroth, Kenneth. "*Macbeth.*" *Saturday Review* 17 (1966).
Reynolds, Edgar. Personal report, Ellis Rabb *Macbeth*, San Diego, California, 1969.
Reynolds, Sir Joshua. "Discourse No. 8." *Sir Joshua Reynolds: Discourses on Art.*
    1778. Reprinted 1905.
Ribner, Irving. (1) "*Macbeth:* The Pattern of Idea and Action." *Shakespeare Quarterly* 10
    (1959) 147–159.
———. (2) *Patterns in Shakespearean Tragedy.* 1960.
———. (3) "Political Doctrine in *Macbeth.*" *Shakespeare Quarterly* 4 (1953) 202–205.
Richards, I. A. *The Meaning of Meaning.* 1956.
Richardson, Ian. Personal discussion.
Richmond, Velma Bourgeois. "Lady Macbeth: Feminine Sensibility Gone Wrong."
    CEA Critic 24 (1973) 20–24.
Ridler, Anne, ed. *Shakespeare Criticism 1935–1960.* 1970.
Ridley, M. R. *Shakespeare's Plays. A Commentary.* 1937. See also Shakespeare, editions.
Righter, Anne. *Shakespeare and the Idea of the Play.* 1969.
Rissanen, Matti. " 'Nature's Copy,' 'Great Bond' and 'Lease of Nature' in *Macbeth.*"
    Neuphilologische Mitteilungen 70 (1969) 714–723.
Ristori, Adelaide. *Studies and Memoirs.* 1888. (Translated.)
Robbins, Rossell Hope. *The Encyclopedia of Witchcraft and Demonology.* 1963.
Robertson, J. M. *Shakespeare and Chapman.* 1917.
Robins, Edward. *Twelve Great Actresses.* 1900.
Robinson, Eileen. Personal report of the 1955 Olivier *Macbeth* and others performed
    in Stratford, England.
Robinson, Henry Crabbe. *The Diary, Reminiscences and Correspondence of Henry Crabbe
    Robinson.* T. Sadler, ed. 2 vols. 1869, 1872.
Robinson, Ian. "The Witches and Macbeth." *Critical Review* 11 (1968) 101–105.
Robson, Flora. *Notes on Macbeth:* Introduction to Laurel Edition, 1959.
Robson, William. *The Old Play-Goer.* 1846.
Rogers, Harold Leslie. "Double Profit in *Macbeth.*" *Review of English Studies,* 1965,
    44–49.
Rogers, Paul. Letter on acting Macbeth, 1973.
Roppolo, Joseph Patrick. "Hamlet in New Orleans." *Tulane Studies,* 1956, 71–86.
Rosen, Barbara. *Witchcraft.* 1969.
Rosen, William. *Shakespeare and the Craft of Tragedy.* 1960.
Rosenberg, Marvin. (1) "Lady Macbeth's Indispensable Child." *Educational Theatre
    Journal,* Spring 1974.
———. (2) "*Macbeth* in Rehearsal, a Journal." *Shakespeare Jahrbuch,* 1973.
———. (3) "Poetry of the Theatre." *Costerus, Essays in English and American Litera-
    ture* 3 (1972) 211–220.
———. (4) *The Masks of King Lear.* 1972.
———. (5) *The Masks of Othello.* 1963.
———. (6) "Public Night Performances in Shakespeare's Time." *Theatre Notebook*
    8 (1954) 44–46.
———. (7) Personal report, James Dunn staging of *Macbeth.*

Ross, Douglas. "The Craig-Shakespeare *Macbeth.*" *Drama* 19 (Dec., 1928) 69–71.
Rossi, Ernesto. (1) *Quarant'anni de Vita Artistica.* Vol. 1. 1887.
――――. (2) *Studii Drammatici e Lettere Autobiografiche.* 1885.
――――. (3) *L'Arte Drammatica.* 1882.
Rossiter, A. P. *Angel with Horns.* 1961.
Rothe, Hans. *Max Reinhardt.* 1920.
Rowse, Alfred Leslie. *Simon Forman: Sex and Society in Shakespeare's Age.* 1974.
Royd-Smith, Naomi. *The Private Life of Mrs. Siddons.* 1939.
Rudd, Dorothy. "The Witches." *The Quarterly Review* 269 (1937) 24–38.
Russell, Charles Edward. *Julia Marlowe, Her Life and Art.* 1926.
Russell, Sir Edward R. (1) "Henry Irving's Interpretation of *Macbeth.*" *Fortnightly Review* 40 (1883) 466–81.
――――. (2) *The Life of Henry Irving.* 1896.
――――. (3) Review in *Liverpool Daily Post*, Dec. 31, 1888.
Russell, Jeffery Burton. *Witchcraft and the Middle Ages.* 1972.
Russell, William C. *Representative Actors.* n.d.
Salvini, Tommaso. (1) *Leaves from the Autobiography of . . . Salvini.* 1893.
――――. (2) "My Interpretation of Macbeth." *Putnam's Monthly* 3 (1907) 211–213.
Sanders, Wilbur. (1) *The Dramatist and the Received Idea.* 1968.
――――. (2) "The 'Strong Pessimism' of *Macbeth.*" *Critical Review* 9 (1966) 38–54.
Santayana, George. *Essays in Literary Criticism.* 1956.
Sarbin, Theodore, and Joseph B. Juhasz. "The Historical Background of the Concept of Hallucination." *Journal of the History of Behavioral Science* 3 (1967) 339–358.
Sarcey, Francisque. "Chronique Theatrale." *Le Temps*, March 4, 1889.
Sargeaunt, W. D. *Macbeth: A New Interpretation.* 1937.
Satin, Joseph. "*Macbeth* and the *Inferno* of Dante." *Forum* 9 (1971) 18–23.
Sava, Jon. "*Macbeth.*" *Secolul* 20 (1964).
Saxon, A. H. "Shakespeare and Circuses." *Theatre Survey* 12 (1966) 59–79.
Sayler, Oliver M., ed. *Max Reinhardt and His Theatre.* 1924. Reprinted 1969.
Schanzer, Ernest. "Four Notes on *Macbeth.*" *Modern Language Review* 52 (1957) 223–227.
Schiff, Gert. *Johann Heinrich Fuseli.* 2 vols. 1973.
Schink, Johann Friedrich. *Zusätze und Berichtigungen zu der Galerie der Deutscher Schauspieler.* R. N. Werner, ed. 1910.
Schlegel, Augustus. *A Course of Lectures on Dramatic Art.* 1815.
Schmetz, Lotte. "Die Charakterisierung der Personen durch die Sprache in Macbeth." *Shakespeare Jahrbuch*, 1951, 97–113.
Schneider, Daniel. *The Psychoanalyst and the Artist.* 1950.
Schoff, Francis G. "Shakespeare's 'Fair is Foul'." *Notes and Queries* n.s. 1 (1954) 241–242.
Schücking, Levin Ludvig. (1) "The Baroque Character of the Elizabethan Tragic Hero." Annual Shakespeare Lecture, *Proceedings of the British Academy.* Vol. 24. 1938.
――――. (2) *Character Problems in Shakespeare's Plays.* 1922.
Schoenbaum, Samuel. *Shakespeare's Lives.* 1970.
Schumacher, Erich. *Shakespeare's Macbeth auf der deutschen Bühne.* 1938.
Scofield, Paul. Personal discussion, 1967.
Scot, Reginald. *Discoverie of Witchcraft.* 1584.
Scott, Clement W. *From "The Bells" to "King Arthur."* 1897.
Scott, Sir Walter. "The Life of J. P. Kemble." *Quarterly Review*, June and Sept., 1826, 215–228.
Scott-Giles, C. W. "Martlets in *Macbeth.*" Letters to the Editor, *Times Literary Supplement*, April 13, 1951.

Scragg, Leah. "Macbeth on Horseback." *Shakespeare Survey* 26 (1973) 81–88.
Segond-Weber, Mme. "Interpretation du rôle de Lady Macbeth." *Revue d'Art Dramatique* 13 (1889) 300–308.
Sewell, Arthur. (1) *Character and Society in Shakespeare.* 1951.
———. (2) "Tragedy and the 'Kingdom of Ends'." In *Shakespeare: Modern Essays in Criticism.* Leonard F. Dean, ed. 1967.
Shakespeare, William. *Macbeth.* A chronological list of editions consulted.
———. ed. Nicholas Rowe. 1709.
———. ed. Alexander Pope. 1723.
———. ed. Lewis Theobald. 1733.
———. ed. T. Hanmer. 1744.
———. ed. A. Pope and W. Warburton. 1747.
———. ed. H. Blair. *Works.* 1753.
———. ed. Samuel Johnson. 1765.
———. ed. G. Steevens. 1793.
———. (acting edition) J. P. Kemble. 1794.
———. (acting edition) J. P. Kemble. Second edition. 1794.
———. (acting edition) J. P. Kemble. 1803.
———. (revised edition) J. P. Kemble. 1814.
———. ed. C. Knight. 1841.
———. ed. Alexander Dyce. 1847.
———. ed. Hastings Elwin. 1853.
———. (acting edition) Henry Irving. Music by Arthur Sullivan. 1888.
———. ed. F. A. Marshall. 1888.
———. ed. E. K. Chambers. 1896.
———. ed. A. W. Verity. 1901.
———. ed. M. H. Liddell. 1903.
———. ed. T. M. Parrott. 1904.
———. ed. H. N. Hudson. 1909.
———. ed. H. Cunningham. Arden edition. 1912.
———. ed. E. K. Chambers. 1915.
———. ed. F. A. Lombard. 1922.
———. (acting version) Gordon Craig. Unpublished. In the possession of Edward Carrick Craig. 1928.
———. ed J. Dover Wilson. "A Facsimile of the First Folio Text." 1928.
———. ed. Joseph Quincey Adams. 1931.
———. ed. M. R. Ridley. 1935.
———. ed. G. L. Kittredge. 1939.
———. ed. W. A. Neilson. Revised Cambridge edition. 1942.
———. 1946. Twelve plates by Salvador Dali.
———. ed. J. Dover Wilson. 1947.
———. ed. Hardin Craig. 1951.
———. ed. Alfred Harbage. Penguin edition. 1956.
———. ed. Kenneth Muir. Arden edition. 1962.
———. ed. R. A. Foakes. 1968.
———. ed. R. W. Dent. Blackfriar's Shakespeare. 1969.
———. (acting edition) Orson Welles. Filmscript. UCLA Library. 1969.
———. ed. J. L. Halio. 1972.
———. ed. Maynard Mack and Robert W. Boynton. 1973.
Shakespeare, William. *Macbeth.* Translations, German Promptbooks.
———. Maurice Maeterlinck, translator. 1909.
———. (Regiebuch). Erwin Piscator. 1953.
———. (Regiebuch) Max Reinhardt. 1916.

————. Jean Richepin, translator. 1780.
————. (Regiebuch) Jocza Savits. 1891.
————. Friedrich Schiller, translator. In *Sämtliche Werke*, 1810–1811.
Shakespeare, William
Promptbooks in English consulted, cited according to the numbering used in Charles
  H. Shattuck's *The Shakespeare Promptbooks: A Descriptive Catalogue*. 1965.

1. Padua Folio (See Evans, G. B.). A pre-Restoration promptbook?
2. Smock Alley, Dublin. c. 1670.
4. Salmon, Edward. 1753.
5. Salmon, Edward. 1753.
7. Edinburgh Theatre. 1761.
8. Garrick, David. c.1773.
10. Kemble, John Philip. 1785.
11. Palmer, John. 1794.
12. Cooke, George Frederick. 1807.
13. Siddons, Sarah. 1808.
15. Creswick, William. 1820–1837.
16. Macready, William Charles. 1820.
18. Smith, Sol. 1830's.
19. Ludlow, N. M. 1830's.
20. Kean, Charles. 1835.
21. C. Kean. 1838.
22. C. Kean. 1837.
23. C. Kean. n.d.
25. Macready. 1838.
27. Macready. 1842.
28. Faucit, Helen. 1842.
29. Phelps, Samuel. 1844.
31. Betty, Henry. 1845.
32. Murdoch, James. 1845.
35. Phelps. 1847.
36. Phelps. 1847.
37. Cushman, Charlotte. 1849.
38. Moore, John et al. 1850's.
39. Moore. n.d.
42. Cushman. 1850.
44. Macready. c. 1852.
45. Cushman. 1851.
46. Cushman. 1852.
47. Lewis, George W. (includes Forrest, Macready, Booth). 1852.
48. C. Kean. 1853.
49. C. Kean. 1859.
52. C. Kean. n.d.
53. C. Kean. n.d.
54. C. Kean. 1853.
55. Anonymous. c.1853.
56. Phelps. 1853.
57. Wright, J. B. 1854.
59. Roberts, J. B. 1855.
60. Roberts. n.d.
63. Phelps. 1860.
64. Booth, Edwin. 1861.
65. Booth. n.d.
66. Cowper, J. C. 1864.
68. Creswick. 1864.
69. Forrest, Edwin. c.1868.
70. Forrest. n.d.
72. Macready. 1870's.
78. McCullough, John. c.1873.
80. Hackett, Mrs. James. 1875.
81. Irving, Henry. 1875.
86. Salvini, Tommaso. 1880.
87. Ristori, Adelaide. 1884.
89. Salvini. 1884.
90. Irving. 1888.
91. Irving. n.d.
92. Irving. 1888.
93. Irving. 1889.
94. Irving. 1889.
97. Terry. 1888.
98. Terry. 1889.
99. Terry. 1890.
100. Terry. n.d.
101. Terry. 1919.
102. Booth. 1889.
104. Booth. 1878.
105. Booth. 1897.
106. Becks, George. Compilation. 1890's.
108. Bosworth, Hallam. c.1900.
109. Fiske, Minnie Maddern. c.1903.
111. Mantell, Robert B. 1905.
112. Power, Tyrone. 1907.
113. Sothern, E. H. and Julia Marlowe. 1910.
114. Sothern/Marlowe. 1910.
116. Sothern/Marlowe. n.d.
117. Sothern/Marlowe. n.d.
118. Sothern/Marlowe. n.d.
119. Sothern/Marlowe. n.d.
120. Sothern/Marlowe. n.d.
121. Sothern/Marlowe. 1911.
122. Tree, Herbert Beerbohm. 1911.
123. Tree. n.d.
124. Tree. 1911.
125. Tree. n.d.
126. Benson, Frank R. 1917–1918.

127. Benson. c.1903.
128. Ashwell, Lena. 1919–1920.
129. Hackett, James K. 1920.
130. Hackett. 1930.
133. Tyler, George C. (Gordon Craig Production). 1928.
134. Tyler. 1928–1929.
137. Komisarjevsky, Theodore. 1933.
138. Merivale, Philip. 1935.

139. Merivale. 1935.
140. Welles, Orson. 1936.
141. Payne, B. Iden. 1938.
142. Payne. 1942.
144. Quayle, Anthony. 1949.
145. Quayle, Anthony. 1949.
146. Gielgud, John. 1952.
147. Shaw, Glen Byam. 1955.

also:
Hampden, Walter. Players Club, New York.
Gordon Craig Promptbooks, Edward Carrick Craig collection.

Shand, J. "*Macbeth* at the Princess' Theatre." *Adelphi*, 1927, 500–503.
Sharp, William L. "A Play: Scenario or Poem." *Tulane Drama Review* 5 (1960) 73–84.
Shattuck, Charles. *The Shakespeare Promptbooks: A Descriptive Catalogue*. 1965.
Shaw, Glen Byam, Promptbooks and notes.
Shaw, George Bernard. (1) *Bernard Shaw and Mrs. Patrick Campbell: Their Correspondence*. Alan Dent, ed. 1952.
———. (2) *Our Theatres in the Nineties*. 1931.
———. (3) *Ellen Terry and Bernard Shaw: Correspondence*. Christopher St. John, ed. 1931.
Shaw, Katherine. Personal reports on Nicol Williamson's Macbeth. 1974.
Sheppard, Sir John Tresidder. "*Agammemnon* and *Macbeth*." *Proceedings of the Royal Institute of Great Britain* 160 (1955) 560–569.
Sheren, Paul. "Gordon Craig's Only American Production." *Princeton University Library Chronicle* 29 (1968) 163–192.
Shirley, Frances Anne. *Shakespeare's Use of Offstage Sounds*. 1963.
Shumaker, Wayne. *The Occult Sciences in the Renaissance*. 1972.
Shuttleworth, Bertram. "Irving's Macbeth." *Theatre Notebook* 5 (1951).
Siddons, J. H. "Random Recollections of Life." *Harpers*, Dec., 1862, 71–80.
Siddons, Sarah. *The Reminiscences of Sarah Kemble Siddons*. 1942. (See also Sarah Siddons: "Remarks on Lady Macbeth," in Thomas Campbell, above.)
Siegel, Paul N. (1) "Echoes of the Bible Story in *Macbeth*." *Notes and Queries*, n.s. 2 (1955) 142–143.
———. (2) *Shakespearean Tragedy and the Elizabethan Compromise*. 1957.
Sillard, R. M. *Barry Sullivan and His Contemporaries*. 1901.
Simond, Louis. *Journal of a Tour and Residence in Great Britain*. 2 vols. 1815.
Simpson, Lucie. "The Temperance Note in *Othello* and *Macbeth*." *The Secondary Heroes of Shakespeare and Other Essays*. 1950.
Simrock, Karl. *Die Quellen des Shakespeare in Novellen, Märchen und Sagen*. 1872.
Sipe, Dorothy. *Shakespeare's Metrics*. 1968.
Sisson, C. J. *Shakespeare's Tragic Justice*. 1961.
Sitwell, Edith. (1) "*Macbeth*." *Atlantic Monthly*, April, 1950, 43–48.
———. (2) *A Notebook on William Shakespeare*. 1962.
Skinner, Otis. *Footlights and Spotlights*. 1923.
Smidt, Kristian. "Two Aspects of Ambition in Elizabethan Tragedy: *Doctor Faustus* and *Macbeth*." *English Studies* 50 (1969) 235–248.
Smirnov, Aleksandr Aleksandrovich. *Shakespeare, A Marxist Interpretation*. 1936.
Smith, David Nichol. *Shakespearean Criticism*. 1916.
Smith, Grover. "The Naked New-Born Babe in *Macbeth*: Some Iconographical Evidence." *Renaissance Papers*, 1964 (pub. 1965), 21–27.
Smith, Sol. *Theatrical Management in the West and South for Thirty Years*. 1868.

Smith, Warren D. (1) "The Elizabethan Stage and Shakespeare's Entrance Announcements." *Shakespeare Quarterly* 4 (1953) 405–410.

——. (2) "Stage Business in Shakespeare's Dialogue." *Shakespeare Quarterly*, 4 (1953) 311–316.

Soeda, Toru. "On the Changing Character of Lady Macbeth." *Konan Woman's College Studies in English Literature*. n.d.

Sothern, Edward H. *Julia Marlowe's Story*. 1954.

Spargo, John Webster. "The Knocking at the Gate in *Macbeth*: An Essay in Interpretation." *J. Q. Adams Memorial Studies*. 1948.

Speaight, Robert. (1) "Nature and Grace in *Macbeth*." In *Essays by Diverse Hands, Being the Transactions of the Royal Society of Literature*, n.s. 27 (1955) 89–109.

——. (2) *Nature in Shakespearian Tragedy*. 1955.

——. (3) *William Poel and the Elizabethan Revival*. 1954.

——. (4) "Shakespeare in Britain." *Shakespeare Quarterly*, 1976, 15ff.

Spencer, Christopher. (1) "Davenant's *Macbeth*, from the Yale Ms." *Yale Studies in English*, 146 (1961).

——. (2) "*Macbeth* and Davenant's *The Rivals*." *Shakespeare Quarterly* 20 (1969) 225–229.

Spencer, Hazelton. "How Shakespeare Staged His Plays: Some Notes on the Dubiety of Non-textual Evidence." *Johns Hopkins Alumni Magazine* 20 (1932) 205–221.

Spencer, Theodore. *Shakespeare and the Nature of Man*. 1961.

Spender, Stephen. "Books and the War II—Time, Violence and Macbeth." In *Penguin New Writing* III. John Lehman, ed. 1941.

Spevack, Marvin. *A Shakespeare Concordance*. 1968.

Spielman, M. H. "A Shakespearean Revival: *Macbeth*." *Magazine of Art* 12 (1889) 98–100.

Sprague, Arthur Colby. (1) *Shakespeare and the Actors*. 1945.

——. (2) "The Stage Business in Shakespeare's Plays: A Postscript." The Society for Shakespeare Research; Pamphlet Series no. 3. 1953.

——. (3) "Shakespeare on the New York Stage." *Shakespeare Quarterly* 5 (1954) 311–312.

——. (4) *Shakespearian Players and Performances*. 1957.

——. (5) With J. C. Trewin. *Shakespeare's Plays Today*. 1970.

Spurgeon, Caroline. *Shakespeare's Imagery and What It Tells Us*. 1935.

Stackley, Martin Staples. "The Richmond Theatre." *Virginia Magazine of History and Biography* 60 (1952) 421–436.

Stamm, Rudolf. *The Shaping Powers at Work*. 1967.

Starnes, De Witt T. "Acteon's Dogs." *Names* 3 (1955) 19–25.

Stauffer, Donald A. *Shakespeare's World of Images*. 1949.

Stebbins, Emma. *Charlotte Cushman*. 1879.

Stein, Arnold. "Macbeth and Word-Magic." *Sewanee Review* 59 (1951) 271–284.

Sternfeld, F. W. *Music in Shakespearean Tragedy*. 1963.

Stevenson, R. L. *Academy*, April 15, 1876.

Stewart, J. I. M. (1) *Character and Motive in Shakespeare*. 1949.

——. (2) *Julius Caesar* and *Macbeth*. Two Notes on Shakespearean Technique." *Modern Language Review* 40 (1945) 166–173.

Still, Colin. *Shakespeare's Mystery Play*. 1969.

Stirling, Brents. (1) "The Unity of *Macbeth*." *Shakespeare Quarterly* 4 (1953) 385–394.

——. (2) *Unity in Shakespearian Tragedy*. 1956.

Stoddart, James H. *Recollections of a Player*. 1902.

Stoker, Bram. *Personal Reminiscences of Henry Irving*. 2 vols. 1907.

Stoll, Elmer E. "Source and Motive in *Macbeth* and *Othello*." *Review of English Studies* 19 (1943) 25–32.

Stone, George W. (1) "David Garrick's Melancholy." *PMLA* 49 (1934) 896.

———. (2) "Garrick's Handling of *Macbeth.*" *Studies in Philology* 38 (1941) 609–628.

———. (3) "David Garrick's Significance in the History of Shakespearean Criticism." *PMLA* 65 (1950) 183–197.

Stopes, Charlotte. *Poet Lore.* 1896.

Stoqueler, J. H. *Memoirs of A Journalist.* n.d.

Strang, Lewis C. *Famous Actresses of the Day in America.* 1899.

Stratford Scene 1958–1968. Peter Raby, ed. 1968.

Streeth, J. B. "The Durability of Boy Actors." *Notes and Queries,* n.s. 2 (1973) 461–465.

Stříbrný, Dr. Zdenek. (1) Personal reports on Czech *Macbeths.*

———. (2) "Shakespeare in Today's Czechoslovakia." *Czechoslovakian Life,* April 1, 1964.

Strindberg, August. *Open Letters to the Intimate Theatre.* Translated and introduced by Walter Johnson. 1966.

Stroupe, John H. "Shakespeare's *Macbeth.*" *Explicator* 28 (1969) Item No. 30.

Strout, Alan L. "'How Far is't Called to Forres?'" *Notes and Queries* 176 (1939) 330.

Stunz, Arthur. "The Date of *Macbeth.*" *Journal of English Literary History* 9 (1942) 95–105.

Styan, J. L. *Shakespeare's Stagecraft.* 1967.

Swinburne, Algernon. *A Study of Shakespeare.* 1895.

Symons, Arthur. *Great Acting in English.* 1907.

Syrkin, Marie. "Youth and Lady Macduff." *The Use of English* 8 (1957) 257–261.

Talbert, Ernest William. *The Problem of Order: Elizabethan Political Commonplaces and an Example of Shakespeare's Art.* 1962.

Tannenbaum, Samuel A. *Shakespeare's Macbeth, A Concise Bibliography.* 1939.

Taranow, Gerda. *Sara L. Bernhardt.* 1972.

Taylor, John. "On Siddons." *Theatre Quarterly,* vol. 1, no. 3 (1971) 26.

Taylor, Michael. (1) "Ideas of Manhood in *Macbeth.*" *Etudes Anglaises* 21 (1968) 337–348.

———. (2) "Note on Shakespeare's *Macbeth.*" *Humanities Association Bulletin* 20 (1969) 59.

Terry, Ellen. (1) Annotations in Ellen Terry's Copy of *Macbeth,* Smallhythe.

———. (2) "Recollections of Henry Irving." *McClure's* 30 (1907) 131–148.

———. (3) "My First Appearances in America." *McClure's* 31 (1908) 121–132.

———. (4) *Ellen Terry and Bernard Shaw—Correspondence.* 1931.

———. (5) *Four Lectures on Shakespeare.* 1932.

———. (6) Ms. Letters to William Winter, Oct. 29, 1895. In H. H. Furness Library, University of Pennsylvania.

———. (7) *Memoirs.* 1932.

———. (8) *The Story of My Life.* 1908.

Thaler, Alwin. *Shakespeare and Democracy.* 1941.

Theatre Quarterly. "*Macbeth*: Interpretations and Productions from the Elizabethan Period to the Present." Vol. 1, no. 3 (1971) 12–58.

Thomas, Keith. *Religion and the Decline of Magic.* 1971.

Thumboo, Edwin. "Macbeth and the Generous Duncan." *Shakespeare Quarterly* 22 (1971) 181–186.

Thurber, James. "The Macbeth Murder Mystery." In *The Passionate Playgoer.* 1958.

Tieck, Ludwig. (1) *Dramaturgische Blatter.* 1826.

———. (2) *Kritische Schriften.* 1852.

———. (3) See Raumer, 1825, in bibliography of German productions.

Tillyard, E. M. W. (1) *Shakespeare's History Plays.* 1949.

———. (2) *The Elizabethan World Picture.* 1959.

Toliver, H. "Shakespeare and the Abyss of Time." *Journal of English and Germanic Philology*, 1965, 234–254.

Tomory, Peter. *The Life and Art of Henry Fuseli*. 1972.

Toppen, W. H. (1) *Conscience in Shakespeare's "Macbeth."* 1962.

——. (2) "Recent Studies on Shakespeare's Tragedies." In *Revue des Langues Vivantes* 31 (1962) 72–89.

Torbarina, Josip. "Two Notes on *Macbeth*." *Studia Romanica et Anglica Zagrabiensia*. 1974.

Towse, John R. *Sixty Years of the Theatre*. 1916.

Traversi, D. A. An Approach to Shakespeare. 1956.

Traz, R. de. "Lady Macbeth." *Revue de Paris* 54 (1947) 25–38.

Tree, Herbert Beerbohm. *Thoughts and Afterthoughts*. 1913.

Tree, Maud Holt. "Herbert and I." In *Herbert Beerbohm Tree*, Max Beerbohm, ed. 1924.

Trevor-Roper, H. R. *The European Witch-craze of the Sixteenth and Seventeenth Centuries and Other Essays*. 1956.

Trewin, J. C. (1) *The Birmingham Repertory Theatre, 1913–1963*. 1963.

——. (2) *Mr. Macready*. 1955.

——. (3) *Shakespeare on the English Stage, 1900–1964*. 1964.

Tromly, Frederic B. "Macbeth and His Porter." *Shakespeare Quarterly* 26 (1975) 151–156.

Tucker, Susie I. "Johnson and Lady Macbeth." *Notes and Queries* n.s. 3 (1956) 210–211.

Tuveson, Ernest. *The Imagination as a Means of Grace*. 1974.

Tynan, Kenneth. (1) *Curtains*. 1961.

——. (2) Interview of Olivier. See Burton, *Great Acting*, above.

——. (3) *He That Plays The King*. 1950.

Upton, John. *Critical Observations on Shakespeare*. 1746.

Ure, Peter. "*Macbeth* and Warner's *Albion's England*." *Notes and Queries* 194 (1949) 232.

——. (2) "Comment to Richard Flatter's 'The Dumb Show in *Macbeth*.'" *Times Literary Supplement*. March 23, 1951, 213.

Vandenhoff, George. *Leaves From an Actor's Notebook*. 1860.

Van Doren, Mark. *Shakespeare*. 1953.

Van Gyseghem, Andre. *Theatre in Soviet Russia*. 1943.

Veszy-Wagner, L. "*Macbeth*: 'Fair is Foul and Foul is Fair'." *American Imago* 25 (1968) 242–257.

Wain, John. "Guides to Shakespeare." *Encounter* 22 (1964) 53–61.

Waith, Eugene M. (1) "*Macbeth*: Interpretation vs. Adaptation." In *Shakespeare: Of an Age and for all Time*, Charles Tyler Prouty, ed. 1954.

——. (2) "Manhood and Valor in Two Shakespearian Tragedies." *Journal of English Literary History* 17 (1950) 262–273.

Walbrook, H. M. (1) *Nights at the Play*. 1883.

——. (2) "Henry Irving." *Fortnightly Review* 149 (1938) 203–211.

Walker, Roy. (1) *The Time is Free: A Study of Macbeth*. 1949.

——. (2) "Macbeth's Entrance." *Times Literary Supplement*, Aug. 21, 1953.

Walkley, A. B. *Drama and Life*. 1907.

Wallace, H. B. "Mr. Macready's Macbeth." *Literary Criticism*, 1856, 442–448.

Walpole, Horace. *Letters*. Peter Cunningham, ed. 1918.

Waters, Clara Erskine Clement. *Charlotte Cushman*. 1882.

Webster, Margaret. (1) *Shakespeare and the Modern Theatre*. 1944.

——. (2) *Shakespeare Today*. 1957.

——. (3) *Shakespeare Without Tears*. 1942.

Wedmore, F. "*Macbeth* and Irving." *Academy*, Dec., 23, 1876.

Weichmann, Louis. *A True History of the Assassination of Abraham Lincoln and the Conspiracy of 1865*. Floyd Risvold, ed. 1975.

Weilgart, Wolfgang J. "*Macbeth*: Demon and Bourgeois." *Shakespeare Society of New Orleans Publication*. 1946.

Weiner, Albert B. "Samuel Phelps' Staging of *Macbeth*." *Educational Theatre Journal* 16 (1964) 122–133.

Weisinger, Herbert. "The Study of Shakespearian Tragedy Since Bradley." *Shakespeare Quarterly* 6 (1955) 387–396.

West, E. J. "Irving in Shakespeare: Interpretation or Creation." *Shakespeare Quarterly* 6 (1955) 415–422.

West, Robert H. "Night's Black Agents in *Macbeth*." *In Renaissance Papers 1956*, 1957, 17–24.

West, William. *Symboleography*. 1594.

Westbrook, Perry D. "A Note on *Macbeth*, Act II, Scene i." *College English* 7 (1946) 219–220.

W. G. B. "*Macbeth* at Windsor in 1829." *Notes and Queries* 195 (1950) 473.

Whately, T. *Remarks on Some of the Characters of Shakespeare*. (3rd edition) 1839.

Whitaker, Virgil. *Shakespeare's Use of Learning*. 1953.

Whiter, Walter. *A Specimen of Commentary on Shakespeare*. 1794. Alan Over and Mary Bell, eds. 1967.

Whitworth, Geoffrey. "The Making of a Play. I: Audiences and Actors." *The Listener*. March 8, 1933.

Wickham, Glynne W. (1) "Actor and Play in Shakespeare's Theatre." *Mask und Kothurn* (Graz-Wien) 15 (1969) 1–5.

———. (2) "Hell-Castle and Its Door-Keeper." *Shakespeare Survey* 19 (1966) 68–74.

Wilkes, Thomas. *A General View of the Stage*. 1759.

Willan, J. N. First Night Impressions of Mr. Irving's *Macbeth*. 1889.

Willett, John. *The Theatre of Bertolt Brecht*. 1968.

Williams, E. Harcourt. (1) *Four Years at the Old Vic, 1929–1933*. 1935.

———. (2) "The Making of a Play, III: *Macbeth* from the Producer's Point of View." *The Listener*, March 22, 1933.

Williams, Edith Whitehurst. "In Defense of Lady Macbeth." *Shakespeare Quarterly* 24 (1973) 221–223.

Williams, George E. Personal letter on the *Macbeth* text. 1974.

Williamson, Audrey. (1) *The Bristol Old Vic*. 1957.

———. (2) *Contemporary Theatre*. 1956.

———. (3) *Theatres of Two Decades*. 1951.

Wilson, Francis. *Joseph Jefferson*. 1906.

Wilson, Harold S. *On the Design of Shakespearean Tragedy*. 1957.

Wilson, J. Dover., ed. (1) *Of Ghostes and Spirites Walking by Nyght*. 1572.

———. (2) Letters to *Times Literary Supplement*, Sept. 30, 1949.

Wilson, John, cited also as "Christopher North," *Blackwood's Edinburgh Magazine*.

Winer, Anthony. Personal report. 1975.

Wingate, Charles Edgar Lewis. *Shakespeare's Heroines on the Stage*. 1895.

Winter, William. (1) *Between Actor and Critic*. Daniel J. Watermeier, ed. 1971.

———. (2) *Edwin Booth in Twelve Dramatic Characters*. 1872.

———. (3) *Henry Irving*. 1885.

———. (4) *The Life and Art of Edwin Booth*. 1894.

———. (5) "*Macbeth* on the Stage." *Century* 81 (1911) 923–928.

———. (6) *Shadows of the Stage*. 1893.

———. (7) *Shakespeare on the Stage*. Vol. 1 (1911); Vol. 2 (1915).

Winters, Yvor. "Problems for the Modern Critic of Literature." *Hudson Review* 9 (1956) 325–386.

Witte, W. "Time in Wallenstein and *Macbeth*." *Aberdeen University Review* 24 (1952) 217–224.

Wolfit, Donald, (1) *First Interval*. 1954.

———. (2) Personal discussion. 1967.

Wood, James O. (1) "Hecate's Vap'rous Drop, Profound." *Notes and Queries* 9 (1964) 262–264.

———. (2) "Lady Macbeth's Secret Weapon." *Notes and Queries* 12 (March, 1965) 98–100.

———. (3) "Lady Macbeth's Suckling." *Notes and Queries* 13 (1966) 138.

———. (4) "Lost Lore in *Macbeth*." *Shakespeare Quarterly* 24 (1973) 223–226.

Wood, William Burke. *Old Drury of Philadelphia*. 1932.

Woodvine, John. Personal interview. 1976.

Worsley, Thomas Cuthbert. "From Belmont to Forres." *New Statesman and Nation* 45 (1953) 367.

Wren, Robert M. "'The Hideous Trumpet' and Sexual Transformation in *Macbeth*." *Forum* 12 (1967) 18–21.

Wright, Louis. "Animal Actors on the English Stage." *PLMA* 42 (1927) 656–659.

Wyatt, E. V. R. "*Macbeth* Production." *Catholic World* 167 (1948) 168–169.

Young, Julian C. *A Memoir of Charles Mayne Young*. 1871.

Young, Stark. *Immortal Shadows*. 1948.

Zandvoort, R. W. "Dramatic Motivation in *Macbeth*." *Les Languages Modernes* (March–April, 1951) 62–72.

Zarian, Rouben. *Shakespeare and the Armenians*. 1969.

Zukauskas, Vitalis P. Personal reports on *Macbeth* stagings.

Theatre Bibliography

This consists of three parts, as noted earlier:

Part I. Alphabetical lists of significant actors and actresses from English-speaking countries, and distinguished visiting actors from other countries. This includes Canada and Australia; South African stagings are listed in Part III.

Part II. Chronological lists of stagings of *Macbeth* in non-English-speaking countries.

Part III. Stagings of *Macbeth* associated with particular directors, places, or productions, listed alphabetically.

Theatre Bibliography I

The names of (1) actors, (2) actresses, and (3) productions are followed by basic sources of information used for each. Authors of books and articles are identified by last name and initial for location in the main bibliography. Periodicals are identified, where possible, by name and date. All of these sources have been consulted. Some have been referred to specifically in the text; many have contributed to the mass of information which underlies, like the submerged base of an iceberg, the surfaced summary images of characters, meaning and action proposed in my text. Many of these sources, never before cited in scholarly works, are here for any colleagues who can make use of them. London newspapers are identified only by name, thus: *Times*. American counterparts, to avoid confusion, are generally identified thus: *N.Y. Times*. Some of the other newspapers have city names. Where location is relevant, others are also identified by place.

THEATRE BIBLIOGRAPHY I, PART 1, ACTORS

AINLEY, Henry
  See THORNDIKE, *Sybil (1926)*
AKUTAGAWA, Hiroshi
  Interview with Tetsuo Anzai and Peter Milward
  See also foreign bibliography under Japan
ALDRIDGE, Ira Frederick
  Marshall, H.
  See also foreign bibliography under Russia
AYRTON, Randle
  Birmingham Evening Dispatch, April 21, 1931

Birmingham Gazette, April 21, 1931
Birmingham Mail, April 21, 1931
Evesham Journal, May 9, 1931
Stratford-Upon-Avon Herald, April 24, 1931
Stage, April 23, 1931
Unidentified clippings
BAKER, Tom
  Times, Nov. 12, 1973
BARRY, Spranger (acted Macbeth 1746)
  The Dramatic Censor, n.d.
  Examiner, Jan. 15, 1809

Hill, A. (1)
 Theatre Quarterly, vol. 1, no. 3 (1971)
BARRYMORE, Lionel
 Barrymore, L.
 Boston Evening Transcript, Feb. 21, 1921,
  March 18, 1921
 Current Opinion, April 1921
 The Forum, April 21, 1921
 Freeman, March 1921
 Macgowan, K.
 New York Herald, Feb. 18, 1921, Feb. 20,
  1921
 New York Mail, Feb. 18, 1921, April 20, 1921
 New York Post, Feb. 18, 1921
 New York Sun, Feb. 18, 1921
 New York Telegraph, Feb. 18, 1921
 New York Times, Feb. 18, 1921
 New York Tribune, April 20, 1921
 New York World, April 20, 1921
 Theatre Magazine, April, 1921
 Unidentified clippings
BENSON, Frank Robert
 Benson, F.
 Benson, G. C.
 Birmingham Post, April 23, 1896
 Daily Chronicle, April 2, 1900
 Daily Gazette, April 23, 1896
 Daily News, April 2, 1900
 Evening Standard, May 1, 1896, March 2,
  1900
 Globe, Feb. 21, 1905
 Herald, April 24, 1896
 Morning Post, March 2, 1900
 Observer, March 4, 1900
 Stratford-Upon-Avon Herald, May 8, 1908
 Sunday Times, March 4, 1900
 Times, March 3, 1900
BOOTH, Edwin
 Appleton's Journal, Nov. 20, 1875
 Baltimore American, Nov. 26, 1881
 Booth, E. (1), (2), (3), (4)
 Boston Evening Transcript, Jan. 20, 1886
 Boston Herald, May 8, 1885
 Brooklyn Argus, Nov. 2, 1881
 Brooklyn Daily Eagle, Nov. 5, 1881
 Brooklyn Times, Nov. 2, 1881
 Chicago Daily News, March 13, 1890, March
  18, 1890
 Chicago Herald, Oct. 7, 1886
 Chicago Morning News, Oct. 7, 1886
 Chicago Mail, March 18, 1890
 Chicago Record, March 18, 1890
 Chicago Times, April 4, 1882
 Chicago Tribune, April 4, 1882, Oct. 7, 1886
 Clarke, A. B.
 Copeland, C. T.
 Daily Alta California, Oct. 21, 1876, Oct. 22,
  1876, March 8, 1887
 Detroit Tribune, Sept. 18, 1886

 Era, Nov. 6, 1871
 Forum, July, 1893
 Galveston Daily News, Jan. 26, 1882
 Golden Era, Oct. 22, 1876
 Inter Ocean, March 18, 1890
 Louisville Courier Journal, Dec. 16, 1858,
  April 19, 1874
 Louisville Daily Democrat, Dec. 16, 1858,
  Dec. 17, 1858
 New York Daily Mail, May 8, 1885
 New York Evening Telegraph, Oct. 6, 1881
 New York Express, Oct. 6, 1881
 New York Herald, March 29, 1870, May 8,
  1885, Nov. 19, 1889
 New York Post, Oct. 6, 1881
 New York Sun, April 9, 1870
 New York Times, Jan. 24, 1885, Nov. 19,
  1889
 New York Tribune, Oct. 6, 1881, Jan. 1, 1884,
  Nov. 18, 1889
 New York World, Jan. 24, 1885, Nov. 19,
  1889
 Pittsburgh Commercial Gazette, Nov. 25, 1887
 Pittsburgh Daily Post, Nov. 25, 1887
 Roppolo, J. P.
 Salvini, T. (1)
 San Francisco Chronicle, March 15, 1887
 San Francisco Daily Post, Oct. 21, 1876,
  March 15, 1887
 San Francisco Morning Call, March 15, 1887
 St. Louis Republican, Feb. 15, 1882
 Saturday Review, Feb. 19, 1881
 Skinner, O.
 Spirit of the Times, April 2, 1870, April 9,
  1870, April 16, 1870
 Theatre, Aug. 1, 1882
 Times-Star, Nov. 9, 1887
 Towse, J. R.
 Turf, Field and Farm, March 3, 1870
 Winter, W., (1), (2), (5)
 Unidentified clippings*: May 24, 1885, New
  York; 1886, Boston; April 9, 1908; Sept.
  9, 1908
 Other unidentified clippings
 See also MODJESKA, Helena (1889–1890)
 See also CUSHMAN, Charlotte
BOOTH, John Wilkes (1860)
 See WEICHMANN, Louis
BOOTH, Junius Brutus
 Gould, T.
 Theatrical Register, Dec. 25, 1824
 Unidentified clippings
BOURCHIER, Arthur
 Athenaeum, Dec. 15, 1906
 Birmingham Argus, Nov. 14, 1906
 Birmingham Post, Nov. 14, 1906
 Daily Chronicle, Jan. 17, 1907
 Daily Mail, Dec. 12, 1906
 Stratford-Upon-Avon Herald, Nov. 18, 1906

Sunday Times, Dec. 16, 1906
BROOKE, Gustavus Vaughan
  Athenaeum, Oct. 22, 1853
  Bell's Life in Sydney, July 7, 1855
  Illustrated London News, Oct. 22, 1853
  Lawrence, W. J. (5)
  Melbourne Argus, March 14, 1855
  New York Sun, Oct. 20, 1853
  Observer, Oct. 23, 1853
  Sunday Times, Oct. 23, 1853
  Unidentified clippings
CLEMENTS, John
  Birmingham Post, Aug. 3, 1966
  Chicago American, April 9, 1962
  Chicago Daily News, April 9, 1962
  Daily Telegraph, Aug, 3, 1966
  Guardian, April 23, 1964
  New Statesman, Aug. 18, 1966
  New York Daily News, Feb. 7, 1962
  New York Herald Tribune, Feb. 7, 1962
  New York Mirror, Feb. 2, 1962
  New York Post, Feb. 7, 1962
  New York Times, Feb. 7, 1962; Oct. 30, 1966
  New York World Telegram and Sun, Feb. 7, 1962
  Observer, Aug. 7, 1966
  Punch, Aug. 10, 1966
  Spectator, Aug. 12, 1966
  Stage, Aug. 4, 1966
  Sunday Telegraph, Aug. 7, 1966
  Sunday Times, Aug. 7, 1966
  Times, Aug. 3, 1966, Aug. 12, 1966
  Unidentified clippings
CLUNES, Alec (1950)
  Williamson, A. (3)
COGHLAN, Charles F.
  New York Sun, Jan. 22, 1889
  New York Times, Jan. 22, 1889
  New York Tribune, Jan. 22, 1889
  New York World, Jan. 22, 1889
  Winter, W., (4)
  See also LANGTRY, *Lily*
COOKE, George F.
  Daily Telegraph, n.d.
  Lloyd's Weekly London Newspaper, Dec. 7, 1856
  Odell, G. C. (1)
  Port Folio, July, 1811
  Unidentified clippings
COOPER, Thomas Abthorpe
  Dramatic Censor, 1810
  Mirror of Taste, 1810
  Observer, Oct. 3, 1847
  Odell, G. C. (1)
  Port Folio, March 3, 1804; March 1809
  Unidentified clippings
COWPER, J. C. (1864)
  Liverpool Porcupine, n.d.
  See promptbook 66

DANEMAN, Paul (1976)
  See TUTIN, *Dorothy*
DEVLIN, William
  Punch, Jan. 3, 1962
  Williamson, A. (1)
DILLON, Charles
  Marston, J. W.
  See also FAUCIT, *Helen (1869)*
EVANS, Maurice
  Boston Herald, Oct. 28, 1941
  Boston Traveler, Oct. 28, 1941
  Chicago Daily News, April 28, 1942
  Chicago Tribune, April 28, 1942
  Detroit Free Press, March 29, 1942
  Life, Feb. 23, 1942
  Nation, Nov. 29, 1941
  New York Daily News, Nov. 12, 1941
  New York Herald Tribune, Nov. 12, 1941, Nov. 23, 1941
  New York Journal American, Nov. 12, 1941
  New York Post, Nov. 12, 1941
  New York Sun, Nov. 12, 1941, Nov. 14, 1941
  New York Times, Nov. 12, 1941, Nov. 23, 1941, Nov. 24, 1941
  New York World Telegram, Nov. 12, 1941
  Pall Mall Gazette, Nov. 12, 1941
  Philadelphia Bulletin, March 10, 1942, March 15, 1942
  Philadelphia Inquirer, March 15, 1942
  Philadelphia Star, Nov. 16, 1942
  Pittsburgh Post Gazette, March 21, 1942, March 31, 1942
  Pittsburgh Sun-Telegraph, March 31, 1942
  Playgoer, March 9, 1942
  Saturday Review, April 17, 1942
  Theatre Arts, Vol. 26, no. 1 (1942)
  Unidentified clippings: Nov. 12, 1941, Nov. 15, 1941
  Other unidentified clippings
  See also ANDERSON, *Judith (1941)*
FINCH, Jon
  See POLANSKI, *Roman, film production*
FORBES-ROBERTSON, Johnston
  Academy, Sept. 24, 1898
  Athenaeum, Sept. 24, 1898
  Daily Chronicle, Sept. 17, 1898, Sept. 19, 1898
  Daily Mail, Sept. 19, 1898
  Daily News, Sept. 19, 1898
  Daily Telegraph, Sept. 19, 1898
  Era, Sept. 3, Oct. 15, 1898
  Evening Standard, Sept. 19, 1898
  Graphic, Sept. 19, 1898
  Grein, J. T. (2)
  Lloyd's Weekly London Newspaper, Sept. 18, 1898
  Mirror, Oct. 8, 1898
  Observer, Sept. 18, 1898
  Saturday Review, Oct. 1, 1898

Stage, Sept. 22, 1898
Sunday Times, Sept. 18, 1898
Times, Sept. 19, 1898, Sept. 6, 1911
Truth, Sept. 22, 1898
Weekly Dispatch, Sept. 18, 1898
Westminster Budget, Sept. 23, 1898
Unidentified clippings
FORREST, Edwin
Alger, 737–745
Athenaeum, March 1, 1845
Atlas, Dec. 4, 1836
Daily Alta California, June 2, 1866, June 25, 1866, Dec. 13, 1872
Daily Telegraph, Sept. 19, 1898
Era, Sept. 24, 1898
Erskine, C. E.
Evening Standard, Nov. 5, 1836, Dec. 1, 1836
Examiner, March 1, 1845
Forster and Lewes.
Freeman's Journal, May 7, 1845
John Bull, Dec. 4, 1836
Kirk, J. F.
Lloyd's Weekly London Newspaper, Nov. 18, 1898
Manchester Guardian, Jan. 14, 1837
Morning Advertiser, Dec. 1, 1836
Morning Chronicle, Feb. 22, 1845
Murdoch, J.
New York Herald, Sept., 1867, Oct. 29, 1868, Dec. 29, 1868
New York Post, Jan. 22, 1833
New York Semi-Weekly, Nov. 1862
New York Times, Nov. 24, 1862, Nov. 28, 1862
New York Tribune, Nov. 24, 1862, Nov. 26, 1862, Sept. 26, 1867, Oct. 29, 1868, Oct. 31, 1868, Nov. 14, 1905
Observer, Feb. 24, 1845
Pittsburgh Gazette, April 22, 1868
Rees, J.
Roppolo, J P
San Francisco Bulletin, June 1, 1866, June 30, 1866
San Francisco Chronicle, June 30, 1866, Aug. 11, 1866
San Francisco Morning Call, June 2, 1866, June 3, 1866, June 30, 1866
Spirit of the Times, Dec. 8, 1860, March 2, 1861
Times, Dec. 1, 1836
Winter, W (3), (5)
Unidentified clippings: October 1835, Jan. 7, 1837, Oct. 13, 1895
Other unidentified clippings
See also CUSHMAN, *Charlotte (1845)*
See also WARNER, *Mary Amelia (1836)*
GARRICK, David
Anonymous (1); (2)
Appleton, W.

Archer and Lowe (2)
Barton, M.
Blackwood's Magazine, Sept. 1834
Boaden, J. (4)
Burnim, K.
Carlisle, C. (3)
The Connoisseur, Sept. 26, 1754
Cooke, W.
Daily News, Nov. 4, 1864
Daily Telegraph, Sept. 19, 1898
Davies, T. (1); (2)
Donohue, J. (1); (2); (3); (4)
Doran, J.
English Illustrated Magazine, December 1888
Examiner, Jan. 15, 1809
Fitzgerald, P. (3)
Garrick, D. (1); (2); (3); (4)
Gentleman, F. (1), (2)
Hawkins, F. (2)
Hedgecock, F. A.
Hill, A. (1)
Hill, J.
Illustrated London News, Oct. 16, 1875
Kaleidoscope, July 9, 1825
Kelley, J. A.
Lichtenberg, G. C.
Morning Chronicle, Oct. 30, 1773
Morning Post, Sept. 27, 1875
Murphy, A. (2)
New Monthly Magazine, July 1, 1818
Noverre, J. G.
Reader, Nov. 12, 1864
Saint James Chronicle, Jan. 19, 1768, Oct. 30, 1773
Sketch, Sept. 14, 1898
Stone, G. W. (1), (2), (3)
Sunday Times, Dec. 5, 1837
Theatre, Dec. 1, 1888
Theatrical Review, January, 1772
Wilkes, T.
Winter, W. (3), (5)
Inadequately dated clippings. *Dramatic Censor*, 1810; *Gentlemen's Magazine*, 1763; *Mirror of Tastes*, 1810; *Monthly Mirror*, 1799
Other unidentified clippings.
GIELGUD, John
Agate, J. (1)
Birmingham Gazette, July 24, 1942, Oct. 7, 1942
Birmingham Mail, May 15, 1942, May 20, 1942
Birmingham Post, Jan. 2, 1942, Feb. 1, 1942, May 20, 1942, May 22, 1942, May 23, 1942
Bournemouth Daily Echo, March 6, 1942, June 3, 1942
Christian Science Monitor, Aug. 8, 1942
Christian World, July 29, 1942
Country Life, March 29, 1930

Daily Telegraph, March 19, 1930, Jan. 17, 1942
Dukes, A.
Evening Dispatch, May 20, 1942
Gibbs, E. (1)
Gielgud, J. (1), (2), (3), (4)
John O'London's Weekly, July 31, 1942
Listener, March 29, 1933
Manchester Guardian, Jan. 19, 1942, Jan. 26, 1942
New Statesman, July 18, 1942
New York Times, July 26, 1942
Nottingham Journal, July 5, 1942
Observer, March 23, 1930, Jan. 2, 1942, July 12, 1942
Punch, July 22, 1942
Queen, March 26, 1930
Radio Times, March 24, 1933
Saturday Review, Dec. 27, 1958
Sketch, March 28, 1930
Spectator, July 17, 1942
Stage, March 20, 1930, Jan. 22, 1942, July 16, 1942
Sunday Times, March 23, 1930, July 12, 1942
Tablet, July 18, 1942
Theatre Review, Vol. 26 (1942):615–619
Theatre, July 18, 1942
Theatre Arts, October, 1942
Theatre World, August, 1942
Time and Tide, July 18, 1942
Times, March 18, 1930, Jan. 2, 1942, Jan. 9, 1942, Feb. 1, 1942, July 9, 1942, Sept. 7, 1968
Tynan, K. (2)
Williamson, A. (3)
Yorkshire Post, March 18, 1942
Inadequately dated clipping: *Sunday Times*, Dec. 2, year unknown
Other unidentified clippings
GUINNESS, Alec
Daily Telegraph, Oct. 22, 1967
Drama Survey, Vol. 6, no. 1 (1967)
Financial Times, Oct. 21, 1966
Guardian, Oct. 21, 1966, Oct. 28, 1966
Guinness, A.
London Magazine, January, 1967
New Statesman, Oct. 28, 1966
New York Times, Oct. 23, 1966
Observer, Oct. 23, 1966
Plays and Players, December, 1966, February 1967
Sheffield Telegraph, May 5, 1939
Spectator, Oct. 28, 1966
Stage, Oct. 22, 1966, Oct. 25, 1966
Sunday Telegraph, Oct. 23, 1966
Sunday Times, Oct. 23, 1966
Times, May 22, 1966, Oct. 21, 1966
Partially identified clippings: Manchester Examiner, n.d.; Oct. 21, 1966, Oct. 23, 1966

Other unidentified clippings
See also SIGNORET, *Simone*
HACKETT, James K.
Christian Science Monitor, March 17, 1924
Farjeon, H.
Hackett, J. K., Promptbook
Nation, March 19, 1924
New Republic, April 2, 1924
New York American, Feb. 8, 1916
New York Daily News, March 19, 1924
New York Herald, April 6, 1918, March 17, 1924
New York Journal of Commerce, May 17, 1924
New York Post, March 21, 1924
New York Press, Feb. 8, 1916
New York Sun, Feb. 8, 1916, Feb. 18, 1916, March 17, 1924, March 20, 1924
New York Telegram, March 17, 1924
New York Telegraph, Feb. 8, 1916, March 7, 1924, March 17, 1924
New York Times, Feb. 8, 1916, March 12, 1916, March 17, 1924, March 23, 1924
New York Tribune, March 17, 1924
New York World, Feb. 28, 1916, March 14, 1924
Patrician, March, 1921
Sketch, Nov. 3, 1920
The Stage, March 14, 1924
Le Theatre, July 8, 1921
Theatre Arts, May, 1924
Theatre Magazine, March, 1916; May, 1924
Vanity Fair, February, 1921
Weekly Dispatch, Nov. 7, 1920
Partially identified clippings: Shakespeariana, n.d., Nov. 7, 1920
Other unidentified clippings
See also foreign bibliography under France
HAMPDEN, Walter
Boston Evening Transcript, Jan. 5, 1923, May 14, 1934, Dec. 21, 1934
Boston Monitor, Dec. 27, 1934
Chicago Daily News, Jan. 13, 1934
Christian Science Monitor, April 6, 1918, Nov. 19, 1923, Dec. 21, 1934, Dec. 27, 1934
Detroit News, April 26, 1934
Drama Calendar, April 25, 1921
Hampden, W.
Literary Digest, June 4, 1921
New York Daily Mail, April 20, 1921
New York Globe, April 20, 1921
New York Herald, April 20, 1921
New York Post, April 20, 1921, n.d., 1934
New York Telegram, April 20, 1921
New York Telegraph, April 20, 1921
New York Times, April 20, 1921
New York Tribune, April 20, 1921
New York World, April 14, 1921, April 15, 1921, April 20, 1921, April 25, 1921, n.d., 1934

Figaro, Oct. 2, 1875
Filon, A.
Fortnightly Review, Oct. 1, 1883
Fitzgerald, P., (1), (4)
Footlights, April 18, 1896
Foss, G.
Funny Folks, Jan. 5, 1889
Gentleman, Jan. 4, 1889
Gielgud, J.
Gielgud, K. T.
Globe, Sept. 27, 1875, Dec. 31, 1888
Graphic, Oct. 2, 1875, Jan. 5, 1889, Jan. 12, 1889
Grein, J. T.
Hawkins, F., (2)
Hiatt, C.
Illustrated London News, Oct. 2, 1875, Oct. 16, 1875, Dec. 15, 1875, Jan. 5, 1889
Irving, Sir Henry (1), (2), (3), (4), (5), (6)
Irving, L.
James, H.
Kennedy, H. A.
Knight, J.
Lady's Pictorial, Jan. 5, 1889
Licensed Victualler's Gazette and Hotel Courier, Oct. 9, 1875
The Listener, Feb. 2, 1967
Liverpool Daily Post, Dec. 31, 1888
Lloyds Weekly London Newspaper, Oct. 3, 1875, Oct. 9, 1875, Dec. 30, 1888, Jan. 6, 1889
Magazine of Art, 4, 1881
Mail and Express, Oct. 31, 1895
Manchester Guardian, Dec. 8, 1891
Matthews and Hutton
Morning Advertiser, Sept. 27, 1875, Dec. 31, 1888, Oct. 30, 1895
Morning Journal, Oct. 30, 1895
Morning Post, Sept. 27, 1875, Dec. 31, 1888, Dec. 31, 1889, July 25, 1895
New York Daily Mail, Nov. 21, 1895
New York Dispatch, Nov. 3, 1895
New York Herald, Oct. 27, 1895, Nov. 10, 1895, Nov. 21, 1895
New York Post, Oct. 30, 1895
New York Press, Nov. 3, 1895, Nov. 10, 1895
New York Recorder, Nov. 3, 1895
New York Sun, Oct. 30, 1895, Mar. 17, 1924
New York Theatre, April, 1916
New York Times, Dec. 29, 1888, Oct. 30, 1895, Nov. 3, 1895, Nov. 10, 1895
New York Tribune, Oct. 30, 1895
New York World, Oct. 30, 1895, Nov. 2, 1895
Nineteenth Century, Feb. 1879, Feb. 1880
Nottingham Evening Post, Oct. 30, 1895
Observer, Dec. 30, 1888, July 28, 1895
Odell, G. C.
Pall Mall Gazette, Dec. 31, 1888
Penny Illustrated Paper, Jan. 5, 1889

People, Dec. 30, 1888
Philadelphia, April 15, 1896
Philadelphia Times, April 15, 1896
Pictorial News, Jan. 5, 1889
Pictorial World, Jan. 3, 1889
Pitou, A.
The Political World, Jan. 5, 1889
Pollock, W. H.
Punch, Dec. 22, 1888
Queen, Jan. 5, 1889
Referee, Dec. 30, 1888, July 28, 1895
Revue d'art Dramatique, June–Sept. 1889
Russell, E. R.
Saturday Review, Jan. 5, 1889, Jan. 20, 1889, March 30, 1889, April 30, 1889, July 6, 1889
Scott, C. W.
Shuttleworth, B.
Society Times, Jan. 5, 1889
Spectator, Oct. 2, 1875, Jan. 5, 1889
Spielmann, M. H.
Sporting and Dramatic News, Jan. 5, 1889
Sporting Gazette, Oct. 2, 1875
Sporting Life, Dec. 31, 1888
Star, Dec. 31, 1888
Stoker, B.
Terry, E. (1)–(8)
Towse, J. R.
Trade Finance and Recreation, Jan. 2, 1889
Truth, Jan. 3, 1889
Universal Review, Jan. 15, 1889
Vanity Fair, Oct. 2, 1875
Walbrook, H. M.
Wedmore, F.
Weekly Dispatch, Oct. 3, 1875, Oct. 8, 1875, Oct. 9, 1875, Jan. 5, 1889, Sept. 18, 1898
Weekly Times and Echo, Dec. 30, 1888
Whitehall Review, Jan. 3, 1889
Willan, J. N.
Wilson, F.
Wingate, C.
Winter, W., (3), (4), 277–281, 481, (5), 481–485
Women's Magazine, February, 1896
World, Jan. 2, 1889
Unidentified and partially identified clippings: Jan. 15, 1889, n.d., 1895, Oct. 26, 1895, Nov. 10, 1895, Nov. 20, 1895, *Truth*, n.d.
Other unidentified clippings
See also TERRY, *Ellen (1888 et seq.)*
KEAN, Charles
Athenaeum, July 11, 1840, June 9, 1849, Feb. 19, 1853
Atlas, June 11, 1840, July 11, 1840, Feb. 19, 1853
Bath Journal, Jan. 16, 1826, Jan. 26, 1829, Dec. 27, 1830, Feb. 8, 1836, Feb. 27, 1837
"Bede, C."

Boston Herald, Oct. 26, 1895
Britannia, July 4, 1840
Cole, J. W.
Coleman, J. (1)
Critical Review, March, 1861
Daily News, Feb. 15, 1853, Feb. 19, 1853
Daily Telegraph, Sept. 19, 1898
Era, April 10, 1842
Examiner, July 12, 1840, July 19, 1840, April 2, 1842
Flattery and Truth, Feb. 14, 1853
Fontane, T.
Hawkins, F. (1)
Illustrated London News, Oct. 16, 1875
James, H.
John Bull, July 4, 1840, July 12, 1840, April 16, 1842, Feb. 19, 1853
Literary Gazette, Feb. 19, 1846
Marston, W.
Morning Advertiser, July 4, 1840, April 5, 1842
Morning Chronicle, Feb. 16, 1853
Morning Herald, March 15, 1831, July 4, 1840, April 6, 1842, Feb. 14, 1853
Morning Post, July 3, 1840, July 4, 1840, April 5, 1842, Feb. 16, 1853, Sept. 27, 1875
New York Times, May 4, 1853
Notes and Queries, July 13, 1889
Observer, Feb. 26, 1844, Feb. 21, 1853
Opera Glass, Dec. 4, 1830
Robinson, H. C.
Spectator, April 9, 1840, July 18, 1840
Sun, July 4, 1840, April 5, 1842, Feb. 15, 1843
Sunday Times, July 5, 1840, Feb. 20, 1853
Times, July 4, 1840, Feb. 15, 1853
Weekly Dispatch, July 12, 1840, April 10, 1842, Feb. 20, 1853
Winter, W. (4)
Unidentified and partially identified clippings: October, 1840, July 18, 1840, April 16, 18, 1842, Feb. 14, 1853, Oct. 13, 1895, *Atlas*, April 9, n.d.; *Gentleman's Magazine*, n.d.; *Lloyd's Weekly London Newspaper* n.d.
Other unidentified clippings
KEAN, Edmund
Agate, J. (1)
Albion, Nov. 26, 1825, Dec. 3, 1825, Jan. 29, 1826, Feb. 4, 1826, Feb. 11, 1826
Armstrong, C. F.
Aurora, Jan. 23, 1821
Bath Journal, Dec. 27, 1830
Bible Times, Feb. 6, 1817
Champion, Nov. 13, 1814, June 17, 1820, July 17, 1820
Cole, J. W.
Cotton, W.
Critical Review, March 1816

Donohue, J. (4)
The Drama or Theatrical Magazine, n.d.
Dramatic Censor, Sept. 29, 1829
Edinburgh Advertiser, Feb. 26, 1825, Sept. 29, 1829
European Magazine, February 1816, April 1816
Examiner, Nov. 13, 1814, Nov. 15, 1814, Oct. 20, 1817, June 26, 1820
Freeman's Journal, May 27, 1829
Hawkins, F. (1), (2)
Hazlitt, W. (1)
Hillebrand, H.
Hunt, L. (1-4)
Inquirer, or, Literary Miscellany, Nov. 3, 1814
Kaleidoscope, Oct. 26, 1824, Nov. 25, 1828
Literary Gazette, June 17, 1820, Jan. 5, 1822
Liverpool Mercury, Oct. 13, 1820
Marston, W.
Montreal Herald, Aug. 14, 1826
Morning Chronicle, Nov. 7, 1814, Oct. 20, 1817, Oct. 21, 1817
Morning Post, Nov. 7, 1814
Morris, J.
National Register, Nov. 6, 1814
New Monthly Magazine, Dec. 1, 1814
Newcastle Chronicle, April 1, 1815
Newcastle Courant, April 1, 1815
News, Nov. 13, 1814, Oct. 20, 1817, May 4, 1817, Oct. 26, 1817
Perth Courier, Sept. 27, 1822, Oct. 4, 1822
Playfair, G.
Proctor, B. W.
Robinson, H. C.
Sale Room, April 12, 1817
Scotsman, Feb. 28, 1825
St. James Chronicle, Nov. 8, 1814
Sun, Nov. 7, 1814
Theatre, Dec. 1, 1888, Dec. 11, 1888
Theatrical Inquisitor, Nov. 14, 1814, August, 1819
Times, Sept. 19, 1811, Nov. 7, 1814, Feb. 6, 1817, Oct. 20, 1817, Oct. 2, 1835
Winter, W. (5)
York Herald, July 24, 1819
Unidentified and partially identified clippings: Oct. 19, 1817, Oct. 20, 1817, October 1820, October 1835; *Drama, or, Theatrical Magazine*, n.d.; *New York Post*, n.d.
Other unidentified clippings
KEMBLE, John Philip
Baker, H. B. (2)
Bath Journal, March 12, 1832
Bell's Weekly Messenger, July 5, 1812
Boaden, J. (1), (2)
Cabinet, June, 1808
Courier, June 30, 1812

Daily Telegraph, March 10, 1884
Donohue, J. (1), (2)
Drama, vol. 1, 262, vol. 4, 27, 321
Dramatic Censor, Sept. 18, 1811
Dunlap, W.
English Illustrated Magazine, December, 1888
Examiner, Jan. 15, 1809, June 16, 1816, June
   26, 1820, March 20, 1831
Farington, J.
Galt, J.
Hawkins, F. (1)
Hazlitt, W. (1)
Hunt, L., (1), (2)
Illustrated London News, Oct. 16, 1875
Jenkin, F.
John Bull, October 1823
Kemble, J. P. (1), (2)
Lamb, C.
Macready, W. C., (2)
Marston, W.
Martin, T., (2)
Matthews, B., and Hutton, L.
Monthly Mirror, December 1803, November
   1807, October 1808
Morning Chronicle, Sept. 19, 1798
Morning Post, Sept. 19, 1809, June 10, 1812,
   June 10, 1816
Murdoch, J.
New Monthly Magazine, July 1, 1818
News, July 5, 1812, June 16, 1816, July 16,
   1821
New York Tribune, Nov. 14, 1905
Nineteenth Century, February 1880
Oulton, W. C.
Proctor, B. W.
Public Advertiser, Feb. 4, 1785, Feb. 8, 1785
Reader, Nov. 12, 1864
Robinson, H. C.
Sale Room, April 5, 1817
Scott, W.
Simond, L.
Sketch, Sept. 14, 1898
Star, June 10, 1816
Sun, June 10, 1816
Theatre, Dec. 1, 1888
Theatrical Inquisitor, August 1819
Theatre Journal, May, 1764
Times, Nov. 29, 1803, Sept. 19, 1811, Nov.
   17, 1814, June 10, 1816
Winter, W. (3), (5)
World, April 22, 1794
Unidentified and partially identified clippings:
   September 1788; "Critical Observations
   on Mr. Kemble's Performance," n.d.,
   1811; *Blackwood's Edinburgh Magazine*,
   n.d., 1843; *Theatre Journal*, n.d., 1797;
   Monthly Mirror, n.d., 1798, 1804 and
   1809; *Mirror of Taste*, n.d., 1810

Other unidentified clippings
LAUGHTON, Charles
   Agate, J. (1)
   Daily Express, March 4, 1934
   Daily Telegraph, March 4, 1934
   Era, April 4, 1934
   Farjeon, H.
   Lady, April 12, 1934
   Morning Post, April 3, 1934
   Observer, April 8, 1934
   Punch, April 11, 1934
   Queen, April 18, 1934
   Saturday Review, April 14, 1934
   Spectator, April 6, 1934
   Stage, April 5, 1934
   Sunday Times, April 8, 1934
   Times, Nov. 27, 1937
   Unidentified clippings
LEIBER, Fritz
   Daily Texan, Jan. 11, 1929
   New York Times, March 26, 1930
   Pittsburgh Post Gazette, March 7, 1929, Oct.
      25, 1934
   Pittsburgh Sun-Telegraph, May 7, 1929
   Theatre Magazine, May, 1930
MACKLIN, Charles
   Appleton, W.
   Cooke, W.
   London Magazine, n.d.
   Macklin, C.
   Morning Chronicle and London Advertiser, Oct.
      25–30, 1773
   Monthly Mirror, n.s. vol. 4, 1808
   Parry, A.
   St. James Chronicle, Oct. 28–30, 1773
   Sprague, A. C., (4)
   Theatrical Intelligence, Oct. 29, 1773, Nov. 1,
      5, 6, 7, 8, 15, 1773
   Unidentified clippings
MACREADY, William Charles
   Actors by Gaslight, Nov. 3, 1838
   Agate, J. (1)
   Athenaeum, June 1, 1844, June 19, 1847, July
      11, 1857, June 19, 1867
   Archer and Lowe: (2)
   Atlas, July 11, 1840, Oct. 2, 1847, Feb. 26,
      1848
   Bath Journal, May 26, 1823, March 12, 1832,
      Jan. 12, 1835
   Baxter, P.
   Belfast Newsletter, Feb. 20, 1824
   Britannia, Oct. 9, 1847
   Brighton Gazette, Sept. 13, 1849
   Bristol Gazette, Feb. 2, 1823
   Bristol Journal, Jan. 12, 1850
   Bristol Mercury, Jan. 16, 1826, Jan. 23, 1847,
      Jan. 5, 1850, Jan. 12, 1850
   Bristol Mirror, Jan. 12, 1850

Bristol Observer, Feb. 5, 1823
Bristol Standard, Mar. 12, 1850
Bristol Times, Jan. 12, 1850
Cambrian, Sept. 20, 1834
Champion, May 5, 1820, June 17, 1820, July 17, 1820
Charleston Courier, Jan. 8, 1844
Coleman, J. (1)
Le Corsair, April 25, 1828
Court Journal, Oct. 5, 1847, Oct. 9, 1847
Daily Georgian, Nov. 23, 1844
Daily Telegraph, Sept. 19, 1898
Donohue, J. (2)
Downer, A., (1), (2), (3)
Drama, Dec. 1, 1827
Dumfries and Galloway Courier, May 12, 1845
Dundee Advertiser, Aug. 25, 1820
Edinburgh Courant, March 21, 1850
Edinburgh Dramatic Review, April 24, 1824
English Chronicle and Whitehall Evening Post, June 10, 1820
English Illustrated Magazine, December, 1888
Englishman, June 18, 1820
Era, April 3, 1842, Oct. 10, 1847
Examiner, June 25, 1820, June 26, 1820, March 20, 1831, Oct. 4, 1835, Oct. 5, 1835, May 2, 1846, Oct. 9, 1847, Feb. 26, 1848
Finlay, J.
Forster and Lewes
Freeman's Journal, Feb. 7, 1826, Feb. 15, 1826, March 6, 1833, Aug. 10, 1835, Aug. 11, 1835, Feb. 2, 1847
Gautier, T.
Gentleman's Magazine, March, 1889
Glasgow Dramatic Review, April 16, 1845
Le Globe, April 12, 1829, Oct. 5, 1847
Hampshire Advertiser, Dec. 15, 1849
Hazlitt, W. (1)
Hillebrand, H.
Hull Advertiser, March 15, 1850
Hunt, L. (1), (2), (4)
Illustrated London News, Oct. 9, 1847, Oct. 13, 1849, Oct. 16, 1875
John Bull, May 26, 1839, Oct. 9, 1847, March 1, 1851
Journal des Débats, April 14, 1828
Kaleidoscope, Sept. 26, 1820, July 17, 1821, Oct. 21, 1823, June 29, 1824, Nov. 25, 1828
Kirke, J. F.
Lewes, G. H.
Literary Gazette, June 17, 1820, April 12, 1823, Nov. 8, 1823
Liverpool Theatrical Investigator, Sept. 19, 1821
Lloyds Weekly London Newspaper, Oct. 10, 1847, Nov. 13, 1864

Louisville Journal, April 18, 1849, April 19, 1849
Ludlow, N.
Macready, W. C., (1), (2)
Marston, J. W.
Le Mentor, April 14, 1828
Morning Advertiser, Oct. 5, 1847
Morning Chronicle, Oct. 5, 1847, Feb. 22, 1848, Feb. 21, 1857
Morning Herald, March 15, 1831, Oct. 2, 1835, Oct. 5, 1847
Morning Post, Oct. 5, 1847, Sept. 27, 1875
Morris, J.
Murdoch, J.
Pückler-Muskau, H. L. H.
New Mirror, Dec. 9, 1843
New York Literary World, Oct. 14, 1848; Dec. 2, 1848; Dec. 9, 1848
New York Mirror, vol. 4, 95
New York Times, Sept. 21, 1843; Sept. 27, 1843
New York Tribune, April 4, 1870
News, Nov. 15, 1824, Nov. 21, 1824, Oct. 5, 1847
Observer, April 8, 1823, Oct. 11, 1847, Feb. 27, 1848, March 2, 1851
People's Forum, Dec. 19, 1846
Perth Courier, Aug. 31, 1820
Philadelphia Public Ledger, Oct. 23, 1843, Nov. 21, 1848, Nov. 23, 1843
Pilot, July 3, 1844, July 5, 1844, July 8, 1844, July 10, 1844, July 12, 1844, July 15, 1844
Playbill, Nov. 14, 1821, March 9, 1850
Price, W. T. (2)
Reader, Nov. 12, 1864
Roppolo, J. P.
Salisbury and Winchester Journal, March 23, 1835
Scotsman, March 20, 1850, March 29, 1850
Sheffield Iris, n.d.
Smith, S.
Spectator, April 9, 1842
Sprague, A. C. (1), (4)
Stanford Mercury, Nov. 25, 1825
Standard, Oct. 5, 1847
Sun, March 5, 1842
Sunday Times, April 27, 1823, April 5, 1842, Oct. 10, 1847, Feb. 27, 1848
Tallis Dramatic Magazine, Nov., 1850
Theatre, Dec. 1, 1888
Theatrical Inquisitor, July, 1820
Theatrical Journal, Aug. 8, 1840, April 2, 1842, March 16, 1848
Theatrical Observer, April 7, 1828
Theatrical Portrait, Oct. 2, 1835, n.d., 1891
Theatre Quarterly, vol. 1, no. 3 (1971)
Times, Oct. 2, 1835, March 29, 1842, Oct. 5, 1847, Oct. 7, 1847

Olivier, L.
Plays and Players, Aug. 14, 1955
Punch, June 15, 1955
Robinson, E.
Shaw, Glen Byam
Sketch, June 8, 1955
Spectator, June 24, 1955
Stage, Dec. 2, 1937, June 9, 1955, June 11, 1955
Stratford-Upon-Avon Herald, June 10, 1955
Sunday Mercury, June 12, 1955
Sunday Times, Dec. 5, 1937, Dec. 6, 1937, June 12, 1955
Theatre, June 17, 1955
Theatre Quarterly, vol. 1, no. 3 (1971)
Times, June 8, 1955
Time and Tide, Aug. 18, 1955
Tribune, June 8, 1955, July 28, 1955
Truth, June 17, 1955
Tynan, K. (1), (2), (3)
Warwickshire Herald, June 11, 1955
Western Daily Press (Bristol), June 9, 1955
Williamson, A. (3)
Unidentified and partially identified clippings:
June 15, 1955, July 28, 1955; *Voice and Verse*, n.d.
Other unidentified clippings
See also ANDERSON, *Judith (1937)*
See also LEIGH, *Vivian (1955)*
PHELPS, Samuel
Athenaeum, June 1, 1844, Oct. 2, 1847, Oct. 5, 1850
Atlas, Oct. 2, 1847, Nov. 3, 1864
Britannia, Oct. 2, 1847
Coleman, J. (1), (3)
Court Journal, Oct. 2, 1847, Nov. 5, 1864
Daily News, Nov. 4, 1864
Daily Telegraph, Nov. 5, 1864, Sept. 19, 1898
English Illustrated Magazine, December 1888
Era, Oct. 3, 1847, Nov. 6, 1864
Evening Standard, Nov. 7, 1864
Examiner, Oct. 2, 1847, Nov. 5, 1864, Dec. 3, 1864
Fontane, T.
Glasgow Herald, Dec. 22, 1843, Feb. 18, 1861
Globe, Nov. 4, 1864
Illustrated London News, Oct. 2, 1847, Jan. 3, 1851, Sept. 3, 1853, March 3, 1855, Nov. 12, 1864, Nov. 13, 1864, Oct. 2, 1875
John Bull, Oct. 3, 1847, Nov. 5, 1864
Jefferson, J.
Lloyds Weekly London Newspaper, Oct. 3, 1847, Oct. 1, 1847, March 24, 1850, Nov. 13, 1864
Marston, J. W.
Morning Advertiser, Nov. 4, 1864
Morning Herald, Sept. 30, 1847
Morning Post, Sept. 28, 1847, Nov. 7, 1864

Observer, Oct. 3, 1847, Nov. 6, 1864
Queen, Nov. 12, 1864
Reader, Nov. 12, 1864
Spectator, Nov. 3, 1864
Sporting Life, Nov. 9, 1864
Sunday Times, Oct. 3, 1847, Nov. 6, 1864
Sun. Nov. 4, 1864
Theatre, March 1, 1884, June 1, 1887
Times, Sept. 28, 1847, Jan. 23, 1858, Nov. 7, 1864, July 4, 1884
Towse, J. R.
Weekly Dispatch, Oct. 3, 1847, Nov. 6, 1864
Weiner, A. B.
Unidentified clippings
See also FAUCIT, *Helen (1864)*
See also GLYN, *Isabella (1850)*
See also MACREADY, *William Charles (1846)*
See also WARNER, *Mary Amelia (1844)*
PLUMMER, Christopher
Chicago Tribune, June 10, 1962, June 19, 1962
Coghill, N. (1, 3)
Columbus, Ohio, Dispatch, June 20, 1962
Detroit News, June 19, 1962
Le Devoir (Montreal), June 20, 1962
London, Ontario, Evening Free Press, June 19, 1962
Montreal Star, June 19, 1962
New York Herald Tribune, June 2, 1962, June 20, 1962
New York Times, June 20, 1962
Ottawa Citizen, June 19, 1962
Ottawa Le Droit, June 19, 1962
Owen Sound, (Ontario) Sun-Times, June 20, 1962
Port Arthur, (Ontario) News-Chronicle, June 19, 1962 (Canadian Press)
Syracuse (N. Y.) Herald-Journal, June 21, 1962 (Associated Press)
Toronto Daily Star, June 19, 1962
Toronto Telegram, June 19, 1962
Variety, June 20, 1962
Winnipeg Free Press, June 19, 1962
Unidentified clippings
PORTER, Eric
Birmingham Mail, June 6, 1962
Birmingham Post, May 20, June 6, June 8, 1962
Brown, J. R. (1)
Boulton Evening News, June 6, 1962
Daily Express, June 6, 1962
Daily Herald, June 6, 1962
Daily Mail, June 6, 1962
Daily Telegraph, June 6, 1962
Daily Worker, June 7, 1962
Evening Dispatch, June 6, 1962
Financial Times, June 6, 1962
Manchester Guardian, June 7, 1962
Newcastle-Upon Tyne Journal, Aug. 9, 1962

Nottingham Journal, June 6, 1962
Observer, June 6, 1962
Porter, E. (1)
Robinson, E.
Scotsman, July 14, 1962
Stage, June 7, 1962
Stratford-Upon-Avon Herald, June 8, 1962
Sunday Telegraph, June 10, 1962
Sunday Times, June 10, 1962
Tablet, Oct. 27, 1962
Times, June 6, 1962
Western Daily Press, June 6, 1962
Williamson, A., (1)
Wolverhampton Express and Star, June 6, 1962
Yorkshire Post, June 6, 1962
Unidentified clippings
See also WORTH, *Irene*
POWELL, John (acted Macbeth 1768)
Bell's Weekly Messenger, Jan. 5, 1806
Gentleman, F. (1), (2)
Theatre Quarterly, vol. 1, no. 3 (1971)
Unidentified clippings
QUAYLE, Anthony
The Advertiser, Jan. 24, 1950
Age, Nov. 8, 1949
Argus, Nov. 8, 12, 1949
Gaines, B.
The Listener, Nov. 12–18, 1949
The News, Jan. 24, 1950
The Sun, Nov. 8, 1949; Dec. 18, 1949
Sydney Morning Herald, Dec. 13, 1949
Unidentified clippings
See also QUAYLE, *Anthony*, *Production*
QUILLEY, Denis
Catholic Herald, April 27, 1973
Daily Mail, April 5, 1973
Daily Telegraph, April 5, 1973
Financial Times, April 7, 1973
Guardian, April 6, 1973
Observer, April 8, 1973
Plays and Players, April 1973
Spectator, April 14, 1973
Stage, April 1973
Times, April 4, 1973
Unidentified clippings
See also RIGG, *Diana*
QUIN, James (acted Macbeth 1723)
Theatre Quarterly, vol. 1, no. 3 (1971)
RANKIN, McKee
Overland Monthly, Feb. 1886, 186ff
REDGRAVE, Michael
Birmingham Gazette, Dec. 20, 1947
Birmingham Mail, Dec. 2, 1947
Birmingham Post, Dec. 2, 1947
Burton, H., 106
Clurman, H.
Commonweal, April 23, 1944
Evening Dispatch, Dec. 2, 1947

Evening Standard, Dec. 19, 1947
Findlater, R.
Garrett, J.
Gibbs, W. (2)
John O'London's Weekly, Jan. 9, 1948
Manchester Guardian, Dec. 20, 1947
Nathan, G. J.
Nation, April 17, 1948
News Chronicle, Dec. 20, 1947
New Statesman, Dec. 27, 1947, April 23, 1948
New York Daily Mirror, April 1, 1948
New York Daily News, April 1, 1948
New York Herald Tribune, April 1, 1948,
    April 4, 1948
New York Journal-American, April 1, 1948
New York Post, April 1, 1948
New York Sun, April 1, 1948
New York Times, March 28, 1948, April 1,
    1948, April 11, 1948
New York World Telegram, April 1, 1948
Observer, Dec. 21, 1947
Punch, Dec. 31, 1947
Queen, Jan. 7, 1948
Redgrave, M.
Saturday Review, (U.S.) April 17, 1948
Shakespeare Survey, vol. 2 (1949)
Stage, Dec. 24, 1947
Sunday Times, Dec. 21, 1947
Time and Tide, Dec. 27, 1947
Time, April 12, 1948
Wyatt, E. V. R.
Unidentified and partially identified clippings:
    April 11, 1948; *New Theatre*, n.d.; *The-
    atre*, n.d.
Other unidentified clippings
See also ROBSON, *Flora*
RICHARDSON, Ralph
Birmingham Gazette, June 11, 1952
Birmingham Mail, June 11, 1952
Birmingham News, June 16, 1952; June 14,
    1952
Birmingham Post, June 11, 1952, June 18,
    1952
Burton, H.
Coventry Evening Telegraph, June 11, 1952
Daily Mail, June 11, 1952
Daily Telegraph, June 11, 1952
Daily Worker, June 13, 1952, June 15, 1952
Evening Dispatch, June 11, 1952
Evening News, June 11, 1952
Evening Standard, June 11, 1952, June 13,
    1952
Evesham Journal, June 11, 1952, June 14,
    1952
Illustrated London News, May 7, 1952, July 5,
    1952
John O'London's Weekly, June 27, 1952
Lady, June 26, 1952

Leamington Spa Courier, June 13, 1952
Manchester Daily Express, June 11, 1952
News Chronicle, June 11, 1952
New Statesman, June 21, 1952
Nottingham Guardian, June 12, 1952
Observer, June 15, 1952
Punch, June 25, 1952
Sketch, July 2, 1952
Solihull and Warwick County News, June 14, 1952
Spectator, June 20, 1952
Stage, June 12, 1952
Stratford-Upon-Avon Herald, June 13, 1952
Sunday Times, June 15, 1952
Theatre World, July 17, 1952
Times, June 11, 1952
Truth, June 20, 1952
Tynan, K. (2)
Undated clipping: Times Weekly
RIGNOLD, George
Athenaeum, July 8, 1882
Daily Telegraph, July 5, 1882
James, H.
Lloyds Weekly London Newspaper, July 9, 1882
Observer, July 9, 1882
Saturday Review, July 8, 1882
Sunday Times, July 9, 1882
Weekly Dispatch, July 9, 1882
See also RISTORI, *Adelaide*
ROBARDS, Jason
Boston Record, July 31, 1959
New York Times, Aug. 1, 1959
ROGERS, Paul
Birmingham Post, Aug. 25, 1954, Sept. 15, 1954
Chicago American, Feb. 13, 1957
Chicago Daily News, Feb. 13, 1957
Chicago Sun-Times, Feb. 13, 1957
Chicago Tribune, Feb. 13, 1957
Daily Telegraph, Aug. 25, 1954, Sept. 10, 1954
David, R.
Edinburgh Evening Dispatch, Aug. 24, 1954
Edinburgh Evening News, Aug. 24, 1954
Evening Standard, Sept. 10, 1954
Financial Times, Aug. 25, 1954
Manchester Guardian, Sept. 11, 1954
New York Times, Oct. 30, 1956
Observer, Aug. 29, 1954
Rogers, P.
Scotsman, Aug. 25, 1954
Star, Sept. 10, 1954
Sydney Morning Herald, April 29, 1957, June 4, 1957
Times, Aug. 25, 1954, Aug. 29, 1954, Sept. 10, 1954, Oct. 1, 1954
Tribune, Oct. 1, 1954
Truth, Sept. 3, 1954

Tynan, K. (2)
Williamson, A. (2)
Unidentified clippings
ROSSI, Ernesto
Academy, May 13, 1876
Athenaeum, May 2, 1876, May 20, 1876
Bell's Life in London, May 20, 1876
Bell's Weekly Messenger, May 13, 1876
Era, May 14, 1876
James, H.
Knight, J.
Il Piccolo Faust, June 9, 1896
Rossi, E. (1), (3)
Saturday Review, May 20, 1876
Times, May 12, 1876
Unidentified clippings
See also main bibliography, and foreign bibliography under Italy and Sweden
SALVINI, Tommaso
Academy, April 15, 1876
Athenaeum, March 15, 1884
Belgravia, November 1875
Boston Daily Advertiser, April 22, 1881
Chicago Tribune, Dec. 14, 1882, Dec. 17, 1882
Cincinnati Commercial, Jan. 2, 1910
Coleman, J. (1)
Daily News, March 10, 1884
Daily Telegraph, March 10, 1884
Edinburgh Courant, April 6, 1876
Era, March 15, 1884
Evening News, March 10, 1884, March 15, 1884
Figaro, March 15, 1884
Het Toneel, Dec. 1882
Illustrated London News, March 15, 1884
Illustrated Sporting and Dramatic News, March 15, 1884
James, H.
Lazarus, E.
Life, March 13, 1884
Morning Advertiser, March 10, 1884, Oct. 13, 1895
Morning Post, March 3, 1884
New York Clipper, Feb. 19, 1881
New York Herald, Feb. 11, 1881, May 12, 1881
New York Times, Feb. 2, 1881
Observer, March 9, 1884
Salvini, T. (1), (2)
Saturday Review, March 10, 1884, March 15, 1884
Scotsman, April 6, 1876
Scribner's, December 1873
Stage, March 14, 1884
Stevenson, R. L.
Times, June 4, 1875, March 10, 1884, April 10, 1884

Tribune, April 30, 1876
Towse, J. R.
Weekly Dispatch, March 16, 1884
Whitehall Review, March 6, 1884, March 13, 1884
Winter, W. (5)
Unidentified clippings: Oct., 1877 (Paris), Oct. 13, 1895
Other unidentified clippings
See also foreign bibliography under Italy
SCOFIELD, Paul
Financial Times, Aug. 17, 1967
Guardian, Aug. 17, 1967, Jan. 5, 1968
Illustrated London News, Aug. 27, 1967, Jan. 13, 1968
New Statesman, Aug. 25, 1967, Jan. 12, 1968
Observer, Aug. 20, 1967, Jan. 7, 1968
Rosenberg, M. (2)
Scofield, P.
Spectator, Aug. 25, 1967, Jan. 12, 1968, Jan. 21, 1968
Sunday Telegraph, Aug. 20, 1967, Jan. 7, 1968
Sunday Times, Aug. 20, 1967, Jan. 7, 1968
Theatre Quarterly, vol. 1, no. 3 (1971)
Times, Jan. 5, 1968
Unidentified clippings
SMITH, William
Morning Post, Feb. 3, 1785
Public Advertiser, Feb. 8, 1785
Unidentified clippings
See also SIDDONS, *Sarah (1785)*
SOTHERN, Edward Hugh
Baltimore News, Jan. 31, 1911
Boston Advertiser, Nov. 15, 1910
Boston Evening Transcript, Nov. 15, 1910, Nov. 16, 1910, Dec. 9, 1910, Dec. 12, 1911
Boston Globe, Dec. 23, 1911
Boston Herald, Nov. 5, 1910
Boston Traveller, Dec. 23, 1911
Chicago Daily News, Jan. 10, 1913
Chicago Examiner, April 11, 1911
Chicago Record, March 15, 1911
Cincinnati Commercial, Feb. 26, 1911
Commercial Tribune, Jan. 21, 1901, Jan. 22, 1901
Minneapolis Journal, June 18, 1911, June 25, 1911
New Orleans Daily Picayune, March 6, 1912
New York Dramatic Mirror, Nov. 13, 1910, Dec. 7, 1910, Dec. 11, 1898
New York Review, June 24, 1911, July 1, 1911
New York Sun, Feb. 11, 1910, Dec. 9, 1910, Dec. 8, 1910
Philadelphia Times, Jan. 17, 1911
Pittsburgh Post, Feb. 14, 1911
Rochester Democrat, Jan. 6, 1911

Russell, C. E.
Sothern, E.
Symonds, A.
Unidentified and partially identified clippings: Dec. 11, 1910; Jan. 31, 1911; *Los Angeles Examiner*, n.d.; *Rochester Times*, n.d.; *Syracuse Post*, n.d.; *Utah Post*, n.d.
Other unidentified clippings
SULLIVAN, Barry
Lawrence, W. J. (1)
Pittsburgh Post, April 2, 1859, April 4, 1859
Sillard, R. M.
Saturday Review, Dec., 1861
Unidentified clippings
TEARLE, Godfrey
Age, Nov. 8, 1949
Birmingham Gazette, April 18, 1949
Birmingham Mail, April 4, 1949, April 18, 1949, May 5, 1949
Birmingham Post, April 18, 1949, April 22, 1949
Coventry Evening Telegraph, April 18, 1949
Empire News, May 1, 1949
Evening Dispatch, April 18, 1949
Evening Standard, April 22, 1949
Evesham Journal, April 23, 1949
Graphic, April 18, 1949
Illustrated London News, April 24, 1949, May 7, 1949
John O'London's Weekly, May 13, 1949
Leamington Spa Courier, April 23, 1949
Liverpool Post, April 18, 1949
Manchester Guardian, April 18, 1949, April 24, 1949
News Chronicle, April 23, 1949, April 25, 1949
New Statesman, April 23, 1949
Shaw Journal, April 23, 1949, April 28, 1949
Spectator, April 22, 1949
Stage, April 21, 1949, April 29, 1949
Stratford-Upon-Avon Herald, April 17, 1949, April 22, 1949
Sunday Chronicle, April 24, 1949
Sunday Mercury, April 17, 1949
Sunday Times, April 17, 1949
Theatre World, April 24, 1949, June 29, 1949
Times, April 18, 1949, April 20, 1949
Truth, April 29, 1949
Williamson, A. (3)
Unidentified clipping: Herald (?), April 18, 1949
See also WYNYARD, *Diana*
THORNDIKE, Russell
Byrne, Myrtle St. Clare (2)
TREE, Herbert Beerbohm
Aberdeen Journal, July 6, 1911, Sept. 5, 1911, Sept. 6, 1911

Murdoch, J.
  Unidentified clippings
WALLACK, James William
  Athenaeum, March 22, 1821
  Kaleidoscope, July 17, 1821
  Liverpool Theatrical Investigator, July 4, 1821
  Odell, G. C. (1)
  Unidentified clippings
WALLACK, James William, Jr.
  Pittsburgh Gazette, Dec. 15, 1866
  Pittsburgh Morning Post, Oct. 6, 1857
  Odell, G. C. (1)
  Unidentified clippings
WALTER, Wilfrid
  Birmingham Gazette, April 20, 1927
  Birmingham Mail, April 20, 1927
  Daily News, July 15, 1927
  Daily Telegraph, April 20, 1927
  Leamington Spa Courier, July 29, 1927
  Stage, April 28, 1927
  Stratford-Upon-Avon Herald, April 22, 1927
  Times, April 20, 1927, April 21, 1927
  Unidentified clippings
  See also GREEN, *Dorothy*
WANAMAKER, Sam
  Chicago American, Dec. 2, 1964
  Chicago Daily News, Dec. 2, 1964
  Chicago Sun-Times, Dec. 2, 1964
  Chicago Tribune, Dec. 2, 1964
WEAVER, Fritz
  See KAHN, *Michael, production*
WILLIAMSON, Nicol
  Abingdon Herald, Nov. 14, 1974, Nov. 21, 1974
  Birmingham Mail, Oct. 30, 1974
  Birmingham Post, Oct. 31, 1974
  Coventry Evening Telegraph, Oct. 30, 1974, Nov. 1, 1974
  Cross, R. and L.
  Didcot Herald, Nov. 7, 1974
  Drama, Summer, 1975
  Evening News, Oct. 31, 1974
  Gibbs, E. (2)
  Gloucester Citizen, Oct. 30, 1974
  Illustrated London News, Jan., 1975
  Irish Times, Nov. 1, 1974
  Jewish Chronicle, Nov. 1, 1974
  Lady, Nov. 14, 1974
  Malvern Gazette, Oct. 31, 1974
  New Statesman, Nov. 8, 1974
  Northampton Chronicle and Echo, Oct. 31, 1974
  Observer, Nov. 3, 1974
  Plays and Players, May, 1974, Dec., 1974
  Punch, Nov. 13, 1974
  Redditch Indicator, Nov. 1, 1970
  Scotsman, Nov. 2, 1974
  Shaw, K.
  Stage, Nov. 7, 1974

Stratford-Upon-Avon Herald, Nov. 1, 1974, Nov. 8, 1974, Nov. 29, 1974
Sunday Mercury, Nov. 3, 1974
Sunday Telegraph, Nov. 3, 1974
Sunday Times, March 11, 1974
Telegraph, Oct. 30, 1974
Times, Oct. 31, 1974
Time, March 31, 1975
Wolverhampton Express and Star, Oct. 31, 1974
Yorkshire Post, Oct. 31, 1974
WOLFIT, Donald
  Agate, J. (1)
  Birmingham Gazette, Dec. 2, 1937, Nov. 30, 1938
  Birmingham Mail, Dec. 2, 1937, Nov. 24, 1938, Sept. 24, 1947
  Birmingham Post, Nov. 24, 1938, Nov. 30, 1938, Sept. 24, 1947, Oct. 21, 1947
  Catholic Herald, March 26, 1953, March 27, 1953
  Daily Telegraph, Feb. 13, 1945
  Evening Dispatch, Dec. 2, 1937, Sept. 24, 1947
  Evening News, March 20, 1953
  Evening Standard, Dec. 19, 1947, April 22, 1949
  Gloucester Echo, Dec. 9, 1938
  Harwood, R. (1), (2)
  Ilfracombe Chronicle, March 27, 1937
  Jewish Chronicle, March 27, 1953
  Manchester Guardian, Nov. 23, 1937, Nov. 25, 1937, Nov. 27, 1950, March 21, 1953
  News Chronicle, March 20, 1953, March 21 1953
  New Statesman, March 28, 1953
  Observer, Feb. 18, 1945
  Sitwell, E., in Harwood (1)
  Stage, Feb. 15, 1945, March 26, 1953
  Star, March 20, 1953
  Sunday Times, Feb. 18, 1945
  Theatre World, March 1945, May 1953
  Time, Nov. 3, 1937, Feb. 13, 1945, Feb. 14, 1945, March 20, 1953
  Williamson, A. (3)
  Unidentified clippings
YOUNG, Charles Mayne
  Dramatic Censor, September 1811
  Dramatic Magazine, Oct. 1829, November 1829
  Examiner, Jan. 15, 1809
  Kaleidoscope, July 9, 1822, July 13, 1822
  New Monthly Magazine, July 1, 1828
  Observer, June 11, 1822
  Sprague, A. C. (4)
  Theatre, June 13, 1822
  Partially identified clippings: Kaleidoscope, c. 1827.

ALLEN, Sheila
Interview, 1968
Letter, 1976
Times, Nov. 12, 1973
Unidentified clippings
ALLEN, Viola
New York Times, March 5, 1916, April 16, 1916
Promptbook, Folger Library
Strang, L. C.
See also HACKETT, *James K. (1916)*
ANDERSON, Judith
New York Times, Nov. 12, 1941
Personal Interview
See also EVANS, *Maurice*
See also OLIVIER, *Laurence (1937)*
ANGLIN, Margaret
Craig, G.
See CRAIG, *Gordon, production*
ANNIS, Francesca
Aberdeen Press and Journal, Feb. 9, 1972
Observer, Feb. 6, 1972
See also POLANSKI, *Roman, film production*
ARTHUR, Julia
See BARRYMORE, *Lionel*
ATKINSON, Miss
The Stage, n.d.
See also PHELPS, *Samuel (1857)*
BATEMAN, Kate Josephine
See IRVING, *Henry (1875)*
BENSON, Mrs. Gertrude Constance
Benson, G. C.
Stopes, C.
Unidentified clippings
See also BENSON, *Frank R.*
BERNHARDT, Sarah
Academy, July 12, 1884
Agate, May
Athenaeum, July 12, 1884
Bell's Life in London, July 9, 1884
Birmingham Post, May 26, 1884
Bradley, A. C.
Court Circular, July 12, 1884
Daily Chronicle, May 22, 1884
Daily News, July 5, 1884, Aug. 19, 1884
Daily Telegraph, May 23, 1884, July 5, 1884, Oct. 13, 1884
Edinburgh Courant, June 25, 1884
Edinburgh Times, June 24, 1884
Era, July 5, 1884, July 12, 1884
Evening News, July 5, 1884, July 15, 1884
Evening Standard, May 23, 1884, July 5, 1884, July 15, 1884
Figaro, May 22, 1884
Freeman's Journal, July 22, 1884
Gazette de France, May 24, 1884

Glasgow Herald's, June 26, 1884, June 27, 1884
Globe, May 21, 1884, May 23, 1884, May 24, 1884, July 5, 1884
Grandstand, May 24, 1884
Illustrated Sporting and Dramatic News, July 1884
Journal des Débats, May 9, 1884
Lady's Pictorial, July 19, 1884
Land and Water, July 12, 1884
Life, July 10, 1884
Liverpool Daily Post, May 28, 1884, June 28, 1884, Dec. 31, 1888
Lloyd's Weekly London Newspaper, July 13, 1884
Lyon-Revue, Nov. 1884
Manchester Courier, July 7, 1884
Morning Advertiser, July 5, 1884
Morning Post, May 24, 1884, May 27, 1884, Dec. 31, 1888
Pall Mall Gazette, July 5, 1884
Queen, May 24, 1884
Saint James Gazette, May 17, 1884
Saturday Review, June 14, 1884
Scotsman, June 25, 1884
Le Siècle, May 26, 1884
Stage, July 11, 1884
Summary, July 10, 1884, July 12, 1884
Sunday Times, May 27, 1884, July 7, 1884
Sussex Daily News, July 8, 1884
Taranow, G.
Les Temps, May 26, 1884, March 4, 1889
Theatre Magazine, March 1905
Times, March 10, 1884, June 5, 1884, June 24, 1884, June 25, 1884, July 5, 1884, Sept. 31, 1888
Torquay Times, June 11, 1884
Truth, June 26, 1884, July 10, 1884
Under the Clock, July 9, 1884
Vanity Fair, July 12, 1884
Weekly Dispatch, July 13, 1884
Western Daily Mercury, July 7, 1884
Western Morning News, July 7, 1884
Whitehall Review, July 10, 1884
World, May 28, 1884
Unidentified and partially identified clippings:
July 4, 1884, *Studio*, n.d.; *Der Tag*, n.d.
Other unidentified clippings
BROWNE, Coral
See ROGERS, *Paul (1956–1957)*
BURRILL, Ena
See REDGRAVE, *Michael (1947)*
BUTLER, Mrs.
See KEMBLE, *Fanny*
CALHOUN, Eleanor
Calhoun, E.
New York Times, April 16, 1916

Hawkins, F. W. (1)
Illustrated London News, Oct. 16, 1875
Journal, March 16, 1848
Kemble, F. (1)
MacMillan's Magazine, May, 1867
Marston, J. W.
Morning Chronicle, Feb. 22, 1848
New York Tribune, April 4, 1870
Notes and Queries, July 10, 1852
Observer, Feb. 26, 1844, Feb. 27, 1848
Sprague, A. C. (4)
Sketch, Sept. 14, 1898
Sunday Times, Feb. 27, 1848
Times, April 16, 1832, July 24, 1867
Theatre Magazine, Dec. 1, 1888
Theatre Quarterly, vol. 1, no. 3 (1971)
Unidentified clippings
See also MACREADY, *William Charles (1848)*
KENDAL, Madge
See Kendal, main bibliography
LANGTRY, Lily
Chicago News, March 10, 1896
New York Sun, Jan. 22, 1889
New York Times, Jan. 22, 1889
New York Tribune, Jan. 22, 1889
New York World, Jan. 22, 1889
San Francisco Alta, Feb. 8, 1889
Wingate, C.
See also COGHLAN, *Charles*
LEBLANC, Georgette (Mme. Maeterlinck)
See MAETERLINCK, *Maurice, production*
LEHMANN, Beatrix
See Hordern, M.
LEIGH, Vivien
David, 127–129
Gibbs, Evelyn (1), passim
See also OLIVIER, *Laurence (1955)*
LEIGHTON, Margaret
See RICHARDSON, *Ralph*
MAETERLINCK, Mme., see LEBLANC, above
MARLOWE, Julia
Greenbook, n.d.
Redbook, n.d.
Russell, C. E.
Sothern, E. H.
Theatre Magazine, n.d.
See also SOTHERN, *E. H.*
MASSINGHAM, Dorothy
Era, Dec. 1, 1926
The Stage, Dec. 2, 1926
See also AYRTON, *Randle*
See also MILTON, *Ernest*

MCKENNA, Siobhan (1959)
See ROBARDS, *Jason*

MERCHANT, Vivien
See SCOFIELD, *Paul*

MERRALL, Mary
See MATURIN, *Eric*
MIRREN, Helen
See WILLIAMSON, *Nicol*
MODJESKA, Helena
Augusta Herald, April 7, 1906
Boston Evening Journal, Jan. 4, 1896
Boston Evening Transcript, April 9, 1909
Chicago Daily News, March 18, 1890, Nov. 8, 1899
Chicago Mail, March 18, 1890
Chicago Record, March 18, 1890
Fresno Morning Republican, Jan. 24, 1906, Jan. 25, 1906
Galveston Daily News, Dec. 24, 1893
Gronowicz, A.
Got, J. (1), (2)
Indianapolis Star, Jan. 2, 1907
Inkersley, A.
Inter Ocean (Chicago), March 18, 1890
Louisville Courier Journal, March 9, 1899, Dec. 28, 1906
Louisville Herald, Dec. 28, 1906
Národní Listy, Apr. 23, 1891
New York Herald, Nov. 19, 1889, Oct. 24, 1897, Feb. 16, 1898
New York Star, May 8, 1909
New York Times, Feb. 19, 1898, Feb. 20, 1898
New York Tribune, Oct. 24, 1897, Nov. 18, 1889, Nov. 19, 1889, Feb. 16, 1898
Pacific Monthly, May 1909
Rochester Post Express, Nov. 26, 1906
Spirit of the Times, Nov. 16, 1889, Nov. 23, 1889
Springfield Union, Nov. 2, 1906
Stage, June 10, 1881
Strang, L. C.
Swiat asterski meich czasow Warszawa, 1957
Towse, J. R.
Winter, W. (4)
World, Nov. 19, 1889
Partially identified clippings: El Giornale d'Italia, n.d.; *L'Europa*, n.d.
Other unidentified clippings
See also BOOTH, *Edwin (1889–1890)*
See also foreign bibliography under Poland and Czechoslovakia
MORRIS, Clara
Arcadian (New York), Dec. 12, 1874
Boston Daily Advertiser, Nov. 15, 1910
Brooklyn Daily Eagle, Nov. 25, 1874, Nov. 27, 1874, Nov. 28, 1874
Brooklyn Sunday Sun, Nov. 29, 1874
Current Literature, Aug. 1906
Morris, C. (1), (2)
New York Daily Mail, Nov. 26, 1874
New York Herald, Nov. 26, 1874
New York Times, Nov. 26, 1874

New York Tribune, Nov. 26, 1874, Nov. 30, 1874
Pittsburgh Evening Telegraph, Dec. 12, 1874
Spirit of the Times, Nov. 21, 1874, Nov. 28, 1874, Dec. 5, 1874, May 15, 1875, May 22, 1875
Sun, May 1875
Towse, J. R.
Winter, W. (5)
Unidentified clippings: "Mr. and Mrs. Macbeth," May 22, 1875; "Mrs. Conway's Brooklyn Theatre," Dec. 3, 1874, Nov. 26, 1877
Other unidentified clippings
MURPHY, Rosemary
See KAHN, *Michael, production*
OGILVIE, Mrs.
See MACREADY, *William Charles (1823, 1826)*
O'NEIL, Nance
Boston Evening Transcript, April 29, 1904
Unidentified clipping, n.d.
PIAMONTI, T.
See SALVINI, *Tommaso (1884)*
PONISI, Mme.
See FORREST, *Edwin*
PRITCHARD, Hannah
Baker, H. B. (2), (3)
Davies, T. (1)
Doran, J.
English Illustrated Magazine, Dec., 1888
Monthly Mirror, May 10, 1810
Murphy, A. (2)
Reader, Nov. 12, 1864, Nov. 19, 1864
Theatre, Dec. 1, 1888
Winter, W. (3), (5)
Unidentified clippings
See also GARRICK, *David*

RAWLINGS, Margaret
See CLUNES, *Alec*
REDGRAVE, Vanessa
See HESTON, *Charlton*
REED, Florence
See CRAIG, *Gordon, production*
REID, Kate
See PLUMMER, *Christopher*
RIGG, Diana
See HOPKINS, *Anthony*
See also QUILLEY, *Denis*
RISTORI, Adelaide
Academy, July 8, 1882, Oct. 27, 1886
Albion, Oct. 20, 1866, Oct. 27, 1866
Arthur, G.
Ashwell, L.
Athenaeum, July 11, 1857, July 19, 1873, July 8, 1882
Atlantic Monthly, March, 1867
Boston Daily Advertiser, Nov. 7, 1866

Boston Evening Transcript, Nov. 7, 1866
Boston Herald, May 8, 1885
Chicago Record, March 18, 1890
Coleman, J. (1)
Daily Chronicle, July 4, 1882
Daily News, July 4, 1857, July 4, 1882, July 5, 1882
Daily Post, Nov. 1, 1882
Daily Telegraph, July 5, 1882
Deutsche Zeitung, March 7, 1867
Era, July 8, 1882
Examiner, July 11, 1857, July 25, 1857, Nov. 5, 1864
Figaro, July 8, 1882
Freeman's Journal, Aug. 31, 1857
Frenzel, K.
Göteborgs Handels och Sjofarts Tidning, Nov. 15, 1880
Graphic, July 8, 1882
Illustrated London News, July 11, 1857, July 8, 1882
Illustrated Sydney News, Nov. 12, 1875
James, H.
John Bull, July 4, 1857
Leslie's Illustrated Newspaper, Oct. 20, 1866, Nov. 3, 1866, May 11, 1867, May 18, 1867, May 25, 1867
Lloyd's Weekly London Newspaper, July 9, 1882
Manchester Guardian, July 11, 1857, July 8, 1882, Oct. 29, 1883
Morning Post, July 4, 1857, May 7, 1882, July 5, 1887
New South Wales Agriculturist and Grazier, Oct., 1875
New York Commercial Advertiser, Oct. 20, 1866
New York Herald, Jan. 3, 1885, Jan. 11, 1885, Jan. 21, 1885, May 4, 1885, May 11, 1885
New York Tribune, Oct. 19, 1866, Oct. 27, 1866, May 17, 1867
Observer, July 5, 1857, July 9, 1882
Pall Mall Gazette, July 7, 1882
Queen, June 8, 1882
Ristori, A.
Robins, E.
Saturday Review, July 11, 1857, Aug. 11, 1857, Aug. 11, 1867, July 8, 1882
Scotsman, Nov. 27, 1883, June 25, 1884
Scott, C.
Spectator, Jan. 5, 1889
Spirit of the Times, Oct. 20, 1866, Oct. 27, 1866, Nov. 3, 1866
Stage, July 7, 1882
Summary, July 10, 1884, July 12, 1884
Sunday Times, July 9, 1882
Sydney Mail, Oct. 30, 1875
Sydney Morning Herald, Aug. 20, 1875, Oct. 23, 1875

Brereton, A. (1)
Cassell's Weekly, Feb. 18, 1928
Craig, E. C.
Daily Telegraph, Dec. 31, 1888
Detroit Free Press, Oct. 27, 1895
Dramatic Review, Jan. 5, 1889
Drew, E.
Irving, Henry, letter dated Feb. 7, 1889, in the Folger Library
Irving, L.
Leslie, A.
Revue d'Art Dramatique, June–Sept., 1889
Scott, C.
Terry, E. (1–6)
Winter, W. (4), (5)
See also IRVING, *H. (1888 et seq.)*
THORNDIKE, Sybil
Agate, James (1), 220
Bartholomeusz, D.
Crosse, G. (1)
Daily Mail, Dec. 28, 1926
Daily News, Dec. 28, 1926
Daily Telegraph, Dec. 28, 1926
Eastern Daily Press, Dec. 5, 1969
Era, Dec. 23, 1926, Dec. 29, 1926
Farjeon, H. 135
Morning Post, Dec. 28, 1926
New York Times, Jan. 16, 1927
Observer, Dec. 26, 1926
Spectator, Jan. 1, 1927
Stage, Dec. 30, 1926
Sunday Times, Dec. 26, 1926
Sydney Morning Herald, Oct. 8, 1932
Theatre Quarterly, vol. 1, no. 3 (1971)
Times, Dec. 24, 1926, Jan. 6, 1937
Tynan, K. (3)
TODD, Ann
Agate, J. (1)
Birmingham Post, Aug. 25, 1954, Sept. 15, 1954
Daily Telegraph, Aug. 25, 1954, Sept. 10, 1954
Edinburgh Evening Dispatch, Aug. 24, 1954
Edinburgh Evening News, Aug. 24, 1954
Evening Standard, Sept. 10, 1954
Financial Times, Aug. 25, 1954
Manchester Guardian, Sept. 11, 1954
Observer, Aug. 29, 1954
Scotsman, Aug. 25, 1954
Star, Sept. 10, 1954
Times, Aug. 25, 1954
Tribune, Oct. 1, 1954
Truth, Sept. 3, 1954
Tynan, K. (3)
Williamson, A. (2)
See also ROGERS, *Paul, (1954)*
TUTIN, Dorothy
Daily Telegraph, Oct. 19, 1976
Epsom and Ewell Herald, Oct. 21, 1976

Financial Times, Oct. 19, 1976
Guardian, Oct. 20, 1976
Stage, Oct. 28, 1976
Sunday Telegraph, Oct. 24, 1976
Woking News, Oct. 21, 1976
Unidentified clippings
VANBRUGH, Violet
Enthoven collection
London Magazine, Sept. 6, 1911
See also BOURCHIER, *Arthur (1906)*
See also TREE, *Herbert Beerbohm (1911)*
WARD, Geneviève
Wingate, C. E. L.
Winter, W. (7)
WARNER, Mary Amelia (neé Huddart)
Athenaeum, June 19, 1847
Atlas, July 11, 1840
Downer, A. (1)
Forster and Lewes
John Bull, July 12, 1840
Marston, J. W.
Morning Chronicle, Feb. 27, 1857
Morning Post, July 4, 1840
Observer, March 2, 1851
Reader, Nov. 12, 1864
Spectator, July 18, 1840, April 9, 1842
Sun, April 5, 1842
Theatre Journal, April 2, 1842
Times, March 12, 1842
Unidentified clippings
See also FORREST, *Edwin (1837)*
See also MACREADY, *William Charles (1831, 1837, 1842, 1851)*
See also PHELPS, *Samuel (1845)*
WILSON, Josephine
See CLEMENTS, *John (1964)*
WORTH, Irene
Birmingham Mail, June 6, 1962
Birmingham Post, June 6, 1962, June 8, 1962
Bolton Evening News, June 6, 1962
Brown, J. R. (1)
Daily Express, June 6, 1962
Daily Herald, June 6, 1962, June 8, 1962
Daily Mail, June 6, 1962
Daily Telegraph, June 6, 1962
Daily Worker, June 6, 1962
Evening Dispatch, June 6, 1962
Financial Times, June 6, 1962
Manchester Guardian, June 7, 1962
Newcastle-Upon-Tyne Journal, Aug. 9, 1962
Nottingham Journal, June 6, 1962
Observer, June 10, 1962
Scotsman, July 14, 1962
Stage, June 7, 1962
Stratford-Upon-Avon Herald, June 8, 1962
Sunday Telegraph, June 10, 1962
Sunday Times, June 10, 1962
Tablet, Oct. 27, 1962
Times, June 6, 1962

Western Daily Express, June 6, 1962
Wolverhampton Express and Star, June 6, 1962
Yorkshire Post, June 6, 1962
Unidentified clippings
See also PORTER, *Eric*

WYNYARD, Diana
Advertiser, Jan. 24, 1950
Argus, Nov. 8, 1949, Nov. 12, 1949
Listener, Nov. 12, 1949, Nov. 18, 1949
See also TEARLE, *Godfrey*

Theatre Bibliography II

The stagings of *Macbeth* in non-English speaking countries are listed here chronologically, as the most practical way of dealing with material from many languages. I include unidentified and partially identified references that may be of use to specialists in these languages. Again, I could not have assembled this depository of theatre history without the devoted help of colleagues throughout the world.

ARGENTINA

1973
Buenos Aires
Roberto DURÁN, Director
Lautaro MURUA, Macbeth
Inda LEDESMA, Lady Macbeth
Clarin, June 3.
Kibrick, R., personal report.
Panorama, June 7.
La Prensa, May 6.

AUSTRIA

Austrian stagings are listed with those of Germany, as German-speaking productions.

BELGIUM

1970–1971
Brussels, Koninklijke Vlaamse Schouburg
Jo DUA, Director
Senne ROUFFAER, Macbeth
De Vos, Josef, *Shakespeare in Flanders*. See main
  bibliography.
Wetenschappelijke Tijdingen, vol. 30, Sept.-Oct.
  1971

CZECHOSLOVAKIA

1852
KOLAROVÁ, Lady Macbeth
Lumír, 1852.

1858
KOLÁŘ, Macbeth
Lumír, 1858.

1864
SIMONOVSKÝ, Macbeth
LIPSOVÁ, Lady Macbeth
Hlas, Feb. 23 (Jan Neruda).
Rodinna Kronika, June 4, Aug. 27.

1865
SIMONOVSKÝ, Macbeth
Hlas, Feb. 11.

1871
KOLÁŘ, Macbeth
SAMBERKOVÁ, Lady Macbeth
Národní Listy, Oct. 31.

1875
KOLÁŘ, Macbeth
ŠAMBERKOVÁ, Lady Macbeth
Národní Listy, Oct. 21.

1876
KOLÁŘ, Macbeth
Osvěta, No. 12.

1881
SLUKOV, Macbeth
SKLENÁŘOVÁ, Lady Macbeth
Národní Listy, Mar. 18.

1891
SLUKOV, Macbeth
MODJESKA, Lady Macbeth
Cěská Thalia, n.d.
Národní Listy, Apr. 23.

1902
VOYAN, Macbeth
DANZEROVÁ, Lady Macbeth
Čas, Apr. 5, 8.
Divadelní Listy, n.d.
Lumír, 1902.

1916
VOYAN, Macbeth
DOSTALOVÁ, Lady Macbeth
Lidové Noviny, Feb. 2, 29, Mar. 2.
Lumír.
Národní Listy, Nov. 29.
Osvěta, Nov. 26.

1925
VOYAN, Macbeth
Národní Osvobozeni, Oct. 22.
Národní Politika, Oct. 22.

1927
ŠIMČEK, Macbeth
URBÁNKOVÁ, Lady Macbeth
Lidové Noviny, Nov. 15.

1939
BAR, Director
ŠTĚPÁNEK, Macbeth
SCHEINPFLUGOVÁ, Lady Macbeth
České Slovo, Oct. 31, 1939; Jan. 1, 1940.
Lidové Noviny, 1939, n.d.
Národní Listy, Oct. 31.

1946
FREJKA, Director
HEGERLÍKOVÁ, Lady Macbeth
KREJČA, Macbeth
B. Hodek, personal report.

1950
BOROVY, Director
ŠTĚPÁNEK, Macbeth
České Slovo, Jan. 9.

1952
KOLÁŘOVÁ, Lady Macbeth
Lumír, n.d.

1957
PALOUŠ, Director
KORÁK, Macbeth
PEŠKOVÁ, Lady Macbeth

Lidová demokracie, May 7.
Literární noviny, May 18.
Obrana Lidu, May 7.
Práce, May 8.
Svobodné Slovo, May 8.
Večérní Praha, May 8.

1958 (June)
DVOŘÁK, Director
BRZOBOHATÝ, Macbeth
TOLAROVÁ, Lady Macbeth
Divadelní Noviny, July 16.
Literární Noviny, June 7.
Proboj, June 12.

1958
JURDA, Director
VLČEK, K. Macbeth
VOTRUBOVÁ, Lady Macbeth
Svobodne Slovo, March 9.

1959 (January)
JURDA, Director
MEISTER, Macbeth
KRŮZÍKOVÁ, Lady Macbeth
Lidová demokracie, Jan. 17.
Mladá Fronta, Jan. 27.
Práce, Jan. 20.
Svobodné Slovo, Jan. 17.

1959
NAVRATIL, Macbeth
LÁZNIČKOVÁ, Lady Macbeth
(Double casting with above)
Práce, Feb. 24.
Rovnost, Jan. 18.

1959
BUDSKÝ, Director
CHUDÍK, Macbeth
KRISTINOVÁ, Lady Macbeth
Práce, Feb. 5.
Večerník, Jan. 28.

1962
ŠEBESTA, Macbeth
DERKOVÁ, Lady Macbeth
Lidová demokracie, May 25.
Pochodeň, June 14.

1963
ŠPIDLA, Director
KRAHULÍK, Macbeth
JIRÁKOVÁ, Lady Macbeth
Divadelní Noviny, March 6.
Kulturní Tvorba, Feb. 14.
Pravda, Feb. 12.

1967
POKORNÝ, Director
HRADILÁK, Macbeth
HLIŇÁKÓVÁ, Lady Macbeth
Lidová demokracie, Dec. 29.

1969 (June)
PLESKOT, Director
MACHÁČEK, Macbeth
BOHDANOVÁ, Lady Macbeth
Lidová demokracie, June 6.
Mladá Fronta, June 12.
Svět Práce, Sept. 6.
Večerní Praha, June 5.

1970
PLESKOT, Director
B. Hodek, Personal report.

1971
See Germany, April
See Main Bibliography for letters from Hodek,
    Stříbrný.
Help in translation: Walter
    Schamschula

DENMARK

1860
HEIBERG, Johanne Louise, Lady Macbeth
See Krabbe (2), main bibliography

1972
Kai WILTON, Director
B. W. BOOLSEN, Macbeth
Grete HOLMER, Lady Macbeth
Aktuelt, Nov. 11.
Berlingske Tidende, Nov. 11.
Information, Nov. 13.
Kristeligt Dagblad, Nov. 13.
Politiken, Nov. 12.
Stiftstidende, Nov. 11.
Tyllandsposten, Nov. 11.

FRANCE

ca. 1780
Mme. VESTRIS, Lady Macbeth
Lemazurier, Pierre David, *La Galerie His-
    torique*, vol. 2, 1810.
Lyonnet, Henry, (pseud. for Alfred Henri
    Copin), *Dictionnaire des Comédiens Français*,
    vol. 2, 1902.
Lyonnet, Henry, *Les Vestris*, 1908.

ca. 1810
Mlle. GEORGE, Lady Macbeth

Cheramy, A., *A Favorite of Napoleon: Memoirs
    of Mlle. George*, 1908.
Fleischmann, H., *Un Maîtress de Napoléon: Mlle.
    George*, 1908.
Lucas, H., *Galerie des Artistes Dramatiques*,
    1842.
Lyonnet, Henry, op. cit.
Thierry, A. Augustine, *Mlle. George: Maîtress
    d'Empereur*, 1936.
Tieck, Ludwig, *Dramaturgische Blätter*, 1826.

1828
MACREADY in Paris
Le Corsaire, April 25.
Kaleidoscope, "English Actors in France," Nov.
    25.
Unidentified clippings.

1863
L'Odéon
M. TAILLADE, Macbeth
Mme. KAROLY, Lady Macbeth

1883
Mme. SEGOND-WEBER, Lady Macbeth
Gautier, T.
Le Temps, Mar. 4.
Revue D'Art Dramatique, n.d., 304–307.
P. Vierge. *Monographie de Mme. Segond-Weber*.
    n.d.
Clippings, collection of the Bibliothéque de
    l'Arsenal. (Hereafter cited as L'Arsenal.)

1884
Paul MOUNET, Macbeth
Mme. TESSANDIER, Lady Macbeth
Le Siècle, May 26.
Blair Fortescue, "A French Macbeth." Un-
    identified source.

1884
Leon-Hyacinth MARAIS, Macbeth
Sarah BERNHARDT, Lady Macbeth
(See also actress bibliography)
Figaro, May 22.
Gazette de France, May 24.
L'Echo du Parlement, Oct. 8.

1885
L'Arsenal, unidentified clippings.
Moniteur Universel, Sept. 14.

1909
Maurice MAETERLINCK, translator (see also main
    bibliography)
M. SEVERIN-MARS, Macbeth
Georgette LEBLANC, Lady Macbeth
Comoedia Illustré, 1909–1910; 1910–1911.

Figaro, Aug. 30.
Le Théatre, vol. 2, 1909.
Unidentified clippings.
See also Maeterlinck, Theatre Bibliography
    III

1910

Henri ALBERS, Macbeth
Lucienne BRÉVAL, Lady Macbeth
Albert CARRÉ, Director
Comoedia Illustré, 1910–1911.
Le Théatre, 1910.

1914

Paul MOUNET, Macbeth
Mme. BARTET, Lady Macbeth
Albert CARRÉ, Director
Comoedia Illustré, June 20.
Blair Fortescue, "A French *Macbeth*." Uniden-
    tified source.

1921

James HACKETT, Macbeth
Sybil THORNDIKE, Lady Macbeth
Le Théatre, June 8.

1921

Georges PITOËFF, prod.
Hort, J.
Pitoëff, G., see main bibliography
Unidentified source, "Georges Pitoëff, Plain-
    palais, Salle Municipale."
Unidentified clippings.

1942

Gaston BATY, Director
Pierre RENOIR, Macbeth
M. JAMOIS, Lady Macbeth
Comoedia, Dec. 12.
Craig, Gordon, notes on Baty Production in
    l'Arsenal.
Unidentified clippings.

1952

Jean DASTÉ, Director
Rene LESAGÉ, Macbeth
Marie-Hélène DASTÉ, Lady Macbeth
Combat, April 26.
Figaro, June 16.
Lettres Françaises, June 29.
Le Monde, June 19.
Nouvelles Littéraires, June 26.

1954

Jean VILAR, Director
Jean VILAR, Macbeth
Maria CASARÈS, Lady Macbeth
L'avant Scène, 95, 1954.
Casarès, film clip of Act V, Scene i.

Combat, July 23.
Études, July–Dec.
Études Anglaises, vol. 8, I, 1955.
Figaro, July 22.
Figaro Littéraire, July 31.
Jacquot, Jean, *Shakespeare Survey*, 1956.
Lettres Françaises, July 29.

1955

Reprise of above production
Jean VILAR, Macbeth (replaced by Alain CUNY)
Maria CASARÈS, Lady Macbeth
L'Aurore, Jan. 24.
Combat, n.d.
La Croix, Jan. 28.
Jacquot, Jean, letter.
Jacquot, Jean, *Shakespeare Survey*, 1957.
Les Nouvelles Littéraires, Jan. 27.

1958

Festival d'Angers
Jean MARCHAT, Macbeth
Annie DUCAUX, Lady Macbeth
Figaro, June 23.

1959

Théâtre de Ménilmontant
Raymond GARRIVIER, Macbeth
Adette TÉPHANY, Lady Macbeth
Guy RÉTORÉ, Director
Arts, July 2.
Combat, April 10.
Figaro Littéraire, June 20.
London Times, April 14.

1962

Saint-Malo
Jacques DACQMINE, Macbeth
Lise DELAMARE, Lady Macbeth
Jean DARNEL, Director
Figaro, July 30.
Figaro Littéraire, August 11.

1964 (January)

Claude CHABROL, Director
Roger HANIN, Macbeth
L'Aurore, Jan. 20.
Figaro Littéraire, Jan. 30.
L'Humanité, Jan. 20.
Nouvelles Littéraires, Jan. 23.
Témoignage Chrétien, Feb. 13.

1965

Guy RÉTORÉ, Director
Raymond GARRIVIER, Macbeth
Arlette TÉPHANY, Lady Macbeth
Arts, May 5.
Aspects de la France, June 13.

L'Aurore, April 30.
Combat, April 23.
Figaro, n.d.
Figaro Littéraire, May 6.
La Gazette de Lausanne, May 15.
L'Humanité, April 30.
Lettres Françaises, May 13.
Le Monde, April 30.
Nouvelles Littéraires, n.d.
Le Nouvel Observateur, May 6.
Le Parisien Libéré, March 26.
Paris-Presse, April 29.
Le Soir, May 19.
Le Théâtre, May 6, May 13.
Tribune de Genève, May 14.

1969

HERMANTIER Production
Dutourd, Jean, *Le Paradoxe de la Critique*, n.d.,
pp. 330–331.
Figaro, Dec. 15.

1973

Guy RÉTORÉ, Director
L'Éducation, March 22.
Express, March 5.
Figaro, Feb. 23.
Martinet, M. M., personal report.

GERMANY AND AUSTRIA

1771 (December 26)
Biberach, Komödiantenverein
Schumacher, Erich. *Shakespeare's Macbeth auf
der Deutschen Bühne*, 1938, 15–17.

1772 (November 3)
Vienna, Kärntnertortheater
STEPHANIE Production
Historisch-Kritische Theaterchronik von Wien, vol.
1, part 3, 135.
Neue Schauspiele, "Theatern zu Wien," vol. 5,
1773, 3.
Schmids, Christian Heinrich, *Chronologie des
Deutschen Theaters* in *Schriften der Gesellschaft
für Theatergeschichte*, ed. Paul Legband, vol.
1, Berlin, 1902, 207.
Schumacher, 18–37.
Stephanie, Gottlieb, *Sämtliche Schauspiele*, vol.
2, Vienna, 1774.
Theaterjournal für Deutschland, no. 9, 1779, 27.

1777
Prague
R. F. REINECKE, Macbeth
Litteratur und Theater-Zeitung, vol. 3, no. 1,
Berlin, 1780, 363–364.
Schumacher, 37–42, 45, 52.

Shakespeare, William, *Macbeth, ein Trauerspiel
in 5 Aufzügen von Shakespeare fürs hiesig Theater*, adaptirt und herausgegeben von F. J.
Fischer, 1777.

1778 (October 3)
Berlin, Theater in der Behrenstrasse
Rosalie Caroline NOUSEUL, Lady Macbeth
Blöcher, G., "Playdoyer für Lady Macbeth,"
in *Der Tagespiegel*, no. 8, n.d., 1951.
Chodwiecki, Daniel, Engravings in Institut für
Theaterwissenschaft, Cologne.
Drozd, A. Y., "Rosalie Nouseul," in *Jahrbuch
für Wiener Theaterforschung*.
Eisenberg, Ludwig, *Grosses Biographisches Lexi-
kon der Deutschen Bühne im XIX Jahrhundert*,
1903.
Goethe, J. W. von, *Goethe-Zelter Briefwechsel*,
ed. L. Georger, Leipzig, 1902, vol. 2, 301;
vol. 12, 182.
Kauerhowen, Kurt, "J.K.G. Wernichs Mac-
beth-Bearbeitung," *Shakespeare-Jahrbuch*, vol.
54, 50 ff.
Kosch, Wilhelm, *Deutsches Theaterlexikon*, vol.
2, 1960.
Litteratur und Theater-Zeitung, vol. 1, no. 42,
1778, 667–668.
Ibid., vol. 2, no. 1, Berlin, 1779, 16.
Schink, Johann Friedrich, *Zusätze und Berichtigungen zu der Galerie der Deutschen Schauspieler*,
ed. R. N. Werner, 1910, 222 f.
Schumacher, 65–70.

1779 (June 21)
Hamburg
Friedrich Ludwig SCHRÖDER, Macbeth
Meyer, F. L. W., *Friedrich Ludwig Schröder*,
vol. 1, 1823, 317.
Schumacher, 73 f.

1787 (December 28)
Berlin, Nationaltheater
Doebbelin Company
Johann Friedrich FLECK, Macbeth
Annalen des Theaters, I., 1788, 67.
Gross, Edgar, *J. F. Fleck* in *Schriften der Gesell-
schaft für Theatergeschichte*, vol. 22, 1914.
Kauerhowen, Kurt, *Bürgers Macbeth-Bearbei-
tung*, dissertation, 1915.
Kosmann, J. W. A., *Denkwürdigkeiten und Tages-
geschichten der Preuss. Staaten*, part 3, 1802,
817.
Reichardt, J. F. von, *Einige Hexenszenen aus
Shakespeares Macbeth nach Bürgers Verdeutschung
in Musik gesetzt und fürs Klavier ausgezogen*,
Berlin, n.d.
Schumacher, 85, 87.
Tieck, Ludwig, *Dramaturgische Blätter*, part 2,
1826, 87.

Tieck, Ludwig, *Phantasus*, ed. K. G. Wend-
riner, vol. 3, 1911, 455, 507.

1800 (May 14)
Weimar
Friedrich Schiller's translation: first produc-
tion
Deetjen, W., *Shakespeare-Aufführung unter
Goethe*, 1932.
"Deutsche Theaterausstellung Wien," *Schriften
der Gesellschaft für Theatergeschichte*, 1911, fig.
12.
Journal des Luxus und der Moden, vol. 15, 1800,
310.
Niessen, Carl, "Goethe als Bühnenbildner,"
*Die Tribühne: Halbmonatschrift der Städtischen
Bühnen*, vol. 5, 302.
Schumacher, 113–115.

1808 (February 13)
Vienna, Burgtheater and Kärntnertortheater
Josef LANGE, Macbeth
Sophie SCHRÖDER, Betty ROSE, Julie GLEY-
RETTICH, Lady Macbeth
*Allgemeine Theaterzeitung und Originalblatt für
Künst, Literatur, Mode und Geselliges Leben*,
vol. 24, 1832, 618; vol. 25, 8.
Bauer, Caroline, *Aus meinem Bühnenleben:
Eine Auswahl aus den Lebenserinnerungen der
Künstlerin*, ed. K. Hollander, 1917, 17.
Jahrbuch der Deutschen Shakespeare Gesellschaft,
vol. 50, 63.
Kindermann, Heinz, *Shakespeare und das Burg-
theater*, n.d.
Lange, Josef, *Biographie des Josef Lange*, 1808,
237–243.
Sannens, Friedrich, *Wiener Hoftheater Taschen-
buch*, Vienna, 1809, 24.
Schumacher, 128–130, 146 ff., 237–243 ff.
Re Sophie SCHRÖDER:
Bauer, Caroline, *Aus meinem Bühnenleben* . . .
1917, 17.
Müllner, Adolph, *Wie*, no. 37, 1819, 852 ff.
re Julie GLEY-RETTICH:
Klingemann, August, *Wie*, no. 66, 1817.

1809 (December 11)
Berlin, Nationaltheater
Franz MATTAUSCH, Macbeth
Friederike BETHMANN, Lady Macbeth
Bethmann, portraits of, in the Catalogue
for the 400th Anniversary of Shakespeare,
Cologne (Institut für Theaterwissenschaft),
25.
Devrient, Eduard, *Geschichte der Deutschen Schau-
spielkunst*, vol. 2, 1848, 95.

Klingemann, August, *Kunst und Natur, Blätter
aus meinem Reisetagebuche*, vol. 2, 2nd edition,
1823–1828, 21.
Müllner, A. *op. cit.* 851 ff.
"Erinnerungen an Friederike Bethmann," *Zeitung für die Elegante Welt*, no. 174, Sept. 4,
1819.

1820 (March 3)
Stuttgart, Hoftheater
Allgemeine Theaterzeitung . . . vol. 27, 192.
Schumacher, pp. 140, 155.

1822
Ferdinand ESSLAIR, Macbeth
Allgemeine Theaterzeitung . . . *loc. cit.*
Klingemann, A., *Allegemeiner deutscher Theater-
almanach für das Jahr 1822*, 295 ff.

1825
Berlin, Königliches Schauspielhaus
Allgemeine Theater-Chronik, vol. 3, 1834, 143.
Allgemeine Theaterzeitung und Unterhaltungsblatt,
vol. 26, 1833.
Goethe, *op. cit.*
Raumer, see Tieck below.
Schumacher, 126, 134 ff., 139, 142, 160.
Tieck, Ludwig, in Friedrich Raumer's *Leben-
serinnerungen und Briefwechsel*, Leipzig, 1861,
234.

1834 (November 2)
Düsseldorf
REUSSLER, Macbeth
Allgemeine Theater-Chronik, vol. 3, 1834, 143.
Grabbe, Christian Heinrich, *Theater zu Düssel-
dorf mit Rückblick auf die übrige deutsche
Schaubühne* in *Gesammelte Werke*, vol. 5, 1908,
41.
Ibid., vol. 6, 199.
Puttlitz, G. Z., *Theaterbriefe von Karl Immer-
mann*, Berlin 1851, 86.

1836 (March)
Dresden Königliches Hoftheater
Ludwig TIECK Production
Promptbook of the Dresden performance of
1836, quoted by Schumacher, 166 ff.

1851
Berlin, Königliche Schauspiele, Opernhaus
Auguste STICH-CRELINGER, Lady Macbeth
Schumacher, 163.
Ibid., "Berlin-Archive der Staatsoper," quoted,
168 f.
Smidt, Heinrich, *Allgemeine Theater-Chronik*,
nos. 124–126, Leipzig, Oct. 17, 1851, 493 ff.

Re Auguste STICH-CRELINGER

Heine, Heinrich, *Mädchen und Frauen*, Hamburg, 1839, 163.

Horn, F., see main bibliography.

Monatsschrift für Theater und Musik, ed. Josef Klemm, vol. 3, 1847, 254.

1855 (October 1)

Dresden Königliches Hoftheater

Franz von KINGELSTEDT, Director

Bogumil DAWISON (Born in Poland), Macbeth

Auerbach, Berthold, *Dramatische Eindrücke: Aus dem Nachlasse*, Stuttgart, 1893.

Monatsschrift für Theater und Musik, op. cit. vol. 2, 533.

1856 (November)

Vienna, Burgtheater

Josef WAGNER, Adolf von SONNENTHAL, Macbeth

Monatsschrift für Theater und Musik, op. cit., vol. 2, 653–654.

Recensionen und Mitteilungen über Theater und Musik, no. 8, Feb. 22, 1860, 110.

Schumacher, 224 ff.

1871 (March)

Breslau, Stadttheater

Clara ZIEGLER, Lady Macbeth

Breslauer Nachrichten, vol. 3, 1871.

"Clara Ziegler in Breslau," *Schleisische Chronik*, vol. 3, 1871, 190 ff.

Savits, Regiebuch [promptbook], Hoftheater München, March 24, 1886.

1875

Meiningen, Hoftheater

Max GRUBE and Georg II von MEININGEN, Directors

Georg II von MEININGEN Production

Schumacher, 177, 198.

Wiener Allgemeine Theaterzeitung: Centralblatt für Künst, Literatur, Mode und Geselliges Leben, n.d., 183.

Illustrated London News, March 6, 1880.

Grube, M., see main bibliography.

Ochelhäuser Wilhelm, "Shakespeare-Aufführungen in Meiningen," *Shakespeare Jahrbuch*, vol. 3, 383 ff.

Stahl, S., *Shakespeare und die Deutsche Bühne*, Stuttgart, 1967, 454.

1877 (October 10)

Vienna, Burgtheater

Friedrich MITTERWURZER, Macbeth

Charlotte WOLTER, Lady Macbeth

Bab, Julius, *Der Mensch auf der Bühne*. n.d.

Guglia, Eugene, *Friedrich Mitterwurzer*, 1896, *passim*.

Minor, Jakob, *Deutsche Schauspielkunst*, ed. M. Jacobs, 1914, 238 ff.

Neue Freie Presse, Oct. 10, 1877.

Ibid., July 20, 1888.

Niederle, B., *Charlotte Wolter*, 1948, 52 ff.

Richter, Helene, *Shakespeare Jahrbuch*, 43, 185–203.

1877

Berlin

Marie SEEBACH-NIEMANN, Lady Macbeth

Berliner Tageblatt, Nekrolog, Aug. 4, 1897.

Fontane, Theodor, *Causerin über Theater*, ed. Paul Schlenter, 1905, 331.

Schumacher, 230.

1891

Vienna

Adolph SONNENTHAL, Macbeth

Wie, no. 140a, 14.

1891 (October 28)

Munich, Hofschauspiel

Jocza SAVITS, Director

Durian, H., *Jocza Savits und die Münchner Shakespearebühne*, Emsdetten, 1937, 61–64.

Savits, Jocza, Regiebuch.

1901

Berlin

Adalbert MATKOWSKY, Macbeth

Bab, Julius, *Adalbert Matkowsky*, Berlin, 1932, *passim*.

Unidentified clippings.

1906

Louise DUMONT, Lady Macbeth

Brües, Otto, *Louise Dumont, Leben und Werk*, 1956.

Stahl, Ernst, L., "Louise Dumont", *Shakespeare Jahrbuch*, 45, 355–57.

1913 (March 26)

Berlin, Theater in der Königgrätzerstrasse

Rudolf BERNAUER, Director

Paul WEGENER, Macbeth

Helene TRIESCH, Lady Macbeth

Die Schaubühne, vol. 12, no. 1, 1916, 332–333.

Schumacher, 240.

Der Tag, Berlin, March 2, 1916.

Vossische Zeitung, Berlin, March 27, 1913.

Unidentified clippings.

1914 (July 8)

Düsseldorf, Rheinische Goethefestspiele

Paul WEGENER, Macbeth
Helene TRIESCH, Lady Macbeth
Unidentified clippings

1916 (February 29)
Berlin, Deutsches Theater
Max REINHARDT, Director
Paul WEGENER, Macbeth
Hermine KÖRNER, Lady Macbeth
Berliner Börsen Courier, March 1.
Breslauer Zeitung, March 4.
Der Tag, Berlin, March 1, May 2.
Frankfurter Zeitung, March 2.
Freyhan, Max, *Wegener's Shakespeare-Kunst*, 1919.
Handl, Willi, "Macbeth in 1916," in *Paul Wegener: Sein Leben und Seine Rollen*, ed. Kai Möller, Hamburg, 1954, 84 ff.
Jacobsohn, Siegfried, *Max Reinhardt*, 120 ff.
———. *Die Schaubühne*, vol. 12, no. 1, 1916, 236 ff.
Kölnische Zeitung, n.d.; July 9.
Möller, Kai, letter on Paul Wegener, 1975.
Reinhardt, M. Regiebuch
Schumacher, 242, 246.
Vossische Zeitung, Berlin, March 27.
Unidentified press clippings from the Steinfeld collection, Institut für Theaterwissenschaft der Universität Köln.

1920 (February 16)
Vienna, Burgtheater
Albert HEINE, Director
Max DEVRIENT, Macbeth
Neue Freie Presse, Vienna, Feb. 19.
Neues Wiener Tagblatt, Vienna, Feb. 19.

1922 (November 10)
Berlin, Preussisches Staatstheater
Leopold JESSNER, Director
Fritz KORTNER, Macbeth
Gerda MÜLLER, Lady Macbeth
Akademie der Künste: playbill.
Berliner Börsen-Zeitung, Berlin, Nov. 12.
Neue Freie Presse, Nov. 24.
Die Schaubühne, vol. 18, Charlottenburg, 1922, 551.
Sternaux, L., "*Macbeth* im Schauspielhaus," no source.
Vossische Zeitung, Berlin, Feb. 12.

1927 (July)
Heidelberg, Schlossfestspiele
Gustav HARTUNG, Director
Heinrich GEORGE, Macbeth
Darmstädter Zeitung, Darmstadt, Aug. 16.
Kölner Volkszeitung, Cologne, July 31.

1927
Bertolt Brecht, adaptation of *Macbeth* for radio
———. "Vorrede zu *Macbeth*" in *Schriften zum Theater, 1819–1923*, vol. 1, Frankfurt, 1963, 101 ff.

1928 (November 28)
Berlin, Volksbühne
Theater am Bülowplatz
Leo REUSS, Director
Heinrich GEORGE, Macbeth
Agnes STRAUB, Lady Macbeth
Engel, Fritz, *Theaterbibliothek*, Feb. 28, 1928, 563.
Falk, N. "*Macbeth* im Staatlichen Schauspielhaus," n.s.
Ihering, H., Feb. 28, n.s.
Morgenpost, Feb. 28.

1937 (January 15)
Vienna, Burgtheater
Ida ROLAND, Lady Macbeth
Die Presse, March 2, 1964.
Unidentified press clipping, dated Jan. 17, 1937, from the Institut für Theaterwissenschaft, Köln.
Other unidentified clippings.

1942 (March 27)
Munich, Residenztheater
Stahl, E. L., Niessen, C., Papsdorf, W., "Shakespeare auf der Deutschen Bühne, 1940–1942," in *Shakespeare-Jahrbuch*, 78–79, Weimar, 1943

1944 (March)
Hamburg, Staatliches Schauspielhaus
Maria WIMMER, Lady Macbeth
Hamburger Fremdenblatt, Hamburg, March 30.

1946
Graz Opera House
Paula NOVA, Lady Macbeth
Das Steirerblatt, Graz, Sept. 26.
Die Wahrheit, Graz, Sept. 26.

1948
Innsbruck
Paul SCHMID, Macbeth
Neuigkeits-Weltblatt, Vienna, Dec. 19.
Tiroler Nachrichten, Innsbruck, Dec. 19.
Tiroler Neue Zeitung, Innsbruck, n.d.
Tiroler Tageszeitung, Innsbruck, Dec. 19.

1952
Munich
Giorgio STREHLER, Director
Neue Zeitung, June 5.

1953 (September 3)
Oldenburg, Niedersächsisches Staatstheater
Erwin PISCATOR, Director
Bremer Nachrichten, Sept. 3.
General-Anzeiger, Wuppertal, Sept. 3.
Piscator, Erwin, Regiebuch.
See also Piscator, main bibliography

1953 (November 13)
Hamburg, Staatliches Schauspielhaus
Heinrich KOCH, Director
Will QUADFLIEG, Macbeth
Anne RÖMER, Lady Macbeth
Frankfurter Allgemeine Zeitung, Nov. 17.
Hamburger Abendblatt, Nov. 13.
Schüddekopf, J. "Der Hamburger *Macbeth*,"
    Frankfurter Allgemeine Zeitung, n.d.
Süddeutsche Zeitung, Munich, Nov. 18.
Die Welt, Hamburg, Nov. 14.
Unidentified press clippings.

1953
Salzburg
Heinrich ORTMAYR, Macbeth
Demokratisches Volksblatt, Salzburg, Nov. 20.
Kulturnachrichten, Salzburg, Nov. 20.

1955 (December 5)
Darmstadt, Hessisches Staatstheater
Claus HOFER, Macbeth
Charlotte JOERES, Lady Macbeth
Frankfurter Allemeime Zeitung, Dec. 5.
Münchner Merkur, Dec. 8.
Die Welt, Hamburg, Dec. 6.

1955
Vienna, Scala
Wolfgang HEINZ, Macbeth
Hortense RAKY, Lady Macbeth
Der Abend, "*Macbeth* 1773–1955," Vienna, n.d.
Ibid., n.d.
Neues Oesterreich, n.d.
Noerdlinger Nachrichten, Dec. 23.
Oesterreichische Volksstimme, n.d.
Die Union, Jan. 7.
Weltpresse, Dec. 27.
Unidentified clippings.

1957 (October 20)
Stuttgart, Württembergisches Staatstheater
Günther RENNERT, Director
Walter RICHTER, Macbeth
Stuttgarter Nachrichten, Oct. 21.
Tagespiegel, Berlin, Oct. 26.

1958 (June 26)
Munich, Kammerspiele

Hans SCHWEIKART, Director
Hannes MESSEMER, Macbeth
Maria WIMMER, Lady Macbeth
Die Andere Zeitung, Hamburg, July 10.
Frankfurter Allgemeine Zeitung, July 2.

1959 (February)
Bochum, Spielhaus
Rolf BOYEN, Macbeth
Margaret CARL, Lady Macbeth
Der Mittag, Düsseldorf, Feb. 21.
Ruhr-Nachrichten, Essen, Feb. 19.

1959 (March)
Vienna, Volkstheater
Otto WOEGERER, Macbeth
Hilde KRAHL, Lady Macbeth
Neuer Kurier, Vienna, March 11.
Neues Oesterreich, March 1.
Die Presse, March 12.
Volksstimme, March 14.
Welt am Montag, Graz, March 16.

1959 (September)
East Berlin, Volksbühne
Wilfried ORTMANN, Macbeth
Susanne SCHALLER, Lady Macbeth
Frankfurter Rundschau, Frankfurt, Sept. 16.

1960 (May)
Berlin, Theater at the Kurfürstendamm
Stephan SCHNABEL, Macbeth
Claudie LOSCH, Lady Macbeth
Der Abend, Berlin, May 9.
Berliner Stimme, May 14.
Echo der Zeit, Recklinghausen, n.d.
Frankfurter Rundschau, n.d.
Der Kurier, Berlin, May 9.
Spandauer Volksblatt, Berlin, May 10.
Der Tagesspiegel, May 11.

1960 (June)
Recklinghausen, Ruhrfestspiele
Heinrich KOCH, Director
Ernst SCHRÖDER, Macbeth
Hilde KRAHL, Lady Macbeth
Allgemeine Zeitung, Mainz, June 7.
Deutsche Zeitung und Wirtschaftszeitung, June 7.
Düsseldorfer Nachrichten, June 4.
Echo der Zeit, June 12.
Neue Rhein-Zeitung, Düsseldorf, June.
Neue Zeit, Graz, June 10.
Stuttgarter Zeitung, June 8.
Westdeutsches Tageblatt, Dortmund, June 6.

1960 (June)
Heidelberg
Düsseldorfer Nachrichten, June 4.

Frankfurter Zeitung, June 4.
Neue Ruhr-Zeitung, Essen, June 6.
Nürnberger Zeitung, June 9.

1960 (September 10)
Zurich
Leopold LINDBERG, Director
Ernst SCHRÖDER, Macbeth
Margrit WINTER, Lady Macbeth
Basler Zeitung, n.d.
Die Tat, Zurich, Sept. 12.
Unidentified clippings

1963 (September)
Wuppertal, Städtische Bühnen
Peter PALITZSCH, Director
Richard LAUFFER, Macbeth
Ursula VON REIBNITZ, Lady Macbeth
Oberbergische Volkszeitung, Sept. 21.
Unidentified clippings.

1964 (March)
Vienna, Burgtheater
Guenter RENNERT, Director
Will QUADFLIEG, Macbeth
Heidemarie HATHEYER, Lady Macbeth
Express, March 2.
Express am Abend, March 2.
Neuer Kurier, March 2.
Oesterreichische Neue Tageszeitung, March 3.
Die Presse, March 2.
Rheinische Post, Düsseldorf, March 14.
Volksblatt, Vienna, March 3.
Volksstimme, March 3.

1964 (March)
Linz, Austria
Georg MATTHES, Macbeth
Elfriede GOLLMAN, Lady Macbeth
Kultur und Kritik, March 3.
Linzer Tageblatt, March 2.
Linzer Volksblatt, March 3.
Neues Oesterreich, March 3.

1966 (May)
Düsseldorf, Schauspielhaus
Hans REINCKE, Macbeth
Nicole HEESTERS, Lady Macbeth
Frankfurter Allgemeine Zeitung, May 5.
Kölnische Rundschau, May 4.
Schulze, A., letter in *Frankfurter Allgemeine Zeitung*, May 4.
Süddeutsche Zeitung, May 18.
Theater Heute, June, 1966.

1966
Bremen (December)
Kurt HÜBNER, Director

Bruno GANZ, Macbeth
Gisela TROWE, Lady Macbeth
Frankfurter Allgemeine Zeitung, Jan. 2, 1967.
Unidentified clipping.

1971 (March 19)
Oldenburg
Horst MEHRING, Macbeth
Christine SCHRADER, Lady Macbeth
Nordwest-Zeitung Oldenburger Nachrichten, March 22, April 1.

1971 (April)
Bregenz
Alex FREIHART, Macbeth
Gerda ZANGER, Lady Macbeth
Vorarlberger Nachrichten, April 13, April 23.
Vorarlberger Volksblatt, April 13.

1971 (April)
Klagenfurt, Slovenian National Theater
KRALJ, Macbeth
POCKAJEVA, Lady Macbeth
Kärtner Tagezeitung, April 17.
Volkswille, Klagenfurt, April 17.

1972 (March)
Brandenburg
Heiner Müller adaptation
Bernt BARTOSZEWSKI, Director
F. DÜREN, Macbeth
Dublin Evening Herald, June 6.
Frankfurter Rundschau, March 29.
Reading Evening Post, June 6.

1972 (April)
Basel
Müller adaptation
Hans HOLLMANN, Director
Gerhard FRIEDRICH, Macbeth
Monika KOCH, Lady Macbeth
Frankfurter Allgemeine Zeitung, n.d.
Mittwoch, April 26.
Theater Heute, vol. 13, no. 6.

1972 (December)
Ludwigschafen
Konrad HÖLLERS, Director
Michael MENDEL, Macbeth
Ellen SCHWIERS, Lady Macbeth
Die Rheinpfalz, Dec. 5.
Die Rheinpfalz Unterhaardter Rundschau, Dec. 9.
Rhein-Zeitung, Dec. 20.

1972 (December)
Karlsruhe
Müller adaptation
Bert LEDWOCH, Director

Friedhelm BECKERS, Macbeth
Christiane PAULI, Lady Macbeth
Abendpost-Nachtausgabe, Dec. 1.
Bremer Nachrichten, Dec. 1.
Frankfurter Rundschau, Dec. 5.
Neue Osnabrücker Zeitung, Nov. 30.
Schauspiele, Dec. 22.
Südkurier, Nov. 29.
Die Welt, Dec. 2.

1973 (October)
Berlin
Kurt HÜBNER, Director
Dieter LASER, Macbeth
Margit CARSTENSEN, Lady Macbeth
Der Abend, Oct. 13, 1975.
Berliner Morgenpost, Oct. 14.
Frankfurter Allgemeine Zeitung, Oct. 18.
Frankfurter Rundschau, Oct. 15.
Salzburger Volksblatt, Oct. 15.
Spandauer Volksblatt, Sept. 12.
Stuttgarter Zeitung, Nov. 30.
Süddeutsche Zeitung, Oct. 16.
Der Tagesspiegel, Oct. 13, 16.
Unidentified clippings.

1973 (November)
Baden
Günther PENZOLDT, Director
Peter-Uwe ARNDT, Macbeth
Brigitte WALTER, Lady Macbeth
Frankfurter Allgemeine Zeitung, Nov. 27.
Offenburger Tageblatt, Nov. 8.

1974 (May)
Recklinghausen
Müller adaptation
Hansgünther HEYME, Director
Hans SCHULZE, Macbeth
Veronika BAYER, Lady Macbeth
Bremer Nachrichten, May 16, May 21.
Deutsches Allgemeine Sonntagsblatt, May 26.
Deutsche Volkszeitung, May 26.
Flensburger Tageblatt, May 17.
Frankfurter Rundschau, May 18, Sept. 10.
Frankfurter Allgemeine Zeitung, May 18.
Frankenpost, May 23.
Göttinger Tageblatt, May 22.
Hannoversche Allgemeine Zeitung, May 18.
Kölnische Rundschau, May 18.
Münchner Merkur, May 18.
National-Zeitung, June 26.
Neue Osnabrücker Zeitung, May 18.
Neue Rhein-Zeitung, May 18.
Neue Westfälische, May 14.
Rhein-Main-Nahe Allgemeine Zeitung, May 22.
Rhein-Neckar-Zeitung, May 20.

Stuttgarter Nachrichten, May 18.
Stuttgarter Zeitung, May 18.
Süddeutsche Zeitung, May 21, Sept. 12.
Der Tagesspiegel, May 23, Sept. 8.
Vorwärts, May 23.
Die Welt, May 20.
Weser-Kurier, May 18.
Westdeutsche Allgemeine, May 18.
Wiesbadener Tageblatt, May 22.
Die Zeit, May ,24.

1975 (October)
Hannover
Günter KRÄMER, Director
Udo THOMER, Macbeth
Joanna LIEBENEINER, Lady Macbeth
Göttinger Tageblatt, Nov. 12.
Hannoversche Allgemeine Zeitung, Oct. 28.
Neue Hannoversche Presse, Oct. 28.
Nordwest-Zeitung Oldenburger Nachrichten, Nov. 4.
Wilhelmshavener Zeitung, Dec. 23.

1975 (November)
Peter BORCHARDT, Director
Jürgen SCHORNAGEL, Macbeth
Dagmar GABRIEL, Lady Macbeth
Schwäbische Zeitung, Nov. 27.
Südwest Presse, Nov. 20.

1976 (March)
Düsseldorf
Hermann WETZKE, Director
Günther MACH, Macbeth
Ingrid STEIN, Lady Macbeth
Rheinische Post, March 9.

1977 (March)
Munich
Klausjürgen WUSSOW, Macbeth
Ursula LINGEN, Lady Macbeth
Dietrich HAUGK, Director
Süddeutsche Zeitung, Nr. 53

HUNGARY

1812
Kolozsvár, Transylvania
Bayer, József, *The Plays of Shakespeare in Hungary*. (Title translated)

1822 (Dec. 29)
Székesfehérvár
Bayer, op. cit.

1825 (October)
Pozsony
Mrs. KÁNTOR, Lady Macbeth

Bayer, op. cit.

1832 (Oct. 29)
Debrecen
Letter from Klara Bódis, describing the use of "Laterna Magica."

1833 (June 17)
Buda
Mrs. KÁNTOR, Lady Macbeth
Bayer, op. cit.

1843 (Aug. 19)
Pest
EGRESSY, Macbeth and Director
Régelo, *The Story Teller*, cited by Bódis, K.
Bayer, op. cit.

1860 (Oct. 29)
J. R. LENDVAY, Macbeth
Bayer, op. cit.

ca. 1939 (Nov. 18)
Antal NÉMETH, Director
Aurel Kárpáthy, *Theatre*. n.d.

1950 (April 22)
Tamás MAJÓR, Macbeth
Dénes RÁTAI, Director
Friss Ujság, April 29.
New World, ed. by Miklós Gyárfas. n.d.
Theatre and Art. n.d.
Letter from Klara Bódis.

1963 (October 18)
Imre SINKOVITS, Macbeth
Margit LUKACS, Lady Macbeth
Tamás MAJÓR, Director
Letter from Klara Bódis.
Majór, see main bibliography.

INDIA
Kantak, V. Y., personal report.

ITALY
1849
Milan
Almanno MORELLI, Macbeth
Unidentified clippings.

1857 (June)
London
Sr. VITALIANI, Macbeth
Adelaide RISTORI, Lady Macbeth
Il Trovatore, July 18.
See also main bibliography and actresses' bibliography under Ristori.

1866
New York
Adelaide RISTORI, Lady Macbeth
Il Trovatore, n.d.

1876
Mme. PARETI, Lady Macbeth
Times, May 12.

1877
Tommaso SALVINI, Macbeth
Unidentified review, Paris, October 1877.
Celso Salvini, *Tommaso Salvini nella Storia del Teatro Italiano*, 1955.
See also main bibliography and actors' bibliography under Salvini.

1882
London
Adelaide RISTORI, Lady Macbeth
L'Arte Drammatica, n.d.,

1887
Rome
Ernesto ROSSI, Macbeth
Gazzetta Ferrarese, June 22, 1904.
See also main bibliography and actors' bibliography under Rossi.

1908
Ermete NOVELLI, Macbeth
Olga GIANNINI, Lady Macbeth
Unidentified, "A New Macbeth", Jan. 2.

1918
Ermete ZACCONI, Macbeth
G. Pardieri, *Ermete Zacconi*, 1960, p. 49.

1938
Ruggero RUGGIERI, Macbeth
Corriere della Sera, 1938–1939, *passim*.
L. Bragaglia, *Ruggero Ruggieri*, 1968.

1948 (April)
Milan
Renzo RICCI, Macbeth
Eva MAGNI, Lady Macbeth
Renzo RICCI, Director
Bis, April 27, 1948.
Risorgimente Liberale (Rome), Dec. 12, 1947.

1952 (February)
Giorgio STREHLER, Director
Gianni SANTUCCIO, Macbeth
Lilla BRIGNONE, Lady Macbeth
Castello, G. C., unidentified source.
Corriere d'informazione, n.d.
Corriere della Sera, n.d.

Libertà, Feb. 8.
Milano Sera, Feb. 2.
Il Popolo, n.d.
Terron, Carlo, unidentified source.

1953 (February)
Rome
Antonio CRAST, Macbeth
Evi MALTAGLIATI, Lady Macbeth
Orazio COSTA, Director

L'Europa, March 12.
Il Giornale d'Italia, Feb. 26.
Giustizia, Feb. 27.
Il Lavoro Illustrato, March 15.
Il Messaggero, Feb. 25.
Il Momento, Feb. 26.
Momento Sera, Feb. 26.
Il Mondo, March 8.
Il Tempo, Feb. 25.

1966 (October)
Milan
Tino BUAZZELLI, Macbeth
Paola MANNONI, Lady Macbeth
Tino BUAZZELLI, Director

Corriere della Sera, Oct. 6.
La Notte, Oct. 6.
La Stampa, Oct. 6.

1967 (October)
Rome
Same production
Il Messaggero, Oct. 7.
Il Tempo, Oct. 7.

1971 (July 9)
Verona
Glauco MAURI, Macbeth
Valeria MORICONI, Lady Macbeth
Franco ENRIQUEZ, Director

Alessandro Giupponi, program notes.
G. Melchiori, personal report.

1974
Milan
Andree Ruth SCHAMMAH, Director
Neue Zûricher Zeitung, April 6.

Additional information on Italian *Macbeths* in personal reports from Marisa Sestito and G. Melchiori.
See also *Enciclopedia della Spettacolo*, 1958.

JAPAN

1927
Sadao MARUYAMA, Macbeth
Chieko HIGASHIYAMA, Lady Macbeth
Letter from Peter Milward.

1957
Hiroshi AKUTAGAWA, Macbeth
Haroku SUGIMURA, Lady Macbeth
Tsuneari FUKUDA, Director
Peter Milward, interview with Akutagawa.

1972
Kumo Troupe Production
Shigeru KAMIYAMA, Macbeth
Imaiko KISHIDA, Lady Macbeth
Tetsuo ARAKAWA, Director
Japan Times, Sept. 15.
Peter Milward, personal report.

1976
Mikijiro HIRA, Macbeth
Tamasaburo BANDO, Lady Macbeth
Toshikiyo MASUMI, Director
Koshi Nakanori, personal report.
Peter Milward, personal report.
Toshihiko Shibata, personal report.
Unidentified clipping.

MEXICO

1967
SOLE Production
Christian Science Monitor, June 3.

THE NETHERLANDS

1909 (September)
Company: Die Haghespelers
Eduard VERKADE, Director
Het Nieuws van de Dag, Sept. 7.

1916 (November)
Company: Die Haghespelers
Eduard VERKADE, Director
De Groene Amsterdammer, Nov. 25.

1937 (February)
Company: De Amsterdamse Toneelvereniging
August DEFRESNE, Director
De Tijd, Feb. 24, 1937
Erenstein, Marianne, personal report.
Ogden, D.

NORWAY

1972
Espen SKJONBERG, Macbeth
Mona HOFLAND, Lady Macbeth
Casper WREDE, Director
Bergens Tidende, March 3.
Ibid., March 6.
Haugesund Avis, n.d.

Personal report from Grete Lausund
Personal report from Casper Wrede.

POLAND

1812–1830
Marcin Szymanowski, Macbeth
Józefa Ledóchowska, Lady Macbeth
Jerzy Got, "Polish Actors in Shakespearean
   Roles", in *The Neophilological Committee of the
   Polish Academy of Sciences: Poland's Homage
   to Shakespeare*. 1965.

1817–1859
Witalis Smochowski, Macbeth
Ibid.
Dziennik Literacki, 1859, Nr. 26–27.

ca. 1890
Helena Modjeska (Modrzejewska), Lady
Macbeth
Czas, 1891, Nr. 121.
Dziennik Polski, 1902, Nr. 569.
Gazeta Lwowska, 1890, Nr. 271.
Got, *op. cit.*
A. Grzymala-Siedlecki, *Świat aktorski moich
   czasów*, 1957, 83–85.
Przegląd Polski, 1895, Nr. 343; 1903, Nr. 440.
Tygodnik Ilustrowany, 1891, Nr. 62.
See also under Lady Macbeth and in main
   bibliography

1819–1916
Roman ŻELAZOWSKI, Macbeth
Got, *op. cit.*

1904–1929
Stanislawa Wysocka, Lady Macbeth
Got, *op. cit.*
Przegląd Polski, 1904, Nr. 453; 1910, Nr. 533.

1958
Zygmunt Hübner, Director
Przegląd Kulturalny, 1958, Nr. 25.

1960
Jan Świderski, Macbeth
Halina Mikolajska, Lady Macbeth
Jan Kott, *Miarka za miarkę*, 1962, 314–318.
Teatr, 1960, Nr. 24.
Życie Warszawy, 1960, Nr. 273.

1964
Maria Chwalibóg, Lady Macbeth
Teatr, 1964, Nr. 15.

1964
Teresa Mikolajczuk, Lady Macbeth

Kurier Lubelski, 1964, Nr. 90.
Trybuna Ludu, 1964, Nr. 165.

1964
Michal Pawlicki, Macbeth
Nina Andrycz, Lady Macbeth
Otto Axer, Director
Slowo Powszechne, 1964, Nr. 113.
Życie Warszawy, 1964, Nr. 111.

1966
Lidia Zamkow, Lady Macbeth and Director
Teatr, 1966, Nr. 23.
Tygodnik Powszechny, 1966, Nr. 44.

1971
Andrzej Przybylski, Director
Grzgorz Sinko, *Teatr*, 1971, Nr. 23.

1972
Wojciech Pszoniak, Macbeth
Zofia Kucówna, Lady Macbeth
Adam Hanuszkiewicz, Director
Argumenty, 1973, Nr. 1.
Kultura, 1972, Nr. 53.
Literatura, 1973, Nr. 2.
Tygodnik Powszechny, 1973, Nr. 6.
Personal reports on Polish productions by
   Jerzy Got. See also main bibliography.

PORTUGAL

F. De Mello Moser, personal report.

RUSSIA

1861
St. Petersburg, Alexandrinian Theatre
LEONIDOV, Macbeth
ZHULEVA, Lady Macbeth
Russky Mir, Nov. 1861, no. 93, 1553–1556.
Zh. Levin, "Shakespeare and the czarist cen-
   sorship," *Zvezda*, 1964, no. 4.

1861
Moscow, Bolshoy Theatre
I. ALDRIDGE, Macbeth
A. Bazhenov, "Aldridge on the Moscow Stage,"
   Moskovskie Vedomosti, Oct. 27, 1862, no. 234,
   1976–1977.
Other Russian comments on Aldridge have
   been supplied—in translation—by Herbert
   Marshall of the Center for Russian Studies.

1890
Moscow, Maly Theatre
YUZHIN, Macbeth
FEDOTOVA, Lady Macbeth
Teatr i Zhizň, Jan. 19, no. 456.

A. R. Kugel, *Teatralnye Portrety*, 1967.
Unidentified clippings.

1890
ROSSI, Macbeth (see Italy)
See Juriev, Recollections, 1918, below.
Unidentified reports.

1896
Maly Theatre
YUZHIN, Macbeth
ERMOLOVA, Lady Macbeth

Y. Belyaev, *Peterburgskaya Gazeta*, Feb. 23, 1904.
S. N. Durylin, *Maria Nicolaevna Ermolova*, ("Ermolova in Shakespeare's plays," 323–325), 1953.
Petr Kicheev, *Russkoe Slovo*, 1899, no. 257.
A. R. Kugel, *Teatralnye portrety*, 1967.
Kuryer, Sept. 19, 1899

1914
Maly Theatre
YUZHIN, Macbeth
SMIRNOVA, Lady Macbeth
I. Ivanov, *Artist*, 1890, Feb. 6, 94–101.

1918
Petrograd, Tragedy Theatre
JURIEV, Macbeth
ANDREEVA, Lady Macbeth
Novaya Petrogradskaya Gazeta, July 26.
Petrogradskaya Pravda, Sept. 29. no. 212.
Recollections of Juriev published in *The Theatrical Almanac (Teatralny Almanakh)*, Moscow-Leningrad, 1947.

1918–19
Petrograd, Bolshoy Dramaticheskiy
"V. R.", *The Life of Art (Zhizń Iskusstva)*. no. 92, Mar. 6, 1919.

1936
Baku Turkish Theatre
SHARIFOV, Macbeth
MARZIA, Lady Macbeth
Literartuny Azerbaydzhan, 1936, no. 4–5.
V. Rogovsky, *Teatr i Dramaturgia*, 1936, no. 6.

1936
Azerbaydzhan Azisbekov Dramatic Theatre
Notes by director-producer A. Tuganov.

1938
Kirov
Review by Morozov of Kirov *Macbeth*.

1940
Leningrad, Pushkin State Academic Theatre

SIMONOV, Macbeth
ZHIKHAREVA, Lady Macbeth
Sovetskoe Iskusstvo, Apr. 22, 1940.
Teatr, 1940, no. 7.

1955
Maly Theatre
TSAREV, Macbeth
GOGOLEVA, Lady Macbeth

M. Croft, *Sovetskaya Kultura*, Dec. 20, 1956.
E. Loginova, "The Friends of Shakespeare," *Ogonek*, March, 1956, no. 13, 20 ff.
Yu. Malashev, *Sovetskaya Kultura*, May, 1956.
I. Selvinsky, "Zametki Poeta," *Teatr*, 1956, no. 6, 66–74.
A. Shtein, *Ezhegodnik Malogo Teatra*, 1955–56 (*Yearbook of the Maly Theatre, 1955–56*)
K. Zubov, "Makbet v Malom Theatre," *Shekspirovsky sbornik*, vol. 10, 1958, 453–58.

1975
Minsk
Sovetskaia Belorussia, Feb. 8.

SOUTH AFRICA

1967 (January)
Maynardville, South Africa
Michael ATKINSON, Macbeth
Cecilia SONNENBERG, Lady Macbeth
Leslie FRENCH, Director
Cape Times, Jan. 6, 1967.

1970
Johannesburg.
Beverley SKUTELSKY, Lady Macbeth
Rand Daily Mail. Aug. 21, 1970.

SWEDEN

1838
Olov Ulrik TORSSLOW, Macbeth, Director
Sara TORSSLOW, Lady Macbeth
Nils Molin, "Shakespeare i Sverige," in *Studiekameraten*, 1964.

1858
Olov Ulrik TORSSLOW, Macbeth, Director

1880
Sr. UDINA, Macbeth
Adelaide RISTORI, Lady Macbeth
Göteborgs Handels och Sjöfarts Tidnings, Nov. 15.
Ristori, *Memoirs*, 129–132.
See also under Italy and main bibliography.

1886
Ernesto ROSSI, Macbeth
Elise HWASSER, Lady Macbeth

1909
August LINDBERG, Macbeth, Director
Gerda LUNDEQUIST, Lady Macbeth
Svenska Dagbladet, May 15.
Dagens Nyheter, May 15.

1944
Sture ERICSSON, Macbeth
Ingrid LUTERKORT, Lady Macbeth
Ingmar BERGMAN, Director
Aftonbladet, Nov. 20.
Claus Lauréns, personal report.
Henrik Sjögren, *Ingmar Bergman Pa Teatern*,
   1968.
Dagens Nyheter, Nov. 20.
Stockholmstidningen, Nov. 20.
Sydsvenska Dagbladet, Nov. 20.

1948
Anders EK, Macbeth
Karin KAVLI, Lady Macbeth
Ingmar BERGMAN, Director
Bonniers Litterära Magazin, March.
Dagens Nyheter, Mar. 13.
Expressen, Mar. 13.
Göteborgs Handels och Sjofarts Tidning, Mar. 13.
Göteborgs Morgonpost, Mar. 13.
Göteborgs Posten, Mar. 13.
Göteborgs Tidningen, Mar. 13.
Stockholmstidningen, Mar. 13.
Svenska Dagbladet, Mar. 13.
Claus Lauréns, personal report.
Sjögren, *Ingmar Bergman*.

1967
Lennart LUNDH, Macbeth
Kerstin TIDELIUS, Lady Macbeth
Herman AHLSELL, Director
Dagens Nyheter, Mar. 18.
Göteborgs Handels och Sjöfarts Tidning, Mar. 18.
Göteborgs Posten, n.d.
Göteborgs Tidning, Mar. 18.
Svenska Dagbladet, Mar. 18.

1973
Erik APPELGREN, Macbeth
Kim ANDERZON, Lady Macbeth
Claes von RETTIG, Director
Aftonbladet, n.d.
Dagens Nyheter, May 21.
Expressen, May 28.
Svenska Dagbladet, May 22.

1975
Erik APPELGREN, Macbeth
Kim ANDERZON, Lady Macbeth
Claes von RETTIG, Director
Svenska Dagbladet, April 24.

Personal reports on Swedish *Macbeths* from
   Claus Lauréns and Nigel Rollison.

TURKEY

1936
Muhsin ERTUĞRUL, Director
Sami AYANOĞLU, Macbeth
N. NEYIR, Lady Macbeth
Aksam, October 6.
Kurum, October 3.
Son Posta. 1972.
Tan, October 4.
Letter from Özedemir Nutku.

1962
Beklan ALGÂN, Director
Agâh HÜN, Macbeth
Şirin DEVRIM, Lady Macbeth
Milliyet, August 19.
Ulus, September 27.
Son Posta, August 18.
Letter from Özedemir Nutku.
See also Metin And, "Shakespeare in Turkey,"
   in main bibliography.
Help in translation: Grace Smith.

YUGOSLAVIA

1871
Zagreb (Croatia), National Theater
Laza TELEČKI, Macbeth
Maca PERIS, Lady Macbeth

1956
Beograd (Serbia), Yugoslav Drama Theater
Milivoje ŽIVANOVIĆ, Macbeth
Marija CRNOBORI, Lady Macbeth
Mata MILOŠEVIĆ, Director

1957
Celje (Slovenia), National Theater
Andrej HEING, Director

1957
Zagreb (Croatia), National Theater
Drago KRĔA, Macbeth
Vjera ZAGAR-NARDELLI, Lady Macbeth
Branko GAVELLA, Director

1958
Rijeka (Croatia), National Theater
Veljko MARIČIĆ, Macbeth
Branka VERDONIK, Lady Macbeth
Andjelko ŠTIMAC, Director

1962
Sarajevo (Bosnia), National Theater
Dragče POPOVIĆ, Macbeth

Marija DANIRA, Lady Macbeth
Boro DRAŠKOVIĆ, Director

1969

Skopje (Macedonia), National Theater
Kiril KORTOŠFV, Macbeth
Milica STOJANOVA, Lady Macbeth
Gerett MORGAN, Director

1970

Dubrovnik (Croatia), Summer festival
Tonko LONZA, Macbeth
Neva ROŠIĆ, Lady Macbeth
Vlado HABUNEK, Director
Letter from Mladen Engelsfeld.
Letter from Slobodan Jovanović.
Interview between Vlado Habunek and Mladen
Engelsfeld.

1970

Kragujevac (Serbia), National Theater
Ljuba KOVACEVIĆ, Macbeth
Mila STOJADINOVIĆ, Lady Macbeth
Petar GOVEDAREVIĆ, Director

1970

Ljubljana (Slovenia), Slovenian National
Theatre
Boris KRALJ, Macbeth

Duša POČKAJEVA, Lady Macbeth
Žarko PETAN, Director.
See also Germany (1971).

Sources of information on Macbeth in Yugoslavia:
Batušić, Slavko "Šekspir i Zagreb" ("Shakespeare and Zagreb"), *Tuzla* 6 (1964) 75–94.
Mihailović, Dušan, "Šekspir na beogradskoj
sceni, 1869–1900" ("Shakespeare on the Bel-
grade Stage, 1869–1900"), in *Zbornik
muzeja pozorišne umetnosti, I*, Beograd,
1962, 127–150.
———., "Šekspir na sceni narodnog pozorišta" ("Shakespeare on the Stage of the
Serbian National Theatre in Novi Sad"),
in *Spomenica*, 1861–1961, 106–150.
———., "Sto godina sa Šekspirom" ("One
Hundred Years with Shakespeare"), in *Jedan
vek Narodnog pozorišta u Beogradu*, Beograd,
1968, 262–307.
Moravec, Dušan, *Shakespeare pri Slovencih (Shakespeare among Slovenes)*, Ljubljana, 1965.

Additional information on Yugoslavian Macbeths in personal reports from Slobodan
Jovanović and Mladen Engelsfeld.

Theatre Bibliography III

Some stagings of *Macbeth* have been associated with particular directors, producers, or places, and are so identified below. Where relevant, cross-reference to actors or actresses is indicated.

ASTLEY'S HIPPODROME
(EQUESTRIAN *MACBETH*)
  Era, Dec. 7, 1856
  Lady's Newspaper, Dec. 6, 1856
  Punch, Jan. 10, 1857
  Sunday Times, Dec. 7, 1856
  Times, Dec. 4, 1856

BERGMAN, Ingmar
  See Sweden

BLAKEMORE, Michael (1972–1973)
  See HOPKINS, *Anthony*
  See also QUILLEY, *Denis*

BRIDGES-ADAMS, William
  Birmingham Daily Post, April 20, 1920, Aug. 5, 1920
  Birmingham Mail, Aug. 7, 1920
  Morning Post, Sept. 6, 1920
  Oxford Chronicle, Aug. 13, 1920
  Stage, Aug. 12, 1920
  Stratford-Upon-Avon Herald, Aug. 6, 1920, Aug. 13, 1920, Aug. 27, 1920

CASSON, Lewis T. (1926)
  Introduction to Folio Society edition of *Macbeth*.

CRAIG, Edward (Carrick)
  Daily Telegraph, Nov. 22, 1932
  Era, Nov. 23, 1932
  Observer, Nov. 27, 1932
  Personal Discussions, 1973–1976
  Stage, Nov. 24, 1932
  Times, Nov. 22, 1932

CRAIG, (Edward) Gordon, production
  American Hebrew, Dec. 21, 1928
  American Mercury, January 1929
  Anglin, M.
  Boston Evening Transcript, Oct. 1, 1928
  Bridlington Free Press, Oct. 3, 1928
  Catholic World, Nov., 1928, Jan., 1929
  Chicago American, Nov. 20, 1928
  Chicago Daily News, Jan. 29, 1929
  Chicago Journal, Nov., 1928
  Drama, Dec., 1928
  Craig, Gordon, (1–6)
  Daily Telegraph, Oct. 11, 1928, Nov. 22, 1928
  Dial, Feb., 1929
  Evening Post, Nov. 20, 1928
  Freeman, March 16, 1928
  Hamilton, C.
  Literary Digest, Nov. 17, 1928, Dec. 19, 1928, Dec. 24, 1928
  New Republic, April 2, 1929
  New York Times Magazine, Nov. 11, 1928
  New York Times, Nov. 20, 1928
  New York Tribune, Oct. 20, 1928, Nov. 20, 1928
  Mask, vol. 15 (1929)
  Observer, Feb. 13, 1928
  Pittsburgh Post Gazette, Mar. 2, 1929, Feb. 1, 1928, April 2, 1929
  Pittsburgh Sun-Telegraph, April 2, 1929
  Ross, D.
  Stage, Dec. 6, 1928
  Sun, Nov. 20, 1928

Times, July 24, 1967
World, Nov. 21, 1928
Wyatt, E. V. R.
Young, S.
DUNLOP, Frank
  Birmingham Post, Jan. 16, 1975
  Daily Express, Jan. 16, 1975
  Daily Mail, Jan. 17, 1975
  Evening News, Jan. 16, 1975
  Financial Times, Jan. 16, 1975
  Guardian, Jan. 16, 1975
  Hodgkinson, Joseph, personal report
  Lady, Jan. 30, 1975
  Listener, Jan. 23, 1975
  New Statesman, Feb. 7, 1975
  South London Press, Feb. 4, 1975
  Stage, Jan. 23, 1975
  Sunday Telegraph, Jan. 19, 1975
  Sunday Times, Jan. 19, 1975
  Times, Jan. 7, 1975
DUNN, James (California, 1971)
  Personal reports
GUTHRIE, Tyrone (1934)
  See LAUGHTON, *Charles*
HALL, Peter (1967–1968)
  Plays and Players, March, 1968
  Rosenberg (2)
  See also SCOFIELD, *Paul*
HOPKINS, Arthur (1921)
  See BARRYMORE, *Lionel*
HOUGHTON, Norris (1947–1948)
  See REDGRAVE, *Michael*
JACKSON, Sir Barry (1928)
("Modern dress" *Macbeth)*
  See MATURIN, *Eric*
JONES, Robert Edmond (1921)
  See BARRYMORE, *Lionel*
KAHN, Michael
(Fritz Weaver, Macbeth; Rosemary Murphy,
Lady Macbeth)
  Huffman, Richard, personal report
  National Observer, Oct. 6, 1973
  National Review, Aug. 17, 1973
  New York Daily News, July 16, 1973
  New York Post, July 16, 1973
  New York Times, July 15, 1973; July 16, 1973
  Philadelphia Inquirer, July 15, 1973
KOMISARJEVSKY, Theodore
  Birmingham Gazette, April 19, 1933
  Birmingham Mail, April 19, 1933
  Birmingham Post, April 19, 1933
  Gibbs, E. (1)
  Manchester Guardian, April 20, 1933
  Midland Daily Telegraph, April 19, 1933
  Morning Post, April 19, 1933
  Mullin, M.
  The Scotsman, April 21, 1933
  The Stage, April 27, 1933

Stratford-Upon-Avon Herald, April 21, 1933
Times, April 19, 1933
LITTLEWOOD, Joan
("Modern Dress Macbeth")
  Birmingham Post, Sept. 5, 1957, Sept. 11,
    1957
  Daily Express, Sept. 4, 1957
  Daily Herald, Sept. 4, 1957
  Daily Worker, Sept. 5, 1957, Sept. 9, 1957
  Evening Standard, Sept. 4, 1957
  Hackney Gazette, Sept. 9, 1957
  Illustrated London News, Sept. 21, 1957
  Jewish Chronicle, Sept. 13, 1957
  Johannesburg Star, Sept. 6, 1957
  Liverpool Daily Post, Sept. 7, 1957
  Manchester Guardian, Sept. 5, 1957
  Natal Daily News, Sept. 6, 1957
  News Chronicle, Sept. 4, 1957
  New Statesman, Sept. 14, 1957
  Northern Echo, Sept. 5, 1957
  Observer, Sept. 8, 1957
  Oxford Mail, Sept. 7, 1957
  Plays and Players, Oct., 1957
  Punch, Sept. 11, 1957
  Scotsman, Sept. 9, 1957
  Spectator, Sept. 13, 1957
  Stage, Sept. 5, 1957
  Tablet, Sept. 21, 1957
  Theatre World, Oct., 1957
  Times, Sept. 5, 1957
  Tribune, Sept. 13, 1957
MAETERLINCK, Maurice
  Bühne und Welt, vol. 23, 1909–1910
  Comoedia Illustré, 1909–1910, 1910–1911
  Daily Chronicle, Aug. 25, 1909
  Figaro, Aug. 30, 1909
  Fortescue, "A French Macbeth," unidenti-
    fied source, L'Arsenal collection.
  New York Times, Sept. 8, 1909
  New York Tribune, Aug. 29, 1909
  Public Ledger, Sept. 12, 1909
  Schaubühne, Sept. 30, 1909
  Le Théâtre, Oct., 1909
  Theatre Magazine, Nov., 1909
  Unidentified clippings
  See also main bibliography and Theatre Bibli-
    ography II, under France
MILES, Bernard
  Guardian, April 23, 1964
  Sunday Times, April 26, 1964
  Times, April 23, 1964
  Tynan, K. (2)
NUNN, Trevor
  See WILLIAMSON, N (1974)
  See McKELLEN, I. (1976)
POLANSKI, Roman, film
  Auckland Star (New Zealand), Nov. 11, 1972
  Christian Science Monitor, Dec. 20, 1971

Daily Mail, Feb. 9, 1973
Daily News, Dec. 21, 1971, Dec. 24, 1971
Ellsmere Port News, (Cheshire), March 28,
   1973
Irish Press, (Dublin), Oct. 13, 1973
New York Post, Dec. 21, 1971
New York Times, Feb. 28, 1971, Dec. 21, 1971,
   March 15, 1972
Personal reports
Sipario, 1973
Unidentified clippings
See also ANNIS, *Francesca*
QUAYLE, Anthony (1949)
   See TEARLE, *Godfrey*
   See also WYNYARD, *Diana*
RABB, Ellis
   Reynolds, Edgar, personal report
REINHARDT, Max (1916)
(Wegener, Macbeth)
   See Main and German bibliographies
SAVITS, Jocza (1891)
   See German bibliography
SEALE, Douglas (1958)
   See HORDERN, *Michael*
SHAW, Glen Byam (1955)
   See OLIVIER, *Laurence*
   See also LEIGH, *Vivien*
WEBSTER, Margaret (1941)
   See EVANS, *Maurice*
   See also ANDERSON, *Judith*

WELLES, Orson
(WPA "Black *Macbeth*," 1936)
(Film production, 1950)
   Amsterdam News (New York), April 18, 1936
   Catholic World, June, 1936
   Commonweal, July 24, 1936
   Daily Post, June 23, 1936
   Era, April 22, 1936
   Evening Advertiser, June 30, 1936
   Figaro, June 23, 1950
   Library, Feb. 1, 1961
   Life and Letters Today, Summer 1938
   Macbeth filmscript, University of California
      at Los Angeles Library
   New Republic, Jan. 15, 1951
   Newsweek, April 25, 1936, Jan. 23, 1937
   New York Herald Tribune, April 16, 1936
   New York Post, April 15, 1936
   New York Times, April 5, 1936, April 15, 1936,
      May 30, 1947, Dec. 28, 1950
   New York World Telegram, April 15, 1936
   New Yorker, Dec. 30, 1950
   Sight and Sound, March 1950, July–Sept.,
      1952
   Spectator, July 10, 1936
   Stage, July, 1936
   Times, April 16, 1936, Nov. 1, 1948
   Variety, April 22, 1936
   Yale/Theatre, vol. 5, no. 3 (1974)
   Wyatt, E. V. R.

Index